Financial Theory and Corporate Policy

FOURTH EDITION

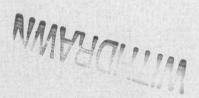

The Addison-Wesley Series in Finance

Copeland/Weston/Shastri
Financial Theory and Corporate Policy

Dufey/Giddy
Cases in International Finance

Eakins
Finance: Investments, Institutions, and Management

Eiteman/Stonehill/Moffett
Multinational Business Finance

Gitman
Principles of Managerial Finance

Gitman
Principles of Managerial Finance— Brief Edition

Gitman/Joehnk
Fundamentals of Investing

Gitman/Madura
Introduction to Finance

Hughes/MacDonald
International Banking: Text and Cases

Madura
Personal Finance

Marthinsen
Risk Takers: Uses and Abuses of Financial Derivatives

McDonald
Derivatives Markets

Megginson
Corporate Finance Theory

Melvin
International Money and Finance

Mishkin/Eakins
Financial Markets and Institutions

Moffett
Cases in International Finance

Moffett/Stonehill/Eiteman
Fundamentals of Multinational Finance

Rejda
Principles of Risk Management and Insurance

Solnik/McLeavey
International Investments

Financial Theory and Corporate Policy

FOURTH EDITION

Thomas E. Copeland

Managing Director of Corporate Finance
Monitor Group, Cambridge, Massachusetts

J. Fred Weston

Professor of Finance Recalled, The Anderson School
University of California at Los Angeles

Kuldeep Shastri

Roger S. Ahlbrandt, Sr. Endowed Chair in Finance
and Professor of Business Administration
Joseph M. Katz Graduate School of Business
University of Pittsburgh

PEARSON

Addison
Wesley

Boston San Francisco New York
London Toronto Sydney Tokyo Singapore Madrid
Mexico City Munich Paris Cape Town Hong Kong Montreal

Editor-in-Chief: Denise Clinton
Senior Acquisitions Editor: Donna Battista
Editorial Assistant: Deborah Tokars
Marketing Manager: Deborah Meredith
Production Supervisor: Meredith Gertz
Project Management and Composition: Windfall Software
Cover and Interior Design: Leslie Haimes
Design Manager: Regina Hagen Kolenda
Copyeditor: Ken DellaPenta
Technical Illustrations: Horizon Design
Proofreader: MaryEllen N. Oliver
Indexer: Ted Laux
Cover Imagery: © Digital Vision and KPT Power Photos
Supplements Editor: Jason Miranda
Senior Manufacturing Buyer: Hugh Crawford

Many of the designations used by manufacturers and sellers to distinguish their products are claimed as trademarks. Where those designations appear in this book, and Pearson Addison Wesley was aware of a trademark claim, the designations have been printed in initial caps or all caps.

This book was composed with the ZzTEX typesetting system on a PC. The text is set in Times Roman and Scala Sans. The math is set in MathTime.

ISBN 0-321-22353-5
    4 5 6 7 8 9 10—PH—07 06 05

Each of us has special people in our lives to whom we would dedicate this book. Fred wishes to thank his wife Bernadine, with love. Kuldeep wishes to thank his wife Karen and son Joey for their support and dedicates this book to the memory of his father N. V. Shastri. And Tom dedicates this book to his beautiful and talented wife Maggie, his sons Tim and Mike, and to the memory of his mother Irene. We also want to dedicate this book to those scholars from whom we have learned the most. Among them are Franco Modigliani and Merton Miller, Jacob Marshack, Kenneth Arrow and Gerard Debreau, Jack Hirshleifer, Bill Sharpe, Jan Mossin, John Lintner, Jack Treynor, Fisher Black, Myron Scholes, and Bob Merton, Gene Fama, Steve Ross, Richard Roll, John Cox, Mark Rubinstein, Jonathan Ingersoll, Hayne Leland, Michael Brennan, Mike Jensen, Stuart Myers, Marti Gruber and Ned Elton, Hans Stoll, Sandy Grossman, and Eduardo Schwartz. To our colleagues and friends who are missing from this pantheon, we apologize.

Contents

8   The Term Structure of Interest Rates, Forward Contracts, and Futures   259

9   Multiperiod Capital Budgeting under Uncertainty: Real Options Analysis   305

10   Efficient Capital Markets: Theory   353

Preface

It has been over 10 years since the third edition of *Financial Theory and Corporate Policy* was published. We have received feedback from many sources that confirms our original judgment that there is a need for a book like *Financial Theory and Corporate Policy*, and so in response to the feedback and many requests for a new edition, we have taken the book out of a long hibernation and present to you this revised and updated edition. For the fourth edition we welcome a third author, Kuldeep Shastri, who holds the Roger S. Ahlbrandt, Sr. Endowed Chair in Finance at the Katz Graduate School of Business at the University of Pittsburgh. Kuldeep is an internationally known scholar and honored teacher who brings greater coverage and mathematical sophistication to the fourth edition.

Our primary aim for the fourth edition remains true to the original objective of the book: to provide a bridge to the more theoretical articles and treatises on finance theory. For doctoral students the book provides a framework of conceptual knowledge, enabling them to understand what the literature on financial theory is trying to do and how it all fits together. For MBAs it provides an in-depth experience with the subject of finance. Our aim here is to equip the MBA for his or her future development as a practicing executive. We seek to prepare the MBA for reading the significant literature of the past, present, and future. This will help practicing financial executives keep up to date with developments in finance theory, particularly as they affect the financial executive's own thinking processes in making financial decisions.

As with the earlier editions, our emphasis is on setting forth clearly and succinctly the most important concepts in finance theory. We have given particular attention to testable propositions and to the literature that has developed empirical tests of important elements of finance theory. In addition, we have emphasized applications so that the nature and uses of finance theory can be better understood.

Purpose and Organization

Over the past 45 years a branch of applied microeconomics has been developed and specialized into what is known as modern finance theory. The historical demarcation point was roughly 1958, when Markowitz and Tobin were working on the theory of portfolio selection and Modigliani and Miller were working on capital structure and valuation. Prior to 1958, finance was largely a descriptive field of endeavor. Since then major theoretical thrusts have transformed the field into a positive science. As evidence of the changes that have taken place we need only look at the types of people who teach in the schools of business. Fifty years ago the faculty were drawn from the ranks of business and government. They were respected and experienced statesmen within their fields. Today, finance faculty are predominantly academicians in the traditional sense of the word. The majority of them have no business experience except for consulting. Their interest and training is in developing theories to explain economic behavior, then testing them with the tools provided by statistics and econometrics. Anecdotal evidence and individual business experience have been superseded by the analytic approach of modern finance theory.

The rapid changes in the field of finance have profound implications for management education. As usual, the best students (and the best managers) possess rare intuition, initiative, common sense, strong reading and writing skills, and the ability to work well with others. But those with the greatest competitive advantage also have strong technical training in the analytical and quantitative skills of management. Modern finance theory emphasizes these skills. It is to the students and faculty who seek to employ them that this textbook is addressed.

The six seminal and internally consistent theories upon which modern finance is founded are (1) utility theory, (2) state-preference theory, (3) mean-variance portfolio theory, (4) the capital asset pricing model and arbitrage pricing theory, (5) option pricing theory, and (6) the Modigliani-Miller theorems. They are discussed in Chapters 3 through 9 and in Chapter 15. Their common sense theme is "How do individuals and society allocate scarce resources through a price system based on the valuation of risky assets?" Utility theory establishes the basis of rational decision making in the face of risky alternatives. It focuses on the question "How do people make choices?" The objects of choice are described by state-preference theory, mean-variance portfolio theory, arbitrage pricing, and option pricing theory. When we combine the theory of choice with the objects of choice, we are able to determine how risky alternatives are valued. When correctly assigned, asset prices provide useful signals to the economy for the necessary task of resource allocation. Finally, the Modigliani-Miller theory asks the question "Does the method of financing have any effect on the value of assets, particularly the firm?" The answer to this question has important implications for the firm's choice of capital structure (debt-to-equity mix) and dividend policy.

It is important to keep in mind that what counts for a positive science is the development of theories that yield valid and meaningful predictions about observed phenomena. The critical first test is whether the hypothesis is consistent with the evidence at hand. Further testing involves deducing new facts capable of being observed but not previously known, then checking those deduced facts against additional empirical evidence. As students of finance, we must not only understand the theory, but also review the empirical evidence to determine which hypotheses have been validated. Consequently, every effort has been made to summarize the empirical evidence related to the theory of finance. Chapter 6 discusses empirical evidence on the capital asset pricing model and the arbitrage pricing theory. Chapter 7 includes studies of how alternative option pricing models perform. Chapter 9, newly added to this edition, discusses the theory and application of real options—a decision tool that is well on its way to replacing net present value. Chapters 10 and 11 cover the theory and evidence on the efficient markets hypothesis. Chapter 12 covers agency costs and signaling theory. Chapter 15 reviews evidence on capital structure. Chapter 16 covers the theory and empirical evidence on dividend policy. Chapter 18 has changed from mergers and acquisitions to acquisitions and divestitures to reflect that the firm can shrink as well as grow in order to create value. Chapter 19 covers international finance.

Finally, in addition to the theory and empirical evidence, there is always the practical question of how to apply the concepts to difficult and complex real-world problems. Toward this end, Chapter 2 is devoted to capital budgeting. Chapter 13 discusses the role of the CFO and performance measurement. Chapter 14 shows how to value companies and discusses tax policy. Chapter 17 emphasizes the theory and evidence on topics of interest to chief financial officers: pension fund management, interest rate swaps, risk management, and leveraged buyouts. Throughout the text we attempt, wherever feasible, to give examples of how to apply the theory. Among other things we show how the reader can estimate his or her own utility function, calculate portfolio means and variances, set up a cross-hedge to reduce the variance of equity returns, value a call option, determine the terms of a merger or acquisition, and use international exchange rate relationships.

In sum, we believe that a sound foundation in finance theory requires not only a complete presentation of the theoretical concepts, but also a review of the empirical evidence that either supports or refutes the theory as well as enough examples to allow the practitioner to apply the validated theory.

Changes in the Fourth Edition

We have tried to move all the central paradigms of finance theory into the first half of the book—the first 12 chapters. In the second edition this motivated our shifting the option pricing material into (what was then) Chapter 8. In this fourth edition we decided to rewrite the chapter on forward contracts and futures markets—a new Chapter 8. It covers traditional material on pricing both commodity and financial futures, as well as newer issues: why futures markets exist, why there are price limits in some markets but not others, and empirical evidence on normal backwardation and contango. We also added several new chapters. Chapter 9 is about real options—the theory, of course, and equally important, the applications. It is a soup-to-nuts presentation that will hopefully fill a void that one finds in most corporate finance textbooks. The new Chapter 12 provides a full development of agency and signaling theories. Throughout both parts of the book, we have updated the literature to include recent developments.

In the materials on portfolio theory we have added a section on how to use T-bond futures contracts for cross-hedging. In Chapter 6 we have updated the literature review on the capital asset pricing model and the arbitrage pricing model. Chapter 7 contains new evidence on option pricing. The materials on capital structure (Chapter 15) and on dividend policy (Chapter 16) have been rewritten to summarize the latest thinking in these rapidly changing areas of research.

Chapters 13 and 14 are completely new. Chapter 13 defines the role of the chief financial officer and discusses performance measurement and incentive design. Chapter 14 shows the details of how to do a discounted cash flow valuation of a company and discusses tax policy.

Chapter 18 covers mergers and acquisitions, divestitures, restructuring, and corporate control and represents up-to-date coverage on the burgeoning literature. Similarly, Chapter 19 reflects the latest thinking in the field of international financial management. Finally, Chapter 20 speculates on the future of research in finance and should be fun reading for faculty, doctoral students who are looking for thesis topics, and MBAs who need a paper topic.

We made numerous other minor changes. In general, we sought to reflect all of the new important literature of finance theory—published articles and treatises as well as working papers. Our aim was to keep the book as close as possible to the frontiers of the state of the art in the literature of finance theory.

Suggested Use in Curriculum

We suggest that the text be used as a second course in finance for MBA students and as the first finance course for doctoral students. When this book was used as a text at UCLA, we found that requiring all finance majors to take a theory-of-finance course before proceeding to upper-level courses eliminated a great deal of redundancy. For example, a portfolio theory course that uses the theory of finance as a prerequisite does not have to waste time with the fundamentals. Instead, after a brief review, most of the course can be devoted to more recent developments and applications.

Because finance theory has developed into a cohesive body of knowledge, it underlies almost all of what had formerly been thought of as disparate topics. The theory of finance, as presented in this text, is prerequisite to security analysis, portfolio theory, money and capital markets, commercial banking, speculative markets investment banking, international finance, insurance, case courses in corporation finance, and quantitative methods of finance. The theory of finance can be, and is, applied to all of these courses. That is why, at UCLA, it was a prerequisite to all the aforementioned course offerings.

The basic building blocks that will lead to the most advantageous use of this text include algebra and elementary calculus; basic finance skills such as discounting, the use of cash flows, pro forma income statements, and balance sheets; elementary statistics; and an intermediate-level microeconomics course.

Use of the Solutions Manual

The end-of-chapter problems and questions ask the students not only to feed back what they have just learned, but also to take the concepts and extend them beyond the material covered directly in the body of the text. Consequently, we hope that the solutions manual will be employed almost as if it were a supplementary text. It should not be locked up in the faculty member's office, as so many instructor's manuals are. It is not an instructor's manual in a narrow sense. Rather, it is a solutions manual, intended for use by the students. Anyone (without restriction) can order it from the publisher. We order it, through the bookstore, as a recommended supplemental reading.

Understanding of the theory is increased by efforts to apply it. Consequently, most of the end-of-chapter problems are oriented toward applications of the theory. They require analytical thinking as well as a thorough understanding of the theory. If the solutions manual is used, as we hope it will be, then students who learn how to apply their understanding of the theory to the end-of-chapter problems will at the same time be learning how to apply the theory to real-world tasks.

Acknowledgments

We have received help from many people on the four editions of the book. We especially benefited from the insightful corrections, clarifications, and suggestions of Eugene Fama and Herb Johnson. Nai-fu Chen and Ronald Bibb wrote Appendices B and D, respectively. Ron Masulis rewrote Chapter 4. Paul Alapat and Juan Siu contributed to Chapters 18 and 19.

Those who reviewed and commented on the fourth edition include Dwight C. Anderson, Eric Bentzen, Alexander W. Butler, Charles Q. Cao, Dr. Mukesh K. Chaudhry, James Conover, Craig G. Dunbar, André Farber, Paolo Fulghieri, Satyananda J. Gabriel, Lawrence R. Glosten, Aditya Goenka, Bing Han, Mark Holder, Michael S. Long, Antonio S. Mello, Nandu Nagarajan, Thomas H. Noe, Arun J. Prakash, Thomas Renstrom, Gary Sanger, Jay Shanken, Laura Starks, John Teall, Christian Weber, Yangru Wu, and Yihong Xia.

We also wish to acknowledge the help of the following on earlier editions: Ed Altman, Enrique Arzac, Dan Asquith, Warren Bailey, Gerry Bierwag, Diran Bodenhorn, Jim Brandon, Michael Brennan, William Carleton, Don Chance, Nai-fu Chen, Don Chew, Kwang S. Chung, Halimah

Clark, Peter Clark, S. Kerry Cooper, Larry Dann, Harry and Linda E. DeAngelo, Dirk Davidson, David Eiteman, Chapman Findlay, Kenneth French, Dan Galai, Robert Geske, Mark Grinblatt, C. W. Haley, Ronald Hanoian, Iraj Heravi, David Hirshleifer, Tom Ho, Chi-Cheng Hsia, William C. Hunter, Ashok Korwar, Clement Krouse, Steven Lippman, Stephen Magee, Dubos Masson, Bill Margrabe, Charles Martin, Ronald Masulis, David Mayers, Guy Mercier, Edward Miller, Merton Miller, Timothy J. Nantell, Ron Necoechea, Jorgen Nielson, R. Richardson Petit, Richard Pettway, Richard Roll, Shigeki Sakakibara, Eduardo Schwartz, Jim Scott, Jandhyala Sharma, Kilman Shin, Ron Shrieves, Keith Smith, Dennis Soter, Joel Stern, Sheridan Titman, Brett Trueman, Jim Wansley, Marty Weingartner, Richard West, Randy Westerfield, Robert Whaley, Stuart Wood, and Bill Ziemba.

For her considerable help in the preparation of this edition, we wish to thank Betsy Seybolt, and for earlier editions, Susan Hoag and Marilyn McElroy. We also express appreciation for the cooperation of Donna Battista and Meredith Gertz, and their associates from Addison Wesley; and Paul Anagnostopoulos from Windfall Software.

There are undoubtedly errors in the final product, both typographical and conceptual as well as differences of opinion. We invite readers to send suggestions, comments, criticisms, and corrections to the authors: Tom Copeland, Monitor Group, Two Canal Park, Cambridge, MA 02141; Kuldeep Shastri, University of Pittsburgh, 368B Mervis Hall, Katz Graduate School of Business, Pittsburgh, PA 15260; or J. Fred Weston at the Anderson Graduate School of Management, University of California, 258 Tavistock Ave., Los Angeles, CA 90049-3229. Any form of communication will be welcome.

T.E.C.
J.F.W.
K.S.

Financial Theory
and Corporate Policy

FOURTH EDITION

The Theory of Finance

P ART I OF THIS TEXT covers what has come to be the accepted theory of financial decision making. Its theme is an understanding of how individuals and their agents make choices among alternatives that have uncertain payoffs over multiple time periods. The theory that explains how and why these decisions are made has many applications in the various topic areas that traditionally make up the study of finance. The topics include security analysis, portfolio management, financial accounting, corporate financial policy, public finance, commercial banking, and international finance.

Chapter 1 shows why the existence of financial marketplaces is so important for economic development. Chapter 2 describes the appropriate investment criterion in the simplest of all possible worlds—a world where all outcomes are known with certainty. For many readers, they will represent a summary and extension of material covered in traditional texts on corporate finance. Chapter 3 covers utility theory. It provides a model of how individuals make choices among risky alternatives. An understanding of individual behavior in the face of uncertainty is fundamental to understanding how financial markets operate. Chapter 4 introduces the objects of investor choice under uncertainty in the most general theoretical framework—state preference theory. Chapter 5 describes the objects of choice in a mean-variance partial equilibrium framework. In a world of uncertainty each combination of assets provides risky outcomes that are assumed to be described in terms of two parameters: mean and variance. Once the opportunity set of all possible choices has been described, we are able to combine Chapter 3, "The Theory of Choice," with Chapter 5, "Objects of Choice," in order to predict exactly what combination of assets an individual will choose. Chapter 6 extends the study of choice into a market equilibrium framework, thereby closing the cycle of logic. Chapter 1 shows why capital markets exist and assumes that all outcomes are known with certainty. Chapter 6 extends the theory of capital markets to include equilibrium with uncertain outcomes and, even more importantly, describes the appropriate concept of risk and shows how it will be priced in equilibrium, including the very general arbitrage pricing theory. Chapter 7 on the option pricing model includes a treatment of the equilibrium prices of contingent claim assets that depend on the outcome of another risky asset. Therefore these materials provide a framework for decision making under uncertainty that can be applied by financial managers throughout the economy. Chapter 8 introduces commodity and financial futures contracts and how they are priced in equilibrium. Chapter 9 applies option pricing to multiperiod investment decisions under uncertainty—real options. Chapter 10 discusses the concept of efficient capital markets. It serves as a bridge between theory and reality. Most of the theory assumes that markets are perfectly frictionless, that is, free of transactions costs and other "market imperfections" that cannot easily be modeled. The questions arise: What assumptions are needed to have efficient (but not necessarily frictionless) capital markets? How well does the theory fit reality? The empirical evidence on capital market efficiency is discussed in Chapter 11. The last chapter of Part I, Chapter 12, discusses principal-agent theory and signaling equilibrium.

Part II of the text focuses on applications of financial theory to corporate policy issues such as capital budgeting, the cost of capital, capital structure, dividend policy, leasing, mergers and acquisitions, and international finance. For almost every topic, there is material that covers the implications of theory for policy and the empirical evidence relevant to the theory, with detailed examples of applications.

Chapter 1

... Through the alterations in the income streams provided by loans or sales, the marginal degrees of impatience for all individuals in the market are brought into equality with each other and with the market rate of interest.

—Irving Fisher,
The Theory of Interest, Macmillan,
New York, 1930, 122.

Introduction: Capital Markets, Consumption, and Investment

A. Introduction

THE OBJECTIVE OF THIS CHAPTER is to study consumption and investment decisions made by individuals and firms and to understand the role of interest rates in making these decisions. The decision about what projects to undertake and which to reject is perhaps the single most important decision that a firm can make. Logical development is facilitated if we begin with the simplest of all worlds, a one-person/one-good economy with no uncertainty. The decision maker, Robinson Crusoe, must choose between consumption now and consumption in the future. Of course, the decision not to consume now is the same as investment. Thus Robinson Crusoe's decision is simultaneously one of consumption and investment. In order to decide, he needs two types of information. First, he needs to understand his own subjective trade-offs between consumption now and consumption in the future. This information is embodied in the utility and indifference curves depicted in Figs. 1.1 through 1.3. Second, he must know the feasible trade-offs between present and future consumption that are technologically possible. These are given in the investment and production opportunity sets of Figs. 1.4 and 1.5.

From the analysis of a Robinson Crusoe economy we will find that the optimal consumption/investment decision establishes a subjective interest rate for Robinson Crusoe. Shown in Fig. 1.5, it represents his (unique) optimal rate of exchange between consumption now and in the future. Thus interest rates are an integral part of consumption/investment decisions. One can think of the interest rate as the price of deferred consumption or the rate of return on investment. Individuals having different subjective interest rates (shown in Fig. 1.6) will select different consumption/investment choices. After the Robinson Crusoe economy we will introduce opportunities to exchange consumption across time by borrowing or lending in a multiperson economy (shown in Fig. 1.7). The introduction of these exchange opportunities results in a single market interest rate that everyone can use as a signal for making optimal consumption/investment decisions

(Fig. 1.8). Furthermore, no one is worse off in an exchange economy when compared with a Robinson Crusoe economy, and almost everyone is better off (Fig. 1.9). Thus an exchange economy that uses market prices (interest rates) to allocate resources across time will be seen to be superior to an economy without the price mechanism.

The obvious extension to the introductory material in this chapter is the investment decisions made by firms in a multiperiod context. Managers need optimal decisions to help in selecting those projects that maximize the wealth of shareholders. We shall see that market-determined interest rates play an important role in the corporate investment and production decisions. This material will be discussed in depth in Chapter 2 given the assumption of certainty, then in Chapter 9 given uncertainty.

B. *C*onsumption and Investment without Capital Markets

The answer to the question "Do capital markets benefit society?" requires that we compare a world without capital markets to one with them and show that no one is worse off and that at least one individual is better off in a world with capital markets. To make things as simple as possible, we assume that all outcomes from investment are known with certainty, that there are no transaction costs or taxes, and that decisions are made in a one-period context. Individuals are endowed with income (manna from heaven) at the beginning of the period, y_0, and at the end of the period, y_1. They must decide how much to actually consume now, C_0, and how much to invest in productive opportunities in order to provide end-of-period consumption, C_1. Every individual is assumed to prefer more consumption to less. In other words, the marginal utility of consumption is always positive. Also, we assume that the marginal utility of consumption is decreasing. The total utility curve (Fig. 1.1) shows the utility of consumption at the beginning of the period, assuming that the second-period consumption is held constant. Changes in consumption have been marked off in equal increments along the horizontal axis. Note that equal increases in consumption cause total utility to increase (marginal utility is positive), but that the increments in utility become smaller and smaller (marginal utility is decreasing). We can easily construct a similar graph to represent the utility of end-of-period consumption, $U(C_1)$. When combined with Fig. 1.1, the result (the three-dimensional graph shown in Fig. 1.2) provides a description of trade-offs between

Figure 1.1 Total utility of consumption.

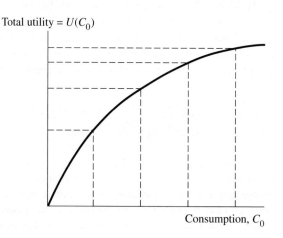

Total utility = $U(C_0)$

Consumption, C_0

Figure 1.2 Trade-offs between beginning and end-of-period consumption.

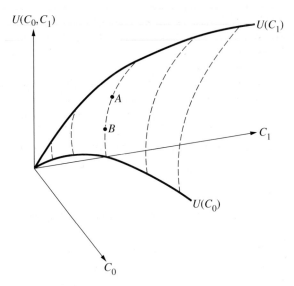

consumption at the beginning of the period, C_0, and consumption at the end of the period, C_1. The dashed lines represent contours along the utility surface where various combinations of C_0 and C_1 provide the same total utility (measured along the vertical axis). Since all points along the same contour (e.g., points A and B) have equal total utility, the individual will be indifferent with respect to them. Therefore the contours are called *indifference curves*. Looking at Fig. 1.2 from above, we can project the indifference curves onto the consumption argument plane (i.e., the plane formed by the C_0, and C_1 axes in Fig. 1.3). To reiterate, all combinations of consumption today and consumption tomorrow that lie on the same indifference curve have the same total utility. The decision maker whose indifference curves are depicted in Fig. 1.3 would be indifferent as to point A with consumption (C_{0a}, C_{1a}) and point B with consumption (C_{0b}, C_{1b}). Point A has more consumption at the end of the period but less consumption at the beginning than point B does. Point D has more consumption in both periods than do either points A or B. Point D lies on an indifference curve with higher utility than points A and B; hence curves to the northeast have greater total utility. The slope of the straight line just tangent to the indifference curve at point B measures the rate of trade-off between C_0 and C_1 at point B. This trade-off is called the *marginal rate of substitution* (MRS) between consumption today and consumption tomorrow. It also reveals how many extra units of consumption tomorrow must be received in order to give up one unit of consumption today and still have the same total utility. Mathematically it's expressed as[1]

$$MRS_{C_1}^{C_0} = \left. \frac{\partial C_1}{\partial C_0} \right|_{U=const.} = -(1 + r_i). \tag{1.1}$$

---

[1] Equation (1.1) can be read as follows: The marginal rate of substitution between consumption today and end-of-period consumption, $MRS_{C_1}^{C_0}$, is equal to the slope of a line tangent to an indifference curve given constant total utility $\left[\partial C_1 / \partial C_0\right]|_{U=const.}$. This in turn is equal to the individual's subjective rate of time preference, $-(1 + r_i)$.

Figure 1.3 Indifference curves representing the time preference of consumption.

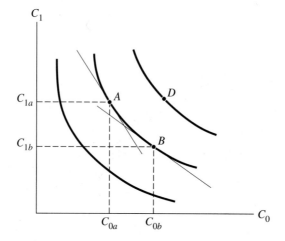

Figure 1.4 An individual's schedule of productive investment opportunities.

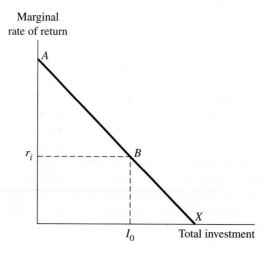

Note that the subjective rate of time preference is greater at point A than at point B due to the convexity of the indifference curve. The individual has less consumption today at point A and will therefore demand relatively more future consumption in order to have the same total utility.

Thus far we have described preference functions that tell us how individuals will make choices among consumption bundles over time. What happens if we introduce productive opportunities that allow a unit of current savings/investment to be turned into more than one unit of future consumption? We assume that each individual in the economy has a schedule of productive investment opportunities that can be arranged from the highest rate of return down to the lowest (Fig. 1.4). Although we have chosen to graph the investment opportunities schedule as a straight line, any decreasing function would do. This implies diminishing marginal returns to investment because the more an individual invests, the lower the rate of return on the marginal investment. Also, all investments are assumed independent of one another and perfectly divisible.

An individual will make all investments in productive opportunities that have rates of return higher than his or her subjective rate of time preference, r_i. This can be demonstrated if we

Figure 1.5 The production opportunity set.

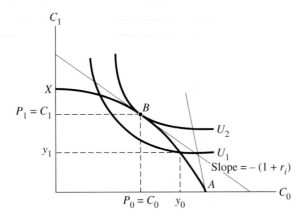

transform the schedule of productive investment opportunities into the consumption argument plane (Fig. 1.5).[2] The slope of a line tangent to curve ABX in Fig. 1.5 is the rate at which a dollar of consumption foregone today is transformed by productive investment into a dollar of consumption tomorrow. It is the *marginal rate of transformation* (MRT) offered by the production/investment opportunity set. The line tangent to point A has the highest slope in Fig. 1.5 and represents the highest rate of return at point A in Fig. 1.4. An individual endowed with a resource bundle (y_0, y_1) that has utility U_1 can move along the production opportunity set to point B, where the indifference curve is tangent to it and he or she receives the maximum attainable utility, U_2. Because current consumption, C_0, is less than the beginning-of-period endowment, y_0, the individual has to invest. The amount of investment is $y_0 - C_0$. Of course, if $C_0 > y_0$, he or she will disinvest.

Note that the marginal rate of return on the last investment made (i.e., MRT, the slope of a line tangent to the investment opportunity set at point B) is exactly equal to the investor's subjective time preference (i.e., MRS, the slope of a line tangent to his or her indifference curve, also at point B). In other words, the investor's subjective marginal rate of substitution is equal to the marginal rate of transformation offered by the production opportunity set:

$$MRS = MRT.$$

This will also be true in a Robinson Crusoe world where there are no capital markets (i.e., no opportunities to exchange). The individual decision maker starts with an initial endowment (y_0, y_1) and compares the marginal rate of return on a dollar of productive investment (or disinvestment) with his or her subjective time preference. If the rate on investment is greater (as it is in Fig. 1.5), he or she will gain utility by making the investment. This process continues until the rate of return on the last dollar of productive investment just equals the rate of subjective time preference (at point B). Note that at point B the individual's consumption in each time period is exactly equal to the output from production (i.e., $P_0 = C_0$ and $P_1 = C_1$).

Without the existence of capital markets, individuals with the same endowment and the same investment opportunity set may choose completely different investments because they have different

---

[2] See Problem 1.6 at the end of the chapter for an example of how to make the transition between the schedule of productive investment opportunities and the consumption argument plane.

Figure 1.6 Individuals with different indifference curves choose different production/consumption patterns.

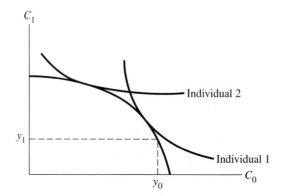

indifference curves. This is shown in Fig. 1.6. Individual 2, who has a lower rate of time preference (Why?), will choose to invest more than individual 1.

C. Consumption and Investment with Capital Markets

A Robinson Crusoe economy is characterized by the fact that there are no opportunities to exchange intertemporal consumption among individuals. What happens if—instead of one person—many individuals are said to exist in the economy? Intertemporal exchange of consumption bundles will be represented by the opportunity to borrow or lend unlimited amounts at r, a market-determined rate of interest.[3]

Financial markets facilitate the transfer of funds between lenders and borrowers. Assuming that interest rates are positive, any amount of funds lent today will return interest plus principal at the end of the period. Ignoring production for the time being, we can graph borrowing and lending opportunities along the *capital market line* in Fig. 1.7 (line $W_0 A B W_1$). With an initial endowment of (y_0, y_1) that has utility equal to U_1, we can reach any point along the market line by borrowing or lending at the market rate plus repaying the principal amount, X_0. If we designate the future value as X_1, we can write that the future value is equal to the principal amount plus interest earned,

$$X_1 = X_0 + rX_0, \qquad X_1 = (1+r)X_0.$$

Similarly, the present value, W_0, of our initial endowment, (y_0, y_1), is the sum of current income, y_0, and the present value of our end-of-period income, $y_1(1+r)^{-1}$:

$$W_0 = y_0 + \frac{y_1}{(1+r)}. \tag{1.2}$$

Referring to Fig. 1.7, we see that with endowment (y_0, y_1) we will maximize utility by moving along the market line to the point where our subjective time preference equals the market interest rate. Point B represents the consumption bundle on the highest attainable indifference curve. At the initial endowment (point A), our subjective time preference, represented by the slope of a

---

[3] The market rate of interest is provided by the solution to a general equilibrium problem. For simplicity, we assume that the market rate of interest is given.

Figure 1.7 The capital market line.

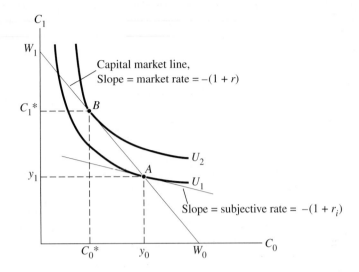

Capital market line,
Slope = market rate = $-(1+r)$

Slope = subjective rate = $-(1+r_i)$

line tangent to the indifference curve at point A, is less than the market rate of return. Therefore we will desire to lend because the capital market rate offers a rate of return higher than what we subjectively require. Ultimately, we reach a consumption decision where we maximize utility. The utility, U_2, at point B is greater than the utility, U_1, at our initial endowment, point A. The present value of this consumption bundle is also equal to our current wealth, W_0:

$$W_0 = C_0^* + \frac{C_1^*}{1+r}. \tag{1.3}$$

This can be rearranged to give the equation for the capital market line:

$$C_1^* = W_0(1+r) - (1+r)C_0^*, \tag{1.4}$$

and since $W_0(1+r) = W_1$, we have

$$C_1^* = W_1 - (1+r)C_0^*. \tag{1.5}$$

Thus the capital market line in Fig. 1.7 has an intercept at W_1 and a slope of $-(1+r)$. Also note that by equating (1.2) and (1.3) we see that the present value of our endowment equals the present value of our consumption, and both are equal to our wealth, W_0. Moving along the capital market line does not change one's wealth, but it does offer a pattern of consumption that has higher utility.

What happens if the production/consumption decision takes place in a world where capital markets facilitate the exchange of funds at the market rate of interest? Figure 1.8 combines production possibilities with market exchange possibilities. With the family of indifference curves U_1, U_2, and U_3 and endowment (y_0, y_1) at point A, what actions will we take in order to maximize our utility? Starting at point A, we can move either along the production opportunity set or along the capital market line. Both alternatives offer a higher rate of return than our subjective time preference, but production offers the higher return (i.e., a steeper slope). Therefore we choose to invest and move along the production opportunity frontier. Without the opportunity to borrow or lend along the capital market line, we would stop investing at point D, where the marginal rate of

Figure 1.8 Production and consumption with capital markets.

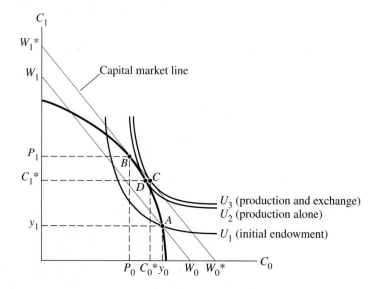

return on productive investment equals our subjective time preference. This was the result shown for consumption and investment in a Robinson Crusoe world without capital markets in Fig. 1.5. At this point, our level of utility has increased from U_1 to U_2. However, with the opportunity to borrow, we can actually do better. Note that at point D the borrowing rate, represented by the slope of the capital market line, is less than the rate of return on the marginal investment, which is the slope of the production opportunity set at point D. Since further investment returns more than the cost of borrowed funds, we will continue to invest until the marginal return on investment is equal to the borrowing rate at point B. At point B, we receive the output from production (P_0, P_1), and the present value of our wealth is W_0^* instead of W_0. Furthermore, we can now reach any point on the market line. Since our time preference at point B is greater than the market rate of return, we will consume more than P_0, which is the current payoff from production. By borrowing, we can reach point C on the capital market line. Our optimal consumption is found, as before, where our subjective time preference just equals the market rate of return. Our utility has increased from U_1 at point A (our initial endowment) to U_2 at point D (the Robinson Crusoe solution) to U_3 at point C (the exchange economy solution). We are clearly better off when capital markets exist since $U_3 > U_2$.

The decision process that takes place with production opportunities and capital market exchange opportunities occurs in two separate and distinct steps: (1) choose the optimal production decision by taking on projects until the marginal rate of return on investment equals the objective market rate; (2) then choose the optimal consumption pattern by borrowing or lending along the capital market line to equate your subjective time preference with the market rate of return. The separation of the investment (step 1) and consumption (step 2) decisions is known as the Fisher separation theorem.

FISHER SEPARATION THEOREM   Given perfect and complete capital markets, the production decision is governed solely by an objective market criterion (represented by maximizing attained wealth) without regard to individuals' subjective preferences that enter into their consumption decisions.

Figure 1.9 The investment decision is independent of individual preferences.

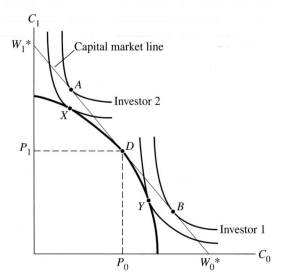

An important implication for corporate policy is that the investment decision can be delegated to managers. Given the same opportunity set, every investor will make the same production decision (P_0, P_1) regardless of the shape of his or her indifference curves. This is shown in Fig. 1.9. Both investor 1 and investor 2 will direct the manager of their firm to choose production combination (P_0, P_1). They can then take the output of the firm and adapt it to their own subjective time preferences by borrowing or lending in the capital market. Investor 1 will choose to consume more than his or her share of current production (point B) by borrowing today in the capital market and repaying out of his or her share of future production. Alternately, investor 2 will lend because he or she consumes less than his or her share of current production. Either way, they are both better off with a capital market. The optimal production decision is separated from individual utility preferences. Without capital market opportunities to borrow or lend, investor 1 would choose to produce at point Y, which has lower utility. Similarly, investor 2 would be worse off at point X.

In equilibrium, the marginal rate of substitution for all investors is equal to the market rate of interest, and this in turn is equal to the marginal rate of transformation for productive investment. Mathematically, the marginal rates of substitution for investors i and j are

$$MRS_i = MRS_j = -(1+r) = MRT.$$

Thus all individuals use the same time value of money (i.e., the same market-determined objective interest rate) in making their production/investment decisions.

The importance of capital markets cannot be overstated. They allow the efficient transfer of funds between borrowers and lenders. Individuals who have insufficient wealth to take advantage of all their investment opportunities that yield rates of return higher than the market rate are able to borrow funds and invest more than they would without capital markets. In this way, funds can be efficiently allocated from individuals with few productive opportunities and great wealth to individuals with many opportunities and insufficient wealth. As a result, all (borrowers and lenders) are better off than they would have been without capital markets.

Figure 1.10 A primitive exchange economy with no central marketplace.

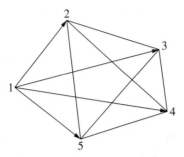

Figure 1.11 The productivity of a central marketplace.

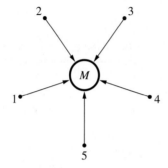

D. $\mathcal{M}$arketplaces and Transaction Costs

The foregoing discussion has demonstrated the advantages of capital markets for funds allocation in a world without transaction costs. In such a world, there is no need for a central location for exchange; that is, there is no need for a marketplace per se. But let us assume that we have a primitive economy with N producers, each making a specialized product and consuming a bundle of all N consumption goods. Given no marketplace, bilateral exchange is necessary. During a given time period, each visits the other in order to exchange goods. The cost of each leg of a trip is T dollars. If there are five individuals and five consumption goods in this economy, then individual 1 makes four trips, one to each of the other four producers. Individual 2 makes three trips, and so on. Altogether, there are $[N(N-1)]/2 = 10$ trips, at a total cost of $10T$ dollars. This is shown in Fig. 1.10. If an entrepreneur establishes a central marketplace and carries an inventory of each of the N products, as shown in Fig. 1.11, the total number of trips can be reduced to five with a total cost of $5T$ dollars. Therefore if the entrepreneur has a total cost (including the cost of living) of less than $10T - 5T$ dollars, he or she can profitably establish a marketplace and everyone will be better off.[4]

This example provides a simple explanation for the productivity in marketplaces. Among other things, they serve to efficiently reduce transaction costs. Later on, we shall refer to this fact

---

[4] In general, for N individuals making two-way exchanges, there are $\binom{N}{2} = N(N-1)/2$ trips. With a marketplace the number of trips is reduced to N. Therefore the savings is $[N(N-1)/2 - N]T$.

as the *operational efficiency* of capital markets. The lower the transaction costs are, the more operationally efficient a market can be.

E. $\mathcal{T}$ransaction Costs and the Breakdown of Separation

If transaction costs are nontrivial, financial intermediaries and marketplaces will provide a useful service. In such a world, the borrowing rate will be greater than the lending rate. Financial institutions will pay the lending rate for money deposited with them and then issue funds at a higher rate to borrowers. The difference between the borrowing and lending rates represents their (competitively determined) fee for the economic service provided. Different borrowing and lending rates will have the effect of invalidating the Fisher separation principle. As shown in Fig. 1.12, individuals with different indifference curves will now choose different levels of investment. Without a single market rate they will not be able to delegate the investment decision to the manager of their firm. Individual 1 would direct the manager to use the lending rate and invest at point B. Individual 2 would use the borrowing rate and choose point A. A third individual might choose investments between points A and B, where his or her indifference curve is directly tangent to the production opportunity set.

The theory of finance is greatly simplified if we assume that capital markets are perfect. Obviously they are not. The relevant question then is whether the theories that assume frictionless markets fit reality well enough to be useful or whether they need to be refined in order to provide greater insights. This is an empirical question that will be addressed later on in the text.

Throughout most of this text we shall adopt the convenient and simplifying assumption that capital markets are perfect. The only major imperfections to be considered in detail are the impact of corporate and personal taxes and information asymmetries. The effects of taxes and imperfect information are certainly nontrivial, and as we shall see, they do change the predictions of many models of financial policy.

Figure 1.12 Markets with different borrowing and lending rates.

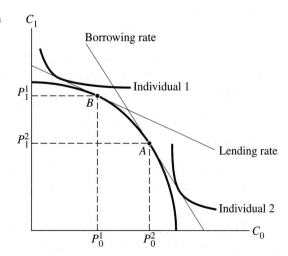

ℐummary

Chapter 2 examines the mechanics of multiperiod investments given the assumption of certainty. The rest of the text follows almost exactly the same logic of this chapter, except that from Chapter 3 onward it focuses on decision making under uncertainty. The first step is to develop indifference curves to model individual decision making in a world with uncertainty. Chapter 3 is analogous to Fig. 1.3. It will describe a theory of choice under uncertainty. Next, the portfolio opportunity set, which represents choices among combinations of risky assets, is developed. Chapters 4 and 5 are similar to Fig. 1.5. They describe the objects of choice—the portfolio opportunity set. The tangency between the indifference curves of a risk-averse investor and his or her opportunity set provides a theory of individual choice in a world without capital markets (this is discussed in Chapter 5). Finally, in Chapter 6, we introduce the opportunity to borrow and lend at a riskless rate and develop models of capital market equilibrium. Chapter 6 follows logic similar to Fig. 1.8. In fact, we show that a type of separation principle (two-fund separation) obtains, given uncertainty and perfect capital markets. Chapters 7 through 9 discuss what are called derivative securities—contracts like options and futures—where value is contingent on the equilibrium value of the underlying securities as described in Chapter 6. Chapters 10 and 11 take a careful look at the meaning of efficient capital markets and at empirical evidence that relates to the question of how well the perfect capital market assumption fits reality. Chapter 12 covers the effects of information asymmetry and agency costs on the theory of decision-making. The remainder of the book, following Chapter 12, applies financial theory to corporate policy decisions.

PROBLEM SET

1.1 Graphically demonstrate the Fisher separation theorem for the case where an individual ends up lending in financial markets. Label the following points on the graph: initial wealth, W_0; optimal production/investment (P_0, P_1); optimal consumption (C_0^*, C_1^*); present value of final wealth, W_0^*.

1.2 Graphically analyze the effect of an exogenous decrease in the interest rate on (a) the utility of borrowers and lenders, (b) the present wealth of borrowers and lenders, and (c) the investment in real assets.

1.3 The interest rate cannot fall below the net rate from storage. True or false? Why?

1.4 Graphically illustrate the decision-making process faced by an individual in a Robinson Crusoe economy where (a) storage is the only investment opportunity and (b) there are no capital markets.

1.5 Suppose that the investment opportunity set has N projects, all of which have the same rate of return, R^*. Graph the investment opportunity set.

1.6 Suppose your production opportunity set in a world of perfect certainty consists of the following possibilities:

Project	Investment Outlay	Rate of Return (%)
A	$1,000,000	8
B	1,000,000	20
C	2,000,000	4
D	3,000,000	30

(a) Graph the production opportunity set in a C_0, C_1 framework.

(b) If the market rate of return is 10%, draw in the capital market line for the optimal investment decision.

REFERENCES

Alderson, W., "Factors Governing the Development of Marketing Channels," reprinted in Richard W. Clewett, *Marketing Channels for Manufactured Products*. Irwin, Homewood, Ill., 1954.

Fama, E. F., and M. H. Miller, *The Theory of Finance*. Holt, Rinehart, and Winston, New York, 1972.

Fisher, I., *The Theory of Interest*. Macmillan, New York, 1930.

Hirshleifer, J., *Investment, Interest, and Capital*. Prentice-Hall, Englewood Cliffs, N.J., 1970.

Chapter 2

. . . When the first primitive man decided to use a bone for a club instead of eating its marrow, that was investment.

—Anonymous.

Investment Decisions: The Certainty Case

A. Introduction

THE INVESTMENT DECISION is essentially how much not to consume in the present in order that more can be consumed in the future. The optimal investment decision maximizes the expected satisfaction (expected utility) gained from consumption over the planning horizon of the decision maker. We assume that all economic decisions ultimately reduce to questions about consumption. Even more fundamentally, consumption is related to survival.

The consumption/investment decision is important to all sectors of the economy. An individual who saves does so because the expected benefit of future compensation provided by an extra dollar of saving exceeds the benefit of using it for consumption today. Managers of corporations, who act as agents for the owners (shareholders) of the firm, must decide between paying out earnings in the form of dividends, which may be used for present consumption, and retaining the earnings to invest in productive opportunities that are expected to yield future consumption. Managers of not-for-profit organizations try to maximize the expected utility of contributors—those individuals who provide external funds. And public sector managers attempt to maximize the expected utility of their constituencies.

The examples of investment decisions in this chapter are taken from the corporate sector of the economy, but the decision criterion, which is to maximize the present value of lifetime consumption, can be applied to any sector of the economy. For the time being, we assume that intertemporal decisions are based on knowledge of the market-determined time value of money—the interest rate. Furthermore, the interest rate is assumed to be known with certainty in all time periods. It is nonstochastic. That is, it may change over time, but each change is known in advance with certainty. In addition, all future payoffs from current investment decisions are known with certainty. And finally, there are no imperfections (e.g., transaction costs) in capital markets. These assumptions are obviously an oversimplification, but they are a good place to start. Most of the

17

remainder of the text after this chapter is devoted to decision making under uncertainty. But for the time being it is useful to establish the fundamental criterion of economic decision making—the maximization of the net present value of wealth, assuming perfect certainty.

The most important theme of this chapter is that the objective of the firm is to maximize the wealth of its shareholders. This will be seen to be the same as maximizing the present value of shareholders' lifetime consumption and no different than maximizing the price per share of stock. Alternative issues such as agency costs are also discussed. Then the maximization of shareholder wealth is more carefully defined as the discounted value of future cash flows. Finally, techniques for project selection are reviewed, and the net present value criterion is shown to be consistent with shareholder wealth maximization in a world with no uncertainty.

B. *F*isher Separation: The Separation of Individual Utility Preferences from the Investment Decision

To say that the goal of the firm is the maximization of shareholders' wealth is one thing, but the problem of how to do it is another. We know that interpersonal comparison of individuals' utility functions is not possible. For example, if we give individuals A and B \$100 each, they will both be happy. However, no one, not even the two individuals, will be able to discern which person is happier. How then can a manager maximize shareholders' utility when individual utility functions cannot be compared or combined?

The answer to the question is provided if we turn to our understanding of the role of capital markets. If capital markets are perfect in the sense that they have no frictions that cause the borrowing rate to be different from the lending rate, then (as we saw in Chapter 1) Fisher separation obtains. This means that individuals can delegate investment decisions to the manager of the firm in which they are owners. Regardless of the shape of the shareholders' individual utility functions, the managers maximize the owners' individual (and collective) wealth positions by choosing to invest until the rate of return on the last favorable project is exactly equal to the market-determined rate of return. This result is shown in Fig. 2.1. The optimal production/investment decision, (P_0, P_1), is the one that maximizes the present value of the shareholders' wealth, W_0. The appropriate decision rule is the same, independent of the shareholders' time preferences for consumption. The manager will be directed, by all shareholders, to undertake all projects that earn more than the market rate of return. The slope of line $W_1 W_0$ in Fig. 2.1 is equal to $-(1 + r)$, where r is the market rate of return.

If the marginal return on investment equals the market-determined opportunity cost of capital, then shareholders' wealth, W_0, is maximized. Individual shareholders can then take the optimal production decision (P_0, P_1) and borrow or lend along the *capital market line* in order to satisfy their time pattern for consumption. In other words, they can take the cash payouts from the firm and use them for current consumption or save them for future consumption, according to their individual desires.

The separation principle implies that the maximization of the shareholders' wealth is identical to maximizing the present value of their lifetime consumption. Mathematically, this was demonstrated in Eq. (1.3):

$$W_0 = C_0^* + \frac{C_1^*}{1+r}.$$

Figure 2.1 Separation of shareholder preferences from the production/investment decision.

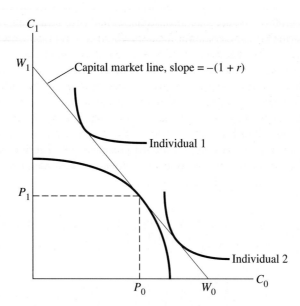

Even though the two individuals in Fig. 2.1 choose different levels of current and future consumption, they have the same current wealth, W_0. This follows from the fact that they receive the same income from productive investments (P_0, P_1).

Because exchange opportunities permit borrowing and lending at the same rate of interest, an individual's productive optimum is independent of his or her resources and tastes. Therefore if asked to vote on their preferred production decisions at a shareholders' meeting, different shareholders of the same firm will be unanimous in their preference. This is known as the *unanimity principle*. It implies that the managers of a firm, in their capacity as agents of the shareholders, need not worry about making decisions that reconcile differences of opinion among shareholders. All shareholders will have identical interests. In effect, the price system by which wealth is measured conveys the shareholders' unanimously preferred productive decisions to the firm.

C. The Agency Problem

So far, we have shown that in perfect markets all shareholders will agree that managers should follow a simple investment decision rule: Take projects until the marginal rate of return equals the market-determined discount rate. Therefore the shareholders' wealth is seen to be the present value of cash flows discounted at the opportunity cost of capital (the market-determined rate).

Shareholders can agree on the decision rule that they should give to managers. But they must be able to costlessly monitor management decisions if they are to be sure that management really does make every decision in a way that maximizes their wealth. There is obviously a difference between ownership and control, and there is no reason to believe that the manager, who serves as an agent for the owners, will always act in the best interest of the shareholders. In most agency relationships the owner will incur nontrivial monitoring costs in order to keep the agent in line. Consequently, the owner faces a trade-off between monitoring costs and forms of compensation that will cause the agent to always act in the owner's interest. At one extreme, if the agent's compensation were in the form of shares in the firm, then monitoring costs would be zero. Unfortunately, this type of scheme is practically impossible because the agent will always be able to receive some compensation in the form of nonpecuniary benefits such as larger office space, expensive lunches, an executive jet, and so on. At the opposite extreme, the owner would have to incur inordinate monitoring costs in order to guarantee that the agent always makes the decision the owner would prefer. Somewhere between these two extremes lies an optimal solution. The agency cost theme is explored in greater depth in Chapter 12 of this text.

In spite of the above discussion, we shall assume that managers always make decisions that maximize the wealth of the firm's shareholders. To do so, they must find and select the best set of investment projects to accomplish their objective.

D. $\mathscr{S}$hareholder Wealth Maximization

1. Dividends vs. Capital Gains

Assuming that managers behave as though they were maximizing the wealth of the shareholders, we need to establish a usable definition of what is meant by shareholders' wealth. We can say that shareholders' wealth is the discounted value of after-tax cash flows paid out by the firm.[1] After-tax cash flows available for consumption can be shown to be the same as the stream of dividends, Div_t, paid to shareholders. The discounted value of the stream of dividends is

$$S_0 = \sum_{t=1}^{\infty} \frac{Div_t}{(1+k_s)^t}, \tag{2.1}$$

where S_0 is the present value of shareholders' wealth (in Fig. 2.1 it is W_0) and k_s is the market-determined required rate of return on equity capital (common stock).

Equation (2.1) is a multiperiod formula that assumes that future cash flows paid to shareholders are known with certainty and that the market-determined discount rate is nonstochastic and constant over all time periods. These assumptions are maintained throughout this chapter because our main objective is to understand how the investment decision, shown graphically in Fig. 2.1 in a one-period context, can be extended to the more practical setting of many time periods in a manner consistent with the maximization of the shareholders' wealth. For the time being, we shall ignore the effect of personal taxes on dividends, and we shall assume that the discount rate, k_s, is the market-determined opportunity cost of capital for equivalent income streams. It is determined by the slope of the market line in Fig. 2.1.

One question that often arises is: What about capital gains? Surely shareholders receive both capital gains and dividends; why then do capital gains not appear in Eq. (2.1)? The answer to this question is that capital gains *do* appear in Eq. (2.1). This can be shown by use of a simple example. Suppose a firm pays a dividend, Div_1, of $1.00 at the end of this year and $1.00 $(1+g)^t$ at the end of each year t thereafter, where the growth rate of the dividend stream is g. If the growth rate of

---

[1] Since much of the rest of this chapter assumes familiarity with discounting, the reader is referred to Appendix A at the end of the book, for a review.

dividends, g, is 5% and the opportunity cost of investment, k_s, is 10%, how much will an investor pay today for the stock? Using the formula for the present value of a growing annuity stream, we get[2]

$$S_0 = \frac{Div_1}{k_s - g} = \frac{\$1.00}{.10 - .05} = \$20.00.$$

Next, suppose that an investor bought the stock today for $20 and held it for five years. What would it be worth at the end of the fifth year?

$$S_5 = \frac{Div_6}{k_s - g}.$$

The dividend, Div_6, at the end of the sixth year is

$$Div_6 = Div_1(1 + g)^5, \qquad Div_6 = \$1.00(1.05)^5 = \$1.2763.$$

Therefore the value of the stock at the end of the fifth year would be

$$S_5 = \frac{\$1.2763}{.10 - .05} = \$25.5256.$$

The value of the stock at the end of the fifth year is the discounted value of all dividends from that time on. Now we can compute the present value of the stream of income of an investor who holds the stock only five years. He or she gets five dividend payments plus the market price of the stock in the fifth year. The discounted value of these payments is S_0.

$$S_0 = \frac{Div_1}{1 + k_s} + \frac{Div_1(1 + g)}{(1 + k_s)^2} + \frac{Div_1(1 + g)^2}{(1 + k_s)^3} + \frac{Div_1(1 + g)^3}{(1 + k_s)^4} + \frac{Div_1(1 + g)^4}{(1 + k_s)^5} + \frac{S_5}{(1 + k_s)^5}$$

$$= \frac{1.00}{1.1} + \frac{1.05}{1.21} + \frac{1.10}{1.33} + \frac{1.16}{1.46} + \frac{1.22}{1.61} + \frac{25.52}{1.61}$$

$$= .91 + .87 + .83 + .79 + 15.85$$

$$= 20.01.$$

Except for a one-cent rounding difference, the present value of the stock is the same whether an investor holds it forever or for only, say, five years. Since the value of the stock in the fifth year is equal to the future dividends from that time on, the value of dividends for five years plus a capital gain is exactly the same as the value of an infinite stream of dividends. Therefore, Eq. (2.1) is the discounted value of the stream of cash payments to shareholders and is equivalent to the shareholders' wealth. Because we are ignoring the taxable differences between dividends and capital gains (this will be discussed in Chapter 16, "Dividend Policy"), we can say that Eq. (2.1) incorporates all cash payments, both dividends and capital gains.

---

[2] The formula used here, sometimes called the Gordon growth model, is derived in Appendix A. It assumes that the dividend grows forever at a constant rate, g, which is less than the discount rate $g < k_s$.

2. The Economic Definition of Profit

Frequently there is a great deal of confusion over what is meant by profits. An economist uses the word *profits* to mean rates of return in excess of the opportunity cost for funds employed in projects of equal risk. To estimate *economic profits*, one must know the exact time pattern of *cash flows* provided by a project and the opportunity cost of capital. As we shall see below, the pattern of cash flows is the same thing as the stream of dividends paid by the firm to its owners. Therefore the appropriate profits for managers to use when making decisions are the discounted stream of cash flows to shareholders—in other words, dividends. Note, however, that *dividends* should be interpreted broadly. Our definition of dividends includes any cash that could be paid out to shareholders. In addition to what we ordinarily think of as dividends, the general definition includes capital gains, spin-offs to shareholders, payments in liquidation or bankruptcy, repurchase of shares, awards in shareholders' lawsuits, and payoffs resulting from merger or acquisition. Stock dividends, which involve no cash flow, are *not* included in our definition of dividends.

We can use a very simple model to show the difference between the economic definition of profit and the accounting definition. Assume that we have an all-equity firm and that there are no taxes.[3] Then sources of funds are revenues, *Rev,* and sale of new equity (on *m* shares at *S* dollars per share). Uses of funds are wages, salaries, materials, and services, *W&S*; investment, *I*; and dividends, *Div.* For each time period, *t*, we can write the *equality between sources and uses of funds* as

$$\text{sources} = \text{uses}$$

$$Rev_t + m_t S_t = Div_t + (W\&S)_t + I_t. \tag{2.2}$$

To simplify things even further, assume that the firm issues no new equity (i.e., $m_t S_t = 0$). Now we can write dividends as

$$Div_t = Rev_t - (W\&S)_t - I_t, \tag{2.3}$$

which is the *simple cash flow definition of profit*. Dividends are the cash flow left over after costs of operations and new investment are deducted from revenues. Using Eq. (2.3) and the definition of shareholders' wealth in Eq. (2.1), we can rewrite shareholders' wealth as

$$S_0 = \sum_{t=1}^{\infty} \frac{Rev_t - (W\&S)_t - I_t}{(1 + k_s)^t} \tag{2.4}$$

The accounting definition of profit does not deduct gross investment, I_t, as investment outlays are made. Instead the book value of new investment is capitalized on the balance sheet and written off at some depreciation rate, *dep.* The *accounting definition of profit* is net income,

$$NI_t = Rev_t - (W\&S)_t - dep_t. \tag{2.5}$$

---

[3] The conclusions to be drawn from the model do not change if we add debt and taxes, but the arithmetic becomes more complex.

Let ΔA_t be the net change in the book value of assets during a year. The net change will equal gross new investment during the year, I_t, less the change in accumulated depreciation during the year, dep_t :

$$\Delta A_t = I_t - dep_t. \tag{2.6}$$

We already know that the accounting definition of profit, NI_t, is different from the economic definition, Div_t. However, it can be adjusted by subtracting net investment. This is done in Eq. (2.7):

$$S_0 = \sum_{t=1}^{\infty} \frac{Rev_t - (W\&S)_t - dep_t - (I_t - dep_t)}{(1+k_s)^t}$$

$$= \sum_{t=1}^{\infty} \frac{NI_t - \Delta A_t}{(1+k_s)^t} \tag{2.7}$$

The main difference between the accounting definition and the economic definition of profit is that the former does not focus on cash flows when they occur, whereas the latter does. The economic definition of profit, for example, correctly deducts the entire expenditure for investment in plant and equipment at the time the cash outflow occurs.

Financial managers are frequently misled when they focus on the accounting definition of profit, or earnings per share. The objective of the firm is *not* to maximize earnings per share. The correct objective is to maximize shareholders' wealth, which is the price per share that in turn is equivalent to the discounted cash flows of the firm. There are two good examples that point out the difference between maximizing earnings per share and maximizing discounted cash flow. The first example is the difference between FIFO (first-in, first-out) and LIFO (last-in, first-out) inventory accounting. The reason is that the cost of manufacturing the oldest items in inventory is less than the cost of producing the newest items. Consequently, if the cost of the oldest inventory (the inventory that was first in) is written off as expense against revenue, earnings per share will be higher than if the cost of the newest items (the inventory that was in last) is written off. A numerical example is given in Table 2.1. It is easy to see that managers might be tempted to use FIFO accounting techniques. Earnings per share are higher. However, FIFO is the wrong technique to use in an inflationary period because it minimizes cash flow by maximizing taxes. In our example, production has taken place during some previous time period, and we are trying to make the correct choice of inventory accounting in the present. The sale of an item from inventory in Table 2.1 provides $100 of cash inflow (revenue) regardless of which accounting system we are using. Cost of goods sold involves no current cash flow, but taxes do. Therefore, with FIFO, earnings per share are $0.45, but cash flow per share is ($100 − $30)/100 shares, which equals $0.70 per share. On the other hand, with LIFO inventory accounting, earnings per share are only $0.06, but cash flow is ($100 − $4)/100 shares, which equals $0.96 per share. Since shareholders care only about discounted cash flow, they will assign a higher value to the shares of the company using LIFO accounting. The reason is that LIFO provides higher cash flow because it pays lower taxes to the government.[4] This is a good

---

[4] In 1979 the Internal Revenue Service estimated that if every firm that could have switched to LIFO had actually done so, approximately $18 billion less corporate taxes would have been paid.

Table 2.1 LIFO vs. FIFO (numbers in dollars)

	LIFO	FIFO	Inventory at Cost
Revenue	100	100	4th item in 90 → LIFO
Cost of goods sold	−90	−25	3rd item in 60
Operating income	10	75	2nd item in 40
Taxes at 40%	−4	−30	1st item in 25 → FIFO
Net income	6	45	
Earnings per share (100 shs)	.06	.45	

example of the difference between maximizing earnings per share and maximizing shareholders' wealth.[5]

It is often argued that maximization of earnings per share is appropriate if investors use earnings per share to value the stock. There is good empirical evidence to indicate that this is not the case. Shareholders do in fact value securities according to the present value of discounted cash flows. Evidence that substantiates this is presented in detail in Chapter 11.

E. Capital Budgeting Techniques

Having argued that maximizing shareholders' wealth is equivalent to maximizing the discounted cash flows provided by investment projects, we now turn our attention to a discussion of investment decision rules. We assume, for the time being, that the stream of cash flows provided by a project can be estimated without error (i.e., that there is no uncertainty), and that the opportunity cost of funds provided to the firm (this is usually referred to as the *cost of capital*) is also known. We also assume that capital markets are frictionless, so that financial managers can separate investment decisions from individual shareholder preferences, and that monitoring costs are zero, so that managers will maximize shareholders' wealth. All that they need to know are cash flows and the required market rate of return for projects of equivalent risk.

Three major problems face managers when they make investment decisions. First, they have to search out new opportunities in the marketplace or new technologies. These are the basis of growth. Unfortunately, the theory of finance cannot help with this problem. Second, the expected cash flows from the projects have to be estimated. And finally, the projects have to be evaluated according to sound decision rules. These latter two problems are central topics of this text. In the remainder of this chapter we look at project evaluation techniques assuming that cash flows are known with certainty, and in Chapter 9 we will assume that cash flows are uncertain.

Investment decision rules are usually referred to as *capital budgeting techniques*. The best technique will possess the following essential property: It will maximize shareholders' wealth. This essential property can be broken down into separate criteria:

---

[5] See Chapter 11 for a discussion of empirical research on this issue.

- All cash flows should be considered.
- The cash flows should be discounted at the opportunity cost of funds.
- The technique should select from a set of mutually exclusive projects the one that maximizes shareholders' wealth.
- Managers should be able to consider one project independently from all others (this is known as the *value-additivity principle*).

The last two criteria need some explanation. *Mutually exclusive projects* are a set from which only one project can be chosen, at the current time. In other words, if a manager chooses to go ahead with one project from the set, he or she cannot choose to take on any of the others. For example, there may be three or four different types of bridges that could be constructed to cross a river at a given site. Choosing a wooden bridge excludes other types (e.g., steel). Projects are also categorized in other ways. *Independent projects* are those that permit a manager to undertake any or all, and *contingent projects* are those that have to be carried out together or not at all. For example, if building a tunnel also requires a ventilation system, then the tunnel and ventilation system should be considered as a single, contingent project.

The fourth criterion, *the value-additivity principle*, implies that if we know the value of separate projects accepted by management, then simply adding their values, V_j, will give us the value of the firm, V. In mathematical terms, if there are N projects, then the value of the firm is

$$V = \sum_{j=1}^{N} V_j. \tag{2.8}$$

This is a particularly important point because it means that projects can be considered on their own merit without the necessity of looking at them in an infinite variety of combinations with other projects.

There are four widely used capital budgeting techniques: (1) the payback method, (2) the accounting rate of return, (3) the net present value, and (4) the internal rate of return. Our task is to choose the technique that best satisfies the four desirable properties discussed above. It will be demonstrated that only one technique—the net present value method—is correct. It is the only technique that (in a world of certainty) is consistent with shareholder wealth maximization.

To provide an example for discussion, Table 2.2 lists the estimates of cash flow for four projects, each of which has a five-year life. Since they are mutually exclusive, there is only one that will maximize shareholders' wealth. We would normally assume at this point that all four projects are equally "risky." However, according to the assumption used throughout this chapter, their cash flows are known with certainty; therefore their risk is zero. The appropriate discount rate in a world with no risk is the risk-free rate (e.g., the Treasury bill rate).

1. The Payback Method

The payback period for a project is simply the number of years it takes to recover the initial cash outlay on a project. The payback period for the four projects in Table 2.2 are:

Project A,   2 years;
Project B,   4 years;
Project C,   4 years;
Project D,   3 years.

Table 2.2 Four Mutually Exclusive Projects

	Cash Flows				
Year	A	B	C	D	PV Factor at 10%
0	−1,000	−1,000	−1,000	−1,000	1.000
1	100	0	100	200	.909
2	900	0	200	300	.826
3	100	300	300	500	.751
4	−100	700	400	500	.683
5	−400	1,300	1,250	600	.621

If management were adhering strictly to the payback method, it would choose project A, which has the shortest payback period. Casual inspection of the cash flows shows that this is clearly wrong. The difficulty with the payback method is that it does not consider all cash flows and it fails to discount them. Failure to consider all cash flows results in ignoring the large negative cash flows that occur in the last two years of project A.[6] Failure to discount them means that management would be indifferent in its choice between project A and a second project that paid $900 in the first year and $100 in the second. Both projects would have the same payback period. We reject the payback method because it violates (at least) the first two of the four properties that are desirable in capital budgeting techniques.[7]

2. The Accounting Rate of Return

The *accounting rate of return* (ARR) is the average after-tax profit divided by the initial cash outlay. It is very similar to (and in some uses exactly the same as) the return on assets (ROA) or the return on investment (ROI); they suffer from the same deficiencies. Assuming for the sake of convenience that the numbers in Table 2.2 are accounting profits, the average after-tax profit for project A is

$$\frac{-1,000 + 100 + 900 + 100 - 100 - 400}{5} = -80,$$

and the ARR is

$$ARR = \frac{\text{Average after-tax profit}}{\text{Initial outlay}} = \frac{-80}{1,000} = -8\%. \tag{2.9}$$

The ARRs for the four projects are

Project A,   ARR = −8%;

Project B,   ARR = 26%;

---

[6] It is not too hard to find real-world examples of projects that have negative future cash flows and cannot be abandoned. A good example is nuclear power plants; at the end of their useful life they must be decommissioned at considerable expense.

[7] See Problem 2.10 at the end of the chapter. It demonstrates that the payback technique also violates the value-additivity principle.

Project C,   ARR = 25%;

Project D,   ARR = 22%.

If we were using the ARR, we would choose project B as the best. The problem with the ARR is that it uses accounting profits instead of cash flows and it does not consider the time value of money. The difference between accounting profits and cash flows has been discussed at length, and it is therefore unnecessary to repeat here why it is incorrect to use the accounting definition of profits. In fact, if the numbers in Table 2.2 were accounting profits, we would need to convert them to cash flows before using the ARR. A second deficiency of ARR is that failure to use the time value of money (i.e., failure to discount) means that managers would be indifferent in their choice between project B and a project with after-tax profits that occur in the opposite chronological order because both projects would have the same accounting rate of return.

3. Net Present Value

The *net present value* (NPV) criterion will accept projects that have an NPV greater than zero. The NPV is computed by discounting the cash flows at the firm's opportunity cost of capital. For the projects in Table 2.2, we assume that the cost of capital is 10%. Therefore the present value of project A is[8]

(Cash Flow)	×	PV Factor	=	PV
−1,000		1.000		−1,000.00
100		.909		90.90
900		.826		734.40
100		.751		75.10
−100		.683		−68.30
−400		.621		−248.40

NPV= −407.30

We have discounted each of the cash flows back to the present and summed them. Mathematically, this can be written as

$$NPV = \sum_{t=1}^{N} \frac{FCF_t}{(1+k)^t} - I_0,$$
(2.10)

where FCF_t is the free cash flow in time period t, I_0 is the initial cash outlay, k is the firm's weighted average cost of capital, and N is the number of years in the project. The net present values of the four projects are

Project A,   NPV = −407.30;

Project B,   NPV = 510.70;

Project C,   NPV = 530.85;

Project D,   NPV = 519.20.

---

[8] The reader who wishes to brush up on the algebra of discounting is referred to Appendix A at the end of the book.

Table 2.3 IRR for Project C

Year	Cash Flow	PV at 10%		PV at 20%		PV at 25%		PV at 22.8%	
0	−1,000	1.000	−1,000.00	1.000	−1,000.00	1.000	−1,000.00	1.000	−1,000.00
1	100	.909	90.90	.833	83.33	.800	80.00	.814	81.40
2	200	.826	165.20	.694	138.80	.640	128.00	.663	132.60
3	300	.751	225.30	.579	173.70	.512	153.60	.540	162.00
4	400	.683	273.20	.482	192.80	.410	163.84	.440	176.00
5	1,250	.621	776.25	.402	502.50	.328	410.00	.358	447.50
			530.85		91.13		−64.56		−.50

If these projects were independent instead of mutually exclusive, we would reject project A and accept B, C, and D. (Why?) Since they are mutually exclusive, we select the project with the greatest NPV, project C. The NPV of the project is exactly the same as the increase in shareholders' wealth. This fact makes it the correct decision rule for capital budgeting purposes. More will be said about this when we compare the NPV rule with the internal rate of return.

4. Internal Rate of Return

The *internal rate of return* (IRR) on a project is defined as that rate which equates the present value of the cash outflows and inflows. In other words, it is the rate that makes the computed NPV exactly zero. Hence this is the rate of return on invested capital that the project is returning to the firm. Mathematically, we solve for the rate of return where the NPV equals zero:

$$NPV = 0 = \sum_{t=1}^{N} \frac{FCF_t}{(1+IRR)^t} - I_0. \tag{2.11}$$

We can solve for the IRR on project C by trial and error. (Most pocket calculators have programs that can quickly solve for the IRR by using iterative techniques.) This is done in Table 2.3 and graphed in Fig. 2.2.

Figure 2.2 shows that the NPV of the given set of cash flows decreases as the discount rate is increased. If the discount rate is zero, there is no time value of money, and the NPV of a project is simply the sum of its cash flows. For project C, the NPV equals $1,250 when the discount rate is zero. At the opposite extreme, if the discount rate is infinite, then future cash flows are valueless, and the NPV of project C is its current cash flow, −$1,000. Somewhat between these two extremes is a discount rate that makes the present value equal to zero. Called the IRR on the project, this rate equates the present value of cash inflows with the present value of cash outflows. The IRRs for the four projects are

Project A,   IRR = −200%;

Project B,   IRR = 20.9%;

Project C,   IRR = 22.8%;

Project D,   IRR = 25.4%.

Figure 2.2 NPV of project C at different discount rates.

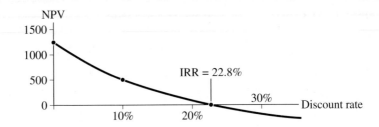

If we use the IRR criterion and the projects are independent, we accept any project that has an IRR greater than the opportunity cost of capital, which is 10%. Therefore, we would accept projects B, C, and D. However, since these projects are mutually exclusive, the IRR rule leads us to accept project D as the best.

F. Comparison of Net Present Value with Internal Rate of Return

As the example shows, the net present value and the internal rate of return can favor conflicting project choices. The net present value favors project C, but the IRR favors project D. Both techniques consider all cash flows and both use the concept of the time value of money in order to discount cash flows. However, we must choose from among the four mutually exclusive projects the one project that maximizes shareholders' wealth. Consequently, only one of the techniques can be correct. We shall see that the NPV criterion is the only one that is necessarily consistent with maximizing shareholders' wealth, given the current set of assumptions.

Figure 2.3 compares projects B, C, and D. For very low discount rates, project B has the highest net present value; for intermediate discount rates, project C is best; and for high discount rates, project D is best. The NPV rule compares three projects at the same discount rate. Remember, 10% was not arbitrarily chosen. It is the market-determined opportunity cost of capital. We saw earlier in the chapter that this market-determined discount rate is the one managers should use if they desire to maximize the wealth of all shareholders. Consequently, no other discount rate is appropriate. Project C is the best project because it gives the greatest NPV when the opportunity cost of funds invested is 10%.

The IRR rule does not discount at the opportunity cost of capital. Instead, it implicitly assumes that the time value of money is the project specific IRR, since all cash flows are discounted at that rate. This implicit assumption has come to be called the *reinvestment rate assumption.*

1. The Reinvestment Rate Assumption

The correct interpretation for the *reinvestment rate* is that it is really the same thing as the opportunity cost of capital. Both the NPV rule and the IRR rule make implicit assumptions about the reinvestment rate. The NPV rule assumes that shareholders can reinvest their money at the *market-determined* opportunity cost of capital, which in our example was 10%. Because 10% is the market-determined opportunity cost of funds, the NPV rule is making the correct reinvestment rate assumption. The projects have the same risk, and therefore their cash flows should be discounted at the same rate (10%).

Figure 2.3 Comparison of three mutually exclusive projects.

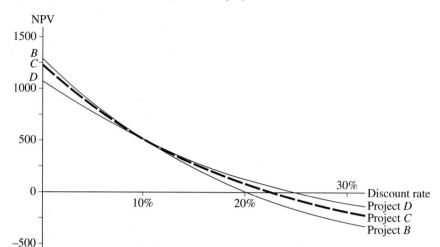

On the other hand, the IRR rule assumes that investors can reinvest their money at the IRR for each project. Therefore, in our example, it assumes that shareholders can reinvest funds in project C at 22.8% and in project D at 25.4%. But we have been told that both projects have the same risk (namely, cash flows are known with certainty). Why should investors be able to reinvest at one rate for project C and at another for project D? Obviously, the implicit reinvestment rate assumption in the IRR rule defies logic. Although the IRR does discount cash flows, it does not discount them at the opportunity cost of capital. Therefore it violates the second of the four properties mentioned earlier. It also violates the Fisher separation theorem discussed in Chapter 1.

2. The Value-Additivity Principle

The fourth of the desirable properties of capital budgeting rules demands that managers be able to consider one project independently of all others. This is known as the *value-additivity principle*, and it implies that the value of the firm is equal to the sum of the values of each of its projects, as in Eq. (2.8). To demonstrate that the IRR rule can violate the value-additivity principle, consider the three projects whose cash flows are given in Table 2.4. Projects 1 and 2 are mutually exclusive, and project 3 is independent of them. If the value-additivity principle holds, we should be able to choose the better of the two mutually exclusive projects without having to consider the independent project. The NPVs of the three projects as well as their IRR are also given in Table 2.4. If we use the IRR rule to choose between projects 1 and 2, we would select project 1. But if we consider combinations of projects, then the IRR rule would prefer projects 2 and 3 to projects 1 and 3. The IRR rule prefers project 1 in isolation but project 2 in combination with the independent project. In this example, the IRR rule does not obey the value-additivity principle. The implication for management is that it would have to consider all possible combinations of projects and choose the combination that has the greatest internal rate

Table 2.4 Example of Value-Additivity

Year	Project 1	Project 2	Project 3	PV Factor at 10%	1 + 3	2 + 3
0	−100	−100	−100	1.000	−200	−200
1	0	225	540	.909	450	675
2	530	0	0	.826	550	0

Project	NPV at 10%	IRR
1	354.30	134.5%
2	104.53	125.0%
3	309.05	350.0%
1 + 3	663.35	212.8%
2 + 3	413.58	237.5%

of return. If, for example, a firm had only five projects, it would need to consider 32 different combinations.[9]

The NPV rule always obeys the value-additivity principle. Given that the opportunity cost of capital is 10%, we would choose project 1 as being the best either by itself or in combination with project 3. Note that the combinations of 1 and 3 or 2 and 3 are simply the sums of the NPVs of the projects considered separately. Consequently, if we adopt the NPV rule, the value of the firm is the sum of the values of the separate projects. Later (in Chapter 6) we shall see that this result holds even in a world with uncertainty where the firm may be viewed as a portfolio of risky projects.

3. Multiple Rates of Return

Still another difficulty with the IRR rule is that it can result in *multiple rates of return* if the stream of estimated cash flows changes sign more than once. A classic example of this situation has come to be known as the *oil well pump problem*. An oil company is trying to decide whether or not to install a high-speed pump on a well that is already in operation. The estimated incremental cash flows are given in Table 2.5. The pump will cost $1,600 to install. During its first year of operation it will produce $10,000 more oil than the pump that is currently in place. But during the second year, the high-speed pump produces $10,000 less oil because the well has been depleted. The question is whether or not to accept the rapid pumping technique, which speeds up cash flows in the near term at the expense of cash flows in the long term. Figure 2.4 shows the NPV of the project for different discount rates. If the opportunity cost of capital is 10%, the NPV rule would reject the project because it has negative NPV at that rate. If we are using the IRR rule, the project has

---

[9] The number of combinations for five projects is

$$\binom{5}{0} + \binom{5}{1} + \binom{5}{2} + \binom{5}{3} + \binom{5}{4} + \binom{5}{5} = 32.$$

Imagine the number of combinations that would have to be considered if there were 50 projects.

Table 2.5 Oil Well Pump Incremental Cash Flows

Year	Estimated Cash Flow
0	−1,600
1	10,000
2	−10,000

Figure 2.4 Multiple internal rates of return.

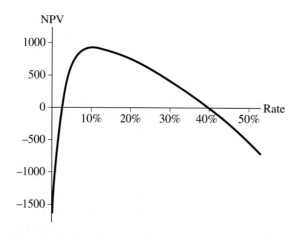

two IRRs, 25% and 400%. Since both exceed the opportunity cost of capital, the project would probably be accepted.

Mathematically, the multiple IRRs are a result of Descartes's rule of signs, which implies that every time the cash flows change signs, there may be a new (positive, real) root to the problem solution. For the above example, the signs of cash flows change twice. The IRR is the rate that causes the discounted value of the cash flows to equal zero. Hence we solve the following equation for IRR:

$$NPV = 0 = \frac{-1,600}{(1+IRR)^0} + \frac{10,000}{(1+IRR)^1} + \frac{-10,000}{(1+IRR)^2}$$

$$0 = \frac{-1,600(1+IRR)^2 + 10,000(1+IRR) - 10,000}{(1+IRR)^2}$$

$$0 = 1,600(1+IRR)^2 - 10,000(1+IRR) + 10,000.$$

This is clearly a quadratic equation and has two roots. It has the general form

$$ax^2 + bx + c = 0$$

and can be solved using the quadratic formula

$$x = \frac{-b \pm \sqrt{b^2 - 4ac}}{2a}.$$

Therefore for our example the roots are

$$(1 + IRR) = x = \frac{10,000 \pm \sqrt{10,000^2 - 4(1,600)10,000}}{2(1,600)}$$

$$(1 + IRR) = \frac{10,000 \pm 6,000}{3,200}$$

$$IRR = 25\% \quad \text{or} \quad 400\%.$$

An *economic interpretation of the multiple root problem* is that we can think of the project as an investment, with the firm putting money into it twice: $-1,600$ at the time of the initial investment, and $-10,000$ in the second time period. Let us assume that the positive cash flows provided by the project to the firm are lent at 10%, which is the opportunity cost of capital. This assumption makes sense because the +10,000 received by the firm cannot be invested in another oil well pump (only one is available). Therefore it is appropriate to assume that the +10,000 received by the firm in the first period is reinvested at the opportunity cost of capital, namely, 10%. On the other hand, the firm expects to earn the IRR (whatever it is) on the cash flows it puts into the project. Therefore the firm invests $-1,600$ now and expects to earn the IRR at the end of the first time period. Mathematically, the value at the end of the first period should be

$$1,600(1 + IRR).$$

The difference between this result and the amount of money (+10,000) that the project lends to the firm at the opportunity cost of capital, 10%, in the second period is the amount borrowed at rate k. The net amount lent to the firm is given in brackets below. The future value of this amount in the second period is the net amount multiplied by $(1 + k)$:

$$[10,000 - 1,600(1 + IRR)](1 + k).$$

The firm then invests $-10,000$ at the end of the second period. This is set equal to the future value of the project that was given above. The result is

$$10,000 = [10,000 - 1,600(1 + IRR)](1 + k).$$

Recalling that the opportunity cost of capital, k, is 10%, we can solve for the rate of return on investment:

$$\frac{10,000 - 11,000}{-1,760} = 1 + IRR$$

$$-43.18\% = IRR.$$

This way of looking at the cash flows of the project solves the multiple root problem because the cash flows lent to the firm are assumed to be provided at a known rate of return equal to the opportunity cost of capital. This makes it possible to isolate the rate of return on money invested in the project. This rate can be thought of as the IRR. For the example of the oil well pump, we see that when it is viewed properly, the IRR gives the same answer as the NPV. We should reject the project because internal rate of return is less than the opportunity cost of capital.

4. Summary of Comparison of IRR and NPV

The IRR rule errs in several ways. First it does not obey the value-additivity principle, and consequently managers who use the IRR cannot consider projects independently of each other. Second, the IRR rule assumes that funds invested in projects have opportunity costs equal to the IRR for the project. This implicit reinvestment rate assumption violates the requirement that cash flows be discounted at the market-determined opportunity cost of capital. Finally, the IRR rule can lead to multiple rates of return whenever the sign of cash flows changes more than once. However, we saw that this problem can be avoided by the simple expedient of assuming that all cash flows are loaned to the firm by the project at the market opportunity cost, and that the rate of return on cash flows invested in the project is the IRR.

The NPV rule avoids all the problems the IRR is heir to. It obeys the value-additivity principle, it correctly discounts at the opportunity cost of funds, and most important, it is precisely the same thing as maximizing the shareholders' wealth.

G. *C*ash Flows for Capital Budgeting Purposes

Up to this point we have made the implicit assumptions that the firm has no debt and that there are no corporate taxes. This section adds a note of realism by providing a definition of cash flows for capital budgeting purposes, given debt and taxes. In particular, we shall see that some cash flows, such as interest paid on debt and repayment of principal on debt, should not be considered *cash flows for capital budgeting purposes*. At the same time, we shall demonstrate, by using an example, that there is only one definition of cash flows that is consistent with shareholder wealth maximization. Later on, in Chapter 14, we will provide an even more detailed definition of cash flows that starts with the public accounting statements of a company, extracts the correct definition of cash flows, and uses them to value the company.

To understand discounted cash flows it is necessary to have a rudimentary understanding of the opportunity cost of capital of the firm. Chapter 15 discusses the cost of capital in great depth; however, the basics will be given here. The firm receives its investment funds from two classes of investors: creditors and shareholders. They provide debt and equity capital, respectively. Both groups expect to receive a rate of return that compensates them for the level of risk they accept.[10] Debt holders receive a stream of fixed payments and can force the firm to receivership or bankruptcy if they do not receive payment. On the other hand, shareholders receive the firm's residual cash flows that remain after all other payments are made. Consequently, the interest paid to debt holders is less than the required rate of return on equity because debt is less risky.

It is important to understand that projects undertaken by the firm must earn enough cash flow to provide the required rate of return to creditors, repayment of the face amount of debt, and payment of expected dividends to shareholders. Only when cash flows exceed these amounts will there be any gain in shareholders' wealth. When we discount cash flows at the weighted average cost of capital, this is exactly what we are saying. A positive NPV is achieved only after creditors and shareholders receive their expected risk-adjusted rates of return.

In order to provide an example of this very important concept, consider the following (somewhat artificial) situation. A firm is going to be created from scratch. It will require an initial investment,

---

[10] The assumption that future cash flows are known with certainty must be relaxed at this point, in order to allow risk-free debt and risky equity.

Table 2.6 Pro Forma Income Statement

Rev	Revenue	1,300
− VC	Variable costs	−600
− FCC	Fixed cash costs	0
− dep.	Noncash charges (depreciation)	−200
EBIT	Earnings before interest and taxes	500
− $k_d D$	Interest expenses	−50
EBT	Earnings before taxes	450
− T	Taxes @ 50%	−225
NI	Net income	225

I, of $1,000 for equipment that will depreciate at the rate of $200 per year. The owners have decided to borrow $500 at 10% interest. In other words, the before-tax coupon rate on debt capital, k_d, is 10%. The expected annual cash flows for the project are implicit in the pro forma income statement given in Table 2.6. We shall assume that shareholders require a rate of return of 30% in order to compensate them for the riskiness of their position. Thus, the cost of equity, k_s, is 30%.

To provide the simplest possible example, assume that all cash flows are perpetual (i.e., the firm has no growth). This assumption has the effect of keeping the firm's market value debt-to-equity ratio constant through time.[11] Perpetual cash flows are obtained, first, by writing a consol bond that never matures and pays a coupon of $50 each year, and second, by investing $200 annually to replace the depreciation of the equipment.

Table 2.7 details the exact cash flows assuming that the project is held for five years. At the end of five years the firm will be sold for its market value. Shareholders will receive cash, use some of it ($500) to pay off bondholders, and keep the remainder.

Current cash flows are $500 provided by creditors and $500 from equity holders; outflows are $1,000 paid for the equipment. In years 1 through 5 the project returns $700 in cash after the cash costs of production ($600) are subtracted from revenues ($1,300). Then depreciation, a noncash charge ($200), is deducted, leaving $500 in earnings before interest and taxes. The deduction of $50 of interest expenses leaves taxable income of $450. After taxes (at a 50% rate), there is $225 in net income. To compute *free cash flows* available for payment to shareholders, depreciation ($200), a noncash charge, must be added back, and replacement investment ($200), a cash outflow, must be subtracted. Thus residual cash flow available to shareholders is $225 per year.

Shareholders' wealth, S, is the present value of their stream of residual cash flows, discounted at the cost of equity capital, $k_s = 30\%$. Recalling that their stream of residual cash flows continues forever, we can compute their wealth as[12]

$$S = \frac{\text{Residual cash flow}}{k_s} = \frac{\$225}{.3} = \$750.$$

---

[11] Without constant debt-to-equity ratio, the weighted average cost of capital would change through time, and the problem would become much more complex.

[12] This formula is exact for perpetual cash flows. See Appendix A at the end of the book.

Table 2.7 Total Cash Flows for the Project

Year	Inflow	Outflow	Depre- ciation	Replacement Investment	EBIT	Interest	Taxable Income	Tax	Net Income	Residual Cash Flow
0	1,000	−1,000								
1	700		200	−200	500	−50	450	−225	225	225
2	700		200	−200	500	−50	450	−225	225	225
3	700		200	−200	500	−50	450	−225	225	225
4	700		200	−200	500	−50	450	−225	225	225
5	700	−500	200	−200	500	−50	450	−225	225	225 + 1,250

The present value of bondholders' wealth, B, is the present value of their perpetual stream of coupon payments discounted at the market cost of debt, k_b:

$$B = \frac{\text{Interest payments}}{k_b} = \frac{\$50}{.10} = \$500.$$

Thus we see that the market value of the firm, V, is expected to be

$$V = B + S = \$500 + \$750 = \$1,250.$$

Note that the present value of debt and equity are not affected by the fact that they will be sold at the end of year 5. The new bondholders and shareholders simply take ownership of their streams of cash, paying $500 and $750, respectively. As shown in the last row of Table 2.7, the shareholders receive $1250 in year 5 for the firm but must pay $500 to bondholders. Note also that the present value of shareholders' wealth is $750, but they had to put up $500 of the initial investment. Therefore their change in wealth, ΔS, is $750 minus $500, which equals $250. We shall see that this is exactly the same thing as the NPV of the project.

Instead of working through the complicated procedure given above, it will be easier to analyze *capital budgeting projects* by defining cash flows for capital budgeting purposes and discounting them at the firm's weighted average cost of capital. First, what is the weighted average cost of capital ($k = WACC$)? As shown in Eq. (2.12), it is the after-tax market cost of debt capital ($k_b(1 - \tau_c)$), multiplied by the percentage of the market value of the firm owned by creditors, $B/(B + S)$, plus the cost of equity, k_s, multiplied by the percentage of the firm's value owned by shareholders, $S/(B + S)$. Note that τ_c is the firm's marginal tax rate.

$$k = WACC = k_b(1 - \tau_c)\frac{B}{B + S} + k_s\frac{S}{B + S} \tag{2.12}$$

$$= .10(1 - .5)(.4) + .30 (.6) = 20\%$$

In a world without any taxes, the cost of capital would simply be a weighted average of the costs of debt and equity. However, in the real world, the government allows corporations to deduct the interest paid on debt as an expense before paying taxes. This tax shield on interest payments makes the cost of debt even less expensive from the firm's point of view. The weighted average cost of capital is the same as the after-tax market-determined opportunity cost of funds provided to the firm.

After determining the after-tax weighted average cost of capital, we need to find a definition of cash flow for use in standard capital budgeting procedures that is consistent with maximizing shareholders' wealth. The appropriate definition of *net cash flow for capital budgeting purposes* is after-tax cash flows from operations, assuming that the firm has no debt and net of gross investment, ΔI. This investment includes any changes in operating working capital (e.g., an increase in inventories), but our simple example has no working capital, so turn to Chapter 14 for a more detailed exposition. Marginal operating cash flows for a project are the change in revenues, ΔRev, minus the change in the direct costs that include variable costs of operations, ΔVC, and the change in fixed cash costs, ΔFCC, such as property taxes and administrative salaries and wages:

$$\text{Marginal (before tax) operating cash flows} = \Delta Rev - \Delta VC - \Delta FCC.$$

But to maintain the operating capacity of a firm it is necessary to invest; therefore not all cash flows are available for payment to the suppliers of capital. Investment must be subtracted from operating cash flows. Operating cash flows net of investment, ΔI, are called *free operating cash flows:*

$$\text{Free operating cash flows (before tax)} = \Delta Rev - \Delta VC - \Delta FCC - \Delta I.$$

Taxes on operating cash flows are the tax rate, τ_c, times the change in revenues minus the change in direct cash costs and depreciation (Δdep).[13]

$$\text{Taxes on operating cash flows} = \tau_c(\Delta Rev - \Delta VC - \Delta dep - \Delta FCC).$$

Therefore the correct definition of cash flows for capital budgeting purposes is free operating cash flows minus taxes on free operating cash flows.[14]

$$
\begin{aligned}
\text{FCF for cap. budgeting} &= (\Delta Rev - \Delta VC - \Delta FCC) \\
&\quad - \tau_c(\Delta Rev - \Delta VC - \Delta FCC - \Delta dep) - \Delta I \\
&= (\Delta Rev - \Delta VC - \Delta FCC)(1 - \tau_c) + \tau_c(\Delta dep) - \Delta I \\
&= (\Delta Rev - \Delta VC - \Delta FCC - \Delta dep)(1 - \tau_c) + \Delta dep - \Delta I \\
&= EBIT(1 - \tau_c) + \Delta dep - \Delta I
\end{aligned}
\tag{2.13}
$$

Note that *EBIT* is defined as earnings before interest and taxes. The definition of free cash flow is very different from the accounting definition of net income. Cash flows for capital budgeting purposes can be thought of as the after-tax cash flows the firm would have if it had no debt. Interest

---

[13] Depreciation is a noncash charge against revenues. If there are other noncash charges, they should also be included here.

[14] An equivalent definition is

$$\text{FCF for capital budgeting} = \Delta NI + \Delta dep + (1 - \tau_c)\Delta(k_d D) - \Delta I, \tag{2.13a}$$

where ΔNI stands for the change in net income, the accounting definition of profit, and $\Delta k_d D$ is the change in the coupon rate, k_d, on debt times the change in the face value of debt, D. Although sometimes easier to use, it obscures the difference between cash flows for budgeting purposes and the accounting definition of profit.

Table 2.8 Cash Flows for Capital Budgeting

Year	Operating Cash Flow	Subtract Depreciation	EBIT	Tax* on EBIT	Add Back Depreciation	Investment	Free Cash Flow
0	−1,000						−1,000
1	700	(200)	500	250	200	(200)	250
2	700	(200)	500	250	200	(200)	250
3	700	(200)	500	250	200	(200)	250
4	700	(200)	500	250	200	(200)	250
5	700	(200)	500	250	200	(200)	250

* The tax on operating income, also called EBIT, earnings before interest and taxes, that is, .5(500).

expenses and their tax shield are not included in the definition of cash flow for capital budgeting purposes. The reason is that when we discount at the weighted average cost of capital we are implicitly assuming that the project will return the expected interest payments to creditors and the expected dividends to shareholders. Hence inclusion of interest payments (or dividends) as a cash flow to be discounted would be double counting. Furthermore, the tax shield provided by depreciation, $\tau_c(\Delta dep)$, is treated as if it were a cash inflow. Table 2.8 shows the appropriate cash flows for budgeting purposes using the numbers from the example we have been using. To demonstrate that these are the correct cash flows, we can discount them at the weighted average cost of capital. The resulting number should exactly equal the increment to the shareholders' wealth, that is, $250 (see Table 2.9). It is no coincidence that it works out correctly. We are discounting the after-tax cash flows from operations at the weighted average cost of capital. Thus the NPV of the project is exactly the same thing as the increase in shareholders' wealth.

One of the advantages of discounting the firm's free cash flows at the after-tax weighted average cost of capital is that this technique separates the investment decisions of the firm from its financing decisions. The definition of free cash flows shows what the firm will earn after taxes, assuming that it has no debt capital. Thus changes in the firm's debt-to-equity ratio have no effect on the definition of cash flows for capital budgeting purposes. The effect of financial decisions (e.g., changes in the ratio of debt to equity) is reflected in the firm's weighted average cost of capital.

The theory of the firm's cost of capital is discussed in greater detail in Chapter 15. In most applications it is assumed that the firm has an optimal ratio of debt to equity, which is called the *target capital structure*. For the firm as a whole, the ratio of debt to equity is assumed to remain constant across time even though the financing for individual projects may require that debt be paid off over the life of the project. Without this assumption, the cost of capital would have to change each time period.

Another relevant issue worth pointing out is that the definition of cash flows for capital budgeting purposes includes all incremental cash flows attributable to a project. Too often, analysts forget that the total investment in a project includes working capital requirements as well as the cash outlays for buildings and equipment. Working capital includes any changes in short-term balance sheet items such as increases in inventories, accounts receivable, and accounts payable that are expected to result from undertaking a project. Net working capital requirements are the difference between changes in short-term assets and short-term liabilities.

Table 2.9 NPV of Free Cash Flows

Year	Free Cash Flow	PV Factor at 20%	PV
0	−1,000	1.000	−1,000.00
1	250	.833	208.33
2	250	.694	173.61
3	250	.579	144.68
4	250	.482	120.56
5	250	.401	100.47
5*	1,250	.401	502.35
			250.00

* Recall that in year 5 the firm was sold for a market value of $1,250. This amount is the present value of cash flows from year 5 on, that is, $250 \div .20 = 1,250$.

H. Relaxing the Assumptions

It is useful to give a preview of things to come—the next steps in making the analysis of investment decisions more and more realistic. Although the net present value criterion is certainly multiperiod in scope, we must relax the assumption of certainty in order to make it more realistic. Implicitly, we have also assumed that the only decision that can be made is to either accept or reject the project today—call it a precommitment assumption. This precommitment is equivalent to assuming that there is no flexibility in decision making. This is a major shortcoming of the NPV decision tool that has been described in this chapter—a flaw that is rectified in Chapter 9.

Managers often decide to actually accept negative NPV projects. Why? Their intuition tells them that they can manage the project, once it gets started, in ways that alter the expected cash flows that were used in the NPV analysis. For example, once the project begins, if it turns out to be more profitable than expected, the manager can expand it by spending further investment. As we shall see, this expansion option is an American call on the value of the project and the new investment is its exercise price. Another option that the manager has is to extend the life of the project. If the project turns out to be worse than expected, the manager can decrease its scale, or abandon it altogether. Finally, there is an option to defer the start of the project—a deferral option. Every project has these options to respond to the resolution of uncertainty in the future. Unfortunately NPV analysis, as described in this chapter, implicitly assumes precommitment and therefore ignores these sources of additional value that are contained in managerial flexibility. Therefore, NPV systematically undervalues every project, the only question is by how much. Chapter 9 introduces the reader to the use of what is called real options analysis—a somewhat more complicated but much more realistic decision tool.

$\mathcal{S}$ummary

The objective of the firm is assumed to be the maximization of shareholders' wealth. Toward this end, managers should take projects with positive NPV. Other decision criteria, such as the payback method, the accounting rate of return, and the IRR, do not necessarily guarantee undertaking projects that maximize shareholders' wealth.

PROBLEM SET

2.1 *Basic capital budgeting problem with straight-line depreciation.* The Roberts Company has cash inflows of $140,000 per year on project A and cash outflows of $100,000 per year. The investment outlay on the project is $100,000. Its life is 10 years. The tax rate, τ_c, is 40%. The opportunity cost of capital is 12%.

> **(a)** Present two alternative formulations of the net cash flows adjusted for the depreciation tax shelter.
> **(b)** Calculate the net present value for project A, using straight-line depreciation for tax purposes.

2.2 *Basic capital budgeting problem with accelerated depreciation.* Assume the same facts as in Problem 2.1 except that the earnings before depreciation, interest, and taxes is $22,000 per year.

> **(a)** Calculate the net present value, using straight-line depreciation for tax purposes.
> **(b)** Calculate the net present value, using the sum-of-the-years digits method of accelerated depreciation, for tax purposes.[15]

2.3 *Basic replacement problem.* The Virginia Company is considering replacing a riveting machine with a new design that will increase earnings before depreciation from $20,000 per year to $51,000 per year. The new machine will cost $100,000 and has an estimated life of eight years, with no salvage value. The applicable corporate tax rate is 40%, and the firm's cost of capital is 12%. The old machine has been fully depreciated and has no salvage value. Should it be replaced with a new machine?

2.4 *Replacement problem when old machine has a positive book value.* Assume the same facts as in Problem 2.3 except that the new machine will have a salvage value of $12,000. Assume further that the old machine has a book value of $40,000, with a remaining life of eight years. If replaced, the old machine can, at present, be sold for $15,000. Should the machine replacement be made?

2.5 *Cash flows.* The Cary Company is considering a new investment that costs $10,000. It will last five years and has no salvage value. The project would save $3,000 in salaries and wages each year and would be financed with a loan with interest costs of 15% per year and amortization costs (repayment of principal on the loan) of $2,000 per year. If the firm's tax rate is 40% and its after-tax cost of capital is 20%, what is the net present value of the project? (*Note:* The annuity factor for five years at 20% is 2.991.)

---

[15] Depreciation in year 1 of a 5-year project is 5 divided by the sum of the digits for years 1 through 5, that is, 15.

2.6 Calculate the internal rate of return for the following set of cash flows:

$$t_1: \qquad 400$$
$$t_2: \qquad 400$$
$$t_3: \quad -1,000$$

If the opportunity cost of capital is 10%, should the project be accepted?

2.7 Calculate the internal rate of return on the following set of cash flows:

$$t_0: \quad -1,000$$
$$t_1: \qquad 100$$
$$t_2: \qquad 900$$
$$t_3: \qquad 100$$
$$t_4: \quad -100$$
$$t_5: \quad -400$$

2.8 The Ambergast Corporation is considering a project that has a three-year life and costs $1,200. It would save $360 per year in operating costs and increase revenue by $200 per year. It would be financed with a three-year loan with the following payment schedule (the annual rate of interest is 5%):

Payment	Interest	Repayment of Principal	Balance
440.65	60.00	380.65	819.35
440.65	40.97	399.68	419.67
440.65	20.98	419.67	0
	121.95	1,200.00	

If the company has a 10% after-tax weighted average cost of capital, has a 40% tax rate, and uses straight-line depreciation, what is the net present value of the project?

2.9 The treasurer of United Southern Capital Co. has submitted a proposal to the board of directors that, he argues, will increase profits for the all-equity company by a whopping 55%. It costs $900 and saves $290 in labor costs, providing a 3.1-year payback even though the equipment has an expected 5-year life (with no salvage value). If the firm has a 50% tax rate, uses straight-line depreciation, and has a 10% weighted average cost of capital, should the project be accepted? Income statements before and after the project are given in Tables Q2.9A and Q2.9B, respectively.

2.10 The cash flows for projects A, B, and C are given below. Calculate the payback period and net present value for each project (assume a 10% discount rate). If A and B are mutually exclusive and C is independent, which project, or combination of projects, is preferred using (a) the payback method or (b) the net present value method? What do the results tell you about the value-additivity properties of the payback method?

Table Q2.9A

Before	Year 1	Year 2	Year 3	Year 4	Year 5
Revenue	1,000	1,000	1,000	1,000	1,000
Variable cost	500	500	500	500	500
Depreciation	300	300	300	300	300
Net operating income	200	200	200	200	200
Interest expense	0	0	0	0	0
Earnings before taxes	200	200	200	200	200
Taxes	−100	−100	−100	−100	−100
Net income	100	100	100	100	100

Table Q2.9B

After	Year 1	Year 2	Year 3	Year 4	Year 5
Revenue	1,000	1,000	1,000	1,000	1,000
Variable cost	210	210	210	210	210
Depreciation	480	480	480	480	480
Net operating income	310	310	310	310	310
Interest expense	0	0	0	0	0
Earnings before taxes	310	310	310	310	310
Taxes	−155	−155	−155	−155	−155
Net income	155	155	155	155	155

	Project		
Year	A	B	C
0	−1	−1	−1
1	0	1	0
2	2	0	0
3	−1	1	3

2.11 Calculate the internal rate of return on the following set of cash flows, according to the economic interpretation of internal rate of return near the end of Section F.3. Assume that the opportunity cost of capital is $k = 10\%$.

Year	Cash Flow
0	−5,000
1	10,000
2	−3,000

REFERENCES

Alchian, A., and H. Demsetz, "Production, Information Costs, and Economic Organization," *American Economic Review*, 1972, 777–795.

Bierman, H., Jr., and S. Smidt, *The Capital Budgeting Decision*, 4th ed. Macmillan, New York, 1975.

Bodenhorn, D., "A Cash Flow Concept of Profit," *Journal of Finance*, March 1964, 16–31.

Coase, R. H., "The Nature of the Firm," *Economica*, 1937, 386–405.

Cyert, R. M., and J. G. March, *A Behavioral Theory of the Firm*. Prentice-Hall, Englewood Cliffs, N.J., 1963.

Gagnon, J. M., "The Purchase-Pooling Choice: Some Empirical Evidence," *Journal of Accounting Research*, Spring 1971, 52–72.

Hirshleifer, J., *Investment, Interest, and Capital*. Prentice-Hall, Englewood Cliffs, N.J., 1970.

Hong, J, R. S. Kaplan, and G. Mandelker, "Pooling vs. Purchase: The Effects of Accounting Mergers on Stock Prices," *Accounting Review*, January 1978, 31–47.

Jensen, M., and W. Meckling, "Theory of the Firm: Managerial Behavior, Agency Costs and Ownership Structure," *Journal of Financial Economics*, October 1976, 305–360.

Machlup, F., "Theories of the Firm: Marginalist, Behavior, Managerial," *American Economic Review*, March 1967, 1–33.

Marschak, J., and R. Radner, *Economic Theory of Teams* (Cowles Foundation Monograph 22). Yale University Press, New Haven, Conn., 1972.

Stern, J., "Earnings per Share Doesn't Count," *Financial Analysts Journal*, July–August 1974, 39–43.

Sunder, S., "Relationship between Accounting Changes and Stock Prices: Problems of Measurement and Some Empirical Evidence," *Empirical Research in Accounting: Selected Studies*, 1973, 1–45.

———, "Stock Price and Risk Related to Accounting Changes in Inventory Valuation," *Accounting Review*, April 1975, 305–315.

Teichroew, D., *An Introduction to Management Science: Deterministic Models*. Wiley, New York, 1964, 78–82.

Williamson, O. E., *The Economics of Discretionary Behavior: Managerial Objectives in a Theory of the Firm*. Prentice-Hall, Englewood Cliffs, N.J., 1964.

The Theory of Choice: Utility Theory Given Uncertainty

ECONOMICS IS THE STUDY of how people and societies choose to allocate scarce resources and distribute wealth among one another and over time. Therefore one must understand the objects of choice and the method of choice. The following two chapters (Chapters 4 and 5) are devoted to the objects of choice faced by an investor. Here, we focus on the theory of how people make choices when faced with uncertainty. Later on—once the theory of choice and the objects of choice are understood—we shall combine them in order to produce a theory of optimal decision-making under uncertainty. In particular, we shall study the allocation of resources in an economic society where prices provide a system of signals for optimal allocation. There are, however, other means of allocation. Instead of using prices, we might allow an individual or committee to make all the allocation decisions, or we might program allocational rules into an algorithm run by machine.

We shall begin with a discussion of the axioms of behavior used by economists. However, before rushing into them, we must recognize that there are other theories of behavior. Social sciences such as anthropology, psychology, political science, sociobiology, and sociology also provide great insight into the theory of choice. And very early in this chapter we shall be forced to recognize that individuals have different tastes for the time preference of consumption and different degrees of risk aversion. Economic theory recognizes these differences but has little to say about why they exist or what causes them.[1] The other social sciences study these problems. However, as we shall see, there is much one can say about the theory of choice under uncertainty without, for example, understanding why a 70-year-old person is more or less risk averse than the same person at 20, or why some people prefer meat, whereas others prefer vegetables.

The theory of investor choice is only one corner of what has come to be known as utility theory. Most students are already familiar with the microeconomic price theory treatment of choices

---

[1] An interesting exception is an article by Rubin and Paul [1979] that suggests a theory of why people exhibit different attitudes toward risk at different stages in their lives.

Figure 3.1 Indifference curves for various types of choices between: (a) consumption goods under certainty; (b) consumption and investment under certainty; (c) risk and return.

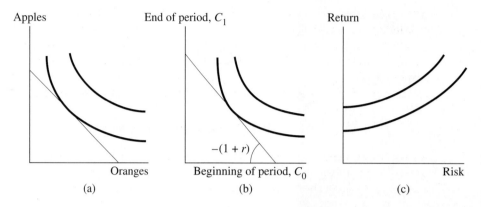

(a)   (b)   (c)

among various bundles of perishable commodities such as apples and oranges at an instant in time. The indifference curves that result are shown in Fig. 3.1(a). Another type of choice available to individuals is whether to consume now or to save (invest) and consume more at a later date. This is the utility theory of choices over time, which is fundamental for understanding interest rates. This type of one-period consumption/ investment decision was discussed in Chapter 1 and is illustrated in Fig. 3.1(b). Our main concern here is the choice between timeless risky alternatives, which we call the theory of investor choice. The theory begins with nothing more than five assumptions about the behavior of individuals when confronted with the task of ranking risky alternatives and the assumption of nonsatiation (i.e., greed). The theory ends by parameterizing the objects of choice as the mean and variance of return and by mapping trade-offs between them that provide equal utility to investors. These mappings are indifference curves for timeless (or one-period) choices under uncertainty. They are shown in Fig. 3.1(c) and are used extensively in Chapters 5 and 6.

A. $\mathscr{F}$ive Axioms of Choice under Uncertainty

To develop a theory of rational decision making in the face of uncertainty, it is necessary to make some precise assumptions about an individual's behavior. Known as the *axioms of cardinal utility*, these assumptions provide the minimum set of conditions for consistent and rational behavior. Once they are established, all the remaining theory must follow.[2]

> **AXIOM 1** *Comparability (sometimes called completeness).* For the entire set, S, of uncertain alternatives, an individual can say either that outcome x is preferred to outcome y (we write this as $x \succ y$) or y is preferred to x ($y \succ x$) or the individual is indifferent as to x and y ($x \sim y$).[3]

> **AXIOM 2** *Transitivity (sometimes called consistency).* If an individual prefers x to y and y to z, then x is preferred to z. (If $x \succ y$ and $y \succ z$, then $x \succ z$.) If an individual is indifferent as to

---

[2] The notation and much of the conceptual outline follow the development found in Fama and Miller [1972].

[3] The symbol used to indicate preference ($\succ$) is not a mathematical inequality. It can rank only preferences. For example, an individual may prefer one Picasso to two Rembrandts, or vice versa.

x and y and is also indifferent as to y and z, then he or she is indifferent as to x and z. (If $x \sim y$ and $y \sim z$, then $y \sim z$.)

AXIOM 3 *Strong independence.* Suppose we construct a gamble where an individual has a probability α of receiving outcome x and a probability of $(1 - \alpha)$ of receiving outcome z. We shall write this gamble as $G(x, z : \alpha)$. Strong independence says that if the individual is indifferent as to x and y, then he or she will also be indifferent as to a first gamble, set up between x with probability α and a mutually exclusive outcome, z, and a second gamble, set up between y with probability α and the same mutually exclusive outcome, z.

$$\text{If } x \sim y, \text{ then } G(x, z : \alpha) \sim G(y, z : \alpha)$$

AXIOM 4 *Measurability.* If outcome y is preferred less than x but more than z, then there is a unique α (a probability) such that the individual will be indifferent between y and a gamble between x with probability α and z with probability $(1 - \alpha)$.[4]

$$\text{If } x \succ y \succeq z \text{ or } x \succeq y \succ z, \text{ then there exists a unique } \alpha, \text{ such that } y \sim G(x, z : \alpha).$$

AXIOM 5 *Ranking.* If alternatives y and u both lie somewhere between x and z and we can establish gambles such that an individual is indifferent between y and a gamble between x (with probability α_1) and z, while also indifferent between u and a second gamble, this time between x (with probability α_2) and z, then if α_1 is greater than α_2, y is preferred to u.

$$\text{If } x \succeq y \succeq z \text{ and } x \succeq u \succeq z, \text{ then if } y \sim G(x, z : \alpha_1)$$

$$\text{and } u \sim G(x, z : \alpha_2), \text{ it follows that if } \alpha_1 > \alpha_2, \text{ then } y \succ u,$$

$$\text{or if } \alpha_1 = \alpha_2, \text{ then } y \sim u.$$

These axioms of cardinal utility boil down to the following assumptions about behavior. First, all individuals are assumed to always make completely rational decisions. A statement that "I like Chevrolets more than Fords and Fords more than Toyotas but Toyotas more than Chevrolets" is not rational. Second, people are assumed to be able to make these rational choices among thousands of alternatives—not a very simple task.

The axiom of strong independence is usually the hardest to accept. To illustrate it, consider the following example. Let outcome x be winning a left shoe, let y be a right shoe, and let z also be a right shoe. Imagine two gambles. The first is a 50/50 chance of winning x or z (i.e., a left shoe or a right shoe). The second gamble is a 50/50 chance of winning x or z (i.e., a right shoe or a right shoe). If we were originally indifferent between our choice of a left shoe (by itself) or a right shoe (by itself), then strong independence implies that we will also be indifferent between the two gambles we constructed. Of course, left shoes and right shoes are complementary goods, and we would naturally prefer to have both if possible. The point of strong independence is that outcome z in the above examples is always mutually exclusive. In the first gamble, the payoffs are the left shoe or a right shoe but never both. The mutual exclusiveness of the third alternative z is critical to the axiom of strong independence.

---

[4] The reason for bounding y on only one side or the other is to eliminate the possibility of $x \sim y \sim z$, in which case any α would satisfy the indifference condition required by the gamble.

Next, we need to answer the question, How do individuals rank various combinations of risky alternatives? We can use the axioms of preference to show how preferences can be mapped into measurable utility. How do we establish a utility function that allows the assignment of a unit measure (a number) to various alternatives so that we can look at the number and know that if, for example, the utility of x is 35 and the utility of y is 27, then x is preferred to y? To do this we need to discuss two properties of utility functions.

B. $\mathcal{D}$eveloping Utility Functions

The utility function will have two properties. First, it will be order preserving. In other words, if we measure the utility of x as greater than the utility of y, $U(x) > U(y)$, it means that x is actually preferred to y ($x \succ y$). Second, expected utility can be used to rank combinations of risky alternatives. Mathematically, this means that

$$U[G(x, y : \alpha)] = \alpha U(x) + (1 - \alpha)U(y). \tag{3.1}$$

To prove that utility functions are order preserving, consider the set of risky outcomes, S, which is assumed to be bounded above by outcome a and below by outcome b. Next consider two intermediate outcomes x and y such that

$$a \succ x \succeq b \quad \text{or} \quad a \succeq x \succ b$$

and

$$a \succ y \succeq b \quad \text{or} \quad a \succeq y \succ b.$$

By using Axiom 4 (measurability), we can choose unique probabilities for x and y in order to construct the following gambles:

$$x \sim G(a, b : \alpha(x)), \qquad y \sim G(a, b : \alpha(y)).$$

Then we can use Axiom 5 (ranking) so that the probabilities $\alpha(x)$ and $\alpha(y)$ can be interpreted as numerical utilities that uniquely rank x and y. By Axiom 5:

$$\text{If } \alpha(x) > \alpha(y), \text{ then } x \succ y.$$
$$\text{If } \alpha(x) = \alpha(y), \text{ then } x \sim y.$$
$$\text{If } \alpha(x) < \alpha(y), \text{ then } x \prec y.$$

In this way, we have developed an order-preserving utility function. The maximum and minimum outcomes, a and b, may be assigned any number at all (e.g., let $a = 100$ and $b = 0$). Then by forming simple gambles, we can assign cardinal utility numbers to the intermediate outcomes x and y.

Next it is important to show that expected utility can be used to rank risky alternatives. This is the second property of utility functions. Let us begin by establishing the elementary gambles in exactly the same way as before. This is illustrated in Fig. 3.2. Next, consider a third alternative, z. Note that we can rely on Axiom 3 (strong independence) to say that the choice of z will not affect the relationship between x and y. Next, by Axiom 4, there must exist a unique probability, $\beta(z)$,

Figure 3.2 Elementary gambles.

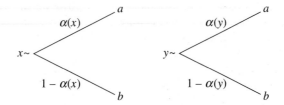

Figure 3.3 Outcome z compared with a gamble between x and y.

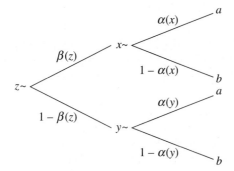

that would make us indifferent as to outcome z and a gamble between x and y (see Fig. 3.3). Now we can relate z to the elemental prospects a and b. If we can trace the branches in the decision tree represented by Fig. 3.3, we will be indifferent between z and outcome a with probability $\gamma = \beta(z)\alpha(x) + (1 - \beta(z))\,\alpha(y)$ and outcome b with probability $(1 - \gamma)$. This is shown in Figure 3.4. We can write the gamble as follows:

$$z \sim G[a, b : \beta(z)\alpha(x) + (1 - \beta(z))\alpha(y)].$$

Now, we have already established, by Axioms 4 and 5, that utilities of x and y can be represented by their probabilities; that is, $U(x) = \alpha(x)$ and $U(y) = \alpha(y)$. Therefore the above gamble can be written as

$$z \sim G[a, b : \beta(z)U(x) + (1 - \beta(z))U(y)].$$

Finally, by using Axioms 4 and 5 a second time, it must be true that the unique probability of outcome z can be used as a cardinal measure of its utility relative to the elemental prospects of a and b. Therefore we have

$$U(z) = \beta(z)U(x) + (1 - \beta(z))U(y). \tag{3.2}$$

In this way we have shown that the correct ranking function for risky alternatives is *expected utility*. Equation (3.1) says that the utility of z is equal to the probability of x times its utility plus the probability of y times its utility. This is an expected utility that represents a linear combination of the utilities of outcomes.

In general, we can write the expected utility of wealth as follows:

$$E[U(W)] = \sum_i p_i U(W_i).$$

Figure 3.4 Outcome z related to elementary prospects a and b.

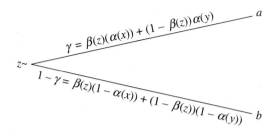

$$\gamma = \beta(z)(\alpha(x)) + (1 - \beta(z))\alpha(y)$$

$$1 - \gamma = \beta(z)(1 - \alpha(x)) + (1 - \beta(z))(1 - \alpha(y))$$

Given the five axioms of rational investor behavior and the additional assumption that all investors always prefer more wealth to less, we can say that investors will always seek to maximize their expected utility of wealth. In fact, the above equation is exactly what we mean by the theory of choice. All investors will use it as their objective function. In other words, they will seem to calculate the expected utility of wealth for all possible alternative choices and then choose the outcome that maximizes their expected utility of wealth.

Now, we can use the properties of utility functions to demonstrate how our utility function might be constructed. Suppose we arbitrarily assign a utility of -10 utiles to a loss of \$1,000 and ask the following question: When we are faced with a gamble with probability α of winning \$1,000 and probability $(1 - \alpha)$ of losing \$1,000, what probability would make us indifferent between the gamble and \$0 with certainty? Mathematically, this problem can be expressed as

$$0 \sim G(1,000, -1,000 : \alpha)$$

or

$$U(0) = \alpha U(1,000) + (1 - \alpha)U(-1,000).$$

Suppose that the probability of winning \$1,000 must be .6 in order for us to be indifferent between the gamble and a sure \$0. By assuming that the utility of \$0 with certainty is zero and substituting $U(-1,000) = -10$ and $\alpha = .6$ into the above equation, we can solve for the utility of \$1,000:

$$U(1,000) = \frac{(1 - \alpha)U(-1,000)}{\alpha}$$

$$= -\frac{(1 - .6)(-10)}{.6} = 6.7 \text{ utiles.}$$

By repeating this procedure for different payoffs it is possible to develop a utility function. Table 3.1 shows various gambles, their probabilities, and the utility of payoffs for a risk-averse investor. The cardinal utility function that obtains for the set of preferences indicated in Table 3.1 is given in Fig. 3.5.[5]

An important thing to keep in mind is that utility functions are specific to individuals. There is no way to compare one individual's utility function to another's. For example, we could perform an experiment by giving two people \$1,000. We would see that they are both happy, having just experienced an increase in utility. But whose utility increased more? It is impossible to say!

---

[5] This example can be found in Walter [1967].

Table 3.1 Payoffs, Probabilities, and Utilities

Loss	Gain	Profitability of Gain	Utility of Gain	Utility of Loss
−1,000	1,000	.60	6.7	−10.0
−1,000	2,000	.55	8.2	−10.0
−1,000	3,000	.50	10.0	−10.0
−1,000	4,000	.45	12.2	−10.0
−1,000	5,000	.40	15.0	−10.0
−1,000	6,000	.35	18.6	−10.0
−1,000	7,000	.30	23.3	−10.0
−2,000	2,000	.75	8.2	−24.6
−3,000	3,000	.80	10.0	−40.0
−4,000	4,000	.85	12.2	−69.2
−5,000	5,000	.90	15.0	−135.0

From *Dividend Policy and Enterprise Valuation,* by James E. Walter. © 1967 by Wadsworth Publishing Company, Inc., Belmont, Calif. Reprinted by permission of the publisher.

Interpersonal comparison of utility functions is impossible. If it were not, we could establish a social welfare function that would combine everyone's utility, and we could then use it to solve such problems as the optimal distribution of wealth. We could maximize society's utility by taking wealth away from individual I and giving it to individual J. However, it is not possible to know how real-world utility functions for different individuals should be aggregated. It follows that group utility functions, such as the utility function of a firm, have no meaning.

Another important property of cardinal utility functions is that we can sensibly talk about increasing or decreasing marginal utility. This can best be illustrated with an example taken from the Celsius and Fahrenheit temperature scales. Consider two outcomes: the freezing point of water and its boiling point. Call them x and y, respectively. Each scale may be likened to a function that maps various degrees of heat into numbers. Utility functions do the same thing for risky alternatives. The difference between two outcomes is marginal utility. On the Celsius scale the difference between freezing and boiling is 100°C. On the Fahrenheit scale the difference is 180° Fahrenheit. The ratio of the "changes" is

$$\frac{212° - 32°}{100° - 0°} = 1.8.$$

If the two scales really do provide the same ranking for all prospects, then the ratio of changes should be the same for all prospects. Mathematically,

$$\frac{U(x) - U(y)}{\psi(x) - \psi(y)} = \text{constant},$$

where $U(\cdot)$ and $\psi(\cdot)$ are the two utility functions. Compare any two points on the two temperature scales and you will see that the ratio of changes between them is a constant (i.e., 1.8). Hence changes in utility between any two wealth levels have exactly the same meaning on the two utility functions; that is, one utility function is just a "transformation" of the other.

Figure 3.5 Cardinal utility function.

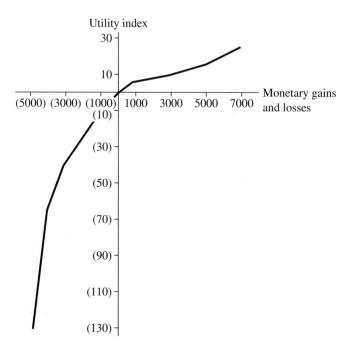

Utility index

C. $\mathcal{E}$stablishing a Definition of Risk Aversion

Having established a way of converting the axioms of preference into a utility function, we can make use of the concept to establish definitions of risk premia and also precisely what is meant by *risk aversion*. A useful way to begin is to compare three simple utility functions (Fig. 3.6) that assume that more wealth is preferred to less; in other words, the marginal utility of wealth is positive: $MU(W) > 0$. Suppose that we establish a gamble between two prospects, a and b. Let the probability of receiving prospect a be α and prospect of b be $(1 - \alpha)$. The gamble can be written as before: $G(a, b : \alpha)$. Now the question is this: Will we prefer the actuarial value of the gamble (i.e., its expected or average outcome) with certainty—or the gamble itself? In other words, would we like to receive $10 for sure, or would we prefer to "roll the dice" in a gamble that pays off $100 with a 10% probability and $0 with a 90% probability? A person who prefers the gamble is a risk lover; one who is indifferent is risk neutral; and one who prefers the actuarial value with certainty is a risk averter. In Fig. 3.7, we have graphed a logarithmic utility function: $U(W) = \ln(W)$. The gamble is an 80% chance of a $5 outcome and a 20% chance of a $30 outcome. The *actuarial value of the gamble* is its expected outcome. In other words, the expected wealth is

$$E(W) = .8(\$5) + .2(\$30) = \$10.$$

The utility of the expected wealth can be read directly from the utility function: $U[E(W)] = 2.3$. That is, if an individual with a logarithmic utility function could receive $10 with certainty, it would provide him or her with 2.3 utiles. The other possibility is the utility of the gamble. We know from Eq. (3.1) that it is equal to the expected utility of wealth provided by the gamble.

Figure 3.6 Three utility functions with positive marginal utility: (a) risk lover; (b) risk neutral; (c) risk averter.

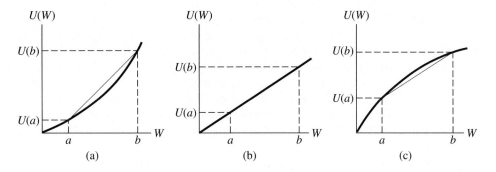

 (a)   (b)   (c)

Figure 3.7 Logarithmic utility function.

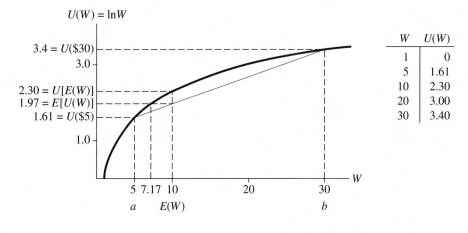

W	U(W)
1	0
5	1.61
10	2.30
20	3.00
30	3.40

$$E[U(W)] = .8U(\$5) + .2U(\$30)$$

$$= .8(1.61) + .2(3.40) = 1.97.$$

Because we receive more utility from the actuarial value of the gamble obtained with certainty than from taking the gamble itself, we are risk averse. In general, if the utility of expected wealth is greater than the expected utility of wealth, the individual will be risk averse. The three definitions are[6]

> If $U[E(W)] > E[U(W)]$, then we have risk aversion.

> If $U[E(W)] = E[U(W)]$, then we have risk neutrality.

> If $U[E(W)] < E[U(W)]$, then we have risk loving.

Note that if our utility function is strictly concave, we will be risk averse; if it is linear, we will be risk neutral; and if it is convex, we will be risk lovers (see Fig. 3.6).

---

[6] These definitions can be found in Markowitz [1959].

It is even possible to compute the maximum amount of wealth an individual would be willing to give up in order to avoid the gamble. This is called the *risk premium*. Suppose that Mr. Smith is faced with the gamble illustrated in Fig. 3.7, has a current level of wealth of $10, and has a logarithmic utility function. How much will he pay to avoid the gamble? If he does nothing, he has an 80% chance of ending up with $5 (a decline of $5) and a 20% chance of ending up with $30 (an increase of $20). The expected utility of the gamble has already been determined to be 1.97 utiles. From the logarithmic utility function in Fig. 3.7 we see that the level of wealth that provides 1.97 utiles is $7.17. On the other hand, Smith receives an expected level of wealth of $10 (equal to his current wealth) if he accepts the gamble. Therefore, given a logarithmic utility function, he will be willing to pay up to $2.83 in order to avoid the gamble. We shall call this the *Markowitz risk premium*. If Smith is offered insurance against the gamble that costs less than $2.83, he will buy it.

We shall adopt the convention of measuring the risk premium as the difference between an individual's expected wealth, given the gamble, and the level of wealth that individual would accept with certainty if the gamble were removed, that is, his or her *certainty equivalent wealth*. There is another convention that might be called the cost of the gamble. It is defined as the difference between an individual's current wealth and his or her certainty equivalent wealth. Note that in the first example, given above, expected wealth and current wealth were identical because the expected change in wealth was zero. Thus there was no difference between the risk premium and the cost of the gamble. To illustrate the difference between the two definitions, consider the following example. A risk-averse individual has the same logarithmic utility function as in Fig. 3.7 and the same current wealth (i.e., $10), but the gamble is a 10% chance of winning $10 and a 90% chance of winning $100. We can compute the following numbers:[7]

$$\text{current wealth} = \$10,$$

$$\text{expected wealth} = \$101,$$

$$\text{certainty equivalent wealth} = \$92.76.$$

Our convention will be to define the risk premium as the difference between expected wealth and certainty equivalent wealth:

$$\text{risk premium} = \text{expected wealth} - \text{certainty equivalent wealth}$$

$$= \$101 - \$92.76 = \$8.24.$$

This measures, in dollars, the risk premium associated with the gamble. Note, however, that since the gamble is favorable (we can only win if we take it), we would be willing to pay a positive amount to take the gamble. The cost of the gamble is

$$\text{cost of the gamble} = \text{current wealth} - \text{certainty equivalent wealth}$$

$$= \$10 - \$92.76 = \$-82.76.$$

In other words, we would be willing to pay up to $82.76 in order to take a gamble that has a 10% chance of increasing our wealth from $10 to $20, and a 90% chance of increasing it from $10 to $110. We would pay even more if we were less risk averse. Note that for a risk averter the

---

[7] Expected wealth equals current wealth, $10, plus the expected outcome of the gamble, $.1(\$10) + .9(\$100) = \$91$. $E(W) = \$101$.

risk premium as defined above is always positive, whereas the cost of the gamble can be positive, negative, or zero, depending on the risk of the gamble and how much it is expected to change one's current wealth.

Throughout the remainder of this text we shall assume that all individuals are risk averse. Their utility functions are assumed to be strictly concave and increasing. Mathematically, this implies two things: (1) they always prefer more wealth to less (the marginal utility of wealth is positive, $MU(W) > 0$) and (2) their marginal utility of wealth decreases as they have more and more wealth $(dMU(W)/dW < 0)$.[8]

Now we know how to characterize a risk-averse utility function and how to measure a risk premium for a given gamble, but it is even more interesting to provide a specific definition of *risk aversion*. This was done by Pratt [1964] and Arrow [1971]. Take an individual, say, Ms. Torres, with a current amount of wealth, W, and present her with an actuarially neutral gamble of $\tilde{Z}$ dollars (by *actuarially neutral* we mean that $E(\tilde{Z}) = 0$). What risk premium, $\pi(W, \tilde{Z})$, must be added to the gamble to make her indifferent between it and the actuarial value of the gamble? In Fig. 3.7, which illustrates our first example, the risk premium is analogous to the difference between $U[E(W)]$ and $E[U(W)]$ if it is measured in utiles, or the difference between \$10 and \$7.17 if measured in dollars. Presumably, the risk premium will be a function of the level of wealth, W, and the gamble, $\tilde{Z}$. Mathematically, the risk premium, π, can be defined as the value that satisfies the following equality:

$$E[U(W + \tilde{Z})] = U[W + E(\tilde{Z}) - \pi(W, \tilde{Z})]. \tag{3.3}$$

The left-hand side is the expected utility of the current level of wealth, given the gamble. Its utility must equal the utility of the right-hand side, that is, the current level of wealth, W, plus the utility of the actuarial value of the gamble, $E(\tilde{Z})$, minus the risk premium, $\pi(W, \tilde{Z})$. We can use Taylor's series approximation to expand the utility function of wealth (whatever it might be) around both sides of Eq. (3.3).[9] Working with the right-hand side of (3.3), we have

$$U[W + E(\tilde{Z}) - \pi(W, \tilde{Z})] = U[W - \pi(W, \tilde{Z})].$$

Since $E(\tilde{Z}) \equiv 0$, an actuarially neutral risk, the Taylor's series expansion is[10]

$$U(W - \pi) = U(W) - \pi U'(W) + \text{ terms of order at most } (\pi^2). \tag{3.4}$$

The Taylor's series expansion of the left-hand side of (3.3) is

$$E[U(W + \tilde{Z})] = E[U(W) + \tilde{Z}U'(W) + \frac{1}{2}\sigma\tilde{Z}^2 U''(W) + \text{ terms of order at most } \tilde{Z}^3]$$

$$= U(W) + \frac{1}{2}\sigma_Z^2 U''(W) + \text{ terms of smaller order than } \sigma_Z^2. \tag{3.5}$$

The above result may require a little explanation. It is true because

---

[8] Decreasing marginal utility is probably genetically coded because without it we would exhibit extreme impulsive behavior. We would engage in the activity with the highest marginal utility to the exclusion of all other choices.

[9] Students not familiar with Taylor's series approximations are referred to Appendix D at the end of the book.

[10] We assume that the third absolute central moment of $\tilde{Z}$ is of smaller order than σ_z^2 (normally it is of the order of σ_z^3).

$$E[U(W)] = U(W), \qquad \text{current wealth is not random;}$$

$$E[\widetilde{Z}] \equiv 0, \qquad \text{the risk is actuarilly neutral;}$$

$$E[\widetilde{Z}^2] = \sigma_Z^2, \qquad \text{because } \sigma_Z^2 \equiv E[(\widetilde{Z}) - E(\widetilde{Z})]^2.$$

Next we can equate (3.4) and (3.5):

$$U(W) - \pi U'(W) + \cdots = U(W) + \frac{1}{2}\sigma_Z^2 U''(W) + \cdots. \tag{3.6}$$

Solving (3.6) for the risk premium, we obtain

$$\pi = \frac{1}{2}\sigma_Z^2 \left(-\frac{U''(W)}{U'(W)} \right). \tag{3.7}$$

This is the *Pratt-Arrow measure* of a local risk premium. Since $\frac{1}{2}\sigma_Z^2$ is always positive, the sign of the risk premium is always determined by the sign of the term in parentheses. We shall define the measure of *absolute risk aversion* (ARA) as

$$\text{ARA} = -\frac{U''(W)}{U'(W)} \tag{3.8}$$

It is called absolute risk aversion because it measures risk aversion for a given level of wealth. The Pratt-Arrow definition of risk aversion is useful because it provides much more insight into people's behavior in the face of risk. For example, how does ARA change with one's wealth level? Casual empiricism tells us that ARA will probably decrease as our wealth increases. A \$1,000 gamble may seem trivial to a billionaire, but a pauper would probably be risk averse toward it. On the other hand, we can multiply the measure of absolute risk aversion by the level of wealth to obtain what is known as relative risk aversion (RRA):

$$\text{RRA} = -W\frac{U''(W)}{U'(W)} \tag{3.9}$$

Constant relative risk aversion implies that an individual will have constant risk aversion to a proportional loss of wealth even though the absolute loss increases as wealth does.

We can use these definitions of risk aversion to provide a more detailed examination of various types of utility functions to see whether or not they have decreasing ARA and constant RRA. The quadratic utility function has been widely used in academic literature. It can be written (for $W \leq a/2b$) as

$$\text{Quadratic utility function:} \qquad U(W) = aW - bW^2;$$

$$\text{First derivative, marginal utility:} \quad U'(W) = a - 2bW;$$

Second derivative, change in MU

with respect to change in wealth: $U''(W) = -2b.$ $\tag{3.10}$

For the quadratic utility function, ARA and RRA are

$$\text{ARA} = -\frac{2b}{a - 2bW}, \qquad \frac{d(\text{ARA})}{dW} > 0,$$

$$\text{RRA} = \frac{2b}{(a/W) - 2b}, \qquad \frac{d(\text{RRA})}{dW} > 0.$$

Unfortunately, the quadratic utility function exhibits increasing ARA and increasing RRA. Neither of these properties makes sense intuitively. For example, an individual with increasing RRA would become more averse to a given percentage loss in wealth as wealth increases. A billionaire who loses half his wealth, leaving $500 million, would lose more utility than the same person who started with $20,000 and ended up with $10,000. This result is simply not intuitive.

Friend and Blume [1975] have used Internal Revenue Service data to replicate, from reported dividends, the portfolios held by individual investors. Sophisticated econometric techniques were used to estimate changes in ARA and RRA as a function of wealth of investors. The results were consistent with a power utility function with $a = -1$ (for $W > 0$). It can be written as

$$U(W) = -W^{-1}, \qquad U'(W) = W^{-2} > 0, \qquad U''(W) = -2W^{-3} < 0. \qquad (3.11)$$

For this power utility function, ARA and RRA are

$$\text{ARA} = -\frac{-2W^{-3}}{W^{-2}} = \frac{2}{W}, \qquad \frac{d(\text{ARA})}{dW} < 0,$$

$$\text{RRA} = W\frac{2}{W} = 2, \qquad \frac{d(\text{RRA})}{dW} = 0$$

The power function given by Eq. (3.11) is consistent with the empirical results of Friend and Blume and exhibits all the intuitively plausible properties: the marginal utility of wealth is positive, it decreases with increasing wealth, the measure of ARA decreases with increasing wealth, and RRA is constant.

D. $\mathscr{C}$omparison of Risk Aversion in the Small and in the Large

The Pratt-Arrow definition of risk aversion provides useful insights into the properties of ARA and RRA, but it assumes that risks are small and actuarially neutral. The Markowitz concept, which simply compares $E[U(W)]$ with $U[E(W)]$, is not limited by these assumptions.

An interesting comparison of the two measures of risk premiums is offered in the following example. An individual with a logarithmic utility function and a level of wealth of $20,000 is exposed to two different risks: (1) a 50/50 chance of gaining or losing $10 and (2) an 80% chance of losing $1,000 and a 20% chance of losing $10,000. What is the risk premium required by the individual faced with each of these risks? Note that the first risk is small and actuarially neutral, so that it approximates the assumptions that were used to derive the Pratt-Arrow risk premium. The second risk, however, is large and very asymmetric.

The Pratt-Arrow measure is

$$\pi = -\frac{1}{2}\sigma_Z^2 \frac{U''(W)}{U'(W)}.$$

The variance of the first risk is

$$\sigma_Z^2 = \sum p_i (X_i - \bar{E}(X))^2$$

$$= \frac{1}{2}(20{,}010 - 20{,}000)^2 + \frac{1}{2}(19{,}990 - 20{,}000)^2$$

$$= 100.$$

The ratio of the second and the first derivatives of a logarithmic utility function evaluated at a level of wealth of \$20,000 is

$$U'(W) = \frac{1}{W}, \qquad U''(W) = -\frac{1}{W^2}, \qquad \frac{U''(W)}{U'(W)} = -\frac{1}{W} = -\frac{1}{20{,}000}.$$

Combining these results, we obtain an estimate of the Pratt-Arrow risk premium:

$$\pi = -\frac{100}{2}\left(-\frac{1}{20{,}000}\right) = \$.0025$$

The Markowitz approach requires computation of the expected utility of the gamble as follows:

$$E[U(W)] = \sum p_i U(W_i)$$

$$= \frac{1}{2}U(20{,}010) + \frac{1}{2}U(19{,}990)$$

$$= \frac{1}{2}\ln(20{,}010) + \frac{1}{2}\ln(19{,}990) = 9.903487428.$$

The certainty equivalent wealth level that would make us indifferent to our current level of wealth, given the gamble and a lower but certain level of wealth, is the level of wealth that has utility of 9.903487428. This is

$$W = e^{\ln(W)} = \$19{,}999.9974998.$$

Therefore we would pay a risk premium as large as \$.0025002. The difference between the Pratt-Arrow risk premium and that of Markowitz is negligible in this case.

   If we repeat similar computations for the second risk in the above example, the Pratt-Arrow assumptions of a small, actuarially neutral risk are not closely approximated. Nevertheless, if we apply the Pratt-Arrow definition, the risk premium is calculated to be \$324. The Markowitz risk premium for the same risk is the difference between expected wealth, \$17,200, and the certainty equivalent wealth, \$16,711, or \$489. Now the dollar difference between the two risk premia is much larger.[11]

   The above example illustrates the difference between risk aversion for small, actuarially neutral risks, where the Pratt-Arrow assumptions are closely approximated, and risk aversion in the large,

---

[11] Had we calculated the cost of the gamble instead of the risk premium, we would have subtracted the certainty equivalent wealth, \$16,711, from the individual's current wealth, \$20,000, to find that the individual would have paid up to \$3,289 to avoid the gamble.

where the magnitude of the gamble is large or where it is not actuarially neutral. In general, the Markowitz measure of a risk premium is superior for large or asymmetric risks. This does not mean that the Pratt-Arrow definition of risk aversion was not useful. As we have seen, the intuition provided by the definition of risk aversion was useful for distinguishing between various types of concave utility functions.

E. *S*tochastic Dominance

So far we have discussed the axioms of investor preference, then used them to develop cardinal utility functions, and finally employed the utility functions to measure risk premia and derive measures of risk aversion. Clearly, any investor, whether risk averse or not, will seek to maximize the expected utility of his or her wealth. The expected utility role can be used to introduce the economics of choice under uncertainty. An asset (or portfolio) is said to be stochastically dominant over another if an individual receives greater wealth from it in every (ordered) state of nature. This definition is known as *first-order stochastic dominance*. Mathematically, asset x, with cumulative probability distribution $F_x(W)$, will be stochastically dominant over asset y, with cumulative probability $G_y(W)$, for a set of all nondecreasing utility functions if

$$F_x(W) \leq G_y(W) \quad \text{for all } W, \quad \textit{first-order stochastic dominance}$$

$$F_x(W_i) < G_y(W_i) \quad \text{for some } W_i. \tag{3.12}$$

In other words, the cumulative probability distribution (defined on wealth, W) for asset y always lies to the left of the cumulative distribution for x. If true, then x is said to dominate y. Figure 3.8 shows an example of first-order stochastic dominance assuming that the distribution of wealth provided by both assets is a (truncated) normal distribution. It is obvious from the figure that x dominates y because the cumulative distribution of y always lies to the left of x.

First-order stochastic dominance applies to all increasing utility functions. This means that individuals with any of the three utility functions in Fig. 3.6 would prefer asset x to asset y because

Figure 3.8 An example of first-order stochastic dominance.

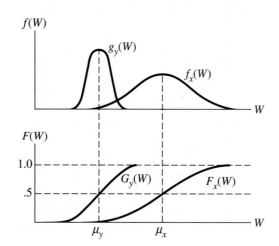

Figure 3.9 First-order stochastic dominance and expected utility.

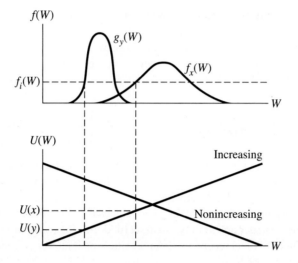

first-order stochastic dominance guarantees that the expected utility of wealth offered by x will be greater than that offered by y for all increasing utility functions. This fact can be illustrated by using Fig. 3.9 and the definition of expected utility:

$$E[U(W)] \equiv \int_{-\infty}^{\infty} U(W)f(W)dW, \tag{3.13}$$

where

$$U(W) = \text{the utility function,}$$

$$W = \text{the level of wealth,}$$

$$f(W) = \text{the frequency distribution of wealth.}$$

The utility functions in Fig. 3.9 are linear, but they could just as easily be any of the set of increasing functions that we are comparing with any set of nonincreasing functions. Expected utility is the sum of utilities of all possible levels of wealth weighted by their probability. For a given frequency of wealth, $f_i(W)$, in the top half of Fig. 3.9, the increasing utility function assigns higher utility to the level of wealth offered by asset x than by asset y. This is true for every frequency. Consequently, the expected utility of wealth from asset x is greater than that from asset y for the set of increasing utility functions (i.e., all utility functions that have positive marginal utility of wealth). Of course, the opposite would be true for utility functions nonincreasing in wealth.

Second-order stochastic dominance not only assumes utility functions where marginal utility of wealth is positive; it also assumes that total utility must increase at a decreasing rate. In other words, utility functions are nondecreasing and strictly concave. Thus individuals are assumed to be risk averse. Asset x will be stochastically dominant over asset y for all risk-averse investors if

$$\int_{-\infty}^{W_i} [G_y(W) - F_x(W)]\,dW \geq 0 \quad \text{for all } W, \quad \text{second-order stochastic dominance}$$

$$G_y(W_i) \neq F_x(W_i) \qquad\qquad \text{for some } W_i. \tag{3.14}$$

Figure 3.10 An example of second-order stochastic dominance.

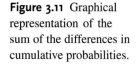

Figure 3.11 Graphical representation of the sum of the differences in cumulative probabilities.

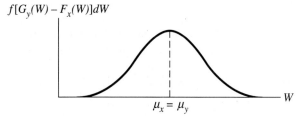

$$f[G_y(W) - F_x(W)]dW$$

This means that in order for asset x to dominate asset y for all risk-averse investors, the accumulated area under the cumulative probability distribution of y must be greater than the accumulated area for x, below any given level of wealth. This implies that, unlike first-order stochastic dominance, the cumulative density functions can cross. Figure 3.10 provides a graphic example, this time assuming normal distributions. Obviously, asset x will dominate asset y if an investor is risk averse because they both offer the same expected level of wealth ($\mu_x = \mu_y$) because y is riskier. It has greater variance. The second-order stochastic dominance criterion requires that the difference in areas under the cumulative density functions be positive below any level of wealth, W_i. Up to the mean, $G_y(W)$ is strictly greater than $F_x(W)$. Beyond the mean, the opposite is true. Figure 3.11 shows that the sum of the differences between the two cumulative density functions is always greater than or equal to zero; therefore x dominates y.

Figure 3.10(b) ties the concept of second-order stochastic dominance back to the notion of maximizing expected utility.[12] The concave utility function of a risk averter has the property that the increase in utility for constant changes in wealth declines as a function of wealth. Therefore if we select a given frequency of wealth such as $f_i(W)$, it maps out equal changes in wealth, ΔW_1 and ΔW_2. The difference in utility between x and y below the mean is much greater than the difference in utility for the same change in wealth above the mean. Consequently, if we take the expected utility by pairing all such differences with equal probability, the expected utility of x is seen as greater than the expected utility of y. If the individual were risk neutral, with a linear utility function, the differences in utility above and below the mean would always be equal. Hence a risk-neutral investor would be indifferent between alternatives x and y.

Stochastic dominance is an extremely important and powerful result. It is properly founded on the basis of expected utility maximization, and even more important, it applies to any probability distribution whatsoever. This is because it takes into account every point in the probability distribution. Furthermore, we can be sure that if an asset demonstrates second-order stochastic dominance, it will be preferred by all risk-averse investors, regardless of the specific shape of their utility functions. We could use stochastic dominance as the basis of the complete theory of how risk-averse investors choose among various risky alternatives. All we need to do is find the set of portfolios that is stochastically dominant and then select a portfolio from among those in the set.[13]

F. $\mathcal{U}$sing Mean and Variance as Choice Criteria

If the distribution of returns offered by assets is jointly normal, then we can maximize expected utility simply by selecting the best combination of mean and variance.[14] This is computationally much simpler than stochastic dominance but requires that we restrict ourselves to normal distributions. Every normal distribution can be completely described by two parameters: its mean and variance—return and risk. If we adopt utility functions that maximize expected utility of end-of-period wealth (assuming a single-period model), it is easy to show the relationship between wealth and return:

$$\widetilde{R}_j = \frac{\widetilde{W}_j - W_0}{W_0}.$$

If the end-of-period wealth from investing in asset j is normally distributed with mean $\overline{W}$ and variance σ_W^2, then the return on asset j will also be normally distributed with mean $E(R_j) = [(E(W_j)/W_0) - 1]$ and variance $\sigma_R^2 = (\sigma_W^2/W_0^2)$.

---

[12] The graphical presentation given here is intuitive and not meant to be proof of the fact that second-order stochastic dominance maximizes expected utility for risk-averse investors. For proof, the reader is referred to Hanoch and Levy [1969].

[13] For a body of literature that uses this concept, the interested reader is referred to Bawa [1975], Whitmore [1970], Porter, Wart, and Ferguson [1973], Levy and Kroll [1976], Vickson and Altman [1977], Jean [1975], and Kira and Ziemba [1977].

[14] By "jointly normal" we mean that all assets are individually normally distributed, and in addition, their interrelationships (covariances) obey the normal probability laws. This concept is developed further in Chapter 5.

Figure 3.12 Indifference curves for a risk-averse investor.

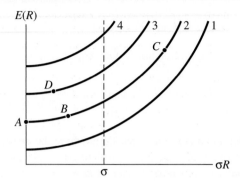

Assuming that the return on an asset is normally distributed with mean E and variance σ^2, we can write our utility function as[15]

$$U = U(R_j; E, \sigma).$$

Our expected utility is

$$E(U) = \int_{-\infty}^{\infty} U(R) f(R; E, \sigma) dR. \tag{3.15}$$

We would like to express the indifference curve of a risk-averse investor as a function of the mean and standard deviation of a distribution of returns. The indifference curve is a mapping of all combinations of risk and return (standard deviation or variance) that yield the same expected utility of wealth. Obviously, if the combinations offer identical expected utility, the investor will be indifferent between them. Figure 3.12 shows the end result of the following proofs (i.e., the indifference curves of a risk-averse investor).

We want to show that the marginal rate of substitution between return and risk is positive and that the indifference curves are convex. This can be done, first by converting the random return into a unit normal variable, Z, which has a mean of zero and variance of one:

$$\tilde{Z} = \frac{\tilde{R} - E}{\sigma}. \tag{3.16}$$

From this we see that

$$\tilde{R} = E + \sigma \tilde{Z}, \qquad \frac{dR}{dZ} = \sigma, \qquad dR = \sigma dZ,$$

and when $R = -\infty$, then $Z = -\infty$, and when $R = \infty$, then $Z = \infty$. Now, by using the change-in-variables technique from integral calculus, we can rewrite (3.15) as[16]

---

[15] This proof can be found in Tobin [1958]. Also note that the proof applies equally well to any continuous, symmetric two-parameter distribution.

[16] Since $f(R; E, \sigma) = (1/\sigma) f(Z; 0, 1)$, it follows that

$$E(U) = \int_{-\infty}^{\infty} U(E + \sigma \tilde{Z}) f(Z; 0, 1) \frac{\sigma}{\sigma} dZ.$$

$$E(U) = \int_{-\infty}^{\infty} U(E + \sigma \widetilde{Z}) f(Z; 0, 1) dZ. \tag{3.17}$$

Next, we take the derivative of the expected utility with respect to a change in the standard deviation of return:[17]

$$\frac{dE(U)}{d\sigma} = \int_{-\infty}^{\infty} U'(E + \sigma \widetilde{Z}) \left(\frac{dE}{d\sigma} + \widetilde{Z} \right) f(Z; 0, 1) dZ = 0. \tag{3.18}$$

An indifference curve is defined as the locus of points where the change in the expected utility is equal to zero. Therefore (3.18) has been set equal to zero, and the solution of the equation represents an indifference curve. Separating terms, we have

$$0 = \frac{dE}{d\sigma} \int_{-\infty}^{\infty} U'(E + \sigma \widetilde{Z}) f(Z; 0, 1) dZ + \int_{-\infty}^{\infty} U'(E + \sigma \widetilde{Z}) Z f; (Z; 0, 1) dZ.$$

Therefore, the slope of the indifference curve is

$$\frac{dE}{d\sigma} = -\frac{\int U'(E + \sigma Z) Z f(Z; 0, 1) dZ}{\int U'(E + \sigma Z) f(Z; 0, 1) dZ} > 0. \tag{3.19}$$

The denominator must be positive because of the assumption that marginal utility, $U'(E + \sigma \widetilde{Z})$, must always be positive. People always prefer more return to less. The numerator will be negative (and therefore the entire ratio will be positive) if we have a risk-averse investor with a strictly concave utility function. The marginal utility of every negative value of Z in Fig. 3.13 is greater than the marginal utility of an equally likely positive value of Z. Because this is true for every pair of outcomes, $\pm Z$, the integral in the numerator of Eq. (3.19) is negative, and the (entire) numerator is positive. Consequently, the slope of a risk averter's indifference curve in Fig. 3.12 (i.e., his or her marginal rate of substitution between mean and variance) is everywhere positive, excepting when $\sigma = 0$ where the slope is also zero.[18]

The indifference curves in Figure 3.12 will be used throughout the remainder of the text to represent the theory of choice for risk-averse investors. Any points along a given indifference curve provide us with equal total utility. For example, we would not care whether we were at point A in Fig. 3.12, which has no risk, at point B with higher risk and return, or at point C. They all lie on the same indifference curve. Moving from right to left across the family of indifference curves provides us with increasing levels of expected utility. We would prefer point D on indifference curve 3 to point C on indifference curve 2, even though D has a lower return. The reason, of course,

---

[17] $\partial(Z)/\partial\sigma = 0$.

[18] The convexity of the utility function can be shown as follows. Let (E_1, σ_1) and (E_2, σ_2) be two points on the same indifference curve so that they have the same expected utility. If a third point is constructed to be a weighted average of the first two, $(E_1 + E_2)/2$, $(\sigma_1 + \sigma_2)/2$, the indifference curve is convex, if for every Z,

$$\frac{1}{2} U(E_1 + \sigma_1 Z) + \frac{1}{2} U(E_2 + \sigma_2 Z) < U\left(\frac{E_1 + E_2}{2} + \frac{\sigma_1 + \sigma_2}{2} Z \right).$$

In the case of the declining marginal utilities, this is obviously true because the utility of the second point, (E_2, σ_2), will be less than twice the utility of the first. Consequently,

$$E\left[U\left(\frac{E_1 + E_2}{2}, \frac{\sigma_1 + \sigma_2}{2} \right) \right] > E[U(E_1, \sigma_1)] = E[U(E_2, \sigma_2)],$$

Figure 3.13 Graphic representation for $\int U'(E + \sigma Z)Zf(Z;0,1)dZ < 0$.

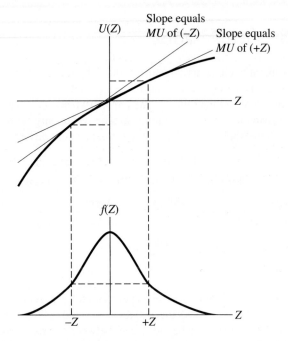

is that it has a much lower risk, which more than makes up for the lower return. The easiest way to see that expected utility increases from right to left is to fix the level of risk at $\bar{\sigma}$ and then note that the expected return increases as we move from curve 1 to curve 4. Although the indifference curves in Fig. 3.12 appear to be parallel, they need not be. The only requirement is that they never touch or cross.

and the third point, which is a weighted average of the two, lies above the indifference curve. This is shown graphically here:

Figure 3.F18 Convexity of the risk averter's indifference curve.

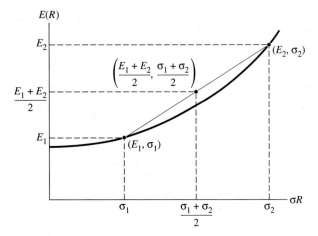

G. 𝒜 Mean Variance Paradox

Although it is convenient to characterize return and risk by the mean and variance of distributions of return offered by assets, it is not always correct. In fact, it is correct only when the returns have a normal distribution. Consider the following example. Two companies with equal total assets and exactly the same distribution of net operating income differ only with regard to their financial leverage. Table 3.2 shows their respective income statements in different, equally likely, states of nature.

	Firm A			**Firm B**	
Assets		**Liabilities**	**Assets**		**Liabilities**
	Debt	0		Debt	10,000
	Equity	20,000		Equity	10,000
$20,000		$20,000	$20,000		$20,000

The mean and standard deviation of earnings per share for firm A are $5 and $1.41, respectively. For firm B, they are $7 and $2.82. These alternatives are plotted in Fig. 3.14. According to the mean-variance criterion, individual I would be indifferent between the risk-return combinations offered by A and B. Individual II, who is less risk averse, would prefer alternative B, which has a greater

Table 3.2 Mean-Variance Paradox

	Economic State of Nature				
	Horrid	**Bad**	**Average**	**Good**	**Great**
Net operating income	$1,200	$1,600	$2,000	$2,400	$2,800
Probability	.2	.2	.2	.2	.2
Firm A					
Interest expense	0	0	0	0	0
Earnings before tax	1,200	1,600	2,000	2,400	2,800
Tax at 50%	−600	−800	−1,000	−1,200	−1,400
Net income	$600	800	1,000	1,200	1,400
Earnings per share (200 shares)	$3.00	$4.00	$5.00	$6.00	$7.00
Firm B					
Interest expense	−600	−600	−600	−600	−600
Earnings before tax	600	1,000	1,400	1,800	2,200
Tax at 50%	−300	−500	−700	−900	−1,100
Net income	300	500	700	900	1,100
Earnings per share (100 shares)	$3.00	$5.00	$7.00	$9.00	$11.00

Figure 3.14 A mean variance paradox.

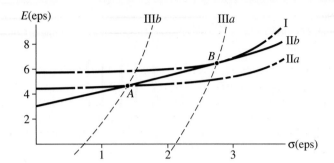

Table 3.3 Using Second-Order Stochastic Dominance

EPS	Prob. (B)	Prob. (A)	F(B)	G(A)	$F - G$	$\sum(F - G)$
3.00	.2	.2	.2	.2	0	0
4.00	0	.2	.2	.4	−.2	−.2
5.00	.2	.2	.4	.6	−.2	−.4
6.00	0	.2	.4	.8	−.4	−.8
7.00	.2	.2	.6	1.0	−.4	−1.2
8.00	0	0	.6	1.0	−.4	−1.6
9.00	.2	0	.8	1.0	−.2	−1.8
10.00	0	0	.8	1.0	−.2	−2.0
11.00	.2	0	1.0	1.0	0	−2.0
	1.0	1.0				

return. Finally, individual III would prefer alternative A, which has lower risk. The paradox arises when we reexamine the earnings per share offered by the two firms. The earnings per share for firm B are equal to or greater than the earnings per share for firm A in every state of nature. Obviously, the mean-variance criterion provides misleading results. No investor with positive marginal utility would prefer firm A.

The trouble with trying to apply the mean-variance criterion to the above problem is that the distribution of outcomes is not normal. Instead, it is a rectangular distribution with equal probabilities for each state of nature. However, we can use second-order stochastic dominance regardless of the shape of the probability distribution.[19] This is done in Table 3.3. Because the accumulated area under the distribution of earnings per share offered by firm B is always less than or equal to the accumulated distribution for firm A, we can say that B clearly dominates A. The density functions and cumulative density functions are shown in Fig. 3.15.

---

[19] First-order stochastic dominance also obtains in this example. We have used second-order dominance because we assume a risk-averse decision maker.

Figure 3.15 Stochastic dominance applied to the mean-variance paradox.

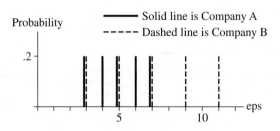

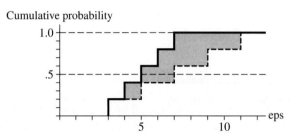

This mean-variance paradox example demonstrates very clearly the shortcomings of a theory of choice that relies on the (somewhat heroic) assumption that returns are normally distributed. Nevertheless, much of the remainder of this text will assume that returns are in fact normally distributed.

H. Recent Thinking and Empirical Evidence

Utility theory is founded on the axioms of Von Neumann and Morgenstern [1947] and the elegant mathematics that follows logically from them. Furthermore, the basic results—increasing marginal utility, risk aversion, and decreasing absolute risk aversion—seem to conform to economists' causal empiricism. There has been almost no empirical testing of the axioms or of their implications, at least not by economists. Psychologists, however, have been busy testing the validity of the axioms. Do individuals actually behave as described by the axioms? The answer seems to be a resounding no—they do not.

Kahneman and Tversky [1979, 1986] point out that the way decisions are framed seems to matter for decision making. They give the following example where people are asked to decide between surgery and radiation therapy for cancer treatment:

Survival Frame
Surgery: Of 100 people having surgery, 90 live through the postoperative period, 68 are alive at the end of the first year, and 34 are alive at the end of five years.
Radiation therapy: Of 100 people having radiation therapy, all live through the treatment, 77 are alive at the end of one year, and 22 are alive at the end of five years.
Mortality Frame
Surgery: Of 100 people having surgery, 10 die during surgery or the postoperative period, 32 die by the end of the first year, and 66 die by the end of five years.
Radiation therapy: Of 100 people having radiation therapy, none die during treatment, 23 die by the end of one year, and 78 die by the end of five years.

The information in both frames is exactly the same, yet when presented with the survival frame, 18 percent preferred radiation, and when presented with the mortality frame, 44 percent preferred radiation—a significant difference. The framing effect was not smaller for experienced physicians or for statistically sophisticated students.

If individual decision making is not adequately described by Von Neumann and Morgenstern's axioms, then it becomes necessary to rethink the descriptive validity of expected utility theory. No widely accepted answer to this problem has appeared, but it is safe to say that the foundations of mathematical utility theory have been shaken by the empirical evidence. Much work remains to be done.

$\mathscr{S}$ummary

The logic of the theory of investor choice can best be summarized by listing the series of logical steps and assumptions necessary to derive the indifference curves of Fig. 3.12:

- First, the five axioms of rational behavior were described.
- The expected utility rule was derived from the axioms.
- Cardinal utility functions were derived from the axioms.
- We assumed positive marginal utility. This and the expected utility rule were used to argue that individuals will always maximize the expected utility of wealth.
- Risk premia were defined, and a Pratt-Arrow measure of local risk aversion was developed.
- Stochastic dominance was shown to be a general theory of choice that maximizes expected utility for various classes of utility functions.
- Mean-variance indifference curves (which exhibit second-order stochastic dominance for normally distributed returns) were developed as a parametric theory of choice.

In Chapter 5 we shall use the mean-variance theory of choice as embodied in the mean-variance indifference curves to describe the manner in which investors actually choose optimal portfolios.

PROBLEM SET

3.1 State in your own words the minimum set of necessary conditions needed to obtain mean variance indifference curves like those graphed in Fig. Q3.1.

Figure Q3.1 Mean variance indifference curves.

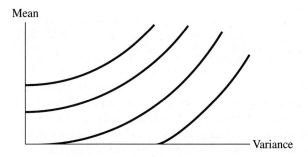

3.2 Figure 3.6(a) shows the utility of a risk lover. What does the indifference curve of a risk lover look like?

3.3 You have a logarithmic utility function $U(W) = \ln W$, and your current level of wealth is $5,000.

> **(a)** Suppose you are exposed to a situation that results in a 50/50 chance of winning or losing $1,000. If you can buy insurance that completely removes the risk for a fee of $125, will you buy it or take the gamble?
>
> **(b)** Suppose you accept the gamble outlined in (a) and lose, so that your wealth is reduced to $4,000. If you are faced with the same gamble and have the same offer of insurance as before, will you buy the insurance the second time around?

3.4 Assume that you have a logarithmic utility function for wealth $U(W) = \ln(W)$ and that you are faced with a 50/50 chance of winning or losing $1,000. How much will you pay to avoid risk if your current level of wealth is $10,000? How much would you pay if your level of wealth were $1,000,000?

3.5 Given the exponential utility function $U(W) = -e^{-aW}$:

> **(a)** Graph the function, assuming $a < 0$.
> **(b)** Does the function exhibit positive marginal utility and risk aversion?
> **(c)** Does the function have decreasing absolute risk aversion?
> **(d)** Does the function have constant relative risk aversion?

3.6 What kind of utility function of wealth might be consistent with an individual gambling and paying insurance at the same time?

3.7 Suppose that $A > B > C > D$ and that the utilities of these alternatives satisfy $U(A) + U(D) = U(B) + U(C)$. Is it true that $U\left(\frac{1}{2}B + \frac{1}{2}C\right)$ is greater than $U\left(\frac{1}{2}A + \frac{1}{2}D\right)$ because the former has a smaller variance? Why or why not?

3.8 A small businesswoman faces a 10% chance of having a fire that will reduce her net worth to $1.00, a 10% chance that fire will reduce it to $50,000, and an 80% chance that nothing detrimental will happen, so that her business will retain its worth of $100,000. What is the maximum amount she will pay for insurance if she has a logarithmic utility function? In other words, if $U(W) = \ln W$, compute the cost of the gamble. (*Note:* The insurance pays $99,999 in the first case; $50,000 in the second; and nothing in the third.)

3.9 If you are exposed to a 50/50 chance of gaining or losing $1,000 and insurance that removes the risk costs $500, at what level of wealth will you be indifferent relative to taking the gamble or paying the insurance? That is, what is your certainty equivalent wealth? Assume your utility function is $U(W) = -W^{-1}$.

3.10 Consider a lottery that pays $2 if n consecutive heads turn up in $(n + 1)$ tosses of a fair coin (i.e., the sequence of coin flips ends with the first tail). If you have a logarithmic utility function, $U(W) = \ln W$, what is the utility of the expected payoff? What is the expected utility of the payoff?

3.11 (Our thanks to David Pyle, University of California, Berkeley, for providing this problem.) Mr. Casadesus's current wealth consists of his home, which is worth $50,000, and $20,000 in savings, which are earning 7% in a savings and loan account. His (one-year) homeowner's insurance is up for renewal, and he has the following estimates of the potential losses on his house owing to fire, storm, and so on, during the period covered by the renewal:

Value of Loss ($)	Probability
0	.98
5,000	.01
10,000	.005
50,000	.005

His insurance agent has quoted the following premiums:

Amount of Insurance ($)	Premium ($)
30,000	$30 + AVL_1^*$
40,000	$27 + AVL_2$
50,000	$24 + AVL_3$

where AVL = actuarial value of loss = expected value of the *insurer's* loss.

Mr. Casadesus expects neither to save nor to dissave during the coming year, and he does not expect his home to change appreciably in value over this period. His utility for wealth at the end of the period covered by the renewal is logarithmic; that is, $U(W) = \ln(W)$.

(a) Given that the insurance company agrees with Mr. Casadesus's estimate of his losses, should he renew his policy (1) for the full value of his house, (2) for $40,000, or (3) for $30,000, or (4) should he cancel it?

(b) Suppose that Mr. Casadesus had $320,000 in a savings account. Would this change his insurance decision?

(c) If Mr. Casadesus has $20,000 in savings, and if his utility function is

$$U(W) = -200,000^{-1},$$

should he renew his home insurance? And if so, for what amount of coverage?

[Note: Insurance covers the first x dollars of loss. For simplicity, assume that all losses occur at the end of the year and that the premium paid is paid at the beginning of the year.]

3.12 Assume that security returns are normally distributed. Compare portfolios A and B, using both first- and second-order stochastic dominance:

Case 1	Case 2	Case 3
$\sigma_A > \sigma_B$	$\sigma_A = \sigma_B$	$\sigma_A < \sigma_B$
$E_A = E_B$	$E_A > E_B$	$E_A < E_B$

3.13 Given the following probability distributions for risky assets X and Y:

Probability X_i	X_i	Probability Y_i	Y_i
.1	−10	.2	2
.4	5	.5	3
.3	10	.2	4
.2	12	.1	30

(a) If the only available choice is 100% of your wealth in X or 100% in Y and you choose on the basis of mean and variance, which asset is preferred?

(b) According to the second-order stochastic dominance criterion, how would you compare them?

3.14 You have estimated the following probabilities for earnings per share of companies A and B:

Probability	A	B
.1	0.00	−.50
.2	.50	−.25
.4	1.00	1.50
.2	2.00	3.00
.1	3.00	4.00

(a) Calculate the mean and variance of the earnings per share for each company.

(b) Explain how some investors might choose A and others might choose B if preferences are based on mean and variance.

(c) Compare A and B, using the second-order stochastic dominance criterion.

3.15 Answer the following questions either true or false:

(a) If asset A is stochastically dominant over asset B according to the second-order criterion, it is also dominant according to the first-order criterion.

(b) If asset A has a higher mean and higher variance than asset B, it is stochastically dominant, according to the first-order criterion.

(c) A risk-neutral investor will use second-order stochastic dominance as a decision criterion only if the return of the underlying assets are normally distributed.

(d) A second-order stochastic dominance is consistent with utility functions that have positive marginal utility and risk aversion.

3.16 Consider the following risky scenarios for future cash flows for a firm:

Project 1		Project 2	
Probability	**Cash Flow ($)**	**Probability**	**Cash Flow ($)**
.2	4,000	.4	0
.6	5,000	.2	5,000
.2	6,000	.4	10,000

Given that the firm has fixed debt payments of $8,000 and limited liability, which scenario will shareholders choose and why? How would your answer change if there were not limited liability?

3.17 (Our thanks to Nils Hakansson, University of California, Berkeley, for providing this problem.) Two widows, each with $10,000 to invest, have been advised by a trusted friend to put their money into a one-year real estate trust that requires a minimum investment of $10,000. They have been offered a choice of six trusts with the following estimated yields:

Probability That Yield Will Be

Trust	−2	−1	0	1	2	3	4	5	6	7	8	9	10	11	12	13	14
A							.4	.2	.2	.2							
B	.1		.1	.1		.1	.1				.1		.1	.1	.1	.1	
C							.2	.2	.2	.2	.2						
D		.2			.2				.1	.1		.1	.1				.2
E								.4		.6							
F		.2			.2				.1	.1	.1	.1	.1			.1	.1

Before making up their minds, they have called on you for advice.

    (a) The first widow leaves you unsure as to whether she is risk averse. What advice can you give her?

    (b) The second widow shows definite risk aversion. What is your advice to her?

3.18 **(a)** Reorder the six real estate trusts in Problem 3.17, using the mean-variance criterion.

    (b) Is the mean-variance ranking the same as that achieved by second-order stochastic dominance?

REFERENCES

Arrow, K. J., *Essays in the Theory of Risk-Bearing*. North-Holland, Amsterdam, 1971.

Bawa, V. J., "Optimal Rules for Ordering Uncertain Prospects," *Journal of Financial Economics*, March 1975, 95–121.

Fama, E. F., and M. H. Miller, *The Theory of Finance*, Chapter 5. Holt, Rinehart, and Winston, New York, 1972.

Friedman, M., and L. J. Savage, "The Utility Analysis of Choices Involving Risk," *Journal of Political Economy,* August 1948, 279–304.

Friend, I., and M. Blume, "The Demand for Risky Assets," *American Economic Review*, December 1975, 900–922.

Hanoch, G., and H. Levy, "The Efficiency Analysis of Choices Involving Risk," *Review of Economic Studies*, 1969, 335–346.

Herstein, I. N., and J. Milnor, "An Axiomatic Approach to Expected Utility," *Econometrica*, April 1953, 291–297.

Jean, W., "Comparison of Moment and Stochastic Dominance Ranking Methods," *Journal of Financial and Quantitative Analysis*, March 1975, 151–162.

Kahneman, D., and A. Tversky, "Prospect Theory: An Analysis of Decision Under Risk," *Econometrica*, March 1979, 263–291.

Keeney, R. L., and H. Raiffa, *Decisions with Multiple Objectives: Preferences and Value through Tradeoffs*. John Wiley and Sons, New York, 1976.

Kira, D., and W. T. Ziemba, "Equivalence among Alternative Portfolio Selection Criteria," in Levy and Sarnat, eds., *Financial Decision Making under Uncertainty*, Academic Press, New York, 1977, 151–161.

Levy, H., and Y. Kroll, "Stochastic Dominance with Riskless Assets," *Journal of Financial and Quantitative Analysis*, December 1976, 743–778.

Markowitz, H., *Portfolio Selection*. Yale University Press, New Haven, Conn., 1959.

Porter, R. B., J. R. Wart, and D. L. Ferguson, "Efficient Algorithms for Conducting Stochastic Dominance Tests of Large Numbers of Portfolios," *Journal of Financial and Quantitative Analysis*, January 1973, 71–82.

Pratt, J. W., "Risk Aversion in the Small and in the Large," *Econometrica*, January–April, 1964, 122–136.

Rubin, P. H., and C. W. Paul II, "An Evolutionary Model of Taste for Risk," *Economic Inquiry*, October 1979, 585–596.

Tobin, J., "Liquidity Preference as a Behavior toward Risk," *Review of Economic Studies*, February 1958, 65–86.

Tversky, A., and D. Kahneman, "Rational Choice and the Framing of Decisions," *Journal of Business*, October 1986, S251–S278.

Vickson, R. G., "Stochastic Dominance for Decreasing Absolute Risk Aversion," *Journal of Financial and Quantitative Analysis*, December 1975, 799–812.

Vickson, R. G., and M. Altman, "On the Relative Effectiveness of Stochastic Dominance Rules: Extension to Decreasingly Risk-Averse Utility Functions," *Journal of Financial and Quantitative Analysis*, March 1977, 73–84.

Von Neumann, J., and O. Morgenstern, *Theory of Games and Economic Behavior*. Princeton University Press, Princeton, N.J., 1947.

Walter, J. E., *Dividend Policy and Enterprise Valuation*. Wadsworth, Belmont, Calif., 1967.

Whitmore, G. A., "Third Degree Stochastic Dominance," *American Economic Review*, June 1970, 457–459.

Whitmore, G. A., and M. C. Findlay, *Stochastic Dominance*. Lexington Books, D.C. Heath and Co., Lexington, Mass., 1975.

Ziemba, W. T., and R. G. Vickson, eds., *Stochastic Optimization Models in Finance*. Academic Press, New York, 1975.

Chapter 4

In this formulation the objects of choice are not derivative statistical measures of the probability distribution of consumption opportunities but rather the contingent consumption claims themselves set out in extensive form.

—J. Hirshleifer, "Efficient Allocation of Capital in an Uncertain World," *American Economic Review,* May 1964, 80.

State Preference Theory

F INANCE DEALS WITH INVESTMENT DECISIONS of individuals and firms linked through the supply and demand for securities in the capital market.[1] Firms borrow capital for investment in real assets by *selling* securities; individuals obtain claims to firms' real assets by *investing* in securities. Thus securities present opportunities for intertemporal shifts of consumption through the financing of productive activities. Individual consumption/investment decisions that determine aggregate security supply are both affected by security prices. By equating security supply and demand, security prices yield a consistent set of firm and individual investment decisions. In this chapter, we will analyze how optimal individual investment decisions and optimal firm investment decisions are determined under uncertainty for a given set of security prices.

In Chapter 3 we found that, under specified conditions, individual decision making under uncertainty is accomplished by maximizing *expected* utility of end-of-period wealth. This decision criterion was shown to be valid when individuals are rational, prefer more wealth to less, and follow the five axioms of choice under uncertainty. Implicitly, it was also assumed that individuals can assess a security's probability distribution of end-of-period payoffs. It was shown that the expected utility criterion is a very simple way of choosing among mutually exclusive investments having different probability distributions of end-of-period payoffs. By choosing the investment with the highest expected utility, the optimal investment is determined, thus condensing a choice across N probability distributions of end-of-period payoffs into a comparison among N expected utility values.

In this and in the following chapter, we wish to move beyond the individual's choice problem of mutually exclusive investments to the more general problem of portfolio decision making, that is, the optimal choice of investing in more than one risky security. This is equivalent to the problem of choosing an individual's probability distribution of end-of-period wealth that is consistent with the

---

[1] Ronald W. Masulis was the primary author of this chapter and has benefited from lecture notes on this topic by Herbert Johnson.

Figure 4.1 Elementary state-contingent claim.

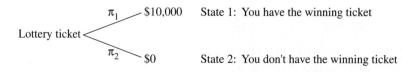

π_1 — $10,000   State 1: You have the winning ticket

Lottery ticket

π_2 — $0   State 2: You don't have the winning ticket

set of available risky securities and the individual's initial wealth. The individual's choice problem is to find that portfolio or linear combination of risky securities that is optimal, given his or her initial wealth and tastes. We assume a perfect capital market to ensure that there are no costs of portfolio construction.

A. Uncertainty and Alternative Future States

Securities inherently have a time dimension. The securities investment decisions of individuals are determined by their desired consumption over future time intervals. The passage of time involves uncertainty about the future and hence about the future value of a security investment. From the standpoint of the issuing firm and the individual investors, the uncertain future value of a security can be represented as a vector of probable payoffs at some future date, and an individual's portfolio of investments is a matrix of possible payoffs on the different securities that compose the portfolio.

In the state preference model, uncertainty takes the form of not knowing what the state of nature will be at some future date. To the investor a security is a set of possible payoffs, each one associated with a mutually exclusive state of nature. Once the uncertain state of the world is revealed, the payoff on the security is determined exactly. Thus a security represents a claim to a vector (or bundle) of state-contingent payoffs.

In the simplest case, there are two possible outcomes with probabilities π_1 and π_2 and therefore two mutually exclusive states of nature with probabilities π_1 and π_2. Take as an example an investment in a lottery ticket with outcomes ($10,000, $0). With probability π_1, state 1 is realized and the lottery ticket pays off $10,000; with probability $\pi_2 = 1 - \pi_1$, state 2 is realized and the lottery ticket pays off nothing (Fig. 4.1).

The probability of a state of nature occurring is thus equal to the probability of the associated end-of-period security payoff. The states of nature are assumed to capture the fundamental causes of economic uncertainty in the economy; for example, state 1 could represent peace and state 2 could represent war, or state 1 could represent prosperity and state 2 could represent depression. Once the state of nature is known, the end-of-period payoff at each risky security is also known. By summing over individual security holdings and then over individuals, it follows that once the state of nature is known, individual and aggregate end-of-period wealth are also known.

In principle, there can be an infinite number of states of nature and thus an infinite number of end-of-period payoffs for a risky asset. This set of states must meet the critical properties of being mutually exclusive and exhaustive. That is to say, one and only one state of nature will be realized at the end of the period, and the sum of the probabilities of the individual states of nature equals one. It is also assumed that (1) individuals can associate an outcome from each security's probability distribution of its end-of-period payoff with each state of nature that could occur, and (2) individuals are only concerned about the amount of wealth they will have if a given state occurs;

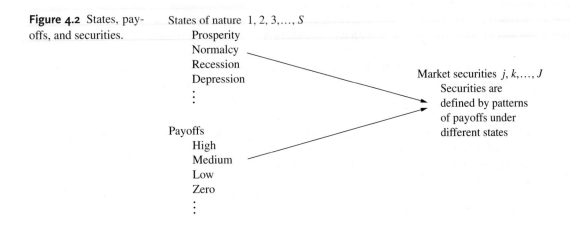

Figure 4.2 States, pay-offs, and securities.

once their wealth is known they are otherwise indifferent as to which state of nature occurs (i.e., individuals have state-independent utility functions).[2]

B. Definition of Pure Securities

Analytically, the generalization of the standard, timeless, microeconomic analysis under certainty to a multiperiod economy under uncertainty with securities markets is facilitated by the concept of a pure security. A *pure* or *primitive security* is defined as a security that pays $1 at the end of the period if a given state occurs and nothing if any other state occurs. The concept of the pure security allows the logical decomposition of market securities into portfolios of pure securities.[3] Thus every market security may be considered a combination of various pure securities.

In terms of state preference theory, a security represents a position with regard to each possible future state of nature. In Fig. 4.2, market securities are defined with respect to the characteristics of their payoffs under each alternative future state. A market security thus consists of a set of payoff characteristics distributed over states of nature. The complexity of the security may range from numerous payoff characteristics in many states to no payoff at all in all but one state.

C. Complete Capital Market

In the state preference framework, uncertainty about securities' future values is represented by a set of possible state-contingent payoffs. Linear combinations of this set of state-contingent *security* payoffs represent an individual's opportunity set of state-contingent *portfolio* payoffs. An important property of this opportunity set is determined by whether or not the capital market is *complete*. When the number of unique linearly independent securities is equal to the total number of alternative future states of nature, the market is said to be complete. For the case of three states of

---

[2] For example, if an individual's utility were a function of other individuals' wealth positions as well as one's own, then the utility function would generally be state dependent.

[3] Pure or primitive securities are often called Arrow-Debreu securities, since Arrow [1964] and Debreu [1959] set forth their original specification.

nature, suppose that a risk-free asset with payoff $(1,1,1)$, an unemployment insurance contract with payoff $(1,0,0)$, and risky debt with payoff $(0,1,1)$ all exist, but no other securities can be traded. In this case we have three securities and three states of nature, but we do not have a complete market since the payoff on the risk-free asset is just the sum of the payoffs on the other two market securities; that is, the three securities are not linearly independent. If the market is incomplete, then not every possible security payoff can be constructed from a portfolio of the existing securities. For example, the security payoff $(0,1,0)$ cannot be obtained from $(1,1,1)$, $(1,0,0)$, and $(0,1,1)$. The existing securities will, of course, have well-defined prices, but any possible new security not *spanned* by these securities (i.e., cannot be created from the existing securities) will not have a unique price.[4]

Suppose now that in addition to the security payoffs $(1,1,1)$, $(1,0,0)$, and $(0,1,1)$, a stock with payoff $(0,1,3)$ also exists. Then among these four securities there are three that are linearly independent state-contingent payoffs, and with three states the market is complete. Assuming the market is perfect, any pattern of returns can be created in a complete market. In particular, a complete set of pure securities with payoffs $(1,0,0)$, $(0,1,0)$, and $(0,0,1)$ can be created as linear combinations of existing securities. It takes some linear algebra to figure out how to obtain the pure securities from any arbitrary complete set of market securities, but once we know how to form them, it is easy to replicate any other security from a linear combination of the pure securities. For example: a security with a payoff (a,b,c) can be replicated by buying (or short selling if a, b, or c is negative) a of $(1,0,0)$, b of $(0,1,0)$, and c of $(0,0,1)$.[5]

Given a complete securities market, we could theoretically reduce the uncertainty about our future wealth to zero. It does not make any difference which uncertain future state of nature will actually occur. That is, by dividing our wealth in a particular way among the available securities, we could, if we chose, construct a portfolio that was equivalent to holding equal amounts of all the pure securities. This portfolio would have the same payoff in every state even though the payoffs of individual securities varied over states.[6]

Without going through a complex solution process to attain the general equilibrium results that the concept of a pure security facilitates, we shall convey the role of the concept of a pure security in a more limited setting. We shall demonstrate how in a perfect and complete capital market the implicit price of a pure security can be derived from the prices of existing market securities and how the prices of other securities can then be developed from the implicit prices of pure securities.

D. *Derivation of Pure Security Prices*

Given that we know the state-contingent payoff vectors of both the market securities and the pure securities, we wish to develop the relationship between the *prices* of the market securities and pure securities in a perfect and complete capital market.

---

[4] One person might think the security with payoff $(0,1,0)$ is worth more than someone else does, but if the security cannot be formed from a portfolio of existing market securities, then these virtual prices that different people would assign to this hypothetical security need not be the same.

[5] See Appendix 4A for a general method of determining whether a complete market exists.

[6] While a complete market may appear to require an unreasonably large number of independent securities, Ross [1976] showed that in general if option contracts can be written on market securities and market securities have sufficiently variable payoffs across states, an infinite number of linearly independent security and option payoffs can be formed from a small number of securities.

Table 4.1 Payoffs in Relation to Prices of Baskets of Fruit

	Bananas	Apples	Prices*
Basket 1	10	20	$8
Basket 2	30	10	$9

* The probabilities of the states are implicit in the prices.

The following notation will be used throughout this chapter:

$p_s =$ prices of pure securities,

$p_j =$ prices of market securities,

$\pi_s =$ state probabilities—individuals' beliefs about the relative likelihoods of states occurring,

$Q_s =$ number of pure securities.

Let us begin with an analogy. The Mistinback Company sells baskets of fruit, limiting its sales to only two types of baskets. Basket 1 is composed of 10 bananas and 20 apples and sells for $8. Basket 2 is composed of 30 bananas and 10 apples and sells for $9. The situation may be summarized by the payoffs set forth in Table 4.1.

Using the relationships in Table 4.1, we can solve for the prices of apples and bananas separately. Let us denote apples by A, bananas by B, the baskets of fruit by 1 and 2, and the quantity of apples and bananas in a basket by Q_{jA} and Q_{jB}, respectively. Using this notation, we can express the prices of the two baskets as follows:

$$p_1 = p_A Q_{1A} + p_B Q_{1B}, \qquad p_2 = p_A Q_{2A} + p_B Q_{2B}.$$

Only p_A and p_B are unknown. Thus there are two equations and two unknowns, and the system is solvable as follows (substitute the known values in each equation):

$$\$8 = p_A 20 + p_B 10, \text{ (a)} \qquad \$9 = p_A 10 + p_B 30. \text{ (b)}$$

Subtract three times Eq. (a) from Eq. (b) to obtain p_A:

$$\$9 = p_A 10 + p_B 30$$
$$-\$24 = -p_A 60 - p_B 30$$
$$\overline{-\$15 = -p_A 50}$$
$$p_A = \$.30$$

Then substituting the value p_A into Eq. (a), we have

$$\$8 = (\$.30)20 + p_B 10 = \$6 + p_B 10$$
$$\$2 = p_B 10$$
$$p_B = \$.20.$$

Given that we know the prices of the market securities, we may now apply this same analysis to the problem of determining the implicit prices of the pure securities. Consider security j, which

Table 4.2 Payoff Table for Securities j and k

Security	State 1	State 2	
j	$10	$20	$p_j = \$8$
k	$30	$10	$p_k = \$9$

pays $10 if state 1 occurs and $20 if state 2 occurs; its price is $9. Note that state 1 might be a gross national product (GNP) growth of 8% in real terms during the year, whereas state 2 might represent a GNP growth rate of only 1% in real terms. This information is summarized in Table 4.2.

Any individual security is similar to a mixed basket of goods with regard to alternative future states of nature. Recall that a pure security pays $1 if a specified state occurs and nothing if any other state occurs. We may proceed to determine the price of a pure security in a matter analogous to that employed for the fruit baskets.

The equations for determining the price for two pure securities related to the situation described are

$$p_1 Q_{j1} + p_2 Q_{j2} = p_j,$$

$$p_1 Q_{k1} + p_2 Q_{k2} = p_k,$$

where Q_{j1} represents the quantity of pure securities paying $1 in state 1 included in security j. Proceeding analogously to the situation for the fruit baskets, we insert values into the two equations. Substituting the respective payoffs for securities j and k, we obtain $.20 as the price of pure security 1 and $.30 as the price of pure security 2:

$$p_1 10 + p_2 20 = \$8,$$

$$p_1 30 + p_2 10 = \$9,$$

$$p_1 = \$.20, \qquad p_2 = \$.30.$$

It should be emphasized that the p_1 of $.20 and the p_2 of $.30 are the prices of the two pure securities and not the prices of the market securities j and k. Securities j and k represent portfolios of pure securities. Any actual security provides different payoffs for different future states. But under appropriately defined conditions, the prices of market securities permit us to determine the prices of pure securities. Thus our results indicate that for pure security 1 a $.20 payment is required for a promise of a payoff of $1 if state 1 occurs and nothing if any other states occur. The concept of pure security is useful for analytical purposes as well as for providing a simple description of uncertainty for financial analysis.

E. No-Arbitrage Profit Condition

Capital market equilibrium requires that market prices be set so that supply equals demand for each individual security. In the context of the state preference framework, one condition necessary for market equilibrium requires that any two securities or portfolios with the same state-contingent payoff vectors must be priced identically.[7] Otherwise, everyone would want to buy the security or portfolio with the lower price and to sell the security or portfolio with the higher price. If both securities or portfolios are in positive supply, such prices cannot represent an equilibrium. This condition is called the *single-price law of markets*.

If short selling is allowed in the capital market, we can obtain a second related necessary condition for market equilibrium—the absence of any riskless arbitrage profit opportunity. To short-sell a security, an individual borrows the security from a current owner and then immediately sells the security in the capital market at the current price. Then, at a later date, the individual goes back to the capital market and repurchases the security at the then-current market price and immediately returns the security to the lender. If the security price falls over the period of the short sale, the individual makes a profit; if the security price rises, he or she takes a loss. In either case the short seller's gain or loss is always the negative of the owner's gain or loss over this same period.

When two portfolios, A and B, sell at different prices, where $p_A > p_B$, but have identical state-contingent payoff vectors, we could short-sell the more expensive portfolio and realize a cash flow of p_A, then buy the less expensive portfolio, for a negative cash flow of p_B. We would realize a positive net cash flow of $(p_A - p_B)$, and at the end of the period, we could at no risk take our payoff from owning portfolio B to *exactly* repay our short position in portfolio A. Thus the positive net cash flow at the beginning of the period represents a riskless arbitrage profit opportunity. Since all investors are assumed to prefer more wealth to less, this arbitrage opportunity is inconsistent with market equilibrium.

In a perfect and complete capital market, any market security's payoff vector can be exactly replicated by a portfolio of pure securities. Thus, it follows that when short selling is allowed, the no-arbitrage profit condition requires that the price of the market security be equal to the price of any linear combination of pure securities that replicates the market security's payoff vector.

F. *Economic Determinants of Security Prices*

To gain an understanding of what determines the price of a market security, we will first consider what determines the price of individual pure securities. Since a market security can always be constructed from the set of pure securities in a complete market, we can then answer the first question as well.

The prices of the pure securities will be determined by trading among individuals. Even if these pure securities themselves are not directly traded, we can still infer prices for them in a complete market from the prices of the market securities that *are* traded. The prices of pure securities will be shown to depend on

1. time preferences for consumption and the productivity of capital;

2. expectations as to the probability that a particular state will occur;

3. individuals' attitudes toward risk, given the variability across states of aggregate end-of-period wealth.

---

[7] This condition implies the absence of any first-order stochastically dominated market securities. Otherwise the former payoff per dollar of investment would exceed the latter payoff per dollar of investment in every state. The latter security would be first-order stochastically dominated by the former security.

To understand how time preferences and the productivity of capital affect security prices, we need to recognize that a riskless security can always be constructed in a complete capital market simply by forming a portfolio composed of one pure security for each state. The payoff on this portfolio is riskless since a dollar will be paid regardless of what state is realized. In the case of three states the price of this riskless portfolio is the sum of the prices of the three individual pure securities (e.g., $p_1 + p + p_3 = .8$). The price of a riskless claim to a dollar at the end of the period is just the present value of a dollar discounted at the risk-free rate r_f, that is to say, $1/(1 + r_f) = \sum p_s$. If there is a positive time value of money, the riskless interest rate will be positive. The actual size of this interest rate will reflect individual time preferences for consumption and the productivity of capital, just as is the case in a simple world of certainty.[8] Thus one determinant of the price of a pure security paying a dollar if state s occurs is the market discounted rate on certain end-of-period dollar payoff.

The second determinant of a pure security's price, and a cause for differences in security prices, is individuals' beliefs concerning the relative likelihood of different states occurring. These beliefs are often termed *state probabilities*, π_s. Individuals' subjective beliefs concerning state probabilities can differ in principle. However, the simplest case is one in which individuals agree on the relative likelihoods of states. This assumption is termed *homogeneous expectations* and implies that there is a well-defined set of state probabilities known to all individuals in the capital market. Under the assumption of homogeneous expectations, the price of a pure (state-contingent) security, p_s, can be decomposed into the probability of the state, π_s, and the price, θ_s, of an expected dollar payoff contingent on state s occurring, $p_s = \pi_s \cdot \theta_s$. This follows from the fact that pure security s pays a dollar only when s is realized. Thus the expected end-of-period payoff on pure security s is a dollar multiplied by the probability of state s occurring. This implies that we can decompose the end-of-period expected payoff into an expected payoff of a dollar and the probability of state s. Even when prices contingent on a particular state s occurring are the same across states ($\theta_s = \theta_t$, for all s and t), the prices of pure securities will differ as long as the probabilities of states occurring are not all identical ($\pi_s \neq \pi_t$, for all s and t).

A useful alternative way to see this point is to recognize that the price of a pure security is equal to its *expected* end-of-period payoff discounted to the present at its expected rate of return:

$$p_s = \frac{\$1 \cdot \pi_s}{1 + E(R_s)},$$

where $0 < p_s < 1$. Thus the pure security's expected rate of return is

$$E(R_s) = \frac{\$1 \cdot \pi_s}{p_s} - 1 = \frac{\$1}{\theta_s} - 1, \quad \text{where } 0 < \theta_s < 1,$$

since $p_s = \pi_s \theta_s$ under the assumption of homogeneous expectations. So if the θ_s's were identical across states, the expected states of return would be equal for all pure securities. But given that

---

[8] The property that individuals prefer to consume a dollar of resources today, rather than consume the same dollar of resources tomorrow, is called the time preference for consumption. As discussed in Chapter 1, an individual's marginal rate of time preference for consumption is equal to his or her marginal rate of substitution of current consumption and *certain* end-of-period consumption. In a perfect capital market, it was also shown that the marginal rates of time preference for all individuals are equal to the market interest rate.

the probabilities across states differ, the expected payoffs across pure securities must also differ. If expected payoffs vary, expected rates of return can be the same only when the prices of the pure securities vary proportionally with the state probabilities.

The third determinant of security prices, and a second cause for differences in these prices, is individuals' attitudes toward risk when there is variability in aggregate wealth across states. Assuming that individuals are risk averse, they will diversify by investing in some of each pure security to ensure that they are not penniless regardless of what state is realized.[9] In fact, if the prices, θ_s's, of expected payoffs of a dollar contingent on a particular state occurring were the same for all states (and thus the expected rates of return of pure securities are all equal), then each risk-averse individual would want to invest in an equal number of each pure security so as to eliminate all uncertainty about his or her future wealth. Not everyone can do this, however, in the economy, and it must be borne by someone. Consider the following example. End-of-period aggregate wealth can be one, two, or three trillion dollars, depending on whether the depressed, normal, or prosperous state occurs; then the average investor must hold a portfolio with a payoff vector of the form $(X, 2X, 3X)$. Because individuals are risk averse, dollar payoffs are more valuable in states where they have relatively low wealth, which in this example is state 1. In order for people to be induced to bear the risk associated with a payoff vector of the form $(X, 2X, 3X)$, pure security prices must be adjusted to make the state 1 security relatively expensive and the state 3 security relatively cheap. In other words, to increase demand for the relatively abundant state 3 securities, prices must adjust to lower the expected rate of return on state 1 securities and to raise the expected rate of return on state 3 securities.

If aggregate wealth were the same in some states, then risk-averse investors would want to hold the same number of pure securities for these states and there would be no reason for prices of expected dollar payoffs to be different in these states. Investors would not want to hold unequal numbers of claims to the states with the same aggregate wealth because this would mean bearing risk that could be diversified away, and there is no reason to expect a reward for bearing *diversifiable risk*. So it is the prospect of a higher portfolio expected return that induces the risk-averse investors to bear nondiversifiable risk. Thus risk aversion combined with variability in end-of-period aggregate wealth causes variation in the prices (θ_s's) of dollar expected payoffs across states, negatively related to the aggregate end-of-period wealth or aggregate payoffs across states. This in turn causes like variations in the pure security prices.

There is a very important condition implicit in the previous discussion. We found that when investors are risk averse, securities that pay off relatively more in states with low aggregate wealth have relatively low expected rates of return, whereas securities that pay off relatively more in states with high aggregate wealth have relatively high expected rates of return. Since aggregate wealth is equal to the sum of the payoffs on all market securities, it is also termed the payoff on the *market portfolio*. Securities with state-contingent payoffs positively related to the state-contingent payoffs on the market portfolio, and which therefore involve significant nondiversifiable risk bearing, have higher expected rates of return than securities that have payoffs negatively or less positively related to the payoffs on the market portfolio, and which therefore involve little diversifiable risk bearing. We will return to this important condition in Chapter 6.

It follows from this analysis that a pure security price can be decomposed into three factors:

---

[9] This also requires the utility function to exhibit infinite *marginal* utility at a zero wealth level.

$$p_s = \pi_s \theta_s = \frac{\$1\pi_s}{1 + E(R_s)} = \left[\frac{\$1}{1 + r_f}\right] \pi_s \left[\frac{1 + r_f}{1 + E(R_s)}\right]$$

$$= \left[\frac{\$1}{1 + r_f}\right] \pi_s \left[1 - \frac{E(R_s) - r_f}{1 + E(R_s)}\right], \quad \text{where } E(R_s) \geq r_f.$$

The first factor is an end-of-period dollar payoff discounted to the present at the riskless rate. It is multiplied by the second factor, which is the probability of payoff. The third factor is a risk adjustment factor. Note that if investors are all risk neutral, the expected rate of return on all securities will be equal to the riskless interest rate, in which case the above risk adjustment factor (i.e., the third factor) becomes one. In summary, security prices are affected by (1) the time value of money, (2) the probability beliefs about state-contingent payoffs, and (3) individual preferences toward risk and the level of variability in aggregate state-contingent payoffs or wealth (i.e., the level of nondiversifiable risk in the economy).

G. Optimal Portfolio Decisions

Now that we have developed the basic structure of state preference theory, we will return to the problem of optimal portfolio choice in a perfect and complete capital market. This will then be followed by an analysis of a firm's optimal investment problem, also in a perfect and complete capital market. Since any portfolio payoff pattern can be constructed from the existing market securities or from a full set of pure securities in a complete capital market, we can obtain the same optimal portfolio position whether we frame the analysis in terms of market securities or pure securities. Since pure securities are much simpler to analyze, we will phrase the optimal portfolio problem in terms of these securities. Thus we can write an individual's expected utility of end-of-period wealth as $\sum \pi_s U(Q_s)$, where Q_s = number of pure securities paying a dollar if state s occurs. In this context, Q_s represents the number of state s pure securities the individual buys as well as his or her end-of-period wealth if state s occurs.

Now consider the problem we face when we must decide how much of our initial wealth, W_0, to spend for current consumption, C, and what portfolio of securities to hold for the future. We wish to solve the problem[10]

$$\max \left[u(C) + \sum_s \pi_s U(Q_s)\right] \tag{4.1}$$

subject to

$$\sum_s p_s Q_s + \$1C = W_0. \tag{4.2}$$

That is, we are maximizing our expected utility of current and future consumption (Eq. 4.1) subject to our wealth constraint (Eq. 4.2). Our portfolio decision consists of the choices we make

---

[10] This formulation assumes that the utility function is separable into utility of current consumption and utility of end-of-period consumption. In principle, the utility functions $u(C)$ and $U(Q_s)$ can be different functions.

for Q_s, the number of pure securities we buy for each state s. Note that there is no explicit discounting of future utility, but any such discounting could be absorbed in the functional form for $U(Q_s)$. In addition, the p_s's include an implicit market discount rate. There is no need to take an expectation over $u(C)$, our utility of current consumption, since there is no uncertainty concerning the present.

There are two ways to maximize expected utility subject to a wealth constraint. We could solve (4.2) for one of the Q_s's, say Q_1, and then eliminate this variable from (4.1). Sometimes this is the easiest way, but more often it is easier to use the Lagrange multiplier method (see Appendix D at the end of the book):

$$L = u(C) + \sum_s \pi_s U(Q_s) - \lambda \left(\sum_s p_s Q_s + \$1C - W_0 \right), \tag{4.3}$$

where λ is called a Lagrange multiplier. The Lagrange multiplier λ is a measure of how much our utility would increase if our initial wealth were increased by \$1 (i.e., the shadow price for relaxing the constraint). To obtain the investor's optimal choice of C and Q_s's, we take the partial derivatives with respect to each of these variables and set them equal to zero. Taking the partial derivative with respect to C yields

$$\frac{\partial L}{\partial C} = u'(C) - \$1\lambda = 0, \tag{4.4}$$

where the prime denotes partial differentiation with respect to the argument of the function. Next, we take partial derivatives with respect to Q_1, Q_2, and so on. For each Q_t, we will pick up one term from the expected utility and one from the wealth constraint (all other terms vanish):

$$\frac{\partial L}{\partial Q_1} = \pi_t U'(Q_t) - \lambda p_t = 0, \tag{4.5}$$

where $\pi_t U'(Q_t)$ = expected marginal utility of an investment Q_t in pure security s. We also take the partial derivative with respect to λ:

$$\frac{\partial L}{\partial \lambda} = \left(\sum_s p_s Q_s + \$1C - W_0 \right) = 0. \tag{4.6}$$

This just gives us back the wealth constraint. These first-order conditions allow us to determine the individual's optimal consumption/investment choices.[11]

As an example, consider an investor with a logarithmic utility function of wealth and initial wealth of \$10,000. Assume a two-state world where the pure security prices are .4 and .6 and the state probabilities are $\frac{1}{3}$ and $\frac{2}{3}$, respectively. The Lagrangian function is

$$L = \ln C + \frac{1}{3} \ln Q_1 + \frac{2}{3} \ln Q_2 - \lambda(.4Q_1 + .6Q_2 + C - 10{,}000),$$

and the first-order conditions are

---

[11] We are also assuming that the second-order conditions for a maximum hold.

$$\frac{\partial L}{\partial C} = \frac{1}{C} - \lambda = 0, \qquad\qquad \text{which implies} \quad C = \frac{1}{\lambda}, \tag{a}$$

$$\frac{\partial L}{\partial Q_1} = \frac{1}{3Q_1} - .4\lambda = 0, \qquad\qquad \text{which implies} \quad Q_1 = \frac{1}{1.2\lambda}, \tag{b}$$

$$\frac{\partial L}{\partial Q_1} = \frac{2}{3Q_2} - .6\lambda = 0, \qquad\qquad \text{which implies} \quad Q_2 = \frac{1}{.9\lambda}, \tag{c}$$

$$\frac{\partial L}{\partial \lambda} = 10{,}000 - C - .4Q_1 - .6Q_2 = 0. \tag{d}$$

Substituting Eqs. (a), (b), and (c) into (d) yields

$$\frac{1}{\lambda} + \frac{.4}{1.2\lambda} + \frac{.6}{.9\lambda} = 10{,}000, \tag{d$'$}$$

and multiplying by λ yields

$$1 + \frac{1}{3} + \frac{2}{3} = 10{,}000\lambda, \quad \text{which yields} \quad \lambda = \frac{1}{5{,}000}. \tag{d$''$}$$

Now, substituting this value of λ back into Eqs. (a), (b), and (c) yields the optimal consumption and investment choices, $C = \$5{,}000$, $Q_1 = 4{,}166.7$, and $Q_2 = 5{,}555.5$. Substituting these quantities back into the wealth constraint verifies that this is indeed a feasible solution. The investor in this problem divides his or her wealth equally between current and future consumption, which is what we should expect since the risk-free interest rate is zero—that is, $\sum p_s = 1 = 1/(1 + r)$—and there is no time preference for consumption in this logarithmic utility function. However, the investor does buy more of the state 2 pure security since the expected rate of return on the state 2 pure security is greater. Because the utility function exhibits risk aversion, the investor also invests some of his or her wealth in the state 1 pure security.

In this example we assumed that the investor is a price taker. In a general equilibrium framework, the prices of the pure securities would be determined as part of the problem; that is, they would be *endogenous*. The prices would be determined as a result of the individuals' constrained expected utility maximization (which determines the aggregate demands for securities). The critical condition required for equilibrium is that the supply of each market security equal its aggregate demand. In a complete capital market this equilibrium condition can be restated by saying that the aggregate supply of each pure security is equal to its aggregate demand.

H. The Efficient Set with Two Risky Assets (and No Risk-Free Asset)

In a complete capital market, we can obtain a number of important portfolio optimality conditions. These conditions hold for any risk-averse expected utility maximizer. Rewriting Eq. (4.4) and Eq. (4.5) in terms of λ and eliminating λ yields two sets of portfolio optimality conditions:

$$\frac{\pi_t U'(Q_t)}{u'(C)} = \frac{p_t}{\$1} \quad \text{for any state } t \tag{4.7}$$

Figure 4.3 Optimal consumption/investment decisions.

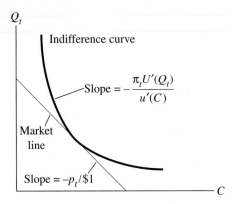

and

$$\frac{\pi_t U'(Q_t)}{\pi_s U'(Q_s)} = \frac{p_t}{p_s} \quad \text{for any two states } s \text{ and } t. \tag{4.8}$$

In both cases, the optimal allocation of wealth represents choosing C and the Q_s's so that the ratio of expected marginal utilities equals the ratio of market prices for the C and the Q_s's. That is, the optimal consumption and investment choices involve choosing points on the various indifference curves (curves of constant *expected* utility) that are tangent to the associated market lines. This is equivalent to choosing consumption and investment weights so that the slopes of the indifference curves (which are defined as the negative of the marginal rates of substitution) representing current consumption and future consumption contingent on state t (as in Fig. 4.3) or representing future consumption contingent on state t (as in Fig 4.4) are equal to the slopes of the respective market lines (representing the market exchange rates, e.g., $-p_t/p_s$).

An alternative way of stating the optimality conditions of the above portfolio is that the expected marginal utilities of wealth in state s, divided by the price of the state s pure security, should be equal across all states, and this ratio should also be equal to the marginal utility of current consumption. This is a reasonable result; if expected marginal utility per pure security price were high in one state and low in another, then we must not have maximized expected utility. We should increase investment in the high expected marginal utility security at the expense of the security yielding low expected marginal utility. But as we do that, we lower expected marginal utility where it is high and raise it where it is low, because a risk-averse investor's marginal utility decreases with wealth (his or her utility function has a positive but decreasing slope). Finally, when Eq. (4.8) is satisfied, there is no way left to provide a further increase of expected utility.[12]

When investors' portfolio choices over risky securities are independent of their individual wealth positions, we have a condition known as *portfolio separation*. This condition requires that there are either additional restrictions on investor preferences or additional restrictions on

---

[12] This entire procedure will ordinarily not work if the investor is risk neutral instead of risk averse. A risk-neutral investor will plunge entirely into the security with the highest expected return. He or she would like to invest more in this security, but, being already fully invested in it, cannot do so. Equation (4.8) will not hold for risk neutrality.

Figure 4.4 Optimal
portfolio decisions.

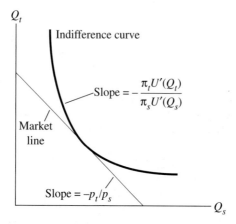

security return distributions.[13] Under portfolio separation, investors choose among only a few basic portfolios of market securities. Thus the importance of having a complete market is greatly decreased. Recall that when capital markets are incomplete, individuals are limited in their choices of state-contingent payoff patterns to those payoff patterns that can be constructed as linear combinations of existing market securities. However, with portfolio separation, investors will often find that the infeasible payoff opportunities would not have been chosen even if they were available. Thus under portfolio separation, investor portfolio decisions will often be unaffected by whether or not the capital market is complete.

Portfolio separation has been shown to depend on the form of the utility function of individuals and the form of the security return distributions. In the special case where investor utility functions of wealth are quadratic, or security returns are joint-normally distributed, portfolio separation obtains. With the addition of homogeneous expectations, portfolio separation provides sufficient conditions for a security-pricing equation. This security-pricing relationship can be expressed in terms of means and variances and is called the *capital asset pricing model*.[14] The resulting form of the security-pricing equation is particularly convenient for formulating testable propositions and conducting empirical studies. As we shall discuss in the following chapters, many of the implications of portfolio separation in capital markets appear to be consistent with observed behavior and have been supported by empirical tests.

---

[13] Cass and Stiglitz [1970] proved that for arbitrary security return distributions, utility functions with the property of linear risk tolerance yield portfolio separation. The risk tolerance of the utility function is the reciprocal of the Pratt-Arrow measure of the absolute risk aversion discussed in Chapter 3. Thus a linear risk-tolerance utility function can be expressed as a *linear* function of wealth:

$$-u(W)/U''(W) = a + bW. \tag{4.9}$$

If investors also have homogeneous expectations about state probabilities and all investors have the same b, then there is *two-fund separation*, where all investors hold combinations of two basic portfolios.

Utility functions exhibiting linear risk tolerance include the quadratic, logarithmic, power, and exponential functions. Ross [1976] proved that for arbitrary risk-averse utility functions a number of classes of security return distributions (including the normal distribution, some stable Paretian distributions, and some distributions that are not stable Paretian, e.g., fat-tailed distributions with relatively more extreme values) yield portfolio separation.

[14] The capital asset pricing model is discussed in detail in Chapter 6.

I. $\mathscr{F}$irm Valuation, the Fisher Separation Principle, and Optimal Investment Decisions[15]

In state preference theory, individuals save when they purchase a firm's securities. Firms obtain resources for investment by issuing securities. Securities are precisely defined as conditional or unconditional payoffs in terms of alternative future states of nature. All individual and firm decisions are made, and all trading occurs at the beginning of the period. Consumers maximize their expected utility of present and future consumption and are characterized by their initial endowments (wealth) and their preferences. Firms are characterized by production functions that define the ability to transform current resources into state-contingent future consumption goods; for example, where I_j is the initial investment, $Q_{sj} = \phi(I_j, s)$. Total state-contingent output produced by a firm must equal the sum of the payoffs from all securities issued by a firm.

A firm maximizes an objective function that, in its most general form, is maximization of the expected utility of its current shareholders. To do this it may appear that a firm would need to know the utility functions of all its current shareholders. However, in Chapter 1 it was shown that in a perfect capital market (a frictionless and perfectly competitive market) under certainty, actions that maximize the price of the firm's shares maximize both the wealth and the utility of each current shareholder. So managers need only know the market discount rate and the cash flows of their investment projects to make optimal investment decisions. This separation of investment/operating decisions of firms from shareholder preferences or tastes is termed the *Fisher separation principle.*

In shifting from a firm's decision making under certainty to a world with uncertainty, it is important to know under what conditions, if any, Fisher separation continues to hold. It can be shown that firms that are maximizing the price of current shares are also maximizing current shareholders' *expected* utility when the capital market is (1) perfectly competitive and frictionless and (2) complete. The first condition ensures that one firm's actions will not be perceived to affect other firms' market security prices, whereas the second ensures that the state space "spanned" by the existing set of linearly independent market securities (i.e., the set of risky opportunities) is unaffected by the firm's actions. Thus the firm's actions affect shareholders' expected utility only by affecting their wealth through changes in the firm's current share price. This is analogous to the certainty case in Chapter 1.

The two conditions of a perfect and complete capital market ensure that the prices of a full set of pure securities can be obtained from the prices of the market securities, and vice versa, given the state-contingent payoff vectors of the market securities. As a result, the firm's objective function to maximize current share price can be phrased in terms of a portfolio of pure securities that replicates its shares. The firm's objective function then becomes $\sum Q_{js} p_s$, where Q_{js} is defined as the state s–contingent end-of-period payoff on firm j's existing securities. In this formulation, the price of a firm's current shares is determined by (1) the firm's state-contingent production function $Q_{js} = \phi_j(I_j, s)$, which transforms current resources into state-contingent future payoffs, and (2) the initial investment I_j, which represents the current cost to the firm of producing its state-contingent payoff. It follows that the price Y_j, for which the current

---

[15] Hirshleifer [1964, 1965, 1966] and Myers [1968] were among the first papers to apply state preference theory to corporate finance problems.

Table 4.3 Firm A's Stock and Investment Project Payoffs

States of Nature	Stock Payoff	State-Contingent Payoff on Firm A's Proposed Investment Project
State 1	100	10
State 2	30	12

Firm A's stock price = 62; initial investment cost of its project = 10.

Table 4.4 Firm B's Stock and Investment Project Payoffs

States of Nature	Stock Payoff	State-Contingent Payoff on Firm B's Proposed Investment Project
State 1	40	12
State 2	90	6

Firm B's stock price = 56; initial investment cost of its project = 8.

owners could sell the firm prior to making the investment I_j, is

$$Y_j = \sum_s p_s Q_{js} - I_j. \tag{4.10}$$

For indivisible investment projects with finite scale, the optimal investment rule is to accept all projects with positive net present value. In this context, Eq. (4.10) represents the net present value of the project's state-contingent net cash flow.

It is important to note that acceptance of positive NPV investments increases the price of the firm's current stock and therefore the wealth and expected utility of all current shareholders in a perfect and complete capital market. Since all shareholders are made better off by these investment decisions, these firm investment decisions are unanimously supported by all the firm's current shareholders. However, if the capital market is incomplete or imperfect, this is not necessarily true, because the firm's investment decisions may affect the price of other firms' shares or the feasible set of state-contingent payoffs. As a result, increasing the price of a firm's shares may *not* increase the wealth of all current shareholders (since the prices of some of their other shareholdings may fall) and may not maximize shareholder expected utility (since the opportunity set of feasible end-of-period payoffs may have changed).[16]

Let us now consider an example of a firm investment decision in a two-state world of uncertainty. Assume that all investors are expected utility maximizers and exhibit positive marginal utility of wealth (i.e., more wealth is preferred to less). Consider the following two firms and their proposed investment projects described in Tables 4.3 and 4.4.

To determine whether either firm should undertake its proposed project, we need to first determine whether the capital market is complete. Since the state-contingent payoffs of the two firms' stocks are linearly independent, the capital market is complete. In a complete market, the Fisher separation principle holds, so that the firm need only maximize the price of current shares

---

[16] See DeAngelo [1981] for a critical analysis of the unanimity literature and a careful formulation of the conditions under which it holds in incomplete and complete capital markets.

to maximize its current shareholders' expected utility. This requires that the firm invest only in positive net present value investment projects, which requires knowing the pure security prices in the two states. These two prices can be obtained from the market prices of the two firms' stocks and their state-contingent payoffs by solving the two simultaneous equations

$$100p_1 + 30p_2 = 62,$$
$$40p_1 + 90p_2 = 56,$$

to obtain the solution $p_1 = .5$ and $p_2 = .4$. To calculate the net present value of the two projects, we use the NPV definition in (4.10):

$$NPV_A = 10p_1 + 12p_2 - I_0^A = 10(.5) + 12(.4) - 10 = -.2$$

and

$$NPV_B = 12p_1 + 6p_2 - I_0^B = 12(.5) + 6(.4) - 8 = .4.$$

Since firm A's project has a negative NPV, it should be rejected, whereas firm B's project should be accepted since it has a positive NPV.

In examining this optimal investment rule, it should be clear that the prices of the pure securities affect the firm's investment decisions. It follows that since these security prices are affected by (1) time preference for consumption and the productivity of capital, (2) the probability of state-contingent payoffs, and (3) individual preferences toward risk and the level of nondiversifiable risk in the economy, firm investment decisions are also affected by these factors.

We have applied state preference theory to the firm's optimal investment decision while assuming that the firm has a simple capital structure represented by shares of stock. However, it is also possible to allow the firm to have a more complicated capital structure, which may include various debt, preferred stock, and warrant contracts. In doing this, state preference theory can be used to address the important question of a firm's optimal financing decision.[17] For this purpose it has been found useful to order the payoffs under alternative states. One can think of the payoffs for future states as arranged in an ordered sequence from the lowest to the highest payoff. Keeping in mind the ordered payoffs for alternative future states, we can specify the conditions under which a security such as corporate debt will be risk free or risky.[18]

The state preference model has also been very useful in developing option pricing theory. By combining securities with claims on various portions of the ordered payoffs and by combining long and short positions, portfolios with an infinite variety of payoff characteristics can be created. From such portfolios various propositions with regard to option pricing relationships can be developed.[19]

---

[17] There are many examples of the usefulness of state-preference theory in the area of optimal capital structure or financing decisions; see, for example, Stiglitz [1969], Mossin [1977], and DeAngelo and Masulis [1980a, 1980b].

[18] For applications of this approach, see Kraus and Litzenberger [1973] and DeAngelo and Masulis [1980a].

[19] For some further applications of state preference theory to option pricing theory, see Merton [1973] and Ross [1976], and for application to investment decision making, see Appendix B at the end of this chapter.

$\mathcal{S}$ummary

Wealth is held over periods of time, and the different future states of nature will change the value of a person's wealth position over time. Securities represent positions with regard to the relation between present and future wealth. Since securities involve taking a position over time, they inherently involve risk and uncertainty.

The states of nature capture a wide variety of factors that influence the future values of risky assets. Individuals must formulate judgements about payoffs under alternative future states of nature. From these state-contingent payoffs and market prices of securities, the prices of the underlying pure securities can be developed in a complete and perfect capital market. Given these pure security prices, the price of any other security can be determined from its state-contingent payoff vector. Conceptually, the equilibrium prices of the pure securities reflect the aggregate risk preferences of investors and investment opportunities of firms. Furthermore, the concept of a pure security facilitates analytical solutions to individuals' consumption/portfolio investment decisions under uncertainty.

The state preference approach is a useful way of looking at firm investment decisions under uncertainty. In a perfect and complete capital market the net present value rule was shown to be an optimal firm investment decision rule. The property that firm decisions can be made independently of shareholder utility functions is termed the Fisher separation principle. State preference theory also provides a conceptual basis for developing models for analyzing firm capital structure decisions and the pricing of option contracts. Thus the state preference approach provides a useful way of thinking about finance problems both for the individual investor and for the corporate manager.

The state-preference model has been shown to be very useful in a world of uncertainty. It can be used to develop optimal portfolio decisions for individuals and optimal investment rules for firms. We have found that in perfect and complete capital markets a set of equilibrium prices of all outstanding market securities can be derived. Further, these prices have been shown to be determined by (1) individual time preferences for consumption and the investment opportunities of firms, (2) probability beliefs concerning state-contingent payoffs, and (3) individual preferences toward risk and the level of nondiversifiable risk in the economy.

A number of important concepts developed in this chapter will be found to be very useful in the analysis to follow. In Chapter 5 we develop the fundamental properties of the mean-variance model, where the concept of diversifiable and nondiversifiable risk takes on added importance. In Chapter 6 the mean-variance framework is used to develop market equilibrium relationships that provide an alternative basis for pricing securities. Known as the capital asset pricing model, this model, like the state preference model, has the property that securities having relatively high levels of nondiversifiable risk have relatively higher expected rates of return. The concept of arbitrage is fundamental to the development of arbitrage pricing theory (APT) in Chapter 6 and the option pricing model (OPM) in Chapter 7.

PROBLEM SET

4.1 Security A pays \$30 if state 1 occurs and \$10 if state 2 occurs. Security B pays \$20 if state 1 occurs and \$0 if state 2 occurs. The price of security A is \$5, and the price of security B is \$10.

    (a) Set up the payoff table for securities A and B.

    (b) Determine the prices of the two pure securities.

4.2 You are given the following information:

	Payoff		
Security	**State 1**	**State 2**	**Security Prices**
j	$12	$20	$p_j = \$22$
k	24	10	$p_k = 20$

(a) What are the prices of pure security 1 and pure security 2?

(b) What is the initial price of a third security i, for which the payoff in state 1 is $6 and the payoff in state 2 is $10?

4.3 Interplanetary starship captain José Ching has been pondering the investment of his recent pilot's bonus of 1,000 stenglers. His choice is restricted to two securities: Galactic Steel, selling for 20 stenglers per share, and Nova Nutrients, at 10 stenglers per share. The future state of his solar system is uncertain. If there is a war with a nearby group of asteroids, Captain Ching expects Galactic Steel to be worth 36 stenglers per share. However, if peace prevails, Galactic Steel will be worth only 4 stenglers per share. Nova Nutrients should sell at a future price of 6 stenglers per share in either eventuality.

(a) Construct the payoff table that summarizes the starship captain's assessment of future security prices, given the two possible future states of the solar system. What are the prices of the pure securities implicit in the payoff table?

(b) If the captain buys only Nova Nutrients shares, how many can he buy? If he buys only Galactic Steel, how many shares can he buy? What would be his final wealth in both cases in peace? At war?

(c) Suppose Captain Ching can issue (sell short) securities as well as buy them, but he must be able to meet all claims in the future. What is the maximum number of Nova Nutrients shares he could sell short to buy Galactic Steel? How many shares of Galactic Steel could he sell short to buy Nova Nutrients? What would be his final wealth in both cases and in each possible future state?

(d) Suppose a third security, Astro Ammo, is available and should be worth 28 stenglers per share if peace continues and 36 stenglers per share if war breaks out. What would be the current price of Astro Ammo?

(e) Summarize the results of (a) through (d) on a graph with axes W_1 and W_2.

(f) Suppose the captain's utility function can be written as $U = W_1^{.8}W_2^{.2}$. If his investment is restricted to Galactic Steel and/or Nova Nutrients, what is his optimal portfolio (i.e., how many shares of each security should he buy or sell)?

4.4 Ms. Mary Kelley has initial wealth $W_0 = \$1,200$ and faces an uncertain future that she partitions into two states, $s = 1$ and $s = 2$. She can invest in two securities, j and k, with initial prices of $p_j = \$10$ and $p_k = \$12$, and the following payoff table:

	Payoff	
Security	**S = 1**	**S = 2**
j	$10	$12
k	20	8

(a) If she buys only security j, how many shares can she buy? If she buys only security k, how many can she buy? What would her final wealth, W_s, be in both cases and each state?
(b) Suppose Ms. Kelley can issue as well as buy securities; however, she must be able to meet all claims under the occurrence of either state. What is the maximum number of shares of security j she could sell to buy security k? What is the maximum number of shares of security k she could sell to buy security j? What would her final wealth be in both cases and in each state?
(c) What are the prices of the pure securities implicit in the payoff table?
(d) What is the initial price of a third security i for which $Q_{i1} = \$5$ and $Q_{i2} = \$12$?
(e) Summarize the results of (a) through (d) on a graph with axes W_1 and W_2.
(f) Suppose Ms. Kelley has a utility function of the form $U = W_1^{.6}W_2^{.4}$. Find the optimal portfolio, assuming the issuance of securities is possible, if she restricts herself to a portfolio consisting only of j and k. How do you interpret your results?

4.5 Two securities have the following payoffs in two equally likely states of nature at the end of one year:

	Payoff	
Security	S = 1	S = 2
j	$10	$20
k	30	10

Security j costs $8 today, whereas k costs $9, and your total wealth is currently $720.

(a) If you wanted to buy a completely risk-free portfolio (i.e., one that has the same payoff in both states of nature), how many shares of j and k would you buy? (You may buy fractions of shares.)
(b) What is the one-period risk-free rate of interest?
(c) If there were two securities and three states of nature, you would not be able to find a completely risk-free portfolio. Why not?

4.6 Suppose that there are only two possible future states of the world, and the utility function is logarithmic.[20] Let the probability of state 1, π_1, equal $\frac{2}{3}$, and the prices of the pure securities, p_1 and p_2, equal $0.60 and $0.40, respectively. An individual has an initial wealth or endowment, W_0, of $50,000.

(a) What amounts will the risk-averse individual invest in pure securities 1 and 2?
(b) How will the individual divide his or her initial endowment between current and future consumption?

(*Hint:* Use the wealth constraint instead of the Lagrange multiplier technique.)

REFERENCES

Arrow, K. J., "The Role of Securities in the Optimal Allocation of Risk-Bearing," *Review of Economic Studies*, 1964, 91–96.

———, *Theory of Risk-Bearing*. Markham, Chicago, 1971.

---

[20] Problem 4.6 was suggested by Professor Herb Johnson of the University of California, Davis.

Banz, R. W., and M. Miller, "Prices for State-Contingent Claims: Some Estimates and Applications," *Journal of Business*, October 1978, 653–672.

Breeden, D. T., and R. H. Litzenberger, "Prices of State-Contingent Claims Implicit in Option Prices," *Journal of Business*, October 1978, 621–651.

Brennan, M. J., and A. Kraus, "The Geometry of Separation and Myopia," *Journal of Financial and Quantitative Analysis,* June 1976, 171–193.

Cass, D., and J. E. Stiglitz, "The Structure of Investor Preferences and Asset Returns, and Separability in Portfolio Allocation: A Contribution to the Pure Theory of Mutual Funds," *Journal of Economic Theory*, June 1970, 122–160.

DeAngelo, H. C., "Competition and Unanimity," *American Economic Review*, March 1981, 18–28.

DeAngelo, H. C., and R. W. Masulis, "Leverage and Dividend Irrelevance under Corporate and Personal Taxation," *Journal of Finance*, May 1980a, 453–464.

———, "Optimal Capital Structure under Corporate and Personal Taxation," *Journal of Financial Economics*, March 1980b, 3–29.

Debreu, G., *The Theory of Value*. Wiley, New York, 1959.

Dreze, J. H., "Market Allocation under Uncertainty," *European Economic Review*, Winter 1970–1971, 133–165.

Fama, E. F., and M. H. Miller, *The Theory of Finance*. Holt, Rinehart, and Winston, New York, 1972.

Fisher, Irving, *The Theory of Interest*. Macmillan, London, 1930.

Garman, M., "The Pricing of Supershares," *Journal of Financial Economics*, March 1978, 3–10.

Hirshleifer, J., "Efficient Allocation of Capital in an Uncertain World," *American Economic Review*, May 1964, 77–85.

———, "Investment Decision under Uncertainty: Choice-Theoretic Approaches," *Quarterly Journal of Economics*, November 1965, 509–536.

———, "Investment Decision under Uncertainty: Application of the State-Preference Approach," *Quarterly Journal of Economics*, May 1966, 252–277.

——, *Investment, Interest, and Capital*. Prentice-Hall, Englewood Cliffs, N.J., 1970, 215–276.

Kraus, A., and R. Litzenberger, "A State-Preference Model of Optimal Financial Leverage," *Journal of Finance,* September 1973, 911–922.

Krouse, C. G., *Capital Markets and Prices*. Elsevier Science Publishers B.V., Amsterdam, 1986.

Leland, H. E., "Production Theory and the Stock Market," *Bell Journal of Economics and Management Science*, Spring 1973, 141–183.

Merton, R., "The Theory of Rational Option Pricing," *Bell Journal of Economics and Management Science*, 1974, 125–144.

Mossin, J., *The Economic Efficiency of Financial Markets*. D.C. Heath, Lexington, 1977, 21–40.

Myers, S. C., "A Time-State Preference Model of Security Valuation," *Journal of Financial and Quantitative Analysis,* March 1968, 1–33.

Ross, S. A., "Options and Efficiency," *Quarterly Journal of Economics*, February 1976, 75–86.

———, "Return, Risk and Arbitrage," in Friend and Bicksler, eds., *Risk and Return in Finance, Volume 1*. Ballinger Publishing Company, Cambridge, Mass., 1977, 189–218.

———, "Mutual Fund Separation in Financial Theory—The Separating Distributions," *Journal of Economic Theory*, December 1978, 254–286.

Sharpe, W. F., *Portfolio Theory and Capital Markets*, Chapter 10, "State-Preference Theory." McGraw-Hill, New York, 1970, 202–222.

Stiglitz, J. E., "A Re-examination of the Modigliani-Miller Theorem," *American Economic Review*, December 1969, 784–793.

Appendix 4A. Forming a Portfolio of Pure Securities

If we have n market securities and n states of the world, and we are not sure the n market securities are independent, we can find out by taking the determinant of the payoffs from the securities: a nonzero determinant implies independence. For example, the set of pure securities is independent since

$$\begin{vmatrix} 1 & 0 & 0 \\ 0 & 1 & 0 \\ 0 & 0 & 1 \end{vmatrix} = 1;$$

but

$$\begin{vmatrix} 1 & 0 & 0 \\ 0 & 1 & 1 \\ 1 & 1 & 1 \end{vmatrix} = \begin{vmatrix} 1 & 1 \\ 1 & 1 \end{vmatrix} = 0$$

implies that the security payoffs $(1, 0, 0)$, $(0, 1, 1)$, and $(1, 1, 1)$ are not linearly independent.

We can use Appendix B, "Matrix Algebra," found at the end of the book, to form a portfolio of pure securities from an arbitrary complete set of market securities. This involves computing the inverse of the payoff matrix for the actual securities. For example, if $(1, 0, 0)$, $(0, 1, 1)$, and $(0, 1, 3)$ are available, then define

$$A = \begin{pmatrix} 1 & 0 & 0 \\ 0 & 1 & 1 \\ 0 & 1 & 3 \end{pmatrix}$$

as the payoff matrix. Thus the determinant of A is

$$|A| = \begin{vmatrix} 1 & 0 & 0 \\ 0 & 1 & 1 \\ 0 & 1 & 3 \end{vmatrix} = \begin{vmatrix} 1 & 1 \\ 1 & 3 \end{vmatrix} = 2 \neq 0.$$

Let X_{ij} be the amount of the jth security one buys in forming the ith pure security, and let X be the matrix formed from the X_{ij}. Then we require that

$$XA = I \quad \text{where} \quad I = \begin{pmatrix} 1 & 0 & 0 \\ 0 & 1 & 0 \\ 0 & 0 & 1 \end{pmatrix}$$

is the identity matrix and also the matrix of payoffs from the pure securities. Hence $X = A^{-1}$. In the present example

$$A^{-1} = \frac{1}{2} \begin{pmatrix} 2 & 0 & 0 \\ 0 & 3 & -1 \\ 0 & -1 & 1 \end{pmatrix} = \begin{pmatrix} 1 & 0 & 0 \\ 0 & \frac{3}{2} & -\frac{1}{2} \\ 0 & -\frac{1}{2} & \frac{1}{2} \end{pmatrix}.$$

We then multiply X times A or equivalently $A^{-1}A$ to obtain a matrix of payoffs from the pure securities. We have

$$
\begin{pmatrix} 1 & 0 & 0 \\ 0 & \frac{3}{2} & -\frac{1}{2} \\ 0 & -\frac{1}{2} & \frac{1}{2} \end{pmatrix} \begin{pmatrix} 1 & 0 & 0 \\ 0 & 1 & 1 \\ 0 & 1 & 3 \end{pmatrix} = \begin{pmatrix} 1 & 0 & 0 \\ 0 & 1 & 0 \\ 0 & 0 & 1 \end{pmatrix}.
$$

We can now see that the purpose of finding the inverse of A is to obtain directions for forming a portfolio that will yield a matrix of payoffs from the pure securities—the identity matrix. Recall that the three securities available are $(1, 0, 0)$, $(0, 1, 1)$, and $(0, 1, 3)$. To obtain the pure security payoff $(1, 0, 0)$, we buy the security with that pattern of payoffs under the three states. To obtain $(0, 1, 0)$, we buy $\frac{3}{2}$ of $(0, 1, 1)$ and sell short $\frac{1}{2}$ of $(0, 1, 3)$. To obtain $(0, 0, 1)$, we sell short $\frac{1}{2}$ of $(0, 1, 1)$ and buy $\frac{1}{2}$ of $(0, 1, 3)$.

Appendix 4B. Use of Prices of State-Contingent Claims in Capital Budgeting

Banz and Miller [1978] develop estimates of prices for state-contingent claims that can be applied in capital budgeting problems of the kind discussed in Chapter 9. Similar methodologies were developed about the same time by Garman [1978] and by Breeden and Litzenberger [1978].

Banz and Miller note that a fundamental breakthrough was provided in Ross [1976], who demonstrated that by selling or buying options on a portfolio of existing securities, investors could obtain any desired pattern of returns—"investors could span the return space to any degree of fineness desired" [Banz and Miller, 1978, 658].

Banz and Miller present their estimates of state prices in a format similar to standard interest tables. Like other interest tables, the estimates of state prices can in principle be used by any firm in any industry or activity (subject to some important cautions and qualifications). Thus the reciprocals (minus one) of the state prices computed are analogous to single-period interest rates. Banz and Miller handle the multiperiod case by assuming stability in the relations between initial states and outcome states. Thus the two-period matrix is simply the square of the one-period matrix and the two-period matrix, the four-period matrix is the product of the one-period matrix and the three-period matrix, and so on. In equation form,

$$
V^n = V \cdot V^{n-1}. \tag{4B.1}
$$

The perpetuity matrix is the one-period matrix times the inverse of the identity matrix minus the one-period matrix, or $V(I - V)^{-1}$.

Their computations for a V matrix of real discount factors for three states of the world is provided in Table 4B.1. In the definition of states in Table 4B.1 the state boundaries are defined over returns on the market.

The conditional means are expected market returns under alternative states. The elements of any matrix V may be interpreted by use of the first group of data. The .5251 represents the outcome for state 1 when the initial state was also state 1. The .2935 represents the outcome for state 2 when state 1 was the initial state. By analogy the .1612 represents an outcome for state 3 when state 3 was the initial state.

For equal probabilities the current price of a claim to funds in a state in which funds are scarce (a depression) will be higher than in a boom state when returns are more favorable. Thus a project with most of its payoffs contingent on a boom will have a lower value per dollar of expected returns than a project whose payoffs are relatively more favorable during a depression.

Table 4B.1 Three-State Matrix of State Prices and Matrix Powers

Definition of States		
State	**State Boundaries** *	**Conditional Mean** $(\overline{R}_{i,mr})$
1	$-.8647 - +.0006$	$-.1352$
2	$+.0006 - +.2042$	$+.0972$
3	$+.2042 - +1.7183^{\dagger}$	$+.3854$

State Prices					
State	**1**	**2**	**3**	**Row Sum**	**Implied Annual Real Riskless Rate**
1 year (V):					
1	.5251	.2935	.1735	.9921	.0079
2	.5398	.2912	.1672	.9982	.0018
3	.5544	.2888	.1612	1.0044	$-.0044$
2 years (V^2):					
1	.5304	.2897	.1681	.9882	.0056
2	.5333	.2915	.1693	.9941	.0030
3	.5364	.2934	.1705	1.0003	$-.0001$
3 years (V^3):					
1	.5281	.2886	.1676	.9843	.0053
2	.5313	.2903	.1686	.9902	.0033
3	.5345	.2921	.1696	.9962	.0013
4 years (V^4):					
1	.5260	.2874	.1669	.9803	.0050
2	.5291	.2892	.1679	.9862	.0035
3	.5324	.2909	.1689	.9922	.0026
5 years (V^5):					
1	.5239	.2863	.1662	.9764	.0048
2	.5270	.2880	.1672	.9822	.0036
3	.5302	.2897	.1682	.9881	.0024
6 years (V^6):					
1	.5217	.2851	.1655	.9723	.0047
2	.5249	.2968	.1665	.9782	.0037
3	.5281	.2886	.1676	.9843	.0027
7 years (V^7):					
1	.5197	.2840	.1649	.9685	.0046
2	.5228	.2857	.1659	.9744	.0043
3	.5260	.2874	.1669	.9803	.0033

Table 4B.1 *(continued)*

8 years (V^8):					
1	.5176	.2828	.1642	.9646	.0045
2	.5207	.2845	.1652	.9704	.0038
3	.5239	.2863	.1662	.9764	.0030
9 years (V^9):					
1	.5155	.2817	.1636	.9608	.0045
2	.5186	.2823	.1639	.9627	.0038
3	.5197	.2840	.1649	.9686	.0031
10 years (V^{10}):					
1	.5134	.2806	.1629	.9569	.0044
2	.5165	.2823	.1639	.9627	.0038
3	.5197	.2840	.1649	.9686	.0032
Perpetuity: $\left[V(I-V)^{-1}\right]$:					
1	132.50	72.41	42.05	246.96	.0040
2	133.31	72.85	42.30	248.46	.0040
3	134.14	73.29	42.55	249.98	.0040

* Chosen to yield ranges of R_{mr} that are approximately equally probable.
† Arbitrary truncations.

Table 4B.2 Cash Flow Patterns for an Investment

State of the Economy	Range of Rates of Return on the Market Portfolio	Cash Flow before Competition Enters $\overline{X}_m$	Steady-State Cash Flow after Competition Enters X_c
Depression	$-.8647 - +.0006$	300	-20
Normal	$+.0006 - +.2042$	400	20
Boom	$+.2042 - +1.7183$	500	40

The vector of gross present values of the project, G_k, will be

$$G_k = \sum_{t=1}^{p} V^t \overline{X}_k(t), \tag{4B.2}$$

where $\overline{X}_k(t)$ is a vector whose elements represent the expected real cash flows of project k in year t, assuming the economy is in state i. The summation is performed over time periods ending in p, the last period during which the project's cash flows are nonzero in any state.

An example of how the "interest factors" in Table 4B.1 can be applied is based on the illustration presented by Banz and Miller. The Omega Corporation is analyzing an investment project whose cash flow pattern in constant 1980 dollars (ignoring taxes and shields) is presented in Table 4B.2.

The Banz-Miller example is sophisticated in illustrating that both the level and risk of the cash flows vary with the degree of competition. In our example we modify their estimates of the cumulative probabilities of competitive entry, using 0 in the year of introduction, .3 one year later, .6 two years later, and 1 three years later. The risk-adjusted gross present value vector for the project was set forth in Eq. (4B.2). For the assumptions of our example, the particular gross present value vector is

$$G_k = V\overline{X}_m + V^2 \left(0.7\overline{X}_m + 0.3\overline{X}_c\right) + V^3 \left(0.4\overline{X}_m + 0.6\overline{X}_c\right) + V^4 \left[V\left(I - V\right)^{-1}\right]\overline{X}_c.$$

We use the values of V and its powers as presented in Table 4B.1 to obtain the following results:

$$
\begin{bmatrix} g_D \\ g_N \\ g_B \end{bmatrix} = \begin{bmatrix} .5251 & .2935 & .1735 \\ .5398 & .2912 & .1672 \\ .5544 & .2888 & .1612 \end{bmatrix} \begin{bmatrix} 300 \\ 400 \\ 500 \end{bmatrix}
$$

$$
+ \begin{bmatrix} .5304 & .2897 & .1681 \\ .5333 & .2915 & .1693 \\ .5364 & .2934 & .1705 \end{bmatrix} \begin{bmatrix} 204 \\ 286 \\ 362 \end{bmatrix} \begin{bmatrix} .5281 & .2886 & .1676 \\ .5313 & .2903 & .1686 \\ .5345 & .2921 & .1696 \end{bmatrix} \begin{bmatrix} 108 \\ 172 \\ 224 \end{bmatrix}
$$

$$
+ \begin{bmatrix} .5260 & .2874 & .1669 \\ .5291 & .2892 & .1679 \\ .5324 & .2909 & .1689 \end{bmatrix} \begin{bmatrix} 132.50 & 72.41 & 42.05 \\ 133.31 & 72.85 & 42.30 \\ 134.14 & 73.29 & 42.55 \end{bmatrix} \begin{bmatrix} -20 \\ 20 \\ 40 \end{bmatrix}
$$

$$
= \begin{bmatrix} 1230.09 \\ 1235.68 \\ 1241.48 \end{bmatrix}
$$

If the initial investment were \$1,236 in every state of the economy, the project would not have a positive net present value if the economy were depressed or normal. However, the net present value would be positive if the economy were strong. If initial investment costs had cyclical behavior, particularly if supply bottlenecks developed during a boom, investment outlays might vary so strongly with states of the world that net present values could be positive for a depressed economy and negative for a booming economy.

The Banz-Miller use of state prices in capital budgeting is a promising application of the state preference model. Further applications will provide additional tests of the feasibility of their approach. More work in comparing the results under alternative approaches will provide increased understanding of the advantages and possible limitations of the use of state prices as discount factors in capital budgeting analysis.

Chapter 5

Objects of Choice: Mean-Variance Portfolio Theory

> The results of a portfolio analysis are no more than the logical consequence of its information concerning securities.
>
> —Harry Markowitz, *Portfolio Selection*, Yale University Press, New Haven, 1959, 205.

C HAPTER 3 INTRODUCED THE THEORY of how risk-averse investors make choices in a world with uncertainty. Chapter 4 used a state preference framework to show that the fundamental objects of choice are payoffs offered in different states of nature. While this is a very general approach, it lacks empirical content. It would be difficult, if not impossible, to list all payoffs offered in different states of nature. To provide a framework for analysis where objects of choice are readily measurable, this chapter develops mean-variance objects of choice. Investors' indifference curves are assumed to be defined in terms of the mean and variance of asset returns. While much less general than state preference theory, the mean-variance portfolio theory introduced here is statistical in nature and therefore lends itself to empirical testing. Some of the empirical tests of a mean-variance equilibrium pricing model are discussed in Chapter 6.

One of the most important developments in finance theory in the last few decades is the ability to talk about risk in a quantifiable fashion. If we know how to measure and price financial risk correctly, we can properly value risky assets. This in turn leads to better allocation of resources in the economy. Investors can do a better job of allocating their savings to various types of risky securities, and managers can better allocate the funds provided by shareholders and creditors among scarce capital resources.

This chapter begins with simple measures of risk and return for a single asset and then complicates the discussion by moving to risk and return for a portfolio of many risky assets. Decision rules are then developed to show how individuals choose optimal portfolios that maximize their expected utility of wealth, first in a world without riskless borrowing and lending, then with such opportunities.

A. *M*easuring Risk and Return for a Single Asset

Suppose the task at hand is to describe the relevant features of a common stock to a friend who is an investor. What are the really crucial facts that you should communicate? You could start off by giving the company's name, say, Bayside Smoke Co. Then you would discuss the financial ratios of the company: its earnings per share, its inventory turnover, its financial leverage, its interest coverage, and so on. All these data are merely one way of getting at what is crucial: How will your friend's wealth position be affected if he or she invests in Bayside Smoke Co.? Consequently, it is wise to talk about measures of the effect on relative wealth at the end of an investment period. The terminology used is *end-of-period wealth.*

The link between end-of-period wealth and an initial dollar investment is the *rate of return.* For the time being, we will not specify what calendar interval we are working with except to say that it is a single time period. If the initial investment is I and the final wealth is W, then the investor's rate of return, R, is

$$R = \frac{W - I}{I}. \tag{5.1a}$$

As you see, this is the same expression as that used for the present or future value formulas for one time period:

$$W = (1 + R)I, \qquad \text{future value formulation;} \tag{5.1b}$$

$$I = (1 + R)^{-1}W, \qquad \text{present value formulation.} \tag{5.1c}$$

If end-of-period wealth is known with certainty, then so is the present value of the investment and the rate of return. However, this is seldom the case in the real world. Even short-term default-free bonds such as U.S. Treasury bills are not completely risk free (although later on we shall use them as a close approximation to a risk-free security).

For risky assets often the best that can be done is to assign probabilities to various possible outcomes. Suppose the current price (P_0) of Bayside Smoke is $25 per share and you tell your friend that after a careful analysis the best estimate of the price per share at the end of the time period is given in Table 5.1.

Table 5.1 Hypothetical Prices for Bayside Smoke Co.

p_i = Probability	End-of-Period Price per Share	R_i = Return (%)
.1	$20.00	−20
.2	22.50	−10
.4	25.00	0
.2	30.00	+20
.1	40.00	+60
1.0		

1. Measures of Location

It is desirable to develop some statistics that can summarize a wide set of possible outcomes. The most commonly used statistics are measures of location and dispersion. Measures of location are intended to describe the most likely outcome in a set of events. The most often used measure of location is the mean or expectation. It is defined as

$$E(\widetilde{X}) = \sum_{i=1}^{N} p_i X_i, \tag{5.2}$$

where p_i is the probability of a random event, X_i; N is the total number of possible events; and the tilde ($\sim$) is used to designate randomness. Hence the mean weights each event by its probability, then sums all events. For Bayside Smoke the expected end-of-period price is

$$E(\widetilde{P}) = .1(20) + .2(22.5) + .4(25) + .2(30) + .1(40) = \$26.50.$$

The expected or mean return is the expected price less the current price divided by the current price:

$$E(\widetilde{R}) = \frac{E(\widetilde{P}) - P_0}{P_0} = \frac{26.50 - 25}{25} = .06 \quad \text{or} \quad 6\%. \tag{5.3}$$

Implicitly, we have used two probability properties of the expected value operator to obtain Eq. (5.3).

PROPERTY 1   The expected value of a random variable $\widetilde{X}$ plus a constant a is equal to the expected value of the random variable plus the constant:

$$E(\widetilde{X} + a) = E(\widetilde{X}) + a. \tag{5.4}$$

Property 1 can be proved by using the definition of expected value. Since the random variable is $(\widetilde{X} + a)$, we take its expectation by substituting $(X_i + a)$ for X_i in Eq. (5.2):

$$E(\widetilde{X} + a) = \sum_{i=1}^{N} p_i(X_i + a).$$

Writing out all the terms in the sum, we have

$$E(\widetilde{X} + a) = \left[p_1(X_1 + a) + p_2(X_2 + a) + \cdots + p_n(X_n + a) \right].$$

By simply collecting terms, we get

$$E(\widetilde{X} + a) = \sum_{i=1}^{N} p_i X_i + a \sum_{i=1}^{N} p_i.$$

And since we know that the sum of the probabilities of all events must add to 1, ($\sum p_i \equiv 1$), we have proven Property 1:

$$E(\tilde{X} + a) = \sum_{i=1}^{N} p_i(X_i) + a,$$

$$E(\tilde{X} + a) = E(\tilde{X}) + a. \qquad \text{QED}$$

PROPERTY 2 The expected value of a random variable $\tilde{X}$ multiplied by a constant a is equal to the constant multiplied by the expected value of the random variable:

$$E(a\tilde{X}) = aE(\tilde{X}). \tag{5.5}$$

Property 2 can also be proved by using the definition of the expected-value operator. Substituting aX_i for X_i in Eq. (5.2), we get

$$E(a\tilde{X}) = \sum_{i=1}^{N} p_i(aX_i).$$

Then by expanding the sum, we have

$$E(a\tilde{X}) = p_1 a X_1 + p_2 a X_2 + \cdots + p_n a X_n.$$

Next, a can be factored out:

$$E(a\tilde{X}) = a \sum_{i=1}^{N} p_i X_i.$$

And finally, recognizing that $\sum p_i X_i = E(\tilde{X})$, we have

$$E(a\tilde{X}) = aE(\tilde{X}). \qquad \text{QED}$$

When we used the definition of return and the expected end-of-period price to derive the expected return, we were using both properties of the expected-value operator described above. In the numerator of (5.3) the price of Bayside Smoke today, P_0, is known and is a constant. The end-of-period price is random variable. Therefore, the numerator is multiplied by ($1/P_0$), a constant.

The expected outcome, or *the average*, is the most frequently used statistical measure of location, but it is not the only one. Before moving on to measures of dispersion, we should also mention the *median* and *mode*, which are also measures of location. The median is defined as the outcome in the middle, often referred to as the 50th percentile. Consider the set of numbers (which are equally likely, i.e., $p_i = 1/N$) given in Table 5.2.

Figure 5.1 is a histogram for a set of numbers. Note that most of the probability (in fact 53.3%) lies between -1 and 20. However, the mean, which assigns equal weight to all observations in this case, gives 28.13 as the best measure of location. The median is 13. Clearly, in this case, where we have a distribution of outcomes that is skewed to the right, the median is a better measure of location than the mean is. Later on, when we actually look at empirical distributions of security returns, the choice of mean return as the best measure of central tendency will depend a great deal on whether or not the actual distributions are skewed.

Table 5.2 Set of Numbers with Equal Probability

17	0	7	10	13	3
15	−4	6	−1	17	13
13	25	13	150	−1	6
−8	2	54	32	202	16
13	21	120	24	29	37

Figure 5.1 Histogram.

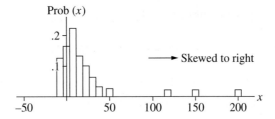

The last measure of location to be considered is the mode. It is defined as the most frequent outcome. In the above example it is the number 13, which occurs five times, or the interval between 6 and 13, which contains 23.3% of the probability. The mode is not often used as a measure of location for empirical distributions of security returns because security returns are real numbers (i.e., they can take on any decimal value) and consequently do not repeat themselves frequently.

2. Measures of Dispersion

So far we have looked at statistical measures that can be used to best describe the most likely outcome when our friend invests in Bayside Smoke. An investment of $1,000 can be expected to bring an end-of-period wealth of $1,060. (Why?) But the question still remains: What risk is being taken? There are five measures of dispersion we could use: the range, the semi-interquartile range, the variance, the semivariance, and the mean absolute deviation. Each of these has slightly different implications for risk.

The *range* is the simplest statistic and is defined as the difference between the highest and lowest outcomes. For an investment in one share of Bayside Smoke (see Table 5.1), the worst outcome is $20 and the best outcome is $40. Therefore the range is $20. However, the range is a very poor descriptive statistic because it becomes larger as sample size increases. Whenever the underlying probability distribution of investment outcomes is being estimated (e.g., by looking at observations of past performance), the estimated range will increase as more observations are included in the sample.

The *semi-interquartile range* is the difference between the observation of the 75th percentile, $X_{.75}$, and the 25th percentile, $X_{.25}$, divided by 2:

$$\text{Semi-interquartile range} = \frac{X_{.75} - X_{.25}}{2}. \tag{5.6}$$

Unlike the range, this statistic does not increase with sample size and is therefore much more reliable.[1] For the set of 30 numbers that we were using earlier (in Table 5.2) the semi-interquartile range is

$$\text{Semi-interquartile range} = \frac{27.0 - 4.5}{2} = 11.25.$$

This statistic is frequently used as a measure of dispersion when the variance of a distribution does not exist.

The *variance* is the statistic most frequently used to measure the dispersion of a distribution, and later on in this chapter it will be used as a measure of investment risk. It is defined as the expectation of the squared differences from the mean:

$$\text{VAR}(\tilde{X}) = E\left[(X_i - E(\tilde{X}))^2 \right]. \tag{5.7a}$$

Recalling the definition of the mean as the sum of the probabilities of events times the value of the events, the definition of variance can be rewritten as

$$\text{VAR}(\tilde{X}) = \sum_{i=1}^{N} p_i (X_i - E(\tilde{X}))^2. \tag{5.7b}$$

Therefore for Bayside Smoke the variance of end-of-period prices is

$$\text{VAR}(\tilde{P}) = .1(20 - 26.5)^2 + .2(22.5 - 26.5)^2 + .4(25 - 26.5)^2$$

$$+ .2(30 - 26.5)^2 + .1(40 - 26.5)^2$$

$$= .1(42.25) + .2(16) + .4(2.25) + .2(12.25) + .1(182.25)$$

$$= 29.00.$$

Note that the variance is expressed in dollars squared. Since people do not usually think in these terms, the *standard deviation*, which is the positive square root of the variance, is often used to express dispersion:

$$\sigma(\tilde{P}) = \sqrt{\text{VAR}(\tilde{P})} = \$5.39.$$

The variance of the return from investing in Bayside Smoke is

$$\text{VAR}(\tilde{R}) = \frac{\text{VAR}(\tilde{P})}{P_0^2} = \frac{29}{(25)^2} = 4.64\%,$$

and the standard deviation is

$$\sigma(\tilde{R}) = \sqrt{\text{VAR}(\tilde{R})} = 21.54\%.$$

---

[1] The interested reader is referred to Crámer [1961, 367–370] for proof that sample quartiles converge to consistent estimates as sample sizes increase.

The result is derived by using two properties of the variance in much the same way as properties of the mean were used earlier.

PROPERTY 3   The variance of the random variable plus a constant is equal to the variance of the random variable.

It makes sense that adding a constant to a variable would have no effect on the variance because the constant by itself has zero variance. This is demonstrated by using the definition of variance in Eq. (5.7a) and substituting $(X_i + a)$ for X_i as follows:

$$\text{VAR}(\tilde{X} + a) = E[((X_i + a) - E(\tilde{X} + a))^2].$$

From Property 1 of the expected-value operator, we know that

$$E(\tilde{X} + a) = E(\tilde{X}) + a;$$

therefore

$$\text{VAR}(\tilde{X} + a) = E[((X_i) + a - E(\tilde{X}) - a)^2].$$

Because the constant terms cancel out, we have

$$\text{VAR}(\tilde{X} + a) = E[(X_i - E(\tilde{X}))^2] = \text{VAR}(\tilde{X}). \qquad \text{QED} \qquad (5.8)$$

PROPERTY 4   The variance of a random variable multiplied by a constant is equal to the constant squared times the variance of the random variable.

For proof we again refer to the definition of variance and substitute aX_i for X_i in Eq. (5.7a):

$$\text{VAR}(a\tilde{X}) = E\left[aX_i - a(\tilde{X}))^2\right].$$

The constant term can be factored out as follows:

$$\text{VAR}(a\tilde{X}) = E\left[\left(a\left[X_i - E(\tilde{X})\right]\right)^2\right]$$

$$= E\left[a^2(X_i - E(\tilde{X}))^2\right]$$

$$= a^2 E\left[\left(X_i - E(\tilde{X})\right)^2\right] = a^2\text{VAR}(X). \qquad \text{QED} \qquad (5.9)$$

Going back to the example where we computed the variance of return on Bayside Smoke directly from the variance of its price, we can readily see how Properties 3 and 4 were used. Let us recall that the definition of return is

$$R_i = \frac{P_i - P_0}{P_0},$$

and that the expected return is

$$E(\tilde{R}) = \frac{E(\tilde{P}) - P_0}{P_0}.$$

Therefore the variance of return is

$$\text{VAR}(\tilde{R}) = E\left[(R_i - E(\tilde{R}))^2\right]$$

$$= E\left[\left(\frac{P_i - P_0}{P_0} - \frac{E(\tilde{P}) - P_0}{P_0}\right)^2\right].$$

Because P_0 is a constant, we can use Property 4 to write

$$\text{VAR}(\tilde{R}) = \frac{1}{P_0^2} E\left[(P_i - E(\tilde{P}))^2\right]$$

$$= \frac{\text{VAR}(\tilde{P})}{P_0^2}$$

and of course this is exactly the formula used earlier to compute the variance of return from our knowledge of the variance of prices.

The next section of this chapter uses the properties of the mean and variance that we have developed here in order to discuss the mean and variance of a portfolio of assets. At this point we could summarize the investment opportunity offered by Bayside Smoke by saying that the expected price is $26.50 with a standard deviation of $5.39. Or else we could say that the expected return on this investment is 6%, with a standard deviation of 21.54%. However, before moving on, it will be useful to contrast the variance as a measure of risk with the semivariance and the average absolute deviation.

One problem with the variance is that it gives equal weight to possibilities above as well as below the average. However, suppose that risk-averse investors are more concerned with downside risk. The *semivariance* is a statistic that relates to just that risk. It is defined as the expectation of the mean differences *below* the mean, squared. Mathematically, the definition is as follows. Let

$$X_i = \begin{cases} X_i - E(\tilde{X}) & \text{if } X_i < E(\tilde{X}) \\ 0 & \text{if } X_i \geq E(\tilde{X}) \end{cases},$$

then

$$\text{SEMIVAR} = E\left[(X_i)^2\right]. \tag{5.10}$$

If the semivariance is used as a measure of risk, an increase in the probability of events above the mean will change risk only slightly because the only effect would be to increase the mean slightly. For example, the semivariance of return for Bayside Smoke is

$$\text{SEMIVAR} = .1(-.20 - .06)^2 + .2(.10 - .06)^2 + .4(0 - .06)^2$$

$$= 1.332\%.$$

But if the probability of a 60% return (in Table 5.1) were to increase to .2 while the probability of a 20% return fell to .1, the impact on semivariance would be slight. The new expected return would be 10%, and the semivariance would increase to 2.1%. Given the same change in probabilities, the variance would increase from 4.64% to 7.2%.

Both the variance and the semivariance are sensitive to observations distant from the mean because the mean differences are squared. Squaring gives them greater weight. A statistic that avoids this difficulty is the *average absolute deviation* (AAD), which is defined as the expectation of the absolute value of the differences from the mean:

$$\text{AAD} = E\left[\left|X_i - E(\tilde{X})\right|\right]. \tag{5.11}$$

For the Bayside Smoke example, the average absolute deviation is

$$\text{AAD} = .1\left|(-.2 - .06)\right| + .2\left|(-.1 - .06| + .4|0 - .06)\right|$$
$$+ .2\left|(.2 - .06)\right| + .1\left|(.6 - .06)\right|$$
$$= 16.4\%.$$

Although for the most part we shall measure risk and return by using the variance (or standard deviation) and the mean return, it is useful to keep in mind that there are other statistics that, in some situations, may be more appropriate. An understanding of these statistics helps to put the mean and variance into proper perspective.

B. Measuring Portfolio Risk and Return

From this point we assume that investors measure the expected utility of choices among risky assets by looking at the mean and variance provided by combinations of those assets. For a financial manager, the operating risk of the firm may be measured by estimating the mean and variance of returns provided by the portfolio of assets that the firm holds: its inventory, cash, accounts receivable, marketable securities, and physical plant. For a portfolio manager, the risk and return are the mean and variance of the weighted average of the assets in his or her portfolio. Therefore, in order to understand how to manage risk, it becomes necessary to explore the risk and return provided by combinations of risky assets.

1. The Normal Distribution

By looking only at mean and variance, we are necessarily assuming that no other statistics are necessary to describe the distribution of end-of-period wealth. Unless investors have a special type of utility function (quadratic utility function), it is necessary to assume that returns have a normal distribution, which can be completely described by mean and variance. This is the bell-shaped probability distribution that many natural phenomena obey. For example, measures of intelligence quotients (IQs) follow this distribution. An example is given in Fig. 5.2. The frequency of a return is measured along the vertical axis, and the returns are measured along the horizontal axis. The normal distribution is perfectly symmetric, and 50% of the probability lies above the mean, 15.9% above a point one standard deviation above the mean, and 2.3% above a point two standard deviations above the mean. Because of its symmetry the variance and semivariance are equivalent measures of risk for the normal distribution. Furthermore, if you know the mean and standard deviation (or semivariance) of a normal distribution, you know the likelihood of every point in the distribution. This would not be true if the distribution were not symmetric. If it were skewed to the right, for example, one would also need to know a measure of skewness in addition to the mean and standard deviation, and the variance and semivariance would not be equivalent.

Figure 5.2 A normal distribution $[E(R) = .1, \sigma = .2]$.

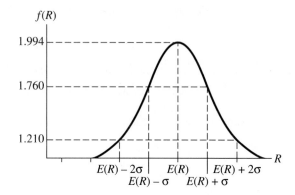

The equation for the frequency of returns, R, that are normally distributed is[2]

$$f(R) = \frac{1}{\sigma\sqrt{2\pi}}e^{-(1/2)[(R-E(R))/\sigma]^2}. \tag{5.12}$$

If we know the mean, $E(R)$, and the standard deviation, σ, of the distribution, then we can plot the frequency of any return. For example, if $E(R) = 10\%$ and $\sigma = 20\%$, then the frequency of a 13% rate of return is

$$f(.13) = \frac{1}{.2\sqrt{2\pi}}e^{-(1/2)[(.13-.10)/.2]^2}$$

$$= 1.972.$$

Often a normal distribution is converted into a unit normal distribution that always has a mean of zero and a standard deviation of one. Most normal probability tables (like that given at the end of Chapter 7) are based on a unit normal distribution. To convert a return, R, into a unit normal variable, z, we subtract the mean, $E(R)$, and divide by the standard deviation, σ:

$$z = \frac{R - E(R)}{\sigma}. \tag{5.13}$$

The frequency function for a unit normal variable is

$$f(z) = \frac{1}{\sqrt{2\pi}}e^{-(1/2)z^2}. \tag{5.14}$$

This could be plotted in Fig. 5.2. Of course the scales would change.

2. Calculating the Mean and Variance of a Two-Asset Portfolio

Consider a portfolio of two risky assets that are both normally distributed. How can we measure the mean and standard deviation of a portfolio with $a\%$ of our wealth invested in asset X, and $b\% = (1 - a\%)$ invested in asset Y? Mathematically, the portfolio return can be expressed as the

---

[2] Of course π is "pi," the ratio of the circumference and the diameter of a circle, and e is the base of natural logarithms.

weighted sum of two random variables:

$$\tilde{R}_p = a\tilde{X} + b\tilde{Y}.$$

By using the properties of mean and variance derived earlier, we can derive the mean and variance of the portfolio. The mean return is the expected outcome:

$$E(\tilde{R}_p) = E\left[a\tilde{X} + b\tilde{Y}\right].$$

Separating terms, we have

$$E(\tilde{R}_p) = E(a\tilde{X}) + E(b\tilde{Y}).$$

Using Property 2, that is, $E(a\tilde{X}) = a E(\tilde{X})$, we have

$$E(\tilde{R}_p) = a E(\tilde{X}) + b E(\tilde{Y}). \tag{5.15}$$

Thus the portfolio mean return is seen to be simply the weighted average of returns on individual securities, where the weights are the percentage invested in those securities.

The variance of the portfolio return is expressed as

$$\text{VAR}(\tilde{R}_p) = E[\tilde{R}_p - E(\tilde{R}_p)]^2$$

$$= E[(a\tilde{X} + b\tilde{Y}) - E(a\tilde{X} + b\tilde{Y})]^2.$$

Again, using Property 2 and rearranging terms, we have

$$\text{VAR}(\tilde{R}_p) = E\left[(a\tilde{X} - a E(\tilde{X})) + (b\tilde{Y} - b E(\tilde{Y}))\right]^2.$$

By squaring the term in brackets and using Property 4, we have

$$\text{VAR}(\tilde{R}_p) = E\left[a^2(\tilde{X} - E(\tilde{X}))^2 + b^2(\tilde{Y} - E(\tilde{Y}))^2 + 2ab(\tilde{X} - E(\tilde{X}))(\tilde{Y} - E(\tilde{Y}))\right].$$

You will recall that from the definition of variance and by Property 4,

$$\text{VAR}(a\tilde{X}) = a^2 E\left[(\tilde{X} - E(\tilde{X}))^2\right] = a^2 \text{VAR}(\tilde{X}).$$

Also,

$$\text{VAR}(b\tilde{Y}) = b^2 E\left[(\tilde{Y} - E(\tilde{X}))^2\right] = b^2 \text{VAR}(\tilde{Y}).$$

Therefore the portfolio variance is the sum of the variances of the individual securities multiplied by the square of their weights plus a third term, which includes the *covariance*, $\text{COV}(\tilde{X}, \tilde{Y})$:

$$\text{VAR}(\tilde{R}_p) = a^2 \text{VAR}(\tilde{X}) + b^2 \text{VAR}(\tilde{Y}) + 2ab E\left[(\tilde{X} - E(\tilde{X}))(\tilde{Y} - E(\tilde{Y}))\right],$$

$$\text{COV}(\tilde{X}, \tilde{Y}) \equiv E\left[(\tilde{X} - E(\tilde{X}))(\tilde{Y} - E(\tilde{Y}))\right].$$

The covariance is a measure of the way in which the two random variables move in relation to each other. If the covariance is positive, the variables move in the same direction. If it is negative, they move in opposite directions. The covariance is an extremely important concept because it is the appropriate measure of the contribution of a single asset to portfolio risk. The variance of a random variable is really the same thing as its covariance with itself:[3]

$$\text{COV}(aX, aX) = a \cdot aE\left[(X - E(X))(X - E(X))\right]$$

$$= a^2 E\left[(X - E(X))^2\right] = a^2 \text{VAR}(X).$$

We now see that the variance for a portfolio of two assets is

$$\text{VAR}(R_p) = a^2 \text{VAR}(X) + b^2 \text{VAR}(Y) + 2ab\,\text{COV}(X, Y). \tag{5.16}$$

To provide a better intuitive feel for portfolio variance and for the meaning of covariance, consider the following set of returns for assets X and Y:

Probability	X_i (%)	Y_i (%)
.2	11	−3
.2	9	15
.2	25	2
.2	7	20
.2	−2	6

To simplify matters we have assumed that each pair of returns $[X_i Y_i]$ has equal probability (Prob. = .2). The expected value of X is 10%, and the expected value of Y is 8%. Then the variances are

$$\text{VAR}(X) = .2(.11 - 10)^2 + .2(.09 - 10)^2 + .2(.25 - 10)^2$$
$$+ .2(.07 - .10)^2 + .2(-.02 - .10)^2$$
$$= .0076;$$

$$\text{VAR}(Y) = .2(-.03 - .08)^2 + .2(.15 - .08)^2 + .2(.02 - .08)^2$$
$$+ .2(.20 - .08)^2 + .2(.06 - .08)^2$$
$$= .00708.$$

The covariance between X and Y is

$$\text{COV}(X, Y) = E\left[(X - E(X))(Y - E(Y))\right]$$
$$= .2(.11 - .10)(.03 - .08) + .2(.09 - .10)(.15 - .08)$$
$$+ .2(.25 - .10)(.02 - .08) + .2(.07 - .10)(.20 - .08)$$
$$+ .2(-.02 - .10)(.06 - .08)$$
$$= -.0024.$$

---

[3] From this point on, the tilde (~) will be used in the text to designate a random variable only when it is needed to prevent ambiguity.

Table 5.3 Mean and Standard Deviation of Returns

Percentage in X	Percentage in Y	$E(\widetilde{R}_p)$ (%)	$\sigma(\widetilde{R}_p)$ (%)
100	0	10.0	8.72
75	25	9.5	6.18
50	50	9.0	4.97
25	75	8.5	5.96
0	100	8.0	8.41

Negative covariance implies that the returns on assets X and Y tend to move in opposite directions. If we invest in both securities at once, the result is a portfolio that is less risky than holding either asset separately: while we are losing with asset X, we win with asset Y. Therefore our investment position is partially hedged, and risk is reduced.

As an illustration of the effect of diversification, suppose we invest half our assets in X and half in Y. By using Eqs. (5.15) and (5.16) we can compute portfolio return and risk directly.

$$E(R_p) = aE(X) + bE(Y) \tag{5.15}$$

$$= .5(.10) + .5(.08) = 9\%.$$

$$VAR(R_p) = a^2 VAR(X) + b^2 VAR(Y) + 2ab COV(X, Y) \tag{5.16}$$

$$= (.5)^2(.0076) + (.5)^2(.00708) + 2(.5)(.5)(-.0024)$$

$$= .00247 \quad \text{or} \quad \sigma(R_p) = 4.97\%.$$

The advantage of portfolio diversification becomes clear in this example. With half our assets in X and half in Y, the expected return is halfway between that offered by X and by Y, but the portfolio risk is considerably less than either VAR(X) or VAR(Y).

Of course, we may choose any combination of X and Y. Table 5.3 gives the mean and standard deviation of returns for some of the possibilities.

Figure 5.3(a) shows the relationship between (1) the expected return on the portfolio and (2) the percentage of the portfolio, a, that is invested in risky asset X. Note that the portfolio expected return is a linear function of the weight in asset X.

$$\frac{dE(R_p)}{da} = E(X) - E(Y) = 10.0\% - 8.0\% = 2\%.$$

For each 1% decline in a there will be a 2% decline in expected return. The relationship between the portfolio standard deviation, $\sigma(R_p)$, and the weight in asset X is nonlinear and reaches a minimum. Later on, we will show how to determine the portfolio weights that will minimize portfolio risk.

Figure 5.4 plots the portfolio mean and standard deviation on a single graph. Each point represents a different weight in asset X. The solid portion of the line represents all combinations where the weights in asset X range between 0% and 100%.

If we can sell an asset short without restriction, then the dashed portions of the lines in Fig. 5.4 are feasible. Selling short means that you sell an asset that you do not already have. For example, it might be possible to sell short 50% of your wealth in asset X (even though you do not already own

Figure 5.3 The portfolio return mean and standard deviation as a function of the percentage invested in risky asset X.

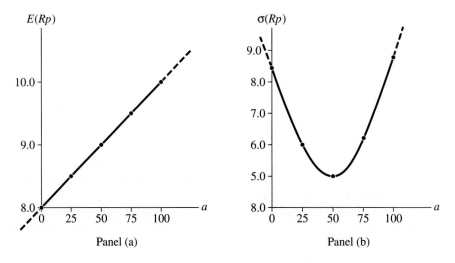

Panel (a)   Panel (b)

Figure 5.4 Trade-off between mean and standard deviation.

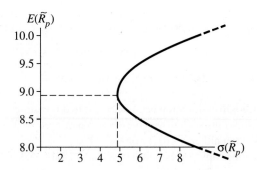

shares of asset X) and buy 150% of asset Y. If you sell X short, you should receive the proceeds, which you can then use to buy an extra 50% of Y. This is not possible in the real world because investors do not receive funds equal to the value of securities in which they sell short. Nevertheless, for expositional purposes, we assume that short sales are not constrained. The mean and variance of the above short position are

$$E(R_p) = -.5E(X) + 1.5E(Y)$$

$$= -.5(.10) + 1.5(.08) = 7.0\%.$$

$$VAR(R_p) = (-.5)^2 VAR(X) + (1.5)^2 VAR(Y) + 2(-.5)(1.5)COV(X, Y)$$

$$= .25(.0076) + (2.25)(.00708) + 2(-.75)(-.0024) = .02143.$$

$$\sigma(R_p) = \sqrt{VAR(R_p)} = 14.64\%.$$

Figure 5.5 Independent returns.

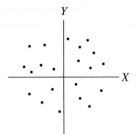

Figure 5.6 Perfectly correlated returns.

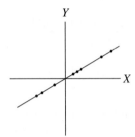

Now that we have developed ways of measuring the risk (variance) and return (mean) for a portfolio of assets, there are several interesting questions to explore. For example, what happens if the covariance between X and Y is zero—that is, what happens if the two securities are independent? On the other hand, what happens if they are perfectly correlated? How do we find the combination of X and Y that gives minimum variance?

3. The Correlation Coefficient

To answer some of these questions, it is useful to explain the concept of correlation, which is similar to covariance. The *correlation*, r_{xy}, between two random variables is defined as the covariance divided by the product of the standard deviations:

$$r_{xy} \equiv \frac{\text{COV}(X, Y)}{\sigma_x \sigma_y}. \tag{5.17}$$

Obviously, if returns on the two assets are independent (i.e., if the covariance between them is zero), then the correlation between them will be zero. Such a situation is shown in Fig. 5.5, which is the scatter diagram of two independent returns.

The opposite situation occurs when the returns are perfectly correlated, as in Fig. 5.6, in which the returns all fall on a straight line. Perfect correlation will result in a correlation coefficient equal to 1. To see that this is true we can use the fact that Y is a linear function of X. In other words, if we are given the value X, we know for sure what the corresponding value of Y will be. This is expressed as a linear function:

$$Y = a + bX.$$

We also use the definition of the correlation coefficient. First, we derive the expected value and standard deviation of Y by using Properties 1 through 4:

$$E(Y) = a + bE(X),$$

$$\text{VAR}(Y) = b^2\text{VAR}(X),$$

$$\sigma_y = b\sigma_x.$$

The definition of the correlation coefficient is

$$r_{xy} = \frac{\text{COV}(X, Y)}{\sigma_x\sigma_y} = \frac{E\left[(X - E(X))(Y - E(Y))\right]}{\sigma_x\sigma_y}.$$

By substituting the mean and variance of Y, we obtain

$$r_{xy} = \frac{E\left[(X - E(X))(a + bX - a - bE(X))\right]}{\sigma_x b\sigma_x}$$

$$= \frac{E\left[(X - E(X))b(X - E(X))\right]}{b\sigma_x^2} = \frac{b\sigma_x^2}{b\sigma_x^2} = 1.$$

Therefore the correlation coefficient equals +1 if the returns are perfectly correlated, and it equals −1 if the returns are perfectly inversely correlated.[4] It is left as an exercise for the student to prove that the latter is true. The correlation coefficient ranges between +1 and −1 :

$$-1 \le r_{xy} \le 1. \tag{5.18}$$

For the example we have been working with, the correlation between X and Y is

$$r_{xy} = \frac{\text{COV}(X, Y)}{\sigma_x\sigma_y} = \frac{-.0024}{(.0872)(.0841)} = -.33.$$

By rearranging the definition of the correlation coefficient in Eq. (5.17), we get another definition of covariance whereby it is seen to be equal to the correlation coefficient times the product of the standard deviations:

$$\text{COV}(X, Y) - r_{xy}\sigma_x\sigma_y. \tag{5.19}$$

This in turn can be substituted into the definition of the variance of a portfolio of two assets. Substituting (5.19) into (5.16), we have

$$\text{VAR}(R_p) = a^2\text{VAR}(X) + b^2\text{VAR}(Y) + 2abr_{xy}\sigma_x\sigma_y. \tag{5.20}$$

4. The Minimum Variance Portfolio

This reformulation of the variance definition is useful in a number of ways. First, it can be used to find the combination of random variables, X and Y, that provides the portfolio with minimum variance. This portfolio is the one where changes in variance (or standard deviation) with respect to changes in the percentage invested in X are zero.[5] First, recall that since the sum of weights

---

[4] The linear relationship between X and Y for perfect inverse correlation is $Y = a - bX$.
[5] To review the mathematics of maximization refer to Appendix D at the end of the book.

must add to 1, $b = 1 - a$. Therefore the variance can be rewritten as

$$\text{VAR}(R_p) = a^2\sigma_x^2 + (1-a)^2\sigma_y^2 + 2a(1-a)r_{xy}\sigma_x\sigma_y.$$

We can minimize portfolio variance by setting the first derivative equal to zero:

$$\frac{d\text{VAR}(R_p)}{da} = 2a\sigma_x^2 - 2\sigma_y^2 + 2a\sigma_y^2 + 2r_{xy}\sigma_x\sigma_y - 4ar_{xy}\sigma_x\sigma_y = 0$$

$$a(\sigma_x^2 + \sigma_y^2 - 2r_{xy}\sigma_x\sigma_y) + r_{xy}\sigma_x\sigma_y - \sigma_y^2 = 0$$

Solving for the optimal percentage to invest in X in order to obtain the minimum variance portfolio, we get

$$a^* = \frac{\sigma_y^2 - r_{xy}\sigma_x\sigma_y}{\sigma_x^2 + \sigma_y^2 - 2r_{xy}\sigma_x\sigma_y}. \tag{5.21}$$

Continuing with the example used throughout this section, we see that the minimum variance portfolio is the one where

$$a^* = \frac{.00708 - (-.33)(.0872)(.0841)}{.0076 + .00708 - 2(-.33)(.0872)(.0841)} = .487.$$

The portfolio return and variance for the minimum variance portfolio are

$$E(R_p) = aE(X) + (1-a)E(Y)$$

$$= .487(.10) + (.513)(.08) = 8.974\%.$$

$$\text{VAR}(R_p) = a^2\text{VAR}(X) + (1-a)^2\text{VAR}(Y) + 2a(1-a)r_{xy}\sigma_x\sigma_y$$

$$= (.487)^2(.0076) + (.513)^2(.00708) + 2(.487)(.513)(-.33)(.0872)(.0841)$$

$$= .0018025 + .0018632 - .0012092 = .0024565.$$

$$\sigma_p = 4.956\%.$$

The minimum variance portfolio is represented by the intersection of the dashed lines in Fig. 5.4.

5. Perfectly Correlated Assets

Up to this point, we have considered an example where the returns of the two risky assets had a negative correlation. What happens if they are perfectly correlated? Suppose $r_{xy} = 1$. Table 5.4 gives an example of security returns where $X = 1.037Y + 1.703$. All combinations of X and Y lie along a straight line and hence are perfectly correlated.

Since we have used the same numbers for the returns on asset Y as were used in the previous example, its standard deviation is 8.41%. We can derive the standard deviation of X by using Property 4, and the covariance between X and Y by using the definition of covariance in Eq. (5.19). It is also interesting to look at the graph of mean versus variance (Fig. 5.7). Point A represents the risk and return for a portfolio consisting of 100% of our investment in X, and B represents 100% in Y. The dashed line represents the risk and return provided for all combinations of X and Y

Table 5.4 Perfectly Correlated Security Returns

Probability	X (%)	Y (%)
.2	−1.408	−3
.2	17.258	15
.2	3.777	2
.2	22.443	20
.2	7.925	6

$$\sigma_x = 1.037\sigma_y = 8.72\%,$$
$$\sigma_y = 8.41\%,$$
$$\text{COV}(X, Y) = r_{xy}\sigma_x\sigma_y = .007334.$$

Figure 5.7 Risk-return trade-offs for two assets.

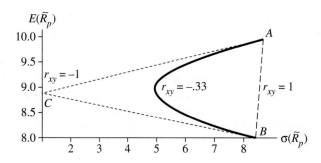

when they are perfectly correlated. To see that this trade-off is a straight line, in the mean-variance argument plane, we take a look at the definitions of mean and variance when $r_{xy} = 1$:

$$E(R_p) = aE(X) + (1 - a)E(Y),$$
$$\text{VAR}(R_p) = a^2\sigma_x^2 + (1 - a)^2\sigma_x^2 + 2a(1 - a)\sigma_x\sigma_y. \tag{5.22}$$

Note that the variance can be factored:

$$\text{VAR}(R_p) = [a\sigma_x + (1 - a)\sigma_y]^2;$$

therefore the standard deviation is

$$\sigma(R_p) = a\sigma_x + (1 - a)\sigma_y. \tag{5.23}$$

The easiest way to prove that the curve between A and B is a straight line is to show that its slope does not change as a, the proportion of the portfolio invested in X, changes. The slope of the line will be the derivative of expected value with respect to the weight in X divided by the derivative of standard deviation with respect to the weight in X:

$$\text{Slope} = \frac{dE(R_p)}{d\sigma(R_p)} = \frac{dE(R_p)/da}{d\sigma(R_p)/da}.$$

The derivative of the expected portfolio return with respect to a change in a is

$$\frac{dE(R_p)}{da} = E(X) - E(Y),$$

and the derivative of the standard deviation with respect to a is

$$\frac{dE(R_p)}{da} = \sigma_x - \sigma_y.$$

Therefore the slope is

$$\frac{dE(R_p)}{d\sigma(R_p)} = \frac{E(X) - E(Y)}{\sigma_x - \sigma_y} = \frac{.10 - .08}{.0872 - .0841} = 6.45.$$

This proves that AB is a straight line because no matter what percentage of wealth, a, we choose to invest in X, the trade-off between expected value and standard deviation is constant.

Finally, suppose the returns on X and Y are perfectly inversely correlated; in other words, $r_{xy} = -1$. In this case the graph of the relationship between mean and standard deviation is the dotted line ACB in Fig. 5.7. We should expect that if the assets have perfect inverse correlation, it would be possible to construct a perfect hedge. That is, the appropriate choice of a will result in a portfolio with zero variance. The mean and variance for a portfolio with two perfectly inversely correlated assets are

$$E(R_p) = aE(X) + (1-a)E(Y), \tag{5.24}$$

$$VAR(R_p) = a^2\sigma_x^2 + (1-a)^2\sigma_y^2 - 2a(1-a)\sigma_x\sigma_y, \quad \text{since} \quad r_{xy} = -1.$$

The variance can be factored as follows:

$$VAR(R_p) = [a\sigma_x - (1-a)\sigma_y]^2,$$

$$\sigma(R_p) = \pm[a\sigma_x - (1-a)\sigma_y]. \tag{5.25a}$$

Note that Eq. (5.25a) has both a positive and a negative root. The dotted line in Fig. 5.7 is really two line segments, one with a positive slope and the other with a negative slope. The following proofs show that the signs of the slopes of the line segments are determined by Eq. (5.25a) and that they will always intersect the vertical axis in Fig. 5.7 at a point where the minimum variance portfolio has zero variance.

To show this result, we can use Eq. (5.21) to find the minimum variance portfolio:

$$a^* = \frac{\sigma_y^2 - r_{xy}\sigma_x\sigma_y}{\sigma_x^2 + \sigma_y^2 - 2r_{xy}\sigma_x\sigma_y}.$$

Because $r_{xy} = 1$, we have

$$a^* = \frac{\sigma_y^2 + \sigma_x\sigma_y}{\sigma_x^2 + \sigma_y^2 + 2\sigma_x\sigma_y} = \frac{\sigma_y}{\sigma_x + \sigma_y} = \frac{.0841}{.0872 + .0841} = 49.095\%.$$

By substituting this weight into the equations for mean and standard deviation, we can demonstrate that the portfolio has zero variance:

$$E(R_p) = .49095(.10) + (1 - .49095)(.08) = 8.92\%,$$

$$\sigma(R_p) = .49095(.0872) - (1 - .49095)(.0841) = 0\%.$$

This result is represented by point C in Fig. 5.7.

Next, let us examine the properties of the line segments AC and CB in Fig. 5.7. To do so it is important to realize that the expression for the standard deviation in Eq. (5.25a) for a portfolio with two perfectly inversely correlated assets has both positive and negative roots. In our example, suppose that none of the portfolio is invested in X. Then $a = 0$, and the standard deviation is a negative number,

$$\sigma(R_p) = -(1 - 0)\sigma_y < 0.$$

Because standard deviations cannot be negative, the two roots of Eq. (5.25a) need to be interpreted as follows. So long as the percentage invested in X is greater than or equal to 49.095% (which is a^*, the minimum variance portfolio), the standard deviation of the portfolio is

$$\sigma(R_p) = a\sigma_x - (1 - a)\sigma_y \quad \text{if} \quad a \geq \frac{\sigma_y}{\sigma_x + \sigma_y}. \tag{5.25b}$$

On the other hand, if less than 49.095% of the portfolio is invested in X, the standard deviation is

$$\sigma(R_p) = (1 - a)\sigma_y - a\sigma_x \quad \text{if} \quad a < \frac{\sigma_y}{\sigma_x + \sigma_y}. \tag{5.25c}$$

We can use these results to show that the line segments AC and CB are linear. The proof proceeds in precisely the same way that we were able to show that AB is linear if $r_{xy} = 1$. For the positively sloped line segment, AC, using Eq. (5.24), we have

$$\frac{dE(R_p)}{da} = E(X) - E(Y),$$

and using Eq. (5.25b), we have

$$\frac{d\sigma(R_p)}{da} = \sigma_x + \sigma_y \quad \text{if} \quad a \geq \frac{\sigma_y}{\sigma_x + \sigma_y}.$$

Therefore the slope of the line is

$$\frac{dE(R_p)}{d\sigma(R_p)} = \frac{dE(R_p)/da}{d\sigma(R_p)/da} = \frac{E(X) - E(Y)}{-(\sigma_y + \sigma_x)} = \frac{.10 - .08}{-(.0872 + .0841)} = -.117 < 0.$$

The slope of CB is negative and CB is linear.

6. The Minimum Variance Opportunity Set

Line AB in Fig. 5.7 shows the risk-return trade-offs available to the investor if the two assets are perfectly correlated, and line segments AC and CB represent the trade-offs if the assets are perfectly inversely correlated. However, these are the two extreme cases. Usually assets are less than perfectly correlated (i.e., $-1 < r_{xy} < 1$). The general slope of the mean-variance opportunity set is the solid line in Fig. 5.7. The opportunity set can be defined as follows:

> **MINIMUM VARIANCE OPPORTUNITY SET**   The minimum variance opportunity set is the locus of risk and return combinations offered by portfolios of risky assets that yields the minimum variance for a given rate of return.

In general the minimum variance opportunity set will be convex (as represented by the solid line in Fig. 5.7). This property is rather obvious because the opportunity set is bounded by the triangle ACB. Intuitively, any set of portfolio combinations formed by two risky assets that are less than perfectly correlated must lie inside the triangle ACB and will be convex.

The concepts developed in this section can now be used to discuss the way we, as investors, are able to select portfolios that maximize our expected utility. The portfolio mean return and variance are the measures of return and risk. We choose the percentages of our wealth that we want to invest in each security in order to obtain the required risk and return. We have shown the choices that are possible if two risky assets are perfectly correlated, perfectly inversely correlated, and where their correlation lies between -1 and $+1$. We have also seen how we can find the minimum variance portfolio. Later in this chapter these results will be extended from the two-asset case to portfolios of many assets, and we will discuss an example wherein a corporate treasurer may use portfolio theory to reduce the risk (variability) of shareholders' wealth.

C. The Efficient Set with Two Risky Assets (and No Risk-Free Asset)

The assumption of no risk-free asset is the same as saying that there are no borrowing or lending opportunities. In other words, this section shows how a single individual (Robinson Crusoe) will choose his optimal portfolio of risky assets in a world where there is no opportunity for exchange. As we shall see, the following discussion is analogous to the Robinson Crusoe economy described in Chapter 1 except that the objects of choice are risk and return rather than consumption and investment. The results are also similar. Robinson Crusoe's optimal portfolio will be that where his subjective marginal rate of substitution between risk and return is exactly equal to the objectively determined marginal rate of transformation (along his mean-variance opportunity set) between risk and return. At this optimal portfolio the equality between MRS and MRT determines his subjective price of risk. Later on, in Section E.5, we shall introduce a marketplace with opportunities to exchange by borrowing and lending unlimited amounts of money at the risk-free rate. This exchange economy setting will show the existence of a single market-determined price of risk. All individuals and their agents (firms, for example) will use the market price of risk for optimal decisions in the face of uncertainty.

In the chapter on utility theory we saw that indifference curves for the risk-averse investor were convex in the mean-variance plane. Figure 5.8 shows a family of indifference curves as well as the convex set of portfolio choices offered by various percentages of investment in two risky assets. If we know our risk-return trade-off and also know the possibilities offered by combinations of risky assets, we will maximize our expected utility at point C in Fig. 5.8. This is where our indifference curve is tangent to the opportunity set offered by combinations of X and Y. Each indifference curve maps out all combinations of risk and return to provide us with the same total utility. Moving from

Figure 5.8 Optimal portfolio choice for a risk-averse investor and two risky assets.

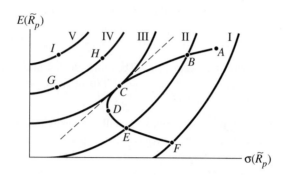

right to left in Fig. 5.8, we know (from Chapter 3) that indifference curve I has less total utility than indifference curve II, and so on. We could put all our money in one asset and receive the risk and return at point F, which is on indifference curve I, but of course we can do better at points B and E, and best at point C (on indifference curve III). Points G, H, and I have higher total utility than point C, but they are not feasible because the opportunity set offered by the risky assets does not extend that far.

An important feature of the optimal portfolio that we choose in order to maximize our utility is that the marginal rate of substitution between our preference for risk and return represented by our indifference curves must equal the marginal rate of transformation offered by the minimum variance opportunity set. The slope of the dashed line drawn tangent to our indifference curve at point C is our marginal rate of substitution between risk and return. This line is also tangent to the opportunity set at point C. Hence its slope also represents the trade-off between risk and return offered by the opportunity set. Therefore the way we can find a utility-maximizing portfolio is to try different portfolios along the opportunity set until we find the one where the marginal rate of transformation between risk and return along the minimum variance opportunity set just equals the marginal rate of substitution along our indifference curve:

$$\text{MRS}_{\sigma(R_p)}^{E(R_p)} = \text{MRT}_{\sigma(R_p)}^{E(R_p)}.$$

The fact that this point is unique is guaranteed by the convexity of our indifference curve and the convexity of the upper half of the minimum variance opportunity set.

Let us take a look at Fig. 5.9. Suppose we find ourselves endowed with a portfolio that has the mean-variance opportunities at point A. By changing the percentage of our wealth in each of the risky assets, we can reach any point along the minimum variance opportunity set. At point A the marginal rate of transformation between return and risk along the minimum variance opportunity set is equal to the slope of the line DAF. The low slope indicates that we will get rid of a lot of risk in exchange for giving up only a little return. On the other hand, the slope of our indifference curve, U_1, the slope of the line CAB at point A, indicates our subjective trade-off between return and risk (i.e., our marginal rate of substitution). At point A, where we already have a relatively high level of risk, we are willing to give up a lot of return in order to get rid of a little risk. If we can move along the opportunity set toward point E without incurring any cost, we will clearly do so because the opportunity set at point A allows us to trade off return and risk at a more favorable rate than we require (according to our indifference curve). We will continue to move along the opportunity set until we reach point E. At this point we attain the highest possible expected utility on indifference

Figure 5.9 The utility-maximizing choice equates the marginal rates of substitution and transformation.

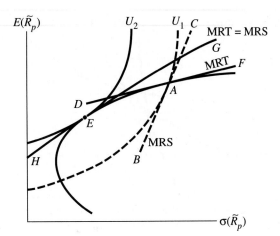

curve U_2. Furthermore, the marginal rate of transformation between return and risk along the opportunity set (the slope of line HEG) is exactly equal to the marginal rate of substitution along the indifference curve (also, the slope of tangent HEG). Thus we have shown that a necessary condition for expected utility maximization is that the marginal rate of substitution must equal the marginal rate of transformation. This also implies that at the optimum portfolio choice, we have a linear trade-off between return, $E(R_p)$, and risk, $\sigma(R_p)$.[6]

Even though different investors may have the same assessment of the return and risk offered by risky assets, they may hold different portfolios. Later we shall discover that when a riskless asset is introduced into the opportunity set, investors will hold identical combinations of risky assets even though they have different attitudes toward risk. However, in the current framework for analysis, we assume that investors have homogeneous beliefs about the opportunity set, that no risk-free asset exists, and that investors have different indifference curves, which reflect their differing attitudes toward risk.[7] Figure 5.10 shows three different indifference curves and the investment opportunity set. Investor III is more risk averse than investor II, who in turn is more risk averse than investor I. (Why is this true?) Consequently, they each will choose to invest a different percentage of their portfolio in the risky assets that make up the opportunity set.

Note that rational investors will never choose a portfolio below the minimum variance point. They can always attain higher expected utility along the positively sloped portion of the opportunity set represented by the line segment $EDCBA$. This concept leads to the definition of the efficient set.

> **EFFICIENT SET**   The efficient set is the set of mean-variance choices from the investment opportunity set where for a given variance (or standard deviation) no other investment opportunity offers a higher mean return.

The notion of an efficient set considerably narrows the number of portfolios from which an investor might choose. In Fig. 5.10, for example, the portfolios at points B and F offer the same

---

[6] For an excellent mathematical development of this fact, see Fama and Miller [1972, Chapter 6].

[7] Homogeneous beliefs mean simply that everyone has exactly the same information so that they all perceive exactly the same opportunity set.

Figure 5.10 Choices by investors with different indifference curves.

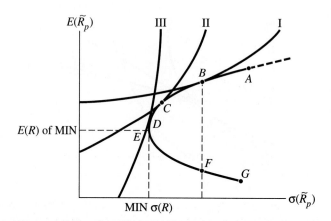

Figure 5.11 Two perfectly correlated assets.

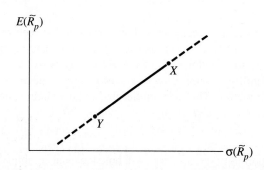

standard deviation, but B is on the efficient set because it offers a higher return for the same risk. Hence no rational investor would ever choose point F over point B, and we can ignore point F. Point B is stochastically dominant over point F. It is interesting to note, however, that investors will hold positions in an asset or portfolio at point F. No one will hold F by itself; rather it will be held as part of portfolios that lie along the efficient set.

Interesting special cases of the efficient set for two risky assets occur when their returns are perfectly correlated. Figure 5.11 shows perfect correlation, and Fig. 5.12 shows perfect inverse correlation. In both cases, the efficient set is linear. In Fig. 5.11 it is line XY, and in Fig. 5.12 it is line XZ.

In general the locus of feasible mean-variance opportunities can be found by solving either of the following two mathematical programming problems. The first defines the minimum variance opportunity set, and the second defines the efficient set:

Programming Problem 1:

$$\text{MIN } \sigma^2(R_p) \quad \text{subject to} \quad E(R_p) = K. \tag{5.26a}$$

Programming Problem 2:

$$\text{MAX } E(R_p) \quad \text{subject to} \quad \sigma^2(R_p) = K. \tag{5.26b}$$

Figure 5.12 Two assets with perfect inverse correlation.

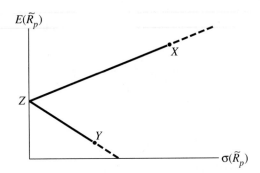

Note that the minimum variance opportunity set is found by finding all combinations that give the lowest risk for a given return. The efficient set is the locus of highest returns for a given risk. If we write out the first problem at greater length,

$$\text{MIN}\left\{\sigma^2(R_p) = \left[a^2\sigma_x^2 + (1-a)^2\sigma_y^2 + 2a(1-a)r_{xy}\sigma_x\sigma_y\right]\right\},$$

subject to

$$E(R_p) = aE(X) + (1-a)E(Y) = K,$$

we see that it is a quadratic programming problem because the objective function contains squared terms in the choice variable, a. The decision variable in either problem, of course, is to choose the percentage, a, to invest in asset X that minimizes variance subject to the expected return constraint. Markowitz [1959] was the first to define the investor's portfolio decision problem in this way and to show that it is equivalent to maximizing the investor's expected utility. The interested student is referred to his book for an excellent exposition. However, it is beyond the scope of the present text to explore the details of a quadratic programming solution to the efficient set. Furthermore, the problem can be simplified greatly by introducing a risk-free asset into the analysis.

D. *The* Efficient Set with One Risky and One Risk-Free Asset

If one of the two assets, R_f, has zero variance, then the mean and variance of the portfolio become

$$E(R_p) = aE(X) + (1-a)R_f,$$

$$\text{VAR}(R_p) = a^2\text{VAR}(X).$$

We have assumed that the risk-free asset is R_f. Its variance and its covariance with the risky asset are zero; therefore the second and third terms in the general expression for variance, Eq. (5.20), are equal to zero, and portfolio variance is simply the variance of the risky asset.

Knowledge of the mean and variance of a portfolio with one risk-free and one risky asset allows us to plot the opportunity set in Fig. 5.13. It is linear. Proof of linearity proceeds in the same way as earlier proofs. All we need to do is show that the slope is independent of a, the percentage of the

Figure 5.13 Opportunity set with one risky and one risk-free asset.

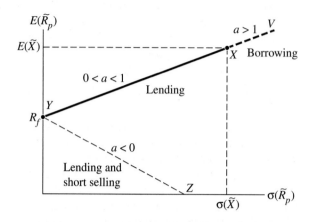

portfolio invested in the risky asset. The change in expected return with respect to the percentage invested in X is

$$\frac{dE(R_p)}{da} = E(X) - R_f.$$

Therefore the slope of the line is

$$\frac{dE(R_p)}{d\sigma(R_p)} = \frac{dE(R_p)/da}{d\sigma(R_p)/da} = \frac{E(X) - R_f}{\sigma_x}.$$

Consequently, the line VXY must be linear because its slope does not change with the percentage invested in X.

It is usually assumed that the rate of return on the risk-free asset is equal to the borrowing and lending rate in the economy. In the real world, of course, the borrowing and lending rates are not equal. One possible cause is transaction costs (i.e., frictions in the marketplace). However, like physicists who assume that friction does not exist in order to derive the laws of mechanics, economists assume that asset markets are frictionless in order to develop price theory. A frictionless world to an economist is one where all assets are infinitely divisible and where there are no transaction costs. In such a world, the borrowing rate would equal the lending rate for risk-free assets. We shall use this assumption to develop a theory for the equilibrium price of risk, then provide empirical evidence that indicates that in spite of several unrealistic assumptions, the theory describes reality surprisingly well.

Given the assumption that the borrowing rate equals the lending rate, YXV is a straight line. To reach portfolios along the line segment XV, it is necessary to borrow in order to invest more than 100% of the portfolio in the risky asset. Note that borrowing is analogous to selling short the risk-free asset. Therefore along the line segment XV the percentage invested in X is greater than 1; in other words, $a > 1$. The mean and standard deviation of the portfolio along this portion of the line are

$$E(R_p) = aE(X) + (1-a)R_f,$$

$$\sigma(R_p) = a\sigma_x.$$

On the other hand, when we decide to invest more than 100% of our portfolio in the risk-free asset, we must sell short the risky asset. Assuming no restrictions on sort sales (another assumption necessary for frictionless markets), the mean and variance of the portfolio for $a < 0$ are

$$E(R_p) = (1-a)R_f + aE(X),$$

$$\sigma(R_p) = |a|\,\sigma_x.$$

Note that because negative standard deviations are impossible, the absolute value of a is used to measure the standard deviation of the portfolio when the risky asset is sold short. The line segment YZ represents portfolio mean and variance in this case.

What about the efficient set for portfolios composed of one risk-free and one risky asset? Clearly no risk-averse investor would prefer line segment YZ in Fig. 5.13 because he or she can always do better along the positively sloped line segment XYV. Therefore the efficient set is composed of long positions in the risky asset combined with borrowing or lending. Why then do we observe short sales in the real world? The answer, of course, is that not all people hold the same probability beliefs about the distributions of returns provided by risky assets. Some investors may believe that the expected return on asset X is negative, in which case they would sell short. In equilibrium, however, we know that so long as investors are risk averse, the final price of the risky asset X must be adjusted so that its expected rate of return is greater than the risk-free rate. In equilibrium, assets of higher risk must have higher expected return.

E. *O*ptimal Portfolio Choice: Many Assets

Until now it has been convenient to discuss portfolios of only two assets. By generalizing the argument to many assets, we can discuss several important properties such as portfolio diversification, the separation principle, and the Capital Market Line. We can also provide a realistic example of how a corporate chief financial officer who views his or her firm as a portfolio can control the risk exposure of shareholders. We begin by developing the mean and variance for portfolios of many assets.

1. Portfolio Mean, Variance, and Covariance with *N* Risky Assets

Suppose we wish to talk about the mean and variance of portfolios of three assets instead of just two. Let w_1, w_2, and w_3 be the percentages of a portfolio invested in the three assets; let $E(R_1)$, $E(R_2)$, and $E(R_3)$ be the expected returns; let σ_1^2, σ_2^2, σ_3^2 be the variances; and let σ_{12}, σ_{23}, and σ_{13} be the covariances. Finally, let R_1, R_2, R_3 be the random returns. The definition of the portfolio mean return is

$$E(R_p) = E\left[w_1R_1 + w_2R_2 + w_3R_3\right],$$

and using Property 1, we have

$$E(R_p) = w_1E(R_1) + w_2E(R_2) + w_3E(R_3).$$

As was the case for a portfolio with two assets, the expected portfolio return is simply a weighted average of the expected return on individual assets. This can be written as

$$E(R_p) = \sum_{i=1}^{3} w_i E(R_i). \tag{5.27}$$

The definition of portfolio variance for three assets is the expectation of the sum of the mean differences squared:

$$
\begin{aligned}
\text{VAR}(R_p) &= E\left\{\left[(w_1 R_1 + w_2 R_2 + w_3 R_3) - (w_1 E(R_1) + w_2 E(R_2) + w_3 E(R_3))\right]^2\right\} \\
&= E\left\{\left[w_1(R_1 - E(R_1)) + w_2(R_2 - E(R_2)) + w_3(R_3 - E(R_3))\right]^2\right\} \\
&= \{E w_1^2(R_1 - E(R_1))^2 + w_2^2(R_2 - E(R_2))^2 + w_3^2(R_3 - E(R_3))^2 \\
&\quad + 2w_1 w_2(R_1 - E(R_1))(R_2 - E(R_2)) \\
&\quad + 2w_1 w_3(R_1 - E(R_1))(R_3 - E(R_3)) \\
&\quad + 2w_2 w_3(R_2 - E(R_2))(R_3 - E(R_3))\} \\
&= w_1^2 \text{VAR}(R_1) + w_2^2 \text{VAR}(R_2) + w_3^2 \text{VAR}(R_3) + 2w_1 w_2 \text{COV}(R_1, R_2) \\
&\quad + 2w_1 w_3 \text{COV}(R_1, R_3) + 2w_2 w_3 \text{COV}(R_2, R_3).
\end{aligned}
$$

The portfolio variance is a weighted sum of variance and covariance terms. It can be rewritten as

$$\text{VAR}(R_p) = \sum_{i=1}^{3} \sum_{j=1}^{3} w_i w_j \sigma_{ij}, \tag{5.28}$$

where w_i and w_j are the percentages invested in each asset, and σ_{ij} is the covariance of asset i with asset j. You will recall from the discussion of covariance earlier in the text that the variance is really a special case of covariance. The variance is the covariance of an asset with itself. For example, when $i = 2$ and $j = 2$, then we have $w_2 w_2 \sigma_{22}$, which is the same thing as $w_2^2 \text{VAR}(R_2)$. Therefore Eq. (5.28) contains three variance and six covariance terms.

If we replace the three assets with N, Eqs. (5.27) and (5.28) can be used as a general representation of the mean and variance of a portfolio with N assets. We can also write Eqs. (5.27) and (5.28) in matrix form,[8] which for two assets looks like this:

$$E(R_p) = \left[E(R_1) E(R_2)\right] \begin{bmatrix} w_1 \\ w_2 \end{bmatrix} = \mathbf{R'W},$$

$$\text{VAR}(R_p) = [w_1 w_2] \begin{bmatrix} \sigma_{11} & \sigma_{12} \\ \sigma_{21} & \sigma_{22} \end{bmatrix} \begin{bmatrix} w_1 \\ w_2 \end{bmatrix} = \mathbf{W'} \sum \mathbf{W}.$$

The expected portfolio return is the $(1 \times N)$ row vector of expected returns, $\left[E(R_1), E(R_2)\right] = \mathbf{R'}$ postmultiplied by the $(N \times 1)$ column vector of weights held in each asset, $[w_1 \, w_2] = \mathbf{W}$. The variance is the $(N \times N)$ variance-covariance matrix, $\sum$, premultiplied and postmultiplied by the

---

[8] The reader is referred to Appendix B at the end of the book for a review of matrix algebra.

vector of weights, $\mathbf{W}$. To see that the matrix definition of the variance is identical to Eq. (5.28), first postmultiply the variance-covariance matrix by the column vector of weights to get

$$\text{VAR}(R_p) = \begin{bmatrix} w_1 & w_2 \end{bmatrix} \begin{bmatrix} w_1\sigma_{11} + w_2\sigma_{12} \\ w_1\sigma_{21} + w_2\sigma_{22} \end{bmatrix}.$$

Postmultiplying the second vector times the first, we have

$$\text{VAR}(R_p) = w_1^2\sigma_{11} + w_1 w_2\sigma_{12} + w_2 w_1\sigma_{21} + w_2^2\sigma_{22}.$$

Finally, collecting terms, we see that this is equal to

$$\text{VAR}(R_p) = \sum_{i=1}^{N}\sum_{j=1}^{N} w_i w_j \sigma_{ij}, \quad \text{where} \quad N = 2.$$

This shows that the matrix definition of variance is equivalent to Eq. (5.28).

Suppose we want to express the covariance between two portfolios, A and B, using matrix notation. This will prove to be an extremely powerful and useful tool later on. Let $\mathbf{W}_1'$ be the $(1 \times N)$ row vector of weights held in portfolio A. For example, we might construct portfolio A by holding 50% of our wealth in asset X and the remaining 50% in asset Y. Next, let $\mathbf{W}_2$ be the $(N \times 1)$ column vector of weights used to construct portfolio B. For example, we might have 25% in X and 75% in Y. If $\sum$ is the $(N \times N)$ variance-covariance matrix, then the covariance between the two portfolios is defined as

$$\text{COV}(R_A, R_B) = \mathbf{W}_1' \sum \mathbf{W}_2$$

$$= \begin{bmatrix} w_{1a} & w_{2a} \end{bmatrix} \begin{bmatrix} \sigma_{11} & \sigma_{12} \\ \sigma_{21} & \sigma_{22} \end{bmatrix} \begin{bmatrix} w_{1b} \\ w_{2b} \end{bmatrix}. \tag{5.29}$$

Postmultiplying the variance-covariance matrix, $\sum$, by the column vector, $\mathbf{W}_2$, we have

$$\text{COV}(R_A, R_B) = \begin{bmatrix} w_{1a} & w_{2a} \end{bmatrix} \begin{bmatrix} w_{1b}\sigma_{11} + w_{2b}\sigma_{12} \\ w_{1b}\sigma_{21} + w_{2b}\sigma_{22} \end{bmatrix},$$

and postmultiplying the row vector, $\mathbf{W}_1'$, by the column vector above, we obtain

$$\text{COV}(R_A, R_B) = w_{1a}w_{1b}\sigma_{11} + w_{1a}w_{2b}\sigma_{12} + w_{2a}w_{1b}\sigma_{21} + w_{2a}w_{2b}\sigma_{22}.$$

To show that this matrix result is indeed the same as the traditional definition, we begin with the usual covariance equation:

$$\text{COV}(R_A, R_B) = E\left[(R_A - E(R_A))(R_B - E(R_B))\right].$$

We know that

$$R_A = w_{1a}R_x + w_{2a}R_y,$$

$$R_B = w_{1b}R_x + w_{2b}R_y.$$

Substituting these expressions as well as their expected values into the covariance definition, we have

$$COV(R_A, R_B) = [E \left(w_{1a}R_x + w_{2a}R_y - w_{1a}E(R_x) - w_{2a}E(R_y)\right)$$
$$\times (w_{1b}R_x + w_{2b}R_y - w_{1b}E(R_x) - w_{2b}E(R_y))]$$
$$= E \left\{ \left[w_{1a}(R_x - E(R_x)) + w_{2a}(R_y - E(R_y)) \right] \right.$$
$$\left. \times \left[w_{1b}(R_x - E(R_x)) + w_{2b}(R_y - E(R_y)) \right] \right\}$$
$$= w_{1a}w_{1b}\sigma_{11} + w_{1a}w_{2b}\sigma_{12} + w_{2a}w_{1b}\sigma_{21} + w_{2a}w_{2b}\sigma_{22}.$$

Note that this is exactly the same as the expanded covariance expression obtained from the matrix definition, Eq. (5.29).

The matrix definitions of portfolio mean, variance, and covariance are particularly powerful and useful because the size of the vectors and matrices can easily be expanded to handle any number of assets. The matrix form also lends itself naturally to computer programs.

2. An Application: Cross Hedging with Futures Contracts

Every corporation is really a portfolio. Take a look at the market value balance sheet in Table 5.5. The assets of NR Inc. are primarily buildings and land, dispersed geographically, but with market values that are sensitive to changes in inflation. Long-term debt is Baa rated, with roughly 10 years before maturity. Its market value is sensitive to changes in interest rates. The shareholders' position may be conceptualized as a portfolio that is long in the firm's assets and short in liabilities. It can be written as

$$\tilde{R}_S = w_{STA}\tilde{R}_{STA} + w_{LTA}\tilde{R}_{LTA} - w_{STL}\tilde{R}_{STL} - w_{LTD}\tilde{R}_{LTD}, \qquad (5.30)$$

where

$$\tilde{R}_S = \text{the risky return on shareholders' wealth,}$$

$$w_{STA}\tilde{R}_{STA} = \text{the weight and return on short-term assets,}$$

$$w_{LTA}\tilde{R}_{LTA} = \text{the weight and return on the firm's portfolio of long-term assets,}$$

$$w_{STL}\tilde{R}_{STL} = \text{the weight and return on the firm's short-term liabilities,}$$

$$w_{LTD}\tilde{R}_{LTD} = \text{the weight and return on the firm's long-term debt.}$$

Table 5.5 Market Value Balance Sheet for NR Inc.

Assets (in millions)		Liabilities (in millions)	
Short-term	239	Short-term	77
Long-term	200	Long-term debt	96
	439	Equity	266
			439

Suppose that the firm's chief financial officer (CFO) is concerned that a tough anti-inflationary policy will cause a decline in inflation and in interest rates. The result would be a decline in the market value of the property held by the company (its major asset) and an increase in the market value of the firm's long-term debt. The net effect would be a dramatic rise in the firm's debt-to-assets ratio and a drop in the market value of equity. To hedge against this risk the CFO has decided to buy T-bond futures contracts (an investment that we shall assume, for the sake of convenience, requires no cash outlay).[9] A long position in T-bond futures is expected to be a hedge for two reasons. First, when inflation and interest rates fall, the market value of the T-bond futures will rise to offset an expected decline in the market value of the firm's assets. Second, the T-bond position will hedge against an increase in the market value of the firm's debt liabilities.

Given that T-bond futures will provide a hedge, the CFO must determine the optimal number, N, of T-bond futures contracts to buy. Too few will not provide an adequate hedge. Too many will overhedge. If P_{TB} is the current price of a \$100,000 face value T-bond contract, V is the market value of the firm, and $\widetilde{R}_{TB}$ is the return on T-bond futures, then the return on equity, given the hedge position, becomes

$$\widetilde{R}_S = w_{STA}\widetilde{R}_{STA} + w_{LTA}\widetilde{R}_{LTA} - w_{STL}\widetilde{R}_{STL} - w_{LTD}\widetilde{R}_{LTD} + \frac{NP_{TB}}{V}\widetilde{R}_{TB} \tag{5.31}$$

The variance of the equity return, expressed in matrix form, is

$$\mathrm{VAR}(R_S) = \mathbf{W}' \sum \mathbf{W}, \tag{5.32}$$

where:

$$\mathbf{W}' = \left[w_{STA}, \; w_{LTA} - w_{STL}, \; -w_{LTD}, \; \frac{NP_{TB}}{V} \right],$$

$\sum$ = the variance-covariance matrix of all assets and liabilities in the firm's hedge portfolio.

To find the optimal hedge portfolio, we can take the derivative of Eq. (5.32) with respect to N and set the result equal to zero:

$$\frac{d\mathrm{VAR}(R_S)}{dN} = \frac{2P_{TB}}{V} \sum_i w_i r_{i,TB}\sigma_i\sigma_{TB} + 2\frac{P_{TB}^2}{V^2}\sigma_{TB}^2 N = 0.$$

Note that $r_{i,TB}$ is the correlation between the ith portfolio asset (or liability) and T-bond futures contracts, σ_i is the standard deviation of the ith asset, and σ_{TB} is the standard deviation of the T-bond futures contract return. Solving for N, the optimal number of futures contracts, we have

$$N = -\sum_i \frac{V_i r_{i,TB}\sigma_i}{P_{TB}\sigma_{TB}}. \tag{5.33}$$

Equation (5.33) shows that the hedging asset, T-bond futures, affects shareholders' risk through the correlation between T-bond futures returns and the returns on the firm's other assets and liabilities, $r_{i,F}$.[10] The actual values for the parameters involved are:

---

[9] Chapter 8 provides a complete description of futures contracts.

[10] The expression $r_{i,TB}\sigma_i/\sigma_{TB}$ is equal to the slope in a linear regression of the returns on the ith asset or liability on T-bond futures.

$$r_{STA,TB} = 0, \qquad r_{STL,TB} = 0,$$
$$r_{LTA,TB} = -.6725, \quad r_{LTD,TB} = .7834,$$
$$\sigma_{LTD} = .0908, \qquad \sigma_{LTA} = .0482,$$
$$\sigma_{TB} = .0766 \qquad V_{TB} = \$70,250.$$

The correlations confirm the CFO's suspicion that T-bond futures will be a good hedge against changes in the market value of long-term assets and long-term debt. T-bond futures returns are negatively correlated with debt. Substituting the above values into Eq. (5.33), we have

$$N = \frac{-V_{LTA}r_{LTA,TB}\sigma_{LTA}}{P_{TB}\sigma_{TB}} + \frac{-V_{LTD}r_{LTD,TB}\sigma_{LTD}}{P_{TB}\sigma_{TB}}$$

$$= \frac{-(200 \times 10^6)(-.6725)(.0482)}{(70.25 \times 10^3)(.0766)} + \frac{-(-96 \times 10^6)(.7834)(.0908)}{(70.25 \times 10^3)(.0766)}$$

$$= 1,205 \text{ contracts} + 1,269 \text{ contracts}.$$

The numbers reveal that the CFO needs to buy 1,205 contracts as a hedge against changes in the values of assets and 1,269 contracts to hedge against changes in the value of long-term debt.

There are, of course, many ways a CFO might choose to reduce the risk of shareholders. This example shows that a total of 2,474 T-bond contracts (i.e., $247.4 million worth) provides the optimal hedge, and illustrates one way of conceptualizing the firm as a portfolio of risky assets. Whether or not the CFO should hedge in the first place and the set of other possible hedge techniques are topics that will be discussed in Chapter 17.

3. The Opportunity Set with *N* Risky Assets

When considering portfolios with many assets, we can discover the opportunity set and efficient set if we know the expected returns and the variances of individual assets as well as the covariances between each pair of assets. There were not many assets to consider in the hedging example, but an investor can choose literally any combination of securities. This requires a great deal of information. The New York Stock Exchange alone lists at least 2,000 securities. To determine the opportunity set, it would be necessary to estimate 2,000 mean returns, 2,000 variances, and 1,999,000 covariances.[11] Fortunately, we shall soon see that there are ways around this computational nightmare.

The investment opportunity set has the same shape with many risky assets as it did with two.[12] The only difference is that with many assets to be considered some will fall in the interior of the opportunity set (Fig. 5.14). The opportunity set will be composed of various portfolios and of some individual assets that are mean-variance efficient by themselves. As long as there is no riskless asset, a risk-averse investor would maximize his or her expected utility in the same way as before—by finding the point of tangency between the efficient set and the highest indifference curve. But in order to do so, he or she would have to estimate all the means, variances, and covariances mentioned earlier.

---

[11] In general, if N securities are analyzed, the variance-covariance matrix will have $\frac{1}{2}(N-1)N$ *different* covariance elements and N variance elements.

[12] For proof, see Merton [1972].

Figure 5.14 The investment opportunity set with many risky assets.

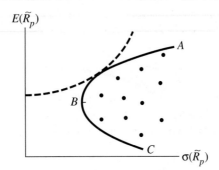

Figure 5.15 The efficient set with one risk-free and many risky assets.

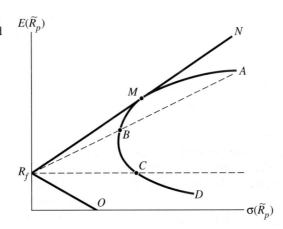

4. The Efficient Set with *N* Risky Assets and One Risk-Free Asset

Once the risk-free asset is introduced into the analysis, the problem of portfolio selection is simplified. If, as before, we assume that the borrowing rate equals the lending rate, we can draw a straight line between any risky asset and risk-free asset. Points along the line represent portfolios consisting of combinations of the risk-free and risky assets. Several possibilities are graphed in Fig. 5.15. Portfolios along any of the lines are possible, but only one line dominates. All investors will prefer combinations of the risk-free asset and portfolio *M* on the efficient set. (Why?) These combinations lie along the positively sloped portion of line NMR_fO. Therefore the efficient set (which is represented by line segment R_fMN) is linear in the presence of a risk-free asset. All an investor needs to know is the combination of assets that makes up portfolio *M* in Fig. 5.15 as well as the risk-free asset. This is true for any investor, regardless of his or her degree of risk aversion. Figure 5.16 clarifies this point. Investor III is the most risk averse of the three pictured in Fig. 5.16 and will choose to invest nearly all of his or her portfolio in the risk-free asset. Investor I, who is the least risk averse, will borrow (at the risk-free rate) to invest more than 100% of his or her portfolio in the risky portfolio *M*. However, no investor will choose to invest in any other risky portfolio except portfolio *M*. For example, all three could attain the minimum variance portfolio at point *B*, but none will choose this alternative because all do better with some combination of the risk-free asset and portfolio *M*. Next, we shall see that portfolio *M* can be identified as the market portfolio of all risky assets. All risky assets are held as part of risky portfolio *M*.

Figure 5.16 Dominance of the linear efficient set.

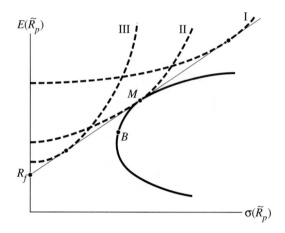

5. A Description of Equilibrium

In Section C we analyzed a Robinson Crusoe economy where there was no opportunity for exchange. Robinson Crusoe's optimal portfolio resulted from maximizing his expected utility, given his risk preferences, subject to the feasible set of mean-variance trade-offs offered by a combination of two risky assets. In Section D we saw how a linear efficient set could be formed from one risky and one risk-free asset. So far in Section E, we have first described the opportunity set with risky assets, then with one risk-free asset and many risky assets.

The introduction of a risk-free asset may be thought of as creating an exchange or market economy where there are many individuals. Each of them may borrow or lend unlimited amounts at the risk-free rate. With the introduction of an exchange economy, we shall be able to describe a fundamental principle called *two-fund separation*. Analogous to Fisher separation found in Chapter 1 (where everyone used the market-determined time value of money to determine consumption/investment decisions), two-fund separation implies that there is a single market-determined equilibrium price of risk (which is used in portfolio decisions). This concept will prove extremely useful later on in the text when, for example, we want to conceptualize the opportunity cost of capital for projects of different risk.

If—in addition to the earlier assumption of equality between the borrowing and lending rate that follows, given frictionless capital markets—we add the assumption that all investors have homogeneous (i.e., identical) beliefs about the expected distributions of returns offered by all assets, then all investors will perceive the same efficient set. Therefore they will all try to hold some combination of the risk-free asset, R_f, and portfolio M.

For the market to be in equilibrium, we require a set of market-clearing prices. All assets must be held. In other words the existence of an equilibrium requires that all prices be adjusted so that the excess demand for any asset will be zero. This market-clearing condition implies that an equilibrium is not attained until the single-tangency portfolio, M, which all investors (with homogeneous expectations) try to combine with risk-free borrowing or lending, is a portfolio in which all assets are held according to their market value weights. If V_i is the market value of the ith asset, then the percentage of wealth in each asset is equal to the ratio of the market value of the

Figure 5.17 The Capital Market Line.

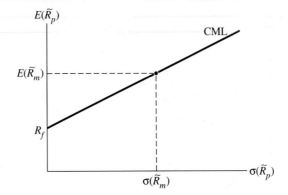

asset to the market value of all assets. Mathematically,

$$w_i = \frac{V_i}{\sum\limits_{i=1}^{N} V_i},$$

where w_i is the weight of the ith asset in the market portfolio and $\sum V_i$ is the total market value of all assets. Market equilibrium is not reached until the tangency portfolio, M, is the market portfolio. Also, the value of the risk-free rate must be such that aggregate borrowing and lending are equal.

The fact that the portfolios of all risk-averse investors will consist of different combinations of only two portfolios is an extremely powerful result. It has come to be known as the two-fund separation principle. Its definition is given below:

TWO-FUND SEPARATION Each investor will have a utility-maximizing portfolio that is a combination of the risk-free asset and a portfolio (or fund) of risky assets that is determined by the line drawn from the risk-free rate of return tangent to the investor's efficient set of risky assets.

The straight line in Fig. 5.16 will be the efficient set for all investors. This line has come to be known as the Capital Market Line. It represents a linear relationship between portfolio risk and return.

CAPITAL MARKET LINE (CML) If investors have homogeneous beliefs, then they all have the same linear efficient set called the Capital Market Line.

Figure 5.17 is a graph of the Capital Market Line. The intercept is the risk-free rate, R_f, and its slope is $[E(R_m) - R_f]/\sigma(R_m)$. Therefore the equation for the Capital Market Line is

$$E(R_p) = R_f + \frac{E(R_m) - R_f}{\sigma(R_m)}\sigma(R_p). \tag{5.34}$$

It provides a simple linear relationship between the risk and return for *efficient portfolios* of assets. Having established the principle of two-fund separation and defined the Capital Market Line, we find it useful to describe the importance of capital market equilibrium from an individual's point of view.

Figure 5.18 Individual expected utility maximization in a world with capital markets.

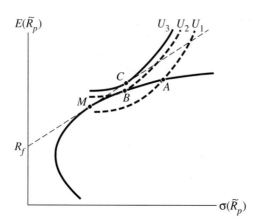

We wish to compare expected utility-maximizing choices in a world without capital markets (as depicted in Fig. 5.9) with those in a world with capital markets (seen in Fig. 5.18). As in Chapter 1, a capital market is nothing more than the opportunity to borrow and lend at the risk-free rate. Chapter 1 emphasized that in a world with certainty everyone was better off, given that capital markets existed and Fisher separation obtained. Now we have extended this result to a world with mean-variance uncertainty. Everyone is better off with capital markets where two-fund separation obtains.

Figure 5.18 shows us endowed with the mean-variance combination at point A. With a capital market, we always have two choices available. We can move along the mean-variance opportunity set (by changing our portfolio of risky assets), or we can move along the Capital Market Line by borrowing or lending. Initially, at point A, the trade-off between return and risk is more favorable along the opportunity set than along the market line. Therefore we will move along the opportunity set toward point B, where the marginal rate of transformation between return and risk on the opportunity set is equal to our subjective marginal rate of substitution along our indifference curve. In the absence of capital markets, we would have maximized our expected utility at point B. This would be the Robinson Crusoe solution, and our level of utility would have increased from U_1 to U_2. However, if we have the opportunity to move along the Capital Market Line, we can be even better off. By moving to point M, then borrowing to reach point C, we can increase our expected utility from U_2 to U_3. Therefore we have three important results. First, nearly everyone is better off in a world with capital markets (and no one is worse off). Second, two-fund separation obtains. This means that everyone, regardless of the shape of his or her indifference curve, will decide to hold various combinations of two funds: the market portfolio and the risk-free asset. And third, in equilibrium, the marginal rate of substitution (MRS) between return and risk is the same for all individuals, regardless of their subjective attitudes toward risk.

If the marginal rate of substitution between risk and return is the same for every individual in equilibrium, then the slope of the Capital Market Line is the market price of risk (MPR):

$$\text{MPR} = \text{MRS}_{\sigma(R_p)}^{E(R_p)} = \frac{E(R_m) - R_f}{\sigma(R_m)}. \tag{5.35}$$

The implication is that decision makers (e.g., managers of firms) can use the market-determined equilibrium price of risk to evaluate investment projects regardless of the tastes of shareholders.

Every shareholder will unanimously agree on the price of risk even though different shareholders have different degrees of risk aversion. Also the marginal rates of substitution between risk and return for the ith and jth individuals in equilibrium will equal the marginal rate of transformation, and both will be equal to the market price of risk:

$$\text{MRS}_i = \text{MRS}_j = \frac{E(R_m) - R_f}{\sigma(R_m)} = \text{MRT}.$$

Next, and in Chapter 6, we turn our attention to the problem of measuring risk. We have already established that variance is an adequate measure of risk for portfolios of assets; however, it is not particularly useful when we wish to evaluate the risk of individual assets that do not lie on the efficient set. Nor is it possible, given our current development of the theory, to compare a single risky asset with a well-diversified portfolio. Therefore it is necessary to distinguish between portfolio risk and the contribution of a single asset to the riskiness of a well-diversified portfolio (such as the market portfolio).

To set the framework for the difference between portfolio risk and individual asset risk, we observe the average return and variance of return calculated for a single asset, Bayside Smoke, and for a 100-stock portfolio of randomly selected common stocks. Return on the assets was defined as total return, that is, dividends, Div_t, plus capital gains, $P_t - P_{t-1}$. The equation for a monthly return is

$$R_t = \frac{P_t - P_{t-1} + Div_t}{P_{t-1}}.$$

Data were collected for the 306 months between January 1975 and June 2000.[13] The average monthly return on Bayside Smoke was .45%, which is approximately 5.4% per year, and the standard deviation was 7.26%. By comparison, the 100-stock portfolio had an average return of .91% per month or 10.9% per year. Its standard deviation was 4.45%. Normally, one would expect the standard deviation of a well-diversified portfolio to be lower than for a single asset, and the empirical results bear this out. But we also know that riskier assets should have higher returns. Therefore if standard deviation is the appropriate measure of risk for an individual asset, then Bayside Smoke should have a higher return. But it does not! We shall see in the next chapter that the resolution to this apparent paradox is that although the standard deviation is appropriate for measuring the risk of an efficient portfolio, it is not the appropriate measure of risk for individual assets or for comparing the riskiness of portfolios with the riskiness of assets.

F. Portfolio Diversification and Individual Asset Risk

We begin by taking a look at what happens to portfolio variance as we increase the number of assets in a portfolio. Equation (5.28),

$$\text{VAR}(R_p) = \sum_{i=1}^{N} \sum_{j=1}^{N} w_i w_j \sigma_{ij},$$

---

[13] See Modigliani and Pogue [1974].

provided an expression for the variance of a portfolio of three assets. Here we generalize it to N assets.

We shall see that as the number of assets in the portfolio increases, the portfolio variance decreases and approaches the average covariance. There are several ways to prove this. The easiest is simply to note that a two-asset portfolio has 2 variance and 2 covariance terms. A three-asset portfolio has 3 variance and 6 covariance terms. In general the number of variance terms equals the number of assets in the portfolio, N, whereas the number of covariance terms equals $(N^2 - N)$, or $N(N-1)$. Suppose that we have an equally weighted portfolio so that $w_i = w_j = 1/N$. Then the portfolio variance can be written from Eq. (5.28) as

$$\text{VAR}(R_p) = \sum_{i=1}^{N} \sum_{j=1}^{N} \frac{1}{N} \frac{1}{N} \sigma_{ij} = \frac{1}{N^2} \sum_{i=1}^{N} \sum_{j=1}^{N} \sigma_{ij}.$$

This expression can be separated into variance and covariance terms as follows:

$$\text{VAR}(R_p) = \frac{1}{N^2} \sum_{i=1}^{N} \sigma_{ii} + \frac{1}{N^2} \sum_{i=1}^{N} \sum_{\substack{j=1 \\ i \neq j}}^{N} \sigma_{ij} \tag{5.36}$$

Suppose that the largest individual asset variance is L. Then the first term, the variance term, is always less than or equal to

$$\frac{1}{N^2} \sum_{i=1}^{N} L = \frac{LN}{N^2} = \frac{L}{N},$$

and as the number of assets in the portfolio becomes large, this term approaches zero:

$$\lim_{N \to \infty} \frac{L}{N} = 0.$$

On the other hand, the covariance terms do not vanish. Let $\overline{\sigma}_{ij}$ be the average covariance. Then in the right-hand term in Eq. (5.36), there are $(N^2 - N)$ covariance terms, all equal to $\overline{\sigma}_{ij}$; therefore the right-hand term can be rewritten as

$$\frac{1}{N^2}(N^2 - N)\overline{\sigma}_{ij} = \frac{N^2}{N^2}\overline{\sigma}_{ij} - \frac{N}{N^2}\overline{\sigma}_{ij},$$

and the limit as N approaches infinity is

$$\lim_{N \to \infty} \left(\frac{N^2}{N^2}\overline{\sigma}_{ij} - \frac{N}{N^2}\overline{\sigma}_{ij} \right) = \overline{\sigma}_{ij} \tag{5.37}$$

Consequently, as we form portfolios that have large numbers of assets that are better diversified, the covariance terms become relatively more important.

Fama [1976] has illustrated this result empirically.[14] His results are shown in Fig. 5.19. He randomly selected 50 New York Stock Exchange (NYSE) listed securities and calculated their

---

[14] See Fama [1976, 253–254].

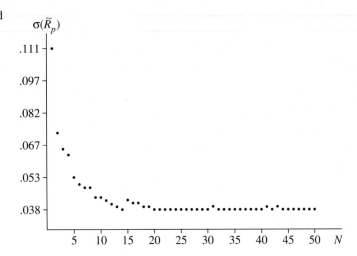

Figure 5.19 The standard deviation of portfolio return as a function of the number of securities in the portfolio. (From Fama, E.F., *Foundations of Finance,* 1976. Reprinted with permission of the author.)

standard deviations using monthly data from July 1963 to June 1968. Then a single security was selected randomly. Its standard deviation of return was around 11%. Next, this security was combined with another (also randomly selected) to form an equally weighted portfolio of two securities. The standard deviation fell to around 7.2%. Step by step more securities were randomly added to the portfolio until 50 securities were included. Almost all the diversification was obtained after the first 10–15 securities were randomly selected. In addition the portfolio standard deviation quickly approached a limit that is roughly equal to the average covariance of all securities. One of the practical implications is that most of the benefits of diversification (given a random portfolio selection strategy) can be achieved with fewer than 15 stocks.

Using monthly data between 1963 and 2002, we have computed the geometric mean and standard deviation of returns for value-weighted portfolios of broad classes of assets, for example, common stocks (the Standard and Poor's 500), small stocks (the smallest quintile on the New York Stock Exchange, Amex, and Nasdaq), and bonds. Table 5.6 summarizes the results. Note that the arithmetic standard deviation of the portfolio of common stocks was 16.6% per year, whereas the standard deviation of small stocks (not a randomly selected portfolio) was about 60% larger at a level of 46.8% per year. These data show the limits of diversification for different classes of securities.

Still another way of looking at the risk of a single asset is to evaluate its contribution to total portfolio risk. This can be done by taking the partial derivative of the expression for portfolio variance, Eq. (5.28), with respect to w_i, the percentage invested in the ith risky asset:

$$\frac{\partial \text{VAR}(R_p)}{\partial w_i} = 2w_i\sigma_i^2 + 2\sum_{j=1}^{N} w_j\sigma_{ij}. \tag{5.38}$$

Again, consider a portfolio where an equal percentage is invested in each asset, $w_i = 1/N$. As the number of assets in the portfolio increases, w_i approaches zero and $\sum w_j$ approaches one. Therefore for well-diversified portfolios the appropriate measure of the contribution of an asset to portfolio risk is its covariance with the other assets in the portfolio. In the marketplace for assets (e.g., the stock market) the number of risky assets is extremely large. We shall see (in Chapter 6) that the contribution of a single asset to market risk is its covariance with the market portfolio.

Table 5.6 Annualized Returns Data 1963–2002

Portfolio	Arithmetic Mean (%)	Arithmetic Standard Deviation (%)	Geometric Mean (%)	Geometric Standard Deviation (%)
Smallest NYSE decile stocks	25.2	41.8	19.6	42.6
S & P 500	11.9	16.6	10.5	16.9
High-grade long-term corporate bonds	8.5	3.2	8.4	3.2
Long-term U.S. government bonds	7.1	3.1	7.0	3.1
U.S. Treasury bills	6.3	2.5	6.3	2.5
Consumer Price Index	4.6	3.1	4.6	N/A

Source: Monitor Group analysis.

Figure 5.20 The Capital Market Line.

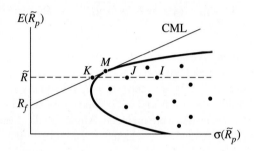

Hence this is the measure of risk appropriate for a single asset even though individual investors may not, in reality, hold well-diversified portfolios. Relationships (5.37) and (5.38) help provide an intuitive appeal for covariance as the appropriate measure of risk for individual assets, but they are not proofs. For proof, we need to consider market equilibrium. In the next chapter we shall show that the covariance risk of an asset is the only portion of an asset's risk that an investor will pay to avoid. This important idea is embodied in what has come to be known as the *Capital Asset Pricing Model*. It is an equilibrium theory of risk and return, which is the main topic of Chapter 6.

But why can variance not be used as a measure of risk? After all, we know that expected utility-maximizing investors choose their optimal portfolios on the basis of mean and variance. The answer lies in Fig. 5.20. Asset I is inefficient because it does not lie on the Capital Market Line. Consequently, even though we know the mean and variance of asset I, we cannot be sure what rate of return the market will require to hold the asset because it is not on the efficient frontier. Investors have available to them other opportunities that have the same expected return but lower variance. Therefore we cannot use our knowledge of the mean and variance of asset I to determine the rate of return that the market will require from asset I in order to hold it in equilibrium. In Chapter 6, given a market equilibrium setting, we shall see that only the portion of total variance that is correlated with the economy is relevant. Any portion of total risk that is not correlated with the economy is irrelevant and can be avoided at zero cost through diversification. Assets I, J, and K have the same expected return, $\overline{R}$, yet they all have different variances. If variance is the correct measure of the riskiness of an individual asset, then the implication is that these three assets, each with different "risk," all have the same expected return. This is nonsense. It would violate what has come to be known as the single-price law of securities:

THE SINGLE-PRICE LAW OF SECURITIES   All securities or combinations of securities that have the same joint distributions of return will have the same price in equilibrium.

Since the three securities clearly have different distributions of return, they also have different prices. Even though we know the mean and variance of return offered by assets I, J, and K, we cannot be sure what prices they will have in equilibrium. The reason is that we do not know their joint distribution with all other assets. The missing information is the variance-covariance matrix of all assets. In Chapter 6 we shall see that variance is not the appropriate measure of risk for an individual asset. This was the point of Eqs. (5.37) and (5.38). As the number of assets in a portfolio increases, the risk that an asset contributes to a portfolio reduces to be exclusively the covariance risk. Therefore the portion of an asset's risk that is uncorrelated with the economy can be avoided at no cost. No rational investor will pay a premium to avoid diversifiable risk. On the other hand, because covariance risk cannot be diversified away, investors will pay a premium to escape it. Therefore covariance is the relevant measure of risk for an asset because it measures the contribution of an individual asset to the variance of a well-diversified portfolio.

*S*ummary

This chapter has combined our knowledge of the theory of investor choice (utility theory) with the objects of investor choice (the portfolio opportunity set) to show how risk-averse investors wishing to maximize expected utility will choose their optimal portfolios. We began with simple measures of risk and return (and simple probability theory) and ended with portfolio theory. Finally, we saw that when a risk-free asset exists, the opportunity set can be reduced to the simple, linear Capital Market Line. Given frictionless capital markets and homogeneous investor expectations, all individuals will choose to hold some combination of the risk-free asset and the market portfolio.

PROBLEM SET

5.1 Historically, the empirical distributions of stock prices on the NYSE have been skewed right. Why?

5.2 Given the following relationship between x and y,

$$y = a + bx \quad b < 0,$$

prove that x and y are perfectly negatively correlated.

5.3 Given the following hypothetical end-of-period prices for shares of the Drill-On Corporation,

Probability	.15	.10	.30	.20	.25
End-of-period price per share	35.00	42.00	50.00	55.00	60.00

and assuming a current price of $50 per share:

(a) Calculate the rate of return for each probability. What is the expected return? The variance of end-of-period returns? The range? The semi-interquartile range?

(b) Suppose forecasting is refined such that probabilities of end-of-period prices can be broken down further, resulting in the following distribution:

Probability		.01	.05	.07	.02	.10	.30	.20	.15	.05	.05
End-of-period price per share	0	35.00	38.57	40.00	42.00	50.00	55.00	57.00	60.00	69.00

Calculate and explain the change in the expected return, the range of returns, and the semi-interquartile range of returns. Calculate the semivariance of end-of-period returns. Why might some investors be concerned with semivariance as a measure of risk?

5.4 Derive an expression for the expectation of the product of two random variables:

$$E(\tilde{x}\tilde{y}) = ?$$

5.5 Using the definition of portfolio variance, prove that a perfectly hedged stock portfolio that is 100 shares long and 100 shares short is perfectly risk free.

5.6 Given Professor Singer's variance-covariance matrix:

$$\begin{bmatrix} 24 & -10 & 9 \\ -10 & 75 & 3 \\ 9 & 3 & 12 \end{bmatrix}$$

(a) Calculate the variance of an equally weighted portfolio.
(b) Calculate the covariance of a portfolio that has 10% in asset 1, 80% in asset 2, and 10% in asset 3 with a second portfolio that has 125% in asset 1, -10% in asset 2, and -15% in asset 3.

5.7 Given two random variables x and y:

Probability of State of Nature	State of Nature	Variable x	Variable y
.2	I	18	0
.2	II	5	-3
.2	III	12	15
.2	IV	4	12
.2	V	6	1

(a) Calculate the mean and variance of each of these variables, and the covariance between them.
(b) Suppose x and y represent the returns from two assets. Calculate the mean and variance for the following portfolios:

% in x	125	100	75	50	25	0	-25
% in y	-25	0	25	50	75	100	125

(c) Find the portfolio that has the minimum variance.
(d) Let portfolio A have 75% in x and portfolio B have 25% in x. Calculate the covariance between the two portfolios.
(e) Calculate the covariance between the minimum variance portfolio and portfolio A, and the covariance between the minimum variance portfolio and portfolio B.

(f) What is the covariance between the minimum variance portfolio and any other portfolio along the efficient set?

(g) What is the relationship between the covariance of the minimum variance portfolio with other efficient portfolios, and the variance of the minimum variance portfolio?

5.8 Prove that for any securities $\widetilde{X}$ and $\widetilde{Y}$:

(a) $E(a\widetilde{X} + b\widetilde{Y}) = aE(\widetilde{X}) + bE(\widetilde{Y})$.

(b) $\mathrm{VAR}(a\widetilde{X} + b\widetilde{Y}) = a^2\mathrm{VAR}(\widetilde{X}) + b^2\mathrm{VAR}(\widetilde{Y}) + 2ab\mathrm{COV}(\widetilde{X}, \widetilde{Y})$.

(c) $\mathrm{COV}\big[(a\widetilde{X} + b\widetilde{Z}), \widetilde{Y}\big] = a\mathrm{COV}(\widetilde{X}, \widetilde{Y}) + b\mathrm{COV}(\widetilde{Z}, \widetilde{Y})$.

(d) $E(\widetilde{X}^2) = (E(\widetilde{X}))^2 + \mathrm{VAR}(\widetilde{X})$.

(e) If $r_{xy} = 1$, then $\sigma(X + Y) = \sigma_x + \sigma_y$. If $r_{xy} = -1$, then $\sigma(\widetilde{X} + \widetilde{Y}) = \sigma_x - \sigma_y$.

5.9 Let R_1 and R_2 be the returns for two securities with $E(R_1) = .03$ and $E(R_2) = .08$, $\mathrm{VAR}(R_1) = .02$, $\mathrm{VAR}(R_2) = .05$, and $\mathrm{COV}(R_1, R_2) = -.01$.

(a) Plot the set of feasible mean-variance combinations of return, assuming that the two securities above are the only investment vehicles available.

(b) If we want to minimize risk, how much of our portfolio will we invest in security 1?

(c) Find the mean and standard deviation of a portfolio that is 50% in security 1.

5.10 (Our thanks to Nils Hakannson, University of California, Berkeley, for providing this problem.) Two securities have the following joint distribution of returns, r_1 and r_2:

$$P\{r_1 = -1.0 \text{ and } r_2 = .15\} = .1,$$
$$P\{r_1 = .5 \text{ and } r_2 = .15\} = .8,$$
$$P\{r_1 = .5 \text{ and } r_2 = 1.65\} = .1.$$

(a) Compute the means, variances, and covariance of returns for the two securities.

(b) Plot the feasible mean–standard deviation $[E(R), \sigma]$ combinations, assuming that the two securities are the only investment vehicles available.

(c) Which portfolios belong to the mean-variance efficient set?

(d) Show that security 2 is mean-variance dominated by security 1, yet enters all efficient portfolios but one. How do you explain this?

(e) Suppose the possibility of lending, but not borrowing, at 5% (without risk) is added to the previous opportunities. Draw the new set of $[E(R), \sigma]$ combinations. Which portfolios are now efficient?

5.11 Suppose a risk-averse investor can choose a portfolio from among N assets with independently distributed returns, all of which have identical means $[E(R_i) = E(R_j)]$ and identical variances $(\sigma_i^2 = \sigma_j^2)$. What will be the composition of his optimal portfolio?

5.12 Given decreasing marginal utility, it is possible to prove that in a mean-variance framework no individual will hold 100% of his or her wealth in the risk-free asset. Why? (*Hint*: The answer requires an understanding of the shape of investors' indifference curves as well as the Capital Market Line.)

5.13 Given that assets X and Y are perfectly correlated such that $Y = 6 + .2X$ and the probability distribution for X is

Probability	X (%)
.1	30
.2	20
.4	15
.2	10
.1	−50

What is the percentage of your wealth to put into asset X to achieve zero variance? Graph the opportunity set and the zero variance point.

5.14 A market value balance sheet for the Carr Commercial Bank is given below in millions of dollars:

Assets		**Liabilities**	
Short-term	100	Short-term	50
U.S. government bonds	200	Deposits	850
Loans	700	Equity	100
	1,000		1,000

The standard deviations and correlations between returns on asset and liability categories (excepting equity) are as follows:

$$\sigma(STA) = .02, \quad r_{STA,US} = 0, \quad r_{STA,L} = 0, \quad r_{STA,STL} = 0,$$
$$r_{STA,D} = 0,$$
$$\sigma(US) = .04, \quad r_{US,L} = .8, \quad r_{US,STL} = 0, \quad r_{US,D} = .3,$$
$$\sigma(L) = .07, \quad r_{L,STL} = 0, \quad r_{L,D} \ .2,$$
$$\sigma(STL) = .02, \quad r_{STL,D} = 0,$$
$$\sigma(D) = .03.$$

(a) What is the standard deviation of the equity holder's position?

(b) Suppose the bank decides to hedge by taking a position in T-bond futures contracts. You are given the following information:

$$V_{TB} = \$90,000 \text{ for a } \$100,000 \text{ face value T-bond contract,}$$
$$\sigma_{TB} = .08, \quad r_{TB,STA} = 0, \quad r_{TB,L} = .5, \quad r_{TB,STL} = 0, \quad r_{TB,D} = .3.$$

Should the bank take a long or short position in T-bond futures? How many futures contracts should they buy/sell? How much is the standard deviation of equity reduced?

REFERENCES

Crámer, H., *Mathematical Methods in Statistics*. Princeton University Press, Princeton, N.J., 1961.

Fama, E. F., *Foundations of Finance*. Basic Books, New York, 1976.

Fama, E. F., and M. Miller, *The Theory of Finance*. Holt, Rinehart, and Winston, New York, 1972.

Ibbotson, R. G., and R. Sinquefield, *Stocks, Bonds, Bills and Inflation: 2002 Yearbook*. Ibbotson Associates, Inc., Chicago, 2002.

Markowitz, H. M., *Portfolio Selection: Efficient Diversification of Investment* (Cowles Foundation Monograph 16). Yale University Press, New Haven, Conn., 1959.

Merton, R., "An Analytic Derivation of the Efficient Set," *Journal of Financial and Quantitative Analysis*, September 1972, 1851–1872.

Modigliani, F., and G. Pogue, "An Introduction to Risk and Return: Concepts and Evidence," *Financial Analysts Journal*, March–April and May–June, 1974, 68–80, 69–85.

Sharpe, W., "A Simplified Model for Portfolio Analysis," *Management Science*, January 1963, 277–293.

———, *Portfolio Theory and Capital Markets*. McGraw-Hill, New York, 1970.

Tobin, J., "Liquidity Preference as Behavior towards Risk," *Review of Economic Studies*, February 1958, 65–86.

Chapter 6

Lucy: "I've just come up with the perfect theory. It's my theory that Beethoven would have written even better music if he had been married."

Schroeder: "What's so perfect about that theory?"

Lucy: "It can't be proved one way or the other!"

—Charles Schulz, *Peanuts*, 1976.

Market Equilibrium: CAPM and APT

A. Introduction

THIS CHAPTER EXTENDS THE CONCEPT of market equilibrium to determine the market price for risk and the appropriate measure of risk for a single asset. One economic model to solve this problem, called the *capital asset pricing model* (CAPM), was developed almost simultaneously by Sharpe [1963, 1964] and Treynor [1961], and then further developed by Mossin [1966], Lintner [1965, 1969], and Black [1972]. It shows that the equilibrium rates of return on all risky assets are a function of their covariance with the market portfolio. A second important equilibrium pricing model, called the *arbitrage pricing theory* (APT), was developed by Ross [1976]. It is similar to the CAPM in that it is also an equilibrium asset pricing model. The return on any risky asset is seen to be a linear combination of various common factors that affect asset returns. It is more general than the CAPM because it allows numerous factors to explain the equilibrium return on a risky asset. However, it is in the same spirit as the CAPM. In fact, the CAPM can be shown to be a special case of the APT.

This chapter first develops the CAPM and its extensions, and then summarizes the empirical evidence relating to its validity. Thereafter, the APT will be developed and the empirical evidence for it will be described. We begin with a list of the assumptions that were first used to derive the CAPM.

The CAPM is developed in a hypothetical world where the following assumptions are made about investors and the opportunity set:

1. Investors are risk-averse individuals who maximize the expected utility of their wealth.

2. Investors are price takers and have homogeneous expectations about asset returns that have a joint normal distribution.

147

3. There exists a risk-free asset such that investors may borrow or lend unlimited amounts at a risk-free rate.

4. The quantities of assets are fixed. Also, all assets are marketable and perfectly divisible.

5. Asset markets are frictionless, and information is costless and simultaneously available to all investors.

6. There are no market imperfections such as taxes, regulations, or restrictions on short selling.

Many of these assumptions have been discussed earlier. However, it is worthwhile to discuss some of their implications. For example, if markets are frictionless, the borrowing rate equals the lending rate, and we are able to develop a linear efficient set called the capital market line (Fig. 5.17 and Eq. 5.34). If all assets are divisible and marketable, we exclude the possibility of human capital as we usually think of it. In other words, slavery is allowed in the model. We are all able to sell (not rent for wages) various portions of our human capital (e.g., typing ability or reading ability) to other investors at market prices. Another important assumption is that investors have homogeneous beliefs. They all make decisions based on an identical opportunity set. In other words, no one can be fooled because everyone has the same information at the same time. Also, since all investors maximize the expected utility of their end-of-period wealth, the model is implicitly a one-period model.

Although not all these assumptions conform to reality, they are simplifications that permit the development of the CAPM, which is extremely useful for financial decision making because it quantifies and prices risk. Most of the restrictive assumptions will be relaxed later on.

B. *The* Efficiency of the Market Portfolio

Proof of the CAPM requires that in equilibrium the market portfolio must be an efficient portfolio. It must lie on the upper half of the minimum variance opportunity set graphed in Fig. 6.1. One way to establish its efficiency is to argue that because investors have homogeneous expectations, they will all perceive the same minimum variance opportunity set.[1] Even without a risk-free asset, they will all select efficient portfolios regardless of their individual risk tolerances. As shown in Fig. 6.1, individual I chooses efficient portfolio B, whereas individual II, who is less risk averse, chooses efficient portfolio C. Given that all individuals hold positive proportions of their wealth in efficient portfolios, then the market portfolio must be efficient because (1) the market is simply the sum of all individual holdings and (2) all individual holdings are efficient.

Thus, in theory, when all individuals have homogeneous expectations, the market portfolio must be efficient. Without homogeneous expectations, the market portfolio is not necessarily efficient, and the equilibrium model of capital markets that is derived in the next section does not necessarily hold. Thus the efficiency of the market portfolio and the capital asset pricing model are inseparable, joint hypotheses. It is not possible to test the validity of one without the other. We shall return to this important point when we discuss Roll's critique later in the chapter.

---

[1] For a more rigorous proof of the efficiency of the market portfolio, see Fama [1976, Chapter 8].

Figure 6.1 All investors select efficient portfolios.

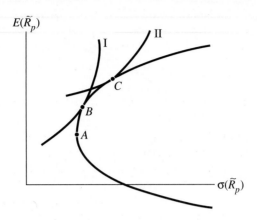

C. $\mathcal{D}$erivation of the CAPM

Figure 6.2 shows the expected return and standard deviation of the market portfolio, M, the risk-free asset, R_f, and a risky asset, I. The straight line connecting the risk-free asset and the market portfolio is the *capital market line* (for example, see Fig. 5.17, in Chapter 5). We know that if a market equilibrium is to exist, the prices of all assets must adjust until all are held by investors. There can be no excess demand. In other words, prices must be established so that the supply of all assets equals the demand for holding them. Consequently, in equilibrium the market portfolio will consist of all marketable assets held in proportion to their value weights. The equilibrium proportion of each asset in the market portfolio must be

$$w_i = \frac{\text{market value of the individual asset}}{\text{market value of all assets}}. \tag{6.1}$$

A portfolio consisting of $a\%$ invested in risky asset I and $(1-a)\%$ in the market portfolio will have the following mean and standard deviation:

$$E(\widetilde{R}_p) = aE(\widetilde{R}_i) + (1-a)E(\widetilde{R}_m), \tag{6.2}$$

$$\sigma(\widetilde{R}_p) = \left[a^2\sigma_i^2 + (1-a)^2\sigma_m^2 + 2a(1-a)\sigma_{im}\right]^{1/2}, \tag{6.3}$$

where

$\sigma_i^2 = $ the variance of risky asset I,

$\sigma_m^2 = $ the variance of the market portfolio,

$\sigma_{im} = $ the covariance between asset I and the market portfolio.

We shall see shortly that the market portfolio already contains asset I held according to its market value weight. In fact the definition of the market portfolio is that it consists of all assets held according to their market value weights. The opportunity set provided by various combinations of the risky asset and the market portfolio is the line IMI' in Fig. 6.2. The change in the mean

Figure 6.2 The opportunity set provided by combinations of risky asset I and the market portfolio, M.

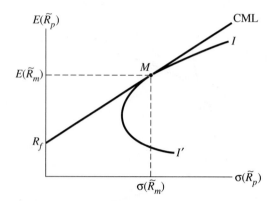

and standard deviation with respect to the percentage of the portfolio, a, invested in asset I is determined as follows:

$$\frac{\partial E(\tilde{R}_p)}{\partial a} = E(\tilde{R}_i) - E(\tilde{R}_m), \tag{6.4}$$

$$\frac{\partial \sigma(\tilde{R}_p)}{\partial a} = \frac{1}{2}\left[a^2\sigma_i^2 + (1-a)^2\sigma_m^2 + 2a(1-a)\sigma_{im}\right]^{-1/2}$$
$$\times \left[2a\sigma_i^2 - 2\sigma_m^2 + 2a\sigma_m^2 + 2\sigma_{im} - 4a\sigma_{im}\right]. \tag{6.5}$$

Sharpe's and Treynor's insight, which allowed them to use the above facts to determine a market equilibrium price for risk, was that in equilibrium the market portfolio already has the value weight, w_i percent, invested in the risky asset I. Therefore the percentage a in the above equations is the excess demand for an individual risky asset. But we know that in equilibrium the excess demand for any asset must be zero. Prices will adjust until all assets are held by someone. Therefore if Eqs. (6.4) and (6.5) are evaluated where excess demand, a, equals zero, then we can determine the equilibrium price relationships at point M in Fig. 6.2. This will provide the equilibrium price of risk. Evaluating Eqs. (6.4) and (6.5) where $a = 0$, we obtain

$$\left.\frac{\partial E(\tilde{R}_p)}{\partial a}\right|_{a=0} = E(\tilde{R}_i) - E(\tilde{R}_m), \tag{6.6}$$

$$\left.\frac{\partial \sigma(\tilde{R}_p)}{\partial a}\right|_{a=0} = \frac{1}{2}(\sigma_m^2)^{-1/2}(-2\sigma_m^2 + 2\sigma_{im}) = \frac{\sigma_{im} - \sigma_m^2}{\sigma_m}. \tag{6.7}$$

The slope of the risk-return trade-off evaluated at point M, in market equilibrium, is

$$\left.\frac{\partial E(\tilde{R}_p)/\partial a}{\partial \sigma(\tilde{R}_p)/\partial a}\right|_{a=0} = \frac{E(\tilde{R}_i) - E(\tilde{R}_m)}{(\sigma_{im} - \sigma_m^2)/\sigma_m}. \tag{6.8}$$

The final insight is to realize that the slope of the opportunity set IMI' provided by the relationship between the risky asset and the market portfolio at point M must also be equal to the slope of the capital market line, $R_f M$.

Figure 6.3 The capital asset pricing model.

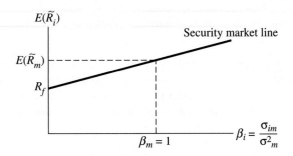

As established in Chapter 5, the capital market line is also an equilibrium relationship. Given market efficiency, the tangency portfolio, M, must be the market portfolio where all assets are held according to their market value weights. Recall that the slope of the market line in Eq. (5.34) is

$$\frac{E(\widetilde{R}_m) - R_f}{\sigma_m},$$

where σ_m is the standard deviation of the market portfolio. Equating this with the slope of the opportunity set at point M, we have

$$\frac{E(\widetilde{R}_m) - R_f}{\sigma_m} = \frac{E(\widetilde{R}_i) - E(\widetilde{R}_m)}{(\sigma_{im} - \sigma_m^2)/\sigma_m}.$$

This relationship can be arranged to solve for $E(\widetilde{R}_i)$ as follows:

$$E(\widetilde{R}_i) = R_f + \left[E(\widetilde{R}_m) - R_f \right] \frac{\sigma_{im}}{\sigma_m^2}. \tag{6.9}$$

Equation (6.9) is known as the *capital asset pricing model*, CAPM. It is shown graphically in Fig. 6.3, where it is also called the *security market line*. The required rate of return on any asset, $E(\widetilde{R}_i)$ in Eq. (6.9), is equal to the risk-free rate of return plus a risk premium. The risk premium is the price of risk multiplied by the quantity of risk. In the terminology of the CAPM, the price of risk is the slope of the line, the difference between the expected rate of return on the market portfolio and the risk-free rate of return.[2] The quantity of risk is often called beta, β_i:

---

[2] Note that the CAPM terminology is somewhat different from that used in Chapter 5. Earlier, the equilibrium price of risk was seen to be the marginal rate of substitution between return and risk and was described as

$$\frac{E(\widetilde{R}_m) - R_f}{\sigma_m}.$$

Using this definition for the price of risk, the quantity of risk is

$$\frac{\text{COV}(\widetilde{R}_i, \widetilde{R}_m)}{\sigma_m}.$$

Because σ_m, the standard deviation of the market, is assumed to be constant, it does not make much difference which terminology we adopt. Hereafter, risk will be β, and the market price of risk will be $\left[E(\widetilde{R}_m) - R_f \right]$.

$$\beta_i = \frac{\sigma_{im}}{\sigma_m^2} = \frac{\text{COV}(\tilde{R}_i, \tilde{R}_m)}{\text{VAR}(\tilde{R}_m)}. \tag{6.10}$$

It is the covariance between returns on the risky asset, I, and market portfolio, M, divided by the variance of the market portfolio. The risk-free asset has a beta of zero because its covariance with the market portfolio is zero. The market portfolio has a beta of one because the covariance of the market portfolio with itself is identical to the variance of the market portfolio:

$$\beta_m = \frac{\text{COV}(\tilde{R}_i, \tilde{R}_m)}{\text{VAR}(\tilde{R}_m)} = \frac{\text{VAR}(\tilde{R}_m)}{\text{VAR}(\tilde{R}_m)} = 1.$$

D. $\mathcal{P}$roperties of the CAPM

There are several properties of the CAPM that are important. First, in equilibrium, every asset must be priced so that its risk-adjusted required rate of return falls exactly on the straight line in Fig. 6.3, which is called the *security market line*. This means, for example, that assets such as I and J in Fig 5.20, which do not lie on the mean-variance efficient set, will lie exactly on the security market line in Fig. 6.3. This is true because not all the variance of an asset's return is of concern to risk-averse investors. As we saw in the previous chapter, investors can always diversify away all risk except the covariance of an asset with the market portfolio. In other words, they can diversify away all risk except the risk of the economy as a whole, which is inescapable (undiversifiable). Consequently, the only risk that investors will pay a premium to avoid is covariance risk. The total risk of any individual asset can be partitioned into two parts—systematic risk, which is a measure of how the asset covaries with the economy, and unsystematic risk, which is independent of the economy:

$$\text{total risk} = \text{systematic risk} + \text{unsystematic risk}. \tag{6.11}$$

Mathematical precision can be attached to this concept by noting that empirically the return on any asset is a linear function of market return plus a random error term $\tilde{\varepsilon}_j$, which is independent of the market:

$$\tilde{R}_j = a_j + b_j \tilde{R}_m + \tilde{\varepsilon}_j.$$

This equation contains three terms: a constant, a_j, which has no variance; a constant times a random variable, $b_j \tilde{R}_m$; and a second random variable, $\tilde{\varepsilon}_j$, which has zero covariance with $\tilde{R}_m$. Using Properties 3 and 4 of random variables (given in Chapter 5), we can immediately write the variance of this relationship as

$$\sigma_j^2 = b_j^2 \sigma_m^2 + \sigma_\varepsilon^2. \tag{6.12}$$

Table 6.1 Risk and Return for Bayside Smokes and a 100-Stock Portfolio

	Annual Return (%)	Standard Deviation (%)	Beta
100-stock portfolio	10.9	4.45	1.11
Bayside Smokes	5.4	7.25	.71

The variance is total risk. It can be partitioned into systematic risk, $b_j^2 \sigma_m^2$, and unsystematic risk, σ_ε^2. It turns out that b_j in the simple linear relationship between individual asset return and market return is exactly the same as β_j in the CAPM.[3]

If systematic risk is the only type of risk that investors will pay to avoid, and if the required rate of return for every asset in equilibrium must fall on the security market line, we should be able to go back to the example of Bayside Smokes Company and resolve the paradox introduced in Chapter 5. Table 6.1 summarizes the empirical findings. We know that if investors are risk averse, there should be a positive trade-off between risk and return. When we tried to use the standard deviation as a measure of risk for an individual asset, Bayside Smokes, in comparison with a well-diversified portfolio, we were forced to make the inappropriate observation that the asset with higher risk has a lower return. The difficulty was that we were using the wrong measure of risk. One cannot compare the variance of return on a single asset with the variance for a well-diversified portfolio. The variance of the portfolio will almost always be smaller. The appropriate measure of risk for a single asset is beta, its covariance with the market divided by the variance of the market. This risk is nondiversifiable and is linearly related to the rate of return—$E(R_i)$ in Eq. (6.9)—required in equilibrium. When we look at the appropriate measure of risk, we see that Bayside Smokes is *less risky* than the 100-stock portfolio, and we have the sensible result that lower risk is accompanied by lower return.

Table 6.2 shows the realized rates of return and the betas of many different assets between January 1945 and June 1970. The calculations are taken from an article by Modigliani and Pogue [1974] that used monthly observations. In most cases the risk-return relationships make sense. Consumer product companies such as Swift and Co., Bayside Smokes, and American Snuff are all less risky than the market portfolio (represented here by the NYSE index). On the other hand, steel, electronics, and automobiles are riskier. Fig. 6.4 plots the empirical relationship between risk (measured by beta) and return for the companies listed in Table 6.2. The linearity of the relationship appears to be reasonable, and the trade-off between risk and return is positive. A more thorough discussion of empirical tests of the CAPM will be given later in this chapter.

A second important property of the CAPM is that the measure of risk for individual assets is linearly additive when the assets are combined into portfolios. For example, if we put $a\%$ of our wealth into asset X, with systematic risk of β_x, and $b\%$ of our wealth into asset Y, with systematic risk of β_y, then the beta of the resulting portfolio, β_p, is simply the weighted average of the betas of the individual securities:

$$\beta_p = a\beta_x + b\beta_y. \tag{6.13}$$

---

[3] The interested reader is referred to Appendix C on linear regression at the end of the book for proof that the slope coefficient, b_j, equals

$$b_j = \text{COV}(R_j, R_m)/\text{VAR}(R_m) = \sigma_{im}/\sigma_m^2$$

Table 6.2 Rates of Return and Betas for Selected Companies, 1945–1970

	Average Annual Return (%)	Standard Deviation (%)	Beta
City Investing Co.	17.4	11.09	1.67
Radio Corporation of America	11.4	8.30	1.35
Chrysler Corporation	7.0	7.73	1.21
Continental Steel Co.	11.9	7.50	1.12
100-stock portfolio	10.9	4.45	1.11
NYSE index	8.3	3.73	1.00
Swift and Co.	5.7	5.89	.81
Bayside Smokes	5.4	7.26	.71
American Snuff	6.5	4.77	.54
Homestake Mining Co.	4.0	6.55	.24

From F. Modigliani and G. Pogue, "An Introduction to Risk and Return," reprinted from *Financial Analysts Journal*, March–April 1974, 71.

Figure 6.4 An empirical security market line.

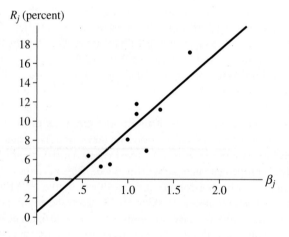

Proof of this follows from the definition of covariance and the properties of the mean and variance. The definition of the portfolio beta is

$$\beta_p = \frac{E\left\{[aX + bY - aE(X) - bE(Y)]\left[R_m - E(R_m)\right]\right\}}{\text{VAR}(R_m)}.$$

Rearranging terms, we have

$$\beta_p = \frac{E\left\{[a[X - E(X)] + b[Y - E(Y)]]\left[R_m - E(R_m)\right]\right\}}{\text{VAR}(R_m)}.$$

Next, we factor out a and b:

$$\beta_p = a \frac{E[(X - E(X))(R_m - E(R_m))]}{\text{VAR}(R_m)} + b \frac{E[(Y - E(Y))(R_m - E(R_m))]}{\text{VAR}(R_m)}.$$

Finally, using the definition of β,

$$\beta_p = a\beta_x + b\beta_y. \qquad \text{QED}$$

The fact that portfolio betas are linearly weighted combinations of individual asset betas is an extremely useful tool. All that is needed to measure the systematic risk of portfolios is the betas of the individual assets. It is not necessary to solve a quadratic programming problem (see Eqs. 5.26a and 5.26b) to find the efficient set.

It is worth reiterating the relationship between individual asset risk and portfolio risk. The correct definition of an individual asset's risk is its contribution to portfolio risk. Referring to Eq. (5.28), we see that the variance of returns for a portfolio of assets is

$$\text{VAR}(R_p) = \sigma^2(R_p) = \sum_{i=1}^{N} \sum_{j=1}^{N} w_i w_j \sigma_{ij},$$

which can be rewritten as[4]

$$\sigma^2(R_p) = \sum_{i=1}^{N} \left(\sum_{j=1}^{N} w_j \sigma_{ij} \right) = \sum_{i=1}^{N} w_i \text{COV}(R_i, R_p). \tag{6.14}$$

One could interpret

$$w_i \text{COV}(R_i, R_p) \tag{6.15}$$

as the risk of security i in portfolio p. However, at the margin, the change in the contribution of asset i to portfolio risk is simply

$$\text{COV}(R_i, R_p). \tag{6.16}$$

---

[4] To see that $\sum w_i (\sum w_j \sigma_{ij}) = \sum w_i \text{COV}(R_i, R_p)$, consider a simple three-asset example. Rewriting the left-hand side, we have

$$\sum w_i (\sum w_j \sigma_{ij}) = w_1(w_1\sigma_{11} + w_2\sigma_{12} + w_3\sigma_{13})$$
$$+ w_2(w_1\sigma_{21} + w_2\sigma_{22} + w_3\sigma_{23})$$
$$+ w_3(w_1\sigma_{31} + w_2\sigma_{32} + w_3\sigma_{33}).$$

From the definition of covariance, we have

$$\text{COV}(R_1, R_p) = [1 \quad 0 \quad 0] \begin{bmatrix} \sigma_{11} & \sigma_{12} & \sigma_{13} \\ \sigma_{21} & \sigma_{22} & \sigma_{23} \\ \sigma_{31} & \sigma_{32} & \sigma_{33} \end{bmatrix} \begin{bmatrix} w_1 \\ w_2 \\ w_3 \end{bmatrix}$$
$$= w_1\sigma_{11} + w_2\sigma_{12} + w_3\sigma_{13}.$$

Then by multiplying by the weight in the first asset, we obtain

$$w_1 \text{COV}(R_1, R_p) = w_1(w_1\sigma_{11} + w_2\sigma_{12} + w_3\sigma_{13}).$$

Finally, by repeating this procedure for each of the three assets, we can demonstrate the equality in Eq. (6.14).

Therefore covariance risk is the appropriate definition of risk since it measures the change in portfolio risk as we change the weighting of an individual asset in the portfolio.

Although the terms *systematic risk* and *undiversifiable risk* have arisen in the literature as synonyms for covariance risk, they are somewhat misleading. They rely on the existence of costless diversification opportunities and on the existence of a large market portfolio. The definition of covariance risk given above does not. It continues to be relevant, even when the market portfolio under consideration has few assets.

E. $\mathcal{U}$se of the CAPM for Valuation: Single-Period Models with Uncertainty

Because it provides a quantifiable measure of risk for individual assets, the CAPM is an extremely useful tool for valuing risky assets. For the time being, let us assume that we are dealing with a single time period. This assumption was built into the derivation of the CAPM. We want to value an asset that has a risky payoff at the end of the period. Call this $\widetilde{P}_e$. It could represent the capital gain on a common stock or the capital gain plus a dividend. If the risky asset is a bond, it is the repayment of the principal plus the interest on the bond. The expected return on an investment in the risky asset is determined by the price we are willing to pay at the beginning of the time period for the right to the risky end-of-period payoff. If P_0 is the price we pay today, our risky return, $\widetilde{R}_j$, is

$$\widetilde{R}_j = \frac{\widetilde{P}_e - P_0}{P_0}. \tag{6.17}$$

The CAPM can be used to determine what the current value of the asset, P_0, should be. The CAPM is

$$E(R_j) = R_f + \left[E(R_m) - R_f\right] \frac{\text{COV}(R_j, R_m)}{\text{VAR}(R_m)},$$

which can be rewritten as

$$E(R_j) = R_f + \lambda \text{COV}(R_j, R_m), \quad \text{where} \quad \lambda = \frac{E(R_m) - R_f}{\text{VAR}(R_m)}. \tag{6.18}$$

Note that λ can be described as the market price per unit risk. From Eq. (6.17) and the properties of the mean, we can equate the expected return from Eq. (6.17) with the expected return in Eq. (6.18):

$$\frac{E(P_e) - P_0}{P_0} = R_f + \lambda \text{COV}(R_j, R_m).$$

We can now interpret P_0 as the equilibrium price of the risky asset. Rearranging the above expression, we get

$$P_0 = \frac{E(P_e)}{1 + R_f + \lambda \text{COV}(R_j, R_m)}, \tag{6.19}$$

which is often referred to as the *risk-adjusted rate of return valuation formula*. The numerator is the expected end-of-period price for the risky asset, and the denominator can be thought of as a discount rate. If the asset has no risk, then its covariance with the market will be zero, and the appropriate one-period discount rate is $(1 + R_f)$. For assets with positive systematic risk, a risk premium, $\lambda \text{COV}(R_j, R_m)$, is added to the risk-free rate so that the discount rate is risk adjusted.

An equivalent approach to valuation is to deduct a risk premium from $E(P_e)$ in the numerator, then discount at $(1 + R_f)$. The covariance between the risky asset and the market can be rewritten as

$$\text{COV}(R_j, R_m) = \text{COV}\left[\frac{P_e - P_0}{P_0}, R_m\right]$$

$$= E\left[\left(\frac{P_e - P_0}{P_0} - \frac{E(P_e) - P_0}{P_0}\right)(R_m - E(R_m))\right]$$

$$= \frac{1}{P_0}\text{COV}(P_e, R_m).$$

By substituting this into the risk-adjusted rate of return equation, Eq. (6.19),

$$P_0 = \frac{E(P_e)}{1 + R_f + \lambda(1/P_0)\text{COV}(P_e, R_m)},$$

we can derive the *certainty equivalent valuation formula* from

$$P_0 = \frac{E(P_e) - \lambda\text{COV}(P_e, R_m)}{1 + R_f}. \tag{6.20}$$

The risk-adjusted rate of return and the certainty equivalent approaches are equivalent for one-period valuation models. It is important to realize that in both cases value does not depend on the utility preferences of individuals. All one needs to know in order to determine value is the expected end-of-period payoff, the quantity of risk provided by the asset, the risk-free rate, and the price of risk (which are market-determined variables). Consequently, individuals who perceive the same distribution of payoffs for a risky asset will price it exactly the same way regardless of their individual utility functions. The separation of valuation from attitudes toward risk is a consequence of two-fund separation. This was discussed in Chapter 5, Section E.5.

F. Applications of the CAPM for Corporate Policy

In the second half of this book, when we focus on corporate policy, these one-period valuation models will be used to develop decision-making rules for the selection of investment projects by the firm, for measurement of the firm's cost of capital, and for capital structure (optimal debt/equity ratio) decisions. However, for the sake of curiosity, we shall take a quick look at the implications of the CAPM for some corporate policy decisions, assuming that our firm has no debt and that there are no corporate or personal taxes. The complex results in a world with debt and taxes are left to Chapter 15.

Figure 6.5 The cost of equity using the CAPM.

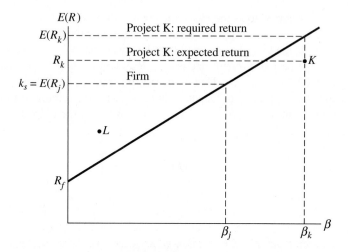

The cost of equity capital for a firm is given directly by the CAPM. After all, the company's beta is measured by calculating the covariance between the return on its common stock and the market index. Consequently, the beta measures the systematic risk of the common stock, and if we know the systematic risk, we can use the CAPM to determine the required rate of return on equity. Equation (6.21) is the capital asset pricing model:

$$E(R_j) = R_f + \left[E(R_m) - R_f\right] \beta_j. \tag{6.21}$$

If it is possible to estimate the systematic risk of a company's equity as well as the market rate of return, the $E(R_j)$ is the required rate of return on equity, that is, the cost of equity for the firm. If we designate the cost of equity as k_s, then

$$E(R_j) = k_s.$$

This is shown in Fig. 6.5. As long as projects have the same risk as the firm, then k_s may also be interpreted as the minimum required rate of return on new capital projects.

But what if the project has a different risk from the firm as a whole? Then all that is necessary is to estimate the systematic risk of the project and use the appropriate rate of return, $E(R_k)$. For example, in Fig. 6.5 the expected rate of return on project K, R_k, is higher than the cost of equity for the firm, $E(R_j)$. But the project also is riskier than the firm because it has greater systematic risk. If the managers of the firm were to demand that it earn the same rate as the firm $\left[k_s = E(R_j)\right]$, the project would be accepted since its expected rate of return, R_k, is greater than the firm's cost of equity. However, this would be incorrect. The market requires a rate of return, $E(R_k)$, for a project with systematic risk of β_k, but the project will earn less. Therefore since $R_k < E(R_k)$, the project is clearly unacceptable. (Is project L acceptable? Why?)

Because the CAPM allows decision makers to estimate the required rate of return for projects of different risk, it is an extremely useful concept. Although we have assumed no debt or taxes in the above simple introduction, Chapter 15 will show how the model can be extended to properly conceptualize more realistic capital budgeting and cost of capital decisions.

G. $\mathscr{E}$xtensions of the CAPM

Virtually every one of the assumptions under which the CAPM is derived is violated in the real world. If so, then how good is the model? There are two parts to this question: (1) Is it possible to extend the model to relax the unrealistic assumptions without drastically changing it? (2) How well does the model stand up to empirical testing? The first part is the subject of this section of the chapter. Surprisingly, the model is fairly resilient to various extensions of it.

1. No Riskless Asset

First, how will the model change if investors cannot borrow and lend at the risk-free rate? In other words, how is the CAPM affected if there is no risk-free asset that has constant returns in every state of nature? This problem was solved by Black [1972]. His argument is illustrated in Fig. 6.6. Portfolio M is identified by the investors as the market portfolio that lies on the efficient set.[5] Now, suppose that we can identify all portfolios that are uncorrelated with the true market portfolio.[6] This means that their returns have zero covariance with the market portfolio, and they have the same systematic risk (i.e., they have zero beta). Because they have the same systematic risk, each must have the same expected return. Portfolios A and B in Fig. 6.6 are both uncorrelated with the market portfolio M and have the same expected return $E(R_z)$. However, only one of them, portfolio B, lies on the opportunity set. It is the *minimum-variance zero-beta portfolio,* and it is unique. Portfolio A also has zero beta, but it has a higher variance and therefore does not lie on the minimum-variance opportunity set.

We can derive the slope of the line $E(R_z)M$ by forming a portfolio with $a\%$ in the market portfolio and $(1-a)\%$ in the minimum-variance zero-beta portfolio. The mean and standard deviation of such a portfolio can be written as follows:

$$E(R_p) = aE(R_m) + (1-a)E(R_z),$$

$$\sigma(R_p) = \left[a^2\sigma_m^2 + (1-a)^2\sigma_z^2 + 2a(1-a)r_{zm}\sigma_z\sigma_m\right]^{1/2}.$$

---

[5] Note, however, that the extension of the CAPM that follows can be applied to *any* efficient portfolio, not just the market portfolio.

[6] As an example of how to calculate the vector of weights in a world with only two assets, see Problem 6.13. For portfolios with many assets, we are interested in identifying the portfolio that (a) has zero covariance with the market portfolio and (b) has the mimimum variance. The solution will be the vector of the weights that satisfies the following quadratic programming problem:

$$\text{MIN}\,\sigma_p^2 = W_1' \sum W_1$$

$$\text{Subject to } W_1' \sum W_m = \sigma_{1m} = 0$$

$$W_1'\mathbf{e} = 1,$$

where σ_p^2 = the variance of the zero-beta portfolio,

W_1' = the row vector of weights in the mimimum-variance zero-beta portfolio (W_1 is a column vector with the same weights),

$\sum$ = the variance/covariance matrix for all N assets in the market,

W_m = the vector of weights in the market portfolio,

σ_{1m} = the covariance between the zero-beta portfolio and the market—which must always equal zero,

$\mathbf{e}$ = a column vector of ones.

Figure 6.6 The capital market line with no risk-free rate.

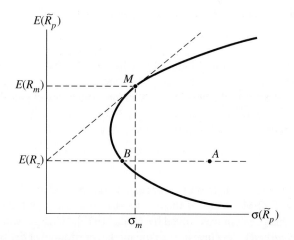

But since the correlation, r_{zm}, between the zero-beta portfolio and the market portfolio is zero, the last term drops out. The slope of a line tangent to the efficient set at point M, where 100% of the investor's wealth is invested in the market portfolio, can be found by taking the partial derivatives of the above equations and evaluating them where $a = 1$. The partial derivative of the mean portfolio return is

$$\frac{\partial E(R_p)}{\partial a} = E(R_m) - E(R_z),$$

and the partial derivative of the standard deviation is

$$\frac{\partial \sigma(R_p)}{\partial a} = \frac{1}{2}\left[a^2\sigma_m^2 + (1-a)^2\sigma_z^2\right]^{-1/2}\left[2a\sigma_m^2 - 2\sigma_z^2 + 2a\sigma_z^2\right].$$

Taking the ratio of these partials and evaluating where $a = 1$, we obtain the slope of the line $E(R_z)M$ in Fig. 6.6:

$$\frac{\partial E(R_p)/\partial a}{\partial \sigma(R_p)/\partial a} = \frac{E(R_m) - E(R_z)}{\sigma_m}. \tag{6.22}$$

Furthermore, since the line must pass through the point $\left[E(R_m), \sigma(R_m)\right]$, the intercept of the tangent line must be $E(R_z)$. Consequently, the equation of the line must be

$$E(R_p) = E(R_z) + \left[\frac{E(R_m) - E(R_z)}{\sigma_m}\right]\sigma_p. \tag{6.23}$$

This is exactly the same as the capital market line in Eq. (5.34) except that the expected rate of return on the zero-beta portfolio, $E(R_z)$, has replaced the risk-free rate.

   Given the above result, it is not hard to prove that the expected rate of return on *any* risky asset, whether or not it lies on the efficient set, must be a linear combination of the rate of return on the zero-beta portfolio and the market portfolio. To show this, recall that in equilibrium the slope of a line tangent to a portfolio composed of the market portfolio and any other asset at the point represented by the market portfolio must be equal to Eq. (6.8):

$$\left.\frac{\partial E(R_p)/\partial a}{\partial \sigma(R_p)/\partial a}\right|_{a=0} = \frac{E(R_i) - E(R_m)}{(\sigma_{im} - \sigma_m^2)/\sigma_m}.$$

If we equate the two definitions of the slope of a line tangent to point M, that is, if we equate (6.8) and (6.22), we have

$$\frac{E(R_m) - E(R_z)}{\sigma_m} = \frac{\left[E(R_i) - E(R_m)\right]\sigma_m}{\sigma_{im} - \sigma_m^2}.$$

Solving for the required rate of return on asset i, we have

$$E(R_i) = (1 - \beta_i)E(R_z) + \beta_i E(R_m), \tag{6.24}$$

where

$$\beta_i = \sigma_{im}/\sigma_m^2 = \text{COV}(R_i, R_m)/\sigma_m^2. \tag{6.25}$$

Equation (6.24) shows that the expected rate of return on any asset can be written as a linear combination of the expected rate of return of any two assets—the market portfolio and the unique minimum-variance zero-beta portfolio (which is chosen to be uncorrelated with the market portfolio). Interestingly, the weight to be invested in the market portfolio is the beta of the ith asset. If we rearrange (6.24), we see that it is exactly equal to the CAPM (Eqs. 6.9 and 6.21) except that the expected rate of return on the zero-beta portfolio has replaced the rate of return on the risk-free asset:

$$E(R_i) = E(R_z) + \left[E(R_m) - E(R_z)\right]\beta_i. \tag{6.26}$$

The upshot of this proof is that the major results of the CAPM do not require the existence of a pure riskless asset. Beta is still the appropriate measure of systematic risk for an asset, and the linearity of the model still obtains. The version of the model given by Eq. (6.26) is usually called the *two-factor model*.[7]

2. The Existence of Nonmarketable Assets

Suppose that the cost of transacting in an asset is infinite or that by law or regulation the asset is not marketable. Perhaps the most important example of such an asset is human capital. You can rent your skills in return for wages, but you cannot sell yourself or buy anyone else. Slavery is forbidden. This has the effect of introducing a nondiversifiable asset into your portfolio—your human asset capital. Because you cannot divide up your skills and sell them to different investors, you are forced into making portfolio decisions where you are constrained to hold a large risky

---

[7] One limitation of the two-factor model is that it relies rather heavily on the assumption that there are no short sales constraints. In general, zero-beta portfolios would have to be composed of both long and short positions of risky assets. Ross [1977] has shown that in a world with short sales restrictions and no riskless asset the linear CAPM is invalid. Thus to obtain the CAPM in a linear form (Eqs. 6.9 and 6.25) we require either (1) a risk-free asset that can be freely short sold or (2) no constraints on short sales.

component of your wealth in the form of your own human capital. What impact does this have on portfolio decisions and the CAPM?

We saw earlier that if there are no transaction costs and if all assets are perfectly divisible, two-fund separation obtains (see Chapter 5). Every investor, regardless of the shape of his or her indifference curve, will hold one of two assets: the risk-free asset or the market portfolio. Of course, casual empiricism tells us that this is not what actually happens. People do hold different portfolios of risky assets. There are many reasons why this may be true, and the existence of nonmarketable assets is a good possibility.

Mayers [1972] shows that when investors are constrained to hold nonmarketable assets that have risky (dollar) rates of return, R_H, the CAPM takes the following form:

$$E(R_j) = R_f + \lambda \left[V_m \text{COV}(R_j, R_m) + \text{COV}(R_j, R_H) \right], \tag{6.27}$$

where

$$\lambda = \frac{E(R_m) - R_f}{V_m \sigma_m^2 + \text{COV}(R_m, R_H)},$$

V_m = the current market value of all marketable assets,

R_H = the total dollar return on all nonmarketable assets.

In this version of the model, λ may be interpreted as the market price per unit risk where risk contains not only the market variance, σ_m^2, but also the covariance between the rate of return on marketable assets and the aggregate dollar return on nonmarketable assets. This result is obtained by first deriving an individual's demand curves for holding marketable assets, then aggregating them to obtain Eq. (6.26), which is the return on a marketable asset required by the market equilibrium. There are three important implications. First, individuals will hold different portfolios of risky assets because their human capital has differing amounts of risk. Second, the market equilibrium price of a risky asset may still be determined independently of the shape of the individual's indifference curves. This implies that the separation principle still holds. There is still an objectively determined market price of risk that is independent of individual attitudes toward risk. No variable in Eq. (6.26) is subscripted for the preference of the ith individual. Both the price of risk and the amount of risk depend only on properties of the jth asset, the portfolio of all marketable assets, and the portfolio of aggregated nonmarketable assets. Third, the appropriate measure of risk is still the covariance, but we must now consider the covariance between the jth risky asset and two portfolios, one composed of marketable and a second of nonmarketable assets.[8]

3. The Model in Continuous Time

Merton [1973] has derived a version of the CAPM that assumes (among other things) that trading takes place continuously over time, and that asset returns are distributed lognormally. If the risk-free rate of interest is nonstochastic over time, then (regardless of individual preferences, the distribution of individuals' wealth, or their time horizon) the equilibrium returns must satisfy

$$E(R_i) = r_f + \left[E(R_m) - r_f \right] \beta_i. \tag{6.28}$$

---

[8] See Fama and Schwert [1977] for an empirical test of the model set forth by Mayers.

Eq. (6.28) is the continuous-time analogy to the CAPM. In fact, it is exactly the same as the CAPM except that instantaneous rates of return have replaced rates of return over discrete intervals of time, and the distribution of returns is lognormal instead of normal.

If the risk-free rate is stochastic, investors are exposed to another kind of risk, namely, the risk of unfavorable shifts in the investment opportunity set. Merton shows that investors will hold portfolios chosen from three funds: the riskless asset, the market portfolio, and a portfolio chosen so that its returns are perfectly negatively correlated with the riskless asset. This model exhibits three-fund separation. The third fund is necessary to hedge against unforeseen changes in the future risk-free rate. The required rate of return on the jth asset is

$$E(R_j) = r_f + \gamma_1 \left[E(R_m) - r_f \right] + \gamma_2 \left[E(R_N) - r_f \right], \tag{6.29}$$

where

$R_N =$ the instantaneous rate of return on a portfolio that has perfect
   negative correlation with the riskless asset,

$$\gamma_1 = \frac{\beta_{jm} - \beta_{jN}\beta_{Nm}}{1 - \rho_{Nm}^2}, \qquad \gamma_2 = \frac{\beta_{jn} - \beta_{jm}\beta_{Nm}}{1 - \rho_{Nm}^2},$$

$\rho_{Nm} =$ the correlation between portfolio N and the market portfolio, M,

$$\beta_{ik} = \frac{\mathrm{COV}(R_i, R_k)}{\sigma_k^2}.$$

Merton argues that the sign of γ_2 will be negative for high-beta assets and positive for low-beta assets. As we shall see in the next section, which discusses the empirical tests of the CAPM, Merton's argument is consistent with the empirical evidence.

4. The Existence of Heterogeneous Expectations and Taxes

If investors do not have the same information about the distribution of future returns, they will perceive different opportunity sets and will obviously choose different portfolios. Lintner [1969] has shown that the existence of heterogeneous expectations does not critically alter the CAPM except that expected returns and covariances are expressed as complex weighted averages of investor expectations. However, if investors have heterogeneous expectations, the market portfolio is not necessarily efficient. This makes the CAPM nontestable. In fact, as we shall see when we discuss Roll's critique later in this chapter, the only legitimate test of the CAPM is a joint test to determine whether or not the market portfolio is efficient.

No one has investigated the equilibrium model in a world with personal as well as corporate taxes. However, Brennan [1970] has investigated the effect of differential tax rates on capital gains and dividends. Although he concludes that beta is the appropriate measure of risk, his model includes an extra term that causes the expected return on an asset to depend on dividend yield as well as systematic risk:

$$E(R_j) = \gamma_1 R_f + \gamma_2 \beta_j + \gamma_3 DY_j \tag{6.30}$$

where

$DY_j =$ the dividend yield on asset j.

We shall leave a complete discussion of the Brennan model to Chapter 16, which will cover the theory and empirical evidence related to the corporate dividend policy decision. For now it is sufficient to note that Brennan's model predicts that higher rates of return will be required on assets with higher dividend yields. In other words, investors do not like dividends because they must pay ordinary income tax rates on dividends but only capital gains rates on stock price increases.

H. *E*mpirical Tests of the CAPM

We begin the discussion of empirical tests with Table 6.3, which clearly shows that riskier (well-diversified) portfolios have higher returns over very long periods of time. *Geometric returns* are measured as the geometric average holding period return, r_g, calculated as follows for a portfolio that is reweighted at the beginning of each period:

$$r_g = [\prod(1+r_{pt})]^{1/N} - 1 \tag{6.31}$$

Arithmetic returns for the same portfolio are

$$r_a = 1/N[\sum(1+r_{pt})] - 1 \tag{6.32}$$

The CAPM is a simple linear model that is expressed in terms of expected returns and expected risk. In its ex ante form, we have

$$E(R_j) = R_f + [E(R_m) - R_f]\beta_j. \tag{6.33}$$

If the CAPM is a better model of the reward-risk trade-off for individual securities, it should be an improvement over Table 6.3 because it predicts that beta, not the standard deviation, should be a better measure of risk. Although many of the aforementioned extensions of the CAPM model support its simple linear form, others suggest that it may not be linear, that factors other than beta are needed to explain $E(R_j)$, or that R_f is not the appropriate risk-free rate. Therefore with so many alternative possibilities a great deal of energy has been devoted to the empirical question: How well does the model fit the data? In fact, researchers have been working on tests of the CAPM for nearly 40 years, and no conclusive evidence has been published to date—the jury is still out.

Table 6.3 Annual Average Market Data U.S. 1963–2002 (Percent)

	Geometric Return	Arithmetic Return	Geometric Standard Deviation	Arithmetic Standard Deviation
Stocks of smaller companies	19.6	25.2	42.6	41.8
S & P 500	10.5	11.9	16.9	16.6
Long-term corporate bonds	8.4	8.5	3.2	3.2
Long-term U.S. government bonds	7.0	7.1	3.1	3.1
Short-term U.S. Treasury bills	6.3	6.3	2.5	2.5

Source: Monitor Group analysis.

There have been numerous empirical tests of the CAPM, so many in fact that it would be fruitless to mention all of them. Also, the literature is interwoven with many serious and difficult econometric problems that must be confronted in order to provide the best empirical tests of the model.[9] However, in the opinion of the authors, the tests of the CAPM summarized below represent the best of the work that has been done to date.

The first step necessary to empirically test the theoretical CAPM is to transform it from expectations or ex ante form (expectations cannot be measured) into a form that uses observed data. This can be done by assuming that the rate of return on any asset is a *fair game*.[10] In other words, on average the realized rate of return on an asset is equal to the expected rate of return. We can write the fair game as follows:

$$R_{jt} = E(R_{jt}) + \beta_j \delta_{mt} + \varepsilon_{jt}, \tag{6.34}$$

where

$$\delta_{mt} = R_{mt} - E(R_{mt}),$$

$$E(\delta_{mt}) = 0,$$

$$\varepsilon_{jt} = \text{a random-error term,}$$

$$E(\varepsilon_{jt}) = 0$$

$$\text{COV}(\varepsilon_{jt}, \delta_{mt}) = 0,$$

$$\beta_j = \text{COV}(R_{jt}, R_{mt})/\text{VAR}(R_{mt})$$

Equation (6.34) is seen to be a fair game because if we take the expectation of both sides, the average realized return is equal to the expected return. In other words, on average you get the return you expected:

$$E(R_{jt}) = E(R_{jt}).$$

By substituting $E(R_j)$ from the CAPM into Eq. (6.34), we obtain

$$R_{jt} = R_{ft} + [E(R_{mt}) - R_{ft}]\beta_j + \beta_j[R_{mt} - E(R_{mt})] + \varepsilon_{jt}$$

$$= R_{ft} + (R_{mt} - R_{ft})\beta_j + \varepsilon_{jt}.$$

Finally, by subtracting R_{ft} from both sides, we have

$$R_{jt} - R_{ft} = (R_{mt} - R_{ft})\beta_j + \varepsilon_{jt}, \tag{6.35}$$

which is the ex post form of the CAPM. We derived it by simply assuming that returns are normally distributed and that capital markets are efficient in a fair game sense. Now we have an empirical version of the CAPM that is expressed in terms of ex post observations of return data instead of ex ante expectations.

---

[9] For papers that discuss some of the econometric problems involved in testing the CAPM, the reader is referred to Miller and Scholes [1972], Roll [1977, 1981], Scholes and Williams [1977], Dimson [1979], and Gibbons [1982].

[10] Chapter 10 explains the theory of efficient capital markets that describes a fair game at length. Also, empirical evidence is presented that suggests that the market is in fact a fair game.

Figure 6.7 (a) Ex post CAPM; (b) ex ante CAPM.

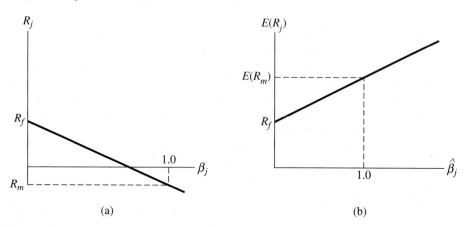

(a)   (b)

One important difference between the ex post empirical model and the ex ante theoretical model is that the former can have a negative slope, whereas the latter cannot. After the fact we may have experienced a state of nature where the market rate of return was negative. When this happens the empirical security market line will slope downward as in Fig. 6.7(a). On the other hand, the theoretical CAPM always requires the ex ante expected return on the market to be higher than the risk-free rate of return as shown in Fig. 6.7(b). This is because prices must be established in such a way that riskier assets have higher expected rates of return. Of course, it may turn out that after the fact their return was low or negative, but that is what is meant by risk. If a risky asset has a beta of 2.0, it will lose roughly 20% when the market goes down by 10%.

When the CAPM is empirically tested, it is usually written in the following form:

$$R'_{pt} = \gamma_0 + \gamma_1 \beta_p + \varepsilon_{pt}, \tag{6.36}$$

where

$$\gamma_1 = R_{mt} - R_{ft},$$

$$R'_{pt} = \text{the excess return on portfolio } p = (R_{pt} - R_{ft}).$$

This is the same as Eq. (6.35) except that a constant term, γ_0, has been added.

Exactly what predictions made by the CAPM are tested in Eq. (6.36)?

1. The intercept term, γ_0, should not be significantly different from zero. If it is different from zero, then there may be something "left out" of the CAPM that is captured in the empirically estimated intercept term.

2. Beta should be the only factor that explains the rate of return on the risky asset. If other terms such as residual variance, dividend yield, price/earnings ratios, firm size, or beta squared are included in an attempt to explain return, they should have no explanatory power.

3. The relationship should be linear in beta.

4. The coefficient of beta, γ_1, should be equal to $(R_{mt} - R_{ft})$.

5. When the equation is estimated over very long periods of time, the rate of return on the market portfolio should be greater than the risk-free rate. Because the market portfolio is riskier, on average it should have a higher rate of return.

The major empirical tests of the CAPM were published by Friend and Blume [1970], Black, Jensen, and Scholes [1972], Miller and Scholes [1972], Blume and Friend [1973], Blume and Husick [1973], Fama and Macbeth [1973], Basu [1977], Reinganum [1981b], Litzenberger and Ramaswamy [1979], Banz [1981], Gibbons [1982], Stambaugh [1982], Shanken [1985b], Fama and French [1992], and Kothari, Shanken, and Sloan [1995]. Most of the studies use monthly total returns (dividends are reinvested) on listed common stocks as their database. A frequently used technique is to estimate the betas of every security during a five-year holding period, by computing the covariance between return on the security and a market index that is usually an equally weighted index of all listed common stocks. The securities are then ranked by beta and placed into N portfolios (where N is usually 10, 12, or 20). By grouping the individual securities into large portfolios chosen to provide the maximum dispersion in systematic risk, it is possible to avoid a good part of the measurement error in estimating betas of individual stocks. Next, the portfolio betas and returns are calculated over a second five-year period and a regression similar to Eq. (6.33) is run.

With few exceptions, the empirical studies prior to Fama and French [1992] agree on the following conclusions:

1. The intercept term, γ_0, is significantly different from zero, and the slope, γ_1, is less than the difference between the return on the market portfolio minus the risk-free rate.[11] The implication is that low-beta securities earn more than the CAPM would predict and high-beta securities earn less.

2. Versions of the model that include a squared-beta term or unsystematic risk find that at best these explanatory factors are used only in a small number of the time periods sampled. Beta dominates them as a measure of risk.

3. The simple linear empirical model of Eq. (6.36) fits the data best. It is linear in beta. Also, over long periods of time the rate of return on the market portfolio is greater than the risk-free rate (i.e., $\gamma_1 > 0$).

4. Factors other than beta are successful in explaining that portion of security returns not captured by beta. Basu [1977] found that low price/earnings portfolios have rates of return higher than could be explained by the CAPM. Banz [1981] and Reinganum [1981b] found that the size of a firm is important. Smaller firms tend to have high abnormal rates of return. Litzenberger and Ramaswamy [1979] found that the market requires higher rates of return on equities with high dividend yields. Keim [1983, 1985] reports seasonality in stock returns—a January effect, where most of excess returns are earned in one month. Fama and French [1992] conclude that market capitalization (a measure of size) and the ratio of the book to the market value of equity should replace beta altogether.

Figure 6.8 shows the average monthly returns on 10 portfolios versus their systematic risk for the 35-year period 1931–1965 (taken from the Black-Jensen-Scholes study [1972]). The results shown

---

[11] Empirical studies have used 90-day Treasury bills as a proxy for the risk-free rate, and they have also laboriously calculated the return on the zero-beta portfolio. Either approach results in an intercept term significantly different from zero.

Figure 6.8 Average monthly returns vs. systematic risk for 10 portfolios, 1931–1965. (From *Studies in the Theory of Capital Markets*, edited by Michael C. Jensen. Copyright ©1972 by Praeger Publishers, Inc. Reprinted with permission of Holt, Rinehart, and Winston.)

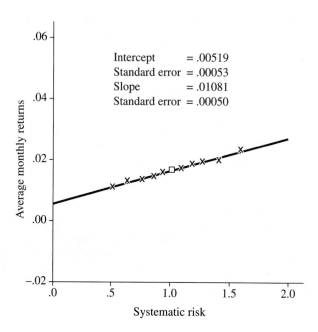

here are typical. The empirical market line is linear with a positive trade-off between return and risk, but the intercept term is significantly different from zero. In fact, it is 9.79 standard deviations away. This forces us to reject the CAPM, given the empirical techniques of the previously mentioned studies. In addition, the ability of the other variables such as price/earnings ratios to explain the portion of returns that are unexplained by the CAPM suggests either (1) that the CAPM is misspecified and requires the addition of factors other than beta to explain security returns or (2) that the problems in measuring beta are systematically related to variables such as firm size. Work that is consistent with this second point of view has been published by Rosenberg and Marathe [1977], who find that beta can be predicted much better if variables such as dividend yield, trading volume, and firm size are added to the predictive model. Roll [1981] suggests that infrequent trading of shares in small firms may explain much of the measurement error in estimating betas.

Gibbons [1982], Stambaugh [1982], and Shanken [1985b] test the CAPM by first assuming that the market model is true—that is, the return on the ith asset is a linear function of a market portfolio proxy such as an equally weighted market portfolio:

$$R_{it} = \alpha_i + \beta_i R_{mt} + \varepsilon_{it}. \tag{6.37}$$

The market model, Eq. (6.37), is merely a statistical statement. It is not the CAPM. The CAPM—for example, Black's [1972] two-factor version—actually requires the intercept term, $E(R_z)$, in Eq. (6.37) to be the same for all assets. The two-factor CAPM is true across all assets at a point in time,

$$E(R_i) = E(R_z) + \left[E(R_m) - E(R_z) \right] \beta_i. \tag{6.38}$$

Table 6.4 Portfolio Monthly Rate of Return, Sorted on Size and Beta 1963–1990

	1A	1B	2	3	4	5	6	7	8	9	10A	10B
Portfolios Formed on Size												
Average monthly return	1.64	1.16	1.29	1.24	1.25	1.29	1.17	1.07	1.10	0.95	0.88	0.90
Beta	1.44	1.44	1.39	1.34	1.33	1.24	1.22	1.16	1.08	1.02	0.95	0.90
ln(market equity)	1.98	3.18	3.63	4.10	4.50	4.89	5.30	5.73	6.24	6.82	7.39	8.44
Number of companies	722	189	236	170	144	140	128	125	119	114	60	64
Portfolios Formed on Beta												
Average monthly return	1.20	1.20	1.32	1.26	1.31	1.30	1.30	1.23	1.23	1.33	1.34	1.18
Beta	0.81	0.79	0.92	1.04	1.13	1.19	1.26	1.32	1.14	1.52	1.63	1.73
ln (market equity)	1.98	3.18	3.63	4.10	4.50	4.89	5.30	5.73	6.24	6.82	7.39	8.44
Number of companies	116	80	185	181	179	182	185	205	227	267	165	291

Source: Fama and French [1992]. (© 1992 Blackwell Publishing. Reprinted with permission.)

Gibbons [1982] points out that the two-factor CAPM implies the following constraint on the intercept of the market model:

$$\alpha_i = E(R_z)(1 - \beta_i) \tag{6.39}$$

for all securities during the same time interval. When he tests restriction (6.39), he finds that it is violated and that the CAPM must be rejected.

Fama and French [1992] published a landmark study on the cross-sectional relationship between return and risk, as a test of the CAPM. They used larger databases then ever before, starting with daily individual stock returns from 1963 to 1990 for all NYSE and AMEX listed stocks, then adding all NASDAQ-listed stocks from 1973 to 1990. Cognizant of the strong negative correlation between size and beta (−0.988), they designed an empirical test that carefully separated the two. Table 6.4 shows simple sorts based on size (measured as the natural logarithm of the equity market capitalization of a company) and beta (estimated using the value-weighted portfolio of NYSE, AMEX, and after 1973, NASDAQ stocks). The results clearly show that when portfolios are arranged by size there is a visible relationship between monthly returns and both size and beta, but when the portfolios are arranged by beta, the relationship becomes tenuous.

Therefore, Fama and French ran a two-pass sort to attempt to separate the effect of beta from size. The results are shown in Table 6.5. The numbers in each cell are the percentage average monthly returns. If we scan down the columns, we see the relationship between return and company size. It is fairly clear. If we read across the rows, we are seeing the relationship between return and beta, holding size constant. For the small and the large equity rows, the relationship between beta and return goes in the wrong direction and is not very strong in the remaining rows. Finally, Fama and French ran multiple regressions with the individual stock returns as the dependent variable. Beta was not statistically significantly related to the average returns of individual securities, either by itself, or when combined with size in a multiple regression. The strongest model did not include beta at all. It explained the return as a negative function of size (measured as the natural logarithm of market capitalization) and a positive function of the logarithm of the ratio of the book to the market value of equity. However, when they exclude the NASDAQ stocks and extend their data back to include the period 1941–1990, then beta is significant and positively related to returns both for portfolios and for individual stocks.

Table 6.5 Two-Pass Sort by Size and Beta Average Monthly Returns, 1963–1990 (percent)

	Low Beta	Third Decile	Average of Fifth and Sixth	Eighth Decile	High Beta
Small equity	1.71	1.79	1.50	1.63	1.42
Third decile	1.12	1.17	1.19	1.36	0.76
Average of fifth and sixth deciles	1.21	1.33	1.25	1.16	1.05
Eighth decile	1.09	1.37	1.13	1.02	0.94
Large equity	1.01	1.10	0.91	0.71	0.56

Source: Fama and French [1992]. (© 1992 Blackwell Publishing. Reprinted with permission.)

The Fama and French [1992] results were soon followed by others. Roll and Ross [1994] showed that even small departures of the index portfolio from ex post market efficiency can easily result in empirical results that show no relationship between beta and average cross-sectional returns. Kothari, Shanken, and Sloan [1995] study the same relationship between beta, size, and the ratio of book to market value of equity. They conclude that "examination of the cross-section of expected returns reveals economically and statistically significant compensation (about 6–9% per annum) for beta risk." They note that annual returns are used to avoid the seasonality of returns, there is a significant linear relationship between returns and beta between 1941 and 1990, that size is also related to returns but the incremental economic contribution is small (less than 1 percent), and that the book to market results are the result of survivorship bias in the Compustat database and are not economically significant.[12]

Fama and French [1996] update their work and present a three-factor model that, when fit to data for NYSE, AMEX, and NASDAQ stock returns for 366 months from July 1963 to December 1993, provides the best explanation of excess returns. Their model, written below, says that the excess return of the ith security over the risk-free rate is a linear function of three factors: the excess return of the market portfolio over the risk-free rate, the difference between the returns on a portfolio of small stocks and large stocks, $E(SMB)$, and the difference between the returns on a portfolio of high and low book-to-market stocks, $E(HML)$:

$$E(R_i) - R_f = b_i[E(R_m) - R_f] + s_i E(SMB) + h_i E(HML). \tag{6.40}$$

The debate concerning the empirical validity of the CAPM continues today and may be summarized by three lines of thinking. First are research studies that look for misspecification of the simple linear two-factor model. Some, like Fama and French [1992] or Roll and Ross [1980] suggest a multifactor model. Others look for errors in the execution and design of the empirical tests (e.g., the survivorship bias problem discussed in Kothari, Shanken, and Sloan [1995]), frictions in capital markets (Amihud and Mendelsohn [1986]), or simply irrational behavior (Lakonishok, Shleifer, and Vishny [1994]). Finally is the possibility that the market risk premium and betas change over time (e.g., papers by Jagannathan and Wang [1996], Scruggs [1998], and Ferson and

---

[12] Selection bias is found in Compustat and results in upward-biased returns for high book/market equity portfolios for several reasons: In 1978 Compustat expanded its database from 2,700 to 6,000 companies, adding five years of data going back to 1973 with the likely effect that high book-to-market companies (in 1973) that did poorly or failed were unlikely to be found in the 1978 database, and vice versa. Kothari, Shanken, and Sloan [1995] found that the returns for the set of companies that were included on the CRSP data but not on Compustat were in fact lower than average.

Harvey [1999]). Gradual progress is being made, and most scholars believe that the notion of systematic risk is intuitive and important, but much remains to be done.

Berk, Green, and Naik [1999] present a dynamic theory of the firm that provides some intuition behind the empirical results of Fama and French [1996]. Each company is viewed as creating value through its stewardship of assets in place and discovery of valuable growth options. Good news about profitable growth drives up the share price but is also associated with relatively lower betas. Berk et al. describe the book-to-market ratio as a state variable that summarizes a firm's risk relative to the scale of its asset base. Strong profitable growth drives the book-to-market ratio down, drives beta down, and drives the required return down. Hence we would expect high book-to-market stocks to have lower cross-sectional returns than low book-to-market stocks—consistent with the empirical results. Also, in Berk et al., market capitalization is described as a state variable that captures the relative importance of existing assets versus growth options. Small stocks have higher expected returns than large because expected growth options are riskier and have a greater weighting in the present value of the company.

I. $\mathcal{T}$he Market Risk Premium

One of the most important numbers in financial economics is the market risk premium. If we are using a CAPM framework, it is the difference between the expected rate of return on the market portfolio and the expected return on the minimum-variance zero-beta portfolio (usually assumed to be the same as the risk-free rate). The market risk premium is a benchmark for required returns of index funds (and other mutual funds), and for the required returns on corporate capital investments. Practitioners are constantly confronted with how to estimate it. This turns out to be a thorny problem, interwoven with empirical tests of the CAPM as discussed in Section H.

The definition of the market risk premium, λ_1, is deceptively simple:

$$\lambda_1 = E(R_m) - E(R_z). \tag{6.41}$$

But over what interval of time should expectations be measured, how do we interpret ex post data, how do we account for sample selection biases, and should we use nominal or real rates of return? Not all of these questions are resolved. What follows is a discussion of some of the more important issues.

How do we interpret ex post data, when the definition of the risk premium is based on forward-looking expected returns on two portfolios, one with zero beta and the other with a beta of one? Normally, one assumes that the ex ante and ex post betas are identical, and proceeds to calculate arithmetic rather than geometric returns. To illustrate why, consider the following simple example. You invest $100 at time zero, and there is a 50% chance that it can rise to $200 or fall to $50 in one year. After two years, it can rise to $400, return to $100, or fall to $25. This event tree is illustrated in Fig. 6.9.

The usual calculation of the realized rate of return is the ex post geometric rate, defined as

$$R_p = [\Pi(1 + r_{pt})]^{1/T} - 1. \tag{6.42}$$

Note that there are no probabilities involved, because ex post the portfolio return has only one realization. For example, suppose that it followed the middle path in Fig. 6.9, where the stock price starts at $100, climbs to $200, then falls to $100 at the end. The geometric average rate of

Figure 6.9 Example used to contrast arithmetic and geometric rates of return.

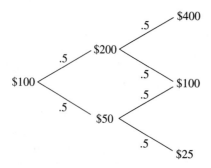

return along this path is 0%:

$$R_p = (1 + 100\%)(1 - 50\%) - 1 = (2)(1/2) - 1 = 0\%. \qquad (6.43)$$

When attempting to evaluate the event tree of Fig. 6.9, ex ante, the problem is different because all branches are possible. Therefore we have to probability weight the outcomes of each branch in order to obtain the ex ante expected return, as an arithmetic average:

$$E(R_p) = \left[\sum p_i (1 + r_{pi})\right]^{1/T} - 1$$

$$E(R_p) = [.25(400/100) + 2(.25)(100/100) + .25(25/100)]^{1/2} - 1$$

$$= 1.5625^{1/2} - 1$$

$$= 25\% \text{ per year.}$$

Thus, while it is appropriate to use geometric averages when measuring historical portfolio performance, the asset pricing models are forward looking and therefore are based on arithmetic averages that are representative of expected returns.

The arithmetic average of the difference between the annual return on a value-weighted index of U.S. equities and returns on short-term U.S. Treasury bills has been 7.7 percent over the period 1926–1999 according to Ibbotson [2000]. But as Brown, Goetzmann, and Ross [1995] point out, this statistic includes survivorship bias and is biased upward. The intuition is fairly straightforward. Over the time interval 1926–2001, the U.S. index has not only been continuously traded, but also has been perhaps the single most successful of all indices that might have been chosen for investment in 1926. But what is the probability that over the next 76 years the U.S. markets will experience the same rate of success? Because of survivorship bias, many benchmarks of portfolio performance are upward biased, especially those whose weightings are chosen ex post—such as the Dow 30 Industrials, and the Standard & Poor's 500. No company in either index has ever been delisted or gone into Chapter 11. One estimate of the survivorship bias in the U.S. equity market index is 2%.

Another issue is how to define the risk-free rate. If we assume, for the time being, that interest rates are a fundamental factor that is not wholly captured in the CAPM, then portfolios with different interest rate sensitivity may have expected returns that differ as a function of their interest rate sensitivity. In this case, it is better to choose a risk-free rate that is zero default risk, namely, the rate on a U.S. government obligation, but with approximately the same sensitivity to interest rates

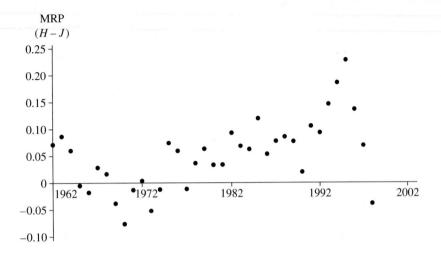

Figure 6.10 The market risk premium 1963–2002. *Source:* Monitor Group analysis.

as the equity (or market) index. Figure 6.10 shows the annual arithmetic market risk premium for an index of large company stocks minus the rate of return on an index of U.S. government bonds of intermediate maturity (which should have closer sensitivity to interest rates than an index based on short-term Treasury bills). If we were to use this data (1963–2002), our estimate of the market risk premium would be 11.9% (the average arithmetic return on the S & P 500 index) minus 7% (the average arithmetic return on intermediate-term U.S. government bonds). Thus, our estimate of the market risk premium would be roughly 5%, in nominal terms. We would obtain the same estimate in real terms if the expected inflation in our estimate of the risk-free rate is the same as the expected inflation in the index of large company stocks.

A time-series regression of the *market risk premium, MRP*, provides the following results (40 observations):

$$MRP = .041 + .0002\,(year)$$

$$(0.77) \quad (0.44) \tag{6.44}$$

The *t*-statistics are given in parentheses. The slope is not statistically different from zero. Consequently, there is absolutely no evidence of a trend in the market risk premium over time. Were the regression run on data from 1926 to 2002, the conclusion would be the same.

Fama and French [2002] estimate the market risk premium differently and use a longer time period, 1872–2000. Their logic is that the average stock return is the average dividend yield plus the average rate of capital gain:

$$A(R_t) = A(D_t/P_{t-1}) + A(GP_t). \tag{6.45}$$

If the dividend price ratio is stationary over time, then the rate of dividend growth approaches the compound rate of capital gain; therefore the annual growth in dividends can be substituted in place of the annual capital gain (in the equation above). Fama and French use this dividend growth model (and an earnings growth model) to estimate the unconditional expected stock return for the *i*th stock. Thus, they do not use ex post historical realizations of the difference between the return on the market portfolio and the risk-free rate. Instead they model ex ante differences between the expected return on the market portfolio and the risk-free rate. The simple arithmetic average for the period 1872–1950 is 4.40%, and the estimate from their dividend growth model is about the same, namely, 4.17%. However, for the period 1950–2000 the difference is large—7.43 versus 2.55%. There are several issues, however, for example, the growing use of stock repurchases and the declining use of dividends to deliver value to shareholders.

J. The Empirical Market Line

The empirical evidence has led scholars to conclude that the pure theoretical form of the CAPM does not agree well with reality. However, the empirical form of the model, which has come to be known as the *empirical market line,*

$$R_{it} = \widehat{\gamma}_{0t} + \widehat{\gamma}_{1t}\beta_{it} + \varepsilon_{it}, \qquad (6.46)$$

does provide an adequate model of security returns. Obviously, if one can estimate a security's beta for a given time period, then by knowing the empirical market line parameters, one can estimate the security's required rate of return from Eq. (6.46).

Some (e.g., Ibbotson) have gone so far as to employ a version that does not use beta. For example, the expected rate of return on the equity of a company is argued to be a log-linear function of the size of the company and its book-to-market ratio:

$$R_{it} = \gamma_{0t} + \gamma_{1t} \ln(Size)_i + \gamma_{2t}(Book/Market)_i + \varepsilon_{it}. \qquad (6.47)$$

Obvious questions facing a practitioner who attempts to use this version are "How do I apply it to projects that are obviously and significantly different in their total and systematic risk, although they have the same size?" or "What are the implications for the merger of two large companies?"

K. The Problem of Measuring Performance: Roll's Critique

One of the potentially most useful applications of the securities market line in its ex post form, Eq. (6.35), or the empirical market line, Eq. (6.46), is that they might be used as benchmarks for security performance. The residual term, ε_{jt}, has been interpreted as abnormal because, as shown in Fig. 6.11, it represents return in excess of what is predicted by the security market line.

Roll [1977] takes exception to this interpretation of cross-section abnormal performance measures and to empirical tests of the CAPM in general. In brief, his major conclusions are

1. The only legitimate test of the CAPM is whether or not the market portfolio (which includes *all* assets) is mean-variance efficient.

2. If performance is measured relative to an index that is ex post efficient, then from the mathematics of the efficient set no security will have abnormal performance when measured as a departure from the security market line.[13]

---

[13] It is important to note that Roll does not take exception to time-series measures of performance such as those described by the market model in Chapter 11.

Figure 6.11 Abnormal return.

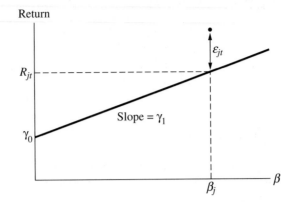

3. If performance is measured relative to an ex post inefficient index, then any ranking of portfolio performance is possible, depending on which inefficient index has been chosen.

This is a startling statement. It implies that even if markets are efficient and the CAPM is valid, then the cross-section security market line cannot be used as a means of measuring the ex post performance of portfolio selection techniques. Furthermore, the efficiency of the market portfolio and the validity of the CAPM are joint hypotheses that are almost impossible to test because of the difficulty of measuring the true market portfolio.

To understand Roll's critique, we must go back to the derivation of the zero-beta portfolio. Recall that if there is no risk-free asset, it is still possible to write the security market line as a combination of the market portfolio and a zero-beta portfolio that is uncorrelated with the market index. Therefore the expected return on any asset could be written as a two-factor model:

$$E(R_i) = E\left(R_z\right) + [E(R_m) - E(R_z)]\beta_i. \tag{6.48}$$

Roll points out that there is nothing unique about the market portfolio. It is always possible to choose any efficient portfolio as an index, then find the minimum-variance portfolio that is uncorrelated with the selected efficient index. This is shown in Fig. 6.12. Once this has been done, then Eq. (6.37) can be derived and written as

$$E(R_i) = E(R_{z,I}) + \left[E(R_I) - E(R_{z,I})\right]\beta_{i,I}. \tag{6.49}$$

Note that the market portfolio, R_m, has been replaced by any efficient index, R_I, and the beta is measured relative to the selected efficient index, $\beta_{i,I}$. Also, the zero-beta portfolio is measured relative to the index $R_{z,I}$. Because the expected return on any asset can be written as a linear function of its beta measured relative to any efficient index, it is not necessary to know the market index. One only need know the composition of an efficient index in order to write Eq. (6.49). Furthermore, if the index turns out to be ex post efficient, then every asset will fall exactly on the security market line. There will be no abnormal returns. If there are systematic abnormal returns, it simply means that the index that has been chosen is not ex post efficient.

The Roll critique does not imply that the CAPM is an invalid theory. However, it does mean that tests of the CAPM must be interpreted with great caution. The fact that portfolio residuals exhibited no significant departures from linearity merely implies that the market index that was selected

Figure 6.12 Two index portfolios with their respective orthogonal portfolios.

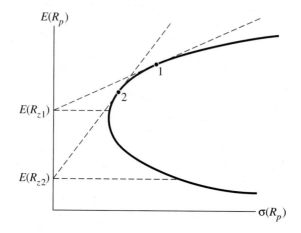

(usually an equally weighted index of all listed shares of common stock) was ex post efficient. In fact, the only way to test the CAPM directly is to see whether or not the true market portfolio is ex post efficient. Unfortunately, because the market portfolio contains all assets (marketable and nonmarketable, e.g., human capital, coins, houses, bonds, stocks, options, land, etc.), it is impossible to observe.

L. *The* Arbitrage Pricing Theory

1. The Theory

Formulated by Ross [1976], the *arbitrage pricing theory* (APT) offers a testable alternative to the capital asset pricing model. The CAPM predicts that security rates of return will be linearly related to a single common factor—the rate of return on the market portfolio. The APT is based on similar intuition but is much more general. It assumes that the rate of return on any security is a linear function of k factors:

$$\widetilde{R}_i = E(\widetilde{R}_i) + b_{i1}\widetilde{F}_1 + \cdots + b_{ik}\widetilde{F}_k + \widetilde{\varepsilon}_i, \qquad (6.50)$$

where

$$\widetilde{R}_i = \text{the random rate of return on the } i\text{th asset,}$$

$$E(\widetilde{R}_i) = \text{the expected rate of return on the } i\text{th asset,}$$

$$b_{ik} = \text{the sensitivity of the } i\text{th asset's returns to the } k\text{th factor,}$$

$$\widetilde{F}_k = \text{the mean zero } k\text{th factor common to the returns of all assets,}$$

$$\widetilde{\varepsilon}_i = \text{a random zero mean noise term for the } i\text{th asset.}$$

As we shall see later on, the CAPM may be viewed as a special case of the APT when the market rate of return is assumed to be the single relevant factor.

The APT is derived under the usual assumptions of perfectly competitive and frictionless capital markets. Furthermore, individuals are assumed to have homogeneous beliefs that the random returns for the set of assets being considered are governed by the linear k-factor model given in Eq. (6.50). The theory requires that the number of assets under consideration, n, be much larger than the number of factors, k, and that the noise term, $\tilde{\varepsilon}_i$, be the unsystematic risk component for the ith asset. It must be independent of all factors and all error terms for other assets.

The most important feature of the APT is reasonable and straightforward. In equilibrium all portfolios that can be selected from among the set of assets under consideration and that satisfy the conditions of (1) using no wealth and (2) having no risk must earn no return on average. These portfolios are called *arbitrage portfolios*. To see how they can be constructed, let w_i be the *change* in the dollar amount invested in the ith asset as a percentage of an individual's total invested wealth. To form an arbitrage portfolio that requires no change in wealth (or is said to be self-financing), the usual course of action would be to sell some assets and use the proceeds to buy others. Mathematically, the zero change in wealth is written as

$$\sum_{i=1}^{n} w_i = 0. \tag{6.51}$$

If there are n assets in the arbitrage portfolio, then the additional portfolio return gained is

$$\tilde{R}_p = \sum_{i=1}^{n} w_i \tilde{R}_i$$

$$= \sum_i w_i E(\tilde{R}_i) + \sum_i w_i b_{i1} \tilde{F}_1 + \cdots + \sum_i w_i b_{ik} \tilde{F}_k + \sum_i w_i \tilde{\varepsilon}_i. \tag{6.52}$$

To obtain a riskless arbitrage portfolio it is necessary to eliminate both diversifiable (i.e., unsystematic or idiosyncratic) and undiversifiable (i.e., systematic) risk. This can be done by meeting three conditions: (1) selecting percentage changes in investment ratios, w_i, that are small, (2) diversifying across a large number of assets, and (3) choosing changes, w_i, so that for each factor, k, the weighted sum of the systematic risk components, b_k, is zero. Mathematically, these conditions are

$$w_i \approx 1/n, \tag{6.53a}$$

$$n \text{ chosen to be a large number,} \tag{6.53b}$$

$$\sum_i w_i b_{ik} = 0 \quad \text{for each factor.} \tag{6.53c}$$

Because the error terms, ε_i, are independent, the law of large numbers guarantees that a weighted average of many of them will approach zero in the limit as n becomes large. In other words, costless diversification eliminates the last term (the unsystematic or idiosyncratic risk) in Eq. (6.50). Thus, we are left with

$$\tilde{R}_p = \sum_i w_i E(\tilde{R}_i) + \sum_i w_i b_{i1} \tilde{F}_1 + \cdots + \sum_i w_i b_{ik} \tilde{F}_k. \tag{6.54}$$

At first glance the return on our portfolio appears to be a random variable, but we have chosen the weighted average of the systematic risk components for each factor to be equal to zero ($\sum w_i b_{ik} = 0$). This eliminates all systematic risk. One might say that we have selected an arbitrage portfolio with zero beta in each factor. Consequently, the return on our arbitrage portfolio becomes a constant. Correct choice of the weights has eliminated all uncertainty, so that R_p is not a random variable. Therefore Eq. (6.52) becomes

$$R_p = \sum_i w_i E\left(\tilde{R}_i\right).$$

(6.55)

Recall that the arbitrage portfolio, so constructed, has no risk (of any kind) and requires no new wealth. If the return on the arbitrage portfolio were not zero, then it would be possible to achieve an infinite rate of return with no capital requirements and no risk. Such an opportunity is clearly impossible if the market is to be in equilibrium. In fact, if the individual arbitrageur is in equilibrium (hence content with his or her current portfolio), then the return on any and all arbitrage portfolios must be zero. In other words,

$$R_p = \sum_i w_i E\left(\tilde{R}_i\right) = 0.$$

(6.56)

Eqs. (6.51), (6.53c), and (6.56) are really statements in linear algebra. Any vector that is orthogonal to the constant vector, that is,[14]

$$\sum_{i=1}^{n} (w_i) \cdot \mathbf{e} = 0,$$

and to each of the coefficient vectors, that is,

$$\sum_i w_i b_{ik} = 0 \quad \text{for each } k,$$

must also be orthogonal to the vector of expected returns, that is,

$$\sum_i w_i E\left(\tilde{R}_i\right) = 0.$$

An algebraic consequence of this statement is that the expected return vector must be a linear combination of the constant vector and the coefficient vectors. Algebraically, there must exist a set of $k + 1$ coefficients, $\lambda_0, \lambda_1, \ldots, \lambda_k$ such that

$$E(\tilde{R}_i) = \lambda_0 + \lambda_1 b_{i1} + \cdots + \lambda_k b_{ik}.$$

(6.57)

Recall that the b_{ik} are the "sensitivities" of the returns on the ith security to the kth factor. If there is a riskless asset with a riskless rate of return, R_f, then $b_{0k} = 0$ and

$$R_f = \lambda_0.$$

Hence Eq. (6.45) can be rewritten in "excess returns form" as

$$E(R_i) - R_f = \lambda_1 b_{i1} + \cdots + \lambda_k b_{ik}.$$

(6.58)

----

[14] Note that Eq. (6.40) says that the sum of the investment weights equals zero. This is really a no-wealth constraint. No new wealth is required to take an arbitrage position. Recall that $\mathbf{e}$ is a column vector of ones.

Figure 6.13 The arbitrage pricing line.

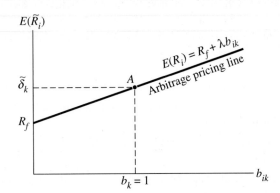

Figure 6.13 illustrates the arbitrage pricing relationship (6.58) assuming that there is only a single stochastic factor, k. In equilibrium, all assets must fall on the *arbitrage pricing line*. A natural interpretation for λ_k is that it represents the risk premium (i.e., the price of risk), in equilibrium, for the kth factor. Because the arbitrage pricing relationship is linear, we can use the slope-intercept definition of a straight line to rewrite Eq. (6.58) as

$$E(R_i) = R_f + \left[\overline{\delta}_k - R_f\right]b_{ik},$$

where $\overline{\delta}_k$ is the expected return on a portfolio with unit sensitivity to the kth factor and zero sensitivity to all other factors. Therefore the risk premium, λ_k, is equal to the difference between (1) the expectation of a portfolio that has unit response to the kth factor and zero response to the other factors and (2) the risk-free rate, R_f:

$$\lambda_k = \overline{\delta}_k - R_f.$$

In general the arbitrage pricing theory can be rewritten as

$$E(R_i) - R_f = \left[\overline{\delta}_1 - R_f\right]b_{i1} + \cdots + \left[\overline{\delta}_k - R_f\right]b_{ik}. \tag{6.59}$$

If Eq. (6.59) is interpreted as a linear regression equation (assuming that the vectors of returns have a joint normal distribution and that the factors have been linearly transformed so that their transformed vectors are orthonormal), then the coefficients, b_{ik}, are defined in exactly the same way as beta in the capital asset pricing model, that is,

$$b_{ik} = \frac{\text{COV}(R_i, \delta_k)}{\text{VAR}(\delta_k)} \tag{6.60}$$

where

$$\text{COV}(R_i, \delta_k) = \text{the covariance between the } i\text{th asset's returns and the linear}$$
$$\text{transformation of the } k\text{th factor,}$$

$$\text{VAR}(\delta_k) = \text{the variance of the linear transformation of the } k\text{th factor.}$$

Hence the CAPM is seen to be a special case of the APT (where asset returns are assumed to be joint normal).

The arbitrage pricing theory is much more robust than the capital asset pricing model for several reasons:

1. The APT makes no assumptions about the empirical distribution of asset returns.

2. The APT makes no strong assumptions about individuals' utility functions (at least nothing stronger than greed and risk aversion).

3. The APT allows the equilibrium returns of assets to be dependent on many factors, not just one (e.g., beta).

4. The APT yields a statement about the relative pricing of any subset of assets; hence one need not measure the entire universe of assets in order to test the theory.

5. There is no special role for the market portfolio in the APT, whereas the CAPM requires that the market portfolio be efficient.

6. The APT is easily extended to a multiperiod framework (see Ross [1976]).

Suppose that asset returns are determined by two underlying factors such as unanticipated changes in real output and unanticipated inflation. The arbitrage pricing theory can easily account for the effect of changes in both factors on asset returns. Because the capital asset pricing model relies on a single factor (the market index), it cannot do as well. Using the CAPM is a little like being lost in the clouds while piloting a private plane. You call the air controller and ask, "Where am I?" If the controller is using a unidimensional model like the CAPM, he or she is likely to respond, "Two hundred miles from New York City." Obviously, this is not a very helpful answer. A multidimensional model like the APT would be more useful. It would be nice to know latitude, longitude, and altitude.

Figure 6.14 illustrates the same point. The factor loadings (or factor sensitivities), b_{i1} and b_{i2}, for our two hypothetical factors—changes in unanticipated real output and changes in unanticipated inflation—are plotted on the axes. The origin represents the risk-free rate that is the rate of return received when an asset has zero beta in both factors. Points along the diagonal dashed lines have equal expected return but not the same risk. For example, all points along the line OJ have an expected rate of return equal to the risk-free rate but are not riskless portfolios. If the risk-free rate is 10%, one can obtain that rate either with a truly riskless portfolio that pays 10% in every state of nature or with a second portfolio that has positive sensitivity to one factor and negative sensitivity to the other factor.

Suppose the arbitrage pricing model, Eq. (6.59),

$$E(R_i) - R_f = \left[\bar{\delta}_1 - R_f\right] b_{i1} + \left[\bar{\delta}_2 - R_f\right] b_{i2},$$

is estimated to have the following numerical values: $R_f = 10\%$, $\bar{\delta}_1 = 20\%$, and $\bar{\delta}_2 = 15\%$. If b_{i1} is plotted on the vertical axis, then the vertical intercept for a given return $E(R_i)$ is

$$\alpha = \text{vertical intercept} = \frac{E(R_i) - R_f}{\bar{\delta}_1 - R_f},$$

Figure 6.14 A graph of the CAPM and the APT.

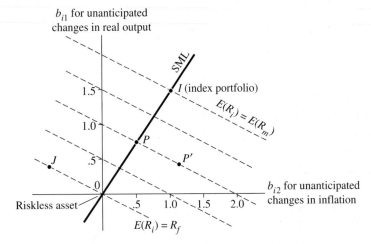

and the slope of the equal return line is

$$m = \text{slope} = -\frac{\bar{\delta}_2 - R_f}{\bar{\delta}_1 - R_f},$$

where the equation for the return line is $b_{i1} = \alpha + m b_{i2}$.

Next, suppose that we know that a CAPM efficient index portfolio has been chosen, that its expected return is 30%, and that its sensitivity to changes in unanticipated real output and changes in unanticipated inflation are $b_{i1} = 1.5$ and $b_{i2} = 1.0$. The CAPM index portfolio is plotted at point I in Fig. 6.14. We know from the CAPM, Eq. (6.9), that the security market line is represented by all linear combinations of the risk-free asset and the market index portfolio. Therefore the security market line is represented by the ray OI from the origin (which is the risk-free asset) to the efficient index portfolio (point I).

The CAPM measures risk only in one dimension, rather than two. If we are told that the portfolio's CAPM β is .5, then it will plot at point P in Fig. 6.14, halfway between the riskless asset and the index portfolio. However, according to the APT there are an infinite number of portfolios, all with the same expected return as portfolio P and each having a different sensitivity to the APT risk parameters b_{i1} and b_{i2}. If people are in fact sensitive to more than one type of risk when choosing among portfolios of equal return, then the APT is superior to the CAPM because the CAPM is unidimensional in risk. It is perfectly reasonable that portfolio P' might be preferred to portfolio P by some investors because it has the same return as portfolio P but a preferable combination of sensitivities to the underlying factors. For example, a public pension fund manager might not care much about the sensitivity of the value of the fund to industrial production but might be very concerned about hedging against unexpected changes in inflation. Later on we shall discuss some empirical work that provides evidence that more than one factor is significant in explaining security returns.

2. A Numerical Example

To illustrate how arbitrage pricing might be employed in practice, suppose that empirical work reveals that the expected returns on assets can be explained by two factors, F_1 and F_2. Table 6.6

Table 6.6 Data for an APT Example

State of Nature	Prob.	Asset Returns (%)			Transformed Factor Changes (%)	
		$\widetilde{X}$	$\widetilde{Y}$	$\widetilde{Z}$	$\overline{\delta}_1$	$\overline{\delta}_2$
Horrid	.2	−55.23	623.99	53.00	−10.00	−5.00
Bad	.2	70.70	10.00	413.37	−5.00	38.48
Average	.2	−9.00	25.00	−1493.12	25.00	8.00
Good	.2	−12.47	−3771.42	1058.75	40.00	−1.44
Great	.2	61.00	3237.44	83.00	50.00	0.00

shows the subjectively estimated returns on three assets (X, Y, and Z) and the changes in (orthogonal transformations of) the two factors for five equally likely states of nature. To make the problem tractable, assume that all factors and returns are normally distributed. In addition, suppose we know that the expected return on the risk-free asset, R_f, is 10%.

One of the requirements of the factor analysis program usually used to test the arbitrage pricing model is that we are working with linear transformations of the underlying factors. The transformations must be orthogonal (i.e., the product of their row and column vectors must equal zero). This is shown below for the transformed factors in Table 6.6:

$$[-10 \quad -5 \quad 25 \quad 40 \quad 50] \begin{bmatrix} -5.00 \\ 38.48 \\ 8.00 \\ -1.44 \\ 0 \end{bmatrix} = 0.$$

How can we tell from the bewildering set of numbers in Table 6.6 whether or not there are any arbitrage opportunities? And if there are, how can we take advantage of them by forming an arbitrage portfolio?

If there are only two factors that govern all returns, then the APT becomes

$$E(R_i) = R_f + \left[\overline{\delta}_1 - R_f \right] b_{i1} + \left[\overline{\delta}_2 - R_f \right] b_{i2}.$$

The data from Table 6.6 can be used to compute all the terms on the right-hand side of this equation. The factor loadings (or sensitivities) are the same as beta, Eq. (6.60), given the assumption of normally distributed returns and orthogonal transformations of the factors. Using asset X as an example, we need to calculate

$$b_{x1} = \frac{\text{COV}(X, \delta_1)}{\text{VAR}(\delta_1)} = \frac{285.0}{570.0} = .5.$$

The computations are done in Table 6.7. Given that $b_{x1} = .5$, we know that a 1% increase in factor 1 will result in a .5% increase in the return on security X. We can think of the factor loadings (or sensitivities) in exactly the same way as we thought of beta (systematic risk) in the CAPM. The expectations of each asset and transformed factor and the factor loadings (sensitivities) are given in Table 6.8. By substituting these data into the APT equation, we can determine the market

Table 6.7 Calculating b_{x1} from the Data in Table 6.6

$p_i X_i$	$p_i \delta_{1i}$	$p_i(\delta_{1i} - \bar{\delta}_1)^2$
$.2(-55.23) = -11.046$	$.2(-10) = -2.0$	$.2(-10 - 20)^2 = 180$
$.2(70.70) = 14.140$	$.2(-5) = -1.0$	$.2(-5 - 20)^2 = 125$
$.2(-9.00) = -1.800$	$.2(25) = 5.0$	$.2(25 - 20)^2 = 5$
$.2(-12.47) = -2.494$	$.2(40) = 8.0$	$.2(40 - 20)^2 = 80$
$.2(-61.00) = 12.200$	$.2(50) = 10.0$	$.2(50 - 20)^2 = 180$
$\bar{X} = 11.000$	$\bar{\delta}_1 = 20.0$	$\mathrm{VAR}(\delta_1) = 570$

$p_i(X_i - \bar{X})(\delta - \bar{\delta}_1)$

$.2(-66.23)(-30) = 397.38$
$.2(59.70)(-25) = -298.50$
$.2(-20.00)(5) = -20.00$
$.2(-23.47)(20) = -93.98$ $b_{x1} = \frac{285.00}{570.00} = .5$
$.2(50.00)(30) = 300.00$

$\mathrm{COV}(X, \delta_1) = 285.00$

Table 6.8 Statistics Computed from Table 6.6

Asset	R_1	Factor Loadings b_{i1}	Factor Loadings b_{i2}	Transformed Factor Expectations
X	11%	.5	2.0	$\bar{\delta}_1 = 20\%$
Y	25	1.0	1.5	$\bar{\delta}_2 = 8\%$
Z	23	1.5	1.0	

equilibrium rate of return, $E(R_i)$, for each of the three assets. This is done below:

$$E(R_x) = .10 + [.20 - .10]0.5 + [.08 - .10]2.0 = 11\%,$$

$$E(R_y) = .10 + [.20 - .10]1.0 + [.08 - .10]1.5 = 17\%,$$

$$E(R_z) = .10 + [.20 - .10]1.5 + [.08 - .10]1.0 = 23\%.$$

Note that the equilibrium return, $E(R_i)$, on assets X and Z is the same as the projected return, $\bar{R}_i$, computed from the data. Hence no arbitrage opportunities exist for trading in these two assets. On the other hand the projected return on asset Y, $\bar{R}_y$, is 25% when computed from the data, and the market equilibrium return, $E(R_y)$, is only 17%. Therefore by selling the correct proportions of assets X and Z and buying asset Y, we can form an arbitrage portfolio that requires no new capital, has no change in risk, and earns a positive rate of return.

Suppose that we currently have one third of our wealth in each of the three assets. How should we change our portfolio to form a riskless arbitrage position? It turns out that so long as there are more assets than factors, there are virtually an infinite number of ways of forming arbitrage portfolios. But let us suppose that we desire to put the maximum investment into asset Y without actually selling short either X or Z. Our investment proportion in Y would go from one third to one; thus the change in holdings of asset Y would be $w_y = \frac{2}{3}$. We also require that the change portfolio have zero beta in each factor and that it need no net wealth. These conditions are stated in Eqs. (6.51) and (6.53c), which are repeated below:

$$\left(\sum_{i=1}^{3} w_i \right) \cdot \mathbf{e} = \mathbf{0}.$$

$$\sum_{i=1}^{3} w_i b_{ik} = 0 \quad \text{for each } k.$$

Expanding these equations, we have

$$w_x + w_y + w_z = 0,$$

$$w_x b_{x1} + w_y b_{y1} + w_z b_{z1} = 0 \quad \text{for factor 1,}$$

$$w_x b_{x2} + w_y b_{y2} + w_z b_{z2} = 0 \quad \text{for factor 2.}$$

And substituting in the numbers of our problem, we get

$$w_x + \frac{2}{3} + w_z = 0,$$

$$w_x(.5) + \frac{2}{3}(1.0) + w_z(1.5) = 0,$$

$$w_x(2.0) + \frac{2}{3}(1.5) + w_z(1.0) = 0.$$

Solving, we find that

$$w_x = -\frac{1}{3}, \qquad w_y = \frac{2}{3}, \qquad w_z = -\frac{1}{3}.$$

Thus we would sell all our holdings in assets X and Z and invest the proceeds in asset Y.

This strategy would require no new wealth and would have no change in risk. Note that our risk position before making the change was

$$\frac{1}{3}(.5) + \frac{1}{3}(1.0) + 0(1.5) = 1.0 \quad \text{for factor 1,}$$

$$\frac{1}{3}(2) + \frac{1}{3}(1.5) + \frac{1}{3}(1.0) = 1.5 \quad \text{for factor 2.}$$

Figure 6.15 Arbitrage pricing plane for two factors.

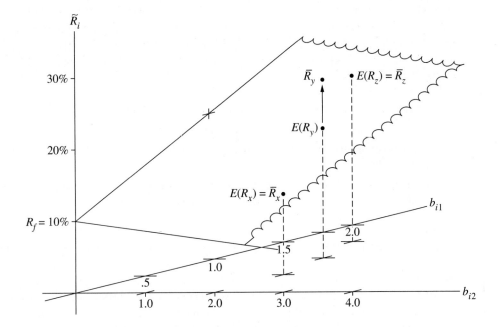

Since our systematic risk has not changed, the extra systematic risk created by the arbitrage portfolio is zero.[15] Our originally projected portfolio return was

$$\frac{1}{3}(11\%) + \frac{1}{3}(25\%) + \frac{1}{3}(23\%) = 19.67\%.$$

But after investing in the arbitrage portfolio, we project a rate of return of

$$0(11\%) + 1(25\%) + 0(23\%) = 25\%.$$

Thus the arbitrage portfolio increases our return by 5.33% without changing our systematic risk.

Figure 6.15 provides a visual description of the example problem. Expected rates of return are plotted on the vertical axis, and asset betas in each of the two factors are plotted along the horizontal axes. Note that the expected returns for assets X and Z plot exactly on the arbitrage pricing plane. They are in equilibrium. But asset Y plots above the plane. Its return lies considerably above what the market requires for its factor loadings, b_{y1} and b_{y2}. Hence an arbitrage opportunity exists. If enough people take advantage of it, the price of asset Y will rise, thereby forcing its rate of return down and back into equilibrium.

---

[15] Because there is idiosyncratic risk to contend with, total risk will in fact change. However, with well-diversified arbitrage portfolios this problem vanishes because diversification reduces idiosyncratic risk until it is negligible.

M. $\mathcal{E}$mpirical Tests of the Arbitrage Pricing Theory

Papers by Gehr [1975], Roll and Ross [1980], Reinganum [1981a], Chen [1983], Chen, Roll, and Ross [1986], and Conner and Korajczyk [1993] have tested the APT using data on equity rates of return for New York and American Stock Exchange listed stocks. The usual empirical procedure has the following steps:

1. Collect a time series of stock returns data for a group of stocks.
2. Compute the empirical variance-covariance matrix from the returns data.
3. Use a (maximum-likelihood) factor analysis procedure to identify the number of factors and their factor loadings, b_{ik}.
4. Use the estimated factor loadings, b_{ik}, to explain the cross-sectional variation of individual estimated expected returns and to measure the size and statistical significance of the estimated risk premia associated with each factor.

The Roll and Ross [1980] study used daily returns data for NYSE and AMEX companies listed on the exchanges on both July 3, 1962, and December 31, 1972. There were a maximum of 2,619 daily returns for each stock. The 1,260 securities selected were divided alphabetically into groups of 30. For each group of 30 the procedure described above was carried out. The analysis showed that there are at least three and probably four "priced" factors. There may be other zero-priced factors, but this procedure cannot identify them because their regression coefficients in step 4 would be zero.

One of the frustrating things about using factor analysis to test the APT is that this procedure cannot tell us what the factors are. However, we can reject the APT if a specified alternative variable such as the total variance of individual returns, firm size, or the asset's last period return were to be significant in explaining the expected returns. Roll and Ross [1980], after correcting for the problem that positive skewness in lognormal returns can create dependence between the sample mean and the sample standard deviation, found that the total variance of security returns does not add any explanatory power for estimated expected returns. Therefore the APT could not be rejected on this basis. Although a different procedure was employed by Chen [1983], he was able to confirm this result. He also found that the asset's last period return added no explanatory power.

Currently there is a question whether or not firm size can be used to refute the APT because it adds explanatory power to the factor loadings. Reinganum [1981a] finds that it does. His test consisted of estimating the factor loadings in year $(t - 1)$ for all securities, then combining securities with similar loadings into control portfolios. In year t, excess security returns are computed by subtracting the daily control portfolio returns from the daily security returns. Finally, with excess returns in hand, the securities are ranked on the basis of the market value of all the firm's outstanding common stock at period $(t - 1)$. The APT predicts (if factor loadings are stationary across time) that all deciles of the market value ranked excess returns should have the same mean. Reinganum finds that there are significant differences between the mean excess returns and rejects the APT. Chen [1983], on the other hand, finds that firm size adds no explanatory power. His procedure uses Reinganum's data for the market value of each firm's equity. He divides the sample of firms into two groups—those with greater than the median market value and those with less. Then portfolios are formed from the high- and low-value firms so that the following conditions are satisfied: (1) each security in the portfolio has nonnegative weight and the weight should not be too far from $1/n$, where n is the number of securities in the portfolio, and (2) the resultant two portfolios have exactly the same factor loadings (arbitrage risk factors) in each factor. The factor loadings are determined by using returns data from odd days during each test period; the even-days returns from the same test period are used for measuring the average portfolio returns of the high- and low-valued portfolios. If the APT is correct, the returns of the two portfolios should not be statistically different because they are selected to have the same "risk" as determined by the factor loadings. In only one of the four periods tested is the difference in returns statistically different at the 95% confidence level. Therefore Chen argues that firm size effects have insufficient explanatory power to reject the APT.

There is one parameter in the APT, namely the intercept term, $\lambda_0 = R_f$, that should be identical across groups of securities when the model is estimated separately for each group during a time period. Other factors need not be the same because the factor loadings are not unique from group to group. For example, factor 1 in group A might correspond to factor 3 in group B. The intercept term, λ_0, however, has the same meaning in each group because it is the return on an asset that has no sensitivity to the common factors. Roll and Ross [1980] tested for the equivalence of the $\widehat{\lambda}_0$ terms across 38 groups and found absolutely no evidence that the intercept terms were different. Again, the APT could not be rejected.

A direct comparison of the APT and the CAPM was performed by Chen [1983]. First, the APT model was fitted to the data as in the following equation:

$$\widetilde{R}_i = \widehat{\lambda}_0 + \widehat{\lambda}_1 b_{i1} + \cdots + \widehat{\lambda}_n b_{in} + \widehat{\varepsilon}_i. \qquad \text{(APT)}$$

Then the CAPM was fitted to the same data:

$$\widetilde{R}_i = \widehat{\lambda}_0 + \widehat{\lambda}_1 \widehat{\beta}_i + \widetilde{\eta}_i. \qquad \text{(CAPM)}$$

Next the CAPM residuals, η_i, were regressed on the arbitrage factor loadings, $\widehat{\lambda}_k$, and the APT residuals, ε_i, were regressed on the CAPM coefficients. The results showed that the APT could explain a statistically significant portion of the CAPM residual variance, but the CAPM could not explain the APT residuals. This is strong evidence that the APT is a more reasonable model for explaining the cross-sectional variance in asset returns.

Although it is mathematically impossible to use factor analysis to unambiguously identify the underlying factors that drive security returns, Chen, Roll, and Ross [1986] have correlated various macroeconomic variables with returns on five portfolios that mimic what the underlying factors might be. Four macroeconomic variables were significant:

1. An index of industrial production
2. Changes in a default risk premium (measured by the differences in promised yields to maturity on AAA versus Baa corporate bonds)
3. Twists in the yield curve (measured by differences in promised yields to maturity on long- and short-term government bonds)
4. Unanticipated inflation

The economic logic underlying these variables seems to make sense. Common stock prices are the present values of discounted cash flows. The industrial production index is obviously related to profitability. The remaining variables are related to the discount rate. Conner and Korajczyk [1993] find evidence supporting the existence of one to six factors in a data set consisting of monthly returns of NYSE and AMEX stocks from 1967 to 1991.

The intuition behind these factors is useful for portfolio management. For example, it has often been stated that common stocks are not a good hedge against inflation. Although it is true if one holds an equally weighted portfolio of all stocks, the logic of factor analysis suggests that there is a well-diversified subset of common stocks that is in fact a good hedge against inflation. Since the factors are mutually orthogonal, one can (at least in principle) choose a portfolio that is hedged against inflation risk without changing the portfolio sensitivity to any of the other three above-mentioned factors.

*S*ummary

This chapter has derived two theoretical models, the CAPM and the APT, that enable us to price risky assets in equilibrium. Within the CAPM framework the appropriate measure of risk is the covariance of returns between the risky asset in question and the market portfolio of all assets. The APT model is more general. Many factors (not just the market portfolio) may explain asset returns. For each factor the appropriate measure of risk is the sensitivity of asset returns to changes in the factor. For normally distributed returns the sensitivity is analogous to the beta (or systematic risk) of the CAPM.

The CAPM was shown to provide a useful conceptual framework for capital budgeting and the cost of capital. It is also reasonably unchanged by the relaxation of many of the unrealistic assumptions that made its derivation simpler. Finally, although the model is not perfectly validated by empirical tests, its main implications are upheld—namely, that systematic risk (beta) is a valid measure of risk, that the model is linear, and that the trade-off between return and risk is positive.

The APT can also be applied to cost of capital and capital budgeting problems. The earliest empirical tests of the APT have shown that asset returns are explained by three or possibly more factors and have ruled out the variance of an asset's own returns as one of the factors.

PROBLEM SET

6.1 Let us assume a normal distribution of returns and risk-averse utility functions. Under what conditions will all investors demand the same portfolio of risky assets?

6.2 The following data have been developed for the Donovan Company, the manufacturer of an advanced line of adhesives:

State	Probability	Market Return, R_m	Return for the Firm, R_j
1	.1	−.15	−.30
2	.3	.05	.00
3	.4	.15	.20
4	.2	.20	.50

The risk-free rate is 6%. Calculate the following:

  (a) The expected market return.
  (b) The variance of the market return.
  (c) The expected return for the Donovan Company.

(d) The covariance of the return for the Donovan Company with the market return.

(e) Write the equation of the security market line.

(f) What is the required return for the Donovan Company? How does this compare with its expected return?

6.3 The following data have been developed for the Milliken Company:

Year	Market Return	Company Returns
1978	.27	.25
1977	.12	.05
1976	−.03	−.05
1975	.12	.15
1974	−.03	−.10
1973	.27	.30

The yield to maturity on Treasury bills is .066 and is expected to remain at this point for the foreseeable future. Calculate the following:

(a) The expected market return.

(b) The variance of the market return.

(c) The expected rate of return for the Milliken Company.

(d) The covariance of the return for the Milliken Company with the return on the market.

(e) Write the equation of the security market line.

(f) What is the required return for the Milliken Company?

6.4 For the data in Table Q6.4 (page 190), perform the indicated calculations.

6.5 For the data in Table Q6.5 (page 191), calculate the items indicated.

6.6 What are the assumptions sufficient to guarantee that the market portfolio is an efficient portfolio?

6.7 In the CAPM is there any way to identify the investors who are more risk averse? Explain. How would your answer change if there were not a riskless asset?

6.8 Given risk-free borrowing and lending, efficient portfolios have no unsystematic risk. True or false? Explain.

6.9 What is the beta of an efficient portfolio with $E(R_j) = 20\%$ if $R_f = 5\%$, $E(R_m) = 15\%$, and $\sigma_m = 20\%$? What is its σ_j? What is its correlation with the market?

6.10 Given the facts of Problem 6.9, and that the common stock of the Rapid Rolling Corporation has $E(R_k) = 25\%$ and $\sigma_k^2 = 52\%$, what is the systematic risk of the common stock? What is its unsystematic risk?

6.11 (a) If the expected rate of return on the market portfolio is 14% and the risk-free rate is 6%, find the beta for a portfolio that has expected rate of return of 10%. What assumptions concerning this portfolio and/or market conditions do you need to make to calculate the portfolio's beta?

(b) What percentage of this portfolio must an individual put into the market portfolio in order to achieve an expected return of 10%?

Table Q6.4 Estimates of Market Parameters

Year	S&P 500 Index	Percentage Change in Price	Dividend Yield	Percentage Return	Return Deviation	Market Variance	
	P_t	$\dfrac{P_t}{P_{t-1}} - 1$	$\dfrac{Div_t}{P_t}$	R_{mt} $(3+4)$	$(R_{mt} - \overline{R}_m)$ $(5 - R_m)$	$(R_{mt} - \overline{R}_m)^2$ (6^2)	R_f
(1)	(2)	(3)	(4)	(5)	(6)	(7)	(8)
1960	55.84						
1961	66.27		.0298				.03
1962	62.38		.0337				.03
1963	69.87		.0317				.03
1964	81.37		.0301				.04
1965	88.17		.0300				.04
1966	85.26		.0340				.04
1967	91.93		.0320				.05
1968	98.70		.0307				.05
1969	97.84		.0324				.07
1970	83.22		.0383				.06

a. $\overline{R}_m = ?$
b. $VAR(R_m) = ?$
c. $\sigma(R_m) = ?$

6.12 You believe that the Beta Alpha Watch Company will be worth $100 per share one year from now. How much are you willing to pay for one share today if the risk-free rate is 8%, the expected rate of return on the market is 18%, and the company's beta is 2.0?

6.13 Given the following variance-covariance matrix and expected returns vector (for assets X and Y, respectively) for a two-asset world:

$$\Sigma = \begin{bmatrix} .01 & 0 \\ 0 & .0064 \end{bmatrix}, \quad \overline{R}'_I = [.2 \quad .1]$$

(a) What is the expected return of a zero-beta portfolio, given that 50% of the index portfolio is invested in asset X and asset Y?
(b) What is the vector of weights in the global minimum-variance portfolio?
(c) What is the covariance between the global minimum-variance portfolio and the zero-beta portfolio?
(d) What is the equation of the market line?

6.14 Given the following variance-covariance matrix, calculate the covariance between portfolio A, which has 10% in asset 1 and 90% in asset 2, and portfolio B, which has 60% in asset 1 and 40% in asset 2:

Table Q6.5 Calculations of Beta for General Motors

Year	GM Price	Percentage Change in Price	Dividend Yield	Percentage Return	Deviation of Returns	Variance of Returns	Covariance with Market
				R_{jt}	$(R_{jt} - \overline{R}_j)$	$(R_{jt} - \overline{R}_j)^2$	$(R_{jt} - \overline{R}_j)(R_{mt} - \overline{R}_m)$
	P_t	$\dfrac{P_t}{P_{t-1}} - 1$	$\dfrac{Div_t}{P_t}$	$(3 + 4)$	$(5 - \overline{R}_j)$	(6^2)	**(Col. 6 × Q6.4 Col. 6)**
(1)	(2)	(3)	(4)	(5)	(6)	(7)	(8)
1960	48						
1961	49		.05				
1962	52		.06				
1963	74		.05				
1964	90		.05				
1965	102		.05				
1966	87		.05				
1967	78		.05				
1968	81		.05				
1969	74		.06				
1970	70		.05				

a. $\overline{R}_j = ?$
b. $VAR(R_j) = ?$
c. $COV(R_j, R_m) = ?$
d. $\beta_j = ?$

$$\Sigma = \begin{bmatrix} .01 & -.02 \\ -.02 & .04 \end{bmatrix}$$

6.15 Suppose that securities are priced as if they are traded in a two-parameter economy. You have forecast the correlation coefficient between the rate of return on Knowlode Mutual Fund and the market portfolio at .8. Your forecast of the standard deviations of the rates of return are .25 for Knowlode, and .20 for the market portfolio. How would you combine the Knowlode Fund and a riskless security to obtain a portfolio with a beta of 1.6?

6.16 You currently have 50% of your wealth in a risk-free asset and 50% in the four assets below:

Asset	Expected Return on Asset i (%)	β_i	Percentage Invested in Asset i (%)
$i = 1$	7.6	.2	10
$i = 2$	12.4	.8	10
$i = 3$	15.6	1.3	10
$i = 4$	18.8	1.6	20

If you want an expected rate of return of 12%, you can obtain it by selling some of your holdings of the risk-free asset and using the proceeds to buy the equally weighted market portfolio. If this is the way you decide to revise your portfolio, what will the set of weights in your portfolio be? If you hold only the risk-free asset and the market portfolio, what set of weights would give you an expected 12% return?

6.17 The market price of a security is $40, the security's expected rate of return is 13%, the riskless rate of interest is 7%, and the market risk premium, $[E(R_m) - R_f]$, is 8%. What will be the security's current price if its expected future payoff remains the same but the covariance of its rate of return with the market portfolio doubles?

6.18 Suppose you are the manager of an investment fund in a two-parameter economy. Given the following forecast:

$$E(R_m) = .16, \qquad \sigma(R_m) = .20, \qquad R_f = .08$$

(a) Would you recommend investment in a security with $E(R_j) = .12$ and $\text{COV}(R_j, R_m) = .01$? (*Note:* Assume that this price change has no significant effect on the position of the security market line.)

(b) Suppose that in the next period security R_j has earned only 5% over the preceding period. How would you explain this ex post return?

6.19 Why is the separation principle still valid in a world with

(a) nonmarketable assets?

(b) a nonstochastic risk-free rate?

6.20 Assume that the mean-variance opportunity set is constructed from only two risky assets, A and B. Their variance-covariance matrix is

$$\Sigma = \begin{bmatrix} .0081 & 0 \\ 0 & .0025 \end{bmatrix}.$$

Asset A has an expected return of 30%, and Asset B has an expected return of 20%. Answer the following questions:

(a) Suppose investor I chooses his "market portfolio" to consist of 75% in asset A and 25% in asset B, whereas investor J chooses a different "market portfolio" with 50% in asset A and 50% in asset B.

Weights chosen by I are $[.75 \quad .25]$.

Weights chosen by J are $[.50 \quad .50]$.

Given these facts, what beta will each investor calculate for asset A?

(b) Given your answer to part (a), which of the following is true and why?

1. Investor I will require a higher rate of return on asset A than will investor J.

2. They will both require the same return on asset A.

3. Investor J will require a higher rate of return on asset A than will investor I.

(c) Compute the zero-beta portfolios and the equations for the security market line for each investor.

6.21 Ms. Bethel, manager of the Humongous Mutual Fund, knows that her fund currently is well diversified and that it has a CAPM beta of 1.0. The risk-free rate is 8% and the CAPM risk premium,

$\left[E(R_m) - R_f \right]$, is 6.2%. She has been learning about measures of risk and knows that there are (at least) two factors: changes in industrial production index, $\bar{\delta}_1$, and unexpected inflation, $\bar{\delta}_2$. The APT equation is

$$E(R_i) - R_f = \left[\bar{\delta}_1 - R_f \right] b_{i1} + \left[\bar{\delta}_2 - R_f \right] b_{i2},$$

$$E(R_i) = .08 + [.05]b_{i1} + [.11]b_{i2}.$$

(a) If her portfolio currently has a sensitivity to the first factor of $b_{p1} = -.5$, what is its sensitivity to unexpected inflation?

(b) If she rebalances her portfolio to keep the same expected return but reduce her exposure to inflation to zero (i.e., $b_{p2} = 0$), what will its sensitivity to the first factor become?

REFERENCES

Amihud, Y., and H. Mendelson, "Asset Pricing and the Bid-Ask Spread," *Journal of Financial Economics,* 1986, Vol. 17, 223–250.

Bansal, R., and S. Viswanathan, "No Arbitrage and Arbitrage Pricing," *Journal of Finance,* Vol. 48, 1993, 1231–1262.

Banz, R. W., "The Relationship between Return and Market Value of Common Stocks," *Journal of Financial Economics*, March 1981, 3–18.

Basu, S., "Investment Performance of Common Stocks in Relation to Their Price-Earnings Ratios: A Test of the Efficient Markets Hypothesis," *Journal of Finance*, June 1977, 663–682.

Berk, J., R. Green, and V. Naik, "Optimal Investment, Growth Options, and Security Returns," *Journal of Finance,* 1999, Vol. 54, No. 5, 1553–1607.

Black, F., "Capital Market Equilibrium with Restricted Borrowing," *Journal of Business*, July 1972, 444–455.

Black, F., M. C. Jensen, and M. Scholes, "The Capital Asset Pricing Model: Some Empirical Tests," in M. C. Jensen, ed., *Studies in the Theory of Capital Markets*. Praeger, New York, 1972, 79–124.

Blume, M., "Portfolio Theory: A Step toward Its Practical Application," *Journal of Business*, April 1970, 152–173.

————, "On the Assessment of Risk," *Journal of Finance*, March 1971, 1–10.

Blume, M., and I. Friend, "A New Look at the Capital Asset Pricing Model," *Journal of Finance*, March 1973, 19–34.

Blume, M., and F. Husick, "Price, Beta and Exchange Listing," *Journal of Finance*, May 1973, 283–299.

Blume, M., and R. Stambaugh, "Biases in Computed Returns: An Application to the Size Effect," *Journal of Financial Economics*, November 1983, 387–404.

Bower, D., R. Bower, and D. Logue, "Arbitrage Pricing Theory and Utility Stock Returns," *Journal of Finance*, September 1984, 1041–1054.

Breeden, D. T., "An Intertemporal Asset Pricing Model with Stochastic Consumption and Investment Opportunities," *Journal of Financial Economics*, September 1979, 265–296.

Brennan, M. J., "Taxes, Market Valuation and Corporation Financial Policy," *National Tax Journal,* December 1970, 417–427.

Brennan, M. J., T. Chordra, and A. Subrahmanyam, "Alternative Factor Specifications, Security Characteristics, and the Cross-Section of Expected returns," *Journal of Financial Economics,* 1998, Vol. 49, 345–373.

Brown, S., W. Goetzman, and S. Ross, "Survival," *Journal of Finance*, July 1995, Vol. 50, No. 3, 853–873.

Chamberlain, G., and M. Rothschild, "Arbitrage, Factor Structure, and Mean-Variance Analysis on Large Asset Markets," *Econometrica*, September 1983, 1281–1304.

Chen, N. F., "Some Empirical Tests of the Theory of Arbitrage Pricing," *Journal of Finance*, December 1983, 1393–1414.

Chen, N. F., and J. Ingersoll, Jr., "Exact Pricing in Linear Factor Models with Finitely Many Assets," *Journal of Finance*, June 1983, 985–988.

Chen, N. F., R. Roll, and S. Ross, "Economic Forces and the Stock Market," *Journal of Business,* 1986, Vol. 59, 383–403.

Chordra, T., A. Subrahmanyam, and V. R. Anshuman, "Trading Activity and Expected Stock Returns," *Journal of Financial Economics,* 2001, Vol. 59, 3–32.

Clark, P. K., "A Subordinated Stochastic Process Model with Finite Variance for Speculative Prices," *Econometrica*, January 1973, 135–155.

Conner, G., and R. Korajczyk, "Risk and Return in an Equilibrium APT: Application of a New Test Methodology," *Journal of Financial Economics,* 1988, Vol. 21, 255–290.

———, "A Test for the Number of Factors in an Approximate Factor Model," *Journal of Finance,* 1993, Vol. 48, 1263–1291.

Copeland, T. E., and D. Mayers, "The Value Line Enigma (1965–1978): A Case Study of Performance Evaluation Issues," *Journal of Financial Economics*, November 1982, 289–322.

Cornell, B., "Asymmetric Information and Portfolio Performance Measurement," *Journal of Financial Economics*, December 1979, 381–390.

Daniel, K., and S. Titman, "Evidence on the Characteristics of Cross-Sectional Variation in Stock Returns," *Journal of Finance,* 1997, Vol. 52, 1–33.

Dhrymes, P., I. Friend, and B. Bultekin, "A Critical Reexamination of the Empirical Evidence on the Arbitrage Pricing Theory," *Journal of Finance*, June 1984, 323–346.

Dimson, E., "Risk Management When Shares Are Subject to Infrequent Trading," *Journal of Financial Economics*, June 1979, 197–226.

Dybvig, P., "An Explicit Bound on Individual Assets' Deviations from APT Pricing in a Finite Economy," *Journal of Financial Economics*, December 1983, 483–496.

Dybvig, P., and S. Ross, "Yes, the APT Is Testable," *Journal of Finance*, September 1985, 1173–1188.

Fama, E. F., "The Behavior of Stock Market Prices," *Journal of Business*, January 1965a, 34–105.

———, "Portfolio Analysis in a Stable Paretian Market," *Management Science*, January 1965b, 404–419.

———, "Risk, Return and Equilibrium: Some Clarifying Comments," *Journal of Finance*, March 1968, 29–40.

———, "Risk, Return and Equilibrium," *Journal of Political Economy*, January–February 1971, 30–55.

———, *Foundations of Finance*, Basic Books, New York, 1976.

Fama, E. F., and K. French, "On the Cross-Section of Expected Stock Returns," *Journal of Finance,* 1992, Vol. 47, 427–466.

———, "Size and Book-to-Market Factors in Earnings and Returns," *Journal of Finance,* 1995, Vol. 50, 131–155.

———, "Multifactor Explanations of Asset Pricing Analomies," *Journal of Finance,* 1996, Vol. 51, 55–84.

———, "The Equity Premium," *Journal of Finance,* 2002, Vol. 57, No. 2, 637–659.

Fama, E. F., and J. MacBeth, "Risk, Return and Equilibrium: Empirical Test," *Journal of Political Economy*, May–June 1973, 607–636.

Fama, E. F., and G. W. Schwert, "Human Capital and Capital Market Equilibrium," *Journal of Financial Economics*, January 1977, 95–125.

Ferson, W., and C. Harvey, "Conditioning Variables and the Cross-Section of Stock Returns," *Journal of Finance,* 1999, Vol. 54, 1325–1360.

Friend, I., and M. Blume, "Measurement of Portfolio Performance under Uncertainty," *American Economic Review*, September 1970, 561–575.

Friend, I., R. Westerfield, and M. Granito, "New Evidence on the Capital Asset Pricing Model," *Journal of Finance*, June 1978, 903–917.

Gehr, A., Jr., "Some Tests of the Arbitrage Pricing Theory," *Journal of Midwest Financial Economics*, March 1973, 91–135.

Gehr, A., Jr., and W. Ferson, "Testing Asset Pricing Models with Changing Expectations and an Unobservable Market Portfolio," *Journal of Financial Economics*, June 1985, 217–236.

Gibbons, M., "Multivariate Tests of Financial Models: A New Approach," *Journal of Financial Economics*, 1982, Vol. 10, No. 1, 3–28.

Grinblatt, M., and S. Titman, "Factor Pricing in a Finite Economy," *Journal of Financial Economics*, December 1983, 497–507.

Hamada, R. S., "The Effect of the Firm's Capital Structure on the Systematic Risk of Common Stocks," *Journal of Finance*, May 1972, 435–452.

Hansen, L., J. Heaton, and E. Luttmer, "Econometric Evaluation of Asset Pricing Models," *Review of Financial Studies,* 1995, Vol. 8, 237–274.

Hodrick, R., and X. Zhang, "Evaluating the Specification Errors of Asset Pricing Models," *Journal of Financial Economics,* 2001, Vol. 62, 327–376.

Huberman, G., "A Simple Approach to Arbitrage Pricing Theory," *Journal of Economic Theory*, 1982, 183–191.

Ibbotson, R., and R. Sinqefield, "Stocks, Bonds, Bills and Inflation: Year-by-Year Historical Returns (1926–1974)," *Journal of Business*, January 1976, 11–47.

Ibbotson Associates, *Ibbotson 2002 Stocks, Bonds, Bills and Inflation (SBBI) Year Book.*

Jaganathan, R., and Z. Wang, "The Conditional CAPM and the Cross-Section of Returns," *Journal of Finance*, Vol. 51, 1996, 3–53.

Jensen, M. C., "Capital Markets: Theory and Evidence," *Bell Journal of Economics and Management Science*, Autumn 1972a, 357–398.

———, ed., *Studies in the Theory of Capital Markets*. Praeger, New York, 1972b.

Keim, D., "Size-Related Anomalies and Stock-Market Seasonality: Further Empirical Evidence," *Journal of Financial Economics*, June 1983, 13–32.

———, "Dividend Yields and Stock Returns," *Journal of Financial Economics*, September 1985, 474–489.

Knez, P., and M. Ready, "On the Robustness of Size and Book-to-Market in Cross-Sectional Regressions," *Journal of Finance*, 1997, Vol. 52, 1355–1382.

Kothari, S., and J. Shanken, "Book-to-Market, Dividend Yield, and Expected Market Returns: A Time-Series Analysis," *Journal of Financial Economics,* 1997, Vol. 44, 169–204.

Kothari, S., J. Shanken, and R. Sloan, "Another Look at the Cross-Section of Expected Returns," *Journal of Finance,* 1995, Vol. 50, 185–224.

Lakonishok, J., A. Schleifer, and R. Vishny, "Contrarian Investment, Extrapolation and Risk," *Journal of Finance*, 1994, Vol. 49, No. 5, 1541–1578.

LaPorta, R., "Expectations and the Cross-Section of Stock Returns," *Journal of Finance,* 1996, Vol. 51, 1715–1742.

Lawley, D. N., and A. E. Maxwell, "Mutual Fund Performance Evaluation: A Comparison of Benchmarks and Benchmark Comparisons," working paper, Columbia University, 1985.

Lewellen, J., "The Time-Series Relations among Expected Return, Risk and Book-to-Market," *Journal of Financial Economics,* 1999, Vol. 54, 5–44.

Lintner, J., "Security Prices and Maximal Gains from Diversification," *Journal of Finance*, December 1965a, 587–616.

———, "The Valuation of Risk Assets and the Selection of Risky Investments in Stock Portfolios and Capital Budgets," *Review of Economics and Statistics*, February 1965b, 13–37.

———, "The Aggregation of Investor's Diverse Judgements and Preferences in Purely Competitive Security Markets," *Journal of Financial and Quantitative Analysis*, December 1969, 347–400.

Litzenberger, R., and K. Ramaswamy, "The Effect of Personal Taxes and Dividends and Capital Asset Prices: Theory and Empirical Evidence," *Journal of Financial Economics*, June 1979, 163–195.

Lo, A., and A. C. MacKinlay, "Data Snooping Biases in Tests of Financial Asset Pricing Models," *Review of Financial Studies,* 1990, Vol. 3, 431–468.

MacKinlay, A. C., "Multifactor Models Do Not Explain Deviations from the CAPM," *Journal of Financial Economics,* 1995, Vol. 38, 3–28.

Mayers, D., "Non-Marketable Assets and the Capital Market Equilibrium under Uncertainty," in M. C. Jensen, ed., *Studies in the Theory of Capital Markets*. Praeger, New York, 1972, 223–248.

Mayers, D., and E. Rice, "Measuring Portfolio Performance and the Empirical Content of Asset Pricing Models," *Journal of Financial Economics*, March 1979, 3–28.

Mehra, R., and E. Prescott, "The Equity Premium: A Puzzle," *Journal of Monetary Economics,* 1985, Vol. 15, 145–161.

Merton, R., "An Intertemporal Capital Asset Pricing Model," *Econometrica*, September 1973, 867–888.

———, "On Estimating the Expected Return on the Market: An Exploratory Investigation," *Journal of Financial Economics*, December 1980, 323–361.

Miller, M., and M. Scholes, "Rates of Return in Relation to Risk: A Re-examination of Some Recent Findings," in M. C. Jensen, ed., *Studies in the Theory of Capital Markets*. Praeger, New York, 1972, 47–78.

Modigliani, F., and G. Pogue, "An Introduction to Risk and Return," *Financial Analysts Journal*, March–April and May–June 1974, 68–80 and 69–85.

Mossin, J., "Equilibrium in a Capital Asset Market," *Econometrica*, October 1966, 768–783.

Oldfield, G., Jr. and R. Rogalski, "Treasury Bill Factors and Common Stock Returns," *Journal of Finance*, May 1981, 337–350.

Pettit, R. R., and R. Westerfield, "Using the Capital Asset Pricing Model and the Market Model to Predict Security Returns," *Journal of Financial and Quantitative Analysis*, September 1974, 579–605.

Reinganum, M. R., "The Arbitrage Pricing Theory: Some Empirical Results," *Journal of Finance*, May 1981a, 313–321.

———, "Misspecification of Capital Asset Pricing: Empirical Anomalies Based on Earnings Yields and Market Values," *Journal of Financial Economics*, March 1981b, 19–46.

Roll, R., "A Critique of the Asset Pricing Theory's Tests," *Journal of Financial Economics*, March 1977, 129–176.

———, "A Possible Explanation of the Small Firm Effect," *Journal of Finance*, September 1981, 879–888.

———, "A Note on the Geometry of Shanken's CSR Tsquared Test for Mean/Variance Efficiency," *Journal of Financial Economics*, September 1985, 349–357.

Roll, R., and S. Ross, "On the Cross-Sectional Relation between Expected Returns and Betas," *Journal of Finance*, March 1994, 102–121.

———, "An Empirical Investigation of the Arbitrage Pricing Theory," *Journal of Finance*, December 1980, 1073–1103.

———, "A Critical Reexamination of the Empirical Evidence on the Arbitrage Pricing Theory: A Reply," *Journal of Finance*, June 1984, 347–350.

Rosenberg, B., and V. Marathe, "Tests of Capital Asset Pricing Hypotheses," unpublished manuscript, University of California at Berkeley, 1977.

Ross, S. A., "Return, Risk and Arbitrage," in Friend, I., and J. Bicksler, eds., *Risk and Return in Finance*, Heath Lexington, New York, 1974.

———, "The Arbitrage Theory of Capital Asset Pricing," *Journal of Economic Theory*, December 1976, 343–362.

———, "The Capital Asset Pricing Model (CAPM), Short Sales Restrictions and Related Issues," *Journal of Finance*, March 1977, 177–184.

———, "A Simple Approach to the Valuation of Risky Streams," *Journal of Business*, July 1978, 453–475.

Rubinstein, M. E., "A Mean Variance Synthesis of Corporate Financial Theory," *Journal of Finance*, March 1973, 167–182.

Scholes, M., and J. Williams, "Estimating Betas from Non-synchronous Data," *Journal of Financial Economics*, December 1977, 309–327.

Scruggs, J., "Resolving the Puzzling Intertemporal Relation between the Market Risk Premium and Conditional Market Variance: A Two-Factor Approach," *Journal of Finance,* 1998, Vol. 53, 575–603.

Shanken, J., "Multi-Beta CAPM or Equilibrium in APT?: A Reply," *Journal of Finance*, September 1985a, 1189–1196.

———, "Multivariate Tests of the Zero-beta CAPM," *Journal of Financial Economics*, September 1985b, 327–348.

Sharpe, W. F., "A Simplified Model for Portfolio Analysis," *Management Science*, January 1963, 277–293.

———, "Capital Asset Prices: A Theory of Market Equilibrium under Conditions of Risk," *Journal of Finance*, September 1964, 425–442.

Stambaugh, R., "On the Exclusion of Assets from Tests of the Two Parameter Model: A Sensitivity Analysis," *Journal of Financial Economics*, November 1982, 237–268.

Treynor, J., "Towards a Theory of the Market Value of Risky Assets," unpublished manuscript, 1961.

Vasicek, O. A., "Capital Market Equilibrium with No Riskless Borrowing," mimeograph available from the Wells Fargo Bank, March 1971.

Verrecchia, R. E., "The Mayers-Rice Conjecture—A Counterexample," *Journal of Financial Economics*, March 1980, 87–100.

... option pricing theory is relevant to almost every area of finance. For example, virtually all corporate securities can be interpreted as portfolios of puts and calls on the firm.

—J. C. Cox, S. A. Ross, and M. Rubinstein, "Option Pricing: A Simplified Approach," *Journal of Financial Economics*, September 1979, 230. .

Pricing Contingent Claims: Option Pricing Theory and Evidence

A. *Introduction*

ON APRIL 26, 1973, THE CHICAGO BOARD OF OPTIONS EXCHANGE (CBOE) became the first organized exchange for trading standardized options contracts in the United States. Initially trading was limited to call options on 16 underlying stocks, but over time the list of underlying instruments has expanded to include many more individual equities, indices, foreign currency, interest rates, volatility, and energy products, to name a few. In 2002, the monthly trading volume in equity and index options was 63.8 million contracts with a dollar value of 20.9 billion. In 1997, a seat on the CBOE sold for $727,500, an increase of 1,144% from a seat price in 1976.[1] This tremendous increase in interest in trading in options has also generated rapid advances in the theory of option pricing and a recognition of the importance of this theory.

There are many types of options, and at first the terminology is confusing, with calls, puts, straps, strips, straddles, spreads, in-the-money options, out-of-the-money options, and so forth. This nomenclature can be greatly simplified if we recognize that all contracts are made up of four basic securities: puts, calls, stocks (the underlying asset), and default-free bonds. A *call option* gives its holder the right but not the obligation to purchase a share of stock in the underlying company at a fixed price, usually called the *exercise price* or the *strike price*, for a fixed length of time, called the *maturity of the option*. Table 7.1 is a clipping from the *Wall Street Journal* of July 18, 2002. We see, for example, that two Amgen call options were being traded based on the value of their common stock, which closed that day at $33.92 per share. The options had an exercise price of $35 and two maturity dates, the Saturday following the third Friday in July 2002 and August 2002.

---

[1] Although a full membership in the CBOE in 2003 sold for $343,000 (another demonstration that the only thing that is certain is uncertainty).

Table 7.1 CBOE Option Price Listing (Copyright 2002 by Dow Jones & Co. Inc. Reproduced with permission of Dow Jones & Co. Inc.)

LISTED OPTIONS QUOTATIONS

Thursday, July 18, 2002

Composite volume and close for actively traded equity and LEAPS, or long-term options, with results for the corresponding put or call contract. Volume figures are unofficial. Open interest is total outstanding for all exchanges and reflects previous trading day. Close when possible is shown for the underlying stock or primary market. **XC**-Composite. **p**-Put. **o**-Strike price adjusted for split.

Most Active Contracts

OPTION/STRIKE				VOL	EXCH	LAST	NET CHG	CLOSE	OPEN INT
Nasd100Tr	Sep	23	p	93,674	XC	1.30	0.15	24.73	24,138
Nasd100Tr	Jul	25		73,480	XC	0.35	-0.60	24.73	149,571
Nasd100Tr	Jul	25	p	50,849	XC	0.60	0.30	24.73	78,562
Nasd100Tr	Jul	26		33,690	XC	0.05	-0.35	24.73	137,011
Nasd100Tr	Jul	22.50	p	25,344	XC	0.20	0.10	24.73	57,706
Nasd100Tr	Aug	27		25,237	XC	0.70	-0.40	24.73	79,931
Nasd100Tr	Sep	30		23,467	XC	0.45	-0.20	24.73	94,446
Microsft	Jul	50	p	21,193	XC	1	0.25	51.11	61,980
Nasd100Tr	Aug	25		19,841	XC	1.45	-0.55	24.73	67,360
Lucent	Jan 05	2.50	p	17,866	XC	1.65	0.10	2.26	58,341
Nasd100Tr	Aug	26		17,671	XC	1	-0.55	24.73	58,636
Nasd100Tr	Jul	26	p	16,955	XC	1.30	0.50	24.73	53,572
Nasd100Tr	Sep	25	p	16,755	XC	2.15	0.30	24.73	62,902
Nasd100Tr	Aug	25	p	16,733	XC	1.65	0.30	24.73	54,975
Microsft	Jul	55		15,645	XC	0.20	-0.20	51.11	60,140
Nasd100Tr	Jul	22.50		15,490	XC	0.90	-0.80	24.73	66,616
Nasd100Tr	Jan 04	35		15,334	XC	1.90	-0.30	24.73	109,550
I B M	Jul	75		12,719	XC	0.15	-0.50	72.05	41,221
Nasd100Tr	Aug	22	p	12,131	XC	0.60	0.10	24.73	42,911
Nasd100Tr	Aug	26	p	12,035	XC	2.20	0.35	24.73	30,962
Nasd100Tr	Jul	27	p	12,017	XC	2.25	0.75	24.73	40,585
Motorola	Jul	15		11,015	XC	0.15	-0.25	15	47,725
Nasd100Tr	Aug	22.50	p	10,942	XC	1.25	0.25	24.73	55,849
AOL TW	Jan	20		10,066	XC	0.45	-0.15	12.45	38,759
Nasd100Tr	Sep	32		10,030	XC	0.25	-0.20	24.73	30,521
Nasd100Tr	Jul	27		9,919	XC	0.05	-0.05	24.73	132,869
Nasd100Tr	Sep	25		8,874	XC	2.05	-0.35	24.73	25,973
Nasd100Tr	Jul	23		8,620	XC	1.90	-0.80	24.73	20,728
Microsft	Aug	50	p	8,481	XC	2.70	0.25	51.11	16,853
Calpine	Oct	5	p	8,464	XC	1.45	0.10	4.91	12,613
AppldMat	Jul	17.50	p	8,224	XC	0.60	0.20	17.15	19,381
Cisco	Jul	15	p	7,505	XC	0.60	0.15	14.34	64,896
JohnJn	Aug	50	p	7,471	XC	2.80	0.75	49.73	5,068
Xilinx	Jul	20	p	7,009	XC	1.30	0.40	19.52	9,301
CIGNA	Aug	90	p	6,862	XC	6.80	-0.10	82.80	2,013
Intel	Jul	20		6,820	XC	0.10	-0.15	19.19	54,738
TycoIntl	Jul	85		6,817	XC	0.20	-0.25	11.92	41,143
Intel	Jul	17.50		6,773	XC	1.80	-0.15	19.19	28,375
Microsft	Jul	47.50	p	6,610	XC	0.35	...	51.11	14,087
Nasd100Tr	Sep	27	p	6,477	XC	3.30	0.30	24.73	36,588

OPTION/STRIKE		EXP	-CALL- VOL	-CALL- LAST	-PUT- VOL	-PUT- LAST
AOL TW	7.50	Jan	1	6	2783	0.80
12.45	10	Aug	215	3.10	4483	0.65
12.45	12.50	Jul	2183	0.30	1918	0.45
12.45	12.50	Aug	4543	1.40	1823	1.45
12.45	12.50	Jan	1197	2.60	151	2.50
12.45	15	Aug	3840	0.45	121	3
12.45	20	Jan	10066	0.45	67	7.80
AmOnline	35	Jan	1072	0.05	1012	22.50
AT&T	10	Jul	3710	0.35	500	0.05
10.28	10	Aug	2959	0.90	158	0.60
10.28	10	Oct	50	1.40	5026	1.20
ATI Tech	7.50	Aug	1520	0.90	50	0.55
AldWaste	7.50	Dec	1000	1.40	...	...
Allste	37.50	Oct	3026	1.05	...	...
AmIntGp	60	Aug	1635	2	1195	5
Amgen	35	Jul	5091	0.45	1051	1.25
33.92	35	Aug	1792	2.60	974	3.40
AppleC	27.50	Oct	1650	0.10	...	...
AppldMat	17.50	Jul	3212	0.30	8224	0.60
17.15	17.50	Aug	876	1.55	437	1.80
17.15	25	Jul	...	...	981	7.90
AutoNatn	15	Oct	2000	0.60	...	...
12.35	17.50	Oct	2000	0.25	...	...
•BEA Sys	7.50	Aug	1595	0.85	113	0.95
BJ Svc	32.50	Jul	660	0.55	2051	0.55
Bk of Am	65	Jul	706	0.20	4127	2.35
62.61	65	Feb	19	4.80	5651	8.10
62.61	70	Jul	1	0.05	1096	7.50
62.61	70	Aug	472	0.55	1830	7.70
62.61	75	Aug	1446	0.10	23	11.80
Baxter	35	Aug	1948	1.60	1304	4.20
32.00	40	Aug	651	0.70	2101	7.70
Block	40	Oct	...	...	3026	1.30
Boeing	42.50	Jul	121	0.15	1947	1.05
BrMySq	22.50	Jul	1513	0.70	1840	0.70
Broadcom	17.50	Jul	538	1.90	1690	0.30
19.00	20	Jul	4713	0.50	3030	1.40
19.00	20	Aug	1710	1.80	2842	2.60
19.00	25	Aug	261	0.40	1129	6.30
Brocade	30	Oct	1276	0.85	...	...
19.31	35	Oct	2801	0.45	...	...
CDW Cpt	45	Aug	1455	4.40	19	2.90
46.67	50	Aug	933	1.90	20	5.40
CIGNA	90	Aug	20	1.60	6862	6.80
CV Thera	15	Aug	1000	6.40	20	0.45
20.55	20	Jul	84	1.45	1225	0.90
Calpine	5	Jul	95	0.15	2241	0.25
4.91	5	Oct	1550	1.45	8464	1.45
4.91	10	Oct	2673	0.30	80	5
CapOne	30	Aug	383	6.40	3457	2.90
33.31	35	Aug	1686	3.40	57	4.80
33.31	40	Aug	3722	1.60	38	8.60
33.31	42.50	Aug	2017	1	...	...
33.31	45	Aug	997	0.70	...	...
33.31	45	Sep	1692	1.55	...	...
33.31	45	Dec	1544	2.65	...	...
33.31	50	Aug	1340	0.25	1200	17
CaremkRx	15	Aug	3316	0.60	3510	1.35
Carnvl	22.50	Jan	1000	5.30	...	...
Cendant	17.50	Feb	4261	0.95	3	5.10
Chubb	65	Oct	125	2.35	2463	9
58.09	70	Jan	1760	2.50	...	...
58.09	80	Jan	1252	0.65	...	...
Cisco	12.50	Jul	978	2.05	300	0.05
14.34	15	Jul	4769	0.05	7505	0.60
19.19	20	Jul	6820	0.10	3467	0.85
19.19	20	Aug	3693	1.05	519	1.85
19.19	20	Oct	1278	2.05	304	2.75
19.19	20	Jan	1004	2.90	1460	3.50
19.19	22.50	Aug	2525	0.30	143	3.60
19.19	22.50	Jan	945	1.95	31	4.80
19.19	25	Aug	5298	0.10	33	5.80
I B M	60	Oct	3	15	3127	1.95
72.05	65	Jul	1350	7.60	752	0.05
72.05	65	Aug	58	8.10	1725	1.10
72.05	70	Jul	2005	2.45	6403	0.20
72.05	70	Aug	1061	4.40	1766	2.40
72.05	70	Oct	1064	7.10	761	4.70
72.05	75	Jul	12719	0.15	1648	3
72.05	75	Aug	2156	1.90	1077	4.80
72.05	75	Oct	1973	4.40	329	7
72.05	75	Jan	1133	6.50	104	8.90
72.05	80	Aug	3396	0.65	205	7.80
72.05	80	Oct	1470	2.65	97	10
72.05	80	Jan	3874	4.60	605	12.10
72.05	85	Oct	5841	1.30	32	13.50
72.05	85	Jan	3643	3	30	15.30
Intuit	40	Jul	534	2	972	0.35
41.69	45	Jul	1189	0.10	154	3.90
41.69	45	Aug	1684	1.65	117	5.10
Ixia	10	Feb	1000	0.50	...	...
JPMorgCh	25	Aug	...	...	2297	1.30
27.20	25	Dec	...	...	3799	2.85
27.20	27.50	Jul	124	0.30	1726	0.80
27.20	30	Jul	562	0.05	1022	2.75
27.20	30	Dec	2047	2.65	120	5.20
Jabil	17.50	Aug	1235	3	4	0.90
JHFnSrv	30	Aug	1008	1.90	10	1.45
JohnJn	50	Aug	2339	2.40	7471	2.80
JnprNtw	10	Aug	895	0.55	133	1.65
KLA Tnc	45	Jul	1621	0.35	948	1.80
43.30	50	Aug	123	1.65	1520	8.10
Kohls	55	Oct	...	...	921	2.40
KrspKrm	30	Aug	2855	5.10	13	0.95
34.65	35	Jul	156	0.20	1307	0.75
34.65	35	Aug	2465	1.90	56	2.60
34.65	45	Aug	1723	0.15	...	...
LTX	7.50	Nov	...	...	916	0.90
9.67	10	Nov	...	...	916	1.90
Lennar	55	Aug	1351	3.10	54	5
Level3	7.50	Aug	3402	0.50	10	2.15
Lexmark	50	Oct	1150	6.20	...	...
47.96	55	Oct	6001	3.20	...	...
Lilly	50	Jul	889	0.45	1421	1.70
48.54	50	Aug	1374	2.25	1436	3.60
LockhdM	60	Aug	49	4.20	3030	3.20
60.60	65	Aug	3288	1.70	68	6
LaPac	7.50	Feb	...	...	2000	1.10
Lowes	17.50	Jan	970	1.85	...	...
37.85	47.50	Jan	1195	1.80	...	...
Lucent o	5	Jan	26	0.40	1001	2.85
MedImun	25	Jul	5135	0.75	183	0.20
25.40	25	Aug	5091	2.50	164	1.70
Merck	60	Jan	883	0.55	11	18.40
Mercint	20	Jul	117	3.90	1089	0.55
23.60	22.50	Jul	1179	2	1078	1.20
23.60	22.50	Aug	1668	2.95	236	2.35
23.60	25	Jul	2023	0.75	82	2.40
23.60	25	Aug	1328	2.15	81	3.90
23.60	45	Oct	1601	0.40	...	...
10.05	12.50	Sep	1174	0.40	291	2.80
Paychex	25	Jul	2320	0.20	389	1.15
Peoplesoft	12.50	Jul	34	2.10	1316	0.20
14.51	15	Jul	2108	0.55	2438	1
14.51	25	Oct	6016	0.45	3	10.70
PepsiCo	40	Jul	1487	0.95	1447	0.55
40.30	40	Aug	1423	2.35	268	2
40.30	42.50	Jul	6317	0.20	3302	2.60
Pfizer	25	Sep	3	4.60	1057	1
27.98	35	Sep	1146	0.25	110	6.30
PhmHldTr	65	Aug	...	...	3073	2.95
Pharmacia	40	Jul	5149	0.25	406	0.65
39.50	40	Aug	5035	2	63	2
Ph Mor	42.50	Jul	90	0.40	1344	0.50
Placer	10	Dec	150	1.85	3010	1.30
PrpdLeg	20	Jul	80	0.10	1544	1.70
17.95	22.50	Nov	3105	3.10	...	...
17.95	25	Jul	20	0.10	3140	6.60
17.95	25	Nov	1200	2.70	3100	10
ProcG o	80	Jul	967	1.15	140	0.50
80.39	85	Jan	908	5.60	...	...
Qlogic	30	Jul	337	12.20	1732	0.10
41.23	35	Jul	1334	6.60	1443	0.30
41.23	40	Jul	1656	2.35	3196	1.10
41.23	40	Aug	1320	5	980	3.80
41.23	45	Jul	2344	0.30	1067	4
41.23	65	Jul	1500	0.05	...	...
41.23	70	Jan	1665	2.20	...	...
Qualcom	25	Aug	27	6.60	1931	0.95
30.37	30	Jul	3250	0.85	1499	0.40
30.37	30	Aug	700	3	3891	2.50
30.37	35	Aug	5240	1	33	5.50
QwestCom	2.50	Jul	1810	0.25	264	0.10
2.74	5	Oct	898	0.50	238	2.65
Raytheon	32.50	Aug	2998	2.80	180	2.20
Rowan	25	Jan	1004	1.40	...	...
RoyDut	40	Aug	7	7.30	2574	1
46.00	45	Jul	185	1.40	3522	0.55
46.00	45	Aug	623	2.90	1703	2.35
46.00	45	Oct	565	4.20	2161	3.90
46.00	50	Jul	140	0.10	3113	4.30
SBC Cm	30	Aug	1089	0.70	36	2.90
Schering	22.50	Jul	1087	0.30	3302	0.50
Sears	45	Jul	2682	1.50	325	0.40
SemiHTr	30	Aug	1203	2.30	8	2.20
SempraEn	17.50	Jan	3015	3.10	...	...
SiebelSys	10	Jul	2786	0.15	4893	0.50
9.62	10	Aug	4355	0.95	4150	1.30
9.62	12.50	Jul	252	0.05	1212	2.80
9.62	12.50	Nov	1807	1.10	25	4
Smthln.	32.50	Aug	...	...	3005	2.30
SprintPCS	5	Aug	781	1.10	3229	0.70
5.50	7.50	Aug	3336	0.40	30	2
SP Mid	79	Aug	...	...	1150	2.70
SunMicro	5	Jul	1765	0.85	696	0.05
5.80	5	Aug	3085	1.10	785	0.30
Symntc	30	Jul	147	1.60	1083	0.40
Synops	55	Dec	3305	2.90	...	...
TenetHlt	45	Jul	1007	2.15	1	0.10
46.93	45	Aug	1000	4.30	90	1.65
TexasInst	25	Jul	951	0.80	446	0.30
3M Co	120	Jul	891	0.30	284	3.10
TycoIntl	5	Oct	25	7.50	2962	0.85
11.92	5	Jan	2310	8.30	2289	1.20
11.92	7.50	Jan	2652	6.80	1491	2
11.92	10	Jul	2054	2.10	4602	0.10

Should the price of the common stock have climbed above $35 per share, a trader who held the call option with an exercise price of $35 could have exercised his or her option and kept the difference between the exercise price and the stock price. A *put* is exactly the opposite of a call option. The holder of a put has the right to sell the stock at the exercise price any time up to and including the maturity date of the put. For example, the holder of an October put option on AT&T with the exercise price of $10 could have made a profit if the stock, which was then selling for $10.28 per share, fell below $10 before the Saturday following the third Friday in October.

B. A Description of the Factors that Affect Prices of European Options

To keep the theory simple for the time being, we assume that all options can be exercised only on their maturity date. Options of this type are called *European* options. They are considerably easier to price than their *American* counterparts, which can be exercised at any date up to maturity. We also assume that there are no cash payments (such as dividends) made by the underlying asset.

A quick look at the option prices in Table 7.1 shows at least three factors are important for the market value of an option. For ease of exposition, we shall, for the moment, confine our discussion to the determination of the value of call options. Similar arguments would apply to the value of put options. The higher the value of the *underlying asset*, S, the greater the value of a call option written on it, ceteris paribus. Baxter, Capital One, PepsiCo, Pharmacia, Qlogic, and Royal Dutch Petroleum all have call options with an *exercise price*, X, of $40 and a maturity date on the Saturday following the third Friday in August. Figure 7.1 clearly shows that the value of the call increases as a function of the value of the stock for a given exercise price and *maturity date*, T. Note also that the options have positive values even though for some of them the stock price is less than the exercise price. As long as investors believe that there is a chance that the stock price will exceed the exercise price before the option matures, the option will be valuable. Two of these companies,

Figure 7.1 The relationship between the call price and the stock price.

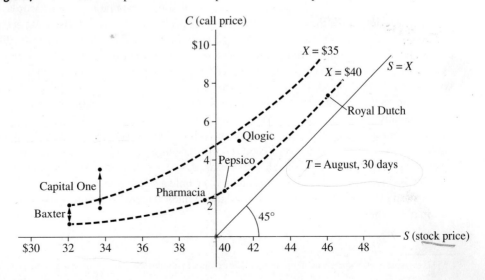

Figure 7.2 Hypothetical distributions of stock prices.

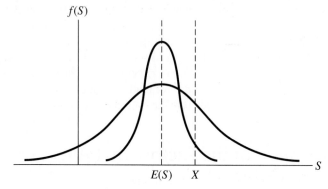

Baxter and Capital One, have a second call option with a lower exercise price of $35. Note that the relationship between the call price and the stock price has shifted upward. The lower the exercise price, the greater the value of the call option. The third factor that affects call prices is the length of time to maturity, T. A quick look at any option in Table 7.1 shows that the longer the time to maturity, the higher the value of the call option. For example, the July 40 call options on PepsiCo, Pharmacia, and Qlogic are priced at 0.95, 0.25, and 2.35, respectively, and each value is lower than its August counterpart. The reason is that with more time to maturity there is a greater chance that the stock will climb above the exercise price. Hence options with longer maturity have higher value. In fact, a call option that has an infinite maturity date will have the same value as the (non-dividend-paying) stock, regardless of its exercise price. This is because the option will never be exercised.

In addition to the stock price, the exercise price, and the time to maturity, there are two other important (but less obvious) factors that affect the option's value: (1) the *instantaneous variance of the rate of return on the underlying asset* (common stock) and (2) the risk-free rate of return. The holder of a call option will prefer more variance in the price of a stock to less. The greater the variance, the greater the probability that the stock price will exceed the exercise price, and this is of value to the call holder. A call option is a type of contingent claim. In other words, the option holder gains only under the condition that the stock price exceeds the exercise price at the maturity date. Suppose we hold options and are faced with the two hypothetical stock price distributions shown in Fig. 7.2. Both distributions have identical means, but one has a larger variance. Which would we prefer if both have an identical exercise price, X? Recalling that call option holders gain only when the stock price is greater than the exercise price, it becomes clear that we will prefer the option on the security that has the higher variance (given that the stock price is fixed) because the cumulative probability of receiving a gain is greater for a security of this sort.[2] This points out an important difference between the value of options and the value of the underlying asset. If we hold the asset, we receive the payoffs offered by the entire probability distribution of outcomes. If we are risk averse, we will dislike higher variance, which means that we will require high returns along with high variance. On the other hand, if we hold a call option, we receive payoffs only from the upper tail of the distribution. The contingent-claim feature of options makes higher variance desirable.

---

[2] This example is given merely as an illustration. The example that follows is more accurate and more general.

The value of higher variance is also illustrated in the following example. Suppose that a company has borrowed long-term debt with fixed interest payments of $8,000 per year and that it finds itself with one of the two investment projects below:

Project 1		Project 2	
Probability	Cash Flow	Probability	Cash Flow
.2	4,000	.4	0
.6	5,000	.2	5,000
.2	6,000	.4	10,000

Both projects have identical expected cash flows of $5,000. However, if the shareholders accept project 1, the firm will surely go bankrupt because all possible cash flows are less than the debt commitment of $8,000. On the other hand, if they accept project 2, which has a higher variance, there is a 40% chance that they will be able to pay off their debt obligation and have $2,000 left over. Obviously they will choose the riskier project because it offers them a 40% chance of a positive value. This example further illustrates the fact that holders of contingent claims (i.e., holders of options) will prefer more variance to less. It also introduces the notion that the shareholders of a firm are really holders of call options on the market value of the firm. If the value of the firm is less than the required debt payoff (the exercise price on the option), shareholders will allow their option to expire unexercised and turn over the assets of the firm to bondholders. If the value of the firm exceeds the debt payoff, they will exercise their option by paying off the debt holders and keeping any excess for themselves. In many of the chapters that follow we shall utilize option pricing theory for applications in corporate financial policy.

The final factor in determining the value of an option is the *risk-free rate* of interest. Of all the factors it is the least intuitive. Black and Scholes [1973] have shown that it is possible to create a risk-free hedged position consisting of a long position in the stock and a short position (where the investor writes a call) in the option. This insight allows them to argue that the rate of return on the equity in the hedged position is nonstochastic. Therefore the appropriate rate is the risk-free rate of return. The mechanics of forming the risk-free hedge, as well as a more precise exposition of the logic, will be given later in the chapter.

The preceding intuitive description shows that five factors are important in determining the value of a European call option: the price of the underlying asset, S; the exercise price of the option, X; the instantaneous variance of the returns of the underlying asset, σ^2; the time to maturity of the option, T; and the risk-free rate, r_f. This may be written in functional form as

$$c = f(S, X, \sigma^2, T, r_f), \tag{7.1}$$

and the partial derivatives of the call price, c, with respect to its various arguments are

$$\frac{\partial c}{\partial S} > 0, \qquad \frac{\partial c}{\partial X} < 0, \qquad \frac{\partial c}{\partial \sigma^2} > 0, \qquad \frac{\partial c}{\partial T} > 0, \qquad \frac{\partial c}{\partial r_f} > 0. \tag{7.2}$$

Using similar arguments and denoting the value of a put option as $p = f(S, X, \sigma^2, T, r_f)$, the partial derivatives of the put price, p, with respect to its various arguments are

$$\frac{\partial p}{\partial S} < 0, \qquad \frac{\partial p}{\partial X} > 0, \qquad \frac{\partial p}{\partial \sigma^2} > 0, \qquad \frac{\partial p}{\partial T} \leq \text{ or } > 0, \qquad \frac{\partial p}{\partial r_f} < 0. \tag{7.3}$$

The logic behind the signs of the partial derivatives with respect to the price of the underlying asset, S; the exercise price of the option, X; the instantaneous variance of the returns of the underlying asset, σ^2; and the risk-free rate, r_f, follow that used for call options. The ambiguous sign of the partial derivative of the put value with respect to the time to maturity of the option, T, follows from that fact that put options on non-dividend-paying stocks may be exercised early (as will be shown in a later section of this chapter). As a result if we force a delay in exercise by increasing the expiration date, the value of the put may decrease. This would imply that put option values could decrease with increases in time to expiration.

C. Combining Options: A Graphic Presentation

One of the most fascinating features of options is that they can be combined in many different ways to provide almost any desired pattern of payoffs. For the sake of simplicity, assume that European put and call options have the same maturity date on the same underlying asset, and that the exercise price is set equal to the asset price.[3] A graphic representation of the value of buying or selling a call option as a function of changes in the stock price is given in Fig. 7.3. When selling a call, we receive the call price now. If the stock price stays the same or falls, the option will mature unexpired, and we keep the future value of the sale price, $+e^{r_f T}C$. If the stock price rises, we lose a dollar for each dollar it rises. This is the portion of the dashed line with an intercept at $+e^{r_f T}C$ and a slope of -1. Buying a call is the opposite of selling a call. If we sell a put, we receive $+P$ dollars now and lose a dollar for every dollar the stock price falls below the exercise price. This is represented by the dashed line in Fig. 7.3(b). The solid line, which represents buying a put, is just the opposite.

The payoffs for long and short positions for stocks and risk-free pure discount bonds are shown in Fig. 7.4. If we hold a long position in a stock, we gain or lose a dollar for every dollar the stock price changes. If we hold a bond, we receive the same payoff regardless of changes in the stock price because a risk-free bond is presumed to have identical payoffs irrespective of which state of the world obtains.

These elemental securities may be combined in various ways according to the following relationship:

$$S + P = B + C. \tag{7.4}$$

Buying a share of stock and buying a put written on that share yield the same payoff as holding a bond and buying a call. Alternatively, holding a portfolio made up of long positions in the stock and the put and a short position in the call is equivalent to the perfectly risk-free payoff offered by holding the bond (Fig. 7.5).

The reader may use this graphic analysis to investigate the profit patterns of many different securities. One often hears of straddles, strangles, straps, and strips. They are defined as follows:

- *Straddle.* A combination of put and call options in the same contract where the exercise price and maturity date are identical for both options. A straddle is graphed in Fig. 7.6.

---

[3] We also assume that capital markets are frictionless and there are no taxes. This implies, among other things, that the risk-free borrowing rate equals the risk-free lending rate.

Figure 7.3 Profits from put and call options given that $S = X$.

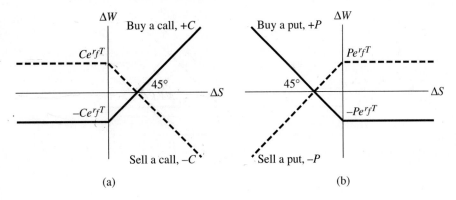

(a)   (b)

Figure 7.4 Payoffs from stock or bond.

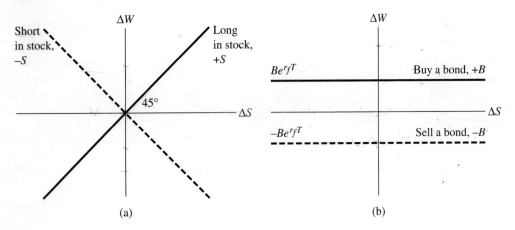

(a)   (b)

- *Strangle.* A combination of put and call options in a single contract, with the exercise price of the put usually less than the exercise price of the call.

- *Straps and strips.* Combinations of two calls and one put, and two puts and one call, respectively.

A straddle or a strangle loses money for small changes in the stock price and gains money for large changes. This may seem to be "a good deal," but let us keep in mind that the market values of the put and call options are determined in a way that already incorporates the market's best estimate of the variance in the price of the underlying security. The greater the variance, the more we have to pay for the put and call options. Therefore greater price fluctuations will be needed to make a profit. In the final analysis the securities will always be priced to yield a fair return for their riskiness.

Figure 7.5 Graphical representation of $S + P - C = B$ (given that $S = X$).

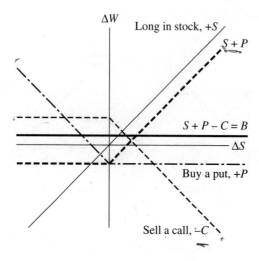

Figure 7.6 Profits on a straddle.

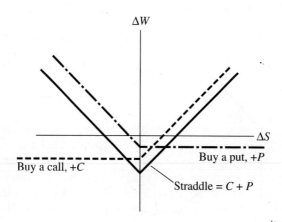

D. $\mathcal{E}$quity as a Call Option

Option pricing theory has many applications in corporate finance. Black and Scholes [1973] were the first to point out that the equity in a levered firm is really a call option on the value of the firm. Later articles have shown how option pricing applies to many different corporate finance topics such as dividend policy, capital structure, mergers and acquisitions, investment policy, spin-offs, divestitures, convertible debt and warrants, and abandonment decisions. Needless to say, the more we know about option pricing theory, the better we shall understand corporate financial management.

To introduce equity as a call option on the assets of a levered firm, assume that the firm has only two sources of capital: equity and *risky* debt. The debt is a zero coupon bond, has a face value D, and matures T years from now. It is secured by the assets of the firm, but bondholders may not force the firm into bankruptcy until the maturity date of the bond. The firm pays no dividends.

We saw, in Eq. (7.4), that any risky portfolio can be constructed from the four basic building blocks:

$$S + P = B + C.$$

For a CBOE call option the underlying asset is a share of stock, S. For our current discussion, it is the market value of the firm, V. The equity in a levered firm, S, is really a call option on the value of the firm. If, on the maturity date, the value of the firm, V, exceeds the face value of the bonds, D, the shareholders will exercise their call option by paying off the bonds and keeping the excess. On the other hand, if the value of the firm is less than the face value of the bonds, the shareholders will default on the debt by failing to exercise their option. Therefore at maturity the shareholders' wealth, S, is

$$S = \text{MAX}[0, V - D]. \tag{7.5}$$

If we substitute V for S, and S for C in Eq. (7.4), we have

$$V = (B - P) + S. \tag{7.6}$$

Equation (7.6) tells us that the value of a risky asset, the levered firm, can be partitioned into two parts. The equity position, S, is a call option, and the risky debt, $(B - P)$, is equivalent to the present value of the risk-free debt, B, minus the value of a European put option, P. At maturity the bondholders receive

$$B - P = \text{MIN}[V, D]. \tag{7.7}$$

Table 7.2 shows how the payoffs to equity and risky debt add up to equal the value of the firm at maturity. We are assuming that there are no taxes and no bankruptcy costs paid to third parties (e.g., lawyers and courts). At maturity the entire value of the firm is divided between bondholders and shareholders. If the firm is successful (i.e., if $V \geq D$), the bondholders receive the face value of the riskless bond, D, and their put option is worthless. If the firm is bankrupt, they still receive the face value of the riskless bond, but a put option has in effect been exercised against them because they lose the difference between the face value of the riskless debt, D, and the market value of the

Table 7.2 Stakeholders' Payoffs at Maturity

	Payoffs at Maturity	
	If $V \leq D$	If $V > D$
Shareholders' position:		
Call option, S	0	$(V - D)$
Bondholders' position:		
Default-free bond	D	D
Put option, P	$-(D - V)$	0
Total for bondholders	V	D
Sum of stakeholder positions	$0 + V = V$	$V - D + D = V$

firm, V. They gain D but lose $(D - V)$; therefore their net position is V, the market value of the firm in bankruptcy.

The fact that the equity in a levered firm is really a call option on the value of the firm's assets will provide many insights throughout this chapter and in the remainder of the text. Now let us turn our attention to the problem of how to value a call option.

E. Put-Call Parity

Table 7.1 shows some securities with both put and call options written against them. For example, Calpine has puts and calls with exercise prices of $5 and $10. We show below that for European options there is a fixed relationship between the price of put and call options with the same maturity date that are written on a single underlying security. This relationship, derived by Stoll [1969], is called *put-call parity*. It implies that if we know the price of a European call on an asset, we can easily determine the price of a European put on the same asset.

Suppose we have a portfolio where we purchase one share of stock, one put option, and sell (write) one call option. Both options are written on the share of stock. Also, they have the same maturity date, T, and the same exercise price, X. At maturity all states of the world can be divided into those where the stock price is less than the exercise price, $S < X$, and those where it is greater than or equal to the exercise price, $S \geq X$. The payoffs from the portfolio in either state are listed below:

If $S < X$:

    a. You hold the stock S

    b. The call option is worthless 0

    c. The put option is worth $X - S$

    d. Therefore, your net position is X

If $S \geq X$:

    a. You hold the stock S

    b. The call option is worth $-(S - X)$

    c. And the put option is worthless 0

    d. Therefore, your net position is X

No matter what state of the world obtains at maturity, the portfolio will be worth X. Consequently, the payoff from the portfolio is completely risk free, and we can discount its value at the risk-free rate, r_f. Using discrete discounting, this is[4]

$$S_0 + p_0 - c_0 = \frac{X}{1 + r_f}.$$

---

[4] Hereafter we adopt the convention that uppercase C and P are American calls and puts while lowercase c and p are European.

This can be rearranged to give the put-call parity formula:

$$c_0 - p_0 = \frac{(1+r_f)S_0 - X}{1+r_f}. \tag{7.8}$$

Note that the interest rate, r_f, is a one-period rate but that the time period need not equal a calendar year. For example, if the option expires in six months and r_f is an annual rate, then we can replace $(1+r_f)$ in Eq. (7.8) with $(1+r_f)^{.5}$. Equation (7.8) is referred to as the put-call parity relationship for European options. A special case occurs when the exercise price, X, is set equal to the current stock price, S_0. When $S_0 = X$, we have

$$c_0 - p_0 = \frac{r_f S_0}{1+r_f} > 0. \tag{7.9}$$

This shows that when the valuation parameters are identical (the stock price, instantaneous variance, exercise price, time to expiration, and risk-free rate) and the exercise price equals the stock price, the call option will have greater present value than the put option. It explains why the dashed call line in Fig. 7.6 lies below the put line.

An equivalent continuous compounding formula for put-call parity is

$$c_0 - p_0 = S_0 - X e^{-r_f T}, \tag{7.10}$$

where r_f is the annual risk-free rate and T is the time to maturity (in years) of the put and call options. The put-call parity relationship is extremely useful for the valuation of European options because if we know the value of a European call, the put-call parity relationship also gives the value of a corresponding put.

F. Some Dominance Theorems that Bound the Value of a Call Option

The value of a call or put option has been described as a function of five parameters: the price of the underlying asset, S; the instantaneous variance of the asset returns, σ^2; the exercise price, X; the time to expiration, T; and the risk-free rate, r_f:

$$c \text{ or } p = f(S, \sigma^2, X, T, r_f).$$

Perhaps even more interesting are some factors that do not affect the value of an option. For example, the option price does not depend on investor attitudes toward risk, nor does it depend on the expected rate of return of the underlying security. This section of the chapter provides a logical, rather than descriptive or intuitive, framework for understanding why these five parameters affect option value and why investor attitudes toward risk and the rate of return on the underlying security do not.

All the following discussion is based on the notion of stochastic dominance, which was introduced in Chapter 3. We shall use first-order stochastic dominance, which says that one asset will be preferred by all investors (be they risk averse, risk neutral, or risk loving) if the return that it offers is superior in every state of nature to the return offered by a second asset. If this is true, we say that the first asset is stochastically dominant over the second. Clearly, if all the following analysis is based on this simple notion, the value of a call option will not depend on individual risk preferences.

Before developing the analysis and some related theorems it is useful to spell out in detail the assumptions that have been used in valuation models for options:

- Frictionless capital markets with no transaction costs or taxes and with information simultaneously and costlessly available to all individuals

- No restrictions on short sales

- Continuous asset trading with all asset prices following continuous and stationary stochastic processes[5]

- Nonstochastic risk-free rate (constant over time)[6]

- No dividends[7]

Most of these assumptions are self-explanatory and are consistent with efficient capital markets. By *continuous stochastic processes* we mean that the price of the underlying asset can vary over time but does not have any discontinuities or jumps. In other words, we could graph the price movement over time without lifting our pen from the paper. A stationary stochastic process is one that is determined the same way for all time periods of equal length. In particular the instantaneous price variance does not change over time. If the underlying asset is a common stock, we assume no dividend payments so that there are no jumps in the stock price. It is well known that the stock price falls by approximately the amount of the dividend on the ex-dividend date.

Our objectives are (1) to show the boundary conditions that limit the values that call and put options can take, (2) to prove that American calls on non-dividend-paying stocks will optimally not be exercised prior to maturity, and (3) to prove that American put options on non-dividend-paying stocks may be exercised early. The reader who wishes to carefully study the theorems of option pricing is referred to the seminal work of Merton [1973b]. We shall adopt the convention that European calls (puts) that can be exercised only at maturity will be written with a lowercase c (p), whereas American calls (puts) that can be exercised at any time will be written with an uppercase C (P).

The profit to a call option at maturity is (1) the maximum of zero if the stock price is less than the exercise price or (2) the difference between the stock price and the exercise price if the stock price exceeds the exercise price, that is,

$$C \geq c = \text{MAX}[0, S - X] \geq 0. \tag{7.11}$$

Clearly, the call price must be nonnegative. Also, because the American call, C, can be exercised prior to maturity, its value must be greater than or equal to the European call value, c.

Also, Eq. (7.11) tells us that the call price can never fall below $(S - X)$. Additionally, the option price will never exceed the price of the stock on which it is written. If the exercise price, X, is zero and the option never matures, it can be worth at most S. Even in this extreme case the option may be worth less than the stock because shareholders have voting rights, whereas option holders do not.

---

[5] Cox and Ross [1975] have relaxed this assumption.

[6] Merton [1976] has relaxed this assumption.

[7] Geske [1977] has relaxed this assumption.

Figure 7.7 Boundaries for the value of a call option.

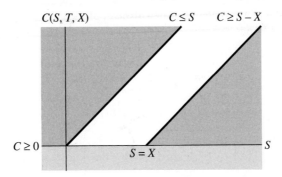

The preceding discussion serves to limit the possible values that option prices may take relative to the stock price. The results are illustrated in Fig. 7.7. The call option is a function of the stock price, S; the time to maturity, T; and the exercise price, $C(S, T, X)$. Its value is nonnegative, less than S, and greater than $S - X$. Note that the boundaries $C \le S$ and $C \ge S - X$ are 45 degree lines.

Next, we shall prove that an American call option written on a non-dividend-paying stock will not be exercised before the expiration date of the option. Along the way we will further bound the value that call options can take and we will see why the call value will increase when the risk-free rate does. The result we wish to prove is stated as Theorem 7.1:

THEOREM 7.1   An American call on a non-dividend-paying stock will not be exercised before the call expiration date.

To prove this, we first assume that $B(T)$ is the current price of a risk-free zero coupon bond. Given positive interest rates and assuming that the bond pays \$1 upon maturity, we have[8]

$$B(T) = (\$1)e^{-r_f T}, \tag{7.12}$$

where r_f is the one-year risk-free rate and T is the number of years (or fraction of a year) to maturity. We shall adopt the convention that $T_1 > T_2 > \cdots > T_n$; therefore

$$0 = B(\infty) < B(T_1) < B(T_2) < \cdots < B(0) = \$1.$$

Now let us consider two portfolios. Portfolio A represents the purchase of one European call for $c(S, T, X)$ dollars and X bonds for $XB(T)$ dollars.[9] Portfolio B is the purchase of one share of stock for S dollars. Table 7.3 demonstrates the relationship between the terminal values for the two portfolios. If the stock price is less than the exercise price at the expiration date, the option will expire unexercised, with no value, and portfolio A will be worth X dollars. But since $X > S$, portfolio A will be worth more than portfolio B, which is one share of stock. On the other hand,

---

[8] This is the continuous discounting version of the more familiar discrete discounting formula

$$B(T) = \frac{\$1}{(1 + r_f)^T} = (\$1)(1 + r_f)^{-T}.$$

[9] In this proof we have defined T as the time to maturity for the call option.

Table 7.3 Relationship Between the Value of a Share of Stock and a Portfolio Made Up of a European Call and X Risk-Free Bonds

Portfolio	Current Value	Portfolio Value, Given Stock Price at T	
		$S < X$	$S \geq X$
A	$c(S, T, X) + XB(T)$	$0 + X$	$S - X + X$
B	S_0	S	S
Relationship between terminal values of A and B		$V_a > V_b$	$V_a = V_b$

when the stock price is greater than the exercise price, portfolios A and B have the same payoff. In any state of nature portfolio A pays an amount greater than or equal to portfolio B. Therefore, in order to prevent dominance, portfolio A must have a higher price than portfolio B:

$$c(S, T, X) + XB(T) \geq S.$$

This restriction may be rearranged to obtain

$$c(S, T, X) \geq \text{MAX}[0, S - XB(T)].$$

Finally, from (7.12) we have

$$c(S, T, X) \geq \text{MAX}[0, S - e^{-r_f T}X]. \tag{7.13}$$

Equation (7.13) applies to a European call, but we have already discussed the fact that an American call is always at least as valuable as an equivalent European call; therefore

$$C(S, T, X) \geq c(S, T, X) \geq \text{MAX}[0, S - e^{-r_f T}X]. \tag{7.14}$$

Furthermore, if exercised, the value of an American call is $\text{MAX}[0, S - X]$, which is less than $\text{MAX}[0, S - XB(T)]$, since $B(T) = e^{-r_f T}$, which is less than one, for positive r_f. Consequently, the holder of an American option can always do better by selling it in the marketplace rather than exercising it prior to expiration. This is an important result because European options are much simpler than American options.

Theorem 7.1 further limits the set of feasible prices for call options because the requirement that

$$c(S, T, X) \geq \text{MAX}[0, S - XB(T)]$$

is more restrictive than

$$c(S, T, X) \geq \text{MAX}[0, S - X].$$

This is shown in Fig. 7.8. Also, it is now possible to demonstrate, in a plausible fashion, that the call price will increase when the risk-free rate increases. Suppose the stock price is $50, the exercise price is $30, and the option expires in one year. If the risk-free rate is 5%, the lower bound on

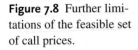

Figure 7.8 Further limitations of the feasible set of call prices.

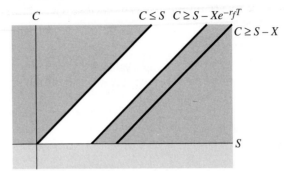

the option price will be $21.46. If the risk-free rate changes to 10%, the lower bound increases to $22.85. Intuitively, the call option is worth more because an investor has to pay less today to acquire the risk-free discount bond that guarantees $1 at the end of the year. This makes portfolio A in Table 7.3 more valuable relative to portfolio B.

Theorem 7.2 introduces more realism into the analysis by showing what happens to the value of an American call option when the underlying stock pays a dividend. Since many firms pay dividends, investors who hold CBOE call options must be careful; the options are not protected against a drop in value when the underlying stock falls in price because it goes ex-dividend.

THEOREM 7.2   Premature exercise of an American call may occur if the underlying security (common stock) pays dividends (and if the option is inadequately protected against the dividend payment).

On May 13, 2002, Consolidated Edison stock was selling at around $44.15 per share. July call options were outstanding with an exercise price of $30. On the next day, the company was scheduled to go ex-dividend with a dividend of $0.56 per share. This implied that the stock price would fall to approximately $43.59 per share. CBOE call options provide no protection against dividend payments, and hence option holders would have found themselves with the following dilemma. Before the ex-dividend date the option price could not fall below its intrinsic value, $S - X$, or $14.15. (Why?) On the following day, everyone knew the stock price would fall to around $43.59 per share and that the option's intrinsic value would also fall with certainty. On one day their option was worth at least $14.15 and on the next they knew it would have a lower minimum price. On the other hand, if they exercised early on May 13, they would face an opportunity cost associated with having to pay the exercise price of $30 on May 13 rather than on July 20 if they waited till expiration. Depending on the relative value of the opportunity cost and the dividend, it could be rational for the call holder to exercise the option prior to the ex-dividend date.

The rationality of the above example can be demonstrated by assuming that a security makes a certain dividend payment, Div, on the expiration date of an option. Consider two portfolios. Portfolio A is one European call and $X + Div$ bonds. Portfolio B is one share of stock. Table 7.4 shows the terminal values of the two portfolios. The value of A is greater than that of B when the stock price is less than the exercise price and equal to it otherwise. Therefore

$$c(S, T, X) + (X + Div)B(T) \geq S.$$

Table 7.4 Call Options on Dividend-Paying Stocks May Be Exercised Prematurely

Portfolio	Current Value	Portfolio Value, Given Stock Price at T	
		$S < X$	$S \geq X$
A	$c(S, T, X) + (X + Div)B(T)$	$0 + X + Div$	$S - X + X + Div$
B	S	$S + Div$	$S + Div$
Relationship between terminal values of A and B		$V_a > V_b$	$V_a = V_b$

By rearranging this and using Eq. (7.12), we obtain

$$c(S, T, X) \geq \text{MAX}\left[0, S - (X + Div)e^{-r_f T}\right]. \qquad (7.15)$$

Depending on the size of the dividend payment and the risk-free rate, it is possible to have the following situation:

$$(X + Div)e^{-r_f T} > S,$$

in which case the value of the call in (7.15) is zero, at best. Therefore, in some cases it may be advantageous to exercise an American call option prematurely.[10]

Let us now consider the same issues as they pertain to put options. The payoff to a put option at maturity is (1) the maximum of the difference between the exercise price and the stock price if the stock price is less than the exercise price or (2) zero if the stock price exceeds the exercise price, that is,

$$P \geq p = \text{MAX}[0, X - S] \geq 0. \qquad (7.16)$$

Clearly, the put price must be nonnegative. Also, because the American put, P, can be exercised prior to maturity, its value must be greater than or equal to the European put value, p.

Equation (7.16) also tells us that the American put price can never fall below $(X - S)$. Additionally, the American option price will never exceed the exercise price of the option. Even if the stock price, S, is zero and the option never matures, it can be worth at most X.

The preceding discussion serves to limit the possible values that put option prices may take relative to the stock price. The results are illustrated in Fig. 7.9. The American put option is a function of the stock price, S; the time to maturity, T; and the exercise price, X, $P(S, T, X)$. Its value is nonnegative, less than X, and greater than $X - S$.

What are the equivalent boundaries for an European put? To determine this consider two portfolios, one that consists of a purchased share of stock and a European put and another that consists of a purchased bond with a face value equal to the exercise price of the option, X. Table 7.5 demonstrates the relationship between the terminal values for the two portfolios. If the stock price is less than the exercise price at the expiration date, the option will be exercised, and portfolio B will be worth X dollars. Thus, portfolio A will be worth the same as portfolio B. On the other hand, when the stock price is greater than the exercise price, the option expires unexercised

---

[10] The reader who is interested in the valuation of call options written on dividend-paying stocks is referred to Roll [1977].

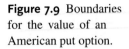

Figure 7.9 Boundaries for the value of an American put option.

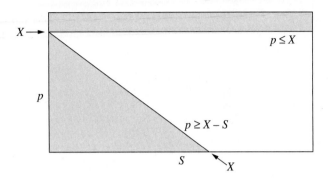

Table 7.5 Relationship between the Value of X Risk-Free Bonds and a Portfolio Made up of a Share of Stock and a European Put

Portfolio	Current Value	Portfolio Value, Given Stock Price at T	
		$S < X$	$S \geq X$
A	$XB(T)$	X	X
B	$S_0 + p$	$S + X - S$	S
Relationship between terminal values of A and B		$V_a = V_b$	$V_a < V_b$

and portfolio B is worth S dollars, which is larger than the payoff from portfolio A. In any state of nature portfolio B pays an amount greater than or equal to portfolio A. Therefore, in order to prevent dominance, portfolio B must have a higher price than portfolio A:

$$p(S, T, X) + S \geq XB(T).$$

This restriction may be rearranged to obtain

$$p(S, T, X) \geq \text{MAX}[0, XB(T) - S].$$

Finally, from (7.12) we have

$$p(S, T, X) \geq \text{MAX}[0, e^{-r_f T} X - S]. \tag{7.17}$$

The limitations this places on European put prices is shown in Fig. 7.10. Recall from Eq. (7.16) that the value of the American put is bounded by the stronger condition that

$$P \geq \text{MAX}[0, X - S]. \tag{7.18}$$

This implies that, in contrast to European calls, European puts may have a value less than their intrinsic value, $X - S$, since it is possible that

$$e^{-r_f T} X - S < p < X - S.$$

Figure 7.10 Limitations of the feasible set of European put prices.

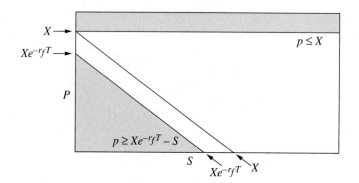

Table 7.6 Put Options on Dividend-Paying Stocks Are Less Likely to Be Exercised Prematurely

| Portfolio | Current Value | Portfolio Value, Given Stock Price at T | |
		$S < X$	$S \geq X$
A	$(X + Div)B(T)$	$X + Div$	$X + Div$
B	$S + p(S, T, X)$	$S + Div + X - S$	$S + Div$
Relationship between terminal values of A and B		$V_a = V_b$	$V_a < V_b$

Next, we shall show that an American put option written on a non-dividend-paying stock may be exercised before the expiration date of the option. To illustrate this consider the situation of Oct 10 put option on Calpine. If Calpine's stock price is close to zero, immediate exercise would result in a cash inflow of $10. If the put holder waits, the gain from exercise would be less than $10 but cannot be more than $10 since the stock price cannot go below zero. It would, therefore, be rational for the holder to exercise the American put early.

Again, in contrast to American calls, dividend payments on the underlying stock make it less likely that an American put may be exercised early. The rationality of this statement can be demonstrated by assuming that a security makes a certain dividend payment, Div, on the expiration date of an option. Consider two portfolios. Portfolio A is $X + Div$ bonds. Portfolio B is one share of stock and one European put. Table 7.6 shows the terminal values of the two portfolios. The value of A is less than that of B when the stock price is greater than the exercise price and equal to it otherwise. Therefore

$$S + p(S, X, T) \geq (X + Div)B(T).$$

By rearranging this and using Eq. (7.12), we obtain

$$p(S, T, X) \geq \text{MAX}\left[0, (X + Div)e^{-r_fT} - S\right]. \tag{7.19}$$

Depending on the size of the dividend payment and the risk-free rate, it is possible to have the following situation:

$$(X + Div)e^{-r_fT} > X.$$

The value of the European put is more than its intrinsic value. Therefore, in some cases it may be advantageous to not exercise an American put option prior to its maturity date, and the range of stock prices for which early exercise is optimal decreases with increases in dividends.

The preceding discussion has served to bound the possible values of call and put prices as shown in Figs. 7.8 and 7.10. This is done without any mention whatsoever of the risk preferences of different individuals. The dominance arguments used in the analysis are very robust. They require only that the absence of arbitrage opportunities in efficient capital markets means that prices are set so that there are no dominated securities. Further, the theorems provide considerable insight into the relationship between option prices; the price of the underlying asset, S; the exercise price, X; the time to maturity, T; and the risk-free rate, r_f. In the next section we demonstrate the call (put) valuation formula, which can be used to determine the price of a European call (put), given that we know about the four parameters and the instantaneous variance of the price of the underlying asset.

G. $\mathcal{D}$erivation of the Option Pricing Formula— The Binomial Approach

We shall discuss two derivations of the (Black-Scholes) option pricing model (OPM). The second, a closed-form solution, was provided by Black and Scholes [1973]. They recognized that, given the assumption of frictionless markets and continuous trading opportunities, it is possible to form a riskless hedge portfolio consisting of a long position in a stock and a short position in a European call written on that stock. As we shall see, this insight is critical for solving the option pricing problem. However, because their derivation requires the use of advanced mathematical tools such as stochastic differential equations, it is relegated to the appendix of this chapter. A somewhat more intuitive approach, and the first that we shall discuss, uses binomial distributions. It was independently derived by Cox, Ross, and Rubinstein [1979] and Rendleman and Bartter [1979]. Besides being easier to understand, the binomial approach provides solutions, not only for a closed-form European option pricing model but also for the more difficult American option problem where numerical simulations must be employed.

Chapter 9 uses the binomial approach repeatedly in real option applications. These multiperiod investment decisions are exemplified by research and development, exploration and development, new product development, phased investment, and entry and exit decisions.

1. The Binomial Model for Pricing Call Options on Stock

In addition to the usual assumption of frictionless and competitive capital markets where no riskless arbitrage opportunities can exist, assume that the stock price, S, obeys a multiplicative binomial generating process as shown in Fig. 7.11, where

S = the stock price,

$q = .5$ = the probability the stock price will move upward,

$1 + r_f = 1.1$ = one plus the annual risk-free rate of interest,

$u = 1.2$ = the multiplicative upward movement in the stock price ($u > 1 + r_f > 1$),

$d = .67$ = the multiplicative downward movement in the stock price ($d < 1 < 1 + r_f$).

Figure 7.11 A one-period binomial process.

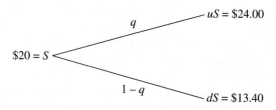

$$uS = \$24.00$$
$$q$$
$$\$20 = S$$
$$1 - q$$
$$dS = \$13.40$$

Figure 7.12 Payoffs for a one-period call option.

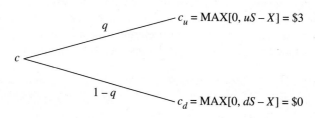

$$c_u = \text{MAX}[0,\, uS - X] = \$3$$
$$q$$
$$c$$
$$1 - q$$
$$c_d = \text{MAX}[0,\, dS - X] = \$0$$

At the end of one time period the stock price may increase to uS with probability q or decrease to dS with probability $1 - q$. Figure 7.11 provides a simple example where the current stock price is $20. There is a 50/50 chance (i.e., $q = .5$) it will increase to $24 or fall to $13.40 by the end of the period. Note that the downward multiplier for the stock price, d, must be less than one and greater than zero. This assumption ensures that the stock price will not fall below a value of $0, no matter how many time periods are eventually added. If there are n periods, then

$$\lim_{n \to \infty} d^n = 0 \quad \text{iff} \quad 0 \le d \le 1.$$

Of course, there is no upper bound on the value that the stock price may take.

Next, denote $1 + r_f$ as one plus the riskless rate of interest over the single time period ($1 + r_f = 1.1$ in our example). The derivation requires that $u > 1 + r_f > d$. If these inequalities did not hold, then riskless arbitrage opportunities would exist. Also, for convenience, we assume that $r_f > 0$.

Now, imagine a call option, c, with an exercise price of $X = \$21$ written on the stock. The payoffs for the call are shown in Fig. 7.12. Given our numerical example, there is a 50/50 chance of ending up with $\text{MAX}[0, uS - X] = \$3$, or $\text{MAX}[0, dS - X] = \$0$. The question is, How much would we pay for the call right now?

To answer the question, we begin by constructing a risk-free hedge portfolio composed of one share of stock, S, and m shares of a call option written against the stock. Figure 7.13 shows the payoffs for the hedge portfolio. If the end-of-period payoffs are equal, the portfolio will be risk free. Equating the payoffs, we have

$$uS - mc_u = dS - mc_d,$$

and solving for m, the number of call options to be written against the share of stock, we have

$$m = \frac{S(u - d)}{c_u - c_d}. \tag{7.20}$$

Figure 7.13 The payoffs for a risk-free hedge portfolio.

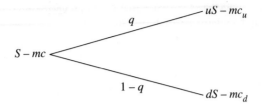

Substituting the numbers from our example problem, we see that the hedge ratio is

$$m = \frac{\$20(1.2 - .67)}{\$3 - \$0} = 3.53.$$

Thus the riskless hedge portfolio consists of buying one share of stock and writing 3.53 call options against it. The payoffs in the two states of nature are identical, as shown below.

State of Nature	Portfolio	Payoff
Favorable	$uS - mc_u$	$1.2(\$20) - 3.53(\$3) = \$13.40$
Unfavorable	$dS - mc_d$	$.67(\$20) - 3.53(\$0) = \$13.40$

Before we can determine what rate of return this payoff represents, we must figure out the call price, c, in order to know exactly what our original investment was.

We also know that because the hedge portfolio is constructed to be riskless, the current value of the portfolio multiplied by one plus the risk-free rate must equal the end-of-period payoff. Mathematically, this is

$$(1 + r_f)(S - mc) = uS - mc_u,$$

$$c = \frac{S\left[(1 + r_f) - u\right] + mc_u}{m(1 + r_f)}. \tag{7.21}$$

Substituting the hedge ratio, m, into this equation and rearranging terms, we can solve for the value of the call option:

$$c = \left[c_u\left(\frac{(1 + r_f) - d}{u - d}\right) + c_d\left(\frac{u - (1 + r_f)}{u - d}\right)\right] \div (1 + r_f). \tag{7.22}$$

It can be simplified by letting

$$p = \frac{(1 + r_f) - d}{u - d} \quad \text{and} \quad 1 - p = \frac{u - (1 + r_f)}{u - d}.$$

Thus we have

$$c = \left[pc_u + (1 - p)c_d\right] \div (1 + r_f). \tag{7.23}$$

We shall call p the *risk-neutral probability*. It is always greater than zero and less than one, so it has all the properties of a probability. In fact p is the value q would have in equilibrium if investors were risk neutral. Referring back to Fig. 7.9, a risk-neutral investor would require only the risk-free rate on an investment in the common stock; hence

$$(1+r_f)S = qS + (1-q)dS,$$

and solving for q, we have

$$q = \frac{(1+r_f) - d}{u - d}.$$

Thus $p = q$ for a risk-neutral investor, and Eq. (7.23), which gives us the value of a call, can be interpreted as the expectation of its discounted future value in a risk-neutral world. Of course, this does not imply that in equilibrium the required rate of return on a call is the risk-free rate. A call option has risk similar to that of buying the stock on margin.[11]

Continuing with our numerical example, we can use Eq. (7.23) to solve for the value of the call option:

$$c = \left[pc_u + (1-p)c_d \right] \div (1+r_f)$$

$$= \left[\left(\frac{1.1 - .67}{1.2 - .67} \right) \$3 + \left(\frac{1.2 - 1.1}{1.2 - .67} \right) \$0 \right] \div 1.1$$

$$= \left[(.8113)\$3 + (.1887)\$0 \right] \div 1.1 = \$2.2126.$$

Referring back to Fig. 7.11, we can now compute the dollar investment required for our hedge portfolio and confirm that the payoff of $13.40 at the end of the period yields the risk-free rate of return. The hedge portfolio consists of one share of stock and 3.53 call options written against it; therefore the dollar investment is

$$S - mc = \$20.00 - 3.53(\$2.2126) = \$12.19$$

and the rate of return on investment is

$$\frac{\$13.40}{\$12.19} = 1.1 = 1 + r_f.$$

The preceding derivation of the value of a call option depends critically on the existence of a hedge portfolio and on the fact that the call option must be priced so that the risk-free hedge earns exactly the risk-free rate of return. If the call had a higher (or lower) price, the hedge portfolio would earn more (or less) than the riskless rate, and opportunities to earn risk-free arbitrage profits would exist.

There are three interesting features of the call pricing formula:

- It does not depend on q, the objective probability of an upward movement in the stock price. Consequently, even though investors might have heterogeneous expectations about q, they will

---

[11] *Buying on margin* means that part of the investment in the stock is borrowed. In fact the exact payoffs of the call option can be duplicated by buying $(c_u - c_d)/[(u - d) S]$ shares of stock and $[uc_d - dc_u]/(u - d)(1 + r_f)$ units of the risk-free bond. See Cox, Ross, and Rubinstein [1979].

Figure 7.14 Stock prices with a two-period binomial process: $S = \$20$, $u = 1.2$, $d = .67$.

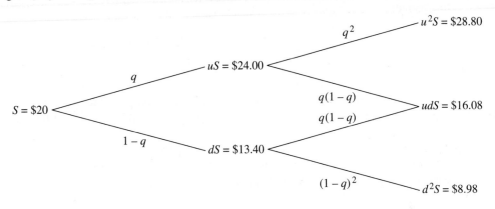

Figure 7.15 Two-period binomial call payoffs: $S = \$20$, $u = 1.2$, $d = .67$, $X = \$21$.

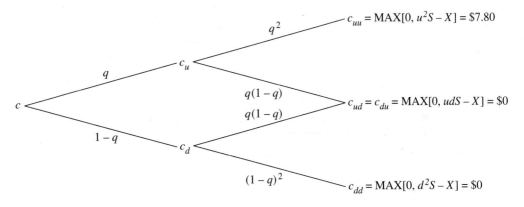

agree on the call value relative to its other parameters, namely, u, S, X, and r_f (in the one-period model). The stock price itself aggregates investors' diverse opinions regarding q.

- Individuals' attitudes toward risk are irrelevant in deriving the call option formula. All that is required for our results is that people prefer more wealth to less so that arbitrage profits are eliminated.

- The only random variable on which the call value depends is the stock itself. It does not depend, for example, on the market portfolio of all securities.

The next logical step is to extend the one-period model to many time periods in order to show how an option's time to maturity affects its value. First consider the two-period graphs of the stock prices and the call option payoffs as shown in Figs. 7.14 and 7.15. We assume that the two-period risk-free rate is simply $(1 + r_f)^2$.[12] Next, we can employ the one-period option pricing model,

---

[12] This is equivalent to assuming a flat term structure of interest rates.

Eq. (7.19), to solve for c_u and c_d, the values of the one-period options that started the end of the first period:

$$c_u = \left[pc_{uu} + (1-p)c_{ud} \right] \div (1+r_f),$$

$$c_d = \left[pc_{du} + (1-p)c_{dd} \right] \div (1+r_f). \qquad (7.24)$$

As before, we can construct a riskless hedge during the first period to prevent riskless arbitrage opportunities. The result gives the following equation for the present value of the call:

$$c = \left[pc_u + (1-p)c_d \right] \div (1+r_f).$$

Substituting the values of c_u and c_d from Eq. (7.24), we have

$$c = \left[p^2 c_{uu} + p(1-p)c_{ud} + (1-p)pc_{du} + (1-p)^2 c_{dd} \right] \div (1+r_f)^2. \qquad (7.25)$$

Equation (7.25) is the result of applying the one-period model twice.[13] The terms within brackets of Eq. (7.25) are a binomial expansion of the terms within brackets in Eq. (7.23), the one-period model. The terms c_{uu}, c_{ud}, and c_{dd} are the three possible values the call can have after two time periods:

$$c_{uu} = \text{MAX}\left[0, u^2 S - X \right],$$

$$c_{ud} = c_{du} = \text{MAX}\left[0, udS - X \right],$$

$$c_{dd} = \text{MAX}\left[0, d^2 S - X \right].$$

Another way of looking at Eq. (7.25) is to say that the call value is equal to the expected two-period payoffs (where the expectation uses the risk-neutral probabilities, p and $1-p$), discounted at the risk-free rate.

2. A Binomial Model for Pricing Call Options on Bonds

The time pattern for bond payouts is just the opposite from stock. While stock prices branch out across time to assume many values, as in Fig. 7.15, bond prices converge toward their face value at maturity. In addition, most bonds have coupon payments.[14] For our example we shall assume that the risk-free interest rate follows a binomial stochastic process as shown in Fig. 7.16. Assume that $r_f = 10\%$, that $u = 1.2$, that $d = .85$, and that there is a 50/50 chance of an up or down movement in interest rates (i.e., $q = .5$). Next, assume a default-free bond that has a face value of $D = \$1,000$, and that pays constant annual coupons of $coup = \$100$ at the end of each year during its three-

---

[13] One can easily imagine how this iterative technique lends itself to a computer program.

[14] One of the problems with the analysis of options on bonds is that when interest rates change, the present values of all coupons shift in a correlated fashion not captured by our simple binomial process. Another problem is that the variance of the interest rate process is not stationary. The simple example given in the text ignores both these important problems.

Figure 7.16 A binomial process for interest rates.

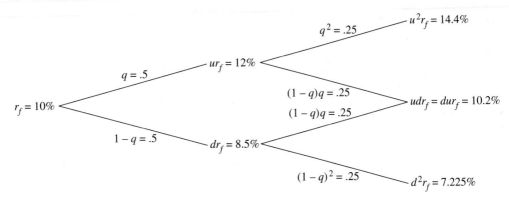

Figure 7.17 Expected bond prices.

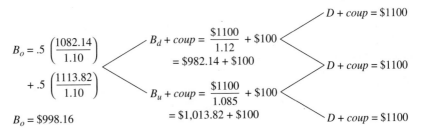

year life. We assume that the bond price is the present value of the expected end-of-period payoffs, that is,

$$B_t = \frac{q B_{d,t+1} + (1-q) B_{u,t+1} + coup}{1 + r_{ft}}. \qquad (7.26)$$

Note that the bond price in the "up" state of nature when interest rates go down, B_u, is greater than when they go up, B_d. Figure 7.17 illustrates the bond valuation tree. The bond price is stochastic until maturity because interest rates are.

Suppose we have a call option, with exercise price $X = \$1,000$, written on the default-free bond. In Part 2 of the book, we shall discuss the cost of capital for callable and convertible bonds. Let c_t be the market value of the call at period t. Its payoffs, if exercised, are illustrated in Fig. 7.18. Note that if the call had the same life as the default-free bond, the call would have the same payout in all final states of nature and would therefore be worthless. The call on a default-free bond must have a shorter life than the bond. Hence the call option illustrated in Fig. 7.18 has a two-period life, whereas the underlying bond matures after three periods.

To value the call option, we have to create a risk-free hedge of one bond minus the value of m calls written against it. A perfect hedge will give the same payoff in each state of nature (up or down); hence we may write

$$B_{d,t+1} + coup - mc_{d,t+1} = B_{u,t+1} + coup - mc_{u,t+1},$$

Figure 7.18 Payoffs of an American call on a risky bond.

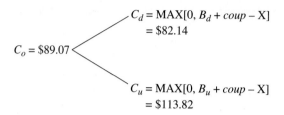

$C_d = \text{MAX}[0, B_d + coup - X]$
$= \$82.14$

$C_o = \$89.07$

$C_u = \text{MAX}[0, B_u + coup - X]$
$= \$113.82$

and the hedge ratio is

$$m = \frac{B_{d,t+1} - B_{u,t+1}}{c_{d,t+1} - c_{u,t+1}}. \tag{7.27}$$

We also know that the current value of the hedge portfolio, multiplied by $1 + r_{ft}$, will equal the end-of-period payoff,

$$(B_t - mc_t)(1 + r_{ft}) = B_{d,t+1} + coup - mc_{d,t+1}. \tag{7.28}$$

Substituting the value of m in Eq. (7.27) into Eq. (7.28) and solving for the call price, c_t, we have

$$c_t = \frac{\left[(B_{d,t+1} + coup) - B_t(1 + r_{ft})\right] c_{u,t+1} - \left[(B_{u,t+1} + coup) - B_t(1 + r_{ft})\right] c_{d,t+1}}{(B_{d,t+1} - B_{u,t+1})(1 + r_{ft})}. \tag{7.29}$$

To evaluate the call formula, Eq. (7.29), one starts at the expiration date of the option and works backward, step by step, until a value for c_0 is obtained. The market value of the call option in our example is

$$c_0 = \frac{[1082.14 - 998.16(1.10)]\,113.82 - [1113.82 - 998.16(1.10)]\,82.14}{(1082.14 - 1113.82)(1.10)}$$

$$c_0 = \$89.069.$$

Later on in the text, we shall use options on bonds to evaluate variable rate loans with CAPS, that is, variable rate loans with an upper bound on the rate of interest. Many corporate loans and mortgage loans have this format.

3. A Digression on the Binomial Distribution

The reader who is familiar with the binomial distribution can skip this section; otherwise a digression is in order. *Binomial trials*, as the name suggests, can take only two values, for example, heads, h, or tails, t, in the flip of a coin. The coin flip need not be fair, so let p be the probability of observing n heads, given T flips of a coin. Designate this probability as $\Pr\{n\,|T\,\}$. A typical question might be, What is the probability, $\Pr\{2\,|3\}$, of observing two heads out of three coin flips? Useful for answering this question is Pascal's triangle. Each row is constructed from the sum of the numbers in the adjacent two columns in the row immediately above it:

Number of Trials	Pascal's Triangle							
$T = 0$				1				
$T = 1$			1		1			
$T = 2$		1		2		1		
$T = 3$	1		3		3		1	
$T = 4$	1	4		6		4		1
Number of heads, $n =$	T		$T - 1$		$\cdots$			$T - T$

The numbers in the rows of Pascal's triangle are the coefficients for a binomial expansion, say, $[p + (1 - p)]^T$. For example, if T is 3 and we want to know the coefficients in $[p + (1 - p)]^3$, they are 1, 3, 3, and 1, as in

$$1 \cdot p^3 + 3 \cdot p^2(1 - p) + 3 \cdot p(1 - p)^2 + 1 \cdot (1 - p)^3.$$

In general the probability of observing n heads in T trials is

$$Pr\,\{n\,|T\,\} = (\text{coef})\,p^n(1 - p)^{T-n},$$

where (coef) is the correct coefficient taken from Pascal's triangle. Thus the probability of observing two heads in three flips of a fair (i.e., $p = .5$) coin is

$$Pr\,\{n = 2\,|T = 3\} = 3(.5)^2(.5) = .375, \quad \text{where coef} = 3.$$

For large numbers Pascal's triangle is cumbersome. Another way of figuring out the coefficient is to use combinatorial notation:

$$\text{coef} = \binom{T}{n} = \frac{T!}{(T - n)!\,n!}.$$

The term in parentheses can be read "The number of combinations of T things chosen n at a time." For example, what are all the possible ways of getting two heads out of three coin flips? There should be three different ways of doing it, and they are: hht, hth, thh. The right-hand term uses factorial notation to compute the number of combinations. The term $T!$ (read "T factorial") is the product of all the numbers from T down to 1. Thus if we want to compute the number of combinations of two heads in three coin flips, we have

$$\frac{T!}{(T - n)!\,n!} = \frac{3!}{(3 - 2)!\,2!} = \frac{3 \cdot 2 \cdot 1}{(1)(2 \cdot 1)} = 3.$$

By the way, 0! is always defined as being equal to 1.

The binomial probability of observing n heads out of T trials, given that the probability of a head is p, can be written

$$B(n\,|T,\,p) = \frac{T!}{(T - n)!\,n!}p^n(1 - p)^{T-n} = \binom{T}{n}p^n(1 - p)^{T-n}.$$

The mean, $E(n)$, of a binomial distribution is the expected number of heads in T trials. It is written

$$E(n) = Tp,$$

and the variance is $\text{VAR}(n) = Tp(1 - p)$.[15]

4. The Complete Binomial Model for Pricing Call Options on Stock

The T-period generalization of the binomial call pricing formula is simply the probability of each final outcome multiplied by the value of the outcome and discounted at the risk-free rate for T time periods. Then the general form of the payoff is

$$\text{MAX}\left[0, u^n d^{T-n} S - X\right],$$

where T is the total number of time periods, and n is the number of upward movements in the stock price ($n = 0, 1, 2, \ldots, T$). The general form of the probabilities of each payoff is given by the binomial distribution

$$B(n \mid T, p) = \frac{T!}{(T - n)! n!} p^n (1 - p)^{T-n}.$$

Multiplying the payoffs by the probabilities and summing across all possible payoffs, we have

$$c = \left\{ \sum_{n=0}^{T} \frac{T!}{(T - n)! n!} p^n (1 - p)^{T-n} \text{MAX}\left[0, u^n d^{T-n} S - X\right] \right\} \div (1 + r_f)^T. \qquad (7.30)$$

Equation (7.30) is a complete expression for binomial option pricing. However, one of our objectives is to compare the binomial model, which is derived in discrete time, with a Black-Scholes model, which is a continuous time model. Therefore the following paragraphs show how to rewrite the binomial model so that it may be easily compared with the Black-Scholes model, which is given in the next section of this chapter.

First, let us make use of the fact that many of the final payoffs for a call option will be zero because the option finishes out-of-the-money. Denote a as the positive integer that bounds those states of nature where the option has a nonnegative value. Then Eq. (7.30) can be rewritten as follows:

$$c = \left\{ \sum_{n=a}^{T} \frac{T!}{(T - n)! n!} p^n (1 - p)^{T-n} \left[u^n d^{T-n} S - X\right] \right\} \div (1 + r_f)^T. \qquad (7.31)$$

The summation in Eq. (7.30) was $n = 0 \ldots T$ and now it is $n = a \ldots T$. Also we are able to drop the notation $\text{MAX}[0, u^n d^{T-n} S - X]$ because we are dealing only with nonnegative payoffs.

---

[15] The reader who wants to read more on binomial trials is referred to Feller [1968, Chapter 6].

Next, separate Eq. (7.31) into two parts as follows:

$$c = S \left[\sum_{n=a}^{T} \frac{T!}{(T-n)!n!} p^n (1-p)^{T-n} \frac{u^n d^{T-n}}{(1+r_f)^T} \right]$$

$$- X(1+r_f)^{-T} \left[\sum_{n=a}^{T} \frac{T!}{(T-n)!n!} p^n (1-p)^{T-n} \right]. \tag{7.32}$$

The second bracketed expression is the discounted value of the exercise price, $X(1+r_f)^{-T}$, multiplied by a complementary binomial distribution, $B(n \geq a \,|T, p)$. The complementary binomial probability is the cumulative probability of having in-the-money options (i.e., where $n \geq a$) where the probabilities are the hedging (or risk neutral) probabilities determined by the risk-free hedge portfolio. The first bracketed expression is the stock price, S, multiplied by a complementary binomial probability. It may be interpreted in the same way if we let

$$p' \equiv \left[u/(1+r_f) \right] p \quad \text{and} \quad 1 - p' = \left[d/(1+r_f) \right] (1-p).$$

We then have

$$p^n (1-p)^{T-n} \frac{u^n d^{T-n}}{(1+r_f)^T} = \left[\frac{u}{(1+r_f)} p \right]^n \left[\frac{d}{(1+r_f)} (1-p) \right]^{T-n} = (p')^n (1-p')^{T-n}.$$

The binomial model for the pricing of a European call option can be summarized as follows:

$$c = SB(n \geq a \,|T, p') - X(1+r_f)^{-T} B(n \geq a \,|T, p), \tag{7.33}$$

where

$$p \equiv \frac{(1+r_f) - d}{u - d} \quad \text{and} \quad p' \equiv \left[\frac{u}{(1+r_f)} \right] p,$$

$a \equiv$ the smallest nonnegative integer greater than $\ln(X/Sd^n)/\ln(u/d)$,

and if $a < T$, then $c = 0$,

$B(n \geq a \,|T, p)$ $=$ the complementary binomial probability that $n \geq a$.

The complementary binomial distribution function is the probability that the sum of n random variables, each of which can take on the value 1 with probability p and 0 with probability $(1 - p)$, will be greater than or equal to $\dot{a}$. Mathematically, it is

$$B(n \geq a \,|T, p) = \sum_{n=a}^{T} \frac{T!}{(T-n)!n!} (p(1-p)^{T-n}),$$

$T =$ the total number of time periods.

It is obvious from (7.33) that the call option increases in value when the stock price, S, rises, and decreases when the exercise price, X, rises. In addition, the risk-free rate, r_f, the number of time periods before the option matures, T, and the variance of the binomial distribution,

$\sigma^2 = Tp(1-p)$, affect the call value. When the risk-free rate increases, its main effect is to decrease the discounted value of the exercise price, $X(1+r_f)^{-n}$, and this increases the call value (although there are secondary effects causing p and p' to decrease as r_f increases). An increase in the number of time periods to maturity, T, clearly increases the call price. Recall that the call value is equivalent to the discounted value of the final payoffs multiplied by their hedging probabilities. The number of time periods does not change the hedging probabilities, p. However, it does increase the number of positive payoffs, because in Eq. (7.32) the integer, a, that bounds the positive payoffs will decrease as T increases. Also the expected value of the binomial payoffs, $E(n) = pT$, increases with T. Finally, the call value will increase with increases in the binomial variance, $\text{VAR}(n) = Tp(1-p)$. This happens because when the size of the stock price change, u, goes up, so does that variance of the binomial distribution. A greater variance increases the chances that the stock price will exceed the exercise price in the final payoffs, and therefore the call price goes up.

In sum, the intuition behind the call pricing formula, Eq. (7.33), is that the value of the call is equal to today's stock price, S, converted into a risk-adjusted position of one call by multiplying it by one over a hedge ratio, $B(n \geq a | T, p')$, then subtracting the present value of the exercise price $X(1+r_f)^{-T}$ weighted by the probability that the option will mature in-the-money, $B(n \geq a | T, p)$. Note that the risk-neutral probability, p', is used for the risk-adjusted position and p for the objective probability of finishing in-the-money.

5. The Black-Scholes Option Pricing Model—Extending the Binomial Model to Continuous Time

The binomial pricing model can be extended to derive a continuous time equivalent if we hold the amount of calendar time (say, one year) constant and divide it into more and more binomial trials. We will define T as the life of the option expressed as a fraction of a year and will divide T into n smaller time intervals. As n becomes larger, the calendar interval between binomial trials becomes shorter and shorter until, in the limit, we have a continuous stochastic process.[16] Note that in this section of the chapter we used T as the number of periods until maturity. A continuous stochastic process has the stock price constantly changing, so its path can be drawn without ever lifting pen from paper.

Of particular concern is the way that the annual risk-free rate, r_f, the up and down movements, u and d, and the binomial processes are to be handled as the number of time intervals, n, becomes infinite. If we define r_f as the rate of return for one year, and let j be the rate that is compounded n times in interval T (where T is a fraction of a year, e.g., six months), then in the limit we have[17]

$$\lim_{n \to \infty} \left(1 + \frac{j}{n/T}\right)^{n/T} = e^j = (1+r_f). \tag{7.34}$$

Equation (7.34) shows how an annual rate of interest can be converted into the rate of interest for a binomial model with n binomial trials per year. Next, we need to know how the up and down movements, u and d, in a single binomial trial relate to the annual standard deviation of a stock's

---

[16] The binomial formula can also be used to model a jump stochastic process as a limiting case. See Cox, Ross, and Rubinstein [1979, 254–255] for the derivation. With a jump process the stock price will usually move in a smooth deterministic way but will occasionally experience sudden discontinuous jumps.

[17] For proof, see Appendix A at the end of the book.

rate of return. Cox, Ross, and Rubinstein [1979] prove the following:

$$u = e^{\sigma \sqrt{T/n}}$$

and

$$d = e^{-\sigma \sqrt{T/n}}. \tag{7.35}$$

The relationships given in Eq. (7.35) are extremely useful for translating continuous time variables such as the annualized standard deviation, σ, into discrete variables such as u and d for use in the binomial option pricing model.

The continuous-time option pricing formula, derived by Black-Scholes [1973], is[18]

$$c = SN(d_1) - Xe^{-r_f T} N(d_2), \tag{7.36a}$$

where

$$d_1 = \frac{\ln(S/X) + r_f T}{\sigma \sqrt{T}} + \frac{1}{2} \sigma \sqrt{T}, \tag{7.36b}$$

$$d_2 = d_1 - \sigma \sqrt{T}. \tag{7.36c}$$

The terms $N(d_1)$ and $N(d_2)$ are the cumulative probabilities for a unit normal variable z where, for example, $N(-\infty) = 0$, $N(0) = .5$, and $N(\infty) = 1.0$. Mathematically, this is

$$N(d_1) = \int_{-\infty}^{d_1} f(z)dz,$$

where z is distributed normally with mean zero and standard deviation one, and $f(z)$ is the normal density.

The binomial model is rewritten below so that it can be readily compared with the Black-Scholes model:

$$c = SB(n \geq a \,|T, \, p') - X(1 + r_f)^{-T} B(n \geq a \,|T, \, p).$$

The two equations look very similar. The variables S and X are exactly the same and Eq. (7.34) shows the relationship between $(1 + r_f)^{-T}$ and $e^{-r_f T}$. Cox, Ross, and Rubinstein [1979] have proved that as n, the number of binomial jumps per year, becomes large, the two formulas converge because

$$B(n \geq a \,|T, \, p') \rightarrow N(d_1) \quad \text{and} \quad B(n \geq a \,|T, \, p) \rightarrow N(d_2).$$

Thus the binomial option pricing formula contains the Black-Scholes formula as a limiting case.

Both formulas will be used throughout the remainder of the text, and the student should be familiar with how to use them. The next section gives a numerical example using both artificial data and data for Krispy Kreme call options. Because Krispy Kreme paid no dividends during the

---

[18] The appendix at the end of this chapter gives the stochastic calculus derivation.

valuation period, the Black-Scholes and binomial pricing models can be used directly, without further modification.

H. Valuation of a Call On a Stock with No Dividends

1. An Example with Artificial Data

To understand the mechanics of using the OPM we can first use a simple example where all the parameters are given. Then we can proceed to a problem that uses real-world data.

Suppose that the current stock price is $50, that the exercise price of an American call written on the stock is $45, that the annual risk-free rate is $r_f = 6\%$, that the option matures in three months, and that the variance of the stock price is estimated to be 20% per year. Given these facts and the assumption that the stock will pay no dividends or undertake any other capital distributions, we can use the Black-Scholes OPM, Eq. (7.36a), to value the call.

To evaluate Eq. (7.36a) we first calculate the value of d_1, a unit normal variable, with a mean of zero and a standard deviation of one. The time to maturity, three months, must be expressed as a fraction of a year (i.e., one fourth of a year). Setting $T = .25$, and substituting in the values of the other parameters, we get

$$d_1 = \frac{\ln(50/45) + .06(.25)}{\sqrt{.2}\sqrt{.25}} + \frac{1}{2}\left(\sqrt{.2}\right)\sqrt{.25}$$

$$= \frac{.12036}{.2236} + .1118 = .65.$$

Using Eq. (7.36c), we can solve for d_2:

$$d_2 = d_1 - \sigma\sqrt{T} = .65 - \sqrt{.2}\sqrt{.25} = .4264.$$

Substituting these values back into Eq. (7.36a), we have

$$c = SN(.65) - e^{-r_f T} XN(.4264).$$

Recall that $N(\cdot)$ are cumulative probabilities for a unit normal variable. Therefore $N(d_1)$ is the cumulative probability from minus infinity to $+.65$ standard deviations above the mean (which is defined to be zero for a unit normal distribution). The probability contained in the shaded area of Fig. 7.19 will give us the value of $N(d_1)$. Table 7.7 shows that if $d_1 = .65$, the cumulative probability from the mean ($\mu = 0$) to .65 is approximately .242. If we add this to the cumulative probability from minus infinity to zero (which equals .5), we get

$$N(d_1) = \int_{-\infty}^{0} f(z)dz + \int_{0}^{d_1} f(z)dz$$

$$= .5 + .242 = .742.$$

Repeating this procedure for $N(d_2)$, we get .6651. Substituting these probabilities into the call valuation formula, we have

Figure 7.19 Illustration of $N(d_1)$.

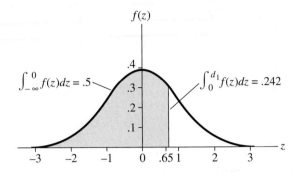

$$c = 50(.742) - e^{-.06(.25)}(45)(.6651)$$

$$= 37.10 - .9851(45)(.6651)$$

$$= 37.10 - 29.48 = \$7.62.$$

Table 7.8 gives the value of the call option for various stock prices, and Fig. 7.20 plots the call price as a function of the stock price. Note that the call has little value until the stock price rises to the point where it is near the exercise price ($X = \$45$). When the stock price is well below the exercise price, the option is said to be "out-of-the-money," and the call will not be worth much. On the other hand, when the stock price is above the exercise price, the option is "in-the-money," and its value increases until in the limit it reaches $S - Xe^{-r_f T}$ for very high stock prices.

When pricing a real-world call it is important to keep in mind (1) that the Black-Scholes formula cannot be used if the common stock is expected to pay a dividend during the life of the option, (2) that a CBOE call option is not really a simple option but rather an option on an option,[19] and (3) that the instantaneous variance is not stationary over time. If the common stock of a firm is really an option on the assets of the firm, then a call option written against the common stock is really an option on an option. The Black-Scholes formula tends to misprice deep out-of-the-money options and deep in-the-money options. One possible reason is that the simple OPM does not accurately price compound options, and that the bias increases as the stock price moves away from the exercise price.

It is also of interest to contrast the call prices obtained from the binomial model with those given by the Black-Scholes model. Suppose we assume there are only two time periods (each six weeks long). How closely does the binomial model with only two periods approximate the Black-Scholes continuous time call price of $7.62, given a $45 exercise price and three months to maturity?

First, we need to convert the annual effective risk-free rate, 6%, into a semiquarterly rate, j. This is done below for $T = $ three months, that is, .25 years:[20]

$$\left(1 + \frac{j}{2/.25}\right)^{2/.25} = 1 + .06,$$

$$j/8 = .731\%.$$

---

[19] Because the equity in a levered firm is a call option on the value of the (unlevered) assets of the firm, and the CBOE call is an option on the equity.

[20] See Eq. (7.30) or Appendix A at the back of the book.

Table 7.7 Areas under the Normal Curve

Areas under the Standard Normal Distribution Function $\int_0^z f(z)dz$									
z	.00	.01	.02	.03	.04	.05	.06	.07	.08	.09
0.0	.0000	.0040	.0080	.0120	.0160	.0199	.0239	.0279	.0319	.0359
0.1	.0398	.0438	.0478	.0517	.0557	.0596	.0636	.0675	.0714	.0753
0.2	.0793	.0832	.0871	.0910	.0948	.0987	.1026	.1064	.1103	.1141
0.3	.1179	.1217	.1255	.1293	.1331	.1368	.1406	.1443	.1480	.1517
0.4	.1554	.1591	.1628	.1664	.1700	.1736	.1772	.1808	.1844	.1879
0.5	.1915	.1950	.1985	.2019	.2054	.2088	.2123	.2157	.2190	.2224
0.6	.2257	.2291	.2324	.2357	.2389	.2422	.2454	.2486	.2517	.2549
0.7	.2580	.2611	.2642	.2673	.2704	.2734	.2764	.2794	.2823	.2852
0.8	.2881	.2910	.2939	.2967	.2995	.3023	.3051	.3078	.3106	.3133
0.9	.3159	.3186	.3212	.3238	.3264	.3289	.3315	.3340	.3365	.3389
1.0	.3413	.3438	.3461	.3485	.3508	.3531	.3554	.3577	.3599	.3621
1.1	.3643	.3665	.3686	.3708	.3729	.3749	.3770	.3790	.3810	.3830
1.2	.3849	.3869	.3888	.3907	.3925	.3944	.3962	.3980	.3997	.4015
1.3	.4032	.4049	.4066	.4082	.4099	.4115	.4131	.4147	.4162	.4177
1.4	.4192	.4207	.4222	.4236	.4251	.4265	.4279	.4292	.4306	.4319
1.5	.4332	.4345	.4357	.4370	.4382	.4394	.4406	.4418	.4429	.4441
1.6	.4452	.4463	.4474	.4484	.4495	.4505	.4515	.4525	.4535	.4545
1.7	.4554	.4564	.4573	.4582	.4591	.4599	.4608	.4616	.4625	.4633
1.8	.4641	.4649	.4656	.4664	.4671	.4678	.4686	.4693	.4699	.4706
1.9	.4713	.4719	.4726	.4732	.4738	.4744	.4750	.4756	.4761	.4767
2.0	.4772	.4778	.4783	.4788	.4793	.4798	.4803	.4808	.4812	.4817
2.1	.4821	.4826	.4830	.4834	.4838	.4842	.4846	.4850	.4854	.4857
2.2	.4861	.4864	.4868	.4871	.4875	.4878	.4881	.4884	.4887	.4890
2.3	.4893	.4896	.4898	.4901	.4904	.4906	.4909	.4911	.4913	.4916
2.4	.4918	.4920	.4922	.4925	.4927	.4929	.4931	.4932	.4934	.4936
2.5	.4938	.4940	.4941	.4943	.4945	.4946	.4948	.4949	.4951	.4952
2.6	.4953	.4955	.4956	.4957	.4959	.4960	.4961	.4962	.4963	.4964
2.7	.4965	.4966	.4967	.4968	.4969	.4970	.4971	.4972	.4973	.4974
2.8	.4974	.4975	.4976	.4977	.4977	.4978	.4979	.4979	.4980	.4981
2.9	.4981	.4982	.4982	.4982	.4984	.4984	.4985	.4985	.4986	.4986
3.0	.4987	.4987	.4987	.4987	.4988	.4989	.4989	.4989	.4990	.4990

Table 7.8 $c(S, T, \sigma^2, X, r_f)$ for Different Stock Prices

Stock Price	d_1	$N(d_1)$	d_2	$N(d_2)$	Call Price	Given
$30	−1.63	.052	−1.85	.032	$.14	
$40	−.35	.363	−.57	.284	$1.93	$T = 3$ months
$50	.65	.742	.43	.665	$7.62	$r_f = .06$
$60	1.47	.929	1.24	.893	$16.15	$\sigma^2 = 20\%$
$70	2.15	.984	1.93	.973	$25.75	$X = \$45$

Figure 7.20 Call pricing example.

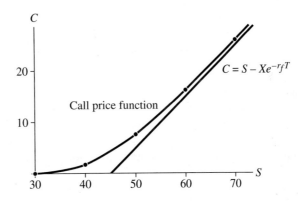

Next, we need to convert the annualized standard deviation, $\sigma = \sqrt{.2} = .4472$, into the up and down variables of the option pricing formula. Using Eq. (7.31) we have

$$u = e^{\sigma\sqrt{T/n}} = e^{.4472\sqrt{.25/2}} = 1.1713,$$

$$d = e^{-\sigma\sqrt{T/n}} = e^{-.4472\sqrt{.25/2}} = .8538.$$

These numbers are needed to estimate the complementary binomial probabilities in the binomial option pricing formula. The easiest way to solve for the value of a call option is to use the iterative approach illustrated in Figs. 7.14 and 7.15 and given algebraically in Eq. (7.25). For the particular example at hand, the call option payoffs are given in Fig. 7.21. First solve for c_u, the option value at the end of the first period, given that the stock price moved up. Using Eq. (7.23) we have

$$c_u[pc_{uu} + (1-p)c_{ud}] \div (1+r_f),$$

where the objective probability is

$$p = (1+r_f - d)/(u - d)$$

$$= (1.00731 - .8538)/(1.1713 - .8538) = .4835$$

and

$$1 - p = .5165.$$

Figure 7.21 Binomial call payoffs.

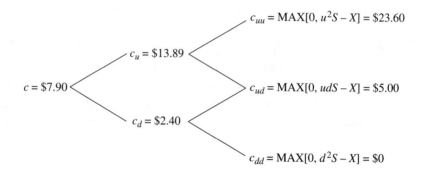

Therefore,

$$c_u = [.4835(23.60) + .5165(5.00)] \div 1.00731 = \$13.8916.$$

A similar calculation reveals that

$$c_d = \left[pc_{du} + (1-p)c_{dd} \right] \div (1 + r_f) = \$2.4000.$$

Now the above results for c_u and c_d can be used to solve for the current call value, c:

$$c = \left[pc_u + (1-p)c_d \right] \div (1 + r_f)$$
$$= [.4835(13.8916) + .5165(2.4000)] \div 1.00731$$
$$= \$7.90.$$

From the same data, the Black-Scholes call value was computed to be $7.62. A two-period binomial approximation is reasonably accurate in this case. However, as the number of binomial trials is increased, the accuracy of the binomial approximation improves considerably. Figure 7.22 shows how the binomial approximation approaches the Black-Scholes answer as n increases. It is fairly easy to write a computer program to estimate the binomial pricing formula using either the iterative technique as illustrated above or Eq. (7.33).[21]

2. An Example Using Real Data

Consider the options on Krispy Kreme Doughnuts that are listed in Table 7.1. Since Krispy Kreme has paid no dividends, the calls are effectively European and can be valued using the Black-Scholes model. Table 7.9 provides most of the information needed to value the call. The stock price, the exercise price, and the number of days to maturity are given for each option. The risk-free rate is estimated by using the average of the bid and ask quotes on U.S. Treasury bills of approximately the same maturity as the option. The only missing piece of information is the instantaneous variance of the stock rate of return. Several different techniques have been suggested for estimating it (e.g., see Latane and Rendleman [1976] or Parkinson [1977]). We shall use the implicit variance estimated

---

[21] See Copeland and Antikarov [2001, Chapter 7] for details.

Figure 7.22 The binomial option pricing closely approximates the Black-Scholes result.

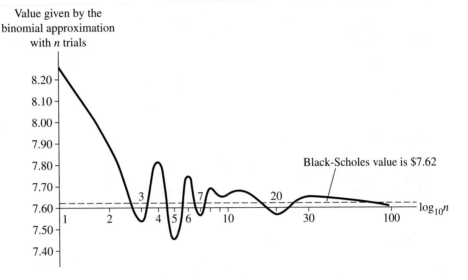

from one call price in valuing the others.[22] The implicit variance is calculated by simply using the actual call price and the four known exogenous parameters in the Black-Scholes formula, Eq. (7.36a), to solve for an estimate of the instantaneous variance. We did this using the August 35s on Krispy Kreme, which were priced at $1.90 on July 18, 2002. The estimate of the instantaneous standard deviation was approximately 51.5%.

Substituting our estimates of the five parameters into the Black-Scholes valuation equation, we can estimate the price of the August 30s as follows:

$$c = SN(d_1) - e^{-r_f T} X N(d_2),$$

where

$$r_f = .0171, \qquad T = 30/365, \qquad S = \$34.65, \qquad X = \$30, \qquad \sigma = .515,$$

$$d_1 = \frac{\ln(S/X) + r_f T}{\sigma\sqrt{T}} + \frac{1}{2}\sigma\sqrt{T}, \qquad d_2 = d_1 - \sigma\sqrt{T}.$$

The estimated call price turns out to be $5.10, which is equal to the actual call price. If we repeat the procedure for the August 45s (now $X = 45$), the estimated call price is $0.09, whereas the actual price is $0.15.

The above examples show how the Black-Scholes valuation model may be used to price call options on non-dividend-paying stocks. Roll [1977] and Geske [1979a] have solved the problem

---

[22] The implied variance is forward looking, but uses the Black-Scholes formula and the market price of one option to estimate the standard deviation—a parameter to be used in Black-Scholes to value another option on the same stock. We might have used the actual return history of the stock and our knowledge of statistics to estimate the variance from historical data—a backward-looking approach.

Table 7.9 Data Needed to Price Krispy Kreme Doughnut Calls

Call Prices, July 18, 2002		
Exercise Price	**Call Price**	**Closing Stock Price**
$30	$5.10	$34.65
35	1.90	34.65
45	0.15	34.65
Maturity date	Aug 17	
Days to maturity	30	

Treasury Bill Rates on July 18, 2002				
Maturity Date	**Bid**	**Ask**	**Average**	r_f
Aug. 16, 2002	1.69%	1.68%	1.685%	1.71%

of valuing American calls when the common stock is assumed to make known dividend payments before the option matures.[23] However, the mathematics involved in the solution is beyond the level of this text.

3. Forming Hedge Portfolios

Suppose we wish to form a riskless hedge portfolio consisting of shares of Krispy Kreme and call options written against them. If we own 100 shares, how many call options should be written? The answer is derived by noting that the Black-Scholes formula is

$$c = SN(d_1) - Xe^{-r_f T} N(d_2),$$

and its partial derivative with respect to a change in the stock price is[24]

$$\frac{\partial c}{\partial S} = N(d_1). \tag{7.37}$$

A riskless hedge portfolio will contain Q_S shares of stock and Q_c call options written against it. Its dollar return per unit time will be approximately

$$Q_S \left(\frac{dS}{dt} \right) - Q_c \left(\frac{dc}{dt} \right).$$

If we write $1/N(d_1)$ call options for each share of stock (i.e., $Q_S = 1$), the return on the hedge is approximately zero, as shown below:

$$1 \cdot \left(\frac{dS}{dt} \right) - \frac{1}{dc/dS} \left(\frac{dc}{dt} \right) = 0.$$

---

[23] Also see Whaley [1981].

[24] Equation (7.33) is the exact solution even though the derivative is complicated by the fact that $N(d_1)$ is a function of S. The curious reader is referred to Galai and Masulis [1976] for the math.

If we use the Krispy Kreme August 35s to hedge against 100 shares of Krispy Kreme common stock, then we would have to write 100 times $1/N(d_1)$ options. Computing $N(d_1)$ we have

$$d_1 = \frac{\ln(S/X) + r_f T}{\sigma\sqrt{T}} + \frac{1}{2}\sigma\sqrt{T}$$

$$= \frac{\ln(34.65/35) + .0171(30/365)}{(.515)\sqrt{30/365}} + \frac{1}{2}(.515)\sqrt{30/365}$$

$$= .0153.$$

And referring to Table 7.7, we see that

$$N(d_1) = .5 + .0161 = .5161.$$

Therefore we want to write 100 times $1/N(d_1)$, or 193.8 call options.

It is important to bear in mind that this type of hedge is riskless only for small changes in the stock price. The hedge ratio must be adjusted whenever the stock price changes.

4. Intuitive Explanations of $N(d_1)$ and $N(d_2)$

The intuition of the call pricing formula is that the call is equal to the stock price, S, minus the discounted value of the exercise price, $Xe^{-r_f T}$. However, each component is weighted by a probability. The stock price is weighted by $N(d_1)$, which is the inverse of the hedge ratio. For each share of stock, a riskless hedge contains $1/N(d_1)$ call options written against the stock. On the other hand, the discounted value of the exercise price is multiplied by $N(d_2)$. We can interpret $N(d_2)$ as the probability that the option will finish in-the-money. The best way to see this is to go back to the binomial option model discussion, Eq. (7.33), and recall that there the discounted exercise price is multiplied by the complementary binomial probability, $B(n \geq a \,|\, T, p)$, which is the probability that the option will finish in-the-money, that is, the probability that it will be exercised.

Thus the Black-Scholes model can be interpreted as the stock price multiplied by the inverse of the hedge ratio, minus the discounted exercise price multiplied by the probability that the option will be exercised.

I. $\mathcal{P}$ricing American Put Options

Knowledge of put-call parity, Eq. (7.10), and the call option pricing formula is sufficient to value a European put option. Unfortunately, American put options can be exercised before maturity. Therefore put-call parity does not hold for them and they must be evaluated directly.

All known solutions to the American put valuation problem involve computerized numerical methods. Solutions have been provided by Parkinson [1977], Brennan and Schwartz [1977], and Cox, Ross, and Rubinstein [1979]. Because we have already made use of the binomial approach to option pricing in Section G of this chapter, the easiest thing to do is to show how it may be employed to value American puts on non-dividend-paying common stock.

Figure 7.23 Payoffs to the American put after one period.

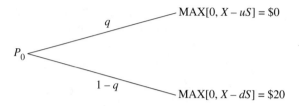

$$MAX[0, X - uS] = \$0$$

$$MAX[0, X - dS] = \$20$$

$X = \$50 =$ the exercise price for the option,
$S = \$50 =$ the current value of the stock,
$P_0 =$ the present value of an American put.

To provide a concrete example, suppose we know the following facts for a two-period American put:

$S = \$50 =$ stock price

$X = \$50 =$ exercise price

$u = 1.2 =$ multiplicative upward movement in the stock price, $u > 1 + r_f > 1$,

$d = .6 =$ multiplicative downward movement in the stock price, $d < 1 + r_f$,

$1 + r_f = 1.1 =$ one plus the annual risk-free rate.

Figure 7.23 shows the payoffs to the holder of an American put at the end of the first of two time periods. A hedge portfolio can be formed by purchasing a fraction, m, of the risky asset and simultaneously buying a put option written against it. The hedge portfolio and its payoffs are given in Fig. 7.24. By equating the end-of-period payoffs, we can solve for the hedging fraction, m, which gives a risk-free hedge:

$$muS + P_u = mdS + P_d,$$

$$m = \frac{P_d - P_u}{S(u - d)} = \frac{20 - 0}{50(1.2 - .6)} = .667. \tag{7.38}$$

The numerical payoffs from using the hedge consisting of (1) two thirds of a share of stock and (2) one put option are given in Fig. 7.25. This risk-free hedge pays $40 regardless of whether the stock price moves up (to $60) or down (to $30). Also note that the proper hedge does not depend on investors' subjective probabilities (q and $1 - q$ in Fig. 7.23) of an upward or downward movement in the stock price.

Next, we can solve for the risk-neutral probabilities (p and $1 - p$) by multiplying the current price of the hedge portfolio by one plus the risk-free rate and equating this to the end-of-period payoff

$$(1 + r_f)(mS + P_0) = muS + P_u.$$

Substituting the value of m, Eq. (7.38), into this equation and solving for the current put price, P_0, gives

$$P_0 = \left[\left(\frac{u - (1 + r_f)}{u - d} \right) P_d + \left(\frac{(1 + r_f) - d}{u - d} \right) P_u \right] \div (1 + r_f),$$

Figure 7.24 One-period hedge portfolio payoffs.

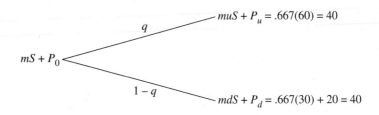

$$muS + P_u = .667(60) = 40$$
$$mdS + P_d = .667(30) + 20 = 40$$

Figure 7.25 Payoffs for a two-period American put.

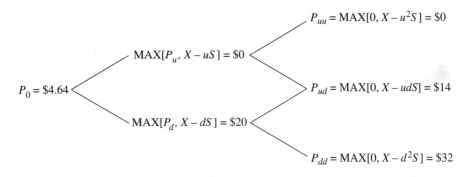

$$P_{uu} = \text{MAX}[0, X - u^2 S] = \$0$$
$$\text{MAX}[P_u, X - uS] = \$0$$
$$P_0 = \$4.64$$
$$P_{ud} = \text{MAX}[0, X - udS] = \$14$$
$$\text{MAX}[P_d, X - dS] = \$20$$
$$P_{dd} = \text{MAX}[0, X - d^2 S] = \$32$$

or

$$P_0 = [p P_d + (1 - p) P_u] \div (1 + r_f), \tag{7.39}$$

where p and $(1 - p)$ are the risk-neutral probabilities:

$$p = \frac{u - (1 + r_f)}{u - d}, \qquad (1 - p) = \frac{(1 + r_f) - d}{u - d}. \tag{7.40}$$

This one-period put valuation equation can easily be extended recursively into a multiperiod framework to derive a binomial pricing equation for European puts similar to that for European calls (Eq. 7.33). However, our objective in this section is to price American puts that may be exercised before maturity. Figure 7.25 shows the payoffs for a two-period American put. Note that the problem is complicated by the fact that the put holder may decide to exercise his or her option at the end of the first period if the value from exercising, say, $X - dS$, is greater than the market value of the put, P_d. Given the numbers chosen for our example, this is exactly what will happen. For example, let's use the one-period put formula to evaluate P_u and P_d, the put values at the end of the first period. First, we know that the risk-neutral probability is

$$p = \frac{u - (1 + r_f)}{u - d} = \frac{1.2 - 1.1}{1.2 - .6} = .167.$$

Substituting this into Eq. (7.39) we have

$$P_u = [p P_{ud} + (1 - p) P_{uu}] \div (1 + r_f)$$
$$= [.167(14) + .833(0)] \div 1.1 = 2.12$$

and

$$P_d = \left[p P_{dd} + (1 - p) P_{ud}\right] \div (1 + r_f)$$

$$= [.167(32) + .833(14)] \div 1.1 = 15.45.$$

Given that the stock price has fallen to $dS = \$30$ at the end of the first period, a rational investor can either exercise the option and receive $X - dS = \$50 - \$30 = \$20$ or hold it, in which case it is worth \$15.45. Obviously it is better to exercise early and not hold the option to the end of the second period. This fact makes it difficult to come up with a closed-form solution to the American put valuation problem (see Geske and Johnson [1984]). However, a computer program that uses an iterative technique starting with the set of possible final payoffs in n periods and working backward, as illustrated in Fig. 7.25, can solve for the present value of American puts.

The opportunity to exercise early makes an American put option have a value equal to or greater than its European counterpart. For the numerical example we have been using, the put option is worth \$4.64 if it is an American put and only \$3.95 if it is a European put.

J. ℰxtensions of the Option Pricing Model

All the models discussed so far have assumed that the stock price is generated by a continuous stochastic process with a constant variance. Changes in the assumptions about the distribution of stock prices that change the model are discussed in Subsection 1. There are also various special circumstances (such as unusual types of contracts) that cause us to consider alterations in the model parameter definitions. For example, the exercise price might be a random variable or it may change in a predetermined fashion over the life of the option. Extensions of this type are discussed in Subsection 2.

1. Changing the Distributional Assumptions

All changes in the distributional assumptions involve either the continuity assumption or the constant variance assumption. Black and Scholes assumed that stock prices are generated according to the following differential equation:

$$\frac{dS}{S} = \mu dt + \sigma dz, \tag{7.41}$$

where

$\mu =$ the instantaneous expected rate of return (measuring the drift on the
random walk of the stock price through time),

$\sigma =$ the instantaneous standard deviation of the rate of return,
assumed constant,

$dt =$ a small increment in time,

$dz =$ a Wiener process.

If the stock price does not follow a continuous path through time, then it follows either a *pure jump process* or a mixed *diffusion-jump model*.

The pure jump model was introduced by Cox and Ross [1975]. The stock price path through time is described as a deterministic movement upon which are superimposed discrete jumps. It can be written as

$$\frac{dS}{S} = \mu dt + (k-1)\, d\pi$$

$$= \mu dt + \begin{matrix} \lambda\, dt & k-1 \\ \diagdown & \\ 1 - \lambda\, dt & 0 \end{matrix} \qquad (7.42)$$

where

$$\pi = \text{a continuous-time Poisson process,}$$
$$\lambda = \text{the intensity of the process,}$$
$$k - 1 = \text{the jump amplitude.}$$

Equation (7.42) says that the percentage jump on the stock price is composed of a drift term, μdt, and a term $d\pi$ that with probability λdt will jump the percentage stock change to $(k-1)$ and with probability $(1 - \lambda dt)$ will do nothing.

The mixed diffusion-jump model, developed by Merton [1976], is something of a mixture of the continuous and pure jump models. Its plausibility comes from the intuition that stock prices seem to have small, almost continuous movements most of the time but sometimes experience large discrete jumps when important new information arrives.

The next three models relax the Black-Scholes assumption that the instantaneous standard deviation is constant through time.

The *constant elasticity of variance model* was derived by Cox [1975] and Cox and Ross [1976]. Its mathematical statement is

$$dS = \mu S dt + \sigma S^{\alpha/2} dz, \qquad (7.43)$$

where

$$\alpha = \text{an elasticity factor } (0 \le \alpha < 2).$$

Note that if $\alpha = 2$, the constant elasticity of variance model reduces to the Black-Scholes model. For $\alpha < 2$ the standard deviation of the return distribution moves inversely with the level of the stock price. The intuitive appeal of such an argument is that every firm has fixed costs that have to be met regardless of the level of its income. A decrease in income will decrease the value of the firm and simultaneously increase its riskiness. Either operating or financial leverage may explain the inverse relationship between variance and stock price.

The *compound option model* of Geske [1977] shows how to price options on options. This may seem to be a complex abstraction until one considers that the equity in a levered firm is really an option on the assets of the firm. An example of this was given in Section D of this chapter. A CBOE-listed call option is therefore an option on the firm's equity, which in turn is an option on the firm's assets. Thus a CBOE call option is really an option on an option. In Geske's model a compound call option is a function of seven variables instead of the usual five variables found in the Black-Scholes model:

$$c = f(S, X, r_f, T, \sigma, D/V, t_B).$$

The two new variables are D/V, the ratio of the face value of debt to the market value of the firm, and t_B, the time to maturity of the firm's debt. Under certain conditions the compound option model can be made equal to the constant elasticity of variance model.

The *displaced diffusion model* by Rubinstein [1983] focuses on the assets side of a firm's balance sheet and divides it into a portfolio of riskless assets and risky assets. Like Geske's model it is a compound option formula and requires two parameters in addition to those of the Black-Scholes model. They are (1) the instantaneous volatility of the rate of return on the firm's risky assets and (2) the proportion of total assets invested in risky assets.

The stochastic volatility model of Hull and White (1987) allows volatility to follow a process similar to stock price with the drift in volatility being such that it reverts to some deterministic level at some nonstochastic rate. They show that if the volatility process is uncorrelated with stock prices, then the option price is the Black-Scholes price integrated over the probability distribution of the average variance rate over the life of the option.

Rubinstein (1994) and others have suggested a model in which the volatility is a deterministic function of stock price and time. In this approach to pricing options, an implied risk-neutral probability distribution of asset prices is implied from an observed cross-section of option prices. This distribution is then used to determine the size of the up and down movements and the probabilities in the binomial lattice. The asset price tree is then used to determine option values in a way similar to the binomial model discussed previously.

One common aspect of many of the above models that introduce additional risk factors is that they assume zero risk premia for these factors. Merton [1973b] solved the problem of pricing options when the value of the underlying asset and the risk-free rate are both stochastic. More recently following the Fourier inversion approach to option pricing as suggested by Stein and Stein [1991] and Heston [1993], there have been a number of papers that are incorporating multiple types of risk without sacrificing the tractability of the resulting option pricing models. Examples of this include papers such as Bakshi, Cao, and Chen [1997], Bakshi and Madan [2000], and Bates [2000]. As pointed out by Bakshi et al., one of the problems with generating and comparing option pricing models is that the number of potential option pricing models is extremely large. Specifically, all models make three sets of assumptions regarding the distribution of the underlying process, the interest rate process, and the market price of risk factors and the various permutations and combination of these three assumptions can yield an intractably large number of models. For example, Bakshi et al. propose a model that incorporates stochastic volatility, stochastic interest rates, and random jumps, the SVSI-J model. The model has a functional form that is similar to the Black-Scholes model in that the value of a call can be written as $c = S\pi_1 - XB(T)\pi_2$, where π_1 and π_2 are risk-neutral probabilities.[25] In this model, the value of an option is a function of a number of variables in addition to those in the Black-Scholes model including the correlation between the stock price and volatility processes; the jump frequency; the mean and standard deviation of jump size; and the speed of adjustment, long-run mean, and variation coefficient of the stock volatility.

Section K of this chapter discusses the empirical evidence on the option pricing formulae discussed above. Much of the research along these lines is very recent and evolving, and therefore the conclusions are tentative. Yet the evidence seems to provide support for the extensions of the Black-Scholes model over the original model.

---

[25] See Bakshi, Cao, and Chen [1997] for more details.

2. Options to Value Special Situations

What happens to the value of an option if the exercise price is stochastic, if the stock price changes in a deterministic fashion, if the risk-free rate is stochastic, or if the payouts are truncated in unusual ways?

Fisher [1978] and Margrabe [1978] solve the problem of valuing an option when the exercise price is uncertain. An example of this type of problem is a stock exchange offer between two unlevered firms.[26] Firm A tenders for the shares of firm B (a much smaller firm) by offering one of its own shares currently priced at, let us say, $S_A = \$50$ for one of firm B's shares priced at $S_B = \$30$. The offer might be good for 30 days. The shareholders of firm B have received an option to exchange one asset for another. The exercise price on the call option is the value of firm B's stock, a random variable.

Margrabe [1978] and Fisher [1978] show that the value of an option to exchange one asset for another depends on the standard deviations of the two assets and the correlations between them. Their formula is

$$C(S_A, S_B, T) = S_A N(d_1) - S_B N(d_2),$$

where

$$d_1 = \frac{\ln(S_A/S_B) + .5V^2 T}{V\sqrt{T}},$$
$$d_2 = d_1 - V\sqrt{T},$$
$$V^2 = V_A^2 - 2\rho_{AB}V_A V_B + V_B^2.$$

Note that V^2 is the instantaneous proportional variance of the change in the ratio of the asset prices, S_A/S_B, and ρ_{AB} is the instantaneous correlation between them. The option is less (more) valuable if the assets are positively (negatively) correlated.

Another interesting option is the *truncated option* discussed by Johnson [1981]. Examples of a truncated option are an option on a firm consisting of two divisions, an option entitling the owner to a choice between two risky assets, and competing tender offers. Consider the case of an option on a firm with two risky divisions. Rubinstein's [1983] displaced diffusion model is a special case because it considers an option on a firm consisting of one riskless and one risky asset. Here we are examining the value of an option on a portfolio of two risky assets. If A_1 and A_2 are the lognormally distributed returns of the two divisions, the payoff to this type of truncated option at maturity is

$$C = \text{MAX}\left[0, A_1 + A_2 - X\right].$$

The actual solution is too complex for this text; however, the interested reader is referred to Johnson [1981] for the mathematics of this and three other truncated option cases. One of the implications is that an option on a portfolio of risky assets is less valuable than the corresponding portfolio of options.

---

[26] If the firms were levered, the problem would be much the same except that we would have to deal with options on options.

K. *E*mpirical Evidence on the Option Pricing Model

Tests of the option pricing model (OPM) are different from those of the CAPM because options are contingent claims on an underlying asset, the stock price, that is directly observable. This fact, however, does not eliminate the problem that empirical tests of the OPM are joint tests of market efficiency and the validity of the model. In addition there are two practical problems: option prices must be recorded synchronously with prices of the underlying asset, and data must allow unbiased estimation of the OPM parameters.

There are three broad categories of OPM empirical tests.[27] The most obvious are tests of the absolute price level of options to determine whether model prices are biased relative to market prices and to investigate the profitability of trading rules based on portfolios of mispriced options. One difficulty with these tests is that taxes and transactions costs must be taken into account in order to determine the net profit from any trading rule. A second form of test is based on violations of option pricing boundary conditions such as those implied by Theorems 7.1 and 7.2. Significant and persistent violations of these boundary conditions would imply either market inefficiency or that the OPM is incorrect. The third form of testing is based on the performance of hedge portfolios, that is, combinations of options and other assets. Riskless hedge portfolios that earn returns above the risk-free rate are indications of a failure of either the OPM being tested or of market efficiency.

The earliest empirical test of the Black-Scholes OPM was done by Black and Scholes themselves [1973]. They used price data from the over-the-counter option market (OTCOM) for contracts written on 545 securities between 1966 and 1969. Options traded on the OTCOM did not have standardized exercise prices or maturity dates; however, they were "dividend protected."[28] Whenever the stock went ex-dividend, the exercise price on outstanding options was lowered by the amount of the dividend.

The secondary market in nonstandardized OTCOM options was virtually nonexistent. Therefore Black-Scholes adopted a test procedure that used the OPM to generate the expected prices of each option on each trading day. By comparing the model prices with actual prices at the issuing date, they divided options into those "overvalued" and those "undervalued" by the market. For each option bought (if undervalued) or sold (if overvalued), a perfectly risk-free hedge portfolio was formed by selling or buying shares in the underlying stock. The excess dollar return on the hedge portfolio was defined as

$$\Delta V_H - V_H r_f \Delta t = \left(\Delta C - \frac{\partial C}{\partial S} \Delta S \right) - \left(C - \frac{\partial C}{\partial S} S \right) r_f \Delta t.$$

The first expression is the dollar return on the hedge portfolio, ΔV_H, where ΔC is the change in the value of a call option and where $\partial C / \partial S = N(d_1)$ is the number of shares multiplied by ΔS, the change in the price per share. The second expression, which is subtracted from the first in order to obtain *excess* returns, is the dollar return on a risk-free position. Theoretically, the difference between the two terms should be equal to zero because the portfolio is chosen to be a risk-free hedge. Therefore the portfolio should have zero beta and earn the risk-free rate.

---

[27] See Bates [1995], Bates [2002], and Garcia, Ghysels, and Renault [2002] for an excellent review of this area.

[28] Of course, there is no such thing as perfect dividend protection. For example, if shareholders were to issue a liquidating dividend equal to the value of the firm's assets, the value of common stock would fall to zero, and no amount of dividend protection could keep the value of a call option from falling to zero.

The option position was maintained throughout the life of the option. The risk-free hedge was adjusted daily by buying or selling shares of stock in order to maintain the proportion $\partial C / \partial S = N(d_1)$. At the end of each day, the hedge position was assumed to be liquidated so that the daily dollar return could be calculated. The option position was then immediately reestablished and a new hedge position constructed.

Black and Scholes computed the systematic risk of the hedge portfolio by regressing its excess returns against a market index. The results verified that it has a beta not significantly different from zero (even though the hedge was not adjusted continuously).

Their results showed that (given ex post estimates of actual variances of the returns on the underlying stock over the holding period), in the absence of transactions costs, buying undervalued contracts and selling overvalued contracts at model prices produced insignificant average profits. However, when ex ante variances were estimated from past stock price histories, buying undervalued contracts and selling overvalued contracts at model prices resulted in significant negative excess portfolio returns. The same procedure, when repeated using market prices, yielded substantial positive excess returns. These results indicate that the market uses more than past price histories to estimate the ex ante instantaneous variance of stock returns. But when actual variances are used in the model, it matches actual option prices quite accurately.

When the transaction costs of trading options were included, the implied profits vanished. Therefore even though the option market does not appear to be efficient before transaction costs are taken into account, there is no opportunity for traders to take advantage of this inefficiency.

Galai [1977] used data from the Chicago Board of Options Exchange (CBOE) for each option traded between April 26, 1973, and November 30, 1973. Option contracts on the CBOE have standardized striking prices and expiration dates. Although the options are not dividend protected, the standardization of contracts has resulted in a substantial volume of trading and lower transaction costs.

The fact that option prices are listed every day allowed Galai to extend the Black-Scholes procedure. Black and Scholes established an initial option position and then maintained a hedge position by buying or selling shares of stock. They could not adjust the option position because they did not have market prices for the options. They were unable to exploit all the information available in the daily deviation of the option's actual prices from the model prices.

Galai duplicated the Black-Scholes tests and extended them by adjusting the option position every day. Undervalued options were bought and overvalued options were sold at the end of each day; in addition, the hedged position was maintained by buying or selling the appropriate number of shares of common stock. Galai used two tests: (1) an ex post test that assumed that traders can use the closing price on day t to determine whether the option is over- or undervalued and that they could transact at the closing prices on day t and (2) a more realistic ex ante test that assumed that the trading rule is determined from closing prices on day t but the transaction is not executed until the closing price at day $t + 1$. Both tests used various estimates of the variance of common stock rates of return that were based on data gathered *before* the trading rule was executed.

The main results of the test were:

1. Using ex post hedge returns, trading strategies (in the absence of transaction costs) that were based on the Black-Scholes model earned significant excess returns.

2. Given 1% transaction costs, the excess returns vanished.

3. The returns were robust to changes in various parameters such as the risk-free rate or instantaneous variance.

4. The results are sensitive to dividend adjustment. Trading in options written on common stocks paying high dividends yielded lower profits than trading in options written on low-dividend stocks. This result, however, simply reflects the fact that the Black-Scholes formula assumes no dividend payments.

5. Deviations from the model's specifications led to worse performance.

6. Tests of spread strategies yielded results similar to those produced by the hedging strategies described above.

Bhattacharya [1983] used CBOE transaction data from August 1976 to June 1977. He looked at three different boundary conditions. An immediate exercise test was composed of situations where the trader could earn more from exercising immediately than from keeping his or her option alive. For a sample of 86,137 transactions there were 1,120 immediate exercise opportunities assuming zero transactions costs. However, after transactions costs, even a member of the CBOE or NYSE would have realized negative average trading profits. Similar results were obtained for tests of dividend-adjusted lower bounds using the lower bound for European call options and for pseudo-American call options. Culumovic and Welsh [1994] found that the proportion of stock option prices violating lower bounds on the CBOE had declined by 1987–89. Evnine and Rudd [1985] found that 2.7% of the calls on the S&P 100 (traded on the CBOE) and 1.6% of the calls on the Major Market Index (traded on the AMEX) violated lower bounds but argue that these violations do not represent trading opportunities because of difficulties associated with trading the underlying.

Taken together, the studies mentioned above seem to indicate that the Black-Scholes OPM predicts option prices very well indeed. So well in fact, that excess returns can only be earned in the absence of transaction costs. However, once transaction costs are introduced into the trading strategies, excess profits vanish. This confirms the usual result that nonmember traders cannot beat the market. Prices are efficiently determined down to the level of transaction costs.

Since June 1977, standardized put options have been offered on the CBOE. Klemkosky and Resnick [1979] collected continuous transactions data for put and call options for each of 15 companies for 12 days (one each month) during the July 1977 to June 1978 interval. A total of 606 long and short hedge portfolios were constructed. The put, call, and underlying stock had to have traded within one minute of each other. The hedge portfolios were based on the following inequalities:

$$(C - P - S)(1 + r_f) + X + \sum_{j=1}^{n} Div_j (1 + r_f)^{\delta j} \leq 0 \qquad \text{long hedge,}$$

$$(S + P - C)(1 + r_f) - X - \sum_{j=1}^{n} Div_j (1 + r_f)^{\delta j} \leq 0 \qquad \text{short hedge.}$$

These hedges are based on the gross terminal profit from engaging in a long or short hedge constructed from American options and the stock. The terms are as defined in the put-call parity equation (Eq. 7.8), where r_f is the risk-free rate of return covering the life of the option. The last term in each equation is the terminal value of the dividends, where Div_j is assumed to be the known stochastic dividend paid during the life of the option, and δj is the length of time between the dividend and the expiration date of the options. The strongest assumption, of course, is that dividends were nonstochastic. However, the virtue of a test based on put-call parity is that it is not necessary to make any assumptions about which version of the option pricing model is best. If put-call parity holds, then there are no arbitrage profits and the market is efficient, regardless of how options are valued.

Klemkosky and Resnick find their results to be consistent with put-call parity and with efficiency for the registered options markets. If $20 is the minimum transactions cost for a member firm to take a hedge position, then only 27% of the hedges were profitable. If $60 is the minimum transactions cost for a nonmember investor, then only 7% of the hedges were profitable.

If one is empirically testing the null hypothesis that observed market prices and the Black-Scholes (B-S) theoretical prices exhibit no systematic differences, the null hypothesis can be rejected for any of three reasons:

1. Inputs to the Black-Scholes model have been incorrectly measured or
2. the options market is inefficient or
3. the mathematical structure of the Black-Scholes model is incorrect.

Bhattacharya [1980] avoids difficulties (1) and (2) by creating hypothetical hedge portfolios based on simulated B-S option values. If a neutral hedge is adjusted daily (continuously would be even better), the excess return should be zero if the B-S formula is correct. The only observed data inputs are the stock price, the stock price variance estimated directly from stock data during the life of the hedge, and the risk-free rate. Bhattacharya's results show no operationally significant mispricing by the B-S formula except for at-the-money options very close to maturity where the B-S model overvalues options.

Using CBOE daily closing prices between December 31, 1975, and December 31, 1976, for all call options listed for six major companies (AT&T, Avon, Kodak, Exxon, IBM, and Xerox), MacBeth and Merville [1979] tested the Black-Scholes model to see whether or not it over- or underpriced options. Using the same data set, MacBeth and Merville [1980] tested the Black-Scholes model against an alternative constant elasticity of variance (CEV) model (derived by Cox [1975] and Cox and Ross [1976]).

In their first paper, MacBeth and Merville [1979] estimate the implied standard deviation of the rate of return for the underlying common stock by employing the Black-Scholes model Eq. (7.36). Then, by assuming that the B-S model correctly prices at-the-money options with at least 90 days to expiration, they are able to estimate the percent deviation of observed call prices from B-S call prices. They conclude that

1. The Black-Scholes model prices are on average less (greater) than market prices for in-the-money (out-of-the-money) options.
2. The extent to which the Black-Scholes model underprices (overprices) an in-the-money (out-of-the-money) option and increases with the extent to which the option is in-the-money (out-of-the-money) and decreases as the time to expiration decreases.
3. The Black-Scholes model prices of out-of-the-money options with less than 90 days to expiration are, on the average, greater than market prices; but there does not appear to be any consistent relationship between the extent to which these options are overpriced by the B-S model and the degree to which these options are out-of-the-money or the time to expiration.

The second MacBeth and Merville paper [1980] compares the Black-Scholes model against the constant elasticity of variance (CEV) model. The primary difference between the two models is that the B-S model assumes the variance of returns on the underlying asset remains constant, whereas the constant elasticity of variance model assumes the variance changes when the stock price does. Empirical evidence on the relationship between the level of stock prices and the rate of return variance is somewhat mixed. Blattberg and Gonedes [1974] suggest that the variance may change randomly through time. Rosenberg [1973] finds that it follows an autoregressive scheme. And Black [1976] observes that the variance of returns varies inversely with stock prices. For the six securities that MacBeth and Merville studied the variance relative to the stock price seems to decrease as the stock price rises. Using their estimates of the constant elasticity of variance, they find that the Cox model fits the data better than the Black-Scholes model. Their empirical results are also consistent with the compound option model of Geske [1979b].

Beckers [1980] also compares the constant elasticity of variance model with the Black-Scholes model. First, however, he uses 1,253 daily observations (September 18, 1972, to September 7, 1977) for 47 different stocks to test the Black-Scholes assumption that the stock variance is not a function of the stock price. The data reject this hypothesis. The variance was an inverse function of the stock price for 38 of the 47 stocks—a result consistent with the constant elasticity of variance model. This is sometimes called the volatility bias. When testing simulated Black-Scholes call prices against the constant elasticity of variance prices, Beckers found that the CEV model gives higher option prices than B-S for in-the-money options. This is consistent with the empirical work of MacBeth and Merville, who found that the B-S model undervalues in-the-money options.

Geske and Roll [1984a] used transactions data for all options traded at midday on August 24, 1976 (a sample of 667 different options on 85 stocks). A subsample of 119 options on 28 different stocks with zero scheduled dividends during their remaining life was identified within the main sample. Using regression analysis, Geske and Roll demonstrate that the original time, in- versus out-of-the-money, and volatility biases are present in the entire sample. Next, they show that for the nondividend sample the time and "money" biases are significantly reduced but the volatility bias remains large. However, by correcting the volatility estimates of all stocks by using a "Stein shrinker" technique, the volatility bias is reduced. Geske and Roll conclude that the time and money biases may be related to improper model treatment of early exercise (the dividend problem), whereas the volatility bias problem may be more related to statistical errors in variance parameter estimates.

Five of the extensions of the option pricing model, discussed in Section J, have been compared by Rubinstein [1985]. He used the MDR (market data report) database of the Chicago Board of Options Exchange, which has been consolidated into the Berkeley Options Database. The data is a time-stamped record, to the nearest second, including option trade prices, quotes, and volume, coupled with the stock price at the corresponding time during the day.

Rubinstein's experimental design was to select matched pairs of options, for example, all options belonging to the same stock, observed on the same day during the same constant stock price interval, having the same exercise price, and falling within a predetermined range of out-of-the-money values (e.g., $S/X = .75$ to $.85$). Pairing in this case was on the basis of different times to maturity. For example, one option might fall within the 71- to 120-day range and another on the 171- to 220-day range. There were actually 373 of these particular matched pairs (overall there were 19,904 pairs based on differences on time to expiration and 12,239 pairs based on equal time to maturity but different exercise prices). If the Black-Scholes formula is unbiased, there should be a 50/50 chance that the implied option variance for the shorter maturity option is higher than for the longer maturity option. In fact, 94.1% of the shorter maturity options had higher variance. Thus in this case the Black-Scholes formula could be rejected.

Nonparametric tests of options paired either by differences in time to maturity or in exercise prices were performed for two time periods: (1) August 21, 1976, to October 21, 1977, and (2) October 24, 1977, to August 31, 1978. Two interesting conclusions were found. First, if the time to maturity is held constant, then the Black-Scholes model is biased, but the direction of the bias is different in the two time periods that were investigated. During the 1976–1977 interval, in-the-money options were undervalued by the Black-Scholes formula. This confirms the work of MacBeth and Merville [1979]. The direction of the bias is reversed during the 1977–1978 period. No one knows why the bias should reverse. The second conclusion was that although some of the alternative pricing models (e.g., the displaced diffusion model) were more compatible with the empirical results, none of them were superior in both time periods.

Ball and Torous [1985] and Trautmann and Reiner [1994] estimate the parameters of a jump-diffusion process for stock prices in the United States and Germany, respectively, and analyze the ability of the jump-diffusion option pricing model to outperform the Black-Scholes model. They find that the option prices resulting from the jump-diffusion model are indistinguishable from those obtained from a no-jump model.

Amin and Ng [1993] test the ability of autoregressive conditionally heteroscedastic (ARCH) models to correct Black-Scholes pricing errors using data from July 1988 to December 1989. They find that the ARCH models display both moneyness- and maturity-related biases. On the other hand, they also find in terms of pricing errors that the EGARCH model performs better than the symmetric GARCH model, while the latter outperforms the Black-Scholes model.

Rubinstein [1994] finds that although the Black-Scholes model seems to perform well in the pre-1987 period, the pricing ability of the model has deteriorated substantially since then. Specifically both Jackwerth and Rubinstein [1996] and Rubinstein [1994] report results that are consistent with implied volatility decreasing with strike price (the smile). Based on these results, Rubinstein and others have suggested that a model where volatility is a deterministic function of stock price and time should outperform the Black-Scholes model. Dumas, Fleming, and Whaley [1998] test this model relative to the Black-Scholes and find that the former performs no better than the latter with some ad hoc strike price and time to expiration adjustments for volatility.

Given the persistence of these empirical biases, more recently a number of papers have started to focus on empirical tests of models that simultaneously incorporate additional priced risk factors such as stochastic volatility, interest rates, and/or jumps. Examples of such papers include Bakshi, Cao, and Chen [1997] and Buraschi and Jackwerth [2001].

Buraschi and Jackwerth argue that the difference between deterministic volatility models and stochastic models that allow for additional risk factors is that in the former framework options are redundant securities, while they are not in the latter framework. They develop statistical tests based on this difference and, using index options data from 1986 to 1995, come to the conclusion that the data is more consistent with models that contain additional risk factors such as stochastic volatility, jumps, or stochastic interest rates.

Bakshi et al. empirically test a model that allows for stochastic volatility, stochastic interest rates, and random jumps (the SVSI-J model) using data on 38,749 S&P 500 call options prices. They compare the performance of this model with the Black-Scholes, the stochastic interest (SI), stochastic volatility (SV), stochastic volatility and stochastic interest (SVSI), and the stochastic volatility random-jump (SVJ) models. Their results indicate that all models are misspecified, with the SVJ being the least misspecified and the Black-Scholes being the most misspecified.

*S*ummary

Closed-form solutions to the option pricing problem have been developed relatively recently. Yet their potential for applications to problems in finance is tremendous. Almost all financial assets are really contingent claims. For example, common stock is really a call option on the value of the assets of a levered firm. Similarly, risky debt, insurance, warrants, and convertible debt may all be thought of as options. Also, option pricing theory has implications for the capital structure of the firm, for investment policy, for mergers and acquisitions, for spin-offs, and for dividend policy. Much of the rest of this book is devoted to exploring applications for the theories discussed so far: state preference theory, the capital asset pricing model, arbitrage pricing theory, and option pricing. As we shall see, option pricing plays a major role in shaping our thinking.

We have established that option prices are functions of five parameters: the price of the underlying security, its instantaneous variance, the exercise price on the option, the time to maturity, and the risk-free rate. Only one of these variables, the instantaneous variance, is not directly observable. Even more interesting is the fact that the option price does not depend (1) on individual risk preferences or (2) on the expected rate of return on the underlying asset. Both results follow from the fact that option prices are determined from pure arbitrage conditions available to the investor who establishes perfectly hedged portfolios.

Much remains to be done to empirically test the validity of the option pricing model in general and of various versions of it such as the Black-Scholes model, and other models that incorporate additional risk factors. The empirical results thus far tend to be mixed. A number of papers have reported that more complex models do not do significantly better than the simple Black-Scholes option pricing model. On the other hand, statistically significant departures from the Black-Scholes model have been discovered, with indications that the departures are consistent with the market pricing additional risk such as stochastic volatility and random jumps.

PROBLEM SET

7.1 What is the value of a European call option with an exercise price of $40 and a maturity date six months from now if the stock price is $28, the instantaneous variance of the return on the price is .5, and the risk-free rate is 6%?

7.2 What is the price of a European put if the price of the underlying common stock is $20, the exercise price is $20, the risk-free rate is 8%, the variance of the return of the underlying stock is .36 (that is, $\sigma = .6$), and the option expires six months from now?

7.3   **(a)** Graph changes in wealth, ΔW, vs. changes in the prices of the underlying security, ΔS, for a portfolio where you sell one call option and sell one put option (both the same X, T, σ, and r_f). Would this be a good strategy if you have private information that leads you to expect the instantaneous variance of the underlying security will increase?

   (b) Graph ΔW against ΔS for a portfolio where you buy a call and sell a put. Would this be a good strategy if you expect an increase in the instantaneous variance?

7.4 Assume you are a senior financial analyst at Morgan Stanley. You are asked by a client to determine the maximum price he or she should be willing to pay to purchase Honeywell call options having an exercise price of $45 and expiring in 156 days. The current price of Honeywell stock is $44\frac{3}{8}$, the riskless interest rate is 7%, and the estimated rate of return variance of the stock is $\sigma^2 = .0961$. No dividends are expected to be declared over the next six months.

7.5 Given two European put options that are identical except that the exercise price of the first put, X_1, is greater than the exercise price of the second put, X_2, use first-order stochastic dominance and equilibrium in a perfect capital market to prove that one of the puts must have a higher price than the other. Which put option has the higher price? (*Hint:* Determine the relevant states of the world.)

7.6 Consider a firm with current value of $5,000,000 and outstanding debt of $4,000,000 that matures in 10 years. The firm's asset rate-of-return variance is .5. The interest on the debt is paid at maturity, and the firm has a policy of not paying cash dividends. Use the OPM to determine the change in the prices of the firm's debt and equity if there is an unanticipated rise in the rate of inflation of 5%, which raises the riskless nominal interest rate from 5% to 10%. Which class of security holders benefits from the rise in r_f?

7.7 Figure 7.3 graphs the value of the call option as a function of the value of the underlying stock. Graph the value of a call option (vertical axis) against

(a) σ, the instantaneous standard deviation of the returns on the underlying asset
(b) r_f, the risk-free rate
(c) T, the time to maturity

7.8 What are the conditions under which an American put would be exercised early on a stock that pays no dividends?

7.9 Consider the case of the firm with secured debt, subordinated debentures, and common stock, where the secured debt and subordinated debentures mature at the same time. Find the equations for the values of the three classes of securities using the OPM framework. Assume no dividends or interest payments prior to the debt's maturity and a lognormal distribution of the future value of the firm's assets, $\tilde{V}_t$, as shown in Fig. Q7.9, where V = market value of the firm, S = market value of the stock, B_S = market value of the senior debt, B_j = market value of the junior debt, D_S = face value of the senior debt, D_j = face value of the junior debt.

Figure Q7.9 A firm with secured debt, subordinated debentures, and common stock.

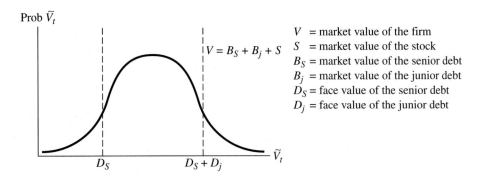

7.10 Why will the value of an American put always be greater than or equal to the value of a corresponding European put?

7.11 Options listed for Krispy Kreme were used in the text as an example of option price estimation using implicit variance. The implicit variance from the August 35 option resulted in estimated call prices lower than actual call prices for the August 45 option. Assuming the Black-Scholes OPM is correct, and that all assumptions of the model are met in the marketplace: What hedge (i.e., riskless) portfolio can be formed to make arbitrage profits with Krispy Kreme August 45 options?

7.12 The share price of Honeybear Inc. is $4.75. Call options written on Honeybear have an exercise price of $40 and mature in 71 days. The risk-free rate is $6\frac{1}{2}\%$, and the instantaneous price variance of Honeybear is 9.61% (i.e., $\sigma = .31$). What actions must you take in order to create a perfect hedge in the following situations:

(a) If you own 100 shares of Honeybear stock, how many call options must you buy (sell)?

(b) If you own five put option contracts, how many shares of stock do you need?

(c) If you own one call contract, how many put options do you need?

7.13 After a call contract is created, the outcome must be a zero-sum game; that is, the call writer may win or lose N, but the call buyer will experience an opposite return of exactly N and consequently their aggregate payoff is zero. Given this fact, can you explain how they could both enter into the contract anticipating a positive return?

7.14 Suppose that the government passes a usury law that prohibits lending at more than 5% interest, but normal market rates are much higher due to inflation. You have a customer, a Ms. Olson, who wants to borrow at 20% and can put up her $100,000 store as collateral. Rather than refusing her request you decide to create a five-year contract with the following terms: You hold title to the store and receive the right to sell her the store for X at the end of five years. If you decide to sell, she *must* buy. In return you give her $80,000 in cash (the amount she wants to borrow) and the right to buy the store from you for X at the end of five years. How can this contract provide you with a 20% annual rate of return on the $80,000?

REFERENCES

Amin, K., and V. Ng, "Option Valuation with Systematic Stochastic Volatility," *Journal of Finance*, 1993, Vol. 48, 881–910.

Bakshi, G., C. Cao, and Z. Chen, "Empirical Performance of Alternative Option Pricing Models," *Journal of Finance*, December 1997, Vol. 52, No. 5, 2003–2049.

Bakshi, G., and D. Madan, "Spanning and Derivative Security Valuation," *Journal of Financial Economics*, February 2000, Vol. 55, No. 2, 205–238.

Ball, C. A., and W. N. Torous, "Bond Price Dynamics and Options," *Journal of Financial and Quantitative Analysis*, 1983, 517–531.

———, "On Jumps in Common Stock Prices and Their Impact on Call Option Pricing," *Journal of Finance*, March 1985, 155–173.

Bates, D., "Testing Option Pricing Models," working paper, The Wharton School, University of Pennsylvania and the National Bureau of Economic Research, 1995.

———, "Post-'87 Crash Fears in the S&P 500 Futures Option Market," *Journal of Econometrics* 94, 181–238, 2000.

———, "Empirical Option Pricing: A Retrospection," working paper, University of Iowa, June 2002.

Beckers, S., "The Constant Elasticity of Variance Model and Its Implications for Option Pricing," *Journal of Finance*, June 1980, 661–673.

————, "A Note on Estimating the Parameters of the Diffusion-Jump Model of Stock Returns," *Journal of Financial and Quantitative Analysis*, March 1981, 127–139.

Bhattacharya, M., "Empirical Properties of the Black-Scholes Formula under Ideal Conditions," *Journal of Financial and Quantitative Analysis*, December 1980, 1081–1106.

————, "Transactions Data Tests on the Efficiency of the Chicago Board of Options Exchange," *Journal of Financial Economics*, August 1983, 161–185.

Black, F., "Studies of Stock Price Volatility Changes," *Proceedings of the Meetings of the American Statistical Association*, Business and Economics Statistics Section, Chicago, 1976.

Black, F., and M. Scholes, "The Valuation of Option Contracts and a Test of Market Efficiency," *Journal of Finance*, May 1972, 399–418.

————, "The Pricing of Options and Corporate Liabilities," *Journal of Political Economy*, May–June 1973, 637–659.

Blattberg, R., and N. Gonedes, "A Comparison of the Stable and Student Distributions as Stochastic Models for Stock Prices," *Journal of Business*, 1974, 244–280.

Boyle, P., and D. Emmanuel, "Discretely Adjusted Option Hedges," *Journal of Financial Economics*, September 1980, 259–282.

Brennan, M., and E. Schwartz, "The Valuation of American Put Options," *Journal of Finance*, May 1977, 449–462.

Buraschi, A., and J. Jackwerth, "Pricing with a Smile: Hedging and Spanning in Option Markets," *Review of Financial Economics*, Summer 2001, Vol. 14, 495–527.

Butler, J., and B. Schachter, "Unbiased Estimation of the Black-Scholes Formula," *Journal of Financial Economics*, March 1986, 341–357.

Chiras, D., and S. Manaster, "The Informational Content of Option Prices and a Test of Market Efficiency," *Journal of Financial Economics*, June–September 1978, 213–234.

Copeland, T., and V. Antikarov, *Real Options: A Practitioner's Guide*. Texere, New York, 2001.

Courtdon, G., "The Pricing of Options on Default-Free Bonds," *Journal of Financial and Quantitative Analysis*, March 1982, 75–100.

Cox, J., "Notes on Option Pricing I: Constant Elasticity of Diffusions," unpublished draft, Stanford University, September 1975.

Cox, J., J. Ingersoll, and S. Ross, "A Theory of the Term Structure of Interest Rates," *Econometrica*, March 1985, 385–407.

Cox, J., and S. Ross, "The Valuation of Options for Alternative Stochastic Processes," *Journal of Financial Economics*, 1976, Vol. 3, pp. 145–166.

————, "The Valuation of Options for Alternative Stochastic Processes," *Journal of Financial Economics*, January–March 1976, 145–166.

Cox, J., S. Ross, and M. Rubinstein, "Option Pricing: A Simplified Approach," *Journal of Financial Economics*, September 1979, 229–263.

Cox, J., and M. Rubinstein, *Options Markets*. Prentice-Hall, Englewood Cliffs, N.J., 1985.

Culumovic, R., and R. L. Welsh, "A re-examination of constant-variance American call mispricing," *Advances in Futures and Options Research* 7, 177–221, 1994.

Dumas, B., J. Fleming, and R. Whaley, "Implied Volatility Functions: Empirical Tests," *Journal of Finance,* 1998, Vol. 53, 2059–2106.

Evnine, J., and A. Rudd, "Index Options: The Early Evidence," *Journal of Finance* 40, 1985, 743–756.

Feller, W., *An Introduction to Probability Theory and Its Applications*, Vol. I, 3rd ed. John Wiley and Sons, New York, 1968.

Finnerty, J., "The Chicago Board of Options Exchange and Market Efficiency," *Journal of Financial and Quantitative Analysis*, March 1978, 29–38.

Fisher, S., "Call Option Pricing When the Exercise Price Is Uncertain and the Valuation of Index Bonds," *Journal of Finance*, March 1978, 169–186.

Galai, D., "Tests of Market Efficiency of the Chicago Board of Options Exchange," *Journal of Business*, April 1977, 167–197.

———, "On the Boness and Black-Scholes Models for the Valuation of Call Options," *Journal of Financial and Quantitative Analysis*, March 1978, 15–27.

Galai, D., and R. Masulis, "The Option Pricing Model and the Risk Factor of Stock," *Journal of Financial Economics*, January–March 1976, 53–82.

Garcia, R., Ghysels, E., Renault, E., "The Econometrics of Option Pricing," *Handbook of Financial Econometrics*, Yacine Aït-Sahalia and Lars Peter Hansen, eds., Elsevier-North Holland, Amsterdam, 2002.

Garman, M., "An Algebra for Evaluating Hedge Portfolios," *Journal of Financial Economics*, October 1976, 403–428.

Geske, R., "The Valuation of Corporate Liabilities as Compound Options," *Journal of Financial and Quantitative Analysis*, November 1977, 541–552.

———, "The Pricing of Options with Stochastic Dividend Yield," *Journal of Finance*, May 1978, 617–625.

———, "A Note on an Analytical Valuation Formula for Unprotected American Call Options on Stocks with Known Dividends," *Journal of Financial Economics*, December 1979a, 375–380.

———, "The Valuation of Compound Options," *Journal of Financial Economics*, March 1979b, 63–81.

Geske, R., and H. Johnson, "The American Put Option Valued Analytically," *Journal of Finance*, December 1984, 1511–1524.

Geske, R., and R. Roll, "Isolating the Obscured Biases in American Call Pricing: An Alternative Variance Estimator," UCLA Working Paper No. 4–84, February 1984a.

———, "On Valuing American Call Options with the Black-Scholes European Formula," *Journal of Finance*, 1984b, 443–455.

Gould, J., and D. Galai, "Transactions Costs and the Relationship between Put and Call Prices," *Journal of Financial Economics*, July 1974, 104–129.

Heston, S., "Invisible Parameters in Option Prices," *Journal of Finance*, July 1993, Vol. 48, No. 3, 933–947.

Hsia, C., "Relationships among the Theories of MM, CAPM, and OPM," mimeograph, UCLA, 1978.

Jackwerth, J., and M. Rubinstein, "Recovering Stochastic Processes from Option Prices," working paper, University of California, Berkeley, 1996.

Johnson, H., "Three Topics in Option Pricing," Ph.D. dissertation, UCLA Graduate School of Management, 1981.

Klemkosky, R., and B. Resnick, "Put-Call Parity and Market Efficiency," *Journal of Finance*, December 1979, 1141–1155.

Kruizenga, R. J., "Introduction to the Option Contract," reprinted in P. H. Cootner, ed., *The Random Character of Stock Market Prices*. MIT Press, Cambridge, Mass., 1964, 377–391.

Latane, H., and R. J. Rendleman, Jr., "Standard Deviations of Stock Price Ratios Implied in Option Prices," *Journal of Finance*, May 1976, 369–382.

MacBeth, J., and L. Merville, "Tests of the Black-Scholes and Cox Call Option Valuation Models," *Journal of Finance*, March 1980, 177–186.

———, "An Empirical Examination of the Black-Scholes Call Option Pricing Model," *Journal of Finance*, December 1979, 1173–1186.

Margrabe, W., "The Value of an Option to Exchange One Asset for Another," *Journal of Finance*, 33(1), 1978, 177–186.

Merton, R., "An Intertemporal Capital Asset Pricing Model," *Econometrica*, September 1973a, 867–887.

———, "The Theory of Rational Option Pricing," *Bell Journal of Economics and Management Science*, Spring 1973b, 141–183.

———, "On the Pricing of Corporate Debt: The Risk Structure of Interest Rates," *Journal of Finance*, May 1974, 449–470.

———, "Option Pricing When Underlying Stock Returns are Discontinuous," *Journal of Financial Economics*, January–March 1976, 125–144.

Parkinson, M., "Option Pricing: The American Put," *Journal of Business*, January 1977, 21–36.

———, "The Valuation of GNMA Options," *Financial Analysts Journal*, September–October 1982, 66–76.

Phillips, S., and C. Smith, "Trading Costs for Listed Options: The Implications for Market Efficiency," *Journal of Financial Economics*, 1980, 197–201.

Rendleman, R., Jr., and B. Bartter, "Two-State Option Pricing," *Journal of Finance*, December 1979, 1093–1110.

———, "The Pricing of Options on Debt Securities," *Journal of Financial and Quantitative Analysis*, March 1980, 11–24.

Roll, R., "An Analytic Valuation Formula for Unprotected American Call Options on Stocks with Known Dividends," *Journal of Financial Economics*, November 1977, 251–258.

Rosenberg, B., "The Behavior of Random Variables with Nonstationary Variance and the Distribution of Security Prices," manuscript, University of California, Berkeley, 1973.

Ross, S., "Options and Efficiency," *Quarterly Journal of Economics*, February 1976, 75–89.

Rubinstein, M., "The Valuation of Uncertain Income Streams and the Pricing of Options," *Bell Journal of Economics*, Autumn 1976, 407–425.

———, "Displaced Diffusion Option Pricing," *Journal of Finance*, March 1983, 213–265.

———, "Nonparametric Tests of Alternative Option Pricing Models," *Journal of Finance*, June 1985, 455–480.

———, "Implied Binomial Trees," *Journal of Finance*, July 1994, Vol. 49, No. 3, 771–818.

Schmalensee, R., and R. Trippi, "Common Stock Volatility Expectations Implied by Option Premia," *Journal of Finance*, March 1978, 129–147.

Smith, C., "Option Pricing Review," *Journal of Financial Economics*, January–March 1976, 1–51.

Stein, E., and J. Stein, "Stock Price Distributions with Stochastic Volatility: An Analytic Approach," *Review of Financial Studies,* 1991, Vol. 4, 717–752.

Stoll, H. R., "The Relationship between Put and Call Option Prices," *Journal of Finance*, December 1969, 802–824.

Trautmann, S., and M. Beinert, "Stock Price Jumps and Their Impact on Option Valuation" working paper, Johannes Gutenberg Universität, Mainz, Germany, 1995.

Whaley, R., "On Valuation of American Call Options on Stocks with Known Dividends," *Journal of Financial Economics*, June 1981, 208–212.

———, "Valuation of American Call Options on Dividend Paying Stocks: Empirical Tests," *Journal of Financial Economics*, 1982, 29–58.

Appendix 7A. Two Alternative Derivations of the Black-Scholes Option Pricing Model

Black and Scholes [1973] were the first to provide a closed-form solution for the valuation of European calls. Their model is the solution to a partial differential equation that governs the value of the option and is derived under the assumption that stock prices follow geometric Brownian motion. Specifically, the stock price process is

$$dS = \mu S dt + \sigma dz, \tag{7A.1}$$

where

μ = the instantaneous expected rate of return (it measures drift in the random

walk through time, dt),

σ = the instantaneous standard deviation of the rate of return,

dt = a small increment of time,

dz = a Wiener process (i.e., dz is normally distributed with mean 0 and variance dt).

In addition, assume that there exists a riskless asset $B(t) = e^{-r_f t}$.

The option price depends on the stock price and time and can be denoted by $c(S, t)$. Employing Ito's lemma, one can express the change in the option price by the following stochastic differential equation:

$$dc = \frac{\partial c}{\partial S} dS + \frac{\partial c}{\partial t} + \frac{1}{2} \frac{\partial^2 c}{\partial S^2} \sigma^2 S^2 dt \tag{7A.2}$$

Substituting Eq. (7A.1) into Eq. (7A.2) and grouping dt and dz terms yields

$$dc = (\frac{\partial c}{\partial t} + \mu S \frac{\partial c}{\partial S} + \frac{1}{2} \sigma^2 S^2 \frac{\partial^2 c}{\partial S^2}) dt + \sigma S \frac{\partial c}{\partial S} dz = \mu_c c \, dt + \sigma_c c \, dz \tag{7A.3}$$

Consider a portfolio with investments Q_S, Q_c, and Q_B, respectively, in the stock, option, and riskless instrument such that $V = Q_S + Q_c + Q_B = 0$. The return on this portfolio is

$$\frac{dV}{V} = Q_S \frac{dS}{S} + Q_c \frac{dc}{c} + Q_B \frac{dB}{B}. \tag{7A.4}$$

Substituting for dS and dc using Eqs. (7A.1) and (7A.3), respectively, and recognizing that $\frac{dB}{B} = r_f dt$ and $Q_B = -Q_S - Q_c$, we obtain

$$\frac{dV}{V} = [Q_S(\mu - r_f) + Q_c(\mu_c - r_f)] dt + [Q_S \sigma + Q_c \sigma_c] dz. \tag{7A.5}$$

Assume that we choose Q_S and Q_c such that the portfolio is riskless. Since the risky part depends on dz, this implies that for the portfolio to be riskless we must have

$$Q_S \sigma + Q_c \sigma_c = 0 \text{ or } Q_S = -\frac{Q_c \sigma_c}{\sigma}. \tag{7A.6}$$

If the portfolio is riskless and has zero initial investment, then to avoid arbitrage opportunities, the expected return on the portfolio has to be zero. This implies that

$$Q_S(\mu - r_f) + Q_c(\mu_c - r_f) = 0 \text{ or } Q_S = -\frac{Q_c(\mu_c - r_f)}{(\mu - r_f)}. \tag{7A.7}$$

Combining Eqs. (7A.6) and (7A.7) and simplifying yields

$$\frac{(\mu - r_f)}{\sigma} = \frac{(\mu_c - r_f)}{\sigma_c}. \tag{7A.8}$$

Substituting $\mu_c = (\frac{\partial c}{\partial t} + \mu S \frac{\partial c}{\partial S} + \frac{1}{2}\sigma^2 S^2 \frac{\partial^2 c}{\partial S^2})/c$ and $\sigma_c = \sigma S \frac{\partial c}{\partial S}/c$ from Eq. (7A.3) into Eq. (7A.8) and simplifying yields

$$\frac{\partial c}{\partial t} = r_f C - r_f S \frac{\partial c}{\partial S} - \frac{1}{2}\sigma^2 S^2 \frac{\partial^2 c}{\partial S^2}. \tag{7A.9}$$

Equation (7A.9) is a nonstochastic differential equation for the value of the option that may be solved subject to the boundary conditions that at the terminal date the option price must be

$$c = \text{MAX}\,[0, S - X]$$

and that, for any date,

$$c(S = 0, T) = 0.$$

Black and Scholes [1973] transform the equation into the heat exchange equation from physics to find the following solution:[29]

$$c = S \cdot N \left\{ \frac{\ln(S/X) + \left[r_f + (\sigma^2/2)\right] T}{\sigma\sqrt{T}} \right\} - e^{r_f T} X \cdot N \left\{ \frac{\ln(S/X) + \left[r_f - (\sigma^2/2)\right] T}{\sigma\sqrt{T}} \right\} \tag{7A.10}$$

where all variables are as defined previously except that

$N(\cdot) =$ the cumulative normal probability of a unit normal variable;
where, for example, $N(-\infty) = 0$, $N(0) = .5$, and $N(\infty) = 1.0$;

$N(\cdot) = \int_{-\infty}^{z} f(z)dz$, where $f(z)$ is distributed normally with mean zero and standard deviation one.

Cox and Ross [1976] provide an alternate approach to deriving the value of an option that is commonly referred to as risk-neutral valuation. They argue that since the Black-Scholes partial differential equation (BSpde) does not contain any parameters that are related to risk preferences, these parameters will not affect the solution to the BSpde. Therefore, any set of risk preferences can be used in obtaining the option pricing equation. Specifically, they suggest that the solution can be obtained in a risk-neutral world where all securities return the risk-free rate, r_f, and all discounting can be done at the risk-free rate. In this framework, the value of the option is $c = e^{-r_f T} E(c_T)$, where c_T is the value of the option at expiration and is given by $MAX[0, S_T - X]$ if the option is a call. If the stock price distribution is denoted by $f(S_T|S)$, then the value of the option can be written as

$$c = e^{-r_f T} \int_X^{\infty} (S_T - X) f(S_T|S)dS_T \tag{7A.11}$$

Note that in Eq. (7A.11), the stock price ranges from X to ∞ since the option is worthless for expiration date stock prices below the exercise price X.

---

[29] Note that once we are given the call pricing solution, Eq. (7A.9), we see that the hedge ratio in terms of the number of calls per share is

$$Q_c = -1/(\partial c/\partial S) = -1/N(d_1),$$

where $N(d_1)$ is the first term in braces in Eq. (7A.9). This fact is needed in order to continuously construct risk-free hedges.

To solve Eq. (7A.11), we need to specify the density function, $f(S_T|S)$. To obtain this density function consider the geometric Brownian motion specification in Eq. (7A.1) for stock price. This specification is equivalent to assuming that the distribution of the natural logarithm of future stock prices, $\ln(S_T)$, conditional on the current stock price is normal with a mean of $[\ln(S) + (r_f - \frac{\sigma^2}{2})T]$ and a variance of $\sigma^2 T$. This implies that the density function, $f(S_T|S)$, can be written as

$$f(S_T|S) = \frac{1}{S_T\sqrt{2\pi\sigma^2 T}} e^{-\frac{1}{2\sigma^2 T}[\ln S_T - \ln S - (r_f - \frac{\sigma^2}{2})T]^2} \qquad (7A.12)$$

Substituting Eq. (7A.11) into Eq. (7A.10) and some extensive algebra yields the Black-Scholes model.

Futures trading would seem to be
one of those marvels that ought
to be invented if it did not already
exist. Yet the number of futures
markets is surprisingly small . . .

—H. S. Houthakker, "The Scope and Limits
of Futures Trading," in M. Abramovitz, ed.,
The Allocation of Economic Resources.
Stanford University Press,
Stanford, 1959, 159.

Chapter 8

The Term Structure of Interest Rates, Forward Contracts, and Futures

A. The Term Structure of Interest Rates

THROUGHOUT CHAPTERS 1–7 THERE HAS BEEN the implicit assumption that interest rates are nonstochastic and constant in a multiperiod setting. This has been a convenient but misleading assumption. Interest rates are not constant through time. The yield on a particular financial investment (a bond, for example) is a function of the length of time to maturity. The yield also depends on the risk of the security, but we shall continue to assume, for the time being, that there is no risk.

Figure 8.1 shows the term structure of interest rates for United States Treasury securities at four points in time, March 1976, August 1981, May 1987, and March 2003. Each point on the graph gives the yield to maturity, $_0R_T$, on a bond that is bought at time zero and matures T years hence. The bond is assumed to be default free. *Default free* means that there is no uncertainty about the nominal payments promised by the bond. There are, however, other kinds of risk. For example, unexpected changes in future interest rates will induce risk because the market value of the bond will change when interest rate expectations do.

1. The Yield to Maturity

The yield to maturity, $_0R_T$, is computed in exactly the same way one would solve for the internal rate of return on a security. Consider the following hypothetical example: A bond promises to pay a 15% coupon at the end of each year for three years, then pay a face value of $1,000. We observe

Figure 8.1 The yield to maturity on U.S. Treasury securities.

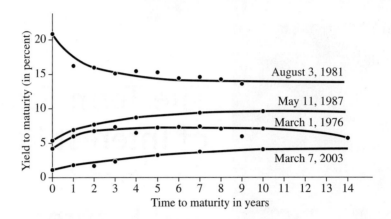

the current market price, B_0, of the bond to be $977.54. The yield to maturity on the bond may be computed by solving for $_0R_T$ in the following present value formula:

$$B_0 = \sum_{t=1}^{T} \frac{coupon}{(1 + {}_0R_T)^t} + \frac{face\ value}{(1 + {}_0R_T)^t}, \tag{8.1}$$

$$977.54 = \sum_{t=1}^{3} \frac{150}{(1 + {}_0R_T)^t} + \frac{1000}{(1 + {}_0R_T)^3}.$$

Solving iteratively, we find that the yield to maturity, $_0R_T$, is 16%.

The term structure shows the yield to maturity for all bonds of all maturities. In March 1976, May 1987, and March 2003, the term structure was upward sloping. Long-term bonds paid higher yields than short-term bonds. In August 1981 the opposite pattern existed. The term structure was downward sloping. One thing that both term structure patterns have in common is that the interest rate is not constant. The yield on securities clearly depends on when they mature.

2. Forward Rates, Future Rates, and Unbiased Expectations

The term structure is said to be unbiased if the *expected future interest rates* are equivalent to the *forward rates* computed from observed bond prices. This is called the *unbiased expectations hypothesis*, which was first postulated by Irving Fisher [1896], then further developed by Friedrich Lutz [1940]. An example will help to clarify the meaning of forward rates and expected future rates.[1] Suppose we have three zero-coupon bonds. They pay a face value of $1,000 upon maturity; mature one, two, and three years hence; and are observed to have current market prices of $826.45, $718.18, and $640.66, respectively. The observed average annual yield to maturity, $_0R_T$, is assumed to be the product of the one-period forward rates, $_tf_{t+1}$, as shown in Eq. (8.2):

$$[(1 + {}_0R_T)]^T = (1 + {}_0R_1)(1 + {}_1f_2) \ldots (1 + {}_{T-1}f_T). \tag{8.2}$$

---

[1] To keep things simple, we assume that forward rates are one-period rates and that all prices and yields are observed at the present time. One could also discuss N-period forward rates observed at any time, t.

Figure 8.2 A simple term structure example (zero coupon bonds).

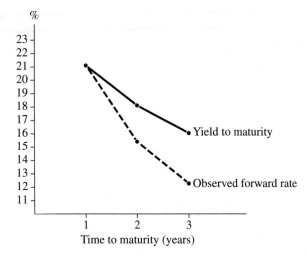

The forward rate, $_1f_2$, is the one-period rate computed for a bond bought at the end of the first period and held to the end of the second period. Hence it is a one-period rate for the second period. Note that the forward rate for the first year can be observed directly. It is $_0R_1$.

To compute the implied forward rates, one would first compute the yields to maturity using Eq. (8.1).[2] For the three bonds in our example, the yields to maturity are 21%, 18%, and 16%, respectively. The term structure for this example is shown in Fig. 8.2. Suppose that we want to know the forward rate implied for the third time period. It can be computed by taking the ratio of the (geometric product of the) yields to maturity on the three- and two-period bonds:

$$1 + {}_2f_3 = \frac{(1 + {}_0R_3)^3}{(1 + {}_0R_2)^2}$$

$$1 + {}_2f_3 = \frac{(1 + {}_0R_1)(1 + {}_1f_2)(1 + {}_2f_3)}{(1 + {}_0R_1)(1 + {}_1f_2)}$$

$$1 + {}_2f_3 = \frac{(1.16)^3}{(1.18)^2} = \frac{1.560895}{1.3294} = 1.121$$

$${}_2f_3 = 12.10\%.$$

Similarly, one can compute the second-period forward rate as 15.07%, and of course the one-period rate is observed directly to be 21%. The pattern of forward rate in this example would be consistent with expectations that future inflation will be less than current inflation.

By itself, the forward rate is merely an algebraic computation from observed bond data. The unbiased expectations theory attempts to explain observed forward rates by saying that expected future rates, $_tr_{t+1}$, will, on average, be equal to the implied forward rates (1) if investors' expectations of future one-period rates are unbiased and (2) if bonds of different maturity are perfect substitutes for each other. Among other things, this second condition requires that the risk

---

[2] Note that like the internal rate of return the yield to maturity implicitly assumes that funds are reinvested at the implied yield. This contrasts with the assumption of discounting at the market-determined rate to get a net present value.

Table 8.1 An Investor's Expectations

Time to Maturity (Years)	Bond Price	Yield (%)	Observed Forward Rate (%)	Investor's Forward Rate (%)
1	$826.45	21	21.0	21.0
2	718.18	18	15.1	17.0
3	640.66	16	12.1	12.1

and transactions cost for a strategy of rolling over a one-period bond three times are the same as holding a three-period bond. If the two strategies are in fact perfect substitutes, investors will keep the rates in line with expectations by forming arbitrage positions whenever interest rates (and bond prices) are "out of line."

To show how arbitrage might work, suppose that we believe that the pattern of future rates in our example is out of line. Table 8.1 shows the actual prices and rates, along with our expectations. We believe that the implied forward rate in the second year is too low—that it should be 17% instead of 15.1%. What should we do?

The logical action would be to sell short the two-year bonds for $718.18. If we are right, interest rates in the second year will be higher than the market expects, and we will make a capital gain. If enough people believe the observed forward rate is too low, the decreased demand for two-year bonds will lower their prices until the implied forward rate rises to 17%. Then interest rates will be in line with revised expectations.

If there were no transactions costs and if there was no uncertainty, then there is every reason to believe that the unbiased expectations theory of the term structure would hold. Implied forward rates would be exact forecasts of expected future rates.

3. A Liquidity Premium in the Term Structure

Future interest rates become more uncertain the further into the future one tries to predict. Attempts to deal with this fact have led to theories of a *liquidity premium* in the term structure of interest rates.[3] Hicks argues that a liquidity premium exists because a given change in interest rates will have a greater effect on the price of long-term bonds than on short-term bonds. Hence there is greater risk of loss (and, one should add, a greater probability of gain) with long-term bonds. Consequently, risk-averse investors will require a higher yield in order to hold longer-term bonds. This extra yield is called a *liquidity premium*.

To illustrate the sensitivity of bond prices to changes in the interest rate, consider two bonds. They both pay $120 per year in coupons and have a $1,000 face value, but one has 5 years to maturity and the other has 10. If current interest rates are 10%, the present value of the 5-year bond, B_5, is

$$B_5 = \sum_{t=1}^{5} \frac{\$120}{(1+.10)^t} + \frac{\$1000}{(1+.10)^5} = \$1075.82,$$

---

[3] For example, see Hicks [1946], Keynes [1936], Kessel [1965], Hirshleifer [1972], and Woodward [1983].

and the present value of the 10-year bond is

$$B_{10} = \sum_{t=1}^{10} \frac{\$120}{(1+.10)^t} + \frac{\$1000}{(1+.10)^{10}} = \$1122.89.$$

What happens to the market prices of the bonds if the interest rate increases from 10% to 15%, a 50% increase? By similar calculations, we find that

$$B_5 = \$899.44 \quad \text{and} \quad B_{10} = \$849.44.$$

The market value of the 5-year bond has decreased 16.4%, whereas the 10-year bond has fallen by 24.4%. Clearly, the 10-year bond is more sensitive to the increase in interest rates. This is the risk Hicks had in mind when he described the liquidity premium.

Figure 8.3 shows how the liquidity premium is posited to change with the time to maturity on bonds. Note that the liquidity premium increases for bonds of longer maturity, but that it increases at a decreasing rate. Figure 8.4 shows how the liquidity premium is added to unbiased expectations in order to arrive at the observed term structure.

Using monthly returns data on U.S. Treasury bills (1964–1982) and on portfolios of U.S. government bonds (1953–1982), Fama [1984b] investigated term premiums in bond returns. He

Figure 8.3 The liquidity premium.

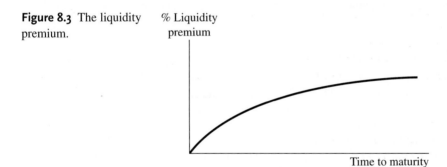

Figure 8.4 The liquidity premium added (a) to a decreasing term structure and (b) to an increasing term structure.

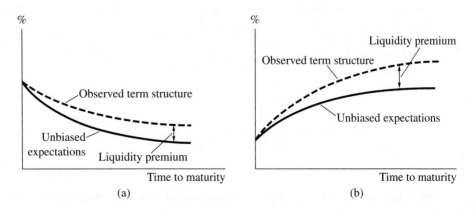

found statistically reliable evidence that expected returns on longer-term bills exceed the returns on one-month bills, but that the premium did not increase monotonically with maturity; rather it tended to peak at around eight or nine months. The high variability of longer-term bond returns made it impossible to draw any conclusions about liquidity premia on their returns.

4. The Market Segmentation Hypothesis

A third theory of the term structure, attributable to Culbertson [1957], Walker [1954], and Modigliani and Sutch [1966], is called the *market segmentation hypothesis*. It is argued that there is relatively little substitution between assets of different maturity because investors have preferred "habitats." For example, a firm that borrows to undertake an investment program will try to tailor its debt payments to the expected cash flows from the project. Capital-intensive firms that construct long-term plant and equipment will prefer to issue long-term debt rather than rolling over short-term debt, and less capital-intensive firms will prefer to borrow short term. Insurance companies with long-term liabilities (their life insurance policies) prefer to lend long term. Thus the market segmentation hypothesis argues that suppliers and users of funds have preferred habitats. Interest rates for a given maturity are explained mainly by the supply and demand for funds of that specific maturity.

While the market segmentation hypothesis can explain why implied forward and expected future rates may differ, the direction and magnitudes are not systematic. Recall that the Hicksian liquidity premium causes forward and future rates to differ systematically, depending on the maturity of the bonds.

5. Implications for Capital Budgeting

Regardless of which theory of the term structure is correct, the fact that one-year forward rates are not constant is relevant for the capital budgeting decision. The cash flows estimated for each year should be discounted to the present, using the information revealed in the term structure of interest rates. Let us use the hypothetical term structure example that was given earlier in the chapter to illustrate the relationship between the term structure and capital budgeting. Table 8.2 gives the yields to maturity, the implied forward rates, and cash flows for two projects. It is not uncommon for corporate treasurers to compute the NPV of these projects by discounting at the cost of capital for "three-year money," that is, 16%. After all, both projects have a three-year life. When the cash flows are discounted at 16%, project A has a NPV of $8.55, whereas B has a lower NPV of $8.21. Project A appears to be superior. Unfortunately, this procedure does not account for the fact that the real opportunity cost of funds is 21% for cash flows received in the first year, 15.07% for second-year cash flows, and 12.1% for third-year cash flows. The correct discount rate for cash flows in each year is the yield to maturity for that year. Note that this is also equal to the product of the implied forward rates from year 1 up to the year of the cash flows. For example, the three-year discount factor is

$$(1.16)^{-3} = [(1.21)(1.1507)(1.1210)]^{-1} = .6407.$$

The correct discount factors are given in the last column of Table 8.2. When the cash flows are appropriately discounted, the NPVs of projects A and B are $5.08 and $5.21, respectively. Now project B is preferred over A.

When the term structure is downward sloping, as in our simple example, a firm that uses the long-term rate (the three-year rate) to discount all cash flows will tend to overestimate the NPVs of

Table 8.2 The Term Structure and Capital Budgeting

Year	Yield to Maturity (%)	Forward Rate (%)	Cash Flow for A	Cash Flow for B	Discount Factor
0	–	–	$-100	$-100	1.0000
1	21	21.00	62	48	.8265
2	18	15.07	50	52	.7182
3	16	12.10	28	44	.6407

projects. Of course, when the term structure is upward sloping, the opposite bias exists. In addition, as the example has shown, it is possible for the wrong project to be selected if the information given in the term structure is ignored.

It has been suggested that the term structure provides the best estimate of expected inflation.[4] If so, a downward-sloping term structure implies that investors expect near-term inflation to be higher than long-term. An upward-sloping term structure (removing the liquidity premium) implies the opposite. If the firm's capital budgeting procedure discounts nominal cash flows (cum inflation) at market rates, the cash flow estimates should reflect inflation on a year-by-year basis.

B. $\mathcal{M}$odels of the Term Structure

Models of the term structure fall into two categories—equilibrium and arbitrage-free. Equilibrium models specify a process for the short-term interest rate that is based on assumptions about economic variables. As a result, they do not automatically fit market data on the term structure of interest rates at any point in time. In contrast, arbitrage-free models are calibrated to fit market data.

1. Equilibrium Models of the Yield Curve

In most one-factor equilibrium models, the stochastic process for the short-term rate, r, is of the form

$$dr = m(r)dt + w(r)dz, \tag{8.3}$$

where the instantaneous drift (m) and standard deviation (w) are related to the short-term rate but are not a function of time, and dz is normally distributed with mean 0 and variance of dt (i.e., z is a Wiener process).

Rendelman and Bartter [1980] assume that r follows a geometric Brownian motion by setting $m(r) = \mu r$ and $w(r) = \sigma r$, the process that stock prices were assumed to follow in Chapter 7. To illustrate the use of this approach, consider the binomial approximation to this continuous time process with an initial short-term rate of 8% and potential up moves of 25% ($u = 1.25$), down moves of 20% ($d = 0.8$), and a 50% probability of an up move. The evolution of short-term rates is given by

---

[4] For empirical evidence consistent with this point of view, see Fama [1975].

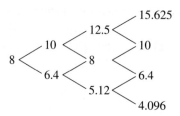

To determine the term structure of interest rates at time 0, we begin by calculating the price of a one-period bond. Specifically, at time 0 the price of the bond is $B(0, 1) = \frac{\$1}{1.08} = \$0.926$.

Similarly, the values in one period at the up and down nodes, respectively, of a bond that expires in one period are

$$B_u(1, 2) = \frac{\$1}{1.1} = \$0.909,$$

$$B_d(1, 2) = \frac{\$1}{1.064} = \$0.940.$$

The value of the bond today would be the discounted expected value in one period, that is,

$$B(0, 2) = \frac{(0.5)(0.9091) + (0.5)(0.9399)}{1.08} = 0.8560.$$

This implies that the two-period interest rate is $8.085\% \left(= \sqrt{\frac{1}{0.8560}} \right)$. Proceeding similarly with three- and four-period bonds would yield three- and four-period interest rates of 8.16% and 8.23%, respectively. The term structure of interest rates implied by this process is

Time to Maturity (periods)	Interest Rate (%)
1	8
2	8.085
3	8.16
4	8.23

The Rendelman-Bartter model has been criticized since it does not account for the empirical observation that interest rates tend to revert to a long-run average level over time.

Vasicek [1977] assumes the following mean-reverting process for the short-term rate:

$$dr = v(\mu - r)dt + \sigma dz, \tag{8.4}$$

where μ is the long-term mean of the short-term rate, v is the speed of adjustment of the short-term rate to the long-term mean, and σ is the instantaneous standard deviation. There is mean reversion in the process specified in Eq. (8.4) since a higher (lower) current short-term rate, r, as compared to the long-run mean, μ, implied a negative (positive) drift, which, in turn, implies that, on average, the short-term rate will decrease (increase) towards the long-run mean.

The price at time t of a zero-coupon bond that pays $1 at time T is then given by

$$B(t, T) = A(t, T)e^{-b(t,T)r(t)}, \tag{8.5}$$

where

$$r(t) = \text{the short rate at } t,$$

$$b(t, T) = \frac{1 - e^{-v(T-t)}}{v},$$

$$A(t, T) = e^{\left[\frac{(b(t,T)-T+t)\left(v^2\mu-\frac{\sigma^2}{2}\right)}{v^2} - \frac{\sigma^2 b^2(t,T)}{4v}\right]}.$$

Since $B(t, T) = e^{-(_tR_T)(T-t)}$, where $_tR_T$ is the interest rate at time t for a term of $(T - t)$, we get

$$_tR_T = \frac{1}{T - t}[b(t, T)r(t) - \ln A(t, T)]. \tag{8.6}$$

Equation (8.6) suggests that the entire yield curve can be obtained as a function of $r(t)$ once the three process parameters (the long-term mean of the short-term rate, μ; the speed of adjustment, v; and the instantaneous standard deviation, σ) are specified. The term structure can be upward sloping, downward sloping, or humped depending on the values of the various parameters.

To illustrate the use of the Vasicek model, consider a situation where the current short-term rate, $r(t)$, is 8%, the long-run mean, μ, is 10%, the instantaneous standard deviation, σ, is 5%, and the rate of adjustment, v, is 0.2. This set of parameters results in the following humped term structure of interest rates:

Time to Maturity in Years $(T - t)$	$b(t, T)$	$A(t, T)$	Value of a Zero-Coupon Bond $[B(t, T)]$	Interest Rate $[_tR_T]$ (%)
1	0.9063	0.9910	0.9217	8.15
2	1.6484	0.9679	0.8483	8.23
3	2.2559	0.9351	0.7807	8.25
4	2.7534	0.8964	0.7192	8.24
5	3.1606	0.8541	0.6633	8.21

One of the problems with the Vasicek model is that it allows the short-term rate to become negative. To rectify this problem, Cox, Ingersoll, and Ross [1985] (CIR) propose a mean reverting process for the short rate where the standard deviation of the changes in interest rates are proportional to the square root of the level of the rate. In the model, the short-term interest rate process is

$$dr = v(\mu - r)dt + \sigma\left(\sqrt{r}\right)dz \tag{8.7}$$

As in the Vasicek model, the price of a zero-coupon bond in this framework is given by the equation

$$B(t, T) = A(t, T)e^{-b(t,T)r(t)}, \tag{8.8}$$

where

$$b(t, T) = \frac{2(e^{r(T-t)} - 1)}{2\gamma + (\upsilon + \gamma)(e^{\gamma(T-t)} - 1)},$$

$$A(t, T) = \left(\frac{2\gamma e^{(\upsilon+\gamma)(T-t)/2}}{2\gamma + (\upsilon + \gamma)(e^{\gamma(T-t)} - 1)} \right)^{2\upsilon\mu/\sigma^2},$$

$$\gamma = \sqrt{\upsilon^2 + 2\sigma^2}.$$

As stated earlier, the price of the zero-coupon bond can be used to determine the interest rate for any term. Specifically, the interest rate from t to T, $_tR_T$, would be given by

$$_tR_T = \frac{1}{T - t}[b(t, T)r(t) - \ln A(t, T)], \tag{8.9}$$

where $b(t, T)$ and $A(t, T)$ are as defined above.

The term structure can be upward sloping, downward sloping, or humped depending on the values of the various parameters. For example, suppose the current short-term rate is 8%, the long-run mean is 10%, the instantaneous standard deviation is 5%, and the rate of adjustment is 0.2. This set of parameters results in the following upward-sloping term structure of interest rates:

Time to Maturity in Years $(T - t)$	$b(t, T)$	$A(t, T)$	Value of a Zero-Coupon Bond $[B(t, T)]$	Interest Rate $[_tR_T]$ (%)
1	0.9061	0.9907	0.9214	8.18
2	1.6462	0.9655	0.8463	8.34
3	2.2497	0.9284	0.7755	8.48
4	2.7411	0.8830	0.7092	8.59
5	3.1406	0.8325	0.6475	8.69

A number of papers have directly tested the CIR model. These include Brown and Dybvig [1986], Gibbons and Ramaswamy [1993], and Pearson and Sun [1994]. Brown and Dybvig find that the CIR model overestimates the short-term rate and "appears to fit Treasury Bills better than it does other Treasury issues." Gibbons and Ramaswamy find that the CIR model performs reasonably well in explaining short-term Treasury bill returns. In contrast, Pearson and Sun conclude that the CIR model "fails to provide a good description of the Treasury market."

Models of the yield curve that assume a mean reverting framework are not restricted to the Vasicek and CIR. There are a number of other versions of the standard deviation function (w) that have appeared in the literature. For example, Courtadon [1982] models the function as σr, Chan et al. [1992] use a constant elasticity of variance assumption and set $w(r) = \sigma r^\alpha$, while Duffie and Kan [1993] specify $w(r)$ to be $\sqrt{\sigma_0 + \sigma_1 r}$. Chan et al. test several one-factor models on one-month Treasury bills. Their results indicate that "the models that best describe the dynamics of interest rates over time are those that allow the conditional volatility of interest rate changes to be highly dependent on the level of the interest rate." More recently, Ait-Sahalia [1996] also empirically tests several of these one-factor models on the seven-day Eurodollar deposit rate. He finds that the linearity of the drift term is the main source of misspecification. He reports that the drift is approximately zero as long as the rate is between 4 and 17% but pulls strongly towards this region whenever rates move out of it. He also finds that volatility is higher when the rate moves away from the mean.

A number of papers including Ahn, Dittmar, and Gallant [2002] (ADG), Dai and Singleton [2000], and Duffie [2000] have examined the applicability of general affine term structure models (ATSMs) that contain Vasicek and CIR as special cases. Dai and Singleton find that these models pass several goodness-of-fit tests when applied to LIBOR-based yields in the ordinary fixed-for-variable rate swap market. On the other hand, Duffie [2000] finds that these models provide poor forecasts of future yield changes. ADG argue that ATSMs have several drawbacks including the fact that they cannot simultaneously allow for negative correlations between the state variables and guarantee that interest rates would be positive and they fail to capture important nonlinearities in the data. ADG suggest that a class of term structure models where yields are specified as quadratic functions of the state variables may be superior to affine term structure models since the former overcome many of the drawbacks of the latter. They estimate the parameters of four versions of the quadratic term structure models and assess their goodness-of-fit using data on 3-month and 12-month Treasury bills and 10-year bonds. They conclude from these tests that quadratic term structure models outperform affine term structure models in explaining historical price behavior in Treasury securities.

2. Arbitrage-Free Models of the Yield Curve

In the discussion of equilibrium models of the yield curve, we started by specifying the evolution process for short-term rate and from that we obtained the term structure of interest rates. In contrast, arbitrage-free models use the market data on yield curves as an input to ensure that the model and future values of the short-term rate are fully consistent with today's term structure. One major implication of this condition is that the drift of the short-term rate in arbitrage-free models is, in general, going to be time dependent. The purpose of arbitrage-free models is to define the price of zero-coupon bonds at some time in the future in terms of today's bond prices and the short-term rate at the future date. Examples of such models include Ho and Lee [1986], Hull and White [1990], and Heath, Jarrow, and Morton [1992].

Ho and Lee propose a binomial model for bond prices of the following form:

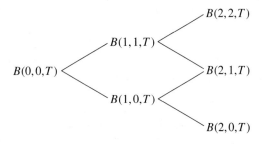

where $B(t, i, T)$ is the price of a bond at time t and state i that pays \$1 at time T. Note that $B(0, 0, T)$ is the initially observed term structure of bond prices. The evolution of bond prices is based on perturbation functions $h(\tau)$ and $h^*(\tau)$ such that

$$B(t, i+1, T) = \frac{B(t-1, i, T)}{B(t-1, i, t)} h(T-t), \tag{8.10a}$$

$$B(t, i, T) = \frac{B(t-1, i, T)}{B(t-1, i, t)} h^*(T-t), \tag{8.10b}$$

$$h(0) = h^*(0) = 1. \tag{8.10c}$$

The above equations when divided imply that

$$\frac{B(t, i+1, T)}{B(t, i, T)} = \frac{h(T-t)}{h*(T-t)}. \tag{8.11}$$

The no-arbitrage condition implies that

$$B(t, i, T) = [\pi B(t+1, i+1, T) + (1-\pi)B(t+1, i, T)]B(t, i, t+1), \tag{8.12}$$

where π is the probability associated with the perturbation $h(\tau)$. Combining the no-arbitrage condition with the perturbation equations yields the following constraint on the perturbation function:

$$\pi h(\tau) + (1-\pi)h^*(\tau) = 1. \tag{8.13}$$

Ho and Lee also show that for path independence to hold such that the order of the perturbations is not important, $h(\tau)$ and $h^*(\tau)$ have to satisfy the following conditions:

$$h(\tau) = \frac{1}{\pi + (1-\pi)\delta^\tau} \text{ and } h^*(\tau) = \frac{\delta^\tau}{\pi + (1-\pi)\delta^\tau} \tag{8.14}$$

for some constant $0 \le \delta \le 1$.

To apply this model, π and δ need to be estimated using market data. These estimates when combined with observed yields provide a future distribution of bond prices and term structures.

Consider the following example that illustrates the use of the Ho-Lee model. Assume that we have estimated π and δ to be 0.5 and 0.95, respectively. Further assume that 1-, 2-, and 3-year rates are at 6, 7, and 8%, respectively. These inputs would result in the following values for $h(T)$, $h^*(T)$, and $B(0, 0, T)$:

Maturity (T)	$h(T)$	$h^*(T)$	$B(0, 0, T)$
1	1.026	0.974	0.9434
2	1.051	0.949	0.8734
3	1.077	0.923	0.7939

Applying the no-arbitrage condition, Eq. (8.12), to $B(0, 0, 2)$, we get

$$B(0, 0, 2) = [0.5B(1, 1, 2) + 0.5B(1, 0, 2)]B(0, 0, 1).$$

The perturbation conditions imply that

$$\frac{B(1, 1, 2)}{B(1, 0, 2)} = \frac{h(1)}{h*(1)}.$$

Substituting values from the table into the above two equations yields $B(1, 1, 2) = 0.9496$ and $B(1, 0, 2) = 0.9021$. This implies that with a perturbation of h or h^*, the value of a bond that pays $1 in two periods is going to be 0.9496, or 0.9021 in one period.

Applying the same logic and process at different nodes yields the following tree of bond prices:

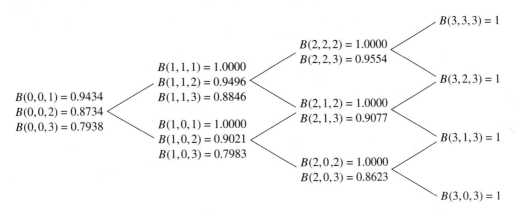

$$B(0,0,1) = 0.9434$$
$$B(0,0,2) = 0.8734$$
$$B(0,0,3) = 0.7938$$

$$B(1,1,1) = 1.0000$$
$$B(1,1,2) = 0.9496$$
$$B(1,1,3) = 0.8846$$

$$B(1,0,1) = 1.0000$$
$$B(1,0,2) = 0.9021$$
$$B(1,0,3) = 0.7983$$

$$B(2,2,2) = 1.0000$$
$$B(2,2,3) = 0.9554$$

$$B(2,1,2) = 1.0000$$
$$B(2,1,3) = 0.9077$$

$$B(2,0,2) = 1.0000$$
$$B(2,0,3) = 0.8623$$

$$B(3,3,3) = 1$$
$$B(3,2,3) = 1$$
$$B(3,1,3) = 1$$
$$B(3,0,3) = 1$$

A drawback of the Ho-Lee model is that it allows interest rates to become negative. Hull and White [1990] address this issue by analyzing an extended version of the Vasicek model that allows for a time-varying drift in the short rate. Specifically, the process for the short rate is given by

$$dr = [\theta(t) - vr] dt + \sigma dz. \tag{8.15}$$

In this framework, the short rate at time t reverts to $\frac{\theta(t)}{v}$ at the rate v. Hull and White show that bond prices at time t are given by

$$B(t, T) = A(t, T)e^{-b(t,T)r(t)}, \tag{8.16a}$$

where

$$b(t, T) = \frac{1 - e^{-v(T-t)}}{v}, \tag{8.16b}$$

$$\ln A(t, T) = \ln \frac{B(0, T)}{B(0, t)} - b(t, T)\frac{\delta B(0, t)}{\delta t} - \frac{1}{4v^3}\sigma^2(e^{-vT} - e^{-vt} - 1). \tag{8.16c}$$

The above equations define the price of a bond at some future time t as a function of the short rate at time t and the current bond prices.[5]

In contrast to Ho and Lee and Hull and White, who model the process for the short rate, Heath, Jarrow, and Morton [1990, 1992] (HJM) model the evolution of forward rates. In their model, the

---

[5] Hull and White [1994] provide a procedure for implementing this approach using trinomial trees.

forward rate process is given by

$$\Delta f(t, T) = \alpha(t, T)\Delta + \sigma(t, T)\Delta z, \tag{8.17}$$

where $f(t, T)$ is *date-t* forward rate for the interval $(T, T + \Delta)$; $\Delta f(t, T) = f(t + \Delta, T) - f(t, T)$; $\alpha(t, T)$ is the drift of the forward process; $\sigma(t, T)$ is its instantaneous volatility; and Δz is normally distributed with mean 0 and a standard deviation of $\sqrt{\Delta}$. The price of a zero-coupon bond in the HJM framework is given by

$$B(t, T) = \frac{B(0, T)}{B(0, t)} e^{[-b(t,T)r(t)+b(t,T)f(0,T)-A(t,T)]}, \tag{8.18a}$$

where

$$b(t, T) = \frac{1 - e^{-\lambda(T-t)}}{\lambda}, \tag{8.18b}$$

$$A(t, T) = \frac{\sigma^2[b(t, T)]^2 \left[1 - e^{-2\lambda t}\right]}{4\lambda}, \tag{8.18c}$$

$$\sigma(t, T) = \sigma e^{-\lambda(T-t)}. \tag{8.18d}$$

The implementation of this model is similar to the binomial approach of Ho and Lee with one major exception. In the Ho-Lee binomial process, the tree is recombining; that is, an up perturbation followed by the down perturbation results in the same bond price as a down perturbation followed by an up perturbation. In contrast, the HJM tree is not recombining. As a result this model is computationally more complicated than the Ho-Lee approach. Specifically, to implement this model, the forward rate is assumed to change as follows:[6]

$$f(t + \Delta t, T) = \begin{cases} f(t, T) + \mu(t, T)\Delta t + \sigma(t, T)\sqrt{\Delta t} \text{ with prob.} \frac{1}{2} \\ f(t, T) + \mu(t, T)\Delta t - \sigma(t, T)\sqrt{\Delta t} \text{ with prob.} \frac{1}{2} \end{cases} \tag{8.19a}$$

where

$$\mu(t, T)\Delta t = \frac{e^\omega - e^{-\omega}}{e^\omega + e^{-\omega}} \sigma(t, T)\sqrt{\Delta t}, \tag{8.19b}$$

$$\omega = \left[\int_{t+\Delta t}^{T} \sigma(t, u)du\right] \sqrt{\Delta t}, \tag{8.19c}$$

$$\sigma(t, T) = \sigma e^{-\lambda(T-t)}. \tag{8.19d}$$

Thus, given today's structure of forward rates $(f(0, T))$, the volatility decay parameter (λ), the volatility (σ), and the time increment (Δt), one can generate a tree of forward rate from time 0 to time T in increments of Δt. These forward rates can then be used to specify the term structure of interest rates and bond prices at future points in time.

---

[6] See Ritchken [1996] for more details

C. $\mathscr{F}$orward and Futures Contracts

In July 2002 the *Wall Street Journal* listed futures contracts on commodities (e.g., grains, livestock, food fiber, metals, petroleum products, and wood), on foreign currencies (e.g., the Australian dollar, British pound, Canadian dollar, Japanese yen, Mexican peso, Swiss franc, and Euro), on financial instruments (e.g., Treasury bonds, notes, and bills, Long Gilt), and on stock indices (e.g., the Standard and Poor's 500, the NYSE Composite index, the Nikkei 225 index, and the NASDAQ 100 index). Figure 8.5 shows a sampling of futures quotations. We can broadly divide futures contracts into three categories: commodities futures, financial futures, and futures on indices.

One chapter alone cannot cover all the details of every futures contract. Our objective is to describe the general features of futures contracts (such as standardization, delivery, clearing, open interest, and price limits) in Section C, the theory of the pricing of futures contracts in Section D, empirical evidence in Section E, and synthetic futures and options on futures in Section F.

1. Definitions

When you buy a *forward contract*, you write a contract today at a stated price—but pay no cash—for promised future delivery of the underlying asset at a specified time and place in the future. At the time of delivery you receive the asset you purchased and pay the contract price. Your profit (or loss) on the delivery date is the difference between the market value of the asset and the contract price. A *futures contract* is similar to a forward contract except that changes in the contract price are settled daily. There is nothing unusual about forward and futures contracts. In fact they are commonplace. For example, when you contract for purchase of a car that will be delivered six weeks from now (at the dealer's lot), you are buying a futures contract. If the future value of the car is known with certainty, the current value of the forward contract is easy to determine. For example, suppose you know the car will be worth $10,000 six weeks from now; then the current price of the contract that delivers at date T, $_0F_T$, is

$$_0F_T = E(S_T), \tag{8.20}$$

where T is the time until delivery of the asset, and $E(S_T)$ is the expected price of the asset (the car) on the delivery date.[7] For our simple example, since there is no uncertainty, the contract price is $10,000. If there were a secondary market for futures contracts on cars, you could resell your contract for future delivery of the car, and the futures contract price would be $10,000.

Alternately, if you were able to purchase the car immediately, you would pay the *spot price*, which is the current market price of the commodity. The spot price today would be the expected spot price six weeks from now, discounted back to the present at the continuous annual risk-free

---

[7] Notation shall be standardized as follows: The T period futures (or forward) contract priced at time t will be written as $_tF_T$, and the spot price at time t as S_t. Whenever it is useful to subscript interest rates, the interest rate between t and T will be written as $_tr_T$.

Figure 8.5 Selected futures contract prices, July 29, 2002. (© by Dow Jones & Co Inc. Reproduced with permission of Dow Jones & Co Inc.)

Exchange Abbreviations

For commodity futures and futures options

CBT-Chicago Board of Trade;
CME-Chicago Mercantile Exchange;
CSCE-Coffee, Sugar & Cocoa Exchange, New York;
CMX-COMEX (Div. of New York Mercantile Exchange);
CTN-New York Cotton Exchange;
DTB-Deutsche Terminboerse;
EUREX-European Exchange;
FINEX-Financial Exchange (Div. of New York Cotton Exchange;
IPE-International Petroleum Exchange;
KC-Kansas City Board of Trade;
LIFFE-London International Financial Futures Exchange;
MATIF-Marche a-Terme International de France;
ME-Montreal Exchange;
MCE-MidAmerica Commodity Exchange;
MPLS-Minneapolis Grain Exchange;
NYFE-New York Futures Exchange (Sub. of New York Cotton Exchange);
NYM-New York Mercantile Exchange;
SFE-Sydney Futures Exchange;
SGX-Singapore Exchange Ltd.;

Futures prices reflect day and overnight trading
Open interest reflects previous day's trading

Monday, July 29, 2002

Grain and Oilseed Futures

Corn (CBT)-5,000 bu.; cents per bu.

	OPEN	HIGH	LOW	SETTLE	CHG	LIFETIME HIGH	LIFETIME LOW	OPEN INT
Sept	238.00	238.75	230.25	231.00	-12.00	262.00	205.25	149,009
Dec	247.50	248.50	239.50	240.25	-12.50	272.00	215.00	244,277
Mr03	253.00	253.75	245.75	246.75	-11.25	264.50	224.00	41,416
May	254.00	255.00	250.25	251.25	-10.00	267.50	229.25	9,873
July	259.50	259.50	253.50	254.25	-9.75	272.00	233.75	16,832
Sept	249.00	249.00	246.00	246.50	-5.25	254.00	233.00	2,258
Dec	243.25	245.00	240.75	241.00	-5.25	269.00	235.00	15,283
Jl04	252.00	252.00	251.00	251.00	-4.50	259.50	247.75	326
Dec	242.75	243.00	241.50	241.50	-2.50	260.00	237.00	1,322

Est vol 109,410; vol Fri 64,053; open int 481,801, +1,656.

Oats (CBT)-5,000 bu.; cents per bu.

	OPEN	HIGH	LOW	SETTLE	CHG	LIFETIME HIGH	LIFETIME LOW	OPEN INT
Sept	165.00	167.00	160.50	163.50	-3.75	186.50	117.50	2,726
Dec	164.00	164.50	161.00	162.75	-5.25	183.25	123.00	6,883
Mr03	168.00	168.00	160.50	164.25	-4.50	183.00	130.00	834

Est vol 1,084; vol Fri 1,536; open int 10,577, -191.

Soybeans (CBT)-5,000 bu.; cents per bu.

	OPEN	HIGH	LOW	SETTLE	CHG	LIFETIME HIGH	LIFETIME LOW	OPEN INT
Aug	544.00	544.00	532.00	534.75	-16.00	605.00	425.00	19,583
Sept	525.00	525.00	514.00	519.50	-13.00	580.00	425.00	27,169
Nov	509.00	550.25	500.00	503.00	-12.25	565.00	428.50	104,324
Ja03	511.00	512.00	503.00	505.75	-12.25	562.75	445.00	17,433
Mar	509.00	514.00	503.00	509.00	-9.75	553.50	449.00	15,405
May	514.25	515.00	507.00	510.25	-9.25	554.00	461.00	27,399
July	510.00	513.00	508.00	510.50	-8.75	554.00	450.00	6,424
Nov	494.00	497.00	492.00	494.00	-5.25	525.00	484.00	2,447

Est vol 71,774; vol Fri 99,411; open int 220,196, -9,232.

Soybean Meal (CBT)-100 tons; $ per ton.

	OPEN	HIGH	LOW	SETTLE	CHG	LIFETIME HIGH	LIFETIME LOW	OPEN INT
Aug	175.50	175.50	171.00	171.20	-6.10	193.00	141.10	16,225
Sept	169.00	169.70	166.10	166.40	-5.40	185.50	139.70	23,398
Oct	163.50	163.50	160.50	160.70	-4.30	180.90	141.50	18,413
Dec	161.60	161.80	159.00	159.20	-4.40	178.00	142.70	52,275
Ja03	159.00	161.30	159.00	159.00	-4.00	175.00	143.50	6,782
Mar	158.50	160.80	158.50	159.00	-3.20	174.60	145.50	5,624
May	159.00	160.00	158.30	158.30	-2.70	172.00	146.00	6,761
July	158.50	160.20	158.40	158.50	-2.70	172.10	147.00	4,493
Aug	158.80	159.50	157.50	157.80	-2.20	170.00	148.00	929
Sept	158.20	158.50	156.00	156.00	-3.10	168.80	148.00	818
Dec	156.00	156.00	156.00	156.00	-1.50	166.00	148.00	1,034

Est vol 48,354; vol Fri 47,038; open int 137,118, -3,182.

Soybean Oil (CBT)-60,000 lbs.; cents per lb.

	OPEN	HIGH	LOW	SETTLE	CHG	LIFETIME HIGH	LIFETIME LOW	OPEN INT
Aug	19.25	19.28	19.02	19.19	-.11	20.38	15.62	13,498
Sept	19.33	19.40	19.14	19.29	-.15	20.50	15.73	26,485
Oct	19.45	19.46	19.25	19.40	-.13	20.48	15.15	10,747
Dec	19.69	19.72	19.46	19.64	-.17	20.90	16.10	59,840
Ja03	19.64	19.78	19.54	19.70	-.19	20.78	16.35	6,418
Mar	19.85	19.85	19.64	19.77	-.23	20.83	16.70	4,618
May	19.84	19.94	19.73	19.83	-.23	20.90	16.80	10,488
July	19.83	19.90	19.73	19.82	-.28	20.90	16.95	3,955

Est vol 37,930; vol Fri 34,415; open int 138,402, -4,188.

Wheat (CBT)-5,000 bu.; cents per bu.

	OPEN	HIGH	LOW	SETTLE	CHG	LIFETIME HIGH	LIFETIME LOW	OPEN INT
Sept	332.00	332.75	324.75	326.50	-8.50	343.00	271.00	45,339
Dec	340.25	341.50	330.50	336.25	-7.75	365.00	283.50	63,880
Mr03	344.00	346.00	332.00	342.25	-8.00	355.50	288.50	9,722
May	334.00	337.00	333.50	334.50	-5.50	365.00	287.00	510

Cotton (NYCE)-50,000 lbs.; cents per lb.

	OPEN	HIGH	LOW	SETTLE	CHG	LIFETIME HIGH	LIFETIME LOW	OPEN INT
Oct	45.25	45.40	44.90	45.25	-.50	65.50	33.85	3,322
Dec	46.70	47.05	46.55	46.75	-.68	64.75	34.65	55,382
Mr03	48.50	48.95	48.41	48.60	-.60	55.25	36.20	8,611
May	50.95	51.30	50.95	51.20	-.50	54.40	38.70	4,754
July	51.60	52.20	52.00	51.90	-.70	54.97	39.50	2,112
Dec	53.30	53.55	53.30	53.30	-.60	55.80	43.80	930

Est vol 3,307; vol Fri 2,747; open int 75,331, -44.

Orange Juice (NYCE)-15,000 lbs.; cents per lb.

	OPEN	HIGH	LOW	SETTLE	CHG	LIFETIME HIGH	LIFETIME LOW	OPEN INT
Sept	99.70	100.20	99.50	99.90	.30	101.10	86.50	18,365
Nov	100.00	100.65	100.00	100.60	.25	101.60	86.50	6,815
Ja03	100.55	100.55	100.55	100.70	.15	102.40	87.80	4,339
Mar	101.00	101.50	101.00	101.60	.15	102.00	88.25	2,399
May	102.20	102.20	102.20	102.45	.25	103.00	91.25	350

Est vol 1,502; vol Fri 1,085; open int 32,280, -80.

Metal Futures

Copper-High (CMX)-25,000 lbs.; cents per lb.

	OPEN	HIGH	LOW	SETTLE	CHG	LIFETIME HIGH	LIFETIME LOW	OPEN INT
July	69.35	69.55	69.15	69.50	0.80	88.90	62.30	1,285
Aug	69.15	69.60	69.15	69.55	0.80	82.90	62.90	4,671
Sept	69.00	70.10	69.00	69.85	0.80	88.00	62.95	53,866
Oct	70.00	70.30	70.00	70.15	0.80	85.50	63.60	1,461
Nov	70.35	70.55	70.35	70.35	0.70	85.50	64.00	1,113
Dec	70.35	70.90	70.25	70.65	0.70	83.00	63.50	13,845
Ja03	71.00	71.15	71.00	71.00	0.70	81.00	64.90	953
Feb	71.35	71.35	71.35	71.25	0.70	79.95	65.10	826
Mar	71.20	71.75	71.20	71.50	0.70	80.70	65.30	3,163
May	71.75	72.15	71.75	72.00	0.70	81.05	65.80	2,773
June	72.40	72.40	72.40	72.20	0.70	78.40	70.80	570
July	72.10	72.60	72.10	72.40	0.70	80.80	66.80	2,110
Aug	72.70	72.70	72.70	72.55	0.70	77.85	67.40	553
Sept	72.90	72.90	72.90	72.75	0.70	81.00	66.00	2,703
Nov	73.10	73.10	73.10	73.10	0.70	81.00	67.00	359
Dec	73.40	73.40	73.40	73.25	0.70	81.60	71.50	3,513

Est vol 27,000; vol Fri 9,721; open int 95,686, +1,887.

Gold (CMX)-100 troy oz.; $ per troy oz.

	OPEN	HIGH	LOW	SETTLE	CHG	LIFETIME HIGH	LIFETIME LOW	OPEN INT
July	301.00	301.00	300.80	302.50	-0.90	326.80	300.80	
Aug	303.20	303.50	301.60	302.40	-0.90	331.50	272.60	32,373
Oct	303.00	305.00	302.50	303.60	-0.80	331.50	274.00	10,775
Dec	305.20	305.60	303.50	304.50	-0.70	358.00	268.10	68,164
Fb03	305.00	306.30	304.20	305.20	-0.70	333.70	286.50	8,264
Apr	307.00	307.00	307.00	305.80	-0.70	332.50	281.50	4,351
June	306.30	307.00	305.80	306.30	-0.70	338.00	280.00	5,902
Dec	307.90	309.50	307.40	309.00	-0.20	359.30	280.00	8,503

Est vol 57,000; vol Fri 90,807; open int 154,149, -3,993.

Platinum (NYM)-50 troy oz.; $ per troy oz.

	OPEN	HIGH	LOW	SETTLE	CHG	LIFETIME HIGH	LIFETIME LOW	OPEN INT
Oct	520.50	523.00	519.00	519.60	-3.60	566.00	400.00	4,938

Est vol 178; vol Fri 949; open int 5,008, -6.

Silver (CMX)-5,000 troy oz.; cents per troy oz.

	OPEN	HIGH	LOW	SETTLE	CHG	LIFETIME HIGH	LIFETIME LOW	OPEN INT
July	468.0	469.0	461.0	463.6	-2.5	559.0	409.5	37
Sept	467.0	469.5	462.0	464.0	-2.5	517.0	412.5	48,554
Dec	469.0	471.0	465.0	466.8	-2.6	613.0	412.0	23,974
Mr03	472.0	472.0	467.5	468.9	-2.6	522.0	417.0	2,097
May	469.0	469.0	469.0	470.0	-2.6	523.0	463.5	1,877
July	472.0	474.0	466.0	471.0	-2.6	551.0	421.0	4,433
Dec	475.0	476.0	475.0	473.9	-2.6	565.0	419.0	2,196
Jl04	490.0	490.0	490.0	475.0	-2.6	570.0	436.0	703

Est vol 14,000; vol Fri 30,955; open int 85,632, -5,761.

Petroleum Futures

Crude Oil, Light Sweet (NYM)-1,000 bbls.; $ per bbl.

	OPEN	HIGH	LOW	SETTLE	CHG	LIFETIME HIGH	LIFETIME LOW	OPEN INT
Sept	26.52	26.66	26.32	26.55	0.01	28.18	19.10	137,443
Oct	26.11	26.18	25.93	26.09	-0.02	27.61	19.50	61,557
Nov	25.84	26.00	25.80	25.94	-0.02	27.25	19.55	23,000
Dec	25.69	25.85	25.64	25.79	...	27.05	15.50	51,685
Ja03	25.54	25.65	25.45	25.57	...	26.40	19.90	20,696
Feb	25.39	25.39	25.30	25.37	0.01	26.25	19.70	9,977
Mar	25.20	25.20	25.20	25.18	0.02	26.00	20.05	8,586
Apr	24.90	25.00	24.90	25.00	0.02	25.75	20.55	6,833
June	24.65	24.65	24.55	24.64	0.02	25.39	19.82	15,121

Est vol 75,560; vol Fri 125,191; open int 430,604, -3,635.

Heating Oil No. 2 (NYM)-42,000 gal.; $ per gal.

	OPEN	HIGH	LOW	SETTLE	CHG	LIFETIME HIGH	LIFETIME LOW	OPEN INT
Aug	.6671	.6715	.6640	.6660	-.0015	.7340	.5300	14,459
Sept	.6779	.6790	.6720	.6751	-.0028	.7300	.5390	38,742
Oct	.6840	.6860	.6800	.6826	-.0028	.7345	.5460	13,948
Nov	.6920	.6935	.6890	.6901	-.0023	.7500	.5570	8,291
Dec	.6980	.7010	.6950	.6971	-.0023	.7500	.5660	16,802
Ja03	.7060	.7060	.7000	.7021	-.0023	.7510	.5680	9,866
Feb	.7000	.7040	.7000	.7001	-.0023	.7441	.5710	8,651
Mar	.6900	.6900	.6885	.6871	-.0018	.7261	.5640	6,094

rate, $r_f = 10\%$, since there is no uncertainty:

$$S_0 = E(S_T)e^{-r_f T}$$

$$= 10{,}000e^{-.10(6/52)}$$

$$= 10{,}000(.988528)$$

$$= \$9{,}885.28.$$

One pays the spot price for immediate delivery and the futures price at the time of future delivery.

When the forward/futures contract matures, six weeks from now, you receive a car worth $10,000 from the dealer and pay $10,000 in cash. Your net profit at delivery is zero because there was no uncertainty in our simple example. Had the future value of the car been uncertain, you could have gained or lost the difference between the market value of the car at the delivery date, T, and the $10,000 contract price that you must pay at T. In Section D we shall examine some of the complications that arise in pricing futures contracts when the future commodity price is uncertain, when storage of the commodity is costly, and when taxes must be taken into consideration.

2. Standardization

Of course, if a secondary market existed, other buyers would like to know exactly what kind of car they would be buying (e.g., a blue four-cylinder Chevrolet with bucket seats and a four-speed manual transmission). The same is true of actual futures markets. The asset to be delivered must be standardized as much as is practical. Standardization helps make the market large enough to attract active trading and to provide liquidity.

As an example of standardization the New York Mercantile Exchange (NYMEX) defines a contract in "light, sweet" crude oil as follows:[8]

1. The seller agrees to deliver 1,000 U.S. barrels (42,000 gallons) of "light, sweet" crude oil meeting the following specifications:
   (a) Sulfur—.42% or less by weight.
   (b) Gravity—not less than 37 degrees nor more than 42 degrees API.
   (c) Domestic crudes that are deliverable include West Texas Intermediate, Low Sweet Mix, New Mexican Sweet, North Texas Sweet, Oklahoma Sweet, and South Texas Sweet.
   (d) Price adjustments can be made for specific foreign crudes of gravity not less than 34 degrees nor more than 42 degrees API.

2. Delivery shall be made FOB (free on board) seller's facility, Cushing, Oklahoma, or any pipeline or storage facility with pipeline access to TEPPCO, Cushing storage, or Equilon Pipeline Co.

3. Delivery shall take place no earlier than the first calendar day and no later than the last calendar day of the delivery month. Delivery months are the 30 consecutive calendar months following the current calendar month as well as long-dated futures initially listed 36, 48, 60, 72, and 84 months prior to delivery.

4. Speculative position limits are imposed. No person shall own or control a net long or short position in all months combined of more than 5,000 contracts and in the month preceding delivery no more than 750 contracts for the delivery month.

---

[8] Actual contract terms have been simplified for expositional purposes. Contact the NYMEX for full details.

Although the definition of the commodity to be delivered seems very precise, to the extent that variations exist, the seller has an *implied delivery option* and will, if possible, deliver the lowest-quality product at the latest possible date. The value of the implied delivery option varies from contract to contract and is implicit in the futures price.[9]

3. Clearing, Volume, and Open Interest

Both standardization of contracts and ease of clearing have helped to provide liquidity to futures markets. The futures *clearinghouse* stands between the buyer and seller in order to facilitate transactions. Think of the clearinghouse as an accounting system for long and short positions in futures contracts. Figure 8.6 illustrates a simple example.

At 11:15 A.M. Mr. A buys two December contracts at a market price of $25.69 per barrel. He never knows the identity of the seller or sellers and probably does not care. The clearinghouse records his purchase along with the fact that one contract was sold at $25.69 per barrel by Mr. B and another by Mr. C. Next, at 1:20 P.M., Mr. A sells a contract at $25.85 per barrel (for a $0.16 gain), and Mr. D is on the buying side. At 1:40 P.M., Mr. D buys another contract at $25.64 with Mr. B on the selling side. Finally, Mr. C sells one contract for $25.79 a barrel to Mr. A at 2:10 P.M. There are no further transactions and the market closes at $25.79 per barrel. The *Wall Street Journal* reports (see Fig. 8.6) that the market for December contracts opened at $25.69, the high was $25.85, the low was $25.64, and the closing price was $25.79. The price change from the previous day's close was $0.00.

At the end of the trading day, each trader's position is *marked to market* by the clearinghouse in its *daily settlement* operation. As shown in Fig. 8.6, Mr. A's net position for the day is a gain of $260. This amount of money is credited to his interest-bearing account at the clearinghouse. On the other hand, Mr. C lost $100 and he must pay the clearinghouse. In actuality, only brokers belong to the clearinghouse, and it is their accounts that are settled daily. Each brokerage firm then acts as a clearinghouse for its clients.

Note that five contracts were traded during the day in our example. Actual trading volume in December contracts is not reported in the *Wall Street Journal*, but total trading volume for all oil contracts was estimated at 75,560. In addition to volume per day, the *Wall Street Journal* reports *open interest*, which is the total number of contracts outstanding as of the previous day. In most futures markets the open interest, as illustrated in Fig. 8.7, is relatively low during the early months of a contract, when it still has a long time before expiration. Then it arises as hedgers and speculators become more active in the market, and finally it falls rapidly as the contract expiration approaches. For example, in crude oil the open interest in April 2003 contracts, which have almost one year to maturity, was only 6,656, whereas for the September 2002 contracts, open interest was 137,443. In some futures markets (e.g., stock index futures), there cannot be any open interest at the contract expiration date because it is not possible to actually deliver the underlying asset—the stock index. Even when the commodity can be delivered, relatively few of the futures positions (less than 3% on average) end in actual delivery of the commodity involved. Later on, in the theory section of the chapter, we shall discuss some reasons why open interest is so high relative to the number of contracts that result in delivery.

---

[9] Chance and Hemler [1993] provide an excellent survey of the literature in this area. They report that most studies estimate that the quality option is worth less than 1–2% of futures price three months prior to delivery. Exceptions include Johnston and McConnell [1989], who obtain values as high as 19% for GNMA CDR futures, and Kane and Marcus [1986], who obtain expiration values exceeding 4% for T-bond futures.

Figure 8.6 A clearinghouse illustration.

Record of Transactions during the Trading Day:

Long Positions				Short Positions			
Buyer	Quantity	Price	Time	Seller	Quantity	Price	Time
Mr. A	2	$25.69	11:15A	Mr. B	1	$25.69	11:15 A
Mr. D	1	25.85	1:20P	Mr. C	1	25.69	11:15 A
Mr. D	1	25.64	1:40P	Mr. A	1	25.85	1:20 P
Mr. A	1	25.79	2:10P	Mr. B	1	25.64	1:40 P
	5			Mr. C.	1	25.79	2:10 P
					5		

Net Positions: **(Market closing price = $25.79 per barrel)**

Mr. A:				
	2 purchased	at $25.69 =	−	$51,380
	1 purchased	at $25.79 =	−	25,790
	1 sold	at $25.85 =	+	25,850
			−	51,320
	2 long	at $25.79 =	+	51,580
	At settlement		+	260
Mr. B	1 sold	at $25.69 =	+	25,690
	1 sold	at $25.64 =	+	25,640
			+	51,330
	2 short	at $25.79	−	51,580
	At settlement		−	250
Mr. C	1 sold	at $25.69 =	+	25,690
	1 sold	at $25.79 =	+	25,790
			+	51,480
	2 short	at $25.79 =	−	51,580
	At settlement		−	100
Mr. D	1 purchased	at $25.85 =	−	25,850
	1 purchased	at $25.64 =	−	25,640
			−	51,490
	2 long	at $25.79 =	+	51,580
	At settlement		+	90

Figure 8.7 Typical pattern for open interest over the life of a futures contract.

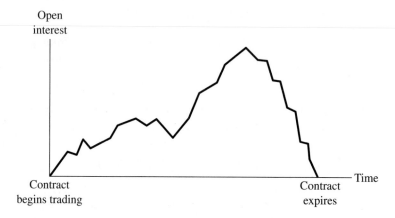

4. Margins

The example in Fig. 8.6 implicitly assumed that all traders invested an amount equal to the full value of the underlying commodity. This is rarely the case. Usually, the futures trader is required to put up only enough money to insure that the probability of reaching a negative equity position in one day is quite small. Each futures market has its own regulations, but the *initial margin* when a position is first opened is usually only 5–10% of the total value of the contract. The *maintenance margin* is the minimum amount of equity that the account may have and is usually set at 75–80% of the initial margin. If losses drive down the value of equity in the account below the maintenance margin, then the investor receives a *margin call* requiring that additional cash (or interest-bearing certificates) be placed into the account to bring the equity in the account above the initial margin. If the investor fails to meet the requirements of the margin call, then the broker may close out the investor's futures position.

There is, of course, nothing that requires an investor to use a margin account. The effect of trading on margin is to leverage any position so that the systematic and unsystematic risks are both greater per dollar of investment. High margin has given commodity futures markets the reputation of being very risky when in fact, as we shall see later on (in Section E), 100% margin positions have about the same variance as common stock portfolios, although they have very different covariances with the market portfolio.

There are commonly cited reasons for having margin requirements. First, a margin on a futures contract represents a performance bond, which serves to protect the integrity and reputation of the futures exchange and to protect the middleman (known as the futures commission merchant) from customer default. Second, it is often argued (by regulators) that higher margin requirements serve to reduce price volatility caused by speculative activity.

Hartzmark [1986] analyzes the effect of changes in margin requirements on futures markets and concludes (1) that when margin levels are raised (lowered) the number of open contracts falls (rises), (2) that there is weak evidence to support the conclusion that there is an inverse relationship between margin changes and trading volume, (3) that there are significant but unpredictable changes in the composition of traders in the market, and (4) that there is no systematic or significant relationship between margin changes and price volatility. More recently Adrangi and Chatrath [1999] report that margin increases have a negative impact on the trading activities of all types of traders, with the closest to delivery contract being the most sensitive. They also find that margins are increased in high-volatility environments, while the reverse occurs in stable or low-volatility environments.

5. Price Limits

Another interesting feature of commodities markets is *price limits*. The U.S. Commodity Futures Trading Commission, which regulates trading on U.S. commodity exchanges, places limits on the extent to which futures prices are allowed to vary from day to day. For example, a simplified description of the price limits on frozen concentrated orange juice futures (after 1979) is that (1) prices may move no more than $0.05 per pound ($750 per contract); (2) when three or more contract months have closed at the limit in the same direction for three successive business days, the limit is raised to $0.08 per pound; and (3) on the last three days before the near contract's expiration, its limit is $0.10 per pound. It is not unusual for the price to move up (or down) the limit (i.e., up or down by $0.10 per pound) for several days without any trading taking place.

There are arguments for and against price limits. For example, Roll [1984] notes that the orange juice futures price is rendered informationally inefficient by the imposition of price limits on price movements because prices respond to weather changes (especially freezes, which damage the crop) slower than they otherwise might in the absence of price limits. Brennan [1986b], however, provides an economic rationale for price limits. Against the clear costs on market participants imposed by prohibiting mutually beneficial trades at prices outside the price limits, he suggests that a benefit of price limits is that their imposition allows lower margin requirements than would otherwise prevail. Margin requirements and price limits are substitutes in ensuring contract performance without costly litigation. If margin requirements are costly, then having lower margin requirements is a benefit that results from price limits.

That margin requirements are costly is itself a debated proposition. Black [1976], for example, argues that the opportunity cost of margins is zero with daily settlement because the value of the futures position goes to zero. This argument, however, fails to account for the costs associated with the initial margin. Others (e.g., Anderson [1981]) believe that the margin positions have no opportunity cost because they can be satisfied with interest-bearing securities. However, Telser [1981a] provides a sensible argument for costly margin requirements, namely, that interest-bearing securities such as Treasury bills are part of the holder's precautionary balance and if they are committed for use as margin, they are unavailable for other uses. Brennan [1986b] also points out that the bonding feature of margin requirements helps to avoid costly litigation that would otherwise be needed to enforce daily settlement on futures contracts.

Brennan [1986b] is also able to explain why some futures markets have price limits while others do not. A futures market with daily price limits helps to prevent default because the losing trader cannot be absolutely certain that defaulting is the best thing to do. For example, if the price moves down the limit, the trader may be subject to a margin call but will not necessarily be wiped out. Furthermore, the trader does not know what the futures price will be when the daily price limits no longer apply. Therefore he will tend to meet the maintenance margin rather than defaulting. An analogy (provided by Phil Dybvig when he was at Yale) is that you take your aging car to the mechanic to ask him to fix it. The car is only worth $4,000 and the mechanic knows it will take $4,500 to complete all repairs. Rather than telling you the total cost of repair, and having you respond by junking the car instead of repairing it, the mechanic gives you a price limit. He says that the first repair will cost $450. Once this is paid for, he announces that the second repair will cost $450. And so it goes. Of course, your ability to estimate the total cost of repairs is crucial. The reason the mechanic can fool you is that on average the total cost of the repair is, let's say, only $550. It pays for you to pay $450 now because you are "saving" $100 on average. But occasionally you have bad luck and can be persuaded to pay up even when the eventual repair is much more. Similar, argues Brennan, is the investor's ability to estimate what the equilibrium futures price will be when the price limits are lifted. If there is an active spot market where spot prices are good predictors of futures prices (e.g., in interest rate, currency, stock index, and possibly metals futures) price limits will serve little use because investors can use the spot prices to learn the bad news. Also, price limits on short-term contracts should be larger or nonexistent because spot and futures prices are equal at maturity. Note that for orange juice futures the price limit is doubled for near-maturity contracts. For agricultural commodities futures with some time before delivery is due, there is usually no spot market (it's hard to trade orange juice when the crop is still in blossom) and price limits serve a useful role.

The evidence on the impact of price limits on price discovery is mixed. Kuserk and Locke [1996] examine the trading activities of floor traders of pork belly futures over the 1990–92 period and conclude that price discovery is suspended rather than aided by price limits. Chen [1998] also finds that price limits delay price discovery and that prices one day after a locked limit day move in the same direction as the locked limit day. On the other hand, in an analysis of NIKKEI futures contracts that trade on both the Osaka Securities Exchange (OSE) and the Singapore International Monetary Exchange (SIMEX), Berkman and Steenbeck [1998] report that prices do not differ substantially across exchanges even as the limit is approached. On the other hand, they find that trading migrated from the stricter price limit exchange (the OSE) to the SIMEX as prices get closer to limits on the OSE price.

6. Taxation of Futures Contracts

The Internal Revenue Service distinguishes between *hedgers* and *speculators* for tax purposes. Hedgers are market participants whose positions are considered to be part of their normal commercial activities. Their profits and losses are treated as ordinary income for tax purposes. All other traders are defined as speculators and are considered to have a capital asset for tax purposes. The capital gain or loss is recorded when the position is closed out. The length of time that the position is maintained determines whether or not the capital gain is short or long term for tax purposes.

In 1982 Congress changed the capital gains treatment by stipulating that all futures positions must be marked to market at year's end. In addition, 40% of any gains or losses are treated as short-term capital gains or losses, with the remaining 60% as long term. The motivation for the change was the elimination of "tax straddles," which were being used for tax avoidance. A tax straddle was established by selling a contract in one commodity and buying a contract in a highly correlated commodity (e.g., corn and wheat). Gains in one contract would presumably offset losses in the other. Near year's end the losses in the declining contract were realized in order to shelter this year's income, and shortly after the end of the year, the winning position would be closed out but not taxed until next year. The only risk involved was the fact that the position was not hedged during the interval between the closing of the loss position and the closing of the gain position shortly thereafter.

Cornell and French [1983b] point out that the 1982 change in the tax code affected the pricing of stock index futures. The portfolio of stocks (e.g., the Standard and Poor's 500) from which the index is constructed does not have to be marked to market at year's end for tax purposes, but the stock futures contract on the index must be. Consequently, the index portfolio contains a valuable tax-timing option (see Constantinides [1983]) that the futures contract does not. A portfolio manager who holds the stock portfolio can hold his or her winning stocks to defer capital gains and sell the losing stocks to receive a tax shelter now. Hence the stock index futures contract should always sell for a discount relative to the stock index portfolio.

D. $\mathcal{T}$he Theory of Futures Markets and Futures Contract Pricing

First, it is interesting to take a look at the fundamental question of why futures markets exist at all. What purpose do they serve, and why have some futures markets prospered while others have withered and failed? Next, how are futures contracts valued? Since there are so many different kinds of contracts, we will try to simplify matters by proceeding in three stages. Initially, we will discuss a generalized model of futures contracts (provided by Samuelson [1965]) to see how expected futures prices should be expected to vary randomly through time even though the variance of futures prices may increase, decrease, or remain constant as the contract life declines. Next we will turn to the pricing of financial futures contracts where arbitrage with the spot financial contracts helps to determine the market price. Finally, we will discuss commodities futures, where arbitrage in the spot contract is not always so easy.

1. Why Do Futures Markets Exist?

A quick look at the *Wall Street Journal* shows that for many commodities there are no existing futures markets. There are futures contracts for wheat, corn, and oats; but none for rye and barley (although rye futures were traded from 1869 to 1970, and barley futures between 1885 and 1940). There was also an active egg futures market at one time. Other commodities, which never had futures contracts, are tobacco, hay, and buckwheat. Why should some commodities have futures contracts while others do not?

There are a number of factors that contribute to the existence of a futures market. First, there must be enough of the underlying standardized commodity (or financial security) so that economies of scale lower transactions costs sufficiently to allow frequent trading. This point is emphasized by Telser [1981b]. Second, there must be sufficient price variability in the commodity to create a demand for risk sharing among hedgers and speculators. The theory of Keynes [1923] and Hicks [1946] is that producers are risk averse and are willing to offer a premium in order to sell futures contracts as a means of hedging against spot price fluctuations at harvest time. Speculators participate in the market in order to gain this premium by sharing risk. Without any price variability there would be no risk to share and no futures market. Third, Working [1953] and Salmon [1985] extend the idea of risk sharing by recognizing that a "core" of trading activity among present and future commodity owners, trading futures contracts among themselves, must be present before speculators can be attracted. The incentive for commodity owners to trade among themselves is provided by uncorrelated production; using the terminology of Hirshleifer [1984], there must be diversity—something like "good-fair-weather farms," "average-market farms," and "good-poor-weather farms." Commodities supplied by farms with very different individual crop outcome covariances with the market crop outcome will be more likely to have futures markets than commodities supplied by farms with very similar private crop outcome covariances with the market. Fourth, as argued by Duffie and Jackson [1989] and Cuny [1993], the contract must provide a hedging ability that is not available in other markets. For example, Nothaft, Lekkas, and Wang [1995] argue that the Mortgage-Backed futures contract failed because of the existence of other interest rate futures contracts that were good cross-hedges for the underlying instrument. Fifth, the

Figure 8.8 A hypothetical spot price that obeys the autoregressive scheme in Eq. (8.21).

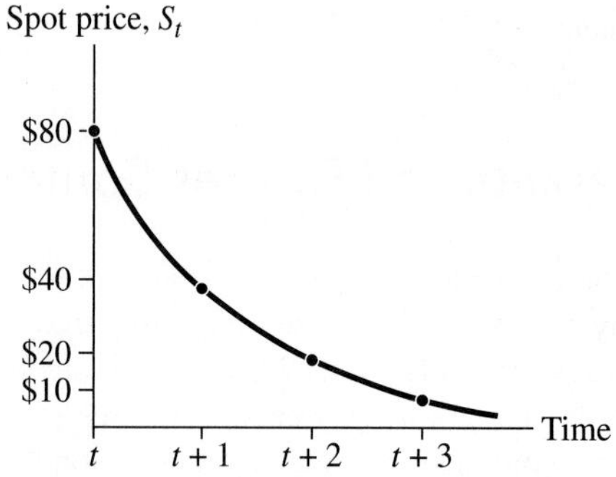

Spot price, S_t

T	$E(S_{t+T})$	$VAR(S_{t+T})$
0	$80	0
1	40	σ_ε^2
2	20	$\sigma_\varepsilon^2(a^2 + 1)$
3	10	$\sigma_\varepsilon^2(a^4 + a^2 + 1)$
⋮	⋮	⋮
∞	0	$\sigma_\varepsilon^2/(1 - a^2)$

contract must be designed accurately and be equally fair for both buyer and seller. A bad contract design in terms of the delivery options is cited by Johnston and McConnell [1989] as the major reason for the failure of the GNMA CDR futures contract.

Given that an active futures market exists, we now turn our attention to the pricing of futures contracts.

2. The Time-Series Behavior of Futures Prices

In his classic paper entitled "Proof That Properly Anticipated Prices Fluctuate Randomly," Samuelson [1965] demonstrates that even though there may be a known seasonal pattern in spot (commodity) prices, the futures will fluctuate randomly. He also shows the intuition for why the variance of futures prices may not be constant over the life of the contract.[10]

To replicate Samuelson's proof, assume that storage costs and interest rates are zero, and that the spot price, S_{t+1}, obeys the following stationary autoregressive scheme:

$$S_{t+1} = aS_t + \varepsilon_t, \quad a < 1. \tag{8.21}$$

For the purposes of numerical example, let the constant a equal $\frac{1}{2}$; the error term, ε_t, be distributed normally with mean zero and standard deviation, σ_t; let the initial spot price be $80; and let the covariance between the error term and the spot price be zero, that is, $COV(S_t, \varepsilon_t) = 0$. Given that $a = \frac{1}{2}$, the expected spot price one period ahead is one half of the previous period's spot price, as illustrated in Fig. 8.8. Needless to say, this is an aberrant example because the spot price does not behave randomly. However, as we shall see, the futures price will in fact be random even though the spot price is not.

Begin by deriving the mean and variance of the spot price. Today's spot price, S_t, is a constant with no variance. Next period's expected spot price, $E(S_{t+1})$, according to Eq. (8.21) is

$$E_t(S_{t+1}) = aE(S_t) \quad \text{since} \quad E(\varepsilon_t) = 0 \tag{8.22}$$

---

[10] The changing variance is important for those who wish to price options on futures contracts. Recall that the Black-Scholes option pricing model assumes a constant variance; hence it may not do well for pricing options on futures contracts. See Section F of this chapter.

and

$$\text{VAR}_t(S_{t+1}) = E[aS_t + \varepsilon_t - aE(S_t)]^2 \tag{8.23}$$

$$= E(\varepsilon_t)^2 = \sigma_\varepsilon^2.$$

The mean and variance of the spot price two periods hence can be derived by substituting Eq. (8.21) into the definition of S_{t+2}, namely,

$$S_{t+2} = aS_{t+1} + \varepsilon_{t+1}$$

$$= a(aS_t + \varepsilon_t) + \varepsilon_{t+1}$$

$$= a^2 S_t + a\varepsilon_{t+1} + \varepsilon_{t+1}.$$

The expected spot price for the second period is

$$E(S_{t+2}) = a^2 E(S_t) \quad \text{since} \quad E(\varepsilon_{t+1}) = E(\varepsilon_t) = 0, \tag{8.24}$$

and the variance is

$$\text{VAR}(S_{t+2}) = E[a^2 S_t + a\varepsilon_t + \varepsilon_{t+1} - a^2 E(S_t)]^2$$

$$= E[a^2 \varepsilon_t^2 + 2a\varepsilon_t\varepsilon_{t+1} + \varepsilon_{t+1}^2]$$

$$= a^2 \sigma_\varepsilon^2 + \sigma_\varepsilon^2$$

$$= \sigma_\varepsilon^2(a^2 + 1) \tag{8.25}$$

since $E(\varepsilon_t\varepsilon_{t+1}) = \text{COV}(\varepsilon_t\varepsilon_{t+1}) = 0$ and $E(\varepsilon_t)^2 = E(\varepsilon_{t+1})^2 = \sigma_\varepsilon^2$.

The progression of expected spot prices and their variances is summarized below and in Fig. 8.9.[11]

T	$E(S_{t+T})$	$\sigma_\varepsilon^2(S_{t+T})$
0	S_t	0
1	$aE(S_t)$	σ_ε^2
2	$a^2 E(S_t)$	$\sigma_\varepsilon^2(a^2 + 1)$
3	$a^3 E(S_t)$	$\sigma_\varepsilon^2(a^4 + a^2 + 1)$
$\vdots$	$\vdots$	$\vdots$
∞	$a^T E(S_t)$	$\sigma_\varepsilon^2/(1 - a^2)$, if $a < 1$

Note that although the expected spot price declines across time, the variance of the expected spot price increases unless $a = 1$. If $a = 1$, then the spot price follows a random walk with the

---

[11] Note that for the third period

$$S_{t+3} = aS_{t+2} + \varepsilon_{t+2}$$

$$= a(a^2 S_t + a\varepsilon_t + \varepsilon_{t+1}) + \varepsilon_{t+2}$$

$$= a^3 S_t + a^2 \varepsilon_t + a\varepsilon_{t+1} + \varepsilon_{t+2}.$$

Figure 8.9 Hypothetical spot and futures prices.

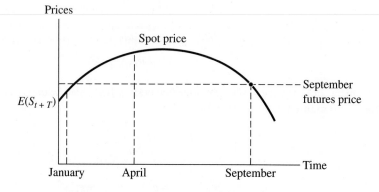

expected spot price equal to the initial spot price, $S_t = E(S_{t+1}) = E(S_{t+2}) = \cdots = E(S_{t+T})$, and the variance is equal to $\text{VAR}(S_{t+T}) = T\sigma_\varepsilon^2$. In other words, the standard deviation of the spot price is $\sigma_\varepsilon\sqrt{T}$. This is the standard square root relationship between the standard deviation of asset prices and time that we found in the Black-Scholes formula in Chapter 7.

Having described the behavior of spot prices, we turn to the problem of pricing futures contracts. The price, $_tF_T$, of the futures contract at the time t (today) on the commodity to be delivered at time T (e.g., three periods hence) in the absence of storage costs, interest rates, and a risk premium will be the expected spot price in period three. This may be written as

$$_tF_3 = E_t(S_{t+3})$$

$$= E_t(a^3 S_t + a^2\varepsilon_{t+1} + a\varepsilon_{t+2} + \varepsilon_{t+3})$$

$$= a^3 S_t \quad \text{since} \quad E_t(a^2\varepsilon_{t+1}) = E_t(a\varepsilon_{t+2}) = E(\varepsilon_{t+3}) = 0. \tag{8.26}$$

The futures price one period hence is still the expected spot price in period three, but the expectation must be made at $t + 1$; therefore

$$_{t+1}F_3 = E_{t+1}(S_{t+3})$$

$$= E_{t+1}(a^3 S_t + a^2\varepsilon_{t+1} + a\varepsilon_{t+2} + \varepsilon_{t+3})$$

$$= a^3 S_t + a^2\varepsilon_{t+1} \quad \text{since} \quad E_{t+1}(a\varepsilon_{t+2}) = E(\varepsilon_{t+3}) = 0. \tag{8.27}$$

Notice that the expectation, taken at $t + 1$, of the error term at $t + 1$ does not vanish because the error already exists at $t + 1$.

Next, Samuelson proves that the expected futures price does not change through time. The change in the futures price from t to $t + 1$ is

$$_{t+1}F_3 - {}_tF_3 = a^3 S_t + a^2\varepsilon_{t+1} - a^3 S_t, \tag{8.28}$$

and the expected futures price change, evaluated at time t, is zero since $E_t(a^2\varepsilon_{t+1}) = 0$. Thus even though the spot price changes in a known fashion, the futures price is not expected to change. Given no storage costs or interest rates, it is a random walk with no drift. The intuition is quite simple. Futures contracts are written for delivery at a single point in time. Hence the pattern of spot prices is irrelevant. All that counts is today's estimate of the expected spot price at maturity. For example, in Fig. 8.8 the futures price today for delivery in period $t + 2$ is $20 even though today's spot price is $80. Since expected information about the spot price at maturity is random and unbiased, $E(\varepsilon_{t+T}) = 0$, the futures price is a random walk with zero drift.

The variance of the futures price from t to $t+1$ is taken from Eq. (8.26) as follows:

$$\text{VAR}\left[_{t+1}F_3 - {_t}F_3\right] = E_{t+1}\left[\left(a^2\varepsilon_{t+1}\right)^2\right]$$

$$= a^4\sigma_\varepsilon^2, \tag{8.29}$$

and in general the futures price variance is

$$\text{VAR}\left[_{t+1}F_3 - {_t}F_3\right] = a^4\sigma_\varepsilon^2,$$

$$\text{VAR}\left[_{t+2}F_3 - {_{t+1}}F_3\right] = a^2\sigma_\varepsilon^2, \tag{8.30}$$

$$\text{VAR}\left[_{t+3}F_3 - {_{t+2}}F_3\right] = \sigma_\varepsilon^2.$$

Thus if $a < 1$, the variance of the future price increases as we get closer to the maturity of the contract, but if $a = 1$, so that the spot price is a random walk, then the standard deviation of the futures prices is $\sigma_\varepsilon\sqrt{T}$, is constant across time, and is equal to the standard deviation of the spot price.

The basic intuition of Samuelson's model is that if we assume a stationary autoregressive process in spot prices, then the variance of futures prices will increase as the contract nears maturity. Far-distant contracts will exhibit relatively lower variances because autoregressive prices will have a long interval to correct themselves. Near-maturity contracts will be more variable because prices have little time to correct. Of course, it may be too much to expect stationarity in the price-generating process. Many commodities, especially grains, have critical points in their growing seasons when weather dramatically affects the potential harvest. One might expect greater variance during these seasons than during other points in time.

Using daily data for 9 commodities between 1966 and 1980, Anderson [1985] finds evidence supporting both hypotheses—the Samuelson hypothesis that the futures price variance increases nearer maturity and the seasonal production hypothesis that variance is higher at critical infor-mation points. Milonas [1986] uses a slightly larger database and, after removing seasonalities, finds a strong maturity effect on variance for 10 of 11 commodities tested—including financial futures (T-bills, T-bonds, and the GNMA, or Government National Mortgage Association) and metals (copper, gold, and silver). In a comprehensive analysis of 45 futures contracts over the 1969–92 period, Galloway and Kolb [1996] find that time to maturity has a significant negative relation to monthly return variance (after controlling for other sources of nonstationarity in prices) for agricultural, energy, and copper futures. They also report that no such relation exists for pre-cious metal and financial futures. Based on this evidence, they suggest that the maturity effect for volatility is important for commodities that experience seasonality in demand but not for those where cost of carry predominantly explains prices. Similar conclusions are reached by Bessem-binder, Coughenour, Seguin, and Smoller [1996], who find that the Samuelson hypothesis is valid for futures markets where the spot price changes have a significant temporary component.

The preceding analysis helps to make the point that there is no necessary relationship between today's spot price and today's futures price, which is the expectation of the spot price at the delivery date.[12] For example, the futures price for September contracts in Fig. 8.9 is the expected September spot price, $E(S_{t+T})$. The January spot price is below the expected September spot price (i.e., the futures price), and the April spot price is above it.

3. Pricing Financial Futures Contracts

Financial instruments are usually traded in very liquid spot markets, and there is virtually no cost of storage. This distinguishes them from commodity markets where the spot market may be thin and storage costs high. It also makes financial futures somewhat easier to price because arbitrage between the spot and futures markets helps to determine the futures price.

To see how riskless arbitrage determines prices of *interest rate futures* such as futures on T-bills and T-bonds, let $_t r_T$ be the riskless T-period interest rate observed at time t, let S_t be the current spot price, and let $_t F_T$ be the price at time t (today) of the T-period futures contract.[13] For riskless securities the futures price is the expectation of the future spot price:

$$_f F_T = E(S_{t+T}).\tag{8.31}$$

This implies that the futures price should be equal to the current spot price multiplied times a compounding factor:

$$_t F_T = S_t e^{t^r T}.\tag{8.32}$$

Equation (8.31) is called the *expectations theory of futures prices*. Suppose Eq. (8.30) does not hold. In particular, suppose that the futures price is higher than the compounded spot price:

$$_t F_T > S_t e^{t^r T}.\tag{8.33}$$

If this happens, a riskless arbitrage opportunity is available if investors short the futures contract and simultaneously buy the asset. At maturity the asset is then delivered to cover the short position in the futures contract. As more and more arbitrageurs sell the futures position, its price will fall. Simultaneously, buying pressure on the underlying asset will raise its price. Arbitrage will continue until the futures price just equals the compounded current spot price, as required by Eq. (8.30).

To make the concept of arbitrage more concrete, consider the following numerical example taken from the 30-day Federal Funds futures market. On July 1, 2002, you observe the following relationships:

	Life	Yield
Futures contract that requires delivery in 6 months of a 30-day deposit	30 days	2.3%
T-bill maturing in 7 months	7 months	1.8%
T-bill maturing in 6 months	6 months	1.6%

What position should you take in order to earn an arbitrage profit? First, remember that the futures contract that matures in 6 months results in the delivery of a 30-day deposit (maturing in January

---

[12] In Section F, we shall prove that, for financial futures at least, the current futures price must be a risk-adjusted expected spot price.

[13] Later on, in Section F, we shall return to the problem of pricing financial futures on risky assets.

Figure 8.10 Time line for arbitrage example.

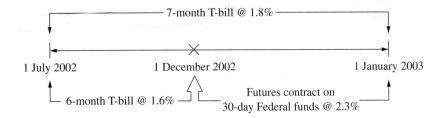

2003 with an expected yield of 2.3%). Therefore if you hold a portfolio consisting of the futures contract and the T-bill maturing in December 2002, your position should be exactly equal to holding the January T-bill, which matures in 7 months. This equivalence is illustrated in Fig. 8.10. In order for there to be no arbitrage, the product of the yields to maturity on the two shorter instruments should equal the yield to maturity on the longer instrument.[14] If there were no arbitrage, then

$$(1.016)^{6/12}(1.023)^{30/360} = (1.018)^{7/12},$$

$$(1.00797)(1.0019) = (1.01046),$$

$$1.00988 \neq 1.01046.$$

The 7-month yield is high relative to the product of the 6- and 1-month yields. Therefore the price of the 7-month T-bill is too low and it should be bought; that is, you should lend money at the 7-month rate. If the futures contract size is $5,000,000, the amount you lend today is

$$PV = \$5,000,000(1.018)^{-7/12}$$

$$= \$5,000,000(0.98965)$$

$$= \$4,948,236.71.$$

The cash necessary for the lending can be raised by borrowing this amount for 6 months at 1.6%, which is the 6-month interest rate currently prevailing in the market. Therefore in 6 months you will pay back a future value of

$$PV = \$4,948,236.71(1.016)^{6/12}$$

$$= \$4,948,236.71(1.00797)$$

$$= \$4,987,665.52.$$

In addition to borrowing, you simultaneously sell short a 30-day Federal Funds futures contract with a $5,000,000 face value. In 6 months when the futures contract matures you will deliver the 7-month T-bill, which will have 30 days to maturity, in order to cover your short position in the futures contract, and you receive the following amount in cash:

$$PV = \$5,000,000(1.023)^{-30/360}$$

$$= \$5,000,000(0.998107)$$

$$= \$4,990,534.19.$$

---

[14] The convention in bond markets is to calculate the yield to maturity on the basis of a 360-day year.

This is more than enough to repay our loan that comes due on December 1. In fact, your net arbitrage profit on December 1 is

$4,990,534.19   proceeds from the short position

−$4,987,665.52   amount due on the loan

$2,868.67   profit

Thus you earn a $2,868.67 arbitrage profit without taking any risk whatsoever and without investing any capital of your own. This is called a *self-financing riskless arbitrage*. There is no risk involved because you locked in the arbitrage by owning the 7-month T-bill and simultaneously borrowing and shorting the futures contract against it. No matter how prices changed in the interim over the next 6 months, your profit was assured. When the loan came due, you received cash for delivering a T-bill that you owned. The deal was self-financing because you put up none of your own money.

Thus given the existence of arbitrage between spot and futures markets, financial futures contracts should be priced according to the expectations theory of Eq. (8.30). Empirical evidence by Rendleman and Carabini [1979] indicates that when brokerage costs, bid-ask spreads, and borrowing costs arc taken into account, no pure arbitrage opportunities could be found. They conclude that "the inefficiencies in the Treasury bill futures market do not appear to be significant enough to offer attractive investment alternatives to the short-term portfolio manager." Capozza and Cornell [1979] concluded that near-term contracts were priced efficiently but that longer-term contracts tended to be underpriced; however, none of these discrepancies could have been arbitraged owing to the cost of shorting the spot bill necessary to establish the appropriate position.

Pricing *stock index futures* is more difficult than pricing interest rate futures for several reasons.[15] First, the market value of the stock index portfolio is affected by the fact that the portfolio of stocks pays dividends, but the index portfolio is only a weighted average of the stock prices. The index does not receive dividends. Therefore the stock index futures price must subtract the present value of expected dividends paid by the index stocks before the futures contract matures. Second, futures are taxed differently than the underlying stock index portfolio. All gains and losses are marked to market at year's end with 40% taxed at the short-term capital gains rate and 60% at the long-term capital gains rate. Hence capital gains taxes cannot be deferred on the futures contract, whereas they may on the underlying securities. Cornell and French [1983b] show how to price futures on stock indices and test their model on data taken from the first seven months of stock index futures trading. Neal [1996] examines 837 S&P 500 futures-index arbitrage trades over the period January 3 to March 31, 1989. He estimates that the average gross profit of these trades is 0.3 percent which is approximately half the spread for the index. More recently, Tse [2001] analyzes the futures-spot relation for the Dow Jones Industrial Average (DJIA) futures contract and reports that information is reflected in the futures market before the spot. On the other hand, Tse does not provide an estimate of the value of this potential arbitrage opportunity.

One of the interesting applications of stock index futures is to select a portfolio of securities that is expected to do better than a set of other companies from the same industries. Against this portfolio, one shorts a stock index futures contract in order to remove market risk. When this is done properly the selected portfolio will do well regardless of whether the stock market goes up

---

[15] Stock index futures are traded on the Standard and Poor's 500 index, the New York Stock Exchange Composite index, and the Value Line index.

or down, because changes in the value of the stock index futures contract offset the market risk in the selected portfolio. All that is left is the idiosyncratic component of returns.

4. Pricing Commodities Futures Contracts

The pricing of commodities futures contracts[16] is complicated by the fact that storage is costly and that spot markets may be nonexistent or too thin for arbitrage. There are two general approaches for explaining returns on commodities futures, one based on convenience yields and storage costs, and the other on risk premia such as the CAPM beta.

FUTURES PRICES AND STORAGE The traditional view explains the current futures price as the expected spot price, minus the cost of storage (interest foregone, warehousing, and shrinkage), and minus a convenience yield. Costs of storage are obvious, but *convenience yield* is much like a liquidity premium, usually described as the convenience of holding inventories because many commodities (e.g., wheat) are inputs in the production process (e.g., bread making) or as the convenience of having inventory to meet unexpected demand. The theory of storage predicts low convenience yields when inventories are plentiful and high convenience yields when stockout is more likely. Telser [1958] and Brennan [1986a] have provided empirical estimates of the convenience yield that are consistent with the theory. Fama and French [1987] have provided evidence that marginal convenience yields vary seasonally for most agricultural and animal commodities but not for metals.

According to the storage theory, the futures price of a T-period contract observed at time t is given by

$$_tF_T = S_t e^{t^rT} + {}_tW_T - {}_tC_T, \tag{8.34}$$

where $S_t e^{t^rT}$ is the current spot price compounded by the interest rate between the current time, t, and the delivery date, T; ${}_tW_T$ is the storage cost between now and delivery; and ${}_tC_T$ is the convenience yield (in dollars) between now and delivery.

If storage costs are low and convenience yields are high, then we would predict that prior to delivery the futures price is below the expected spot price,

$$_tF_T < E(S_T) = S_t e^{t^rT}. \tag{8.35}$$

This relationship, called *normal backwardation*, is graphed in Fig. 8.11. The origin of the idea is that producers (e.g., farmers) normally wish to hedge their risk by shorting the commodity. To attract speculators into the market, they have to sell futures contracts at a discount from the expected spot price. Consequently, futures contracts should yield a rate of return higher than the riskless interest rate, and their prices will rise (on average) through time until, at delivery, the futures price equals the spot price.

Also illustrated in Fig. 8.11 is a situation where the futures price is above the expected spot price:

$$_tF_T > E(S_T) = S_t e^{t^rT}.$$

---

[16] See Carter [1999] for an excellent survey of the literature on commodity futures markets.

Figure 8.11 Normal backwardation and contango.

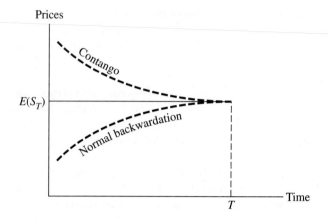

Called *contango*, this is just the opposite of normal backwardation. If hedgers need to go long, or if the convenience yield is negative owing to oversupply, then they must pay a premium for futures contracts in order to induce speculators to go short.

FUTURES PRICES AND THE CAPM   A second way of explaining commodity futures prices posits that the futures price can be divided into the expected future spot price plus an expected risk premium based on the capital asset pricing model. For example, Dusak [1973] relates the CAPM to commodity futures in a one-period framework. Begin by writing out the CAPM:

$$E(R_i) = R_f + \left[\frac{E(R_m) - R_f}{\sigma(R_m)} \right] \frac{\text{COV}(R_i, R_m)}{\sigma(R_m)}, \tag{8.36}$$

where

$$\begin{aligned}
E(R_i) &= \text{the expected return on the } i\text{th asset,} \\
R_f &= \text{the risk-free rate, assumed to be constant over the life of the futures contract,} \\
E(R_m) &= \text{the expected return on the market portfolio,} \\
\sigma(R_m) &= \text{the standard deviation of return on a (single factor) market index portfolio,} \\
\text{COV}(R_i, R_m) &= \text{the expected covariance of returns between the } i\text{th asset and the market index portfolio.}
\end{aligned}$$

Next, write down the definition of a one-period rate of return for an investor who holds the risky commodity. If S_{i0} is the current spot price of the ith commodity and $E(S_{iT})$ is the expected spot price at the time of delivery, T, we have

$$E(R_i) = \frac{E(S_{iT}) - S_{i0}}{S_{i0}}. \tag{8.37}$$

Combining Eq. (8.37) with Eq. (8.36), we have a certainty equivalent model for the spot price of the commodity:

$$S_{i0} = \frac{E(S_{iT}) - [E(R_m) - R_f]S_{i0}\beta_i}{1 + R_f}, \tag{8.38}$$

where

$$\beta_i = \frac{\text{COV}(R_i, R_m)}{\sigma^2(R_m)} = \text{the systematic risk of the } i\text{th commodity.}$$

Finally, a futures contract allows an investor to purchase an asset now but to defer payment for one period; therefore the current price of the futures contract, $_0F_{iT}$, must be the current spot price multiplied by a future value factor:[17]

$$_0F_{iT} = S_{i0}(1 + R_f). \tag{8.39}$$

Multiplying both sides of the certainty equivalent model, Eq. (8.38), by $(1 + R_f)$, and noting that the result is equivalent to Eq. (8.39), we have

$$_0F_{iT} = S_{i0}(1 + R_f) = E(S_{iT}) - \left[E(R_m) - R_f\right]S_{i0}\beta_i. \tag{8.40}$$

The futures price, $_0F_{iT}$, equals the expected spot price minus a risk premium based on the systematic risk of the commodity.

The CAPM approach, Eq. (8.40), argues that systematic risk should be important in the pricing of futures contracts but leaves out storage costs and convenience yields. On the other hand, the traditional approach, Eq. (8.31), ignores the possibility that systematic risk may affect the equilibrium prices of commodity futures contracts. We now turn to the empirical evidence to provide some clues to which theory is correct or whether some combination of them best describes commodities futures prices.

E. *E*mpirical Evidence

There are two interrelated lines of empirical research on futures contracts. One focuses on comparing models of futures prices to see which best explains the data. The other asks how well information is reflected in futures prices: Are they good forecasts of future spot prices? These ideas are interrelated because we need a good model to forecast future spot prices, and because the futures markets must be informationally efficient if the models are to have any hope of working.

Bodie and Rosansky [1980] provide a comprehensive analysis of rates of return on commodities futures prices between 1950 and 1976. Table 8.3 summarizes their results. Perhaps the most interesting fact is that an equally weighted portfolio of 23 commodities futures had roughly the same return and standard deviation as the equally weighted common stock portfolio.[18] Also, the correlation matrix (Panel B) indicates that stocks and futures are negatively correlated with each other. Furthermore, common stock returns are negatively correlated with inflation, whereas commodity futures are positively correlated. One interpretation of these facts is that different factors (in the arbitrage pricing model) affect commodities and stocks. A randomly chosen portfolio of common stock is a bad hedge against unexpected inflation, but a well-diversified commodity portfolio is a good hedge. Apparently, stocks have very different factor sensitivities to the factors in the arbitrage pricing model (APM) (especially unexpected inflation) than do commodities. If this

---

[17] This is the same argument used in Eq. (8.32) for financial futures.

[18] None of the futures positions were bought on margin.

Table 8.3 Rate of Return Data, 1950–1976

Panel A: Comparison Rates of Return				
	Nominal Returns		Real Returns	
	Mean	Std. Dev.	Mean	Std. Dev.
Common stock	13.05	18.95	9.58	19.65
Commodity futures	13.83	22.43	9.81	19.44
Long-term government bonds	2.84	6.53	−.51	6.81
T-bills	3.63	1.95	.22	1.80
Inflation	3.43	2.90	—	—

Panel B: Correlation Matrix of Nominal Returns					
	Common	Futures	Bonds	T-bills	Inflation
Common	1.00	−.24	−.10	−.57	−.43
Futures		1.00	−.16	.34	.58
Bonds			1.00	.20	.03
T-bills				1.00	.76
Inflation					1.00

Adapted from Z. Bodie and V. Rosansky, "Risk and Return in Commodities Futures," *Financial Analysts Journal*, May–June 1980, 27–39.

interpretation is true, then it is not surprising that Bodie and Rosansky [1980] and Dusak [1973] both found that the CAPM does a poor job of explaining commodities returns. After all, a market portfolio of common stock is usually employed as the proxy for the market portfolio (a single-factor model), and commodity returns are negatively correlated with common stock. Bodie and Rosansky found that 15 out of 23 commodities had negative betas and that the security market line, estimated using commodities data, had a negative slope. From these results we must conclude that the CAPM fails to explain (even approximately) the returns on the commodities. We are waiting for someone to apply the APM to this problem.

On a more positive note, Bodie and Rosansky do find evidence of normal backwardation, where Dusak had not, because they used a longer time period. Mean returns in excess of the risk-free rate averaged 9.77% for commodity futures. Chang [1985] also finds evidence of normal backwardation for wheat, corn, and soybeans over the interval 1951 to 1980. Fama and French [1987] find marginal evidence of normal backwardation when commodities are combined into portfolios but conclude that the evidence is not strong enough to resolve the long-standing controversy about the existence of nonzero-risk premia. Kolb [1992] uses a similar methodology on daily returns for 29 commodities and finds very little evidence to support the existence of a risk premium. Similar results are reported by Bessembinder [1993] for 19 of the 22 agricultural, financial, foreign exchange, and mineral futures included in his study. In one of the more comprehensive studies to date, Kolb [1996] examines 4,735 futures contracts on 45 commodities. His results indicate that (a) 29 of the commodities have mean futures returns that are not significantly different from zero; (b) the mean beta for physical commodity futures is 0.0463, for currency futures is zero, for index futures is greater than 1, and for short maturity debt futures is positive but less than 0.05; and (c) there is no positive relation between risk and realized return for the futures contracts. Bessembinder and Chan [1992] and Miffne [2000] suggest that one possible reason for these results is that if there is a risk premium for commodity futures contracts, it may be time varying, and tests that do not explicitly account for this are flawed. Both papers find evidence in support of the hypothesis that futures returns are time varying and the return is related to a time-varying risk premium.

The second interesting question is whether or not futures prices are good forecasts of expected spot prices. The variability of spot prices will depend on seasonal supply and demand shocks, and on the availability of inventory to cushion them. One might expect that commodities with high inventory relative to production—for example, precious metals (gold, silver, and platinum)—allow price shocks to be transmitted freely from one period to another. This implies that a demand shock today will affect both today's spot price and expected spot prices. If spot prices are linked in this fashion, there is little left for futures prices to explain. French [1986] and Fama and French [1987] argue that futures prices cannot provide forecasts that are reliably better than the current spot price unless the variance in the expected spot price changes is a large fraction of the variance of the actual spot price changes. For metals this is not true, and they find that futures prices predict expected spot prices no better than do current spot prices. However, they find reliable evidence that futures prices are good forecasts for animal and agricultural commodity expected spot prices. This is consistent with the role of inventories because commodities are affected by relatively large storage costs and production seasonals.

Miffne [2000] also examines whether futures prices are unbiased estimators of future spot prices by analyzing eight agricultural, five metal, and six financial futures contracts over the period March 1982 to October 1996. He finds very little support for the hypothesis that futures prices are unbiased estimates of future spot prices.

Roll [1984] studied the orange juice futures market. Although the commodity is frozen and therefore not perishable, only a small amount (about 10%) is carried over in inventory from one year to the next. Almost all (98%) of U.S. production takes place in central Florida around Orlando. Short-term variations in supply due to planting decisions are low (because oranges grow on trees that require 5–15 years to mature), and short-term variations in demand are also low. All these facts imply that orange juice futures prices should be heavily influenced by weather, particularly by cold temperatures. Roll reports that the orange juice futures price is a statistically significant predictor of the forecast *error* of the U.S. National Weather Service. That is, futures prices predict the weather better than the weather service. Also, Roll finds (1) that price limits decrease the informational efficiency of the market and (2) that there is much more variability in futures prices than can be explained by the weather or any other measurable short-term supply or demand shock.

In sum, the existing empirical evidence indicates that inventories are important in explaining the ability of futures prices to predict expected spot prices. Also, there is weak evidence to support normal backwardation, but the risk premium may be time varying and is not related to a CAPM beta. In addition, it was reported earlier in the chapter that Brennan [1986a] and Fama and French [1987] have found evidence consistent with the existence of convenience yields that vary through time with inventory levels.

F. *Synthetic* Futures and Options on Futures

1. Synthetic Futures

We can create a *synthetic forward contract* by buying a European call, C, on the underlying risky asset or commodity with time to maturity T and exercise price X, equal to the forward price, $_0F_T$,

Table 8.4 Payouts for a Synthetic Forward Contract

Portfolio	Payouts at Delivery	
	If $S_T < X$	**If $S_T \geq X$**
$V_A = C_0 - P_0$	$0 - (_0F_T - S_T)$	$S_T - _0F_T$
$V_B =$ forward contract	$S_T - _0F_T$	$S_T - _0F_T$
	$V_A = V_B$	$V_A = V_B$

and simultaneously writing a European put, P, with the same time to maturity and exercise price. Table 8.4 shows that the end-of-period payoffs for the synthetic forward contract are equal to the payoffs on an actual forward contract. At maturity, if the price of the risky asset, S, is less than the exercise price, $X = _0F_T$, then the call is worthless and the put is exercised against us, creating a loss of $_0F_T - S_T$ dollars. Had we held the forward contract, we would have lost exactly the same dollar amount. Alternately, if the risky asset is worth more than the exercise price at maturity, the call pays the difference between the asset price and the delivery price, $S_T - _0F_T$, which is the same as the forward contract payout. Either way, the synthetic forward contract and the real forward contract have identical payouts.

The initial investments in the synthetic and real forward contracts must also be identical—they must both have zero initial outlay. This fact allows us to establish an interesting result, namely, the *expectations hypothesis for pricing financial futures*. We begin by writing down the formula for put-call parity from Chapter 7:

$$C_0 - P_0 = S_0 - Xe^{-r_f T}.$$

Next, our synthetic futures position has an exercise price, X, equal to the current forward price, $_0F_T$. Therefore

$$C_0 - P_0 = S_0 - _0F_T e^{-r_f T}. \tag{8.41}$$

We also know that the synthetic forward contract requires zero cash outlay; therefore we can set Eq. (8.41) equal to zero:[19]

$$C_0 - P_0 = S_0 - _0F_T e^{-r_f T} = 0,$$

$$_0F_T = S_0 e^{r_f T}. \tag{8.42}$$

So the forward contract price must be equal to the current spot price multiplied by a riskless compounding factor. The forward price will always be greater than the spot price. Furthermore, the expected spot price is the current spot price multiplied by a risk-adjusted compounding factor, based on the cost of equity, k_s:

$$E(S_T) = S_0 e^{k_s T}. \tag{8.43}$$

---

[19] This is the same as Eq. (8.32).

Figure 8.12 Constructing a synthetic future.

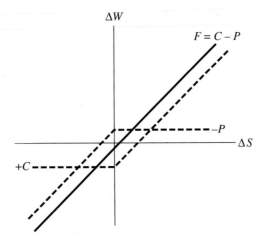

Solving Eq. (8.43) for S_0 and substituting the result into Eq. (8.42), we have

$$_0F_T = E(S_T)e^{-(k_s-r_f)T}. \tag{8.44}$$

Note that if the underlying asset is riskless, then $k_s = r_f$ and the forward price equals the expected spot price, as assumed in Eq. (8.31). Otherwise, if the underlying asset is risky, the forward price is the expected spot price discounted at a risk-adjusted rate, $e^{-(k_s-r_f)T}$.

Figure 8.12 graphs the end-of-period payoffs from our synthetic forward (or futures) contract. The solid line in Fig. 8.12 has the same end-of-period payouts as a futures contract, where delivery is accepted, and it requires no initial cash outlay. Hence when options on an asset or commodity are traded, but there is no futures market, it is always possible to construct a synthetic futures contract. There are problems, however. For example, the options are usually American options, which means the synthetic future can be disrupted if the American put is exercised early. Also, as we have emphasized throughout, the synthetic future is really a forward contract since no daily marking to market is required.

2. Options on Futures

Options are traded on futures in stock market indices, on Treasury instruments, on foreign exchange rates, and on some metals. Since these options are merely contingent claims on the underlying risky assets, one would think that they could be priced using the Black-Scholes formula. Unfortunately, this is not quite true. Ramaswamy and Sundaresan [1985] have shown (1) that even with constant interest rates, premature exercise may be optimal, and (2) that the fact that interest rates are stochastic is crucial for pricing options on futures.

To show why early exercise may be optimal, even with constant interest rates, it is useful to recognize that an option on a futures contract has the same payouts as an option on a portfolio with the same random price realizations as the futures contract but that pays a continuous dividend at the riskless rate of interest. Consider a generalization of Eq. (8.32), where the futures price was shown to be the spot price multiplied by a compounding factor:

$$_tF_T = S_t e^{r_f T}. \tag{8.45}$$

The generalization is to define the rate of compounding as the risk-free rate plus (or minus) a risk premium, δ:

$$_t r_T = r_{f(T,t)} - \delta_{t,t}.$$

Thus the current futures price can be written as

$$_t F_T = S_t e^{(r_{f(T,t)} - \delta_{T,t})}. \tag{8.46}$$

If $r_f > \delta$, the futures price will be at a premium relative to the spot price throughout the contract's life (contango), and if $\delta > r_f$, the futures price will be at a discount (backwardation). Of course, as the contract approaches maturity, the futures and spot prices will become equal. The dynamics of the futures price involve an "implicit dividend" flow, thereby suggesting that it may be optimal to exercise American calls (or puts) prematurely if the value of the exercise price reinvested at the riskless rate exceeds the value of the "implicit dividend" flow. Ramaswamy and Sundaresan [1985] have shown, under a reasonable set of parameters, that the value of early exercise is small.

Stochastic interest rates, however, can have a relatively important effect on the value of options on futures. If the riskless rate is expected to drift upward (because the term structure is upward sloping), then $r_{f(T,t)}$ in Eq. (8.46) will be expected to increase through time, thereby altering the expected implicit dividend and the option value. Numerical solution methods to simulate values for options on futures, employed by Ramaswamy and Sundaresan, show this effect to be relatively important.[20]

Hilliard and Reis [1999] argue that commodity and commodity futures prices exhibit jump risk that cannot be diversified away because of their systematic relation to macro-economic factors. They, therefore, suggest that a jump-diffusion model would be more appropriate for pricing options on futures. They test this hypothesis by analyzing the pricing efficiency of a model developed in Bates [1991] relative to that of the Black [1976] model. Their tests are limited to options on soybean futures and their results indicate that the jump-diffusion model is superior to the pure-diffusion model.

*S*ummary

This chapter discussed the term structure of interest rates on default-free government bonds. We relaxed the implicit assumption that these rates are constant and allowed them (and of course the prices of the bonds) to be stochastic. Models of the term structure were grouped into either equilibrium or arbitrage-free models. Equilibrium models included Rendleman and Bartter [1980], who assume that the short-term risk-free rate follows geometric Brownian motion with a drift; Vasicek [1977], who assumes a mean-reverting process for the short-term rate; and Cox, Ingersoll, and Ross [1985], who also assume mean reversion but require positive rates. Arbitrage-free models use market data on the term structure as an input in an effort to ensure that expected future rates are consistent with the current observed term structure. Examples included Ho and Lee [1986], Hull and White [1990], and Heath, Jarrow, and Morton [1992].

---

[20] Their model assumes the variance of the futures contract price is constant over the life of the contract, but empirical evidence indicates that it increases.

The second half of the chapter used the assumption of stochastic default-free rates to price forward and futures contracts, starting with financial futures, then moving on to somewhat more complex commodity futures contracts. Futures contracts give one the right to receive delivery of a risky asset or commodity at a predetermined future date at a price agreed upon today. No cash changes hands at the time of purchase of the contract. Unlike forward contracts, which are usually bilateral contracts between two parties, futures contracts are marked to market each day via a clearinghouse. This procedure provides liquidity to the market and allows open interest to far exceed the quantity of the underlying asset to be delivered.

Most futures contracts are traded on margin, which has an opportunity cost to investors. Price limits on futures contracts are (imperfect) substitutes for margin levels, and therefore we can predict that contracts on assets with active spot markets will have low margins and no price limits, but when spot markets are thin (as with orange juice futures) price limits will play an important role.

Futures contract prices are determined by storage costs, by convenience yields, and probably by a risk premium, although the risk premium is not a function of the CAPM beta. The variance of futures prices appears to increase as the contract comes closer to maturity. Futures prices provide better forecasts of future spot prices than do current spot prices for those commodities where inventory levels are relatively low (e.g., for agricultural and animal commodities).

PROBLEM SET

8.1 The yields to maturity on five zero-coupon bonds are given below:

Years to Maturity	Yield (%)
1	12.0
2	14.0
3	15.0
4	15.5
5	15.7

(a) What is the implied forward rate of interest for the third year?

(b) What rate of interest would you receive if you bought a bond at the beginning of the second year and sold it at the beginning of the fourth year?

8.2 Consider the Vasicek model where the current short-term rate is 2%, the long-run mean is 6%, the instantaneous standard deviation is 10%, and the rate of adjustment is 0.4. Derive the interest rates for 1, 2, 3, 4, and 5 year maturities.

8.3 Consider the Cox, Ingersoll, and Ross model where the current short-term rate is 2%, the long-run mean is 6%, the instantaneous standard deviation is 10%, and the rate of adjustment is 0.4. Derive the interest rates for 1, 2, 3, 4, and 5 year maturities.

8.4 Consider the Ho-Lee model with $\pi = 0.5$ and $\delta = 0.9$. Further assume that 1-, 2-, and 3-year interest rates are 4, 5, and 6%. Derive the four-period tree of bond prices.

8.5 Most futures contracts have fairly short lives, usually less than 18 months. Why are there not futures contracts with longer lives?

8.6 Suppose you observe the following yields on T-bills and T-bill futures contracts on January 5, 1991:

	Yield (%)
March futures contract on a 90 day T-bill (futures contract matures in 77 days on March 22)	12.5
167-day T-bill	10.0
77-day T-bill	6.0

(a) What arbitrage position should you undertake in order to make a certain profit with no risk and no net investment?

(b) What effect does the trend in spot prices have on the variance of prices for May contracts sold in February?

8.7 Your team of agricultural experts has observed that spot prices of rutabagas show a definite pattern, rising from January through June, then falling toward a December low. You wish to buy contracts for May delivery.

(a) What effect does the trend in spot prices have on the time pattern of the futures price for May contracts?

(b) What effect does the trend in spot prices have on the variance of prices for May contracts sold in February?

8.8 Suppose you can buy or sell European puts and calls on the common stock of XYZ Corporation, which has a current share price of $30, has a rate of return of standard deviation of .3, and pays no dividends. The exercise price on six-month puts and calls is $35, and the risk-free rate is 7% per year. You believe the stock price will rise and wish to create a synthetic forward contract position for delivery of 100 shares six months hence.

(a) How do you construct the synthetic futures position? How much must you borrow or lend?

(b) What is your expected profit if you believe the share price will be $42 six months from now?

8.9 On January 29, 1987, you could buy a March 1987 silver contract for $5.610 per ounce and at the same time sell a March 1988 contract for $6.008 an ounce.

(a) Exactly what would you have done had you taken these positions?

(b) If the annual riskless rate of interest were 8%, would the position be profitable? Why or why not?

8.10 Suppose you believe your portfolio, which has a beta of 1.0, has been selected to outperform other portfolios of similar risk, but you know you cannot predict which way the market will move. If it goes down, you will outperform the market but will still have a negative rate of return. What can you do to alleviate your timing risk?

8.11 Suppose you are convinced that the spread between long- and short-term rates will widen, whereas everyone else thinks it will remain constant. Unfortunately, you do not know whether the general level of interest rates will go up or down. What can you do?

8.12 Your bank is exploring the possibility of using T-bond futures to minimize the exposure of shareholders to changes in the interest rate. The market value of major assets and liabilities is given in the balance sheet below:

Market Value of Assets ($MM)		Market Value of Liabilities ($MM)	
Cash and reserves	180	Demand deposits	900
Loans	820	Equity	100
	1,000		1,000

The economics staff has used the rates of return on the asset and liability positions to compute the following long-run standard deviations and correlations:

	Standard Deviation	Correlation with T-Bond Futures
Cash and reserves	0	0
Loans	0.06	+0.30
Demand deposits	0.02	+0.15
T-bond futures	0.08	1.00

If the current market value is $80,000 for a T-bond futures contract with a $100,000 face value, how many T-bond contracts will be needed to minimize shareholders' risk exposure to interest rate fluctuations?

REFERENCES

Adrangi, B., and A. Chatrath, "Margin Requirements and Futures Activity: Evidence from the Soybean and Corn Markets," *Journal of Futures Markets*, 1999, Vol. 19, 433–455.

Ahn, D., R. Dittmar, and A. Gallant, "Quadratic Term Structure Models: Theory and Evidence," *Review of Financial Studies,* Spring 2002, Vol. 12, 243–288.

Ait-Sahalia, Y., "Testing Continuous Time Models of the Spot Interest Rate," *Review of Financial Studies,* 1996, Vol. 9, 385–426.

Anderson, R., "Comments on 'Margins and Futures Contracts'" *Journal of Futures Markets*, Summer 1981, 259–264.

———, "Some Determinants of the Volatility of Futures Prices," *Journal of Futures Markets*, Fall 1985, 331–348.

Anderson, R., and J. Danthine, "The Time Pattern of Hedging and the Volatility of Futures Prices," *Review of Economic Studies*, April 1983, 249–266.

Ball, C., and W. Torous, "Futures Options and the Volatility of Futures Prices," *Journal of Finance*, September 1986, 857–870.

Bates, D., "The Crash of '87: Was It Expected? The Evidence from Options Markets," *Journal of Finance*, 1991, Vol. 46, 1009–1044.

Berkman, H., and O. Steenbeck, "The Influence of Daily Price Limits on Trading in Nikkei Futures," *Journal of Futures Markets*, 1998, Vol. 18, 265–279.

Bessembinder, H., "Systematic Risk, Hedging Pressure and Risk Premiums in Futures Markets," *Review of Financial Studies,* 1993, Vol. 2, 637–667.

Bessembinder, H., and K. Chan, "Time-Varying Risk Premia and Forecastable Returns in Futures Markets," *Journal of Financial Economics,* 1992, Vol. 32, 169–193.

Bessembinder, H., J. Coughenour, P. Seguin, and M. Smoller, "Is There a Term Structure of Futures Volatilities? Reevaluating the Samuelson Hypothesis," *Journal of Derivatives*, 1996, 45–58.

Black, F., "The Pricing of Commodity Options," *Journal of Financial Economics*, March 1976, 167–179.

Bodie, Z., and V. Rosansky, "Risk and Return in Commodities Futures," *Financial Analysts Journal*, May–June 1980, 27–39.

Breeden, D., "Consumption Risk in Futures Markets," *Journal of Finance*, May 1980, 503–520.

Brennan, M. J., "The Supply of Storage," *American Economic Review*, March 1958, 50–72.

Brennan, M., "The Cost of Convenience and the Pricing of Commodity Contingent Claims," working paper, UCLA, 1986a.

———, "A Theory of Price Limits in Futures Markets," *Journal of Financial Economics*, June 1986b, 213–234.

Brenner, M., G. Courtadon, and M. Subrahmanyam, "Options on the Spot and Options on Futures," *Journal of Finance*, December 1985, 1303–1317.

Brown, S., and P. Dybvig, "Empirical Implications of the Cox, Ingersoll, Ross Theory of the Term Structure of Interest Rates," *Journal of Finance*, 1986, Vol. 41, 616–628.

Capozza, D., and B. Cornell, "Treasury Bill Pricing in the Spot and Futures Markets," *Review of Economics and Statistics*, November 1979, 513–520.

Carlton, D., "Futures Markets: Their Purpose, Their History, Their Growth, Their Successes and Failures," *Journal of Futures Markets*, Fall 1984, 237–271.

Carter, C. A., "Commodity Futures Markets: A Survey," *The Australian Journal of Agricultural and Resource Economics*, 1999, Vol. 43, 209–247.

Carter, C. A., G. C. Rausser, and A. Schmitz, "Efficient Asset Portfolios and the Theory of Normal Backwardation," *Journal of Political Economy*, April 1983, 319–331.

Chan, K. C., A. Karolyi, F. Longstaff, and A. Saunders, "An Empirical Comparison of Alternative Models of Short-term Interest Rates," *Journal of Finance,* 1992, Vol. 47, 1209–1227.

Chance, D. and M. Hemler, "The Impact of Delivery Options on Futures Prices: A Survey," *The Journal of Futures Markets 13,* April 1993, 127–155.

Chang, E., "Returns to Speculators and the Theory of Normal Backwardation," *Journal of Finance*, March 1985, 193–208.

Chen, H., "Price Limits, Overreaction and Price Resolution in Futures Markets," *Journal of Futures Markets*, 1998, Vol. 18, 243–263.

Constantinides, G. M., "Capital Market Equilibrium with Personal Tax," *Econometrica*, May 1983, 611–636.

Cootner, P., "Returns to Speculators: Telser vs. Keynes," *Journal of Political Economy*, August 1960, 396–414.

Cornell, B., and K. French, "The Pricing of Stock Index Futures," *Journal of Futures Markets*, Spring 1983a, 1–14.

———, "Taxes and the Pricing of Stock Index Futures," *Journal of Finance*, June 1983b, 675–694.

Cornell, B., and M. Reinganum, "Forward and Futures Prices: Evidence from the Foreign Exchange Markets," *Journal of Finance*, December 1981, 1035–1045.

Courtadon, G., "The Pricing of Options on Default–Free Bonds," *Journal of Financial and Quantitative Analysis*, 1982, Vol. 17, 75–100.

Cox, J. C., J. E. Ingersoll, and S. A. Ross, "The Relation between Forward Prices and Futures Prices," *Journal of Financial Economics*, December 1981, 321–346.

———, "A Theory of the Term Structure of Interest Rates," *Econometrica*, 1985, Vol. 53, 385–406.

Culbertson, J. M., "The Term Structure of Interest Rates," *Quarterly Journal of Economics*, November 1957, 489–504.

Cuny, C., "The Role of Liquidity in Futures Markets Innovation," *Review of Financial Studies*, 1993, Vol. 6, 57–78.

Dai, Q., and K. Singleton, "Specification Analysis of Affine Term Structure Models," *Journal of Finance*, 2000, Vol. 55, 1943–1978.

Duffie, D., "Term Premia and Interest Rate Forecasts in Affine Models," working paper, Stanford University, 2000.

Duffie, D., and M. Jackson, "Optimal Innovation of Futures Contracts," *Review of Financial Studies*, 1989, Vol. 2, 275–296.

Duffie, D., and R. Kan, "A Yield-Factor Model of Interest Rates," *Mathematical Finance,* 1993, Vol. 6, 379–406.

Dusak, K., "Futures Trading and Investor Returns: An Investigation of Commodity Market Risk Premiums," *Journal of Political Economy*, November–December 1973, 1387–1406.

Fama, E. F., "Short-term Interest Rates as Predictors of Inflation," *American Economic Review*, June 1975, 269–282.

———, "The Information in the Term Structure," *Journal of Financial Economics*, December 1984a, 509–528.

———, "Term Premiums in Bond Returns," *Journal of Financial Economics*, December 1984b, 529–546.

Fama, E., and K. French, "Business Cycles and the Behavior of Metals Prices," Working Paper #31-86, UCLA, 1986.

———, "Commodity Futures Prices: Some Evidence on the Forecast Power, Premiums, and the Theory of Storage," *Journal of Business*, January 1987, 55–73.

Fama, E. F., and G. W. Schwert, "Asset Returns and Inflation," *Journal of Financial Economics*, November 1977, 113–146.

Figlewski, S., "Margins and Market Integrity: Margin Setting for Stock Index Futures and Options," *Journal of Futures Markets*, Fall 1984, 385–416.

Fisher, I., "Appreciation and Interest," *Publications of the American Economic Association*, August 1896, 23–29, 91–92.

French, K., "Detecting Spot Price Forecasts in Futures Prices," *Journal of Business*, April 1986, 539–554.

Galloway, T., and R. Kolb, "Futures Prices and the Maturity Effect," *Journal of Futures Markets*, 1996, Vol. 16, 809–828.

Gay, G., and S. Manaster, "The Quality Option Implicit in Futures Contracts," *Journal of Financial Economics*, September 1984, 353–370.

Gibbons, M., and K. Ramaswamy, "A Test of the Cox, Ingersoll and Ross Model of the Term Structure of Interest Rates," *Review of Financial Studies*, 1993, Vol. 6, 619–658.

Grauer, F., and R. Litzenberger, "The Pricing of Commodity Futures Contracts, Nominal Bonds and Other Assets under Commodity Price Uncertainty," *Journal of Finance*, March 1979, 69–83.

Hansen, L. P., and R. J. Hodrick, "Forward Exchange Rates as Optimal Predictors of Future Spot Rates: An Econometric Analysis," *Journal of Political Economy*, October 1980, 829–853.

Hartzmark, M. L., "The Effect of Changing Margin Levels on Futures Market Activity, the Composition of Traders in the Market, and Price Performance," *Journal of Business*, April 1986, S147–S180.

Hatzuka, T., "Consumption Betas and Backwardation in Commodity Markets," *Journal of Finance*, July 1984, 647–655.

Heath, D., R. Jarrow, and A. Morton, "Bond Pricing and the Term Structure of Interest Rates: A Discrete Time Approximation," *Journal of Financial and Quantitative Analysis*, 1990, Vol. 25, 419–440.

———, "Bond Pricing and the Term Structure of Interest Rates: A New Methodology for Contingent Claims Valuation," *Econometrica*, 1992, Vol. 60, 77–105.

Hemler, M., "The Quality Delivery Option in Treasury Bond Futures Contracts," Ph.D. dissertation, University of Chicago, 1987.

Hicks, J. R., *Value and Capital*, 2nd ed. Oxford University Press, Oxford, 1946.

Hilliard, J., and J. Reis, "Jump Processes in Commodity Futures Prices and Option Pricing," *American Journal of Agricultural Economics*, 1999, Vol. 81, 273–286.

Hirshleifer, D., "Risk, Equilibrium, and Futures Markets," Ph.D. dissertation, University of Chicago, 1984.

———, "Residual Risk, Trading Costs and Commodity Risk Premia," working paper, UCLA, 1986.

Hirshleifer, J., *Investment, Interest, and Capital*. Prentice-Hall, Englewood Cliffs, N.J., 1970.

———, "Liquidity, Uncertainty, and the Accumulation of Information," in Carter and Ford, eds., *Essays in Honor of G. L. S. Shackle*. Basil Blackwell, Oxford, 1972.

Ho, T., and S.-B. Lee, "Term Structure Movements and Pricing Interest Rate Contingent Claims," *Journal of Finance*, 1986, Vol. 41, 1011–1030.

Houthakker, H. S., "The Scope and Limits of Futures Trading," in Abramovitz, ed., *The Allocation of Economic Resources*, Stanford University Press, Stanford, 1959.

Hull, J., and A. White, "Pricing Interest Rate Derivative Securities," *Review of Financial Studies*, 1990, Vol. 3, 573–592.

———, "Numerical Procedures for Implementing Term Structure Models I: Single Factor Models," *Journal of Derivatives*, 1994, Vol. 2, 7–16.

Jagannathan, Ravi, "An Investigation of Commodity Futures Prices Using the Consumption-Based Intertemporal Capital Asset Pricing Model," *Journal of Finance*, March 1985, 175–191.

Johnston, E., and J. McConnell, "Requiem for a Market: An Analysis of the Rise and Fall of a Financial Futures Contract," *Review of Financial Studies*, 1989, Vol. 2, 1–24.

Kaldor, N., "Speculation and Economic Stability," *Review of Economic Studies*, October 1939, 1–27.

Kessel, R. A., *The Cyclical Behavior of the Term Structure of Interest Rates*. National Bureau of Economic Research, New York, 1965.

Keynes, J. M., "Some Aspects of Commodity Markets," *Manchester Guardian Commercial, European Reconstruction Series*, Section 13, March 29, 1923, 784–786.

———, *The General Theory of Employment, Interest and Money*. Harcourt, Brace and World, Inc., New York, 1936.

Kolb, R., *Understanding Futures Markets*, Scott, Foresman and Company, Glenview, Ill., 1985.

———, "Is Normal Backwardization Normal," *Journal of Futures Markets*, 1992, Vol. 12, 75–92.

———, "The Systematic Risk of Futures Contracts," *Journal of Futures Markets*, 1996, Vol. 16, 631–654.

Kolb, R., and R. Chiang, "Improving Hedging Performance Using Interest Rate Futures," *Financial Management*, Autumn 1981, 72–279.

———, "Immunization and Hedging with Interest Rate Futures," *Journal of Financial Research*, Summer 1982, 161–170.

Kolb, R., G. Gay, and J. Jordan, "Are There Arbitrage Opportunities in the Treasury-Bond Futures Market?" *Journal of Futures Markets*, Fall 1982, 217–230.

Kuserk, G., and P. Locke, "Market Making with Price Limits," *Journal of Futures Markets*, 1996, Vol. 16, 677–696.

Lutz, F. A., "The Structure of Interest Rates," *Quarterly Journal of Economics*, November 1940, 36–63.

Malkiel, B. G., "Expectations, Bond Prices, and the Term Structure of Interest Rates," *Quarterly Journal of Economics*, May 1962, 197–218.

McCulloch, J. H., "An Estimate of the Liquidity Premium," *Journal of Political Economy*, January–February 1975, 95–119.

Meiselman, D., *The Term Structure of Interest Rates*. Princeton University Press, Princeton, N.J., 1966.

Miffne, J., "Normal Backwardization Is Normal," *Journal of Futures Markets*, 2000, Vol. 20, 803–821.

Milonas, N., "Price Variability and the Maturity Effect in Futures Markets," *Journal of Futures Markets*, Fall 1986, 443–460.

Modest, D., and S. M. Sundaresan, "The Relationship between Spot and Futures Prices in Stock Index Futures Markets: Some Preliminary Evidence," *Journal of Futures Markets*, Spring 1983, 14–41.

Modigliani, F., and R. Sutsch, "Innovation and Interest Rate Policy," *American Economic Review*, May 1966, 178–197.

Neal, R., "Direct Tests of Arbitrage Index Models," *Journal of Financial and Quantitative Analysis*, 1996, Vol. 41, 541–562.

Nelson, C., *The Term Structure of Interest Rates: An Application of the Efficient Market Model to U.S. Treasury Bills*. Basic Books, New York, 1972.

Nothaft, F., V. Lekkas, and G. Wang, "The Failure of the Mortgage-Backed Futures Contract," *Journal of Futures Markets*, 1995, Vol. 15, 585–603.

Oldfield, G., and C. Rovira, "Futures Contract Options," *Journal of Futures Markets*, Winter 1984, 479–490.

Pashigan, B. P., "The Political Economy of Futures Market Regulation," *Journal of Business*, April 1986, S55–S84.

Pearson, N., and T.-S. Sun, "Exploiting the Conditional Density in Estimating the Term Structure: An Application to the Cox, Ingersoll and Ross Model," *Journal of Finance*, 1994, Vol. 49, 1279–1304.

Ramaswamy, K., and S. M. Sundaresan, "The Valuation of Options on Futures Contracts," *Journal of Finance*, December 1985, 1319–1340.

Rendleman, R., and B. Bartter, "The Pricing of Options on Debt Securities," *Journal of Financial and Quantitative Analysis*, 1980, Vol. 15, 11–24.

Rendleman, R., and C. Carabini, "The Efficiency of the Treasury Bill Futures Market," *Journal of Finance*, September 1979, 895–914.

Richard, S., and S. M. Sundaresan, "A Continuous Time Equilibrium Model of Forward Prices and Futures Prices in a Multigood Economy," *Journal of Financial Economics*, December 1981, 347–371.

Ritchken, P., *Derivative Markets*, Harper-Collins, New York, 1996.

Roll, R., "Orange Juice and Weather," *American Economic Review*, December 1984, 861–880.

———, *The Behavior of Interest Rates: An Application of the Efficient Market Model to U.S. Treasury Bills*. Basic Books, New York, 1970.

Salmon, J. W., "The Emergence of Organized Futures Market: The Distribution of Consumption Risk," Ph.D. dissertation, University of California at Los Angeles, 1985.

Samuelson, P., "Proof That Properly Anticipated Prices Fluctuate Randomly," *Industrial Management Review*, Spring 1965, 41–49.

———, "Proof That Properly Discounted Present Values of Assets Vibrate Randomly," in K. Crowley, ed., *Collected Scientific Papers of Paul A. Samuelson*, Vol. IV. MIT Press, Cambridge, Mass., 1977.

Sargent, T., "Rational Expectations and the Term Structure of Interest Rates," *Journal of Money, Credit and Banking*, February 1972, 74–97.

Shastri, K., and K. Tandon, "Options on Futures Contracts: A Comparison of European and American Pricing Models," *Journal of Futures Markets*, Winter 1986, 593–618.

Telser, L., "Futures Trading and the Storage of Cotton and Wheat," *Journal of Political Economy*, June 1958, 233–255.

———, "Margins and Futures Contracts," *Journal of Futures Markets*, Summer 1981a, 225–253.

———, "Why Are There Organized Futures Markets?" *Journal of Law and Economics*, April 1981b, 1–22.

Tse, Y., "Price Discovery and Volatility Spillovers in the DJIA Index and Futures Markets," *Journal of Futures Markets*, 2001.

Vasicek, O., "An Equilibrium Characterization of the Term Structure," *Journal of Financial Economics*, 1977, Vol. 5, 177–188.

Walker, C. E., "Federal Reserve Policy and the Structure of Interest Rates on Government Securities," *Quarterly Journal of Economics*, February 1954, 22–23.

Wolf, A., "Options on Futures: Pricing and the Effect of an Anticipated Price Change," *Journal of Futures Markets*, Winter 1984, 491–512.

Wood, J. H., "Expectations, Error and the Term Structure of Interest Rates," *Journal of Political Economy*, April 1963, 160–171.

Woodward, S., "The Liquidity Premium and the Solidity Premium," *American Economic Review*, June 1983, 348–361.

Working, H., "Theory of the Price of Storage," *American Economic Review*, June 1953, 312–343.

———, "Economic Functions of Futures Markets," in A. E. Peck, ed., *Selected Writings of Holbrook Working*. Board of Trade of the City of Chicago, 1977.

Former Student: "Professor, this is the same question that you gave our class when I was a student twenty years ago. Don't you ever change the questions?"

Professor: "The questions don't change—just the answers."

Multiperiod Capital Budgeting under Uncertainty: Real Options Analysis

A. Introduction

I N THE FIRST THREE EDITIONS OF OUR BOOK, this chapter was an orphan. We presented some nascent ideas, but somehow everyone knew, as the quotation above says, that the answers would be changing. So this is a completely new chapter. We are concerned with multiperiod investment decisions, that is, with capital budgeting, under uncertainty. Now that we have covered financial options in Chapter 7, we use this background to analyze flexibility in the firm's investment decision. We shall see that the net present value (NPV) rule, which was proven to be wealth maximizing for shareholders in Chapter 2, makes an implicit assumption—namely, precommitment to a deterministic course of action—that invalidates it for multiperiod decision making under uncertainty. It is replaced by a more comprehensive criterion—called real option analysis (ROA)—that properly handles flexibility in making future decisions in the face of uncertainty. NPV is therefore relegated to the status of being a quite limited special case of real options, one where there is no flexibility.

We shall assume that the reader has a basic (but not advanced) knowledge of the mathematical tools that have become the "tools of the trade" for understanding the material. Really, they are not so bad. The chapter assumes basic knowledge of probability theory—especially the binomial distribution.[1] Also, it assumes some basic knowledge of stochastic calculus. We use both tools, although probability theory will be the main workhorse.

The chapter begins with a discussion of the limiting implicit assumptions of traditional net present value analysis and decision trees, and how real options analysis overcomes them. We see that real options are a new and more sophisticated form of net present value analysis, where the value of flexibility is taken into account. Then we are introduced to the role of risk-neutral

---

[1] The binomial distribution was discussed in Chapter 7.

probabilities in ROA, to three key assumptions, and to combinations of simple real options. Next, we discuss what to do when the underlying risky asset pays dividends. With the basics in hand we begin to get more realistic by covering options on options, called compound options, which are important for any phased investment, for example, a research and development program or new product development. Another important class of real options are switching options—the right to switch from one mode of operation to another. Examples are opening and closing operating plants, or exit and reentry into an industry. Then we show how to evaluate an investment program comprised of choices between a large, efficient plant or multiple smaller but less efficient plants. The result is that flexibility is a substitute for economies of scale.

B. *C*omparing NPV with Decision Trees and Real Options

The net present value rule is a model of decision making that is deceptively simple. It estimates the expected cash flows over the life of a project, say, eight years, discounts them at the weighted average cost of capital, *WACC*, then subtracts out the initial investment, I_0, and if the answer is positive, the assumption is that the wealth of shareholders goes up and the project should be accepted. The mathematical representation is

$$NPV = -I_0 + \sum_{t=1}^{N} \frac{E(FCF_t)}{(1 + WACC)^t} > 0$$

Dixit and Pindyck [1994] provide a simple example. You can decide today to invest in a machine that costs $1,600, paid regardless of the state of nature at the end of a year, and at the end of that year, the machine produces one Gigablock (painted yellow and orange). As shown in Fig. 9.1(a), it is expected to be worth $300 or $100 with 50-50 probability. Once the price level becomes known, it stays there forever. The weighted average cost of capital for risks of this type is 10%, according to a panel of experts. Should we invest? Working through the numbers of the NPV calculation, we get

$$NPV_1 = -1,600 + [.5(300) + .5(100)] + \sum_{t=1}^{\infty} \frac{.5(300) + .5(100)}{(1 + .1)^t}$$

$$= -1,600 + 200 + \frac{200}{.1} = 600$$

$$NPV_0 = 600/1.1 = 545.5.$$

According to the NPV criterion that was introduced in Chapter 1, shareholders' wealth increases by $545.50 if we take the project, and so we do. But what if we had a deferral option giving us the right to decide at the end of one year instead of precommitting now? Suppose the cost of investment goes up to $1,800 if we wait to decide. Figure 9.1 shows the decision tree that we face (we shall continue to assume a 10% discount rate until we can provide a better idea). If the price of the Gigablock turns out to be $300, the present value of the investment at that time is $300 + $300/.1 − $1,800 = $1,500. When discounted to the present at 10% and weighted by its 50% probability, it contributes $681.80 to shareholder value. If the price turns out to be $100, we would choose not to invest. Therefore, the net present value of the project with the right to defer is

Figure 9.1 A simple decision tree (assumes $WACC = 10\%$ in either case).*

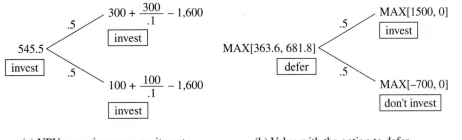

(a) NPV assuming precommitment   (b) Value with the option to defer

*Both cases assume that one unit is produced immediately, followed by a perpetual stream at the rate of one unit per year. The capital outlays at the end of the first period are $1,600 if we precommit and $1,800 if we do not.

$681.80. We would defer, and the value of the right to do so is $136.30—the difference between the value of the project with flexibility (the deferral option) and its value given precommitment.

If you work through the problem given greater uncertainty, the value of the deferral option increases. Suppose that the Gigablock price range widens to $400 or $0 instead of $300 or $100. You will find that the right to defer becomes even more valuable. It is an option, after all. Its value increases with uncertainty because, given the right but not the obligation to invest, we continue to invest when the price is higher, and capture the benefit, but continue to decide not to invest when the price is lower. The net effect is that we can invest to take advantage of the upside without being required to invest on the downside.

1. Recognizing Real Options

In Chapter 7, we studied financial options. They were financial claims, like call and put options, that were side bets traded in an options market (e.g., the CBOE). They gave the holder the right to buy (a call option) or sell (a put option) a share of the underlying common stock of a company, which is itself a financial security. The right was offered at a predetermined price, called the exercise price, for a predetermined period of time, called the time to maturity. The present value of the call option was seen to be a function of the present value of the underlying security, S_0, the standard deviation of the annual rate of return of the underlying security, σ_s, the exercise price, X, the time to maturity, T, and the (nonstochastic) risk-free rate, r_f. We used either the Black-Scholes [1973] model or a binomial approximation derived by Cox, Ross, and Rubinstein [1979] to value the option.

One of the major differences between real and financial options is that the underlying risky asset for a real option is a physical asset whose value can be affected directly by management decisions. The underlying for a financial option is another security. CBOE options are not issued as direct claims on a company by the company—rather they are side bets. For every call option purchased by a market participant, another is sold by a counterparty who writes the call under the protection of the CBOE clearinghouse.

Economic historians have dug back into the distant past to find in the writings of Aristotle, in the second century B.C., the earliest mention of a call option. It seems that a philosopher named

Thales lived on the island of Milos and, upon reading the tea leaves, had reached the conclusion that the olive harvest would be large that year. His scheme to take advantage of the forecast was to offer his meagre life savings to the owners of the olive presses for the right to rent the presses for the normal rental rate during harvest. Having no special prediction of their own, they gladly took his money, reasoning that they could rent the presses and keep Thales' money too. It turned out, sometime later, that the tea leaves were right. The olive growers, blessed by a bountiful harvest and anxious to have the olives pressed for their oil, ran to the presses, where they encountered Thales, who demanded and received a rental price much higher than normal. He took the high rental rate, paid the normal rate, and pocketed the difference for himself—becoming a rich man in the process. This is an example of a European call. What was the underlying risky asset? If you said the olive harvest, you would be wrong. Although the size of the harvest was the source of uncertainty, the underlying asset was the rental price of the presses, and its volatility is not necessarily the same as the volatility of the harvest. The exercise price was the normal rental price, and the maturity was the time to harvest.

It may seem a little strange at first, especially if you are used to the language of financial options, but soon you will recognize that the exercise price of a real option is usually the investment that is required, and the underlying risky asset is the present value of the project itself but without flexibility. And in many cases, the properties of real options make them much more complex than the Black-Scholes model can handle. Remember, Black-Scholes assumes that the underlying pays no dividends (no cash flows), can be exercised only at maturity, and is influenced by only a single source of uncertainty. Furthermore, Black-Scholes assumes a constant exercise price and that the option is a simple option—not an option on an option.

2. Differences between NPV, Decision Trees, and Real Options

We now take the stance that both NPV and decision trees are flawed due to the strong implicit assumptions that they make. Starting with net present value analysis, we note that senior managers have been observed to accept negative NPV projects. Their intuition seems to be that they recognize managerial flexibility that they have that is implicitly assumed away by NPV. For example, if a project turns out to be better than expected, the manager can spend some more money (an exercise price) to expand the project to capture incremental value. Therefore, he has an American expansion option. Similar is the right to extend the life of the project (an extension option). If the project turns out to be worse than expected, he can shrink it (a contraction option), or it can be abandoned altogether (an abandonment option). Finally, the project investment decision can be deferred (a deferral option). Therefore, the manager knows that he or she has at least five types of option embedded in every project, and that none of them are valued by standard NPV. It is not unreasonable to conclude that *NPV systematically undervalues everything.* It is only a question of how much.

You are asked to use NPV analysis to evaluate the following set of facts. A project costs $125, which will be due at the end of the year, and returns either $200 or $80 with 50-50 probability at the end of the year. The risk-free rate of interest is 5%. A quick glance tells you that something is missing, namely, the discount rate. Most corporate finance analysts would, at this juncture, try to estimate the weighted average cost of capital by finding the beta of a firm whose systematic risk is similar to the project, assuming a market risk premium, a tax rate, a target capital structure, and a risk-adjusted cost of debt. But there is another approach—to find a priced security that has perfectly correlated payouts with the project. Suppose that this "twin security" is priced at $24 and is expected to pay out $40 in the up state and $16 in the down state. Notice that these are exactly one-fifth of the payouts of our project. We can construct a portfolio of 5 units of the twin security and it will have exactly the same payments as our project in both states of nature. According to the law of one price, which prevents arbitrage, the current price of the portfolio must equal the present value of our project:

$$PV = 5S_0 = 5(\$24) = \$120.$$

Therefore, the net present value of our project is

$$NPV = V_0 - I = \$120 - \$125 = -\$5,$$

and we would not accept the project. By the way, we can reverse-engineer the weighted average cost of capital as

$$V_0 = \$120 = \frac{.5(\$200) + .5(\$80)}{(1 + WACC)}$$

$$1 + WACC = \$140/\$120$$

$$WACC = 16.7\%.$$

Next, suppose that we have a deferral option that allows us to wait until the end of the year to decide whether to spend \$125, rather than precommitting to do so as assumed with the NPV calculation. In the up state, we would choose to invest, and therefore our payout is \$75. In the down state, we would choose not to invest, and our payout would be \$0. These payouts are not perfectly correlated with the twin security or the project itself. However, we can use put-call parity from Chapter 7 to construct a *replicating portfolio* that is made up of m shares of the twin security and B default-free bonds, each worth \$1 today and paying $\$1(1 + r_f)$ at the end of the period. If u is the multiplier applied to the value of the underlying, V_0, in the up state, and d is the multiplier for the down state, then the payouts of this portfolio must be

$$m(uV_0) + B(1 + r_f) = \$75 = C_u,$$

$$m(dV_0) + B(1 + r_f) = \$0 = C_d.$$

Given two equations and two unknowns, we subtract the second equation from the first and solve for m, the number of units of the twin security in the replicating portfolio:

$$m = \frac{C_u - C_d}{(u - d)V_0} = \frac{\$75 - \$0}{(1.67 - .67)\$24} = 3.125 \text{ units,}$$

and solving for B, the number of default-free bonds, we get

$$3.125(\$40) + B(1.05) = \$75$$

$$B = (\$75 - \$125)/1.05 = -\$47.62.$$

Since the *law of one price* is applicable, the value of the replicating portfolio today must be equal to the value of the call option because they have identical payouts in all states of nature. Therefore the value of the project with the flexibility of deferral is

$$C_0 = mV_0 + B$$

$$= 3.125(\$24) - \$47.62 = \$27.38.$$

The value of the deferral option is the difference between the net present value of the project given precommitment and its net present value given the flexibility of deferral. This amounts to $27.38 − (−$5) = $32.38.

The main difference between NPV methodology and real options is that the former discounts expected cash flows at a constant discount rate. NPV implicitly assumes that no decisions will be made in the future—that all expected cash flows are precommitted. Real options analysis uses decision trees and therefore models optimal actions taken in the future in response to the resolution of uncertainty. By using the concept of replicating portfolios, it insures that there is no arbitrage and that the resulting present value calculations conform to the law of one price.

A second important difference between NPV and real options is that they deal with mutually exclusive opportunities in quite different ways. Take the deferral decision as an example. NPV treats the decision to defer one year as a mutually exclusive alternative from deferring for two years and so on. After all, we can defer for one year or for two years, but not both. The NPV of each possible deferral choice is calculated, and we then choose the maximum of the set. In contrast, real options analysis uses a decision tree and works backward through it, from the future to the present, to calculate a single value—the value of the project with the right to defer until a given date (e.g., five years). Mathematically, it is possible to prove that the real options value is greater than the maximum of the NPV alternatives. Thus, there are no mutually exclusive alternatives if we use a real options approach to the problem, only a single value for the American call (the right to defer) and state-contingent rules for when to defer or invest. Thus, the net present value rule forces us to conceive of false mutually exclusive alternatives when confronted with decisions that could be made in the future, but to which we must precommit now. Real options analysis handles these future decisions on a state-contingent basis as part of a decision tree.

Next, let's compare real options with decision trees. They both make state-contingent future decisions, but there remains an important difference. Decision trees assume a constant discount rate—either the risk-free rate or the weighted average cost of capital—throughout the tree. Real options analysis uses replicating portfolios and obeys the law of one price. Implicitly, it changes the risk-adjusted discount rate at each branch in the tree. If we extend the simple one-period example given above to the two-period example shown in Fig. 9.2, we can illustrate the shortcoming of an approach that assumes a constant ad hoc discount rate. Figure 9.2(a) shows the objective probabilities and payouts for the underlying risky asset in each state of nature for two years. If the required investment of $125, which is also the exercise price on the option, remains constant, then the optimal payouts and decisions at each node are given in Fig. 9.2(b). The value of the twin security is $24 at time zero, and after two periods there is a 25% chance of its value reaching $66.70, a 50% chance that it will be $26.67, and a 25% chance that it will be $10.67. The discount rate, given in the circles at each vertex in the binomial tree, is constant at 16.67%. If we treat the problem as a decision tree, there is a question about what discount rate to use for the state-contingent payouts from the deferral option that are given. Sometimes, it is argued that the risk-free rate is appropriate because the risk of the project is idiosyncratic, and sometimes the analyst advocates the weighted average cost of capital for the underlying project.

If we were to use the risk-free rate, the objective probabilities, and the payouts given the correct state-contingent decision, as given in Fig. 9.2(b), the decision-tree value would be $67, and if discounted at the weighted average cost of capital, it would be $55. Of course, both answers are wrong because the decision tree uses ad hoc assumptions about the riskiness of the option. It violates the law of one price. It is also easy to construct an example where the decision at a given node in the decision tree is different using decision tree analysis than real options analysis, and

Figure 9.2 Two-period deferral option: (a) underlying project and (b) call option.

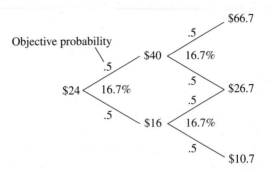

(a) Present value of underlying twin security
(before investment of $125)

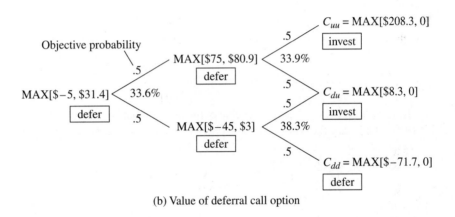

(b) Value of deferral call option

that the rank ordering of mutually exclusive projects can change depending on which method you use. See Question 9.2 at the end of the chapter.

Each of the state-contingent values in Fig. 9.2(b) is calculated using the twin security and forming a replicating portfolio. For example, take the upper state of nature at the end of the first period. The decision is either to exercise the call option by investing $125 when the value of the project is $200, for a net of $75, or deferring the investment decision for another period—that is, keeping the option open. The value if the option is not exercised (if we defer for one more period) is $80.90; therefore we will defer. But how did we estimate this value? First, we calculated the end-of-period payouts. In the upper state the project is worth $333.33 and the exercise price is $125; therefore we would invest because the only alternative is to let the option expire and receive a payout of $0. In the middle state the project is worth $133.33, and we will pay the exercise price of $125 to receive a net of $8.33 rather than nothing. Given these payouts, we form a replicating portfolio of m shares of the twin security and B default-free bonds, each worth $1 at the beginning of the period, and paying $\$1(1+r_f)$ at the end of the period. As a result we have two equations and two unknowns:

$$mu V_1 + B(1+r_f) = \$208.30 = C_{uu},$$

$$md V_1 + B(1+r_f) = \$8.30 = C_{du}.$$

By subtracting the second equation from the first we can solve for m:

$$m = \frac{(C_{uu} - C_{du})}{(u-d)V_1} = \frac{(208.3 - 8.3)}{(1.67 - .67)40} = 5.$$

Think of m as a *hedge ratio*. The numerator of the above equation is the change in the option payouts between the up and down states of nature, and the denominator is the change in the value of the twin security between the two states. In this example one needs 5 units of the twin security to hedge the call. Next, we can substitute m into the first of the two equations to solve for B as follows:

$$mu V_1 + B(1+r_f) = \$208.30 = C_{uu}$$

$$5(\$66.70) + B(1+.05) = \$208.30$$

$$B = (\$208.30 - \$333.30)/1.05$$

$$B = -\$119.10.$$

To prevent arbitrage, the present value of the option must be exactly the same as our replicating portfolio, and since the replicating portfolio is constructed from securities whose prices we know, its beginning-of-period value is

$$m V_1 + B = 5(\$40) - \$119.10 = \$80.90.$$

In a similar fashion, replicating portfolios are used to price the option at other nodes in the tree. Since we know the objective probabilities, the payouts, and the values that obey the law of one price, we can reverse-engineer the risk-adjusted discount rates. For example, the rate at the upper node at the end of the first year is 33.9%, and is very different than either of the ad hoc assumptions used in the decision tree approach.

$$\$80.90 = [.5(\$208.30) + .5(\$8.30)]/(1 + WACC)$$

$$WACC = \$108.30/\$80.90 - 1 = 33.9\%$$

Intuitively, the risk of an option is always greater than the risk of the underlying risky asset. This was discussed in Chapter 7. It also implies that the discount rate for the cash flows of the option must be greater than the discount rate for the underlying. Note also, from Fig. 9.2, that the risk-adjusted discount rate changes depending where you are in the tree, because the risk of the option changes as a function of the life of the option and the value of the underlying.

3. Risk-Neutral Probabilities

There is another method for valuing real options that is mathematically equivalent to the *replicating portfolio approach*, where we calculate *risk-neutral probabilities*. Once the value of the option is estimated at a node, and assuming that we know the objective probabilities and payouts, we showed how to reverse-engineer the risk-adjusted discount rate. We can also decide to discount the cash flows at the risk-free rate and to estimate the risk-neutral probabilities that provide the same value. These were also discussed in Chapter 7. If the objective probability of an up movement is p and the risk-neutral probability is q, then

$$V_0 = \frac{p(uV_0) + (1-p)(dV_0)}{1 + RAR} = \frac{q(uV_0) + (1-q)(dV_0)}{1 + r_f}.$$

Solving for the risk-neutral probability, q:

$$V_0(1+r_f) = V_0(qu) + V_0 d(1-q)$$

$$q = \frac{(1 + r_f - d)}{u - d} \quad \text{and} \quad (1-q) = \frac{u - (1+r_f)}{u - d}.$$

The interesting property of risk-neutral probabilities is that they are not a function of V_0 and do not change depending on where one is in the tree. Note that the risk-neutral probability of an upward move, q, is always less than the corresponding objective probability, p, because the risk-neutral expected payout in the numerator of the equation must always be less than the objectively measured expected payout so that when discounted at a lower rate (the risk-free rate) the resulting value is the same.

C. Three Key Assumptions for Pricing Real Options

The prospect of finding a twin security that is priced in active trading and that has payouts that are perfectly correlated with the project that we are trying to value is about as likely as hitting a hole in one on a 550-yard par 5 in golf. Something more practical would be nice. One suggestion that is gaining greater acceptance is that we can use the present value of the project itself (assuming no flexibility to make future decisions) as a twin security. After all, what is better correlated with the project than the project itself? This assumption has been called the marketed asset disclaimer (MAD) assumption by real option practitioners, and it assumes that we treat the present value of the project *without* flexibility as though it could be bought or sold in an active marketplace. That is the assumption that is already made (at least implicitly) when we use the standard NPV criterion. Consequently, the MAD assumption is no stronger and no worse than the traditional NPV assumptions.

To provide a numerical example, suppose we revisit the two-period deferral option example that was illustrated in Fig. 9.2, except this time we will use the value of the project itself as the underlying risky asset, instead of burdening ourselves with the impossible task of finding a twin security. Figure 9.3(a) has the project values. Figure 9.3(b) has the deferral option values.

None of the option values change because the project values are perfectly correlated with those of the twin security, as shown in Fig. 9.2(a). The value of m in the replicating portfolio turns out to be one-fifth of its former value, while B remains unchanged, as does the value of the option. Here are the two equations for the replicating portfolio at the upper node at the end of the first period:

$$m(uV_1) + B(1+r_f) = C_u = \$208.30,$$

$$m(dV_1) + B(1+r_f) = C_d = \$8.30.$$

Figure 9.3 The value of the deferral option revisited using the MAD assumption.

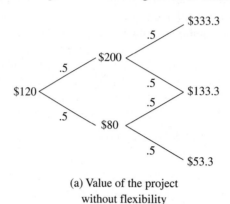

(a) Value of the project
without flexibility

(b) Value of the project
with a deferral option

Subtracting the second equation from the first and solving for m,

$$m = (\$208.30 - \$8.30)/(\$200)(1.67 - .67) = 1,$$

and substituting this into the first equation, solve for B,

$$1(\$333.33) + B(1.05) = \$208.33$$

$$B = (\$208.30 - \$333.30)/1.05 = -\$119.10,$$

and the value of the option if unexercised at this node is

$$C = mV_1 + B = 1(\$200) - \$119.10 = \$80.90.$$

This is the same answer as before. The MAD assumption works. The present value of the project without flexibility may be used as the underlying "twin security" when pricing the option.

The second important assumption is one that we have already discussed—namely, that real option pricing obeys the principle of no arbitrage. This hardly requires explanation or debate. It is why we formed replicating portfolios.

The third assumption comes from Samuelson's paper on the proof that properly anticipated prices fluctuate randomly. This was discussed in Chapter 8 and is one of the earliest mathematical statements of *capital market efficiency*. We need it for valuing real options because the stochastic process for the value of the underlying must be well defined and regular. Project cash flows are anything but that. They definitely cannot be described as a Brownian motion process. They are often autocorrelated, in particular mean-reverting, and often seem to follow other strange patterns such as being "S-shaped." The beauty and simplicity of Samuelson's proof is that the value that an investor receives from a risky project will follow a random walk even though the cash flows are predictable. Why? Because the current value incorporates all information about expected cash flows, and any changes in the current value result from changes in expectations of future cash flows that are random by definition. Since the value follows a Gauss-Wiener process, we can model it so, or as a recombining binomial tree.[2] There is no need to trouble ourselves with a wide variety of complicated assumptions about the stochastic process for the value of the underlying risky asset. It will not be mean-reverting, even though the project cash flows may be. It will not follow a growth curve that is S-shaped, even though the cash flows may.

Figure 9.4 and the accompanying table show an autocorrelated series of cash flows for a project that has a five-year life, their present value as it is expected to change through time, the wealth of the investor, and the investor's expected return through time. Even though the cash flows follow anything but a stationary stochastic process, and the value rises and falls, expected investor wealth rises at a constant rate—namely, the 10% discount rate. It is assumed that all cash put into the project or paid out by the project is "put into investments of equivalent risk" and accumulates through time. For example, the present value of the cash flows from year 1 to year 5 is $2,615.30. But the investor must put $1,000 into the project in order to get it started. Therefore, her wealth is $1,615.30 at time zero. At the end of the first period the project is worth $2,876.80, but the $1,000 investment (a negative cash flow) is now worth $1,100; therefore the investor's accumulated wealth is $1,775.80 for a one-year return of 10%. As shown in the table accompanying Fig. 9.4, the return on the investor's wealth is constant at 10% over the life of the project. Random shocks to the expected cash flows will be reflected as random movements in the investor's wealth and in the return on it. Therefore, we can model the investor's wealth as a Gauss-Wiener process, or as a recombining binomial tree.

The three keystone assumptions are instrumental in the application of option pricing methodology to real option problems. The MAD assumption allows us to use the present value of the project without flexibility as the underlying risky asset, the no-arbitrage assumption implies that the replicating portfolio approach correctly values the real option that is contingent on the underlying, and Samuelson's proof implies that regardless of the pattern of expected cash flows we can use recombining binomial trees (equivalent to geometric Brownian motion) to model the evolution of the value of the project through time.

---

[2] In the limit, as the number of binomial trials per period increases to infinity, the binomial process approaches a Gauss-Wiener process as a limit.

Figure 9.4 Expected cash flow, project value, investor wealth, and return over the life of a project.

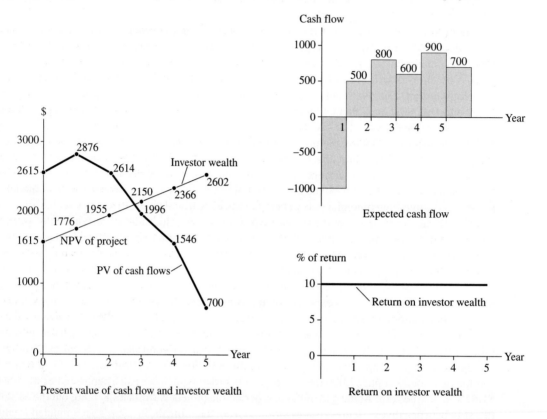

Year	Cash Flow	PV of CF	Investor Wealth	Return on Wealth
0	−$1,000	$2,615.30	$2,615.30 − $1,000.00 = $1,615.30	
1	500	2,876.80	$2,876.80 − 1,000.00(1.1) = 1,775.80$	$1,775.80/$1,615.30 = 1.10
2	800	2,614.50	$2,614.50 − 1,000.00(1.1)^2 + 500(1.1) = 1,954.50$	$1,954.50/1,775.80 = 1.10$
3	600	1,996.30	$1,996.30 − 1,000.00(1.1)^3 + 500(1.1)^2 + 800(1.1) = 2,150.30$	$2,150.30/1,954.50 = 1.10$
4	900	1,536.30	$1,536.30 − 1,000.00(1.1)^4 + 500(1.1)^3 + 800(1.1)^2 + 600(1.1) = 2,365.70$	$2,365.70/2,150.30 = 1.10$
5	700	700.00	$700.00 − 1,000.00(1.1)^5 + 500(1.1)^4 + 800(1.1)^3 + 600(1.1)^2 + 900(1.1) = 2,602.30$	$2,602.30/2,365.70 = 1.10$

D. Valuing Real Options on Dividend-Paying Assets

One of the theorems that we learned in Chapter 7 was that an American call option written on an underlying risky asset that pays out no cash flows or dividends will never be exercised before its maturity date because its market value if not exercised is always greater than its value if exercised. Almost all capital projects do pay out cash flows over the life of the project, and like a dividend-paying stock, any options contingent on them may be exercised prior to expiration. In this section of the chapter, we show how to value an American option—an expansion option—on a typical project that pays out cash flows each period.

Suppose that a project is expected to cost $1,500, to have a three-year life, and to return expected cash flows of $500 the first year, $600 the second year, and $700 the third year. The project value can go up 50% ($u = 1.5$) or down by 66.7% ($d = 1/u$) each year. At the end of each year we have the option to expand the project at a cost of $500, with the result that the value of the project would increase by 50%. The weighted average cost of capital is 12%, and the risk-free rate is 8%.

Figure 9.5(a) graphs what we call the *expected value branch*—the expected value of the project with and without dividends at each point in time. Figure 9.5(b) graphs the project value tree that shows the payoffs given the uncertainty. The value tree is recombining because we have assumed that dividends are proportional to the cash flows in each state of nature.

Remember that expected cash flows are "dividends" because they represent cash that belongs to shareholders, whether actually paid out or not. For example, in the first year, expected cash flow is $500, and the expected value with the dividend is $1,593.70; therefore the dividend payout is 31.4% of value. In the up state 31.4% of $2,134 is $670; therefore the value without the dividend (called the *ex dividend value*) is $1,464. In the down state the value with dividend is $949, and the 31.4% dividend is $298. Proof that the tree is recombining given proportional dividends is that we obtain the same middle state value (with dividend) in period 2. That is, we get $977 = $1,464/1.5 = $651(1.5)$. Note also that the objective probability, p, of an up move is calculated as follows:

$$[puV_0 + (1 - p)dV_0]/(1 + k) = V_0$$

$$p = [V_0(1 + k) - dV_0]/V_0(u - d)$$

$$p = (1 + k - d)/(u - d)$$

$$p = (1 + .12 - .667)/(1.5 - .667) = .544.$$

Using this result, we can demonstrate consistency between the value branch and the value tree. For example, the expected cash flow in the first period is $.544(2,134) + (1 - .544)(949) = 1,593$, and this equals the expected cash flow seen in Fig. 9.5(a), the value branch. In a similar fashion we see that the expected dividend, $.544(669) + (1 - .544)(298) = 500$, in the value tree is the same as the expected dividend in the value branch.

Having developed the value tree for the underlying project, we move on to value the expansion option, as illustrated in Fig. 9.6. Recall that at each decision node, we have the right to exercise our expansion option at a fixed cost of $500 and to increase the value of the project by a factor of 1.5, or to leave the option unexercised. To solve for the option price we must start at the end nodes of the tree and work backward toward the present. At node A, for example, the value of the underlying risky asset, taken from Fig. 9.5, is $1,680 on the upper branch and $747 on the lower branch. If the expansion option is exercised, the payoffs are $1.5($1,680) - $500 = $2,020$ on the

Figure 9.5 Value branch and tree for the underlying risky asset.

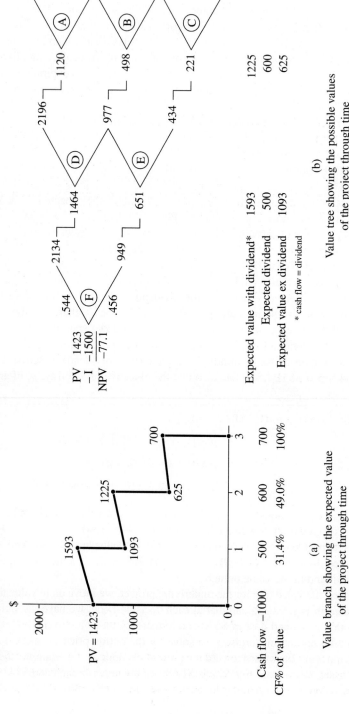

Expected value with dividend*   1593

Expected dividend   500

Expected value ex dividend   1093

* cash flow = dividend

Value tree showing the possible values
of the project through time

(b)

Cash flow	−1000	500	600	700
CF% of value		31.4%	49.0%	100%

Value branch showing the expected value
of the project through time

(a)

upper branch and 1.5($747) − $500 = $621 on the lower branch. Thus, the decision maker will choose to exercise his option on the upper branch, thereby receiving $2,020 rather than $1,680. On the lower branch he chooses to take the value of the underlying risky asset, $747, rather than exercising the expansion option and receiving only $620. Moving back one period to node D in Fig. 9.6, we can either accept the market value or exercise our option. If there were no cash payments, we would always elect to keep our options open. But in this example the cash flows of the project are literally dividends. Note that in order to move back to node D from nodes A and B we must add back the dividend payment, which according to Fig. 9.5 will be 49% of cash flow. Since the value of the underlying was $2,196 in the up state (see Fig. 9.5), dividends are assumed to be .49 × ($2,196) = $1,077. When this is added to the ex-dividend value of $1,276 (the next paragraph explains how to derive $1,276), we obtain a value with dividends in the upper state of nature of $2,353 (see Fig. 9.6, node D). This is the market value of the project assuming that we choose not to exercise our expansion option. However, if we do exercise, we receive 1.5 times the value of the underlying risky asset: 1.5($2,196) minus $500 equals $2,796. Since this is higher than the unexercised value, we would choose to exercise. Similar logic produces a value in the lower state of node D as $977, but in this case we receive higher value if we do not exercise.

The market value of the project if the option is not exercised does not come into play at node D; nevertheless, it is an important number. It is estimated by using replicating portfolios and the MAD assumption. We form two portfolios, each having m shares of the underlying risky project and B default-free bonds. Using the same notation as before, with u as the geometric multiplier for up movements and $d = 1/u$ for down movements, and V as the beginning-of-period value of the underlying risky asset, we have two equations and two unknowns:

$$muV + (1 + r_f)B = \$2,020,$$

$$mdV + (1 + r_f)B = \$747.$$

Subtracting the second from the first, we solve for m:

$$m = (\$2,020 - \$747)/V(u - d)$$

$$m = \$1,273/\$933 = 1.364.$$

Substituting the value of m into the first equation, we solve for B:

$$B = (\$2,020 - muV)/(1 + r_f)$$

$$B = (\$2,020 - \$2,291.50)/(1.08) = -\$251.40.$$

Finally, substituting the values for m and B into the beginning-of-period value of the portfolio, we value the expansion call at node D as follows:

$$C = mV + B = 1.364(\$1,120) - \$251.40 = \$1,276$$

This is the value of the project if we do not exercise our expansion option at node D, given the condition of no arbitrage.

Working back through the tree, we see that we would exercise as early as the first time period if the up state of nature occurs. Also, the value of the project without the expansion option is $1,423, and with it the value is $1,682; therefore the expansion option is worth $199.

Figure 9.6 Valuation of an expansion option.

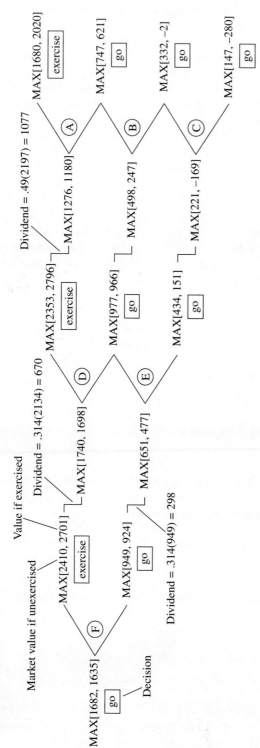

E. *T*ypes of Real Options

Next we expand our vocabulary a little to become familiar with different types of real options and examples of how they are applied. Each paragraph describes a different type, starting with simple options, then becoming more and more complex. The list is not exhaustive. There are simply too many applications.

Expansion options are American calls on an underlying asset that assumes precommitment of a series of investments to growing demand over time. Sometimes called growth options, their exercise price is the cost of the investment to expand, and their value is a multiple of the value of the underlying risky asset. The previous section of this chapter showed an example of how to price them, and that they are usually exercised before the end of the life of the underlying risky asset because the cash flows thrown off by the project have the same effect as dividends, causing the value of the asset to fall without protecting the value of the option. Debottlenecking manufacturing operations may be described as an expansions option.

Contraction options are American puts that give the option to receive cash for giving up the use of part of an asset. An example would be subleasing a part of a manufacturing facility where the owner receives the present value of a stream of lease payments in exchange for allowing a third party to use the facility. The present value of the cash is the exercise price of the put, and the fraction of the value of operations given up is the value of the underlying.

Abandonment options are American options where the owner of an asset has the right to sell it for a given price (which can change through time) rather than continuing to hold it. An example where abandonment is important is research and development programs. When experimental results are unfavorable, the line of research should be abandoned. There are other examples as well. Mines can be abandoned. Factories can be closed permanently. Acquisitions can be sold for a discount should they fail.

Extension options allow the manager to pay a cost for the ability to extend the life of a project— a European call. The exercise price is the cost of the extension. One often sees this type of option in leases of office space.

Deferral options are the right to defer the start of a project. These are quite realistic in situations where competition is not a factor, for example, when a government sells the right to extract minerals from government property (oil, natural gas, copper, iron ore, etc.). Once one acquires the right to develop the leasehold, no one else can do the same, and the right remains good for a fixed period of time, usually five years. The cost of development is the exercise price of the deferral option, and there are at least two important sources of uncertainty—the price of the mineral to be extracted, and the quantity of mineral in the ground. There is an interesting trade-off between them. Greater price uncertainty raises the value of deferral, and greater uncertainty about the reserve size (or reduced costs in obtaining the information) reduces the value of deferral. This means that there is the possibility that there is an optimal deferral decision that results from the trade-off between the two.

Compound options are options on options. There is a broad set of corporate investment decisions that fit into this category. For example, a call option on the stock of a levered firm is a compound option because the equity itself is an option on the unlevered value of the firm. Other examples are phased investments such as research and development programs, exploration and production, and new product development. Most large plant construction plans are phased into design, engineering, preconstruction, and final construction with the ability to defer or abandon at the end of each phase.

Rainbow options have multiple sources of uncertainty. Sometimes it is possible to use Monte Carlo simulation to combine these uncertainties into the standard deviation of the value of the project, and on other occasions it is advisable to keep uncertainties separate and employ a quad-ranomial approach.

F. Valuing Combinations of Simple Real Options

Most projects can be expanded, an American call; contracted, an American put; or abandoned altogether, also an American put. All three options are available to the manager at each node in the decision tree. We talked about this earlier as one of the major differences between NPV applied naively and real options—namely, that managers can make decisions in the future to improve the outcome of the project. This section of the chapter shows how this portfolio of options can be valued using binomial trees.

Suppose a project is valued as worth $200 without flexibility using traditional NPV techniques. Its value can go up by a factor of 1.25 or down by $1/1.25 = .8$ in one time period. The risk-free rate is 5% per year and the weighted average cost of capital is 10%. Figure 9.7 shows the binomial value tree for the underlying project without flexibility. The objective probability, p, of an up movement is determined from our knowledge of the current value, V_0, the up movement, and the weighted average cost of capital, k.

$$V_0 = [puV_0 + (1-p)dV_0]/ (1+k)$$
$$p = [V_0(1+k) - dV_0]/ V_0 (u-d)$$
$$= [1.1 - .8]/[1.25 - .8] = .67.$$

The risk-neutral probability, q, is calculated as follows:

$$V_0 = [quV_0 + (1-q)dV_0]/(1+r_f)$$
$$q = (1+r_f - d)/(u-d)$$
$$q = (1 + .05 - .8)/(1.25 - .8) = .56.$$

As expected, the risk-neutral probability of the favorable payout is lower than the objective probability and has the effect of risk-adjusting the expected payout downward so that the resulting

Figure 9.7 Value of the underlying project (without flexibility).

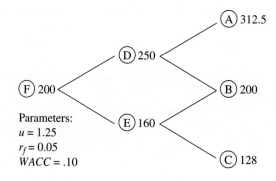

Parameters:
$u = 1.25$
$r_f = 0.05$
$WACC = .10$

(F) 200
(D) 250
(E) 160
(A) 312.5
(B) 200
(C) 128

certainty equivalent values, when discounted at the risk-free rate, provide exactly the same present value as the objectively estimated expected cash flows discounted at the weighted average cost of capital.

Figure 9.8 shows the three options (abandonment, contraction, and expansion) given the assumption that the abandonment value is \$190, that contraction reduces the value of the project 20% and provides \$50 in cash, and that expansion costs \$70 but increases the value of the project by 30%. To keep the analysis as simple as possible, we assume that the exercise price of the abandonment option is unchanged by earlier exercise of the contraction option. We could relax this strong assumption, of course, but then we would have the complication that the decision tree would become path dependent and would not recombine. We will deal with this issue in the section of the chapter that deals with switching options that are also path dependent. Figure 9.8(a) is the value tree for the abandonment option. To value it we begin with the decisions at the end nodes A, B, and C, where we choose the greater of the value of the underlying project or the abandonment value. At nodes A and B we keep the project payout, but at node C we are better off abandoning the project for \$190 rather than keeping it to receive only \$128. The value at node E is the maximum of the market value (MV) of the project if we keep it or its value if exercised. The market value can be estimated in either of two ways—replicating portfolios or risk-neutral probabilities. The simpler approach uses the risk-neutral probability ($q = .56$) as follows:

$$MV = [q(\text{MAX}(uV_0, X) + (1-q)(\text{MAX}(dV_0, X)]/(1+r_f)$$

$$MV = [.56(200) + (1-.56)(190)]/(1.05) = 195.6/1.05 = 186.2.$$

The slightly more cumbersome approach forms two replicating portfolios, one mimicking the up state payout and the other mimicking the down state payout:

$$muV_0 + (1+r_f)B = C_u,$$

$$mdV_0 + (1+r_f)B = C_d.$$

Solving for m by subtracting the second equation from the first, we have

$$m = (C_u - C_d)/V_0 (u - d) = (200 - 190)/160(1.25 - .8) = .139.$$

Then by substituting the solution for m into the first equation, we can solve for B as follows:

$$B = (C_u - muV_0)/(1+r_f) = [200 - .139(200)]/1.05 = 164.$$

And finally, the beginning-of-period value of the portfolio consisting of m shares of the underlying and B bonds must be the same as the value of the real option that we are pricing:

$$C_0 = mV_0 + B = .139(160) + 164 = 186.2.$$

Using either of the two approaches, one can work backward through the tree, node by node, until the current value of the project with flexibility—in this case with an abandonment option—is determined to be \$213. Therefore, the value of the abandonment option, taken alone, is \$13.

Figure 9.8(b) and (c) show the valuation of options to contract the scale of the project and to expand it. Often a project can be contracted in scale by subleasing or selling part of the facilities, and it can be expanded via debottlenecking or by building additions. The solution process is similar to that used above for the abandonment option. Work backward through the tree by making the

Figure 9.8 Three simple options on the underlying.

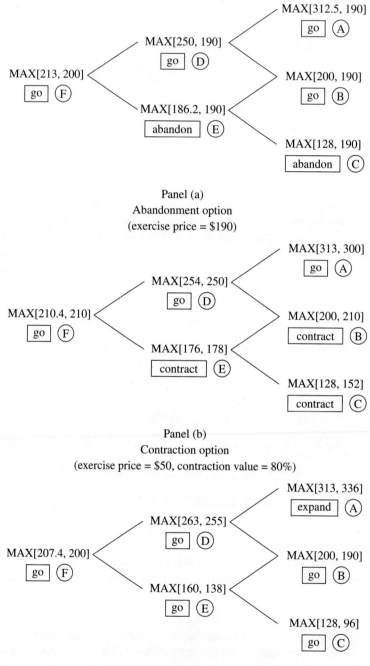

Panel (a)
Abandonment option
(exercise price = $190)

Panel (b)
Contraction option
(exercise price = $50, contraction value = 80%)

Panel (c)
Expansion option
(exercise price = $70, expansion value = 130%)

Figure 9.9 Valuing the combination of three options.

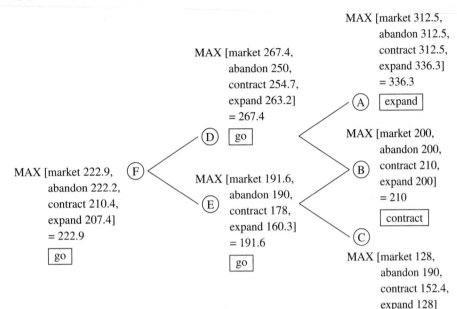

MAX [market 222.9,
abandon 222.2,
contract 210.4,
expand 207.4]
= 222.9

go

MAX [market 191.6,
abandon 190,
contract 178,
expand 160.3]
= 191.6

go

MAX [market 267.4,
abandon 250,
contract 254.7,
expand 263.2]
= 267.4

go

MAX [market 312.5,
abandon 312.5,
contract 312.5,
expand 336.3]
= 336.3

expand

MAX [market 200,
abandon 200,
contract 210,
expand 200]
= 210

contract

MAX [market 128,
abandon 190,
contract 152.4,
expand 128]
= 190

abandon

optimal decision at each node, then by using risk-neutral probabilities or replicating portfolios. We would choose to contract the scale of the project at nodes B, C, and E, and the value of the contraction option is $10.40. We would expand only at node A, and the expansion option is worth $7.40.

Figure 9.9 shows what happens when all three options are combined. Starting at the end of the tree we consider the maximum of each alternative. We can keep the value of the underlying project, expand it, contract it, or abandon it. It turns out in this example that we would choose expansion in the upper state at node A, contraction in the middle state, node B, and abandonment in the lowest state, node C (where we have assumed the exercise price is not contingent on prior decisions). Working back through the tree, we find that the present value of the project with flexibility of all three types is now $222.90. Note that this answer is not simply the sum of the three options taken separately because the abandoned option dominates the contraction option at node C.

G. Valuing Compound Options

Compound options are options on options. They are the most common category of real option, and there are two types. *Simultaneous compound options* are exercisable at the same time. For example, a call option traded on the CBOE is alive at the same time as the share of stock on which it is written, but the stock is an option on the value of the underlying levered firm. The valuation of simultaneous compound options was solved by Geske [1977] using stochastic calculus. We shall re-solve it here

Figure 9.10 Binomial tree for the entity value of a firm that underlies levered equity.

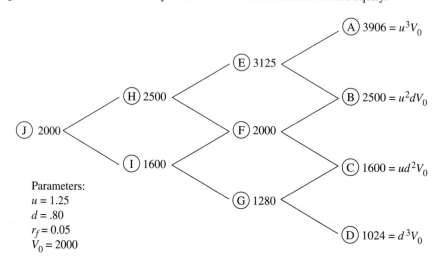

Parameters:
$u = 1.25$
$d = .80$
$r_f = 0.05$
$V_0 = 2000$

using binomial trees. In the limit, as the number of binomial trials per time period approaches infinity, the two approaches converge. *Sequential compound options* are contingent upon each other. For example, FDA drug approval mandates three stages of testing. Drug research can be abandoned after each stage—a European put. But each put is alive only if the put that proceeds it chronologically is not exercised. Therefore, sequential compound options are contingent on each other.

1. Simultaneous Compound Options

Simultaneous compound options are alive at the same time. For example, suppose that we have a firm with an entity value (debt plus equity) of $2,000 and that it could go up by 25% or down by 20% each year. The firm and its equity are both assumed to pay no cash outflows—a no-dividend assumption. Furthermore, the firm has $1,200 of zero-coupon debt (face value) outstanding that matures in three years. The unlevered cost of equity is 7% and the risk-free rate is 5% per year. Finally, there is an American call written on the market value of the firm's equity that has an exercise price of $900 and three years to maturity. What is the current market value of the option?

The call option is a simultaneous call option. It is an option on the equity of the firm, and the equity is an option on the entity value of the firm, with its exercise price the face value of debt. To value the call, we must first value the equity. Then the value of the equity becomes the underlying risky asset that is used to value the call that is written on it. Figure 9.10 shows the binomial tree for the value of the firm. By the third year the entity value could be as high as $3,906 or as low as $1,024.

Figure 9.11 shows the valuation of the equity of the levered firm as an American call with an exercise price equal to the face value of debt, namely, $1,200. Equity payouts at the end nodes are the maximum of zero or the value of the firm minus the face value of debt. Equity holders would rationally decide to default on the debt only in the lowest state of nature at node D, where the value of the firm is $1,024 and the face value of debt is $1,200. In the three higher states of nature the value of the firm exceeds the face value of debt, and it is in the interest of equity holders to pay

Figure 9.11 Equity value event tree.

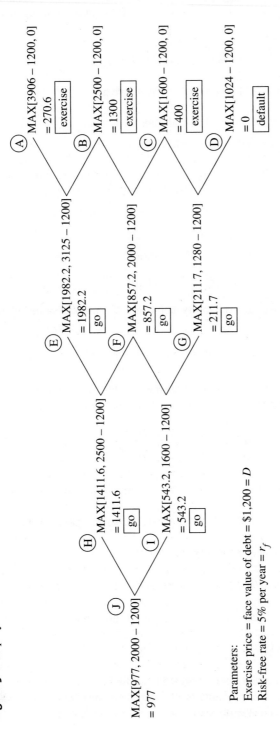

Parameters:
Exercise price = face value of debt = $1,200 = D
Risk-free rate = 5% per year = r_f

off the full face value of the debt and keep the residual value of the firm. At node E we determine the market value of equity either by using risk-neutral probabilities or replicating portfolios. The risk-neutral probability of an up state can be derived from information about the present value of the project as follows:

$$V_0 = [pu V_0 + (1 - p)d V_0]/(1 + k).$$

Solving for the objective probability of an up movement, p, we have

$$p = [V_0(1 + k) - d V_0]/ V_0(u - d)$$
$$p = [1 + .07 - .8]/(1.25 - .8) = 0.6.$$

The risk-neutral probability uses the same valuation equation except that we discount at the risk-free rate and use certainty equivalent or risk-neutral probabilities, q, to weight the cash flows in the numerator:

$$V_0 = [qu V_0 + (1 - q)d V_0]/(1 + r_f)$$
$$q = [V_0(1 + r_f) - d V_0]/ V_0(u - d)$$
$$q = (1.05 - .8)/(1.25 - .8) = 0.5556.$$

Therefore, if we use the risk-neutral probability approach, the market value of the live (i.e., unexercised) option at node E is

$$C = [q C_u + (1 - q)C_d]/(1 + r_f) = [0.5556(2706) + (1 - 0.5556)(1300)]/1.05 = 1982.$$

The other equivalent approach is to assure no arbitrage by forming replicating portfolios consisting of m shares of the underlying and B default-free bonds, as follows:

$$mu V_0 + (1 + r_f)B = C_u$$
$$du V_0 + (1 + r_f)B = C_d.$$

Solving for m, we have

$$m = (C_u - C_d)/ V_0(u - d) = (2,706 - 1,300)/3125(1.25 - .8) = 1.000,$$

and by substituting m into the first equation, we find that B is

$$B = (C_u - mu V_0)/(1 + r_f) = (2,706 - 3,906)/1.05 = -1,142.7.$$

Finally, we solve for the present value of the replicating portfolio at node E:

$$C = m V_0 - B = 1.00(3,125) - 1,142.7 = 1,982.$$

Working back through the binomial tree in Fig. 9.11, we find that the current market value of the equity is $977. Therefore, the market value of the risky debt must be $B_0 = \$2,000 - \$977 = \$1,023$, and the promised yield to maturity, y, must be

$$B_0 = \$1,200/(1+y)^3$$

$$(1+y)^3 = 1,200/1,023$$

$$y = 5.46\%.$$

Note that this is slightly greater than the risk-free rate and reflects the likelihood of default in the worst state of nature but where bondholders would still receive most of the face value (i.e., $1,023 instead of $1,200). We could also compute the cost of levered equity by solving for the rate that equates the expected end-of-period payouts to equity (using the objective probabilities) with the present value of the equity.

The binomial value tree for the equity claims shown in Fig. 9.11 becomes the underlying risky asset for the call option that is written on the equity. The binomial value tree for this compound option is illustrated in Fig. 9.12. Once again, we work from the end nodes of the tree back in time, using risk-neutral probabilities or replicating portfolios to construct market value estimates. The present value of the American call written on the equity of the levered firm is $409.70. Note that because the call is a side bet between two individuals, one who writes the option and the other who buys it, it has no effect on the value of the underlying firm or its equity.

2. Sequential Compound Options

Most applications of real options are sequential compound options where an earlier option must be exercised in order to keep later options open. An example is a research and development program, where there are at least three phases of testing. If the first phase fails and the abandonment option is exercised, then the second and third phases are not going to happen. If further investment is made, the project moves into phase two. Other examples of phased investments that are really sequential compound options are new product development, exploration and production, and the phased construction of manufacturing facilities.

One of the more important aspects of the economics of sequential compound options is that the underlying for each phase is the phase that follows it chronologically in time. (See Copeland and Antikarov [2001].) Let's use a multiphase construction project to illustrate. Suppose a firm is considering whether or not to start construction of a large chemical plant. There will be three phases: the design phase costs $200 million and takes a year to complete, the engineering phase costs $300 million and takes another full year to complete, and the final construction phase costs $700 million and takes a third year to complete. The project can be abandoned at the end of each phase. The decision about whether to abandon or to invest after the design phase depends on the payouts that can be obtained from the engineering phase, and the decision about whether to abandon or invest in the engineering phase depends on the payouts of the construction phase. Therefore, the second phase chronologically (the engineering phase) is the underlying for the first phase (the design phase), and the third phase (construction) is the underlying for the second (engineering).

If the option to abandon at each phase is ignored, then we have a standard NPV analysis:

$$NPV = \$1,000 - 200 - 300(1+k)^{-1} - 700(1+k)^{-2}$$

$$= \$1,000 - 200 - 272.7 - 578.5$$

$$= -\$51.2,$$

Figure 9.12 An American call valued as a simultaneous compound option.

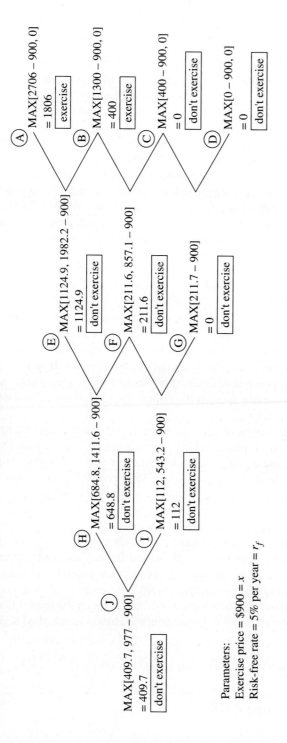

Parameters:
Exercise price = \$900 = x
Risk-free rate = 5% per year = r_f

Figure 9.13 Present value tree for a two-phase project.

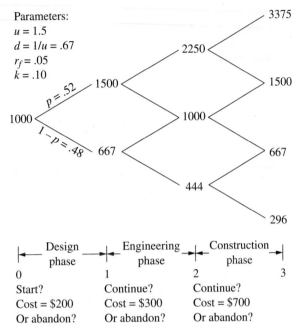

Parameters:
$u = 1.5$
$d = 1/u = .67$
$r_f = .05$
$k = .10$

```
                                                    3375
                                          2250
                                 1500            1500
    p = .52
1000                    1000
    1 − p = .48   667             667
                        444
                                                    296
```

├── Design phase ──┤	├── Engineering phase ──┤	├── Construction phase ──┤
0	1	2	3
Start?	Continue?	Continue?	
Cost = $200	Cost = $300	Cost = $700	
Or abandon?	Or abandon?	Or abandon?	

where the investment costs are discounted to the present at the cost of capital and deducted from the $1,000 present value. The NPV without taking flexibility into account is negative; therefore the project would be rejected.

Figure 9.13 shows the present value of the cash flows of the project if it were completed and in operation. The present value is $1,000, but due to uncertain prices, it could increase by 50% or decrease by 33.3% in a year. The cost of capital is 10%, and the risk-free rate is 5%.

Figure 9.14 is the present value tree for the second option chronologically, that is, the option to construct the project at an expense of $700 or to abandon. The amount of investment is the exercise price on a European call that may be exercised only at the beginning of the third year. Note that the value of the option is calculated all the way back to the present even though the option does not exist until the beginning of year two. This is done because we need to know the hypothetical value of this option during the first year in order to value the first option. At the beginning of the third year (nodes E, F, and G) we would decide to invest in the option only in the two higher states of nature. Because this is a European option, it cannot be exercised at any other time. Using risk-neutral probabilities to work backward in time through the tree, we find that the value of the second option is $497 at present.

Last but not least, we construct the binomial lattice for the first chronological option and use the second option as its underlying risky asset. The result is found in Fig. 9.15(a). At the beginning of the second year we have a European option that allows us to enter the engineering phase at a cost of $300, or to abandon. We will invest if the up state occurs and abandon otherwise. Figure 9.15(b) shows the initial investment decision and that the NPV of the project with flexibility is positive $87. The value of flexibility has added $138 to the project.

Figure 9.14 Value tree for the second chronological option (construction phase).

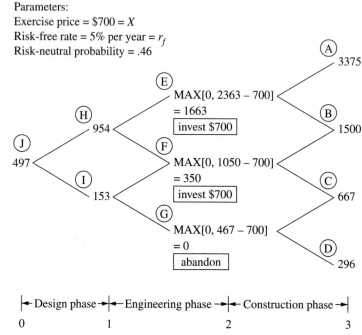

Parameters:
Exercise price = $700 = X$
Risk-free rate = 5% per year = r_f
Risk-neutral probability = .46

(A) 3375

(E)
MAX[0, 2363 − 700]
= 1663
invest $700

(H)
954

(B) 1500

(J)
497

(F)
MAX[0, 1050 − 700]
= 350
invest $700

(I)
153

(C) 667

(G)
MAX[0, 467 − 700]
= 0
abandon

(D) 296

|← Design phase →|← Engineering phase →|← Construction phase →|
0   1   2   3

Figure 9.15 Value trees for the first chronological option (engineering phase) and the initial decision.

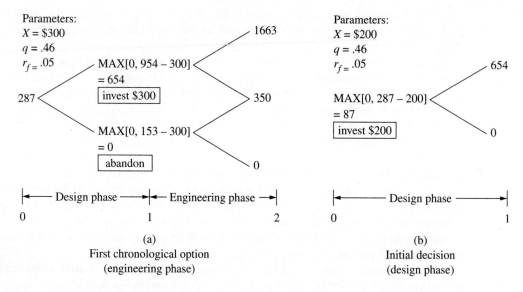

Parameters:
$X = \$300$
$q = .46$
$r_f = .05$

MAX[0, 954 − 300]
= 654
invest $300

287

1663

350

MAX[0, 153 − 300]
= 0
abandon

0

|←——— Design phase ———→|←— Engineering phase —→|
0   1   2

(a)
First chronological option
(engineering phase)

Parameters:
$X = \$200$
$q = .46$
$r_f = .05$

654

MAX[0, 287 − 200]
= 87
invest $200

0

|←——— Design phase ———→|
0   1

(b)
Initial decision
(design phase)

H. $\mathcal{S}$witching Options

Switching options provide the decision maker with the right to switch from one mode of operation to another, usually at a cost. One example is the right to shut down operations when demand shifts down and reopen at a later date. Another is the right to exit and then reenter an industry. Power companies use switching options to value peak load capacity plants because the gas-fired turbines are left idle until the spot price of electricity passes a threshold and are left on to supply electricity during the peak until prices fall to normal levels again.

The extraction of heavy oil (i.e., oil that is too viscous to pump from below ground) is best conceptualized as a switching option. Live steam must be pumped into the oil reservoir to thin it enough for pumping. The cost of the live steam may be considered a fixed cost akin to opening a mine. Basic economics would suggest that if the oil well is currently in operation, it should be shut down when marginal revenue (the price per barrel) is less than marginal cost (the extraction cost per barrel). However, were the operator to do this, the fixed cost would be lost the instant that the price per barrel fell below the extraction cost—an unwise move because there is a 50-50 chance that the marginal revenue will go up in the next instant and the well would have to be reopened. Therefore, our intuition instructs us that we should continue to operate the well at a loss until the marginal revenue falls low enough so that the present value of expected losses from remaining in operation equals the cost of shutting down.

The valuation of switching options follows similar logic, but is somewhat more complicated because when fixed costs of switching are material, the decision tree becomes path dependent. Margrabe [1978] and Fisher [1978] provided the first solution to valuing the right to exchange one risky asset for another in a world without switching costs. The exercise price for a call on the first asset became the random market value of the second asset. Their formula is

$$C(S_A, S_B, T) = S_A N(d_1) - S_B N(d_2), \tag{9.1}$$

where

$$d_1 = [\ln(S_A/S_B) + V^2 T]/V\sqrt{T},$$

$$d_2 = d_1 - V\sqrt{T},$$

$$V^2 = V_A^2 - 2\rho_{AB} V_A V_B + V_B^2.$$

Note that the value of the option depends on the standard deviations of the two assets and the correlation between them. V^2 is the instantaneous proportional variance of the change in the ratio of the asset prices, S_A/S_B, and ρ_{AB} is the instantaneous correlation between them. The option is less (more) valuable as the correlation between them becomes more positive (negative).

Let's return to our lattice approach to deal with the switching option problem when there are switching costs. Suppose a company can build a factory that uses technology X alone, technology Y alone, or build a hybrid, H, that allows switching from mode X to mode Y at a cost of $15 and vice versa at a cost of $10. The initial investment in either X or Y costs $295, but the more flexible hybrid costs more, say, $302. Technology X has higher fixed costs and therefore greater volatility than Y. Figure 9.16 shows the cash flows of X and Y for two time periods. The parameters of Fig. 9.16 are determined to be mutually consistent, so that the probability of an up movement is

Figure 9.16 Cash flows from two modes of operation.

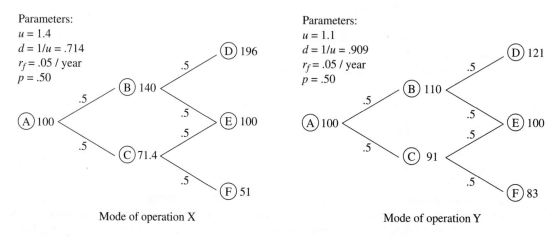

Mode of operation X   Mode of operation Y

50% in both cases, the weighted average cost of capital in mode X is 9% per year, and the risk free rate is 5% per year.

Next, we must convert the cash flows into values because our decisions are based on wealth maximization, not the maximization of cash flow in a given time period. Value trees for both fixed modes of operation are given in Figure 9.17. Starting with the value of X in the left panel, the value at node B is the expected cash flows at nodes D and E discounted at the cost of capital, 9%, that is, $[.5(196) + .5(100)]/(1.09) = 135.78]$. When the cash flow in this state of nature, $140, is added back, we have the predividend value at node B, which is $275.78. Similar calculations complete the value tree for mode of operation X. The present value of mode X is $291, and it costs $295 to construct; therefore its net present value is negative, and we would reject it.

Next, we need to value mode Y in a way that is consistent with our prior valuation of mode X. We require no arbitrage; therefore we value Y by assuming X is the underlying (perfectly correlated) risky asset. To value Y we develop a replicating portfolio with m units of X and B units of a default-free bond that pays back one plus the risk-free rate per dollar of the bond purchased at the beginning of the period. Payouts at the end of the period are the cash flows of mode Y. For example, the value at node B is estimated as follows. First, write down the replicating portfolios:

$$\text{In the up state:}\quad muV + (1+r_f)B = 121,$$

$$\text{In the down state:}\quad mdV + (1+r_f)B = 100.$$

Subtracting the second from the first and solving for m, we have

$$m = [121 - 100]/[196 - 100] = .2187.$$

Substituting into the equation of the upper state, we solve for B as

$$B = [121 - muV]/[1+r_f] = (121 - .2187(196))/(1.05) = 74.41.$$

Figure 9.17 Value tree for two modes of operation.

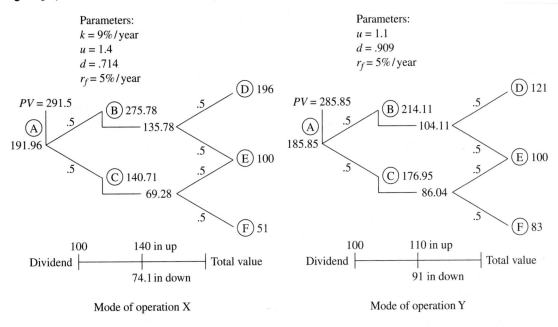

Mode of operation X   Mode of operation Y

Substituting the values of m and B into the expression for the current value of the portfolio, we have the ex-dividend value below node B in Figure 9.17:

$$\text{Ex-dividend value} = mV + B = .2187(135.78) + 74.41 = 104.11.$$

Adding in the dividend cash flow of $110, we see that the value at node B is $214.11. Solving backward through the tree, the present value of mode Y is $285.85, and since the required investment is $295, we will reject mode Y.

Mode H is a more costly hybrid that allows us to switch from mode X to Y at a cost of $15 and from Y to X for $10. These are the exercise prices of a switching option. The solution to a switching option that has positive switching costs starts with the recognition that the value tree will not be recombining, rather it will be *path dependent*. It makes a difference whether the project was operating in mode X or mode Y prior to the current decision node. This is illustrated in Fig. 9.18 at decision node B. If the project was in mode X to start with, and we find ourselves in the up state, then we can stay in mode X and receive $196 of cash, or we can switch to mode Y and receive $121 minus the cost of switching from mode X to Y, namely, $15, for a net of $106. In this case we would choose to stay in X. In the down state of nature, we could receive $100 if we stay in X and $100 minus $15 if we switch to Y. Again, we would receive the higher payout by choosing to stay in X. Next, we must make the alternate assumption—that the project was operating in mode Y—and reexamine our decisions. In the up state, if we stay in mode Y we receive $121, but if we switch to X we receive $196 minus a $10 cost of switching. Thus, if we

Figure 9.18 How to value hybrid technology H at node B.

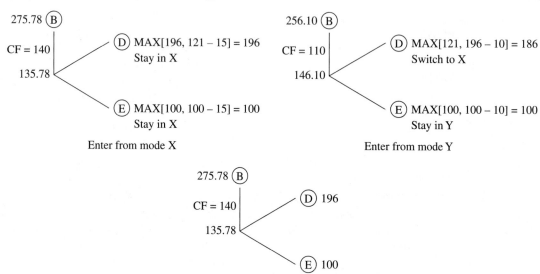

Hybrid technology

enter from Y we would choose to switch to X. In the down state, we would stay in mode Y and receive $100.

Now that we have determined the optimal end-of-period decisions, there still remains the question about whether it is better to enter the last decision state from mode X or Y. To answer this question, we compare the estimates of project value under each assumption—entering from mode X or from mode Y. Since entering from mode X has the higher value ($275.78), we chose to enter from X. The final procedure is to work backward at each node and then forward to choose the higher-valued mode of entry. This is called the *backward-forward algorithm.* The results are shown in Fig. 9.19. The value of the hybrid turns out to be $305.30 if we start operation in mode Y. Since the cost of investing in the hybrid technology is $302, the net present value is $3.30 and we would accept the project. The flexibility to switch between modes of operation is worth $302 − $291 = $11, just enough to turn the NPV positive. The intuition for starting in mode Y is simply that it costs less to switch from Y to X than vice versa.

Of the problems described above in our real options "zoo," switching problems can be among the most difficult to solve because of their path dependency. The number of paths expands rapidly (with 2^n paths given n time intervals), thereby making the problem quickly too large to handle on normal spreadsheets. Also, if the problem involves extracting an exhaustible natural resource, for example, pumping oil fast (mode X) or slow (mode Y), the binomial tree comes quickly to its end point along the uppermost branches where the supply of the resource is quickly exhausted, but may be of infinite length along lower branches where the resource is being extracted slowly or not at all.

Figure 9.19 Valuation of hybrid (switching) technology.

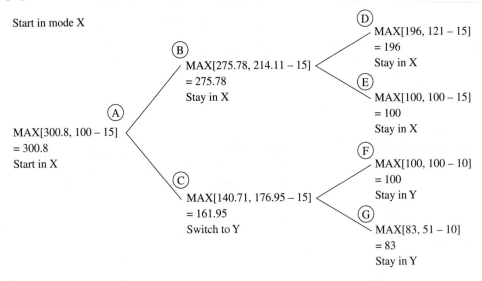

Start in mode X

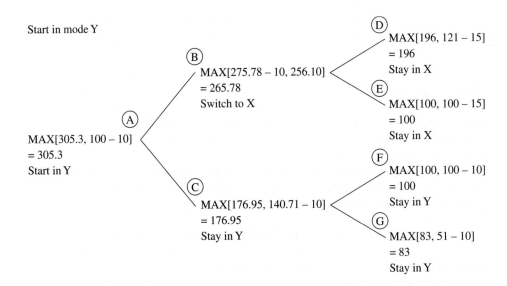

Start in mode Y

I. An Example of How to Evaluate an Investment Program

One can think of a firm as a series of projects that are constructed to provide output needed to meet expected demand. This is in contrast to thinking about projects one at a time in isolation. As usual, an example helps to clarify our point. Suppose that demand for a new type of personal

Table 9.1 Demand Matrix (units in thousands, probability in parentheses)

Present	Year 1	Year 2	Year 3
0	390 (0.435)	1,014 (0.189)	1,977 (0.082)
	231 (0.565)	600 (0.492)	1,170 (0.321)
		355 (0.319)	692 (0.417)
			410 (0.180)

computer is expected to grow rapidly from nothing currently to 300,000 units one year from now, to 600,000 units two years from now, to 900,000 units in the third year, but to fall to zero units per year after that because a new model is expected to make the current model obsolete. Furthermore, we are told that there is enormous uncertainty about demand, as illustrated in Table 9.1. In year 1 it could be as high as 1.3 times its expected value (i.e., 390,000 units), or as low as 1/1.3 times (i.e., 231,000 units).

Engineering explains that we can choose between two modes of operation: a single 900,000-unit plant with a production cost of only $1,200 per unit, or three smaller plants each with capacity of 300,000 units but a higher production cost per unit of $1,450. Note that the objective probabilities of up and down states are consistent with the expected demand. If p is the objective probability of the up state then

$$E(\text{demand}) = p(\text{demand up}) + (1 - p)\,(\text{demand down})$$

$$300 = p390 + (1 - p)(231)$$

$$p = .435.$$

Assuming that the weighted average cost of capital is 9% for the large scale plant and 8% for the three smaller scale plants, that construction costs are $900,000 and $300,000, respectively, that each plant lasts three years, that salvage value equals book, that the price per unit is $2,000, that we use straight-line depreciation, and that the risk-free rate is 5%, the net present value of the two alternatives is given in Tables 9.2 and 9.3.

When reviewing the expected output, notice that it has been calculated by recognizing that the quantity that can be supplied is the quantity demanded less a capacity cap. Formally, if we designate Q_s as the supply and Q_d as the demand, then

$$Q_s = Q_d - \text{MAX}[0,\ Q_d - \text{Capacity}]. \tag{9.2}$$

When the quantity that we are able to supply is weighted by the probability of that event, we have the actual expected output that is used in Tables 9.2 and 9.3. Note, for example, that demand in the up state of nature in year 1 is 390,000 units. If we have built the large plant we can supply all of the demand (as shown in expected output for year 1 of Table 9.2). But if we have built the small plant, we run into the capacity cap and can supply only 300,000 of the 390,000-unit demand. Therefore, in Table 9.3, expected output for year 1 is only .435(300,000) + .565(231,000) = 261,000.

The resulting NPV calculations seem to make sense at first. The larger, more efficient plant wastes some capital at first, but is ultimately of higher value than three of the less efficient smaller plants.

Table 9.2 Standard Net Present Value Calculations, Large Plant (thousands)

	Present	Year 1	Year 2	Year 3
Expected output	–	300	579	725
Price per unit	–	2	2	2
Revenue	–	600	1,158	1,450
Variable cost	–	(360)	(695)	(870)
Depreciation	–	(300)	(300)	(300)
EBIT	–	(60)	163	280
Taxes	–	24	(65)	(112)
Income	–	(36)	98	168
Depreciation	–	300	300	300
Salvage value	–	–	–	0
Capital expense	(900)	–	–	–
Cash flow	(900)	264	398	468
Discount @ 9%	1.000	0.917	0.842	0.772
Present value	(900)	242	335	361
NPV	38			

Recall from our earlier discussion, however, that NPV fails to capture the value of flexibility. There is nothing that says we must precommit to building one of the small plants each year. Instead, we can build more or less of them in response to the evolution of demand. Let's use our knowledge of real options to value the flexibility offered by an investment program that uses smaller plants. The starting point is to choose an underlying risky asset whose value without flexibility is known. For this purpose we select the precommited construction of three plants, one each year. The event tree of free cash flows is given in Fig. 9.20, and the corresponding value tree is shown in Fig. 9.21. Note that the net present value in Fig. 9.21 is the same as the net present value calculated from the expected cash flows of Table 9.3. We build a binomial tree that has the same present value as the base case and up and down movements that are based on the volatility of demand as given in the problem statement, where the state-contingent up movement is 1.3, implying a standard deviation of $\ln(1.3) = .262$, or 26.2% per year. Both the cash flow tree and the value tree for the base case are recombining binomial trees; however, notice that they step up or down at each node to reflect the necessity of putting more cash into the project (an upward step in the tree) or the receipt of cash flow from the project (a downward step). Cash flow at each node is entity cash as in the traditional definition, namely, the operating margin per unit times the number of units supplied, plus depreciation, and if salvage is initiated we also add it. The value at each node is defined as

$$\text{Value} = [(\text{objective probability of an up state} \times \text{payout in up state})$$
$$+ (1 - \text{obj. prob.}) \times (\text{payout in down state})]/(1 + WACC) + CF$$

Table 9.3 Standard Net Present Value Calculations, Three Small Plants (thousands).

	Present	Year 1	Year 2	Year 3
Expected output	–	261	522	725
Price per unit	–	2	2	2
Revenue	–	522	1,044	1,450
Variable cost	–	(378)	(757)	(1,051)
Depreciation	–	(100)	(200)	(300)
EBIT	–	44	87	99
Taxes	–	17	35	39
Income	–	26	52	59
Depreciation	–	100	200	300
Salvage value	–	–	–	300
Capital expense	(300)	(300)	(300)	–
Cash flow	(300)	(174)	(48)	659
Discount @ 8%	1.000	0.926	0.857	0.794
Present value	(300)	(161)	(41)	523
NPV	21.3			

For example, the value at node E (in Fig. 9.21)[3] is

$$\text{Value at E} = [(.435(717) + (1 - .435)(717))/1.08 - 22] = 642.$$

Working backward from its roots to its trunk in the same manner confirms that the value is $21.3 million.

Next, we want to use real options by assuming that a decision can be made at each node to either build one or more new plants, to do nothing, or to contract the scale of operations by selling one or more plants for their salvage value. The results are shown in Fig. 9.22, which gives the cash flows of the optimal solution, and Fig. 9.23, which provides the valuation. Note that the net present value is higher for the flexible solution that allows us to build the smaller, less efficient plants in response to the arrival of information about demand—higher than even the value of the larger, more efficient plant (the NPV of the flexible solution is $81 million versus $38 million for the large plant and $21.3 million for a precommitment to three plants).

The valuation calculations are based on risk-neutral probabilities of the up and down movements that are produced by finding the expected payouts based on risk-neutral probabilities that when discounted at the risk-free rate, 5%, give the same value as the expected payouts based on objective

---

[3] Professor Yihang Xia at the University of Pennsylvania has pointed out that although the calculations of the NPV of the project seem to be correct in terms of DCF valuation, node E in Fig. 9.21 admits an arbitrage opportunity because the end-of-period value will be $717 in both the up and down states. Therefore, the value of the project would be bid up by rational investors to $717/1.05 = $683. This arbitrage is the result of the fact that we chose the cost of capital arbitrarily—another danger with using NPV, and also because we do not price the underlying as the value of the unconstrained investment less the value of a capacity cap (a call). The example is already complicated, so we decided to keep it as is, hoping that our point about the value of flexibility is not lost in the details.

Figure 9.20 Event tree showing the cash flows for the three-plant precommited base case.

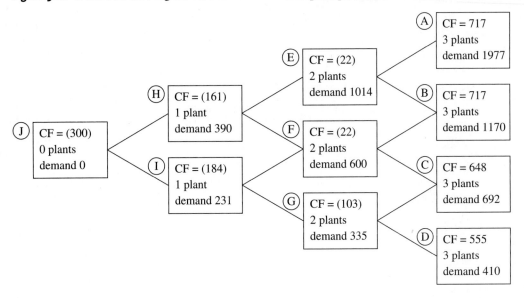

Figure 9.21 Event tree showing the value of the three-plant precommited base case.

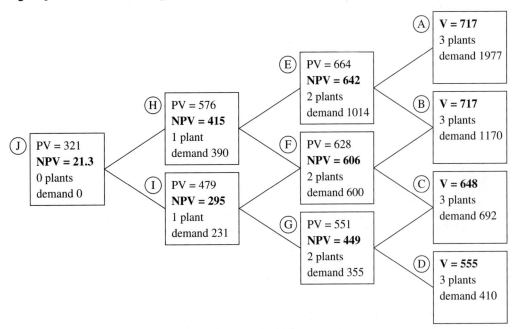

Figure 9.22 Free cash flows for the small plant flexible investment case.

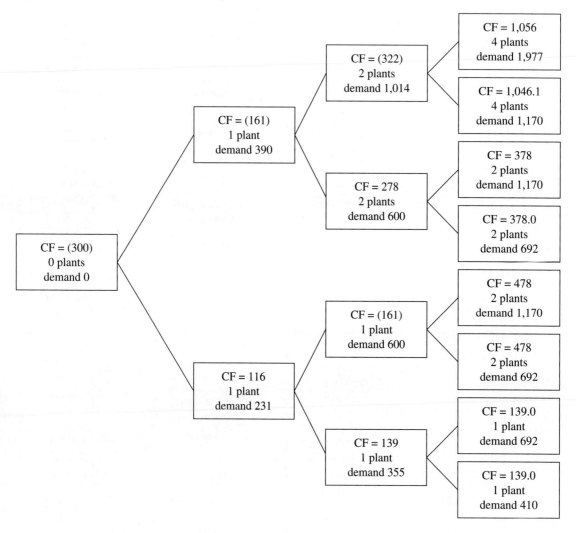

probabilities, discounted at the weighted average cost of capital, 8%. Denoting the risk-neutral up probability as q, we have

$$V = [p(\text{up payout}) + (1 - p)(\text{down payout})]/(1 + WACC) = [q(\text{up}) + (1 - q)(\text{down})]/(1 + r_f).$$

Substituting in numbers from the third and fourth uppermost paths of the three-plant base case (the only states of nature where output is not capped), we have:

$$551 = [.435(648) + .565(555)]/1.08 = [q(648) + (1 - q)(555)]/1.05$$

$$q = .26.$$

Figure 9.23 Valuation of the small plant flexible investment case.

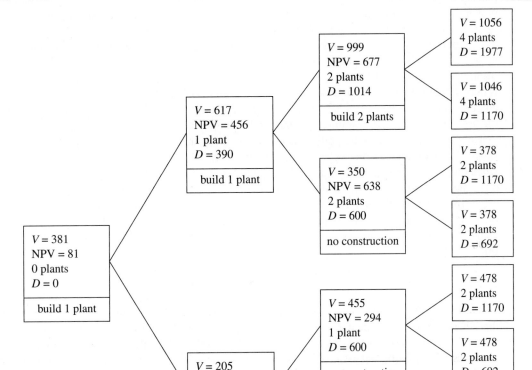

The actual decision tree will be path dependent (i.e., nonrecombining) because the cash flow this year depends on knowing what the investments were in prior years all the way back to the beginning. To decide on how many plants to build this year it becomes necessary to know the depreciation on all plants that were built earlier.

To solve the problem one starts with the optimal solution, N_i plants, at each end node of the eight possible paths in this three-period problem, then goes to the previous node and assumes that there were $N - 1$, $N + 1$, $N - 2$, $N + 2$, etc. plants, resolving the end node problem for each of the possible starting points. This is called a *backward-forward algorithm*. Use the upper path in Fig. 9.23 as an example. In year 3, the top path has a demand of 1,977 in the up state, and 1,170 in the down state. Since the demand is so high in the up state, the firm may decide to operate five plants in this period. In this case, the up state will have a cash flow of 1,395, and the down state will have a cash flow of 1,343.5. Since the firm had two plants in year 2, it had to build three plants for year 3, producing a cash flow of −622. Solving for the value in year 2 using risk-neutral probabilities yields a value of 665. Likewise, if the firm decides to operate only three plants in year 3, the value at year 2 will be 660. As shown in Fig. 9.23, operating four plants in year 3 produces a value of 679. This is the optimal solution for this state, given that there are two plants operating in year 2. Note that if there are three plants operating in year 2, five plants would be the optimal solution for the top branch in year 3. However, using the same mechanism, we find that two plants is the optimal solution for year 2, one plant is the optimal solution for year 1, and so forth. Having completed the analysis for the last period, we move back to the second period and forward from the first, iterating until the optimal sequence is determined along each of the eight paths.

How does the value of flexibility change as we vary the parameters of the problem? First, suppose that we increase the volatility of demand. Surprisingly, the value of flexibility declines when fluctuations in demand increase. This result can be explained by the fact that higher demand on the up side becomes constrained quickly by plant capacity. Thus, the lumpiness of plant capacity provides a "cap" on the supply of output. In effect, the underlying risky asset for our analysis is the distribution of payoffs where every unit of demand is matched by a unit of supply, less the value of a call option whose exercise price is determined by plant capacity. This was explained by Eq. (9.2):

$$Q_s = Q_d - \text{MAX}[0, Q_d - Q_c].$$

The impact on the value of the flexible solution of increasing the operating margin, of increasing the salvage value, and of increasing the growth rate are straightforward and intuitive. Increases in any of these three variables have the effect of increasing value. One interesting observation is that, if we maintain the original assumptions but decrease the salvage value to zero, then the value of the flexible solution declines from $81 million to $62 million, but still is more valuable than the large fixed plant (i.e., $38 million).

J. Empirical Evidence

There is not much empirical evidence concerning the correctness and accuracy of any capital budgeting methodology, let alone real options. However, a survey of roughly 4,000 chief financial officers by Graham and Harvey [2001] reports that 27% of the respondents to their survey used real options for major investment decisions either all of the time or most of the time. While encouraging, this is not even close to the 90+% who use net present value or internal rate of return. The adoption of real options, like the growth in the popularity of spreadsheet-based discounted cash flow valuation before it, seems to be waiting for the development of a truly transparent and useful computerized program to bear the heavy lifting in the analysis.

In order to resolve the debate about whether NPV or real options does a better job of forecasting actual market prices of real options, we searched the literature and found four articles. Chronologically, the first was written by Paddock, Siegel, and Smith [1988]. They collected data on company bids to develop offshore oil leases offered by the government, then calculated the value of each lease using net present value methodology, and compared the result with the real options value—a value based on deferral. The answers provided by the two methodologies were highly correlated, but the real options values came closer to the market transaction price than did the NPV estimate. Yet the evidence is not strong because neither approach was very close to the market price. Some believe that the "winner's curse" drove up the transaction prices, and others believe that the option to prove out the reserves in the ground by drilling—a learning option—outweighed the deferral option, yet was not estimated in the paper.

Bailey [1991] reasoned that the option to close and then reopen commodity plantations producing rubber and palm oil was particularly important in these highly cyclical businesses. Using data from seven companies for the period 1983–1985, he valued them using ordinary DCF and using real options. In six out of seven cases, the real option valuations were closer to the actual market price than DCF-based prices. However, the difference was statistically significant in only two of the seven.

Using a database of 2,700 land transactions in Seattle, Quigg [1993] built a model that incorporates the value of being able to wait to develop the land. The owner of undeveloped property has a perpetual option to decide on exactly the right time to construct an optimal-sized building. Quigg built an option model that used two sources of uncertainty—the development cost (the exercise price) and the price of the building (the underlying asset). The sample of data subdivided transactions into five categories: commercial, business, industrial, and high- and low-density residential. Second, property prices were estimated using regressions containing as independent variables data on building and lot sizes, building height and age, and dummy variables for location and season. A third step used the error terms from the regressions to estimate the variances needed to price the options, and finally she calculated the implied option prices assuming that the building would be built (i.e., that the option to develop would be exercised), when the ratio of its estimated market price relative to its development cost became greater than (one plus) the market rate of interest.

Quigg's results support the real options model vis-a-vis discounted cash flow. The option prices were, on average, 6% above the intrinsic value suggested by the regressions. When the option values were compared to the intrinsic values as explanators of actual transaction prices in the marketplace, the option model had a higher r-squared in 9 of 15 cases. Furthermore, when the option premium was added to the multiple regression, it was significant in 14 out of 15 cases.

Moel and Tufano [2002] studied the opening and closing decisions of 285 developed gold mines in North America during the period 1988–1997. They find strong evidence to support the conclusion that openings and closings are better explained by real (switching) options than other approaches. As predicted by the real options model, mine closings are influenced by the price of gold, its volatility, costs of operating the mine, proxies for closing costs, and the amount of estimated reserves.

Summary

Real options is one of the most important corporate finance decision-making tools to have been introduced in the last 30 or 40 years. It captures the present value of flexibility of managerial decisions at a future date in response to the arrival of new information. Traditional net present value methodology implicitly assumes precommitment—that is, no flexibility. Yet most applications of real options are more realistic and therefore more complicated models of reality. We showed how to value deferral, expansion, contraction, abandonment, compound, and switching options. Our basic assumptions were the MAD (marketed asset disclaimer) assumption that allows us to treat the traditional present value of the project without flexibility as though it were a marketed twin security, the no-arbitrage assumption that allows correct pricing via the formation of replicating portfolios, and the proof that properly anticipated prices fluctuate randomly—a proposition that allows us to model the present value of any pattern of future cash flows whatsoever as a geometric Brownian motion process.

To apply real options in practice, there is much that remains to study. For example, we have not looked at how to develop spreadsheets to do the work. We have not discussed methods for using historical data or forward-looking subjective estimates of risk to provide the crucial "up" and "down" parameters of a binomial tree. We have not covered ways of combining correlated uncertainties via a Monte Carlo process. For coverage of these topics, we refer the interested reader to Copeland and Antikarov [2001].

The theory of real options is not without its own limitations. Most significant among them is the fact that risk is assumed to be exogenous. In other words, decisions made are assumed to be without competitive reaction. While there has been some work on endogenizing elements of game theory into a real options setting, or vice versa (for example, see Smit and Ankum [1993]), much remains to be done.

PROBLEM SET

9.1 A project runs for two periods and then is sold at a fair price. Its present value without flexibility is $30 million, and the initial investment is $20 million. The annual volatility of the project's present value is expected to be 15% and its WACC is 12%. At the end of the second period there is an option to expand, increasing the value of the project by 20% by investing an additional $5 million. The risk-free rate is 5%.

  (a) What is the project's NPV without the option to expand?
  (b) What is its ROA with the option to expand?

9.2 A company operates under a hard budget constraint and has a WACC of 12%. In the current year it can spend a maximum of $80 million on a new investment. The management is considering two alternative projects: project 1 and project 2. Each of the two projects would run for two years and be sold at a fair price. Both of the projects require an $80 million initial investment and have present values without flexibility equal to $100 million. However, project 1 has an annual volatility of 40%, and project 2 has an annual volatility of 20%. Both projects allow the management to contract operations by 40% at any time during the next two years. With project 1 the cash received from contracting would be $33 million, and with project 2 it would be $42 million. The risk-free rate is 5%.

  (a) Using a decision tree analysis (DTA), answer the following questions: Which project should the company select? When and under what conditions would the options to contract be executed with each project? What is the value of the option to contract with project 1? What is the value of the option to contract with project 2?
  (b) Using real option analysis (ROA), answer the following questions: Which project should the company select? When and under what conditions would the options to contract be executed with each project? What is the value of the option to contract with project 1? What is the value of the option to contract with project 2?
  (c) Do the DTA and ROA valuation results suggest the same optimal execution for the options? Do the DTA and ROA valuations show the same value for each of the two projects? Do the DTA and ROA valuations select the same project as a winner?

9.3 Two companies are developing a 50-50 joint venture with an NPV of $25 million. The annual volatility of the venture is 20% and its WACC is 12%. The risk-free rate is 5%. One of the companies wants to buy the right from the other to acquire its 50% share in a year for $15 million.

(a) Using a two-period model (six months per period), what is the maximum price the company should be ready to pay for the option?

(b) Using a three-period model (four months per period), how does the option price change?

(c) How can we use the Black-Scholes formula to solve this problem? What is the option price if we use the Black-Scholes formula?

(d) Which of the three prices would you use to make a decision and why?

(e) What price would you use if the buyer wants the right to buy the share at any time during the year?

9.4 Using simple binomial trees, calculate the value of a European put option with the following characteristics:

Underlying asset current value = 200.
Abandonment value = 175.
Up movement per period = 1.75, $d = 1/u$.
Risk-free rate = 10%.
Time to expiration = 2 years.
Number of time periods per year = 1.

The steps you will need to follow include

Create the event tree for the underlying risky asset.
Calculate whether to exercise the option on the end nodes of the option valuation tree.
Use replicating portfolio technique to value the option.

9.5 Using simple binomial trees, calculate the value of a call option with the following characteristics:

Underlying asset current value = 1,000.
Option exercise price = 1,250.
Per-period dividends = 10% of asset value.
Up movement per period = 1.5, $d = 1/u$.
Risk-free rate = 10%.
Time to expiration = 2 years.
Number of time periods per year = 1.

The steps you will need to follow include

Create the event tree for the underlying risky asset.
Calculate whether to exercise the option on the end nodes of the option valuation tree.
Use replicating portfolio technique to value the option.

9.6 Using simple binomial trees, calculate the value of a call option with the following characteristics:

Underlying asset current value = 100.
Option exercise price in period 1 = 110.
Option exercise price in period 2 = 150.
Up movement in period 1 = 1.2, $d = 1/u$.
Up movement in period 2 = 1.4, $d = 1/u$.
Risk-free rate in period 1 = 10%.
Risk-free rate in period 2 = 8%.
Time to expiration = 2 years.
Number of time periods per year = 1.

The steps you will need to follow include

Create the event tree for the underlying risky asset.
Calculate whether to exercise the option on the end nodes of the option valuation tree.
Use replicating portfolio technique to value the option.

9.7 Using simple binomial trees, calculate the value of a combined call and put option with the following characteristics:

Underlying asset current value = 2,000.
Contraction option = 50% reduction in value.
Savings from contracting = 450.
Expansion option = 15% increase in value.
Exercise price to expand = 100.
Up movement per period = 1.15, $d = 1/u$.
Risk-free rate = 10%.
Time to expiration = 2 years.
Number of time periods per year = 1.

The steps you will need to follow include

Create the event tree for the underlying risky asset.
Calculate whether to exercise either option on the end nodes of the option valuation tree.
Use replicating portfolio technique to value the option.

9.8 The value of a mineral extraction project depends on the inventory in the ground (12,000 tons), the price in the spot market (currently $20 per ton), the cost of capital (12%), the risk-free rate (5% per year), the rate of extraction (4,000 tons per year), and the extraction cost ($22 per ton). Additionally, there is a 50-50 chance the price can go up by 50% or down by $33\frac{1}{3}\%$ in a year. The cost of opening up is $20,000, while the cost of shutting down is $30,000. Should the mine start open or closed, and what is the optimal rule for shutting it down? What is its value? How does the answer change if the price of the mineral is currently $26?

9.9 Suppose that we have a firm whose current value is $1,000 and that (given a multiplicative stochastic process) its value could go up by 12.75% or down by 11.31%—a standard deviation of 12% per annum. The risk-free rate is 8%. The equity of this firm is subordinate to debt that has a face value of $800 maturing in three years and that pays no coupons. What is the value of an American call option written on the equity if its exercise price is $400 and it matures in three years?

9.10 Assume the stochastic process for the value of the firm as shown in Fig. Q9.10 (it might be the present value of a project that has several investment phases). There are two call options in sequence. The first has an exercise price of $400, the investment required to move to the next phase at the end of year 1 when the option expires. It allows us to decide whether to abandon the project or continue by making an additional investment. The second has an exercise price of $800 and expires at the end of year 3. Given this information, solve the problem using a sequential compound option.

Figure Q9.10 Firm value event tree.

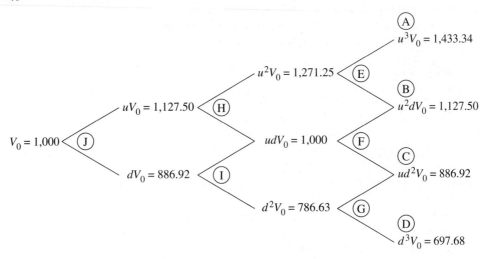

REFERENCES

Abel, A., A. Dixit, J. Eberly, and R. Pindyck, "Options, the Value of Capital, and Investment," *Quarterly Journal of Economics*, August 1996, 753–777.

Bailey, W., "Valuing Agriculture Firms," *Journal of Economic Dynamics and Control*, Vol. 15, 1991, 771–791.

Baldwin, C. Y., "Optimal Sequential Investment When Capital Is Not Readily Reversible," *Journal of Finance*, Vol. 37, No. 3, June 1982, 763–782.

Berger, P., E. Ofek, and I. Swary, "Investor Valuation of the Abandonment Option," *Journal of Financial Economics*, Vol. 42, No. 2, October 1996, 257–287.

Bhattacharya, S., "Project Valuation with Mean-Reverting Cash Flow Streams," *Journal of Finance*, Vol. 33, No. 5, 1978, 1317–1331.

Bjerksund, P., and S. Ekern, "Contingent Claims Evaluation of Mean-Reverting Cash Flows in Shipping," in L. Trigeorgis, ed., *Real Options in Capital Investments*, Praeger, New York, 1995.

———, "Managing Investment Opportunities under Price Uncertainty: From Last Chance to Wait and See Strategies," *Financial Management*, Autumn 1990, 65–83.

Black, F., and M. Scholes, "The Pricing of Options and Corporate Liabilities," *Journal of Political Economy*, May–June 1973.

Bonini, C., "Capital Investment under Uncertainty with Abandonment Options," *Journal of Financial and Quantitative Analysis*, March 1977, 39–54.

Boyle, P., "Options: A Monte Carlo Approach," *Journal of Financial Economics*, May 1977, 323–338.

———, "A Lattice Framework for Option Pricing with Two State Variables," *Journal of Financial and Quantitative Analysis*, Vol. 23, No. 1, 1988, 1–12.

Brennan, M., and E. Schwartz, "Evaluating Natural Resource Investments," *Journal of Business*, Vol. 58, No. 2, 1985, 135–157.

Brennan, M., and L. Trigeorgis, eds., *Product Flexibility, Agency and Product Market Competition: New Development in the Theory and Application of Real Option Analysis*, Oxford University Press, Oxford, 1999.

Capozza, D., and Y. Li, "The Intensity and Timing of Investment: The Case of Land," *American Economic Review*, Vol. 84, No. 4, 1994, 889–904.

Carr, P., "The Valuation of Sequential Exchange Opportunities," *Journal of Finance*, Vol. 43, No. 5, December 1988, 1235–1256.

———, "The Valuation of American Exchange Options with Application to Real Options," in L. Trigeorgis, ed., *Real Options in Capital Investments*, Praeger, New York, 1995.

Chang, C., and J. Chang, "Option Pricing with Stochastic Volatility: Information-time versus Calendar-time," *Management Science*, Vol. 42, No. 7, 1996, 974–991.

Chorn, L., and P. Carr, "The Value of Purchasing Information to Reduce Risk in Capital Investment Projects," SPE Paper No. 37948, presented at SPE Hydrocarbon Economics and Evaluation Symposium, Dallas, March 16–18, 1997.

Copeland, T., and V. Antikarov, *Real Options: A Practitioner's Guide*, Texere, New York, 2001.

Copeland, T., and J. F. Weston, "A Note on the Evaluation of Cancellable Operating Leases," *Financial Management*, Summer 1982, 60–67.

Cortazar, G., and E. Schwartz, "A Compound Option Model of Production and Intermediate Inventories," *Journal of Business*, Vol. 66, No. 4, 1993, 517–540.

Cox, J., S. Ross, and M. Rubinstein, "Option Pricing: A Simplified Approach," *Journal of Financial Economics*, September 1979.

Dixit, A., "Entry and Exit Decisions under Uncertainty," *Journal of Political Economy*, Vol. 97, No. 3, 1989, 620–638.

Dixit, A., and R. Pindyck, *Investment under Uncertainty*, Princeton University Press, Princeton, N.J., 1994.

———, "The Options Approach to Capital Investment," *Harvard Business Review*, May–June 1995, 105–115.

Fisher, S., "Call Option Pricing When the Exercise Price Is Uncertain and the Valuation of Index Bonds," *Journal of Finance*, March 1978, 169–186.

Gesne, R., "The Valuation of Corporate Liabilities as Compound Options," *Journal of Financial and Quantitative Analysis*, November 1977, 541–552.

Graham, J., and C. Harvey, "The Theory and Practice of Corporate Finance: Evidence from the Field," *Journal of Financial Economics*, Vol. 60, 2001, 187–243.

Greenley, D., R. Walsh, and R. Young, "Option Value: Empirical Evidence from a Case Study of Recreation and Water Quality," *Quarterly Journal of Economics*, Vol. 96, 1981, 657–673.

Grenadier, S., "Valuing Lease Contracts: An Real-Options Approach," *Journal of Financial Economics*, No. 38, 1995, 297–331.

Hull, J., and A. White, "The Pricing of Options on Assets with Stochastic Volatilities," *Journal of Finance*, Vol. 42, No. 2, 1987, 281–300.

Hurn, A. S., and R. E. Wright, "Geology or Economics? Testing Models of Irreversible Investment Using North Sea Oil Data," *The Economic Journal*, March 1994.

Ingersoll, J., and S. Ross, "Waiting to Invest: Investment and Uncertainty," *Journal of Business*, Vol. 65, No. 1, 1992, 1–29.

Kaslow, T., and R. Pindyck, "Valuing Flexibility in Utility Planning," *The Electricity Journal*, Vol. 7, March 1994, 60–65.

Kemna, A., "Case Studies on Real Options," *Financial Management*, Autumn 1993, 259–270.

Kester, W., "Today's Options for Tomorrow's Growth," *Harvard Business Review*, Vol. 62, No. 2, March–April 1984, 153–160.

Kogut, B., "Joint Ventures and the Option to Acquire and to Expand," *Management Science*, Vol. 37, No. 1, 1991, 19–33.

Kulatilaka, N., "The Value of Flexibility: The Case of a Dual-Fuel Industrial Steam Boiler," *Financial Management*, Autumn 1993, 271–280.

———, "The Value of Flexibility: A General Model of Real Options," in L. Trigeorgis, ed., *Real Options in Capital Investments*, Praeger Publishing, New York, 1995.

Kulatilaka, N., and A. Markus, "Project Valuation under Uncertainty: When Does DCF Fail?" *Journal of Applied Corporate Finance*, Fall 1992, 92–100.

Majd, S., and R. Pindyck, "Time to Build, Option Value, and Investment Decisions," *Journal of Financial Economics*, No. 18, 1987, 7–27.

McDonald, R., and D. Siegel, "Investment and the Valuation of Firms When There Is an Option of Shutdown," *International Economic Review*, Vol. 28, No. 2, 1985, 331–349.

———, "The Value of Waiting to Invest," *Quarterly Journal of Economics*, November 1986, 707–727.

Margrabe, W., "The Value of an Option to Exchange One Asset for Another," *Journal of Finance*, Vol. 33, No. 1, March 1978, 177–186.

Merville, L., and C. Mishra, "Capital Investment and Firm Leverage: A Corporate Real Options Approach," *Research in Finance*, Vol. 9, JAI Press, 1991, 49–73.

Mitchell, G., and W. Hamilton, "Managing R&D as a Strategic Option," *Research Management*, Vol. 31, May–June 1988, 15–22.

Moel, A., and P. Tufano, "When Are Real Options Exercised: An Empirical Study of Mine Closings," *Review of Financial Studies*, Vol. 15, 2002, 35–64.

Morck, R., E. Schwartz, and D. Strangeland, "The Valuation of Forestry Resources under Stochastic Prices and Inventories," *Journal of Financial and Quantitative Analysis*, No. 24, 473–487.

Myers, S., and S. Majd. "Abandonment Value and Project Life," *Advances in Futures and Operations Research*, Vol. 4, 1990, 1–21.

Omberg, E., "A Note on the Convergence of the Binomial Pricing and Compound Option Models," *The Journal of Finance*, Vol. 42, No. 2, 1987, 463–469.

Paddock, J., J. Siegel, and J. Smith, "Option Valuation of Claims on Real Assets: The Case of Offshore Petroleum Leases," *Quarterly Journal of Economics*, August 1988, 479–508.

Pindyck, R., "Irreversible Investment, Capacity Choice, and the Value of the Firm," *American Economic Review*, Vol. 78, No. 5, December 1988, 969–985.

———, "Irreversibility, Uncertainty and Investment," *Journal of Economic Literature*, Vol. 28, 1991, 1110–1148.

———, "A Note on Competitive Investment under Uncertainty," *American Economic Review*, No. 83, 1993, 273–277.

Quigg, L., "Empirical Testing of Real Option Pricing Models," *Journal of Finance*, Vol. 48, No. 2, 1993, 621–640.

Rao, R., and J. Martin, "Another Look at the Use of Option Pricing Theory to Evaluate Real Asset Investment Opportunity," *Journal of Business Finance and Accounting*, Vol. 8, No. 3, 1981, 421–429.

Ritchkin, P., and G. Rabinowitz, "Capital Budgeting Using Contingent Claims Analysis: A Tutorial," *Advances in Futures and Options Research*, Vol. 3, 1988, 119–143.

Rubinstein, M., "The Valuation of Uncertain Income Streams and the Pricing of Options," *Bell Journal of Economics*, Vol. 7, No. 2, 1976, 407–425.

———, "Implied Binomial Trees," *Journal of Finance*, Vol. 69, No. 3, 1994, 771–818.

Samuelson, P. A., "Proof That Properly Anticipated Prices Fluctuate Randomly," *Industrial Management Review*, Spring 1965, 41–49.

Scarso, E., "Timing the Adoption of a New Technology: An Option-Based Approach," *Management Decision*, Vol. 34, No. 3, 41–48.

Shilling, J., C. Sirmans, G. Turnbull, and J. Benjamin, "A Theory and Empirical Test of Land Option Pricing," *Journal of Urban Economics*, Vol. 28, 1990, 178–186.

Smit, H., and L. Ankum, "A Real-Options and Game-Theoretic Approach to Corporate Investment Strategy under Competition," *Financial Management*, Autumn 1993, 241–250.

Smith, K., and A. Triantis, "The Value of Options in Strategic Acquisitions," in L. Trigeorgis, ed., *Real Options in Capital Investments*, Praeger, New York, 1995.

Stapleton, R., and M. Subrahmanyam, "The Valuation of Options When Asset Returns Are Generated by a Binomial Process," *Journal of Finance*, Vol. 39, No. 5, 1984, 1525–1539.

Titman, S., "Urban Land Prices under Uncertainty," *American Economic Review*, Vol. 75, June 1985, 505–514.

Triantis, A., and J. Hodder, "Valuing Flexibility as a Complex Option," *Journal of Finance*, Vol. 45, No. 2, 1990, 549–565.

Trigeorgis, L., "A Conceptual Options Framework for Capital Budgeting," *Advances in Futures and Options Research*, Vol. 3, 1988, 145–167.

———, "A Real Options Application in Natural Resource Investments," *Advances in Futures and Options Research*, Vol. 4, 1990, 153–164.

———, "Anticipated Competitive Entry and Early Preemptive Investment in Deferrable Projects," *Journal of Economics and Business*, Vol. 43, No. 2, 1991a, 143–156.

———, "A Log-Transformed Binomial Numerical Analysis Method for Valuing Complex Multi-Option Investment," *Journal of Financial and Quantitative Analysis*, 1991b, 309–326.

———, "The Nature of Options Interactions and the Valuation of Investments with Multiple Real Options," *Journal of Financial and Quantitative Analysis*, Vol. 28, No. 1, 1993a, 1–20.

———, "Real Options and Interactions with Flexibility," *Financial Management*, Vol. 22, No. 3, Autumn 1993b, 202–222.

Trigeorgis, L., ed., *Real Options in Capital Investments: Models, Strategies and Applications*, Praeger Publishers, Westport, Conn., 1995.

———, *Real Options: Managerial Flexibility and Strategy in Resource Allocation*, MIT Press, Cambridge, MA, 1996.

Vijverberg, W., "Monte Carlo Evaluation of Multivariate Normal Probabilities," *Journal of Econometrics*, Vol. 76, 1997, 281–307.

Winston, W., *Simulation Modelling Using @Risk*, Duxbury Press, 1996.

Zinkham, F., "Option Pricing and Timberland's Land-Use Conversion Option," *Land Economics*, Vol. 67, 1991, 317–325.

Chapter 10

In a world of uncertainty, information becomes a useful commodity—acquisition of information to eliminate uncertainty should then be considered as an alternative to productive investment subject to uncertainty.

—J. Hirshleifer, *Investment, Interest, and Capital*, Prentice-Hall, Englewood Cliffs, N.J., 1970, 311.

Efficient Capital Markets: Theory

A. Defining Capital Market Efficiency

THE PURPOSE OF CAPITAL MARKETS is to transfer funds between lenders (savers) and borrowers (producers) efficiently. Individuals or firms may have access to productive investment opportunities with anticipated rates of return that exceed the market-determined borrowing rate but not enough funds to take advantage of all these opportunities. However, if capital markets exist, they can borrow the needed funds. Lenders, who have excess funds after exhausting all their productive opportunities with expected returns greater than the borrowing rate, will be willing to lend their excess funds because the borrowing/lending rate is higher than what they might otherwise earn. Therefore both borrowers and lenders are better off if efficient capital markets are used to facilitate fund transfers. The borrowing/lending rate is used as an important piece of information by each producer, who will accept projects until the rate of return on the least profitable project just equals the opportunity cost of external funds (the borrowing/lending rate). Thus a market is said to be *allocationally efficient* when prices are determined in a way that equates the *marginal* rates of return (adjusted for risk) for all producers and savers. In an allocationally efficient market, scarce savings are optimally allocated to productive investments in a way that benefits everyone.

To describe efficient capital markets it is useful, first of all, to contrast them with *perfect capital markets*. The following conditions may be considered as necessary for perfect capital markets:

- Markets are frictionless; that is, there are no transaction costs or taxes, all assets are perfectly divisible and marketable, and there are no constraining regulations.

- There is perfect competition in securities markets. This means that in securities markets all participants are price takers.

- Markets are informationally efficient; that is, information is costless, and it is received simultaneously by all individuals.

- All individuals are rational expected utility maximizers.

Given these conditions, both product and securities markets will be both allocationally and operationally efficient. *Allocational efficiency* has already been defined, but what about *operational efficiency?* Operational efficiency deals with the cost of transferring funds. In the idealized world of perfect capital markets, transaction costs are assumed to be zero and markets are perfectly liquid; therefore we have perfect operational efficiency.[1] However, we shall see later, when we focus on empirical studies of real-world phenomena, that operational efficiency is indeed an important consideration.

Capital market efficiency is much less restrictive than the notion of perfect capital markets outlined above. In an efficient capital market, prices fully and instantaneously reflect all available relevant information. This means that when assets are traded, prices are accurate signals for capital allocation.

To show the difference between perfect markets and efficient capital markets we can relax some of the perfect market assumptions. For example, we can still have efficient capital markets if markets are not frictionless. Prices will still fully reflect all available information if, for example, securities traders have to pay brokerage fees or if an individual's human capital (which, after all, is an asset) cannot be divided into a thousand parts and auctioned off. More importantly, there can be imperfect competition in product markets and we still have efficient capital markets. Hence if a firm can reap monopoly profits in the product market, the efficient capital market will determine a security price that fully reflects the present value of the anticipated stream of monopoly profits. Hence we can have allocative inefficiencies in product markets but still have efficient capital markets. Finally, it is not necessary to have costless information in efficient capital markets. This point is discussed in greater detail in Section E of this chapter.

Still, in a somewhat limited sense, efficient capital markets imply operational efficiency as well as asset prices that are allocationally efficient. Asset prices are correct signals in the sense that they fully and instantaneously reflect all available relevant information and are useful for directing the flow of funds from savers to investment projects that yield the highest return (even though the return may reflect monopolistic practices in product markets). Capital markets are operationally efficient if intermediaries, who provide the service of channeling funds from savers to investors, do so at the minimum cost that provides them a fair return for their services.

Another issue is whether capital markets are efficient even when individual behavior is not rational. What happens for example if information is unbiased, costless, and available to all investors, but they are overconfident? Will current market prices be too high? If so, is there a learning process that drives the market back to a rational market equilibrium?

Fama [1970, 1976] has done a great deal to operationalize the notion of capital market efficiency. He defines three types of efficiency, each of which is based on a different notion of exactly what type of information is understood to be relevant in the phrase "all prices fully reflect all *relevant* information."

---

[1] Note that even in perfect markets the minimum cost of transferring funds may not be zero if the transfer of funds also involves risk bearing.

1. *Weak-form efficiency.* No investor can earn excess returns by developing trading rules based on historical price or return information. In other words, the information in past prices or returns is not useful or relevant in achieving excess returns.

2. *Semistrong-form efficiency.* No investor can earn excess returns from trading rules based on any publicly available information. Examples of publicly available information are annual reports of companies, investment advisory data such as "Heard on the Street" in the *Wall Street Journal*, or tic-to-tic transaction information.

3. *Strong-form efficiency.* No investor can earn excess returns using any information, whether publicly available or not.

Obviously, the last type of market efficiency is very strong indeed. If markets were efficient in their strong form, prices would fully reflect all information even though it might be held exclusively by a corporate insider. Suppose, for example, we know that our company has just discovered how to control nuclear fusion. Even before we have a chance to trade based on the news, the strong form of market efficiency predicts that prices will have adjusted so that we cannot profit.

Rubinstein [1975] and Latham [1985] have extended the definition of market efficiency. The market is said to be efficient with regard to an information event if the information causes no portfolio changes. It is possible that people might disagree about the implications of a piece of information so that some buy an asset and others sell in such a way that the market price is unaffected. If the information does not change prices, then the market is said to be efficient with regard to the information in the Fama [1976] sense but not in the Rubinstein [1975] or Latham [1985] sense. The Rubinstein-Latham definition requires not only that there be no price change but also that there be no transactions. Hence it is a stronger form of market efficiency than even the Fama strong-form efficiency mentioned above.

B. *A* Formal Definition of the Value of Information

The notion of efficient capital markets depends on the precise definition of information and the value of information.[2] An *information structure* may be defined as a message about various events that may happen. For example, the message "There are no clouds in the sky" provides a probability distribution for the likelihood of rain within the next 24 hours. This message may have various values to different people depending on (1) whether or not they can take any actions based on the message and (2) what net benefits (gain in utility) will result from their actions. For example, a message related to rainfall can be of value to farmers, who can act on the information to increase their wealth. If there is no rain, the farmers might decide that it would be a good time to harvest hay. On the other hand, messages about rainfall have no value to deep-pit coal miners because such information probably will not alter the miners' actions at all.

A formal expression of the above concept defines the value of an information structure as

$$V(\eta) \equiv \sum_m q(m) \, \underset{a}{\text{MAX}} \sum_e p(e \mid m) U(a, e) - V(\eta_0), \tag{10.1}$$

---

[2] For an excellent review of the economics of information, see Hirshleifer and Riley [1979].

where

$q(m) = $ the prior probability of receiving a message m;

$p(e \mid m) = $ the conditional probability of an event e, given a message m;

$U(a, e) = $ the utility resulting from an action a if an event e occurs (we shall call this a *benefit function*);

$V(\eta_0) = $ the expected utility of the decision maker without the information.

According to Eq. (10.1), a decision maker will evaluate an information structure (which, for the sake of generality, is defined as a set of messages) by choosing an action that will maximize his or her expected utility, given the arrival of the message. For example, if we receive a message (one of many that we could have received) that there is a 20% chance of rain, we may carry an umbrella because of the high "disutility" of getting drenched and the low cost of carrying it. For each possible message we can determine our optimal action. Mathematically, this is the solution to the problem

$$\underset{a}{\text{MAX}} \sum_{e} p(e \mid m) U(a, e).$$

Finally, by weighting the expected utility of each optimal action (in response to all possible messages) by the probability, $q(m)$, of receiving the message that gives rise to the action, the decision maker knows the expected utility of the entire set of messages, which we call the *expected utility* (or *utility value*) of an information set, $V(\eta)$.

Note that the value of information as defined above in Eq. (10.1) in a one-period setting is very close to the value of a real option in a multiperiod setting, as discussed in Chapter 9. The basic idea is the same. Given the arrival of information a decision maker is assumed to have the right, but not the obligation, to take an action. Hence, the value of information is optimized along three variables, namely, the payoff to the decision maker, the information about the event given the message, and the action assumed to be taken by the decision maker.

To illustrate the value of information, consider the following example. The analysis division of a large retail brokerage firm hires and trains analysts to cover events in various regions around the world. The CIO (Chief Information Officer) has to manage the allocation of analysts and deal with the fact that the demand for analyst coverage is uncertain. To keep it simple, suppose we need 300 analysts or 0 analysts with 50-50 probability for coverage in each of three countries. The CIO is considering three possibilities.

Policy 1: Hire analysts and keep them on their initial allocations.

Policy 2: Switch analysts at a cost of 20 thousand dollars when it makes sense.

Policy 3: Create a catalogue (CAT) that provides better information (e.g., their language capabilities, their technical skills, etc.) for matching analysts to countries when they are switched.

The CIO has assigned project weights to various allocation results:

Outcome	Weight (utility $= U(a, e)$)
Analyst skilled in a job	100 units
Analyst unsatisfactory in job	30 units
Shortage—no one in job	0 units
Excess—no demand for job	−30 units

Table 10.1 CAT Provides Better Information

	Without CAT	With CAT
Probability of being skilled on the job	.7	1.0
Probability of being mismatched	.3	0.0

Figure 10.1 Expected payout from three policies.

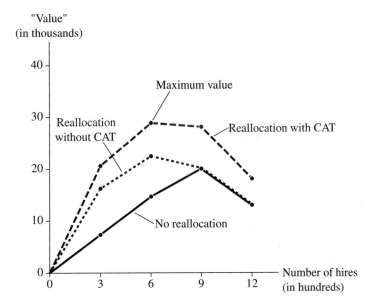

We would like to know which is the best policy, what it implies about the number of analysts to hire initially, and what value should be given to the CAT information. The intuition is reasonably clear. If, for example, the CAT information does not help much to make better job allocations, if the cost of mismatch is relatively low, or if the cost of switching is close to zero, then the value differential between policies 1 and 2 will be low. Table 10.1 shows the probability of getting the right analyst into the right job without having the catalogue information (right-hand side). Assuming that analysts are allocated without the benefit of CAT, there is 70% chance of allocating the analyst with the right skills to the right job. However, if the CAT information is available, the probability of a correct allocation goes up to 100 percent.

Figure 10.1 shows the overall results. If the brokerage company adopts a policy of not retraining and reallocating analysts (policy 1), it should hire 900 analysts for a value of 20,050. This result follows from the fact that there are four states of nature, with demand of 0, 300, 600, and 900 analysts, respectively.

To determine the expected payout from a policy of hiring 600 analysts, but not reallocating them, we can refer to Table 10.2. With 600 analysts we would allocate 200 to each of the countries (A, B, and C). If demand turns out to be 300 in total, the country that has that demand will be 100 analysts short and there will be no reallocation. The payout for 140 of the analysts who turn out to

Table 10.2 Expected Payout from Hiring 600 Analysts and Not Reallocating Them

Demand	Probability	Demand/Supply Country A	Country B	Country C
0	.125	0/200	0/200	0/200
300	.375	300/200	0/200	0/200
600	.375	300/200	300/200	0/200
900	.125	300/200	300/200	300/200
	1.000			

Demand	Payouts Skilled	Mismatch	Shortage	Excess	Contribution
0	0	0	0(0)	600(−30)	−2,250
300	(.7)(200)(100)	(.3)(200)(30)	100(0)	400(−30)	1,425
600	(.7)(400)(100)	2(.3)(400)(30)	200(0)	200(−30)	9,600
900	(.7)(600)(100)	(.3)(600)(30)	100(0)	0	5,925
					14,700

be skilled on the job is 100, and the payout for 60 analysts who are unsatisfactory is 30 each. The shortage of 100 has no cost or benefit and there is no excess. Therefore, the probability-weighted payment is

$$.375 \{[140(100) + 60(30)] + 400(-30)\} = 1,425.$$

Next, if demand turns out to be 600, it would reach that level because two of the three countries have demand of 300. Each would have been allocated 200 and would have a 100-person shortage. The third country would have an excess of 200. The probability-weighted outcome is

$$.375 \{[2 [140(100) + 60(30)] + 200(-30) + 0]\} = 9,600.$$

To complete the analysis of a strategy that consists of hiring 600 people and not reallocating them, we go to the last column in Table 10.2, where the probability-weighted contributions add to 14,700.

The results for all strategies are given in Table 10.3. The value-maximizing strategy without reallocation is to hire 900 people, enough to supply maximum demand for analysts in all three countries. But with the human resources catalogue (CAT) that makes the process of reallocation more accurate, the value-maximizing policy is to hire 600 people with the expectation that many would be reallocated. The difference between the value of reallocation without CAT and reallocation with it is the value of having the CAT (i.e., 28,825 − 22,462).

Table 10.3 Results for All Strategies

		Allocation Policy	
Number Hired	**No Reallocation**	**Reallocation without CAT**	**Reallocation with CAT**
0	0	0	0
300	7,350	16,328	20,625
600	14,700	22,462	28,875
900	22,050	22,050	28,125
1,200	13,050	13,050	19,125

C. The Relationship between the Value of Information and Efficient Capital Markets

Equation (10.1) can be used to evaluate any information structure. It also points out some ideas that are only implicit in the definition of *efficient markets*. Fama [1976] defines efficient capital markets as those where the joint distribution of security prices, $f_m(P_{1t}, P_{2t}, \ldots, P_{nt} \mid \eta^m_{t-1})$, given the set of information that the *market uses* to determine security prices at $t - 1$, is identical to the joint distribution of prices that would exist if *all relevant information* available at $t - 1$ were used, $f(P_{1t}, P_{2t}, \ldots, P_{nt} \mid \eta_{t-1})$. Lewellen and Shanken [2002] point out that the cash flow expectations of the representative investor, η^m_{t-1}, and the expectations given all relevant information, η_{t-1}, may differ, and if so, investors rationally learn over time. Thus it becomes important to understand the equilibrium process. Mathematically, this is

$$f_m(P_{1t}, \ldots, P_{nt} \mid \eta^m_{t-1}) = f(P_{1t}, \ldots, P_{nt} \mid \eta_{t-1}). \tag{10.2}$$

If an information structure is to have value, it must accurately tell us something we do not already know. If the distribution of prices in time period t (which was predicted in the previous time period $t - 1$ and based on the information structure the market uses) is not different from the distribution of prices predicted by using all relevant information from the previous time period, then there must be no difference between the information the market uses and the set of all relevant information. This is the essence of an efficient capital market—it instantaneously and fully reflects all relevant information. Using information theory, this also means that *net of costs*, the utility value of the gain from information to the ith individual, must be zero:

$$V(\eta_i) - V(\eta_0) \equiv 0. \tag{10.3}$$

For example, consider capital markets that are efficient in their weak form. The relevant information structure, η_i, is defined to be the set of historical prices on all assets. If capital markets are efficient, then Eq. (10.2) says that the distribution of security prices today has already incorporated past price histories. In other words, it is not possible to develop trading rules (courses of action) based on past prices that will allow anyone to beat the market. Equation (10.3) says that no one would pay anything for the information set of historical prices. The value of the information is zero. Empirical evidence on trading rules that use past price data is discussed in Section F of this chapter.

It is important to emphasize that the value of information is determined net of costs. These include the cost of undertaking courses of action and the costs of transmitting and evaluating messages. Some of these costs in securities markets are transaction costs: for example, brokerage fees, bid-ask spreads, costs involved in searching for the best price (if more than one price is quoted), and taxes, as well as data costs and analysts' fees. The capital market is efficient relative to a given information set only after consideration of the costs of acquiring messages and taking actions pursuant to a particular information structure.

D. $\mathscr{R}$ational Expectations and Market Efficiency

The value of information in Eq. (10.1) has three parts: (1) the utilities of the payoffs, given an action; (2) the optimal actions, given receipt of a message; and (3) the probabilities of states of nature provided by the messages. We are interested in understanding how the individual's decision-making process, given the receipt of information, is reflected in the market prices of assets. This is not easy because it is impossible to observe the quantity and quality of information or the timing of its receipt in the real world. There is even disagreement among theorists about what information will be used by investors. For example, Forsythe, Palfrey, and Plott [1982] identify four different hypotheses. Each hypothesis assumes that investors know with certainty what their own payoffs will be across time, but they also know that different individuals may pay different prices because of differing preferences.

The first hypothesis is particularly nonsensical (call it the *naïve hypothesis*) in that it asserts that asset prices are completely arbitrary and unrelated either to how much they will pay out in the future or to the probabilities of various payouts. The second hypothesis (call it the *speculative equilibrium hypothesis*) is captured in a quote taken from Keynes's General Theory [1936, 156]:

> Professional investment may be likened to those newspaper competitions in which the competitors have to pick out the six prettiest faces from a hundred photographs, the prize being awarded to the competitor whose choice most nearly corresponds to the average preferences of the competitors as a whole; so that each competitor has to pick, not those faces from which he finds the prettiest, but those which he thinks likeliest to catch the fancy of the other competitors, all of whom are looking at the problem from the same point of view. It is not a case of choosing those which, to the best of one's judgment, are really the prettiest, nor even those which average opinion genuinely thinks the prettiest. We have reached the third degree where we devote our intelligences to anticipating what average opinion expects the average opinion to be. And there are some, I believe, who practice the fourth, fifth and higher degrees.

We might debate about what Keynes really meant, but one interpretation is that all investors base their investment decisions entirely on their anticipation of other individuals' behavior without any necessary relationship to the actual payoffs that the assets are expected to provide. The third hypothesis is that asset prices are systematically related to their future payouts. Called the *intrinsic value hypothesis*, it says that prices will be determined by each individual's estimate of the payoffs of an asset without consideration of its resale value to other individuals. The fourth hypothesis may be called the *rational expectations hypothesis*. It predicts that prices are formed on the basis of the expected future payouts of the assets, including their resale value to third parties. Thus a rational expectations market is an efficient market because prices will reflect all information.

Table 10.4 Parameters for an Experimental Double Auction Spot Market

Investor Type	Initial Working Capital (francs)	Initial Shares Held	Fixed Cost (francs)	Dividends (francs)	
				Period A	Period B
I (3 people)	10,000	2	10,000	300	50
II (3 people)	10,000	2	10,000	50	300
III (3 people)	10,000	2	10,000	150	250

To make these hypotheses more concrete, it is useful to review an experiment by Forsythe, Palfrey, and Plott [1982]. They set up an oral double auction market that had two time periods, one asset, and three "types" of individuals. An oral double auction market is one where individuals can submit both buying and selling prices for an asset. The largest market of this type is the New York Stock Exchange. All participants knew exactly how much the asset would pay them in each time period. They also knew that the asset would pay different amounts to the other market participants, but not how much. Thus the asset had different values to different individuals. Table 10.4 shows the experimental parameters. If you held an asset at the end of the first time period, you received 300, 50, or 150 "francs," depending on whether you were individual type I, II, or III.[3] The differences in the franc payouts across individuals were designed to reflect differences among individual preferences and information sets at an instant in time. Each individual was endowed with 10,000 francs in working capital and two shares.[4] The 10,000 franc endowment was paid back at the end of the second period (this is the fixed cost column in Table 10.4), but any dividends received and any trading profits were kept by the market participants.

The interesting question is, What will the market equilibrium prices be at the end of each of the two time periods? If either of the intrinsic value or rational expectations hypotheses are true, the period B price should be 300 francs (or very close to it) because there are three people competing for that payoff. While the intrinsic value and rational expectations hypotheses agree about the second-period price, they make different predictions concerning the first-period price. The intrinsic value hypothesis predicts that people will bid their own values. For example, if individual type III holds the asset for two periods, he or she can collect 400 francs in dividends (150 in period A and 250 in period B). This will also be the predicted first-period equilibrium price because it represents the high bid. The rational expectations hypothesis predicts that the first-period equilibrium price will be 600 francs because type I individuals can collect a 300 franc dividend in the first time period, then sell the asset for 300 francs to type II individuals in the second time period.

Figure 10.2 shows the results of eight replications of the experiment for two periods each. Note that the period B price quickly converges on the anticipated equilibrium value of 300 francs. This result alone repudiates the naïve value and the speculative equilibrium hypotheses because the asset value is clearly based on its actual second-period payout. The first-period price starts out at 400 francs, seemingly verifying the intrinsic value hypothesis; but it then rises gradually until, by the eighth replication of the experiment ("year" 8), it closes in on the rational expectations value.

The experiment seems to confirm the rational expectations hypothesis, but why did it take so long to do so? The reason is that prices are determined in the first period before second-period

---

[3] Each "franc" was worth $0.002. It was not ever intended to be a French franc.

[4] No short sales were allowed; thus the supply of assets was fixed.

Figure 10.2 Spot price equilibria in an experimental market. (From R. Forsythe, T. Palfrey, and C. R. Plott, "Asset Valuation in an Experimental Market," reprinted from *Econometrica*, May 1982, 550.)

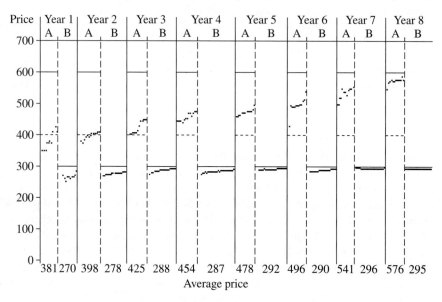

Average price

Table 10.5 Parameters for an Experimental Double Auction Futures Market

Investor Type	Initial Working Capital (francs)	Initial Shares Held	Fixed Cost (francs)	Dividends (francs) Period A	Dividends (francs) Period B
I (3 people)	15,000	2	15,500	403	146
II (3 people)	15,000	2	15,500	284	372
III (3 people)	15,000	2	15,500	110	442

prices are known. In order for type I individuals to bid the full 600 franc value, they need to have the information that the second-period value is really 300 francs. Obviously they do not know this during the first trial of the experiment, but they learn quickly.

If, instead, bidding had taken place in both period A and B markets simultaneously, perhaps the speed of adjustment to a rational expectations equilibrium would have been faster. In another experiment, Forsythe, Palfrey, and Plott [1982] opened a *futures market*. Everything remained the same as before except bidding for period B holdings was held concurrently with the period A spot market, and the payoffs were as shown in Table 10.5.

The rational expectations hypothesis predicts that the period A price will be 845 francs, whereas the intrinsic value hypothesis predicts 656 francs. They both predict a period B price of 442 francs. The results are shown in Fig. 10.3. Even in the first trial, the period A spot price closed at 742 francs, much closer to the rational expectations prediction. In subsequent trials ("years") the closing prices were even closer to the results predicted by the rational expectations hypothesis. Perhaps the most valuable implication of the experiment is that it clearly demonstrates the usefulness of futures markets. By allowing simultaneous trading in both markets, the speed with which information is

Figure 10.3 Rational expectations with a futures market. (From R. Forsythe, T. Palfrey, and C. R. Plott, "Asset Valuation in an Experimental Market," reprinted from *Econometrica*, May 1982, 554.)

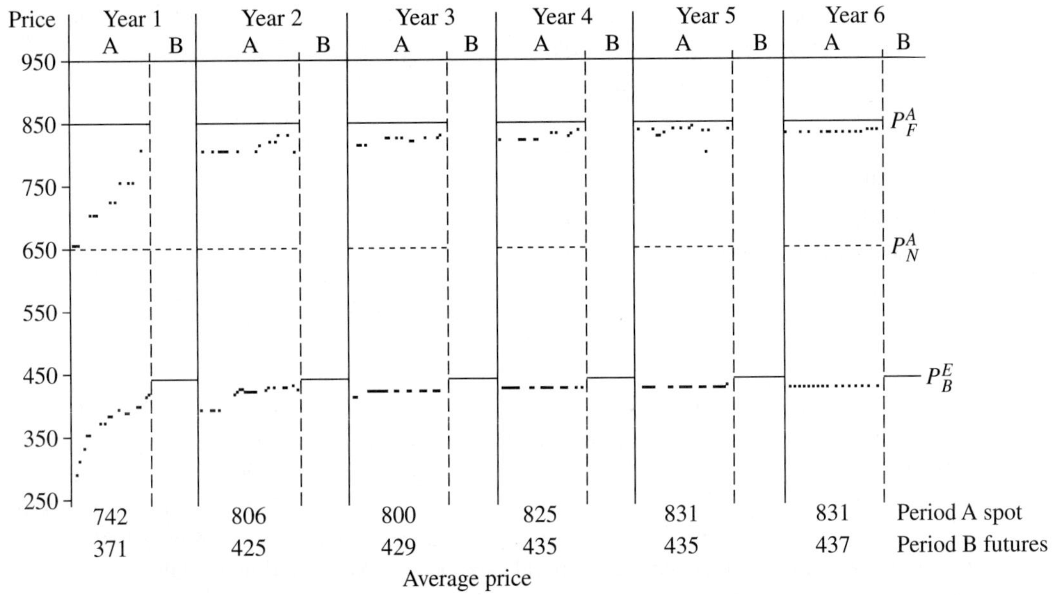

Price	Year 1 A	B	Year 2 A	B	Year 3 A	B	Year 4 A	B	Year 5 A	B	Year 6 A	B	
	742	371	806	425	800	429	825	435	831	435	831	437	Period A spot / Period B futures

Average price

made public is increased through price transactions. Information about the future value of assets is revealed today.

In the rational expectations equilibria described above, all traders knew with certainty what their own payoffs would be in each time period but did not know the asset clearing price because other individuals had different payoffs in the same state of nature. These different payoffs represent a form of heterogeneous expectations. In the above experiments all market participants were equally well informed. There is a different way of looking at heterogeneous expectations, however. Suppose that some traders are better informed about which states of nature will actually occur. Furthermore, suppose that different individuals have different information about which states will occur. For example, suppose investor I knows for sure that a Republican will be elected president but knows nothing else. Investor J, on the other hand, knows that both houses of Congress will be Democratic but knows nothing else. The question is this: Will market prices reflect the full impact of both pieces of information as though the market were fully informed, or will prices reflect only some average of the impact of both pieces of information? If prices reflect all information, the market is said to be *fully aggregating*; otherwise it is only *averaging* prices.

Very little is known about whether real-world capital markets fully aggregate information or merely average it. A fully aggregating market, however, would be consistent with Fama's [1970] definition of strong-form market efficiency. In a fully aggregating market even insiders who possess private information would not be able to profit by it. One mechanism for aggregation has been suggested by Grossman and Stiglitz [1976] and Grossman [1976].[5] In a market with two types of traders, "informed" and "uninformed," informed traders will acquire better estimates of future

---

[5] Actually, this idea can be traced back to Hayek's classic article, "The Use of Knowledge in Society" [1945].

Table 10.6 Net Payoffs, Given Costly Information

		His Opponent Analyzes?	
		Yes	**No**
The Trader	**Yes**	$r - c_2 = -2\%$	$dr - c_2 = 4\%$
Analyzes?	**No**	$r/d - c_1 = -1\%$	$r - c_1 = 2\%$

where

$r =$ normal return $= 6\%$,

$d =$ competitive advantage $= 2\times$,

$c_2 =$ cost of analysis $= 8\%$,

$c_1 =$ cost with no analysis $= 4\%$.

states of nature and take trading positions based on this information. When all informed traders do this, current prices are affected. Uninformed traders invest no resources in collecting information, but they can infer the information of informed traders by observing what happens to prices. Thus the market prices may aggregate information so that all traders (both informed and uninformed) become informed. In Chapter 11 we will suggest that capital markets do not instantaneously and fully aggregate information because empirical evidence on insider trading reveals that insiders can and do make abnormal returns.

E. Market Efficiency with Costly Information

If capital markets are efficient, then no one can earn abnormal returns, but without abnormal returns there is no strong incentive to acquire information. Random selection of securities is just as effective. How, then, can prices reflect information if there is no incentive to search out and use it for arbitrage? How can a securities analysis industry exist?

The above argument may have some merit in a world with costless information because all investors would have zero abnormal returns.[6] However, it is probably premature to predict the demise of the security analysis industry or to argue that prices are uninformative. Grossman and Stiglitz [1976, 1980] and Cornell and Roll [1981] have shown that a sensible asset market equilibrium must leave some room for costly analysis. Their articles make the more reasonable assumption that information acquisition is a costly activity. Because of its simplicity, the Cornell and Roll model is discussed below.

We want to analyze the rational behavior of individuals when information is useful—in the sense that having it will improve one's decisions—but also where information is costly. Imagine two simple strategies. The first is to pay a fee, say, $c_2 = 8\%$, for acquiring valuable information. This is called the *analyst strategy*. The opposing strategy is to pay a minimal fee, say, $c_1 = 4\%$, for the right to trade. Call this the *random selector's strategy*. Table 10.6 shows the net payoffs for various two-way trades involving all combinations of analysts and random selectors. Note that the "normal" rate of return, r, is 6% $(c_1 < r < c_2)$.

---

[6] Abnormal returns are returns in excess of what can be earned for a given level of risk.

The example in Table 10.6 assumes that the costly information doubles the competitive advantage, d, of an analyst whenever he or she trades with a random selector. The analyst, being better informed, grosses 12% and nets 4% after paying 8% for the information. Conversely, the random selector finds his or her gross return halved when trading with an analyst. He or she grosses only 3% and nets -1% after paying 4% on transaction costs. When an analyst trades with another analyst there is no competitive advantage because they possess the same information. Thus their gross return is only 6% and they net -2%.

A stable equilibrium can exist (1) if all trading is anonymous and (2) if the expected payoff to the analysis strategy equals the expected payoff to the random selection strategy.[7] If p is the probability of utilizing an analyst's strategy and $1 - p$ is the probability of random selection, then the equilibrium condition is

$$E(\text{Payoff to analysis strategy}) = E(\text{Payoff to random selection})$$

$$p(r - c_2) + (1 - p)(dr - c_2) = p(r/d - c_1) + (1 - p)(r - c_1). \tag{10.4}$$

The expected payoff to analysis—the left-hand side of Eq. (10.4)—is the probability that an analyst will confront another analyst multiplied by the net payoff given this event, plus the probability of confronting a random selector multiplied by the net payoff in that event. Similar logic produces the expected payoff for a random selector, the right-hand side of Eq. (10.4). Solving Eq. (10.4) for p, the probability of using analysis, we have

$$p = \frac{r(1 - d) + c_2 - c_1}{2r - rd - r/d}. \tag{10.5}$$

A *mixed* strategy is one where $0 < p < 1$, that is, where analysts and random selectors will coexist in equilibrium. The necessary conditions for a mixed stable strategy are

$$r(d - 1) > c_2 - c_1 \quad \text{and} \quad r(1 - 1/d) < c_2 - c_1. \tag{10.6}$$

These conditions can be derived from the definition of the equilibrium probability, p, in Eq. (10.5). We know that the "normal" rate of return, r, is greater than zero and the competitive advantage, d, is greater than one. Therefore the denominator of Eq. (10.5) must be negative:

$$2r - rd - r/d < 0,$$

$$2d - d^2 - 1 < 0,$$

$$(d - 1)^2 > 0, \quad \text{since} \quad d > 1. \quad \text{QED}$$

It follows that the numerator of Eq. (10.5) must also be negative if the probability, p, is to be positive. Therefore

$$r(1 - d) + c_2 - c_1 < 0,$$

$$r(d - 1) > c_2 - c_1,$$

and we have derived the first necessary condition in Eq. (10.6). Also, in order for $p < 1$ the numerator of Eq. (10.5) must be greater than the denominator (since both are negative numbers).

---

[7] Anonymous trading is necessary so that uninformed random selectors will actually consummate a trade with an analyst with superior information. One service provided by brokers is to ensure the anonymity of their clients.

This fact gives us the second necessary condition:

$$r(1 - d) + c_2 - c_1 > 2r - rd - r/d,$$

$$c_2 - c_1 > r(1 - 1/d).$$

If there is no net economic profit when the mixed stable strategy evolves, then there will be no incentive for new entrants to disturb the equilibrium. This zero profit condition is equivalent to setting both sides of Eq. (10.4), the expected payoff equation, equal to zero. This results in two equations, which when equated and simplified give the further result that

$$d = c_2/c_1 \quad \text{and} \quad p = (rd - c_2)/(rd - r)$$

for a stable mixed strategy where all net profits are zero.

Using the numbers in Table 10.6, we see that a stable mixed strategy with $p = \frac{2}{3}$ will exist. Thus with costly information we will observe the analyst strategy being used two thirds and the random selection strategy one third of the time. No one will be tempted to change strategies because there is no incentive to do so. Also, we will observe that the gross return for analysis is higher than for random selection. But once the cost of obtaining information is subtracted, the net rate of return to both strategies is the same.

The simple model of Cornell and Roll [1981] shows that there is nothing inconsistent about having efficient markets and security analysis at the same time. The average individual who utilizes costly information to perform security analysis will outperform other individuals who use less information, but only in terms of gross returns. The net return to both strategies will be identical. Some empirical evidence consistent with this point of view is presented in Chapter 11 where mutual fund performance is discussed.

Copeland and Friedman [1992] designed an experimental market where it was possible to control the sequential arrival of information to individuals trading assets in the market. They then conducted a pretrading auction where prospective traders could bid to know with certainty, before trading started, exactly what information (regarding the state of nature and their payout in it) they would receive. After a learning period, the prices of assets in the market behaved as though there were a fully revealing rational expectations equilibrium—an equilibrium where prices fully reveal all privately held information. The value of information in the premarket fell to zero as participants found that their net profits after paying a cost for information turned out to be zero. These experimental results provide strong support for the efficiency of markets in the presence of costly information.

There is, however, plenty of room for over- or undershooting of what would otherwise be long-term equilibrium prices, because information is constantly being generated and its implications for equilibrium prices are a matter of disagreement among traders.

F. $\mathcal{S}$ tatistical Tests Adjusted for Risk

Historically it was possible to test certain predictions of the efficient markets hypothesis even before a theory of risk bearing allowed comparison of risk-adjusted returns. For example, if the riskiness of an asset does not change over time or if its risk changes randomly over time, then there should be no pattern in the time series of security returns. If there were a recurring pattern of any type, investors who recognize it could use it to predict future returns and make excess profits. However, in their very efforts to use the patterns, they would eliminate them.

Three theories of the time-series behavior of prices can be found in the literature: (1) the *fair-game model*, (2) the *martingale or submartingale*, and (3) the *random walk*. The fair-game model is based on the behavior of average returns (not on the entire probability distribution). Its mathematical expression is

$$\varepsilon_{j,t+1} = \frac{P_{j,t+1} - P_{jt}}{P_{jt}} - \frac{E(P_{j,t+1} \mid \eta_t) - P_{jt}}{P_{jt}} = 0$$

$$= \frac{P_{j,t+1} - E(P_{j,t+1} \mid \eta_t)}{P_{jt}} = 0, \tag{10.7}$$

where

$$P_{j,t+1} = \text{the actual price of security } j \text{ next period,}$$

$$E(P_{j,t+1} \mid \eta_t) = \text{the predicted end-of-period price of security } j \text{ given the current}$$

$$\text{information structure, } \eta_t,$$

$$\varepsilon_{j,t+1} = \text{the difference between actual and predicted returns.}$$

Note that (10.7) is really written in returns form. If we let the one-period return be defined as

$$r_{j,t+1} = \frac{P_{j,t+1} - P_{jt}}{P_{jt}},$$

then (10.7) may be rewritten as

$$\varepsilon_{j,t+1} = r_{j,t+1} - E(r_{j,t+1} \mid \eta_t)$$

and

$$E(\varepsilon_{j,t+1}) = E\left[r_{j,t+1} - E(r_{j,t+1} \mid \eta_t) \right] = 0. \tag{10.8}$$

A fair game means that, on average, across a large number of samples, the expected return on an asset equals its actual return. An example of a fair game would be games of chance in Las Vegas. Because of the house percentage, you should expect to lose, let us say 10%, and sure enough, on the average that is what people actually lose. A fair game does not imply that you will earn a positive return; only that expectations are not biased.

Given the definition of a fair game in Eq. (10.7), a *submartingale* is a fair game where tomorrow's price is expected to be greater than today's price. Mathematically, a submartingale is

$$E(P_{j,t+1} \mid \eta_t) > P_{jt}.$$

In returns form this implies that expected returns are positive. This may be written as follows:

$$\frac{E(P_{j,t+1} \mid \eta_t) - P_{jt}}{P_{jt}} = E(r_{j,t+1} \mid \eta_t) > 0. \tag{10.9a}$$

A *martingale* is also a fair game. With a martingale, however, tomorrow's price is expected to be the same as today's price. Mathematically, this is

$$E(P_{j,t+1} \mid \eta_t) = P_{jt,}$$

or in returns form, it is written as

$$\frac{E(P_{j,t+1} \mid \eta_t) - P_{jt}}{P_{jt}} = E(r_{j,t+1} \mid \eta_t) = 0. \tag{10.9b}$$

A submartingale has the following empirical implication: Because prices are expected to increase over time, any test of the abnormal return from an experimental portfolio must compare its return from a buy-and-hold strategy for a control portfolio of the same composition. If the market is an efficient submartingale, both portfolios will have a positive return, and the difference between their returns will be zero. In other words, we will observe a fair game with positive returns: a submartingale.

Finally, a *random walk* says that there is no difference between the distribution of returns conditional on a given information structure and the unconditional distribution of returns. Equation (10.2) is a random walk in prices. Equation (10.10) is a random walk in returns:

$$f(r_{1,t+1}, \dots, r_{n,t+1}) = f(r_{1,t+1}, \dots, r_{n,t+1} \mid \eta_t) \tag{10.10}$$

Random walks are much stronger conditions than fair games or martingales because they require all the parameters of a distribution (e.g., mean, variance, skewness, and kurtosis) to be the same with or without an information structure. Furthermore, successive drawings over time must (1) be independent and (2) be taken from the same distribution. If returns follow a random walk, then the mean of the underlying distribution does not change over time, and a fair game will result.

Most empirical evidence indicates that security returns do not follow a process that has all the properties of a random walk. This makes sense because the condition that the entire underlying probability distribution of returns remain stationary through time is simply too strong. It is reasonable to believe that because of changes in the risk of the firm, the variance of stock returns will change over time. This, in fact, appears to be the case. The fair-game model makes no statement about the variance of the distribution of security returns, and consequently, the nonstationarity of return variances is irrelevant to its validity.[8]

A statistical difference between fair games and random walks is that the latter hypothesis requires that all drawings be independently taken from the same distribution, whereas the former does not. This means that the random walk requires that serial covariances between returns for any lag must be zero. However, significant covariances of one-period returns are not inconsistent with a fair game. To see this, suppose that the relevant information structure consists of past returns. In other words, assume weak-form market efficiency. When Eq. (10.7) is written in returns form, we have

$$\varepsilon_{j,t+1} = r_{j,t+1} - E(r_{j,t+1} \mid r_{jt}, r_{j,t-1}, \dots, r_{j,t-n}) \tag{10.11}$$

---

[8] For example, consider a situation where random drawings are taken randomly from two normal distributions that have a mean return of zero but different return variances. The expected value of a large sample of alternative drawings would be zero; therefore we have a fair game. However, the experiment violates the random walk requirement that all drawings will be taken from the same distribution.

and

$$E(\varepsilon_{j,t+1}) = 0.$$

Note that the fair game variable, $\varepsilon_{j,t+1}$, is the deviation of the return of period $t + 1$ from its conditional expectation (i.e., the residual). If the residual is fair game, then it must have zero covariance for all lags. Yet even though the residual is a fair game variable, the conditional expectation of returns for $t + 1$ can depend on the return observed for t. Therefore the serial covariances of *returns* need not be zero. The serial covariance for one-period returns is[9]

$$E\left[(r_{j,t+1} - E(r_{j,t+1}))(r_{jt} - E(r_{jt}))\right] = \text{COV}(r_{j,t+1}, r_{jt}) \tag{10.12}$$

$$= \int_{r_{jt}} \left[r_{jt} - E(r_{jt})\right]\left[r_{j,t+1} - E(r_{j,t+1})\right] f(r_{jt}) dr_{jt}.$$

From (10.11) we know that $E\left[r_{j,t+1} \mid r_{jt}\right] = r_{j,t+1}$. Therefore

$$\text{COV}(r_{j,t+1}, r_{jt}) = \int_{r_{jt}} \left[r_{jt} - E(r_{jt})\right]\left[E(r_{j,t+1} \mid r_{jt}) - E(r_{j,t+1})\right] f(r_{jt}) dr_{jt}. \tag{10.13}$$

But the fair game in residuals, Eq. (10.11), does not imply that $E(r_{j,t+1} \mid r_{jt}) = E(r_{j,t+1})$. We have the result that the *deviation* of return for $t + 1$ from its conditional expectation is a fair game, but the conditional expectation of return can depend on the return observed for t. Therefore serial covariances of one-period returns are not inconsistent with a fair-game model. However, they are inconsistent with a random walk because the latter requires that successive drawings be independent (a serial covariance of zero for all lags).

Fama [1965] has presented evidence to show that the serial correlations of one-day changes in the natural logarithm of prices are significantly different from zero for 11 out of 30 of the Dow Jones Industrials.[10] Furthermore, 22 of the 30 estimated serial correlations are positive. This, as well as evidence collected by other authors, shows that security returns are not, strictly speaking, random walks. However, the evidence is not inconsistent with fair-game models or, in particular, the submartingale.

Direct tests of the fair-game model were provided by Alexander [1961] and Fama and Blume [1966]. They used a technical trading filter rule, which states: Using price history, buy a stock if the price rises $x\%$, hold it until the security falls $x\%$, then sell and go short. Maintain the short position until the price rises $x\%$, then cover the short position and establish a long position. This process is repeated for a fixed time interval, and the performance according to the filter rule is then

---

[9] The reader who is unfamiliar with covariances is referred to Chapter 6. In general the covariance between the two random variables, x and y, is

$$\text{COV}(x, y) = E[(x - E(x))(y - E(y))].$$

[10] To show that the logarithm of successive price changes is a good approximation of returns, assume one-period continuous compounding:

$$P_{t+1} = P_t e^{rt}, \quad \text{where} \quad t = 1,$$

$$\ln P_{t+1} - \ln P_t = \frac{P_{t+1} - P_t}{P_t}, \quad \text{where} \quad r = \frac{P_{t+1} - P_t}{P_t}.$$

compared with a buy-and-hold strategy in the same security. Because each security is compared with itself, there is no need to adjust for risk.

Filter rules are designed to make the investor a profit if there are any systematic patterns in the movement in prices over time. It is only a matter of trying enough different filters so that one of them picks up any serial dependencies in prices and makes a profit that exceeds the simple buy-and-hold strategy.

The filter rule tests have three important results. First, they show that even before subtracting transaction costs, filters greater than 1.5% cannot beat a simple buy-and-hold strategy. Second, filters below 1.5%, on the average, make very small profits that because of frequent trading can beat the market. This is evidence of a very short-term serial dependence in price changes. However, it is not necessarily evidence of capital market inefficiency. First one must subtract from gross profits the cost of taking action based on the filter rule. Fama and Blume [1966] show that even a floor trader (the owner of a seat on the NYSE) would at that time in history have had to pay at least .1% per transaction. Once these costs are deducted from the profits of filters that are less than 1.5%, the profits vanish. Therefore the capital market is allocationally efficient down to the level of transactions costs. The smaller the transactions costs are, the more operationally efficient the market is, and smaller price dependencies are eliminated by arbitrage trading. Capital markets are efficient in their weak form because the return on a portfolio managed with price-history information is the same as a buy-and-hold strategy that uses no information. Therefore the value of messages provided by filter rules is zero. Technical trading does not work.[11]

The third inference that can be drawn from filter tests is that the market appears to follow a submartingale. All the securities tested had average positive returns. This makes sense because risky assets are expected to yield positive returns to compensate investors for the risk they undertake.

G. *The* Joint Hypothesis of Market Efficiency and the CAPM

Statistical tests and filter rules are interesting and present evidence of weak-form efficiency but are limited by the fact that they cannot compare assets of different risk. The CAPM provides a theory that allows the expected return of a fair-game model to be conditional on a relevant costless measure of risk.[12] If the CAPM is written as a fair game, we have

$$\varepsilon_{jt} = R_{jt} - E(R_{jt} \mid \widehat{\beta}_{jt}),$$

$$E(R_{jt} \mid \widehat{\beta}_{jt}) = R_{ft} + \left[E(R_{mt} \mid \widehat{\beta}_{mt}) - R_{ft}\right]\widehat{\beta}_{jt}, \tag{10.14}$$

$$E(\varepsilon_{jt}) = 0, \tag{10.15}$$

---

[11] See Ball [1978] for a discussion of filter rules and how to improve them as tests of market efficiency.

[12] Note that the discussion that follows also applies to the arbitrage pricing theory if one allows the expected return to depend on multiple factor loadings (i.e., multiple betas).

Figure 10.4 The CAPM is a fair game.

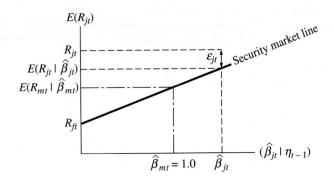

where

$$E(R_{jt} \mid \widehat{\beta}_{jt}) = \text{the expected rate of return on the } j\text{th asset during this time period,}$$
$$\text{given a prediction of its systematic risk, } \widehat{\beta}_{jt},$$

$$R_{ft} = \text{the risk-free rate of return during this time period,}$$

$$E(R_{mt} \mid \widehat{\beta}_{mt}) = \text{the expected market rate of return, given a prediction of its}$$
$$\text{systematic risk, } \widehat{\beta}_{mt},$$

$$\widehat{\beta}_{jt} = \text{the estimated systematic risk of the } j\text{th security based on last time}$$
$$\text{period's information structure } \eta_{t-1}.$$

The CAPM is graphed in Fig. 10.4. According to the theory, the only relevant parameter necessary to evaluate the expected return for every security is its systematic risk.[13] Therefore if the CAPM is true and if markets are efficient, the expected return of every asset should fall exactly on the security market line. Any deviation from the expected return is interpreted as an abnormal return, ε_{jt}, and can be taken as evidence of market efficiency *if* the CAPM is correct.

The CAPM is derived from a set of assumptions that are similar to those of market efficiency. For example, the Sharpe-Lintner-Mossin derivation of the CAPM assumes

- All investors are single-period expected utility of wealth maximizers whose utility functions are based on the mean and variance of return.
- All investors can borrow or lend an indefinite amount at the risk-free rate, and there are no restrictions on short sales.
- All investors have homogeneous expectations of the end-of-period joint distributions of returns.
- Securities markets are frictionless and perfectly competitive.

In Chapter 11 we shall report the results of several empirical studies that use the CAPM and multifactor models as tools for analyzing capital market efficiency. However, one should always keep in mind the fact that the CAPM and capital market efficiency are joint and inseparable hypotheses. If capital markets are inefficient, then the assumptions of the CAPM are invalid and

---

[13] For a detailed explanation of the CAPM and empirical tests of it, see Chapter 6.

a different model is required. And if the CAPM is inappropriate, even though capital markets are efficient, then the CAPM is the wrong tool to use in order to test for efficiency.

Early empirical tests of the CAPM by Black, Jensen, and Scholes [1972], Black and Scholes [1974], and Fama and MacBeth [1973] show that the CAPM fits reality surprisingly well. But later empirical evidence has called it into question (e.g., Fama and French [1992]). For a more complete discussion of tests of the CAPM, however, please refer back to Chapter 6. Because the theoretical CAPM assumes market efficiency, any empirical results that show that, on the average, there are no significant deviations from the model are merely consistent with market efficiency. They do not necessarily prove market efficiency because the model might be wrong. Therefore any test of market efficiency that uses the CAPM to adjust the risk is, as mentioned before, a joint test of the CAPM that assumes market efficiency for its derivation and of market efficiency itself.

One may also ask the question: "If I can accurately predict systematic risk, $\widehat{\beta}_{jt}$, I can also predict the expected rate of return on an asset; doesn't this mean that I can beat the market?" The answer, of course, is "Probably not." If the information necessary to estimate $\widehat{\beta}_{jt}$ is publicly available and if markets are efficient in their semistrong form, then prices will instantaneously and fully reflect all the information relevant for estimates $\widehat{\beta}_{jt}$, the expected return of the security will fall exactly on the security line, and no abnormal returns will be observed.

Perhaps the most interesting use of the CAPM is to examine historical situations to see whether or not the market was efficient for a particular set of information. If the CAPM is valid (we shall assume it is, but keep in mind that it is a joint hypothesis with market efficiency), then any evidence of persistent deviations from the security market line can be interpreted as evidence of capital market inefficiency with regard to a particular information set. Chapter 11 is devoted to tests of market efficiency with regard to various information sets.

Summary

The hypothesis of capital market efficiency has attracted a great deal of interest and critical comment. This is somewhat surprising because capital market efficiency is a fairly limited concept. It says that the prices of securities instantaneously and fully reflect all available relevant information. It does not imply that product markets are perfectly competitive or that information is costless.

Capital market efficiency relies on the ability of arbitrageurs to recognize that prices are out of line and to make a profit by driving them back to an equilibrium value consistent with available information. Given this type of behavioral paradigm, one often hears the following questions: If capital market efficiency implies that no one can beat the market (i.e., make an abnormal profit), then how can analysts be expected to exist since they, too, cannot beat the market? If capital markets are efficient, how can we explain the existence of a multibillion dollar security analysis industry? The answer, of course, is that neither of these questions is inconsistent with efficient capital markets. First, analysts can and do make profits. However, they compete with each other to do so. If the profit to analysis becomes abnormally large, then new individuals will enter the analysis business until, on average, the return from analysis equals the cost (which by the way, includes a fair return to the resources that are employed). As shown by Cornell and Roll [1981], it is reasonable to have efficient markets where people earn different gross rates of return because they pay differing costs for information. However, net of costs their abnormal rates of return will be equal (to zero).

As we shall see in the next chapter, the concept of capital market efficiency is important in a wide range of applied topics, such as accounting information, new issues of securities, and portfolio performance measurement. By and large the evidence seems to indicate that capital markets are efficient in the weak and semistrong forms but not in the strong form.

PROBLEM SET

10.1 Suppose you know with certainty that the Clark Capital Corporation will pay a dividend of $10 per share on every January 1 forever. The continuously compounded risk-free rate is 5% (also forever).

(a) Graph the price path of Clark Capital common stock over time.

(b) Is this (highly artificial) example a random walk? A martingale? A submartingale? (Why?)

10.2 Given the following situations, determine in each case whether or not the hypothesis of an efficient capital market (semistrong form) is contradicted.

(a) Through the introduction of a complex computer program into the analysis of past stock price changes, a brokerage firm is able to predict price movements well enough to earn a consistent 3% profit, adjusted for risk, above normal market returns.

(b) On the average, investors in the stock market this year are expected to earn a positive return (profit) on their investment. Some investors will earn considerably more than others.

(c) You have discovered that the square root of any given stock price multiplied by the day of the month provides an indication of the direction in price movement of that particular stock with a probability of .7.

(d) A Securities and Exchange Commission (SEC) suit was filed against Texas Gulf Sulphur Company in 1965 because its corporate employees had made unusually high profits on company stock that they had purchased after exploratory drilling had started in Ontario (in 1959) and before stock prices rose dramatically (in 1964) with the announcement of the discovery of large mineral deposits in Ontario.

10.3 The First National Bank has been losing money on automobile consumer loans and is considering the implementation of a new loan procedure that requires a credit check on loan applicants. Experience indicates that 82% of the loans were paid off, whereas the remainder defaulted. However, if the credit check is run, the probabilities can be revised as follows:

	Favorable Credit Check	Unfavorable Credit Check
Loan is paid	.9	.5
Loan is defaulted	.1	.5

An estimated 80% of the loan applicants receive a favorable credit check. Assume that the bank earns 18% on successful loans, loses 100% on defaulted loans, and suffers an opportunity cost of 0% when the loan is not granted and would have defaulted. If the cost of a credit check is 5% of the value of the loan and the bank is risk neutral, should the bank go ahead with the new policy?

10.4 Hearty Western Foods, one of the nation's largest consumer products firms, is trying to decide whether it should spend $5 million to test market a new ready-to-eat product (called Kidwich), to proceed directly to a nationwide marketing effort, or to cancel the product. The expected payoffs (in millions of dollars) from cancellation versus nationwide marketing are given below:

		Action	
Market Conditions		**Cancel**	**Go Nationwide**
No acceptance		0	−10
Marginal		0	10
Success		0	80

Prior experience with nationwide marketing efforts has been:

Market Conditions	**Probability**
No acceptance	.6
Marginal	.3
Success	.1

If the firm decides to test market the product, the following information becomes available:

		Probability		
		No Acceptance	**Marginal**	**Success**
Outcome Predicted	**No Acceptance**	.9	.1	0
by the Test Market	**Marginal**	.1	.7	.2
	Success	.1	.3	.6

For example, if the test market results predict a success, there is a 60% chance that the nationwide marketing effort really will be a success but a 30% chance it will be marginal and a 10% chance it will have no acceptance.

(a) If the firm is risk neutral, should it test market the product or not?

(b) If the firm is risk averse with a utility function

$$U(W) = \ln(W + 11),$$

should it test market the product or not?

10.5 The efficient market hypothesis implies that abnormal returns are expected to be zero. Yet in order for markets to be efficient, arbitrageurs must be able to force prices back into equilibrium. If they earn profits in doing so, is this fact inconsistent with market efficiency?

10.6 **(a)** In a poker game with six players, you can expect to lose 83% of the time. How can this still be a martingale?

(b) In the options market, call options expire unexercised over 80% of the time.[14] Thus the option holders frequently lose all their investment. Does this imply that the options market is not a fair game? Not a martingale? Not a submartingale?

10.7 If securities markets are efficient, what is the NPV of any security, regardless of risk?

---

[14] See Chapter 7 for a description of call options.

10.8 From time to time the federal government considers passing into law an excess profits tax on U.S. corporations. Given what you know about efficient markets and the CAPM, how would you define excess profits? What would be the effect of an excess profits tax on the investor?

10.9 State the assumptions inherent in this statement: A condition for market efficiency is that there be no second-order stochastic dominance.

REFERENCES

Alexander, S. S., "Price Movements in Speculative Markets: Trends or Random Walks," *Industrial Management Review*, May 1961, 7–26.

Ball, R., "Filter Rules: Interpretation of Market Efficiency, Experimental Problems and Australian Evidence," *Accounting Education*, November 1978, 1–17.

Black, F., M. Jensen, and M. Scholes, "The Capital Asset Pricing Model: Some Empirical Tests," in Jensen, ed., *Studies in the Theory of Capital Markets*. Praeger, New York, 1972, 79–124.

Black, F., and M. Scholes, "The Effects of Dividend Yield and Dividend Policy on Common Stock Prices and Returns," *Journal of Financial Economics*, May 1974, 1–22.

Copeland, T. E., and D. Friedman, "Partial Revelation of Information in Experimental Asset Markets," *Journal of Finance,* March 1991, 265–295.

———, "The Market for Information: Some Experimental Results," *Journal of Business,* April 1992, 241–266.

Cornell, B., and R. Roll, "Strategies for Pairwise Competitions in Markets and Organizations," *Bell Journal of Economics*, Spring 1981, 201–213.

David, K., D. Hirshleifer, and A. Subrahmanian, "Investor Psychology and Security Market Under- and Over-reactions," *Journal of Finance*, 1998, 1839–1885.

Fama, E. F., "The Behavior of Stock Market Prices," *The Journal of Business*, January 1965, 34–105.

———, "Efficient Capital Markets: A Review of Theory and Empirical Work," *Journal of Finance*, May 1970, 383–417.

———, *Foundations of Finance*. Basic Books, New York, 1976.

Fama, E. F., and M. Blume, "Filter Rules and Stock Market Trading Profits," *Journal of Business*, January (spec. supp.) 1966, 226–241.

Fama, E. F., and K. French, "On the Cross-Section of Expected Returns," *Journal of Finance*, 1992, Vol. 47, 427–466.

Fama, E. F., and J. MacBeth, "Risk Return and Equilibrium: Empirical Test," *Journal of Political Economy*, May–June 1973, 607–636.

Finnerty, J. E., "Insiders and Market Efficiency," *Journal of Finance*, September 1976, 1141–1148.

Forsythe, R., T. Palfrey, and C. R. Plott, "Asset Valuation in an Experimental Market," *Econometrica*, May 1982, 537–567.

Green, J. R., "Information, Efficiency and Equilibrium," Discussion Paper No. 284, Harvard Institute of Economic Research, March 1974.

Grossman, S. J., "On the Efficiency of Competitive Stock Markets Where Trades Have Diverse Information," *Journal of Finance*, May 1976, 573–586.

Grossman, S. J., and J. Stiglitz, "Information and Competitive Price Systems," *American Economic Review*, May 1976, 246–253.

———, "The Impossibility of Informationally Efficient Markets," *American Economic Review*, June 1980, 393–408.

Harrison, J. M., and D. M. Kreps, "Speculative Investor Behavior in a Stock Market with Heterogeneous Expectations," *Quarterly Journal of Economics*, May 1978, 323–336.

Hayek, F. H., "The Use of Knowledge in Society," *American Economic Review*, September 1945.

Hirshleifer, J., *Investment, Interest, and Capital*. Prentice-Hall, Englewood Cliffs, N.J., 1970.

Hirshleifer, J., and J. Riley, "The Analytics of Uncertainty and Information—An Expository Survey," *Journal of Economic Literature*, December 1979, 1375–1421.

Huang, C. C., I. Vertinsky, and W. T. Ziemba, "Sharp Bounds on the Value of Perfect Information," *Operations Research*, January–February 1977, 128–139.

Jaffe, J., "The Effect of Regulation Changes on Insider Trading," *Bell Journal of Economics and Management Science*, Spring 1974, 93–121.

Keynes, J. M., *The General Theory of Employment, Interest and Money*. Harcourt Brace, New York, 1936.

Latham, M., "Defining Capital Market Efficiency," Finance Working Paper 150, Institute for Business and Economic Research, University of California, Berkeley, April 1985.

Lewellen, J., and J. Shanken, "Learning, Asset-Pricing Tests, and Market Efficiency," *Journal of Finance*, Vol. 57, No. 3, 2002, 1113–1145.

Lucas, R. E., "Expectations and the Neutrality of Money," *Journal of Economic Theory*, April 1972, 103–124.

Marschak, J., *Economic Information, Decisions, and Predictions, Selected Essays*, Vol. 2, Reidel, Boston, 1974.

Miller, R. M., C. R. Plott, and V. L. Smith, "Intertemporal Competitive Equilibrium: An Empirical Study of Speculation," *American Economic Review*, June 1981, 448–459.

Plott, C. R., and S. Sunder, "Efficiency of Experimental Security Markets with Insider Information: An Application of Rational Expectations Models," *Journal of Political Economy*, August 1982, 663–698.

Rubinstein, M., "Securities Market Efficiency in an Arrow-Debreu Economy," *American Economic Review*, December 1975, 812–824.

Samuelson, P. A., "Proof That Properly Anticipated Prices Fluctuate Randomly," *Industrial Management Review*, Spring 1965, 41–49.

Smith, V. L., "Experimental Economics: Induced Value Theory," *American Economic Review*, May 1976, 274–279.

Sunder, S., "Market for Information: Experimental Evidence," Working Paper, University of Minnesota, 1984.

Chapter 11

> The only valid statement is that the current price embodies all knowledge, all expectations and all discounts that infringe upon the market.
>
> —C. W. J. Granger and O. Morgenstern,
> *Predictability of Stock Market Prices,*
> Heath Lexington Books,
> Lexington, Mass., 1970, 20.

Efficient Capital Markets: Evidence

EMPIRICAL EVIDENCE FOR OR AGAINST the hypothesis that capital markets are efficient takes many forms. This chapter is arranged in topical rather than chronological order, degree of sophistication, or type of market efficiency being tested. Not all the articles mentioned completely support the efficient capital market hypothesis. However, most agree that capital markets are efficient in the weak and semistrong forms but not in the strong form. The studies that we review span decades, dating from the late 1960s and continuing up to the most recently published papers. Usually capital market efficiency has been tested in the large and sophisticated capital markets of developed countries. Therefore one must be careful to limit any conclusions to the appropriate arena from which they are drawn. Research into the efficiency of capital markets is an ongoing process, and the work is being extended to include assets other than common stock as well as smaller and less sophisticated marketplaces.

A. Empirical Models Used for Residual Analysis

Before discussing the empirical tests of market efficiency, it is useful to review four basic types of empirical models that are frequently employed. The differences between them are important.

The simplest model, called the *market model*, simply argues that returns on security j are linearly related to returns on a "market portfolio." Mathematically, the market model is described by

$$R_{jt} = a_j + b_j R_{mt} + \varepsilon_{jt}. \tag{11.1}$$

The market model is not supported by any theory. It assumes that the slope and intercept terms are constant over the time period during which the model is fit to the available data. This is a strong assumption, particularly if the time series is long.

The second model uses the capital asset pricing theory. It requires the intercept term to be equal to the risk-free rate, or the rate of return on the minimum-variance zero-beta portfolio, both of which change over time. This CAPM-based methodology is given by Eq. (6.21):

$$R_{jt} = R_{ft} + [R_{mt} - R_{ft}] \beta_j + \varepsilon_{jt}.$$

Note, however, that systematic risk is assumed to remain constant over the interval of estimation. The use of the CAPM for residual analysis was explained at the end of Chapter 10.

Third, we sometimes see the *empirical market line*, which was explained in Chapter 6 and was given by Eq. (6.46):

$$R_{jt} = \widehat{\gamma}_{0t} + \widehat{\gamma}_{1t} \beta_{jt} + \varepsilon_{jt}.$$

Although related to the CAPM, it does not require the intercept term to equal the risk-free rate. Instead, both the intercept, $\widehat{\gamma}_{0t}$, and the slope, $\widehat{\gamma}_{1t}$, are the best linear estimates taken from cross-section data each time period (typically each month). Furthermore, it has the advantage that no parameters are assumed to be constant over time.

Finally, there are various multifactor cross-sectional models that have been used to explain returns, for example,

$$R_{jt} = \alpha_j + \beta_{1j}(R_{mt} - R_{ft}) + \beta_{2j}(RLE_t - RSE_t) + \beta_{3j}(HBTM_t - LBTM_t) + \varepsilon_{jt}. \tag{11.2}$$

In this fourth equation, the return of the jth stock in the tth time period is a function of the excess return on the market index over the risk-free rate, the difference in return between a large-capitalization equity portfolio and a small-cap portfolio, and the difference in return between a high and a low book-to-market equity portfolio.

All four models use the residual term, ε_{jt}, as measure of risk-adjusted abnormal performance. However, only one of the models, the second, relies exactly on the theoretical specifications of the Sharpe-Lintner capital asset pricing model.

In each of the empirical studies discussed, we shall mention the empirical technique by name because the market model and the multifactor model are not subject to Roll's critique (discussed in Chapter 6), whereas the CAPM and the empirical market line are. Thus residual analysis that employs the CAPM or the empirical market line may be subject to criticism.

B. Relevant Information (Earnings versus Cash Flow)

Market efficiency requires that security prices instantaneously and fully reflect all available relevant information. But what information is *relevant?* And how *fast* do security prices really react to new information? The answers to these questions are of particular interest to corporate officers who report the performance of their firm to the public; to the accounting profession, which audits these reports; and to the Securities and Exchange Commission, which regulates securities information.

The market value of assets is the present value of their cash flows discounted at the appropriate risk-adjusted rate. Investors should care only about the cash flow implications of various corporate decisions. However, corporations report accounting definitions, not cash flow, and frequently the two are not related. Does an efficient market look at the effect of managerial decisions on earnings per share (EPS) on cash flow? This is not an unimportant question, because frequently managers

Table 11.1 FIFO versus LIFO

	LIFO	FIFO	Inventory at Cost	
Revenue	100	100		
Cost of goods sold	90	25	Fourth item	$90 \rightarrow$ LIFO
Operating income	10	75	Third item	60
Taxes at 40%	4	30	Second item	40
Net income	6	45	First item	$25 \rightarrow$ FIFO
EPS (100 shares)	.06	.45		
Cash flow per share	.96	.70		

are observed to maximize EPS rather than cash flow because they believe that the market value of the company depends on reported EPS, when in fact (as we shall see) it does not.

Inventory accounting provides a good example of a situation where managerial decisions have opposite effects on EPS and cash flow. During an inflationary economy the cost of producing the most recent inventory continues to rise. On the books, inventory is recorded at cost, so that in the example given in Table 11.1 the fourth item added to the inventory costs more to produce than the first. If management elects to use first-in, first-out (FIFO) accounting, it will record a cost of goods sold of $25 against a revenue of $100 when an item is sold from inventory. This results in an EPS of $0.45. On the other hand, if LIFO (last-in, first-out) is used, EPS is $0.06. The impact of the two accounting treatments on cash flow is in exactly the opposite direction. Because the goods were manufactured in past time periods, the actual costs of production are sunk costs and irrelevant to current decision making. Therefore current cash flows are revenues less taxes. The cost of goods sold is a noncash charge. Therefore, with FIFO, cash flow per share is $0.70, whereas with LIFO it is $0.96. LIFO provides more cash flow because taxes are lower.

If investors really value cash flow and not EPS, we should expect to see stock prices rise when firms announce a switch from FIFO to LIFO accounting during inflationary periods. Sunder [1973, 1975] collected a sample of 110 firms that switched from FIFO to LIFO between 1946 and 1966 and 22 firms that switched from LIFO to FIFO. His procedure was to look at the pattern of cumulative average residuals from the CAPM. A residual return is the difference between the actual return and the return estimated by the model

$$\varepsilon_{jt} = R_{jt} - E(R_{jt} \mid \widehat{\beta}_{jt}).$$

The usual technique is to estimate ε_{jt} over an interval surrounding the economic event of interest. Taking monthly data, Sunder used all observations of returns except for those occurring plus or minus 12 months around the announcement of the inventory accounting change. He then used the estimated $\widehat{\beta}_{jt}$, the actual risk-free rate, and the actual market return during the 24-month period around the announcement date to predict the expected return.[1] Differences between estimated and actual returns were then averaged across all companies for each month. The average abnormal return in a given month is

---

[1] Sunder used a moving-average beta technique in his second study [1975]. However, it did not substantially change his results.

$$AR_t = \frac{1}{N} \sum_{j=1}^{N} \varepsilon_{jt},$$

where

$$N = \text{the number of companies.}$$

The cumulative average return (*CAR*) is the sum of average abnormal returns over all months from the start of the data up to and including the current month, T:

$$CAR_T = \sum_{t=1}^{T} AR_t,$$

where

$$T = \text{the total number of months being summed } (T = 1, 2, \ldots, M),$$

$$M = \text{the total number of months in the sample.}$$

If there were no abnormal change in the value of the firm associated with the switch from FIFO to LIFO, we should observe no pattern in the residuals. They would fluctuate around zero and on the average would equal zero. In other words, we would have a fair game. Figure 11.1 shows Sunder's results. Assuming that risk does not change during the 24-month period, the cumulative average residuals for the firms switching to LIFO rise by 5.3% during the 12 months prior to the announcement of the accounting change. This is consistent with the fact that shareholders actually value cash flow, not EPS. However, it does not necessarily mean that a switch to LIFO causes higher value. Almost all studies of this type, which focus on a particular phenomenon, suffer from what has come to be known as *postselection bias*. In this case, firms may decide to switch to LIFO because they are already doing well, and their value may have risen for that reason, not because of the switch in accounting method. Therefore, there are two explanations for the big run-up prior to the announcement of a switch from FIFO to LIFO. One is that firms that were doing well were more likely to switch in spite of the lower earnings effect. This interpretation implies higher than expected free cash flow (FCF). Cash flow matters. Alternatively, it could be that news of the decision leaked out via the rumor mill, and the market reacted to higher expected FCF before the announcement. Either way, since FCF is higher, the evidence supports FCF versus earnings as the variable of interest to the market. Either way, Sunder's results are inconsistent with the fact that shareholders look only at changes in EPS in order to value common stock. He finds no evidence that the switch to LIFO lowered value even though it did lower EPS.

Ricks [1982] studied a set of 354 NYSE- and AMEX-listed firms that switched to LIFO in 1974. He computed their earnings "as if" they never switched and found that the firms that switched to LIFO had an average 47% increase in their as-if earnings, whereas a matched sample of no-change firms had a 2% decrease. Ricks also found that the abnormal returns of the switching firms were significantly lower than the matched sample of no-change firms. These results are inconsistent with those reported by Sunder.

The studies above indicate that investors in efficient markets attempt to evaluate news about the effect of managerial decisions on cash flows—not on EPS. The empirical studies of Sunder [1973, 1975] provide evidence of what is meant by *relevant* accounting information. By relevant we mean any information about the *expected distribution of future cash flows*. Next, a study by Ball

Figure 11.1 Cumulative residuals for 24 months around the accounting change. (From S. Sunder, "Relationship between Accounting Changes and Stock Prices: Problems of Measurement and Some Empirical Evidence," reprinted from *Empirical Research in Accounting: Selected Studies*, 1973, 18.)

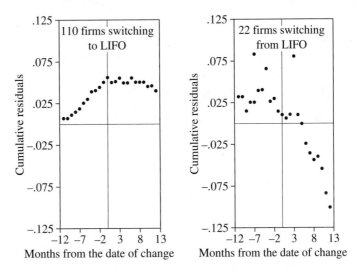

and Brown [1968] provides some evidence about the speed of adjustment as well as the information context of annual reports.

Earnings data and cash flows are usually highly correlated. The examples discussed above merely serve to point out some situations where they are not related and therefore allow empiricists to distinguish between the two. Ball and Brown used monthly data for a sample of 261 firms between 1946 and 1965 to evaluate the usefulness of information in annual reports. First, they separated the sample into companies that had earnings that were either higher or lower than those predicted by a naive time series model. Their model for the change in earnings was

$$\Delta N I_{jt} = \widehat{a} + \widehat{b}_j \Delta m_t + \varepsilon_{jt}, \tag{11.3}$$

where

$$\Delta N I_{jt} = \text{the change in earnings per share for the } j\text{th firm,}$$

$$\Delta m_t = \text{the change in the average EPS for all firms (other than firm } j) \text{ in the market.}$$

Next, this regression was used to explain next year's change in earnings, $\Delta \widehat{N I}_{j,t+1}$:

$$\Delta \widehat{N I}_{j,t+1} = \widehat{a} + \widehat{b}_j \Delta m_{t+1}, \tag{11.4}$$

where

$$\widehat{a}, \widehat{b} = \text{coefficients estimated from time-series fits of Eq. (11.2) to the data,}$$

$$\Delta m_{t+1} = \text{the actual change in market average EPS during the } (t+1)\text{th time period.}$$

Figure 11.2 Abnormal performance index of portfolios chosen on the basis of differences between actual and predicted accounting income. (From R. Ball and P. Brown, "An Empirical Evaluation of Accounting Income Numbers," reprinted with the permission of *Journal of Accounting Research*, Autumn 1968, 169.)

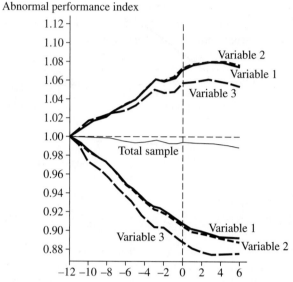

A quick look at Fig. 11.2 shows that when earnings are higher than predicted, returns are abnormally high. Furthermore, returns appear to adjust gradually until, by the time of the annual report, almost all the adjustment has occurred. Most of the information contained in the annual report is anticipated by the market *before* the annual report is released. In fact, anticipation is so accurate that the actual income number does not appear to cause any unusual jumps in the API in the announcement month. Most of the content of the annual report (about 85% to 90%) is captured by more timely sources of information. Apparently market prices adjust continuously to new information as it becomes publicly available throughout the year. The annual report has little new information to add.

Finally, estimated changes were compared with actual earnings changes. If the actual change was greater than estimated, the company was put into a portfolio where returns were expected to be positive, and vice versa.

Figure 11.2 plots an abnormal performance index (API) that represents the value of \$1 invested in a portfolio 12 months before an annual report and held for T months (where $T = 1, 2, \ldots, 12$). It is computed as follows:

$$ API = \frac{1}{N} \sum_{j=1}^{N} \prod_{t=1}^{T} (1 + \varepsilon_{jt}), $$

where

N = the number of companies in a portfolio,

$T = 1, 2, \ldots, 12,$

ε_{jt} = abnormal performance measured by deviations from the market model.

These results suggest that prices in the marketplace continuously adjust in an unbiased manner to new information. Two implications for chief financial officers are (1) significant new information, which will affect the future cash flows of the firm, should be announced as soon as it becomes available so that shareholders can use it without the (presumably greater) expense of discovering it from alternative sources, and (2) it probably does not make any difference whether cash flows are reported in the balance sheet, the income statement, or the footnotes—the market can evaluate the news as long as it is publicly available, whatever form it may take.

C. Speed of Adjustment

1. Quarterly Earnings and Dividends

The Ball and Brown study raised the question of whether or not annual reports contain any new information. Studies by Aharony and Swary [1980], Joy, Litzenberger, and McEnally [1977], and Watts [1978] have focused on quarterly earnings reports, where information revealed to the market is (perhaps) more timely than annual reports.[2] They typically use a time-series model to predict quarterly earnings, then form two portfolios of equal risk, one consisting of firms with earnings higher than predicted and the other of firms with lower than expected earnings. The combined portfolio, which is long in the higher than expected earnings firms and short in the lower than expected earnings firms, is a zero-beta portfolio that (in perfect markets) requires no investment. It is an arbitrage portfolio and should have zero expected return. Watts [1978] finds a statistically significant return in the quarter of the announcement—a clear indication that quarterly earnings reports contain new information. However, he also finds a statistically significant return in the following quarter and concludes that "the existence of those abnormal returns is evidence that the market is inefficient."

Quarterly earnings reports are sometimes followed by announcements of dividend changes, which also affect the stock price. To study this problem, Aharony and Swary [1980] examine all dividend and earnings announcements within the same quarter that are at least 11 trading days apart. They conclude that both quarterly earnings announcements and dividend change announcements have significant effects on the stock price. But more importantly they find no evidence of market inefficiency when the two types of announcement effects are separated. They used daily data and Watts [1978] used quarterly data, so we cannot be sure that the conclusions of the two studies regarding market inefficiency are inconsistent. All we can say is that unexpected changes in quarterly dividends and in quarterly earnings both have significant effects on the value of the firm and that more research needs to be done on possible market inefficiencies following the announcement of unexpected earnings changes.

Using intraday records of all transactions for the common stock returns of 96 (large) firms, Patell and Wolfson [1984] were able to estimate the speed of market reaction to disclosures of dividend and earnings information. In a simple trading rule, they bought (sold short) stocks whose dividend or earnings announcements exceeded (fell below) what had been forecast by Value Line Investor Service. The initial price reactions to earnings and dividend change announcements begin with the first pair of price changes following the appearance of the news release on the Broad Tape monitors. Although there was a hint of some activity in the hour or two preceding the Broad Tape

---

[2] See also articles by Brown [1978], Griffin [1977], and Foster [1977].

news release, by far the largest portion of the price response occurs in the first 5 to 15 minutes after the disclosure. Thus, according to Patell and Wolfson, the market reacts to unexpected changes in earnings and dividends, and it reacts *very* quickly.

2. Block Trades

During a typical day for an actively traded security on a major stock exchange, thousands of shares will be traded, usually in round lots ranging between one hundred and several hundred shares. However, occasionally a large block, say 10,000 shares or more, is brought to the floor for trading. The behavior of the marketplace during the time interval around the trading of a large block provides a "laboratory" where the following questions can be investigated: (1) Does the block trade disrupt the market? (2) If the stock price falls when the block is sold, is the fall a liquidity effect, an information effect, or both? (3) Can anyone earn abnormal returns from the fall in price? (4) How fast does the market adjust to the effects of a block trade?

In perfect (rather than efficient) capital markets, securities of equal risk are perfect substitutes for each other. Because all individuals are assumed to possess the same information and because markets are assumed to be frictionless, the number of shares traded in a given security should have no effect on its price. If markets are less than perfect, the sale of a large block may have two effects (see Fig. 11.3). First, if it is believed to carry with it some new information about the security, the price will change (permanently) to reflect the new information. As illustrated in Fig. 11.3(c) and (d), the closing price is lower than the opening price and it remains low permanently.[3] Second, if buyers must incur extra costs when they accept the block, there may be a (temporary) decline in price to reflect what has been in various articles described as a price pressure, or distribution effect, or liquidity premium, as shown in Fig. 11.3(a) and (c). Figure 11.3 depicts how hypothesized information or price pressure effects can be expected to show up in continuous transactions data. For example, if the sale of a large block has both effects, as in Fig. 11.3(c), we may expect the price to fall from the price before the trade $(-T)$ to the block price (BP) at the time of the block trade (BT), then to recover quickly from any price pressure effect by the time of the next trade $(+T)$ but to remain at a permanently lower level, which reflects the impact of new information on the value of the security.

Scholes [1972] and Kraus and Stoll [1972] provided the first empirical evidence about the price effects of block trading. Scholes used daily returns data to analyze 345 secondary distributions between July 1961 and December 1965. Secondary distributions, unlike primary distributions, are not initiated by the company but by shareholders who will receive the proceeds of the sale. The distributions are usually underwritten by an investment banking group that buys the entire block from the seller. The shares are then sold on a subscription basis *after* normal trading hours. The subscriber pays only the subscription price and not stock exchange or brokerage commissions. Figure 11.4 shows an abnormal performance index based on the market model and calculated for 40 trading days around the date of a secondary distribution. The abnormal performance index falls from an initial level of 1.0 to a final value of .977 just 14 days after the sale, a decline of 2.2%. On the day of the secondary distribution, the average abnormal performance was −.5%. Because this study uses only close-to-close daily returns data, it focuses only on permanent price changes. We have characterized these as information effects, as in Fig. 11.3(c) and (d). Further evidence that

---

[3] The permanent decline in price is also tested by looking at the pattern of day-to-day closing prices. Evidence on this is reported in Fig. 11.4.

Figure 11.3 Competing hypotheses of price behavior around the sale of a large block.

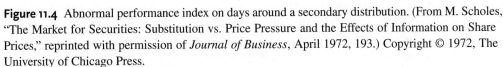

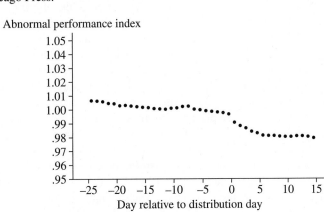

Figure 11.4 Abnormal performance index on days around a secondary distribution. (From M. Scholes, "The Market for Securities: Substitution vs. Price Pressure and the Effects of Information on Share Prices," reprinted with permission of *Journal of Business*, April 1972, 193.) Copyright © 1972, The University of Chicago Press.

the permanent decline in price is an information effect is revealed when the API is partitioned by vendor classification. These results appear in Table 11.2.

On the day of the offering the vendor is not usually known, but we may presume that the news becomes available soon thereafter. One may expect that an estate liquidation or portfolio rebalancing by a bank or insurance company would not be motivated by information about the performance of the firm. On the other hand, corporate insiders as well as investment companies

Table 11.2 Abnormal Performance Index for Secondary Distributions Partitioned by Vendor Category

No. of Observations in Sample	Category	API (%) −10 to +10 Days	API (%) 0 to +10 Days
192	Investment companies and mutual funds	−2.5	−1.4
31	Banks and insurance companies	−.3	−0.0
36	Individuals	−1.1	−.7
23	Corporations and officers	−2.9	−2.1
50	Estates and trusts	−.7	−.5

From M. Scholes, "The Market for Securities: Substitution vs. Price Pressure and the Effects of Information on Share Prices," reprinted with permission of *Journal of Business*, April 1972, 202. Copyright © 1972, The University of Chicago Press.

and mutual funds (with large research staffs) may be selling on the basis of adverse information. The data seem to support these suppositions. Greater price changes after the distribution are observed when the seller is presumed to have a knowledgeable reason for trading.[4]

Mikkelson and Partch [1985] studied a sample of 146 registered and 321 nonregistered secondary offerings between 1972 and 1981. Using daily return data, they find an average statistically significant initial announcement price decline of −2.87% for registered secondaries and −1.96% for nonregistered distributions. The announcement date price declines are permanent, they are positively correlated to the size of the offering, and they are related to the identity of the seller (with the largest declines occurring when the vendors are directors or officers). These results are consistent with a permanent information effect. Mikkelson and Partch also find that the underwriting spread of secondaries is positively related to the relative size of the offering. This is consistent with the argument that the underwriting spread reflects compensation for the underwriter's selling effort or liquidity services. Therefore, even though Mikkelson and Partch find no rebound in market prices following secondary offerings, they cannot conclude that the costs of liquidity are unimportant.

The data available to Kraus and Stoll [1972] pertain to open market block trades. They examined price effects for all block trades of 10,000 shares or more carried out on the NYSE between July 1, 1968, and September 30, 1969. They had prices for the close of day before the block trade, the price immediately prior to the transaction, the block price, and the closing price the day of the block trade. Abnormal performance indices based on daily data were consistent with Scholes's results. More interesting were intraday price effects, which are shown in Fig. 11.5. There is clear evidence of a price pressure or distribution effect. The stock price recovers substantially from the block price by the end of the trading day. The recovery averages .713%. For example, a stock that sold for $50.00 before the block transaction would have a block price of $49.43, but by the end of the day the price would have recovered to $49.79.

The Scholes and Kraus-Stoll studies find evidence of a permanent price decline that is measured by price drops from the closing price the day before the block trade to the closing price the day

---

[4] A second test performed by Scholes showed that there was no relationship between the size of the distribution (as a percentage of the firm) and changes in the API on the distribution date. This would lead us to reject the hypothesis that investment companies and mutual funds may have an impact because they sold larger blocks.

Figure 11.5 Intraday price impacts of block trading. (From A. Kraus and H. R. Stoll, "Price Impacts of Block Trading on the New York Stock Exchange," reprinted with permission of *Journal of Finance*, June 1972, 575.)

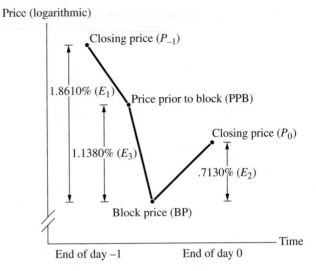

of the block transaction. These negative returns seem to persist for at least a month after the block trade. In addition, Kraus and Stoll found evidence of temporary intraday price pressure effects. The implications of these findings are discussed by Dann, Mayers, and Raab [1977], who collected continuous transactions data during the day of a block trade for a sample of 298 blocks between July 1968 and December 1969. The open-to-block price change is at least 4.56% for each block in their sample. The reason for restricting the sample to blocks with large price declines was to provide the strongest test for market efficiency. If an individual or group of individuals can establish a trading rule that allows them to buy a block whose open-to-block price change is at least 4.56%, then sell at the end of the day, they may be able to earn abnormal profits. This would be evidence of capital market inefficiency.

Testing a trading rule of this type takes great care. Normally, a block trade is not made publicly available until the trade has already been consummated and the transaction is recorded on the ticker. The semistrong form of market efficiency is based on the set of publicly available information. Therefore a critical issue is, exactly how fast must we react after we observe that our −4.56% trading rule has been activated by the first publicly available announcement that occurs on the ticker tape? Figure 11.6 shows annualized rates of return using the −4.56% rule with a purchase made x minutes after the block and the stock then sold at the close. Returns are net of actual commissions and the New York State transfer taxes. For both time periods that are reported, we would have to react in less than five minutes in order to earn a positive return. Such a rapid reaction is, for all practical purposes, impossible. It seems that no abnormal returns are available to individuals who trade on publicly available information about block trades because prices react so quickly. Fifteen minutes after the block trade, transaction prices have completely adjusted to unbiased estimating of closing prices. This gives some idea of how fast the market adjusts to new, unexpected information like a block trade.

What about people who can transact at the block price? Who are they and do they earn an abnormal return? Usually, the specialist, the floor trader (a member of the NYSE), brokerage houses, and favored customers of the brokerage houses can participate in the block price. Dann, Mayers, and Raab show that with a −4.56% trading rule, an individual participating in every

Figure 11.6 Annualized rates of return on the −4.56% rule. (From L. Dann, D. Mayers, and R. Raab, "Trading Rules, Large Blocks, and the Speed of Adjustment," reprinted from *Journal of Financial Economics*, January 1977, 18.)

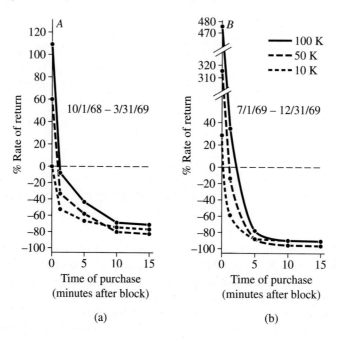

(a)   (b)

block with purchases of $100,000 or more could have earned a net annualized rate of return of 203% for the 173 blocks that activated the filter rule. Of course, this represents the maximum realizable rate of return. Nevertheless, it is clear that even after adjusting for risk, transaction costs, and taxes, it is possible to earn rates of return in excess of what any existing theory would call "normal." This may be interpreted as evidence that capital markets are inefficient in their strong form. Individuals who are notified of the pending block trade and who can participate at the block price before the information becomes publicly available do in fact appear to earn excess profits.

However, Dann, Mayers, and Raab caution us that we may not properly understand all the costs that a buyer faces in a block trade. One possibility is that the specialist (or anyone else) normally holds an optimal utility-maximizing portfolio. In order to accept part of a block trade, which forces the specialist away from that portfolio, he or she will charge a premium rate of return. In this way, what appear to be abnormal returns may actually be fair, competitively determined fees for a service rendered—the service of providing liquidity to a seller.

To date, the empirical research into the phenomenon of price changes around a block trade shows that block trades do not disrupt markets and that markets are efficient in the sense that they very quickly (less than 15 minutes) fully reflect all publicly available information. There is evidence of both a permanent effect and a (very) temporary liquidity or price pressure effect as illustrated in Fig. 11.3(c). The market is efficient in its semistrong form, but the fact that abnormal returns are earned by individuals who participate at the block price may indicate strong-form inefficiency.

D. Rejection of Strong-Form Efficiency

A direct test of strong-form efficiency is whether or not insiders with access to information that is not publicly available can outperform the market.[5] Jaffe [1974] collected data on insider trading from the *Official Summary of Security Transactions and Holdings,* published by the Securities and Exchange Commission. He then defined an intensive trading month as one during which there were at least three more insiders selling than buying, or vice versa. If a stock was intensively traded during a given month, it was included in an intensive-trading portfolio. Using the empirical market line, Jaffe then calculated cumulative average residuals. If the stock had intensive selling, its residual (which would presumably be negative) was multiplied by -1 and added to the portfolio returns, and conversely for intensive buying. For 861 observations during the 1960s, the residuals rose approximately 5% in eight months following the intensive-trading event, with 3% of the rise occurring in the last six months. These returns are statistically significant and are greater than transactions costs. A sample of insider trading during the 1950s produces similar results. These findings suggest that insiders do earn abnormal returns and that the strong-form hypothesis of market efficiency does not hold.

A study by Finnerty [1976] corroborates Jaffe's conclusions. The major difference is that the Finnerty data sample was not restricted to an intensive trading group. By testing the entire population of insiders, the empirical findings allow an evaluation of the "average" insider returns. The data include over 30,000 individual insider transactions between January 1969 and December 1972. Abnormal returns computed from the market model indicated that insiders are able to "beat the market" on a risk-adjusted basis, both when selling and when buying.

A study by Givoly and Palmon [1985] correlates insider trading with subsequent news announcements to see if insiders trade in anticipation of news releases. The surprising result is that there is no relationship between insider trading and news events. Although insiders' transactions are associated with a strong price movement in the direction of the trade during the month following the trade, these price movements occur independently of subsequent publication of news. This leads to the conjecture that outside investors accept (blindly) the superior knowledge and follow in the footsteps of insiders.

E. Common Errors of Empirical Studies

The design and interpretation of empirical studies of market efficiency is a tricky business. This brief section lists the common pitfalls. Unless research is carefully conducted, results that indicate possible market inefficiencies may simply be faulty research.

1. *Biased model of equilibrium returns*—Remember that any test of market efficiency is a joint test of the model that defines "normal" returns. If the model is misspecified, then it will not estimate

---

[5] The Securities and Exchange Commission defines *insiders* as members of the board of directors, corporate officers, and any beneficial owner of more than 10% of any class of stock. They must disclose, on a monthly basis, any changes in their stock holdings.

the correct normal returns, and the so-called abnormal returns that result are not evidence of market inefficiency—only a bad model.

2. *Specification searches*—It is always possible, if one tries long enough, to find a model that seems to beat the market during a test period. However, the acid test of whether there is a market inefficiency is to test the model on a different holdout sample period (or periods).

3. *Sample selection bias*—A portfolio of stocks that split will always show positive abnormal returns prior to the split announcement date. Why? Because only stocks whose prices have risen will decide to split. The very fact that one chooses to study stock splits means that the presplit characteristics of the sample stocks are abnormal. Modeling their behavior relative to the market presplit and expecting their postsplit behavior to be similar is a heroic assumption that is usually wrong.

4. *Survivorship bias*—If we study the behavior of mutual funds by gathering a list of funds that exist today, then collect data about their historical performance for analysis, we are designing survivorship bias into our research. Why? Because we are looking at only those funds that survived up to today. To avoid survivorship bias we should collect a sample of all funds that existed on a given date in the past, and then collect data about their performance from that date forward. By so doing we will capture all of the funds that ceased to exist between then and now. They probably have lower excess returns, and failure to include them in our sample implies upward-biased results.

5. *Biased measures of return*—As Fama [1998] points out, the calculation of geometric returns over a long period of time can overstate performance. For example, suppose that an abnormal return of 10% is recorded in year 1 on a test portfolio and then compounded, doubling over an additional four years. The cumulative return would be $(1.1)(2.0) = 2.2$. A benchmark portfolio would earn no abnormal return the first year and would also double over the following four years with a cumulative return of $(1.0)(2.0) = 2.0$. If we were to take the difference between the two, we would conclude that the test portfolio earned an abnormal return of 20 percent over the four years following year 1. This false conclusion can be avoided by measuring cumulative abnormal return as the ratio of geometric returns on the test portfolio to the geometric returns on the benchmark portfolio, for example, $[(1.1)(2.0)/(1.0)(2.0) -1] = 10\%$. This approach provides the correct conclusion that 10% abnormal return was earned in year 1 and no abnormal return thereafter.

6. *Inappropriate portfolio weightings*—The economic interpretation of market inefficiency depends on value weightings of outcomes. Often equally weighted abnormal returns are reported with the average being driven by small firms. The researcher then concludes the market is inefficient when in fact only the pricing of small illiquid stocks is inefficient.

7. *Failure to distinguish between statistical and economic significance*—Many studies conclude that the market is inefficient on a statistical basis without actually going the next step. To be economically significant, a trading rule must show arbitrage profits after transaction costs that include paying half of the bid-ask spread, brokerage fees, and net of any price pressure effects. A market is inefficient only if there is both statistical and economic proof of inefficiency.

8. *Overestimating the frequency of opportunities for arbitrage*—In practice, arbitrage opportunities do not appear every day. For example, transactions involving very large blocks may offer arbitrage profits, but they do not happen frequently. For the market to be inefficient, the frequency of opportunities must be high enough to allow economically significant arbitrage returns.

F. *S*emistrong-Form Anomalies: Long Term

1. New Issues (IPOs)

There has been a long history of articles that have studied the pricing of the common stock of companies that is issued to the public for the first time in transactions called initial public offerings (IPOs). To mention a few, the list includes papers by the Securities and Exchange Commission [1963], Reilly and Hatfield [1969], Stickney [1970], McDonald and Fisher [1972], Logue [1973], Stigler [1964], Shaw [1971], Loughran and Ritter [1995], Brav and Gompers [1997], Mitchell and Stafford [1997], Lowrey and Schwert [2002], and Ritter and Welch [2002]. The unadjusted returns show positive abnormal returns of 19% at the end of the first day of trading and negative abnormal returns in the long run (underperforming the market index over the next three years by 23%, and underperforming a benchmark portfolio of similar size and book-to-market ratio by 5%). Hence there is a two-part puzzle broken down into short-run positive and long-run negative abnormal returns.

Studies of long-run returns (e.g., Loughran and Ritter [1995]) report that IPO'd equities under-perform benchmark portfolios by approximately 30% over the five-year period following listing. All of these studies faced the same seemingly insoluble problem: How could returns on unseasoned issues be adjusted for risk if time-series data on preissue prices was nonexistent?

Any CAPM-based estimate of risk-adjusted returns requires the computation of the covariance between time-series returns for a given security and returns on a market portfolio. But new issues are not priced until they become public. An ingenious way around this problem was employed by Ibbotson [1975]. Portfolios of new issues with identical seasoning (defined as the number of months since issue) were formed. The monthly return on the XYZ Company in March 1964, say, two months after its issue, was matched with the market return that month, resulting in one pair of returns for a portfolio of two months' seasoning. By collecting a large number of return pairs for new issues that went public in different calendar months but all with two months' seasoning, it was possible to form a vector of returns of issues of two months' seasoning for which Ibbotson could compute a covariance with the market. In this manner, he estimated the systematic risk of issues with various seasoning. Using the empirical market line, he was able to estimate abnormal performance indices in the month of initial issue (initial performance from the offering date price to the end of the first month) and in the aftermarket (months following the initial issue). From 2,650 new issues between 1960 and 1969, Ibbotson randomly selected one new issue for each of the 120 calendar months.

The estimated systematic risk (beta) in the month of issue was 2.26, and the abnormal return was estimated to be 11.4%. Even after transaction costs, this represents a statistically significant positive abnormal return. Therefore, either the offering price is set too low or investors systematically overvalue new issues at the end of the first month of seasoning. We shall return to this short-term anomaly a little later. What about new issue performance in the aftermarket, that is, for prices from the first market price onward? Figure 11.7 shows abnormal returns (based on the empirical market line) in the aftermarket for six-month holding periods and the significance tests (t-tests). The 9 periods other than the initial offering period include only 2 periods with results that are statistically different from zero (and returns in these 2 periods are negative). Ibbotson concludes that the evidence cannot allow us to reject the null hypothesis that *aftermarkets* are efficient, although it is interesting to note that returns in 7 out of 10 periods show negative returns. Figure 11.8 shows plots of changes in systematic risk in the aftermarket; note the decline. The

Figure 11.7 Abnormal returns for issues of different seasoning. (From R. Ibbotson, "Price Performance of Common Stock New Issues," reprinted from *Journal of Financial Economics*, September 1975, 254.)

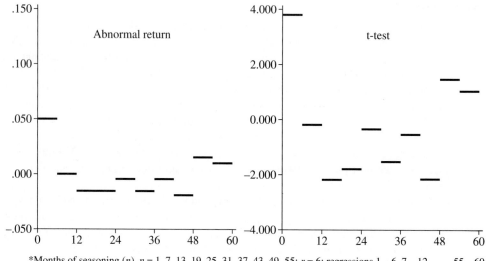

*Months of seasoning (n), $n = 1, 7, 13, 19, 25, 31, 37, 43, 49, 55$; $r = 6$; regressions $1 - 6, 7 - 12, \ldots, 55 - 60$

results show that the systematic risk of new issues is greater than the systematic risk of the market (which always has a beta equal to one) and that the systematic risk is not stable in that it drops as the new issue becomes seasoned.

Loughran and Ritter [1995] do not use a CAPM risk adjustment; rather they control for size (a variable that is easier to measure yet highly correlated with beta). They found that IPOs underperform the benchmark by 30% over the five-year period following issuance. If valid, this result would imply the market is inefficient in its semistrong form. A follow-up study by Brav and Gompers [1997] uses the Fama-French [1992] cross-sectional explanation of security returns to form benchmarks that control for size and for the book-to-market ratio. Instead of declining 30%, the IPO portfolio stays even with the benchmark and the anomaly disappears. As Fama [1998] points out, IPOs are typically small high-growth stocks, and such stocks have low returns in the post-1963 period. Therefore, the problem of low returns is not specific to IPOs, but is common to all small high-growth stocks.

Studies of short-term returns (e.g., Ibbotson [1975]) provide several possible explanations of the short-term underpricing of IPOs (i.e., the fact that offering prices determined by the investment banking firm are systematically set below the fair market value of a security). Regulations of the SEC require a maximum offering price for a new issue, which is usually filed two weeks in advance of the actual offering, although it can be adjusted in some cases.[6] The actual offering price is set immediately after the offering. The existence of a regulation that requires the actual offering price to be fixed creates the possibility of a "heads I lose, tails you win" situation for the underwriter. Table 11.3 shows the four possibilities that can occur in a firm commitment offering

---

[6] In most cases the maximum offering price is set high enough to cause little concern that it may actually constrain the actual offering price.

Figure 11.8 Systematic risk of issues with different seasoning. (From R. Ibbotson, "Price Performance of Common Stock New Issues," reprinted from *Journal of Financial Economics*, September 1975, 260.)

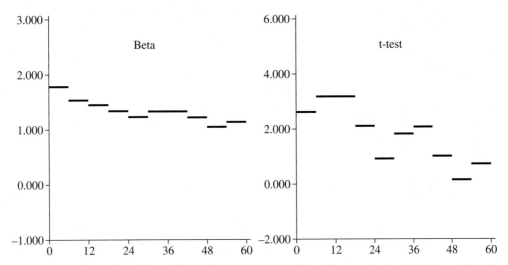

*Months of seasoning (*n*), *n* = 1, 7, 13, 19, 25, 31, 37, 43, 49, 55; *r* = 6; regressions 1 – 6, 7 – 12, . . . , 55 – 60.
These *t*-statistics are designed to test if $\beta_{x,r0} > 1$.

Table 11.3 Gain and Loss Situations for a New Issue

	Situation	Investors	Investment Banker
I	Maximum offering price ≥ market price ≥ offering price	Gain	Parity
II	Maximum offering price ≥ offering price ≥ market price	Parity	Loss
III	Maximum offering price = offering price ≥ market price	Parity	Loss
IV	Market price ≥ maximum offering price = offering price	Gain	Parity

(the underwriter syndicate buys the issue from the firm for the offering price less an underwriting spread, then sells the issue to the public at the fixed offering price). The best the underwriter can do is achieve a parity situation with no gain or loss. This happens whenever the market price turns out to be above the offering price (situations I and IV). Obviously, the investment banker does not want the market price to equal or exceed the *maximum* offering price (situations III and IV). This would infuriate the issuing firm and lead to a loss of future underwriting business. Therefore we usually observe situations I and II.

But if the investment banking firm receives adequate compensation from its underwriting spread for the risk it undertakes, and if it cannot gain by setting the offer price lower than the market price, then why do we not observe offer prices (which, after all, are established only moments before the issues are sold to the public) set equal to the market value? Why can investors systematically earn an abnormal return of 11.4% during the first month of issue? A possible explanation is information asymmetry between the insiders of the issuing company and investors in the market. For a complete discussion see Ritter and Welch [2002]. Think of a bid-ask spread. When a large block is being sold by an informed seller, the market is willing to pay a bid price significantly below the intrinsic value of the stock. The magnitude of the discount depends on the size of the block relative to expected normal trading volume, and on the extent of information asymmetry between the seller and the buyer. If, for example, the childless owner of a company is selling his controlling interest of a company in order to retire, the underpricing may be considerably less than it might be in an alternate scenario where an otherwise wealthy and sophisticated entrepreneur convinces the board to IPO the company in the midst of a hot market for new issues. In the first instance, the amount of information asymmetry is presumably low because the IPO is motivated more by the retiring owner's need for liquidity than anything else. In the second instance, the IPO may well be motivated by inside information. Needless to say, there remains considerable debate among researchers about whether the systematic short-term underpricing of IPOs is rational or not.

Weinstein [1978] studied the price behavior of newly issued corporate bonds by measuring their excess holding period returns. Excess returns were defined as the difference between the return on the ith newly issued bond and a portfolio of seasoned bonds with the same (Moody's) bond rating. Data were collected for 179 new issues between June 1962 and July 1974. Weinstein's conclusions for newly issued bonds are similar to those of Ibbotson [1975] for newly issued stock, namely, that the offering price is below the market equilibrium price but that the aftermarket is efficient. Weinstein found a .383% rate of return during the first month and only a .06% rate of return over the next six months.

2. Stock Splits

Why do stocks split, and what effect, if any, do splits have on shareholder wealth? The best-known study of stock splits was conducted by Fama, Fisher, Jensen, and Roll [1969]. Cumulative average residuals were calculated from the simple market model, using monthly data for an interval of 60 months around the split ex date for 940 splits between January 1927 and December 1959. Figure 11.9 shows the results. It plots the cumulative average return for the stock split sample. Positive abnormal returns are observed *before* the split but not afterward. This would seem to indicate that splits are the cause of the abnormal returns. But such a conclusion has no economic logic to it. The run-up in the cumulative average returns prior to the stock split in Fig. 11.9 can be explained by selection bias. Stocks split because their price has increased prior to the split date. Consequently, it should hardly be surprising that when we select a sample of split-up stocks, we observe that they have positive abnormal performance prior to the split date. Selection bias occurs because we are studying a selected data set of stocks that have been observed to split.

Fama et al. [1969] speculated that stock splits might be interpreted by investors as a message about future changes in the firm's expected cash flows. Specifically, they hypothesized that stock splits might be interpreted as a message about dividend increases, which in turn imply that managers of the firm feel confident that it can maintain a permanently higher level of cash flows. To test this hypothesis the sample was divided into those firms that increased their dividends beyond the average for the market in the interval following the split and those that paid out lower dividends. The results, shown in Fig. 11.10, reveal that stocks in the dividend "increased" class have slightly positive returns following the split. This is consistent with the hypothesis that splits are interpreted

Figure 11.9 Cumulative average residuals for 60 months around stock splits. (From E. F. Fama, L. Fisher, M. Jensen, and R. Roll, "The Adjustment of Stock Prices to New Information," reprinted with permission of *International Economic Review*, February 1969, 13. Copyright © *International Economic Review*.)

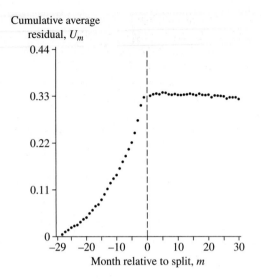

Cumulative average residual, U_m

Month relative to split, m

as messages about dividend increases.[7] Of course, a dividend increase does not always follow a split. Hence the slightly positive abnormal return for the dividend-increase group reflects small price adjustments that occur when the market is absolutely sure of the increase. On the other hand, the cumulative average residuals of split-up stocks with prior dividend performance decline until about a year after the split, by which time it must be very clear that the anticipated dividend increase is not forthcoming. When we combine the results for the dividend increases and decreases, these results are consistent with the hypothesis that on the average the market makes unbiased dividend forecasts for split-up securities and these forecasts are fully reflected in the price of the security by the end of the split month.

A study by Grinblatt, Masulis, and Titman [1984] used daily data and looked at shareholder returns on the split announcement date as well as the split ex date. They examined a special subsample of splits where no other announcements were made in the three-day period around the split announcement and where no cash dividends had been declared in the previous three years.[8] For this sample of 125 "pure" stock splits they found a statistically significant announcement return of 3.44%. They too interpret stock split announcements as favorable signs about the firm's future cash flows. Surprisingly, they also find statistically significant returns (for their entire sample of 1,360 stock splits) on the ex date. At that time there was no explanation for this result, and it is inconsistent with the earlier Fama et al. study that used monthly returns data.

In the same study, Grinblatt, Masulis, and Titman [1984] confirm earlier work on stock dividends by Foster and Vickrey [1978] and Woolridge [1983a, 1983b]. The announcement effects for stock dividends are large, 4.90% for a sample of 382 stock dividends and 5.89% for a smaller sample of 84 stock dividends with no other announcements in a three-day period around the stock dividend announcement. One possible reason for the announcement effect of a stock dividend

---

[7] This does not imply that higher dividend payout per se causes an increase in the value of the firm. In Chapter 16 we shall see that higher dividends are interpreted as signals that the future cash flows from the firm will increase.

[8] However, 11% of the pure samples declared a dividend within one year of the stock split.

Figure 11.10 Cumulative average residuals for splits with (a) dividend increases and (b) decreases. (From E. F. Fama, L. Fisher, M. Jensen, and R. Roll, "The Adjustment of Stock Prices to New Information," reprinted with permission of *International Economic Review*, February 1969, 15. Copyright © *International Economic Review*.)

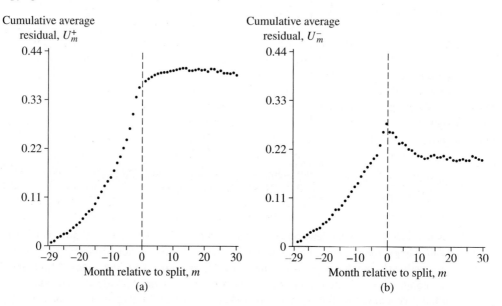

is that retained earnings must be reduced by the dollar amount of the stock dividend. Only those companies that are confident they will not run afoul of debt restrictions that require minimum levels of retained earnings will willingly announce a stock dividend. Another reason is that convertible debt is not protected against dilution caused by stock dividends. As with stock splits, there was a significant positive return on the stock dividend ex date (and the day before). No explanation is offered for why the ex date effect is observed.

The results of Fama et al. [1969] are consistent with the semistrong form of market efficiency. Prices appear to fully reflect information about expected cash flows. The split per se has no effect on shareholder wealth. Rather, it merely serves as a message about the future prospects of the firm. Thus splits have benefits as signaling devices. There seems to be no way to use a split to increase one's expected returns, unless, of course, inside information concerning the split or subsequent dividend behavior is available.

One often hears that stocks split because there is an "optimal" price range for common stocks. Moving the security price into this range makes the market for trading in the security "wider" or "deeper"; hence there is more trading liquidity. Copeland [1979] reports that contrary to the above argument, market liquidity is actually lower following a stock split. Trading volume is proportionately lower than its presplit level, brokerage revenues (a major portion of transaction costs) are proportionately higher, and bid-ask spreads are higher as a percentage of the bid price.[9]

---

[9] The bid price is the price that a potential buyer offers, say, $20, and the ask price is what the seller requires, suppose it is $20\frac{1}{2}$. The bid-ask spread is the difference, specifically $\frac{1}{2}$.

Taken together, these empirical results point to lower postsplit liquidity. Hence we can say that the market for split-up securities has lower operational efficiency relative to its presplit level. Ohlson and Penman [1985] report that the postsplit return standard deviation for split-up stocks exceeds the presplit return standard deviation by an average of 30%. Lower liquidity and higher return variance are both costs of splitting.

Brennan and Copeland [1988] provide a costly signaling theory explanation for stock splits and show that it is consistent with the data. The intuition can be explained as follows. Suppose that managers know the future prospects of their firm better than the market does. Furthermore, assume that there are two firms with a price of $60 per share that are alike in every way except that the managers of firm A know it has a bright future while the managers of firm B expect only average performance. Managers of both firms know that if they decide to announce a split, their shareholders will suffer from the higher transaction cost documented by Copeland [1979]. However, the successful firm A will bear these costs only temporarily (because its managers have positive information about its future), while firm B will bear them indefinitely. Hence firm A will signal its bright future with a stock split, and the signal will not be mimicked by firm B. Costly signaling creates a separating equilibrium. As a result, A's price will rise at the time of the announcement so as to reflect the present value of its future prospects. Furthermore, the lower the target price to which the firm splits, the greater confidence management has, and the larger will be the announcement residual. Empirical results by Brennan and Copeland [1987] confirm this prediction.

Dharan and Ikenberry [1995] and Ikenberry, Rankine, and Stice [1996] have reported roughly 7% positive abnormal returns in the year after the split ex date. If valid, these results would be inconsistent with semistrong-form market efficiency. Fama [1998] notes that these studies use buy-and-hold returns for the sample of split-up stocks and for the comparable stocks used as benchmarks. According to an earlier paper by Mitchell and Stafford [1997], this can lead to biased measurement of long-term returns in the following way. Suppose that the test group of firms record a 10% abnormal return during the announcement year and the benchmark portfolio records a 0% abnormal return. Then assume that both portfolios record a cumulative 100% buy-and-hold return (BAHR) over the next four years. The BAHR for the test group will be $1.1 \times 2.0 = 2.20$ and the BAHR for the benchmark group will be $1.0 \times 2.0 = 2.0$, leading to the mistaken conclusion that an abnormal return of 20% had been earned over the five-year period including the year of the announcement. One way to correct this problem is to take the ratios of the cumulative returns rather than their difference. In this case we are back to a ratio of 1.1, that is, to a 10% abnormal return (in the announcement year).

3. The Value Line Investor Survey

Hundreds of investment advisory services sell advice that predicts the performance of various types of assets. Perhaps the largest is the Value Line Investor Survey. Employing over 200 people, it ranks around 1,700 securities each week. Securities are ranked 1 to 5 (with 1 being highest), based on their expected price performance relative to the other stocks covered in the survey. Security rankings result from a complex filter rule that utilizes four criteria: (1) the earnings and price rank of each security relative to all others, (2) a price momentum factor, (3) year-to-year relative changes in quarterly earnings, and (4) an earnings "surprise" factor. Roughly 53% of the securities are ranked third, 18% are ranked second or fourth, and 6% are ranked first or fifth.

The Value Line predictions have been the subject of many academic studies because they represent a clear attempt to use historical data in a complex computerized filter rule to try to predict future performance.[10] Figure Q11.8 (Problem 11.8 in the problem set at the end of this chapter) shows an 18-year price performance record assuming that all Value Line ranking changes had been followed between April 1965 and December 1983. Group 1 had price appreciation of 1,295%, whereas group 5 increased in price only 35%. However, this is only the realized *price* appreciation. The rates of return reported in Fig. Q11.8 are not total returns because they do not include dividends. Furthermore, they are not adjusted for risk. The problem is how to measure the performance of a portfolio of securities assuming that the Value Line recommendations are used for portfolio formation.

Black [1971] performed the first systematic study utilizing Jensen's abnormal performance measure, which will be given later in Eq. (11.7). Black's results indicate statistically significant abnormal performance for equally weighted portfolios formed from stocks ranked 1, 2, 4, and 5 by Value Line and rebalanced monthly. Before transactions costs, portfolios 1 and 5 had risk-adjusted rates of return of $+10\%$ and -10%, respectively. Even with round-trip transaction costs of 2%, the net rate of return for a long position in portfolio 1 would still have been positive, thereby indicating economically significant performance. One problem with these results is the Jensen methodology for measuring portfolio performance. It has been criticized by Roll [1977, 1978], who argues that any methodology based on the capital asset pricing model will measure either (1) no abnormal performance if the market index portfolio is ex post efficient or (2) a meaningless abnormal performance if the index portfolio is ex post inefficient.[11]

Copeland and Mayers [1982] and Chen, Copeland, and Mayers [1987] measured Value Line portfolio performance by using a *future benchmark technique* that avoids selection bias problems associated with using historic benchmarks as well as the known difficulties of using capital asset pricing model benchmarks.[12] The future benchmark technique uses the market model (described in Section A of this chapter) fit using data after the test period where portfolio performance is being measured. The steps in the procedure are

1. Using the sample from after the test period, calculate the market model equation for the portfolio being evaluated.

2. Use the parameters of the model as a benchmark for computing the portfolio's unexpected return during a test period.

3. Repeat the procedure and the test to see whether the mean unexpected return is significantly different from zero.

In other words, rather than using a particular (perhaps suspect) model (such as the CAPM) of asset pricing as a benchmark, estimate the expected returns directly from the data. The future benchmark technique is not without its problems, however. It assumes that the portfolio characteristics (e.g., risk and dividend yield) remain essentially the same throughout the test and benchmark periods.

---

[10] A partial list of Value Line–related studies is Shelton [1967], Hausman [1969], Black [1971], Kaplan and Weil [1973], Brown and Rozeff [1978], Holloway [1981], Copeland and Mayers [1982], and Chen, Copeland, and Mayers [1987].

[11] For a more complete discussion of Roll's critique, see Chapter 6.

[12] Using historic benchmarks creates a selection bias problem because Value Line uses a variant of the "relative strength" criterion to choose rankings. Portfolio 1 stocks tend to have abnormally high historic rates of return; thus subtracting these rates from test period returns would tend to bias the results against Value Line.

Copeland and Mayers find considerably less abnormal performance than Black, who uses the Jensen methodology. Where Black reported (roughly) 20% per year for an investor who was long on portfolio 1 and short on portfolio 5, Copeland and Mayers find an annual rate of return of only 6.8%. Moreover, only portfolio 5 had statistically significant returns. Nevertheless, any significant performance is a potential violation of semistrong market efficiency. Thus Value Line remains an enigma.

Stickel [1985] uses the future benchmark methodology to measure the abnormal performance resulting from changes in Value Line rankings. He finds statistically significant returns for reclassifications from rank 2 to rank 1 that are three times as large as the returns from reclassifications from 1 to 2. Upgradings from 5 to 4 were not associated with significant abnormal returns. He concludes that the market reacts to Value Line reclassifications as news events and that the price adjustment is larger for smaller firms.

4. Self-Tenders and Share Repurchases

Lakonishok and Vermaelen [1990], Ikenberry, Lakonishok, and Vermaelen [1995], and Mitchell and Stafford [1997] all find abnormal returns from a trading rule where one purchases a stock on the day following the announcement of a planned self-tender or open-market repurchase plan. For example, Mitchell and Stafford report three-year buy-and-hold returns of 9% for 475 self-tenders during the 1960–1993 time period, after controlling for size and for book-to-market. They also report a 19% abnormal return for a portfolio of 2,542 open-market repurchase plans. These abnormal returns are statistically and economically significant and would be consistent with market inefficiency. However, most of the abnormal returns vanish when they use a three-factor benchmark that includes as independent variables (1) the difference between the return on the market portfolio and the risk-free rate, (2) the difference between the returns on a small-cap portfolio minus a large-cap portfolio, and (3) the difference between returns on a high book-to-market and a low book-to-market portfolio. Furthermore, the abnormal returns disappear completely if the portfolio of repurchases is value weighted rather than equally weighted. The lesson learned from these results is that measurement of abnormal returns is extremely sensitive to apparently minor changes in technique.

G. Semistrong-Form Anomalies: Short Term

1. Mutual Funds

Mutual funds allege that they can provide two types of service to their clients. First, they minimize the amount of unsystematic risk an investor must face. This is done through efficient diversification in the face of transaction costs. Second, they may be able to use their professional expertise to earn abnormal returns through successful prediction of security prices. This second claim is contradictory to the semistrong form of capital market efficiency unless, for some reason, mutual fund managers can consistently obtain information that is not publicly available.

A number of studies have focused their attention on the performance of mutual funds. A partial list includes Friend and Vickers [1965], Sharpe [1966], Treynor [1965], Farrar [1962], Friend, Blume, and Crockett [1970], Jensen [1968], Mains [1977], Henricksson [1984], and

Grinblatt and Titman [1989]. Various performance measures are used. Among them are

$$\text{Sharpe ratio} = \frac{R_{jt} - R_{ft}}{\sigma_j}, \tag{11.5}$$

$$\text{Treynor index} = \frac{R_{jt} - R_{ft}}{\widehat{\beta}_j}, \tag{11.6}$$

$$\text{Abnormal performance} = \alpha_{jt} = (R_{jt} - R_{ft}) - \left[\widehat{\beta}_j(R_{mt} - R_{ft})\right], \tag{11.7}$$

where

$R_j = $ the return of the jth mutual fund,

$R_f = $ the return on a risk-free asset (usually Treasury bills),

$\sigma_j = $ the estimated standard deviation of return on the jth mutual fund,

$\widehat{\beta}_j = $ the estimated systematic risk of the jth mutual fund.

Of these, the abnormal performance measure of Eq. (11.7) makes use of the CAPM. It was developed by Jensen [1968], who used it to test the abnormal performance of 115 mutual funds, using annual data between 1955 and 1964. If the performance index, α, is positive, then after adjusting for risk and for movements in the market index, the abnormal performance of a portfolio is also positive. The average α for returns measured net of costs (such as research costs, management fees, and brokerage commissions) was -1.1% per year over the 10-year period. This suggests that on the average the funds were not able to forecast future security prices well enough to cover their expenses. When returns were measured gross of expenses (except brokerage commissions), the average α was $-.4\%$ per year. Apparently the gross returns were not sufficient to recoup even brokerage commissions.

In sum, Jensen's study of mutual funds provides evidence that the 115 mutual funds, on the average, were not able to predict security prices well enough to outperform a buy-and-hold strategy. In addition, there was very little evidence that any individual fund was able to do better than what might be expected from mere random chance. These conclusions held even when fund returns were measured gross of management expenses and brokerage costs. Results obtained are consistent with the hypothesis of capital market efficiency in its semistrong form, because we may assume that, at the very least, mutual fund managers have access to publicly available information. However, they do not necessarily imply that mutual funds will not be held by rational investors. On the average the funds do an excellent job of diversification. This may by itself be a socially desirable service to investors.

Mains [1977] reexamined the issue of mutual fund performance. He criticized Jensen's work on two accounts. First, the rates of return were underestimated because dividends were assumed to be reinvested at year's end rather than during the quarter they were received and because when expenses were added back to obtain gross returns, they were added back at year's end instead of continuously throughout the year. By using monthly data instead of annual data, Mains is able to better estimate both net and gross returns. Second, Jensen assumed that mutual fund betas were stationary over long periods of time; note that $\widehat{\beta}_j$ has no time subscript in Eq. (11.7). Using monthly data, Mains observes lower estimates of $\widehat{\beta}_j$ and argues that Jensen's estimates of risk were too high.

The abnormal performance results calculated for a sample of 70 mutual funds indicate that as a group the mutual funds had neutral risk-adjusted performance on a net return basis. On a gross return basis (i.e., before operating expenses and transaction costs), 80% of the funds sampled performed positively. This suggests that mutual funds are able to outperform the market well enough to earn back their operating expenses. It is also consistent with the theory of efficient markets given costly information. Recall from Chapter 10 that the theoretical work of Cornell and Roll [1981] and Grossman [1980] predicts a market equilibrium where investors who utilize costly information will have higher gross rates of return than their uninformed competitors. But because information is costly, the equilibrium net rates of return for informed and uninformed investors will be the same. This is just what Main's work shows. Mutual funds' gross rates of return are greater than the rate on a randomly selected portfolio of equivalent risk, but when costs (transaction costs and management fees) are subtracted, the net performance of mutual funds is the same as that for a naive investment strategy.

There have been several studies of mutual fund performance that have seemingly found evidence of market inefficiency because there is persistence, or autocorrelation, in the abnormal performance of mutual funds over time. Stickel [1992] and Grinblatt and Titman [1992] approach the question in different ways in the same issue of the *Journal of Finance*. Stickel compares the accuracy of analyst recommendations for two groups, an award-winning All-American Research Team, selected by the *Institutional Investor* magazine, and all others. The abnormal returns for the first 11 days following large upward forecast revisions indicates that the All-American portfolio has a 0.21% greater average impact on security prices than the non-All-Americans, after controlling for the size of the firm and the magnitude of the revision. There is no difference between the two groups when there are downward revisions. Grinblatt and Titman [1992] study the persistence of mutual fund performance. They find that, after controlling for firm size, dividend yield, past returns, interest rate sensitivity, beta, and skewness, there is statistically significant persistence in returns over time and evidence that mutual fund managers can earn abnormal returns. Carhart [1997] reexamines the issue using a sample that is free of survivorship or selection bias, and demonstrates that the persistence in returns is completely explained by common factors in stock returns and investment expenses. His results do not provide evidence of the existence of skilled or informed mutual fund portfolio managers.

2. Dual-Purpose Funds

Dual-purpose funds are companies whose only assets are the securities of other companies. However, unlike open-end funds, closed-end dual-purpose funds neither issue new shares nor redeem outstanding ones. Investors who wish to own shares in a closed-end fund must purchase fund shares on the open market. The shares are divided into two types, both of which have claim on the same underlying assets. The *capital shares* of a dual fund pay no dividends and are redeemable at net asset value at the (predetermined) maturity date of the fund.[13] The *income shares* receive any dividends or income that the fund may earn, subject to a stated minimum cumulative dividend, and are redeemed at a fixed price at the fund's maturity date. Dual funds were established on the premise that some investors may wish to own a security providing only income, whereas other investors may desire only potential capital gains.

---

[13] The net asset value received at maturity is the market value of the securities in the fund at that date, less the promised repayment of capital to income shares.

There are two very interesting issues that are raised when one observes the market price of closed-end shares. First, the market value of the fund's capital shares does not equal the *net asset value*.[14] Most often, the net asset value per share exceeds the actual price per share of the dual fund. In this case the dual fund is said to sell at a discount. Given that a speculator (especially a tax-exempt institution) could buy all of a fund's outstanding shares and liquidate the fund for its net asset value, it is a mystery why a discount (or premium) can persist. The second issue has to do with whether or not risk-adjusted abnormal rates of return accrue to investors who buy a dual fund when it is selling at a discount, then hold it for a period of time, possibly to maturity.

Ingersoll [1976] shows that the capital shares of a dual fund are analogous to call options written on the dividend-paying securities held by the fund. Holders of income shares are entitled to all income produced by the portfolio plus an amount equal to their initial investment payable when the fund matures. If S is the value of the fund at maturity and X is the promised payment to income shares, then capital shareowners receive the maximum of $(S - X)$ or zero, whichever is larger, at maturity. This payoff can be written as

$$\text{MAX}\,[S - X, 0]$$

and is exactly the same as the payoff to a call option.[15] We know, from option pricing theory, that the present value of a call option is bounded from below by $S - Xe^{-r_f T}$. However, dual funds are characterized by the fact that cash disbursements in the form of dividends and management fees are made over the life of the fund. If these disbursements are assumed to be continuous, then the present value of the fund is $Se^{-\gamma T}$, where γ is the rate of payment. Ingersoll shows that, given the cash disbursements, the lower bound on the value of the capital shares must be $Se^{-\gamma T} - Xe^{-r_f T}$, as shown in Fig. 11.11. The dashed line, $S - X$, is the net asset value of the capital shares.[16] When the fund value is above a critical level, S_c, the capital shares will sell at a discount. Below S_c they sell at a premium.

When Ingersoll used the option pricing model to estimate the market value of capital shares, he found that it tracked actual prices very well in spite of the fact that no tax effects were taken into account. The data consisted of prices for seven funds on a weekly basis between May 1967 and December 1973. Furthermore, he simulated a trading rule that bought (sold) capital shares when the option model price was above (below) the market price and financed the investment by an opposite position in the securities of the fund and borrowing or lending at a riskless rate. Thus a hedged portfolio was created that required no investment and that had very low risk.[17] The returns on the hedge portfolio were (almost always) insignificantly different from zero. This suggests that even though the capital shares may sell for a discount or premium, they are efficiently priced in a semistrong-form sense.

Thompson [1978] measures the performance of closed-end dual funds by using all three versions of the empirical models described at the beginning of this chapter. He used monthly data for 23 closed-end funds. The longest-lived fund was in existence from 1940 until 1975 (when the data

---

[14] The net asset value is the value to shareholders measured as the market value of the securities held by the fund at a given point in time.

[15] See, for example, Eq. (7.11).

[16] Figure 11.11 is very similar to Fig. 7.20. The valuation of dual fund capital shares is an application of option pricing theory.

[17] Not all risk could be eliminated because of (1) weekly rather than continuous adjustment of the hedge position, (2) changes in the model deviation, and (3) improper hedge ratios if the option model of capital shares is incorrect.

Figure 11.11 Capital share price as a function of asset value. (From J. Ingersoll, Jr., "A Theoretical and Empirical Investigation of Dual Purpose Funds," reprinted from *Journal of Financial Economics*, January–March 1976, 87.)

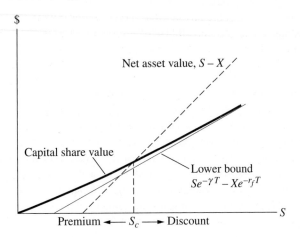

set ended). A trading rule purchased shares in each fund that was selling at a discount at the previous year's end, then held the fund and reinvested all distributions until the end of the year. The procedure was repeated for each year that data existed, and abnormal returns were then calculated for a portfolio based on this trading strategy. Thompson found that discounted closed-end fund shares tend to outperform the market, adjusted for risk. By one performance measure the annual abnormal return (i.e., the return above that earned by NYSE stocks of equivalent risk) was in excess of 4%. It is interesting to note that a trading strategy that purchased shares of funds selling at a premium would have experienced a −7.9% per year abnormal return, although the results were not statistically significant.

There are several explanations for Thompson's results. First, the market may be inefficient, at least for tax-exempt institutions that could seemingly be able to profit from the above-mentioned trading rule. Second, so long as taxable investors persist in holding closed-end shares, the gross rates of return before taxes may have to exceed the market equilibrium rate of return in order to compensate for unrealized tax liabilities. Third, abnormal return measures based on the capital asset pricing model may be inappropriate for measuring the performance of closed-end fund capital shares that are call options.

An interesting paper by Brauer [1984] reports on the effects of open-ending 14 closed-end funds between 1960 and 1981. Funds that were open-ended had larger discounts from net asset value (23.6% versus 16.2%) and lower management fees (.78% versus 1.00%) than funds that were not open-ended. Large discounts provide shareholders with greater incentive to open-end their funds, and lower management fees imply less management resistance. These two variables were actually able to predict which funds would be open-ended. In addition, Brauer reports that most of the (large) abnormal returns that resulted from the announcement of open-ending were realized by the end of the announcement month—a result consistent with semistrong-form market efficiency.

The problem of analyzing dual funds is not yet completely resolved. The observed discounts (premia) on capital shares may be attributable to (1) unrealized capital gains tax liabilities, (2) fund holdings of letter stock, (3) management and brokerage costs, or (4) the option nature of capital shares. The relative importance of these factors has not yet been completely resolved. There is no good explanation for why all funds selling at a discount have not been open-ended. In addition, there remains some question about whether or not abnormal returns can be earned by utilizing trading rules based on observed discounts (premia). Thompson's [1978] work suggests that abnormal returns are possible, whereas Ingersoll [1976] finds no evidence of abnormal returns.

3. Timing Strategies

If it were possible to reweight away from high-risk stocks during market downturns and toward them during upturns, it would be possible to outperform a buy-and-hold strategy. Also, timing would be possible if the market or segments of it were to overreact or underreact to the arrival of new information (e.g., earnings news or macroeconomic indicators). Empirical evidence of timing is difficult to find because the decisions of fund managers simultaneously include both the selection of individual stocks for their own merit as well as reweighting for timing reasons. A few studies, however, examine trading rules directly. Graham and Harvey [1996] and Copeland and Copeland [1999] examine trading rules designed to exploit new information about volatility. Copeland and Copeland find that when an index of forward-looking implied volatility, called VIX, increases unexpectedly from its current level, it is possible to earn statistically significant returns by buying futures on large-cap stocks and selling futures on low-cap stocks. Busse [1999] finds that a significant proportion of mutual fund managers reduce their market exposure during periods of increased market volatility. Fleming, Kirby, and Ostdiek [2001] find that volatility-timing strategies earn economically and statistically significant returns. These timing anomalies, although statistically significant, are usually small in magnitude. Nevertheless they represent evidence of semistrong-form inefficiency that has not yet been explained away.

4. Stocks That Over- or Undershoot

It is also widely believed that instead of adjusting smoothly, stocks tend to overshoot the equilibrium price. If so, a strategy that is based on this idea might easily earn significant excess returns. Chopra, Lakonishok, and Ritter [1992], like DeBondt and Thaler [1985] before them, report that stocks that are extreme losers at time zero outperform those that were extreme winners over the following five years. The extent of abnormal performance ranges from 6.5% per year using annual data to 9.5% per year using monthly data. After adjusting for size but before adjusting for beta, extreme losers outperform extreme winners by 9.7% per year. In the context of multiple regressions that control for size, beta, and prior returns, there still remains an economically significant overreaction of 5% per year. However, much of this excess return is seasonal, being earned in January, and seems to be more pronounced among smaller firms. There was no evidence of overreaction among a set of large market cap firms. Furthermore, Bell, Kothari, and Shanken [1995] report that abnormal returns from the strategy become statistically insignificant when changes in the betas of winners and losers are taken into account.

H. Cross-Sectional Puzzles

Any predictable pattern in asset returns may be exploitable and therefore judged as evidence against weak-form market efficiency. Even if the pattern cannot be employed directly in a trading rule because of prohibitive transaction costs, it may enable people who were going to trade anyway to increase their portfolio returns over what they otherwise may have received without knowledge of the pattern. Two statistically significant patterns in stock market returns are the weekend effect and the turn-of-the-year effect.

Table 11.4 Summary Statistics for Daily Returns on the S&P 500 Stock Index, 1953–1977

Means, Standard Deviations, and t-Statistics of the Percent Return from the Close of the Previous Trading Day to the Close of the Day Indicated [a]

		Monday	Tuesday	Wednesday	Thursday	Friday
1953–1977	Mean	−0.1681	0.0157	0.0967	0.0448	0.0873
	Standard-deviation	0.8427	0.7267	0.7483	0.6857	0.6600
	t-statistic	−6.823[c]	0.746	4.534[c]	2.283[b]	4.599[c]
	Observations	1,170	1,193	1,231	1,221	1,209

a. Returns for periods including a holiday are omitted. These returns are defined as $R_t = \ln(P_t/P_{t-1}) \cdot 100$.
b. 5% significance level.
c. 0.5% significance level.
From K. French, "Stock Returns and the Weekend Effect," reprinted from the *Journal of Financial Economics*, March 1980, 58.

1. Day-of-the-Week Effect

French [1980] studied daily returns on the Standard and Poor's composite portfolio of the 500 largest firms on the New York Stock Exchange over the period 1953 to 1977. Table 11.4 shows the summary statistics for returns by day of the week. The negative returns on Monday were highly significant. They were also significantly negative in each of the five-year subperiods that were studied.

An immediate natural reaction to explain this phenomenon is that firms wait until after the close of the market on Fridays to announce bad news. The problem is that soon people would anticipate such behavior and discount Friday prices to account for it. In this way negative returns over the weekend would soon be eliminated. Another explanation is that negative returns are caused by a general "market-closed" effect. French eliminated this possibility by showing that for days following holidays, only Tuesday returns were negative. All other days of the week that followed holidays had positive returns.

At present there is no satisfactory explanation for the weekend effect. It is not directly exploitable by a trading rule because transaction costs of even .25% eliminate all profits. However, it may be considered a form of market inefficiency because people who were going to trade anyway can delay purchases planned for Thursday or Friday until Monday and execute sales scheduled for Monday on the preceding Friday.

2. Year-End Effect

Another interesting pattern in stock prices is the so-called year-end effect, which has been documented by Dyl [1973], Branch [1977], Keim [1983], Reinganum [1983], Roll [1983], and Gultekin and Gultekin [1983]. Stock returns decline in December of each year, especially for small firms and for firms whose price had already declined during the year. The prices increase during the following January. Roll [1983] reported that for 18 consecutive years from 1963 to 1980, average returns of small firms have been larger than average returns of large firms on the first trading day of the calendar year. That day's difference in returns between equally weighted indices of AMEX- and NYSE-listed stocks averaged 1.16% over the 18 years. The t-statistic of the difference was 8.18.

Again quoting Roll [1983]:

> To put the turn-of-the-year period into perspective, the annual return differential between equally-weighted and value-weighted indices of NYSE and AMEX stocks was 9.31% for calendar years 1963–1980 inclusive. During those same years, the average return for the five days of the turn-of-the-year (last day of December and first five days of January) was 3.45%. Thus, about 37% of the annual differential is due to just five trading days, 67% of the annual differential is due to the first twenty trading days of January plus the last day of December.

The most likely cause of the year-end effect is tax selling. At least there is a significant correlation between the realized rates of return during the year and the size of the turn-of-the-year price recovery. Whether or not this phenomenon is exploitable with a trading rule remains to be seen. However, an individual who is going to transact anyway can benefit by altering his or her timing to buy late in December and to sell in early January. Bhardwaj and Brooks [1992] looked at net returns after transaction costs and bid-ask spreads for turn-of-the-year trading strategies for 300 NYSE stocks during the 1982–1986 time period. They conclude that after transactions costs "the January anomaly of low-price stocks outperforming high-price stocks cannot be used to earn abnormal returns."

Summary

Most (but not all) evidence suggests that capital markets are efficient in their weak and semistrong forms, that security prices conform to a fair-game model but not precisely to a random walk because of small first-order dependencies in prices and nonstationarities in the underlying price distribution over time, and that the strong form of market efficiency does not hold. However, any conclusions about the strong form of market efficiency need to be qualified by the fact that capital market efficiency must be considered jointly with competition and efficiency in markets for information. If insiders have monopolistic access to information, this fact may be considered an inefficiency in the market for information rather than in capital markets. Filter rules (described in Chapter 10) have shown that security prices exhibit no dependencies over time, at least down to the level of transaction costs. Thus capital markets are allocationally efficient up to the point of operational efficiency. If transaction costs amounted to a greater percentage of value traded, price dependencies for filter rules greater than 1.5% might have been found.

Most of the studies reviewed in this chapter have used data from the stock market. However, there is evidence that other markets are also efficient. Roll [1970] showed that prices in the Treasury bill market obey a fair-game model. Schwert [1977] concluded that the prices of the New York Stock Exchange seats follow a multiplicative random walk. Stein [1977] examined the auction market for art and found it efficient. Larson [1964] looked at corn futures, and Mandelbrot [1964] investigated spot prices in cotton. In addition to these studies, we should mention in passing that there are many other topics related to the question of market efficiency that have not been discussed here.

PROBLEM SET

11.1 Roll's critique of tests of the CAPM shows that if the index portfolio is ex post efficient, it is mathematically impossible for abnormal returns, as measured by the empirical market line, to be statistically different from zero. Yet the Ibbotson study on new issues uses the cross-section empirical market line and finds significant abnormal returns in the month of issue and none in the following months. Given Roll's critique, this should have been impossible. How can the empirical results be reconciled with the theory?

11.2 In a study on corporate disclosure by a special committee of the Securities and Exchange Commission, we find the following statement (177, D6):

> The "efficient market hypothesis"—which asserts that the current price of a security reflect all publicly available information—even if valid, does not negate the necessity of a manda-tory disclosure system. This theory is concerned with how the market reacts to disclosed information and is silent as to the optimum amount of information required or whether that optimum should be achieved on a mandatory or voluntary basis; market forces alone are insufficient to cause all material information to be disclosed.

Two questions that arise are

(a) What is the difference between efficient markets for securities and efficient markets for information?

(b) What criteria define "material information"?

11.3 In your own words, what does the empirical evidence on block trading tell us about market efficiency?

11.4 Which of the following types of information provides a likely opportunity to earn abnormal returns on the market?

(a) The latest copy of a company's annual report.

(b) News coming across the NYSE ticker tape that 100,000 shares of Oracle were just traded in a single block.

(c) Advance notice that the XYZ Company is going to split its common stock three for one but not increase dividend payout.

(d) Advance notice that a large new issue of common stock in the ABC Company will be offered soon.

11.5 Mr. A has received, over the last three months, a solicitation to purchase a service that claims to be able to forecast movements in the Dow Jones Industrial index. Normally, he does not believe in such things, but the service provides evidence of amazing accuracy. In each of the last three months, it was always right in predicting whether or not the index would move up more than 10 points, stay within a 10-point range or go down by more than 10 points. Would you advise him to purchase the service? Why or why not?

11.6 The Ponzi Mutual Fund (which is not registered with the SEC) guarantees a 2% per month (24% per year) return on your money. You have looked into the matter and found that they have indeed been able to pay their shareholders the promised return for each of the 18 months they have been in operation. What implications does this have for capital markets? Should you invest?

11.7 Empirical evidence indicates the mutual funds that have abnormal returns in a given year are successful in attracting abnormally large numbers of new investors the following year. Is this consistent with capital market efficiency?

11.8 The Value Line Investment Survey publishes weekly stock performance forecasts. Stocks are grouped into five portfolios according to expected price performance, with Group 1 comprising the most highly recommended stocks. The chart of each portfolio's actual performance over an 18-year period (Fig. Q11.8) assumes that each of the five portfolios was adjusted on a weekly basis in accordance with Value Line's stock ratings. The chart shows that the portfolios' actual

Figure Q11.8 Eighteen-year record of actual forecasts assumes all rank changes have been followed. (From A. Bernhard, "The Value Line Investment Survey," *Investing in Common Stock*, Arnold Bernhard and Company, Inc. © Value Line, Inc. Reprinted with permission.)

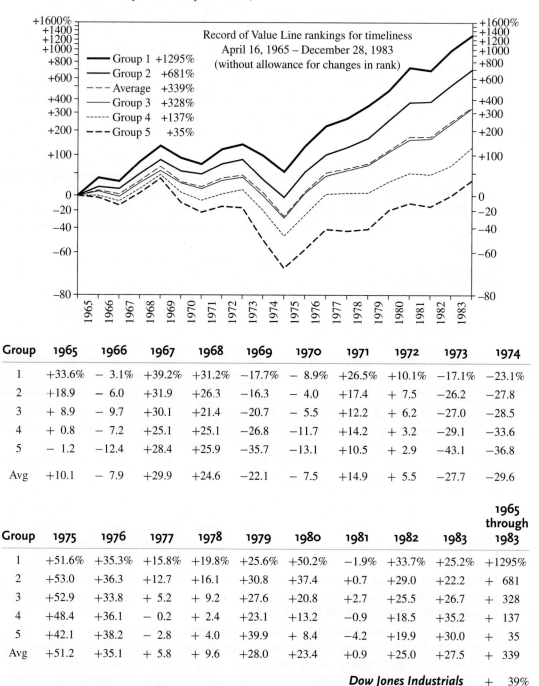

Group	1965	1966	1967	1968	1969	1970	1971	1972	1973	1974
1	+33.6%	− 3.1%	+39.2%	+31.2%	−17.7%	− 8.9%	+26.5%	+10.1%	−17.1%	−23.1%
2	+18.9	− 6.0	+31.9	+26.3	−16.3	− 4.0	+17.4	+ 7.5	−26.2	−27.8
3	+ 8.9	− 9.7	+30.1	+21.4	−20.7	− 5.5	+12.2	+ 6.2	−27.0	−28.5
4	+ 0.8	− 7.2	+25.1	+25.1	−26.8	−11.7	+14.2	+ 3.2	−29.1	−33.6
5	− 1.2	−12.4	+28.4	+25.9	−35.7	−13.1	+10.5	+ 2.9	−43.1	−36.8
Avg	+10.1	− 7.9	+29.9	+24.6	−22.1	− 7.5	+14.9	+ 5.5	−27.7	−29.6

Group	1975	1976	1977	1978	1979	1980	1981	1982	1983	1965 through 1983
1	+51.6%	+35.3%	+15.8%	+19.8%	+25.6%	+50.2%	−1.9%	+33.7%	+25.2%	+1295%
2	+53.0	+36.3	+12.7	+16.1	+30.8	+37.4	+0.7	+29.0	+22.2	+ 681
3	+52.9	+33.8	+ 5.2	+ 9.2	+27.6	+20.8	+2.7	+25.5	+26.7	+ 328
4	+48.4	+36.1	− 0.2	+ 2.4	+23.1	+13.2	−0.9	+18.5	+35.2	+ 137
5	+42.1	+38.2	− 2.8	+ 4.0	+39.9	+ 8.4	−4.2	+19.9	+30.0	+ 35
Avg	+51.2	+35.1	+ 5.8	+ 9.6	+28.0	+23.4	+0.9	+25.0	+27.5	+ 339

Dow Jones Industrials + 39%

N.Y. Stock Exchange Composite + 101%

performances are consistent with Value Line's forecasts. Is this evidence against an efficient securities market?

11.9 In each of the following situations, explain the extent to which the empirical results offer reliable evidence for (or against) market efficiency.

(a) A research study using data for firms continuously listed on the Compustat computer tapes from 1953 to 1973 finds no evidence of impending bankruptcy cost reflected in stock prices as a firm's debt/equity ratio increases.

(b) One thousand stockbrokers are surveyed via questionnaire, and their stated investment preferences are classified according to industry groupings. The results can be used to explain rate of return differences across industries.

(c) A study of the relationships between size of type in the *New York Times* headline and size of price change (in either direction) in the subsequent day's stock index reveals a significant positive correlation. Further, when independent subjects are asked to qualify the headline news as good, neutral, or bad, the direction of the following day's price change (up or down) is discovered to vary with the quality of news (good or bad).

(d) Using 25 years of data in exhaustive regression analysis, a *Barron's* writer develops a statistical model that explains the 25-year period of stock returns (using 31 variables) with miniscule error.

REFERENCES

Aharony, J., and I. Swary, "Quarterly Dividend and Earnings Announcements and Stockholders' Returns: An Empirical Analysis," *Journal of Finance*, March 1980, 1–12.

Alexander, S. S., "Price Movements in Speculative Markets: Trends or Random Walks," *Industrial Management Review*, May 1961, 7–26.

Ball, R., and P. Brown, "An Empirical Evaluation of Accounting Income Numbers," *Journal of Accounting Research*, Autumn 1968, 159–178.

Barker, A., "Evaluation of Stock Dividends," *Harvard Business Review*, July–August 1958, 99–114.

Bell, R., S. P. Kothari, and J. Shanken, "Problems in Measuring Portfolio Performance: An Application to Contrarian Investment Strategies," *Journal of Financial Economics*, May 1995, 79–107.

Bernhard, A., *Investing in Common Stocks*. Arnold Bernhard & Co., Inc., New York, 1975.

———, *Value Line Methods of Evaluating Common Stocks*. Arnold Bernhard & Co., Inc., New York, 1975.

Bhardwaj, R., and L. Brooks, "The January Anomaly: Effects of Low Share Price, Transaction Costs, and Bid-Ask Bias," *Journal of Finance*, June 1992, 553–575.

Black, F., "Yes Virginia, There is Hope: Tests of the Value Line Ranking System," *Financial Analysts Journal* (September/October) 1973, Vol 29, 10–14.

Black, F., M. Jensen, and M. Scholes, "The Capital Asset Pricing Model: Some Empirical Tests," in M. Jensen, ed., *Studies in the Theory of Capital Markets*, Praeger, New York, 1972, 79–121.

Black, F., and M. Scholes, "The Effects of Dividend Yield and Dividend Policy on Common Stock Prices and Returns," *Journal of Financial Economics*, May 1974, 1–22.

Boudreaux, K., "Discounts and Premiums on Closed-End Funds: A Study on Valuation," *Journal of Finance*, May 1973, 515–522.

Branch, B., "A Tax Loss Trading Rule," *Journal of Business*, April 1977, 198–207.

Brauer, G., "'Open-Ending' Closed-End Funds," *Journal of Financial Economics*, December 1984, 491–508.

Brav, A., and P. Gompers, "Myth or Reality? The Long-Term Underperformance of Initial Public Offerings: Evidence from Venture and Nonventure Capital-Backed Companies," *Journal of Finance,* 1997, Vol. 52, 1791–1821.

Brennan, M., and T. Copeland, "Beta Changes around Stock Splits," *Journal of Finance,* September 1988a, 1009–1013.

———, "Stock Splits, Stock Prices, and Transactions Costs," *Journal of Financial Economics,* December 1988b.

Brimmer, A., "Credit Conditions and Price Determination in the Corporate Bond Market," *Journal of Finance,* September 1960, 353–370.

Brown, L., and M. Rozeff, "The Superiority of Analyst Forecasts as Measures of Expectations: Evidence from Earnings," *Journal of Finance,* March 1978, 2–16.

Brown, S., "Earnings Changes, Stock Prices and Market Efficiency," *Journal of Finance,* March 1978, 17–28.

Busse, J., "Volatility Timing in Mutual Funds, Evidence from Daily Returns," *Review of Financial Studies,* 1999, 1009–1041.

Carhart, M., "On Persistence of Mutual Fund Performance," *Journal of Finance,* March 1997, 57–82.

Chen, N. F., Copeland, T. E., and Mayers, D., "A Comparison of Single and Multifactor Portfolio Performance Methodologies," *Journal of Financial and Quantitative Analysis,* December 1987, Vol. 22, No. 4, 401–417.

Chopra N., J. Lakonishok, and J. Ritter, "Do Stocks Overrreact?" *Journal of Financial Economics,* April 1992, 235–268.

Chottiner, S., and A. Young, "A Test of the AICPA Differentiation between Stock Dividends and Stock Splits," *Journal of Accounting Research,* Autumn 1971, 367–374.

Copeland, M., and T. Copeland, "Market Timing: Style and Size Rotation Using VIX," *Financial Analysts Journal,* 1999, 73–81.

Copeland, T. E., "Liquidity Changes Following Stock Splits," *Journal of Finance,* March 1979, 115–141.

Copeland, T. E., and D. Mayers, "The Value Line Enigma (1965–1978): A Case Study of Performance Evaluation Issues," *Journal of Financial Economics,* November 1982, 289–321.

Cornell, B., and R. Roll, "Strategies for Pairwise Competitions in Markets and Organizations," *Bell Journal of Economics,* Spring 1981, 201–213.

Dann, L., D. Mayers, and R. Raab, "Trading Rules, Large Blocks and the Speed of Adjustment," *Journal of Financial Economics,* January 1977, 3–22.

DeBondt, W., and R. Thaler, "Does the Stock Market Overreact?" *Journal of Finance,* 1985, 793–805.

Dharan, B., and D. Ikenberry, "The Long-Run Negative Drift of Post-Listing Stock Returns," *Journal of Finance,* 1995, Vol. 50, 1547–1574.

Dyl, E., *The Effect of Capital Gains Taxation on the Stock Market,* Ph.D. dissertation, Stanford University Graduate School of Business, August 1973.

Erdington, L., "The Yield Spread on New Issues of Corporate Bonds," *Journal of Finance,* December 1974, 1531–1543.

Fama, E. F., "The Behavior of Stock Market Prices," *Journal of Business,* January 1965, 34–105.

———, "Efficient Capital Markets: A Review of Theory and Empirical Work," *Journal of Finance,* May 1970, 383–417.

———, *Foundations of Finance.* Basic Books, New York, 1976.

———, "Market Efficiency, Long-Term Returns, and Behavioral Finance," *Journal of Financial Economics,* September 1998, 283–306.

Fama, E. F., and M. Blume, "Filter Rules and Stock Market Trading Profits," *Journal of Finance,* May 1970, 226–241.

Fama, E. F., L. Fisher, M. Jensen, and R. Roll, "The Adjustment of Stock Prices to New Information," *International Economic Review,* February 1969, 1–21.

Fama, E., and K. French, "The Cross-Section of Expected Stock Returns," *Journal of Finance,* June 1992, 427–465.

Fama, E. F., and J. MacBeth, "Risk, Return and Equilibrium: Empirical Test," *Journal of Political Economy,* May–June 1973, 607–635.

Farrar, D. E., *The Investment Decision under Uncertainty*. Prentice-Hall, Englewood Cliffs, N.J., 1962.

Finnerty, J. E., "Insiders and Market Efficiency," *Journal of Finance*, September 1976, 1141–1148.

Fleming, J., C. Kirby, and B. Ostdiek, "The Economic Value of Volatility Timing," *The Journal of Finance,* February 2001, 329–352.

Foster, G., "Quarterly Accounting Data: Time Series Properties and Predictive Ability Results," *Accounting Review*, January 1977, 1–21.

Foster, T., III, and D. Vickrey, "The Information Content of Stock Dividend Announcements," *Accounting Review*, April 1978, 360–370.

French, D., "The Weekend Effect on the Distribution of Stock Prices," *Journal of Financial Economics*, December 1984, 547–560.

French, K., "Stock Returns and the Weekend Effect," *Journal of Financial Economics*, March 1980, 55–69.

Friend, I., M. Blume, and J. Crockett, *Mutual Funds and Other Institutional Investors*. McGraw-Hill, New York, 1970.

Friend, I., and D. Vickers, "Portfolio Selection and Investment Performance," *Journal of Finance*, September 1965, 391–415.

Gibbons, M., and P. Hess, "Day of the Week Effects and Asset Returns," *Journal of Business*, October 1981, 579–596.

Gibbons, M. R., and K. Ramaswamy, "A Test of the Cox, Ingersoll, and Ross Model of the Term Structure," *Review of Financial Studies*, 1993, Vol. 6, 619–658.

Givoly, D., and D. Palmon, "Insider Trading and the Exploitation of Inside Information: Some Empirical Evidence," *Journal of Business*, January 1985, 69–87.

Graham, J., and C. Harvey, "Market Timing Ability and Volatility Implied by the Investment Newsletters' Asset Allocation Recommendations," *Journal of Financial Economics,* 1996, 397–421.

Granger, C. W. J., and O. Morgenstern, *Predictability of Stock Market Prices*. Heath Lexington Books, Lexington, Mass., 1970.

Griffin, P., "The Time-Series Behavior of Quarterly Earnings: Preliminary Evidence," *Journal of Accounting Research*, Spring 1977, 71–83.

Grinblatt, M., R. Masulis, and S. Titman, "The Valuation Effects of Stock Splits and Stock Dividends," *Journal of Financial Economics*, December 1984, 461–490.

Grinblatt, M., and S. Titman, "Portfolio Performance Evaluation: Old Issues and New Insights," *Review of Financial Studies,* 1989, 393–416.

———, "The Persistence of Mutual Fund Performance," *Journal of Finance,* December 1992, 1977–1984.

Grossman, S., "The Impossibility of Informationally Efficient Markets," *American Economic Review*, June 1980, 393–408.

Gultekin, M., and N. B. Gultekin, "Stock Market Seasonality: International Evidence," *Journal of Financial Economics*, December 1983, 469–481.

Hausman, W., "A Note on the Value Line Contest: A Test of the Predictability of Stock Price Changes," *Journal of Business*, July 1969, 317–320.

Henricksson, R., "Market Timing and Mutual Fund Performance: An Empirical Investigation," *Journal of Business*, January 1984, 73–96.

Holloway, C., "A Note on Testing in Aggressive Investment Strategy Using Value Line Ranks," *Journal of Finance*, June 1981, 711–719.

Hong, H., R. S. Kaplan, and G. Mandelker, "Pooling vs. Purchase: The Effects of Accounting for Mergers on Stock Prices," *Accounting Review*, January 1978, 31–47.

Ibbotson, R., "Price Performance of Common Stock New Issues," *Journal of Financial Economics*, September 1975, 235–272.

Ikenberry, D., J. Lakonishok, and T. Vermaelen, "Market Underreaction to Open Market Share Repurchases," *Journal of Financial Economics*, 1995, Vol. 39, 181–208.

Ikenberry, D., G. Rankine, and E. Stice, "What Do Stock Splits Really Signal?" *Journal of Financial and Quantitative Analysis*, 1996, Vol. 31, 357–377.

Ingersoll, J., Jr., "A Theoretical and Empirical Investigation of the Dual Purpose Funds: An Application of Contingent Claims Analysis," *Journal of Financial Economics*, January–March 1976, 83–124.

Jaffe, J., "The Effect of Regulation Changes on Insider Trading," *Bell Journal of Economics and Management Science*, Spring 1974, 93–121.

Jensen, M., "The Performance of Mutual Funds in the Period 1945–64," *Journal of Finance*, May 1968, 389–416.

———, "Risk, the Pricing of Capital Assets, and the Evaluation of Investment Portfolios," *Journal of Business*, April 1969, 167–247.

———, "Capital Markets: Theory and Evidence," *Bell Journal of Economics and Management Science*, August 1972, 357–398.

Joy, M., R. Litzenberger, and R. McEnally, "The Adjustment of Stock Prices to Announcements of Unanticipated Changes in Quarterly Earnings," *Journal of Accounting Research*, Autumn 1977, 207–225.

Kaplan, R. S., and R. Roll, "Investor Evaluation of Accounting Information: Some Empirical Evidence," *Journal of Business*, April 1972, 225–257.

Kaplan, R. S., R. Roll, and R. Weil, "Risk and the Value Line Contest," *Financial Analysts Journal*, July–August 1973, 56–60.

Keim, D., "Size-Related Anomalies and Stock Return Seasonality: Further Empirical Evidence," *Journal of Financial Economics*, June 1983, 13–32.

Kraus, A., and H. R. Stoll, "Price Impacts of Block Trading on the New York Stock Exchange," *Journal of Finance*, June 1972, 569–588.

Lakonishok, J., and T. Vermaelen, "Anomalous Price Behavior around Repurchase Tender Offers," *Journal of Finance*, 1990, Vol. 45, 455–477.

Larson, A. B., "Measurement of a Random Process in Futures Prices," in J. Cootner, ed., *The Random Character of Stock Market Prices*, MIT Press, Cambridge, Mass., 1964, 219–230.

Lindvall, J., "New Issue Corporate Bonds, Seasoned Market Efficiency, and Yield Spreads," *Journal of Finance*, September 1977, 1057–1067.

Lintner, J., "The Valuation of Risky Assets and the Selection of Risky Investments in Stock Portfolios and Capital Budgets," *Review of Economics and Statistics*, February 1965, 13–37.

Litzenberger, R., and H. Sosin, "The Structure and Management of Dual Purpose Funds," *Journal of Financial Economics*, March 1977, 203–230.

Logue, D. E., "On the Pricing of Unseasoned Equity Offerings: 1965–1969," *Journal of Financial and Quantitative Analysis*, January 1973, 91–104.

Loughran, T., and J. Ritter, "The New Issues Puzzle," *Journal of Finance,* 1995, Vol. 50, 23–51.

Lowrey, M., and G. W. Schwert, "IPO Market Cycles: Bubbles or Sequential Learning?" *Journal of Finance,* June 2002, 1171–1200.

Mains, N. E., "Risk, the Pricing of Capital Assets, and the Evaluation of Investment Portfolios: Comment," *Journal of Business*, July 1977, 371–384.

Malkiel, B., "The Valuation of Closed-End Investment Company Shares," *Journal of Finance*, June 1977, 847–859.

Mandelbrot, B., "The Variation of Certain Speculative Prices," in J. Cootner, ed., *The Random Character of Stock Market Prices*, MIT Press, Cambridge, Mass., 1964, 307–332.

McDonald, J. G., and A. K. Fisher, "New Issue Stock Price Behavior," *Journal of Finance*, March 1972, 97–102.

Mikkelson, W., and M. Partch, "Stock Price Effects and the Costs of Secondary Distribution," *Journal of Financial Economics*, June 1985, 165–194.

Mitchell, M., and E. Stafford, "Managerial Decisions and Long-Term Stock Price Performance," working paper, Graduate School of Business, University of Chicago, 1997.

Mossin, J., "Security Pricing and Investment Criteria in Competitive Markets," *American Economic Review*, December 1969, 749–756.

Ohlson, J., and S. Penman, "Volatility Increases Subsequent to Stock Splits: An Empirical Aberration," *Journal of Financial Economics*, June 1985, 251–266.

Patell, J., and M. Wolfson, "Anticipated Information Releases Reflected in Call Option Prices," *Journal of Accounting and Economics*, August 1979, 117–140.

———, "The Intraday Speed of Adjustment of Stock Prices to Earnings and Dividend Announcements," *Journal of Financial Economics*, June 1984, 223–252.

Pratt, E., "Myths Associated with Closed-End Investment Company Discounts," *Financial Analysts Journal*, July–August 1966, 79–82.

Reilly, F. K., and K. Hatfield, "Investor Experience with New Stock Issues," *Financial Analysts Journal*, September–October 1969, 73–80.

Reinganum, M., "The Anomalous Stock Market Behavior of Small Firms in January: Empirical Tests for Tax-Loss Selling Effects," *Journal of Financial Economics*, June 1983, 89–104.

Report of the Advisory Committee on Corporate Disclosure to the Securities and Exchange Commission. U.S. Government Printing Office, Washington, D.C., November 1977.

Ricks, W., "The Market's Responses to the 1974 LIFO Adoptions," *Journal of Accounting Research*, Autumn 1982, 367–387.

Ritter, J., and I. Welch, "A Review of IPO Activity, Pricing, and Allocations," *Journal of Finance,* August 2002, 1795–1828.

Roendfelt, R., and D. Tuttle, "An Examination of Discounts and Premiums of Closed-End Investment Companies," *Journal of Business Research*, Fall 1973, 129–140.

Roll, R., *The Behavior of Interest Rates*. Basic Books, New York, 1970.

———, "A Critique of the Asset Pricing Theory's Tests," *Journal of Financial Economics*, March 1977, 129–176.

———, "Ambiguity When Performance Is Measured by the Securities Market Line," *Journal of Finance*, September 1978, 1051–1069.

———, "The Turn-of-the-Year Effect and the Return Premia of Small Firms," *Journal of Portfolio Management*, Winter 1983, 18–28.

Scholes, M., "The Market for Securities: Substitution vs. Price Pressure and the Effects of Information on Share Prices," *Journal of Business*, April 1972, 179–211.

Schwert, W., "Stock Exchange Seats as Capital Assets," *Journal of Financial Economics*, January 1977, 51–78.

Securities and Exchange Commission, *Report of the Special Study on Securities Markets*. U.S. Government Printing Office, Washington, D.C., 1963.

Sharpe, W. F., "Mutual Fund Performance," *Journal of Business*, January 1966, 119–138.

Shaw, D., "The Performance of Primary Stock Offerings: A Canadian Comparison," *Journal of Finance*, December 1971, 1103–1113.

Shelton, J., "The Value Line Contest: A Test of the Predictability of Stock Price Changes," *Journal of Business*, July 1967, 251–269.

Sherman, A., "The Pricing of Best Efforts New Issues," *Journal of Finance,* June 1992, 781–790.

Stein, J. P., "The Monetary Appreciation of Paintings," *Journal of Political Economy*, October 1977, 1021–1036.

Stickel, S., "The Effect of Value Line Investment Survey Rank Changes on Common Stock Prices," *Journal of Financial Economics*, March 1985, 121–144.

———, "Reputation Performance Among Security Analysts," *Journal of Finance,* December 1992, 1811–1836.

Stickney, C. P., Jr., *A Study of the Relationships of Accounting Principles and Common Stock Prices of Firms Going Public*, Ph.D. dissertation, Florida State University, Tallahassee, 1970.

Stigler, G., "Public Regulation of Security Markets," *Journal of Business*, April 1964, 117–142.

Sunder, S., "Relationship between Accounting Changes and Stock Prices: Problems of Measurement and Some Empirical Evidence," *Empirical Research in Accounting: Selected Studies*, 1973, 1–45.

———, "Stock Price and Risk Related Accounting Changes in Inventory Valuation," *Accounting Review*, April 1975, 305–315.

Thompson, R., "The Information Content of Discounts and Premiums on Closed-End Fund Shares," *Journal of Financial Economics*, June–September 1978, 151–186.

Treynor, J. L., "How to Rate Mutual Fund Performance," *Harvard Business Review*, January–February 1965, 63–75.

Watts, R., "Systematic 'Abnormal' Returns after Quarterly Earnings Announcements," *Journal of Financial Economics*, June–September 1978, 127–150.

Weinstein, M., "The Seasoning Process of New Corporate Bond Issues," *Journal of Finance*, December 1978, 1343–1354.

Woolridge, J. R., "Ex-date Stock Price Adjustment to Stock Dividends: A Note," *Journal of Finance*, March 1983a, 247–255.

———, "Stock Dividends as Signals," *Journal of Financial Research*, Spring 1983b, 1–12.

Information Asymmetry and Agency Theory

NFORMATION ASYMMETRY AND AGENCY THEORY play a central role in corporate finance and have their roots in the information economics literature. Information asymmetry occurs when one group of participants has better or more timely information than other groups. A signal is an action taken by the more informed that provides credible information to the less informed. Typically, the source of the information asymmetry is the superior knowledge that managers have about the firm's prospects, while the investors in the firms comprise the uninformed group. Agency theory derives from the fact that decisions within firms are made by management, who are agents for the investors. Conflicting interests between management and investors can lead to suboptimal allocation of resources within the firm. As stated by Lambert [2001], agency theory evaluates the impact of the conflict of interest between principals and agents because of (1) shirking by the agent, (2) diversion of resources by the agent for private consumption, (3) differential time horizon of the agent and principal, and (4) differential risk aversion of the agent and the principal. The purpose of this chapter is to provide a foundation for the role of information asymmetry and agency theory in corporate finance. Specifically, signaling provides testable empirical implications for firm decisions about capital structure, dividend policy, new investments, and stock splits. Agency theory provides its own explanation for the same decisions. Empirical testing is still trying to wring out the separable implications of these two fundamental theories.

A. Information Asymmetry

This section provides a discussion of information asymmetry and signaling. Specifically, consider a world in which there are two types of firms—low and high quality. The managers of the high-quality firms would like to signal their superiority to the market. These signals can either have exogenous costs associated with them (costly signals) or have costs that are endogenous (costless or cheap-talk signals). Examples of such signals include the level of investment in the firm, the amount of debt issued, the size of the dividend declared, the type of financing used for an investment, and the decision to split the stock. Regardless of the choice of the signaling mechanism, high-quality firms can separate themselves from low-quality firms as long as the low-quality firm cannot mimic the actions of a high-quality firm. Such a separating equilibrium requires that the gain to the low-quality firms from mimicking must be lower than the cost associated with signaling falsely. If the cost is lower than the gain, low-quality firms would mimic the signaling actions of high-quality firms, thus leading to a pooling equilibrium where the market would be unable to distinguish between them.

1. Costly Signaling

One of the first papers that explicitly related uncertainty with price and quality is Akerlof [1970]. He examines the market for automobiles where there are four types of cars available—new or used and good or bad. In his framework, individuals buy new cars without knowing whether they are good or bad. On the other hand, after owning the car for some time, the owners get a better idea of the quality of the car; that is, information asymmetry develops since the owners (potential sellers) have more knowledge about the car than the potential buyers. Since the potential buyers cannot tell the difference between good and bad cars, they are willing to offer the same amount for both and, therefore, the good and bad cars sell for the same price. As a result, a potential seller of a used car cannot receive the true value since the true quality is not known to the potential buyer. In addition, since the seller would always find it beneficial to sell a bad car and buy a new one if the price of a used car is more than the expected value of a new car, this would imply that a used car will never be priced above this expected value. As a result, it is predicted that good cars may not be traded at all while bad cars will drive the good cars out of the market.

Spence [1973] extends the logic of Akerlof's argument by formally examining a market in which signaling takes place, there are a relatively large number of signalers, and the signalers do not acquire signaling reputation. He demonstrates the existence of a signaling equilibrium with a specific example in the context of job market signaling. Specifically, there are two groups of job seekers within the population and they both face one employer. The two groups differ in productivity, with that of group A being 1 and that of group B being 2. Group A represents a fraction q of the population and a potential signal (for example, years of education) is available at a cost. The cost for group A to acquire y units of education is y (that is, \$1 per unit), while the cost for group B is $0.5y$.

Now suppose that the employer believes that there is a level of education, $y*$, such that if $y < y*$, she expects the employee's productivity to be equal to 1 with probability one, and if $y \geq y*$, then the productivity will be equal to 2 with probability one. Therefore, his wage schedule $W(y)$ would be 1 if $y < y*$ and would be 2 if $y \geq y*$.

In this framework, each group will select their education level at either 0 or $y*$, since acquiring education between 0 and $y*$ or beyond $y*$ does not provide any marginal benefits (wage) but has a marginal cost. For this to be a separating equilibrium with group A selecting an education level of 0 and group B selecting a level of $y*$, we must have $1 > 2 - y*$ and $2 - \frac{y*}{2} > 1$ or $1 < y* < 2$. This follows from the fact that if group A (B) selects an education of 0, their gain is 1 (1), while the gain is $2 - y*(2 - \frac{y*}{2})$ if an education of $y*$ is selected. It should be noted that there are an infinite number of equilibrium values for $y*$ since for any $y*$ in the range of 1 to 2, the employer can perfectly distinguish between the two groups.

Spence then proceeds to show that group A is worse off with the existence of signaling since they would be paid more than 1 $[q + 2(1 - q) = 2 - q]$ in the no-signaling case. On the other hand, group B is not always better off with the signaling. For example, if 50% of the population is group 1 (q is 0.5), then the no-signaling wage for both groups is 1.5 (with no associated cost) while the signaling wage for group B is 2 at a cost of $\frac{y*}{2}$. Therefore the net benefit to group B from signaling is $0.5 - \frac{y*}{2}$. Since $y* > 1$, this implies the net benefit from signaling is negative, and group B would prefer a solution without signaling. Finally Spence shows that under certain circumstances (for example, different wage functions), pooling equilibria exist with both groups either selecting an education level of 0 or an education level of $y*$. In such pooling equilibria, education levels convey no useful information.

Using a similar framework, Rothschild and Stiglitz [1976] and Wilson [1978] analyze a model of information transformation in insurance markets. They show that in a market with two classes of customers, high risk and low risk, there is a separating equilibrium where the two groups buy different insurance contracts. Specifically they show that rather than offering a single price per unit of coverage, firms have incentives to charge a higher price for increased coverage. This causes high-risk individuals to be separated from low-risk individuals since the additional coverage yields greater marginal benefits for the high-risk individuals but not for low-risk individuals. They also show that a Nash equilibrium may also fail to exist.[1] Riley [1975, 1979] confirms that a Nash equilibrium does not exist for this class of models with a continuum of types of informed participants. Riley also provides formal conditions under which signaling equilibria exist. Specifically he shows that the multiple signaling equilibria in the Spence model reduce to a single equilibrium that is Pareto optimal.

Applications of the costly signaling model of Spence to issues in corporate finance include Leland and Pyle [1977], Ross [1977], and Bhattacharya [1979, 1980] in the context of entrepreneurs seeking financing for projects that only they know the value of, managers of firms signaling their firm's better prospects with debt financing, and managers signaling firm cash flows by pre-committing to higher levels of dividends, respectively.

SIGNALING PROJECT QUALITY WITH INVESTMENT In the Leland and Pyle [1977] analysis, an entrepreneur plans to invest in a project by retaining fraction α of the project's equity and raising the remainder from other investors. The project involves a capital outlay of $\$X$ and a future value of $\mu + \tilde{\varepsilon}$, where μ is the expected end-of-period value and $\tilde{\varepsilon}$ is a random variable with a mean of 0 and a standard deviation of σ_ε. The entrepreneur has information that allows her to assign a particular value to the expected end-of-period value but has no credible way to convey this information to other investors who have a probability distribution for μ. However, these investors are assumed to respond to a signal from the entrepreneur regarding her knowledge of μ. The signal is the fraction of the project that the entrepreneur retains, α; that is, investors perceive that μ is a function of α.

In this framework, the market value of the project, V, given a signal α, is

$$V(\alpha) = \frac{1}{(1+r)} [\mu(\alpha) - \lambda], \tag{12.1}$$

---

[1] A Nash equilibrium is a set of strategies for participants in a noncooperative game. The equilibrium strategies have the property that no participant can do better than choose her equilibrium strategy holding the strategies of all other participants fixed. Therefore, no participant would want to change her strategy once she has seen what the other participants have done. For example, consider a two-person game in which the persons (A and B) can take either action x or y. If they both take action x (y), they each receive a payoff of $4 (2). If one takes action x and the other takes action y, the payoffs are $1 for the one choosing x and $3 for the one choosing y. This game has two Nash equilibria—one in which they both choose action x and the other in which they both choose action y.

where

$$r = \text{the risk-free rate of return,}$$

$$\mu(\alpha) = \text{the valuation schedule used by the market to infer the expected}$$
$$\text{end-of-period value from the signal, } \alpha,$$

$$\lambda = \text{the market's adjustment for the risk of the project.}$$

The entrepreneur is assumed to maximize her expected utility of terminal wealth subject to a budget constraint; that is,

$$\text{maximize } E\left[U\left(\tilde{W}_1\right)\right] \tag{12.2}$$

$$\text{subject to } W_0 = X + \beta V_M + Y - (1-\alpha)V(\alpha), \tag{12.3}$$

where

$$W_0 = \text{the entrepreneur's initial wealth,}$$

$$V_M = \text{the value of the market portfolio,}$$

$$\beta = \text{the fraction of the market portfolio owned by the entrepreneur,}$$

$$Y = \text{the amount invested in the risk-free asset,}$$

$$\alpha = \text{the fraction of the project the entrepreneur retains.}$$

The uncertain end of period wealth of the entrepreneur, $\tilde{W}_1$, is given by

$$\tilde{W}_1 = \alpha\left(\mu + \tilde{\varepsilon}\right) + \beta\tilde{M} + (1+r)Y$$
$$= \alpha\left[\mu + \tilde{\varepsilon} - \mu(\alpha) + \lambda\right] + \beta\left[\tilde{M} - (1+r)V_M\right] + (1+r)(W_0 - X) + \mu(\alpha) - \lambda \tag{12.4}$$

and $\tilde{M}$ is the gross return of the market portfolio.[2]

The first-order conditions for the maximization imply that

$$\frac{\partial E\left[U\left(\tilde{W}_1\right)\right]}{\partial\alpha} = E\left[U'\left(\tilde{W}_1\right)\left[\mu + \tilde{\varepsilon} - \mu(\alpha) + \lambda + (1-\alpha)\mu_\alpha\right]\right] = 0 \tag{12.5}$$

and

$$\frac{\partial E\left[U\left(\tilde{W}_1\right)\right]}{\partial\beta} = E\left[U'\left(\tilde{W}_1\right)\left[\tilde{M} - (1+r)V_M\right]\right] = 0, \tag{12.6}$$

where

$$\mu_\alpha = \frac{\partial\mu}{\partial\alpha}.$$

---

[2] The second equality in the definition of $\tilde{W}_1$ is obtained by substituting the definitions of $V(\alpha)$ and Y (from the definition of W_0).

Assuming the existence of an equilibrium valuation schedule, $\mu(\alpha) = \mu$, Eq. (12.5) can be written as

$$(1 - \alpha)\,\mu_\alpha = -\frac{E\left[U'\left(\widetilde{W}_1\right)[\widetilde{\varepsilon} + \lambda]\right]}{E\left[U'\left(\widetilde{W}_1\right)\right]}. \tag{12.7}$$

Equation (12.6) can be used to solve for the entrepreneur's optimal holdings of the market portfolio, $\beta^*(\alpha, \mu)$. Substituting this relation for β in Eq. (12.7) provides a differential equation relating μ to α with any equilibrium schedule satisfying this differential equation.

Leland and Pyle proceed to show, based on the condition defined by Eq. (12.7) and the second-order conditions for the maximization, that for entrepreneurs with normal demand for equity in the project (1) the equilibrium valuation schedule, $\mu(\alpha)$ is strictly increasing in α and (2) in equilibrium with signaling through α, an entrepreneur would hold a larger fraction of the project as compared to the case that they can communicate the true value costlessly to investors.[3] The first result implies that an entrepreneur with a higher-value project will retain a larger share of the project compared to an entrepreneur with a low-value project. The second result suggests that entrepreneurs suffer a welfare loss by being forced to hold a fraction of equity that is larger than what they would have optimally held if the value of the project could be communicated costlessly. The cost of the signal represents this welfare loss. This is a separating equilibrium since the gain to a entrepreneur of a low-value project of signaling falsely—that is, retaining a larger fraction of the project than implied by Eq. (12.7)—is smaller than the welfare loss sustained by deviating even more from the "costless communication" holding.

Grinblatt and Hwang [1989] generalize the Leland and Pyle model by assuming that both the mean and the variance of the project's cash flows are unknown. As a result, the fraction of the project that the entrepreneur retains is not sufficient by itself to signal the expected value of the project. A second signal is needed to infer the variance of the project's cash flows since the equilibrium signaling schedule is a function of both the variance and the fraction retained by the entrepreneur. This second signal is observed when the offering price of the issue is announced and is the degree of underpricing per share. The Grinblatt and Hwang model has a number of empirical implications, with some of them being consistent with the Leland and Pyle model. Specifically, their model predicts that (1) holding the degree of underpricing constant, the variance of a project's cash flows is negatively related to the fraction retained by the entrepreneur, (2) holding the fraction retained by the entrepreneur constant, the value of the project is positively related to its variance, (3) holding the project's variance constant, its value is positively related to the fraction retained by the entrepreneur, (4) holding the project's value constant, the variance of a project's cash flows is negatively related to the fraction retained by the entrepreneur, (5) holding the fraction retained by the entrepreneur constant, the degree of underpricing is positively related to its variance, (6) holding the project's variance constant, the degree of underpricing is positively related to the fraction retained by the entrepreneur, (7) holding the fraction retained by the entrepreneur constant, the value of the project is positively related to the degree of underpricing, and (8) holding the project's variance constant, its value is positively related to the degree of underpricing.

SIGNALING FIRM QUALITY WITH DEBT Ross [1977] considers a market with two types of firms, A and B, in a two-date world.[4] At time 1, type A firms have a value, V_a (= 100), greater

---

[3] The second-order conditions are $\frac{\partial^2 E[\bullet]}{\partial \alpha^2} < 0$, $\frac{\partial^2 E[\bullet]}{\partial \beta^2} < 0$, and $\left[\frac{\partial^2 E[\bullet]}{\partial \alpha^2}\right]\left[\frac{\partial^2 E[\bullet]}{\partial \beta^2}\right] - \left[\frac{\partial^2 E[\bullet]}{\partial \alpha \partial \beta}\right]^2 > 0.$

[4] A discussion of the Ross model is also contained in Chapter 15.

than type B firms with value V_b ($= 50$) $< V_a$. If there is no uncertainty in the market and pricing is risk neutral, the time 0 values of the two types of firms would be given by

$$V_{0a} = \frac{V_{1a}}{1+r} = \frac{100}{1} = 100 \tag{12.8}$$

and

$$V_{0b} = \frac{V_{1b}}{1+r} = \frac{50}{1} = 50 < V_{0a}, \tag{12.9}$$

where

$$r = \text{the risk-free interest rate } (= 0\%).$$

Now suppose there is uncertainty and investors cannot differentiate between the two types of firms. If q ($= 0.4$) is the proportion of type A firms and investors assume that firms are type A with probability q and type B with probability $(1 - q)$, then all firms in the market will have the same value given by

$$V_0 = \frac{qV_{1a} + (1-q)V_{1b}}{1+r} = \frac{(0.4)(100) + (0.6)(50)}{1} = 70. \tag{12.10}$$

In this framework, if type A firms would attempt to signal that they are of type A, B firms would give the same signal, resulting in no discrimination between firms in the market (a pooling equilibrium).

Ross suggests that one way to resolve this issue (that is, create a separating equilibrium) is to assume that the manager of a firm is accountable for financing decisions made at time 0. Specifically, assume that managers know the true quality of their firms, they are not allowed to trade in their firm's securities, they issue debt at time 0, they are compensated by an incentive schedule that is known to investors, and they act to maximize their incentive compensation. The compensation schedule is given by

$$M = (1+r)\gamma_0 V_0 + \gamma_1 \begin{cases} V_1 & \text{if } V_1 > D \\ V_1 - C & \text{if } V_1 \leq D \end{cases}, \tag{12.11}$$

where γ_0, γ_1 are positive weights, V_1 is the value of the firm at time 1, D is the face value of debt issued by the firm at time 0, and C is a penalty imposed on the manager if $V_1 < D$. For example, assume that $\gamma_0 = 0.1$ and $\gamma_1 = 0.2$. Thus the manager's compensation is

$$M = 0.1V_0 + 0.15 \begin{cases} V_1 & \text{if } V_1 > D \\ V_1 - C & \text{if } V_1 \leq D \end{cases}. \tag{12.12}$$

Ross shows that the compensation schedule as defined in Eq. (12.11) can be used to establish a Spence-style signaling equilibrium. Assume that D^* is the maximum amount of debt a type B firm can carry without going into bankruptcy. Further assume that if $D > D^*$, investors perceive the firm to be of type A and if $D \leq D^*$, investors perceive the firm to be of type B. For this to be established as a signaling equilibrium, the signal has to be unambiguous and managers must have the incentive to always issue the correct signal, that is, to tell the truth rather than lie.

Based on the signal (debt level) chosen by the manager of a type A firm, her compensation would be

$$M^A(D) = \begin{cases} \gamma_0 V_{1a} + \gamma_1 V_{1a} & \text{if } D^* < D \le V_{1a} \\ \gamma_0 V_{1b} + \gamma_1 V_{1a} & \text{if } D \le D^* \end{cases} = \begin{cases} 25 & \text{if } D^* < D \le V_{1a} \\ 20 & \text{if } D \le D^* \end{cases}. \quad (12.13)$$

The manager of a type A firm would have the incentive to issue the correct signal (choose a debt level higher then D^*) as long as her compensation from signaling correctly is greater than her compensation based on an false signal. In this case, since the marginal payoff from telling the truth is greater than that from a lie, that is, $(\gamma_0 V_{1a} + \gamma_1 V_{1a}) = 25 > 20 = (\gamma_0 V_{1b} + \gamma_1 V_{1a})$, she will give the correct signal.

The compensation of the manager of a type B firm is given by

$$M^B(D) = \begin{cases} \gamma_0 V_{1a} + \gamma_1 (V_{1b} - C) & \text{if } D^* < D \le V_{1a} \\ \gamma_0 V_{1b} + \gamma_1 V_{1b} & \text{if } D \le D^* \end{cases} = \begin{cases} 17.5 - 0.15C & \text{if } D^* < D \le V_{1a} \\ 12.5 & \text{if } D \le D^* \end{cases}. \quad (12.14)$$

Again, the manager of a type B firm will have the incentive to signal correctly if $[\gamma_0 V_{1a} + \gamma_1 (V_{1b} - C)] = 17.5 - 0.15C < 12.5 = (\gamma_0 V_{1b} + \gamma_1 V_{1b})$ or if $\gamma_0 (V_{1a} - V_{1b}) = 5 < 0.15C = \gamma_1 C$ or if $C > 33.33$. Therefore, the managers of type B firms would signal correctly if their marginal gain is less than the cost they bear for signaling falsely. In the example we have used, the manager of the type B firms chooses to signal correctly if the cost imposed on him for lying is larger than 33.33. As in the Spence paper, there are multiple equilibrium values for D^* in this case. The main empirical implication of the Ross model is that firms with larger expected future cash flows should issue more debt.

Guedes and Thompson [1995] develop a model based on the Ross model in which the choice between fixed-rate and floating-rate debt serves as a signal of firm quality. In their model, costs of financial distress provide an incentive for managers to choose borrowing strategies that stabilize net income. They show that a separating equilibrium exists where firms above a minimum quality issue high default risk debt and those below this minimum issue low default risk debt. This equilibrium, in conjunction with the result that there is a unique threshold for the volatility of expected inflation at which fixed- and variable-rate debt have the same default risk, implies that fixed-rate financing is a favorable signal above the volatility threshold, while variable-rate debt is a favorable signal below the volatility threshold.

The empirical evidence on the use of debt as a signal of firm quality is mixed. Studies that have focused on decisions by firms to change leverage and analyzed the impact of the announcement of these decisions on stock value have found evidence consistent with the signaling role of debt. Specifically, they find that leverage-increasing transactions are associated with increases in stock price while the opposite is true for leverage-decreasing transactions. On the other hand, many cross-sectional studies have found that firm profitability is negatively related to debt, indicating that more profitable firms carry less debt. This result is not consistent with higher-quality firms being associated with larger amounts of debt. A more detailed review of the empirical evidence on capital structure is provided in Chapter 15.

SIGNALING EXPECTED CASH FLOWS WITH DIVIDENDS Bhattacharya [1979] develops a dividend-signaling model in which the liquidation value of a firm is related to the actual dividend paid.[5] In his model, a firm is considering a new (perpetual) project with end-of-period cash flows

---

[5] A discussion of the Bhattacharya model is also provided in Chapter 16.

denoted by X. The firm signals information about the cash flows associated with the project by declaring an incremental dividend of D. The signaling response of the incremental dividend commitment is an incremental liquidation value of $V(D)$. If the project cash flow is larger than the committed dividend $(X > D)$, then the firm can reduce the amount of external financing it needs by the amount $(X - D)$. If, on the other hand, the cash flow is less than the dividend $(X < D)$, the dividend is still paid but the firm faces a shortfall. Bhattacharya assumes that the cost of making up the shortfall is more than the benefit of the cash flow surplus because of costs associated with raising external funds. Specifically, he assumes that in the case of a shortfall the cost to the firm (shareholders) is $(1 + \beta)\,[X - D]$. Finally, he also assumes that shareholders pay a personal tax of τ_p on dividends and pay no tax on capital gains.

In this framework, the shareholders receive the incremental liquidation value that results from the response to the signal, $V(D)$, and the after-tax value of the committed dividend, $(1 - \tau_p)D$. In addition, if the cash flow, X, is more than the committed dividend, the shareholders receive the residual, $X - D$. On the other hand, if the cash flow is less than the committed dividend, the shareholders face a shortfall of $(1 + \beta)(X - D)$. Therefore, the incremental objective function of the shareholders is

$$E(D) = \frac{1}{1+r}\left[V(D) + (1 - \tau_p)D + \int_D^{\overline{X}}(X - D)f(X)dX + \int_{\underline{X}}^D(1 + \beta)(X - D)f(X)dX\right]$$

$$= \frac{1}{(1+r)}\left[V(D) + \mu - \tau_p D - \beta\int_{\underline{X}}^D(X - D)f(X)dX\right], \tag{12.15}$$

where r is the after-tax rate of interest, the cash flow X is distributed over the range $\left(\underline{X}, \overline{X}\right)$, and μ is the expected cash flow. The intuitive explanation of Eq. (12.15) is that the value to the shareholder is the sum of the incremental liquidation value and the expected cash flow less the amount of taxes paid on the dividend received and the cost borne to fund the cash flow shortfall.

Managers choose D to maximize $E(D)$ given a market signaling value function $V(D)$. Now consider a project with cash flows uniformly distributed over the range $[0, t]$. Substituting the density function for this uniform distribution in Eq. (12.15) implies that managers choose D to maximize

$$E(D) = \frac{1}{1+r}\left[V(D) + \frac{t}{2} - \tau_p D - \beta\frac{D^2}{2t}\right]. \tag{12.16}$$

The first-order condition associated with this maximization is

$$V'(D^*) = \tau_p + \beta\frac{D^*}{t}. \tag{12.17}$$

Equation (12.17) states that at the optimal dividend, the marginal benefit from signaling has to equal its marginal cost. The marginal benefit, $V'(D^*)$, is the change in the liquidation value from a unit change in the dividend, while the marginal cost, $\tau_p + \beta\frac{D^*}{t}$, is the sum of the marginal tax rate (the tax paid for a unit change in dividend) and the change in the cost borne to fund a cash flow shortfall.

The market signaling value function $V(D)$ is an equilibrium schedule only if $V[D^*(t)]$ is the true value of future cash flows for the project whose cash flows are being signaled by the dividend commitment of $D^*(t)$. Given the assumptions that the project is perpetual, the dividend is stationary, and that no learning takes place over time, then the equilibrium market signaling value function is given by

$$V\left[D^*(t)\right] = \frac{1}{r}\left[\frac{t}{2} - \tau_P D^*(t) - \beta\frac{[D^*(t)]^2}{2t}\right]. \tag{12.18}$$

Equations (12.17) and (12.18) can be solved for the equilibrium $D^*(t)$ and $V(D)$ schedules. Specifically, they imply that

$$D^*(t) = At \tag{12.19}$$

and

$$V\left[D^*(t)\right] = (\tau_P + \beta A)\, D^*(t), \tag{12.20}$$

where A determines the response of value, $V(D)$, to the committed dividend, D, and is given by

$$A = -\left[\frac{\tau_P}{\beta}\right]\left[\frac{1+r}{1+2r}\right] + \left[\frac{\tau_P}{\beta}\right]\left[\frac{1+r}{1+2r}\right]\sqrt{1 + \frac{\beta(1+2r)}{\tau_P^2(1+r)^2}}. \tag{12.21}$$

Bhattacharya's results imply that the equilibrium response of value, $V(D)$, to the committed dividend, D, namely, the value of A, is a decreasing function of the personal dividend tax rate, τ_P, the cost associated with a cash flow shortfall, β, and the rate of interest, r. The first two results follow from the argument that if for a higher tax rate or cash flow shortfall cost, $V(D)$ responded to τ_P or β only, the optimizing dividend will be the same. As a result, $V(D)$ would overestimate the true value of future cash flows. This implies that, in equilibrium, A would have to be lower. Similarly, if the rate of interest increases, the present value of future cash flows decreases. Thus, in equilibrium this requires a lower response of $V(D)$ to D, implying a lower A.

To illustrate these results numerically, consider a situation in which the personal tax rate is 40% ($= \tau_P$), the shortfall penalty is 60% ($= \beta$), the upper bound of the cash flow is $100 ($= t$) and the after-tax rate of interest is 25%. In this case the value of A is 0.64, the optimal dividend is to pay $64, and the value response to this dividend is $50. If the tax rate is increased to 50%, the corresponding figures are 0.57, $57, and $48, respectively. On the other hand, decreasing the shortfall penalty to 40% increases A to 0.7, increases the dividend to $70, but decreases the value response to $48. Finally a decrease in interest rates to 10% increases all three variables, with A being .72, the dividend being $72, and the value response being $59.

John and Williams [1985] provide an alternate model for the use of dividends as a signal of private information held by insiders. They consider a two-date (one-period) model in which insiders of an all-equity firm commit to an investment of I at time 0. Conditional on this investment, they select a dividend D. Funds for the investment and dividends are raised by cash held by the firm (C) or selling new shares of stock (N) at the ex-dividend price per share (p_e). Thus the sources and uses of funds satisfy

$$I + D = C + Np_e = C + P_e, \tag{12.22}$$

where $P_e = Np_e$. Dividends are costly to stockholders in the sense that they have to pay tax on the dividend at the marginal personal tax rate of τ_P. At time 1, each firm realizes its cash flows, and stockholders receive a liquidating dividend. Shareholders do not pay taxes on the liquidating dividend. The present value of the future cash flows is denoted by X, $1 \leq X < \infty$. Insiders have private information about X that they are attempting to signal with the selection of the aggregate dividend D. If there are Q shares of stock outstanding prior to the issue of new equity, the cum-dividend price per share (p) and the ex-dividend price per share (p_e) have to be related by

$$p = p_e + \frac{(1 - \tau_P)D}{Q}$$

to preclude arbitrage. Finally, it is assumed that shareholders have a demand for liquidity (L), and they meet this demand through the dividend and the sale of M shares of stock at the ex-dividend price of p_e, that is, $L = D + p_e M$. In this framework, insiders select the optimal dividend to maximize the firm's true value to its current stockholders, that is,

$$\underset{D}{\text{maximize}} \left[(1 - \tau_P)D + p_e M + \frac{Q - M}{Q + N} X \right]. \tag{12.23}$$

In the above expression, the first term is the after-tax dividend receipt, the second term represents the process of the sale of M shares of stock at the ex-dividend price of p_e, and the last term is the value of the $Q - M$ shares they are left with after the sale. Substitution of the source and use of funds, and the no-arbitrage and the liquidity constraints, into Eq. (12.23) yields the alternate objective function

$$\underset{D}{\text{maximize}} \, L - \tau_P D + \left[\frac{P + \tau_P D - L}{P + \tau_P D + I - C} \right] X, \tag{12.24}$$

where $P = Qp$. The first-order condition for this maximization is

$$\tau_P = \left(\tau_P + \frac{\partial P}{\partial D} \right) \frac{L + I - C}{(P + \tau_P D + I - C)} X. \tag{12.25}$$

The first-order condition in Eq. (12.25) states that at the optimal dividend the marginal cost of the dividend to the shareholder (τ_P) is equal to the marginal benefit to the current shareholder from signaling. Solving this first-order condition along with the normalizing assumption that the dividend for the firm with the most unfavorable information $(X = 1)$ is zero yields the following optimal dividend:

$$D(X) = \frac{1}{\tau_P} \max (I - C + L, 0) \ln X. \tag{12.26}$$

As can be seen from Eq. (12.26), the optimal dividend increases in the present value of the cash flows and shareholders' liquidity demands and decreases in the personal tax rate and the supply of cash. John and Williams also show that the market value of the firm's stock is the net value of the firm minus the optimal signaling costs, that is,

$$P[D(X)] = C + X - I - \tau_P D(X), \tag{12.27}$$

and the impact of announced increments in dividends is

$$\frac{\partial P}{\partial D} = \tau_P \frac{P[D(X)] + \tau_P D(X) - L}{I - C + L}. \tag{12.28}$$

Thus increments in dividends cause an increase in market price.

Empirical evidence on the relation between dividend changes and stock values and future earnings changes provides support for the signaling role of dividends. Specifically, it has been reported that the announcement of increases in dividends is associated with stock price increases while the reverse holds true for dividend decreases. In addition, it has been shown that the announcements of dividend initiations are associated with increases in stock price. Finally, when tracking earnings announcements two years following a dividend increase, studies have reported unexpected positive earnings changes. Chapter 16 provides a more detailed discussion on the empirical evidence associated with dividend policy.

SIGNALING AND THE ISSUE-INVEST DECISION Myers and Majluf [1984] consider a three-date model (time -1, 0, and 1) of a firm that has assets in place and a valuable investment opportunity (project).[6] At time -1, the market has the same information about the assets in place and the project as the management of the firm. Specifically, both management and the market know the distributions of the future value of the assets in place ($\widetilde{A}$) and the net present value (NPV) of the project ($\widetilde{B}$). At time 0, management receives additional information about the value of the assets in place and the NPV of the project. In particular, they observe the realization of $\widetilde{A}$ ($= a$) and $\widetilde{B}$ ($= b$). The market receives this information at time $+1$. The project requires an investment of I and can be financed by issuing stock, selling marketable securities (short-term assets of the company), and/or drawing down on the firm's holding of cash. The total amount of cash that can be obtained from the last two options is S and is referred to as *financial slack*. The amount of slack available is known at time 0 to the market. It is further assumed that the investment required is greater than the financial slack available ($S < I$). Thus investing in the project requires an equity issue of E ($= I - S$) at time 0. Management is assumed to act in the best interest of shareholders who own stock at time 0 by maximizing the value of the old shares conditional on the issue-invest decision and their knowledge of a and b, that is, maximize $V_0^{old} = V(a, b, E)$. Since the market does not know the values of a and b at time 0, the market value of their shares will not necessarily be equal to V_0^{old}.

If the management of the firm decides not to issue new equity, it foregoes the project and the value of the old shares would be

$$V_0^{old} = S + a. \qquad (12.29)$$

If, on the other hand, management issues equity and invests in the project, the value of the old shares would be

$$V_0^{old} = \frac{P'}{P' + E}(E + S + a + b), \qquad (12.30)$$

where P' is the market price of old shares if stock is issued.

The old shareholders will not be worse off under the condition that

$$\frac{P'}{P' + E}(E + S + a + b) \geq S + a \qquad (12.31)$$

---

[6] A discussion of the Myers-Majluf model is also provided in Chapter 15.

or when

$$\frac{P'}{P' + E}(E + b) \geq \frac{E}{P' + E}(S + a)$$

$$(E + b) \geq \frac{E}{P'}(S + a) .\tag{12.32}$$

The condition specified in Eq. (12.32) states that management should issue and invest for combinations of a and b such that the gain to the old shareholders from investing is not less than the fraction of the no-invest value that is captured by new shareholders.[7] Specifically, the lower the value of a and the higher the value of b, the more the firm is likely to invest. This condition also implies that under certain circumstances, a firm may give up on good investment opportunities rather than issuing new equity to raise funds. The loss in share value as a result of this is $L = P(\text{do not issue and invest})E(\widetilde{B}|\text{do not issue and invest})$. This loss decreases with the slack (S) and increases with the investment required (I) and the amount of equity that needs to be raised to fund the investment (E).

If a is known to all investors and managers, then stock is always issued as long as $b \geq 0$. To see this, consider the share price if a is known. Specifically, it is given by

$$P' = S + a + E(\widetilde{B}|\text{issue and invest})\tag{12.33}$$

Since $E(\widetilde{B}|\text{issue and invest}) > 0$, this implies that $P' > S + a$ or $\frac{S+a}{P'} < 1$ or $\frac{E}{P}(S + a) < E$. If $b \geq 0$, then $E + b > E$. Combining these two inequalities yields $\frac{E}{P}(S + a) < E < E + b$. Equation (12.32) always holds if a is known to all market participants and $b \geq 0$. Therefore, the firm will always issue equity and invest if faced with a nonnegative NPV project.

If the firm has no investment opportunities available, this model suggests that the firm will issue and invest only in bad states of the world. To see this, consider a situation where a has a lower bound of a_{min} and all market participants know that a cannot be lower than a_{min}. This implies that the price of old shares cannot be less than $S + a_{min}$. Assume that $P' = S + a_{min} + \epsilon$. Substituting this expression for P' into Eq. (12.32) yields the condition that the firm issues equity only if

$$\frac{S + a}{S + a_{min} + \epsilon} < 1$$

or if $a < a_{min} + \epsilon$. This implies that $E(\widetilde{A}|\text{issue and invest}) < a_{min} + \epsilon$. Combining this condition with the definition of $P' = S + a_{min} + \epsilon$ yields $P' > S + E(\widetilde{A}|\text{issue and invest})$, a contradiction to the definition of the price of the stock. Therefore if the firm has no investment opportunities available, $P' = S + a_{min}$. Substituting this expression for P' in the condition defined by Eq. (12.32) implies that the firm issues equity only if

$$\frac{S + a}{S + a_{min}} \leq 1.\tag{12.34}$$

Equation (12.34) only holds if $a = a_{min}$. Thus with no investment opportunities, the firm issues equity only if the value of assets in place is at its lower bound.

---

[7] The price P' is given by $P' = S + E(\widetilde{A}|\text{issue and invest}) + E(\widetilde{B}|\text{issue and invest})$.

In the Myers-Majluf model, the decision to issue new equity always reduces stock prices unless the firm is going to issue new equity with a probability of one. To see this, consider the condition in Eq. (12.32). The firm chooses not to issue equity if there exist combinations of a and b such that

$$(E + b) < \frac{E}{P'} (S + a) \text{ or} \tag{12.35}$$

$$a > P' \left(1 + \frac{b}{E}\right) - S.$$

Since $\frac{b}{E} \geq 0$, the firm would choose not to issue equity as long as $a > P' - S$ or $P' < S + a$. If the firm decides not to issue new equity, the share price is given by $P = S + E(\widetilde{A}|\text{do not issue}$ and invest$) \geq S + a > P'$. Therefore, the price must fall when the firm chooses to issue and invest. Intuitively, this result follows from the fact that the decision to issue signals to the market that the realization of $\widetilde{A}$ is such that the value of assets in place are in a region with relatively low values for a.

To consider the potential impact of debt financing on this equilibrium, assume that the firm can raise the funding it needs with debt or equity, and that the financing policies are announced at time -1 and adhered to at time 0. Suppose the firm issues equity. Then the value with the equity issue is $V^{old}_{issue} = a + b + I - E_1$, where E_1 is the value of the newly issued shares at time 1. Since $I = S + E$, this implies that

$$V^{old}_{issue} = S + a + b - (E_1 - E) = S + a + b - \Delta E = V^{old}_{no\ issue} + b - \Delta E.$$

Since the firm will choose to issue only if $V^{old}_{issue} \geq V^{old}_{no\ issue}$, this implies that for the "issue equity and invest" decision to be made, the project's NPV should not be lower than the gain to the new shareholders, that is, $b \geq \Delta E$. On the other hand, if the firm issues debt to finance the project, the same logic leads to the conclusion that the firm would issue debt and invest as long as $b \geq \Delta D$. If debt is risk-free, then $\Delta D = 0$ and the firm issues risk-free debt and invests as long as the project has nonnegative NPV, that is, $b \geq 0$. If debt is risky, then ΔD is not zero but $|\Delta D| < |\Delta E|$. This implies that if a firm chooses to issue equity it will also be willing (and, in fact, would prefer) to issue debt. In addition, when $\Delta D < b < \Delta E$, the firm would issue debt but not issue equity. This suggests that firms would follow a pecking order in financing—internal funds followed by risk-free debt, risky debt, and equity. The "pecking order" theory of capital structure and empirical tests of it are also discussed in Chapter 15.

Krasker [1986] extends the Myers and Majluf model to allow firms to choose the size of the new investment project and the equity issue. In addition to obtaining the same result as Myers and Majluf, he also shows that the larger the equity issue the worse the signal.

Cooney and Kalay [1993] extend the Myers and Majluf model to allow for the existence of negative NPV projects. Using the same structure as the Myers and Majluf model, they argue that the value of the old shares if the firm issues and invests can be either greater or smaller than the preannouncement value. As a result the decision to issue does not always result in a stock price decrease. Specifically, if the preannouncement value of the old stock is the weighted average of the value if the firm "issued and invested" and the value if the firm "did not issue," where the weights are the probabilities of issuing and not issuing, respectively, then the announcement to issue will be associated with a price increase if and only if the value if the firm issued equity is larger than the value if the firm did not issue. If the firm is restricted to nonnegative NPV projects, this will never hold true. On the other hand, if the firm is faced with both nonnegative and negative NPV projects, Cooney and Kalay show that there are combinations of a and b for which the value if the firm issued is larger than the value if the firm did not issue, and the announcement of the issue would be associated with an increase in stock price.

Stein [1992] uses an adaptation of the Myers and Majluf model to examine the role of convertible bonds in the pecking order theory of capital structure. He considers a three-date model (time 0, 1, and 2) with three types of firms (good, medium, and bad). Each firm has access to a project with required investment at time 0 of I and expected net present value of B. The discount rate is assumed to be zero, all agents are risk neutral, the amount required for investment has to be raised from external sources, and the firm is completely owned by its manager prior to the infusion of capital. Each firm receives a cash flow from the investment of either b_L or b_H at time 2 ($b_L < I < b_H$). Firms differ in the ex ante probability of receiving b_H, with good types receiving b_H with certainty, medium types receiving b_H with probability p, and bad types receiving b_H with probability q ($q < p < 1$). Firm types are private information at time 0, and the true value of bad firms is volatile between time 0 and time 1. At time 1, the firm type is revealed, and for bad firms, the value of the probability q is updated to either 0 or p. The probability of deterioration is assumed to be z and for consistency $q = (1 - z)p$. The firm has three financing options at time 0—straight debt that matures at time 2, convertible debt that matures at time 2 but can be called to force conversion at time 1 at a predetermined conversion ratio, and equity. Debt financing is associated with a potential for costly financial distress where a deadweight cost of c is imposed on the owner-manager.

Stein shows that if the costs of financial distress are such that $c > (I - b_L)$, then there is a separating equilibrium in which good firms issued debt with face value I, bad firms issue a fraction

$$\frac{I}{qb_H + (1 - q)b_L}$$

of equity, and medium firms issue convertible bonds with face value $F > b_L$, a call price K, $b_L < K < I$, and convertible to

$$\frac{I}{pb_H + (1 - p)b_L}$$

of equity. For this to be a separating equilibrium, the firms should not want to mimic each other. For example, consider a situation in which the bad firm issues convertible debt. If it does so, there is a probability of z that the firm will deteriorate and will, therefore, not be able to force conversion at time 1. This follows from the fact that if the firm deteriorates, the conversion value of the bond is

$$\frac{Ib_L}{pb_H + (1 - p)b_L},$$

which is below the call price K. Since the cash flow for the deteriorated bad firm is b_L with probability 1 and this cash flow is less than the face value of debt (F), the bad firm would be forced into financial distress at time 2 with probability z, and the expected cost of distress would be zc. On the other hand, the bad firm would be issuing an overpriced security at time 0 and would receive a gain from the overpricing. Specifically, the bad firm raises I with a security that will become a straight debt claim with probability z and become an equity claim with probability $(1 - z)$. The payoff on the security would be b_L and I, respectively. This implies that the expected payoff is $zb_L + (1 - z)I$ and the overpricing is $z(I - b_L)$ $[= I - (zb_L + (1 - z)I)]$. This overpricing is less than the expected cost of financial distress, that is, $z(I - b_L) < zc$, since it has been assumed that $c > (I - b_L)$. Therefore, a bad firm will not mimic a medium firm. Using a similar argument it can be shown that a bad firm will not mimic a good firm by issuing straight debt, a medium firm will not want to mimic a bad or good firm, and there is no reason for a good firm to deviate from the policy of issuing straight debt. Thus, a convertible debt issue allows a medium firm to get equity into its capital structure while conveying positive news to the market.

The pecking order hypothesis predicts that, holding investment constant, leverage should decrease with profitability since more profitable firms have more access to internal capital. Similarly, leverage should increase with investments, holding profitability constant. Consistent with the pecking order hypothesis, a number of empirical studies have reported a negative relation between leverage and profitability. In addition, Fama and French [2002] report that short-term variations in investments are absorbed by changes in debt, a result consistent with the pecking order hypothesis. On the other hand, they also report that firms with higher investments have less leverage. Minton and Wruck [2002] find for a group of conservatively financed firms that they do not exhaust all internal funds before they seek external funds. Lemmon and Zender [2002] find for a sample of firms that are likely to gain most from debt financing that they are no less likely to issue equity when seeking outside financing. These results are not consistent with the pecking order hypothesis.

COSTLY SIGNALING AND STOCK SPLITS Copeland and Brennan [1988] consider a two-period world where a stock split may reveal private information held by management about the future prospects of the firm. Specifically, assume that the manager of an all-equity firm has private information at time 0 about its true expected future cash flows at time 1, X. At time 0, the firm has m shares outstanding, and the manager can announce a split factor, s. Therefore, after the split the number of shares outstanding becomes $n = ms$. At time 0, the value of the firm as assessed by investors is denoted by $\overline{P}(z)$ if no split is announced and $\widehat{P}(n, z)$ if a split is announced, where z is a vector of observable firm characteristics (e.g., cash flows) that affect value. At time 1, the value of the cash flows, P, is revealed, and the value at which the firm will trade is $P - T(m, P)$ if no split is announced and $P - T(n, P)$ if a split is announced. $T(a, B)$, the transaction cost incurred by the shareholder when there are a shares outstanding and the value of the cash flows is B, is defined as $t_1 B + t_2 \frac{a}{B^{\gamma - 1}}$ with $t_1, t_2 > 0$ and $\gamma > 1$.

The wage paid to the manager is assumed to be a linear function of the market's assessment of value, the value itself, and the transactions costs faced by the shareholder.[8] Specifically, if a split is not announced, the manager's wage is given by

$$W^0(z) = \alpha \overline{P}(z) + \beta P - T(m, P). \tag{12.36}$$

On the other hand, the manager's wage with a split announcement is

$$W^S(n, z) = \alpha \widehat{P}(n, z) + \beta P - T(n, P). \tag{12.37}$$

The manager will decide to split only if $W^S(n^*, z) > W^0(z)$, where n^* maximizes the wage as defined in Eq. (12.37). The first-order condition for the maximization is

$$W_n = \alpha \widehat{P}_n - \frac{t_2}{P^{\gamma - 1}} = 0. \tag{12.38}$$

---

[8] Copeland [1979] documents higher transactions costs per dollar of transaction for lower-priced stocks.

Since the manager's private information is fully revealed by the split announcement, the value assessed by investors after the split announcement must equal true value, that is, $\widehat{P}(n, z) = P$. Substituting this consistency condition in Eq. (12.38) yields the following differential equation for the market assessment:

$$\alpha \widehat{P}_n P^{\gamma-1} = t_2. \tag{12.39}$$

The solution to Eq. (12.39) is

$$\widehat{P}(n, z) = k[n + c(z)]^{1/\gamma}, \tag{12.40}$$

where $k = (t_2 \gamma / \alpha)^{1/\gamma}$ and $c(z)$ is a constant of integration. Therefore, the market value of a firm after it announces a split is

$$M(n, z) = \widehat{P}(n, z) - T(n, P) = k(1 - t_1)[n + c(z)]^{1/\gamma} - t_2 n k^{1-\gamma}[n + c(z)]^{(1-\gamma)/\gamma}. \tag{12.41}$$

Equation (12.41) implies that the value of the firm increases in the number of shares outstanding. This follows from the fact that even though both the intrinsic value and the total transactions costs increase with the number of shares outstanding, the incremental transactions cost due to an increase in the number of shares outstanding is lower than the incremental intrinsic value.

Equation (12.41) has a number of testable empirical implications. Specifically, consider the situation where $c(z) = 0$, that is, where the constant of integration is zero. In that case, Eq. (12.41) can be written as

$$M(n, z) = \left[k(1 - t_1) - t_2 k^{1-\gamma} \right] n^{1/\gamma}. \tag{12.42}$$

Equation (12.42) implies that the return after the announcement of a split can be written as

$$u = M(n, z)/\overline{M}(z) = \left[k(1 - t_1) - t_2 k^{1-\gamma} \right] n^{1/\gamma}/\overline{M}(z) = K \left[\frac{n}{\overline{M}(z)} \right]^{1/\gamma} \left[\overline{M}(z) \right]^{1/\gamma - 1}, \tag{12.43}$$

where $\overline{M}(z)$ is the presplit value of the firm and $K = \left[k(1 - t_1) - t_2 k^{1-\gamma} \right]$.

Taking the log of Eq. (12.43) yields

$$\ln u = \ln K - \left(\frac{1}{\gamma} \right) \ln \left[\frac{\overline{M}(z)}{n} \right] + \left(\frac{1}{\gamma} - 1 \right) \ln \left[\overline{M}(z) \right]. \tag{12.44}$$

Equation (12.44) implies that a regression of the return associated with the announcement of a stock split should be a decreasing function of the logs of the target share price $\left(= \frac{\overline{M}(z)}{n} \right)$ and the presplit market capitalization of the stock $(= \overline{M}(z))$. In other words, the announcement date return for a stock that splits 2 for 1 from \$100 per share to \$50 will be smaller than the announcement date return of another firm that splits 2 for 1 from \$30 per share to \$15. The equation also implies that the coefficients of the two variables should sum to -1. Copeland and Brennan estimate Eq. (12.44) for 967 stock splits over the period 1967 to 1976. They find that the coefficient of the target share price is negative and significant while that of market capitalization is negative but not significant. They also reject the hypothesis that the two coefficients sum to -1. They also report that these two variables explain about 15% of the variation in announcement returns. Their model also predicts that the growth in earnings postsplit for firms that actually decided to split will be higher than for similar firms that decided not to split. McNichols and Dravid [1990] report results that are consistent with this prediction. Overall, these results support the prediction of the signaling model that the number of shares outstanding after the split provides new information to investors.

2. Costless Signaling (Cheap Talk)

In the previous section, we considered signaling models that have exogenously specified signaling costs. Crawford and Sobel [1982] consider a model in which they consider a costless message (cheap talk) as a signal. Specifically they consider a situation in which a sender has private information in that she observes the value of a random variable (information type) and sends a signal about this to a receiver. The receiver, in turn, takes an action in response to the signal. This action then determines the payoff to both sender and receiver. The equilibrium in this model consists of a family of signaling rules for the sender and action rules for the receiver such that (1) the sender's signaling rule yields an expected utility maximizing action for each of her information types taking receiver's action rules as given and (2) the receiver responds optimally to each possible signal using Bayes's law to update his priors taking account of the sender's signaling strategy and the signal he receives. The model, therefore, has an *endogenous signaling cost* since the utility of the sender can be affected by action taken by the receiver in response to the signal he receives. Crawford and Sobel demonstrate the existence of equilibria where this endogenous signaling cost is such that it is optimal for the sender to tell the truth.

In an extension of the Crawford and Sobel model, Austen-Smith and Banks [2000] also allow the sender to have the ability to accept some direct loss in utility to transmit information in a more credible manner (costly signals) than employing cheap talk (costless signals) alone. They show that the set of equilibria can be dramatically increased when costly signals can be used. They also show that the availability of costly signals can improve the precision of cheap talk communications.

COSTLESS SIGNALING WITH STOCK SPLITS Brennan and Hughes [1991] consider a situation where the manager of a firm has private information about its future cash flows and wants to communicate it to the market. They assume that there is no credible and costless way to communicate the information. They consider a situation in which managers use splits to change stock price since these splits affect the incentives of brokerage houses to provide earnings forecasts that reveal the manager's private information.[9]

Brennan and Hughes have a four-date world where at time 0 investors and managers have homogenous prior beliefs about the firm's future value, X. At time 1, the manager receives private information about X and announces the number of new shares, n, through a stock split. At time 2, N analysts gather information and announce earnings forecasts. At time 3, cash flow/value is realized and analysts are paid their commission. All individuals are assumed to be risk neutral and the priors on X are that it is normally distributed with mean X_0 and variance $1/s_0$ (precision s_0). Assuming a zero interest rate, the market value of the firm at time 0 is

$$V_0 = (1-t)X_0, \tag{12.45}$$

---

[9] It is not clear, however, what mechanism explains just how brokerage houses discover private information held by managers.

where t is the brokerage commission rate that is assumed to depend on stock price. At time 1, the manager receives a noisy signal about the firm's value, $Y_m = X + \tilde{\epsilon}_m$, where $\tilde{\epsilon}_m$ is normally distributed with mean zero and precision s_m. The manager then announces n, and investors infer that the manager's signal was $\widehat{Y}_m(n)$ and revise their beliefs about X to

$$E(X|n) = \widehat{X}(n) = \frac{X_0 s_0 + \widehat{Y}_m(n) s_m}{s_0 + s_m}. \tag{12.46}$$

The new market value of the firm is

$$V_1(n) = \widehat{X}(n) - T(n) - C, \tag{12.47}$$

where C is the cost of executing the split and $T(n)$ is the expected total brokerage commission $(= E\left[Xt(X/n)|n\right])$.

Brennan and Hughes argue that if $T(n)$ is monotonic, the information contained in the announcement of n is equivalent to that contained in the announcement of T. Therefore, they assume that the manager announces T, and the market value of the firm after the managerial announcement can be written as

$$V_1(n) = \widehat{X}(T) - T - C, \tag{12.48}$$

where $\widehat{X}(T) = E(X|T)$. If the cost to an individual analyst of making an earnings forecast is f, the number of analysts who make forecasts is

$$N(T) = T/f = FT, \tag{12.49}$$

where $F = 1/f$. The forecast of an analyst i is $Y_i = X + \tilde{\epsilon}_i$, where ϵ_i is normally distributed with mean 0 and precision s. The value of the firm after the forecasts have been released will be given by

$$V_2(T, \overline{Y}) = \frac{X_0 s_0 + \widehat{Y}_m s_m + \overline{Y} FTs}{s_0 + s_m + FTs} - E\left[Xt(X/n)|T, \widehat{Y}_m, \overline{Y}\right] - C, \tag{12.50}$$

where $\overline{Y}$ is the average value of Y_i. Equation (12.50) indicates that as the number of analysts making forecasts increases, the greater the weight attached to the average analyst's forecast. Thus managers with good news would be motivated to attract the attention of more analysts.

The objective of the manager is to choose n or T at time 1 in order to maximize the expected value of the firm at time 2, with this expectation being conditioned on the manager's private information. Specifically, the manager wants to maximize

$$E[V_2(T)|Y_m] = \frac{X_0 s_0 + \widehat{Y}_m s_m + \left(\frac{X_0 s_0 + Y_m s_m}{s_0 + s_m}\right) FTs}{s_0 + s_m + FTs} - T - C, \tag{12.51}$$

since

$$E\left[\overline{Y}|Y_m\right] = \frac{X_0 s_0 + Y_m s_m}{s_0 + s_m}$$

and

$$E\left(\left[X_t(X/n)|T, \widehat{Y}_m, \overline{Y}\right]|Y_m\right) = T.$$

The first-order condition for this maximization along with the consistency condition that $Y_m = \widehat{Y}_m(T)$ yields the following differential equation for the investor's valuation schedule:

$$\widehat{Y}'_m(T) = \frac{s_0 + s_m + FTs}{s_m}. \tag{12.52}$$

The solution to this differential equation is

$$Y_m(T) = \frac{s_0 + s_m}{s_m}T + \frac{Fs}{2s_m}T^2 + K, \tag{12.53}$$

where K is a constant of integration. The investor's valuation schedule is an increasing function of the aggregate brokerage commission.

To summarize, in this section we presented a model developed by Brennan and Hughes in which managers with private information have an incentive to attract the attention of analysts so that they will discover the value of this private information and transmit it to investors using earnings forecasts. Specifically, the manager achieves this by announcing a stock split that reduces stock price and thereby increasing brokerage commissions that result from the research conducted by the analysts in the brokerage house. Knowing this, investors interpret stock splits as a signal that the manager has favorable information.

Two direct empirical implications of this model are that the number of analysts following a firm should be negatively related to share price and the change in the number of analysts should be positively related to the magnitude of the stock split. Both these implications are empirically supported by the data.

COSTLESS SIGNALING WITH DEBT AND EQUITY Heinkel [1982] develops a costless separating equilibrium in which the amount of debt used by a firm is monotonically related to its unobservable firm value.[10] In his model, each firm consists of a single one-period project that requires financing. The optimal investment amount is the same for all projects, and financing is available from perfectly competitive debt and equity markets. Denote V as the value of the project that requires an investment of I, D as the face value of debt issued to fund the project, B as the current value of debt, E as the value of equity issued to fund the project, S as the market value of equity after the financing and investment is completed, and α as the proportion of equity that is retained by insiders. Insiders are assumed to know the random function that will generate the project's future cash flows, while outsiders (capital suppliers) know only the distribution of functions across the economy, with each return generating function referenced by the quality rating of the firm, n. It is further assumed that the value of the project is decreasing in n, $(dV/dn < 0)$, the value of debt is increasing in n $(\partial B/\partial n > 0)$, and $\partial^2 B/\partial n \partial D \geq 0$. These conditions imply that high-n (high-quality) firms have safer debt but are less valuable. Therefore, high-quality (low-quality) firms can benefit from misrepresentation in the debt (equity) market.

---

[10] See Chapter 15 for a more detailed description of the theory and empirical evidence on capital structure.

Insiders know the true value of the firm's debt claim, $B = B(n, D)$, and the value of the equity position they retain, $\alpha(D)[V(n) - B(n, D)]$. They choose D to maximize this value. The first-order condition for this optimization is

$$(d\alpha/dD)\,[V(n) - B(n, D)] - \alpha(D)\,(\partial B/\partial D) = 0. \tag{12.54}$$

The second-order condition is

$$\left(d^2\alpha/dD^2\right)[V(n) - B(n, D)] - 2(d\alpha/dD)\,(\partial B/\partial D) - \alpha(D)\left(\partial^2 B/\partial D^2\right) < 0. \tag{12.55}$$

For this signaling equilibrium to be costless, insiders of a quality n firm should receive the net present value of the project, $V(n) - I$, or

$$\alpha\left(D^*(n)\right)\left[V(n) - B\left(n, D^*(n)\right)\right] - [V(n) - I] = 0, \tag{12.56}$$

where $D^*(n)$ is the optimal value of D for insiders of a firm of quality n as determined by Eqs. (12.54) and (12.55).

Equations (12.54), (12.55), and (12.56) define a costless signaling equilibrium in which the insiders determine $D^*(n)$ and the market interprets the signal according to Eq. (12.48). It can be shown that Eqs. (12.54) and (12.55) imply that low-quality firms issue more debt than high-quality firms, that is, $dD^*(n)/dn < 0$. To see this, take the total differential of Eq. (12.55) to get

$$\left[\frac{d^2\alpha}{dD^2}(V - B) - 2\frac{d\alpha}{dD}\frac{\partial B}{\partial D} - \alpha\frac{\partial^2 B}{\partial D^2}\right]\frac{dD}{dn} = \frac{d\alpha}{dD}\left(\frac{\partial B}{\partial n} - \frac{dV}{dn}\right) + \alpha\left(\frac{\partial^2 B}{\partial n\partial D}\right). \tag{12.57}$$

Since it has been assumed that $\partial B/\partial n > 0$, $\partial V/\partial n < 0$, $\partial^2 B/\partial n\partial D \geq 0$, and $d\alpha/dD > 0$ from Eq. (12.54), the right-hand side of Eq. (12.57) is positive. In addition, since the bracketed term on the left-hand side of Eq. (12.57) is negative according to Eq. (12.55), this implies that $dD^*(n)/dn < 0$.

The intuition behind this result follows from the restriction on the joint distribution between firm value and credit risk where high-quality firms have safer debt but are less valuable. As a result of this restriction, insiders face opposing incentives in the equity and debt markets. If they misrepresent the equity claims as being of high value, then the debt claims will be overvalued. As a result of this trade-off, insiders have the incentive not to sell overvalued claims. Therefore, low-quality firms will issue more debt than high-quality firms.

Brennan and Kraus [1987] extend Heinkel's model and derive conditions under which the adverse selection problem can be costlessly overcome by an appropriate choice of financing strategy. In Heinkel's analysis, he takes the security types as given and demonstrates a fully revealing equilibrium for a particular type of information asymmetry. In contrast, Brennan and Kraus derive the properties the securities must have to be informative. The Brennan and Kraus results are best illustrated by two examples they present in the paper.

In the first example, consider a firm that has the opportunity to invest 10 at time 0. The distribution of returns on the investment depends on the current state of the world, denoted by A and B. The current state of the world is private information to the firm. If the firm does not make the investment, it earns 100 or 140 at time 1, each with probability of 0.5. If the firm makes the investment, the time 1 payoffs are 100 and 200 if the current state is A, and 80 and 195 if the current state is B. As in the no-investment case, the probabilities are 0.5 each. The firm is currently financed with 100 in debt that matures at time 1 and 40 shares of equity. Since valuation is assumed to be by expected value, the full information value of the firm with no investment is 120, with 100 being the value of debt and 20 the value of equity. Similarly with the investment, the full information value of the firm is 150 in state A, with debt being worth 100 and equity valued at 40. The corresponding figures for state B are 137.5, 90, and 37.5, respectively.

Consider the following fully revealing equilibrium. If state A occurs, the firm retires its debt at its full information value of 100 and issues 110 shares of equity at the full information value of 1 per share. The true full information value of the old equity is 40. If state B occurs, the firm issues 10.67 shares of new equity at the full information value of 0.9375. The true full information value of the old equity is 37.50 $(= (40/50.67)(47.5))$. For this equilibrium to be feasible, there should be no incentive for the firm to misrepresent the state at time 0 by adopting the strategy for the other state. Therefore, if state A occurs, the firm does not have an incentive to issue equity only since the value of old equity would be $(40/50.67)(50)$ or $39.47 < 40$, the value with repurchasing debt and issuing equity. Similarly, if state B occurs, the firm does not have an incentive to retire debt and issue 110 in new equity since the original equity would be worth $(40/150)(137.5)$ or $36.67 < 37.5$, the value with issuing equity only. Thus, in this case the firm repurchases debt and issues equity in the better state and issues equity only in the worse state and the equilibrium is fully revealing. This would imply that the announcement of a pure equity issue should be associated with a decrease in stock value while a combination announcement of a debt repurchase and an equity issue should be associated with an increase in stock value.

In the second example, assume that the density function for a firm's cash flows is uniformly distributed over $(a - \varepsilon, a + \varepsilon)$. At time 0, a is known to all participants, but ε is private information to the firm. The firm has outstanding bonds that mature at time 1 with face value D_0. The firm can finance its capital needs by issuing junior subordinated convertible debt with face value D and conversion ratio α. Brennan and Kraus show that, under certain conditions, a revealing equilibrium is possible where the firm type that investors can infer from the financing (α, D) is

$$\widehat{\varepsilon}(\alpha, D) = \left[(a - D_0)^2 + D^2 (1 - \alpha) / \alpha^2 \right]. \qquad (12.58)$$

Equation (12.58) implies that higher conversion ratios and lower convertible bond face values are associated with safer firms since $\partial \widehat{\varepsilon}/\partial \alpha < 0$ and $\partial \widehat{\varepsilon}/\partial D > 0$.

Constantinides and Grundy [1989] consider a three-date model where firms have assets in place at time 0 and the only claim to the firm is common stock with management owning a fraction of the outstanding equity. Management also announces the planned investment and how it will be financed at time 0. The financing instrument is issued at time 1, matures at time 2, and can be equity, a straight bond, a convertible bond, or some combination. If the amount the firm raises is more than the investment required, the firm repurchases stock from the outside shareholders. The firm's value becomes common knowledge at time 2. At time 0, the firm value is a random variable with a density function that depends on the investment and a parameter, θ, that represents the information that the management has at time 0 and the market does not. The market has a prior distribution for θ and updates its beliefs using Bayes's rule based on the investment and financing announced by management.

In the case that the investment amount is fixed, Constantinides and Grundy show that there is a separating equilibrium that is fully revealing in which all firms make the investment and issue convertible debt. The convertible debt issue is sufficient to cover the investment and repurchase of some of the existing equity. The repurchase assures that the management has no incentive to overvalue while the convertible debt issue removes the incentive to undervalue. If different firms are allowed to have different optimal investment amounts and if investment is observable,

Constantinides and Grundy show that firms can fully separate using the investment amount and the size of a straight bond issue with some share repurchase.

Noe [1988] considers a sequential game model of debt-equity choice in a two-date framework. In his model, at time 0 the firm has assets in place that are expected to generate a time 1 cash flow of x_1. The firm also has access to a project that requires an investment (I) that is common knowledge at time 0. The project yields a cash flow of x_2 at time 1. The quality of the firm is defined by $x = (x_1, x_2)$. Insiders know the quality of the firm, and outsiders have a common probability distribution $f(\bullet)$ over firm types. Noe considers two cases regarding the relation between knowledge of quality and cash flows—one in which knowledge of quality provides perfect foresight on cash flows and another in which the cash flow is equal to the perfect foresight values plus a zero-mean random variable. Insiders must raise funds through debt or equity to finance the project. He presents an example with three firm types, low, medium, and high. The high type firm is assumed to be much better than the medium type firm, and the probability of the firm being a low type is the lowest of the three probabilities.[11] He shows that, in equilibrium, all three firms accept the positive NPV projects, with the low and high type firms pooling and issuing debt to finance the project while the middle type firm separates and issues equity. Investors correctly identify the quality of the firm issuing equity, and consequently the equity issue by the medium type firm is priced correctly by the market. In contrast, either security issued by the low-quality firm will be overpriced since it will be pooled with the medium type firm (if it issues equity) and the high type firm (if it issues debt). Since the high type firm is much better than the medium type firm, the overpricing is more severe for debt, and the low type firm chooses to issue debt. For the high type firm, either issue is going to be underpriced, with the underpricing of debt being less since the probability of being a low type firm is small. Consequently, the high type firm chooses to issue debt. Noe's model suggests that some firms may actually prefer to issue equity over debt, and issuance of equity is not necessarily associated with the lowest-quality firm.

Nachman and Noe [1994] derive necessary and sufficient conditions for the issuance of securities to be an equilibrium outcome of raising external capital. They show that debt financing is a pooling equilibrium outcome if and only if firm types are strictly ordered by conditional stochastic dominance, a strong version of first-order stochastic dominance.

In a recent paper, Heider [2002] presents a model in which combinations of debt and equity can be used to convey credible information to the markets. Heider argues that the different results across papers are special cases of his model by using specific parameter values to describe the quality of the firm. Heider's model is best explained by an example he presents in his paper. In a two-date framework, consider a situation in which a firm needs to raise 10 units of outside capital at time 0 to invest in a project. The firm has no financial slack and cannot sell its assets in place that are worth 100 units. There are two types of investment projects, 1 and 2. A type 2 project returns nothing with a probability of 0.25 and returns 18 units with a probability of 0.75. A type 1 project returns 0 with a probability of 0.15 and 13 units with a probability of 0.85. Thus the expected rate of return for a type 1 project is 10.5% and that for a type 2 project is 35%.

Assume first that there is no information asymmetry regarding project type. Thus if we finance a type 1 project with debt, the "fair-price" repayment on debt would be 11.765 units since the expected payment would be $10 [= (0.15)(0) + (0.85)(11.765)]$. If the type 1 project is financed with equity, the firm would have to issue 9.005% of the equity of the firm since the expected payoff

---

[11] For example, he assumes that the assets in place generate cash flows of 0.3, 1.5, and 20 for low, medium, and high type firms, respectively. The corresponding probabilities of firm type are 0.001, 0.991, and 0.008, respectively.

on this would be 10 [= (0.09)(100 + (0.85)(13))]. The corresponding figures for a type 2 project are 13.333 and 8.811%. The value of the firm is independent of financing in this case. Specifically, regardless of the method of financing, the value of the firm with the type 1 project is 101.05 and that with the type 2 project is 103.5.

Now consider the situation in which the firm knows more about the investment projects than outsiders do. Suppose that firms use debt to finance type 1 projects and equity to finance type 2 projects. In that case, when outsiders observe a debt issue, they infer that the firm is investing in a type 1 project, and they are willing to accept a "fair-price" repayment on debt of 11.765. On the other hand, when they observe an equity issue, they expect an equity stake of 8.811%. Firms knowing this have an opportunity to sell overvalued claims. Specifically, if a firm investing in a type 2 project mimics the issue decision of a firm that invests in a type 1 project, they can issue debt with a repayment of 11.765 rather than the 13.333 they would have to offer under conditions of information symmetry. Similarly firms that invest in type 1 projects mimic the issue decision of firms with type 2 projects by selling 8.811% of the equity rather than 9.005%. Since investors know that firms have an incentive to sell overvalued claims, they would not accept the offered claims, and this cannot be an equilibrium.

Now consider the reverse system of financing where equity is used to finance type 1 projects and debt is used for type 2 projects. Therefore for type 1 projects, the firm issues 9.005% of its equity, while for type 2 projects it uses debt with a repayment of 13.333. In this situation a firm has no incentive to mimic, and they obtain the same prices as in the full information situation. Thus the use of equity financing for safer projects and debt financing for riskier projects is an equilibrium. Heider argues that the driving force behind the pecking order and underinvestment argument in Myers and Majluf is that equity financing of riskier projects by firms gives firms with less risky projects the incentive to mimic the former.

In a more formal model, Heider [2002] considers firms with access to two types of projects, $T = 1, 2$, with both projects requiring an investment of I. The projects return X_T with probability p_T and zero with probability $(1 - p_T)$ with $p_1 \geq p_2$ and $X_1 \leq X_2$. The net present value of all projects is positive, that is, $p_T X_T > I$. Denote the relative difference in success probabilities as $\gamma = (p_1 - p_2) / p_1$ and the relative difference in returns as $\epsilon = (X_2 - X_1) / X_2$. Therefore, if $\epsilon = 0$, project 1 dominates project 2 by first-order stochastic dominance (FOSD); project 2 dominates project 1 by FOSD if $\gamma = 0$. If $\gamma \geq \epsilon$, project 1 dominates project 2 by second-order stochastic dominance (SOSD), while neither dominates by FOSD or SOSD if $\epsilon > \gamma$. Finally, the projects are mean-preserving spreads (MPS) if $\epsilon = \gamma$. According to Heider, many of the papers discussed above are special cases of his model since they consider particular combinations of ϵ and γ. For example, he argues that Heinkel's model fits into the situation where $\epsilon > \gamma$, while Myers and Majluf considered situations where $\gamma = 0$. He also suggests that Brennan and Kraus in the first example above, Constantinides and Grundy, and Nachman and Noe consider situations in which either $\epsilon = 0$ or $\gamma = 0$, while the second example from Brennan and Kraus assumes MPS.

Heider shows that some financing contracts give the outside investor the same payoff regardless of the quality of the project. Specifically he shows that these *belief-independent contracts* must satisfy the condition

$$\overline{D} = X_1 \left[\frac{\overline{\alpha}(\epsilon - \gamma)}{(1 - \overline{\alpha})(1 - \epsilon)\gamma} \right], \tag{12.59}$$

where $\overline{D}$ is the belief-independent amount of debt and $\overline{\alpha}$ is the belief-independent fraction of equity.

Equation (12.59) implies that when projects are MPS ($\epsilon = \gamma$), the belief-independent contract is pure equity. If $\gamma = 0$, pure debt is the belief independent contract. On the other hand, if $\epsilon < \gamma$, the belief-independent contract involves debt repurchases. Heider also shows that if debt repurchases are allowed, then there exists a continuum of separating equilibria in which (1) safer projects are financed with more equity and less debt than riskier projects, that is, $\alpha_1 \geq \bar{\alpha} \geq \alpha_2$ and $D_1 \leq \bar{D} \leq D_2$ with at least one strict inequality each, and (2) a deviation with more equity than $\bar{\alpha}$ is interpreted as coming from firms with a type 1 project and vice versa. In addition, he shows that when repurchases of debt are allowed there exists a unique pooling equilibrium in which all projects are financed with belief-independent combinations of debt and equity. Again, any deviations with more equity than $\bar{\alpha}$ are interpreted as coming from firms with type 1 projects and vice versa.

Consider the equilibria derived by Heider relative to those derived in previous work. If $\gamma = 0$ (the Myers and Majluf case), the belief-independent contract is pure debt, and there is a pooling equilibrium on pure debt. As stated earlier, Heider suggests that Heinkel's model is analogous to his model with $\epsilon > \gamma$ and no repurchase of debt. Therefore his model would imply that riskier firms would issue more debt than less risky firms. This is consistent with Heinkel's argument that more valuable (less risky) firms would issue less debt. In the first example from Brennan and Kraus discussed above, with FOSD ($\epsilon = 0$ or $\gamma = 0$), the separating equilibrium requires firms to repurchase debt and issue equity, the result in the Heider model if $\epsilon = 0$. On the other hand, if $\gamma = 0$, the pooling equilibrium is pure debt, the result in Nachman and Noe. If $\gamma = 0$, the Constantinides and Grundy result corresponds to the separating equilibrium that requires a repurchase of equity by firms with riskier projects. Specifically, when $\gamma = 0$, the belief-independent equity contract is $\bar{\alpha} = 0$. Thus, if firms with less risky projects issue debt only, ones with more risky projects have to repurchase equity. Finally, in the second example of Brennan and Kraus, projects are MPS and convertible bonds financing riskier projects require higher debt face value and lower equity into which debt can be converted. Heider argues that this is analogous to his separating result that with $\epsilon = \gamma$ (MPS), riskier firms are financed with more debt and firms with safer projects issue more equity and buy back debt. Therefore, Heider's analysis suggests that even though various models in the literature on signaling with debt and equity seem to have conflicting implications, they can be reconciled by recognizing that they have a common logic.

3. Summary of Signaling Theory

This section has provided an overview of information asymmetry and signals that could potentially be used by insiders to reduce this asymmetry. These signals can either be costly (i.e., have exogenous costs associated with them) or be costless (i.e., have costs that are endogenous). Examples of costly signals considered include the amount of the firm's equity that is retained by an entrepreneur, the amount of debt issued by the firm, the size of the dividend declared, the type of financing used for an investment, and the decision to split the stock. Examples of costless signals considered include stock splits, the amount of equity issued or repurchased, and the type of debt issued or repurchased. Regardless of the choice of the signaling mechanism, the equilibria achieved from signaling can be of the separating kind, where high-quality firms cannot be mimicked by low-quality firms, or the pooling kind, where outsiders cannot differentiate between the two types of firms.

B. *A*gency Theory

The separation of ownership from control is one of the basic tenets of a free-market society because it allows specialization.[12] For example, Ms. Smith may have enough wealth to own a farm but lacks the skill to run it. Mr. Jones, a farmer with years of experience, may lack the wealth to own a farm and can earn his highest income by operating a farm. Ms. Smith, the principal, can hire Mr. Jones, the agent, and they can both be better off. But when ownership and control are separated, agency costs arise. Ms. Smith wants to maximize the value of the land, which depends on its ability to produce crops over a long period of time minus the cost of production (e.g., fertilizer, seed, machinery, and Mr. Jones's share of the crop each year) while Mr. Jones wants to maximize his share of the crop. Agency costs include the cost of monitoring, losses due to the choice of objective function, and informational asymmetries.

Agency problems arise in firms because corporate decisions are made by managers (agents) on behalf of the firm's capital suppliers (principals). In most agency models, the sequence of events starts with the principal choosing the agent's compensation system, which depends on the performance measures that the principal specifies as well as the final outcome, $c(s, p)$, where s is the final outcome and p are the performance measures. Based on this contract, the agent chooses an action a, for example, decisions of financing and investment. This action along with some exogenous (random) factors determines the final outcome. Next, the performance measures p and final outcome s are observed, the agent is paid according to his compensation contract $c(s, p)$, and the principal gets to keep the difference between the final outcome and the agent's compensation, $s - c(s, p)$.

Consider a principal whose utility function is defined as $U(s - c)$. The principal is assumed to exhibit greed; that is, he has positive marginal utility of wealth ($U' > 0$). The principal is risk neutral or risk averse; that is, he has either constant or decreasing marginal utility ($U'' \leq 0$). The principal's utility is affected by the compensation paid to the agent both directly and indirectly. The indirect effect is from the impact of the compensation function on the action chosen by the manager, which in turn affects the distribution of the outcomes. Let $f(s, p|a)$ represent the joint probability distribution of outcomes and performance measures conditional on the agent's actions. Let us assume that both the agent and the principal have homogeneous beliefs regarding $f(s, p|a)$. Finally, denote the agent's utility function as $V(c) - G(a)$.

In the remainder of the chapter, we tackle various principal-agent issues one at a time.[13] What is the optimal contract when monitoring is the issue, that is, when

- the agent's actions are observable (no monitoring problem),
- are not observable,
- only the final outcome can be observed,
- the content can depend on both the final outcome and other performance measures,
- there are multiple actions by the agent?

---

[12] The analysis and discussion in this section borrows heavily from Lambert [2001].

[13] See Pendergast [1999] and Laffont and Martimort [2002] for excellent reviews of the literature.

Next, suppose information asymmetry between the principal and the agent is at the heart of the problem. What is the optimal contract? Finally, we address corporate finance specific issues. How does agency theory affect the mix of debt and equity, dividend policy, and investment decisions?

1. The Optimal Compensation Contract When the Agent's Actions Are Observable

As a first step in the analysis of this model consider a situation in which a incentive problem does not exist.[14] In the aforementioned farm example, Mr. Jones, the farmer, has incentive to overfarm the land, and therefore to destroy its value, because he receives a share of the crop, not a share of the land value. In this framework, we would choose a compensation contract and an action to maximize the principal's utility subject to the agent achieving a minimum acceptable level of utility, $\underline{V}$. Specifically, we can write the problem as

$$\underset{c(s,p),a}{\text{maximize}} \iint U\left[s - c(s, p)\right] f(s, p|a) \, ds \, dp \tag{12.60}$$

subject to

$$\iint V\left[c(s, p)\right] f(s, p|a) \, ds \, dp - G(a) \geq \underline{V}. \tag{12.61}$$

The first part of the above equation represents the expected utility of the principal for a given compensation contract and action. The expectation is based on the utility of the payoff to the principal, $U\left[s - c(s, p)\right]$, and the joint density function for the final outcome and the performance measure subject to the action taken, $f(s, p|a)$. The second part of the equation specifies that the difference between the agent's expected utility from compensation and that from the action chosen has to be larger than the minimum level acceptable to the agent. Again, the expectation is over the joint density function for the final outcome and the performance measure subject to the action taken.

If λ denotes the Lagrangian multiplier associated with the constraint, the problem can be written as

$$\underset{c(s,p),a}{\text{maximize}} \iint U\left[s - c(s, p)\right] f(s, p|a) \, ds \, dp + \lambda \left[\iint V\left[c(s, p)\right] f(s, p|a) \, ds \, dp - G(a) - \underline{V}\right].$$

$$\tag{12.62}$$

The first-order condition for this optimization is

$$-U'\left[s - c(s, p)\right] + \lambda V'\left[c(s, p)\right] = 0 \text{ or}$$

$$\frac{U'\left[s - c(s, p)\right]}{V'\left[c(s, p)\right]} = \lambda. \tag{12.63}$$

The above condition states that optimal risk sharing condition is such that the agent's compensation is set so that the ratio of the marginal utility of the principal to the marginal utility of the agent is equal to a constant for all possible realizations of $\left[s, p\right]$. This solution is generally referred to as the "first-best" solution.

---

[14] The incentive problem arises because the principal cannot observe the agent's actions.

Equation (12.63) has a number of implications. For example, if the agent is risk neutral and the principal is risk averse, Eq. (12.63) becomes $U'\left[s - c(s, p)\right] = \lambda$. Since λ is a constant, this implies that marginal utility U' is a constant. Therefore, the optimal compensation contract is for the principal to bear no risk and conversely for the agent to bear all the risk. The optimal compensation contract in this case would be $c(s, p) = s - k$, where k is a constant. On the other hand, if the principal is risk neutral and the agent is risk averse, Eq. (12.63) becomes $V'\left[c(s, p)\right] = \frac{1}{\lambda}$, and the optimal compensation contract would be $c(s, p) = k$, with the principal bearing all the risk and the agent bearing none.

When both the agent and the principal are risk averse, the optimal contract will incorporate some risk sharing with the exact form of the risk-sharing function depending on the two utility functions. For example, Wilson [1968] shows that if both parties have negative exponential utility function, the optimal compensation contract is linear in the final outcome s with a slope coefficient equal to the ratio of the risk tolerances of the agent and the principal.[15] Specifically, consider an agent and a principal with utility functions given by $U_i(W) = -\alpha_i e^{-W/\alpha_i}$, $i = agent, principal$, and α_i is i's risk tolerance. Substituting these utility functions in Eq. (12.63) yields the optimal compensation contract

$$c = \beta + \left(\frac{\alpha_{agent}}{\alpha}\right) s,$$

where $\alpha = \alpha_{agent} + \alpha_{principal}$ and $\beta = \frac{\lambda}{\alpha}$. Figure 12.1(a) provides a plot of this optimal compensation function. As can be seen from this plot, the slope of the compensation function increases with the risk tolerance of the agent; that is, the more risk the agent is willing to tolerate, the more risk he bears in the optimal compensation contract.

Compensation contracts that deviate from the linear structure specified above can lead to conflicts of interest between the agent and the principal. For example, consider the compensation contract in Fig. 12.1(b), which can be defined as

$$c(s) = \begin{cases} \beta_0 & \text{if } s \leq s_0 \\ \left(\frac{\beta_0 s_1 - \beta_1 s_0}{s_1 - s_0}\right) + \left(\frac{\beta_1 - \beta_0}{s_1 - s_0}\right) s & \text{if } s_0 < s < s_1 \\ \beta_1 & \text{if } s \geq s_1 \end{cases} \tag{12.64}$$

As can be seen from the figure, the agent receives a fixed payment if the final outcome is below s_0 or above s_1 and receives a payment that is linearly related to the final outcome if it is between s_0 and s_1. Further assume that the outcome is measured and compensation paid at the end of a period, while the agent expends effort over the period at a rate that can vary over the period. Consider the situation in which the agent has expended effort over three-fourths of a period and is relatively certain that the final outcome will be above s_1. In this case, the agent has an incentive to stop expending any more effort since any outcome above s_1 provides him with the same compensation, β_1. On the other hand, if the outcome is close to (and below) s_0, the agent has the incentive to take large risks since his compensation cannot fall below β_0. This suggests that compensation contracts that deviate from the first-best solution can induce conflicts of interest between the principal and agent.

---

[15] Recall from Chapter 3 that the negative exponential is $U(x) = -\alpha e^{-X/\alpha}$, where α is a measure of the individual's risk tolerance.

Figure 12.1 (a) The first-best compensation contract when the principal and agent have exponential utility, $U(W) = -\alpha e^{-W/\alpha}$. (b) An alternate compensation contract.

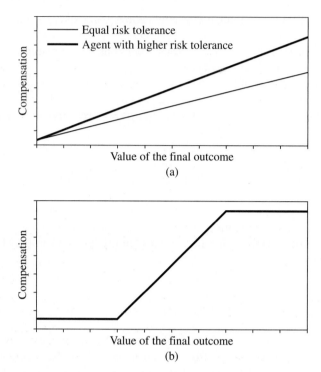

AN OPTIMAL COMPENSATION CONTRACT WHEN THE AGENT'S ACTIONS ARE NOT OBSERVABLE

Let us now assume that the agent will select actions that are in his best interests given the compensation contract that is offered to him by the principal. As a link to the discussion in the previous section, first consider the situations under which the principal can design a compensation contract that shares the risk optimally between the principal and the agent and provides an incentive to the agent to select a "first-best solution" action. If the agent is risk neutral, the optimal risk-sharing contract is for the principal to receive a fixed payment k and for the agent to bear all the risk and receive the residual value $s - k$. In this case the "first-best solution" action can be viewed as the solution to

$$\underset{a}{\text{maximize}}\; U(k) + \lambda \left[\iint V\left[c(s, p)\right] f(s, p|a) ds dp - G(a) - \underline{V} \right]. \tag{12.65}$$

Specifically, this implies the "first-best solution" action is chosen to maximize the agent's expected utility. Therefore, this action is identical to what the agent would select given his own incentives. Thus, when the firm is "owned" by the agent because of the structure of the compensation contract, he chooses an action that represents the first-best solution.

The first-best solution also obtains if the agent is risk averse and the principal can invert the outcome function to infer the agent's action. In this case, the principal can offer the agent a compensation contract that contains the optimal risk-sharing terms if the first-best action has been selected by the agent and substantially penalize any deviation from the first-best action.

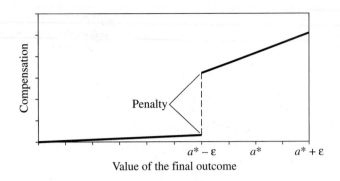

Figure 12.2 A compensation contract with penalties for shirking when the principal and agent have exponential utility, $U(W) = -\alpha e^{-W/\alpha}$.

Finally, first-best solutions can also be achieved if the set of possible outcomes changes with the action selected. For example, consider a situation in which the outcome is uniformly distributed between $[a - \varepsilon, a + \varepsilon]$ if the agent picks action a. If the first-best action is a^*, then any realized outcome that falls in the range $[a^* - \varepsilon, a^* + \varepsilon]$ is consistent with the agent having selected action a^*. This implies that if the final outcome is below $(a^* - \varepsilon)$, the principal knows with certainty that the agent did not choose the first-best action a^*. Assume that the principal offers the agent a compensation contract that contains the optimal risk-sharing terms if the final outcome is in the range $[a^* - \varepsilon, a^* + \varepsilon]$ and imposes a large penalty on the agent if the outcome is below $(a^* - \varepsilon)$. In this case, if the penalty is large enough, the agent will pick the first-best action a^* since he knows that while he could put out an effort less than a^* and have a good chance of the outcome being in the range $[a^* - \varepsilon, a^* + \varepsilon]$, there is some probability that the final outcome will be below $a^* - \varepsilon$ and he would suffer the penalty. Figure 12.2 provides an example of a compensation contract with such penalties built in.

THE IMPACT OF CONTRACTING ON OBSERVABLE FINAL OUTCOME ONLY

Holmstrom [1979] considers a principal-agent model where the compensation contract depends on the final outcome only. The structure of the game is Stackelberg in that the principal moves first and makes a "take it or leave it" offer to the agent. If the agent accepts the contract, it is assumed that he is able to select a level of effort (action) a belonging to a set of feasible actions A. The outcome s is a continuous random variable that increases in the level of effort. The density function for the outcome conditional on the effort is denoted by $f(s|a)$. The density function is assumed to have the property that if $f(s|a) > 0$ for some effort a, then it is positive for all $a \in A$.[16] Finally, it is assumed that the agent's utility decreases with increasing effort, that is, $G'(a) < 0$ and $G''(a) > 0$. In this scenario, the principal's problem is

$$\underset{c(s),a}{\text{maximize}} \int U[s - c(s)] f(s|a) \, ds \qquad (12.66)$$

subject to

$$\int V[c(s)] f(s|a) \, ds - G(a) \geq \underline{V},$$

---

[16] The condition ensures that the principal cannot infer the level of effort from the outcome.

while for the agent,

$$\text{maximize}_{c(s),a} \int V\,[c(s)]\,f(s|a)\,ds - G(a).$$

The difference between the above formulation and the formulation for the first-best solution is that in this problem a constraint is added where it is assumed that the agent selects an action that maximizes his expected utility given the compensation contract offered by the principal (the *incentive compatibility constraint*). To make this problem more tractable, the incentive compatibility constraint as stated above is replaced by the first-order condition for the maximization by the agent. Specifically, the first-order condition is

$$\int V\,[c(s)]\,f_a(s|a)\,ds - G'(a) = 0. \tag{12.67}$$

If λ is the Lagrangian multiplier for the acceptable utility constraint and μ is the multiplier associated with the first-order condition in Eq. (12.67), the principal's problem can be written as

$$\text{maximize}_{c(s),a} \int U\,[s - c(s)]\,f(s|a)\,ds + \lambda \left[\int V\,[c(s)]\,f(s|a)\,ds - G(a) - \underline{V} \right]$$

$$+ \mu \left[\int V\,[c(s)]\,f_a(s|a)\,ds - G'(a) \right]. \tag{12.68}$$

The first-order condition for the above maximization is

$$-U'\,[s - c(s)]\,f(s|a) + \lambda V'\,[c(s)]\,f(s|a) + \mu V'\,[c(s)]\,f_a(s|a). \tag{12.69}$$

The condition in Eq. (12.69) can be rearranged as

$$\frac{U'\,[s - c(s)]}{V'\,[c(s)]} = \lambda + \mu \frac{f_a(s|a)}{f(s|a)}. \tag{12.70}$$

A comparison of Eq. (12.63), the condition for the first-best solution, and Eq. (12.70) indicates that if μ is nonzero, the first-best solution is not achievable. Holmstrom shows that μ has to be positive as long as the principal wants the agent to expend more than the minimal level of effort possible. In this case, if the principal gives the agent an optimal risk-sharing contract, this does not provide incentive to the agent to expend a high enough level of effort. By imposing more risk on the agent, the principal provides more incentive to increase effort, but this increased effort decreases the agent's utility. To compensate for this decrease and maintain utility at the acceptable level $\underline{V}$, the principal has to offer a higher expected compensation to the agent. Figure 12.3 provides a comparison of the first-best contract and a potential solution to Eq. (12.70). As can be seen from the figure, the contract has a higher intercept and a larger slope than the first-best contract. The higher slope imposes more risk on the agent, while the higher intercept provides a larger expected compensation.

Equation (12.70) indicates that the shape of the optimal contract depends on the shapes of the principal's and agent's utility functions and the shape of the likelihood ratio function

Figure 12.3 A compensation contract when only the final outcome is observable and the principal and agent have exponential utility, $U(W) = -\alpha e^{-W/\alpha}$.

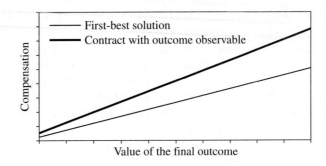

Figure 12.4 A compensation contract when only the final outcome is observable, the principal is risk neutral, and the agent has a utility function, $U(W) = [1/(1-\gamma)](\delta_0 + \delta_1 W)^{(1-\gamma)}$.

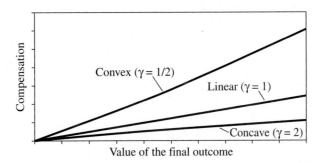

$f_a(s|a)/f(s|a)$.[17] In general, a sufficient condition for the contract to be nondecreasing in the outcome s is for $f_a(s|a)/f(s|a)$ to increase in s; that is, the outcome density satisfies the monotone likelihood ratio property (MLRP).[18] On the other hand, a linear likelihood ratio function does not guarantee an optimal contract that is linear in the outcome. For example, consider a risk-neutral principal and the agent's utility function is $V(c) = [1/(1-\gamma)](\delta_0 + \delta_1 c)^{(1-\gamma)}$. In this case, $V'(c) = \delta_1/(\delta_0 + \delta_1 c)^{\gamma}$, and Eq. (12.70) can be written as

$$\left(\frac{1}{\delta_1}\right)(\delta_0 + \delta_1 c)^{\gamma} = \lambda + \mu \frac{f_a(s|a)}{f(s|a)}. \tag{12.71}$$

Solving Eq. (12.71) for the compensation function yields

$$c(s) = -\frac{\delta_0}{\delta_1} + (\delta_1)^{\left(\frac{1}{\gamma}-1\right)}\left(\lambda + \mu\frac{f_a(s|a)}{f(s|a)}\right)^{\left(\frac{1}{\gamma}\right)}. \tag{12.72}$$

Even if μ is positive and the likelihood ratio function is linear in s, the compensation function can be concave, linear, or convex in s. Specifically if $0 < \gamma < 1$, the compensation function is a convex function of s. It is linear if γ is 1 and concave if γ is larger than 1. Figure 12.4 provides an example of concave, linear, and convex contracts.

---

[17] $f_a(s|a)/f(s|a)$ is a likelihood ratio since it is equal to $\partial \ln f(s|a)/\partial a$ and the latter represents the term that is set equal to zero to obtain the maximum likelihood estimate of a.

[18] See Milgrom [1981] for more details.

**THE IMPACT OF CONTRACTING ON THE FINAL OUTCOME AND OTHER PERFOR-
MANCE MEASURES** Since contracting on outcomes alone can result in deviations from the
first-best contract, this implies that the addition of other performance measures into the compensation contract can improve utilities if they improve incentives and risk sharing. Consider a
situation in which the final outcome s and an additional performance measure p are observable.
Let $f(s, p|a)$ denote the joint density function for the final outcome and the performance measure
conditional on the effort a. In this case, the principal's problem can be written as

$$\underset{c(s,p),a}{\text{maximize}} \iint U\left[s - c(s, p)\right] f(s, p|a) \, ds \, dp$$

$$+ \lambda \left[\iint V\left[c(s, p)\right] f(s, p|a) \, ds \, dp - G(a) - \underline{V}\right]$$

$$+ \mu \left[\iint V\left[c(s, p)\right] f_a(s, p|a) \, ds \, dp - G'(a)\right]. \tag{12.73}$$

The first-order condition for the above maximization is

$$\frac{U'\left[s - c(s, p)\right]}{V'\left[c(s, p)\right]} = \lambda + \mu \frac{f_a(s, p|a)}{f(s, p|a)}. \tag{12.74}$$

As with the case where only the final outcome is observable, μ is greater than zero if both the final
outcome and another performance measure is observable. This implies that the optimal contract
depends on the performance measure p if the likelihood ratio function $f_a(s, p|a)/f(s, p|a)$
depends on p. Holmstrom shows that the likelihood ratio function depends on p as long as the final
outcome s is not a sufficient statistic for s and p with respect to the agent's effort a. This follows
from the fact that if s is a sufficient statistic, then even though p contains information about the
effort a, it does not provide any information in addition to what is provided by the final outcome s.
To generalize, Holmstrom's informativeness condition suggests that any additional performance
measures will be a valuable addition to a compensation contract as long as other available variables
are not sufficient statistics for this measure regardless of the noise associated with the measure.

Banker and Datar [1989] take the Holmstrom informative condition a step further by deriving
conditions under which multiple performance measures can be aggregated into one measure,
with the compensation contract being based on this one aggregate performance metric. They
show that if the principal is risk neutral, then multiple performance measures can be aggregated
linearly if the joint density function of the performance measures conditional on the agent's effort
a belongs to the exponential family of distributions.[19] In addition, they show that the weight
attached to each performance measure in the aggregation is proportional to the sensitivity of
the performance measure to the agent's effort and the precision of the measure. This suggests
that performance measures that are more sensitive to a will be weighted more in the aggregate
measure of performance. In addition, more noisy measures would have lower weights as compared
to measures that are more precise.

---

[19] As pointed out by Banker and Datar, the exponential family of distributions includes many common distributions such
as the (truncated) normal, exponential, gamma, chi-squared, and inverse gaussian.

THE IMPACT OF ALLOWING MULTIPLE ACTIONS BY THE AGENT As suggested by Lambert [2001], Eq. (12.74) can easily be extended to a multiple-action framework. Specifically, the optimal contract will be the solution to the first-order condition

$$\frac{U'\left[s - c(\mathbf{p})\right]}{V'\left[c(\mathbf{p})\right]} = \lambda + \mu_1 \frac{f_{a_1}(\mathbf{p}|\mathbf{a})}{f(\mathbf{p}|\mathbf{a})} + \mu_2 \frac{f_{a_2}(\mathbf{p}|\mathbf{a})}{f(\mathbf{p}|\mathbf{a})} + \cdots + \mu_n \frac{f_{a_n}(\mathbf{p}|\mathbf{a})}{f(\mathbf{p}|\mathbf{a})}, \tag{12.75}$$

where μ_i is the Lagrangian multiplier associated with action a_i, $i = 1, \ldots, m$; $\mathbf{a}$ represents the set of actions; and $\mathbf{p}$ represents the set of observable performance measures (that could include the final outcome s). The results of Banker and Datar as related to linear aggregation continue to apply to this case, with the weights associated with each performance measure being proportional to the sensitivity of the performance measure to the agent's effort and the precision of the measure. The sensitivity of the performance measure is defined as the weighted average of the sensitivities of the performance measure to each individual action $[\partial E(p_j|\mathbf{a})/\partial a_i]$, where the weight is the Lagrangian multiplier μ_i. One major problem with this result in this multiple-action framework is that, in contrast to the single-action framework, other features of the model other than the sensitivities of the performance measure to each individual action and the precisions affect the relative weights. This requires a solution to the Lagrangian multipliers and makes the model intractable since these multipliers are generally difficult to solve for.

Holmstrom and Milgrom [1987] have proposed an alternate formulation to the multiple-action problem that is more tractable. In this model, the agent is responsible for an m-dimensional effort $\mathbf{a} = (a_1, \ldots, a_m)$ that is not observed by the principal both at the individual and the aggregate levels. The principal bases the agent's compensation contract on K observed performance measures, $\mathbf{p} = (p_1, \ldots, p_K)$. One of the performance measures may be the final outcome, but it is also possible for the final outcome to be unobservable to the principal. The performance measures are assumed to be normally distributed with the agent's actions affecting only the means of the distributions. The expected values of the final outcome and the performance measures are assumed to be linear functions of the agent's efforts. Specifically, the outcome function is

$$s = \sum_{j=1}^{m} b_j a_j + \epsilon_s, \tag{12.76}$$

and the performance measures are

$$p_i = \sum_{j=1}^{m} q_{ij} a_j + \epsilon_i \quad \text{for } i = 1, \ldots, K, \tag{12.77}$$

where ϵ_s and ϵ_i, $i = 1, \ldots, K$, are jointly normal with means of zero. Denote σ_{ii} as the variance of p_i and σ_{ij} as the covariance between p_i and p_j. In the above definitions of the outcome and the performance measures, the b_js and the q_{ij}s measure the sensitivity of the final outcome and performance measure p_i to action a_j, respectively.

The principal is assumed to be risk neutral, and the agent's utility function is of the form $V(W) = -e^{-\rho W}$, where $W = c(\mathbf{p}) - G(\mathbf{a})$, ρ is the coefficient of absolute risk aversion, and

$$G(\mathbf{a}) = 0.5 \sum_{j=1}^{m} a_j^2$$

is the monetary value associated with effort **a**. Finally, the compensation contract is assumed to be a linear function of the performance measures and is given by

$$c(p_1, \ldots, p_K) = \beta_0 + \sum_{i=1}^{K} \beta_i \tilde{p}_i. \tag{12.78}$$

Based on these assumptions, it can be shown that the principal's optimization problem can be written as

$$\underset{\beta_0, \ldots, \beta_K}{\text{minimize}} \sum_{j=1}^{m} \left[b_j - \sum_{i=1}^{K} \beta_i q_{ij} \right]^2 + \rho \left[\sum_{i=1}^{K} \sum_{j=1}^{K} \beta_i \beta_j \sigma_{ij} \right]. \tag{12.79}$$

In Eq. (12.79), the first term reflects the principal's desire to pick weights in the compensation contract that minimize the difference between the sensitivity of the final outcome to agent's actions (b_j) and the sensitivity of the compensation to the agent's actions

$$\sum_{i=1}^{K} \beta_i q_{ij},$$

the congruity effect. On the other hand, the second term reflects the desire to minimize the risk in the agent's compensation since the agent would have to be compensated more for bearing added risk, *the sensitivity-precision effect.*

In the case where there are two performance measures, p_1 and p_2, Datar, Kulp, and Lambert [2001] show that the ratio of the weights of p_1 and p_2 in the compensation contract are

$$\frac{\beta_1}{\beta_2} = \frac{\sum_{j=1}^{m} b_j q_{1j} \sum_{j=1}^{m} q_{2j}^2 - \sum_{j=1}^{m} b_j q_{2j} \sum_{j=1}^{m} q_{1j} q_{2j} + \rho \sigma_{12} \sum_{j=1}^{m} b_j q_{2j} - \rho \sigma_{22} \sum_{j=1}^{m} b_j q_{1j}}{\sum_{j=1}^{m} b_j q_{2j} \sum_{j=1}^{m} q_{1j}^2 - \sum_{j=1}^{m} b_j q_{1j} \sum_{j=1}^{m} q_{1j} q_{2j} + \rho \sigma_{12} \sum_{j=1}^{m} b_j q_{1j} - \rho \sigma_{11} \sum_{j=1}^{m} b_j q_{2j}}. \tag{12.80}$$

The first two terms in both the numerator and the denominator reflect the congruity effect while the second two terms reflect the sensitivity-precision effect. Thus, if the agent is risk neutral ($\rho = 0$) or if the performance measures are noiseless ($\sigma_{ij} = 0$ for all i, $j = 1, \ldots, K$), then the principal's problem is to design a contract that makes the agent's overall performance measure

$$\sum_{i=1}^{K} \beta_i p_i$$

as congruent as possible to the final outcome s. On the other hand, if the agent's overall performance measure is perfectly aligned with the final outcome, the model is essentially the same as the single-action model where the weight assigned to each performance measure is related to the sensitivity and noise of the measure.

2. The Impact of Information Asymmetry between the Agent and the Principal

Consider a situation in which an agent receives an information signal m with a probability density function of $g(m)$ and uses the signal to update the density function of the final outcome and other performance measures to $h(s, \mathbf{p}|a, m)$. Further assume that the agent receives the signal after signing his compensation contract but before selecting his action, that he can leave the firm after observing the signal, and that he can communicate the signal to the principal. In this case the principal's problem can be written as

$$\underset{c(s,\mathbf{p},m),a(m),m(m)}{\text{maximize}} \quad E_{s,\mathbf{p},m} \left[U \left[s - c(s, \mathbf{p}, m) \right] \mid a(m) \right]$$

subject to (for all m)

$$E_{s,\mathbf{p}|m} \left[\left[V \left[c(s, \mathbf{p}, m) \right] - G \left[a(m) \right] \right] | a(m) \right] \geq \underline{V}, \tag{12.81}$$

where

$$a(m) = \text{the } a \text{ that maximizes } E_{s,\mathbf{y}|m} \left[V \left[c(s, p, m) \right] | a \right] - G(a) \text{ for each } m,$$

$$m(m) = \text{the } \widehat{m}(m) \text{ that maximizes } E_{s,\mathbf{y}|m} \left[V \left[c(s, p, \widehat{m}) \right] | a \right] - G(a) \text{ for each } m.$$

We define $\widehat{m}(m)$ as the agent's message to the principal after observing the signal m, which by the *revelation principle* is assumed to be the true signal $m(m)$.[20] The revelation principle establishes that by recognizing the agent's rational behavior, one can restrict oneself, without loss of generality, to the class of truthful messages. Specifically, it assumes that the principal is able to credibly commit to not opportunistically use the information revealed by the message and can get the agent to truthfully signal his private information by promising the agent whatever he would have received by lying.

In the above formulation, the optimal compensation contract is based not only on the final outcome s and the performance measures p but also on the message sent by the agent. The major differences between this formulation and that presented earlier under conditions of symmetric information are in the *agent's minimum acceptable utility* (AU) and *incentive compatibility* (IC) constraints. Specifically in the symmetric information case, the AU constraint is based on expected utility, but in this case it is replaced by a set of AU constraints, one for each signal m. This change is necessary to ensure that the agent is prevented from leaving after observing the signal for all realizations of m. Similarly, the single IC constraint is replaced by a set of IC constraints, one for each signal m. In general, these models demonstrate that the principal will be worse off in the presence of private information since the agent is likely to earn rents from his superior information.[21]

C. $\mathcal{A}$gency Theory and Finance

Agency theory has been applied to a number of different areas in finance. Although the economic theory of agency is mainly focused on the structure of managerial compensation contracts that mitigate agency problems, the financial theory of agency also analyzes the impact of the conflict between managers and a firm's claimholders and the conflict between claimholders on issues related to optimal levels of investment and risk bearing by the firm and optimal capital structure. In this section, we discuss the financial theory of agency by first looking at the impact of manager-claimholder conflicts on firm value, investment decisions, and compensation contracts. We will

---

[20] See Myerson [1979] for more details on the revelation principle.
[21] See Sappington [1983] for more details.

then offer an analysis of stockholder-bondholder conflicts and its impact on various financial decisions including capital structure and structure of investments by firms.

1. Conflicts between Managers and Stockholders

As stated by Jensen and Smith [1985], there are three main sources of conflict between managers and claimholders. The first is the choice of effort by managers and has been discussed extensively in the previous section. The second stems from the fact that since investment in firm-specific human capital represents a significant portion of the manager's wealth, she is concerned about the total risk of the firm even though the shareholder can diversify away most of that risk. As a result, a manager may make investment decisions that help diversify the firm but may not be in the best interest of shareholders. Finally, the third source of conflict arises from the differential horizons of the managers and claimholders. A manager's claim on the firm is limited to their tenure with the firm, but a firm's life is infinite. As a result, managers would tend to place less weight on cash flows occurring after their horizon in making decisions.

Jensen and Meckling [1976] analyze the impact of the first source of conflict by comparing the behavior of a manager who owns 100% of a firm's equity with that of a manager who sells a portion of the equity to outsiders. Specifically, consider a firm in which X is a vector of activities from which the manager derives nonpecuniary benefits.[22] Assume that the present value of cost of generating X is $C(X)$, and the total dollar present value to the firm of the productive benefit of X is $P(X)$. Therefore, the net dollar gain to the firm of X is $V(X) = P(X) - C(X)$.[23] The optimal level of factors and activities X^* that is picked by a manager that is a 100% owner is defined by

$$\frac{\partial V\left(X^*\right)}{\partial X} = \frac{\partial P\left(X^*\right)}{\partial X} - \frac{\partial C\left(X^*\right)}{\partial X} = 0. \tag{12.82}$$

Thus for any $X > X^*$, the net dollar gain to the firm must be lower than that at the optimal, that is, $V(X) < V\left(X^*\right)$. Define the dollar cost to the firm of providing the increment $X - X^*$ of activities as $F = V\left(X^*\right) - V(X)$. Figure 12.5 provides a plot of the trade-offs between the value of the firm, V, and the value of the nonpecuniary benefits, F. In particular, the line $\overline{VF}$ defines the possible combinations of V and F that are available to the firm and its owners. Since it has been assumed that an increase of one unit in F causes a decrease of 1 unit in V, the slope of $\overline{VF}$ is -1. Consider a manager whose utility function, $U(V, F)$, is defined in terms of the indifference curves U_1, U_2, and U_3. If the manager owned 100% of the firm, the manager would pick a level of F such that her indifference curve is tangent to the line $\overline{VF}$. This is represented by A in the figure and results in the value of the firm being V^*. If the manager sells 100% of the firm to outsiders and if the first-best solution can be achieved, then the outsiders should be willing to pay V^* for the firm.

Assume that the first-best solution cannot be achieved and the manager retains a fraction α of this firm. Further assume that the outsiders pay the manager $(1 - \alpha)V^*$ for their share of the firm. Given the change in ownership, the cost to the manager of consuming 1 more unit of nonpecuniary benefits is no longer 1 unit. Specifically, although the decision to consume more than one unit in nonpecuniary benefits reduces firm value by one unit, the cost to the manager is only α since the remaining $(1 - \alpha)$ is borne by the outsiders. Thus the new (V, F) constraint faced by the manager

---

[22] This corresponds to what has been previously referred to as the manager's action or effort.

[23] This assumes that X has no impact on the equilibrium wage of the manager.

Figure 12.5 The value of the firm (V) and the value of nonpecuniary benefits consumed (F) when the manager owns a fraction α of the firm and has indifference curves denoted by U.

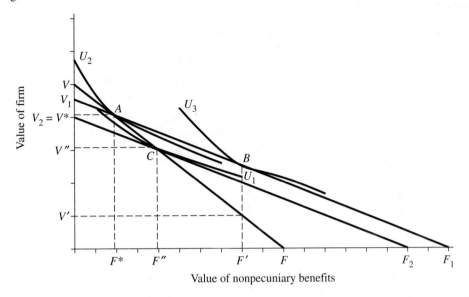

is defined by a line that passes through A but has a slope of $-\alpha$, the line $V_1 F_1$ in Fig. 12.5. If the owner-manager is free to choose the level of nonpecuniary benefits subject only to the loss she incurs as a partial owner, she will move to point B, where the value of the firm will fall to V' and the value of the nonpecuniary benefits consumed increases to F'. Since the outside investors are aware of this incentive to increase consumption of nonpecuniary benefits, they will not pay $(1 - \alpha)V^*$ for their share of the firm. Specifically, assume that the outsiders pay S for their share of the firm. The wealth of the manager is then given by $W = S + \alpha V(F, \alpha)$, where $V(F, \alpha)$ represents the value of the firm given a nonpecuniary benefit consumption of F and managerial ownership of a fraction α of the firm. Based on this level of wealth, the manager will select a level of F at a point where the (V, F) constraint faced by the manager is tangent to an indifference curve. In addition, the value of F will also lie along the line $\overline{VF}$. This implies that the (V, F) constraint faced by the manager given that she has sold a fraction $(1 - \alpha)$ of the firm for S will be given by the line $V_2 F_2$ in Fig. 12.5. In this scenario, the manager's optimal choice is denoted by the point C, where the value of the firm is V'' and the value of the nonpecuniary benefits is F''. The result that point C represents the point of tangency follows from the fact that, if the optimal point is to the left of C, this implies that the outsider is paying less than the value of the claim he acquires. On the other hand, if the optimal is to the right of C, the outsider is paying more than the value of the claim. Therefore, if the outsider pays an amount equal to the value of the claim he acquires, the solution has to be represented by point C and $S = (1 - \alpha)V(F, \alpha) = (1 - \alpha)V''$. This also implies that the manager bears the full cost of reduction in firm value since her wealth is given by $W = S + \alpha V(F, \alpha) = (1 - \alpha)V'' + \alpha V'' = V''$. The manager incurs a welfare loss in this case since the decreased utility associated with the reduction in firm value is more than the added utility associated with the consumption of additional nonpecuniary benefits. The reduction in market value represents the agency cost caused by the sale of equity to outsiders.

Figure 12.6 The optimal scale of the firm when the manager owns a fraction α of the firm.

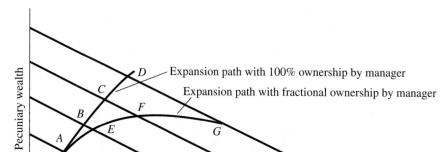

Jensen and Meckling also show that the agency problem associated with effort can impact the optimal scale of investment by the firm. Specifically consider an entrepreneur with initial (pecuniary) wealth of W and monopoly access to an project requiring an investment of I and value $V(I)$, with the project being subject to diminishing returns to scale in I. Figure 12.6 provides a graphical solution to the optimal scale of the firm. In this figure, the total wealth of the entrepreneur is plotted along the vertical axis, where total wealth is defined as $W + [V(I) - I]$, while the horizontal axis plots the value of nonpecuniary benefits. The market value of the firm is a function of the level of investment and the value of the nonpecuniary benefits consumed by the manager and is denoted by $V(I, F)$. Let $\overline{V}(I)$ denote the value of the firm when the nonpecuniary benefits consumed are zero. Consider potential combinations of the manager's wealth and value of nonpecuniary consumption by the manager for various levels of investment, $I_1, I_2, I_3, \ldots, I_N$, where I_N represents the value-maximizing investment level, that is,

$$\frac{\partial \overline{V}(I)}{\partial I} = 1$$

at $I = I_N$. For example, at an investment level of I_3, the potential combinations lie on a line joining the point $(W + [\overline{V}(I_3) - I_3])$ along the vertical axis and point F_3 along the horizontal axis. At each investment level, the manager chooses a level of nonpecuniary benefits based on the tangency between his indifference curves and the line representing potential combinations of the manager's wealth and value of nonpecuniary consumption by the manager. For example, for investment level I_3, the manager chooses to consume F_3^* in nonpecuniary benefits and have a pecuniary wealth of $W + [V(I_3, F_3) - I_3]$. Therefore, the path ABCD represents the equilibrium combinations of wealth and nonpecuniary benefits that the manager would choose if he could finance all levels of investments till I_N.

Now consider the situation in which the manager can finance investments up to a level of I_1 only and has to obtain outside financing for all levels of investments above I_1. Note that this implies that the fraction of the firm that the manager retains decreases with the scale of the investment, from 100% at an investment level of I_1 down to (I_1/I_N) percent for an investment level of I_N. If the first-best solution could be achieved, then the expansion path would still be ABCD even when the manager obtains outside financing. If the first-best solution cannot be achieved, then the manager will choose to consume more nonpecuniary benefits when outside financing funds part of the firm's investments. The deviation from the first-best solution will be larger the larger the fraction of outside financing. This follows from the argument that the larger the fraction of outside finance the lower the cost to the manager of $1 of nonpecuniary benefits. As a result, the manager would choose an expansion path denoted by AEFG, where at each point his indifference curve is tangent to a line with a slope equal to $-\alpha$, the fraction of the firm owned by the manager. Since α decreases with increasing investment, the tangency point would move further away from the first-best solution as the level of investment increases. In Fig. 12.6, the manager maximizes his utility at point F, where he consumes F_3' and the value of the firm is $V(I_3, F_3') - I_3$. Thus, the manager chooses a suboptimal level of investment because of the agency problem associated with effort.

To see this more formally, consider the conditions under which the optimal investment level is chosen if the first-best solution can be achieved. Specifically, the manager chooses the level of investment at which

$$\frac{\partial \overline{V}(I)}{\partial I} = 1.$$

If the first-best solution cannot be achieved, the manager chooses an investment level I at which

$$\frac{\partial V(I, F)}{\partial I} + \alpha \frac{\partial F}{\partial I} = 1,$$

where $\alpha = I_1/I$. Since $V(I, F) = \overline{V}(I) - F$, this implies that the investment level chosen satisfies

$$\frac{\partial \overline{V}(I)}{\partial I} - (1 - \alpha)\frac{\partial F}{\partial I} = 1$$

or

$$\frac{\partial \overline{V}(I)}{\partial I} = 1 + (1 - \alpha)\frac{\partial F}{\partial I} > 1$$

since the level of nonpecuniary benefits consumption increases with scale, that is, $\frac{\partial F}{\partial I} > 0$. Since the project is subject to diminishing returns to scale in I and the first-best solution is a level of investment I_N that solves

$$\frac{\partial \overline{V}(I)}{\partial I} = 1,$$

the level of investment I' that solves

$$\frac{\partial \overline{V}(I)}{\partial I} > 1$$

has to be such that $I' < I_N$. This implies that the manager chooses a suboptimal level of investment.

As stated earlier, since investment in firm-specific human capital represents a significant portion of the manager's portfolio, she is concerned about the total risk of the firm even though the shareholder can diversify away some of that risk. Reagan and Stulz [1986] provide a detailed analysis of the risk-sharing incentives between shareholders and employees (managers). Consider a manager who earns a compensation c and holds nontradeable assets with end-of-period value of W.[24] The manager's expected utility is given by

$$E(V) = aE(W + c) - bVar(W + c) = a\,[E(w) + E(c)] - b\,[Var(W) + 2Cov(W, c) + Var(c)],$$

where $E(W)$ is the expected value of the asset, $E(c)$ is the expected compensation, $Var(W)$ is the variance of the asset, $Var(c)$ is the variance of compensation, $Cov(W, c)$ is the covariance of the asset, and compensation and a and b are positive constants. The objective of shareholders is to maximize the market value of their share of firm revenues (s). The compensation contracts of the managers are assumed to be linear in revenues, that is, $c = \alpha + \beta s$ ($\alpha, \beta \geq 0$), and managers require that the expected utility from compensation received is at least as high as what they could obtain from other alternatives, that is, $E(V) \geq \underline{V}$.[25] Based on these assumptions, the capital asset pricing model suggests that the present value of the shareholder's position in the firm is given by

$$S = \frac{(1 - \beta)E(s) - \alpha - \lambda(1 - \beta)Cov(s, R_M)}{1 + r_f}, \tag{12.83}$$

where $E(s)$ is the expected revenue, R_M is the return on the market portfolio, r_f is the risk-free rate of return, λ is the market price of risk

$$\frac{E(R_M) - r_f}{r_m},$$

and $Cov(s, R_M)$ is the covariance between revenue and the market return.

The maximization problem faced by the shareholder is

$$\underset{\alpha, \beta}{\text{maximize}} \quad \frac{(1 - \beta)E(s) - \alpha - \lambda(1 - \beta)Cov(s, R_M)}{1 + r_f} \tag{12.84}$$

subject to the constraint

$$a\left[E(W) + \alpha + \beta E(s)\right] - b\left[Var(W) + 2\beta Cov(W, s) + \beta^2 Var(s)\right] \geq \underline{V}. \tag{12.85}$$

If μ denotes the Lagrangian multiplier associated with the constraint, the problem can be written as

$$\underset{\alpha, \beta}{\text{maximize}} \quad \frac{(1 - \beta)E(s) - \alpha - \lambda(1 - \beta)Cov(s, R_M)}{1 + r_f} \tag{12.86}$$

$$+ \mu\left(a[E(W) + \alpha + \beta E(s)] - b[Var(W) + 2\beta Cov(W, s) + \beta^2 Var(s)] - \underline{V}\right).$$

The first-order conditions for this maximization are

$$\mu a - \frac{1}{1 + r_f} = 0 \tag{12.87}$$

---

[24] For example, this nontradeable asset could be the manager's firm-specific human capital.

[25] The disutility associated with effort is ignored in this analysis since the level of effort is assumed to be given.

$$\mu \left[aE(s) - 2b \left(Cov(W, s) + \beta Var(s) \right) \right] - \frac{E(s) - \lambda Cov(s, R_M)}{1 + r_f} = 0 \tag{12.88}$$

$$a \left[\alpha + \beta E(s) \right] - b \beta^2 Var(s) - \underline{V} = 0. \tag{12.89}$$

Substituting for μ from Eq. (12.87) into Eq. (12.88) yields the following expression for β:

$$\beta = \frac{\lambda a Cov(s, R_M)}{2b Var(s)} - \frac{Cov(W, s)}{Var(s)}. \tag{12.90}$$

Equation (12.90) implies that if the manager owns no risky asset other than their contract, the optimal risk-bearing coefficient (β) depends on the market price of risk and the systematic risk of the firm. Thus if the market price of risk is zero or if the firm has no systematic risk, the managers bear no risk. Conversely, under these two conditions, the shareholders bear all the risk. If the manager does own risky assets, then the optimal risk-bearing coefficient depends on the covariance between the assets and the firm. If the covariance between the two is negative, the asset holdings act as a partial hedge against compensation risk and the manager is willing to take more risk in the compensation contract. On the other hand, the opposite is true if the asset held by the manager is positively correlated with the firm, for example, the asset is firm-specific human capital. Thus, in this situation the manager is less willing to bear compensation risk. It is, therefore, consistent with this model that the managers would be concerned about the total risk of the firm and they would attempt to diversify the risk associated with their contracts by diversifying the firm itself.

Finally, another source of conflict arises from the differential horizons of the managers and claimholders. This conflict can also result in managers investing at levels below the optimum. To see this, consider the following modified example from Jensen and Meckling [1979]. Consider a firm in which the manager invests (his human) capital in the firm and receives nontradeable claims on the cash flows contingent on employment. Let us assume that the opportunity cost faced by the manager is i per annum and the expected tenure of the manager is T. Consider a perpetual project with a cash flow normalized to 1 and an annual rate of return of r. The value of the project to the firm is $\frac{1}{r}$. In contrast, the value of the project from the manager's point of view is

$$\left\{ \frac{1}{i} \left[1 - (1 + i)^{-T} \right] \right\}.$$

This implies that a manager will be indifferent to investing in the project or not investing if the rate of return from the project is such that its value is equal to the value from the manager's viewpoint. This implies that given a tenure of T and an opportunity cost of i, the manager will use a hurdle rate of r^* for project accept/reject decisions, where r^* is given by

$$r^* = \frac{i}{1 - (1 + i)^{-T}}. \tag{12.91}$$

Equation (12.91) indicates that the hurdle rate used for the project decreases with tenure, with the limit being the manager's opportunity cost when the tenure becomes infinite. Table 12.1 provides a numerical example for the relation between the tenure of the manager and the hurdle rate employed for an opportunity cost of 10% ($= i$). As can be seen from this table, the shorter the tenure, the higher the hurdle rate. This implies that managers will tend to underinvest because of their

Table 12.1 The Relation between Manager Tenure and Project Hurdle Rates for an Opportunity Cost of 10%

Manager Tenure (*T* years)	Project Hurdle Rate (*r** percent)
2	58
5	26
10	16
15	13
20	12
40	10

shorter horizon as compared to shareholders and the problem of underinvestment gets attenuated the shorter the time horizon of the manager.

Rational shareholders will recognize the incentives facing managers to shirk, diversify, and underinvest. Therefore, they would forecast the potential impact of these decisions and incorporate it into the value they attach to the stock. Therefore, the firm would suffer losses from these decisions, and these losses would represent the agency costs of outside equity financing. These agency costs of outside equity would have an impact on the amount of equity financing a firm chooses to use. Chapter 15 contains a detailed description on the relation between the agency costs of equity and the capital structure of the firm.

2. Conflicts between a Firm's Bondholders and Stockholders

Conflicts arise between the bondholders and stockholders when managers make decisions that benefit stockholders at the cost of bondholders. Smith and Warner [1979] identify four major sources of conflict between these two claimholders—dividend payout, claim dilution, asset substitution, and underinvestment. Dividend payout becomes a source of conflict if a firm unexpectedly changes its dividend payout and finances this increase by reducing the asset base or by reducing planned investments. If a firm chooses to issue new debt with equal or higher priority than existing debt, the claim of the existing debtholders is diluted. Prior to the new issue of debt, the existing debt had sole priority in its claim on the firm's assets and revenues. With the new debt issue the existing debt has to share the claim, and this causes a reduction in debt value. Asset substitution reduces the value of debt by making it more risky. Specifically, if a firm decided to substitute a high-risk investment for a low-risk investment, the risk faced by debtholders increases, and this results in a reduction in debt value. Finally, consider a situation in which a firm can potentially invest in a positive net present value project with the benefits of the investment accruing to bondholders. Under certain circumstances, a firm may choose to pass up on this project (underinvest), thus causing bonds to suffer an opportunity loss.

To illustrate the conflict of interest arising from the dividend payout decision, consider a firm that has assets in place that are valued today at $220. $20 of these assets are in cash (with a return of 0%), while $200 is the value of a project that is expected to return 20% or −10% with equal probability in one period. Assume that the firm has debt that matures in one period and has a face value of $200 and pays no dividends to its stockholders. In this scenario, debt is riskless and will be valued at $200. Specifically, if the project returns 20%, the value of the firm's assets are $260

($20 in cash and $240 from the project) and debt is paid its face value of $200. On the other hand, if the project returns -10%, the firm's assets are valued at $200 and debt is paid in full. Now consider the scenario in which the firm decides to pay a dividend of $10 to shareholders from its cash holdings. This implies that the assets in place are now valued at $210 with potential payoffs of $250 and $190 next period. If the value of the firm is $250 next period, the bondholders still get paid in full. On the other hand, if the firm is valued at $190, the payoff to the bondholders is $10 less than the promised amount of $200. Since debt was riskless before the decision to pay the dividend, this implies that the change in dividend payout causes a reduction in the value of debt.

A more general way of viewing the impact of changes in dividend policy is based on the insight in Black and Scholes [1973] that corporate securities can be viewed as options on the assets of the firm. Denote V_t as the value of the firm at time t. Assume that the firm consists of equity and one issue of zero-coupon debt that has a face value of D and a maturity of T. Further assume that there are no dividends paid to stockholders. This implies that the maturity date payoff on debt will be given by

$$B_t = \begin{cases} V_t & \text{if } V_t < D \\ D & \text{if } V_t \geq D \end{cases} = D - \begin{cases} D - V_t & \text{if } V_t < D \\ 0 & \text{if } V_t \geq D \end{cases} \tag{12.92}$$

Equation (12.92) indicates that the payoff on risky debt can be written as a combination of the payoff on risk-free debt and a written put option on the firm's assets with the exercise price and maturity of the option being the face value and maturity of debt, respectively. Thus the value of risky debt would be the value of risk-free debt minus a put option on the firm's assets with an exercise price of D and a maturity of T, that is,

$$B = \frac{D}{(1+r_f)^t} - P(V, D, T, r_f, \sigma_V),$$

where $P(\bullet)$ is the value of the put option, r_f is the risk-free rate of interest, and σ_V is the volatility of returns on the firm. An unexpected increase in the dividends paid by the firm can be viewed as a decrease in the current value of the firm's assets. The impact of a decrease in firm value on debt can be determined by examining the partial derivative of B with respect to V. Specifically,

$$\frac{\partial B}{\partial V} = -\frac{\partial P}{\partial V}.$$

Since put values decrease with increases in the value of the underlying, this implies that

$$\frac{\partial P}{\partial V} < 0$$

and

$$\frac{\partial B}{\partial V} > 0.$$

Therefore, the value of a risky bond increases with firm value. This implies that the value of the bond would decrease with decreases in firm value caused by unexpected increases in dividends paid.

To illustrate the claim substitution problem, consider again the bond with a payoff described in Eq. (12.92). As stated earlier, the value of the bond is

$$B = \frac{D}{(1+r_f)^t} - P(V, D, T, r_f, \sigma_V).$$

Now assume that a firm issues new debt with the same priority as existing debt, a face value of dD, and a market value of dB. Since the debt is risky, we would expect the market value to be less than face value, that is, $dB < dD$. Since the new bond has the same priority as the old debt, the total market value of the debt in this firm is

$$B' = \frac{D+dD}{(1+r_f)^t} - P(V+dB, D+dD, T, r_f, \sigma_V),$$

and the new value of the existing debt is

$$B_{NEW} = \left(\frac{D}{D+dD}\right) B' = \frac{D}{(1+r_f)^t} - \left(\frac{D}{D+dD}\right) \left[P(V+dB, D+dD, T, r_f, \sigma_V)\right].$$

Since option prices are homogeneous in the value of the underlying and the exercise price, the value of the put option, $\left[P(V+dB, D+dD, T, r_f, \sigma_V)\right]$ can be written as

$$(D+dD) \, P \left(\frac{V+dB}{D+dD}, 1, T, r_f, \sigma_V\right).$$

Substituting this expression for the value of the put in the new value of existing debt provides the following expression for its value:

$$B_{NEW} = \frac{D}{(1+r_f)^t} - (D) \left[P(\frac{V+dB}{D+dD}, 1, T, r_f, \sigma_V)\right]. \tag{12.93}$$

Equation (12.93) indicates that the change in value of existing debt is given by

$$B_{NEW} - B = D \left\{-\left[P(\frac{V+dB}{D+dD}, 1, T, r_f, \sigma_V)\right] + P(\frac{V}{D}, 1, T, r_f, \sigma_V)\right\} = D \left(-P_X + P_Y\right). \tag{12.94}$$

Equation (12.94) suggests that the change in the value of existing debt is proportional to the difference in the values of two put options (call them X and Y) that are identical in all respects except for the values of the underlying. Put option X is valued for an underlying value of

$$\frac{V+dB}{D+dD},$$

while put option Y is based on an underlying value of $\frac{V}{D}$. Since $dB < dD$ and put values decrease with increases in firm value, put X is worth more than put Y and $D \left(-P_X + P_Y\right) < 0$. Therefore, the value of existing debt falls with the issue of new debt with equal priority, that is, $B_{NEW} - B < 0$. The intuition behind this result is that the new claim shares payoffs with the existing claims when the value of the firm is below the promised payment. If the sharing rule is such that the existing debtholders get less in every state of the world where the value of the firm is below the promised payment, then the value of debt would fall.

The asset substitution effect follows directly from examining the impact of change in volatility on the value of risky debt. In particular, a change in the volatility of returns on the firm would induce the following change in the value of debt:

$$\frac{\partial B}{\partial \sigma_V} = -\frac{\partial P(V, D, T, r_f, \sigma_V)}{\partial \sigma_V}. \tag{12.95}$$

Since option values increase with volatility, this implies that $\frac{\partial P}{\partial \sigma_V}$ is positive and $\frac{\partial B}{\partial \sigma_V}$ is negative. Thus, a decision to substitute less risky with more risky assets results in a decrease in bond value and, conversely, an increase in stock value.

The asset substitution effect can also be illustrated with a simple example. Consider a firm that is currently planning to invest in a project with end-of-period payoffs of $200 and $180 with equal probability. The firm is financing this investment with a debt issue with a face value of $170. Given the expected payoffs on the project and the promised payment to debt, holders of this debt would expect $170 in each state of the world. Now assume that after issuing the debt, the firm switches to another project with end-of-period payoffs of $230 and $150 with equal probability. The payment to debt would no longer be riskless since the bonds would receive either $170 or $150 with equal probability. Therefore, bondholders incur a loss of $30 with a 50% probability, and this would result in a reduction in bond value. In contrast, if shareholders are the only other claimants in this firm, they would now receive an extra $30 with a 50% probability, and this would result in an increase in stock value that exactly offsets the decrease in bond value.

Myers [1977] provides a detailed analysis of the underinvestment problem. Consider an all-equity firm with no assets in place and one future investment opportunity. The firm has to decide whether to invest I one period from now (at $t = 1$). If the firm invests, it obtains an asset worth $V(s)$ at $t = 1$, where s is the state of nature that occurs at $t = 1$. Thus at time $t = 1$, the value of the firm is $V(s)$. Assume that for states $s < s_a$, the value of the investment is less than the amount of investment, that is, $V(s) < I$. Therefore, the firm will not invest in these states, and the value of the firm at time $t = 0$ is given by

$$V = \int_{s_a}^{\infty} q(s)[V(s) - I] \, ds, \tag{12.96}$$

where $q(s)$ is the value today of a dollar delivered at $t = 1$ if and only if state s occurs. Since this is an all-equity firm, the value of equity is equal to the value of the firm, that is, $V_E = V$.

Now consider the situation where the firm can issue risky debt with a promised payment of D and debt matures before the investment is made. The proceeds of the debt issue are used to reduce the required initial equity investment. In this case, if the value of the investment is above the face value of debt, equity holders would pay off the debt and make the investment. This follows from the fact that if $V(s) - I > D$, then by paying the debtholders D and making the investment of I, the stockholders are left with $V(s) - I - D > 0$. If $s > s_b$ defines the states for which $V(s) - I > D$, the value of equity would be given by

$$V_E = \int_{s_b}^{\infty} q(s)[V(s) - I - D] \, ds. \tag{12.97}$$

On the other hand, if $V(s) - I \leq D$, the stockholders will turn the firm over to the bondholders. The bondholders will choose to exercise the investment option as long as they receive positive value from it. Therefore, the bondholders will invest as long as $V(s) - I > 0$. The value of the bonds will be given by

$$V_D = \int_{s_a}^{s_b} q(s)[V(s) - I]\,ds + \int_{s_b}^{\infty} q(s)D\,ds. \tag{12.98}$$

The total value of the firm in this scenario can be obtained from the sum of Eqs. (12.97) and (12.98) and is identical to that defined in Eq. (12.96). Therefore, in this case the existence of debt financing has no impact on the firm.

Now assume that the debt matures after the investment decision. Consider the situation where the value of the investment is positive but is less than the promised payment to the debtholders, that is, $0 < V(s) - I < D$. In this case, the shareholders would not make the investment since their payoff from the investment is negative after accounting for the payment to debtholders, that is, $V(s) - I - D < 0$. Thus, the shareholders will forego the investment in all states below s_b, and the value of the firm be

$$V = \int_{s_b}^{\infty} q(s)[V(s) - I]\,ds. \tag{12.99}$$

This implies that the existence of debt that expires after the time the firm has to make an investment decision can result in an incentive to underinvest.

The fact that stockholders face these incentives to expropriate debt value would be recognized by rational bondholders. As a result, they will forecast the impact of these potential decisions and incorporate them into their pricing decision. Therefore, the firm would suffer losses from these decisions, and these losses would represent the agency costs of debt financing. These agency costs of debt would have an impact on the amount of debt financing a firm chooses to use. Chapter 15 contains a detailed description on the relation between the agency costs of debt and the capital structure of the firm.

ummary

In this chapter, we have examined various principal-agent issues related to the design of the optimal contract when monitoring is the issue. Specifically, we have examined the structure of the contract when the agent's actions are observable (no monitoring problem), when the agent's actions are not observable, when only the final outcome can be observed, when the content can depend on both the final outcome and other performance measures, where there are multiple actions available to the agent, and when information asymmetry between the principal and the agent is at the heart of the problem. In the case where there is no monitoring problem and both the principal and the agent have exponential utility functions, we showed that the optimal compensation contract is linear in the final outcome with the slope of the function depending on the risk tolerance of the agent relative to the principal. If only the final outcome is observable, we show that the optimal compensation contract is going to involve more risk taking being imposed on the agent to provide an incentive for the agent to increase effort and a higher expected compensation to offset the impact of the risk. In the case where the contract is based on multiple performance measures, the optimal compensation contract is shown to have higher weights attached to performance measures that are more sensitive to the action taken by the agent and are less noisy. Similar results are shown to hold when the agent can take multiple actions.

Finally, we addressed issues specific to corporate finance. In particular we discussed how agency theory affects the mix of debt and equity, dividend policy, and investment decisions. We argue that the presence of agency conflicts between managers and stockholders, and stockholders and bondholders, impose costs that increase with the amount of debt and equity in the firm. This suggests that there would exist an optimal mix of debt and equity that would minimize the overall agency costs faced by the company. A more detailed description of the impact of agency costs on capital structure is contained in Chapter 15.

It should be recognized that even though we have focused on agency theory and its relation to optimal contracting and corporate finance, this theory has been applied to a number of other areas, for example, accounting, insurance, and property rights. As stated in Lambert [2001], agency theory has been used in the accounting area to answer two questions. First, how do accounting and compensation systems affect managerial incentives? And second, how do these incentive problems affect the design of these systems? Mayers and Smith [1981, 1982] argue that "the differing costs of controlling incentive conflicts between residual claimants and managers, and between policyholders and residual claimants lead to different ownership structures" in the insurance industry. The property rights literature focuses on how costs and rewards are allocated among various participants in an organization and how the specification of these rights is affected by contracting.

PROBLEM SET

12.1 In the context of the Ross [1977] model, assume that managers are paid 20% of the time 0 and time 1 values of the firm. Further assume good firms are worth 250, bad firms are worth 150, and the risk-free rate is 10%. What is the minimum cost of false signaling that has to be imposed on management to ensure that all managers signal correctly?

12.2 In the context of the Bhattacharya [1979] model, assume that the personal tax rate is 25%, the penalty associated with a shortfall is 50%, the project cash flows are uniformly distributed over $(0, 500)$, and the appropriate discount rate is 20%. What is the optimal dividend and value response to this dividend? What is the impact of changing the personal tax rate to 30%? Changing the cost of a shortfall to 70%? Changing the discount rate to 40%?

12.3 In the context of the Stein [1992] paper, show that (1) a bad firm will not mimic a good firm by issuing straight debt and (2) a medium firm will not mimic either a bad or good firm.

12.4 Assume that both the principal and agent have negative exponential utility and that the actions of the agent are observable. What is the optimal contract?

12.5 Consider a risk-neutral principal and an agent with utility function

$$V(c) = \left[1/ \left(1 - \gamma \right) \right] \left(\delta_0 + \delta_1 c \right)^{(1-\gamma)}.$$

Assume that the contract being provided to the agent is based on the final outcome only and that the outcome density satisfies the monotone likelihood ratio property (MLRP). What is the optimal contract? Under what circumstances is the optimal contract linear in the final outcome? Convex? Concave?

12.6 Assume that the opportunity cost of capital is 25%. Provide a plot of the relation between the hurdle rate used by a manager for projects and the manager's tenure.

REFERENCES

Akerlof, G., "The Market for 'Lemons': Qualitative Uncertainty and the Market Mechanism," *Quarterly Journal of Economics*, 1970, Vol. 85, 488–500.

Austen-Smith, D., and J. Banks, "Cheap Talk and Burned Money," *Journal of Economic Theory*, 2000, Vol. 91, 1–16.

Banker, R., and S. Datar, "Sensitivity, Precision and Linear Aggregation of Signals for Performance Evaluation," *Journal of Accounting Research*, 1989, Vol. 27, 21–39.

Bhattacharya, S., "Imperfect Information, Dividend Policy and the 'Bird in the Hand' Fallacy," *Bell Journal of Economics*, 1979, Vol. 10, 259–270.

———, "Nondissipative Signaling Structures and Dividend Policy," *Quarterly Journal of Economics*, 1980, Vol. 95, 1–24.

Black, F., and M. Scholes, "The Pricing of Options and Corporate Liabilities," *Journal of Political Economy*, 1973, Vol. 81, 637–659.

Brennan, M., and P. Hughes, "Stock Prices and the Supply of Information," *Journal of Finance*, 1991, Vol. 46, 1665–1691.

Brennan, M., and A. Kraus, "Efficient Financing under Asymmetric Information," *Journal of Finance*, 1987, Vol. 42, 1225–1243.

Constantinides, G., and B. Grundy, "Optimal Investment with Stock Repurchase and Financing as Signals," *Review of Financial Studies*, 1989, Vol. 2, 445–465.

Cooney, J., and A. Kalay, "Positive Information from Equity Issue Announcements," *Journal of Financial Economics*, 1993, Vol. 33, 149–172.

Copeland, T., "Liquidity Changes Following Stock Splits," *The Journal of Finance*, March 1979, Vol. 34, No. 1, 115–141.

Copeland, T., and M. Brennan, "Stock Splits, Stock Prices and Transactions Costs," *Journal of Financial Economics*, 1988, Vol. 22, 83–102.

Crawford, V. P., and J. Sobel, "Strategic Information Transmission," *Econometrica*, 1982, Vol. 50, 1431–1451.

Datar, S., S. Kulp, and R. A. Lambert, "Balancing Accounting Measures," *Journal of Accounting Research*, 2001, Vol. 39, 75–92.

Fama, E., and K. French, "Testing Trade-off and Pecking Order Predictions about Dividends and Debt," *Review of Financial Studies*, 2002, Vol. 15, 1–33.

Grinblatt, M., and C. Y. Hwang, "Signaling and the Pricing of New Issues," *Journal of Finance*, 1989, Vol. 44, 393–420.

Guedes, J., and R. Thompson, "Tests of a Signaling Hypothesis: The Choice between Fixed- and Adjustable-Rate Debt," *Review of Financial Studies*, 1995, Vol. 8, 605–636.

Heider, F., "Signalling with Debt and Equity," working paper, New York University, 2002.

Heinkel, R., "A Theory of Capital Structure Relevance under Imperfect Information," *Journal of Finance*, 1982, Vol. 37, 1141–1150.

Holmstrom, B., "Moral Hazard and Observability," *Bell Journal of Economics*, 1979, Vol. 10, 74–91.

Holmstrom, B., and P. Milgrom, "Aggregation and Linearity in the Provision of Intertemporal Incentives," *Econometrica*, 1987, 303–328.

Jensen, M., *A Theory of the Firm*, Harvard University Press, Cambridge, Mass., 2000.

Jensen, M., and W. Meckling, "Theory of the Firm: Managerial Behavior, Agency Costs and Ownership Structure," *Journal of Financial Economics*, 1976, Vol. 3, 305–360.

———, "Rights and Production Functions: An Application to Labor Managed Firms and Codetermination," *Journal of Business*, 1979, Vol. 52, 469–506.

Jensen, M., and C. Smith, "Stockholder, Manager and Creditor Interests: Applications of Agency Theory," *Recent Advances in Corporate Finance*, 1985, 93–131.

John, K., and J. Williams, "Dividends, Dilution and Taxes: A Signalling Equilibrium," *Journal of Finance*, 1985, Vol. 40, 1053–1070.

Krasker, W., "Stock Price Movements in Response to Stock Issues under Asymmetric Information," *Journal of Finance*, 1986, Vol. 41, 93–106.

Laffont, J., and D. Martimort, *The Theory of Incentives*, Princeton University Press, Princeton, N.J., 2002.

Lambert, R. A., "Contracting Theory and Accounting," *Journal of Accounting and Economics*, 2001, Vol. 32, 1–87.

Leland, H., and D. H. Pyle, "Informational Asymmetries, Financial Structure and Financial Intermediation," *Journal of Finance*, 1977, Vol. 32, 371–387.

Lemmon, M. L., and J. F. Zender, "Looking under the Lamppost: An Empirical Examination of the Determinants of Capital Structure," working paper, University of Utah, 2002.

Mayers, D., and C. Smith, "Contractual Provisions, Organizational Structure, and Conflict Control in Insurance Markets," *Journal of Business* 1981, Vol. 54, 407–434.

———, "On the Corporate Demand for Insurance," *Journal of Business* 1982, Vol. 55, 281–296.

McNichols, M., and A. Dravid, "Stock Dividends, Stock Splits, and Signaling," *Journal of Finance*, July 1990, Vol. 45, 857–879.

Milgrom, P., "Good News and Bad News: Representation Theorem and Applications," *Bell Journal of Economics*, 1981.

Minton, B., and K. Wruck, "Financial Conservatism: Evidence on Capital Structure from Low Leverage Firms," working paper, Ohio State University, 2002.

Myers, S., "Determinants of Corporate Borrowing," *Journal of Financial Economics*, 1977, Vol. 9, 147–176.

Myers, S., and N. Majluf, "Corporate Financing and Investment Decisions When Firms Have Information Investors Do Not Have," *Journal of Financial Economics*, 1984, Vol. 13, 187–221.

Myerson, R., "Incentive Compatibility and the Bargaining Problem," *Econometrica*, 1979, 61–74.

Nachman, D., and T. Noe, "Optimal Design of Securities under Asymmetric Information," *Review of Financial Studies*, 1954, Vol. 7, 1–44.

Noe, T., "Capital Structure and Signaling Game Equilibria," *Review of Financial Studies*, 1988, Vol. 1, 331–355.

Pendergast, C., "The Provision of Incentives in Firms," *Journal of Economic Literature*, 1999, 7–63.

Reagan, P., and R. Stulz, "Risk-Bearing, Labor Contracts and Capital Markets," *Research in Finance*, 1986, Vol. 6, 217–231.

Riley, J., "Competitive Signalling," *Journal of Economic Theory*, 1975, Vol. 10, 174–186.

———, "Informational Equilibrium," *Econometrica*, 1979, Vol. 47, 331–360.

Ross, S., "The Determination of Financial Structure: The Incentive Signalling Approach," *Bell Journal of Economics*, 1977, Vol. 8, 23–40.

Rothschild, M., and J. Stiglitz, "Equilibrium in Competitive Insurance Markets," *Quarterly Journal of Economics*, 1976, Vol. 90, 629–650.

Sappington, D., "Limited Liability Contracts between Principal and Agent," *Journal of Economic Theory*, 1983, 1–21.

Smith, C., and J. Warner, "On Financial Contracting: An Analysis of Bond Covenants," *Journal of Financial Economics*, 1979, Vol. 7, 117–161.

Spence, A. M., "Job Market Signaling," *Quarterly Journal of Economics*, 1973, Vol. 87, 355–379.

Stein, J., "Convertible Bonds as Backdoor Equity Financing," *Journal of Financial Economics*, 1992, Vol. 32, 3–21.

Wilson, C., "A Model of Insurance Markets with Incomplete Information," *Journal of Economic Theory*, 1978, Vol. 6, 167–207.

Wilson, R., "On the Theory of Syndicates," *Econometrica*, 1968, 119–132.

Part II

Corporate Policy: Theory, Evidence, and Applications

T HE FIRST 12 CHAPTERS OF THIS BOOK covered the theory of finance, starting with a world of certainty and discussing objects of choice, the theory of choice, and the separation theorem that resulted in a decision rule for optimal choice, namely, that regardless of their individual time preferences all shareholders of a firm will unanimously support the proposition that investment should be undertaken up to the point where the marginal return exactly equals the market-determined opportunity cost of capital. This simple foundation was quickly extended to a world with uncertainty. The theory of choice was developed to include the general proposition of stochastic dominance, and in a world of normally distributed returns, mean-variance indifference curves. Investment opportunity sets were then described as the efficient mean-variance frontier, and a second separation theorem (one appropriate for a world of uncertainty, but not yet a multiperiod world) was derived—a theorem that implied a market price of risk that would be accepted unanimously by all investors, who would then choose their optimal portfolio from a weighted combination of two funds: a zero-beta portfolio and an efficient market portfolio. Two nontrivial corollaries of this equilibrium theory are the capital asset pricing model and the arbitrage pricing theory. They have become widely used tools for practitioners of corporate finance, especially when estimating the equilibrium required rate of return on a risky asset, whether it be a corporate project or a mutual fund. We completed the theory part of the book by discussing contingent claims in the form of both financial and real options, forward and futures contracts, the theory and evidence of market efficiency, agency costs, and signaling theory.

Given the set of theoretical concepts and frameworks that were developed in the first part of the book, we now apply them to corporate policy in the second part. Traditionally, corporate finance has been considered to be about two types of decisions—what investments should the firm undertake, and how should they be financed? In particular, do the mix of debt and equity, and dividend payout policy, affect the value of the firm? Although these are undeniably the central issues, we believe that they are inadequate to prepare modern students of corporate finance for the wide set of decisions that chief financial officers must face in today's multibusiness and multinational world. CFOs are interested in a variety of issues that are not often covered in corporate finance texts. We intend to cover them here, in Part II of the book. They include performance measurement, or what drives the total return to shareholders from a business perspective? How should one value companies? What tax policy maximizes value? What is the optimal capital structure and dividend policy to maximize the value of the firm? How can the value of the firm be enhanced through better risk management? How should pension funds be managed? How should the firm think about the lease versus own decision? How can value be increased via better working capital management? How should the firm approach mergers, acquisitions, and divestitures? What special issues are faced by a multinational firm? How should management be compensated?

As we shall see, the theoretical answer to the question "Does financing matter?" is often a loud and resounding "Maybe." Often the answer depends on the assumptions of the model employed to study the problem. Under different sets of assumptions, different and even opposite answers are possible. This is extremely disquieting to the student of finance. Fortunately, there is enough data available to test and actually reject improper theories. Therefore, we have done our best to synthesize the empirical evidence related to each of the theoretical issues.

It is important to remember that hypotheses cannot be tested by the realism of the assumptions used to derive them. What counts for a positive science is the development of theories that yield valid and meaningful predictions about observed phenomena. On the first pass, what counts is whether or not the hypothesis is consistent with the evidence at hand. Further testing involves deducing new facts capable of being observed but not previously known, then checking those deduced facts against additional empirical evidence. As students of finance, which seeks to be a positive science, we must not only understand the theory, but also study the empirical evidence in order to determine which hypothesis is validated.

Chapter 13 sets the tone for Part II by describing the role of chief financial officer in a large multibusiness, multinational company. Over the last 30–40 years this role has changed from being largely an accountant and record keeper with few decision rights to being a decision maker who is part of the top management team, and who is often chosen for the role of chief executive officer. Chapter 13 also discusses performance measurement, public relations, the budget process, and incentive design.

Chapter 14 discusses the theory and practice of valuing companies using formulas and discounted cash flow forecasts. A plain-vanilla industrial DCF spreadsheet model is discussed in detail, and an overview of banking and insurance models is also provided. Tax policy is also discussed in the context of valuation because many corporate tax policy decisions are best made in a multiperiod setting.

Chapter 15 covers the theory and empirical evidence relating to the effect of capital structure and the cost of capital on the value of the levered firm. This is the first of the questions that relate to whether or not the value of the firm is affected by its mix of debt and equity financing. We simultaneously discuss the estimation of the weighted average cost of capital both at the corporate and the business unit level, as well as the opportunity cost of various types of capital such as risky debt, callable and convertible debt, preferred stock, warrants, and equity. To clearly develop the capital structure theme in Chapter 15, we use an historical perspective, starting with the work of Franco Modigliani and Merton Miller [1958], from which we can date the beginning of modern corporate finance and for which they won the Nobel prize in economics. We investigate capital structure in a world without corporate taxes, then with them, then with personal as well as corporate taxes, and finally with business disruption costs. Chapter 15 then moves on to discuss the empirical evidence regarding capital structure. This is one of the most difficult areas in corporate finance. Although not conclusive, the evidence indicates that the value of the firm increases as it takes on higher amounts of debt—up to some range.

Chapter 16 covers corporate dividend policy, both the theory and the empirical evidence. There are several competing theories. The most common point of view is that the percentage of cash flow paid out to shareholders in the form of dividends is irrelevant because it makes very little difference whether the cash is kept in the firm and put into marketable securities, or paid out and invested (after taxes) in the same marketable securities. Said another way, the dominant argument seems to be that the value of an all-equity firm depends on the expected returns from current and future investment and not on the form in which the returns are paid out. As long as investment plans are unaffected, it makes no difference how much is paid out in the form of dividends. The second most prevalent point of view is that dividend payments are a poor way to deliver value to shareholders because the tax burden on dividend payments is greater than on share repurchases. Interestingly, any changes in dividends from their expected level is viewed by the marketplace as a favorable signal concerning the future rate of return on investment, and that good news drives the share price up. The empirical evidence regarding dividend policy supports the point of view that dividend policy has no measurable effect on the total return to shareholders, but that unexpected changes in dividend payout are viewed as signals by the market.

Chapter 17 is a potpourri of applied corporate finance topics—risk management, the lease or borrow decision, working capital management, how to achieve capital efficiency, ESOPs, interest rate swaps, and pension fund management.

Chapter 18 deals with deals—mergers, acquisitions, divestitures, joint ventures, spin-offs, and tracking stock. It discusses the success rate of mergers from the point of view of both the acquiring and the acquired companies, deal structure, goodwill accounting, tax rules governing mergers, antitrust laws, and the managerial aspects of how to make mergers work.

Chapter 19 discusses the rapidly advancing topic of international finance. We cover the traditional theory (e.g., interest rate parity and purchasing power parity), but also evidence on the efficiency of the capital markets of developing countries and ownership structure (e.g., stakeholder claims). Among topics of interest to practitioners are how to estimate the cost of capital and the market risk premium when local data is inadequate, how to account for country risk, project financing, and a review of foreign exchange hedging.

Chapter 20 is our brief attempt to suggest the direction of future research in the field of financial economics. We hope that you find it interesting.

Chapter 13

Market-based compensation provisions are well-suited to control the effort and horizon problems, since the market value of the stock reflects the present value of the entire future stream of expected cash flows.

—Michael Jensen, *A Theory of the Firm*, 2000, Harvard University Press, 146.

Not everything that can be counted counts, and not everything that counts can be counted.

—Albert Einstein

The Role of the CFO, Performance Measurement, and Incentive Design

THE FIRST PART OF THE BOOK developed the theory of finance from first principles—the theory of choice (utility theory) and objects of choice (investment frontiers that were constructed of uncertain choices in a multiperiod setting). The equilibrium asset pricing theories that resulted are extremely useful tools for financial decision makers at the microeconomic level and shall be used throughout the remainder of the book. Now, however, we shift our orientation to the practitioner. We take the decision maker's point of view. In this chapter, we tackle three questions. How should I measure the performance of my company vis-à-vis competitors? What drives my stock price? How shall I design incentives to reduce the agency costs between owner, manager, and other stakeholders? In the remaining chapters we discuss the financial economics of the following questions (as well as many others). How much is a target company worth in a takeover? How can I legally avoid taxes and how much is it worth to do so? How should I manage the mix of debt and equity to maximize the value of my firm? What dividend or share repurchase policy should I recommend? Is leasing better than borrowing? How do I manage my company's pension fund? How do I make decisions about allocating our resources abroad? How should I manage my company's risk?

The two parts of the book are interactive and reflective. Whenever possible, we shall point out where the theory of finance helps practitioners and where there are gaps—either because the theory is inconsistent with practice or where the theory simply is devoid of content to aid day-to-day decisions. For multiperiod investment decisions in the face of uncertainty, the developments made in the application of real options (Chapter 9) have helped enormously. We seriously considered moving that material to this part of the book, but it is so fundamental we put it up front.

This chapter starts with the role of the chief financial officer (CFO) of a large multibusiness, multinational company in order to describe the wide variety of decisions and responsibilities that he or she may have. Most of these fall squarely in the domain of financial economics, for example, capital structure and dividend policy. Others are closely related, but somehow missing from textbooks, for example, performance measurement and incentive design. Others are learned on the job, for example, investor relations and how to manage the budgeting process. So let's begin. What does a CFO do anyway?

A. *T*he Role of the Chief Financial Officer

In the middle of the last century, the 1950s and 1960s, the CFO was primarily a financial record keeper, in charge of internal accounts and of the company's financial reporting to shareholders and regulators. This role is still common in family-owned businesses in Asia, Latin America, Africa, and Eastern Europe. But in large multibusiness, multinational companies such as Toyota, International Business Machines, British Air, Deutsche Bank, CVRD, Telefonica, and Norilsk, the CFO is one of the top three decision makers, standing alongside the chief executive officer (CEO) and the chief operating officer (COO). Figure 13.1 attempts to display the decisions for which the CFO may be responsible. Most finance textbooks stress the first two categories: investment and financing. However, there is an important third category, namely, managerial decisions such as performance measurement and incentive design. Let's review each category in greater detail.

Figure 13.1 Decisions for which the CFO may be responsible.

Investment decisions
- Large capital expenditures
- Research and development
- Mergers and acqusitions
- Ownership structure
- Capital efficiency
- Working capital management

CFO

Financing decisions
- Capital structure
- Dividend policy
- Lease vs. borrow
- Risk management
- Auditing and reporting
- Planning (business, tax)

- Performance measurement
- Budget
- Incentive design
- Investor relations
- Regulatory requirements

Management decisions

Managerial decisions made by the CFO include the performance measurement of the business units of the firm, setting and reviewing budgets, designing incentives that are performance compatible, and investor relations to communicate aspirations and results to the external community. The CFO is also usually responsible for being sure that the company conforms to all regulations (environmental, health and safety, tax, agency, and legal). Other top executives from planning, budgeting, human resources, and legal staff will report to the CFO on these matters. Much of the remainder of this chapter will deal with performance measurement and incentive design.

The second area is financial decisions. The CFO is responsible for the audited financial statements of the firm; hence the comptroller reports to him as do the external auditors. He is also responsible for the sources and uses of funds. This means that he must recommend capital structure (the mix of debt and equity) and dividend policy (the percentage of dividends paid out) to the board of directors. For this purpose, the corporate treasurer usually reports to the CFO. Closely related is the risk management function, which of course includes financial risk. The CFO is usually responsible for the insurance position, the hedging position, and the net risk exposure of shareholders. He will also deal with bond rating agencies that provide an assessment of the credit risk of the company. Also, the chief planning officer often reports to the CFO. There are many types of plans, for example, tax plans, short-term (annual and quarterly) budgets, and strategic and long-range plans.

Finally, there are investment decisions. The CFO is often responsible for reviewing all capital expenditures above a certain limit, say, $2 million. A myriad of details are involved: What methodology should be used (traditional net present value or real options analysis)? How should the cost of capital be adjusted for differences in project and country risk? How should cash flows be defined? For firms with substantial research and development budgets, the CFO is often assigned the responsibility for final allocations. In addition to internally generated growth, most firms have a development officer in charge of mergers and acquisitions, joint ventures, and divestitures, who reports to the CFO. Closely related are issues that affect the ownership structure of the firm—dilution of ownership value, violation of debt covenants, equity carveouts (initial public offerings of ownership in a business unit), issuance of tracking stock (whose value is based on the income of a business unit), and issuance of executive stock options. Finally, there is working capital management (inventory, payables, and receivables policy).

The remainder of this chapter covers performance measurement, budgeting, communicating with the external investment community, and incentive design. The remainder of Part II of the book covers most of the other topics.

B. Performance Measurement

1. Measures Based on Earnings

Performance measurement is one of the most important management responsibilities of the CFO because it subtly affects the way people behave. Owners of the firm want performance measures to be aligned with maximizing shareholder wealth, a goal that is easy to articulate but difficult to implement.

Figure 13.2 defines a wide variety of performance measures that companies can use. Choice of the one to actually use is not immediately obvious. Let's go through them one by one. First, we have earnings per share or growth in earnings per share. It suffers from every knock-out criterion. It contains no balance sheet information—a deficiency that implies that if one firm requires two

Figure 13.2 Comparison of performance metrics.

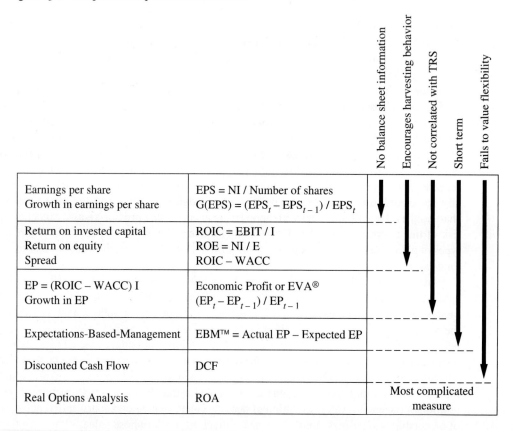

dollars of capital to generate one dollar in earnings while at the same time another requires only one dollar of capital to produce the same earnings, then the market would assign the same value to both because they report identical earnings. Take a look at Figure 13.3 for an example.

The first company, called Longlife, invests $3,000 every three years in equipment that lasts three years. The other company, called Shortlife, invests $1,000 every year. They also have timing differences in working capital investments, but other than that they are identical. They both are assumed to have a 10% cost of capital. In particular, their net income is exactly the same each year. Therefore, if one were to believe that value depended only on net income, then they should have the same value.

We have already shown, in Chapter 2, that value depends on discounted cash flows (net income plus depreciation minus capital expenditures minus investment in working capital). Although the undiscounted total cash flows are $1,800 for both companies, there are significant timing differences. Consequently, the DCF value of Longlife is $808, while for Shortlife it is $1,296— a 60% difference. This clearly illustrates why net income or earnings per share is an inadequate performance measure.

Another problem is that earnings is short term in nature. We once sat in a division manager's office while she received a phone call from her CEO asking that her division supply more fourth-quarter earnings so that the firm could meet its year-end consolidated earnings target. After hanging

Figure 13.3 Two companies with identical earnings but a 60% difference in value.

Longlife	1	2	3	4	5	6	Total
Revenues	4,000	4,000	4,000	4,000	4,000	4,000	24,000
Cash costs	2,000	2,000	2,000	2,000	2,000	2,000	12,000
Depreciation	1,000	1,000	1,000	1,000	1,000	1,000	6,000
Taxes @ 50%	500	500	500	500	500	500	3,000
Net income	500	500	500	500	500	500	3,000
Capital expenditure	3,000	0	0	3,000	0	0	6,000
Increase in working capital	600	50	50	300	100	100	1,200
Cash flow	−2,100	1,450	1,450	−1,800	1,400	1,400	1,800
Discount factor	.909	.826	.751	.683	.621	.564	
Present value	−1,909	1,198	1,089	−1,229	869	790	

Value of Longlife given 10% cost of capital = 808

Shortlife	1	2	3	4	5	6	Total
Revenues	4,000	4,000	4,000	4,000	4,000	4,000	24,000
Cash costs	2,000	2,000	2,000	2,000	2,000	2,000	12,000
Depreciation	1,000	1,000	1,000	1,000	1,000	1,000	6,000
Taxes @ 50%	500	500	500	500	500	500	3,000
Net income	500	500	500	500	500	500	3,000
Capital expenditure	1,000	1,000	1,000	1,000	1,000	1,000	6,000
Increase in working capital	200	250	250	100	200	200	1,200
Cash flow	300	250	250	400	300	300	1800
Discount factor	.909	.826	.751	.683	.621	.564	
Present value	273	207	188	273	186	169	

Value of Shortlife given 10% cost of capital = 1,296

up the phone she remarked that she would supply the earnings by slashing advertising expenses, but would lose customers during the following year and would have to pay great expense to win them back. Although she believed the dictum from above would destroy value, she did in fact produce the required extra earnings. Finally, as we shall soon see, neither earnings per share nor the growth in earnings per share is highly correlated with the total return to shareholders.

2. Measures Based on Rates of Return

Return on invested capital (ROIC) is comprehensive because it is the product of two key value drivers (operating margin and capital turnover). The definition of pretax ROIC is

$$ROIC = \frac{EBIT}{sales} \times \frac{sales}{invested\ capital} \tag{13.1}$$

Figure 13.4 ROIC tree.

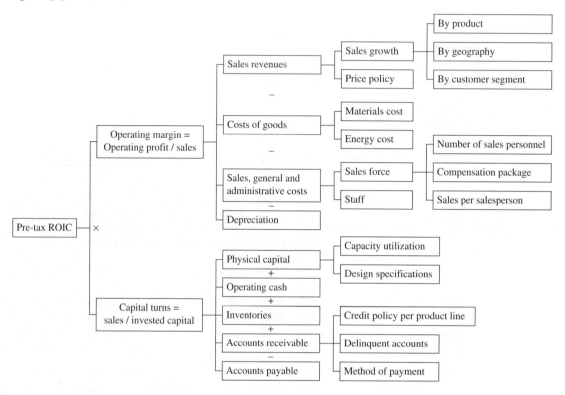

where *EBIT* is earnings before interest and taxes. When used to evaluate business unit performance, however, ROIC encourages capital harvesting behavior. It is easier for a manager to allow the capital under her control to depreciate than it is to invest new capital profitably. As she harvests the business, ROIC rises because the amount of invested capital is assumed to drift upward. What happens, however, before much time passes, is that the capital base devalues and, assuming that the decline in sales is not as bad as the decline in the capital base, then ROIC will be fine. The spread of the ROIC over the weighted average cost of capital (*WACC*) has the same problem. Management cannot influence *WACC,* so the easiest thing to do to raise ROIC is to allow the base of invested capital to depreciate—that is, to harvest the business.

As part of expectations-based management, however, ROIC is useful because it traces back into all of the line items in the income statement and balance sheet as shown in Figure 13.4. It is possible to trace individual lines on the financial statement all the way down to individual product line information for the purpose of performance measurement.

Return on equity (ROE) is also a poor performance measure. First, it is possible to artificially raise the return on equity by using 100% debt to purchase another company that earns less than its cost of capital but more than the cost of debt. The result will be to increase the return on equity, but to increase risk faster, thereby decreasing the price per share of the company:

$$ROE = (EBIT - k_b D)(1 - T)/E, \qquad (13.2)$$

where

$$k_b = \text{the interest rate good on the face value of debt,}$$

$$D = \text{the face value of debt,}$$

$$T = \text{the cash tax rate,}$$

$$E = \text{the book value of equity.}$$

3. An Economic Profit Measure

The definition of EVA®, a trademark of Stern Stewart, also called economic profit (EP), is the spread between the return on invested capital (*ROIC*) and the weighted average cost of capital (*WACC*) multiplied by the dollar amount of invested capital (*I*). $EP = EVA^{®} = (ROIC - WACC)I$. It helps to alleviate harvesting behavior by multiplying the spread by the amount of invested capital. One often reads that when economic profit is positive, that is, when a business unit earns more than its weighted average cost of capital, the business unit in question creates value for shareholders. It turns out that positive EVA® is neither a necessary nor sufficient condition for creation of shareholder value either at the company or the business unit level. Furthermore, the level of EVA® as well as the growth in EVA® are not highly correlated with the total return to shareholders (TRS). More detail will be given shortly. Perhaps an example will suffice in the meantime. In October 1998, Intel, a computer processor manufacturer, which was earning roughly 50% return on invested capital, and which had a cost of capital equal to roughly 10%, reported that its earnings were up 19% over the year before. Clearly, Intel's EVA® was positive, as was its growth in EVA®. Yet on the announcement, its share price fell 6%. Why? Because the consensus analyst expectation was that earnings were to have gone up 24%. Hence, expectations were not met, and Intel's price was adjusted downward. EVA® does not attempt to incorporate expectations.

Chapter 14 shows that the discounted value of EP, when added to the book value of assets in place, equals the DCF value of the firm. A short example is shown in Table 13.1. Either way, whether we look at DCF or at discounted EP plus assets in place, the value of the entity is $1,088.60. Given this value, the expected return to investors is 10% (i.e., *WACC*). To create value in year 1, for example, EP must exceed the $50 that is expected, or EBIT $(1 - T)$ must exceed $150. The same requirement is true for any and all years. For example, in year 2 if EBIT $(1 - T)$ turns out to be $200 instead of $220, the value of the firm will fall, even though $ROIC > WACC$ and EP is positive.

4. Measurement Based on Expectations

To create shareholder value it is necessary and sufficient for a company or a business unit to exceed shareholder expectations. As shown in Figure 13.2, expectations-based management (EBM™ is a trademark of the Monitor Group) is defined as the difference between actual and expected economic profit:

$$\text{Actual EP} - \text{Expected EP} = [\text{Actual ROIC} - \text{Expected ROIC}] \times I$$

$$- [\text{Actual } WACC - \text{Expected } WACC] \times I$$

$$+ [ROIC - WACC][\text{Actual } I - \text{Expected } I]. \tag{13.3}$$

Equation 13.3 has three parts. The first may be interpreted as earning more than expected on the company's invested capital, I. The second says that value is created when the actual cost of capital is lower than the expected cost of capital. The third term says value is created when the company

Table 13.1 Comparison of EP with DCF for Valuation

Year	After-tax ROIC	I	EBIT$(1 - T)$	WACC	EP	FCF	Discount Factor	PV(FCF)	PV(EP)
0		$1,000		10%			1.000		$1,000.0
1	15%	$1,100	$150	10%	$50	$50	0.909	$45.5	$45.5
2	20%	$1,300	$220	10%	$110	$20	0.826	$16.5	$90.9
3	10%	$1,400	$130	10%	$0	$30	0.757	$22.5	$0.0
4	5%	$1,800	$70	10%	-$70	-$330	0.683	-$225.4	-$47.8
5	10%	$2,000	$180	10%	$0	-$20	0.621	-$12.4	$0.0
CV	10%		$200	10%	$0	$2,000	0.621	$1,241.8	$0.0
								$1,088.6	$1,088.6

Notes:

$g_{CV} = $ 5.0% (continuing value growth)

FCF $= $ free cash flow = EBIT $(1 - T)$ − changes in new (I) investment

CV $= $ continuing value = EBIT $(1 - T)(1 - g_{CV}/r)/(WACC - g_{CV})$

$= $ $200(1 - .05/.10)/(.1 - .05) = $2,000$

$I = $ book value of assets

$WACC = $ 10% (weighted average cost of capital)

invests more than expected and does so profitably. In other words, it earns more than the cost of capital on new capital invested. Overall, expectations-based management is the best short-term measure of management performance. It is also the measure that is most highly correlated with the total return to shareholders.

Table 13.2 shows the results of regressions where the annual market-adjusted total return to shareholders is the dependent variable and the independent variables are the earnings per share (EPS) scaled by the share price at the beginning of the year in the first row, the growth in EPS scaled by the beginning-of-the-year share price in the second row, the economic value added (scaled) in the third row, and the growth in economic value added (scaled) in the fourth row. The sample was taken from the S&P 500 for the years 1992–1998. None of the r-squared statistics exceed 6%, although according to the t-statistics that are shown in parentheses, all of the independent variables are statistically significant.

Table 13.3 brings analyst expectations into the picture. As before, the dependent variable is the total return to shareholders, adjusted for the market return the same year. The equation for the market-adjusted return, MAR_{it},

$$MAR_{it} = \frac{\Pi(1 + r_{it})}{\Pi(1 + r_{mt})} \tag{13.4}$$

takes the ratio of the product of the one-month returns for the ith stock in a given year and divides it by the product of the monthly market returns in the same year. This is then regressed against three expectations-based variables in the following structural equation:

$$MAR_{it} = a + b \ln[E(1, 1)/E(1, 0)] + c \ln[E(2, 1)/E(2, 0)] + d[E(L, 1) - E(L, 0)] + \epsilon_{i,t}. \tag{13.5}$$

Table 13.2 Market-Adjusted Total Return to Shareholders and One-Period Return Measures

	A	B	C	D
Intercept	−0.099	−0.0441	−0.003	−0.004
	(14.02)	(−8.33)	(−5.59)	(−6.87)
EPS_t/S_{t-1}	1.086			
	(12.89)			
$\Delta EPS_t/S_{t-1}$		0.669		
		(11.10)		
EVA/S_{t-1}			0.001	
			(6.786)	
$\Delta EVA/S_{t-1}$				0.003
				(10.02)
Number of observations	2,582	2,579	2,194	2,185
Adjusted R-squared	0.06	0.05	0.02	0.04
F-statistic	166.1	123.3	46.1	100.4

Source: Copeland, Dolgoff, and Moel (2003)
Panel data for the S&P 500 companies for the years 1992–1998. EVA® data from *Stern Stewart.* Company EPS and EPS growth data from Compustat, market return data from CRSP. *t*-statistics in parentheses.

The first term is analyst expectations about this year's earnings as revised this year (between time 0 and time 1). The second term is the revision of analyst expectations of earnings next year, but observed this year. In other words it is the difference between analyst expectations of next year's earnings at the end of this year versus the expectations of earnings next year at the beginning of this year. The natural logarithm of the first two terms is used because the data are supplied in units of dollars per share and we wanted to convert to percentages. The third term, the change in expectations about long-term growth as observed this year, was already given as a percentage. The results of this multiple regression are given in Table 13.3.

In this regression the *r*-squared is 47% when all variables are included (column 1). When only two independent variables at a time are included, the lowest *r*-squared is 28%. Clearly, the total return to shareholders and changes in analyst expectations are closely related with each other. Upon further examination, the first column of Table 13.3 tells us that there is no significant relationship between changes in expectations this year about this year's earnings and TRS, when longer-term expectations are also in the multiple regression. However, changes in expectations this year about next year's earnings and about long-term earnings growth are both highly significant. Even more interesting is the fact that the impact of changes in expectations regarding long-term growth (3.269) is 8.4 times larger than the impact of changes in expectations about earnings next year. If the value of a company in the market is conceptualized as a discounted cash flow, the multiple regression makes perfect sense because most of the value is derived from cash flows beyond the first two years.

So far we have only looked at changes in earnings expectations. What about the cost of capital and capital expenditures? They also appear in Eq. (13.3). Unfortunately, most analysts do not record their expectations about these two additional variables. Therefore, we have to build our own expectation models. The CAPM was used to estimate the difference between the beginning and end-of-year cost of equity and that was assumed to be the change in expectations about the cost

Table 13.3 Market-Adjusted Total Return to Shareholders and Changes in Analyst Expectations

	A	B	C	D
Intercept	0.360	0.430	0.420	0.461
	(18.108)	(19.81)	(18.88)	(20.74)
$\ln[E(1, 1)/E(1, 0)]$	0.018	0.324		
	(0.94)	(22.25)		
$\ln[E(2, 1)/E(2, 0)]$	0.389		0.280	
	(18.22)		(23.25)	
$E(L, 1) - E(L, 0)$	3.269			4.105
	(16.08)			(19.79)
$\ln(1/S_{t-1})$	0.117	0.142	0.139	0.159
	(18.82)	(20.80)	(19.88)	(22.85)
Number of observations	2,318	2,491	2,365	2,560
Adjusted R-squared	0.47	0.31	0.32	0.28
F-statistic	512.9	567.7	562.1	489.3

Source: Copeland, Dolgoff, and Moel (2003).
Panel data for the S&P 500 companies for the years 1992–1998.
Expectations data from Zacks, market return data from CRSP. t-statistics in parentheses.

of capital. Changes in expectations about capital expenditures were estimated by calculating the difference between actual capital expenditures as a percentage of sales and capital expenditures predicted by a simple time-series regression based on the last five years of history. The results, shown in Table 13.4, indicate that percentage changes in expectations of the cost of equity $k_{s,t+1}$ are statistically significant and have a negative sign as predicted. Unexpected changes in capital expenditures, however, are not significant.

What are the implications of expectations-based management for CFOs? First of all, *performance of business units must exceed expectations in order to create shareholder value.* Consider the following example. Two business units have the same cost of capital, let's say 10%. During the past year business unit A earned 8% ROIC and business unit B earned 15%. Which created more value for shareholders? The answer is that we cannot make any judgment unless we know what the business units were expected to earn. If, for example, unit A was expected to lose 5%, then it has exceeded expectations by 13% and created shareholder value. On the other hand, if unit B was expected to earn 25%, then it has fallen short of expectations by 10% and destroyed shareholder value. Slightly more subtle are decisions that involve new investment. Again, let's take a simple example. Suppose that a company has informed the market that it has two new investments, each expected to earn 30% while the cost of capital is 10%. The market believes what it has heard and incorporates the good news into the share price, which has risen as a consequence. Suddenly, management learns that one of the two projects will earn only 15% instead of the expected 30%. Should management cancel the new project? This is a thorny problem, requiring careful thought. If management does proceed to undertake the project, then the market's expectations will be revised downward and surely the stock price will fall. Remember though, that every decision in economics must be weighed in light of the next-best alternative, which in this case is deciding not to go ahead with the 15% return project. If management decides not to invest, then shareholders are presumed to earn exactly the opportunity cost of capital, namely, 10%. Consequently, if the 15% project

Table 13.4 Market-Adjusted Return and Expectations, the Cost of Equity, and Capital Expenditures

Independent Variable	A	B	C	D	E	F	G
Intercept	0.009	0.360	0.359	0.358	0.359	0.361	0.361
	(2.23)	(18.11)	(17.73)	(17.96)	(17.74)	(13.33)	(13.67)
$\ln[E(1, 1)/E(1, 0)]$	−0.006	0.018	0.026	0.017	0.026	0.011	0.007
	(−0.34)	(0.94)	(1.39)	(0.92)	(1.37)	(0.48)	(0.33)
$\ln[E(2, 1)/E(2, 0)]$	0.465	0.389	0.391	0.391	0.390	0.416	0.421
	(22.30)	(18.22)	(18.19)	(18.28)	(18.15)	(15.89)	(16.26)
$E(L, 1) - E(L, 0)$	3.492	3.269	3.263	3.273	3.260	2.771	2.679
	(17.73)	(16.08)	(15.27)	(16.10)	(15.27)	(10.36)	(10.38)
$\ln(1/S_{t-1})$		0.117	0.118	0.118	0.118	0.123	0.123
		(18.82)	(18.60)	(18.83)	(18.59)	(14.70)	(15.06)
$(k_{t+1} - k_t)/k_t$		−0.087				−0.014	
		(−2.30)				(−0.30)	
$(r_{f,t+1} - E(r_{f,t+1}))/E(r_{f,t+1})$				−0.036			
				(−1.53)			
$(\beta_{t+1} - \beta_t)/\beta_t$					−0.128		
					(−2.99)		
UCAPEX						−0.002	−0.002
						(−0.38)	(−0.40)
Number of observations	2,699	2,318	2,185	2,318	2,185	1,384	1,457
Adjusted *R*-squared	0.38	0.47	0.48	0.47	0.48	0.47	0.47
F-statistic	558.7	512.9	403.8	411.0	405.2	206.0	254.6

Source: Copeland, Dolgoff, and Moel (2003).
Panel data for the S&P 500 companies for the years 1992–1998. k, is the market cost of equity. $r_{f,t+1}$ is the actual 10-year Treasury spot rate at the end of the year, $E(r_{f,t+1})$ is the one year forward 10-year rate as of the beginning of the year. Betas are BARRA betas. *UCAPEX* stands for scaled unexpected capital expenditures. Expectations data from Zacks, market return data from CRSP. *t*-statistics in parentheses.

is rejected, shareholders will earn only 10% and the stock price will fall even more. Therefore, when it comes to new investments, the rule of thumb remains the same as in Chapter 1. *Maximize shareholder wealth by accepting all new investments that earn more than the market-determined opportunity cost of capital.*

Figure 13.5 shows a chart with data for Chevron, one of the world's largest integrated oil companies from 1990 to 2000. Notice that in 1994–95 earnings rose from approximately $2.50 per share to $3.00 per share. Normally, we would expect this to be good news, but the total return to shareholders, relative to the market, fell the whole year. The rationality of this is difficult to understand until analyst expectations are plotted on the same chart. The squiggly line that starts in January 1993 and ends in the square earnings box in December 1995 represents consensus analyst expectations. In January 1993 analysts were expecting about $3.50 per share for 1995. During the two years that followed they continuously reduced their expectations, and it was this downward revision that matched the decline in the market-adjusted total return to shareholders. Note also that during 1995, expectations of earnings the following year (1996) were also adjusted downward, although in early 1996 they began to turn around.

Figure 13.5 Chevron 1990–1998: TSR, annual earnings, and market expectations. *Source:* Monitor Analysis, Zacks, Compustat.

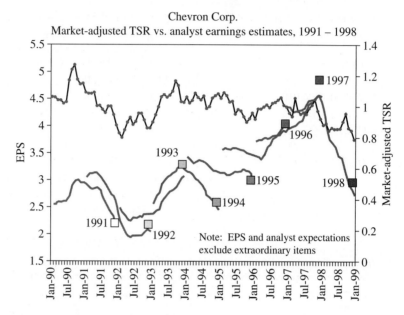

The art of setting expectations requires that management communicate appropriately with investors in the market place, and formulate and monitor performance vis-à-vis expectations internally. Let's discuss external communications first. Define the signal-to-noise ratio as

$$SNR = [\text{actual EP} - \text{expected EP}]/\sigma\,(\text{analyst}). \qquad (13.6)$$

The signal, in the numerator, is the difference between actual and expected economic profit. Noise, in the denominator, is the dispersion of analyst expectations (measured by the standard deviation).

For a given strength signal, we hypothesize that as the amount of noise increases, there will be three effects. First, greater noise implies greater variation in the resulting message, namely, the total return to shareholders. Second, the reaction of share prices to any single message becomes smaller because the information in the message becomes obscured by the noise. For time-series data these two effects will be difficult if not impossible to separate. The third effect is the relationship between the signal-to-noise ratio and the level of TRS. Since greater noise implies greater variance in TRS and greater difficulty interpreting the signal, we expect that the market will require higher returns on average in order to be compensated for poorer-quality signals. The conclusion is that if management seeks to maximize shareholder wealth, it should attempt to reduce noise when communicating with the market. In practice this implies an unbiased signal. If there is a bias (e.g., consistently setting expectations lower than management expects it can achieve), and if the bias is constant, then the market simply adjusts for it and the resulting signal is the same as if there had been no bias at all. The opposite is an uncertain bias—sometimes pessimistic and at other times optimistic. This lack of constancy results in a noisier signal and consequently a lower share price as investors require a higher expected return.

Not only is it advisable to have an unbiased signal, but it is wise to pay attention to other attributes. If multiple members of the top management team are responsible for communicating with the market, their messages should be mutually consistent—to reduce noise. The messages should be verifiable through independent sources (such as customers, suppliers, competitors, regulators, and former employees of the company). And there should be "color" to the signal. In other words it should contain in-depth explanations for what is being communicated.

The complement to external communications with investors is the process of building and monitoring internal performance expectations. Finally, it is desirable to align compensation with performance—a topic that is discussed in greater detail later in this chapter. Usually the budgeting process is the way that expected performance is established and monitored. Without delving far into an unnecessary level of granularity, it is worth simply stating a few rules of thumb that set apart good from bad budgeting practices:

1. Redo the budget whenever the operating environment changes.
2. Work to set reasonable stretch targets.
3. Assign decision rights to the people who have the right skills and necessary information.
4. Don't overreach a manager's span of control.
5. Be aware that the process of setting expectations is not necessarily incentive compatible with actual performance.
6. When decision rights are assigned, be sure to assign responsibility and accountability with them.
7. Be aware of externalities among business units and seek market-based solutions.
8. Be aware of multiperiod problems with measuring performance and designing incentives.

The first of the eight rules of thumb is almost always violated by bureaucrats who insist that budgets be submitted at the same time each year whether revision is needed or not. The reality is that when information arrives that materially changes the opportunity set facing a company, then it is time to revise the plans that are embedded in the budget and to resubmit. An annual budgeting cycle is meaningless most of the time. Rules 2 and 5 are closely related. Michael Jensen [2002] has been quoted as saying that "the budgeting process is just an incentive for lying." The logic is straightforward, but not compelling. Lower-level management has an incentive to set expectations low—low enough that it becomes easy to surpass easy benchmarks—a process called *sandbagging*. There are two ways to overcome this problem. The first is to be better informed. In order to have a two-way discussion between top management who must set expected performance standards, and lower-level management who must perform, it becomes necessary for top management to take the time and effort to understand the business that they are evaluating. Critical information may be gathered from former managers of the business, from suppliers, from customers, from engineers, and from government agencies. An informed discussion helps to reduce sandbagging. The second piece of advice is to create an incentive-compatible compensation design. There is more on this point later on in the chapter. Rules 3, 4, and 6 are also related. Together they imply that the manager of a business unit should have complete control over its resources. For example, a performance measurement system based on earnings assigns no responsibility for managing capital efficiently. It is hardly surprising that when managers are not charged for using the firm's capital, that the sales revenue per dollar of capital employed begins to decline. Rules 7 and 8 are easy to state but difficult to implement.

5. Measurement Based on DCF Valuation

The main shortcoming of all of the aforementioned performance measures is that they are basically one-period views of the world. Consequently, at the corporate level and the business unit level, where it is reasonable to assume that forecasts of both the income statement and of the balance sheet information are available, it is advisable to take a look at discounted cash flow valuations. The expected cash flows in these models might be based on analyst forecasts and provide a market perspective of the company's value, or they might be based on management forecasts to provide an inside-out perspective. If the difference between the two is significant, it may lead to board-level decisions. For example, if the market value is less than management believes the stock is worth, then a share repurchase program can be initiated.

Because valuations are multiperiod in nature, they are also useful for setting one-period performance targets, when one is using an expectations-based management system. To create value it is necessary to exceed expectations, and these are not always constant over the life of a business unit. Often there is a start-up period following a major capital expenditure when the expected ROIC is low or negative, followed by a normal return period, followed by higher expected returns when the capital base depreciates. If these life cycle stages are predictable, then it is not difficult to set expectations of performance in an appropriate manner. A similar story can be told for turn-around activities and cyclical businesses. Still other businesses perpetually earn high ROIC because they do not use much capital, for example, a consulting firm. In all instances, the multiperiod aspect of DCF is useful when used in conjunction with the short-term measures listed earlier in the chapter.

6. Measurement Based on Real Options

Real options analysis is a superset of DCF, and all that was said there is applicable here. Most companies gain insight from ROA primarily at the project level, although decisions concerning whether to exit and reenter a line of business, and certain aspects of mergers and acquisitions (the option to expand or abandon an acquired business), are common applications.

C. *I*ncentive Design

This section discusses the design of incentive systems. Given that there is often a separation of ownership from the control of operations, how can incentive design help to alleviate the resulting agency cost? For example, you might own a farm, but fail to possess the farming skills necessary to own it. Naturally, you hire a farmer to run the day-to-day operations. How should you compensate her? If you use a form of profit sharing, the farmer will maximize this year's crop output. But as owner that may not be in your best interest because it requires overfarming the land and therefore exhausting it for future use. The result is that there is a conflict between maximizing this year's crop yield and maximizing the value of the farm for resale.

There is a short list of thorny issues in incentive design. First, how should pay be linked to performance, given the objective of shareholder (i.e., owner) wealth maximization? Second, given that executives change jobs frequently, how should compensation be distributed over time? Third, how should incentive design vary between line officers and staff, and as one moves from top management to middle-level management and lower?

1. Why Maximize Shareholder Wealth?

Before diving into these topics, there is first the question of why it makes sense to organize resources into corporations with a limited liability residual claimant called the shareholder. Why not organize as an Athenian democracy where all stakeholders can vote on policies and decisions, or into an autocracy run by an absolute dictator, or into a socialist firm where all ownership rests in the hands of workers who are represented by decision-making committees? The broad answer is that a firm may be thought of as a set of contracts designed to share risk and maximize output. As residual claimants (with limited liability) the shareholders need to satisfy all other higher-priority claimants and to accept all residual risk. In order to maximize their own wealth, shareholders must be sure that customers are well cared for, that the appropriate labor force can be recruited and retained, that suppliers are content, that bank covenants are adhered to, that interest and debt principal payments are made as promised, and that the government receives the taxes that are due. Suppose that there were no residual claimant to whom decision rights are assigned. If so, then stakeholders with limited information might take the helm. For example, employees who are typically risk averse find it difficult to separate the risk of their human capital (e.g., losing their jobs) from risk taking in business and, consequently, they might be overly conservative decision makers. The assignment of residual risk to shareholders who are free to sell their shares in an open market and free to spread their company-specific risk across diversified portfolios, and who do not have their human capital tied up in the corporation, results in efficient risk sharing. The fact that they have control of the company that they are said to own gives them decision rights that are aligned with the interests of all of the stakeholders ahead of their residual claim.

Jensen [1998] adds four related attributes to these basic themes. First, when risk changes over time (as it always does), then it is costly to write and rewrite contracts for sharing rules among the diverse claimants of the firm. Second, shareholders who are not employees, and who are granted limited liability by the government, find that it is easier and less costly for them to bear the company risk than it is to write detailed contracts regarding risk sharing. It has been argued that common stock (i.e., wealth from residual claimants) is ideal for outright ownership of assets by a firm, having lower transactions costs than rental contracts for use of the same assets. Third, residual claims that are alienable (i.e., that can be sold and bought) make it easier to separate ownership from control. This, in turn, makes it easier to hire managers with firm-specific skills because they are not required to tie up both their human and their financial capital under the roof of the firm for which they work. Finally, the existence of shares as residual claims does not hamper decision making of management because the separation theorem discussed in Chapter 1 of this textbook can be applied—namely, take all projects until the marginal rate of return on the last dollar spent just equals the market-determined cost of capital.

Often it is alleged that the existence of residual claims held by shareholders creates conflicts with other stakeholders, especially labor. The allegation is that greater profits for shareholders are obtained by laying off labor. Copeland, Koller, and Murrin [1994] study the relationship between employment growth and shareholder wealth creation over the 1983–1991 time interval. Their sample is collected at the company level and aggregated by industry in three countries: Japan, Germany, and the United States. They find no evidence that labor suffers to benefit shareholders. Within an industry, and in the long run, companies that are winners are more productive, create more shareholder wealth, and experience greater growth in employment. In the auto assembly industry, for example, all countries experienced growth in employment, but the Japanese, who were the most productive, had the greatest growth in employment. Similarly, in steel, an industry with overcapacity and shrinking employment due to technological changes, Germany had greater shareholder wealth creation and better employment results than the United States. The empirical evidence clearly indicates that creating an organization where residual claims and control of the company both are held by shareholders actually aligns the economic interests of all stakeholders. All are afloat in the same ship, and prosper or sink with it.

2. Alignment of Pay with Performance

The first half of this chapter makes a strong case that the performance measure most closely related to the total return to shareholders is the difference between actual and expected (i.e., forecasted) results. This is without doubt a subjective measure, and it becomes necessary to deal with its subjectivity. Jensen [1998, p. 206] argues that "performance in most jobs cannot be measured objectively because joint production and unobservability mean that individual output is not quantifiable." He goes on to criticize objective merit systems because (1) any misspecification of the performance measurement system can be easily gamed by employees, (2) the measurement system becomes difficult to change because inevitably any alteration is detrimental to some employees, and (3) the threat of increasing objective standards higher in response to better-than-expected performance this year—the so-called expectations treadmill—causes a behavioral reaction where employees deliberately restrict output so that they can earn their bonuses. There are reasons against subjective systems as well. Subjective systems are unpopular because employees may not trust superiors to evaluate their performance accurately. Given the negative attributes of objective systems and the lack of trust that defeats subjective systems, Jensen concludes: "The compensation system that results from this set of forces appears to be one with little or no pay for performance."

There are, however, some basic principles that help to link pay with performance. The first is to keep the relationship between performance and compensation as linear as possible. Figure 13.6 illustrates a "kinked" relationship between pay and performance that is typical. Although the relationship is linear around the average or expected level of performance, there is a lower bound represented by basic salary, and an upper bound that represents salary plus maximum bonus. To understand how the kinks in the curve, combined with the one-period nature of compensation, result in perverse behavior, suppose that a manager finds herself at point A on the curve near the end of the year. It makes sense to take large risks because she cannot do worse on the downside, and if the risk pays off she can earn much more on the upside. If we study her behavior at point B instead, and if it is early in the year, then from her point of view she is incented to be very conservative because she can lose a lot on the downside and gain little on the upside because she is already at the maximum bonus point. Clearly, a linear pay schedule is much better because she gets a constant percentage of the value created through her actions. By the way, we note that if performance is measured relative to expectations, it is just as easy to construct a linear pay schedule.

Figure 13.6 "Kinked" relationship between pay and performance.

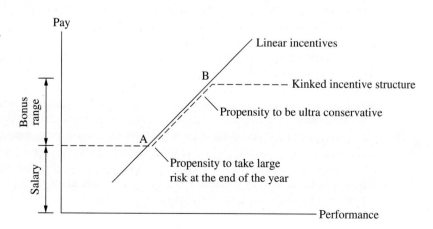

3. The Use of Stock Options

It is often argued that if enough of an executive's wealth is tied to the performance of the company, then there is no agency problem between the owner and the managers of the firm. The manager will want to join the owner in seeking to maximize the value of the stock. Some would say that the manager should invest a substantial portion of his wealth in the stock or in call options on it to align the manager's interests with their own. An executive stock option plan is a form of long-term compensation contract that depends on corporate performance. It usually gives managers the right to purchase a specified number of shares for a specified period of time (called the maturity date of the option) for a specified price (called the exercise price). The first stock option plan to receive favorable tax treatment was called the Restricted Stock Option plan of the Revenue Act of 1950. There have been many changes since then, but since 1994 the tax laws govern two types of plan: incentive stock options (ISOs) and nonqualified stock options (NQSOs).

Tax consequences are as follows: At the time of the grant there are no tax consequences for either the executive or the company. At exercise, the executive who was granted NQSOs pays the ordinary income tax on the spread $(S_X - X)$ between the stock price and the exercise price; the company reduces X and can deduct $S - X$. When the stock is sold, the executive pays a capital gains tax on $S_T - S_X$, and there is no consequence for the company. If the executive was granted an ISO, taxation is deferred until the stock is sold, when the capital gains rate is applied to $S_T - S_0$, the gain from the time of grant, and there is no tax consequence for the company.

The accounting treatment is also important. Both NQSOs and ISOs must be exercised sequentially. There is a definite drawback to the sequential exercise requirement. Suppose the firm's share price was $50, fell back to $30, then rose again to $40. If options were issued at each stage with the exercise price equal to the stock price, executives would be required to exercise the earlier $50 options (that are $10 out-of-the-money) before they could exercise the options that were issued at $30 (that are $10 in-the-money).

Both ISOs and NQSOs have a maximum life of 10 years from the date of issue. The exercise price of ISOs must be greater than or equal to the stock price at the time of issue, but NQSOs can have an exercise price as low as 50 percent of the stock price.

Two reasons for using stock options at all are (1) that they augment salaries with a call option that makes executives' total compensation more closely tied to shareholder wealth creation and (2) that stock options are a more tax-efficient way of delivering after-tax dollars to executives. Nevertheless, options pay off on the upside and are simply left unexercised on the downside; consequentially they are part of a compensation schedule that is "kinked" on the downside. However, it can be argued that the practice of resetting the exercise price after the stock price declines has the effect of straightening the kinks, for example, cash payments.

Miller and Scholes [1982] demonstrate that, when compared with salaries, options are tax neutral from the firm's point of view and are tax dominant from the manager's point of view. To illustrate their argument, suppose that a firm expects $140 million of cash flow in a good state of nature before paying management salaries, and $120 million in a bad state. The firm's tax rate is 50%, and management salaries amount to $100 million. Table 13.5 shows the firm's net payoffs after management salaries and taxes.

If the probability of the good state is 50% and if we assume a zero discount rate, then the present value of the firm in this one-period example is $15 million. Assume 10 million shares outstanding so that the price per share is $1.50. An at-the-money call option will sell for $0.25, the average of its good and bad state payouts, as shown in Table 13.6.

Table 13.5 Expected Cash Flows of the Firm (millions of dollars)

	Good State	Bad State
Cash flow before salaries	$140	$120
Salaries	−100	−100
Cash flow before taxes	40	20
Taxes @ 50%	−20	−10
Net cash flow	$20	$10

Table 13.6 Call Option Payouts at Time 1

	Good State	Bad State
Share price	$2.00	$1.00
Less the exercise price	−1.50	−1.50
Payout	$0.50	$0.00

Table 13.7 Subsidiary Balance Sheet (millions of dollars)

Beginning			Good State			Bad State		
Assets $15	Debt	$12.5	Assets $15	Debt	$15	Assets $10	Debt	$10
	Equity	2.5		Equity	0		Equity	0
Total $15	Total	$15.0	Total $15	Total	$15	Total $10	Total	$10

Now, suppose that the company offers managers an option plan that is tax neutral from the firm's point of view. What will its terms be? The plan will need to have a present value of $2.5 million and will be constructed from a portfolio of 10 million at-the-money options granted to management. In return, management would have to agree to reduce its salary by $2.5 million—an equal dollar amount.

To handle the potential liability created by the plan, we assume that the firm creates a subsidiary that will have a balance sheet with $2.5 million in equity (the salary expense reduction) and will borrow $12.5 million via a zero-coupon bond with a face value of $15 million. The $15 million in cash is used to purchase 10 million shares of stock. Table 13.7 shows the current balance sheet of the subsidiary as well as its balance sheet in the good and bad states of nature. If the good state occurs, the options will be exercised, whereupon the subsidiary receives $15 million in cash and delivers stock worth $20 million. The $15 million in cash is used to pay off the loan and the equity in the subsidiary is worthless, leaving the parent firm with a $2.5 million tax-deductible loss. If the bad state occurs, the options will not be exercised, and the stock held by the subsidiary will be worth $10 million and turned over to the bank. The equity in the subsidiary will be worthless, once again leaving the parent with a tax-deductible loss. The bank lends $12.5 million, and its expected payoff is $12.5 million. The parent ends up with a $2.5 million loss either way.

Table 13.8 The Firm's Cash Flow, Given the SAR Plan (millions of dollars)

	Good State	Bad State
Cash flow before salaries	$140.0	$120.0
Salaries	−97.5	−97.5
Cash flow after salaries	42.5	22.5
Investment loss	−2.5	−2.5
Cash flow before taxes	40.0	20.0
Taxes	−20.0	−10.0
Net cash flow	$20.0	$10.0

Table 13.8 shows the firm's expected cash flows given the terms of the option plan and its payouts from the subsidiary. Comparing the net cash flows of Tables 13.8 and 13.5, we see that the firm is completely indifferent between the two alternatives.[1]

From the management perspective, after-tax salary could be invested in stock options in order to have the same pattern of future risky payouts. The main advantage of the stock option plan is that taxes are deferred. Given that the plan is tax neutral from the firm's perspective and tax preferred by management, there is a strong incentive to use stock option plans.

Management, whose compensation is based on straight salary, cannot benefit from undertaking risky positive net present value projects unless their salaries are adjusted ex post to reflect good decisions. Stock option plans can help to correct this underinvestment problem because the options, and the stock, are immediately more valuable when risky positive net present value projects are initiated. There are several possible drawbacks, however. Management cannot easily diversify the greater firm-specific risk imposed by stock option plans and may require a higher level of expected compensation. From the shareholders' point of view, the cost of higher expected compensation may offset the benefit of reducing the underinvestment problem. Furthermore, stock options are not protected against dividend payments. This may change the behavior of management to have a bias against the payment of dividends and in favor of share repurchases. This may conflict with the wishes of some groups of shareholders and support the desires of others. Stock option plans may also bias management toward decisions that increase the variability of the stock price in an effort to increase the value of their stock options.

Studies of the announcement effect of the inception of stock option plans for management indicate that shareholders react favorably, considering the plan to be a net benefit. Larker [1983] finds a significant positive residual on the day following receipt of the first shareholder proxy statement. Brickley, Bhagat, and Lease [1985] find a significant positive 2.4% cumulative return between the board of directors meeting and the Security and Exchange Commission stamp date for the proxy statement. Lemgruber [1986] used monthly return data for a sample of 119 firms with no other information in their proxy statements except for the election of board members. For the interval between the board meeting and the release of the proxy statement, he found a significant 2.7% abnormal return.

---

[1] Note that we have not argued that the firm will use the tax shelter that has been created if it can write off the difference between the stock price and the exercise price in the good state of nature.

That the market reacts favorably to the inception of executive stock option plans is consistent with the benefits of the plan exceeding its costs from the shareholders' point of view. Call this the *incentive hypothesis*. It is also consistent with a *signaling hypothesis*. If managers have superior information concerning the future prospects of the firm, they would desire the implementation of a stock option plan when they believe the firm will do well. The market would respond favorably to their action. Positive announcement effects are also consistent with a *tax hypothesis*, namely, that the after-tax payoffs of a salary plus the stock option plan dominate those for a salary and bonus plan. Consequently, the value of the firm will rise following the inception of a stock option plan because total costs fall.

It is not easy to separate the three aforementioned hypotheses. They are all consistent with the observation of positive abnormal returns at the inception of a stock option plan. They do, however, make different predictions regarding management behavior. For example, the incentive hypothesis predicts greater investment and higher leverage once the plan is started. The signaling and tax hypotheses predict greater earnings. All three hypotheses predict lower dividend payout. The empirical evidence seems to lend little support to the incentive hypothesis. For example, although Lemgruber [1986] found positive announcement returns, he found no significant changes in the rate of investment, in financial leverage, or in the variance of the stock price. Lambert and Larcker [1985] found that the variance decreased (a result that is inconsistent with Lemgruber). Lemgruber did, however, find significant decreases in dividend payout after the beginning of stock option plans. Tehranian and Waegelein [1985] find that abnormal returns after the adoption of short-term compensation plans are associated with positive unexpected earnings. In sum, the empirical work suggests that stock option plans are adopted more for tax or signaling reasons than to reduce agency costs between owners and managers.

Although options are a tax-efficient way of delivering compensation to executives, and help to align the interests of owners and managers, a problem arises, namely, that a manager who has accumulated a sizeable amount of wealth in the form of options has an incentive to manipulate the market based on his inside information. If he can convince the market that he has received good news, the stock price will rise, thereby giving him the opportunity to exercise his options at a higher price. To mitigate this problem it is advisable to make the options exercisable only at certain points of time during the year. This separates the manager's ability to exercise the options from the freshness of inside information that he might have. Even better are "clawback" provisions that empower the board of directors to take back all gains from the exercise of stock options.

Very large stock option awards also become material for accounting reporting of earnings. FASB now requires that the present value of option plans be estimated and reported in a footnote, and that a fully diluted earnings estimate also be reported.

4. Total CEO Compensation

Total CEO compensation has many separate components: salary, stock grants, stock options, pension and health benefits, perquisites, and the duration of the CEO's time in office. Additionally, there are contingent payment schemes such as evergreen contracts, golden parachutes, and golden handcuffs. Let's review the whole package.

Graef Crystal [1988] studied the top 100 of Fortune's 500 companies and found that CEO pay (including salary, bonus, the value of perquisites when available, and 20% of realized gains from long-term incentives, e.g., stock options) varies in line with a number of seemingly rational factors. See Table 13.9. The only problem is that shareholder returns is not one of them. The variables in his index of company performance (profits, return on equity, the market-to-book value of equity,

Table 13.9 Poor Alignment between CEO Pay and Shareholder Returns

Factor	Definition/Comment	Effect of a 10% Increase on CEO Pay
Company size	Index combining sales, assets, book equity, and number of employees	+2.0%
Company performance	Index based on profits, 5-year average ROE, market-to-book value of equity, and 5-year average total return to investors	+31.0%
Company risk	Beta	+5.0%
Government regulation	Regulated companies pay less	N/A
Tenure of CEO	Longer tenure results in relatively lower pay	−1.2%
Location	More pay in high cost-of-living areas (e.g., + 7% for New York and 10% for Los Angeles)	N/A
CEO age	No effect on pay	0.0%
Shares owned by CEO	No effect on pay	0.0%

Note: CEO compensation includes salary, bonus, value of perquisites when available, and 20% of realized gains from long-term incentives (e.g., stock options).
Source: Graef Crystal, *Fortune*, June 1988.

and the historic return to investors) are virtually uncorrelated with shareholder returns. Of course, he did not test to see whether changes in expectations regarding these variables had an impact mainly because he had no data on expectations.

Research by Jensen and Murphy [1990] studies the relationship between CEO bonus and salary compensation and various explanatory factors including the change in shareholder wealth. Table 13.10 shows the results. First, there is a statistically significant relationship between CEO compensation and firm-specific changes in shareholder wealth, even after accounting for the company performance relative to the industry (row 3) and relative to the economy (row 4). Second, the change in CEO compensation is incredibly small relative to what happens to the firm. For example, a $1,000 change in accounting profits results in a 17.7 cent increase in CEO pay (row 5, column 3). Overall, the results in Table 13.10 indicate that CEO compensation is linked (but not very strongly) to changes in shareholder wealth, changes in accounting income, and changes in sales, but not to performance relative to the market or industry. Holding the effects of accounting profit and sales constant, a $1,000 increase in shareholder's wealth results in a .74 cent increase in CEO compensation.

The relationship between the level of CEO compensation and the size of the company is much stronger, as shown in Table 13.11. The r-squared is between 50 and 70%. The average elasticity is 30%. Thus, a CEO of a $200 million sales revenue company earns about 30% more than the CEO of a $100 million company.

Jensen and Murphy [1990] also estimate the total effects of all estimatable origins on CEO wealth. Note this is not salary and wage, but an estimate of the wealth of the CEO. Note that it includes the wealth effect of not being dismissed due to poor performance. Also, the relationship between pay and performance seems to be much larger for small firms than large. The largest single effect is changes in value of the company's stock with respect to stock ownership by the CEO, who had considerable skin in the game.

Table 13.10 Sensitivity of CEO Pay to Changes in Various Stock and Accounting-Related Measures of Performance (© 1990 by The University of Chicago Press. Reprinted with permission.)

Independent Variable [a]	Regression Coefficients [b]				
	(1)	(2)	(3)	(4)	(5)
Intercept	31.5	31.9	32.5	31.0	32.8
Δ(shareholder wealth)	.0000140	.0000126	.0000074	.0000120	.0000074
	(7.5)	(4.8)	(4.3)	(7.1)	(4.4)
Δ(wealth net-of-industry) [c]	−.0000012	—	—	—	—
	(−.7)				
Δ(wealth net-of-market) [c]	—	.0000013	—	—	—
		(.4)			
Δ(accounting profits)	—	—	.000177	—	.000187
	—	—	(17.2)		(15.7)
Δ(sales)	—	—	—	.0000122	−.0000034
				(7.2)	(−1.7)
R^2	.0083	.0082	.0449	.0148	.0453
Sample size	7,747	7,747	7,721	7,721	7,721

Note: The sample is constructed from longitudinal data reported in *Forbes* on 1,668 CEOs serving in 1,049 firms, 1974–1986; t-statistics are in parentheses.
a. The variables are all measured in thousands of 1986 dollars.
b. The dependent variable is Δ(salary + bonus), measured in thousands of 1986 constant dollars. The qualitative results are unchanged when Δ(total pay) is used as the dependent variable.
c. Δ(wealth net-of-industry) is defined as $(r_t - i_t)V_{t-1}$, where r_t is shareholder return, V_{t-1} is beginning-of-period market value, and i_t is the value-weighted return for all other firms in the same two-digit industry. Similarly, Δ(wealth net-of-market) is defined as $(r_t - m_t)V_{t-1}$, where m_t is the value-weighted return for all NYSE stocks.
Source: Jensen and Murphy (1990).

Table 13.11 Estimated Elasticity of CEO Pay with Respect to Sales (© 1990 by The University of Chicago Press. Reprinted with permission.)

	Year					R^2
	1973	1975	1979	1981	1983	
Manufacturing	.313	.296	.297	.287	.285	.60
Retail trade	.253	.271	.230	.306	.298	.53
Gas and electric utilities	.331	.236	.347	.313	.314	.67
Commerical banking	.337	.329	.367	.372	.404	.68
Insurance	.313	.277	.299	.372	.345	.69

5. Set Stretch Targets

In 1986 the board of directors of Ralston Purina announced that 491,000 shares of stock would be awarded to Ralston's top 14 executives (160,000 to the CEO) if the stock closed at or above $100 per share for 10 consecutive days any time within the next 10 years. The current stock price was $63. An increase from $63 to $100 represents a wealth gain of $811 million for shareholders, and the stock awarded to management would represent 6.05% of the gain in shareholder wealth. Is this

Figure 13.7 Cumulative abnormal performance of Ralston Purina. (Reprinted from Campbell and Wasley [1999], with permission from Elsevier.)

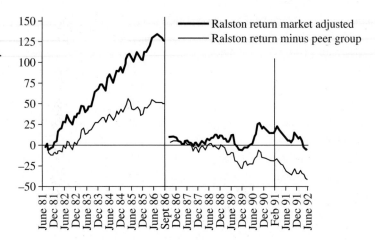

an appropriate incentive for management? At first it seems so because both parties (management and shareholders) would gain—a win-win proposition.

Campbell and Wasley [1999] use the CAPM to estimate that had Ralston Purina merely earned its cost of equity, it would have taken four years and ten months to achieve the target share price. It actually took four years and five months. During the expected time to the award, Ralston's stock slightly underperformed the S&P 500 and greatly underperformed comparables. Figure 13.7 shows the cumulative abnormal performance starting in June of 1981, five years prior to the announcement of September 1986, and continuing beyond the time of the award in February 1991 up to June of 1992, which was the expected time of the award.

During the four years and five months that it took to earn the award, Ralston announced share repurchases seven times amounting to $1.541 billion. Dividends plus share repurchases averaged 140% of net income between 1987 and 1990. As before, and once again, the moral of the story is that performance should be set relative to expectations. In this case management received a handsome reward for earning less than the cost of equity, for performance that fell below expectations. Stretch targets need to be set relative to expectations.

6. Incentive Design across Multiple Time Periods

The multiperiod aspects of decison making are what make incentive design so difficult. Managers change jobs frequently, thereby creating the problem of giving proper attribution during the current compensation period for the effect of their decisions made years earlier in a different business unit. Managers vary in the number of years before retirement, and this creates an end-game problem. Incentives based on the company's stock price may be less important for executives near the end of their career than those who are just starting. Also, one-year performance measures should be "guided" by a long-term view to avoid behavior that maximizes short-term performance at the expense of the long-run.

There is not much good theory to provide advice about a solution for this multiperiod problem. We offer two thoughts—creation of a "compensation bank" system, and control of share ownership based on expected time to retirement.

The compensation bank concept takes the awarded bonus received by an executive this year and puts it into a corporate trust (or makes it a general obligation of the firm), where it vests to the

Table 13.12 An Example of a Compensation Bank

	Year 1	Year 2	Year 3
Bonus award	$500	$100	$300
Cash paid out [a]	$100	$ 20	$ 60
Deposit to compensation bank	$400	$ 80	$240
Amount in bank (end-of-year)	$400	$520	$622
Less withdrawal [b]	$ 0	$173	$207
Total cash compensation	$100	$193	$267
Bank balance forward [c]	$400	$347	$415

a. 20% bonus
b. 33.3% of balance
c. Earns 10% interest

executive over a period of time. Vesting may be granted by a review board or be automatic over time. Table 13.12 provides a short example.

7. Designing Incentives for Different Layers of Management

The incentive structure that is appropriate for top management is quite different than that of successively lower layers of management. Top management can directly impact the share price of the company. Business unit leadership cannot, nor can sub–business unit, project, or plant management. Everyone, of course, will be happy to accept a stock option plan if the grants are supplementary to their existing level of compensation, but when faced with the more difficult choice of whether they want to give up an amount of existing income in order to receive an equivalent value of stock options, few employees decide to switch. The most important reason is that further down in the organization, managers have little or no direct influence on the company's stock price. They would rather have their bonus compensation tied to something that they control and where they have a reasonable chance of exceeding expectations. A second reason is that they cannot separate the value of their human capital from the value of the company; therefore stock options do not allow them to diversify, whereas a cash bonus for superior performance on their value drivers can be reinvested elsewhere, thereby allowing diversification.

Middle management usually receives a salary plus bonus. The problem with most bonus systems is that they do not require forced ranking, and consequently everyone is placed in the top two or three categories. A study by Medoff and Abraham [1980] surveyed two large companies and found that the first, with 4,788 employees, placed 94.5% in the top two of four ratings. The second company rated 2,841 managers into six categories and 98.8% fell into the highest three ratings. Further analysis indicated that earnings differentials between jobs were much more significant than earnings differentials (i.e., bonus differences) within job categories. In other words, promotion is much more important as a differentiator than are bonuses. Murphy [1985] found that for a sample of vice presidents of large companies, promotion implied an average 18.8% pay increase while the average pay increase given no promotion was only 3.3%. There are two implications. First, bonus systems can be more effective signals if rank ordering is required. But since the more meaningful economic signal is promotion, it is wise to place a great deal of effort in doing the evaluation well.

Lower-level management incentive pay, called gain sharing, actually results in productivity gains. Mitchell, Lewin, and Lawler [1990] study the relationship between the hourly wages earned (the dependent variable in a multiple regression) and two independent variables, the proportion of workers with incentives and the existence of an incentive plan. Based on 716 companies they obtained a cross-sectional r-squared of 68%, and both independent variables were highly significant. The concept of linking the performance of employees to value drivers under their control actually works quite well.

8. The Issue of Relative Performance—Who Is Responsible?

Arguably, one drawback of incentive plans tied to changes in the stock price is that not all stock price movements are attributable to management decisions. Why should management be responsible for a change in the market rate of interest as driven by the Federal Reserve Bank? One point of view would argue that senior management should, in fact, be held responsible for the total movement in stock prices. It is possible to hedge. For example, a gold mine can be thought of as a portfolio of risky assets that is long in gold and other precious metals. An offsetting position can be created by shorting futures on gold. The net effect would be to reduce the mining company's exposure to fluctuations in the price of gold—and were the hedge perfect, the equity of the gold mining company could theoretically be turned into a low-risk or even risk-free bond. In a sense, if management decides to be in the gold business, it is making a conscious decision to do so on behalf of shareholders. There is no risk that cannot be managed in the long run—if not by hedging or diversifying, then by simply deciding to get out of the business. Therefore, there is a strong philosophical point of view that favors total management responsibility for any movement in the stock price, whatever the cause. The maxim is simple. Maximize shareholder wealth.

An alternative point of view argues that management of a gold mine should have a comparative advantage in operating gold mines and in finding and developing new sources of gold. Management should not be expected to also specialize in hedging. Therefore, if the stock price of the gold mining company changes because interest rates rise or because the economy goes into a recession, management should be indemnified. One of the implications, of course, is that if management is compensated on its relative (not on its absolute) performance, then it may receive high compensation in a depressed economy or low compensation in a buoyant economy.

To some extent it is possible to measure the performance of a company after removing the effect of exogenous factors that are judged to be beyond the control of management. We show, in Chapter 14, the details of how to build a spreadsheet discounted cash flow model of a company. It is based on assumptions made by analysts concerning value drivers such as the nominal rate of growth in revenues, operating margins, capital turns, and the cost of capital. This type of model typically produces a valuation that is 85% (or higher) correlated with the actual market price. Given this degree of accuracy, the DCF model can then be manipulated to show the separate effects of exogenous variables on the stock from management performance relative to expectations. While still more an art than a science, nevertheless, this process is one way of informing the judgment of the decision makers who arbitrate the level of total compensation for relative performance. In this way, if so desired, it is possible to remove the effect of a change in the price of gold from the actual change in the stock price of a gold mine.

*S*ummary

We started this chapter with the role of the chief financial officer—a role that has increased in complexity with the emergence of multibusiness, multinational companies. Years ago the CFO was an accountant, but today he or she is one of the top decision makers in the company and often is elevated to the role of CEO. The CFO's responsibilities are broad, including managerial decisions such as performance measurement, incentive design, public relations, and the management of human resources. Financial decisions include risk management, capital structure and the cost of capital, dividend policy, tax policy, and working capital management. The CFO is also usually responsible for major investment decisions including research and development spending, large internal projects, and mergers and acquisitions.

The CFO is confronted with the problem of choosing a measure of performance that is highly correlated with the change in shareholders' wealth. We saw that for one-year time intervals the best measure was the difference between actual and expected economic profit, the keystone for expectations-based management. Closely related is a multiperiod measure, namely, discounted cash flow valuation. In the next chapter we shall prove that the sum of discounted economic profits, when added to the book value of assets, equals the discounted cash flow value of the company.

Given that expectations drive the share price of companies, we then discussed the myriad of thorny problems concerning the design of incentive programs—what the agency problems are, how they are usually handled, and the realization that there is no perfect solution.

PROBLEM SET

13.1 Prove the following theorem: "The present value of forecasted economic profit, when discounted at the weighted average cost of capital, plus the book value of assets, equals the DCF value of the firm."

13.2 Suppose that a firm has a project that was started last year, and it is expected to earn less than its cost of capital if left unchanged. Management comes up with these suggestions.

(a) Invest in a debottlenecking project that will raise economic profit, but not up to the cost of capital.
(b) Cut operating costs but not enough to earn the cost of capital.
(c) Sell the unprofitable business unit for a premium over its book value.

Some numbers are given in Table Q13.2. Value each alternative and compare them in terms of value creation.

13.3 Some companies measure performance by requiring both "top line" growth and "bottom line" growth (i.e., growth in revenues and growth in net income). Is this performance measure consistent with shareholder value creation? Why or why not ?

13.4 Why are EPS, the percent change in EPS, EVA®, and the change in EVA® unrelated to TRS (total return to shareholders) in Table 13.2?

13.5 Management has informed the market that it expects to earn 30% on project A and 40% on project B, and these expectations are already baked into the firm's current stock price. The cost of capital for both projects is 10%. The amount of investment required for project A is $5 million, and project B requires $30 million. Just before it is about to invest in project B, the company learns that the expected rate on the project will be 30%, not 40%.

Table Q13.2 Data for Q13.2

	Base Case	(a) Debottleneck	(b) Cut Costs	(c) Sell for 10% Premium
WACC	10%	10%	10%	10%
I_o	$1,000	$1,000	$1,000	$1,000
ΔI_o	0	400	0	0
CF_1	$300	500	350	—
CF_2	$300	500	350	—
CF_3	$300	500	350	—
Sale price	—	—	—	$1,100

(a) Should management still make the investment in project B?

(b) What will happen to the company's stock price if management invests in B?

(c) What will happen to the stock price if management does not invest in B?

13.6 Jensen criticizes "kinked" relationships between pay and performance (see Fig. 13.6). How well do the following compensation schemes fit a linear relationship?

(a) Stock option growth

(b) Stock growth

(c) Fixed salary plus variable bonus based on exceeding expectations

REFERENCES

Brickley, J., S. Bhagat, and R. Lease, "Incentive Effects of Stock Purchase Plans," *Journal of Financial Economics*, June 1985, Vol. 14, 115–129.

Campbell, C., and J. Wasley, "Stock Price-Based Incentive Contracts and Managerial Performance: The Case of Ralston-Purina Company," *Journal of Financial Economics*, February 1999, Vol. 51, 195–217.

Copeland, T., A. Dolgoff, and A. Moel, "The Role of Expectations in the Cross-Section of Returns," working paper, Monitor Group, Cambridge, Mass., 2003.

Copeland, T., T. Koller, and J. Murrin, *Valuation: Measuring and Managing the Value of Companies*, 2nd edition, John Wiley & Sons, New York, 1994.

Crystal, G., "The Wacky, Wacky World of Executive Pay," *Fortune*, June 6, 1988, Vol. 117, No. 12, pp. 68–78.

Jensen, M., *Foundations of Organizational Strategy*, Harvard University Press, Cambridge, Mass., 1998.

———, *A Theory of the Firm: Managerial Behavior, Agency Costs and Ownership Structure*, Harvard University Press, Cambridge, Mass., 2000.

Jensen, M., and K. Murphy, "Performance Pay and Top Management Incentives," *Journal of Political Economy*, 1990, Vol. 98, 225–264.

Lambert, R., and D. Larcker, "Executive Compensation, Corporate Decision-Making and Shareholder Wealth: A Review of the Evidence," *Midland Corporate Finance Journal*, Winter 1985, 6–22.

Larcker, D., "The Association between Performance Plan Adoption and Corporate Capital Investment," *Journal of Accounting and Economics*, April 1983, 3–30.

Lemgruber, E., *Stock Option Plans and Corporate Behavior*, Ph.D. dissertation, University of California, Los Angeles, 1986.

Medoff, J., and K. Abraham, "Experience, Performance and Earnings," *Quarterly Journal of Economics*, December 1980, 703–736.

Miller, M., and M. Scholes, "Dividends and Taxes: Some Empirical Evidence," *Journal of Political Economy*, December 1982, 1118–1141.

Mitchell, D., F. Lewin, and D. Lawler, "Alternative Pay Systems, Firm Performance and Productivity," in A. Blinder, ed., *Paying for Productivity*, 1990, Brookings Institution.

Murphy, K., "Corporate Performance and Managerial Remuneration," *Journal of Accounting and Economics*, April 1985, 11–42.

Smith, C., and R. Watts, "Incentive and Tax Effects of Executive Compensation Plans," *Australian Journal of Management*, 1982, Vol. 7, No. 2, 139–157.

Tehranian, H., and J. Waegelein, "Market Reaction to Short-Term Executive Compensation Plan Adoption," *Journal of Accounting and Economics*, April 1985, 131–144.

Most companies already use the same discounted cash flow techniques used in the shareholder value approach to assess the attractiveness of capital investment projects and to value potential acquisition targets. As it will be shown, this approach can be extended to estimate the value creation potential of individual business units and the strategic plan for the entire company.

—Alfred Rappaport, *Creating Shareholder Value*, 1986, The Free Press, New York, 11.

Valuation and Tax Policy

VALUATION IS AT THE VERY HEART of financial economics and especially of corporate finance. The first half of this chapter shows the details of valuing companies—how to define cash flows, how to calculate a discount rate, what goes into the continuing or terminal value, and some tricks of the trade. First, there is a brief section that works through the math for using formulas for company valuation. Before the advent of spreadsheets as a tool for valuation, formula approaches proved easier and were useful for providing insight into the fundamentals. Unfortunately, the assumptions of formula approaches are more confining than those in spreadsheets; therefore we go into the details of spreadsheet valuation. As our example we shall value Coca-Cola Enterprises (CCE).

The second half of the chapter introduces the interested reader to corporate tax policy. And who would not be interested? The only sure things in life are death and taxes. Corporations that are aggressive in using all of the legal means of avoiding taxes that are available to them are worth hundreds of millions of dollars more than less aggressive competitors. Most corporate finance textbooks, with the exception of Scholes, Wolfson, Erikson, Maydew, and Shevlin [2002] have little content on tax policy except insofar as it affects capital structure and dividend policy. Oddly, we shall refrain from covering these tax-related topics (as well as leasing versus borrowing) until the next few chapters. Instead, we shall investigate the value implications of net operating loss carry forwards, alternative minimum tax credits, accelerated depreciation, write-offs, transfer pricing, foreign tax credits, offshore operations, the write-off of goodwill, the realization of capital gains, the tax effects of diversification, and tax policy as it relates to mergers and acquisitions and to refinancing debt.

A. Formula Approach for Valuing Companies

The advantage of a formulaic approach to valuation is that it is compact and requires only a few input variables that are assumed to remain constant for all time. The disadvantage is that the

Figure 14.1 Time pattern of cash flows for a growing firm.

$$V_0 \qquad EBIT_1(1-T_c)-I_1 \qquad \begin{matrix} EBIT_2(1-T_c)-I_2 = \\ EBIT_1(1-T_c)+r_1I_1-I_2 \end{matrix} \qquad \cdots \qquad EBIT_1(1-T_c)+\sum_{t=1}^{N-1}r_tI_t-I_N$$

$$t_0 \qquad\qquad t_1 \qquad\qquad\qquad t_2 \qquad\qquad\qquad\qquad t_N$$

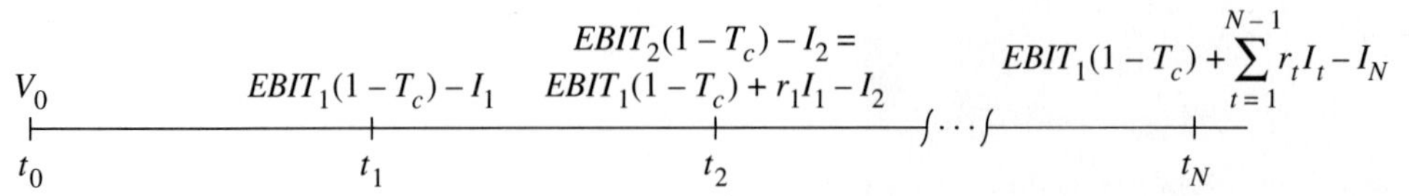

assumptions are too rigid to model reality as well as we would like. Nevertheless, the formulas provide clear demonstrations that the value of a firm can be partitioned into the value of assets in place plus the discounted value of future economic profits, that earnings growth per se is not an appropriate objective for the firm, and that firms that earn supernormal rates of return forever require use of a "value driver" or "supernormal growth" formula.

1. The Valuation of an All-Equity Firm with Growth

Figure 14.1 is a simple time line that graphically represents the pattern of cash flows for a growing firm. Note that there is a current level of cash flow from operations, $EBIT$, that is expected to be received at the end of each year forever. If the firm were to make no new capital investments, just maintain its current level of capital by making new investments that are equal to depreciation, then the firm would receive a constant perpetuity of $EBIT$ at the end of each year. Growth comes from new investment, not replacement investment. The value of new investment comes from both the rate of return (after taxes), r, and the amount, I, of new investment. For the current analysis we make the simplifying assumption that the firm has no debt. Therefore Eq. 14.1 discounts the firm's operating cash flows at the cost of capital, k_u, for the entity—the unlevered firm.[1]

$$V_0 = \frac{EBIT_1(1-T_c)-I_n}{1+k_u} + \frac{V_1}{1+k_u}. \tag{14.1}$$

The first term has expected cash flows in its numerator, reduced to an after-tax basis by multiplying $EBIT$ by one minus the cash tax rate, T_c.[2] If we simply make replacement equal to depreciation, then the capital stock is maintained. Note that since depreciation is a noncash charge, it would be added back to the numerator but would then be eliminated by subtraction of replacement investment. Thus I_n is interpreted as net new investment. The entity cash flows in the numerator of the first term are discounted one year by dividing by one plus the cost of capital for the unlevered cash flows, k_u. The second term is the value, V_1, of all of the cash flows received at the end of the second year and beyond, recorded as of the end of the first year and discounted for one year.

Next, we extend Eq. (14.1) by assuming that the discount rate remains constant. This is reasonable if all new investments have exactly the same risk as existing investments. The N-period extension can be written as follows:

$$V_0 = \frac{EBIT_1(1-T_c)-I_1}{1+k_u} + \frac{EBIT_2(1-T_c)-I_2}{(1+k_u)^2} + \cdots + \frac{EBIT_N(1-T_c)-I_N}{(1+k_u)^N}. \tag{14.2}$$

---

[1] Note that $EBIT_2(1-T_c) = EBIT_1(1-T_c)+r_1I_1$, where r_1 is the return on new capital invested.
[2] The cash tax rate is the average rate that would be levied on operating income (before interest income or expense). It is discussed in greater detail later in the chapter.

Table 14.1 Cash Flows for a Growing Firm

Time Period	Cash Inflow	Cash Outflow
1	$EBIT_1(1 - T_c)$	$-I_1$
2	$EBIT_2(1 - T_c) = EBIT_1(1 - T_c) + r_1I_1$	$-I_2$
3	$EBIT_3(1 - T_c) = EBIT_1(1 - T_c) + r_1I_1 + r_2I_2$	$-I_3$
$\vdots$	$\vdots$	$\vdots$
N	$EBIT_N(1 - T_c) = EBIT_1(1 - T_c) + \sum\limits_{t=1}^{N-1} r_tI_t$	$-I_N$

A reasonable assumption is that the value of the firm is finite in any time period.[3] Therefore, given a model with an infinite horizon, Eq. (14.2) becomes

$$V_0 = \lim_{N \to \infty} \sum_{t=1}^{N} \frac{EBIT_t \left(1 - T_c\right) - I_t}{(1 + k_u)^t}. \tag{14.3}$$

Equation (14.3) is exactly the same as the approach used in Chapter 2 on capital budgeting. The present value of the firm as an entity is the sum of its discounted cash flows from operations less the new investment outlays (for property, plant and equipment, and additions to operating working capital) necessary to provide for expected growth.

Referring to Table 14.1, we can see that the average return on new investment, r_t, is assumed to continue forever at a constant rate. Each project is assumed to generate enough cash to cover payments to suppliers of capital and to recover the initial investment. Thus, the cash flows from each year's investment are assumed to be sufficient to provide the necessary replacement investment to sustain the project at a constant level forever. The stream of cash flows for the growing firm in Figure 14.1 is shown in Table 14.1.

Substituting the cash flows of Table 14.1 into Eq. (14.3), we can express the present value of a growing firm as

$$V_0 = \frac{EBIT_1(1 - T_c) - I_1}{1 + k_u} + \frac{EBIT_1(1 - T_c) + r_1I_1 - I_2}{(1 + k_u)^2}$$

$$+ \frac{EBIT_1(1 - T_c) + r_1I_1 + r_2I_2 - I_3}{(1 + k_u)^3}$$

$$+ \cdots + \frac{EBIT_1(1 - T_c) + \sum\limits_{\tau=1}^{N-1} r_\tau I_\tau - I_N}{(1 + k_u)^N}. \tag{14.4}$$

---

[3] After all, no one has yet observed a firm with infinite value to date.

This extended equation can be simplified greatly. First, rewrite it by rearranging terms as follows:

$$V_0 = \frac{EBIT_1(1-T_c)_1}{1+k_u} + \frac{EBIT_1(1-T_c)}{(1+k_u)^2} + \cdots + \frac{EBIT_1(1-T_c)}{(1+k_u)^N}$$

$$+ I_1 \left[\frac{r_1}{(1+k_u)^2} + \frac{r_1}{(1+k_u)^3} + \cdots + \frac{r_1}{(1+k_u)^N} - \frac{1}{1+k_u} \right] \qquad (14.5)$$

$$+ I_2 \left[\frac{r_2}{(1+k_u)^3} + \frac{r_2}{(1+k_u)^4} + \cdots + \frac{r_2}{(1+k_u)^N} - \frac{1}{(1+k_u)^2} \right] + \cdots$$

This result can be generalized as

$$V_0 = \sum_{t=1}^{N} \frac{EBIT_1(1-T_c)}{(1+k_u)^t} + \sum_{t=1}^{N} I_t \left[\sum_{\tau=t+1}^{N} \frac{r_t}{(1+k_u)^\tau} - \frac{1}{(1+k_u)^t} \right]. \qquad (14.6)$$

We can simplify Eq. (14.6) further by recognizing that the first term is an infinite annuity with constant payments of $EBIT_1(1-T_c)$ per period. Therefore,

$$\lim_{N\to\infty} \sum_{t=1}^{N} \frac{EBIT_1(1-T_c)}{(1+k_u)^t} = \frac{EBIT_1(1-T_c)}{k_u}. \qquad (14.7)$$

Next, the second term in Eq. (14.6) can be simplified as follows:

$$\sum_{\tau=t+1}^{N} \frac{r_t}{(1+k_u)^\tau} = \frac{1}{(1+k_u)^t} \sum_{\tau=1}^{N-t} \frac{r_t}{(1+k_u)^\tau},$$

$$\frac{1}{(1+k_u)^t} \lim_{N\to\infty} \frac{r_t}{(1+k_u)^\tau} = \frac{1}{(1+k_u)^t} \frac{r_t}{k_u}. \qquad (14.8)$$

Substituting Eqs. (14.8) and (14.7) back into (14.6), we obtain a simplified expression for the present value of the firm:

$$V_0 = \lim_{N\to\infty} \left\{ \frac{EBIT_1(1-T_c)}{k_u} + \sum_{t=1}^{N} I_t \left[\left(\frac{r_t}{k_u(1+k_u)^t} \right) - \frac{1}{(1+k_u)^t} \right] \right\}$$

$$= \frac{EBIT_1(1-T_c)}{k_u} + \sum_{t=1}^{\infty} \frac{I_t(r_t - k_u)}{k_u(1+k_u)^t}$$

$$= \text{value of assets in place} + \text{value of future growth.} \qquad (14.9)$$

The interpretation of this formula is interesting. It can be thought of as proof that there are two mathematically equivalent ways of valuing the firm. First, we know that the value is equal to the sum of the firm's discounted free cash flows. That is the straightforward definition that we started with in Eq. (14.1). But an equivalent definition arises from Eq. (14.9). It says that the first term can be thought of as the book value of assets in place. The second term is the value of growth. Note that if the return on new investment, r_t, equals the cost of capital, k_u, no value is created and the value of growth will be zero. The numerator in the value of growth has been labeled "economic profit" in honor of Lord Alfred Marshall, who first described it in 1896, or EVA®, economic value added, as service-marked by Stern Stewart somewhat later. Economic profit, as we shall refer to it, is the spread over the cost of capital multiplied by the amount of new capital invested, I_n. For an all-equity firm it is defined as

$$\text{economic profit [given all equity]} = (r_t - k_u)I,$$

and for a levered firm it is defined as

$$\text{economic profit [for a levered firm]} = (ROIC - WACC)I. \qquad (14.10)$$

In order for a new investment to create value, it must earn a rate of return greater than the weighted average cost of capital (that is appropriate for the riskiness of the investment).

2. Why Maximizing the Growth in Earnings per Share Is an Inappropriate Goal

This form of valuation equation provides important insights into the much abused term *growth stock*. The first term in Eq. (14.9) is the present value of a firm that makes no investments. It is the present value of an infinite stream of constant cash flows. In other words it is the value of the firm that is not growing. It is the value of assets in place. But what about the firm that makes new investments? The present value of new investment is shown in the second term of Eq. (14.9). It is the present value of expected future growth. The *value* of new investment depends on two things: (1) the amount of investment made and (2) the difference between the average rate of return on the investment, r_t, and the market-required rate of return, k_u. The assets of a firm may grow, but they do not add anything to value unless they earn a rate greater than what the market requires for assets of equivalent risk. For example, supposing that the market requires a 10% rate of return (i.e., $k_u = 10\%$), consider the three situations in Table 14.2.

Firm 3 has the greatest "growth" in earnings ($\Delta(EBIT(1 - T_c) = 5,000)$). But which firm has the greatest increase in value? Obviously firm 1 does. The reason is that it is the only firm that has new investments that earn more than the required rate of return of 10%. Therefore the objective of a firm should *never* be to simply maximize growth in earnings or cash flows. The objective should be to maximize the market value of the firm, which is equivalent to maximizing wealth.

Another feature of Eq. (14.9) is that dividend policy is irrelevant and appears nowhere in the fundamental valuation of the firm. All that counts is cash flows from investment, namely, free cash flows. Later on we shall see that free cash flows from operations can be delivered to shareholders in a variety of ways, including dividends, but the choice of delivery is not what creates value.

Table 14.2 Earnings Growth Does Not Always Create Value

	ΔI	%r	$\$\Delta EBIT(1 - T_c)$	$\$\Delta V$
Firm 1	10,000	20	2,000	9,090
Firm 2	30,000	10	3,000	0
Firm 3	100,000	5	5,000	−45,454

Note: WACC = 10%.

3. The Value of an All-Equity Firm That Grows at a Constant Rate Forever

Equation (14.9) is elegant but somewhat cumbersome to use.[4] It has two useful variations. The first, which is developed below, assumes that the firm experiences a constant rate of growth forever. We shall call it the *infinite constant growth model*. The second, developed later on, assumes that the firm can maintain a supernormal rate of growth (where $r_t > k_u$) for a finite period of time, T, and realizes a normal rate of growth thereafter. It is called the *finite supernormal growth model*.

The constant growth model can be derived from (14.9) if we assume that a constant fraction, K, of earnings is retained for investment and the average rate of return, r_t, on all projects is the same. The fraction of $EBIT(1 - T_c)$ to be retained for investment is usually called the *retention ratio;* however, there is no reason to restrict it to be less than 100% of cash flows from operations. Rather than calling K the retention rate, we shall call it the *investment rate*. The firm can invest more than cash flow from operations if it provides for the funds by issuing new equity. If investment is a constant proportion of cash flows, we have

$$I_t = K(EBIT_t(1 - T_c)). \tag{14.11}$$

And if the rate of return on investment, r_t, is the same for every project, then

$$EBIT_t(1 - T_c) = EBIT(1 - T_c) + rI_{t-1}$$

$$= EBIT(1 - T_c) + rK(EBIT_{t-1}(1 - T_c))$$

$$= EBIT_{t-1}(1 - T_c)(1 + rK). \tag{14.12}$$

By successive substitution, we have

$$EBIT_t(1 - T_c) = EBIT_1(1 - T_c)(1 + rK)^{t-1}. \tag{14.13}$$

Note that rK is the same as the rate of growth, g, for cash flows. In other words, *EBIT* in the tth time period is the future value of *EBIT* in the first time period, assuming that cash flows grow at a constant rate, g:

$$EBIT(1 - T_c) = EBIT_1(1 - T_c)(1 + g)^{t-1}. \tag{14.14}$$

By substituting (14.11) into (14.9) and maintaining the assumption that $r_t = r$, we have

$$V_0 = \frac{EBIT(1 - T_c)}{k_u} + \sum_{t=1}^{\infty} \frac{K(EBIT_t(1 - T_c))(r - k_u)}{k_u(1 + k_u)^t}. \tag{14.15}$$

Then by using (14.13) in (14.15) we obtain

$$V_0 = \frac{EBIT(1 - T_c)}{k_u} + K\left[EBIT_1(1 - T_c)\right]\left(\frac{r - k_u}{k_u}\right)\sum_{t=1}^{\infty}\frac{(1 + rK)^{t-1}}{(1 + k_u)^t}$$

$$= \frac{EBIT_1(1 - T_c)}{k_u}\left[1 + \frac{K(r - k_u)}{1 + rK}\sum_{t=1}^{\infty}\left(\frac{1 + rK}{1 + k_u}\right)^t\right]. \tag{14.16}$$

---

[4] However, do not underestimate the usefulness of Eq. (14.9). It is the basis for most commonly used valuation models, for example, ALCAR, which is a personal-computer-based model designed by Professor Al Rappaport of Northwestern.

If $rK < k_u$, then the last term in (14.16) will have a finite limit:[5]

$$\lim_{N \to \infty} \sum_{t=1}^{N} \left(\frac{1+rK}{1+k_u} \right)^t = \frac{1+rK}{k_u - rK} \quad \text{iff} \quad k_u > rK. \tag{14.16a}$$

Substituting (14.16a) into (14.16) and simplifying, we have an equation for the value of the firm, assuming infinite growth at a rate less than the opportunity cost of capital, k_u:

$$V_0 = \frac{EBIT_1(1 - T_c)}{k_u} \left[1 + \frac{K(r - k_u)}{1 + Kr} \frac{1 + Kr}{k_u - rK} \right]$$

$$= \frac{EBIT_1(1 - T_c)(1 - K)}{k_u - Kr}. \tag{14.17}$$

Equation (14.17), rewritten in a somewhat different form, is frequently referred to as the *Gordon growth model*. Note that since K is the investment rate (although K need not be less than one), the numerator of (14.17) is the same as dividends paid at the end of the first time period:

$$EBIT_1(1 - T_c)(1 - K) = Div_1.$$

Also, as was shown earlier, the product of the investment rate and the average rate of return on investment is the same as the growth rate, g, in cash flows; therefore

$$Kr = g. \tag{14.17a}$$

Given these facts and the necessary condition that $g < k_u$, the infinite growth model, Eq. (14.17) can be rewritten as

$$V_0 = \frac{Div_1}{k_u - g}, \tag{14.17b}$$

which is called the Gordon growth model.

4. Finite Supernormal Growth Model for an All-Equity Firm

Perhaps the most useful variation of the valuation equation is one that assumes that the rate of return on investment is greater than the market-required rate of return for a finite number of years, T, and from then on is equal to the market-required rate of return. In other words the firm experiences supernormal growth for a short period of time, then settles down and grows at a rate that is equal to the rate of growth in the economy. Obviously a firm cannot grow faster than the economy forever or it would soon be larger than the economy.

---

[5] For proof let $(1 + rK)/(1 + k_u) = U$. This can be written as

$$S = U + U^2 + \cdots + U^N.$$

Multiplying this by U and subtracting the result from the above, we have

$$S = U/(1 - U) - U^{N+1}/(1 - U).$$

The second term approaches zero in the limit as N approaches infinity. By substituting back the definition of U, we get (14.16a).

To derive the finite supernormal growth model, we start with Eq. (14.16). Note that the summation is no longer infinite:

$$V_0 = \frac{EBIT_1(1 - T_c)}{k_u} \left[1 + \frac{K(r - k_u)}{1 + rK} \sum_{t=1}^{N} \left(\frac{1 + rK}{1 + k_u} \right)^t \right].$$

Instead, growth lasts for only N years. After year N, we assume that $r = k_u$, which means that the second term adds nothing to the present value of the firm. Whenever a firm is earning a rate of return just equal to its cost of capital, the net present value of investment is zero.

The summation term in Eq. (14.16) can be evaluated as follows. Let

$$U = [(1 + rK)/(1 + k_u)].$$

We can then expand the sum:

$$S = U + U^2 + \cdots + U^N.$$

Multiplying this by U and subtracting the result, we have

$$S - US = U - U^{N+1}.$$

Solving for S and substituting back for U, we obtain

$$S = \frac{U - U^{N+1}}{1 - U} = \frac{\left[(1 + Kr)/(1 + k_u) \right] - \left[(1 + Kr)/(1 + k_u) \right]^{N+1}}{1 - \left[(1 + Kr)/(1 + k_u) \right]}$$

$$= \frac{(1 + Kr)\left\{ 1 - \left[(1 + Kr)/(1 + k_u) \right]^N \right\}}{k_u - Kr}.$$

(14.16b)

Substituting (14.16b) into (14.16) yields

$$V_0 = \frac{EBIT_1(1 - T_c)}{k_u} \left\{ 1 + \frac{Kr - k_u K}{k_u - Kr} \left[1 - \left(\frac{1 + Kr}{1 + k_u} \right)^N \right] \right\}.$$

(14.18)

As long as Kr is approximately equal to k_u and N is small, we can approximate the last term as[6]

$$\left(\frac{1 + Kr}{1 + k_u} \right)^N \approx 1 - N \left(\frac{k_u - Kr}{1 + k_u} \right).$$

(14.19)

---

[6] The binomial expansion can be used to derive the approximation in the following way. Let $(1 + Kr)/(1 + k_u) = 1 + \Delta$. Then, recalling that $Kr = g$, we have

$$\left(\frac{1 + g}{1 + k_u} \right)^N = (1 + \Delta)^N = \sum_{K=0}^{N} \binom{N}{K} (1)^{N-K} \Delta^K$$

$$= 1 + N\Delta + \sum_{K=2}^{N} \binom{N}{K} \Delta^K \approx 1 + N\Delta.$$

By substituting the approximation (14.19) into the valuation equation (14.18), we have an approximate valuation formula for finite supernormal growth:[7]

$$V_0 = \frac{EBIT_1(1 - T_c)}{k_u} + \frac{K(r - k_u)}{k_u - Kr} N \left(\frac{k_u - Kr}{1 + k_u}\right) \frac{EBIT_1(1 - T_c)}{k_u}$$

$$= \frac{EBIT_1(1 - T_c)}{k_u} + K(EBIT_1(1 - T_c))N \left[\frac{r - k_u}{k_u(1 + k_u)}\right]. \tag{14.20}$$

5. Finite Supernormal Growth Model for a Firm with Debt and Taxes

Up to this point, we have maintained the assumption that we are dealing with an all-equity firm. To extend the above valuation equation into a world where firms have debt as well as equity, we discount at the weighted average cost of capital, *WACC*, rather than the unlevered cost of equity, k_u. Therefore, the value of a levered firm with finite supernormal growth can be written as follows:

$$V_0 = \frac{EBIT_1(1 - T_c)}{k_u}$$

$$+ T_c B + K \left[EBIT_1(1 - T_c)\right] N \left[\frac{r - WACC}{WACC(1 + WACC)}\right], \tag{14.21}$$

Solving for Δ, we have

$$\Delta = \frac{1 + Kr}{1 + k_u} - 1 = \frac{Kr - k_u}{1 + k_u}.$$

Therefore the correct approximation is

$$1 + N\Delta = 1 - N \left(\frac{k_u - Kr}{1 + k_u}\right).$$

[7] To simulate the validity of the approximation, assume that the investment rate, K, is 50%, the rate of return on investment, r, is 20%, and the market-required rate of return is 15%. The following figure is a plot of $[(1 + Kr)/(1 + k_u)]$. We can see visually that the linear approximation is reasonable.

Figure 14A
The linear approximation of the growth term.

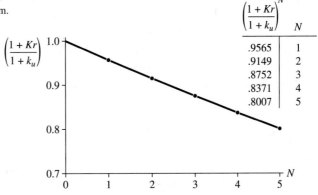

$\left(\dfrac{1 + Kr}{1 + k_u}\right)^N$	N
.9565	1
.9149	2
.8752	3
.8371	4
.8007	5

where

$$EBIT_1(1 - T_c) = \text{end-of-year earnings before interest and taxes, times } (1 - T_c)_1$$

$$WACC = \text{weighted average cost of capital,}$$

$$B = \text{market value of debt,}$$

$$K = \text{investment rate,}$$

$$N = \text{the number of years that } r > WACC,$$

$$r = \text{the average rate of return on investment,}$$

$$k_u = \text{the cost of equity capital for an all-equity firm.}$$

The first two terms in (14.21) add up to the value of a levered firm with no growth (i.e., the value of assets in place). The third term in Eq. (14.21) is the value of growth for the levered firm. It depends on the amount of investment, $I_t = K(EBIT_1(1 - T_c))$; the difference between the expected average rate of return on investment and the weighted average cost of capital, $r - WACC$; and the length of time, N, that the new investment is expected to earn more than the weighted average cost of capital.

B. $\mathcal{S}$preadsheet Approach for Valuing Companies

Before the advent of personal computers the amount of work needed to complete a thorough discounted cash flow analysis of a company was much too time-consuming to be practical in most applications. Very few companies actually tried to implement value-based planning, and most DCF valuations utilized primitive versions of the formula approach that was described in the prior section of this chapter. Since the 1990s, given the easy access to spreadsheets on personal computers, more and more managers are using value-based approaches to planning and control because the greater complexity of managing value has been overcome. This section of the chapter provides sufficient detail to allow the reader to value a company using explicitly forecasted spreadsheets.[8] Figure 14.2 shows the steps involved.

1. The Entity Approach

We are using the *entity approach* to valuation. We first value the free cash flows from operations by discounting them at the weighted average cost of capital. The result is the value of the entity that arises from normal operations. To this is added the present value nonoperating cash flows, for example, marketable securities. The result is the total entity value. We then subtract the market value of debt and other liabilities (e.g., unfunded pension plan liabilities and preferred stock) in order to estimate the market value of equity (see Figure 14.3).

The entity approach to valuing a company is the same as the capital budgeting approach for valuing projects that was described in Chapter 2—free cash flows are defined as after-tax operating cash flows net of gross investment and net increases in working capital. They are assumed to be completely independent of choices about how the company (or the project) is financed and are

---

[8] For a more complete presentation, the reader is referred to T. Copeland, T. Koller, and J. Murrin, *Valuation: Measuring and Managing the Value of Companies*, 3rd edition, John Wiley & Co., New York, 2001.

Figure 14.2 Steps in performing a spreadsheet DCF valuation.

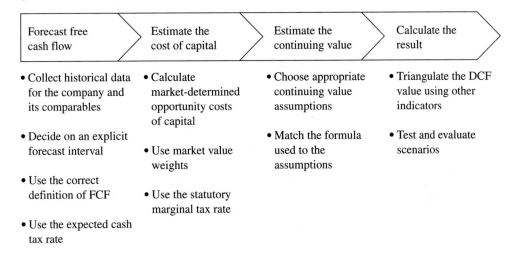

Forecast free cash flow	Estimate the cost of capital	Estimate the continuing value	Calculate the result
• Collect historical data for the company and its comparables	• Calculate market-determined opportunity costs of capital	• Choose appropriate continuing value assumptions	• Triangulate the DCF value using other indicators
• Decide on an explicit forecast interval	• Use market value weights	• Match the formula used to the assumptions	• Test and evaluate scenarios
• Use the correct definition of FCF	• Use the statutory marginal tax rate		
• Use the expected cash tax rate			

Figure 14.3 The entity approach to valuation.

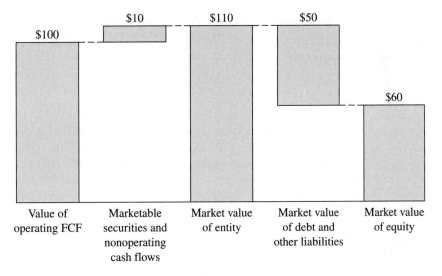

discounted at the weighted average cost of capital. Operating cash flows exclude any financial flows such as interest income and interest expense. The value impact of financing, if any, is reflected entirely in the weighted average cost of capital. As we shall see, operating cash flows and financial cash flows are equal and opposite.

2. Components of Operating Free Cash Flows

Table 14.3 gives the income statements for a hypothetical company, and Table 14.4 gives its balance sheets.

Table 14.3 ABC Company Income Statements

	2003	2004
Revenues	$14,500	$15,000
− Cost of goods sold	(9,667)	(10,000)
− Selling, general, and administrative expense	(2,667)	(3,100)
− Depreciation	(387)	(400)
− Goodwill amortization*	(20)	(20)
= Operating income	$1,430	$1,480
+ Interest income	15	17
− Interest expense	(404)	(434)
= Income before income taxes	$1,011	$1,066
− Provision for income taxes	(495)	(426)**
= Net income	$516	$640
− Dividends	(161)	(200)
= Addition to retained earnings	$355	$440

* Not a deductible expense for tax purposes; therefore, in 2004, *EBIT* = operating income plus goodwill = $1,500.
** Remember that depreciation on a company's tax books is often different than its annual report (e.g., accelerated vs. straight line). Therefore the tax rate implied by the income statement (i.e., $426/$1066 = .40) is usually different from the actual marginal rate (i.e., .42).

These statements are used to estimate free cash flows both historically and during the explicit forecast period that is chosen for analysis. Table 14.5 shows the estimated free cash flows. Note that the cash flows are estimated two ways. First are cash flows from operations, and second are financial flows. These two independent estimates must equal each other. Cash flows from operations are used to make financial payments to providers of debt and equity. Financial flows include all interest-earning or interest-paying financial securities as well as equity. The following paragraphs define each of the major components of operating free cash flows.

EARNINGS BEFORE INTEREST AND TAXES (EBIT) EBIT is the pretax income that a company would have earned if it had no debt. It includes all types of "operating" income (the distinction between operating and nonoperating cash flows is described later). It is often equal to the line "operating income" on the company's income statement. Depreciation should be subtracted in calculating EBIT, but goodwill amortization should not.

TAXES ON EBIT Taxes on EBIT represent the income taxes that are attributable to EBIT. They were represented as T_c in the formula approach earlier in the chapter. They are the taxes the company would pay if it had no debt or excess marketable securities. They equal the total income tax provision (current and deferred) adjusted for the income taxes attributed to interest expense, interest income, and nonoperating items. Using figures for our ABC Company, 2004 taxes on EBIT are calculated as follows:

Table 14.4 ABC Company Balance Sheets

	2002	2003	2004
Cash	$87	$90	$100
+ Excess marketable securities	308	320	300
+ Accounts receivable	2,800	2,900	3,000
+ Inventories	3,200	3,310	3,400
= Short-term assets	$6,395	$6,620	$6,800
Gross property, plant, and equipment	7,000	7,500	8,000
− Accumulated depreciation	(2,400)	(2,700)	(3,000)
= Net property, plant, and equipment	$4,600	$4,800	$5,000
+ Goodwill	540	520	500
+ Other assets	920	950	1,000
= Total assets	$12,455	$12,890	$13,300
Short-term debt	$1,060	$1,030	$1,000
+ Accounts payable	1,980	2,050	2,000
+ Accrued liabilities	880	900	1,000
= Short-term liabilities	$3,920	$3,980	$4,000
+ Long-term debt	3,400	3,500	3,500
+ Accumulated deferred taxes	380	400	500
= Total liabilities	7,700	7,880	8,000
Common shares	1,250	1,150	1,000
+ Retained earnings	3,505	3,860	4,300
= Total shareholders' equity	$4,755	$5,010	$5,300
Total liabilities and shareholders' equity	$12,455	$12,890	$13,300

Total income tax provision from income statement	$426
+ Tax shield on interest expense (.42 × 434)	181
− Tax on interest income (.42 × 17)	(7)
− Tax on nonoperating income	0
= Taxes on EBIT	$600

The taxes related to interest expense, interest income, and nonoperating items are calculated by multiplying the marginal tax rate by the item. (The marginal tax rate is generally the statutory marginal rate, including state and local taxes. However, companies with tax loss carry-forwards or those subject to the alternative minimum tax may have different marginal rates.)

Table 14.5 ABC Company Free Cash Flows

Operating Cash Flows	2003	2004
Earnings before interest and taxes (EBIT)	$1,450	$1,500
− Taxes on EBIT	(701)	(600)
+ Change in deferred taxes	20	100
= Net operating profit less adjusted taxes (NOPLAT)	$769	$1,000
+ Depreciation	387	400
= Gross cash flow	$1,156	$1,400
Increase in working capital	123	150
+ Capital expenditures	587	600
+ Investment in goodwill	0	0
+ Increase in net other assets	30	50
= Gross investment	$740	$800
Gross cash flow	1,156	1,400
− Gross investment	(740)	(800)
= Free cash flow from operations	$416	$600
+ Nonoperating cash flow	0	0
= Total free cash flow	$416	$600
Financial Flows		
Change in excess marketable securities	$12	$(20)
− After-tax interest income*	(8)	(10)
+ Decrease in debt	(70)	30
+ After-tax interest expense*	221	250
+ Dividends	161	200
+ Share repurchase	100	150
= Total financial flow	$416	$600

* Marginal tax rates of 53% in 2003 and 42% in 2004 were used to calculate after-tax interest income and expense.

CHANGE IN DEFERRED TAXES For valuation purposes, taxes should be stated on a cash basis. The provision for income taxes in the income statement generally does not equal the actual taxes paid in cash by the company due to differences between GAAP accounting and accounting for taxes. The adjustment to a cash basis can be calculated from the change in accumulated deferred income taxes on the company's balance sheet. An increase in deferred taxes is a source of cash.

NET OPERATING PROFIT LESS ADJUSTED TAXES (NOPLAT) NOPLAT represents the after-tax operating profits of the company after adjusting taxes to a cash basis. It is important because it is used in the calculation of the rate of the return on invested capital. NOPLAT is equal to EBIT$(1 - T_c)$ in the formula valuation model we discussed in the previous section of this chapter. The EBIT cash tax rate, T_c, is $\$600/\$1,500 = 40\%$.

DEPRECIATION Depreciation includes all the noncash charges deducted from EBIT except goodwill amortization (which is not added back to NOPLAT because it was not deducted in calculating NOPLAT). It also includes the amortization of intangible assets with definite lives such as patents and franchises.

GROSS CASH FLOW Gross cash flow represents the total cash flow thrown off by the company. It is the amount available to reinvest in the business for maintenance and growth without relying on additional capital.

CHANGE IN WORKING CAPITAL The change in operating working capital is the amount the company invested in working capital during the period. Only *operating* capital should be included. Nonoperating assets, excess marketable securities, and interest-bearing liabilities (short-term debt and the current portion of long-term debt) are excluded because they are financing flows, not operating cash flows. The measure is the change in current assets (excluding marketable securities) less current liabilities (excluding short-term debt and the current portion of long-term debt).

CAPITAL EXPENDITURES Capital expenditures include expenditures on new and replacement property, plant, and equipment. Capital expenditures can be calculated as the increase in *net* property, plant, and equipment on the balance sheet plus depreciation expense (taken from the income statement) for the period. (Technically, this calculation results in capital expenditures less the net book value of retired assets.) Capital expenditures are estimated this way (rather than by looking at the changes in gross PP&E) because assets sold during the year are removed from the balance sheet but their depreciation up to the time of sale remains on the income statements.

INVESTMENT IN GOODWILL The investment in goodwill equals the amount of expenditure to acquire another company in excess of the book value of its net assets. Theoretically, goodwill has an indefinite life and should always be stated on a gross basis—that is, before accumulated amortization. In any year, the investment in goodwill is best calculated as the net change in the goodwill account on the balance sheet plus the amortization of goodwill in that period. This ensures that goodwill amortization does not affect free cash flow in either gross cash flow or gross investment.

In 2001 the passage of Financial Accounting Standards Board (FASB) statement 142 required that although goodwill will still be recognized as an asset, it will not be amortized. Instead, goodwill and other intangibles will be subjected to an annual test of impairment of value. If the carrying amount of the goodwill is deemed to exceed its fair value, then an impairment loss is recognized as a separate line item.

INCREASE IN NET OTHER ASSETS The increase in net other assets equals the expenditure on all other operating assets including capitalized intangibles (patents, trademarks), deferred expenses, and net of increases in noncurrent, noninterest-bearing liabilities. These can be calculated directly from the change in the balance sheet accounts plus any amortization included in depreciation.

GROSS INVESTMENT Gross investment is the sum of the company's expenditures for new capital, including working capital, capital expenditures, goodwill, and other assets.

3. Nonoperating Cash Flow

Nonoperating cash flow represents the after-tax cash flow from items not related to operations. Free cash flow does not include nonoperating cash flow. Any nonoperating cash flow must be reflected in the value of the company explicitly. We do this by defining the total value of the company as the discounted present value of the company's free cash flow plus the value of its after-tax nonoperating cash flow.

$$\begin{array}{ccc}
\text{present value of} & & \text{present value of} & & \\
\text{company's free} & + & \text{after-tax nonoperating} & = & \text{total value} \\
\text{cash flow} & & \text{cash flow} & & \text{of company}
\end{array}$$

Cash flow items that are sometimes considered nonoperating include cash flow from discounted operations, extraordinary items, and the cash flow from investments in unrelated subsidiaries. Remember, though, that the present value of any nonoperating cash flow must be reflected in the total value of the company.

It is generally not advisable to consider a recurring cash flow as nonoperating. The company's risk and therefore its cost of capital reflects all its assets and its cash flow. Arbitrarily excluding items from free cash flow may violate the principle of consistency between free cash flow and the cost of capital. The lower half of Table 14.5 shows the calculation of financial flows. For every dollar of operating free cash flows, there is an equal and opposite dollar of financial flows. If operating free cash flow is positive, then it is available for payment to financial claimants (e.g., as dividends, share repurchases, or debt repayment). Of course, the opposite is true if operating free cash flow is negative. When this happens, financing must flow into the firm.

4. Components of Financial Flows

CHANGE IN EXCESS MARKETABLE SECURITIES

Changes in excess marketable securities and the related interest income are considered financial cash flows for two reasons:

1. Excess marketable securities generally represent temporary imbalances in the company's cash flow. For example, the company may build up cash while deciding what to do with it. These excess marketable securities are not generally directly related to the company's operating decisions.

2. Considering these changes as financial cash flow makes valuation easier. Marketable securities are generally much less risky than the operations of the firm. As marketable securities grow or decline in relation to the size of the company, the company's overall level of risk and its cost of capital should rise or fall. Modeling the change in the cost of capital is complex. It is much easier to consider the value of a company as the sum of the value of its operating free cash flow plus the present value of the cash flow related to its excess marketable securities, where the risk of each component is relatively stable over time.

Excess marketable securities are the short-term cash investments that the company holds over and above its target cash balances to support operations. The target balances can be estimated by observing the variability in the company's cash and marketable security balances over time and by comparing against similar companies.

Excess marketable securities and their counterpart, unscheduled debt, are used as "plug" figures in the balance sheet forecasts. When your forecasts imply that the company is generating positive cash flows, then excess marketable securities will go up. Conversely, if your forecasts imply that the company is in trouble, then excess marketable securities will fall to zero and unscheduled debt will build up.

Recognize also that the investment in marketable securities or the buildup of unscheduled debt (government securities and commercial paper) is a zero net present value investment. The return on this investment just compensates for its risk. Therefore, the present value of the cash flow related to these marketable securities must equal the market value of the excess marketable securities on the company's books at the time of the valuation.

AFTER-TAX INTEREST INCOME   The after-tax income on excess marketable securities equals the pretax income times one minus the firm's marginal statutory income tax rate, T_m. The marginal tax rate should be consistent with the rate used for the adjustment of the provisions for income taxes when calculating the EBIT cash tax rate.

CHANGE IN DEBT   The change in debt represents the net borrowing or repayment on all the company's debt, including short-term debt.

AFTER-TAX INTEREST EXPENSE   The after-tax interest expense equals the pretax interest expense times one minus the company's statutory marginal income tax rate ($T_m = 42\%$ in 2004). The marginal tax rate should be consistent with the rate used for the adjustment of taxes on EBIT.

DIVIDENDS   Dividends include all cash dividends on common and preferred shares.

SHARE ISSUES/REPURCHASES   Share issues/repurchases include both preferred and common shares and the effects of conversions of debt to equity. This figure can be calculated by taking the change in total equity plus dividends less net income.

5. Special Items

The foregoing items are fairly standard for most companies. A number of special items may also be relevant, including operating leases, pensions, minority interest, investments in unconsolidated subsidiaries, and foreign currency translation gains/losses.

Operating leases are any lease obligations that the company has not capitalized. Operating leases represent a type of financing and should be treated as such. Therefore, we often adjust the company's financial statements to treat operating leases as if they were capitalized. First, reclassify the implied interest expense portion of the lease payments from an operating expense (usually in cost of goods sold, or selling, general, and administrative expense) to an interest expense. This increases EBIT by the amount of implied interest. Do not forget to adjust the EBIT taxes as well.

Also, reflect changes in the implied principal amount of the leases in gross investment and the change in debt. This mimics the effects that would have occurred had the leases been capitalized. The principal amount of the leases must be estimated by discounting expected future operating lease expenses at the before-tax cost of debt. The implied interest expense is the principal amount times an appropriate interest rate. Next, change the cost of capital by adding the amount of capitalized operating lease to debt. This will lower your estimate of WACC. Note that so far the changes from capitalizing operating leases have increased EBIT and decreased the WACC. The net effect is to increase our estimate of the entity value. Offsetting this result will be the subtraction of the amount of the capitalized operating lease from the higher entity value (because the capitalized operating lease is now treated, like debt, as financing).

The company's *pension costs* are included in the cost of goods sold, or selling, general, and administrative expense. Normally, nothing special need be done in the free cash flow or the valuation related to pensions. If the company has a significant overfunded or underfunded plan, however, care must be taken to ensure that the related cash flow is treated consistently in the valuation. Overfunded or underfunded pension plans can be handled in one of two ways:

1. Adjust the forecasted pension expense so that the overfunded or underfunded pension is eliminated over time. Do not treat the current amount of overfunding or underfunding as a separate item in the valuation because that would be double counting.

2. Do not reflect the overfunding or underfunding in the pension expense forecast. The current amount of the after-tax overfunding or underfunding must be included as a separate item added to or subtracted from the entity valuation.

A *minority interest* occurs when a third party owns some percentage of one of the company's consolidated subsidiaries. The related cash flow should be included as part of the company's financial flow since a minority interest is simply another form of financing. The relevant cash flow amount equals the income statement amount less the change in the minority interest on the balance sheet. This should equal the dividends paid to the minority shareholder less any capital contributions received by the company from the minority shareholders.

The cash flow associated with *unconsolidated subsidiaries* can be handled in one of two ways:

1. Include the cash flow in the free cash flow forecast.

2. Exclude the cash flow from free cash flow but include the present value of the cash flow as a separate item in the valuation.

The first approach is simpler and should be used unless the amount of cash flow is material in size, and the operations of the subsidiary are not related to the core operations of the company. The first approach is recommended because the company's cost of capital probably reflects its holdings in these subsidiaries. Excluding the subsidiaries could violate the consistency between free cash flow and cost of capital.

The related cash flow can be calculated by subtracting the balance sheet increases in the investment-in-subsidiaries account from the income related to the subsidiaries (this works whether they are accounted for on the equity or cost method). The cash flow should also be adjusted for related income taxes.

The change in the cumulative *foreign currency translation gains or losses* account is driven by the changes in translation rates applied to both assets and debt. As a practical matter, you generally cannot separate the asset and the debt gains or losses without good historical internal information. Therefore, treat these gains/losses as nonoperating cash flow in the free cash flow. If you have the information needed to separate the asset from the debt effects, treat the gains/losses on assets as adjustments to free cash flows and the gains/losses on debt as financial cash flow. (See Financial Accounting Standards Board Statement No. 52 for a complete discussion of foreign currency accounting.)

Your forecast of expected future foreign exchange gains or losses should be zero. If you really can make an accurate forecast of foreign exchange gains or losses you do not need to worry about valuing companies because you can make a fortune speculating in foreign currency markets. If markets are reasonably efficient, it should not be possible to forecast abnormal returns.

6. The Equivalence of Economic Profit and DCF Approaches

Recall that Chapter 13 recommended using the difference between actual and expected economic profit as the best short-term measure of performance. Equation (14.10) linked economic profit to the formula approach to valuation, and this section of Chapter 14 shows how to link economic profit to the discounted cash flow valuation of a company using spreadsheets. A simple example will suffice. A firm invests $1,000 then earns $EBIT(1 - T_c)$ of $100 per year forever by investing an amount equal to depreciation in order to maintain its capital base. Its cost of capital is 8%. If we use the entity approach and calculate free cash flow, we will get

$$FCF = EBIT(1 - T_c) + \text{depreciation} - \text{investment}$$

$$= \$100 \quad \text{since depreciation} = \text{investment}$$

$$\text{value} = FCF/WACC = \$100/.08 = \$1,250.$$

Economic profit looks at the same valuation a different but equivalent way. It discounts the forecasted economic profit and adds back the amount of original invested capital at the beginning of the period. Economic profit is defined as

$$EP = (ROIC - WACC)(\text{invested capital})$$

$$= (10\% - 8\%)(\$1,000) = \$20.$$

If we discount the perpetual stream of economic profit at the cost of capital and add back the original book value of invested capital, we have

$$\text{value} = (ROIC - WACC)(\text{invested capital})/WACC + WACC(\text{invested capital})/WACC$$

$$= [ROIC(\text{invested capital}) - WACC(\text{invested capital}) + WACC(\text{invested capital})]/WACC$$

$$= ROIC(\text{invested capital})/WACC$$

$$= EBIT(1 - T_c)/WACC$$

$$= FCF/WACC.$$

Thus, the two approaches always provide the same value. If we substitute the numbers into the first line of the above equation, we get a value of $1,250 as before:

$$\text{value} = EP/WACC + \text{invested capital}$$

$$\text{value} = (.10 - .08)(\$1,000)/.08 + \$1,000 = \$20/.08 + \$1,000 = \$250 + \$1,000 = \$1,250.$$

A more realistic spreadsheet example is provided in the next section, where we value Coca-Cola Enterprises (CCE).

7. An Example DCF: Coca-Cola Enterprises

Coca-Cola is a beverage company with one of the strongest brand names anywhere. The parent company produces syrup using a formula that is a closely guarded trade secret and owns interests in bottling and distribution companies located all around the globe. Our valuation was done at the end of March 2000; although the market price per share was $47.43, our discounted cash flow estimate of the price per share was $49.38—a difference of 3.9%. If you want to construct your own valuation model, you can copy our format that is in the tables below and then fill in the numbers for the company that you wish to value. During our discussion of the DCF model, we will cover forecasts of expected free cash flows (to the entity) during an explicit 10-year forecast period, estimating the weighted average cost of capital that is used to discount the free cash flows, and the

Figure 14.4 Valuation summary of Coca-Cola (billions of dollars).

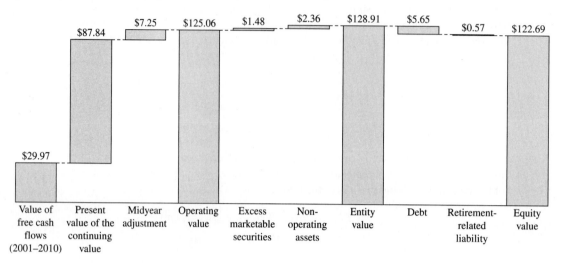

Value of free cash flows (2001–2010)	Present value of the continuing value	Midyear adjustment	Operating value	Excess marketable securities	Non-operating assets	Entity value	Debt	Retirement-related liability	Equity value
$29.97	$87.84	$7.25	$125.06	$1.48	$2.36	$128.91	$5.65	$0.57	$122.69

use of a continuing (or terminal) value formula to value cash flows beyond the explicit forecast period.

FORECASTING FREE CASH FLOWS Figure 14.4 summarizes our approach and the results. The first two bars are the present value of operating cash flows. The first, amounting to $29.97 billion, is the present value of the cash flows during the explicit forecast period. The second is the present value of cash flows during the so-called continuing value period (i.e., years 2011 and beyond), amounting to $87.84 billion. Thus, 74.6% of the total value of Coke is derived from cash flows that are forecasted to occur after 2010. It is not unusual to have 50% or more of the total value of a company come from the continuing value period.

The third bar is called the midyear adjustment factor. It can be explained as a timing shift that accounts for the fact that we are valuing the company at the end of March 2000 while the model assumes that free cash flows arrive at midyear. Figure 14.5 shows that the midyear cash flows are then discounted at an annual rate (the weighted average cost of capital) in yearly increments back to the middle of 1999. Therefore, the DCF model provides a base case valuation, V_0, as of July 1, 1999. But we want a valuation as of March 31, 2000—nine months later. The value that we want is estimated as the base case value multiplied by a factor that is equal to the nine-month cost of capital, namely, $(1.083)^{9/12} = 1.062$. Of course this is an approximation because it implicitly assumes that all cash flows remain in the firm.

To derive an estimate of free cash flows it is necessary to forecast the income statement and balance sheet. Doing so in a way that insures that they are mutually consistent can be quite a challenge. Most of our assumptions are embedded in Table 14.6, the income statement; Table 14.7, the balance sheet; and Table 14.8, the free cash flows. Wherever possible we compared our forecasts with those of analysts. For example, the average revenue growth forecast, taken from reports by Credit Suisse First Boston, Morgan Stanley Dean Witter, and Value Line, was 4.8% for 2000, 8.5% for 2001, 8.9% for 2002, and 7.5% for the next three years. We assumed rates of 4.8%, 8.0%, 7.0% for 2000–2002, and then 6.2% for two years. The analysts' operating margin was 28.3% in the long run—ours was 27.7%. A common forecasting error is the failure to adequately

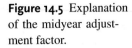

Figure 14.5 Explanation of the midyear adjustment factor.

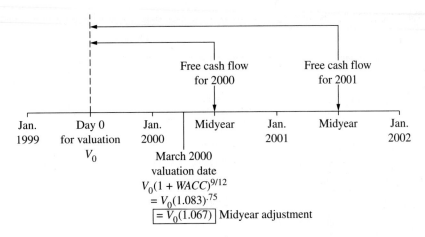

Free cash flow for 2000   Free cash flow for 2001

Jan. 1999   Day 0 for valuation V_0 Jan. 2000   Midyear   Jan. 2001   Midyear   Jan. 2002

March 2000 valuation date
$$V_0(1 + WACC)^{9/12}$$
$$= V_0(1.083)^{.75}$$
$$\boxed{= V_0(1.067)} \text{ Midyear adjustment}$$

tie capital expenditures to sales growth. When this happens, the turnover ratio (sales per dollar of invested capital) increases rapidly, as does the estimated return on invested capital (ROIC). This implies that there is inadequate investment to actually support the forecasted sales growth. As a result free cash flows are overestimated and the company is overvalued. It is nearly impossible to diagnose this problem without forecasting a complete balance sheet, because invested capital must be calculated before one can examine the capital turnover ratio. In Table 14.8, after-tax ROIC stays relatively constant at 37–38% throughout the forecast period, indicating that the forecasts of revenue on the income statement and invested capital on the balance sheet are consistent with each other.

One of the "tricks" of building a balance sheet is the addition of two special lines. On the assets side of the balance sheet, Table 14.7, there is a line item called excess cash/marketable securities. It grows whenever the firm is generating cash and shrinks whenever it needs to go to the capital markets as a source of cash. On the liabilities side is a line called short-term debt (sometimes called "unscheduled" debt). It is the contra account to excess marketable securities. When the firm needs cash, unscheduled (or short-term) debt increases, and when the firm generates excess cash it decreases. These two lines insure that the balance sheet will balance. Neither of these "plugs" is included in operating free cash flows, nor is the interest income or expense that they generate. They are financial cash flows that neither create nor destroy value. Only their current balances are added to the entity valuation, in the case of marketable securities, or subtracted, in the case of debt. Note also that dividend payout (assumed to be 65% of net income) is a financial use of cash that will affect the amount of excess marketable securities or unscheduled debt. This will, in turn, affect the net income per share because it affects interest income and expense indirectly. It will not, however, affect the entity value of the firm because dividends, interest expense, and interest income are all financial flows—not part of operating free cash flows.

Table 14.8 provides the calculation of free cash flows as derived from the projected income statement and balance sheets. Note that although the foreign currency translation effect has been relevant as part of historical free cash flows, it cannot be forecasted and therefore has no effect going forward in time. Also note that the sum of all financial flows equals the sum of all operating cash flows. They are opposite sides of the same coin.

Table 14.6 Pro Forma Income Statements for Coca-Cola, 1996–2010 ($ millions; read across)

Income Statement	History				Forecast		
	1996	1997	1998	1999	2000	2001	2002
Revenues	18,546.0	18,868.0	18,813.0	19,805.0	20,458.0	21,440.0	23,155.2
Cost of goods sold	(6,296.0)	(5,631.0)	(5,181.0)	(5,571.0)	(5,739.0)	(6,003.2)	(6,414.0)
Selling, general and administrative expenses	(7,317.5)	(7,550.0)	(7,947.0)	(8,647.0)	(8,812.0)	(9,219.2)	(9,887.3)
Depreciation expense	(442.0)	(384.0)	(381.0)	(438.0)	(465.0)	(489.0)	(558.8)
Other operating income expense	(385.0)	(60.0)	(73.0)	(813.0)	(1,443.0)	(0.0)	(0.0
Equity income from bottlers	211.0	155.0	32.0	(184.0)	(289.0)	135.1	161.8
Operating income	4,316.5	5,398.0	5,263.0	4,152.0	3,710.0	5,863.7	6,456.9
Amortization of goodwill	(191.0)	(242.0)	(264.0)	(354.0)	(308.0)	(308.0)	(308.0)
Nonoperating income	87.0	75.0	39.0	98.0	99.0	104.0	109.1
Interest income	238.0	211.0	219.0	260.0	345.0	278.3	150.4
Interest expense	(286.0)	(258.0)	(277.0)	(337.0)	(447.0)	(329.5)	(331.2)
Special items	431.5	871.0	218.0	0.0	0.0	0.0	0.0
Earnings before taxes	4,596.0	6,055.0	5,198.0	3,819.0	3,399.0	5,608.6	6,077.3
Income taxes	(1,104.0)	(1,926.0)	(1,665.0)	(1,388.0)	(1,222.0)	(1,782.5)	(1,935.5)
Minority interest	0.0	0.0	0.0	0.0	0.0	0.0	0.0
Income before extra items	3,492.0	4,129.0	3,533.0	2,431.0	2,177.0	3,826.0	4,141.8
Extraordinary items	0.0	0.0	0.0	0.0	0.0	0.0	0.0
Net income	3,492.0	4,129.0	3,533.0	2,431.0	2,177.0	3,826.0	4,141.8

Statement of Retained Earnings

	1996	1997	1998	1999	2000	2001	2002
Beginning retained earnings	12,964.0	15,283.0	17,927.0	19,933.0	20,807.0	21,265.0	22,604.3
Net income	3,492.0	4,129.0	3,533.0	2,431.0	2,177.0	3,826.0	4,141.8
Common dividends	(1,247.0)	(1,387.0	(1,480.0)	(1,580.0)	(1,580.0)	(2,486.7)	(2,691.9)
Preferred dividends	0.0	0.0	0.0	0.0	0.0	0.0	0.0
Adjustment to retained earnings	74.0	(98.0)	(47.0)	23.0	(139.0)	0.0	0.0
Ending retained earnings	15,283.0	17,927.0	19,933.0	20,807.0	21,265.0	22,604.3	24,054.2

Table 14.6 *(continued)*

| | | | Forecast | | | | | |
2003	2004	2005	2006	2007	2008	2009	2010	Perpetuity
24,776.0	26,312.2	27,953.8	29,631.1	31,349.7	33,105.3	34,892.9	36,742.3	38,579.4
(6,838.2)	(7,235.8)	(7,687.3)	(8,148.5)	(8,621.2)	(9,103.9)	(9,595.6)	(10,104.1)	(10,609.3)
(10,480.3)	(11,103.7)	(11,768.6)	(12,474.7)	(13,198.2)	(13,937.3)	(14,689.9)	(15,468.5)	(16,241.9)
(628.2)	(644.0)	(694.4)	(747.3)	(802.9)	(861.1)	(921.9)	(985.2)	(1,051.2)
0.0	0.0	0.0	0.0	0.0	0.0	0.0	0.0	0.0
173.1	183.8	195.3	207.0	219.0	231.3	243.8	256.7	269.5
7,002.5	7,512.4	7,998.9	8,467.5	8,946.4	9,434.2	9,929.3	10,441.1	10,946.4
(308.0)	(200.0)	(100.0)	(50.0)	(50.0)	(50.0)	(50.0)	(50.0)	(50.0)
114.6	120.3	126.4	132.7	139.3	146.3	153.6	161.3	169.3
104.0	88.5	331.5	430.4	558.4	721.7	923.2	1,166.1	1,452.0
(332.5)	(329.5)	(409.7)	(443.1)	(481.8)	(525.4)	(574.3)	(628.7)	(689.0)
0.0	0.0	0.0	0.0	0.0	0.0	0.0	0.0	0.0
6,580.6	7,191.7	7,947.1	8,537.4	9,112.3	9,726.7	10,381.9	11,089.8	11,828.8
(2,082.0)	(2,211.3)	(2,426.9)	(2,597.4)	(2,780.8)	(2,979.5)	(3,194.2)	(3,428.6)	(3,676.5)
0.0	0.0	0.0	0.0	0.0	0.0	0.0	0.0	0.0
4,498.6	4,980.4	5,520.1	5,940.1	6,331.4	6,747.1	7,187.7	7,661.2	8,152.3
0.0	0.0	0.0	0.0	0.0	0.0	0.0	0.0	0.0
4,498.6	4,980.4	5,520.1	5,940.1	6,331.4	6,747.1	7,187.7	7,661.2	8,152.3
24,054.2	25,629.0	27,372.5	29,304.9	31,384.2	33,600.6	35,962.6	38,478.7	41,160.6
4,498.6	4,980.4	5,520.1	5,940.1	6,331.4	6,747.1	7,187.7	7,661.2	8,152.3
(2,923.8)	(3,237.0)	(3,587.7)	(3,860.7)	(4,115.0)	(4,385.2)	(4,671.6)	(4,979.3)	(5,298.5)
0.0	0.0	0.0	0.0	0.0	0.0	0.0	0.0	0.0
0.0	0.0	0.0	0.0	0.0	0.0	0.0	0.0	0.0
25,629.0	27,372.5	29,304.9	31,384.2	33,600.6	35,962.6	38,478.7	41,160.6	44,014.4

Table 14.7 Pro Forma Balance Sheets for Coca-Cola, 1996–2010 ($ millions; read across)

Balance Sheet	History			Forecast			
	1996	1997	1998	1999	2000	2001	2002
Operating cash	370.9	377.4	376.3	396.1	409.2	428.8	463.1
Excess cash/marketable securities	1,287.1	1,465.6	1,430.7	1,415.9	1,482.8	801.4	554.2
Accounts receivable	1,641.0	1,639.0	1,666.0	1,798.0	1,757.0	1,895.5	2,047.1
Inventories	952.0	959.0	890.0	1,076.0	1,066.0	1,098.8	1,186.7
Other current assets	1,659.0	1,528.0	2,017.0	1,794.0	1,905.0	2,079.1	2,245.4
Total current assets	5,910.0	5,969.0	6,380.0	6,480.0	6,620.0	6,303.5	6,496.4
Gross property plant equipment	5,581.0	5,771.0	5,685.0	6,471.0	6,614.0	7,228.1	7,806.5
Accumulated depreciation	(2,031.0)	(2,028.0)	(2,016.0)	(2,204.0)	(2,446.0)	(2,601.8)	(2,796.4)
Net property plant and equipment	3,550.0	3,743.0	3,669.0	4,267.0	4,168.0	4,626.3	5,010.1
Goodwill	753.0	727.0	547.0	1,960.0	1,917.0	1,609.0	1,301.0
Other operating assets (bottlers)	4,169.0	4,894.0	6,686.0	6,792.0	5,765.0	6,041.7	6,525.1
Investment & advances	1,779.0	1,607.0	1,863.0	2,124.0	2,364.0	2,482.2	2,606.3
Other nonoperating assets	0.0	0.0	0.0	0.0	0.0	0.0	0.0
Total assets	16,161.0	16,940.0	19,145.0	21,623.0	20,834.0	21,062.7	21,938.9
Short-term debt	3,397.0	3,074.0	4,462.0	5,373.0	4,816.0	5,000.0	5,175.0
Accounts payable	2,055.0	2,279.0	1,811.0	2,144.0	2,123.0	2,203.3	2,379.5
Other current liabilities	1,954.0	2,026.0	2,367.0	2,339.0	2,382.0	2,575.3	2,781.3
Total current liabilities	7,406.0	7,379.0	8,640.0	9,856.0	9,321.0	9,778.6	10,335.9
Long-term debt	1,116.0	801.0	687.0	854.0	835.0	681.0	528.0
Deferred income taxes	301.0	448.0	424.0	498.0	358.0	377.8	399.8
Other operating liabilities	892.0	692.0	492.0	366.0	434.0	0.0	0.0
Retirement-related liabilities	290.0	309.0	499.0	536.0	570.0	570.0	570.0
Minority interest	0.0	0.0	0.0	0.0	0.0	0.0	0.0
Preferred stock	0.0	0.0	0.0	0.0	0.0	0.0	0.0
Common stock & paid-in capital	1,855.0	2,338.0	2,976.0	3,392.0	4,066.0	4,066.0	4,066.0
Retained earnings	15,283.0	17,927.0	19,933.0	20,807.0	21,265.0	22,604.3	24,054.2
Treasury stock	(10,320.0)	(11,582.0)	(13,145.0)	(13,160.0)	(13,293.0)	(14,293.0)	(15,293.0)
Cumulative transactions and other adjustments	(662.0)	(1,372.0)	(1,361.0)	(1,526.0)	(2,722.0)	(2,722.0)	(2,722.0)
Total common equity	6,156.0	7,311.0	8,403.0	9,513.0	9,513.0	9,655.3	10,105.2
Total liabilities and equity	16,161.0	16,940.0	19,145.0	21,623.0	20,834.0	21,062.7	21,938.9
Assets (liabilities + equity)	0.0	0.0	0.0	0.0	0.0	0.0	0.0

Table 14.7 (*continued*)

	Forecast							
2003	2004	2005	2006	2007	2008	2009	2010	Perpetuity
495.5	526.2	559.1	592.6	627.0	662.1	697.9	734.8	771.6
471.6	1,765.9	2,292.7	2,974.8	3,844.7	4,918.5	6,212.4	7,735.7	9,524.2
2,190.4	2,326.2	2,471.3	2,619.6	2,771.6	2,926.8	3,084.8	3,248.3	3,410.7
1,269.7	1,348.4	1,432.6	1,518.5	1,606.6	1,696.6	1,788.2	1,883.0	1,977.1
2,402.6	2,551.5	2,710.7	2,873.4	3,040.0	3,210.3	3,383.6	3,562.9	3,741.1
6,829.8	8,518.4	9,466.5	10,579.0	11,889.9	13,414.2	15,166.9	17,164.8	19,424.7
8,337.9	8,989.8	9,675.7	20,395.3	11,148.7	11,935.7	12,755.8	13,610.0	14,496.0
(3,031.3)	(3,255.2)	(3,496.6)	(3,756.5)	(4,035.6)	(4,335.0)	(4,655.6)	(4,998.2)	(5,363.7)
5,306.7	5,734.6	6,179.0	6,638.8	7,113.1	7,600.6	8,100.2	8,611.8	9,132.3
993.0	793.0	693.0	643.0	593.0	543.0	493.0	443.0	393.0
6,981.8	7,414.7	7,877.3	8,349.9	8,834.2	9,329.0	9,832.7	10,353.9	10,871.5
2,736.6	2,873.5	3,017.1	3,168.0	3,326.4	3,492.7	3,667.3	3,850.7	4,043.2
0.0	0.0	0.0	0.0	0.0	0.0	0.0	0.0	0.0
22,847.9	25,334.1	27,232.9	29,378.7	31,756.6	34,379.5	37,260.2	40,424.2	43,864.8
5,125.0	6,500.0	7,030.5	7,644.7	8,336.8	9,111.8	9,974.5	10,931.5	11,986.3
2,546.1	2,703.9	2,872.7	3,045.0	3,221.6	3,402.0	3,585.7	3,775.8	3,964.6
2,976.0	3,160.6	3,357.7	3,559.2	3,765.6	3,976.5	4,191.3	4,413.4	4,634.1
10,647.1	12,364.5	13,260.9	14,248.9	15,324.1	16,490.3	17,751.5	19,120.6	20,584.9
527.0	527.0	570.0	619.8	675.9	738.8	808.7	886.3	971.8
423.7	449.1	476.1	504.7	534.9	566.8	600.4	635.6	672.6
0.0	0.0	0.0	0.0	0.0	0.0	0.0	0.0	0.0
570.0	570.0	570.0	570.0	570.0	570.0	570.0	570.0	570.0
0.0	0.0	0.0	0.0	0.0	0.0	0.0	0.0	0.0
0.0	0.0	0.0	0.0	0.0	0.0	0.0	0.0	0.0
4,066.0	4,066.0	4,066.0	4,066.0	4,066.0	4,066.0	4,066.0	4,066.0	4,066.0
25,629.0	27,372.5	29,304.9	31,384.2	33,600.6	35,962.6	38,478.7	41,160.6	44,014.4
(16,293.0)	(17,293.0)	(18,293.0)	(19,293.0)	(20,293.0)	(21,293.0)	(22,293.0)	(23,293.0)	(24,293.0)
(2,722.0)	(2,722.0)	(2,722.0)	(2,722.0)	(2,722.0)	(2,722.0)	(2,722.0)	(2,722.0)	(2,722.0)
10,680.0	11,423.5	12,355.9	13,435.2	14,651.6	16,013.6	17,529.7	19,211.6	21,065.4
22,847.9	25,334.1	27,232.9	29,378.7	31,756.6	34,379.5	37,260.2	40,424.2	43,864.8
0.0	0.0	0.0	0.0	0.0	0.0	0.0	0.0	0.0

Table 14.8 Free Cash Flows for Coca-Cola, 1996–2010 ($ millions; read across)

Free Cash Flow	History				Forecast		
	1996	1997	1998	1999	2000	2001	2002
EBIT	4,316.5	5,398.0	5,263.0	4,152.0	3,710.0	5,863.7	6,456.9
Taxes on EBIT	(911.1)	(1,557.4)	(1,583.4)	(1,379.4)	(1,223.2)	(1,760.9)	(1,964.8)
Changes in deferred taxes	107.0	147.0	(24.0)	74.0	(140.0)	19.8	22.1
NOPLAT	3,512.4	3,987.6	3,655.6	2,846.6	2,346.8	4,122.6	4,514.1
Depreciation	442.0	384.0	381.0	438.0	465.0	489.0	558.8
Gross cash flow	3,954.4	4,371.6	4,036.6	3,284.6	2,811.8	4,611.6	5,072.9
Increase in working capital	543.6	(415.6)	572.9	(190.2)	51.1	91.4	57.9
Capital expenditures	(344.0)	577.0	307.0	1,036.0	366.0	947.3	942.6
Increase in other assets	2,054.0	925.0	1,992.0	232.0	(1,095.0)	710.7	483.3
Investment in operating leases	0.0	0.0	0.0	0.0	0.0	0.0	0.0
Gross investment	2,253.6	1,086.4	2,871.9	1,077.8	(677.9)	1,749.4	1,483.9
Investment in goodwill	0.0	(216.0)	(84.0)	(1,767.0)	(265.0)	0.0	0.0
Operating investment	2,253.6	870.4	2,787.9	(689.2)	(942.9)	1,749.4	1,483.9
Free cash flow after goodwill	1,700.8	3,069.2	1,080.7	439.8	3,224.7	2,862.3	3,589.1
Nonoperating cash flow	921.9	730.1	(104.4)	(203.2)	(181.6)	(56.9)	(59.7)
Foreign currency translation effect	(238.0)	(710.0)	11.0	(165.0)	(1,196.0)	0.0	0.0
Cash flow available to investors	2,384.8	3,089.3	987.3	71.6	1,847.1	2,805.4	3,529.4

Financing Flows

	1996	1997	1998	1999	2000	2001	2002
After-tax interest income	(140.4)	(124.5)	(129.2)	(153.4)	(203.6)	(164.2)	(88.8)
Increase (decrease) in excess cash	332.4	178.6	(34.9)	(14.8)	66.9	(681.4)	(247.2)
After-tax interest expense	168.7	152.2	163.4	198.8	263.7	194.4	195.4
Decrease (increase) in debt	(449.0)	638.0	(1,274.0)	(1,078.0)	576.0	(30.0)	(22.0)
Decrease (increase) in pension liabilities	(17.0)	(19.0)	(190.0)	(37.0)	(34.0)	0.0	0.0
Decrease (increase) in preferred stock	0.0	0.0	0.0	0.0	0.0	0.0	0.0
Common dividends	1,247.0	1,387.0	1,480.0	1,580.0	1,580.0	2,486.7	2,691.9
Decrease (increase) in common and treasury stock	1,243.0	877.0	972.0	(424.0)	(402.0)	1,000.0	1,000.0
Financing flows total	2,384.8	3,089.3	987.3	71.6	1,847.1	2,805.4	3,529.4

Table 14.8 *(continued)*

			Forecast					
2003	**2004**	**2005**	**2006**	**2007**	**2008**	**2009**	**2010**	**Perpetuity**
7,002.5	7,512.4	7,998.9	8,467.5	8,946.4	9,434.2	9,929.3	10,441.1	10,946.4
(2,128.7)	(2,260.8)	(2,407.2)	(2,548.2)	(2,692.3)	(2,839.1)	(2,988.1)	(3,142.1)	(3,294.2)
23.9	25.4	27.0	28.6	30.2	31.9	33.5	35.3	37.0
4,897.6	5,277.0	5,618.7	5,947.9	6,284.3	6,626.9	6,974.7	7,334.2	7,689.2
628.2	644.0	694.4	747.3	802.9	861.1	921.9	985.2	1,051.2
5,525.8	5,921.0	6,313.1	6,695.2	7,087.2	7,488.0	7,896.6	8,319.5	8,740.4
54.7	51.8	55.4	56.6	58.0	59.2	60.3	62.4	62.0
924.7	1,071.9	1,138.8	1,207.1	1,277.1	1,348.7	1,421.5	1,496.8	1,571.7
456.8	432.9	462.6	472.6	484.3	494.7	503.8	521.1	517.7
0.0	0.0	0.0	0.0	0.0	0.0	0.0	0.0	0.0
1,436.2	1,556.6	1,656.8	1,736.4	1,819.4	1,902.6	1,985.6	2,080.4	2,151.4
0.0	0.0	0.0	0.0	0.0	0.0	0.0	0.0	0.0
1,436.2	1,556.6	1,656.8	1,736.4	1,819.4	1,902.6	1,985.6	2,080.4	2,151.4
4,089.7	4,364.4	4,656.3	4,958.9	5,267.8	5,585.4	5,911.1	6,239.1	6,589.1
(62.7)	(65.8)	(69.1)	(72.6)	(76.2)	(80.0)	(84.0)	(88.2)	(92.6)
0.0	0.0	0.0	0.0	0.0	0.0	0.0	0.0	0.0
4,027.0	4,298.5	4,587.1	4,886.3	5,191.6	5,505.4	5,827.0	6,150.9	6,496.4
(61.4)	(52.2)	(195.6)	(253.9)	(329.5)	(425.8)	(544.7)	(688.0)	(856.7)
(82.6)	1,294.4	526.8	682.1	869.9	1,073.7	1,294.0	1,523.3	1,788.5
196.2	194.4	241.7	261.4	284.3	310.0	338.8	370.9	406.5
51.0	(1,375.0)	(573.5)	(664.0)	(748.2)	(837.8)	(932.6)	(1,034.6)	(1,140.4)
0.0	0.0	0.0	0.0	0.0	0.0	0.0	0.0	0.0
0.0	0.0	0.0	0.0	0.0	0.0	0.0	0.0	0.0
2,923.8	3,237.0	3,587.7	3,860.7	4,115.0	4,385.2	4,671.6	4,979.3	5,298.5
1,000.0	1,000.0	1,000.0	1,000.0	1,000.0	1,000.0	1,000.0	1,000.0	1,000.0
4,027.0	4,298.5	4,587.1	4,886.3	5,191.6	5,505.4	5,827.0	6,150.9	6,496.4

Table 14.9 Forecast Assumptions and Key Operating Ratios for Coca-Cola, 1996–2010 (read across)

Operations Ratios/Assumptions	History				Forecast		
	1996	1997	1998	1999	2000	2001	2002
Revenue growth	2.9%	1.7%	−0.3%	5.3%	3.3%	4.8%	8.0%
COGS/revenues	33.9%	29.8%	27.5%	28.1%	28.1%	28.0%	27.7%
SG&A/revenues	39.5%	40.0%	42.2%	43.7%	43.1%	43.0%	42.7%
Other operating income	−2.1%	−0.3%	−0.4%	−4.1%	−7.1%	0.0%	0.0%
Equity income from bottlers/revenue	1.1%	0.8%	0.2%	−0.9%	−1.4%	0.6%	0.7%
EBDIT margin	24.5%	29.8%	29.8%	24.1%	21.8%	29.0%	29.6%
Depreciation-revenues	2.4%	2.0%	2.0%	2.2%	2.3%	2.3%	2.4%
Operating margin (EBIT%)	22.1%	27.8%	27.8%	21.9%	19.5%	26.7%	27.2%
Working capital/revenues							
Operating cash	2.0%	2.0%	2.0%	2.0%	2.0%	2.0%	2.0%
Accounts receivable	8.8%	8.7%	8.9%	9.1%	8.6%	8.8%	8.8%
Inventories	5.1%	5.1%	4.7%	5.4%	5.2%	5.1%	5.1%
Other current assets	8.9%	8.1%	10.7%	9.1%	9.3%	9.7%	9.7%
Accounts payable	11.1%	12.1%	9.6%	10.8%	10.4%	10.3%	10.3%
Other current liabilities	10.5%	10.7%	12.6%	11.8%	11.6%	12.0%	12.0%
Net working capital	3.3%	1.1%	4.1%	2.9%	3.1%	3.4%	3.4%
Property plant equipment							
Capital expenditures/revenues	−1.9%	3.1%	1.6%	5.2%	1.8%	4.4%	4.1%
Depreciation/last year's GPPE	6.6%	6.9%	6.6%	7.7%	7.2%	7.4%	7.7%
Retirements/last year's GPPE	11.0%	6.9%	6.8%	4.4%	3.4%	5.0%	5.0%
Gross PPE/revenues	30.1%	30.6%	30.2%	32.7%	32.3%	33.7%	33.7%
NPPE/revenues	19.1%	19.8%	19.5%	21.5%	20.4%	21.6%	21.6%

Tables 14.9 through 14.13 are useful ratios and backup calculations that show where some of the numbers in the free cash flow statement come from. Table 14.9 provides forecast assumptions and key operating ratios.

8. Estimating the Weighted Average Cost of Capital

Table 14.14 shows the estimation of Coke's weighted average cost of capital as of March 2000. Non-interest-bearing liabilities, accounts payable for example, are given no weight in the calculation because their costs, if any, are already included in the estimation of free cash flows. Although

Table 14.9 *(continued)*

		Forecast						
2003	**2004**	**2005**	**2006**	**2007**	**2008**	**2009**	**2010**	**Perpetuity**
7.0%	6.2%	6.2%	6.0%	5.8%	5.6%	5.4%	5.3%	5.0%
27.6%	27.5%	27.5%	27.5%	27.5%	27.5%	27.5%	27.5%	27.5%
42.3%	42.2%	42.1%	42.1%	42.1%	42.1%	42.1%	42.1%	42.1%
0.0%	0.0%	0.0%	0.0%	0.0%	0.0%	0.0%	0.0%	0.0%
0.7%	0.7%	0.7%	0.7%	0.7%	0.7%	0.7%	0.7%	0.7%
30.1%	30.3%	30.4%	30.4%	30.4%	30.4%	30.4%	30.4%	30.4%
2.5%	2.4%	2.5%	2.5%	2.6%	2.6%	2.6%	2.7%	2.7%
27.6%	27.9%	27.9%	27.9%	27.8%	27.8%	27.8%	27.7%	27.7%
2.0%	2.0%	2.0%	2.0%	2.0%	2.0%	2.0%	2.0%	2.0%
8.8%	8.8%	8.8%	8.8%	8.8%	8.8%	8.8%	8.8%	8.8%
5.1%	5.1%	5.1%	5.1%	5.1%	5.1%	5.1%	5.1%	5.1%
9.7%	9.7%	9.7%	9.7%	9.7%	9.7%	9.7%	9.7%	9.7%
10.3%	10.3%	10.3%	10.3%	10.3%	10.3%	10.3%	10.3%	10.3%
12.0%	12.0%	12.0%	12.0%	12.0%	12.0%	12.0%	12.0%	12.0%
3.4%	3.4%	3.4%	3.4%	3.4%	3.4%	3.4%	3.4%	3.4%
3.7%	4.1%	4.1%	4.1%	4.1%	4.1%	4.1%	4.1%	4.1%
8.0%	7.7%	7.7%	7.7%	7.7%	7.7%	7.7%	7.7%	7.7%
5.0%	5.0%	5.0%	5.0%	5.0%	5.0%	5.0%	5.0%	5.0%
33.7%	34.2%	34.6%	35.1%	35.6%	36.1%	36.6%	37.0%	37.6%
21.4%	21.8%	22.1%	22.4%	22.7%	23.0%	23.2%	23.4%	23.7%

trade credit pays no specific finance charges, its cost is implicit in the price that is charged for the goods and services—namely, the trade credit discount. We make no distinction between short- and long-term debt because 1-year debt has approximately the same cost as 10-year debt when it is rolled over 10 times during the explicit forecast period. The before-tax cost of all interest-bearing debt capital was about 9.88%, given that Coca-Cola had an A+ bond rating at the time and that the marginal tax rate (after accounting for federal taxes and for the effect of state and local taxes after federal taxes) was 41%. Coca-Cola had no convertible debt, no warrants, and no preferred stock outstanding. If it did, Chapter 15 is a good reference for techniques on how to estimate their opportunity cost. This can be a tricky issue, especially when the security has options embedded in

Table 14.10 Operating Ratios and Assumptions for Coca-Cola, 1996–2010 (read across)

Key Operating Ratios	History				Forecast		
	1996	1997	1998	1999	2000	2001	2002
ROIC							
EBIT/revenues	23.3%	28.6%	28.0%	21.0%	18.1%	27.3%	27.9%
Revenues/invested capital	2.51	2.21	1.88	1.62	1.62	1.71	1.74
Pretax ROIC	58.5%	63.3%	52.5%	34.0%	29.3%	46.8%	48.5%
After-tax ROIC (including goodwill)	47.6%	46.7%	36.5%	23.3%	18.6%	32.9%	33.9%
After-tax ROIC (excluding goodwill)	53.7%	51.2%	38.9%	26.0%	21.9%	38.3%	38.1%
Growth Rates							
Revenue growth rate	2.9%	1.7%	−0.3%	5.3%	3.3%	4.8%	8.0%
EBIT growth rate	−1.9%	25.1%	−2.5%	−21.1%	−10.6%	58.1%	10.1%
NOPLAT growth rate	13.2%	13.5%	−8.3%	−22.1%	−17.6%	75.7%	9.5%
Invested capital growth rate	32.2%	9.4%	30.6%	6.0%	−10.1%	12.4%	8.1%
Investment Rates							
Gross investment rate	57.0%	24.9%	71.1%	32.8%	−24.1%	37.9%	29.3%
Net investment rate	51.6%	17.6%	68.1%	22.5%	−48.7%	30.6%	20.5%
Financing							
Coverage (EBIT/interest)	15.1	20.9	19.0	12.3	8.3	17.8	19.5
Debt/total cap (book)	41.2%	33.7%	36.6%	38.3%	35.9%	35.7%	34.8%
Average ROE	60.5%	61.3%	45.0%	27.1%	22.9%	39.9%	41.9%

it. For example, convertible debt can be thought of as a portfolio of straight debt plus an American call option. Therefore, standard calculation of the yield to maturity on convertible debt is a totally bogus way to think about its true opportunity cost.

The capital asset pricing model was used to estimate Coca-Cola's cost of equity:

$$k_s = r_f + [E(r_m) - r_f]Beta_s. \tag{14.22}$$

In March 2000 the risk-free rate on 10-year government bonds was 4.8%, we assumed a market risk premium, $E(R_m) - r_f$, of 5.5 percent, and used the BARRA estimate of beta that they call the "predicted" beta, which was 0.68. Taken together, these assumptions, and the weights shown in Table 14.14, implied a weighted average cost of capital of 8.3%. There was nothing in the forecast that indicated that the risk profile of Coca-Cola would change over time; therefore we assumed a constant cost of capital for the explicit forecast period and for the continuing value as well.

Table 14.10 *(continued)*

			Forecast					
2003	2004	2005	2006	2007	2008	2009	2010	Perpetuity
28.3%	28.6%	28.6%	28.6%	28.5%		28.5%	28.4%	28.4%
1.79	1.82	1.83	1.83	1.83	1.83	1.83	1.83	1.82
50.5%	51.9%	52.4%	52.4%	52.3%	0.0%	52.0%	51.9%	51.7%
35.3%	36.5%	36.8%	36.8%	36.7%	0.0%	36.5%	36.4%	36.3%
38.5%	38.9%	38.7%	38.4%	38.1%	37.8%	37.5%	37.3%	37.0%
7.0%	6.2%	6.2%	6.0%	5.8%	5.6%	5.4%	5.3%	5.0%
8.4%	7.3%	6.5%	5.9%	5.7%	5.5%	5.2%	5.2%	4.8%
8.5%	7.7%	6.5%	5.9%	5.7%	5.5%	5.2%	5.2%	4.8%
6.6%	7.0%	6.9%	6.6%	6.4%	6.1%	5.9%	5.7%	5.4%
26.0%	26.3%	26.2%	25.9%	25.7%	25.4%	25.1%	25.0%	24.6%
16.5%	17.3%	17.1%	16.6%	16.2%	15.7%	15.3%	14.9%	14.3%
21.1	22.8	19.5	19.1	18.6	18.0	17.3	16.6	15.9
33.4%	36.9%	37.0%	37.1%	37.2%	37.3%	37.3%	37.4%	37.5%
43.3%	45.1%	46.4%	46.1%	45.1%	44.0%	42.9%	41.7%	40.5%

9. Estimating the Continuing Value

Earlier in the chapter we showed how to use a formula approach for entity valuation. Now we use Eq. (14.17) in the context of valuing the free cash flows from year 11 to infinity. When rewritten for a levered firm, Eq. (14.17) becomes

$$V_0 = \frac{NOPLAT_T(1+g)[1-g/r]}{WACC - g}. \tag{14.23}$$

Note that *NOPLAT* is net operating profit less adjusted taxes, the same as *EBIT* multiplied by $(1 - T_c)$, where T_c is the effective cash tax rate on operating income (i.e., the rate the company would pay if it had no interest expense or interest income). We grow *NOPLAT* in the last year of the explicit forecast period for one year so that it becomes the first payment in an infinite growing annuity. As noted in Eq. (14.17a), the rate of growth in *NOPLAT* is determined by the rate of

Table 14.11 Financing Ratios and Forecasting Assumptions for Coca-Cola, 1996–2010 (read across)

Financing/Other Ratios and Forecast Assumptions	History				Forecast		
	1996	1997	1998	1999	2000	2001	2002
Taxes							
EBIT tax rate	21.1%	28.9%	30.1%	33.2%	33.0%	30.0%	30.4%
Marginal tax rate	41.0%	41.0%	41.0%	41.0%	41.0%	41.0%	41.0%
Increase in deferred tax/tax on EBIT	11.7%	9.4%	−1.5%	5.4%	−11.4%	1.1%	1.1%
Interest rate on excess marketable securites	18.5%	14.4%	15.3%	18.4%	23.3%	18.8%	18.8%
Interest rate on existing debt	7.0%	5.7%	7.1%	6.5%	7.2%		
Interest rate on short-term debt						5.8%	5.8%
Interest rate on long-term debt						5.8%	5.8%
Interest rate on new long-term debt						5.8%	5.8%
Dividend payout ratio	35.7%	33.6%	41.9%	65.0%	65.0%	65.0%	65.0%
Other Ratios							
Nonoperating income growth	335.0%	−13.8%	−48.0%	151.3%	1.0%	5.0%	5.0%
Other assets/revenues	22.5%	25.9%	35.5%	34.3%	28.2%	28.2%	28.2%
Investments & advances growth rate	−25.7%	−9.7%	15.9%	14.0%	11.3%	5.0%	5.0%
Nonoperating assets growth rate	0.0%	0.0%	0.0%	0.0%	0.0%	0.0%	0.0%
Other liabilities/revenues							
Capitalized operating leases/revenue	0.0%	0.0%	0.0%	0.0%	0.0%	0.0%	0.0%
Other Values ($)							
Amortization of goodwill ($)	191.0	242.0	264.0	354.0	308.0	308.0	308.0
Special items ($)	431.5	871.0	218.0	0.0	0.0	0.0	0.0
Extraordinary items ($)	0.0	0.0	0.0	0.0	0.0	0.0	0.0
Short-term debt ($)	3,397.0	3,074.0	4,462.0	5,373.0	4,816.0	5,000.0	5,175.0
Long-term debt ($)	1,116.0	801.0	687.0	854.0	835.0	681.0	528.0
Retirement-related liabilities	290.0	309.0	499.0	536.0	570.0	570.0	570.0

Table 14.11 (*continued*)

				Forecast				
2003	**2004**	**2005**	**2006**	**2007**	**2008**	**2009**	**2010**	**Perpetuity**
30.4%	30.1%	30.1%	30.1%	30.1%	30.1%	30.1%	30.1%	30.1%
41.0%	41.0%	41.0%	41.0%	41.0%	41.0%	41.0%	41.0%	41.0%
1.1%	1.1%	1.1%	1.1%	1.1%	1.1%	1.1%	1.1%	1.1%
18.8%	18.8%	18.8%	18.8%	18.8%	18.8%	18.8%	18.8%	18.8%
5.8%	5.8%	5.8%	5.8%	5.8%	5.8%	5.8%	5.8%	5.8%
5.8%	5.8%	5.8%	5.8%	5.8%	5.8%	5.8%	5.8%	5.8%
5.8%	5.8%	5.8%	5.8%	5.8%	5.8%	5.8%	5.8%	5.8%
65.0%	65.0%	65.0%	65.0%	65.0%	65.0%	65.0%	65.0%	65.0%
5.0%	5.0%	5.0%	5.0%	5.0%	5.0%	5.0%	5.0%	5.0%
28.2%	28.2%	28.2%	28.2%	28.2%	28.2%	28.2%	28.2%	28.2%
5.0%	5.0%	5.0%	5.0%	5.0%	5.0%	5.0%	5.0%	5.0%
0.0%	0.0%	0.0%	0.0%	0.0%	0.0%	0.0%	0.0%	0.0%
0.0%	0.0%	0.0%	0.0%	0.0%	0.0%	0.0%	0.0%	0.0%
308.0	200.0	100.0	50.0	50.0	50.0	50.0	50.0	50.0
0.0	0.0	0.0	0.0	0.0	0.0	0.0	0.0	0.0
0.0	0.0	0.0	0.0	0.0	0.0	0.0	0.0	0.0
5,125.0	6,500.0	7,030.5	7,644.7	8,336.8	9,111.8	9,974.5	10,931.5	11,986.3
527.0	527.0	570.0	619.8	675.9	738.8	808.7	886.3	971.8
570.0	570.0	570.0	570.0	570.0	570.0	570.0	570.0	570.0

Table 14.12 Working Capital, Capital Expenditures, and Goodwill for Coca-Cola (read across)

	History				Forecast		
Change in Working Capital	**1996**	**1997**	**1998**	**1999**	**2000**	**2001**	**2002**
Increase in operating cash	10.6	6.4	(1.1)	19.8	13.1	19.6	34.3
Increase in accounts receivable	(109.0)	(2.0)	27.0	132.0	(41.0)	138.5	151.6
Increase in inventories	(165.0)	7.0	(69.0)	186.0	(10.0)	32.8	87.9
Increase in other current assets	391.0	(131.0)	489.0	(223.0)	111.0	174.1	166.3
(Increase) in accounts payable	19.0	(224.0)	468.0	(333.0)	21.0	(80.3)	(176.3)
(Increase) in other current liabilities	397.0	(72.0)	(341.0)	28.0	(43.0)	(193.3)	(206.0)
Net change in working capital	543.6	(415.6)	572.9	(190.2)	51.1	91.4	57.9
Capital Expenditures							
Increase in net PPE	(786.0)	193.0	(74.0)	598.0	(99.0)	458.3	383.8
Depreciation	442.0	384.0	381.0	438.0	465.0	489.0	558.8
Capital expenditures (net of disposals)	(344.0)	577.0	307.0	1,036.0	366.0	947.3	942.6
Investment in Goodwill							
Increase/(decrease) balance sheet goodwill	(191.0)	(26.0)	(180.0)	1,413.0	(43.0)	(308.0)	(308.0)
Amortization of goodwill	191.0	242.0	264.0	354.0	308.0	308.0	308.0
Investment in goodwill	0.0	216.0	84.0	1,767.0	265.0	0.0	0.0
Nonoperating Cash Flow							
Extraordinary items	0.0	0.0	0.0	0.0	0.0	0.0	0.0
AT nonoperating income	305.9	558.1	151.6	57.8	58.4	61.3	64.4
Change in investments & advances	616.0	172.0	(256.0)	(261.0)	(240.0)	(118.2)	(124.1)
Change in nonoperating assets	0.0	0.0	0.0	0.0	0.0	0.0	0.0
	921.9	730.1	(104.4)	(203.2)	(181.6)	(56.9)	(59.7)
Employees	26.0	29.5	28.6	37.4	37.4	37.4	37.4
Shares	2,481.0	2,470.6	2,465.5	2,471.6	2,471.6	2,488.5	2,488.5
EPS	1.41	1.67	1.43	0.98	0.88	1.54	1.66
Annual EPS growth	18.06%	18.74%	−14.26%	−31.36%	−10.45%	74.55%	8.25%

Table 14.12 (continued)

				Forecast				
2003	**2004**	**2005**	**2006**	**2007**	**2008**	**2009**	**2010**	**Perpetuity**
32.4	30.7	32.8	33.5	34.4	35.1	35.8	37.0	36.7
143.3	135.8	145.1	148.3	151.9	155.2	158.0	163.5	162.4
83.1	78.7	84.1	86.0	88.1	90.0	91.6	94.8	94.1
157.2	149.0	159.2	162.6	166.7	170.2	173.4	179.3	178.1
(166.6)	(157.9)	(168.7)	(172.4)	(176.6)	(180.4)	(183.7)	(190.0)	(188.8)
(194.7)	(184.5)	(197.2)	(201.5)	(206.4)	(210.9)	(214.7)	(222.1)	(220.7)
54.7	51.8	55.4	56.6	58.0	59.2	60.3	62.4	62.0
296.5	427.9	444.5	459.8	474.2	487.6	499.6	511.6	520.5
628.2	644.0	694.4	747.3	802.9	861.1	921.9	985.2	1,051.2
924.7	1,071.9	1,138.8	1,207.1	1,277.1	1,348.7	1,421.5	1,496.8	1,571.7
(308.0)	(200.0)	(100.0)	(50.0)	(50.0)	(50.0)	(50.0)	(50.0)	(50.0)
308.0	200.0	100.0	50.0	50.0	50.0	50.0	50.0	50.0
0.0	0.0	0.0	0.0	0.0	0.0	0.0	0.0	0.0
0.0	0.0	0.0	0.0	0.0	0.0	0.0	0.0	0.0
67.6	71.0	74.5	78.3	82.2	86.3	90.6	95.1	99.9
(130.3)	(136.8)	(143.7)	(150.9)	(158.4)	(166.3)	(174.6)	(183.4)	(192.5)
0.0	0.0	0.0	0.0	0.0	0.0	0.0	0.0	0.0
(62.7)	(65.8)	(69.1)	(72.6)	(76.2)	(80.0)	(84.0)	(88.2)	(92.6)
37.4	37.4	37.4	37.4	37.4	37.4	37.4	37.4	
2,488.5	2,488.5	2,488.5	2,488.5	2,488.5	2,488.5	2,488.5	2,488.5	
1.81	2.00	2.22	2.39	2.54	2.71	2.89	3.08	
8.61%	10.71%	10.84%	7.61%	6.59%	6.57%	6.53%	6.59%	

Table 14.13 NOPLAT, Tax, and Invested Capital for Coca-Cola (read across)

	History			Forecast			
NOPLAT	**1996**	**1997**	**1998**	**1999**	**2000**	**2001**	**2002**
Net sales	18,546.0	18,868.0	18,813.0	19,805.0	20,458.0	21,440.0	23,155.2
Cost of goods sold	(6,296.0)	(5,631.0)	(5,181.0)	(5,571.0)	(5,739.0)	(6,003.2)	(6,414.0)
Selling, general, & administrative expenses	(7,317.5)	(7,550.0)	(7,947.0)	(8,647.0)	(8,812.0)	(9,219.2)	(9,887.3)
Depreciation expense	(442.0)	(384.0)	(381.0)	(438.0)	(465.0)	(489.0)	(558.8)
Other operating income/expense	(385.0)	(60.0)	(73.0)	(813.0)	(1,443.0)	0.0	0.0
Equity income from bottlers	211.0	155.0	32.0	(184.0)	(289.0)	135.1	161.8
EBIT	4,316.5	5,398.0	5,263.0	4,152.0	3,710.0	5,863.7	6,456.9
Taxes on EBIT	(911.1)	(1,557.4)	(1,583.4)	(1,379.4)	(1,223.2)	(1,760.9)	(1,964.8)
Change in deferred taxes	107.0	147.0	(24.0)	74.0	(140.0)	19.8	22.1
NOPLAT	3,512.4	3,987.6	3,655.6	2,846.6	2,346.8	4,122.6	4,514.1
Taxes on EBIT							
Provision for income taxes	1,104.0	1,926.0	1,665.0	1,388.0	1,222.0	1,782.5	1,935.5
Tax shield on interest expense	117.3	105.8	113.6	138.2	183.3	135.1	135.8
Tax shield on operating lease interest	0.0	0.0	0.0	0.0	0.0	0.0	0.0
Tax shield on retirement-related liabilities interest	0.0	0.0	0.0	0.0	0.0	0.0	0.0
Tax on interest income	(97.6)	(86.5)	(89.8)	(106.6)	(141.5)	(114.1)	(61.7)
Tax on nonoperating income	(212.6)	(387.9)	(105.4)	(40.2)	(40.6)	(42.6)	(44.8)
Taxes on EBIT	911.1	1,557.4	1,583.4	1,379.4	1,223.2	1,760.9	1,964.8
Invested Capital							
Operating current assets	4,622.9	4,503.4	4,949.3	5,064.1	5,137.2	5,502.1	5,942.3
Non-interest-bearing liabilities	(4,009.0)	(4,305.0)	(4,178.0)	(4,483.0)	(4,505.0)	(4,778.6)	(5,160.9)
Operating working capital	613.9	198.4	771.3	581.1	632.2	723.5	781.4
Net property plant and equipment	3,550.0	3,743.0	3,669.0	4,267.0	4,168.0	4,626.3	5,010.1
Other assets net of other liabilities	3,277.0	4,202.0	6,194.0	6,426.0	5,331.0	6,041.7	6,525.1
Value of operating leases	0.0	0.0	0.0	0.0	0.0	0.0	0.0
Operating invested capital	7,440.9	8,143.4	10,634.3	11,274.1	10,131.2	11,391.5	12,316.6
Excess marketable securities	1,287.1	1,465.6	1,430.7	1,415.9	1,482.8	801.4	554.2
Goodwill	753.0	727.0	547.0	1,960.0	1,917.0	1,609.0	1,301.0
Investments & advances	1,779.0	1,607.0	1,863.0	2,124.0	2,364.0	2,482.2	2,606.3
Nonoperating assets	0.0	0.0	0.0	0.0	0.0	0.0	0.0
Total investor funds	11,260.0	11,943.0	14,475.0	16,774.0	15,895.0	16,284.1	16,778.1
Reconciliation							
Equity	6,156.0	7,311.0	8,403.0	9,513.0	9,513.0	9,655.3	10,105.2
Deferred income taxes	301.0	448.0	424.0	498.0	358.0	377.8	399.8
Adjusted equity	6,457.0	7,759.0	8,827.0	10,011.0	9,871.0	10,033.1	10,505.1
Interest-bearing debt	4,513.0	3,875.0	5,149.0	6,227.0	5,651.0	5,681.0	5,703.0
Value of operating leases	0.0	0.0	0.0	0.0	0.0	0.0	0.0
Retirement-related liabilities	290.0	309.0	499.0	536.0	570.0	570.0	570.0
Total investor funds	11,260.0	11,943.0	14,475.0	16,774.0	16,092.0	16,284.1	16,778.1

Table 14.13 *(continued)*

| | Forecast | | | | | | | |
2003	2004	2005	2006	2007	2008	2009	2010	Perpetuity
24,776.0	26,312.2	27,953.8	29,631.1	31,349.7	33,105.3	34,892.9	36,742.3	38,579.4
(6,838.2)	(7,235.8)	(7,687.3)	(8,148.5)	(8,621.2)	(9,103.9)	(9,595.6)	(10,104.1)	(10,609.3)
(10,480.3)	(11,103.7)	(11,768.6)	(12,474.7)	(13,198.2)	(13,937.3)	(14,689.9)	(15,468.5)	(16,241.9)
(628.2)	(644.0)	(694.4)	(747.3)	(802.9)	(861.1)	(921.9)	(985.2)	(1,051.2)
0.0	0.0	0.0	0.0	0.0	0.0	0.0	0.0	0.0
173.1	183.8	195.3	207.0	219.0	231.3	243.8	256.7	269.5
7,002.5	7,512.4	7,998.9	8,467.5	8,946.4	9,434.2	9,929.3	10,441.1	10,946.4
(2,128.7)	(2,260.8)	(2,407.2)	(2,548.2)	(2,692.3)	(2,839.1)	(2,988.1)	(3,142.1)	(3,294.2)
23.9	25.4	27.0	28.6	30.2	31.9	33.5	35.3	37.0
4,897.6	5,277.0	5,618.7	5,947.9	6,284.3	6,626.9	6,974.7	7,334.2	7,689.2
2,082.0	2,211.3	2,426.9	2,597.4	2,780.8	2,979.5	3,194.2	3,428.6	3,676.5
136.3	135.1	168.0	181.7	197.5	215.4	235.5	257.7	282.5
0.0	0.0	0.0	0.0	0.0	0.0	0.0	0.0	0.0
0.0	0.0	0.0	0.0	0.0	0.0	0.0	0.0	0.0
(42.6)	(36.3)	(135.9)	(176.4)	(228.9)	(295.9)	(378.5)	(478.1)	(595.3)
(47.0)	(49.3)	(51.8)	(54.4)	(57.1)	(60.0)	(63.0)	(66.1)	(69.4)
2,128.7	2,260.8	2,407.2	2,548.2	2,692.3	2,839.1	2,988.1	3,142.1	3,294.2
6,358.2	6,752.4	7,173.7	7,604.1	8,045.2	8,495.7	8,954.5	9,429.1	9,900.5
(5,522.1)	(5,864.5)	(6,230.4)	(6,604.2)	(6,987.3)	(7,378.6)	(7,777.0)	(8,189.2)	(8,598.6)
836.1	887.9	943.3	999.9	1,057.9	1,117.2	1,177.5	1,239.9	1,301.9
5,306.7	5,734.6	6,179.0	6,638.8	7,113.1	7,600.6	8,100.2	8,611.8	9,132.3
6,981.8	7,414.7	7,877.3	8,349.9	8,834.2	9,329.0	9,832.7	10,353.9	10,871.5
0.0	0.0	0.0	0.0	0.0	0.0	0.0	0.0	0.0
13,124.6	14,037.2	14,999.7	15,988.7	17,005.2	18,046.7	19,110.4	20,205.6	21,305.7
471.6	1,765.9	2,292.7	2,974.8	3,844.7	4,918.5	6,212.4	7,735.7	9,524.2
993.0	793.0	693.0	643.0	593.0	543.0	493.0	443.0	393.0
2,736.6	2,873.5	3,017.1	3,168.0	3,326.4	3,492.7	3,667.3	3,850.7	4,043.2
0.0	0.0	0.0	0.0	0.0	0.0	0.0	0.0	0.0
17,325.7	19,469.6	21,002.5	22,774.5	24,769.4	27,000.9	29,483.2	32,235.0	35,266.1
10,680.0	11,423.5	12,355.9	13,435.2	14,651.6	16,013.6	17,529.7	19,211.6	21,065.4
423.7	449.1	476.1	504.7	534.9	566.8	600.4	635.6	672.6
11,103.7	11,872.6	12,832.0	13,940.0	15,186.6	16,580.4	18,130.1	19,847.2	21,738.0
5,652.0	7,027.0	7,600.5	8,264.5	9,012.8	9,850.5	10,783.2	11,817.8	12,958.1
0.0	0.0	0.0	0.0	0.0	0.0	0.0	0.0	0.0
570.0	570.0	570.0	570.0	570.0	570.0	570.0	570.0	570.0
17,325.7	19,469.6	21,002.5	22,774.5	24,769.4	27,000.9	29,483.2	32,235.0	35,266.1

Table 14.14 Calculation of the Cost of Capital for Coca-Cola

Barra beta	0.68		Last year of history		2000
Risk-free rate	4.80%				
Market risk premium	5.50%				
Marginal tax rate	41%				

Cost (K)		Market Value (V)		Weights	Contribution
K (debt)	5.83%	V (debt)	5,651.0	4.55%	0.16%
K (equity)	8.55%	V (equity)	117,852.2	94.99%	8.12%
K (preferred)	7.19%	V (preferred)	0.0	0.00%	0.00%
K (retirement liabilities)	5.83%	V (retirement liabilities)	570.0	0.46%	0.02%
K (capitalized leases)	5.83%	V (capitalized leases)	0.0	0.00%	0.00%
K (operating leases)	5.83%	V (operating leases)	0.0	0.00%	0.00%
K (other)	5.83%	V (other)	0.0	0.00%	0.00%
		Total	124,073.2		

Bond rating:	A+		WACC:	8.29%

return on investment, r, and the percent of cash flows that are retained for investment, K; therefore $g = Kr$.

There are a variety of assumptions that can be used when applying the continuing value formula. The most common, and the most conservative, is that competition will drive the return on invested capital down to equal the weighted average cost of capital in the long run. If $r = WACC$ in Eq. (14.23), then it simplifies as follows:

$$V_N = \frac{NOPLAT_{N+1}[1 - g/WACC]}{WACC - g}$$

$$= NOPLAT_{N+1} \left[\frac{(WACC - g)/WACC}{(WACC - g)} \right]$$

$$= \frac{NOPLAT_{N+1}}{WACC}. \tag{14.24}$$

This is called the *perpetuity model* for valuing a company. Interestingly, the nominal rate of growth in cash flows is irrelevant in this case because no value is created by additional growth. Consequently, the present value of all cash flows during the continuing value period as of year 10 is given by Eq. (14.24). For example, had we assumed that CCE could earn only its cost of capital (i.e., that $r = WACC$), the continuing value as of year 10 would be

$$V_{10} = \frac{\$7.6892}{.083} = \$92.641 \text{ billion}, \tag{14.25}$$

and at time zero it would be

$$V_0 = \$92.641(1.083)^{-10} = \$41.737 \text{ billion}. \tag{14.26}$$

The $87.843 billion continuing value that was actually used in the valuation is more than double and is based on the assumption that Coca-Cola Enterprises, because of its strong brand name that serves as an effective deterrent to entry, could continue to earn a return on invested capital of 30% indefinitely. To capture this intuition, we used what we call the *value driver model*, as given in Eq. (14.21), along with the assumption that the long-term rate of growth in *NOPLAT* is strictly less than the cost of capital (*WACC* > *g*). Substituting our assumptions for CCE, namely, that long-term growth in *NOPLAT* is 5%, that $NOPLAT_{T+1}$ is $7.6892 billion, that the long-term rate of return on invested capital is 30%, and that the cost of capital is 8.29%, we see first that the retention rate or reinvestment rate is

$$K = g/r = .05/.30 = 16.7\%. \tag{14.27}$$

In Table 14.10 we see that the net investment rate is roughly 15%; therefore our assumption is consistent with the model. The continuing value as of year 10 is

$$V_{10} = \frac{\$7.6892(1 - .(05/.30))}{.0829 - .05} = \$194.79 \text{ billion}, \tag{14.28}$$

and the present value at time zero is

$$V_0 = (\$194.79 \text{ billion})(1.0829)^{-10} = \$87.843 \text{ billion}. \tag{14.29}$$

There is a third, but inappropriate and illogical, set of assumptions that can be applied to Eq. (14.23) that results in what has been called the *aggressive growth model*. Suppose that we were to assume that *NOPLAT* grows but no investment is required. In this case the reinvestment rate, *K*, equals zero, and the formula becomes

$$V_{10} = NOPLAT_{11}/(WACC - g). \tag{14.30}$$

The problem, of course, is that it requires a truly vivid imagination to conceive of a company that can grow its earnings forever without investing any capital. It implies an infinite rate of return.

We might have simply used the continuing value formula as of the year 2000 to value CCE, and avoided the extra work of forecasting free cash flows during the 10-year explicit forecast period. Had we done so, the entity value estimate would have been based on *NOPLAT* of $2.3468 billion, growth of 5%, a 30% return on invested capital, and a weighted average cost of capital of 8.29%; therefore the entity value would have been

$$V_0 = \frac{\$2,3468(1 - .05/.30)}{.0829 - .05} = \$59.44 \text{ billion}. \tag{14.31}$$

This compares to $117 billion, estimated earlier from the full model. Why the large difference? Because the rate of return and the rate of growth are much different during the explicit forecast period than during the continuing value period. Formula approaches are too limited in their ability to tailor forecasts to the specifics of each company.

10. More on the Equivalence of the DCF and EP Approaches

Table 14.15 shows two valuation summaries for Coca-Cola. The first discounts free cash flows at the weighted average cost of capital over a 10-year explicit discount period, then adds the present value

Table 14.15 A Valuation Summary: Coca-Cola

DCF Valuation Summary for Coca-Cola

Last historical year	Y00		Free Cash Flow	Discount Factor	P.V. of FCF
Current month	3				
		2001	2,862.3	0.923	2,643.2
Operating value	125,065	2002	3,589.1	0.853	3,060.6
		2003	4,089.7	0.787	3,220.5
Excess market securities	1,482.8	2004	4,364.4	0.727	3,173.8
Nonoperating assets	2,364.0	2005	4,656.3	0.672	3,126.8
Excess pension assets	0.0	2006	4,958.9	0.620	3,075.1
Entity value	128,911.7	2007	5,267.8	0.573	3,016.6
Debt	5,651.0	2008	5,585.4	0.529	2,953.7
Capitalized operating leases	0.0	2009	5,911.1	0.488	2,886.6
Retirement-related liability	570.0	2010	6,239.1	0.451	2,813.6
Preferred stock	0.0	Continuing value	194,791.9	0.451	87,843.1
Minority interest	0.0				
Stock options	0.0	Operating value			117,814
Equity value	122,690.7	Midyear adjustment factor			1.062
		Operating value (discounted to current month)			125,065
Most recent shares outstanding	2,484.76				
Value per share	49.38	Present value of nonoperating cash flow			(458.9)
Most recent close price	47.43				
Value difference	–3.9%				
Market value of equity	117,852.2				

Economic Profit Valuation Summary for Coca-Cola

Last historical year	Y00		Economic Profit	Discount Factor	P.V. of EP
Current month	3				
		2001	3,282.8	0.923	3,031.5
Operating value	125,065	2002	3,569.8	0.853	3,044.2
		2003	3,876.7	0.787	3,052.8
Excess market securities	1,482.8	2004	4,189.0	0.727	3,046.3
Nonoperating assets	2,364.0	2005	4,455.1	0.672	2,991.8
Excess pension assets	0.0	2006	4,704.5	0.620	2,917.4
Entity value	128,911.7	2007	4,958.9	0.573	2,839.8
Debt	5,651.0	2008	5,217.3	0.529	2,759.0
Capitalized operating leases	0.0	2009	5,478.8	0.488	2,675.5
Retirement-related liability	570.0	2010	5,750.1	0.451	2,593.0
Preferred stock	0.0	Continuing value	174,586.3	0.451	78,731.2
Minority interest	0.0				
Stock options	0.0	Present value of economic profit			107,682.5
Equity value	122,690.7	Invested capital (beginning of forecast)			10,131.2
		Operating value			117,813.7
Most recent shares outstanding	2,484.8	Midyear adjustment factor			1.062
Value per share	49.38	Operating value (discounted to current month)			125,065
Most recent close price	47.43				
Value difference	–3.9%	Present value of nonoperating cash flow			(458.9)
Market value of equity	117,852.2				

of the continuing value. Using this DCF approach, the entity value (adjusted to the valuation date) is $125.1 billion. The bottom panel shows that the same answer is obtained using the economic profit (EP) approach. The economic profit is estimated each year during the explicit forecast period as

$$EP_t = (ROIC_t - WACC)I_t,$$

and then discounted to the present at the weighted average cost of capital and added to the book value of invested capital and the present value of the continuing value, where

$$CV_{10} = \frac{EP_{11}}{WACC} + \frac{NOPLAT_{11}(g/r)(r - WACC)}{WACC(WACC - g)} \qquad (14.32)$$

adds up to equal the same entity value as the DCF approach.[9] Note that if $r = WACC$ during the continuing value period, the continuing value reduces to a simple perpetuity, that is, to the first term in Eq. (14.23). When the return on new capital invested, r, equals the cost of capital, there is no value to growth.

11. Difficult Issues

As many practitioners know, "Doing a valuation badly can ruin your day." Many investment banks and consulting firms have valuation review committees whose responsibility it is to review valuations done by their staff. All too often practitioners take a shortcut to valuation by using the following formula:

$$V_0 = \sum_{t=1}^{10} \frac{EBIT_1(1 - T_c) + dep - CAPEX - WC}{(1 + WACC)^t} + (multiple)EBITDA_{11}. \qquad (14.33)$$

There are five common errors that arise when using this approach:

1. Failure to forecast complete income statements and balance sheets makes it difficult to forecast *CAPEX* in a way that is consistent with growth in revenues. Consequently, *ROIC* and capital turnover forecasts do not make sense, and without a complete balance sheet, there is no forecast of invested capital—a statistic that is necessary for calculating them. Thus, common-sense consistency checking is impossible.

2. Many analysts interpret the tax rate in the numerator, T_c, as the marginal tax rate, T_m, rather than the cash tax rate on *EBIT*. Furthermore, the increase in accrued taxes due is not added back.

3. Often instead of using operating working capital, analysts will mistakenly use current assets minus current liabilities. Operating working capital leaves out financing, namely, excess marketable securities on the assets side and short-term debt on the liabilities side.

4. Instead of using the continuing value formula, an earnings multiple is multiplied by a convenient earnings surrogate (like earnings before interest, taxes, depreciation and amortization, EBITDA). The problem occurs when the analyst assumes that the multiple that the company currently enjoys is the same multiple that it should have 10 years from now at the end of the explicit forecast period. This is often a problem, especially for high-tech and high-growth companies.

---

[9] When using DCF, Eq. (14.23) becomes

$$CV = \frac{NOPLAT_{11}(1 - g/r)}{WACC - g}.$$

5. The most common mistake forecasting the weighted average cost of capital is to assume that it remains constant even though the risk of the firm changes as it becomes larger and more seasoned.

Other common-sense things to keep in mind include the following. When a business is cyclical, choose an explicit forecast period that ends in midcycle (or is normalized) because the last year of NOPLAT carries into the continuing value formula and it should not be a peak or trough. Make sure that your definition of operating cash flows, the discount rate, and values being estimated are all mutually consistent. If cash flow is to the entity (the enterprise), discount at the weighted average cost of capital. When cash flows are to equity, then discount at the cost of equity. When cash flows are denominated in a foreign currency, use the foreign rates in the weighted average cost of capital. If you are using nominal cash flows (including expected inflation), then WACC should be nominal also. When valuing banks, use an equity model because deposits and certificates of deposit are really part of operations and the bank can earn a spread over the cost of funds that contributes to shareholder value. When valuing insurance companies, estimate the unrealized capital gains or losses embedded in the portfolio of securities held by the institution, and include reserves (a liability) as part of operating cash flows.

12. Empirical Evidence Regarding the Accuracy of DCF

With the emergence of personal computers and user-friendly spreadsheets, the time needed to do a detailed discounted cash flow valuation has decreased dramatically. Furthermore, the models are no longer "black boxes" that reside on mainframe computers, but are under the direct control of top management and its staff. Consequently, DCF is used much more often as a planning and performance evaluation tool. But the question remains: How well do DCF valuations of companies compare with the actual market values? A major issue is whether the marketplace is using the same forecasts of cash flows as the internally generated forecasts that management is using.

To test the validity of the DCF model, we used forecasts made by Value Line Investment Survey (sales growth, operating margins, capital expenditures, and working capital needs) to construct DCF models for 35 companies in 1988 and 30 of the same sample again in 1999. On both occasions we estimated the DCF values in a blind test. We did not look at the actual market values until after having completed the DCF estimate. We did not try to force-fit our DCF valuations to make them close to the market values. It was, however, a laborious task that took at least four hours of work for each company each time that it was valued. Table 14.16 and Figure 14.6 show the results.

The r-squared for the 1988 sample was 94% and for the 1999 sample it was 98%. In both regressions, the intercept is not significantly different from zero, and the slope is not different from 1.0. These are both indications of an unbiased model.

Kaplan and Ruback [1995] compare the market value (transaction value) of 51 highly levered transactions completed between 1983 and 1989 with discounted cash flow estimates of the company value and with valuations based on the transaction multiples of comparables. One of their comparisons was to run a regression similar to those shown in Figure 14.6. Rather than dividing the market and DCF estimates by the book value, to control for size, they used log-log regressions, which have a similar effect. Table 14.17 summarizes their results. Recall that a good model—one that is unbiased—has a slope that is not significantly different from one and an intercept not different from zero. They used three approaches to estimate the cost of capital: an estimate of the firm-specific beta, an average of industry betas, and a beta equal to one (i.e., the market beta). All of these DCF approaches passed the test. None of the t-statistics is significant, indicating an

Table 14.16 Comparison of Market and DCF Values, 1988 and 1999

Company	1988 Results					1999 Results				
	Market	DCF	Mkt/DCF	Error	% Error	Market	DCF	Mkt/DCF	Error	% Error
Abbot Labs	44.63	44.52	1.002471	0.11	0.002465	40.88	39.6	1.032323	1.28	0.031311
American Home Prod	73.13	75.18	0.972732	−2.05	−0.028032	40.88	38.02	1.075224	2.86	0.069961
AMP	47.88	51.62	0.927547	−3.74	−0.078112	—	—	—	—	—
Anheuser Busch	29.75	29.23	1.01779	0.52	0.017479	76.3	60.3	1.26534	16	0.209699
AT&T	—	—	—	—	—	49.25	42.25	1.16568	7	0.142132
Auto Data Processors	38.38	42.09	0.911856	−3.71	−0.096665	40.5	30.31	1.336193	10.19	0.251605
Baxter	20.63	23.83	0.865715	−3.20	−0.155114	66.56	43.11	1.543957	23.45	0.352314
Bristol Myers Squibb	40.13	38.77	1.035079	1.36	0.03389	67.63	66.6	1.015465	1.03	0.01523
Delux	22.88	25.57	0.894799	−2.69	−0.11757	37	36.75	1.006803	0.25	0.006757
Dow Jones	33.13	37.26	0.889157	−4.13	−0.12466	51.38	45.19	1.136977	6.19	0.120475
Dun & Bradstreet	47.63	51.41	0.926473	−3.78	−0.079362	—	—	—	—	—
Eg&G	33.38	27.07	1.233099	6.31	0.189035	33.38	31.2	1.069872	2.18	0.065309
Eli Lilly	84.25	79.65	1.057753	4.60	0.054599	63.06	63.3	0.996209	−0.24	−0.003806
Emerson Electric	29.75	25.38	1.172183	4.37	0.146891	62.5	48.35	1.292658	14.15	0.2264
Gannett	32.13	39.26	0.81839	−7.13	−0.221911	69.94	59.1	1.183418	10.84	0.15499
General Electric	44.13	40.45	1.090977	3.68	0.08339	107.75	95.4	1.129455	12.35	0.114617
Genuine Parts	36.75	36.98	0.99378	−0.23	−0.006259	—	—	—	—	—
Heinz	40.5	37.23	1.087832	3.27	0.080741	47.13	42.22	1.116296	4.91	0.10418
Hewlett Packard	52.5	50.67	1.036116	1.83	0.034857	105.44	79.22	1.330977	26.22	0.248672
IBM	127.63	129.58	0.984951	−1.95	−0.015279	123.38	97.99	1.259108	25.39	0.205787
Johnson & Johnson	77.5	69.77	1.110793	7.73	0.099742	97.31	85.22	1.141868	12.09	0.124242
Masco	27.5	22.87	1.202449	4.63	0.168364	29.38	28.12	1.044808	1.26	0.042886
Maytag	22.13	16.2	1.366049	5.93	0.267962	65.19	61.21	1.065022	3.98	0.061052
McGraw-Hill	60.88	52.4	1.161832	8.48	0.13929	50.56	42.87	1.17938	7.69	0.152097
Merck	54.63	53.59	1.019407	1.04	0.019037	63.75	63.35	1.006314	0.4	0.006275
Nalco	36.5	36.17	1.009124	0.33	0.009041	51.75	43.92	1.178279	7.83	0.151304
Nortel	18.88	16.36	1.154034	2.52	0.133475	84.56	42.15	2.006168	42.41	0.501537
Pepsi	36	31.72	1.134931	4.28	0.118889	38.1	29.29	1.300785	8.81	0.231234
Pfizer	50.38	46.78	1.076956	3.60	0.071457	34.5	32.93	1.047677	1.57	0.045507
Smithkline Becham	45.5	52.29	0.870147	−6.79	−0.149231	—	—	—	—	—
Syntex	38.63	39.49	0.978222	−0.86	−0.022262	—	—	—	—	—
3M	64.65	62.21	1.039222	2.44	0.037742	97.69	80.36	1.215655	17.33	0.177398
Wal-Mart	32.75	30.75	1.065041	2.00	0.061069	44.81	18.17	2.466153	26.64	0.59451
Washington Post	191.5	189.09	1.012745	2.41	0.012585	549.13	612.1	0.897125	−62.97	−0.114672
Waste Management	34.38	30.39	1.131293	3.99	0.116056	—	—	—	—	—
Worthington Ind.	24	18.7	1.283422	5.30	0.220833	15.06	14.6	1.031507	0.46	0.030544
Average percent error					0.029269					0.143985
Number of errors less than 15%					30/35					17/30
Number of errors where market > def					23/35					28/30

Figure 14.6 Regressions of market/book versus DCF/book, 1988 and 1999. (Source: McKinsey analysis, 1988, and Monitor analysis, 1999.)

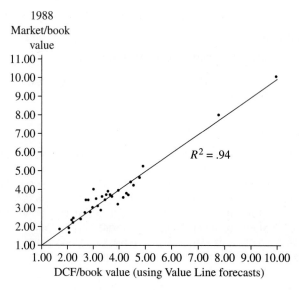

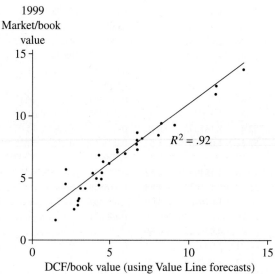

intercept of zero and a slope of one, and the *r*-squareds are quite high, ranging between 95 and 97%. The results of the comparables approach are good but slightly worse than the DCF approach. When multiples of comparable companies were regressed against the transaction multiples, the intercept is significantly different from zero ($t = 3.235$) and the slope is significantly less than one ($t = -2.000$). Comparable transaction multiples fared somewhat better but were not quite as good as the DCF approach. For these and other reasons, Kaplan and Ruback conclude that DCF valuations perform at least as well as valuation methods using comparable companies and transactions.

Table 14.17 Comparison of DCF versus Multiples Based on Comparables for 51 Highly Levered Transactions

	Intercept	t-Test	Slope	t-Test	r-Squared
DCF Approach					
Cost of capital based on					
firm beta	0.060	0.286	0.980	−0.667	0.950
industry beta	0.050	0.263	0.980	−0.667	0.960
market beta	0.220	1.294	0.970	−1.000	0.970
Comparables Approach					
Comparable company	0.550	3.235	0.940	−2.000	0.960
Comparable transaction	0.210	1.313	0.920	−1.500	0.970

Source: Kaplan and Ruback [1995].

C. Corporate Tax Policy and Value

Tax regulations are constantly changing, both by acts of legislatures and via case law as well. It is legal to avoid taxes by aggressive utilization of legal policies but illegal to evade taxes (e.g., by failing to report taxable income). Financial officers of a company can create high value by reducing the firm's effective cash tax rate via legal avoidance. For example, if CCE were to reduce its average EBIT cash tax rate from 30 to 27%, it would increase its equity value roughly $6 billion.

This section of the chapter will focus on corporate tax policy. The equilibrium between personal and corporate rates is important because individuals can choose to leave income inside a corporate legal form where it is exposed to corporate rates or pay it out and therefore expose it to personal income taxes. Aware of this choice, tax authorities try to write tax policy to make tax payers relatively indifferent at the margin whether they receive income on corporate or personal account. Much of the analysis that follows looks at the policy both from the perspective of the employees as well as the corporation. However, we shall leave the analysis of the effect of the tax deductibility of interest expenses to the next chapter—a chapter that discusses optimal capital structure.

Given this preface, what is covered in this section of Chapter 14? First is a refresher of U.S. corporate taxes as the tax code was written as of the fourth quarter of 2002. Next, we discuss tax effects of compensation planning, then the effect of taxes on transactions such as acquisitions, divestitures, and spin-offs. Finally, there is coverage of the multinational aspects of taxes for a U.S. domiciled company.

1. U.S. Corporate Tax Law

For companies with taxable income over $335,000 the federal tax rate is 34%. State and local taxes are deductible against taxable income for federal tax purposes. Therefore, the effective marginal tax rate, T_m, which includes the effect of the federal tax rate, T_f, and state and local tax rates, T_l, is

$$T_m = T_l + T_f \left(1 - T_l\right).$$

Table 14.18 Value of the Interest Tax Shield for Various Depreciation Methods

Year	Discount at 10 %	Straight Line	PV Tax Shield	Sum-of-Years Digits	PV Tax Shield	Double Declining	Balance	PV Tax Shield
0	1.000	0		0			1,000.0	
1	.909	200	181.8	5/15(1,000) = 333.33	302.97	.4(1,000) = 400.00	600.0	363.60
2	.826	200	165.2	4/15(1,000) = 266.67	220.27	.4(600) = 240.00	360.0	198.24
3	.751	200	150.8	3/15(1,000) = 200.00	150.80	.4(360) = 144.00	216.0	108.14
4	.683	200	136.6	2/15(1,000) = 133.33	91.06	.4(216) = 108.0	108.0	73.76
5	.621	200	124.2	1/15(1,000) = 66.67	41.40		108.0	0.0	67.07
		1,000	758.6		1,000.00	805.90	1,000.0		810.81

For example, state and local taxes might be 10% and federal taxes might be 34%. If so, the marginal tax rate, T_m, is 40.6%. Note that in the Coca-Cola valuation we assumed the marginal rate was 41%.

Depreciation is a deductible expense, and companies may choose among a number of depreciation methods: straight-line ($1/N$th of the original book value per year, where N is the allowed life of the project), sum-of-years digits, declining balance, and the units of production approach. Note that real estate must be depreciated only by the straight-line method. Given a positive tax rate, value is maximized by using the depreciation method that accelerates the depreciation tax shield the most. The example given in Table 14.18 shows that double declining depreciation (the 200% declining balance method) creates greater value than the sum-of-years digits and the straight-line method for a hypothetical five-year $1,000 project that can be written off in five years. The present value of the double declining depreciation tax shield (at 10%) is $810.81, while straight-line depreciation for the same project provides a tax shield whose present value is only $758.60. Generally Accepted Accounting Principles (GAAP) allow companies to use straight-line depreciation for their annual reports, while using accelerated depreciation for tax-reporting purposes. The difference between the two is recorded as accrued taxes due.

Corporate capital gains and losses used to be taxed at different rates. Long-term gains were taxed at lower rates than short-term gains, and while this is still true for personal income taxes, it is no longer valid for corporate taxes. All gains and losses are taxed at the ordinary rate.

Interest payments on debt are tax deductible, but dividend payments to equity are not. This distinction plays a major role in the cost of capital and capital structure, as the next chapter will discuss in detail. Dividend income, received from corporate ownership of the stock of another corporation, is 80% exempt from taxation; in other words, ordinary income taxes are paid on only 20% of dividends received from another company.

Net operating loss carryovers are allowed for up to 15 years, and carrybacks for 3 years, subject to the limitations of the Alternate Minimum Tax (AMT). If, for example, a company loses $1,000,000 one year, but made taxable profits of $150,000 for each of the three prior years, then it could go back and reduce its taxable income down to the AMT amount in each year. It could also reduce profits in future years down to the AMT amount until the unused balance of $550,000 of NOL (net operating loss) carry forwards is used up. However, there are limitations to the use of NOLs when there is a change of ownership. The NOL carryover is disallowed if either of the following conditions exist: (1) 50% or more of the company's stock changes hands during a two-year period as a result of share repurchases, or (2) the corporation changes its trade or business. Also, if a company that is profitable purchases one with NOL carry forwards, they may not be used by the surviving entity. However, the opposite is not true. A company that has NOL carry forwards may continue to use them if it acquires a profitable company.

Consolidation of financial statements is necessary when a company owns 50% or more of the voting equity in another company. Income received from the subsidiary is fully included in the income statement but is reduced by a minority interest account that subtracts out the income paid to minority owners of the subsidiary. Pro rata ownership of the balance sheet, both assets and liabilities, is also accounted for. When a company owns less than 50% of another company, only the income that is dividended out is recorded on the income statement, but there are no balance sheet implications.

2. Compensation Design and Corporate Taxes

There are many forms of compensation. Some, like perquisites, are subtle. The building that an employee works in can be decorated sparsely at minimum expense to the company or lavishly at much greater expense. Typically, consumption in this form is not taxed to the employee, and the company deducts the full cost. Many forms of compensation take this form—golf with customers on company time, an expensive dinner, box office tickets at a championship game, and the company picnic are all examples. Since these fringe benefits are not taxable to the employee and are tax deductible to the employer, they are tax-preferred forms of compensation from the employee's perspective. But what about other tax effects on compensation choices? What about deferred compensation, stock grants, stock options, and interest-free loans? An excellent book-length presentation of these and other tax issues can be found in *Taxes and Business Strategy*, co-authored by Scholes, Wolfson, Erickson, Maydew, and Shevlin [2002].

Deferred compensation depends on the relative rate of return that the employee can earn on the deferred amount vis-à-vis the company, and whether the company and individual tax rates are expected to change over time. If, for example, the employee's tax rate is expected to fall, and the company can earn more on investment than the employee, then deferred compensation is preferable.

To demonstrate this result, we begin with the company's point of view. It can pay a salary amount that is fully tax deductible and on an after-tax basis costs $\$Y_0(1 - T_{c0})$ right now, or it can defer payment and pay $D_n(1 - T_{cn})$ in year n. Note that T_{ct} is the corporate tax rate in year t, and later on and T_{px} is the personal tax rate. We assume that the corporation can earn rate $_0r_n$ between now and year n. It would be indifferent if

$$Y_0(1 - T_{c0})(1 + {_0r_n})^n = D_n(1 - T_{cn})$$

$$D_n = Y_0(1 + {_0r_n})^n \frac{(1 - T_{c0})}{(1 - T_{cn})}. \tag{14.34}$$

For example, if CCE can earn 30% on invested capital after taxes, and if the EBIT cash tax rate is expected to remain the same, then the company would be indifferent between paying, for each dollar of current income, a deferred income five years later of $3.71. An employee must decide whether this is better than could be obtained on personal account, where she could earn an equivalent risk-adjusted rate equal to the company's cost of capital, say, 10%. The employee would be indifferent between an after-tax salary of $Y_0(1 - T_{0p})$ today that will earn a rate of return, $_0k_n$, for n years, and a deferred payment of $D_n^*(1 - T_{pn})$ after taxes. Therefore, the employee would be indifferent if

$$Y_0(1 - T_{0p})(1 + {}_0k_n)^n = D_n^*(1 - T_{pn})$$

$$D_n^* = Y_0\left(1 + {}_0k_n\right)^n \frac{(1 - T_{p0})}{(1 - T_{pn})}. \tag{14.35}$$

If the employee can earn a 10% return on the deferred compensation but expects no change in her tax rate, then she would be indifferent between a dollar of current income and $1.61 of deferred compensation paid five years later. However, the company is indifferent between a dollar of current income and $3.71 five years hence. Obviously, the employee will take any deferred compensation from the company that exceeds $1.61. If the company were to offer $3.71, the employee would take it. We might expect, therefore, to see more use of deferred compensation by companies that are expected to earn more than their cost of capital, and that have employees that anticipate a decrease in their personal tax rates in the not-so-distant future.

Fringe benefits, if taxed to the employee, are less desirable than those that are received tax free. But are they still desirable? Take health insurance benefits, for example. Suppose coverage for each employee is $5,000 per year, whether the company pays for it or the employee does. Should the employer pay each employee an additional pretax amount that equals $5,000 after personal taxes, or should it pay for the policy on behalf of the employee and record the benefit as taxable income to the employee? Suppose the employer's tax rate, T_c, is 40% and the employee's rate, T_p, is 30%. If the employee is paid extra income so that after taxes he can pay $5,000, and if the employer deducts the extra income, then the after-tax cost to the employer is

$$C_c = \$5,000 \frac{(1 - T_c)}{(1 - T_p)}. \tag{14.36}$$

The alternative from the employer's point of view is to pay the $5,000 directly to the health insurance company and to deduct it as an expense, with an after-tax cost of $C_c^* = 5,000(1 - T_c)$. This cost is lower; therefore the employer prefers direct payment. If the employee is taxed on the benefit, he receives medical benefits worth $5,000 but pays additional taxes of $5,000T_p = \$1,500$. He is happy to receive the health insurance, of course, but would prefer that the company pay additional salary of $\$1,500/(1 - T_p) = \$2,143$ so that his salary remains the same as it was before adoption of the health plan. Naturally, it turns out that if the company pays the employee $5,000 in benefits plus $2,143, the total after-tax cost to the company is C_c. Tax law says that if the benefits are to be tax deductible, they must be offered equally to all employees. With group health insurance, some employees expect to use the benefits more than others. Those for whom the benefits have relatively low value would prefer extra salary.

Stock appreciation rights and employee stock options. are two types of compensation that are tied to the company's stock price. Stock appreciation rights (SARs) are cash payments that equal the change in the company's stock price over a prespecified period of time. If the stock appreciates, the employee pays personal taxes at the time he elects to exercise his right to receive the appreciation in cash, and the company can deduct the payment. If the stock declines in value, nothing happens— the employee is not required to pay the firm. Thus, an SAR is isomorphic to a call option with equivalent life where the exercise price equals the stock price at the time of grant.

Executive stock options come in two varieties—nonqualified stock options (NQSOs) and incentive stock options (ISOs). In both cases the employee is granted a certain number of American call options to buy shares at a prespecified exercise price for a fixed period of time (often 5 to

Figure 14.7 Tax consequences of NQSOs and
ISOs.

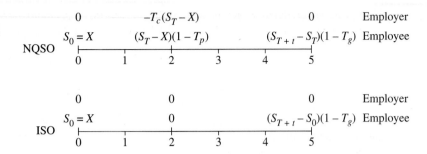

10 years). At the time of exercise (year 2 in Figure 14.7), the gain from NQSOs is taxed to the employee at the ordinary tax rate, T_p, and the taxable basis for the stock that is bought becomes the stock price, S_T, that day.[10] The employer can deduct the full amount of the employee's gain, the stock price minus the exercise price, $S_T - X$. For ISOs there are no taxable events at the time of exercise, either for the employee or the corporation. Instead, taxation is deferred until the date that the stock that was purchased at the exercise date is actually sold. On the date that the stock is sold (year 5 in Figure 14.7), the employee pays a (long-term) capital gains tax on the appreciation of the stock since the date of the original option grant (i.e., $S_T - S_0$). Interestingly, the employer receives no tax deduction for ISOs at any time, neither at the time of the grant, the exercise date, nor the time of sale of the stock.

To determine whether NQSOs are preferable to ISOs or vice versa, we need to compare them both from the employee's and the employer's point of view. Let's use the following example. Suppose the company grants a stock option at time zero when the stock price, S_0, is $20, with an exercise price equal to the stock price (i.e., $S_0 = X$). We assume that it will be exercised two years later at time T when the stock price is $S_T = \$40$, and that the executive then holds the stock for another 3 years when the stock price reaches $S_{T+t} = \$70$. Also, the corporate tax rate is $T_c = 40\%$, and the executive's tax rate is $T_p = 30\%$ on ordinary income and $T_g = 15\%$ on long-term capital gains. Figure 14.7 shows the tax obligations and their timing. Should the firm use NQSOs or ISOs? Let's start from the employee's perspective. The after-tax income from the NQSO at the time of exercise ($t = 2$) is made up of two parts: the gain upon exercise in year 2 less the ordinary income tax, and the gain between the stock price at the time the option was exercised and the price on the date of final sale in year 5. This second term is discounted from year 5 to year 2 at the employee's rate of time preference, k_p, which we assume is 10% per year:

$$NQSO \text{ income as of year 2: } (S_T - X)(1 - T_p) + (S_{T+t} - S_T)(1 - T_g)/(1 + k_p)^3. \quad (14.37)$$

Next, we compare the after-tax income of the ISO, which is the after-tax capital gain from the sale of stock in year 5. We can separate this gain into two parts, namely, the gain from the date of exercise to final sale, and the gain from the time of grant to the time of exercise, and discount the gain to year 2:

$$ISO \text{ income as of year 2: } (S_{T+t} - S_T)(1 - T_g)/(1 + k_p)^3 + (S_T - X)(1 - T_g)/(1 + k_p)^3. \quad (14.38)$$

---

[10] The determination of whether gains or losses from holding the stock (after it is purchased via exercise of the NQSOs) are taxed at the short- or long-term capital gains rate depends on the length of time the stock is held after the exercise date and on the tax code at the time of taxation.

If the capital gains tax rate is less than the ordinary rate and if the employee's rate of time preference is positive, her income from NQSOs will be less than from ISOs, as shown below:

$$\text{ISO income} > \text{NQSO income} \quad \text{if } T_p > T_g \text{ and } k_p > 0$$

$$\frac{(S_{T+t} - S_T)(1 - T_g)}{(1 + k_p)^3} + \frac{(S_T - X)(1 - T_g)}{(1 + k_p)^3} > (S_T - X)(1 - T_p) + \frac{(S_{T+t} - S_T)(1 - T_g)}{(1 + k_p)^3}.$$

Canceling out terms gives:

$$\frac{(1 - T_g)}{(1 + k_p)^3} > (1 - T_p). \tag{14.39}$$

Therefore, we have the result that if the individual's ordinary tax rate, T_p, is greater than the discounted capital gains rate, then ISOs will be preferred to NQSOs by the employee.

In order to make the executive indifferent, the company must gross up the NQSO reimbursement amount by multiplying it by the inverse of the right-hand side of Eq. (14.39). Since NQSO compensation is tax deductible to the employer, the after-tax cost of NQSO compensation becomes

$$(S_T - S_0)\frac{(1 - T_c)}{(1 - T_p)}.$$

The employer will prefer NQSOs to ISOs if the after-tax payment given above is less than the ISO income to the employee given by the left-hand side of Eq. (14.39); therefore we solve the following inequality, and if the left-hand side is greater, the employer will prefer NQSOs:

$$S_T - S_0 > (S_T - S_0)\frac{(1 - T_c)}{(1 - T_p)}\frac{(1 - T_g)}{(1 + k_p)^n}$$

$$\frac{(1 - T_c)}{(1 - T_p)} > 1$$

$$(1 - T_c) > (1 - T_p).$$

The employer is indifferent between NQSOs and ISOs when the firm's marginal tax rate is equal to the marginal ordinary personal rate:

$$T_c = T_p. \tag{14.40}$$

Using the numerical assumptions of this example, the corporate tax rate is 40%, and the personal tax rate is 30%; therefore the company will prefer the NQSO.

3. Tax Planning for Transactions

The different types of transactions that a corporation may enact include an acquisition of the assets of another company for stock or cash, the acquisition of its equity for stock or cash, a joint venture with another company, purchase of minority interest in another company, divestiture of assets, initial public offering (IPO) of part of the company (sometimes called an equity carveout), spin-off of a business unit, and sale of tracking (or letter stock). Other, more financial transactions such

Figure 14.8 Decision tree for tax effects of an acquisition.

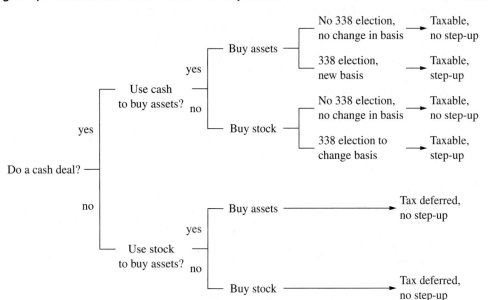

as public issues of debt and equity, repayment or call of debt, repurchase of equity, and swaps are all covered later in the text.

Acquisition and divestiture are the most frequent transactions. The tax status at the time of the deal depends on whether the transaction is for cash or stock. If the acquirer pays mostly with stock, there is no tax at the time of the transaction. Payment is simply deferred until the stock that has been received is sold for cash. When the acquirer pays mostly with cash, the deal is taxable.

A corporate acquirer has several ways to compensate the shareholders of a target. It can create a taxable event either by purchasing the target's assets or its equity with cash. If it purchases assets, it also assumes all of the target's liabilities. If it buys stock, debt is paid off prior to the transaction. If the transaction purchases the target's stock, the target can choose a Section 338 election that will result in a step-up or step-down of the taxable basis of the target firm's assets to their "fair market value." When the target company elects to use Section 338, the taxable basis for items of this type is increased, and the seller must pay taxes on the increase. Figure 14.8 is a decision tree that details the consequences of using cash or stock and of using a Section 338 election.

Cash for assets deal: When the target receives cash for assets, it must pay taxes that are either ordinary or capital gains depending on the assets being sold. For example, the sale of inventory is taxed at the ordinary rate. Property, plant, and equipment that is stepped up via a Section 338 election subjects the target to taxes on the difference (if any) between its sale price and the new basis; however, the difference between the new basis and the original purchase price is also taxable (usually at the capital gains rate). The acquirer takes the stepped-up basis in the target's assets given a Section 338 election.

Cash for stock deal: If the target receives cash for stock, the acquirer's taxable basis in the target's stock generally becomes the purchase price. But if the acquirer has used cash to buy the target's stock and the target elects to use Section 338, then the acquirer can elect to treat its purchase of the target's stock as if it had purchased assets. Consequently, the taxable basis of the target's assets is stepped up to the fair market value (i.e., to the purchase price plus tax liabilities associated with the step-up). Given these circumstances, the target's tax attributes are eliminated (except for its ability to use NOL carry forwards to offset capital gains on the asset sale).

Stock for stock deal: If the acquirer uses stock to purchase the target's stock in a tax-deferred exchange, the target's shareholders will not usually recognize taxable gains at the time of the deal. Also, the acquirer is not permitted to step up the basis of the target's assets. Additionally, the acquirer retains the target's tax attributes.

Stock for assets deal: If the acquirer uses stock to purchase the acquirer's assets in a tax-deferred exchange, the target's shareholders pay no taxes at the time of the deal; rather they pay at a later date when they sell the shares. The acquirer takes a carryover basis in the target's assets, that is, the same tax basis that the target had before the deal. Moreover, the acquirer will not acquire the target's tax attributes.

The tax deductibility of goodwill under Section 197 of the OBRA of 1993 makes goodwill (and nearly all other purchased intangible assets) tax deductible as they are amortized over a 15-year period. However, tax-deductible goodwill arises only from acquisitions where the tax basis of the target's assets had been stepped up. Often the goodwill that is recorded on the balance sheet is not tax deductible; in fact, among freestanding C corporations a stepped-up basis is rare. Scholes et al. [2002] suggest a way of estimating the proportion of total goodwill that cannot be amortized as a tax deductible expense (pp. 328–332).

Taxation of divestitures is also partitioned into those that are tax free at the transaction date, and those that trigger a taxable event. Tax-free events include equity carveouts (the sale of all or part of a business unit) and spin-offs (the distribution of shares in a business unit as a tax-free dividend to existing shareholders that results in the creation of a new stand-alone company).

Table 14.19 shows the accounting and tax treatment of an *equity carveout,* depending on the percentage of the ownership of a business unit that is sold via an initial public offering (IPO). If less than 20% of a unit is IPO'd, the parent can still consolidate the income of the unit for tax purposes as well as for accounting purposes. Between 20 and 50% only consolidation for accounting purposes is allowed, and if controlling interest is sold via the IPO, then no consolidation is allowed. In general the IPO is tax free to the parent if the proceeds of the sale of the unit's shares go to the unit. In spite of this restriction, the parent usually gets cash because it becomes a lender to the unit and the cash from the IPO is often used to pay off the debt, thereby transferring it to the parent. Typically, the transaction does not create a taxable event for either the parent or the IPO'd unit. Often a partial IPO precedes a spin-off.

A *spin-off* is normally a tax-free dividend of 100% of the shares in a new company that was formerly the business unit of a parent company. In order to qualify as tax free under Section 355 of the tax code, certain requirements must be met: The parent company must own 80% of the business unit, the parent must distribute 80% of the ownership in the stock, both the parent and the unit

Table 14.19 Accounting and Tax Treatment of an Equity Carveout

Percent of Ownership Sold	Can Be Consolidated for		Which Entity Receives Proceeds?
	Tax Purposes?	Accounting Purposes?	
50–100%	No	No	IPO'd BU
21–49%	No	Yes	IPO'd BU
0–20%	Yes	Yes	IPO'd BU

must have on-going businesses after the spin-off, the transaction cannot be simply a mechanism for distributing the profits of the parent, the historical shareholders of the parent must maintain a continuing interest in the spin-off, the spin-off cannot have been acquired in a taxable transaction in the last five years, and neither the divesting parent nor the spin-off can be acquired within two years of the spin-off. The taxable basis of the spin-off to the shareholders of the parent company is created by the ratio of the fair market value of the individual shares to the sum of their values at the date of the spin-off, when they are traded separately. If, for example, the shares of the parent were bought for $100 and at the spin-off date the parent shares trade (ex spin-off) at $120 and the spin-off's shares trade at $30, then the tax basis for the parent's shares becomes ($120/$150)($100) = $80 and the tax basis for the spin-off becomes ($30/$150)($100) = $20.

4. Multinational Taxation

The taxation of multinational corporations is complex. Furthermore, tax codes are constantly changing. This textbook cannot be and is not authoritative on the topic, but it can provide an overview of four major topics that confront multinational corporations: foreign tax credits, transfer pricing policies, the use of offshore corporations, and the decision of how and when to repatriate cash from a foreign domicile.

Foreign tax credits are deductions from U.S. federal tax obligations much in the same way that state taxes are. Table 14.20 provides two examples. In both the rule for calculating U.S. taxes is to allow a foreign tax credit that is the lesser of either the U.S. tax rate times consolidated foreign income, or the foreign taxes actually paid on foreign income, whichever is lower. In the first example, foreign tax paid in country A is $40 and in country B it is $180 for a total of $220. The total income earned in countries A and B is $500 and if we multiply by the 34% U.S. federal tax rate, we get $170. Therefore, the foreign tax credit in this case is $170. This amount is a deduction against preliminary U.S. taxes of $510. Therefore, net U.S. taxes due will be $340. Total taxes paid will be $340 in the U.S. and $220 abroad for a total of $560. Since this is the same as the total of all local taxes (countries A and B plus the U.S.), there is no corporate tax penalty that results from the U.S. tax code. This will generally be the result when foreign earnings are located in tax jurisdictions where tax rates are higher than the U.S. (e.g., $300 of foreign income in a 60% tax rate location). If we change the example, as in the bottom half of Table 14.20, so that a larger portion of foreign income is in a low-tax-rate country, the U.S. tax code creates a "corporate tax penalty" because foreign income becomes taxed at the U.S. rate.

In the second example, shown in the bottom half of the table, the U.S. tax code has raised the average effective tax rate to the U.S.-based parent company on income received from country A from 20% (the local rate) to ($30 + $80)/$400 = 27.5%. The marginal effective tax rate in country A has become 34%, the U.S. rate, rather than the local rate of 20%. If this situation were to persist in the long run, and if the company does not wish to move its legal domicile from the U.S. to country A, then it may be advisable to sell the foreign subsidiary to a local owner from country A. The reason, of course, is that after-tax cash flows would be higher for the local owner because his effective tax rate would be only 20%.

Transfer prices are the artificial transfer rates between business units of a company. The objective, at least for tax avoidance, is to reduce profits in high-tax jurisdictions. For example, one can charge out as many headquarters functions as possible, charge foreign business units for research and development expenses, borrow at the subsidiary level, consolidate same-country profitable and unprofitable subsidiaries to take advantage of tax-loss carry forwards, bill back employee stock option expenses to other countries, use cost plus accounting to reduce foreign

Table 14.20 Examples of Use of Foreign Tax Credits by a U.S. Corporation

With Market Prices	U.S.	Subsidiary A	Subsidiary B	Consolidated	U.S. and B Consolidated
Pretax income	$1,000	$200	$300	$1,500	
Local tax rate	× 34%	× 20%	× 60%		
Local taxes	$340	$40	$180		
U.S. tax rate				× 34%	
Preliminary U.S. taxes				$510	
Less: foreign tax credits				− $170	
Net U.S. taxes				$340	
Foreign taxes				+ 220	
Consolidated income taxes				$560	
Less: total local taxes				− $560	
Corporate tax penalty				0	

Using Transfer Prices

	U.S.	Subsidiary A	Subsidiary B	Consolidated	U.S. and B Consolidated
Pretax income	$1,000	$400	$100	$1,500	$1,100
Local tax rate	× 34%	× 20%	× 60%		
Local taxes	$340	$80	$60		
U.S. tax rate				× 34%	34%
Preliminary U.S. taxes				$510	$374
Less: foreign tax credits				− $140	$34
Net U.S. taxes				$370	$340
Foreign taxes				+ $140	+ $60
Consolidated income taxes				$510	$400
Less: total local taxes				− $480	− $400
Corporate tax penalty				$30	$0

Note: The foreign tax credit is the foreign taxes paid or the U.S. tax rate times foreign income, whichever is less.

profit, increase royalty charges and license fees to a foreign subsidiary, establish management fee arrangements, and set low transfer prices for goods and services supplied by the foreign subsidiary to the rest of the company and high transfer prices for goods and services supplied to the subsidiary. Remember that all of these maneuvers are subject to scrutiny by the tax authorities in both jurisdictions. Nevertheless, tax planning can have a significant effect on the market value of a multinational company.

The interrelationship between transfer pricing and effective tax rates is complex. Referring back to Table 14.20, suppose that the profits reflected in the example in the top half of the table are based on market prices. The economics textbooks usually recommend that, tax considerations aside, all decision making should be based on market prices. In this example, however, taxes should not be ignored. Suppose, for example, that the parent is able to use transfer pricing to shift $200 of pretax income from country B, where the tax rate is 60%, to country A, where it is only 20%. The next-to-last column of the bottom half of the table provides the result, namely, that consolidated income taxes have dropped from $560 to $510. However, there is a corporate tax penalty of $30 in this solution. How shall we interpret it?

Given the $30 tax penalty that results from the transfer pricing scheme, it would appear that the parent should consider selling its subsidiary in country A to an owner domiciled in country A. But we have to be careful. If the subsidiary is sold to a local owner, there would be no shift of profits to A from B—and market prices would apply. Therefore, assuming a 10% cost of capital and perpetual cash flows, the subsidiary would be worth

$$[\$200 - .2(\$200)]/.10 = \$1,600$$

to the local owner. Assuming the transfer pricing scheme works for the parent, the country A subsidiary will be worth

$$[\$400 - .2(\$400)/.10 = \$3,200.$$

After consideration of the interaction of transfer pricing and the U.S. tax code for multinationals, the optimum decision for the U.S. parent is to employ transfer pricing to minimize taxes and to retain both of its foreign subsidiaries. Table 14.21 shows the values of various combinations. The highest valued result, namely, keeping both subsidiaries, is calculated as pretax profit of $1,500 less consolidated taxes of $510, capitalized at 10%, for a total of $9,900. If subsidiary A were sold for $1,600 (after taxes), the total value from the sale added to the value of the parent and the value of subsidiary B (which could no longer benefit from transfer pricing) would be only $9,400.

The answer would change if transfer pricing were disallowed and we assumed market prices. Then it would be best to sell subsidiary A while keeping subsidiary B (and the parent, of course). We would receive $1,600 from selling A to a local owner. The preliminary U.S. tax on $1,300 of consolidated profits from the parent and subsidiary B would be .34($1,300) = $442, and the foreign tax credit would be the lesser of the foreign tax paid (i.e., $180) or the U.S. tax rate times profit in country B (which would be $300), that is, $102. Therefore, net U.S. taxes would be $442 less a foreign tax credit of $102, which equals $340. Add taxes paid in country B of $180 and total taxes are $520. The value of the consolidated entity (the parent plus subsidiary B) will be net after tax profit of $1,300 minus total taxes of $520, which equals $790 and when capitalized at 10% provides a value of $7,900. Therefore, the total value obtained from selling A and keeping the

Table 14.21 Value of Various Business Combinations to the Parent Given Transfer Pricing

Business Combination	Using Top Half of Table 14.20	Using Bottom Half of Table 14.20
Keep all three businesses	$9,400	$9,900
Sell A, keep B and parent	$9,500	$9,500
Sell B, keep A and parent	$9,120	$9,120
Sell A and B, keep parent	$9,400	$9,400

Note: Values are estimated assuming no debt, perpetual cash flow, and a 10% cost of capital.

parent and B is $9,500. Table 14.21 shows that, when compared with the other possibilities, this provides the highest value if market prices prevail. If transfer pricing is allowed, the best strategy is to keep all three entities because the value is $9,900.

Some companies build simulation models to deal with the complex combinations of multinational taxation and ownership. It is important to remember, however, that the value of the subsidiary to alternative owners should be taken into consideration.

Repatriation of earnings is often restricted by foreign nations, leading to the need to decide whether to invest in the first place, and how to recover cash from the foreign country given local laws. Let's begin by assuming that all cash flows earned abroad can be repatriated without penalty. In this case one needs to consider the all-in tax effects and the relative rates of return on investments when compared in the same currency. If funds, NI_0, are retained for investment in the foreign subsidiary, they will earn a local after-tax rate, r_l, and be taxed at the local rate, τ_l. Alternately, if we repatriate them, we pay the U.S. tax rate, T_m, and earn the after-tax rate of return, r_{us}, on our U.S.-based operations. We have to consider the fact that the rate of return in the local currency usually translates into a different rate in the home currency over time according to the forward foreign exchange rate (see Chapter 8 for a discussion of forward rates, and Chapter 19 for an application to foreign exchange rates). Let $_0f_T$ be the forward foreign exchange rate between the two currencies expressed in units of foreign currency per dollar (e.g., 125 yen per dollar). The algebra of the decision is whether it is better to repatriate and pay U.S. taxes now or to wait T years, earn the local rate and pay local taxes, and then convert to dollars and pay U.S. taxes at year T. Indifference is achieved if the two alternatives have the same payout after taxes in year T. We will choose to repatriate now if

$$NI_0(_0f_0)(1 - T_m)(1 + r_{us})^T > NI_0(1 + r_l)^T {_0f_T}(1 - T_m)$$

$$(1 + r_{us})^T > (1 + r_l)^T \frac{_0f_T}{_0f_0}.$$

For example, if the after-tax return from investing in the U.S. is 10% and the after-tax rate in Japan is 5%, and if the spot rate of exchange is 125 yen per dollar and the five-year forward rate is 100 yen per dollar, we would have

$$1.61 = (1.1)^5 > (1.05)^5 \frac{100}{125} = 1.021,$$

and we would conclude to repatriate.

If there are restrictions on the amount of funds that can be repatriated, then we would need to build a discounted cash flow model, or even a real options decision tree to assess the conditions under which we would repatriate if we could.

Choice of domicile is becoming less important as the business world becomes more global and governments become more sophisticated in their administration of taxes on foreign income. The United States computes a foreign tax credit (FTC) limitation for each company on a worldwide basis each year in the following way:

FTC limitation = (foreign source income/Worldwide income) × U.S. tax on

worldwide income before FTC

Foreign source income includes all income earned through foreign branches, all income repatriated (or deemed to be repatriated) from foreign subsidiaries, or subpart F income. Worldwide income is all income regardless of where it was earned, and the last term is the U.S. tax liability before foreign tax credits. The implication is that if tax havens, all taxing at a rate lower than the U.S. rate, could be found, it would not do any good due to the FTC limitation rule.

Summary

This chapter has covered the details of valuation and provided an overview of U.S. tax policy. Valuation methodology does not change much over time, but tax laws do. We strongly recommend that you consult legal counsel before making any tax-related decisions. Our intent was merely to point out the effect of tax features such as deferral, different forms of ownership, and foreign taxes. One cannot forget that when management acts on behalf of the shareholders of a company, the tax position of the employees, of other companies, and of other countries is an integral part of deciding who will do what.

PROBLEM SET

14.1 When corporations issue liabilities (debt at a bank or bonds to the public), we assume that they do so at fair market rates. This implies that, on the day the liability is issued, the cash received by the company is equal in value to the debt liability that is recorded on the balance sheet. Except for the possibility of a tax shelter (see Chapter 15), financing creates no value. Banks and insurance companies are different because their liabilities (e.g., demand deposits at a bank, or insurance policy reserves at an insurance company) involve services. Consequently, growth of deposits and of reserves actually creates value for shareholders. How would you construct a DCF valuation differently

    (a) for banks?

    (b) for insurance companies?

14.2 Look at the spreadsheet for Coca-Cola.

    (a) Does the ratio of excess cash marketable securities to total current assets make sense (compare 2003 to 2010)?

    (b) How would you change the model forecasts to make the ratio of excess cash and marketable securities to total current assets more reasonable?

    (c) How would your proposal change affect the value of Coca-Cola?

14.3 Compute the ratio of entity value to EBIT for Coca-Cola in 2000 and again in 2010.

    (a) Do the ratios make sense?

    (b) What do they tell you about the company?

14.4 Substitute reasonable numbers for Coca-Cola (see the suggestions below) into Eq. (14.21).

    (a) What value does the equation provide?

    (b) How do you explain the differences between the formula result and the spreadsheet result?

    (c) Suppose that Coke is able to increase its sales growth rate by an extra 1% every year forever, by accepting a decline in its rate of return. Use Eq. (14.21) to estimate how much return it could give up while maintaining the same value.

Suggested parameter values:

$$EBIT = 4,000 \quad B = 6,000 \quad r = 52\% \text{ pretax}$$
$$T_c = 33\% \quad K = 15\% \quad k_u = 8.45\%$$
$$WACC = 8.3\% \quad N = 10 \text{ years}$$

14.5 The XYZ company is growth oriented, and their return on invested capital is just equal to their cost of capital. Suppose that the company has no debt and

$$NOPLAT_{10} = \$1,000$$
$$EBIT = 1,667$$
$$T = 4$$
$$g = 10\%$$
$$r = 12\%$$
$$WACC = 12\%$$

What happens to its value if the company raises its growth rate from 10% to 15%? What is the new reinvestment rate, K? Explain.

REFERENCES

Ayers, B., C. Lefanowicz, and J. Robinson, "The Effects of Goodwill Tax Deductions on the Market for Corporations Acquisitions," *Journal of the American Taxation Association*, Supplement, 2000, Vol. 22.

Copeland, T., T. Koller, and J. Murrin, *Valuation: Measuring and Managing the Value of Companies*, 3rd edition, John Wiley and Sons, New York, 2001.

Cornell, B., *Corporate Valuation Business*, One Irwin, Homewood, Ill., 1993.

Damodaran, A., *Damodaran on Valuation*, John Wiley & Sons, New York, 1994.

Erickson, M., "The Effect of Taxes on the Structure of Corporate Acquisitions," *Journal of Accounting Research*, 1998, Vol. 36, 279–298.

Erickson, M., and S. Wang, "The Effect of Transaction Structure on Price: Evidence from Subsidiary Sales," *Journal of Accounting and Economics*, 2000, Vol. 30, 59–97.

Fuller, R., and C.-C. Hsia, "A Simplified Common Stock Valuation Model," *Financial Analysts Journal*, Sept.–Oct. 1984, 49–56.

Holt, C., "The Influence of Growth Duration on Share Prices," *Journal of Finance*, September 1962, 465–475.

Kaplan, S., "Management Buyouts: Evidence on Taxes as a Source of Value," *Journal of Finance*, July 1989, 611–632.

Kaplan, S., and R. Ruback, "The Valuation of Cash Flow Forecasts: An Empirical Analysis," *Journal of Finance*, September 1995, 1059–1093.

Landsman, W., and D. Shackelford, "The Lock-In Effect of Capital Gains Taxes: Evidence from the RJR Nabisco Leveraged Buyout," *National Tax Journal*, June 1995, 245–259.

Malkiel, B., "Equity Yields, Growth, and the Structure of Share Prices," *American Economic Review*, December 1963, 467–494.

Maydew, E., K. Schipper, and L. Vincent, "The Effect of Taxes on Divestiture Method," *Journal of Accounting and Economics*, 1999, Vol. 28, 117–150.

Miller, M., and F. Modigliani, "Dividend Policy, Growth and the Valuation of Shares," *Journal of Business*, October 1961, 411–433.

Modigliani, F., "Debt, Dividend Policy, Taxes, Inflation, and Market Valuation," *Journal of Finance*, May 1982, 255–273.

Ohlson, J., and S. Penman, "Disaggregated Accounting Data as Explanatory Variables for Return," *Journal of Accounting, Auditing, and Finance*, Fall 1992, 553–573.

Rappaport, A., *Creating Shareholder Value*, The Free Press, New York, 1986.

Scholes, M., M. Wolfson, M. Erikson, E. Maydew, and T. Shevlin, *Taxes and Business Strategy: A Planning Approach*, 2nd edition, Prentice-Hall, Upper Saddle River, N.J., 2002.

Weston, J. F., and T. E. Copeland, *Managerial Finance*, 9th edition, Dryden Press, 1992.

Chapter 15

The average cost of capital to any firm is completely independent of its capital structure and is equal to the capitalization rate of a pure equity stream of its class.

—F. Modigliani and M. H. Miller, "The Cost of Capital, Corporation Finance, and the Theory of Investment," *American Economic Review*, June 1958, 268.

Capital Structure and the Cost of Capital: Theory and Evidence

F UNDS FOR INVESTMENT are provided to the firm by investors who hold various types of claims on the firm's cash flows. Debt holders have contracts (bonds) that promise to pay them fixed schedules of interest and principal in the future in exchange for their cash now. Equity holders provide retained earnings or buy rights offerings (internal equity provided by *existing* shareholders) or purchase new shares (external equity provided by *new* shareholders). They do so in return for claims on the residual earnings of the firm in the future. Also, shareholders retain control of the investment decision, whereas bondholders have no direct control except for various types of indenture provisions in the bond that may constrain the decision making of shareholders. In addition to these two basic categories of claimants, there are others such as holders of convertible debentures, leases, preferred stock, nonvoting stock, and warrants.

Each investor category is confronted with a different type of risk, and therefore each requires a different expected rate of return in order to provide funds to the firm. The required rate of return is the opportunity cost to the investor of investing scarce resources elsewhere in opportunities with *equivalent risk*. As we shall see, the fact that shareholders are the ones who decide whether to accept or reject new projects is critical to understanding the cost of capital. They will accept only those projects that increase their expected utility of wealth. Each project must earn, on a risk-adjusted basis, enough net cash flow to pay investors (bondholders and shareholders) their expected rates of return, to pay the principal amount that they originally provided, and to have something left over that will increase the wealth of existing shareholders. The cost of capital is the minimum risk-adjusted rate of return that a project must earn in order to be acceptable to shareholders.

The investment decision cannot be made without knowledge of the cost of capital. Consequently, many textbooks introduce the concept of the cost of capital before they discuss investment decisions. It probably does not matter which topic comes first. Both topics are important and they are interrelated. Figure 15.1 shows the investment decision as the intersection of the demand and supply of investment capital. All projects are assumed to have equivalent risk. Also, fund sources have

Figure 15.1 Demand and supply of investment for projects of equal risk.

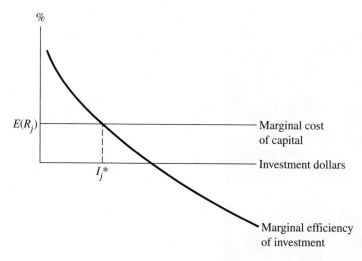

equal risk (in other words, in Fig. 15.1 we make no distinction between equity and debt). Chapter 2 discussed the ranking of projects assuming that the appropriate cost of capital was known. The schedule of projects with their rates of return is sometimes called the *marginal efficiency of investment schedule* and is known as the demand curve in Fig. 15.1. The supply of capital, represented as the marginal cost of capital curve, is assumed to be infinitely elastic. Implicitly, the projects are assumed to have equal risk. Therefore the firm faces an infinite supply of capital at the rate $E(R_j)$ because it is assumed that the projects it offers are only a small portion of all investment in the economy. They affect neither the total risk of the economy nor the total supply of capital. The optimal investment for the firm is I_j^*, and the marginally acceptable project must earn at least $E(R_j)$. All acceptable projects, of course, earn more than the marginal cost of capital.

Figure 15.1 is an oversimplified explanation of the relationship between the cost of capital and the amount of investment. However, it demonstrates the interrelatedness of the two concepts. For a given schedule of investments a rise in the cost of capital will result in less investment. This chapter shows how the firm's mix of debt and equity financing affects the cost of capital, explains how the cost of capital is related to shareholders' wealth, and shows how to extend the cost of capital concept to the situation where projects do not all have the same risk. If the cost of capital can be controlled via some judicious mixture of debt and equity financing, then the financing decision can maximize the value of the firm.

Whether or not an optimal capital structure exists is one of the most important issues in corporate finance—and one of the most complex. This chapter covers the effect of tax-deductible debt on the value of the firm, first in a world with only corporate taxes, then by adding personal taxes as well. Next the effect of business disruption and bankruptcy costs is introduced, and we extend the basic Modigliani-Miller model using the work of Leland. The result is an equilibrium theory of capital structure. The chapter also covers nonequilibrium theories that include the pecking order theory, signaling, and the effect of forgoing profitable investments. There is also a discussion of the effect of risky debt, warrants, convertible bonds, and callable bonds.

Our discussion of optimal capital structure continues by asking two related questions—how can we explain optimal capital structure, if it exists, within an industry, and how can we explain the cross-sectional regularities among industries? Toward this end we survey the empirical evidence. Bankruptcy costs, option pricing effects, agency costs, and the signaling theory are all discussed along with empirical evidence bearing on their validity. Also, the optimal maturity structure of debt is presented. Corporate financial officers must decide not only on how much debt to carry but also its duration. Should it be short-term or long-term debt?

A. The Value of the Firm Given Corporate Taxes Only

1. The Value of the Levered Firm

Modigliani and Miller [1958, 1963] wrote the seminal papers on the cost of capital, corporate valuation, and capital structure. They assumed either explicitly or implicitly the following:

1. Capital markets are frictionless.
2. Individuals can borrow and lend at the risk-free rate.
3. There are no costs to bankruptcy or to business disruption.
4. Firms issue only two types of claims: risk-free debt and (risky) equity.
5. All firms are assumed to be in the same risk class (operating risk).
6. Corporate taxes are the only form of government levy (i.e., there are no wealth taxes on corporations and no personal taxes).
7. All cash flow streams are perpetuities (i.e., no growth).
8. Corporate insiders and outsiders have the same information (i.e., no signaling opportunities).
9. Managers always maximize shareholders' wealth (i.e., no agency costs).
10. Operating cash flows are completely unaffected by changes in capital structure.

It goes without saying that many of these assumptions are unrealistic, but later we can show that relaxing many of them does not really change the major conclusions of the model of firm behavior that Modigliani and Miller provide. Relaxing the assumption that corporate debt is risk-free will not change the results (see Section D). However, the assumptions of no bankruptcy costs (relaxed in Section E) and no personal taxes (relaxed in Section B of this chapter) are critical because they change the implications of the model. The eighth and ninth assumptions rule out signaling behavior (because insiders and outsiders have the same information) and agency costs (because managers never seek to maximize their own wealth). And the tenth assumption is crucial because the operating cash flows are not actually independent of capital structure—with the result that investment and financing decisions should be thought of as codeterminant. These issues are discussed in detail later on.

The fifth assumption requires greater clarification. What is meant when we say that all firms have the same risk class? The implication is that the expected risky future net operating cash flows vary by, at most, a scale factor. Mathematically this is

$$\widetilde{CF}_i = \lambda \widetilde{CF}_j,$$

where

$\widetilde{CF}$ = the risky net cash flow from operations (cash flow before interest and taxes),

λ = a constant scale factor.

This implies that the expected future cash flows from the two firms (or projects) are perfectly correlated.

If, instead of focusing on the level of cash flow, we focus on the returns, the perfect correlation becomes obvious because the returns are identical, as shown below:

$$\tilde{R}_{i,t} = \frac{\widetilde{CF}_{i,t} - CF_{i,t-1}}{CF_{i,t-1}},$$

and because $\widetilde{CF}_{i,t} = \lambda \widetilde{CF}_{j,t}$, we have

$$\tilde{R}_{i,t} = \frac{\lambda \widetilde{CF}_{j,t} - \lambda CF_{j,t-1}}{\lambda CF_{j,t-1}} = \tilde{R}_{j,t}.$$

Therefore if two streams of cash flow differ by, at most, a scale factor, they will have the same distribution of returns, the same risk, and will require the same expected return.

Suppose the assets of a firm return the same distribution of net operating cash flows each time period for an infinite number of time periods. This is a no-growth situation because the average cash flow does not change over time. We can value this after-tax stream of cash flows by discounting its expected value at the appropriate risk-adjusted rate. The value of the unlevered firm (i.e., a firm with no debt) will be

$$V_U = \frac{E(\widetilde{FCF})}{\rho}, \tag{15.1}$$

where

V_U = the present value of an unlevered firm (i.e., all equity),

$E(\widetilde{FCF})$ = the perpetual free cash flow after taxes (to be explained in detail below),

ρ = the discount rate for an all-equity firm of equivalent risk.

This is the value of an unlevered firm because it represents the discounted value of a perpetual, nongrowing stream of free cash flows after taxes that would accrue to shareholders if the firm had no debt. To clarify this point, let us look at the following pro forma statement:

Rev	Revenues
$-VC$	Variable costs of operations
$-FCC$	Fixed cash costs (e.g., administrative costs and real estate taxes)
$-dep$	Noncash charges (e.g., depreciation and deferred taxes)
EBIT	Earnings before interest and taxes
$-k_d D$	Interest on debt (interest rate times principal, D)
EBT	Earnings before taxes
$-T$	Taxes $= \tau_c(EBT)$, where τ_c is the corporate tax rate
NI	Net income

It is extremely important to distinguish between cash flows and the accounting definition of profit. After-tax cash flows from operations may also be calculated as EBIT (earnings before interest and taxes) less cash taxes on EBIT:

$$\widetilde{EBIT} - \tau_c \widetilde{EBIT}.$$

Rewriting this using the fact that $\widetilde{EBIT} = \widetilde{Rev} - \widetilde{VC} - FCC - dep$, we have

$$(\widetilde{Rev} - \widetilde{VC} - FCC - dep)(1 - \tau_c).$$

This is operating income after taxes, but it is not yet a cash flow definition because a portion of total fixed costs are noncash expenses such as depreciation and deferred taxes. Total fixed costs are partitioned in two parts: FCC is the cash fixed costs, and dep is the noncash fixed costs.

To convert after-tax operating income into cash flows, we must add back depreciation and other noncash expenses. Doing this, we have

$$(\widetilde{Rev} - \widetilde{VC} - FCC - dep)(1 - \tau_c) + dep.$$

Finally, by assumption, we know that the firm has no growth; that is, all cash flows are perpetuities. This implies that depreciation each year must be replaced by investment in order to keep the same amount of capital in place. Therefore $dep = I$, and the after-tax free cash flow available for payment to creditors and shareholders is

$$\widetilde{FCF} = (\widetilde{Rev} - \widetilde{VC} - FCC - dep)(1 - \tau_c) + dep - I,$$

$$\widetilde{FCF} = (\widetilde{Rev} - \widetilde{VC} - FCC - dep)(1 - \tau_c) \quad \text{since} \quad dep = I.$$

The interesting result is that when all cash flows are assumed to be perpetuities, free cash flow $(\widetilde{FCF})$ is the same thing as net operating income after taxes (i.e., the cash flow that the firm would have available if it had no debt at all). This is shown below:

$$\widetilde{EBIT}(1 - \tau_c) = \widetilde{FCF} = (\widetilde{Rev} - \widetilde{VC} - FCC - dep)(1 - \tau_c).$$

Note also that this approach to cash flows is exactly the same as that used to define cash flows for budgeting purposes in Chapter 2. The reader should keep in mind that in order to determine the value of the firm correctly, the definition of cash flows and the definition of the discount rate (i.e, the weighted average cost of capital) must be consistent. The material that follows will prove that they are.

Given perpetual cash flows, Eq. (15.1), the value of the unlevered firm, can be written in either of two equivalent ways:[1]

$$V_U = \frac{E(\widetilde{FCF})}{\rho} \quad \text{or} \quad V_U = \frac{E(\widetilde{EBIT})(1 - \tau_c)}{\rho}. \tag{15.2}$$

From this point forward we shall use the net operating income definition of cash flows in order to be consistent with the language originally employed by Modigliani and Miller.

---

[1] The present value of any constant perpetual stream of cash flows is simply the cash flow divided by the discount rate. See Appendix A at the end of the book, Eq. (A.5).

Next assume that the firm issues debt. The after-tax cash flows must be split up between debt holders and shareholders. Shareholders receive $\widetilde{NI} + dep - I$, net cash flows after interest, taxes, and replacement investment; bondholders receive interest on debt, $k_d D$. Mathematically, this is equivalent to total cash flow available for payment to the private sector:[2]

$$\widetilde{NI} + dep - I + k_d D = (\widetilde{Rev} - \widetilde{VC} - FCC - dep - k_d D)(1 - \tau_c) + k_d D.$$

Given that $dep = I$, for a nongrowing firm we can rearrange terms to obtain

$$\widetilde{NI} + k_d D = (\widetilde{Rev} - \widetilde{VC} - FCC - dep)(1 - \tau_c) + k_d D \tau_c. \tag{15.3}$$

The first part of this stream, $\widetilde{EBIT}(1 - \tau_c)$, is exactly the same as the cash flows for the unlevered firm, the numerator of Eq. (15.1), with exactly the same risk. Therefore, recalling that this is a perpetual stream, we can discount it at the rate appropriate for an unlevered firm, ρ. The second part of the stream, $k_d D \tau_c$, is assumed to be risk free. Therefore we shall discount it at the before-tax cost of risk-free debt, k_b. Consequently, the value of the levered firm is the sum of the discounted value of the two types of cash flow that it provides:

$$V^L = \frac{E(\widetilde{EBIT})(1 - \tau_c)}{\rho} + \frac{k_d D \tau_c}{k_b}. \tag{15.4}$$

Note that $k_d D$ is the perpetual stream of risk-free payments to bondholders and that k_b is the current before-tax market-required rate of return for the risk-free stream. Therefore, since the stream is perpetual, the market value of the bonds, B, is

$$B = \frac{k_d D}{k_b}. \tag{15.5}$$

Now we can rewrite Eq. (15.3) as

$$V_L = V_U + \tau_c B. \tag{15.6}$$

The value of the levered firm, V_L, is equal to the value of an unlevered firm, V_U, plus the present value of the tax shield provided by debt, $\tau_c B$. Later on we shall refer to the "extra" value created by the interest tax shield on debt as the *gain from leverage*. This is perhaps one of the most important results in the theory of corporation finance obtained in the last 50 years. It says that in the absence of any market imperfections including corporate taxes (i.e, if $\tau_c = 0$), the value of the firm is completely independent of the type of financing used for its projects. Without taxes, we have

$$V_L = V_U, \quad \text{if} \quad \tau_c = 0. \tag{15.5a}$$

Equation (15.5a) is known as *Modigliani-Miller Proposition I*. "The market value of any firm is independent of its capital structure and is given by capitalizing its expected return at the rate ρ appropriate to its risk class."[3] In other words, the method of financing is irrelevant. Modigliani and Miller went on to support their position by using one of the very first arbitrage pricing arguments

---

[2] The government receives all cash flows not included in Eq. (15.2); that is, the government receives taxes (also a risky cash flow).

[3] Modigliani and Miller [1958, 268].

Table 15.1 Proposition I Arbitrage Example

	Company A	Company B
$EBIT$	10,000	10,000
$-k_dD$	0	1,500
NI	10,000	8,500
k_s	10%	11%
S	100,000	77,272
B	0	30,000
$V = B + S$	100,000	107,272
$WACC$	10%	9.3%
B/S	0%	38.3%

in finance theory. Many say that the arbitrage-free equilibrium was the best of their contributions and the primary reason they deserved the Nobel prize in economics.

One of Professor Miller's favorite jokes was a story about the famous baseball player for the New York Yankees, the catcher Yogi Berra. It seems that after a close game he retired with friends to a local Italian restaurant where he ordered an entire pizza for himself. When the waiter asked if Yogi would like the pizza cut into six slices or eight, the famous humorist replied, "I would like eight slices please. I am very hungry." Of course, the price of the pizza was unchanged by how it was sliced. So too, argued Modigliani and Miller, the value of a firm is independent (aside from tax considerations) of how its liabilities—debt and equity—are partitioned.

Consider the income statements of the two firms given in Table 15.1. Both companies have exactly the same perpetual cash flows from operations, $EBIT$, but company A has no debt, whereas company B has $30,000 of debt paying 5% interest. The example reflects greater risk in holding the levered equity of company B because the cost of equity, $k_s = NI/S$, for B is greater than that of company A. The example has been constructed so that company B has a greater market value than A and hence a lower weighted average cost of capital, $WACC = EBIT/V$. The difference in values is a violation of Proposition I. However, the difference will not persist because if we already own stock in B, we can earn a profit with no extra risk by borrowing (at 5%) and buying company A. In effect, we create homemade leverage in the following way:

1. We sell stock in B (if we own 1%, then we sell $772.72).
2. We borrow an amount equivalent to 1% of the debt in B, that is, $300 at 5% interest.
3. We buy 1% of the shares in A.

Before arbitrage we held 1% of the equity of B and earned 11% on it, that is, .11($772.72) = $85.00. After arbitrage we hold the following position:

1% of A's equity and earn 10%, that is, .10 ($1,000.00)	=	$100.00
pay interest on $300 of debt, that is, .05($300)	=	−15.00
		85.00

This gives the same income as our levered position in company B, but the amount of money we have available is $772.72 (from selling shares in B) plus $300 (from borrowing). So far, in the above calculation, we have used only $1,000.00 to buy shares of A. Therefore we can invest another $72.72 in shares of A and earn 10%. This brings our total income up to $85 + $7.27 = $92.27, and we own $772.72 of *net* worth of equity in A (the bank "owns" $300). Therefore our return on equity is 11.94% (i.e., $92.27/$772.72). Furthermore, our personal leverage is the $300 in debt divided by the equity in A, $772.72. This is exactly the same leverage and therefore the same risk as we started with when we had an equity investment in B.

The upshot of the foregoing arbitrage argument is that we can use homemade leverage to invest in A. We earn a higher rate of return on equity without changing our risk at all. Consequently, we will undertake the arbitrage operation by selling shares in B, borrowing, and buying shares in A. We will continue to do so until the market values of the two firms are identical. Therefore Modigliani-Miller Proposition I is a simple arbitrage argument. In a world without taxes the market values of the levered and unlevered firms must be identical.

However, as shown by Eq. (15.5), when the government "subsidizes" interest payments to providers of debt capital by allowing the corporation to deduct interest payments on debt as an expense, the market value of the corporation can increase as it takes on more and more (risk-free) debt. Ideally (given the assumptions of the model) the firm should take on 100% debt.[4]

2. The Weighted Average Cost of Capital

Next, we can determine the cost of capital by using the fact that shareholders will require the rate of return on new projects to be greater than the opportunity cost of the funds supplied by them and bondholders. This condition is equivalent to requiring that original shareholders' wealth increase. From Eq. (15.3) we see that the change in the value of the levered firm, ΔV^L, with respect to a new investment, ΔI, is[5]

$$\frac{\Delta V_L}{\Delta I} = \frac{(1 - \tau_c)}{\rho} \frac{\Delta E(\widetilde{EBIT})}{\Delta I} + \tau_c \frac{\Delta B}{\Delta I}. \tag{15.7}$$

If we take the new project, the change in the value of the firm, ΔV_L, will also be equal to the change in the value of original shareholders' wealth, ΔS^o, plus the new equity required for the project, ΔS^n, plus the change in the value of bonds outstanding, ΔB^o, plus new bonds issued, ΔB^n:

$$\Delta V_L = \Delta S^o + \Delta S^n + \Delta B^o + \Delta B^n. \tag{15.7a}$$

Alternatively, the changes with respect to the new investment are

$$\frac{\Delta V_L}{\Delta I} = \frac{\Delta S^o}{\Delta I} + \frac{\Delta S^n}{\Delta I} + \frac{\Delta B^o}{\Delta I} + \frac{\Delta B^n}{\Delta I}. \tag{15.7b}$$

Because the old bondholders hold a contract that promised fixed payments of interest and principal, because the new project is assumed to be no riskier than those already outstanding, and especially because both old and new debt are assumed to be risk free, the change in the value

---

[4] We shall see later in this chapter that this result is modified when we consider a world with both corporate and personal taxes, or one where bankruptcy costs are nontrivial. Also, the Internal Revenue Service will disallow the tax deductibility of interest charges on debt if, in its judgment, the firm is using excessive debt financing as a tax shield.

[5] Note that τ_c and ρ do not change with ΔI. The cost of equity for an all-equity firm does not change because new projects are assumed to have the same risk as the old ones.

of outstanding debt is zero ($\Delta B^o = 0$). Furthermore, the new project must be financed with either new debt, new equity, or both. This implies that[6]

$$\Delta I = \Delta S^n + \Delta B^n. \tag{15.8}$$

Using this fact, Eq. (15.7b) can be rewritten as

$$\frac{\Delta V_L}{\Delta I} = \frac{\Delta S^o}{\Delta I} + \frac{\Delta S^n + \Delta B^o}{\Delta I} = \frac{\Delta S^o}{\Delta I} + 1. \tag{15.9}$$

For a project to be acceptable to original shareholders, it must increase their wealth. Therefore they will require that

$$\frac{\Delta S^o}{\Delta I} = \frac{\Delta V_L}{\Delta I} - 1 > 0, \tag{15.10}$$

which is equivalent to the requirement that $\Delta V_L / \Delta I > 1$. Note that the requirement that the change in original shareholders' wealth be positive (i.e., $\Delta S^o / \Delta I > 0$) is a behavioral assumption imposed by Modigliani and Miller. They were assuming (1) that managers always do exactly what shareholders wish and (2) that managers and shareholders always have the same information. The behavioral assumptions of Eq. (15.10) are essential for what follows.

When the assumptions of inequality (15.10) are imposed on Eq. (15.7) we are able to determine the cost of capital[7]

$$\frac{\Delta V_L}{\Delta I} = \frac{(1 - \tau_c)}{\rho} \frac{\Delta E(\widetilde{EBIT})}{\Delta I} + \tau_c \frac{\Delta B}{\Delta I} > 1,$$

or, by rearranging terms, we have

$$\frac{(1 - \tau_c)\Delta E(EBIT)}{\Delta I} > \rho \left(1 - \tau_c \frac{\Delta B}{\Delta I}\right). \tag{15.11}$$

The left-hand side of Eq. (15.11) is the after-tax change in net operating cash flows brought about by the new investment, that is, the after-tax return on the project.[8] The right-hand side is the opportunity cost of capital applicable to the project. As long as the anticipated rate of return on investment is greater than the cost of capital, current shareholders' wealth will increase.

Note that if the corporate tax rate is zero, the cost of capital is independent of capital structure (the ratio of debt to total assets). This result is consistent with Eq. (15.5a), which says that the value of the firm is independent of capital structure. On the other hand, if corporate taxes are paid, the cost of capital declines steadily as the proportion of new investment financed with debt increases. The value of the levered firm reaches a maximum when there is 100% debt financing (so long as all the debt is risk free).

---

[6] Note that Eq. (15.8) does not require new issues of debt or equity to be positive. It is conceivable, for example, that the firm might issue $4,000 in stock for a $1,000 project and repurchase $3,000 in debt.

[7] Note that ($\Delta B = \Delta B^n$) because ΔB^o is assumed to be zero.

[8] Chapter 2, the investment decision, stressed the point that the correct cash flows for capital budgeting purposes were always defined as net cash flows from operations after taxes. Equation (15.11) reiterates this point and shows that it is the *only* definition of cash flows that is consistent with the opportunity cost of capital for the firm. The numerator on the left-hand side, namely, $E(\widetilde{EBIT})(1 - \tau_c)$, is the after-tax cash flows from operations that the firm would have if it had no debt.

3. Two Definitions of Market Value Weights

Equation (15.11) defines what has often been called the weighted average cost of capital, WACC, for the firm:

$$WACC = \rho \left(1 - \tau_c \frac{\Delta B}{\Delta I}\right). \tag{15.12}$$

An often-debated question is the correct interpretation of $\Delta B / \Delta I$. Modigliani and Miller [1963, 441] interpret it by saying:

> If B^*/V^* denotes the firm's long run "target" debt ratio . . . then the firm can assume, to a first approximation at least, that for any particular investment $dB/dI = B^*/V^*$.

Two questions arise in the interpretation of the leverage ratio, $\Delta B / \Delta I$. First, is the leverage ratio marginal or average? Modigliani and Miller, in the above quote, set the marginal ratio equal to the average by assuming the firm sets a long-run target ratio, which is constant. Even if this is the case, we still must consider a second issue, namely: Is the ratio to be measured as *book value leverage, replacement value leverage,* or *reproduction value leverage*? The last two definitions, as we shall see, are both market values. At least one of these three measures, book value leverage, can be ruled out immediately as being meaningless. In particular, there is no relationship whatsoever between book value concepts (e.g., retained earnings) and the economic value of equity.

The remaining two interpretations, replacement and reproduction value, make sense because they are both market value definitions. By replacement value, we mean the economic cost of putting a project in place. For capital projects a large part of this cost is usually the cost of purchasing plant, equipment, and working capital. In the Modigliani-Miller formulation, replacement cost is the market value of the investment in the project under consideration, ΔI. It is the denominator on both sides of the cost of capital inequality (15.11). On the other hand, reproduction value, ΔV, is the total present value of the stream of goods and services expected from the project. The two concepts can be compared by noting that the difference between them is the NPV of the project, that is,

$$NPV = \Delta V - \Delta I.$$

For a marginal project, where $NPV = 0$, replacement cost and reproduction value are equal.

Haley and Schall [1973, 306–311] introduce an alternative cost of capital definition where the "target" leverage is the ratio of debt to reproduction value:

$$WACC = \rho \left(1 - \tau_c \frac{\Delta B}{\Delta V}\right). \tag{15.13}$$

If the firm uses a reproduction value concept for its "target" leverage, it will seek to maintain a constant ratio of the market value of debt to the market value of the firm.

With the foregoing as background, we can now reconcile the apparent conflict in the measurement of leverage applicable to the determination of the relevant cost of capital for a new investment project. Modigliani and Miller define the target L^* as the average, in the long run, of the debt-to-value ratio or B^*/V^*. Then regardless of how a particular investment is financed, the relevant leverage ratio is dB/dV. For example, a particular investment may be financed by debt. But the cost of that particular increment of debt is not the relevant cost of capital for that investment. The debt would require an equity base. How much equity? This is answered by the long-run target

B^*/V^*. So procedurally, we start with the actual amount of investment increment for the particular investment, dI. The L^* ratio then defines the amount of dB assigned to the investment. If the NPV from the investment is positive, then dV will be greater than dI. Hence the debt capacity of the firm will have been increased by more than dB. However, the relevant leverage for estimating the WACC will still be dB/dV, which will be equal to B^*/V^*. We emphasize that the latter is a policy target decision by the firm, based on relevant financial economic considerations. The dV is an amount assigned to the analysis to be consistent with L^*.

The issue is whether to use dB/dV or dB/dI as the weight in the cost of capital formula. The following example highlights the difference between the two approaches. Suppose a firm can undertake a new project that costs \$1,000 and has expected cash flows with a present value of \$9,000 when discounted at the cost of equity for an all-equity project of equivalent risk. If the ratio of the firm's target debt to value is 50% and if its tax rate is 40%, how much debt should it undertake? If it uses replacement value leverage, then $dB/dI = .5$ and $dB = \$500$; that is, half of the \$1,000 investment is financed with debt. Using Eq. (15.5) the value of the levered firm is

$$dV_L = dV_U + \tau_c dB$$

$$= 9,000 + .4(500)$$

$$= 9,200.$$

The same formula can be used to compute the amount of debt if we use reproduction value leverage, that is, $dB/dV_L = .5$, or $dV_L = 2dB$:

$$dV_L = 9,000 + .4dB,$$

$$2dB = 9,000 + .4dB \quad \text{since} \quad dV_L = 2dB,$$

$$dB = 5,625.$$

If our target is set by using reproduction values, then we should issue \$5,625 of new debt for the \$1,000 project, and repurchase \$4,625 of equity. The change in the value of the firm will be

$$dV_L = dV^U + \tau_c dB$$

$$= 9,000 + .4(5625)$$

$$= 11,250.$$

Clearly, the value of the firm is higher if we use the reproduction value definition of leverage. But as a practical matter, what bank would lend \$5,625 on a project that has \$1,000 replacement value of assets? If the bank and the firm have homogeneous expectations, this is possible. If they do not, then it is likely that the firm is more optimistic than the bank about the project. In the case of heterogeneous expectations there is no clear solution to the problem. Hence we favor the original argument of Modigliani and Miller that the long-run target debt-to-value ratio will be close to dB/dI (i.e., use the replacement value definition).

4. The Cost of Equity

If Eqs. (15.12) and (15.13) are the weighted average cost of capital, how do we determine the cost of the two components, debt and equity? The cost of debt is the risk-free rate, at least given the assumptions of this model. (We shall discuss risky debt in Section D.) The cost of equity capital is the change in the return to equity holders with respect to the change in their investment,

$\Delta S^o + \Delta S^n$. The return to equity holders is the net cash flow after interest and taxes, NI. Therefore their rate of return is $\Delta NI/(\Delta S^o + \Delta S^n)$. To solve for this, we begin with identity (15.2),

$$NI + k_d D = EBIT(1 - \tau_c) + k_d D\tau_c.$$

Next we divide by ΔI, the new investment, and obtain

$$\frac{\Delta NI}{\Delta I} + \frac{\Delta(k_d D)}{\Delta I} - \frac{\tau_c \Delta(k_d D)}{\Delta I} = (1 - \tau_c)\frac{\Delta EBIT}{\Delta I}. \tag{15.14}$$

Substituting the left-hand side of (15.14) into (15.6), we get

$$\frac{\Delta V_L}{\Delta I} = \frac{\Delta NI/\Delta I + (1 - \tau_c)\Delta(k_d D)/\Delta I}{\rho} + \tau_c \frac{\Delta B}{\Delta I}. \tag{15.15}$$

From (15.7), we know that

$$\frac{\Delta V_L}{\Delta I} = \frac{\Delta S^o + \Delta S^n}{\Delta I} + \frac{\Delta B^n}{\Delta I}, \quad \text{since} \quad \Delta B^o \equiv 0. \tag{15.16}$$

Consequently, by equating (15.15) and (15.16) we get

$$\frac{\Delta V_L}{\Delta I} = \frac{\Delta S^o + \Delta S^n}{\Delta I} + \frac{\Delta B}{\Delta I} = \frac{\Delta NI/\Delta I + (1 - \tau_c)\Delta(k_d D)/\Delta I}{\rho} + \tau_c \frac{\Delta B}{\Delta I}.$$

Then, multiplying both sides by ΔI, we have

$$\Delta S^o + \Delta S^n + \Delta B = \frac{\Delta NI + (1 - \tau_c)\Delta(k_d D) + \rho\tau_c\Delta B}{\rho}.$$

Subtracting ΔB from both sides gives

$$\Delta S^o + \Delta S^n = \frac{\Delta NI + (1 - \tau_c)\Delta(k_d D) + \rho\tau_c\Delta B - \rho\Delta B}{\rho},$$

$$\rho(\Delta S^o + \Delta S^n) = \Delta NI - (1 - \tau_c)(\rho - k_b)\Delta B, \quad \text{since} \quad \Delta(k_d D) = k_b\Delta B.$$

And finally,

$$\frac{\Delta NI}{\Delta S^o + \Delta S^n} = \rho + (1 - \tau_c)(\rho - k_b)\frac{\Delta B}{\Delta S^o + \Delta S^n}. \tag{15.17}$$

The change in the new equity plus old equity equals the change in the total equity of the firm ($\Delta S = \Delta S^o + \Delta S^n$). Therefore the cost of equity, $k_s = \Delta NI/\Delta S$, is written

$$k_s = \rho + (1 - \tau_c)(\rho - k_b)\frac{\Delta B}{\Delta S}. \tag{15.18}$$

The implication of Eq. (15.18) is that the opportunity cost of capital to shareholders increases linearly with changes in the market value ratio of debt to equity (assuming that $\Delta B/\Delta S = B/S$). If the firm has no debt in its capital structure, the levered cost of equity capital, k_s, is equal to the cost of equity for an all-equity firm, ρ.

Figure 15.2 The cost of capital as a function of the ratio of debt to equity: (a) assuming $\tau_c = 0$; (b) assuming $\tau_c > 0$.

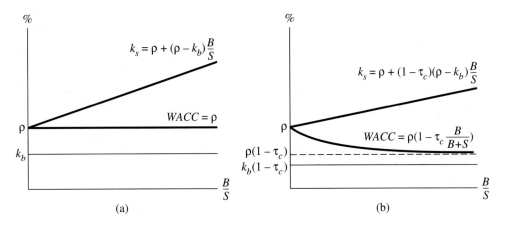

(a)   (b)

5. A Graphical Presentation for the Cost of Capital

Figure 15.2 graphs the cost of capital and its components as a function of the ratio of debt to equity. The weighted average cost of capital is invariant to changes in capital structure in a world without corporate taxes; however, with taxes it declines as more and more debt is used in the firm's capital structure. In both cases the cost of equity capital increases with higher proportions of debt. This makes sense because increasing financial leverage implies a riskier position for shareholders as their residual claim on the firm becomes more variable. They require a higher rate of return to compensate them for the extra risk they take.

The careful reader will have noticed that in Fig. 15.2 B/S is on the horizontal axis, whereas Eqs. (15.13) and (15.18) are written in terms of $\Delta B/\Delta S$ or $\Delta B/\Delta V$, which are changes in debt with respect to changes in equity or value of the firm. The two are equal only when the firm's average debt-to-equity ratio is the same as its marginal debt-to-equity ratio. This will be true as long as the firm establishes a "target" debt-to-equity ratio equal to B/S and then finances all projects with the identical proportion of debt and equity so that $B/S = \Delta B/\Delta S$.

The usual definition of the weighted average cost of capital is to weight the after-tax cost of debt by the percentage of debt in the firm's capital structure and add the result to the cost of equity multiplied by the percentage of equity. The equation is

$$WACC = (1 - \tau_c)k_b \frac{B}{B + S} + k_s \frac{S}{B + S}. \tag{15.19}$$

We can see that this is the same as the Modigliani-Miller definition, Eq. (15.12), by substituting (15.18) into (15.19) and assuming that $B/S = \Delta B/\Delta S$.

$$WACC = (1 - \tau_c)k_b \frac{B}{B+S} + \left[\rho + (1 - \tau_c)(\rho - k_b)\frac{B}{S}\right]\frac{S}{B+S}$$

$$= (1 - \tau_c)k_b \frac{B}{B+S} + \rho\frac{S}{B+S} + (1 - \tau_c)\rho\frac{B}{S}\frac{S}{B+S} - (1 - \tau_c)k_b\frac{B}{S}\frac{S}{B+S}$$

$$= (1 - \tau_c)k_b \frac{B}{B+S} + \rho\left(\frac{S}{B+S} + \frac{B}{B+S}\right) - \rho\tau_c\frac{B}{B+S} - (1 - \tau_c)k_b\frac{B}{B+S}$$

$$= \rho\left(1 - \tau_c\frac{B}{B+S}\right). \qquad \text{QED}$$

There is no inconsistency between the traditional definition and the M-M definition of the cost of capital [Eqs. (15.12) and (15.19)]. They are identical.

B. $\mathcal{T}$he Value of the Firm in a World with Both Personal and Corporate Taxes

1. Assuming All Firms Have Identical Effective Tax Rates

In the original model the *gain from leverage, G,* is the difference between the value of the levered and unlevered firms, which is the product of the corporate tax rate and the market value of debt:

$$G = V_L - V_U = \tau_c B. \tag{15.20}$$

Miller [1977] modifies this result by introducing personal as well as corporate taxes into the model. In addition to making the model more realistic, the revised approach adds considerable insight into the effect of leverage on value in the real world. We do not, after all, observe firms with 100% debt in their capital structure as the original Modigliani-Miller model suggests.

Assume for the moment that there are only two types of personal tax rates: the rate on income received from holding shares, τ_{ps}, and the rate on income from bonds, τ_{pB}. The expected after-tax stream of cash flows to shareholders of an all-equity firm would be $(EBIT)(1 - \tau_c)(1 - \tau_{ps})$. By discounting this perpetual stream at the cost of equity for an all-equity firm, we have the value of the unlevered firm:

$$V_U = \frac{E(EBIT)(1 - \tau_c)(1 - \tau_{ps})}{\rho}. \tag{15.21}$$

Alternatively, if the firm has both bonds and shares outstanding, the earnings stream is partitioned into two parts. Cash flows to shareholders after corporate and personal taxes are

$$\text{payments to shareholders} = (EBIT - k_d D)(1 - \tau_c)(1 - \tau_{ps}),$$

and payments to bondholders, after personal taxes, are

$$\text{payments to bondholders} = k_d D(1 - \tau_{pB}).$$

Adding these together and rearranging terms, we have

$$\begin{matrix} \text{total cash payments} \\ \text{to suppliers of capital} \end{matrix} = EBIT(1 - \tau_c)(1 - \tau_{ps}) - k_d D(1 - \tau_c)(1 - \tau_{ps}) + k_d D(1 - \tau_{pB}). \quad (15.22)$$

The first term on the right-hand side of (15.22) is the same as the stream of cash flows to owners of the unlevered firm, and its expected value can be discounted at the cost of equity for an all-equity firm. The second and third terms are risk free and can be discounted at the risk-free rate, k_b. The sum of the discounted streams of cash flow is the value of the levered firm:

$$V_L = \frac{E(EBIT)(1 - \tau_c)(1 - \tau_{ps})}{\rho} + \frac{k_d D\left[(1 - \tau_{pB}) - (1 - \tau_c)(1 - \tau_{ps})\right]}{k_b}$$

$$= V_U + \left[1 - \frac{(1 - \tau_c)(1 - \tau_{ps})}{(1 - \tau_{pB})}\right] B, \quad (15.23)$$

where $B = k_d D(1 - \tau_{pB})/k_b$, the market value of debt. Consequently, with the introduction of personal taxes, the gain from leverage is the second term in (15.23):

$$G = \left[1 - \frac{(1 - \tau_c)(1 - \tau_{ps})}{(1 - \tau_{pB})}\right] B. \quad (15.24)$$

Note that when personal tax rates are set equal to zero, the gain from leverage in (15.24) equals the gains from leverage in (15.20), the earlier result. This finding also obtains when the personal tax rate on share income equals the rate on bond income. In the United States it is reasonable to assume that the effective tax rate on common stock is lower than that on bonds.[9] The implication is that the gain from leverage when personal taxes are considered (15.24) is lower than $\tau_c B$ (15.20).

If the personal income tax on stocks is less than the tax on income from bonds, then the before-tax return on bonds has to be high enough, other things being equal, to offset this disadvantage. Otherwise the investor would want to hold bonds. While it is true that owners of a levered corporation are subsidized by the interest deductibility of debt, this advantage is counterbalanced by the fact that the required interest payments have already been "grossed up" by any differential that bondholders must pay on their interest income. In this way the advantage of debt financing may be lost. In fact, whenever the following condition is met in Eq. (15.24),

$$(1 - \tau_{pB}) = (1 - \tau_c)(1 - \tau_{ps}), \quad (15.25)$$

the advantage of debt vanishes completely.

Suppose that the personal tax rate on income from common stock is zero. We may justify this by arguing that (1) no one has to realize a capital gain until after death; (2) gains and losses in well-diversified portfolios can offset each other, thereby eliminating the payment of capital gains taxes; (3) 80% of dividends received by taxable corporations can be excluded from taxable income; or (4) many types of investment funds pay no taxes at all (nonprofit organizations, pension funds, trust funds, etc.).[10] Figure 15.3 portrays the supply and demand for corporate bonds. The rate paid on the debt of tax-free institutions (municipal bonds, for example) is r_0. If all bonds paid only r_0,

---

[9] The tax rate on stock is thought of as being lower than that on bonds because of a relatively higher capital gains component of return, and because capital gains are not taxed until the security is sold. Capital gains taxes can, therefore, be deferred indefinitely.

[10] Also, as will be shown in Chapter 17, it is possible to shield up to $10,000 in dividend income from taxes.

Figure 15.3 Aggregate supply and demand for corporate bonds (before tax rates).

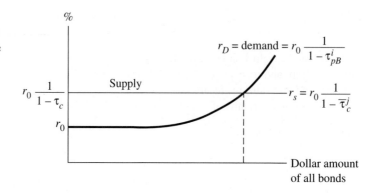

no one would hold them, with the exception of tax-free institutions that are not affected by the tax advantage of holding debt when $\tau_{pB} > \tau_{ps}$. An individual with a marginal tax rate on income from bonds equal to τ_{pB}^i will not hold corporate bonds until they pay $r_0/(1 - \tau_{pB}^i)$, that is, until their return is "grossed up." Since the personal income tax is progressive, the interest rate that is demanded has to keep rising to attract investors in higher and higher tax brackets.[11] The supply of corporate bonds is perfectly elastic, and bonds must pay a rate of $r_0/(1 - \tau_c)$ in equilibrium.

To see that this is true, let us recall that the personal tax rate on stock is assumed to be zero ($\tau_{ps} = 0$) and rewrite the gain from leverage:

$$G = \left(1 - \frac{(1 - \tau_c)}{(1 - \tau_{pB})}\right) B. \tag{15.26}$$

If the rate of return on bonds supplied by corporations is $r_s = r_0/(1 - \tau_c)$, then the gain from leverage, in Eq. (15.26), will be zero. The supply rate of return equals the demand rate of return in equilibrium:

$$r_s = \frac{r_0}{1 - \tau_c} = r_D = \frac{r_0}{1 - \tau_{pB}}.$$

Consequently,

$$(1 - \tau_c) = (1 - \tau_{pB}),$$

and the gain from leverage in (15.26) will equal zero. If the supply rate of return is less than $r_0/(1 - \tau_c)$, then the gain from leverage will be positive, and all corporations will try to have a capital structure containing 100% debt. They will rush out to issue new debt. On the other hand, if the supply rate of return is greater than $r_0/(1 - \tau_c)$, the gain from leverage will be negative and firms will take action to repay outstanding debt. Thus we see that, in equilibrium, taxable debt must be supplied to the point where the before-tax cost of corporate debt must equal the rate that would be paid by tax-free institutions grossed up by the corporate tax rate.

---

[11] Keep in mind that the tax rate on income from stock is assumed to be zero. Therefore the higher an individual's tax bracket becomes, the higher the before-tax rate on bonds must be in order for the after-tax rate on bonds to equal the rate of return on stock (after adjusting for risk).

Miller's argument has important implications for capital structure. First, the gain to leverage may be much smaller than previously thought. Consequently, optimal capital structure may be explained by a trade-off between a small gain to leverage and relatively small costs such as expected bankruptcy costs. This trade-off will be discussed at greater length in the book. Second, the observed market equilibrium interest rate is seen to be a before-tax rate that is "grossed up" so that most or all of the interest tax shield is lost. Finally, Miller's theory implies there is an equilibrium amount of aggregate debt outstanding in the economy that is determined by relative corporate and personal tax rates.

2. Assuming That Firms Have Different Marginal Effective Tax Rates

DeAngelo and Masulis [1980] extend Miller's work by analyzing the effect of tax shields other than interest payments on debt (e.g., noncash charges such as depreciation, oil depletion allowances, and investment tax credits). They are able to demonstrate the existence of an optimal (nonzero) corporate use of debt while still maintaining the assumption of zero bankruptcy (and zero agency) costs.

Their original argument is illustrated in Fig. 15.4. The corporate debt supply curve is downward sloping to reflect the fact that the expected marginal effective tax rate, τ_c^j, differs across corporate suppliers of debt. Investors with personal tax rates lower than the marginal individual earn a consumer surplus because they receive higher after-tax returns. Corporations with higher tax rates than the marginal firm receive a positive gain to leverage, a producer's surplus, in equilibrium because they pay what is for them a low pretax debt rate.

It is reasonable to expect depreciation expenses and investment tax credits to serve as tax shield substitutes for interest expenses. The DeAngelo and Masulis model predicts that firms will select a level of debt that is negatively related to the level of available tax shield substitutes such as depreciation, depletion, and investment tax credits. Also, as more and more debt is utilized, the probability of winding up with zero or negative earnings will increase, thereby causing the interest tax shield to decline in expected value. They further show that if there are positive bankruptcy costs, there will be an optimum trade-off between the marginal expected benefit of interest tax shields and the marginal expected cost of bankruptcy. This issue will be further discussed in the next chapter.

Figure 15.4 Aggregate debt equilibrium with heterogeneous corporate and personal tax rates.

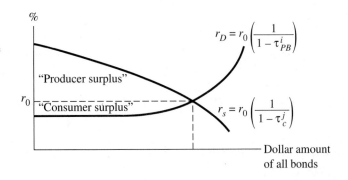

C. $\mathcal{I}$ntroducing Risk—A Synthesis of the Modigliani-Miller Model and CAPM

The CAPM discussed in Chapter 6 provides a natural theory for the pricing of risk. When combined with the cost of capital definitions derived by Modigliani and Miller [1958, 1963], it provides a unified approach to the cost of capital. The work that we shall describe was first published by Hamada [1969] and synthesized by Rubinstein [1973].

The CAPM may be written as

$$E(R_j) = R_f + [E(R_m) - R_f]\beta_j, \tag{15.27}$$

where

$$E(R_j) = \text{the expected rate of return on asset } j,$$

$$R_f = \text{the (constant) risk-free rate,}$$

$$E(R_m) = \text{the expected rate of return on the market portfolio}$$

$$\beta_j = \text{COV}(R_j, R_m)/\text{VAR}(R_m).$$

Recall that all securities fall exactly on the security market line, which is illustrated in Fig. 15.5. We can use this fact to discuss the implications for the cost of debt, the cost of equity, the weighted average cost of capital, and for capital budgeting when projects have different risk.

Figure 15.5 illustrates the difference between the original Modigliani-Miller cost of capital and the CAPM. Modigliani and Miller assumed that all projects within the firm had the same business or operating risk (mathematically, they assumed that $CF_i = \lambda CF_j$). This was expedient because in 1958, when the paper was written, there was no accepted theory that allowed adjustments for differences in systematic risk. Consequently, the Modigliani-Miller theory is represented by the horizontal line in Fig. 15.5. The WACC for the firm (implicitly) does not change as a function of systematic risk. This assumption, of course, must be modified because firms and projects differ in risk.

Figure 15.5 The security market line.

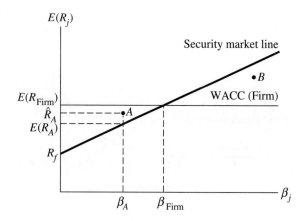

Table 15.2 Comparison of M-M and CAPM Cost of Capital Equations

Type of Capital	CAPM Definition	M-M Definition
Debt	$k_b = R_f + [E\left(R_m\right) - R_f]\beta_b$	$k_b = R_f,\ \beta_b = 0$
Unlevered equity	$\rho = R_f + [E(R_m) - R_f]\beta_U$	$\rho = \rho$
Levered equity	$k_s = R_f + [E(R_m) - R_f]\beta_L$	$k_s = \rho + (\rho - k_b)(1 - \tau_c)\frac{B}{S}$
WACC for the firm	$WACC = k_b(1 - \tau_c)\frac{B}{B+S} + k_s\frac{S}{B+S}$	$WACC = \rho\left(1 - \tau_c\frac{B}{B+S}\right)$

1. The Cost of Capital and Systematic Risk

Table 15.2 shows expressions for the cost of debt, k_b, unlevered equity, ρ, levered equity, k_s, and the weighted average cost of capital, $WACC$, in both the Modigliani-Miller (M-M) and capital asset pricing model frameworks. It has already been demonstrated in the proof following Eq. (15.19), that the traditional and M-M definitions of the weighted average cost of capital (the last line in Table 15.2) are identical. Modigliani and Miller assumed, for convenience, that corporate debt is risk free; that is, its price is insensitive to changes in interest rates and either that it has no default risk or that default risk is completely diversifiable ($\beta_b = 0$). We shall temporarily maintain the assumption that $k_b = R_f$, then relax it a little later in the chapter.

The M-M definition of the cost of equity for the unlevered firm was tautological (i.e., $\rho = \rho$) because the concept of systematic risk had not been developed in 1958. We now know that it depends on the systematic risk of the firm's after-tax operating cash flows, β_U. Unfortunately for empirical work, the unlevered beta is not directly observable. We can, however, easily estimate the levered equity beta, β_L. (This has also been referred to as β_s elsewhere.) If there is a definable relationship between the two betas, there are many practical implications (as we shall demonstrate with a simple numerical example in the next section).

To derive the relationship between the levered and unlevered betas, begin by equating the M-M and CAPM definitions of the cost of levered equity (line 3 in Table 15.2):

$$R_f + \left[E(R_m) - R_f\right]\beta_L = \rho + (\rho - k_b)(1 - \tau_c)\frac{B}{S}.$$

Next, use the simplifying assumption that $k_b = R_f$ to write

$$R_f + \left[E(R_m) - R_f\right]\beta_L = \rho + (\rho - R_f)(1 - \tau_c)\frac{B}{S}.$$

Then substitute into the right-hand side the CAPM definition of the cost of unlevered equity, ρ:

$$R_f + \left[E(R_m) - R_f\right]\beta_L = R_f + \left[E(R_m) - R_f\right]\beta_U$$

$$+ \left\{R_f + \left[E(R_m) - R_f\right]\beta_U - R_f\right\}(1 - \tau_c)\frac{B}{S}.$$

By canceling terms and rearranging the equation, we have

$$[E(R_m) - R_f]\beta_L = [E(R_m) - R_f]\left[1 + (1 - \tau_c)\frac{B}{S}\right]\beta_U,$$

$$\beta_L = \left[1 + (1 - \tau_c)\frac{B}{S}\right]\beta_U. \tag{15.28}$$

The implication of Eq. (15.28) is that if we can observe the levered beta by using observed rates of return on equity capital in the stock market, we can estimate the unlevered risk of the firm's operating cash flows.

2. A Simple Example

The usefulness of the theoretical results can be demonstrated by considering the following problem. The United Southern Construction Company currently has a market value capital structure of 20% debt to total assets. The company's treasurer believes that more debt can be taken on, up to a limit of 35% debt, without losing the firm's ability to borrow at 7%, the prime rate (also assumed to be the risk-free rate). The firm has a marginal tax rate of 50%. The expected return on the market next year is estimated to be 17%, and the systematic risk of the company's equity, β_L, is estimated to be .5.

- What is the company's current weighted average cost of capital? Its current cost of equity?
- What will the new weighted average cost of capital be if the "target" capital structure is changed to 35% debt?
- Should a project with a 9.25% expected rate of return be accepted if its systematic risk, β_L, is the same as that of the firm?

To calculate the company's current cost of equity capital, we can use the CAPM:

$$k_s = R_f + [E(R_m) - R_f]\beta_L$$
$$= .07 + [.17 - .07].5 = .12.$$

Therefore the weighted average cost of capital is

$$WACC = (1 - \tau_c)R_f\frac{B}{B+S} + k_s\frac{S}{B+S}$$
$$= (1 - .5).07(.2) + .12(.8) = 10.3\%.$$

The weighted average cost of capital with the new capital structure is shown in Fig. 15.6.[12] Note that the cost of equity increases with increasing leverage. This simply reflects the fact that shareholders face more risk with higher financial leverage and that they require a higher return to compensate them for it. Therefore in order to calculate the new weighted average cost of

---

[12] Note that if debt to total assets is 20%, then debt to equity is 25%. Also, 35% converts to 53.85% in Fig. 15.6.

Figure 15.6 Changes in the cost of capital as leverage increases.

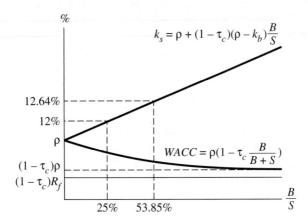

capital we have to use the Modigliani-Miller definition to estimate the cost of equity for an all-equity firm:

$$WACC = \rho \left(1 - \tau_c \frac{B}{B+S}\right)$$

$$\rho = \frac{WACC}{1 - \tau_c \left[B/(B+S)\right]} = \frac{.103}{1 - .5(.2)} = 11.44\%.$$

As long as the firm does not change its business risk, its unlevered cost of equity capital, ρ, will not change. Therefore we can use ρ to estimate the weighted average cost of capital with the new capital structure:

$$WACC = .1144[1 - .5(.35)] = 9.438\%.$$

Therefore, the new project with its 9.25% rate of return will not be acceptable even if the firm increases its ratio of debt to total assets from 20% to 35%.

A common error made in this type of problem is to forget that the cost of equity capital will increase with higher leverage. Had we estimated the weighted average cost of capital, using 12% for the old cost of equity and 35% debt as the target capital structure, we would have obtained 9.03% as the estimated weighted average cost of capital, and we would have accepted the project.

We can also use Eq. (15.28) to compute the unlevered beta for the firm. Before the capital structure change, the levered beta was $\beta_L = .5$; therefore

$$\beta_L = \left[1 + (1 - \tau_c)\frac{B}{S}\right]\beta_U,$$

$$.5 = [1 + (1 - .5)(.25)]\beta_U,$$

$$\beta_U = .4444.$$

Note that the unlevered beta is consistent with the firm's unlevered cost of equity capital. Using the CAPM, we have

$$\rho = R_f + \left[E(R_m) - R_f\right]\beta_U$$

$$= .07 + [.17 - .07].4444$$

$$= 11.44\%.$$

Finally, we know that the unlevered beta will not change as long as the firm does not change its business risk, the risk of the portfolio of projects that it holds. Hence an increase in leverage will increase the levered beta, but the unlevered beta stays constant. Therefore we can use Eq. (15.28) to compute the new levered equity beta:

$$\beta_L = \left[1 + (1 - \tau_c)\frac{B}{S}\right]\beta_U$$

$$= [1 + (1 - 0.5).5385].4444$$

$$= .5641.$$

Hence the increase in leverage raises the levered equity beta from .5 to .5641, and the cost of levered equity increases from 12% to 12.64%.

3. The Cost of Capital for Projects of Differing Risk

A more difficult problem is to decide what to do if the project's risk is different from that of the firm. Suppose the new project would increase the replacement market value of the assets of the firm by 50% and the systematic risk of the operating cash flow it provides is estimated to be $\beta_U = 1.2$. What rate of return must it earn in order to be profitable if the firm has (a) 20% or (b) 35% debt in its capital structure?

Figure 15.7 shows that the CAPM may be used to find the required rate of return given the beta of the project without leverage, $\beta_{U,p}$, which has been estimated to be 1.2. This is the beta for the *unlevered* project, because the beta is defined as the systematic risk of the operating cash flows. By definition this is the covariance between the cash flows *before* leverage and taxes and the market index, divided by the variance of the market portfolio. The required rate of return on the project, if it is an all-equity project, will be computed as

$$E(R_j) = R_f + \left[E(R_m) - R_f\right]\beta_{U,p}$$

$$= .07 + [.17 - .07]1.2 = 19\%.$$

Next we must "add in" the effect of the firm's leverage. If we recognize that 19% is the required rate if the project were all equity, we can find the required rate with 20% leverage by using the Modigliani-Miller weighted average cost of capital, Eq. (15.12):

$$WACC = \rho\left(1 - \tau_c\frac{B}{B + S}\right)$$

$$= .19\,[1 - .5(.2)] = 17.1\%.$$

And if the leverage is increased to 35%, the required return falls to 15.675%:

$$WACC = .19\,[1 - .5(.35)] = 15.675\%.$$

Figure 15.7 Using the CAPM to estimate the required rate of return on a project.

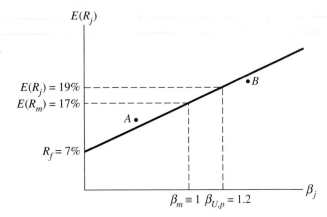

Firms seek to find projects that earn more than the project's weighted average cost of capital. Suppose that, for the sake of argument, the WACC of our firm is 17%. Project B in Fig. 15.7 earns 20%, more than the firm's WACC, whereas project A in Fig. 15.7 earns only 15%, which is less than the firm's WACC. Does this mean that B should be accepted while A is rejected? Obviously not, because they have different risk (and possibly different optimal capital structure) than the firm as a whole. Project B is much riskier and must therefore earn a higher rate of return than the firm. In fact it must earn more than projects of equivalent risk. Since it falls below the security market line, it should be rejected. Alternately, project A should be accepted because its anticipated rate of return is higher than the rate that the market requires for projects of equivalent risk. It lies above the security market line in Fig. 15.7.

The examples above serve to illustrate the usefulness of the risk-adjusted cost of capital for capital budgeting purposes. Each project must be evaluated at a cost of capital that reflects the systematic risk of its operating cash flows as well as the financial leverage appropriate for the project. Estimates of the correct opportunity cost of capital are derived from a thorough understanding of the Modigliani-Miller cost of capital and the CAPM.

D. $\mathcal{T}$he Cost of Capital with Risky Debt

So far it has been convenient to assume that corporate debt is risk free. Obviously it is not. Consideration of risky debt raises several interesting questions. First, if debt is risky, how are the basic Modigliani-Miller propositions affected? We know that riskier debt will require higher rates of return. Does this reduce the tax gain from leverage? The answer is given in Section 1 below. The second question is, How can one estimate the required rate of return on risky debt? This is covered in Section 2.

1. The Effect of Risky Debt in the Absence of Bankruptcy Costs

The fundamental theorem set forth by Modigliani and Miller is that, given complete and perfect capital markets, it does not make any difference how one splits up the stream of operating cash flows. The percentage of debt or equity does not change the total value of the cash stream provided by the productive investments of the firm. Therefore, so long as there are no costs of bankruptcy (paid to third parties like trustees and law firms), it should not make any difference whether debt is risk free or risky. The value of the firm should be equal to the value of the discounted cash flows from an investment. A partition that divides these cash flows into risky debt and risky equity has no impact on value. Stiglitz [1969] first proved this result, using a state preference framework, and Rubinstein [1973] provided a proof, using a mean-variance approach.

Risky debt, just like any other security, must be priced in equilibrium so that it falls on the security market line. Therefore, if we designate the return on risky debt as $\tilde{R}_{bj}$, its expected return is

$$E(\tilde{R}_{bj}) = R_f + \left[E(\tilde{R}_m) - R_f\right]\beta_{bj}, \tag{15.29}$$

where $\beta_{bj} = \text{COV}(\tilde{R}_{bj}, \tilde{R}_m)/\sigma_m^2$. The return on the equity of a levered firm, k_s, can be written (for a perpetuity) as net income divided by the market value of equity:

$$k_s = \frac{(\widetilde{EBIT} - \tilde{R}_{bj}B)(1 - \tau_c)}{S^L}. \tag{15.30}$$

Recall that $\widetilde{EBIT}$ is earnings before interest and taxes, $\tilde{R}_{bj}B$ is the interest on debt, τ_c is the firm's tax rate, and S^L is the market value of the equity in a levered firm. Using the CAPM, we find that the expected return on equity will be[13]

$$E(k_s) = R_f + \lambda^*\text{COV}(k_s, R_m). \tag{15.31}$$

The covariance between the expected rate of return on equity and the market index is

$$\text{COV}(k_s, R_m) = E\left\{\left[\frac{(EBIT - R_{bj}B)(1 - \tau_c)}{S^L} - E\left(\frac{(EBIT - R_{bj}B)(1 - \tau_c)}{S^L}\right)\right]\right.$$
$$\left. \times \left[R_m - E(R_m)\right]\right\}$$
$$= \frac{1 - \tau_c}{S^L}\text{COV}(EBIT, R_m) - \frac{(1 - \tau_c)B}{S^L}\text{COV}(R_{bj}, R_m). \tag{15.32}$$

Substituting the result into (15.31) and the combined result into (15.30), we have the following relationship for a levered firm:

$$R_f S^L + \lambda^*(1 - \tau_c)\text{COV}(EBIT, R_m) - \lambda^*(1 - \tau_c)B[\text{COV}(R_{bj}, R_m)]$$
$$= E(EBIT)(1 - \tau_c) - E(R_{bj})B(1 - \tau_c). \tag{15.33}$$

By following a similar line of logic for the unlevered firm (where $B = 0$, and $S^L = V^U$), we have

$$R_f V^U + \lambda^*(1 - \tau_c)\text{COV}(EBIT, R_m) = E(EBIT)(1 - \tau_c). \tag{15.34}$$

Substituting (15.34) for $E(EBIT)(1 - \tau_c)$ in the right-hand side of (15.33) and using the fact that $V_L = S_L + B$, we have

---

[13] In this instance $\lambda^* \equiv \left[E(R_m) - R_f\right]/\sigma_m^2$.

$$R_f S_L + \lambda^*(1 - \tau_c)\text{COV}(EBIT, R_m) - \lambda^*(1 - \tau_c)B[\text{COV}(R_{bj}, R_m)]$$
$$= R_f V_U + \lambda^*(1 - \tau_c)\text{COV}(EBIT, R_m) - E(R_{bj})(1 - \tau_c),$$
$$[R_f(V_L - B) - \lambda^*(1 - \tau_c)B[\text{COV}(R_{bj}, R_m)]$$
$$= R_f V_U - [R_f + \lambda^*\text{COV}(R_{bj}, R_m)]B(1 - \tau_c),$$
$$V_L = V_U + \tau_c B.$$

This is exactly the same Modigliani-Miller result that we obtained when the firm was assumed to issue only risk-free debt. Therefore the introduction of risky debt cannot, by itself, be used to explain the existence of an optimal capital structure. Later on, we shall see that direct bankruptcy costs such as losses to third parties (lawyers or the courts) or business disruption costs (disruption of services to customers or disruption of the supply of skilled labor) are necessary in conjunction with risky debt and taxes in order to explain an optimal capital structure.

2. The Cost of Risky Debt—Using the Option Pricing Model

Even though risky debt without bankruptcy costs does not alter the basic Modigliani-Miller results, we are still interested in knowing how the cost of risky debt is affected by changes in capital structure. The simple algebraic approach that follows was provided by Hsia [1981], and it combines the option pricing model (OPM), the capital asset pricing model (CAPM), and the Modigliani-Miller theorems. They are all consistent with one another.

To present the issue in its simplest form, assume (1) that the firm issues zero-coupon bonds[14] that prohibit any capital distributions (such as dividend payments) until after the bonds mature T time periods hence, (2) that there are no transactions costs or taxes, so that the value of the firm is unaffected by its capital structure (in other words, Modigliani-Miller Proposition I is assumed to be valid), (3) that there is a known nonstochastic risk-free rate of interest, and (4) that there are homogeneous expectations about the stochastic process that describes the value of the firm's assets. Given these assumptions, we can imagine a simple firm that issues only one class of bonds secured by the assets of the firm.

To illustrate the claims of debt and shareholders, let us use put-call parity from Chapter 7. The payoffs from the underlying risky asset (the value of the firm, V) plus a put written on it are identical to the payoffs from a default-free zero-coupon bond plus a call (the value of shareholders' equity in a levered firm, S) on the risky asset.

Algebraically this is the same put-call parity relationship that was described in Chapter 7:

$$V + P = B + S,$$

or rearranging,

$$V = (B - P) + S. \tag{15.35}$$

Equation (15.35) illustrates that the value of the firm can be partitioned into two claims. The low-risk claim is risky debt that is equivalent to default-free debt minus a put option, that is, $(B - P)$. Thus, risky corporate debt is the same thing as default-free debt minus a put option. The exercise

---

[14] All acclaimed interest on zero-coupon bonds is paid at maturity; hence $B(T)$, the current market value of debt with maturity T, must be less than its face value, D, assuming a positive risk-free rate of discount.

Table 15.3 Stakeholders' Payoffs at Maturity

	Payoffs at Maturity	
Stakeholder Positions	**If $V \leq D$**	**If $V > D$**
Shareholders' position:		
Call option, S	0	$V - D$
Bondholders' position:		
Default-free bond, B	D	D
Minus a put option, P	$-(D - V)$	0
Value of the firm at maturity	V	V

price for the put is the face value of debt, D, and the maturity of the put, T, is the same as the maturity of the risky debt. The higher-risk claim is shareholders' equity, which is equivalent to a call on the value of the firm with an exercise price D and a maturity T. The payoff to shareholders at maturity will be

$$S = \text{MAX}[0, V - D]. \tag{15.36}$$

Table 15.3 shows both stakeholders' payoffs at maturity. If the value of the firm is less than the face value of debt, shareholders file for bankruptcy and allow the bondholders to keep $V < D$. Alternately, if the value of the firm is greater than the face value of debt, shareholders will exercise their call option by paying its exercise price, D, the face value of debt to bondholder, and retain the excess value, $V - D$.

The realization that the equity and debt in a firm can be conceptualized as options allows us to use the insights of Chapter 7 on option pricing theory. For example, if the equity, S, in a levered firm is analogous to a call option, then its value will increase with (1) an increase in the value of the firm's assets, V, (2) an increase in the variance of the value of the firm's assets, (3) an increase in the time to maturity of a given amount of debt with face value, D, and (4) an increase in the risk-free rate. The value of levered equity will decrease with a greater amount of debt, D, which is analogous to the exercise price on a call option.

Next, we wish to show the relationship between the CAPM measure of risk (i.e., β) and the option pricing model. First, however, it is useful to show how the CAPM and OPM are related. Merton [1973] has derived a continuous-time version of the CAPM:

$$E(r_i) = r_f + [E(r_m) - r_f]\beta_i, \tag{15.37}$$

where

$$E(r_i) = \text{the instantaneous expected rate of return on asset } i,$$
$$\beta_i = \text{the instantaneous systematic risk of the } i\text{th asset, } \beta_i = \text{COV}(r_i, r_m)/\text{VAR}(r_m),$$
$$E(r_m) = \text{the expected instantaneous rate of return on the market portfolio,}$$
$$r_f = \text{the nonstochastic instantaneous annualized rate of return on the risk-free asset.}$$

There appears to be no difference between the continuous-time version of the CAPM and the traditional one-period model derived in Chapter 6. However, it is important to prove that the CAPM also exists in continuous time because the Black-Scholes OPM requires continuous trading, and the assumptions underlying the two models must be consistent.

In order to relate the OPM to the CAPM it is easiest (believe it or not) to begin with the differential equation given in Appendix 7A, at the end of Chapter 7, Eq. (7A.2), and to recognize that the call option is now the value of the common stock, S, which is written on the value of the levered firm, V. Therefore Eq. (7A.2) may be rewritten as

$$dS = \frac{\partial S}{\partial V}dV + \frac{\partial S}{\partial t}dt + \frac{1}{2}\frac{\partial^2 S}{\partial V^2}\sigma^2 V^2 dt. \tag{15.38}$$

This equation says that the change in the stock price is related to the change in the value of the firm, dV, movement of the stock price across time, dt, and the instantaneous variance of the firm's value, σ^2. Dividing by S, we have, in the limit as dt approaches zero,

$$\lim_{dt \to 0} \frac{dS}{S} = \frac{\partial S}{\partial V}\frac{dV}{S} = \frac{\partial S}{\partial V}\frac{dV}{V}\frac{V}{S}. \tag{15.39}$$

We recognize dS/S as the rate of return on common stock, r_S, and dV/V as the rate of return on the firm's assets, r_V; therefore

$$r_S = \frac{\partial S}{\partial V}\frac{V}{S}r_V. \tag{15.40}$$

If the instantaneous systematic risk of common stock, β_S, and that of the firm's assets, β_V, are defined as

$$\beta_S \equiv \frac{\text{COV}(r_S, r_m)}{\text{VAR}(r_m)}, \beta_V \equiv \frac{\text{COV}(r_V, r_m)}{\text{VAR}(r_m)}, \tag{15.41}$$

then we can use (15.40) and (15.41) to rewrite the instantaneous covariance as

$$\beta_S \equiv \frac{\partial S}{\partial V}\frac{V}{S}\frac{\text{COV}(r_V, r_m)}{\text{VAR}(r_m)} = \frac{\partial S}{\partial V}\frac{V}{S}\beta_V. \tag{15.42}$$

Now write the Black-Scholes OPM where the call option is the equity of the firm:

$$S = VN(d_1) - e^{-r_f T}DN(d_2), \tag{15.43}$$

where

$S =$ the market value of equity,
$V =$ the market value of the firm's assets,
$r_f =$ the risk-free rate,
$T =$ the time to maturity,
$D =$ the face value of debt (book value),
$N(\cdot) =$ the cumulative normal probability of the unit normal variate d_1,
$$d_1 = \frac{\ln(V/D) + r_f T}{\sigma\sqrt{T}} + \frac{1}{2}\sigma\sqrt{T},$$
$$d_2 = d_1 - \sigma\sqrt{T}.$$

Finally, the partial derivative of the equity value, S, with respect to the value of the underlying assets is

$$\frac{\partial S}{\partial V} = N(d_1), \quad \text{where} \quad 0 \leq N(d_1) \leq 1. \tag{15.44}$$

Substituting this into (15.42), we obtain

$$\beta_S = N(d_1)\frac{V}{S}\beta_V \tag{15.45}$$

This tells us the relationship between the systematic risk of the equity, β_S, and the systematic risk of the firm's assets, β_V. The value of S is given by the OPM, Eq. (15.43), therefore we have

$$\beta_S = \frac{VN(d_1)}{VN(d_1) - De^{-r_fT}N(d_2)}\beta_V$$

$$= \frac{1}{1 - (D/V)e^{-r_fT}[N(d_2)/N(d_1)]}\beta_V. \tag{15.46}$$

We know that $D/V \leq 1$, that $e^{-r_fT} < 1$, that $N(d_2) \leq N(d_1)$, and hence that $\beta_S \geq \beta_V > 0$. This shows that the systematic risk of the equity of a levered firm is greater than the systematic risk of an unlevered firm, a result that is consistent with the results found elsewhere in the theory of finance. Note also that the beta of equity of the levered firm increases monotonically with leverage.

The OPM provides insight into the effect of its parameters on the systematic risk of equity. We may assume that the risks of characteristics of the firm's assets, β_V, are constant over time. Then it can be shown that the partial derivatives of (15.46) have the following signs:

$$\frac{\partial \beta_S}{\partial V} < 0, \quad \frac{\partial \beta_S}{\partial D} > 0, \quad \frac{\partial \beta_S}{\partial r_f} < 0, \quad \frac{\partial \beta_S}{\partial \sigma^2} < 0, \quad \frac{\partial \beta_S}{\partial T} < 0.$$

Most of these have readily intuitive explanations. The systematic risk of equity falls as the market value of the firm increases, and it rises as the amount of debt issued increases. When the risk-free rate of return increases, the value of the equity option increases and its systematic risk decreases. The fourth partial derivative says that as the variance of the value of the firm's assets increases, the systematic risk of equity decreases. This result follows from the contingent claim nature of equity. The equity holders will prefer more variance to less because they profit from the probability that the value of the firm will exceed the face value of the debt. Therefore their risk actually decreases as the variance of the value of the firm's assets increases.[15] Finally, the fifth partial says that the systematic risk of equity declines as the maturity date of the debt becomes longer and longer. From the shareholders' point of view, the best situation would be to never have to repay the face value of the debt. It is also possible to use Eq. (15.45) to view the cost of equity capital in an OPM framework and to compare it with the Modigliani-Miller results.

---

[15] Note that since the value of the firm, V, and the debt equity ratio D/V are held constant, any change in total variance, σ^2, must be nonsystematic risk.

Substituting β_S from (15.45) into the CAPM, we obtain from Eq. (15.37) an expression for k_s, the cost of equity capital:

$$k_s = R_f + (R_m - R_f)N(d_1)\frac{V}{S}\beta_V. \tag{15.47}$$

Note that from Eq. (15.45), $\beta_S = N(d_1)(V/S)\beta_V$. Substituting this into (15.47) yields the familiar CAPM relationship $k_s = R_f + (R_m - R_f)\beta_S$. Furthermore, the CAPM can be rearranged to show that

$$\beta_V = \frac{R_V - R_f}{R_m - R_f},$$

which we substitute into (15.47) to obtain

$$k_s = R_f + N(d_1)(R_V - R_f)\frac{V}{S}. \tag{15.48}$$

Equation (15.48) shows that the cost of equity is an increasing function of financial leverage.

If we assume that debt is risky and assume that bankruptcy costs (i.e., losses to third parties other than creditors or shareholders) are zero, then the OPM, the CAPM, and the Modigliani-Miller propositions can be shown to be consistent. The simple algebraic approach given below was proved by Hsia [1981].

First, note that the systematic risk, β_B, of risky debt capital in a world without taxes can be written in an explanation similar to Eq. (15.42) as[16]

$$\beta_B = \beta_V \frac{\partial B}{\partial V}\frac{V}{B}. \tag{15.49}$$

We know that in a world without taxes the value of the firm is invariant to changes in its capital structure. Also, from Eq (15.44), we know that if the common stock of a firm is thought of as a call option on the value of the firm, then

$$\frac{\partial S}{\partial V} = N(d_1).$$

These two facts imply that

$$\frac{\partial B}{\partial V} = N(-d_1) = 1 - N(d_1). \tag{15.50}$$

In other words, any change in the value of equity is offset by an equal and opposite change in the value of risky debt.

Next, the required rate of return on risky debt, k_b, can be expressed by using the CAPM, Eq. (15.37):

$$k_b = R_f + (R_m - R_f)\beta_B. \tag{15.51}$$

---

[16] See Galai and Masulis [1976, footnote 15].

Substituting Eqs. (15.49) and (15.50) into (15.51), we have

$$k_b = R_f + (R_m - R_f)\beta_V N(-d_1)\frac{V}{B}.$$

From the CAPM, we know that

$$R_V - R_f = (R_m - R_f)\beta_V.$$

Therefore

$$k_b = R_f + (R_V - R_f)N(-d_1)\frac{V}{B}.$$

And since $R_V \equiv \rho$,

$$k_b = R_f + (\rho - R_f)N(d_1)\frac{V}{B}. \tag{15.52}$$

Note that Eq. (15.52) expresses the cost of risky debt in terms of the OPM. The required rate of return on risky debt is equal to the risk-free rate, R_f, plus a risk premium, θ, where

$$\theta = (\rho - R_f)N(-d_1)\frac{V}{B}.$$

A numerical example can be used to illustrate how the cost of debt, in the absence of bankruptcy costs, increases with the firm's utilization of debt. Suppose the current value of a firm, V, is $3 million; the face value of debt is $1.5 million; and the debt will mature in $T = 8$ years. The variance of returns on the firm's assets, σ^2, is .09; its required return on assets is $\rho = .12$; and the riskless rate of interest, R_f, is 5%. From the Black-Scholes option pricing model, we know that

$$d_1 = \frac{\ln(V/D) + R_f T}{\sigma\sqrt{T}} + \frac{1}{2}\sigma\sqrt{T}$$

$$= \frac{\ln(3/1.5) + .05(8)}{.3\sqrt{8}} + .5(.3)\sqrt{8}$$

$$= \frac{.6931 + .4}{.8485} + .4243 = 1.7125.$$

From the cumulative normal probability table (Table 7.7), the value of $N(-1.7125)$ is approximately .0434. Substituting into Eq. (15.33), we see that the cost of debt is increased from the risk-free rate, 5%, to 5.61%:

$$k_b = .05 + (.12 - .05)(.0434)\frac{3}{1.5}$$

$$= .05 + .0061 = .0561.$$

Figure 15.8 shows the relationship of the cost of debt and the ratio of the face value of debt to the current market value of the firm. For low levels of debt, bankruptcy risk is trivial, and therefore the cost of debt is close to the riskless rate. It rises as D/V increases until k_b equals 6.3%, when the face value of debt, due eight years from now, equals the current market value of the firm.

Figure 15.8 The cost of risky debt.

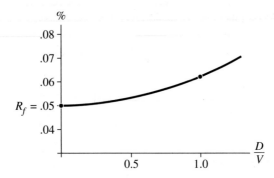

To arrive at a weighted average cost of capital, we multiply Eq. (15.52), the cost of debt, by the percentage of debt in the capital structure, B/V, then add this result to the cost of equity, Eq. (15.48) multiplied by S/V, the percentage of equity in the capital structure. The result is

$$
k_b \frac{B}{V} + k_s \frac{S}{V} = \left[R_f + (\rho - R_f)N(-d_1)\frac{V}{B} \right]\frac{B}{V} + \left[R_f + N(d_1)(\rho - R_f)\frac{V}{S} \right]\frac{S}{V}
$$

$$
= R_f \left(\frac{B+S}{V} \right) + (\rho - R_f)[N(-d_1) + N(d_1)]
$$

$$
= R_f + (\rho - R_f)\left[1 - N(d_1) + N(d_1) \right]
$$

$$
= \rho. \tag{15.53}
$$

Equation (15.53) is exactly the same as the Modigliani-Miller proposition that in a world without taxes the weighted average cost of capital is invariant to changes in the capital structure of the firm. Also, simply by rearranging terms, we have

$$
k_s = \rho + (\rho - k_b)\frac{B}{S}. \tag{15.54}
$$

This is exactly the same as Eq. (15.18), the Modigliani-Miller definition of the cost of equity capital in a world without taxes. Therefore if we assume that debt is risky, then the OPM, the CAPM, and the Modigliani-Miller definition are all consistent with one another.

This result is shown graphically in Fig. 15.9(a). This figure is very similar to Fig. 15.2, which showed the cost of capital as a function of the debt to equity ratio, B/S, assuming riskless debt. The only differences between the two figures are that Fig. 15.9 has the debt to value ratio, $B/(B + S)$, on the horizontal axis and it assumes risky debt. Note that in Fig. 15.9(a) the cost of debt increases as more debt is used in the firm's capital structure. Also, if the firm were to become 100% debt (not a realistic alternative), then the cost of debt would equal the cost of capital for an all-equity firm, ρ. Figure 15.9(b) depicts the weighted average cost of capital in a world with corporate taxes only. The usual Modigliani-Miller result is shown, namely, that the weighted average cost of capital declines monotonically as more debt is employed in the capital structure of the firm. The fact that debt is risky does not change any of our previous results.

Figure 15.9 The cost of capital given risky debt: (a) no taxes; (b) only corporate taxes.

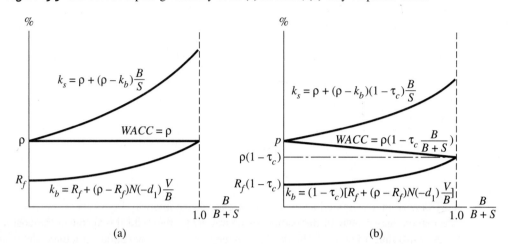

(a)   (b)

3. The Separability of Investment and Financing Decisions

A fundamental assumption of the Modigliani-Miller approach to the capital structure is that the operating cash flows are unaffected or independent of the choice of capital structure. In the last decade or so, this assumption has come into question because the answer changes if it is relaxed. An example, perhaps, was the demise of Allied Federated Department Stores. As they became overburdened with debt, their suppliers began to refuse to extend trade credit. Consequently, the shelves became bare and customers stopped shopping there. This example shows that the financial structure of the firm clearly affects its revenues. These effects have come to be called business disruption costs. They include a wide range of so-called market imperfections ranging from reduced sales to investment opportunities that are foregone.

Next, suppose that projects carry with them the ability to change the optimal capital structure of the firm as a whole.[17] Suppose that some projects have more debt capacity than others (perhaps because they are more flexible due to the real options that are imbedded in them). Then the investment and financing decisions cannot be "handled" as if they were independent. There is very little in the accepted theory of finance that admits of this possibility, but it cannot be disregarded. One reason that projects may have separate debt capacities is that they have different collateral values in bankruptcy, or differences in their ability to respond to new information such as unanticipated demand.

E. 𝒜 Model with Business Disruption and Tax-Deductible Interest

Leland [1994] and Leland and Toft [1996] have modeled the value of a firm assuming that the present value of business disruption costs and the present value of lost interest tax shields are

---

[17] This may be particularly relevant when a firm is considering a conglomerate merger with another firm in a completely different line of business with a completely different optimal capital structure.

affected by the firm's choice of capital structure. The result is an optimal capital structure that is defined by a trade-off between the value created by the present value of the interest tax shield, and the value lost from the present value of business disruption costs as well as the present value of lost interest tax shields. Leland's work begins with the assumption that the value of the unlevered firm, V, follows a diffusion process with a rate of return

$$\frac{dV}{V} = \mu(V, t)dt + \sigma dW. \tag{15.55}$$

Any claim that pays a nonnegative coupon, C, when the firm is solvent, with value $F(V, t)$ must satisfy the partial differential equation

$$\frac{1}{2}\sigma^2 V^2 F_{VV}(V, t) + rV F_V(V, t) - rF(V, t) + F_t(V, t) + C = 0 \tag{15.56}$$

When this security has no explicit time dependence, then $F_t(V, t) = 0$, and the partial differential equation simplifies to be

$$\frac{1}{2}\sigma^2 V^2 F_{VV}(V) + rV F_V(V) - rF(V) + C = 0 \tag{15.57}$$

with a general solution

$$F(V) = A_0 + A_1 V + A_2 V^{-(2r/\sigma^2)}. \tag{15.58}$$

To make Eq. (15.58) more concrete, we can apply it to various securities by specifying the appropriate boundary conditions. Let us start by applying it to the firm's debt. To do so, we define V_B as the level of asset value at which business disruption occurs and α as the fraction of the value of the firm lost to business disruption costs, leaving debt holders with $(1 - \alpha)V_B$, and leaving shareholders with nothing. The boundary conditions are[18]

$$\text{At } V = V_B \qquad B(V) = (1 - \alpha)V_B \tag{15.59a}$$

$$\text{At } V \to \infty \qquad B(V) = C/r. \tag{15.59b}$$

Using the second boundary condition and applying it to the generic valuation Eq. (15.58) we see that $A_1 = 0$ and $A_0 = C/r$, and we can rewrite (15.58) as it applies specifically to risky debt:

$$B(V) = A_0 + A_1 V + A_2 V^{-(2r/\sigma^2)}. \tag{15.60}$$

Next, we observe that as the value of assets approaches infinity at the second boundary condition, $V \to \infty$, the value of debt, $D(V)$, approaches the present value of its perpetual fixed coupon stream:

$$B(V) = A_0 = C/r \quad \text{if and only if} \quad A_1 = 0 \text{ and } \lim V^{-(2r/\sigma^2)} = 0.$$

---

[18] Note that business disruption costs are assumed to be proportional to the asset value where business disruption occurs. Thus, if $V_B = 0$, then business disruption costs are also zero.

At the first boundary condition, we know that $B(V) = (1 - \alpha)V_B$; therefore we can rewrite (15.60) as follows:

$$B(V) = A_0 + A_2 V^{-(2r/\sigma^2)} \qquad\qquad \text{since } A_1 = 0$$

$$= C/r + A_2 V^{-(2r/\sigma^2)} = (1 - \alpha)V_B \qquad \text{since } A_0 = C/r.$$

We can now solve for A_2:

$$A_2 = [(1 - \alpha)V_B - C/r]V_B^{2r/\sigma^2},$$

and since $V = V_B$ at the boundary, Eq. (15.60) reduces to

$$B(V) = C/r + [(1 - \alpha)V_B - C/r](V/V_B)^{-2r/\sigma^2}$$

$$= (1 - p_B)C/r + p_B[(1 - \alpha)V_B], \qquad\qquad (15.61)$$

where

$$p_B \equiv (V/V_B)^{-2r/\sigma^2},$$

and can be interpreted as the present value of \$1 contingent on future business disruption. We can interpret Eq. (15.61) as the present value of risky debt, with two parts, namely, the present value of riskless debt weighted by (one minus) a business disruption factor that reflects both the cost of disruption and its timing, plus the payout if business disruption occurs also weighted by the same business disruption factor.

Next, we examine the effect of the debt tax shield and of expected business disruption costs. First, consider business disruption as a "security" that pays no coupon, but has a value equal to business disruption costs, αV_B, at $V = V_B$. Its value, $DC(V)$, must also satisfy the conditions of Eq. (15.58), but with different boundary conditions:

$$\text{At } V = V_B \qquad DC(V) = \alpha V_B \qquad\qquad (15.62a)$$

$$\text{At } V \to \infty \qquad DC(V) \to 0. \qquad\qquad (15.62b)$$

As before, we start with Eq. (15.58) and interpret it given the boundary conditions for $DC(V)$, as follows:

$$DC(V) = A_0 + A_1 V + A_2 V^{-2r/\sigma^2}.$$

Note that as the value of the assets approaches infinity, then the present value of business disruption costs, $DC(V)$, approaches zero if and only if in the above equation both A_0 and A_1 are equal to zero. At the first boundary condition $V = V_B$; therefore

$$A_2 V^{-2r/\sigma^2} = \alpha V_B,$$

and therefore, at $V = V_B$,

$$A_2 = \left(\frac{V}{V_B}\right)^{-2r/\sigma^2} \equiv p_B.$$

The interpretation of this result is that the present value of expected business disruption costs is their magnitude if business disruption occurs, αV_B, multiplied by the present value of $1 conditional on future business disruption, so that the present value of expected business disruption can be written as

$$DC(V) = \alpha V_B \left(V/V_B\right)^{-2r/\sigma^2}. \tag{15.63}$$

Finally, we must consider the present value of the interest tax shield as a "security" that pays a constant coupon equal to the tax-sheltering value of interest payments ($T_c C$) as long as the firm is solvent. Its value $TB(V)$ also must satisfy Eq. (15.58), but with the following boundary conditions:[19]

$$\text{At } V = V_B \qquad TB(V) = 0 \tag{15.64a}$$

$$\text{At } V \to \infty \qquad TB(V) = T_c(C/r). \tag{15.64b}$$

Rewriting Eq. (15.58) for the present value of the interest tax shield on debt, we have

$$TB(V) = A_0 + A_1 V + A_2 V^{-2r/\sigma^2}. \tag{15.65}$$

Note that as V approaches infinity, the value of the tax shield benefit approaches the tax rate times the present value of debt,

$$\text{As } V \to \infty \quad \text{then } TB(V) \to T_c(C/r) \text{ if and only if } A_0 = T_c(C/r) \text{ and } A_1 = 0.$$

Furthermore, at $V = V_B$ we have

$$TB(V) = 0 = T_c(C/r) - [T_c(C/r)](V/V_B)^{-2r/\sigma^2}. \tag{15.66}$$

Putting this all together, we have the conclusion that the total value of the firm has three parts. First is the firm's asset value (i.e., the value of the firm if it had no debt, the unlevered firm, $V_U(V)$). To this we add the value of the tax benefit from the deductibility of interest payments, $T_c B(V)$, and subtract the present value of business disruption costs, $DC(V)$. Mathematically, this can be written as

$$V_L(V) = V_U(V) + T_c B(V) - DC(V)$$

$$= V_U(V) + T_c(C/r)[1 - (V/V_B)^{-2r/\sigma^2}] - \alpha V_B(V/V_B)^{-2r/\sigma^2}$$

$$= V_U(V) + T_c B - p_B T_c B - \alpha V_B p_B. \tag{15.67}$$

---

[19] Note that Leland [1994] assumes that the firm receives the full tax shelter benefit as long as it is solvent. Actually the boundary should be $EBIT > C$. He handles this case later in his paper. However, since noninterest tax shields are also affected by net operating loss carry forwards, the model becomes even more complicated.

Figure 15.10 Optimal capital structure as a trade-off between the interest tax shield and business disruption costs.

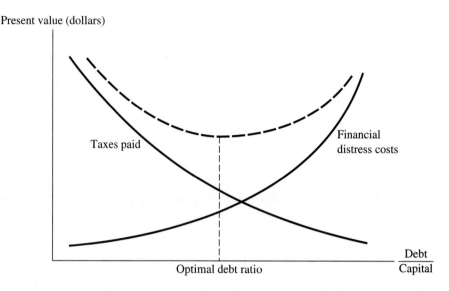

Equation (15.67) has four terms. The first two are the same as the Modigliani-Miller value of a levered firm in a world with corporate taxes. The third is the expected present value of interest tax shields lost as the firm decides to carry more debt and less equity. The fourth is the expected present value of the business disruption costs that are incurred as the firm takes on a greater percentage of debt financing. Leland goes on to examine various types of protective covenants on debt as they impact the value of the firm. He notes that if there are no protective covenants, bankruptcy occurs when the equity holders have no incentive to pay off the face value of debt, that is, when the value of equity falls to zero. With protective covenants, however, bankruptcy occurs when the value of the firm's assets falls below the principal value of debt, D_0—an interpretation that makes sense if the debt is rolled over every day. One consequence is that optimal leverage is much greater for unprotected debt, due to the optionlike nature of the market value of equity.

Figure 15.10 illustrates how an optimal capital structure results from Leland's approach. The present value of business disruption costs, the fourth term in Eq. (15.67), rises when the debt to total capital ratio increases. At the same time, the present value of the interest tax shield, the sum of the second and third terms in Eq. (15.67), declines as a function of the debt to total capital ratio. When the sum of these two costs is minimized, we have the optimal capital structure for the firm.

The empirical implications of equilibrium theories of capital structure are relatively few. As the availability of substitute nondebt tax shields increases, then the value of interest tax shields should decrease, and as business disruption becomes more expensive or more likely (due to the volatility of cash flows), the firm is predicted to carry less debt. These effects are useful for explaining optimal capital structure primarily at the industry level, but are less useful at the individual company level. The section on empirical results goes into greater detail later in this chapter.

F. $\mathcal{B}$usiness Disruption Costs: Evidence

The careful reader will recognize that there is a distinction between bankruptcy costs and business disruption costs. The former is all direct costs associated with Chapter 11 proceedings—lawyer and court fees, consultant fees, and lost management time. Business disruption costs are incurred before as well as during bankruptcy and include lost business and lost investment opportunities. The empirical evidence seems to indicate that direct costs of bankruptcy are relatively trivial, but business disruption costs may average 15% or more.

Warner [1977] collects data for 11 railroad bankruptcies that occurred between 1933 and 1955. He measures only direct costs, such as lawyers' and accountants' fees, other professional fees, and the value of managerial time spent in administering the bankruptcy. He does not estimate indirect costs to creditors, such as the opportunity cost of funds tied up during bankruptcy proceedings and losses in asset value due to forced capital structure changes, or indirect costs to shareholders, such as lost profits created by decreased sales in anticipation of bankruptcy or from disruptions in production during reorganization.[20] The evidence indicates that direct costs are trivial, averaging about 1% of the market value of the firm seven years prior to bankruptcy, and rising to 5.3% of the market value immediately prior to bankruptcy. Furthermore, direct costs as a percentage of value seem to decrease as a function of the size of the bankrupt firm. This would suggest that the direct costs of bankruptcy are less important for the capital structure decisions of large firms than of small firms. Although Warner's evidence is inconclusive because indirect costs are not measured, it does suggest that direct bankruptcy costs may not be sufficiently large to be important determinants of optimal leverage.

Evidence on business disruption costs is provided by Altman [1984].[21] Admittedly, because these costs are opportunity costs (what might have happened in the absence of bankruptcy proceedings), they are difficult to estimate. Altman provides an estimate (for a sample of 19 firms, 12 retailers, and 7 industrials that went bankrupt between 1970 and 1978) that compares expected profits, computed from time-series regressions, with actual profits. The arithmetic average indirect bankruptcy costs were 8.1% of firm value three years prior to bankruptcy and 10.5% the year of bankruptcy. A second method uses unexpected earnings from analysts' forecasts for a sample of 7 firms that went bankrupt in the 1980–1982 interval. Average indirect bankruptcy costs were 17.5% of value one year prior to bankruptcy. Although more research needs to be done on this topic, Altman's evidence suggests that total bankruptcy costs (direct and indirect) are sufficiently large to give credibility to a theory of optimal capital structure based on the trade-off between gains from leverage-induced tax shields and expected bankruptcy costs.

Opler and Titman [1994] attempt to estimate the market impact of business disruption costs by comparing the decline of high-leverage (upper decile debt to equity) with low-leverage (lowest decile) firms in the same industry during a downturn. The sales and the market value of equity of the high-leverage firms both decline an average of 26% more than the low-leverage firms. Their sample consisted of a universe of 46,799 publicly traded firms in the 1972–1991 time period. Their results provide strong evidence consistent with relatively high business disruption costs,

---

[20] Some of the agency costs that are discussed in Section G are closely related to bankruptcy and might also be considered indirect costs. For example, see Titman [1984].

[21] Kalaba, Langetieg, Rasakhoo, and Weinstein [1984] discuss a potentially useful methodology for estimating the expected cost of bankruptcy from bond data but provide no empirical results.

conditional on a downturn in an industry, but cannot establish causality, that is, whether high leverage is a consequence of poor operating performance or contributory to it.

G. Agency Costs—Another Equilibrium Theory of Optimal Capital Structure

Chapter 12 introduced another equilibrium theory—agency theory—that is complementary to what has been discussed above. We saw that if there is a gain from leverage because of the tax deductibility of interest expenses, and if bankruptcy costs are nontrivial, then it is possible to construct a theory of optimal capital structure. One troublesome aspect of this approach is that even before income taxes existed in the United States, firms used debt in their capital structure. Furthermore, the same cross-sectional regularities in financial leverage that exist today can also be observed in data prior to the introduction of corporate taxes. This suggests that optimal leverage (if it exists) may be explained by causes other than debt tax shields and bankruptcy costs.

Jensen and Meckling [1976] use agency costs to argue that the probability distribution of cash flows provided by the firm is not independent of its ownership structure and that this fact may be used to explain optimal leverage. First, there is an incentive problem associated with the issuance of new debt, an *agency cost of debt*. Consider an example where unbeknownst to lenders the firm has two different investment projects (see Table 15.4), both having the same systematic risk but different variances. The first has a 50/50 chance of yielding an end-of-period cash flow of $9,000 or $11,000. The second has a 50/50 chance of yielding $2,000 or $18,000. Both cost $8,000 and both have the same expected return. Suppose the firm shows only project 1 to lenders and asks to borrow $7,000. From the lenders' point of view this request seems reasonable because project 1 will always earn enough to pay off the loan. Of course, if creditors lend $7,000 and if the owners of the firm have the ability to switch to project 2, they will do so. (Why?) The result is the transfer of wealth from bondholders to shareholders. Hence bondholders may insist on various types of protective covenants and monitoring devices in order to protect their wealth from raids made on it by shareholders. However, the costs of writing and enforcing such covenants may well be nontrivial. Debt holders must charge higher ex ante yields to compensate them for possible wealth expropriation by shareholders. Furthermore, these costs may increase with the percentage of financing supplied by bondholders, as illustrated in Fig. 15.11.

On the other hand, there are *agency costs associated with external equity*. Suppose we begin with a firm owned exclusively by a single individual, the owner-manager (O-M). The O-M will obviously take every action possible to increase his or her own wealth. For example, if he or she decides to take Wednesday afternoon off, then as owner-manager he or she bears the full cost of doing so. However, if the O-M sells a portion of the ownership rights by selling external equity to new shareholders, there will arise conflicts in interest. Now the O-M is co-owner with the new shareholders. If the O-M can maximize his or her wealth at the expense of the new shareholders

Table 15.4 Two Investment Projects

Probability	Project 1	Project 2
.5	$ 9,000	$ 2,000
.5	11,000	18,000

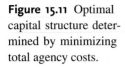

Figure 15.11 Optimal capital structure determined by minimizing total agency costs.

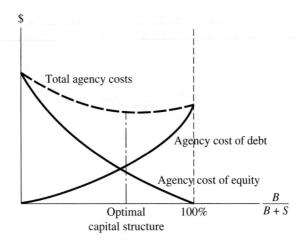

(e.g., by purchasing an executive jet and taking long vacations), then he or she will do so. Co-ownership of equity implies agency problems. The new shareholders will have to incur monitoring costs of one form or another in order to ensure that the original owner-manager acts in their interest. It is assumed, as illustrated in Fig. 15.11, that the agency costs of external equity increase as the percentage of financing supplied by external equity goes up. The agency costs of external equity may be reduced if the management and shareholders agree to hire an independent auditor. For an interesting exposition of this idea, the reader is referred to an article by Watts and Zimmerman [1979].

Jensen and Meckling suggest that, given increasing agency costs with higher proportions of equity on the one hand and higher proportions of debt on the other, there is an optimum combination of outside debt and equity that will be chosen because it minimizes total agency costs. In this way it is possible to argue for the existence of an optimal capital structure even in a world without taxes or bankruptcy costs.

Figure 15.11 illustrates the Jensen-Meckling argument for an optimal capital structure based on the agency costs of external equity and debt (in a world without taxes). Agency costs of external equity are assumed to decrease as the percentage of external equity decreases, and the agency costs of debt are assumed to increase. Figure 15.11 illustrates a case where total agency costs are minimized with an optimal capital structure between 0% and 100%—an interior solution. If the agency costs of external equity are low, as may be the case for a widely held firm, then optimal capital structure can result as a trade-off between the tax shelter benefit of debt and its agency cost.

The discussion of agency costs need not be limited to costs associated with providing debt and equity capital. For example, Titman [1984] suggests that agency costs are important for contracts (whether implied or explicit) between the firm and its customers or between the firm and its employees. Consider the relationship between a firm and its customers. If the firm's product is a durable good and requires future services such as parts and repair, the customer is paying not only for ownership of the product but also for the availability of an expected future stream of services. If the firm goes bankrupt, its customers lose their anticipated services without any hope of being compensated. Consequently, they must assess the probability of bankruptcy and weigh it in their decision to purchase durable goods. Firms that produce durable goods will have lower demand for their products if they increase their probability of bankruptcy by carrying more debt. This is an example of an indirect cost of bankruptcy. Ceteris paribus, we would expect durable goods producers to carry less debt.[22] Agency costs in labor contracts are also important. If a firm's labor force has acquired specialized skills that cannot easily be transferred to alternate employment, then laborers bear nontrivial costs if a firm goes bankrupt. They have to search for new jobs and learn new skills. There is no hope that the bankrupt firm will compensate them for their loss. Consequently, if labor markets are competitive, then laborers will charge lower wages to work for a firm that has a lower probability of bankruptcy. Thus we should expect to find that firms that use a larger percentage of job-specific human capital will also tend to carry less debt, ceteris paribus.

H. Nonequilibrium Effects

We apply the term *nonequilibrium* to mean deviations from permanent influences such as the tax deductibility of interest, business disruption, and agency costs. These factors can change of course, but their effect is industrywide more than it is company specific. Thus, a nonequilibrium effect is primarily company specific, for example, an investment opportunity or anticipated favorable financial results relative to the industry.

1. Signaling

Chapter 12, in addition to agency theory, also introduced signaling theory as a possible explanation for changes in capital structure. Originally introduced by Ross [1977], an incentive-signaling equilibrium separated firms where management was confident of better prospects from those firms where management was not.

Ross suggests that implicit in the Miller-Modigliani irrelevancy proposition is the assumption that the market *knows* the (random) return stream of the firm and values the stream to set the value of the firm. What is valued in the marketplace, however, is the *perceived* stream of returns for the firm. Putting the issue this way raises the possibility that changes in the capital structure (or dividend payout) may alter the market's perception. In the terminology of Modigliani and Miller, by changing its financial structure (or dividend payout) the firm alters its perceived risk class even though the actual risk class remains unchanged.

Managers, as insiders who have monopolistic access to information about the firm's expected cash flows, will choose to establish unambiguous signals about the firm's future if they have the proper incentive to do so. To show how this incentive-signaling process works, let us assume that managers are prohibited (perhaps by SEC regulations) from trading in the securities of their own firm. This keeps them from profiting by issuing false signals such as announcing bad news and selling short even though they know the firm will do well.

In a simple one-period model the manager's compensation, M, paid at the end of the period may be expressed as

$$M = (1+r)\gamma_0 V_0 + \gamma_1 \begin{cases} V_1 & \text{if } V_1 \geq D, \\ V_1 - C & \text{if } V_1 < D, \end{cases} \tag{15.68}$$

---

[22] An exception might be regulated firms. They can carry more debt because regulatory commissions are expected to "guarantee" a reasonable rate of return. Consequently, bankruptcy is very likely.

where

$$\gamma_0, \gamma_1 = \text{positive weights,}$$

$$r = \text{the one-period interest rate,}$$

$$V_0, V_1 = \text{the current and future value of the firm,}$$

$$D = \text{the face value of debt,}$$

$$C = \text{a penalty paid if bankruptcy occurs, that is, if } V < D.$$

This result can be used to establish a signaling equilibrium if we further assume that investors use D, the face value of debt, to tell them whether a firm is successful (type A) or unsuccessful (type B). Assume that $D*$ is the maximum amount of debt that an unsuccessful firm can carry without going bankrupt. If $D > D*$, the market perceives the firm to be successful, and vice versa. For the signaling equilibrium to be established, (1) the signals must be unambiguous (i.e., when investors observe $D > D*$, the firm is always type A), and (2) managers must have incentive to always give the appropriate signal. If the end-of-period value of a successful type-A firm is V_{1a} and is always greater than the value of an unsuccessful type-B firm, V_{1b}, then the compensation of the management of a type-A firm is

$$M_a = \begin{cases} \gamma_0(1+r)\frac{V_{1a}}{1+r} + \gamma_1 V_{1a} & \text{if } D* < D \leq V_{1a} \quad \text{(tell the truth),} \\ \gamma_0(1+r)\frac{V_{1b}}{1+r} + \gamma_1 V_{1a} & \text{if } D < D* \quad \text{(lie).} \end{cases} \tag{15.69}$$

Clearly, management of a type-A firm has incentive to establish a level of debt greater than $D*$ in order to earn maximum compensation. Therefore it will give the correct signal. But what about the management of a type-B firm? Does it not have incentive to lie by falsely signaling that its firm is type A? The answer is found by looking at the management incentive scheme.

$$M_b = \begin{cases} \gamma_0(1+r)\frac{V_{1a}}{1+r} + \gamma_1(V_{1b} - C) & \text{if } D* \leq D \leq V_{1a} \quad \text{(lie),} \\ \gamma_0(1+r)\frac{V_{1b}}{1+r} + \gamma_1 V_{1b} & \text{if } D < D* \quad \text{(tell the truth).} \end{cases} \tag{15.70}$$

In order for management of a type-B firm to have incentive to signal that the firm will be unsuccessful, the payoff from telling the truth must be greater than that produced by telling lies. Mathematically,

$$\gamma_0 V_{1a} + \gamma_1(V_{1b} - C) < \gamma_0 V_{1b} + \gamma_1 V_{1b},$$

which can be rewritten as

$$\gamma_0(V_{1a} - V_{1b}) < \gamma_1 C. \tag{15.71}$$

This condition says that management will give the correct signal if the marginal gain from a false signal, $V_{1a} - V_{1b}$, weighted by management's share, γ_0, is less than the bankruptcy costs incurred by management, C, weighted by its share, γ_1.

The incentive-signaling approach suggests that management might choose real financial variables such as financial leverage or dividend policy as the means of sending unambiguous signals to the public about the future performance of the firm. These signals cannot be mimicked by unsuccessful firms because such firms do not have sufficient cash flow to back them up and because managers have incentives to tell the truth. Without management incentives to signal truthfully there would be no signaling equilibrium.

The concept is easily applied to dividend policy as well as to financial structure. A firm that increases dividend payout is signaling that it has expected future cash flows that are sufficiently large to meet debt payments and dividend payments without increasing the probability of bankruptcy. Therefore we may expect to find empirical evidence that the value of the firm increases, because dividends are taken as signals that the firm is expected to have permanently higher future cash flows. Chapter 16 reviews the empirical evidence relevant to dividend policy.

Ross's paper suggests that greater financial leverage can be used by managers to signal an optimistic future for the firm. Another signaling paper, by Leland and Pyle [1977], focuses on owners instead of managers. They assume that entrepreneurs have better information about the expected value of their venture projects than do outsiders. The inside information held by an entrepreneur can be transferred to suppliers of capital because it is in the owner's interest to invest a greater fraction of his or her wealth in successful projects. Thus the owner's willingness to invest in his or her own projects can serve as a signal of project quality, and the value of the firm increases with the percentage of the equity held by the entrepreneur relative to what he or she otherwise would have held given a lower-quality project. An empirical implication of this signaling argument is that if the original founders of a company going public decide to keep a large fraction of the owner's wealth held as equity in the firm, then the firm will have greater debt capacity and will use greater amounts of debt. Although debt is not a signal in this model, its use will be positively correlated with the firm's value.

Myers and Majluf [1984] present a signaling model that combines investment and financing decisions and that is rich in empirical implications. Managers, better than anyone else, are assumed to know the "true" future value of the firm and of any projects that it might undertake. Furthermore, they are assumed to act in the interest of "old" shareholders, that is, those who hold shares in the firm at the time a decision is made. Finally, "old" shareholders are assumed to be passive in the sense that they do not actively change their personal portfolios to undo the decisions of management.[23] To keep things simple, assume that interest rates are zero and that there are no taxes, transactions costs, or other market imperfections.

To begin the analysis, consider a situation where there are two likely states of nature (good news and bad news). The firm has liquid assets, L_i, and tangible assets in place, A_i, that can take the values illustrated in Table 15.5. It has no positive net present value projects for the time being. (We shall examine the effect of positive NPV projects next.) Also, there is no debt (that will be the third case.) Information asymmetry is created by the fact that insiders are assumed to know which state, good or bad, will turn up for the firm. The market, however, knows nothing except what the value of the firm would be in each state of nature. If the firm does nothing, the market (i.e., outsiders) will compute the current value of the firm as the expected value of its payouts:

$$V_0 = \sum p_i(L_i + A_i) = .5(250) + .5(130) = 190.$$

This is equal to the value of the "old" shareholders' claim.

To establish a rational expectations signaling equilibrium, let us look at the payoffs to "old" shareholders in each state of nature given each of two possible actions: (1) do nothing or (2) issue

---

[23] If shareholders systematically undertake personal portfolio changes to reverse management decisions, then managerial financial decisions become irrelevant.

Table 15.5 Issue Equity, No Positive NPV Projects

	Do Nothing		Issue Equity	
	Good	**Bad**	**Good**	**Bad**
Liquid assets, L_i	50	50	150	150
Assets in place, A_i	200	80	200	80
Value of firm, V_i	250	130	350	230

$100 of new equity to new shareholders. We will see that although "old" shareholders have the incentive to issue new shares when the firm is overvalued—that is, when they know the bad news is coming—the very fact that they try to issue shares will signal their information to the market and consequently destroy their informational advantage. If "old" shareholders know good news (state 1) will occur, their wealth conditional on doing nothing is

$$(V_0 \mid \text{good news, do nothing}) = L_1 + A_1 = 250.$$

Alternately, they can issue $100 of new equity, E, and their value is

$$(V_0 \mid \text{good news, issue equity}) = \frac{V_0}{V_0 + E}(L_1 + A_1 + E) = \frac{190}{290}(350) = 229.31.$$

Their fraction of the firm if they issue the new equity is their current value, 190, divided by 190 plus the cash received from the new equity issue, 100. If "old" shareholders know bad news (state 2) will occur, their payoff from doing nothing is

$$(V_0 \mid \text{bad news, do nothing}) = L_2 + A_2 = 130,$$

and if they issue new equity, it is

$$(V_0 \mid \text{bad news, issue equity}) = \frac{V_0}{V_0 + E}(L_2 + A_2 + E) = \frac{190}{290}(230) = 150.69.$$

The payouts to original shareholders are summarized in Table 15.6. It seems that the optimal actions of the informed "old" shareholders (i.e., the payouts with asterisks) are to do nothing if they think the good news state will occur and to issue equity if the bad news state will occur, because the firm is currently overvalued. Outsiders, however, will not be fooled. When the firm issues new equity they know the firm believes the bad news state will occur, and they impute the bad news value, 130, to the firm. Therefore the expected payout to old shareholders, given that they issue new equity and that the outsiders infer bad news, is

$$(V_0 \mid \text{issue equity}) = \frac{V_2}{V_2 + E}(V_2 + E) = V_2 = 130.$$

The upshot of this argument is that original shareholders cannot take advantage of their inside information because the very act of issuing new shares (when they think the firm is overvalued) will reveal their information to the market. Hence they are indifferent between doing nothing and issuing new equity, and the market will attach no significance to new equity issues.

Table 15.6 "Old" Shareholder Payoffs—Issue vs. Do Nothing

	Do Nothing	Issue Equity
Good news	250.00*	229.31
Bad news	130.00	150.69*

Table 15.7 Positive NPV Project and New Equity

	Do Nothing		Invest and Issue Equity	
	Good	Bad	Good	Bad
Liquid assets, L_i	50	50	50	50
Assets in place, A_i	200	80	300	180
NPV of new project, b_i	0	0	20	10
Value of firm, V_i	250	130	370	240

Next, let us complicate the model slightly by assuming that the firm has a positive net present value project that requires an initial cash outlay of \$100 and that has the state-dependent net present values, b_i, illustrated in Table 15.7. Going through the same type of computations as before, we first compute V_0, the unconditional value of original shareholders' wealth, assuming they do nothing:

$$V_0 = \sum p_i(L_i + A_i) = .5(250) + .5(130) = 190.$$

Alternately, if they issue and invest, their unconditional expected wealth is

$$V_0' = \sum p_i(L_i + A_i + b_i) = .5(270) + .5(140) = 205.$$

Now let us examine their wealth, contingent on each state of nature. If they issue \$100 of new equity and invest the proceeds in the new positive NPV project, their wealth in the good news state is

$$(V_0 \mid \text{good news, invest and issue}) = \frac{V_0'}{V_0' + E}(L_1 + A_1 + b_1 + E)$$

$$= \frac{205}{205 + 100}(370) = 249.69,$$

and if they do nothing, given good news, their wealth is 250. Given bad news, their payout if they issue and invest is

$$(V_0 \mid \text{bad news, invest and issue}) = \frac{V_0'}{V_0' + E}(L_2 + A_2 + b_2 + E)$$

$$= \frac{205}{205 + 100}(240) = 161.31,$$

Table 15.8 "Old" Shareholder Payoffs—Issue and Invest vs. Nothing

	Do Nothing	**Issue and Invest**
Good news	250*	289.69
Bad news	130	161.31*

Table 15.9 Rational Expectations Equilibrium

	Do Nothing	**Issue and Invest**
Good news	250*	248.69
Bad news	130	140.00*

and if they do nothing, given bad news, their wealth is 130. Table 15.8 summarizes the payoffs from the "old" shareholders' point of view. As before, original shareholders are better off doing nothing in the good state because the positive NPV of the project (given good news) is not large enough to offset the fraction of ownership that they must sacrifice by issuing new shares.[24] Hence they desire to issue new equity and invest only if they know the bad state will occur. As before, the market is not fooled. As soon as insiders announce their intention to issue and invest, the market learns that the bad state is forthcoming, and in the bad state the firm is worth only 240, with 100 going to outsiders and the remaining 140 going to original shareholders. The rational expectations equilibrium payoffs are illustrated in Table 15.9. In equilibrium, given the set of numbers we have chosen, the firm issues and invests in the bad news state but not in the good news state.[25] This surprising result implies that the value of the firm may well fall when new equity issues are announced—an important empirical implication.

So far we have examined two cases. First, when the firm had no new projects and the market knew it, then issuing new equity was an unambiguous financial signal that the market could use to discover the inside information held by managers. Hence it was impossible for managers to benefit from issuing new equity when they knew the future prospects of the firm were dismal. Second, when positive NPV projects (good news) were financed with equity issues (bad news), the signal became mixed. The market could not separate information about new projects from information about whether the firm is under- or overvalued. If there were some way to provide two separate signals—one for investment decisions and another for financing decisions—the problem would vanish. If project outcomes were uncorrelated with states of nature (e.g., if the project had the same NPV in both states of nature), the problem would vanish. Or if the firm were to use financing that is not subject to the information asymmetry problem, the problem would vanish.

Harris and Raviv [1990] provide another signaling story, namely, that investors must use information concerning the future prospects of the firm to decide whether to liquidate or to continue operations, but managers who are reluctant to liquidate under any circumstances are unwilling to volunteer information necessary for investors to make their decision. Investors get around this problem by using debt to generate information and to monitor management. Optimal capital

---

[24] It is important to realize that outsiders pay nothing for the expected NPV of the new project. The entire NPV accrues to "old" shareholders.

[25] It is puzzling to understand why shareholders do not provide all investment funds if they know the good state will occur. These funds can come from cash (what Myers and Majluf call slack) or via a rights offering.

structure is the result of a trade-off between the value of information (from more debt) and the probability of incurring investigation costs.

2. Pecking Order

Myers and Majluf point out that if the firm uses its available liquid assets, L_i, to finance positive NPV projects, then all positive NPV projects would be undertaken because no new equity is issued and the information asymmetry problem is thereby resolved. They suggest that this may be a good reason for carrying excess liquid assets. They also suggest that debt financing, which has payoffs less correlated with future states of nature than equity, will be preferred to new equity as a means of financing. Myers [1984] suggests a *pecking order theory* for capital structure. Firms are said to prefer retained earnings (available liquid assets) as their main source of funds for investment. Next in order of preference is debt, and last comes external equity financing. Firms wish to avoid issuing common stock or other risky securities so that they do not run into the dilemma of either passing up positive NPV projects or issuing stock at a price they think is too low.

The pecking order theory is a dynamic story. The observed capital structure of each firm will depend on its history. For example, an unusually profitable firm in an industry with relatively slow growth (few investment opportunities) will end up with an unusually low debt-to-equity ratio. It has no incentive to issue debt and retire equity. An unprofitable firm in the same industry will end up with a high debt ratio. Shyam-Sunder and Myers [1999] provide a test that compares the pecking order theory with the static traditional theory of capital structure by noting that the pecking order theory predicts that the change in debt each year depends on the funds flow deficit that year, a fact that would, if true, result in a zero intercept and slope of 1.0 for the following regression equation:

$$\Delta D_{i,t} = a + b_i DEF_{i,t} + \epsilon_{i,t},$$

where the cash flow deficit is defined as the sum of dividends paid, capital expenditures, the change in working capital, the current portion of debt, and cash flows from operations (i.e., EBIT less taxes plus depreciation and amortization). When the deficit is positive, it is presumed that the firm issues debt, and when it is negative that the firm retires debt.

The traditional static theory assumes a target capital structure. Graham and Harvey [2001] survey 392 chief financial officers and find that although 15% reported that their firms had no target capital structure, 44% said they did. Most of them took into consideration the tax deductibility of interest payments, cash flow volatility, and flexibility—consistent with the static theory. Also, it predicts that if the firm's capital structure lies above its long-term target, it will issue equity, and if it lies below that target, it will issue debt. Although Taggert [1977], Marsh [1982], Auerbach [1985], Jalivand and Harris [1984], and Opler and Titman [1994] all find mean-reverting behavior as the static theory predicts, there is also contradictory evidence finding that firms that were profitable in the past have low current debt-to-equity ratios (see Kester [1986] and Titman and Wessels [1988]). Also, as will be mentioned again later in this chapter, one would expect that overleveraged firms would have positive announcement effects when they issue equity; however, the actual result is quite the opposite. Focusing on the prediction that changes in debt will revert toward the firm's target capital structure, Shyam-Sunder and Myers [1999] fit the following regression:

$$\Delta D_{i,t} = a + b_i(D_{i,t}^* - D_{i,t-1}) + \epsilon_{i,t},$$

where $D_{i,t}^*$ is defined as the firm's target capital structure. The authors try various proxies for the target capital structure on a sample of 157 industrial firms for year endings of 1971, 1981, and 1989. They find that the speed of adjustment coefficient is low in the static theory regression ($b_i = 0.33$) and that the r-squared is only 21%. On the other hand, the coefficient in the pecking order equation is close to one ($b_i = 0.75$) and the r-squared is 68%. They conclude that the evidence provides strong support for the pecking order theory. However, a subsequent paper by Chirinko and Singha [2000] points out that it is difficult to differentiate between the two theories when using the experimental design of Shyam-Sunder and Myers.

Helwege and Liang [1996] test the pecking order hypothesis for a group of firms that went public in 1983. They find, consistent with the hypothesis, that firms with surplus internal funds avoid the external market. On the other hand, the size of the internal cash deficit has no predictive power for the decision to obtain external funds. Finally, for firms that raise external capital they find no evidence of a pecking order.

Frank and Goyal [2003] test the pecking order theory by studying a sample of 768 publicly held U.S. firms with at least 19 years of data (1971–1998). The theory predicts that external financing should be only a small portion of the total capital formation and that external equity should be a small fraction of external finance. Surprisingly, Frank and Goyal find external finance is large, that net equity issues commonly exceed net debt issues, and that net equity issues track the firm's financing deficit much more closely than do net debt issues. They also find that the financing deficit does not challenge the rate of conventional leverage factors (e.g., market to book equity, sales revenue, profitability, fixed to total assets, and lagged leverage) that are proxies for equilibrium factors that explain capital structure. Finally, since the pecking order theory is motivated by adverse selection costs caused by information asymmetry, it should work best in small high-growth firms. Frank and Goyal find quite the opposite. It works the best in large firms that existed continuously during the 1970s and 1980s.

Fama and French [2002] analyze the dividend and debt policies of firms in the context of the static trade-off and pecking order models. They find that firms with larger profits and fewer investments have larger dividend payouts. They also find that more profitable firms and firms with higher investments have lower leverage. They interpret these results as being consistent with both theories. Consistent with the pecking order model, they find that short-term variations in investments and earnings are absorbed by debt.

Lemmon and Zender [2001] examine a sample of firms listed in CRSP and Compustat over the period 1980–1995. They use the Graham [2000] variable entitled "kink" that measures the extent to which a firm can increase its leverage before the marginal expected tax benefits from debt decreases to classify firms. Since the high-kink firms can most benefit from debt issues, they argue that such firms should most likely exhibit pecking order behavior. Specifically, they suggest that this group of firms should predominantly choose debt over equity when they need external funds. They find, contrary to the predictions of the pecking order theory, that these firms were no less likely to issue equity when choosing outside financing.

Minton and Wruck [2001] examine a group of firms that follow financial conservatism. In their analysis financially conservative firms are those with leverage in the lowest 20% of those listed in CRSP and Compustat. Consistent with the pecking order hypothesis, they find that these firms tend to have large levels of internal funds. They also find, as suggested by pecking order, that when the firms seek external funds they tend to choose debt. On the other hand, these firms do not exhaust all internal funds before they seek external funds. Finally, they report that the debt policies of these firms cannot be explained by a low tax benefit from debt (as suggested by the trade-off theory) since they do not have low tax rates or high nondebt tax shields.

3. Foregone Investment Opportunities

Froot, Sharfstein, and Stein [1993] explicitly model the relationship between the firm's investment opportunity set and its financing decisions. They start with the proposition that variability in the cash flows of the firm affects both investment and financing decisions in a way that is costly to the firm. If the firm runs out of internally generated cash flow and if external financing is used to maintain the level of investment unchanged, then it is presumed that the cost of funds goes up. Alternatively, if internally generated funds are insufficient to make all desirable investments and the firm elects not to go to external markets to finance them, the result is suboptimal investment, and that is costly as well.

Although Froot, Sharfstein, and Stein go on to use this argument to motivate the use of hedging to reduce the variance of operating cash flows in order to reduce the expected costs of foregone investment and/or higher cost of capital, their framework is important for two reasons. First, they acknowledge that a major cost of carrying excess debt is the opportunity cost of foregone investment opportunities. Second, they stress the interaction between investment decisions on the one hand and the way they are financed on the other. They provide a plausible rationale for why it is reasonable and realistic to relax and revise the implicit assumption that investment decisions are independent of the mix of debt and equity chosen by the firm.

I. *E*mpirical Evidence Concerning Capital Structure

We have parsed the massive body of empirical evidence into three sections. The first and most generally applicable are cross-sectional studies that look across companies and industries at a point in time (or combine cross-sectional observations into panel data that combines different years into one database). Second are studies that have focused on exchange offers and swaps. They are particularly interesting because the firm's portfolio of operating assets is unaffected. All that happens is that cash is raised by issuing certificates of one type of security (e.g., equity) and the proceeds are then used to retire another class of securities (e.g., debt). Thus, any observed effects are presumably due to a purely financial transaction. Finally, there are time-series studies—primarily event studies of the announcement effects of various types of financial maneuvers.

Capital structure is a difficult issue to test empirically. Often, changes in capital structure are made simultaneously with new investment decisions, thus making it nearly impossible to separate the financial impact on firm value from the effect of the investment decision. Additionally, capital structure is difficult to measure. It is hard enough to get good market value data for publicly held debt, but it is nearly impossible to obtain data on privately held debt. Furthermore, the liabilities of the firm (including subsidiary obligations) include leasing contracts, pension liabilities, deferred compensation to management and employees, performance guarantees, lawsuits that are pending, warranties, and contingent securities such as warrants, convertible debt, and convertible preferred stock. Keeping these difficulties in mind, let us take a look at some of the empirical evidence that reveals something about the way that capital structure affects the value of the firm.

1. Cross-Sectional Studies

Modigliani and Miller [1958] use cross-section equations on data taken from 43 electric utilities during 1947–1948 and 42 oil companies during 1953. They estimate the weighted average cost of capital as net operating cash flows after taxes divided by the market value of the firm.[26] When regressed against financial leverage (measured as the ratio of the market value of debt to the market value of the firm), the results were[27]

$$\text{Electric utilities:} \quad WACC = 5.3 + .006d, \quad r = .12,$$
$$(.008)$$
$$\text{Oil companies:} \quad WACC = 8.5 + .006d, \quad r = .04,$$
$$(.024)$$

where d is the financial leverage of the firm and r is the correlation coefficient. These results suggest that the cost of capital is not affected by capital structure (because the slope coefficients are not significantly different from zero) and therefore that there is no gain to leverage.

Weston [1963] criticizes the Modigliani-Miller results on two counts. First, the oil industry is not even approximately homogeneous in business risk (operating leverage); second, the valuation model from which the cost of capital is derived assumes that cash flows are perpetuities that do not grow. When growth is added to the cross-section regression, the result for electric utilities becomes

$$WACC = 5.91 - .0265d + .00A - .0822E \quad r = .5268.,$$
$$(.0079) \quad (.0001) \quad (.0024)$$

where A is the book value of assets (a proxy for firm size) and E is the compound growth in earnings per share (1949–1959). Since $WACC$ decreases with leverage, Weston's results are consistent with the existence of a gain to leverage (i.e., that the tax shield on debt has value).

Later on, Miller and Modigliani [1966] also found results (based on a sample of 63 electric utility firms in 1954, 1956, and 1957) that were consistent with a gain from leverage. Table 15.10 summarizes their results. The value of the firm is attributed to the present value of the operating cash flows generated by assets in place, by the tax subsidy on debt, by growth potential, and by firm size. For our purposes the important result is that the empirical evidence indicates that the tax subsidy (i.e., the gain from leverage) on debt does contribute a significant amount to the value of the firm, about 26% on average. This is consistent with the notion that the firm's WACC falls as leverage increases.

Cordes and Sheffrin [1983] use Treasury Department data to examine cross-sectional differences in effective tax rates that may be caused by tax carry-backs and carry forwards, by foreign tax credits, by investment tax credits, by the alternate tax on capital gains, and by the minimum tax. They found significant differences across industries, with the highest effective rate for tobacco manufacturing (45%) and the lowest rate (16%) for transportation and agriculture. This tends to support the DeAngelo-Masulis [1980] contention that the gain from leverage-induced tax shields can be positive.

An important part of the Modigliani-Miller theory is that the cost of equity capital increases with higher leverage. Hamada [1972] tests this proposition empirically by combining the Modigliani-Miller theory and the CAPM. He finds that on the average the systematic risk of the levered firm

---

[26] Net operating flows after taxes were actually estimated as net income after taxes plus interest payments on debt. This assumes that there is no growth in earnings and that replacement investment equals depreciation expense.

[27] Standard errors are in parentheses.

Table 15.10 Sources Contributing to the Value of the Firm

Source	Absolute Contribution			Percentage Contribution		
	1957	**1956**	**1954**	**1957**	**1956**	**1954**
1. Value of assets in place	.758	.808	.914	68.1	72.0	75.9
2. Tax subsidy on debt	.262	.254	.258	23.5	22.6	23.7
3. Growth potential	.112	.072	.028	10.0	6.4	2.3
4. Size of firm	−.019	−.008	−.021	−1.7	−.7	−1.7
Average (market/book) value	1.113	1.123	1.204	100.0	100.0	100.0

From M. Miller and F. Modigliani, "Some Estimates of the Cost of Capital to the Electric Utility Industry, 1954–57," *American Economic Review*, June 1966, 373. Reprinted by permission of the authors.

is greater than that for the unlevered firm:

$$\widehat{\beta}_L = .91, \widehat{\beta}_U = .70.$$

This, of course, is consistent with the increased risk associated with higher leverage. However, in order to construct the return on equity for an unlevered firm, Hamada had to assume that the Modigliani-Miller theory was correct. Suppose that it is not correct. Namely, what would happen if the return on equity (i.e., the cost of equity capital) did not increase with increasing leverage? We would expect that for a sample of firms with the same operating risk there would be no increase in systematic risk with higher financial leverage. Because it is almost impossible to find firms with identical operating risk, Hamada suggests that within an industry if the β_U values of individual firms are closer or less scattered than their β_L values, then the Modigliani-Miller theory would be supported. Greater variability in the β_L values implies that the cost of equity changes with financial leverage. In nine industries examined, β_L was greater than β_U in all cases, and the standard deviation of the β_L values was greater than eight out of nine of the β_U values. This may be taken as indirect evidence that the cost of equity increases with higher financial leverage.

Cross-sectional work has been done by Bradley, Jarrell, and Kim [1984], Long and Malitz [1985], and Titman and Wessels [1988]. Bradley, Jarrell, and Kim regressed leverage against (1) earnings volatility as a proxy for bankruptcy risk, (2) the ratio of depreciation plus investment tax credits to earnings as a proxy for nondebt tax shields, and (3) the ratio of advertising plus research and development expenditures to net sales as a proxy for noncollateralizable assets. The first and third variables were significantly negative, supporting the importance of bankruptcy costs and collateral, but the second variable was significantly positive, seeming to be inconsistent with debt as a tax shield. Long and Malitz estimate a similar regression but add several additional variables. They obtain results similar to Bradley, Jarrell, and Kim but find nondebt tax shields to be negatively related to leverage (although not significant).

Titman and Wessels [1988] employ linear structural modeling to explicitly accommodate explanatory variables as proxies for their theoretical counterparts. Their results show that asset uniqueness and profitability were significantly negatively related to leverage. This result supports the Myers-Majluf [1984] pecking order theory because more profitable firms will tend to use less external financing. It also supports the Titman [1984] idea that firms with unique assets can carry less debt owing to agency costs.

Mackie-Mason [1990] examines the incremental financial decisions to analyze whether taxes affect corporate financing decisions. Thus, in contrast to most other empirical work in these areas, Mackie-Mason examines the probability of debt versus equity issuance rather than the debt ratio. He finds that the propensity to issue debt is negatively related to the existence of other tax shields, the probability of financial distress. It is positively related to the level of free cash flow and the fraction of assets that are tangible. He also argues that the tax benefit effects are large since a one standard deviation increase in nondebt tax shield is associated with a 10% reduction of the propensity to issue debt.

Frank and Goyal [2003] examine the relative importance of 39 different factors in the leverage decisions of publicly traded U.S. firms. They find that leverage increases with median industry leverage, firm size, intangibles, collateral, and the top corporate income tax rate. On the other hand, it decreases with bankruptcy risk, whether the firm pays dividends, market-to-book ratio, operating loss carry forward, profitability, and interest rates. They conclude that their results are consistent with the trade-off theory and not consistent with the pecking order model or the market timing theory.

Hovikimian, Opler, and Titman [2001] test the hypothesis that firms tend to move towards their target debt ratios when they raise or retire capital. Their tests explicitly account for the fact that the target capital structure of the firm can change with profitability and stock prices. Their results provide support for this prediction of the static trade-off model, with the effects being more pronounced with the retirement of capital. They also find that stock prices seem to play an important role in the firm's financing decision. Specifically, they report that high stock prices seem to result in debt repurchase and equity issuance.

Kemsley and Nissim [2002] point out a problem with cross-sectional studies that use the debt-equity ratio as a dependent variable and taxes, growth rates, and so on as independent variables. Because it cannot be easily measured, the present value of a firm's operating cash flows is left out of the multiple regression and is correlated with the debt capacity of the firm via causality that is not linked to taxation. One way around this problem is to study the relationship between changes in debt and the level of tax rates. This is done by Graham [1996], who finds a positive relationship in a sample of 10,000 firms in the 1980–1992 time period. Firms with high tax rates issue more straight debt—a result that is consistent with a gain to leverage. Another way around this problem is to test the reverse relationship. Kemsley and Nissim specify the future profitability of the firm as a function of firm value today, debt, and controls for firm-level capitalization rates. Moving future profitability to the left-hand side of the regression puts its measurement error into the residual of the regression, where it can no longer bias the debt coefficient (which is used to estimate the size and significance of the interest tax shield). Moving the market value of the firm out of (the denominator) the left-hand side allows the use of market value variables on the right-hand side to proxy for growth and risk. Using over 42,000 observations they estimate the debt tax shield is 40% of the debt or 10% of the firm value for the average firm. This provides strong evidence of a gain to leverage.

Kahle and Shastri [2003] analyze the relation between the capital structure of the firm and the level of tax benefits realized from the exercise of stock options. The static trade-off hypothesis suggests that firms with tax benefits from the exercise of stock options should carry less debt since these benefits are a nondebt tax shield. They find that both long- and short-term debt ratios are negatively related to the size of tax benefits from option exercise. Their results also indicate that one-year changes in long-term leverage are negatively related to changes in the number of options exercised by employees. Finally, firms with option-related tax benefits tend to issue equity, and the net amount of equity issued is an increasing function of the level of tax benefits from option exercise.

Welch [2003] bifurcates capital structure changes into two components—one related to issuing (net of retirement) activity and another related to stock returns. In other words, high-return companies have high debt loads. He finds that stock returns explain about 40% of capital structure dynamics. He also reports that variables traditionally used in the literature to explain debt-equity ratios such as tax costs, bankruptcy costs, market-to-book ratios, uniqueness, and market timing fail to explain capital structure dynamics once stock returns are accounted for. Based on these results, he concludes "that stock returns are the primary known component of capital structure and capital structure changes."

2. Evidence Based on Exchange Offers and Swaps

In an exchange offer or swap, one class of securities is exchanged for another in a deal that involves no cash. The most important feature is that with exchange offers there is no simultaneous change in the assets structure of the firm. Therefore they represent a relatively pure type of financial event that allows the researcher to isolate the effects of changes in capital structure on the firm. Consequently, exchange offers are one of the most intensely studied financial change phenomena.

For a sample containing 106 leverage-increasing and 57 leverage-decreasing exchange offers during the period 1962 through 1976, Masulis [1980] found highly significant announcement effects. For the *Wall Street Journal* announcement date and the following day, the announcement period return is 7.6% for leverage-increasing exchange offers and −5.4% for leverage-decreasing exchange offers.

These results are possibly consistent with three theories: (1) that there is a valuable tax shield created when financial leverage is increased (and vice versa), (2) that debt holders' wealth is being expropriated by shareholders in leverage-increasing exchange offers, and (3) that higher leverage is a signal of management's confidence in the future of the firm.

A leverage-increasing exchange offer can be damaging to original bondholders if they have imperfect protective covenants in the bond indentures. Masulis [1980] directly examines a sample of 18 nonconvertible debt issues without any covenants to protect against the issuance of new debt with equal seniority. The announcement period return is −.84%, with a statistically significant t-test of 2.7. This result is consistent with expropriation of bondholder wealth. However, a larger sample of all nonconvertible debt issues (with and without protective covenants) experiences a negative .3% two-day announcement return. In general the empirical evidence does not strongly support the bondholder expropriation hypothesis.

Preferred-for-common exchange offers provide an indirect test of the interest tax shield hypothesis because preferred dividends are not tax deductible. Preferred-for-common exchange offers have no tax consequences. Masulis [1980] finds a statistically significant positive 3.3% common stock two-day announcement return for a sample of 43 preferred-for-common exchange offers and a significant positive 3.6% return for 43 debt-for-preferred offers.[28] Pinegar and Lease [1986] find a statistically significant 4.05% positive common stock return for 15 leverage-increasing preferred-for-common exchange offers. The equity return for leverage-decreasing exchange offers is a significantly negative .73% (30 observations). These results favor the signaling hypothesis over the tax hypothesis but cannot be used to reject the tax hypothesis because it may still be relevant to those types of exchange offer where the interest tax shield is affected. Pinegar and Lease also

---

[28] Returns for leverage-decreasing offers were multiplied by −1.0 and added to the returns of leverage-increasing offers.

find that preferred shareholders experience a significant 6.58% positive return during leverage-decreasing exchange offers, although total firm value (equity plus debt plus preferred) is estimated to decrease. They conclude that their results are consistent with the signaling hypothesis (firm value decreases) and with the expropriation hypothesis (preferred stock value increases).

Masulis [1980], in a cross-sectional study of the announcement returns of 133 exchange offers, finds evidence to support the conclusion that stock prices are positively related to leverage changes because of (1) a gain in value induced by tax shields on debt and (2) a positive signaling effect. Also, he concludes that leverage increases induce wealth transfers across security classes, with the greatest effect on unprotected nonconvertible debt.

Copeland and Lee [1991] provide evidence that further strengthens the signaling interpretation of exchange offers. They note that insiders typically do not sell their shares during the offer. Thus, for leverage-increasing exchanges, insiders' ownership in the firm increases when outsiders' shares are repurchased with debt. In support of the signaling hypothesis, they find (1) that 61 of 90 firms with leverage-increasing exchange offers experience decreases in systematic risk following the completion date and that 75 of 127 leverage-decreasing firms experience increases in systematic risk; (2) that earnings, sales, and capital expenditures per share (adjusted for the exchange offer) all increase following leverage-increasing exchange offers; and (3) that there were net insider purchases of stock prior to leverage-increasing exchange offer announcements for 36 of 40 events (where data were available) and net insider sales for 56 of 96 leverage-decreasing events.

On balance the empirical evidence from studying exchange offers is weakly consistent with tax effects (a gain to leverage) and with bondholder expropriation but is strongly consistent with management use of exchange offers to take advantage of superior information concerning the future prospects of the firm. The market interprets leverage-increasing offers as good news and leverage-decreasing offers as bad news.

3. Time-Series Studies: Announcement Effects

Given the plausibility of the signaling hypothesis, it is interesting to take empirical results on dozens of different corporate events and compare them. Smith [1986] suggests that they be compared in two different dimensions—events that increase financial leverage (a favorable signal) and those that imply favorable future cash flow changes.

Table 15.11 and Fig. 15.12 summarize the two-day announcement effects for a wide variety of corporate events. We have already discussed exchange offers, which are purely financial changes. Generally speaking, leverage-increasing exchange offers have significant positive announcement effects. Exchanges of debt for debt, studied by Dietrich [1984], have no significant effect on shareholders' wealth, and leverage-decreasing exchange offers have a significant negative effect.

Stock repurchases and seasoned equity offerings are at the opposite end of the scale. Evidence by Masulis and Korwar [1986], Kolodny and Suhler [1985], and Mikkelson and Partch [1986] indicates that issues of seasoned equity are interpreted as bad news by the marketplace, with significantly negative announcement date effects on equity prices. This result is consistent with the Myers-Majluf pecking order theory of capital structure. Firms will resort to equity issues only as a last resort. It is interesting to note that the negative announcement date residuals are large (−3.2%) for industrial firms that issue equity infrequently and small (−.6%) for utilities that are frequent issuers. This result, too, seems to be consistent with the pecking order theory. Stock repurchases are at the opposite end of the spectrum. They increase leverage, and they are interpreted as favorable signals about the future prospects of the firm. The announcement residuals are extremely large—

Table 15.11 Announcement Effects of Corporate Events

Announcement	Security Issued	Security Retired	Average Sample Size	Two-day Return
Leverage-increasing:				
Stock repurchase	Debt	Common	45	21.9%
Exchange offer	Debt	Common	52	14.0
Exchange offer	Preferred	Common	9	8.3
Exchange offer	Debt	Preferred	24	2.2
Exchange offer	Income bonds	Preferred	24	2.2
Security sale (industrials)	Debt	None	248	−.3*
Security sale (utilities)	Debt	None	140	−1.0*
No-leverage change:				
Exchange offer	Debt	Debt	36	0.6*
Security sale	Debt	Debt	83	0.2*
Equity carveout	Equity	Equity	76	0.7
Security sale (dual offering)	Debt and equity	None	51	−2.6
Security sale	Convertible debt	None	132	−2.3
Security sale	Preferred	None	102	−0.1
Leverage-decreasing:				
Conversion-forcing call	Common	Convertible preferred	57	−0.4
Conversion-forcing call	Common	Convertible bond	113	−2.1
Security sale	Convertible debt	Debt	15	−2.4
Exchange offer	Common	Preferred	30	−2.6
Exchange offer	Common	Debt	20	−9.9
Exchange offer	Preferred	Debt	9	−7.7
Security sale (industrials)	Common	None	388	−3.2
Security sale (utilities)	Common	None	584	−0.6
Investment				
Increases	None	None	510	1.0
Decreases	None	None	111	−1.1
Dividends				
Increases	None	None	280	0.9
Decreases	None	None	48	−3.6

* Interpreted as statistically significant.

Figure 15.12 Two dimensions of announcement effects (two-day abnormal returns in parentheses).

Leverage effect	Worse	No change	Better
Increases	Sale of debt (0.3) Sale of preferred (0.1)	Debt-for-preferred exchange offer (2.2)	Common repurchase (21.9) Debt-for-common exchange offer (14.0)
No change	Investment decreases (−1.1) Dividend decreases (−3.6) Convertible debt sale (−2.4)	Debt-for-debt exchange offer (0.6)	Investment increases (1.0) Dividend increases (0.9)
Decreases	Sale of common (−3.2) Common-for-debt exchange offer (−9.9) Preferred-for-debt exchange offer (−7.7)	Preferred-for-debt exchange offer (−7.7)	Call of convertible bonds (−1.3)

Future prospects of the firm

positive 21.9% for repurchases where debt is issued to retire common and 14.0% for exchange offers of debt for common.

All leverage-decreasing events have negative announcement effects, and all leverage-increasing events, save one, have positive announcement effects. The exception is the new issue of debt securities, where Dann and Mikkelson [1984], Eckbo [1986], and Mikkelson and Partch [1986] found negative but insignificant announcement effects. This result is also consistent with the pecking order theory. The majority of events with no leverage change had insignificant announcement effects.

Announcements with favorable (unfavorable) implications for the future cash flows of the firm such as investment increases (decreases) and dividend increases (decreases) were accompanied by significant positive (negative) effects on shareholders' wealth.

With these results in mind, it is tempting to try to place each type of corporate event into the two dimensions of Figure 15.12. Not all events fit neatly. Yet there does seem to be a convincing pattern. Events that both increase leverage and provide a favorable signal about the future prospects of the firm, common share repurchases and debt-for-common exchange offers, seem to have the largest positive announcement effects.

J. How Does a Practitioner Use the Theory to Determine Optimal Capital Structure?

The answer to this question is the Holy Grail of corporate finance. There is no completely satisfactory answer, and the author of a sound, empirically validated theory will deserve the Nobel prize in economics. At one extreme is the contention first made by Modigliani and Miller [1958] and reiterated by Miller [1977] that capital structure simply does not matter and has no effect on the value of the firm. At the other extreme is the following observation made by Ezra Solomon [1963] around the same time that Modigliani and Miller were publishing their work:

> One kind of evidence in favor of the traditional position is that companies in various industry groups appear to use leverage as if there is some optimal range appropriate to each group. While significant intercompany differences in debt ratios exist within each industry, the average use of leverage by broad industry groups tends to follow a consistent pattern over time.

Figure 15.13 shows industry average and median debt-to-equity ratios (expressed both in market value and book value terms) for companies with A-rated debt, for seven industries in 2002. Clearly, there are significant differences in the debt-to-equity ratio that implies an A rating. Banks have the most debt, and pharmaceutical companies the least. There is not even an overlap between some

Figure 15.13 Industries have significantly different capital structures: (a) market debt-to-equity ratio of A-rated companies; (b) book debt-to-equity ratio of A-rated companies. (Source: Compustat, Monitor analysis.)

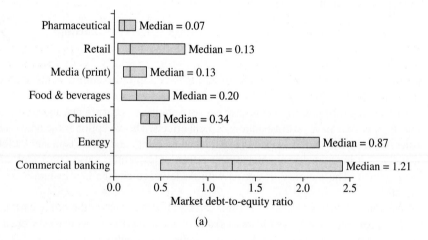

(a)

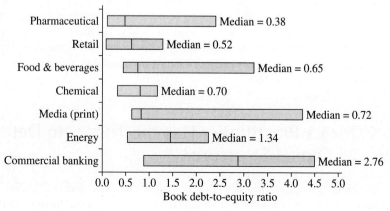

(b)

of the industries; for example, the highest A-rated pharmaceutical leverage ratio is lower than the lowest chemical ratio, and the highest chemical ratio is lower than that of the lowest bank.

The static equilibrium theories predict that we should be able to explain these empirical regularities as trade-offs between the four terms in Eq. (15.66), namely, the trade-off between the present value of the tax shield on debt and the present value of business disruption costs. This is exactly the way that Opler, Saron, and Titman [1997] approach the problem. They construct a discounted cash flow model of the firm, and then introduce uncertainty about its future cash flows via Monte Carlo techniques in an attempt to capture historical volatility relationships as well as mean reversion. For each path of cash flows and in each year, they determine whether business disruption has occurred or not, and if it has, they then introduce business disruption costs. Also they determine cash taxes paid that year given the path that the company is on and what taxes, if any, should be carried forward or back. Figure 15.10 shows the general shape of the relationship between the value of the interest tax shield and business disruption, but it does not help much with the actual parameter estimates. For example, what percentage of the value of a company is appropriate for modeling business disruption costs? Can the approach explain the regularities of Figure 15.13? Perhaps.

Another approach is empirically based and has no strong theoretical framework except that it uses the Modigliani-Miller approach for estimating the cost of equity. It starts with the yield curve that defines the relationship between the yield to maturity on 10-year bonds and their rating (with AAA being the highest). The yield curve for January 2003 is provided in Figure 15.14. All bonds of a given rating trade within a narrow range around the fitted line. Notice that there is an inflection point (or discontinuity between the BBB rating, which is still considered investment grade, and the BB rating, which is speculative), where the promised yield increases due to the threat of business disruption.

Figure 15.14 The yield curve for 10-year bonds (January 2003). (Source: Bloomberg, Monitor analysis.)

10-year U.S. Treasury and industrial corporate bond yield curve

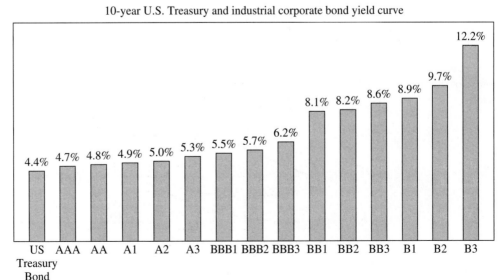

The second step is to run a regression for all of the companies in an industry. The dependent variable is the company's bond rating (numerically scaled), and the independent variable is the debt-to-equity ratio in market value terms (and sometimes other variables such as the volatility of cash flows). An example is shown in Figure 15.15. By combining these first two bits of analysis one can then derive the relationship between the yield to maturity and the debt-to-equity ratio. This is an industry-based pretax cost of debt schedule. Multiplying it by one minus the marginal effective statutory tax rate for a company provides the empirical estimate of the company level cost of debt after taxes.

Next, we can observe the levered equity betas for each company, the tax rate, and the market value debt-to-equity ratio. Equation (15.8) can be used to estimate the business risk, that is the unlevered beta, for each company and we can then use the sample median unlevered beta as representative of our company. The cost of unlevered equity can then be calculated using the CAPM and Eq. (15.18) can be used to construct the relationship between the ratio of debt to equity and the cost of equity.

Figure 15.16 shows the results. The top line is the cost of equity and the bottom line is the after-tax cost of debt. In between them is the weighted average cost of capital. It reaches a minimum around a BBB rating.

Figure 15.15 Linear regression of bond ratings on debt-to-equity ratios.

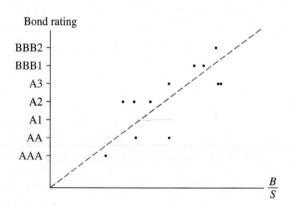

Figure 15.16 Empirical estimate of the cost of capital.

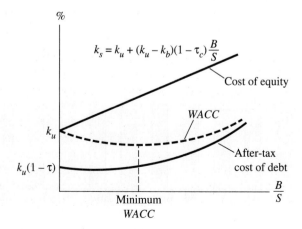

$$k_s = k_u + (k_u - k_b)(1 - \tau_c)\frac{B}{S}$$

Cost of equity

WACC

After-tax cost of debt

k_u

$k_u(1 - \tau)$

Minimum
WACC

$\dfrac{B}{S}$

K. The Maturity Structure of Debt

Optimal capital structure refers not only to the ratio of debt to equity but also to the maturity structure of debt. What portion of total debt should be short term and what portion long term? Should the firm use variable-rate or fixed-rate debt? Should long-term bonds pay annual coupons with a balloon payment, or should they be fully amortized (equal periodic payments)?

There are five approaches to answering the maturity structure problem. The earliest, a cross-hedging argument by Morris [1976], suggests that short-term debt or variable-rate debt can reduce the risk to shareholders and thereby increase equity value if the covariance between net operating income and expected future interest rates is positive. This cross-hedging argument is based on the assumption that unexpected changes in interest rates are a priced (undiversifiable) factor in the arbitrage pricing model. It does not rely directly on bankruptcy costs or on interest tax shields. However, the argument for cross-hedging is only strengthened if it increases debt capacity by reducing the risk of bankruptcy and thereby allowing a greater gain from leverage. Smith and Stulz [1985] support this point of view.

A second approach to optimal debt maturity is based on agency costs. Myers [1977] and Barnea, Haugen, and Senbet [1980] argue that if the shareholders' claim on the assets of a levered firm is similar to a call option, then shareholders have an incentive to undertake riskier (higher-variance) projects because their call option value is greater when the assets of the firm have higher variance. If the firm with long-term risky debt outstanding undertakes positive net present value projects, shareholders will not be able to capture the full benefits because part of the value goes to debt holders in the form of a reduction in the probability of default. Short-term debt may alleviate this problem because the debt may come due before the firm decides to invest. Hence the theory suggests that firms with many investment opportunities that generate higher growth may prefer to use short-term debt (or callable debt).

Third is a liquidity risk argument; for example, see Diamond [1991]. The risk of not being able to refinance (i.e., roll over) short-term debt causes firms to seek longer-maturity obligations. Banks will, however, supply this demand only for higher-quality firms that have higher bond ratings. Consistent with this is the work of Brick and Ravid [1985], who provide a tax-based explanation. Suppose the term structure of interest rates is not flat and there is a gain to leverage in the Miller [1977] sense. Then a long-term maturity is optimal because coupons on long-term bonds are currently higher than coupons on short-term bonds and the tax benefit of debt (the gain to leverage) is accelerated. If the gain to leverage is negative, then the result is reversed.

Fourth are asymmetric information arguments by Flannery [1986], Kale and Noe [1990], and Diamond [1993]. They posit that a firm with prospects more favorable than the market expects will choose short- over long-term debt. Their reasoning is that when, in the course of events, the good news is revealed to the market, short-term debt can be refinanced on favorable terms.

Finally, there are tax-timing arguments (e.g., Brick and Palmon [1992]). Long-term debt becomes more favorable when interest rates are volatile and when the firm expects to have a stream of taxable earnings. They get this result because any increase in the volatility of interest rates reduces the present value of the tax shields on short-term debt. In the limit, rates on overnight debt are adjusted so that they always equal the market rate. In contrast, if interest rates fall and the firm holds long-term debt, it can be refinanced (called) at the option of the firm, and if interest rates rise, the firm can stand pat.

Table 15.12 Distribution of Debt Issues by Maturity and Issue Type across Bond Ratings (7,369 Issues) (1982–1993)

Term to Maturity in Years by Bond Rating									
Term to Maturity (Years)	Unrated	CCC	B	BB	BBB	A	AA	AAA	Total
0–4	32	0	7	25	507	1,124	427	105	2,227
5–9	23	5	129	71	194	376	236	80	1,114
10–14	64	28	385	129	299	478	220	47	1,650
15–19	51	6	122	39	57	124	48	3	450
20–24	45	8	95	35	67	88	31	4	373
25–29	42	6	111	73	72	65	8	1	378
30–100	0	0	1	4	208	395	249	25	882
Mean term to maturity	14	15	14	13	13	12	13	10	
Total number	257	53	850	376	1,404	2,650	1,219	265	

Issue Type by Bond Rating									
Term to Maturity (Years)	Unrated	CCC	B	BB	BBB	A	AA	AAA	Mean Term to Maturity
Foreign notes/bonds	1	0	0	0	0	6	11	4	3
Euronotes/bonds	8	0	2	7	21	151	191	79	8
Medium-term notes	26	0	1	23	477	964	313	40	4
Straight debt	49	18	362	153	531	890	386	98	15
Warrant bonds	9	2	23	4	2	4	8	3	11
Equipment bonds	4	0	10	3	33	162	104	38	11
Mortgage bonds	3	0	7	11	187	284	180	1	21
LYONS	0	0	9	9	13	8	2	0	18
Convertibles	127	21	266	127	76	56	7	3	18

In the third edition of this book, we suggested that there was little research on this topic. Now a paper by Guedes and Opler [1996] has begun to fill the void. They examine the maturity choice for 7,369 U.S. corporate bonds issued between 1982 and 1993 based on a database of corporate debt issues compiled by the Capital Markets Division of the Federal Reserve Board. The mean term to maturity for the entire sample was 12.2 years, and the mean duration was 7 years. The average issuing company was fairly large, with sales revenues of $8.95 billion. Table 15.12 shows details of the relationship between the term to maturity and the bond rating of the issuer, and of the relationship between the type of instrument and the bond rating. The most common rating is "A," and the most common maturity is 0–4 years. Straight debt is the most common type of issue type. Note for later reference that convertible bonds are used predominately by companies with low bond ratings. We will come to the reason why in the next section of the chapter.

Guedes and Opler [1996] conduct several tests including a multiple regression that takes the maturity of the debt issue as the dependent variable and 12 independent variables. They find a highly significant positive relationship between the maturity (economic life) of assets and of debt used to finance them. Also the credit quality of the firm is positively related to the maturity of debt. The results also show that firms with more growth opportunities (proxied by the market-to-book ratio) tend to choose short-term debt, a result that is consistent with Barclay and Smith [1995]. The electric utility industry, which is both capital intensive and regulated, tends to use a greater amount of long-term debt. Most of the remaining variables were statistically insignificant, and the overall r-squared for the multiple regression was only 6%. Still more research needs to be done.

L. $\mathcal{T}$he Effect of Other Financial Instruments on the Cost of Capital

Other than straight debt and equity, firms issue a variety of other securities and contingent claims. The number of different possibilities is limited only by your imagination. However, the actual number of alternative financial instruments is fairly small and their use is limited. A possible explanation for why corporations tend to use only straight debt and equity has been offered by Fama and Jensen [1983]. They argue that it makes sense to separate the financial claims on the firm into only two parts: a relatively low-risk component (i.e., debt capital) and a relatively high-risk residual claim (i.e., equity capital). Specialized risk bearing by residual claimants is an optimal form of contracting that has survival value because (1) it reduces contracting costs (i.e., the costs that would be incurred to monitor contract fulfillment) and (2) it lowers the cost of risk-bearing services.

For example, shareholders and bondholders do not have to monitor each other. It is necessary only for bondholders to monitor shareholders. This form of one-way monitoring reduces the total cost of contracting over what it might otherwise be. Thus it makes sense that most firms keep their capital structure fairly simple by using only debt and equity.

The theory of finance is still developing good explanations for why some firms use alternative financial instruments such as convertible debt, preferred stock, and warrants.

1. Warrants

A warrant is a security issued by the firm in return for cash. It promises to sell m shares (usually one share) of stock to an investor for a fixed exercise price at any time up to the maturity date. Therefore a warrant is very much like an American call option written by the firm. It is not exactly the same as a call because, when exercised, it increases the number of shares outstanding and thus dilutes the equity of stockholders.

The problem of pricing warrants has been studied by Emmanuel [1983], Schwartz [1977], Galai and Schneller [1978], and Constantinides [1984]. The simplest approach to the problem (Galai and Schneller [1978]) assumes a one-period model. The firm is assumed to be 100% equity financed, and its investment policy is not affected by its financing decisions. For example, the proceeds from issuing warrants are immediately distributed as dividends to the old shareholders. Also the firm pays no end-of-period dividends, and the warrants are assumed to be exercised as a block.[29] These somewhat restrictive assumptions facilitate the estimation of the warrant value and its equilibrium rate of return.

---

[29] Block exercise is, perhaps, the most restrictive assumption.

Table 15.13 End-of-Period Payoffs for a Warrant and for a Call Option (Written on a Firm with No Warrants)

	End-of-Period Payoffs	
	If $S \leq X$	**If $S > X$**
Warrant on firm with warrants, W	0	$\dfrac{S+qX}{1+q} - X = \dfrac{1}{1+q}(S-X)$
Call on firm without warrants, C	0	$S - X$

Galai and Schneller show, for the above-mentioned assumptions, that the returns on a warrant are perfectly correlated with those of a call option on the same firm *without* warrants. To obtain this result, let V be the value of the firm's assets (without warrants) at the end of the time period (i.e., on the date when the warrants mature). Let n be the current number of shares outstanding and q be the ratio of warrants to shares outstanding.[30] Finally, let X be the exercise price of the warrant. If the firm had no warrants outstanding, the price per share at the end of the time period would be

$$S = \frac{V}{n}.$$

With warrants, the price per share, assuming that the warrants are exercised, will be

$$S = \frac{V + nqX}{n(1+q)} = \frac{S+qX}{(1+q)}.$$

Of course, nqX is the cash received and $n(1+q)$ is the total number of shares outstanding if the warrants are exercised. The warrants will be exercised if their value when converted is greater than the exercise price, that is, if

$$S = \frac{S+qX}{1+q} > X.$$

This condition is exactly equivalent to $S > X$. In other words the warrant will be exercised whenever the firm's end-of-period share price *without* warrants exceeds the warrant exercise price. Therefore the warrant will be exercised in exactly the same states of nature as a call option with the same exercise price. Also, as shown in Table 15.13, the payoffs to the warrant are a constant fraction, $1/(1+q)$, of the payoffs to the call written on the assets of the firm (without warrants).

Therefore the returns on the warrant are perfectly correlated with the dollar returns on a call option written on the firm without warrants. To prevent arbitrage the warrant price, W, will be a fraction of the call price, C:

$$W = \frac{1}{1+q}C. \tag{15.72}$$

---

[30] The amount of potential dilution can be significant. For example, in July 1977 there were 118 warrants outstanding. Of them 41% had a dilution factor of less than 10%, 25% had a dilution factor between 10 and 19%, 13% between 20 and 29%, and 21% a factor of over 50%.

Because the warrant and the call are perfectly correlated, they will have exactly the same systematic risk and therefore the same required rate of return.[31] This expected return is the before-tax cost of capital for issuing warrants and can easily be estimated for a company that is contemplating a new issue of warrants.

One problem with the above approach is that warrants are not constrained to be exercised simultaneously in one large block. Emmanuel [1983] demonstrated that if all the warrants were held by a single profit-maximizing monopolist, the warrants would be exercised sequentially. Constantinides [1984] has solved the warrant valuation problem for competitive warrant holders and shown that the warrant price, given a competitive equilibrium, is less than or equal to the value it would have given block exercise. Frequently the balance sheet of a firm has several contingent claim securities (e.g., warrants and convertible bonds), with different maturity dates. This means that the expiration and subsequent exercise (or conversion) of one security can result in equity dilution and therefore early exercise of the longer-maturity contingent claim securities. Firms can also force early exercise or conversion by paying a large cash or stock dividend.

2. Convertible Bonds

As the name implies, convertible debt is a hybrid bond that allows its bearer to exchange it for a given number of shares of stock anytime up to and including the maturity date of the bond. Preferred stock is also frequently issued with a convertible provision and may be thought of as a convertible security (a bond) with an infinite maturity date.

A convertible bond is equivalent to a portfolio of two securities: straight debt with the same coupon rate and maturity as the convertible bond, and a warrant written on the value of the firm. The coupon rate on convertible bonds is usually lower than comparable straight debt because the right to convert is worth something. For example, in February 1982, the XYZ Company wanted to raise $50 million by using either straight debt or convertible bonds. An investment banking firm informed the company's treasurer that straight debt with a 25-year maturity would require a 17% coupon. Alternately, convertible debt with the same maturity would require only a 10% coupon. Both debt instruments would sell at par (i.e., $1,000), and the convertible debt could be converted into 35.71 shares (i.e., an exercise price of $28 per share). The stock of the XYZ Company was selling for $25 per share at the time. Later on we will use these facts to compute the cost of capital for the convertible issue. But first, what do financial officers think of convertible debt?

Brigham [1966] received responses from the chief financial officers of 22 firms that had issued convertible debt. Of them, 68% said they used convertible debt because they believed their stock would rise over time and that convertibles would provide a way of selling common stock at a price above the existing market. Another 27% said that their company wanted straight debt but found conditions to be such that a straight bond issue could not be sold at a reasonable rate of interest.

---

[31] From Eq. (15.45) we know that the beta of an option is related to the beta of the underlying asset as follows:

$$\beta_c = N(d_1)\frac{S}{C}\beta_S.$$

From Eq. (15.72) we know that the warrant is perfectly correlated with a call option written on the shares of the company, *ex warrants*; therefore

$$\beta_w = \beta_c.$$

Consequently, it is not difficult to estimate the cost of capital for a warrant because we can estimate $\beta_c = \beta_w$ and then employ the CAPM.

The problem is that neither reason makes much sense. Convertible bonds are not "cheap debt." Because convertible bonds are riskier, their true cost of capital is greater (on a before-tax basis) than the cost of straight debt. Also, convertible bonds are not deferred sale of common stock at an attractive price.[32] The uncertain sale of shares for $28 each at some future date can hardly be compared directly with a current share price of $25.

Brennan and Schwartz [1977a] and Ingersoll [1977] have analyzed the valuation of convertible bonds, assuming that the entire outstanding issue, if converted, will be converted as a block. Constantinides [1984] has extended their work to study the value of convertible debt if conversion does not occur all at once. The reader is referred to these articles for the derivations that show that the market value of convertible debt, CV, is equal to the market value of straight debt, B, and a warrant, W:

$$CV = B + W.$$

Suppose you want to compute the cost of capital for the convertible debt being considered by the XYZ Company as mentioned above. You already know that the maturity date is 25 years, similar straight debt yields 17% to maturity, the convertible bond coupon rate is 10% (with semiannual coupons), the conversion price (exercise price) is $28 per share, the bond will sell at par value (i.e., $1,000), and the current stock price is $25. In addition you need to know that (1) if converted the issue would increase the firm's outstanding shares by 5% (i.e., the dilution factor, q, is 5%); (2) the standard deviation of the firm's equity rate of return is $\sigma = .3$; (3) the risk-free rate is 14.5% for 25-year Treasury bonds; (4) the expected rate of return on the market portfolio is 20.6%; (5) the firm's equity beta is 1.5; and (6) the firm pays no dividends. Given these facts, it is possible to use the capital asset pricing model and the option pricing model to estimate the before-tax cost of capital, k_{CV}, on the firm's contemplated convertible bond issue as a weighted average cost of straight debt, k_b, and the cost of the warrant, k_w,[33]

$$k_{CV} = k_b \frac{B}{B + W} + k_w \frac{W}{B + W}.$$

The value of the straight debt, assuming semiannual coupons of $50, a principal payment of $1,000 twenty-five years hence, and a 17% discount rate, is $B = \$619.91$. Therefore the remainder of the sale price—namely, $\$1,000 - 619.91 = \$380.09$—is the value of the warrant to purchase 35.71 shares at $28 each. The cost of straight debt was given to be $k_b = 17\%$ before taxes. All that remains is to find the cost of the warrant. From Section F.1 we know that the warrant implied in the convertible bond contract is perfectly correlated with a call option written on the firm (without warrants outstanding) and therefore has the same cost of capital. The cost of capital, k_c, for the call option can be estimated from the CAPM:

$$k_c = R_f + [E\,(R_m) - R_f]\beta_c,$$

---

[32] From the theory of option pricing we know that $S + P = B + C$; that is, a bond plus a call option is the same thing as owning the stock and a put option. Thus one could think of a convertible bond as roughly equivalent to the stock plus a put.

[33] Throughout the analysis we asssume that there is no tax gain to leverage. Therefore the conversion of the bond will decrease the firm's debt-to-equity ratio but not change the value of the firm.

where

$$k_c = \text{the cost of capital for a call option with 25 years to maturity,}^{34}$$
$$R_f = \text{the risk-free rate for a 25-year Treasury bond} = 14.5\%,$$
$$E(R_m) = \text{the expected rate of return on the market portfolio} = 20.6\%,$$
$$\beta_c = N(d_1)(S/C)\beta_s = \text{the systematic risk of the call option,}$$
$$\beta_s = \text{the systematic risk of the stock (without warrants)} = 1.5,$$
$$N(d_1) = \text{the cumulative normal probability for option pricing in Chapter 7,}$$
$$C = \text{the value of a call option written on the stock, } ex \text{ } warrants.$$

$$d_1 = \frac{\ln(S/X) + R_f T}{\sigma\sqrt{T}} + \frac{1}{2}\sigma\sqrt{T}.$$

Substituting in the appropriate numbers, we find that $d_1 = 3.09114$ and $N(d_1) = .999$. And using the Black-Scholes version of the option pricing model, we find that $C = \$24.74$. Therefore

$$\beta_c = \frac{S}{C}(d_1)\beta_s$$

$$= \frac{25.00}{24.74}(.999)(1.5) = 1.514,$$

and, substituting into the CAPM, we have

$$k_c = .145 + (.206 - .145)1.514$$

$$= 23.74\%.$$

The cost of capital for the warrant is slightly above the cost of equity for the firm. Actually, the warrant is not much riskier than the equity because its market value is almost equal to the market value of the firm's equity, given a 25-year life and only a $3 difference between the exercise price and the stock price.

Taken together, these facts imply that the before-tax cost of capital for the convertible issue will be

$$k_{CV} = .17\frac{619.91}{1,000.00} + .2374\frac{380.09}{1,000.00}$$

$$= 19.56\%.$$

This answer is almost double the 10% coupon rate that the convertible promises to pay, and it shows that the higher risk of convertible debt requires a higher expected rate of return.

The final point of discussion is why convertible debt is used if financial officers understand its true cost. It certainly is not a cheap form of either debt or equity. Another irrational explanation is that until the accounting rules were changed to require reporting earnings per share on a fully

---

[34] If the firm pays dividends that are large enough, then the convertible debentures may be exercised if the implied warrants are in-the-money. Exercise would occur just prior to the ex dividend date(s). We are assuming, for the sake of simplicity, that the firm pays no dividends.

diluted basis, it was possible for an aggressive firm to acquire another company via convertible debt financing. The lower interest charges of convertible debt meant that earnings of the merged company were often higher than the sum of premerger earnings of the separate entities. Also, the actual number of shares outstanding was lower than the number that would be reported if the conversion were to occur. Given all the evidence in Chapter 11 on the efficiency of markets, it is hard to believe that the market was fooled by the accounting conventions. A possible reason for issuing convertibles is that they are better tailored to the cash flow patterns of rapidly growing firms. The lower coupon rate during the early years keeps the probability of bankruptcy lower than straight debt; then, if the firm is successful, more cash for growth will be available after conversion takes place. Brennan and Schwartz [1986] suggest an alternative rationale—namely, that because of the relative insensitivity of convertible bonds to the risk of the issuing company, it is easier for the bond issuer and purchaser to agree on the value of the bond. This makes it easier for them to come to terms and requires no bonding or underwriting service by investment bankers. Green [1984] shows that agency costs between equity and bondholders are reduced by issuing convertible debt or straight debt with warrants. Bondholders are less concerned about the possibility that shareholders may undertake risky projects (thereby increasing the risk of bankruptcy) because their conversion privilege allows them to participate in the value created if riskier projects are undertaken. Finally, convertible debt may be preferred to straight debt with warrants attached because convertible debt often has a call provision built in that allows a firm to force conversion.

Mayers [1998] provides a theory that explains firms' motivation for issuing callable convertible bonds as a way to lower the issuance costs of what would otherwise be sequential financing. Therefore, callable convertible debt provides the advantages of sequential financing, namely, to help control overinvestment. Think of the growth of an enterprise as a series of risky investments— a compound option where the second investment is made only if the first succeeds. The alternative is to precommit to both projects by raising all of the capital up front. If the first project succeeds, the convertible bond will be converted (because the firm uses its call privilege to force conversion), thereby inserting more cash into the firm at a time when it is needed for investment. If the first project fails, the option built into the bond becomes virtually worthless, the market value of the bond falls below its face value, and there is an incentive for the firm to repurchase the devalued debt in the open market, thereby returning cash to bondholders rather than investing it badly. Mayers goes on to study an empirical prediction of his theory, namely, that firms would be expected to undertake substantial incremental investment and new financing around the time of conversion— and they do.

3. Call Provisions

Many securities have call provisions that allow the firm to force redemption. Frequently, ordinary bonds may be redeemed at a *call premium* roughly equal to 1 year's interest. For example, the call premium on a 20-year $1,000 face value bond with a 12% coupon might be $120 if the bond is called in the first year, $114 is called in the second year, and so on.

The call provision is equivalent to a call option written by the investors who buy the bonds from the firm. The bonds may be repurchased by the firm (at the exercise price, i.e., the call price) anytime during the life of the bond. If interest rates fall, the market price of the outstanding bonds may exceed the call price, thereby making it advantageous for the firm to exercise its option to call in the debt. Since the option is valuable to the firm, it must pay the bondholders by offering a higher interest rate on callable bonds than on similar ordinary bonds that do not have the call feature. New issues of callable bonds must often bear yields from one quarter to one half of a percent higher than the yields of noncallable bonds.

Brennan and Schwartz [1977a] show how to value callable bonds. If the objective of the firm is to maximize shareholders' wealth, then a call policy will be established to minimize the market value of callable debt. The value of the bonds will be minimized if they are called at the point where their uncalled value is equal to the call price. To call when the uncalled value is below the call price is to provide a needless gain to bondholders. To allow the uncalled bond value to rise above the call price is inconsistent with minimizing the bond value. Therefore the firm should call the bond when the market price first rises to reach the call price. Furthermore, we would never expect the market value of a callable bond to exceed the call price plus a small premium for the flotation costs the firm must bear in calling the issue.

Almost all corporate bonds are callable and none are puttable. Why? A plausible answer has been put forth by Boyce and Kalotay [1979]. Whenever the tax rate of the borrower exceeds the tax rate of the lender, there is a tax incentive for issuing callable debt. Since corporations have had marginal tax rates of around 50% while individuals have lower rates, corporations have had an incentive to issue callable bonds.[35] From the firm's point of view the coupons paid and the call premium are both deductible as interest expenses. The investor pays ordinary income taxes on interest received and capital gains taxes on the call premium. If the stream of payments on debt is even across time, then low and high tax bracket lenders and borrowers will value it equally. However, if it is decreasing across time, as it is expected to be with a callable bond, then low tax bracket lenders will assign a higher value because they discount at a higher after-tax rate. Near-term cash inflows are *relatively* more valuable to them. A high tax bracket borrower (i.e., the firm) will use a lower after-tax discount rate and will also prefer a decreasing cash flow pattern because the present value of the interest tax shield will be relatively higher. Even though the firm pays a higher gross rate, it prefers callable debt to ordinary debt because of the tax advantages for the net rate of return.

Brennan and Schwartz [1977a] and Ingersoll [1977] both examined the effect of a call feature on convertible debt and preferred. Unlike simpler option securities, convertible bonds and preferred stocks contain dual options. The bondholder has the right to exchange a convertible for the company's common stock while the company retains the right to call the issue at the contracted call price. One interesting implication of the theory on call policies is that a convertible security should be called as soon as its conversion value (i.e., the value of the common stock that would be received in the conversion exchange) rises to equal the prevailing effective call price (i.e., the stated call price plus accrued interest). Ingersoll [1977] collected data on 179 convertible issues that were called between 1968 and 1975. The calls on all but 9 were delayed beyond the time that the theory predicted. The median company waited until the conversion value of its debentures was 43.9% in excess of the call price.

Mikkelson [1981] discovered that, on average, the common stock returns of companies announcing convertible debt calls fell by a statistically significant -1.065% per day over a two-day announcement period. These results are inconsistent with the idea that optimal calls of convertible debt are beneficial for shareholders.

Harris and Raviv [1985] provide a signaling model that simultaneously explains why calls are delayed far beyond what would seem to be a rational time and why stock returns are negative

---

[35] Interestingly, the opposite is true when the government is lending. The government has a zero tax rate and holders of government debt have positive rates. Consequently, the government has incentive to offer puttable debt and it does. Series E and H savings bonds are redeemable at the lender's option.

at the time of the call. Suppose that managers know the future prospects of their firm better than the marketplace—that is, there is heterogeneous information. Also, assume that managers' compensation depends on the firm's stock price, both now and in future time periods. If the managers suspect that the stock price will fall in the future, conversion will be forced now because what they receive now, given conversion, exceeds what they would otherwise receive in the future when the market learns of the bad news and does not convert. Conversely, managers' failure to convert now will be interpreted by the market as good news. There is incentive for managers not to force conversion early because the market views their stock favorably now, and it will also be viewed favorably in the future when the market is able to confirm the managers' good news. A paper of similar spirit by Robbins and Schatzberg [1986] explains the advantage of the call feature in nonconvertible long-term bonds.

4. Preferred Stock

Preferred stock is much like subordinated debt except that if the promised cash payments (i.e., the preferred coupons) are not paid on time, then preferred shareholders cannot force the firm into bankruptcy. All preferred stocks listed on the New York Stock Exchange must have voting rights in order to be listed. A high percentage of preferred stocks have no stated maturity date and also provide for cumulative dividend payments; that is, all past preferred dividends must be paid before common stock dividends can be paid. Approximately 40% of new preferred stocks are convertible into common stock.

   If preferred stock is not callable or convertible, and if its life is indefinite, then its market value is

$$P = \frac{\text{coupon}}{k_p},$$

where k_p is the before-tax cost of preferred. Of course, the before- and after-tax costs are the same for preferred stock because preferred dividends are not deductible as an expense before taxes. The nondeductibility of preferred dividends has led many companies to buy back their preferred stock and use subordinated debt instead. It is a puzzle why preferred stock is issued at all, especially if there is a gain to leverage from using debt capital as a substitute.

5. Committed Lines of Credit

A committed line of credit is still another form of contingent claim. It does not appear on the firm's balance sheet unless some of the committed line is actually used. Under the terms of the contract a commercial bank will agree to guarantee to supply up to a fixed limit of funds (e.g., up to $1 billion) at a variable rate of interest plus a fixed risk premium (e.g., LIBOR, the London interbank rate plus $\frac{3}{8}$%). In return, the firm agrees to pay a fee, say $\frac{1}{4}$%, on the unused balance. From the borrowing firm's point of view, a committed line may be thought of as the right to put callable debt to the bank. Embedded in this right is an option on the yield spread (i.e., on the difference between the rate paid by high- and low-grade debt). When the committed line is negotiated, the premium above the variable rate ($\frac{3}{8}$% in our example) reflects the current yield spread. If the economy or the fortunes of the firm worsen, the yield spread will probably increase, say to $\frac{5}{8}$%. However, with a committed line the firm can still borrow and pay only $\frac{3}{8}$% yield spread—hence it has an in-the-money option because it is cheaper to borrow on the committed line than in the open market. For a paper analyzing committed lines, see Hawkins [1982].

$\mathcal{S}$ummary

The cost of capital is seen to be a rate of return whose definition requires a project to improve the wealth position of the *current* shareholders of the firm. The original Modigliani-Miller work has been extended by using the CAPM so that a risk-adjusted cost of capital may be obtained for each project. When the expected cash flows of the project are discounted at the correct risk-adjusted rate, the result is the NPV of the project (without flexibility).

In a world without taxes the value of the firm is independent of its capital structure. However, there are several important extensions of the basic model. With the introduction of corporate taxes the optimal capital structure becomes 100% debt. Finally, when personal taxes are also introduced, the value of the firm is unaffected by the choice of financial leverage. Financing is irrelevant!

Empirical results and casual observation both lead to the conclusion that there are cross-sectional regularities in capital structure. Equilibrium approaches contend that optimal capital structure results from a trade-off between the tax deductibility of interest on debt, the fact that tax shields are lost when leverage becomes too high, and business disruption costs. If one relaxes the assumption that operating cash flows of the firm are not independent of its financing, then the theory supports optimal capital structure. It seems to us that a complete theory will soon emerge—one that recognizes that the flexibility of the investment opportunity set is a substitute for flexibility in financing. The investment and financing decisions are codetermined.

PROBLEM SET

15.1 The Modigliani-Miller theorem assumes that the firm has only two classes of securities, perpetual debt and equity. Suppose that the firm has issued a third class of securities—preferred stock—and that $X\%$ of preferred dividends may be written off as an expense ($0 \leq X \leq 1$).

    (a) What is the appropriate expression for the value of the levered firm?

    (b) What is the appropriate expression for the weighted average cost of capital?

15.2 The Acrosstown Company has an equity beta, β_L, of .5 and 50% debt in its capital structure. The company has risk-free debt that costs 6% before taxes, and the expected rate of return on the market is 18%. Acrosstown is considering the acquisition of a new project in the peanut-raising agribusiness that is expected to yield 25% on after-tax operating cash flows. The Carter-nut Company, which is the same product line (and risk class) as the project being considered, has an equity beta, β_L, of 2.0 and has 10% debt in its capital structure. If Acrosstown finances the new project with 50% debt, should it be accepted or rejected? Assume that the marginal tax rate, τ_c, for both companies is 50%.

15.3 The XYZ Company has a current market value of $1,000,000, half of which is debt. Its current weighted average cost of capital is 9%, and the corporate tax rate is 40%. The treasurer proposes to undertake a new project, which costs $500,000 and which can be financed completely with debt. The project is expected to have the same operating risk as the company and to earn 8.5% on its levered after-tax cash flows. The treasurer argues that the project is desirable because it earns more than 5%, which is the before-tax marginal cost of the debt used to finance it. What do you think?

15.4 Given a world with corporate taxes, τ_c, a personal tax rate paid on bonds, τ_{pB}, and a personal tax rate on income from equity, τ_{pS}, what would be the effect of a decrease in the corporate tax rate on

> **(a)** the aggregate amount of debt in the economy, and
> **(b)** the optimal capital structure of firms?

15.5 Congress has proposed to eliminate "double taxation" on dividends by reducing the personal tax on dividend income. At the same time, a compensating increase in taxes on capital gains (traditionally taxed at a much lower percentage than dividend income) has been proposed.

> **(a)** What effect would this joint proposal have on the optimal capital structure of a firm, according to the Miller model?
> **(b)** What effect would it have on the aggregate amount of corporate debt outstanding?

15.6 Consider firm B as an unlevered firm and firm C as a levered firm with target debt-to-equity ratio $(B/S)^* = 1$. Both firms have exactly the same perpetual net operating income, $NOI = 180$, before taxes. The before-tax cost of debt, k_b, is the same as the risk-free rate. The corporate tax rate $= .5$. Given the following market parameters:

$$E(R_m) = .12, \qquad \sigma_m^2 = .0144, \qquad R_f = .06, \qquad \beta_B = 1, \qquad \beta_C = 1.5,$$

> **(a)** Find the cost of capital and value for each firm. (Ignore any effect from personal income taxes.)
> **(b)** Evaluate the following four projects to determine their acceptance (or rejection) by firms B and C. What do the results of this evaluation tell you about leverage in a world with corporate taxes but no personal taxes? (*Note:* r_{jm} is the correlation between the unlevered free cash flows of each project and the market.)

Project j	Cost j	$E(\widetilde{NOI}_j)$ (After-tax)	σ_j	r_{jm} Correlation of j with the Market
1	100	9	.10	.6
2	120	11	.11	.7
3	80	9	.12	.8
4	150	18	.20	.9

15.7 A firm with $1,000,000 in assets and 50% debt in its capital structure is considering a $250,000 project. The firm's after-tax weighted average cost of capital is 10.4%, the marginal cost of debt is 8% (before taxes), and the marginal tax rate is 40%. If the project does not change the firm's operating risk and is financed exclusively with new equity, what rate of return must it earn to be acceptable?

15.8 The firm's cost of equity capital is 18%, the market value of the firm's equity is $8 million, the firm's cost of debt capital is 9%, and the market value of debt is $4 million. The firm is considering a new investment with an expected rate of return of 17%. This project is 30% riskier than the firm's average operations. The riskless rate of return is 5%; the variance of the market return is .08. Is the project profitable? (Assume a world without taxes.)

15.9 Susan Varhard, treasurer of the Gammamax Company, has proposed that the company should sell equity and buy back debt in order to maximize its value. As evidence, she presents the financial statements given in Table Q15.9. The company currently has a price/earnings ratio of 50. Before the change in capital structure it has 10 shares outstanding; therefore its earnings per share are $1.00, and the price per share is $50. If 10 new shares are issued at $50 each, $500 is collected and used to retire $500 of debt (which pays a coupon rate of 8%). After the capital structure change, earnings per share have increased to $1.50 (since there are now 20 shares outstanding); with a price/earnings ratio of 50, presumably the price per share will increase from $50 before the capital structure change to $75 afterward. Given your understanding of modern finance theory, discuss the above proposal.

Table Q15.9

Income Statement	Before	After
Net operating income	100	100
Interest expense	80	40
Earnings before taxes	20	60
Taxes at 50%	10	30
Net income	10	30

Balance Sheet

	Before			**After**	
Assets	**Liabilities**		**Assets**	**Liabilities**	
	Debt	1,000		Debt	500
	Equity	500		Equity	1,000
Total = 1,500	Total =	1,500	Total = 1,500	Total =	1,500

15.10 Community Bank must decide whether to open a new branch. The current market value of the bank is $2,500,000. According to company policy (and industry practice), the bank's capital structure is highly leveraged. The present (and optimal) ratio of debt to total assets is .9. Community Bank's debt is almost exclusively in the form of demand savings and time deposits. The average return on these deposits to the bank's clients has been 5% over the past five years. However, recently interest rates have climbed sharply, and as a result Community Bank presently pays an average annual rate of $6\frac{1}{4}\%$ on its accounts in order to remain competitive. In addition, the bank incurs a service cost of $2\frac{3}{4}\%$ per account. Because federal "Regulation Q" puts a ceiling on the amount of interest paid by banks on their accounts, the banking industry at large has been experiencing disintermediation—a loss of clients to the open money market (Treasury bills, etc.), where interest rates are higher. Largely because of the interest rate situation (which shows no sign of improving), Community Bank's president has stipulated that for the branch project to be acceptable its entire cost of $500,000 will have to be raised by 90% debt and 10% equity. The bank's cost of equity capital, k_s, is 11%. Community Bank's marginal tax rate is .48. Market analysis indicates that the new branch may be expected to return net cash flows according to the following schedule:

Year	0	1	2	3	4	5	6 to ∞
$	−500,000	25,000	35,000	45,000	45,000	50,000	50,000

Should Community Bank open the new branch?

15.11 A not-for-profit organization, such as a ballet company or a museum, usually carries no debt. Also, since there are no shareholders, there is no equity outstanding. How would you go about determining the appropriate weighted average cost of capital for not-for-profit organizations given that they have no debt or equity?

15.12 Firms A and B are each considering an unanticipated new investment opportunity that will marginally increase the value of the firm and will also increase the firm's level of diversification. Firm A is unlevered, and firm B has a capital structure of 50% debt. Assuming that the shareholders control the firm, will either firm make the investment?

15.13 In a world without taxes or transactions costs the Modigliani-Miller model predicts shareholders' wealth invariant to changes in capital structure, whereas the OPM predicts increased shareholder wealth with increased leverage. Given what you know about option pricing, is a 20% increase in the variance of return on the firm's assets more likely to benefit shareholders in a low-leverage or in a high-leverage firm?

15.14 The Sharpe version of the CAPM results in the principle of two-fund separation. Every individual holds the same portfolio of risky assets, namely, the market portfolio. Therefore individuals will be indifferent to redistribution effects caused by imperfect "me-first" rules. True or false? Why?

15.15 Consider a levered firm with $10 million face value of debt outstanding maturing in one year. The riskless rate is 6%, and the expected rate of return on the market is 12%. The systematic risk of the firm's assets is $\beta_V = 1.5$, the total risk of these assets is $\sigma_V = 1.3$, and their market value is $25 million.

(a) Determine the market value of the firm's debt and equity.

(b) Determine the cost of debt and equity capital (assuming a world without taxes).

15.16 (a) True or false? The Modigliani-Miller model of cost of equity is equivalent to the OPM definition of cost of equity for an all-equity firm. Explain.

(b) If we assume that $N(d_1) = 1$ in the OPM, what does this imply about $\partial S / \partial V$? About the firm's capital structure?

15.17 Assume the following:

(a) We are dealing with a world where there are no taxes.

(b) The changes in the parameters affecting value are unanticipated; therefore redistribution effects are possible.

(c) Firms A and B initially have the following parameters:

σ_A	$= \sigma_B = .2$	Instantaneous standard deviation
T_A	$= T_B = 4$ years	Maturity of debt
V_A	$= V_B = \$2,000$	Value of the firm, $V = B + S$
R_f	$= .06$	Risk-free rate
D_A	$= D_B = \$1,000$	Face value of debt

What is the initial market value of debt and equity for firms A and B?

15.18 Make the same assumptions as in Problem 15.17. Firm A decides to use some of its cash in order to purchase marketable securities. This has the effect of leaving its value, V_A, unchanged but increasing its instantaneous standard deviation from .2 to .3. What are the new values of debt and equity?

15.19 What are the empirical problems involved in testing for the effect of capital structure on the value of the firm?

15.20 During recent years your company has made considerable use of debt financing, to the extent that it is generally agreed that the percentage of debt in the firm's capital structure (either in book or market value terms) is too high. Further use of debt will likely lead to a drop in the firm's bond rating. You would like to recommend that the next major capital investment be financed with a new equity issue. Unfortunately, the firm has not been doing very well recently (nor has the market). In fact the rate of return on investment has been just equal to the cost of capital. As shown in the financial statement in Table Q15.20, the market value of the firm's equity is less than its book value. This means that even a profitable project will decrease earnings per share if it is financed with new equity. For example, the firm is considering a project that costs $400 but has a value of $500 (i.e., an NPV of $100), and that will increase total earnings by $60 per year. If it is financed with equity, the $400 will require approximately 200 shares, thus bringing the total shares outstanding to 1,200. The new earnings will be $660, and earnings per share will fall to $0.55. The president of the firm argues that the project should be delayed for three reasons.

(a) It is too expensive for the firm to issue new debt.

(b) Financing the project with new equity will reduce earnings per share because the market value of equity is less than book value.

(c) Equity markets are currently depressed. If the firm waits until the market index improves, the market value of equity will exceed the book value and equity financing will no longer reduce earnings per share.

Critique the president's logic.

Table Q15.20 Balance Sheet as of December 31, 19xx

Assets		Liabilities	
Short-term assets	2,000	Debt	6,000
Plant and equipment	8,000	Equity	4,000
	10,000	Total	10,000
Total market value of equity	=		$2,000.00
Number of shares outstanding	=		1,000
Price per share	=		2.00
Total earnings for the year 19xx	=		600.00
Earnings per share	=		.60

15.21 *Southwestern Electric Company*[36] John Hatteras, the financial analyst for Southwestern Electric Company, is responsible for preliminary analysis of the company's investment projects. He is currently trying to evaluate two large projects that management has decided to consider as a

---

[36] This problem is really a short case. It has a definite answer but requires knowledge of cash flows, discounting, the CAPM, and risky cost of capital.

single joint project, because it is felt that the geographical diversification the joint project provides would be advantageous.

Southwestern Electric was founded in the early 1930s and has operated profitably ever since. Growing at about the same rate as the population in its service areas, the company has usually been able to forecast its revenues with a great deal of accuracy. The stable pattern in revenues and a favorable regulatory environment have caused most investors to view Southwestern as an investment of very low risk.

Hatteras is concerned because one of the two projects uses a new technology that will be very profitable, assuming that demand is high in a booming economy, but will do poorly in a recessionary economy. However, the expected cash flows of the two projects, supplied by the engineering department, are identical. The expected after-tax cash flows on operating income for the joint project are given in Table Q15.21. Both projects are exactly the same size, so the cash flow for one is simply half the joint cash flow.

Table Q15.21

Year	Outflows	Inflows	Interest
1	250	10	7.5
2	250	20	15.0
3	250	25	22.5
4	250	60	30.0
5–30	0	110	30.0
31–40	0	80	30.0
41	0	40	0

In order to better evaluate the project, Hatteras applies his knowledge of modern finance theory. He estimates that the beta of the riskier project is .75, whereas the beta for the less risky project is .4375. These betas, however, are based on the covariance between the return on after-tax operating income and the market. Hatteras vaguely recalls that any discount rate he decides to apply to the project should consider financial risk as well as operating (or business) risk. The beta for the equity of Southwestern is .5. The company has a ratio of debt to total assets of 50% and a marginal tax rate of 40%. Because the bonds of Southwestern are rated AAA, Hatteras decides to assume that they are risk free. Finally, after consulting his investment banker, Hatteras believes that 18% is a reasonable estimate of the expected return on the market.

The joint project, if undertaken, will represent 10% of the corporation's assets. Southwestern intends to finance the joint project with 50% debt and 50% equity.

Hatteras wants to submit a report that answers the following questions:

(a) What is the appropriate required rate of return for the new project?
(b) What are the cost of equity capital and the weighted average cost of capital for Southwestern Electric before it takes the project?
(c) Should the joint project be accepted?
(d) What would the outcome be if the projects are considered separately?
(e) If the joint project is accepted, what will the firm's new risk level be?

REFERENCES

Altman, E., "A Further Empirical Investigation of the Bankruptcy Cost Question," *Journal of Finance*, September 1984, 1067–1089.

Asquith, P., and D. Mullins, Jr., "Equity Issues and Offering Dilution," *Journal of Financial Economics*, January–February 1986, 61–90.

Auerbach, A. J., "Real Determinants of Corporate Leverages," in B. Friedman, ed., *Corporate Capital Structures in the United States*, University of Chicago Press, Chicago, IL, 1985.

Baker, M., and J. Wurgler, "Market Timing and Capital Structure," *Journal of Finance*, 2002, Vol. 57, 1–32.

Barges, A., *The Effect of Capital Structure on the Cost of Capital*. Prentice Hall, Englewood Cliffs, N.J., 1963.

Barclay, M., and C. Smith, "The Maturity Structure of Corporate Debt," *Journal of Finance,* 1995, Vol. 50, 609–631.

Barnea, A., R. Haugen, and L. Senbet, "A Rationale for Debt Maturity Structure and Call Provisions in the Agency Theory Framework," *Journal of Finance*, December 1980, 1223–1243.

———, *Agency Problems and Financial Contracting*, Prentice-Hall, Englewood Cliffs, N.J., 1985.

Baxter, N. D., "Leverage, Risk of Ruin and the Cost of Capital," *Journal of Finance*, September 1967, 395–403.

Beranek, W., "The WACC Criterion and Shareholder Wealth Maximization," *Journal of Financial and Quantitative Analysis*, March 1977, 17–32.

Bierman, H., "The Cost of Warrants," *Journal of Financial and Quantitative Analysis*, June 1973, 499–503.

Black, F., and J. Cox, "Valuing Corporate Securities: Some Effects of Bond Indenture Provisions," *Journal of Finance*, May 1976, 351–367.

Black, F., and M. Scholes, "The Pricing of Options and Corporate Liabilities," *Journal of Political Economy*, May–June 1973, 637–654.

Booth, J., and R. Smith, "Capital Raising, Underwriting and Certification Hypothesis," *Journal of Financial Economics*, January–February 1986, 261–281.

Boyce, W. M., and A. J. Kalotay, "Tax Differentials and Callable Bonds," *Journal of Finance*, September 1979, 825–838.

Bradley, M., G. Jarrell, and E. H. Kim, "On the Existence of an Optimal Capital Structure: Theory and Evidence," *Journal of Finance*, July 1984, 857–878.

Brennan, M. J., and E. S. Schwartz, "Convertible Bonds: Valuation and Optimal Strategies for Call and Conversion," *Journal of Finance*, December 1977a, 1699–1715.

———, "Savings, Bonds, Retractable Bonds and Callable Bonds," *Journal of Financial Economics*, August 1977b, 67–88.

———, "Corporate Income Taxes, Valuation, and the Problem of Optimal Capital Structure," *Journal of Business*, January 1978, 103–114.

———, "Analyzing Convertible Bonds," *Journal of Financial and Quantitative Analysis*, November 1980, 907–929.

———, " Optimal Financial Policy and Firm Valuation," *Journal of Finance*, July 1984, 593–607.

———, "The Case for Convertibles," in Stern, J., and D. Chew, eds., *The Revolution in Corporate Finance*, Basil Blackwell, Oxford, England, 1986.

Brick, I., and O. Palmon, "Interest Rate Fluctuations and the Advantage of Long-Term Debt Financing: A Note on the Effect of the Tax-Timing Option," 1992, *Financial Review,* Vol. 27, 467–474.

Brick, I. E., and A. Ravid, "On the Relevance of Debt Maturity Structure," *Journal of Finance*, December 1985, 1423–1437.

Brigham, E. F., "An Analysis of Convertible Debentures," *Journal of Finance*, March 1966, 35–54.

Chen, A. H. Y., "A Model of Warrant Pricing in a Dynamic Market," *Journal of Finance*, December 1970, 1041–1060.

Chen, A. H. Y., and H. Kim, "Theories of Corporate Debt Policy: A Synthesis," *Journal of Finance*, May 1979, 371–384.

Chirinko, A., and A. Singha, "Testing Static Tradeoff against Pecking Order Models of Capital Structure: A Critical Comment," *Journal of Financial Economics*, December 2000, Vol. 58, No. 3, 412–426.

Constantinides, G., "Warrant Exercise and Bond Conversion in Competitive Markets," *Journal of Financial Economics*, September 1984, 371–398.

Constantinides, G., and B. Grundy, "Optimal Investment with Stock Repurchase and Financing as Signals," *Review of Financial Studies,* 1989, Vol. 2, 445–465.

Copeland, T. E., and W. H. Lee, "Exchange Offers and Stock Swaps: Some New Evidence," *Financial Management*, Autumn 1991, 34–48.

Cordes, J., and S. Sheffrin, "Estimating the Tax Advantage of Corporate Debt," *Journal of Finance*, March 1983, 95–105.

Dann, L., and W. Mikkelson, "Convertible Debt Issuance, Capital Structure Change and Financing-Related Information: Some New Evidence," *Journal of Financial Economics*, June 1984, 157–186.

Darrough, M., and N. Stoughton, "Moral Hazard and Adverse Selection: The Question of Financial Structure," *Journal of Finance*, June 1986, 501–513.

DeAngelo, H., and R. Masulis, "Optimal Capital Structure under Corporate and Personal Taxation," *Journal of Financial Economics*, March 1980, 3–30.

Diamond, D., "Debt Maturity Structure and Liquidity Risk," *Quarterly Journal of Economics,* 1991, Vol. 106, 709–737.

———, "Seniority and Maturity of Debt Contracts," *Journal of Financial Economics,* 1993, Vol. 33, 341–368.

Dietrich, J. R., "Effects of Early Bond Refundings: An Empirical Investigation of Security Returns," *Journal of Accounting and Economics*, April 1984, 67–96.

Dunn, K. B., and C. S. Spatt, "A Strategic Analysis of Sinking Fund Bonds," *Journal of Financial Economics*, August 1983, 211–235.

Dyl, E., and M. Joehnk, "Sinking Funds and the Cost of Corporate Debt," *Journal of Finance*, September 1979, 887–893.

Eckbo, B. E., "Valuation Effects of Corporate Debt Offerings," *Journal of Financial Economics*, January–February 1986, 119–152.

Emmanuel, D. C., "Warrant Valuation and Exercise Strategy," *Journal of Financial Economics*, August 1983, 327–349.

Fama, E., and K. French, "Testing Trade-off and Pecking Order Predictions about Dividends and Debt," *Review of Financial Studies*, 2002, Vol. 15, 1–33.

Fama, E. F., and M. C. Jensen, "Agency Problems and Residual Claims," *Journal of Law and Economics*, June 1983, 327–349.

Fama, E. F., and M. H. Miller, *The Theory of Finance*, Holt, Rinehart and Winston, New York, 1972.

Farrar, D. E., and L. Selwyn, "Taxes, Corporate Financial Policies and Returns to Investors," *National Tax Journal*, December 1967, 444–454.

Finnerty, J., "Stock-for-Debt Swaps and Shareholder Returns," *Financial Management*, Autumn 1985, 5–17.

Flannery, M., "Asymmetric Information and Risky Debt Maturity Choice," *Journal of Finance,* 1986, Vol. 41, 18–38.

Fons, J., "The Default Premium and Corporate Bond Experience," *Journal of Finance*, March 1987, 81–97.

Frank, M., and V. Goyal, "Testing the Pecking Order Theory of Capital Structure," *Journal of Financial Economics*, February 2003a, Vol. 67, No. 2, 217–248.

———, "Capital Structure Decisions," working paper, Hong Kong University of Science and Technology, 2003b.

Froot, K., D. Scharfstein, and J. Stein, "Risk Management: Coordinating Corporate Investment and Financing Policies," *Journal of Finance,* December 1993, Vol. 48, No. 5, 1629–1658.

Galai, D., and R. W. Masulis, "The Option Pricing Model and the Risk Factor of Stock," *Journal of Financial Economics*, January–March 1976, 53–82.

Galai, D., and M. Schneller, "The Pricing of Warrants and the Value of the Firm," *Journal of Finance*, December 1978, 1333–1342.

Graham, J., "Debt and the Marginal Tax Rate," *Journal of Financial Economics*, May 1996a, Vol. 41, No. 1, 41–74.

———, "Proxies for the Corporate Marginal Tax Rate," *Journal of Financial Economics*, October 1996b, Vol. 42, No. 2, 159–186.

Graham, J. R., "How Big Are the Tax Benefits of Debt?" *Journal of Finance*, 2000, Vol. 55, 1901–1941.

Graham, J., and C. Harvey, "The Theory and Practice of Corporate Finance: Evidence from the Field," *Journal of Financial Economics*, 2001, Vol. 60, 187–243.

Green, R., "Investment Incentives, Debt, and Warrants," *Journal of Financial Economics*, March 1984, 115–136.

Grove, M. A., "On Duration and the Optimal Maturity Structure of the Balance Sheet," *Bell Journal*, Autumn 1974, 696–709.

Guedes, J., and T. Opler, "The Determinants of the Maturity Structure of Corporate Debt Issues," *Journal of Finance,* December 1996, Vol. 51, No. 5, 1809–1833.

Haley, C. W., and L. D. Schall, *The Theory of Financial Decisions*, McGraw-Hill, New York, 1973.

Hamada, R. S., "Portfolio Analysis, Market Equilibrium, and Corporation Finance," *Journal of Finance*, March 1969, 13–31.

———, "The Effect of the Firm's Capital Structure on the Systematic Risk of Common Stocks," *Journal of Finance*, May 1972, 435–452.

Harris, M., and A. Raviv, "A Sequential Signalling Model of Convertible Debt Call Policy," *Journal of Finance*, December 1985, 1263–1282.

———, "Capital Structure and the Informational Role of Debt," *Journal of Finance,* June 1990, Vol. 45, No. 2, 321–349.

Hawkins, G. D., "An Analysis of Revolving Credit Agreements," *Journal of Financial Economics*, March 1982, 59–82.

Helwege, J., and N. Liang, "Is There a Pecking Order? Evidence from a Panel of IPO Firms," *Journal of Financial Economics*, 1996, Vol. 40, 429–458.

Ho, T., and R. Singer, "Bond Indenture Provisions and the Risk of Corporate Debt," *Journal of Financial Economics*, December 1982, 375–406.

Hovikimian, A., T. Opler, and S. Titman, "The Debt-Equity Choice," *Journal of Financial and Quantitative Analysis*, 2001, Vol. 36, 1–24.

Hsia, C. C., "Coherence of the Modern Theories of Finance," *Financial Review*, Winter 1981, 27–42.

Ingersoll, J., "A Contingent-Claims Valuation of Convertible Securities," *Journal of Financial Economics,* May 1977, 463–478.

Jalivand, A., and R. S. Harris, "Corporate Behavior in Adjusting to Capital Structure and Dividend Targets: An Econometric Investigation," *Journal of Finance*, 1984, Vol. 39, 611–625.

Jen, F. C., and J. E. Wert, "The Effects of Sinking Fund Provisions on Corporate Bond Yields," *Financial Analysts Journal*, March–April 1967, 125–133.

Jennings, E. H., "An Estimate of Convertible Bond Premiums," *Journal of Financial and Quantitative Analysis*, January 1974, 33–56.

Jensen, M., and W. Meckling, "Theory of the Firm: Managerial Behavior, Agency Costs, and Ownership Structure," *Journal of Financial Economics*, October 1976, 305–360.

Jones, E. P., S. Mason, and E. Rosenfeld, "Contingent Claims Analysis of Corporate Financial Structures: An Empirical Investigation," *Journal of Finance*, July 1984, 611–625.

Kahle, K., and K. Shastri, "Capital Structure, Firm Performance and the Tax Benefits of Employee Stock Options," working paper, 2003.

Kalaba, R., R. Langetieg, N. Rasakhoo, and M. Weinstein, "Estimation of Implicit Bankruptcy Costs," *Journal of Finance*, July 1984, 629–642.

Kale, J., and T. Noe, "Risky Debt Maturity Choice in a Sequential Game Equilibrium," *Journal of Financial Research*, 1990, Vol. 13, 155–166.

Kalotay, A., "On the Advanced Refunding of Discounted Debt," *Financial Management*, Summer 1978, 7–13.

Kane, A., A. Marcus, and R. McDonald, "How Big Is the Tax Advantage to Debt," *Journal of Finance*, July 1984, 841–853.

Kemsley, D., and D. Nissim, "Valuation and the Debt Tax Shield," *Journal of Finance*, October 2002, Vol. 57, No. 5, 2045–2073.

Kim, H., "A Mean-Variance Theory of Optimal Capital Structure and Corporate Debt Capacity," *Journal of Finance*, March 1978, 45–64.

Kim, H., W. Lewellen, and J. McConnell, "Financial Leverage and Clienteles: Theory and Evidence," *Journal of Financial Economics*, March 1979, 83–110.

Kolodny, R., and D. Suhler, "Changes in Capital Structure, New Equity Issues, and Scale Effects," *Journal of Financial Research*, Summer 1985, 127–136.

Kraus, A., and R. Litzenberger, "A State-Preference Model of Optimal Financial Leverage," *Journal of Finance*, September 1973, 911–922.

Leland, H., "Corporate Debt Value, Bond Covenants, and Optimal Capital Structure," *Journal of Finance,* September 1994, Vol. 49, No. 4, 1213–1252.

Leland, H., and D. Pyle, "Informational Asymmetries, Financial Structure, and Financial Intermediation," *Journal of Finance*, May 1977, 371–388.

Leland, H., and K. Toft, "Optimal Capital Structure, Endogenous Bankruptcy, and the Term Structure of Credit Spreads," *Journal of Finance*, 1996, Vol. 51, No. 3, 987–1019.

Lemmon, M. L., and J. F. Zender, "Looking under the Lamppost: An Empirical Examination of the Determinants of Capital Structure," working paper, University of Utah, 2001.

———, "Debt Capacity and Tests of Capital Structure Theories," working paper, University of Utah, 2002.

Long, M., and I. Malitz, "Investment Patterns and Financial Leverage," in B. Friedman, ed., *Corporate Capital Structure in the United States*, University of Chicago Press, Chicago, IL, 1985.

Mackie-Mason, J., "Do Taxes Affect Corporate Financing Decisions?" *Journal of Finance*, 1990, Vol. 45, 1471–1493.

Marsh, P., "The Choice between Equity and Debt: An Empirical Study," *Journal of Finance*, 1982, Vol. 37, 121–144.

Marshall, W., and J. Yawitz, "Optimal Terms of the Call Provision on a Corporate Bond," *Journal of Financial Research*, Summer 1980, 202–211.

Mason, S. P., and S. Bhattacharya, "Risky Debt, Jump Processes, and Safety Covenants," *Journal of Financial Economics*, September 1981, 281–307.

Masulis, R., "The Effects of Capital Structure Change on Security Prices: A Study of Exchange Offers," *Journal of Financial Economics*, June 1980, 139–178.

———, "The Impact of Capital Structure Change on Firm Value, Some Estimates," *Journal of Finance*, March 1983, 107–126.

Masulis, R., and A. Korwar, "Seasoned Equity Offerings: An Empirical Investigation," *Journal of Financial Economics*, January–February 1986, 91–118.

Mauer, D., and A. Triantis, "Interactions of Corporate Financing and Investment Decisions: A Dynamic Framework," *Journal of Finance,* September 1994, Vol. 49, No. 4, 1253–1277.

Mayers, D., "Why Firms Issue Convertible Bonds: The Matching of Financial and Real Investment Options," *Journal of Financial Economics,* 1998, Vol. 47, No. 1, 83–102.

McConnell, J., and G. Schlarbaum, "Evidence on the Impact of Exchange Offers on Security Prices: The Case of Income Bonds," *Journal of Business*, January 1981, 65–85.

Mello, A., and J. Parsons, "Measuring the Agency Cost of Debt," *Journal of Finance,* December 1992, Vol. 47, No. 5, 1887–1904.

Merton, R. C., "An Intertemporal Capital Asset Pricing Model," *Econometrica*, September 1973, 867–887.

Mikkelson, W. H., "Convertible Calls and Security Returns," *Journal of Financial Economics*, September 1981, 237–264.

Mikkelson, W., and W. Partch, "Valuation Effects of Security Offerings and the Issuance Process," *Journal of Financial Economics*, January–February 1986, 31–60.

Miller, M. H., "Debt and Taxes," *Journal of Finance*, May 1977, 261–275.

Miller, M. H., and F. Modigliani, "Some Estimates of the Cost of Capital to the Electric Utility Industry, 1954–1957," *American Economic Review*, June 1966, 333–348.

———, "Some Estimates of the Cost of Capital to the Electric Utility Industry, 1954–57: Reply," *American Economic Review*, June 1958, 261–297.

Minton, B., and K. Wruck, "Financial Conservatism: Evidence on Capital Structure from Low Leverage Firms," working paper, Ohio State University, 2001.

Mitchel, K., "The Call, Sinking Fund, and Term-to-Maturity Features of Corporate Bonds: An Empirical Investigation," *Journal of Financial and Quantitative Analysis,* 1991, Vol. 26, 201–223.

Modigliani, F., and M. H. Miller, "The Cost of Capital, Corporation Finance, and the Theory of Investment," *American Economic Review*, June 1958, 261–297.

———, "Corporate Taxes and the Cost of Capital," *American Economic Review*, June 1963, 433–443.

Morris, J. R., "On Corporate Debt Maturity Policies," *Journal of Finance*, March 1976a, 20–37.

———, "A Model for Corporate Debt Maturity Decisions," *Journal of Financial and Quantitative Analysis*, September 1976b, 339–357.

Myers, S. C., "Determinants of Corporate Borrowing," *Journal of Financial Economics*, November 1977, 147–176.

———, "The Capital Structure Puzzle," *Journal of Finance*, July 1984, 575–592.

Myers, S. C., and N. Majluf, "Corporate Financing and Investment Decisions When Firms Have Information That Investors Do Not Have," *Journal of Financial Economics*, June 1984, 187–221.

Ofer, A., and R. Taggart, Jr., "Bond Refunding: A Clarifying Analysis," *Journal of Finance*, March 1977, 21–30.

Opler, T., M. Saron, and S. Titman, "Designing Capital Structure to Create Shareholder Value," *Journal of Applied Corporate Finance*, 1997, Vol. 7, 21–32.

Opler, T., and S. Titman, "Financial Distress and Corporate Performance," *Journal of Finance,* July 1994, Vol. 49, No. 3, 1015–1040.

Peavy, J., and J. Scott, "The Effect of Stock-for-Debt Swaps on Security Returns," *Financial Review*, November 1985, 303–327.

Peterson, P., D. Peterson, and J. Ang, "The Extinguishment of Debt through In-Substance Defeasance," *Financial Management*, Spring 1985, 59–67.

Pinegar, J., and R. Lease, "The Impact of Preferred-for-Common Exchange Offers on Firm Value," *Journal of Finance*, September 1986, 795–814.

Pye, G., "The Value of a Call Option on a Bond," *Journal of Political Economy*, April 1966, 200–205.

Rajan, R. G., and L. Zingales, "What Do We Know about Capital Structure? Some Evidence from International Data," *Journal of Finance*, 1995, Vol. 50, 1421–1460.

Riley, J., "Competitive Signalling," *Journal of Economic Theory*, April 1975, 174–186.

Robbins, E. H., and J. D. Schatzberg, "Callable Bonds: A Risk-Reducing Signalling Mechanism," *Journal of Finance*, September 1986, 935–949.

Robicheck, A., J. McDonald, and R. Higgins, "Some Estimates of the Cost of Capital to the Electric Utility Industry, 1954–57: Comment," *American Economic Review*, December 1967, 1278–1288.

Robicheck, A., and S. Myers, "Problems in the Theory of Optimal Capital Structure," *Journal of Financial and Quantitative Analysis*, June 1966, 1–35.

Rogers, R., and J. Owers, "Equity for Debt Exchanges and Shareholder Wealth," *Financial Management*, Autumn 1985, 18–26.

Ross, S. A., "The Determination of Financial Structure: The Incentive Signalling Approach," *Bell Journal of Economics*, Spring 1977, 23–40.

Rothschild, M., and J. Stiglitz, "Equilibrium in Competitive Insurance Markets," *Quarterly Journal of Economics*, November 1976, 629–650.

Rubinstein, M. E., "A Mean-Variance Synthesis of Corporate Financial Theory," *Journal of Finance*, March 1973, 167–181.

Samuelson, P. A., "Rational Theory of Warrant Pricing," *Industrial Management Review*, Spring 1965, 13–32.

Schipper, K., and A. Smith, "A Comparison of Equity Carve-outs and Seasoned Equity Offerings: Share Price Effects and Corporate Restructuring," *Journal of Financial Economics*, January–February 1986, 153–186.

Schneller, M., "Taxes and the Optimal Capital Structure of the Firm," *Journal of Finance*, March 1980, 119–127.

Schwartz, E. S., "The Valuation of Warrants: Implementing a New Approach," *Journal of Financial Economics*, January 1977, 79–93.

Scott, J. H., Jr., G. H. Hempel, and J. Peavy III, "The Effect of Stock-for-Debt Swaps on Bank Holding Companies," *Journal of Banking and Finance*, June 1985, 233–251.

Shah, K., "The Nature of Information Conveyed by Pure Capital Structure Changes," *Journal of Financial Economics*, August 1994, Vol. 36, No. 1, 89–126.

Shastri, K., *Two Essays Concerning the Effects of Firm Investment/Financing Decisions on Security Values: An Option Pricing Approach*, Ph.D. dissertation, UCLA Graduate School of Management, 1981.

Shyham-Sunder, L., and S. Myers, "Testing Static Tradeoff against Pecking Order Models of Capital Structure," *Journal of Financial Economics*, February 1999, Vol. 51, No. 2, 219–244.

Smith, C., and R. Stulz, "The Determinants of a Firm's Hedging Policies," *Journal of Financial and Quantitative Analysis*, December 1985, 391–406.

Smith, C., Jr., "Substitute Methods for Raising Additional Capital: Rights Offerings versus Underwritten Issues," *Journal of Financial Economics*, December 1977, 273–307.

———, "Investment Banking and the Capital Acquisition Process," *Journal of Financial Economics*, January–February 1986, 3–30.

Smith, C. J., and J. B. Warner, "On Financial Contracting: An Analysis of Bond Covenants," *Journal of Financial Economics*, June 1979, 117–161.

Solomon, E., *The Theory of Financial Management*, Columbia University Press, New York, 1963.

Stein, J., "Convertible Bonds as Backdoor Equity Financing," *Journal of Financial Economics,* 1992, Vol. 32, 3–21.

Stiglitz, J. E., "A Re-examination of the Modigliani-Miller Theorem," *American Economic Review*, December 1969, 784–793.

———, "Some Aspects of the Pure Theory of Corporate Finance: Bankruptcies and Takeovers," *Bell Journal of Economics and Management Science*, Autumn 1972, 458–482.

———, "On the Irrelevance of Corporate Financial Policy," *American Economic Review*, December 1974, 851–866.

Stone, B. K., "Warrants Financing," *Journal of Financial and Quantitative Analysis*, March 1976, 143–153.

Stultz, R., and H. Johnson, "An Analysis of Secured Debt," *Journal of Financial Economics*, December 1985, 501–521.

Taggert, R. A., Jr., "A Model of Corporate Financing Decisions," *Journal of Finance*, December 1977, 1467–1500.

Titman, S., "The Effect of Capital Structure on a Firm's Liquidation Decision," *Journal of Financial Economics*, March 1984, 137–151.

Titman, S., and R. Wessels, "The Determinants of Capital Structure Choice," *Journal of Finance,* 1988, Vol. 43, 1–19.

Wakeman, L. M., "Bond Rating Agencies and Capital Markets," working paper, Graduate School of Management, University of Rochester, Rochester, N.Y., 1978.

Warner, J., "Bankruptcy, Absolute Priority, and the Pricing of Risky Debt Claims," *Journal of Financial Economics,* May 1977, 239–276.

Watts, R., and J. Zimmerman, "The Demand for and Supply of Accounting Theories: The Market for Excuses," *Accounting Review,* April 1979, 273–305.

Weil, R., J. E. Segall, and D. Green, Jr., "Premiums on Convertible Bonds," *Journal of Finance,* 1968, 445–463.

Welch, I., "Capital Structure and Stock Returns," *Journal of Political Economy,* 2003 (forthcoming).

Weston, J. F., "A Test of Capital Propositions," *Southern Economic Journal,* October 1963, 105–112.

Appendix 15A. Duration and Optimal Maturity Structure of the Balance Sheet

In Chapter 14, we analyzed several aspects of the cost and value of financial instruments. Another aspect of the valuation of securities is the sensitivity of their present values to the unexpected changes in interest rates. We can conceptualize this relationship as the elasticity of the price of securities (particularly bonds) to interest rates. For bonds the elasticity is the ratio of percentage changes in prices to percentage changes in market rates of interest for a given coupon and face value.

DURATION

The *duration* of a payment stream is a measure of elasticity. Thus the duration of bond i can be expressed as follows:

$$D_i = -\frac{dB_i/B_i}{dr/r}, \tag{15A.1}$$

where

$$B_i = \text{price of bond } i,$$

$$r = \text{market yield rate.}$$

For measurement purposes the expression in Eq. (15A.1) would provide only an approximation since it holds strictly for only infinitely small changes in the market yield rate. We can derive a more operational measurement expression. We start with the value of a bond, B_0:

$$B_0 = \frac{I_2}{1+r} + \frac{I_2}{(1+r)^2} + \cdots + \frac{I_T}{(1+r)^T} + \frac{F}{(1+r)^T}, \tag{15A.2}$$

where

$$I_t = \text{dollar value of coupon payment in period } t,$$

$$F = \text{dollar value of maturity payment},$$

$$T = \text{maturity period}.$$

Next we take the derivative of the bond price to the change in the market yield rate:

$$\frac{dB_0}{d(1+r)} = -I(1+r)^{-2} - 2I(1+r)^{-3} - \cdots - TI(1+r)^{-(T+1)} - TF(1+r)^{-(T+1)}$$

$$= -\left[\frac{I}{(1+r)^2} + \frac{2I}{(1+r)^3} + \cdots + \frac{TI}{(1+r)^{T+1}} + \frac{TF}{(1+r)^{T+1}}\right].$$

Divide both sides by B_0 and $(1+r)$:

$$\frac{dB_0/B_0}{d(1+r)/(1+r)} = \frac{dB_0(1+r)}{d(1+r)B_0}$$

$$= -\frac{1}{B_0}\left[\frac{I}{(1+r)} + \frac{2I}{(1+r)^2} + \cdots + \frac{TI}{(1+r)^T} + \frac{TF}{(1+r)^T}\right].$$

Let C represent the appropriate cash flows, and express the result in summation form:

$$D_i = \frac{\displaystyle\sum_{t=1}^{T}\frac{tC_t}{(1+r)^t}}{B_0}. \tag{15A.3a}$$

This result can also be expressed as

$$D_i = \frac{\displaystyle\sum_{t=1}^{T}\frac{tI_t}{(1+r)^t} + \frac{TF}{(1+r)^T}}{\displaystyle\sum_{t=1}^{T}\frac{I_t}{(1+r)^t} + \frac{F}{(1+r)^T}} \tag{15A.3b}$$

From Eq. (15A.3b) we can see that duration is not the same as the time to maturity of the payment stream. Unlike maturity, duration considers all cash flows and gives some weight to their timing.

   Thus duration is calculated as the weighted average of the lengths of time prior to the last cash flows, by using the ratios of the present values of each coupon payment to the present value of the bond as the weights. It identifies the "actual" weighted length of time needed to recover the current cost of the bond. For example, assume a five-year $1,000 bond has a payment of $25 each six months (5% coupon rate), pays $1,000 at the end of the fifth year, and has a yield rate of 12%. The duration of the bond can be calculated as shown in Table 15A.1.

$$D = \frac{\$6,508.0775}{\$742.4050} = 8.7662 \text{ (semiannual)}$$

$$= 4.3831 \text{ years}.$$

Table 15A.1 $1,000 Bond Issue, Five-Year, with 12% Yield Rate and 5% Coupon Rate Paid Semiannually

(1) Period	(2) Cash Payments	(3) Discount Factor at 6% of Semiannual Yield Rate	(4) Present Value of Cash Payments (2) × (3)	(5) (4) × (1)
1	$ 25	.9434	$ 23.5850	$ 23.5850
2	25	.8900	22.2500	44.5000
3	25	.8396	20.9900	62.9700
4	25	.7921	19.8025	79.2100
5	25	.7473	18.6825	93.4125
6	25	.7050	17.6250	105.7500
7	25	.6651	16.6275	116.3925
8	25	.6274	16.6850	125.4800
9	25	.5919	14.7975	133.1775
10	1025	.5584	572.3600	5,723.6000
			PV of bond = $742.4050	$6,508.0775

A short-cut method of calculating duration as originally formulated by Macaulay [1938] is the following:

$$D = \frac{R}{R-1} - \frac{QR + T(1+Q-QR)}{R^T - 1 - Q + QR} \qquad (15A.4)$$

The new terms in Eq. (15A.4) are

$$R = (1+r) = 1.06,$$

$$Q = (F/I_t) = \$1,000/\$25 = 40,$$

$$T = 10.$$

Only for zero-coupon bonds is duration the same as maturity. For other payment streams, duration is shorter than maturity. For a given par value of a bond, the higher the coupon payments and the higher the yield to maturity, the shorter is duration.

The relationship between the bond price and its duration is more complicated. For bonds selling at or above par, the duration increases with maturity, but at a decreasing rate, and is bounded by $(r+p)/rp$ years, where r is the yield to maturity and p is the number of times per year interest is paid and compounded. For discount bonds, duration increases with maturity to a maximum point before it matures, and then declines. For shorter-term bonds, the differences between duration and maturity are small. However, as maturity increases, the differences will be substantially larger.

IMMUNIZATION

Immunization is a technique designed to achieve a specified return target in the face of changes in interest rates. The problem arises because with changing interest rates the reinvestment income will change. However, a bond or a bond portfolio can be immunized against this risk by selecting a maturity or group of maturities whose duration will be equal to the planning horizon of the decision maker. An illustration based on an example by Leibowitz [1981] will convey the ideas involved. The initial facts are these. We have a 9% par bond with a maturity of 6.7 years resulting in a 5-year duration related to the 5-year horizon of the decision maker. With semiannual compounding the bond maturity is 13.4 periods. The simple sum of the coupon income, based on the 9% rate over 5 years (10 periods), is $450.

To verify the relation between the maturity of 6.7 years and the duration of 5 years, we employ the Macaulay formulation. The key inputs are

$$R = 1 + r = 1.045,$$

$$Q = 1000/45 = 22.22,$$

$$T = 13.4.$$

We can now calculate duration, D, as

$$D = \frac{1.045}{.045} - \frac{22.22(1.045) + 13.4[23.22 - 22.22(1.045)]}{(1.045)^{13.4} - 23.22 + 22.22(1.045)}$$

$$= \frac{10.35}{2} = 5.17 \approx 5.$$

Suppose the market yield rate now changes from 9% to 10%. There will be a capital loss because of the rise in the yield rate, but the reinvestment income will be higher. We shall demonstrate that if the investor's planning horizon is 5 years, the yield will remain 9% and the capital gain or loss will be exactly balanced by the present value of the changed reinvestment income. We can demonstrate this by looking at the situation at the end of the fifth year or taking those results and discounting them back to the present. The income at 10% will be

$$= \$45 \times FVIF_a(5\%, 10 \text{ pds})$$

$$= (\$45 \times 12.5779)$$

$$= \$566.$$

However, the interest that would have been earned at a 9% rate would be

$$= (\$45 \times FVIF_a(4\tfrac{1}{2}\%, 10 \text{ pds})$$

$$= (\$45 \times 12.2882)$$

$$= \$553.$$

Thus the gain in interest income is $13 as of the end of the fifth year.

Next we calculate the price that would be received when the bond is sold at the end of the 5-year planning horizon. At the end of 5 years, or 10 periods, the bond had 1.7 years, or 3.4 periods, remaining. Its value and the capital gain (loss) at 10% are

$$V_b = \$45(3.0572) + 1,000(.8471)$$

$$= \$137.57 + \$847.10$$

$$= \$984.67$$

$$\text{capital gain} = \$984.67 - \$1,000 = -\$15.33.$$

Thus we see that the amount of the capital gain or loss is a negative $15. This is slightly different from the $13 gain on interest because we have used approximations for a duration of, for example, 5 years when the exact duration was 5.17 years.

Next we can verify that a 9% yield will actually be achieved and that the current market value of $1,000 is immunized against the rise in the required market yield. In the analysis we use

$$FVIF_a(4\tfrac{1}{2}\%,\ 10\ \text{pds}) = 7.9127,\ \text{and}\ PVIF(4\tfrac{1}{2}\%,\ 10\ \text{pds}) = .6439.$$

So we have

Coupon interest @ 9%	$45 × 7.9127	=	$356.07
Interest @ 10%	$566 × .6439	=	364.45
Capital gain	$985 × .6439	=	634.24
Less*	$533 × .6439	=	(356.08)
			$998.70

The example illustrates that by choosing the duration of the payment stream to be equal to the length of the planning horizon, the present value of the payment stream is immunized against changes in the market rate of interest and the initial yield on the stream is preserved.

Another example of immunization uses the total balance sheet position of a firm. Consider a bank portfolio manager with the following initial position:

	Initial Position	
	Assets	**Liabilities**
Portfolio value	$800,000	$800,000
Portfolio yield	12.0%	8.0%
Portfolio duration	8 years	3 years

With a 1% rise in yields, we can use Eq. (15A.1) to calculate the change in the equity position of the bank. For the asset side we have

$$dP_a = -D_a\left(\frac{dr}{r}\right)P_a$$

$$= -8\frac{.01}{(1.12)}\$800{,}000$$

$$= -\$57{,}142.$$

For the liabilities (or claims on assets) side, we have

$$dP_c = -3\frac{.01}{(1.08)}\$800{,}000$$

$$= -\$22{,}222.$$

---

*To adjust for the 9% interest rate implicit in the interest factor used to discount the present value of the coupon income.

So the decline in the value of assets exceeds the decline in the value of claims on assets by $34,920. By changing the duration of the asset portfolio, the bank can be immunized against a change in the interest rate levels. The required duration for the asset portfolio is

$$dP_a = -D_a \frac{.01}{(1.12)} \$800,000 = -\$22,222.$$

Solving, we have D_a is 3.11, indicating the shorter duration required for immunization of the portfolio.

The examples above illustrate the mechanics of immunization procedures. In actual application immunization involves a wide range of assumptions in connection with its use in immunizing bond portfolios. One assumption is parallel shifts in the yield curve [Yawitz and Marshall, 1981]. The practical effects are small [Kolb and Gay, 1982, 83].

Also, there may be multiple rate changes during the planning horizon. This problem is dealt with by rebalancing the portfolio to maintain a duration matching the remaining life of the planning period. In addition, there are a wide variety of more aggressive approaches to managing the bond portfolio developed under the concept of contingent immunization [Leibowitz and Weinberger, 1982]. Contingent immunization is a form of active portfolio management. It generally involves some degree of rate anticipation reflecting the portfolio manager's judgments about the future direction of interest rates. The procedures are too detailed to be covered in this brief treatment.

APPLICATION OF DURATION TO DEBT MATURITY STRUCTURE

Redington [1952] applied the duration concept to the analysis of investment decisions made by insurance companies. He proposed an immunization rule under which the weighted durations of asset and liability streams are made equal so that the firm's net worth is hedged against interest rate movements. Redington noted that even for insurance companies the concept would be complex in its implementation. Grove [1974] analyzed immunization in a portfolio choice model in a framework of uncertainty of income stream patterns and of interest rate changes.

Morris [1976a, 1976b] sought to apply the duration concept to the problem of corporate debt maturity strategies. Here the problem is even more complex than that faced by insurance companies. In theory, insurance companies can formulate income and repayment streams that are highly predictable by investing in fixed income securities, with payment streams related to the operation of life expectancy tables (which can be further hedged by combining death policies with annuity policies). For the industrial firm the liability structure can be fixed by its corporate debt maturity pattern. However, the income stream varies with the impact of the economy and competition on the firm's revenues and costs.

Morris observes that when the covariance of interest costs with the firm's net operating income is high, a short-term borrowing policy will reduce the variation of net income even though it increases the uncertainty of interest costs in future periods. Thus for a weighted asset life with long duration, immunization through the choice of the duration of the debt structure is not necessarily the least risky maturity policy because of the variability of the income streams from the assets. A shorter debt maturity policy may decrease the uncertainty of net income derived from the asset when there is high covariance between net operating income and interest costs. If the duration of the asset structure is short, immunization calls for a weighted maturity of short-duration debt. But if long-term debt with a longer duration were employed, and if interest rates were negatively correlated with the firm's net operating income, a long-term borrowing policy could reduce the variance of net income. In addition, the level of interest costs would be fixed and certain over the life of the debt. Thus the concept of duration appears to have some potential for developing corporate debt maturity strategies. But the problem is more complex than that encountered in managing portfolios of financial assets and claims.

REFERENCES

Fisher, L., and R. L. Weil, "Coping with the Risk of Interest Rate Fluctuations: Returns to Bondholders from Naive and Optimal Strategies," *Journal of Business*, October 1971, 111–118.

Grove, M. A., "On 'Duration' and the Optimal Maturity Structure of the Balance Sheet," *Bell Journal*, Autumn 1974, 696–709.

Hicks, J. R., *Value and Capital*, Clarendon Press, Oxford, 1946.

Hopewell, M. H., and G. G. Kaufman, "Bond Price Volatility and Term to Maturity: A Generalized Respecification," *American Economic Review*, September 1973, 749–753.

Hsia, C. C., and J. F. Weston, "Price Behavior of Deep Discount Bonds," *Journal of Banking and Finance*, September 1981, 357–361.

Kolb, R. W., *Interest Rate Futures: A Comprehensive Introduction*, Dame, Richmond, Va., 1982.

Kolb, R. W., and G. D. Gay, "Immunizing Bond Portfolios with Interest Rate Futures," *Financial Management*, Summer 1982, 81–89.

Leibowitz, M. L., "Specialized Fixed Income Security Strategies," in E. Altman, ed., *Financial Handbook*, 5th ed., Wiley, New York, 1981, Section 19.

Leibowitz, M. L., and A. Weinberger, *Contingent Immunization: A New Procedure for Structured Active Management*, Salomon, New York, 1982.

Macaulay, F. R., *Some Theoretical Problems Suggested by the Movements of Interest Rates, Bond Yields, and Stock Prices in the U.S. Since 1856*, National Bureau of Economic Research, New York, 1938.

Morris, J. R., "On Corporate Debt Maturity Strategies," *Journal of Finance*, March 1976a, 29–37.

———, "A Model for Corporate Debt Maturity Decisions," *Journal of Financial and Quantitative Analysis*, September 1976b, 339–357.

Redington, F. M., "Review of the Principles of Life Office Valuations," *Journal of the Institute of Actuaries*, 1952, Vol. 78, Part 3, No. 350, 286–340.

Samuelson, P. A., "The Effect of Interest Rate Increases in the Banking System," *American Economic Review*, March 1945, 16–27.

Weil, R. L., "Macaulay's Duration: An Appreciation," *Journal of Business*, October 1973, 589–592.

Yawitz, J. B., and W. J. Marshall, "The Shortcomings of Duration as a Risk Measure for Bonds," *Journal of Financial Research*, Summer 1981, 91–101.

... in the real world a change in the dividend rate is often followed by a change in the market price (sometimes spectacularly so). Such a phenomenon would not be incompatible with irrelevance to the extent that it was merely a reflection of what might be called the "informational content" of dividends ...

—M. Miller and F. Modigliani, "Dividend Policy, Growth, and the Valuation of Shares," *Journal of Business*, October 1961, 431.

Dividend Policy: Theory and Empirical Evidence

I S THE VALUE OF SHAREHOLDERS' WEALTH affected by the dividend policy of the firm? This is another variation on the basic question, Can any financing decision affect the value of the firm? The previous chapter looked at the relationship between capital structure and the value of the firm, using a fairly simple valuation model that assumed a nongrowing stream of cash flows from investment. Capital structure theory shows that, in a world without taxes, agency costs, or information asymmetry, repackaging the firm's net operating cash flows into fixed cash flows for debt and residual cash flows for shareholders has no effect on the value of the firm.

In this chapter, we shall first review the theory. It shows that, in a world without taxes, it makes no difference whether shareholders receive their cash flows as dividends or as capital gains. There is, however, an important distinction between capital structure and dividend policy decisions. Capital structure policy is a way of creating value. Dividend policy is primarily a choice about how to deliver value. Thus in the absence of taxes, agency costs, bond covenants that restrict dividend payout, or information asymmetry, dividend policy is irrelevant. It does not affect shareholders' wealth, namely, the value of the equity of the firm. However, in a world with personal as well as corporate taxes the possibility arises that dividends may affect value because the taxation of various delivery mechanisms (e.g., dividends versus share repurchases) is different. Also, agency costs and information heterogeneity are proposed as possible explanations for dividend policy.

Our discussion of the empirical evidence first deals with models that simply explain the behavior of corporate dividend policy over time. Evidence indicates that U.S. corporations behave as if they had some target dividend payout in mind and that they move toward it with a lag. They also show reluctance to lower dividends. Second, we look at the possibility of clientele effects. Do people in high tax brackets avoid investing in high-dividend companies in order to escape higher income taxes on dividend income? On this question, the empirical evidence is mixed, although it does lean toward the existence of a clientele effect. Third, the information content of dividend increases is tested. There is reasonably strong evidence that leans toward validation of the signaling hypothesis. Fourth, we focus on the relationship between dividend yield and the market value of equity. The best empirical evidence indicates that dividend yield is at most weakly related to the value of the firm. Several explanations are given for why this result is plausible, given our current tax system. Fifth, the empirical literature related to share repurchases via tender offer is reviewed. The announcement of share repurchases tends to be interpreted as unanticipated favorable news about the value of the company.

A. *The* Irrelevance of Dividend Policy in a World without Taxes

Miller and Modigliani [1961] present a cogent argument for the fact that the value of the firm is unaffected by dividend policy in a world without taxes or transactions costs. In a world without taxes it makes no difference whether value is delivered via dividend payout or share repurchase so long as the investment decision is not influenced by payout policy. Miller and Modigliani begin by assuming that two firms are identical in every respect except for their dividend payout in the current time period. Their streams of future cash flows from operations are identical, their planned investment outlays are identical, and all future dividend payments from the second time period on are also identical. We can represent this mathematically as follows:

$$
\begin{aligned}
\widetilde{EBIT}_1(t) &= \widetilde{EBIT}_2(t) & t &= 0, 1, \ldots, \infty, \\
\widetilde{I}_1(t) &= \widetilde{I}_2(t) & t &= 0, 1, \ldots, \infty, \\
\widetilde{Div}_1(t) &= \widetilde{Div}_2(t), & t &= 1, \ldots, \infty, \\
Div_1(0) &\neq Div_2(0),
\end{aligned}
$$

where

$\widetilde{EBIT}_i(t) =$ the random future cash flows from operations for the ith firm in time period t,

$\widetilde{I}_i(t) =$ the variable investment outlay for the ith firm in time period t,

$\widetilde{Div}_i(t) =$ the random dividend payout for firms in period t,

$Div_i(0) =$ the dividend payout for the ith firm during the current time period.

1. A Recursive Valuation Formula

The important question is whether or not the two firms will have different value if their current dividend payouts are different, but everything else is the same. To supply an answer we first need a simple valuation model. Let us begin by assuming that the market-required rates of return for firms in the same risk class are identical.[1] The two firms above obviously have the same risk because their streams of operating cash flows are identical. The rate of return is defined as dividends plus capital gains:

$$
k_u(t + 1) = \frac{div_i(t + 1) + P_i(t + 1) - P_i(t)}{P_i(t)}, \tag{16.1}
$$

---

[1] For the sake of simplicity, we assume that both firms are 100% equity. This avoids the problem of confusing capital structure effects with possible dividend policy effects.

where

$$k_u(t + 1) = \text{the market-required rate of return during the time period } t,$$

$$div_i(t + 1) = \text{dividends per share paid at the end of time period } t,$$

$$P_i(t + 1) = \text{price per share at the end of time period } t,$$

$$P_i(t) = \text{price per share at the beginning of time period } t.$$

If the numerator and denominator of (16.1) are multiplied by the current number of shares outstanding, $n_i(t)$, then by rearranging terms, we have

$$V_i(t) = \frac{Div_i(t + 1) + n_i(t)P_i(t + 1)}{1 + k_u(t + 1)}, \tag{16.2}$$

where

$$Div_i(t + 1) = \text{total dollar dividend payment} = n_i(t)div_i(t + 1),$$

$$V_i(t) = \text{the market value of the firm} = n_i(t)P_i(t).$$

Hence the value of the firm is seen to be equal to the discounted sum of two cash flows: any dividends paid out, $Div_i(t + 1)$, and the end-of-period value of the firm. To show that the present value of the firm is independent of dividend payout, we shall examine the sources and uses of funds for the two firms in order to rewrite (16.2) in a way that is independent of dividends.

2. Sources and Uses of Funds

There are two major sources of funds for an all-equity firm. First, it receives cash from operations, $\widetilde{EBIT}_i(t + 1)$. Second, it may choose to issue new shares, $m_i(t + 1)\widetilde{P}_i(t + 1)$, where $m_i(t + 1)$ is the number of new shares. There are also two major uses of funds: dividends paid out, $\widetilde{Div}_i(t + 1)$, and planned cash outlays for investment, $\widetilde{I}_i(t + 1)$.[2] By definition, sources and uses must be equal. Therefore we have the following identity:

$$\widetilde{EBIT}_i(t + 1) + m_i(t + 1)\widetilde{P}_i(t + 1) \equiv \widetilde{I}_i(t + 1) + \widetilde{Div}_i(t + 1). \tag{16.3}$$

We can use this fact to rewrite the numerator of the valuation equation (16.2). Calling the numerator of (16.2) the dollar return to shareholders, $\widetilde{R}_i(t + 1)$, we have

$$\widetilde{R}_i(t + 1) = \widetilde{Div}_i(t + 1) + n_i(t)\widetilde{P}_i(t + 1). \tag{16.4}$$

We know that if new shares are issued, the total number of shares outstanding at the end of the period, $n(t + 1)$, will be the sum of current shares, $n(t)$, and new shares, $m(t + 1)$:

$$n_i(t + 1) = n_i(t) + m_i(t + 1). \tag{16.5}$$

Using (16.5), we can rewrite (16.4) as

$$\widetilde{R}_i(t + 1) = \widetilde{Div}_i(t + 1) + n_i(t + 1)\widetilde{P}_i(t + 1) - m_i(t + 1)\widetilde{P}_i(t + 1). \tag{16.6}$$

---

[2] This argument assumes, for the sake of convenience, that sources and uses of funds from balance sheet items (e.g., changes in inventory or accounts receivable) are negligible.

Finally, taking Eq. (16.3), which establishes the identity of the sources and uses of funds, to substitute for $m_i(t + 1)\widetilde{P}_i(t + 1)$ in the above equation, we obtain

$$\widetilde{R}_i(t + 1) = \widetilde{Div}_i(t + 1) + \widetilde{V}_i(t + 1) - \widetilde{I}_i(t + 1) + \widetilde{EBIT}_i(t + 1) - \widetilde{Div}_i(t + 1)$$

$$= \widetilde{EBIT}_i(t + 1) - \widetilde{I}_i(t + 1) + \widetilde{V}_i(t + 1), \tag{16.7}$$

where $\widetilde{V}_i(t + 1) = n_i(t + 1)\widetilde{P}_i(t + 1)$. Therefore the valuation equation (16.2) may be rewritten as

$$\widetilde{V}_i(t) = \frac{\widetilde{EBIT}_i(t + 1) - \widetilde{I}_i(t + 1) + \widetilde{V}_i(t + 1)}{1 + k_u(t + 1)}. \tag{16.8}$$

3. Valuation and the Irrelevancy of Dividend Payout

It is no accident that dividends do not appear in the valuation equation (16.8). Given that there are no taxes or transactions costs, the firm can choose any dividend policy whatsoever without affecting the stream of cash flows received by shareholders. It could, for example, elect to pay dividends in excess of cash flows from operations and still be able to undertake any planned investment. The extra funds needed are supplied by issuing new equity. On the other hand, it could decide to pay dividends less than the amount of cash left over from operations after making investments. The excess cash would be used to repurchase shares. It is the availability of external financing in a world without information asymmetry or transactions costs that makes the value of the firm independent of dividend policy.

We can use Eq. (16.8) to prove that two firms that are identical in every respect except for their current dividend payout must have the same value. The equation has four terms. First, the market-required rate of return, k_u, must be the same because both firms have identical risk, $\widetilde{EBIT}_1(t) = \widetilde{EBIT}_2(t)$, for all t. Second, current cash flows from operations and current investment outlays for the two firms have been assumed to be identical:

$$\widetilde{EBIT}_1(1) = \widetilde{EBIT}_2(1), \qquad \widetilde{I}_1(1) = \widetilde{I}_2(1).$$

Finally, the end-of-period values of the two firms depend only on *future* investments, dividends, and cash flows from operations, which also have been assumed to be identical. Therefore the end-of-period values of the two firms must be the same:

$$\widetilde{V}_1(1) = \widetilde{V}_2(1).$$

Consequently, the present values of the two firms must be identical regardless of their dividend payout. Dividend policy is irrelevant because it has no effect on shareholders' wealth in a world without taxes, information asymmetry, or transactions costs, and because, without taxes, the choice to deliver value via cash dividends or using the same cash to repurchase shares is a matter of indifference to shareholders.

Note that the proof of the irrelevancy of dividend policy was made using a multiperiod model whose returns were uncertain. Therefore it is an extremely general argument. In addition to providing insight into what does not affect the value of the firm, it provides considerable insight into what *does* affect value. The value of the firm depends only on the distribution of future cash flows provided by *investment decisions*. The key to the Miller-Modigliani argument is that investment decisions are completely independent of dividend policy. The firm can pay any level of dividends it wishes without affecting investment decisions. If dividends plus desired investment outlays use more cash flow than is provided from operations, the firm should seek external financing (e.g., equity). The desire to maintain a level of dividends need not ever affect the investment decision.

4. Independence between Investment and Dividend Payout

In Chapter 14, we derived the value of an all-equity firm that grows forever at a constant rate, as seen in Eq. (14.17). The form of the valuation model can be used to illustrate the relationship between the result that the value of the firm is independent of dividend policy and the assumption that investment decisions should never be affected by dividend payout. A commonly made error is to implicitly assume that there is some relationship between the amount of cash flow retained and the amount of investment the firm undertakes. Suppose we take the partial derivative of Eq. (14.17) with respect to changes in the investment rate, K:

$$\frac{\partial V_0}{\partial K} = \frac{EBIT_1(1 - T)(r - k_u)}{(k_u - rK)^2} > 0.$$

This suggests that if the rate of return on investments, r, is greater than the market-required rate of return, k_u, the value of the firm will increase as more cash flow is retained, and presumably the increased amount of retained cash flow implies lower dividend payout. This line of reasoning is incorrect for two reasons. First, the amount of cash flow retained has nothing to do with dividend payout. As was shown in the sources and uses of funds, identity (16.3), the firm can arbitrarily set dividend payout at any level whatsoever, and if the sum of funds used for dividends and investment is greater than cash flows from operations, the firm will issue new equity. Second, the investment decision that maximizes shareholder wealth depends only on the market-required rate of return. The amount of cash flow retained could exceed the amount of investment, which would imply that shares be repurchased. Therefore there is no relationship between the value of the firm and either dividend payout or cash flow retention.

5. The Bird-in-Hand Fallacy

A more sophisticated argument for a relationship between the value of the firm and dividend payout is that although the dividend decision cannot change the present value of cash payments to shareholders, it can affect the temporal pattern of payouts. Suppose that investors view distant dividend payments as riskier than current payments. Might they not prefer a bird in the hand to two in the bush? We can represent this argument mathematically by assuming that higher investment rates mean lower current dividend payout, more risk, and therefore an increase in the market rate of return, k_u, as a function of the investment rate, K. A simple example would be to specify the relationship as

$$k_u = \alpha + \beta K^2, \quad \beta > 0.$$

Then we would have

$$\frac{\partial V_0}{\partial K} = \frac{EBIT_1(1 - T)(\beta K^2 - 2\beta K + r - \alpha)}{(\alpha + \beta K^2 - rK)^2}, \quad \alpha + \beta K^2 - rK > 0.$$

This function will have a maximum where

$$EBIT_1(1 - T)(\beta K^2 - 2\beta K + r - \alpha) = 0.$$

To see the error in this line of reasoning, we need only to return to our understanding of valuation under uncertainty. The risk of the firm is determined by the riskiness of the cash flows from its projects. An increase in dividend payout today will result in an equivalent drop in the ex-dividend price of the stock. It will not increase the value of the firm by reducing the riskiness of future cash flows.

B. Dividend Policy in a World with Personal and Corporate Taxes

Up to this point in the chapter, the models of firms that have been introduced assume a world with only corporate taxes. What happens when personal taxes are considered? In particular, how is dividend policy affected by the important fact that in the United States the capital gains tax is less than the personal income tax?[3] An answer to this question is provided by Farrar and Selwyn [1967] and extended into a market equilibrium framework by Brennan [1970].[4]

Farrar and Selwyn use partial equilibrium analysis and assume that individuals attempt to maximize their after-tax income. Shareholders have two choices. They can own shares in an all-equity firm and borrow in order to provide personal leverage, or they can buy shares in a levered firm. Therefore the first choice is the amount of personal versus corporate leverage that is desired. The second choice is the form of payment to be made by the firm. It can pay out earnings as dividends, or it can retain earnings and allow shareholders to take their income in the form of capital gains. Shareholders must choose whether they want dividends or capital gains.

If the firm pays out all its cash flows as dividends, the ith shareholder will receive the following after-tax income, $\widetilde{Y}_{di}$:

$$\widetilde{Y}_{di} = \left[(\widetilde{EBIT} - rD_c)(1 - \tau_c) - rD_{pi}\right](1 - \tau_{pi}), \tag{16.9}$$

where

$\widetilde{Y}_{di} = $ the uncertain income to the ith individual if corporate income is received as dividends,

$\widetilde{EBIT} = $ the uncertain cash flows from operations provided by the firm,

$r = $ the borrowing rate, which is assumed to be equal for individuals and the firm,

$D_c = $ corporate debt,

$D_{pi} = $ personal debt held by the ith individual,

$\tau_c = $ the corporate tax rate,

$\tau_{pi} = $ the personal income tax rate of the ith individual.

The first term within the brackets is the after-tax cash flow of the firm, which is $(\widetilde{EBIT} - rD)$ $(1 - \tau_c)$. All of this is assumed to be paid out as dividends. The before-tax income to the shareholder

---

[3] The 1986 tax code nominally makes the capital gains *rate* equal to the ordinary income rate. However, capital gains taxes are still less than ordinary taxes in effect, because capital gains can be deferred indefinitely, whereas taxes on ordinary taxes cannot.

[4] More recently Miller and Scholes [1978] have also considered a world with dividends and taxes. The implications of this paper are discussed later in this chapter.

is the dividends received minus the interest on debt used to buy shares. After subtracting income taxes on this income, we are left with Eq. (16.9).

Alternatively, the firm can decide to pay no dividends, in which case we assume that all gains are realized *immediately* by investors and taxed at the capital gains rate.[5] In this event the after-tax income of a shareholder is

$$\widetilde{Y}_{gi} = (\widetilde{EBIT} - rD_c)(1 - \tau_c)(1 - \tau_{gi}) - rD_{pi}(1 - \tau_{pi}), \qquad (16.10)$$

where

$\widetilde{Y}_{gi}$ = the uncertain income to the ith individual if corporate income is received as capital gains,

τ_{gi} = the capital gains rate for the ith individual.

Now the individual pays a capital gains tax rate on the income from the firm and deducts after-tax interest expenses on personal debt. The corporation can implement the policy of translating cash flows into capital gains by simply repurchasing its shares in the open market.

We can rewrite Eq. (16.10) as follows:

$$\widetilde{Y}_{gi} = \left[(\widetilde{EBIT} - rD_c)(1 - \tau_c) - rD_{pi}\right](1 - \tau_{gi}) + rD_{pi}(\tau_{pi} - \tau_{gi}). \qquad (16.11)$$

From Eqs. (16.9) and (16.11) the advantage to investors of receiving returns in the form of capital gains rather than dividends should be obvious. So long as the tax rate on capital gains is less than the personal tax rate ($\tau_{gi} < \tau_{pi}$), individuals will prefer capital gains to dividends for any positive operating cash flows, rate of interest, and level of debt (personal or corporate). The ratio of the two income streams,

$$\frac{\widetilde{Y}_{gi}}{\widetilde{Y}_{di}} = \frac{\left[(\widetilde{EBIT} - rD_c)(1 - \tau_c) - rD_{pi}\right](1 - \tau_{gi}) + rD_{pi}(\tau_{pi} - \tau_{gi})}{\left[(\widetilde{EBIT} - rD_c)(1 - \tau_c) - rD_{pi}\right](1 - \tau_{pi})} > 1, \qquad (16.12)$$

is greater than one if $\tau_{gi} < \tau_{pi}$. In general the best form of payment is the one that is subject to least taxation. The implication, of course, is that corporations should never pay dividends. If payments are to be made to shareholders, they should always be made via share repurchase. This allows shareholders to avoid paying income tax rates on dividends. Instead, they receive their payments in the form of capital gains that are taxed at a lower rate.

What about debt policy? Again the same principle holds. The debt should be held by the party who can obtain the greatest tax shield from the deductible interest payments. This is the party with the greatest marginal tax rate. If the firm pays out all its cash flow in the form of dividends, the favorable tax treatment of capital gains is irrelevant. In this case we have the familiar Modigliani-Miller [1963] result that the value of the firm is maximized by taking on the maximum amount of debt (see Chapter 15). Proof is obtained by taking the partial derivative of Eq. (16.12) with respect to personal and corporate debt and comparing the results.

Debt policy becomes more complex when the corporation repurchases shares instead of paying dividends. Taking the partial derivatives of the capital gains income equation, (16.10), we obtain

---

[5] Obviously there is a third possibility that earnings are translated into capital gains and the capital gains taxes are deferred to a later date. This possibility is considered in Farrar and Selwyn [1967]; it does not change their conclusions.

Corporate debt: $\dfrac{\partial \tilde{Y}_{gi}}{\partial D_c} = -r(1 - \tau_c)(1 - \tau_{gi}),$ (16.13)

Personal debt: $\dfrac{\partial \tilde{Y}_{gi}}{\partial D_{pi}} = -r(1 - \tau_{pi}).$ (16.14)

If the effective tax rate on capital gains is zero (as Miller [1977] suggests), then personal debt will be preferred to corporate debt by those individuals who are in marginal tax brackets higher than the marginal tax bracket of the firm. This result allows the possibility of clientele effects where low-income investors prefer corporate debt and high-income investors prefer personal debt. Miller [1977] takes his argument even further. He shows that if the borrowing rate on debt is "grossed up" so that the after-tax rate on debt equals the after-tax rate on other sources of capital, the marginal investor will be indifferent between personal and corporate debt.[6]

Empirical evidence about the existence of debt clienteles is discussed later in this chapter. Some clientele effects are obvious. For example, high-tax-bracket individuals hold tax-free municipal bonds, whereas low-tax-bracket investors like pension funds (which pay no taxes) prefer to invest in taxable corporate bonds. A much more subtle question, however, is whether investors discriminate among various corporate debt issues; that is, do high-tax-bracket investors choose low-leverage firms?

Brennan [1970] extends the work of Farrar and Selwyn into a general equilibrium framework where investors are assumed to maximize their expected utility of wealth. Although this framework is more robust, Brennan's conclusions are not much different from those of Farrar and Selwyn. With regard to dividend payout Brennan concludes that "for a given level of risk, investors require a higher total return on a security the higher its prospective dividend yield is, because of the higher rate of tax levied on dividends than on capital gains." As we shall see, this statement has empirical implications for the CAPM. It suggests that dividend payout should be included as a second factor to explain the equilibrium rate of return on securities. If true, the empirical CAPM would become

$$R_{jt} - R_{ft} = \delta_0 + \delta_1 \beta_{jt} + \delta_2 \left[(div_{jt}/P_{jt} - R_{ft}) \right] + \tilde{\varepsilon}_{jt},$$ (16.15)

where

$\delta_0 =$ a constant,

$\delta_1 =$ influence of systematic risk on R_{jt},

$\delta_2 =$ influence of dividend payout on R_{jt},

$\beta_{jt} =$ the systematic risk of the jth security,

$div_{jt}/P_{jt} =$ the dividend yield of the jth security,

$\tilde{\varepsilon}_{jt} =$ a random error term,

$R_{ft} =$ the risk-free rate.

If the dividend yield factor turns out to be statistically significant, then we might conclude that dividend policy is not irrelevant. Direct empirical tests of the relationship between dividend yield and share value are discussed later.

---

[6] The reader is referred to Chapter 15 for a complete discussion of this point.

Table 16.1 Balance Sheets and Income Statement

Opening Balance Sheet				Closing Balance Sheet			
Assets		**Liabilities**		**Assets**		**Liabilities**	
2,500 shares at $10	= 25,000	Loan	16,667	2,500 shares at $10.60	= 26,500	Loan	16,667
				Accrued dividends	1,000	Accrued interest	1,000
Insurance	16,667	Net Worth	25,000	Insurance	16,667	Net worth	26,500
	41,667		41,667		44,167		44,167

Ordinary Income		Capital Gains	
Dividends received	$1,000	Sale of 2,500 shares at $10.60 =	$26,500
Less interest expense	1,000	Less original basis	25,000
	0		1,500
Nontaxable income	1,000		
	1,000		

A paper by Miller and Scholes [1978] shows that even if the tax on ordinary personal income is greater than the capital gains tax, many individuals need not pay more than the capital gains rate on dividends. The implication is that individuals will be indifferent between payments in the form of dividends or capital gains (if the firm decides to repurchase shares). Thus the firm's value may be unrelated to its dividend policy even in a world with personal and corporate taxes.

To clarify their argument, Miller and Scholes provide the following simple example. Let us suppose we have an initial net worth of $25,000, which is represented wholly by an investment of 2,500 shares worth $10 each in a company that earns $1.00 per share. At the end of the year the company pays $0.40 per share in dividends and retains $0.60. Consequently, its end-of-year price per share is $10.60. In order to neutralize our dividend income for tax purposes, we borrow $16,667 at 6% and invest the proceeds in a risk-free project (such as life insurance or a Keogh account) that pays 6% of tax-deferred interest.[7] Our opening and closing balance sheets and our income statement are given in Table 16.1. Note that by investing in risk-free assets we have not increased the risk of our wealth position. The riskless cash inflows from insurance exactly match the required payments on debt. Our true economic income could be $1,500 in *unrealized* capital gains plus the $1,000 of tax-deferred interest from life insurance or our Keogh account.

Of course, federal tax laws are complex, and these transactions cannot be carried out without some costs.[8] Nevertheless, the above argument is a clever way to demonstrate the fact that ordinary income taxes on dividends can be avoided. The 1986 tax code eliminated interest deductions on all forms of personal debt except housing, where the amount of debt is limited to the original purchase price plus improvements. This shift in the tax code has caused a reorganization of the consumer debt market and made home equity loans a growth business.

---

[7] As of the writing of this book, the interest expense would not be tax deductible to individuals, but the tax rate on dividends has been drastically reduced.

[8] Also the maximum amount of dividends that can be sheltered in this way was $10,000. See Feenberg [1981].

C. $\mathcal{T}$oward a Theory of Optimal Dividend Policy

The Miller-Modigliani [1961] paper proved the irrelevance of dividend policy in a world where there were no taxes or transactions costs and where everyone was fully informed about the distribution of the firm's uncertain future cash flows. Once corporate and personal income taxes were introduced, then the theory (e.g., Farrar and Selwyn [1967] and Brennan [1970]) suggested that perhaps it would be optimal to pay no dividends at all because of the tax disadvantage of ordinary income over capital gains. This point of view was modified somewhat by Miller and Scholes [1978], who showed how dividend income could, to a large extent, be sheltered from taxation. The papers mentioned below go one step further. They provide theories to explain benefits as well as costs of dividend payout in an effort to move toward a theory of optimal dividend policy.

1. A Theory Based on Taxes and Investment Opportunities

The complex individual and corporate tax system in the United States may be an important part of the dividend puzzle. Masulis and Trueman [1988] model the investment and dividend decision under fairly realistic assumptions and show that the cost of deferring dividends may be large enough to induce firms to optimally pay cash dividends. The model assumes the following tax system:

1. Corporations all pay the same effective marginal tax rate, τ_c.
2. Personal tax rates on dividend income, τ_{di}, differ across individuals.
3. Capital gains taxes, τ_g, are effectively zero.
4. The IRS taxes regular corporate repurchases of equity in the same way as dividend payments.
5. There is an 80% dividend exclusion from taxes on all dividends paid by one corporation to another.[9]

In addition, to keep capital structure separate from dividend policy, they assume no debt.

Figure 16.1 illustrates the effect of taxes on the supply and demand for investment funds. Internal capital (retained earnings) and external equity capital (proceeds from new issues) have different costs to the firm. If retained earnings are not reinvested, then the ith shareholder receives the following after-tax return for each dollar paid out as dividends:

$$r_A(1 - \tau_c)(1 - \tau_{di}) = \text{cost of internal funds}, \tag{16.16}$$

where $r_A = $ the pretax return on investments in real assets.

For example, if the pretax return required on investments of equal risk is $r_A = 15\%$, the corporate tax rate is $\tau_c = 50\%$, and the individual's tax rate is 40%, then the individual will be indifferent between (1) earning 9.0% before taxes on corporate investment and (2) receiving dividends.[10] If the individual's tax rate is 20%, a 12% before-tax rate on investment will be required. The higher an individual's tax bracket, the more likely he or she is to want the firm to invest cash flows internally

---

[9] Prior to the 1986 tax code the dividend exclusion rate was 85%.

[10] Given an individual tax rate of 40% and a 15% before-tax rate on investment, the after-tax rate on a dollar paid out as dividends should be

$$r_A(1 - \tau_c)(1 - \tau_{di}) = .15(1 - .5)(1 - .4) = .045.$$

Figure 16.1 Corporate investment and dividend decisions with differing personal tax rates: (a) high tax bracket and (b) low tax bracket.

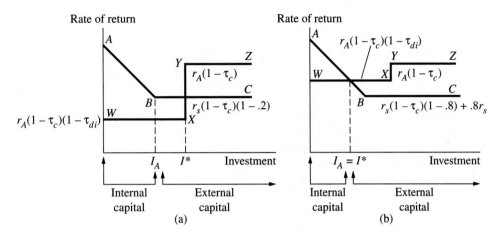

instead of paying dividends, even when investment returns decline with more investment. The line segment WX in Fig. 16.1 represents the cost of capital to current shareholders in different tax brackets. In Fig. 16.1(a) it represents a high-tax-bracket shareholder, and in Fig. 16.1(b), a low-tax-bracket shareholder. At point Y are shareholders who pay no personal taxes at all (e.g., pension funds). They are indifferent between earnings retention and dividend payout because their opportunity cost is the same as the cost of external capital to the firm:

$$r_A(1 - \tau_c) = \text{cost of external funds.} \tag{16.17}$$

External funds are more expensive to the firm because investors do not pay double taxes (corporate and personal) on funds put to other uses. It is assumed that alternative investments earn capital gains only and therefore are not taxed at the personal level. The cost of external equity is illustrated by the horizontal line segment YZ in Fig. 16.1.

The firm has two categories of investment opportunity. First are investments in real assets, represented by line segment AB and assumed to have diminishing returns to scale. Second are investments in securities of other firms. These securities investments have constant returns to scale as illustrated by line segment BC. The before-tax return on investments in securities of other firms is defined as r_s. There is a virtually infinite amount of security investment (in assets of equivalent risk), but their after-tax rate of return to the firm is affected by the fact that it must pay corporate taxes on 20% of the dividends it receives from ownership of other firms. Thus the after-tax return on security investments is

$$r_s(1 - \tau_c)(1 - .80) + .80r_s. \tag{16.18}$$

If the money is kept in the firm, the before-tax return can fall to 9.0% and should give the same after-tax yield, assuming there is no capital gains tax:

$$r_A(1 - \tau_c) = .09(1 - .5) = .045.$$

See Eq. (16.17) for the cost of external equity capital.

To reach its optimal investment/dividend decision the firm in Fig. 16.1(a) uses internal funds to undertake all investments in real assets, I_A, and then invests in securities of other firms up to the amount I^*. At this point it stops because the after-tax return on investing in securities is less than the opportunity cost of capital for externally supplied equity, and we see that the investment in real assets, I_A, is less than total investment, I^*. Since all internal funds have been used, dividends will not be paid out. The high-tax-bracket shareholders in Fig. 16.1(a) prefer low (or zero) dividend payout.

In Fig. 16.1(b), which has the same investment schedule, low-tax-bracket shareholders have a higher opportunity cost for internally generated funds. They will want investment in real assets to stop at $I_A = I^*$. At this point, not all internally generated capital has been spent on real investment and dividends are paid out. For low-tax-bracket shareholders the cost of deferring dividends is sufficiently high that they prefer dividend payout.

One of the implications of this model is that shareholders with different tax rates, τ_{di}, will not unanimously agree on the firm's investment/dividend decision. High-tax-bracket shareholders would prefer the firm to invest more, whereas low-tax-bracket shareholders would prefer less investment and more dividend payout. This lack of unanimity can be diminished somewhat if investors self-select into clienteles with low-tax-bracket individuals purchasing shares of high-dividend firms and vice versa. Empirical evidence on dividend clienteles is reviewed later.

There are (at least) five other implications of the Masulis-Trueman model. (1) Firms are predicted not to externally finance security purchases for investment purposes. However, they are likely to purchase marketable securities with internally generated funds that remain after financing their own profitable production opportunities. (2) Firms with many profitable production opportunities (high-growth firms) will use up all their internally generated funds without paying dividends, but older, more mature firms will pay dividends because not all internally generated funds will be exhausted by investment opportunities. (3) Mergers are predicted between firms where one is internally financing its profitable investments and the other is externally financing. (4) While a decrease in current earnings should leave unchanged the investment expenditures of externally financed firms, it is likely to decrease investment expenditures of firms that initially planned to internally finance all their investments rather than make up the shortfall of funds through external financing. (5) Shareholder disagreement over internally financed investment policy will be more likely the greater the amount of internally generated funds relative to the firm's investment opportunities. In these cases, firms are more likely to experience takeover attempts, proxy fights, and efforts to "go private." Given these tax-induced shareholder conflicts, diffuse ownership is more likely for externally financed firms than for internally financed firms.

2. Theories Based on the Informativeness of Dividend Payout

Ross [1977] suggests that implicit in the Miller-Modigliani dividend irrelevancy proposition is the assumption that the market *knows* the (random) return stream of the firm and values this stream to set the value of the firm. What is valued in the marketplace, however, is the *perceived* stream of returns for the firm. Putting the issue this way raises the possibility that changes in the capital structure (or dividend payout) may alter the market's perception. In the terminology of Modigliani and Miller, a change in the financial structure (or dividend payout) of the firm alters its perceived risk class even though the actual risk class remains unchanged.

Managers, as insiders who have privileged access to information about the firm's expected cash flows, will choose to establish unambiguous signals about the firm's future if they have the proper incentive to do so. We say, in Chapter 15, that changes in the capital structure of the firm may be used as signals. In particular, Ross [1977] proved that an increase in the use of debt can represent an unambiguous signal to the marketplace that the firm's prospects have improved. Empirical evidence seems to confirm the theory.

The signaling concept is easily applied to dividend policy as well as to financial structure. We shall see that a possible benefit of dividends is that they provide valuable signals. This benefit can be balanced against the costs of paying dividends to establish a theory of optimal dividend policy.

A firm that increases dividend payout is signaling that it has expected future cash flows that are sufficiently large to meet debt payments and dividend payments without increasing the probability of bankruptcy. Therefore we may expect to find empirical evidence that shows the value of the firm increases because dividends are taken as signals that the firm is expected to have permanently higher future cash flows. Later on in this chapter, we review the empirical evidence on dividends as signals.

Bhattacharya [1979] develops a model closely related to that of Ross that can be used to explain why firms may pay dividends despite the tax disadvantage of doing so. If investors believe that firms that pay greater dividends per share have higher values, then an unexpected dividend increase will be taken as a favorable signal. Presumably dividends convey information about the value of the firm that cannot be fully communicated by other means such as annual reports, earnings forecasts, or presentations before security analysts. It is expensive for less successful firms to mimic the signal because they must incur extra costs associated with raising external funds in order to pay the dividend.[11] Hence the signaling value of dividends is positive and can be traded off against the tax loss associated with dividend income (as opposed to capital gains). Even firms that are closely held would prefer to pay dividends because the value induced by the signal is received by current owners only when the dividend message is communicated to outsiders. One of the important implications of this signaling argument is that it suggests the possibility of optimal dividend policy. The signaling benefits from paying dividends may be traded off against the tax advantages in order to achieve an optimal payout.

Hakansson [1982] has expanded the understanding of informative signaling to show that in addition to being informative at least one of three sufficient conditions must be met. Either investors must have different probability assessments of dividend payouts, or they must have differing attitudes about how they wish to allocate consumption expenditures over time, or the financial markets must be incomplete. All three of these effects may operate in a complementary fashion, and all three are reasonable.

Miller and Rock [1985] develop a financial signaling model founded on the concept of "net dividends." It is the first theory that explicitly combines dividends and external financing to show that they are merely two sides of the same coin. The announcement that "heads is up" also tells us that "tails is down." As was pointed out in the original Miller-Modigliani [1961] article, every firm is subject to a sources and uses of funds constraint:

$$EBIT + mP + \Delta B = I + Div. \tag{16.19}$$

Recall that sources of funds are $EBIT$, the earnings before interest and taxes; mP, the proceeds from an issue of external equity (the number of new shares, m, times the price per share, P); and ΔB, the proceeds from new debt. Uses of funds are investment, I, and dividends, Div. The sources

---

[11] This suggests that dividend payout and debt level increases are interrelated signals. A firm that simultaneously pays dividends and borrows may be giving a different signal than if it had made the same dividend payment without borrowing.

and uses constraint can be rearranged to have net cash flows from operations on the left-hand side and the firm's "net dividend" on the right-hand side:

$$EBIT - I = Div - \Delta B - mP. \tag{16.20}$$

Now imagine a model where time 1 is the present, time 0 is the past, and time 2 is the future. The present value of the firm, cum dividend, is the value of the current dividend, Div_1, plus the discounted value of cash flows (discounted at the appropriate risk-adjusted rate, k):

$$V_1 = Div_1 + \frac{E(EBIT_2)}{1+k}. \tag{16.21}$$

Original shareholders' wealth is the value of the firm minus the market value of debt and new equity issued:

$$S_1 = V_1 - \Delta B_1 - mP_1 = Div_1 + \frac{E(EBIT_2)}{1+k} - \Delta B_1 - mP_1. \tag{16.22}$$

Using the sources and uses constraint, Eq. (16.20), we have

$$S_1 = EBIT_1 - I_1 + \frac{E(EBIT_2)}{1+k}. \tag{16.23}$$

Without any information asymmetry, this is just the original Miller-Modigliani proposition that dividends are irrelevant. All that counts is the investment decision.

If there is information asymmetry, Eq. (16.23) must be rewritten to show how market expectations are formed. If future earnings depend on current investment, then we can write that net operating income is a function of the amount of investment plus a random error term:

$$EBIT_1 = f(I_0) + \varepsilon_1,$$
$$EBIT_2 = f(I_1) + \varepsilon_2,$$

where ε_1 and ε_2 are random error terms with zero mean, that is, $E(\varepsilon_1) = E(\varepsilon_2) = 0$. We also adopt the special assumption that the expectation of ε_2, given ε_1, is not necessarily zero:

$$E(\varepsilon_2 \mid \varepsilon_1) = \gamma \varepsilon_1.$$

If γ is interpreted as a persistence coefficient, $0 < \gamma < 1$, the market is assumed to only partially adjust to new information (the first-period error). If we use the notation E_0 to remind us that the current value of the firm is based on preannouncement information, then the current expected value of shareholders' wealth is

$$E(S_1) = E_0(EBIT_1) - E_0(I_1) + \frac{E_0\left[f(I_1)\right]}{1+k}$$

$$= f(I_0) - I_1 + \frac{f(I_1)}{1+k}. \tag{16.24}$$

The corresponding postannouncement value of the firm is

$$S_1 = EBIT_1 - I_1 + \frac{E_1(EBIT_2)}{1+k}$$

$$= f(I_0) + \varepsilon_1 - I_1 + \frac{f(I_1) + E_1(\varepsilon_2 \mid \varepsilon_1)}{1+k}$$

$$= f(I_0) + \varepsilon_1 - I_1 + \frac{f(I_1) + \gamma\varepsilon_1}{1+k}. \tag{16.25}$$

Subtracting (16.24) from (16.25) gives the announcement effect

$$S_1 - E(S_1) = \varepsilon_1\left[1 + \frac{\gamma}{1+k}\right]$$

$$= \left[EBIT_1 - E_0(EBIT_1)\right]\left[1 + \frac{\gamma}{1+k}\right]. \tag{16.26}$$

Equation (16.26) says that the announcement effect on shareholders' wealth will depend on the "earnings surprise." Thus we would expect that unexpected changes in earnings will be correlated with share price changes on the announcement date.

Miller and Rock go on to show that the earnings, dividend, and financing announcements are closely related. Assuming that the expected and actual investment decisions are at an optimal level, and are therefore equal, then the difference between the actual and net dividends is

$$Div_1 - \Delta B_1 - m_1 P_1 - E_0(Div_1 - \Delta B_1 - m_1 P_1) = EBIT_1 - I_1 - [E(EBIT_1) - I_1]$$

$$= EBIT_1 - E(EBIT_1).$$

Thus the earnings surprise and the net dividend surprise can convey the same information. The financing announcement effect is merely the dividend announcement effect, but with the sign reversed. An unexpected increase in dividends will increase shareholders' wealth, and an unexpected issue of new equity or debt will be interpreted as bad news about the future prospects of the firm.

The Miller-Rock signaling approach shows that announcement effects (including earnings surprises, unexpected dividend changes, and unexpected external financing) emerge naturally as implications of the basic valuation model rather than as ad hoc appendages.

One problem that the above theories have in common is that although they explain how an optimal dividend policy may arise, none of them can successfully explain cross-sectional differences in dividend payouts across firms.[12]

Brennan and Thakor [1990] note that in spite of the apparent tax advantage of delivering cash to shareholders via share repurchases rather than dividends, firms show little diminished enthusiasm for paying dividends. Signaling to the market about the future prospects of the firms can be accomplished via either delivery mechanism; therefore signaling impact does not appear to be a deciding factor in the choice between repurchases versus dividends.[13] Brennan and Thakor note that dividends are paid pro rata and share repurchases are not (insiders do not participate). Furthermore,

---

[12] A possible exception is the work of Miller and Rock [1985], which suggests that the next theory shows better promise in this regard.

[13] Later in the chapter (see Section H) we present empirical evidence that the signaling impact of dividends actually is stronger than share repurchase—a piece of evidence that Brennan and Thakor did not possess in 1990.

...there is a fixed cost to gathering information, outside shareholders with large positions have more incentive to become informed than outside shareholders with small positions. These uninformed shareholders run the risk of having their wealth expropriated by the better informed shareholders; therefore share repurchases are likely to be associated with a redistribution of wealth from small uninformed shareholders to larger better informed shareholders. The choice of dividends versus repurchase is made by vote with the likely result that small cash distributions will be made by dividends and larger distributions by repurchase.[14]

3. Agency Costs, External Financing, and Optimal Dividend Payout

Rozeff [1982] suggests that optimal dividend policy may exist even though we ignore tax consid-erations. He suggests that cross-sectional regularities in corporate dividend payout ratios[15] may be explained by a trade-off between the flotation costs of raising external capital and the benefit of reduced agency costs when the firm increases the dividend payout. It is not hard to understand that owners prefer to avoid paying the transactions costs associated with external financing.

As discussed earlier (Chapter 15, Section G), there are agency costs that arise when owner-managers sell portfolios of their stockholdings to so-called outside equity owners. The outsiders will charge, ex ante, for the potential problem that owner-managers may increase their personal wealth at the expense of outsiders by means of more perquisites or shirking. To decrease the ex ante charge, owner-managers will find it more in their own interest to agree to incur monitoring or bonding costs if such costs are less than the ex ante charge that outsiders would be forced to request. Thus a wealth-maximizing firm will adopt an optimal monitoring/bonding policy that minimizes agency costs.

Dividend payments may serve as a means of monitoring or bonding management performance. Although greater dividend payout implies costly external financing, the very fact that the firm must go to the capital markets implies that it will come under greater scrutiny. For example, banks will require a careful analysis of the creditworthiness of the firm, and the Securities and Exchange Commission will require prospectus filings for new equity issues. Thus outside suppliers of capital help to monitor the owner-manager on behalf of outside equity owners. Of course, audited financial statements are a substitute means for supplying the same information, but they may not be a perfect substitute for the "adversary" relationship between the firm and suppliers of new capital.

Because of the transactions costs of external financing, Rozeff also argues that the variability of a firm's cash flows will affect its dividend payout. Consider two firms with the same average cash flows across time but different variability. The firm with greater volatility will borrow in bad years and repay in good. It will need to finance externally more often. Consequently, it will tend to have a lower dividend payout ratio.

Rozeff [1982] selected a sample of 1,000 unregulated firms in 64 different industries and examined their average dividend payout ratios during the 1974–1980 interval. Five proxy variables were chosen to test his theory. The results are shown in Table 16.2. The independent variables *GROW*1 and *GROW*2 are an attempt to measure the effect of costly external financing. Firms that grow faster can reduce their need to use external financing by paying lower dividends. *GROW*1

---

[14] The authors of the paper acknowledge that they deliberately ignore the role of management (and other insiders) as informed partners whose percentage ownership unambiguously goes up in repurchase.

[15] The payout ratio is the ratio of dividends to net income.

Table 16.2 Cross-Sectional Dividend Payout Regressions

	CONSTANT	INS	GROW1	GROW2	BETA	STOCK	R^2	F-statistic
(1)	47.81	−0.090	−0.321	−0.526	−26.543	2.584	0.48	185.47
	(12.83)	(−4.10)	(−6.38)	(−6.43)	(−17.05)	(7.73)		
(2)	24.73	−0.068	−0.474	−0.758	—	2.517	0.33	123.23
	(6.27)	(−2.75)	(−8.44)	(−8.28)		(6.63)		
(3)	70.63	—	−0.402	−0.603	−25.409	—	0.41	231.46
	(40.35)		(−7.58)	(−6.94)	(−15.35)			
(4)	39.56	−0.116	—	—	−33.506	3.151	0.39	218.10
	(10.02)	(−4.92)			(−21.28)	(8.82)		
(5)	1.03	−0.102	—	—	—	3.429	0.12	69.33
	(0.24)	(−3.60)				(7.97)		

Note: t-statistics are shown in parentheses under estimated values of the regression coefficients. R^2 is adjusted for degrees of freedom.
From M. Rozeff, "Growth, Beta, and Agency Costs as Determinants of Dividend Payout Ratios," *Journal of Financial Research*, Fall 1982, 249–259. Reprinted with permission.

measures the growth rate in revenues between 1974 and 1979, whereas *GROW*2 is Value Line's forecast of growth of sales revenue over the five-year period 1979–1984. Both variables are negatively related to dividend payout and are statistically significant. The variables *INS* and *STOCK* are proxies for the agency relationship. *INS* is the percentage of insiders; given a lower percentage of outsiders, there is less need to pay dividends to reduce agency costs.[16] On the other hand, if the distribution of outsider holdings is diffuse, then agency costs will be higher; hence one would expect *STOCK*, the number of stockholders, to be positively related to dividend payout. Both *INS* and *STOCK* are statistically significant and of the predicted sign. Finally, the variable *BETA* measures the riskiness of the firm. The prediction that riskier firms have lower dividend payout is verified by the regression.

The best regression in Table 16.2 (regression (1)) explains 48% of the cross-sectional variability in dividend payout across individual firms. Although the results cannot be used to distinguish among various theories of optimal dividend policy, they are consistent with Rozeff's predictions. Furthermore, the very existence of strong cross-sectional regularities suggests that there may be an optimal dividend policy.

D. Behavioral Models of Dividend Policy

Lintner [1956] conducted interviews with 28 carefully selected companies to investigate their thinking on the determination of dividend policy. His fieldwork suggested that (1) managers focused on the change in the existing rate of dividend payout, not on the amount of the newly established payout as such; (2) most managements sought to avoid making changes in their

---

[16] This relationship is also consistent with the tax argument that assumes that high tax bracket insiders prefer to take their return in the form of capital gains rather than dividends.

dividend rates that might have to be reversed within a year or so; (3) major changes in earnings "out of line" with existing dividend rates were the most important determinants of a company's dividend decisions; and (4) investment requirements generally had little effect on modifying the pattern of dividend behavior. Taken together, these observations suggest that most companies had somewhat flexible but nevertheless reasonably well-defined standards regarding the speed with which they would try to move toward a full adjustment of dividend payout to earnings. Lintner suggests that corporate dividend behavior can be described on the basis of the following equation:

$$\Delta Div_{it} = a_i + c_i(Div_{it}^* - Div_{i,t-1}) + U_{it}, \tag{16.27}$$

where

ΔDiv_{it} = the change in dividends,

c_i = the speed of adjustment to the difference between a target dividend payout and last year's payout,

Div_{it}^* = the target dividend payout,

$Div_{i,t-1}$ = last period's dividend payout,

$a_i U_{it}$ = a constant and a normally distributed random error term.

The target dividend payout, Div_{it}^*, is a fraction, r_i, of this period's earnings, NI_{it}. Upon fitting the equations to annual data from 1918 through 1941, Lintner finds that the model explains 85% of the changes in dividends for his sample of companies. The average speed of adjustment is approximately 30% per year, and the target payout is 50% of earnings.

Fama and Babiak [1968] investigate many different models for explaining dividend behavior. They use a sample of 201 firms with 17 years of data (1947–1964), then test each explanatory model by using it (1) to explain dividend policy for a holdout sample of 191 firms and (2) to predict dividend payments one year hence. Of the many models that they try, the two best are Lintner's model in Eq. (16.27) and a similar model that suppresses the constant term and adds a term for the lagged level of earnings. The second model does slightly better than Lintner's.

Brav, Graham, Harvey, and Michaely [2003] survey 384 CFOs and treasurers to determine key factors that drive dividend and repurchase policy. They find that, except under extraordinary circumstances, managers have a strong desire not to cut dividends. As a result, for firms that pay dividends, they tend to be smoothed from year to year and linked to sustainable long-run changes in profitability. They also find that managers are reluctant to increase dividends in conjunction with increases in earnings since they no longer have target payout ratios and are more likely to use repurchases as an alternative. Managers view repurchase decisions as more flexible and tend to repurchase out of temporary earnings after investment and liquidity needs are met and when good investments are hard to find. Managers like to repurchase their stock when they believe their stock price is low, and they are very conscious of the effect of repurchases on EPS.

One can conclude that U.S. corporations seem to increase dividends only after they are reasonably sure that they will be able to maintain them permanently at the new level. However, this does not help to answer the question of why corporations pay dividends in the first place.

E. Clientele Effects and Ex Date Effects

1. The Dividend Clientele Effect

The dividend clientele effect was originally suggested by Miller and Modigliani [1961]:

> If for example the frequency distribution of corporate payout ratios happened to correspond exactly with the distribution of investor preferences for payout ratios, then the existence of these preferences would clearly lead ultimately to a situation whose implications were different, in no fundamental respect, from the perfect market case. Each corporation would tend to attract to itself a "clientele" consisting of those preferring its particular payout ratio, but one clientele would be as good as another in terms of the valuation it would imply for firms.

The clientele effect is a possible explanation for management reluctance to alter established payout ratios because such changes might cause current shareholders to incur unwanted transactions costs.

Elton and Gruber [1970] attempt to measure clientele effects by observing the average price decline when a stock goes ex-dividend. If we were current shareholders and sold our stock the instant before it went ex-dividend, we would receive its price, P_B, and pay the capital gains rate, t_g, on the difference between the selling price and the price at which it was purchased, P_c. Alternatively, we could sell the stock after it went ex-dividend. In this case we would receive the dividend, div, and pay the ordinary tax rate, t_0, on it. In addition, we would pay a capital gains tax on the difference between its ex-dividend price, P_A, and the original purchase price, P_c. To prevent arbitrage profits, our gain from either course of action must be the same, namely,

$$P_B - t_g(P_B - P_c) = P_A - t_g(P_A - P_c) + div(1 - t_0). \tag{16.28}$$

Rearranging (16.28) we get

$$\frac{P_B - P_A}{div} = \frac{1 - t_0}{1 - t_g}. \tag{16.29}$$

Therefore the ratio of the decline in stock price to the dividend paid becomes a means of estimating the marginal tax rate of the average investor, if we assume that the capital gains rate is half the ordinary tax rate, as it was during the time period used by Elton and Gruber for their empirical test.

Using 4,148 observations between April 1, 1966, and March 31, 1967, Elton and Gruber [1970] discovered that the average price decline as a percentage of dividend paid was 77.7%. This implied that the marginal tax bracket of the average investor was 36.4%. They continued by arguing that

> . . . the lower a firm's dividend yield the smaller the percentage of his total return that a stockholder expects to receive in the form of dividends and the larger the percentage he expects to receive in the form of capital gains. Therefore, investors who held stocks which have high dividend yields should be in low tax brackets relative to stockholders who hold stocks with low dividend yield.

Table 16.3 Dividend Yield Statistics Ranked by Decile

| | div/P | $(P^B - P_A)/div$ | | Probability True Mean Is | Implied |
Decile	Mean	Mean	Standard Deviation	One or More	Tax Bracket
1	.0124	.6690	.8054	.341	.4974
2	.0216	.4873	.2080	.007	.6145
3	.0276	.5447	.1550	.002	.5915
4	.0328	.6246	.1216	.001	.5315
5	.0376	.7953	.1064	.027	.3398
6	.0416	.8679	.0712	.031	.2334
7	.0452	.9209	.0761	.113	.1465
8	.0496	.9054	.0691	.085	.1747
9	.0552	1.0123	.0538	.591	†
10	.0708	1.1755	.0555	.999	†

* Spearman's rank correlation coefficient between div/P and $(P_B - P_A)/div$ is .9152, which is significant at the 1% level.
† Indeterminate.
From E. J. Elton and M. J. Gruber, "Marginal Stockholders' Tax Rates and the Clientele Effect," reprinted with permission from *Review of Economics and Statistics*, February 1970, 72.

Table 16.3 shows the dividend payout ranked from the lowest to highest deciles along with (1) the average drop in price as a percentage of dividends and (2) the implied tax bracket. Note that the implied tax bracket decreases when dividend payout increases. Elton and Gruber conclude that the evidence suggests that Miller and Modigliani were right in hypothesizing a clientele effect.

A possible counterargument to this interpretation, provided by Kalay [1977, 1982], is that arbitrage may also be carried out by traders who *do not own* the stock initially. They would not receive favored capital gains treatment but would have to pay ordinary income taxes on short-term gains. Their arbitrage profit, π, may be stated mathematically as

$$\pi = -P_B + div - t_0 div + P_A + t_0(P_B - P_A). \tag{16.30}$$

They spend P_B to acquire the stock before it goes ex-dividend, then receive the dividend and pay ordinary income taxes on it, and finally sell the stock after it goes ex-dividend (receiving P_A dollars) and receive a tax shield from their short-term loss. Rearranging (16.30), we see that their profit is

$$\pi = (1 - t_0)(P_A - P_B + div). \tag{16.31}$$

To prevent arbitrage profits, the price decline must equal the amount of dividend payout (i.e., $P_B - P_A = div$).

The above condition is completely different from Eq. (16.28), proposed by Elton and Gruber. Of course neither model has taken transactions costs into account. Eades, Hess, and Kim [1984] replicate the Elton and Gruber work but report their results in the form of rates of return. If the price decline on the ex-date is less than the amount of the dividend, then the ex-date return,

$$R_t = \frac{P_{t+1} - P_t + div_t}{P_t},$$

will be positive. For the time period July 2, 1962, to April 30, 1975, they find the average ex-date excess return to be .176% (statistically significant). This time interval predates the era of negotiated commissions. On May 1, 1975, all brokerage commissions were competitively negotiated, and presumably transactions costs fell. For the time interval May 1, 1975, to December 31, 1980, Eades, Hess, and Kim found the ex-date return to be significantly lower—only .064%. This result suggests that, given lower transactions costs, it was easier for short-term traders to arbitrage, as was suggested by Kalay and Eq. (16.31).

Bell and Jenkinson [2002] study the July 1997 change in the law in the United Kingdom that increased the taxes on dividend income received by pension funds by approximately £5 billion per year. Prior to 1997 the UK had a dividend imputation tax system where dividend-paying corporations withheld taxes on dividend distributions, then issued a tax credit to investors. Tax-exempt investors (e.g., pension funds) could then receive a full cash refund from the government—a feature that resulted in their strong preference for high dividend yield states. The main effect of the 1997 tax reform was to abolish the right of the exempt investors to reclaim tax credits, thereby causing them to be indifferent between share repurchases and dividend payout. Bell and Jenkinson measure the ex-dividend date drop-off ratio as the slope coefficient, β, in a regression that defines the dependent variable as the percent change in the stock price, measured as the price cum dividend, P_c, minus the price on the ex-dividend day, P_e, divided by P_c:

$$DOR_i = \frac{P_c - P_e}{P_c} = \alpha + \beta \left(\frac{D}{P_c}\right) + \epsilon_i$$

and the independent variable as the dividend divided by the price cum dividend. All median drop-off ratios were significantly lower after the tax reform than before (0.89 before versus 0.78 after), and the largest change was for large companies. They find strong clientele effects with *DOR*s being positively related to the level of dividend yields.

Although there is almost surely a significant drop in price on the ex-dividend date that may be interpreted (in a world without transactions costs) as a tax-affected decline because the drop-off is less than 100%, several authors have pointed out that alternate explanations are also possible. Frank and Jaganathan [1998] study ex-date price declines in Hong Kong, where neither capital gains nor dividends were taxed. The average dividend for the period 1980–1993 was HK $0.12, and the average price drop was HK $0.06. They account for the drop by recognizing that most trades tend to occur at the bid on the last date before the stock goes ex-dividend and at the ask on the ex-date. Bali and Hite [1998] present a similar argument (using U.S. data) based on the fact that quotes were offered in eighths rather than in decimal form.

Eades, Hess, and Kim [1984] also examine ex-date dividend returns for a nonconvertible preferred stock sample, characterized by a relatively large preferred dividend yield. During the sample period, January 1, 1974, to December 31, 1981, these securities had a total of 708 ex-days that occurred on 493 trading days. The average excess return was a significantly negative −.141%. This implies that the stock price fell by more than the amount of the dividend. These results are consistent with tax-induced clienteles if the marginal purchasers are corporations. Corporations are able to exclude 85% of any dividends (80% following the 1986 tax code) received as taxable income, whereas capital gains are taxable at rates as high as 46% (less following the 1986 tax code) if they are short-term capital gains. To see how the price might fall by more than the dividend, suppose the preferred stock is worth $40 and it pays a $4 dividend. If the marginal purchaser is a corporation, it receives the following returns:

$$[div - .46(.15)div] + (P_B - P_A)(1 - .46).$$

The first term is the dividend minus the taxable portion (15% of the dividend times the tax rate); the second term is the tax shelter from the short-term capital loss (taxed at 46%). If we set this return equal to zero and solve, we have

$$\frac{P_B - P_A}{div} = \frac{-[1 - .46(.15)]}{1 - .46} = -172.4\%.$$

Thus the stock price could fall by as much as $4(1.724) = $6.90 in our example before the corporation would not profit. For large dividends and on preferred stock we tend to see security prices bid up prior to ex-dates.

Table 16.4 shows the pattern of excess returns and t-statistics for all taxable distributions on NYSE common stocks. The puzzle here is that abnormal returns are not uniquely associated with the ex-day. No good explanation for this result has yet been proposed.

Finally, Eades, Hess, and Kim report on the ex-date behavior of nontaxable corporate distributions. They find significant positive returns for stock splits and stock dividends (later confirmed by Grinblatt, Masulis, and Titman [1984]) and significant negative returns for nontaxable cash dividends (primarily of high-yielding utilities). Although there is no explanation for the abnormally positive split ex-date returns, we may conjecture that tax arbitrage (short-term capital gains shelters) may explain the negative returns on nontaxable cash dividends.

Lakonishok and Vermaelen [1986] test the hypothesis of tax arbitrage by studying trading volume around the ex-date. If there is tax arbitrage, then volume should be abnormally high around

Table 16.4 Excess Rates of Return for Equally Weighted Ex-Date Portfolios, 1962–1980

Trading Day Relative to Ex-Day	Average Percent Excess Return	t-statistic
−5	.067	4.128
−4	.046	4.155
−3	.061	5.561
−2	.066	5.968
−1	.188	15.647
Ex-day	.142	11.741
+1	−.053	−4.355
+2	−.058	−4.911
+3	−.036	−2.707
+4	−.046	−4.195
+5	−.043	−3.700

From K. Eades, P. Hess, and E. H. Kim, "On Interpreting Security Returns during the Ex-Dividend Period," reprinted with permission from *Journal of Financial Economics*, March 1984, 20. © North-Holland.

ex-dates, and it should be positively related to dividend yield and negatively related to transactions costs. Their results show that trading volume does increase significantly around ex-dates and that it is more pronounced for high-yield, actively traded stocks and during the period following the introduction of negotiated trading commissions.

Pettit [1977] has tested for dividend clientele effects by examining the portfolio positions of approximately 914 individual accounts handled by a large retail brokerage house between 1964 and 1970. He argues that stocks with low dividend yields will be preferred by investors with high incomes, by younger investors, by investors whose ordinary and capital gains tax rates differ substantially, and by investors whose portfolios have high systematic risk. His model is

$$DY_i = a_1 + a_2\beta_i + a_3AGE_i + a_4INC_i + a_5DTR_i + \varepsilon_i, \tag{16.32}$$

where

DY_i = dividend yield for the ith individual's portfolio in 1970,

β_i = the systematic risk of the ith individual's portfolio,

AGE_i = the age of the individual,

INC_i = the gross family income averaged over the last three years,

DTR_i = the difference between the income and capital gains tax rates for the ith individual,

ε_i = a normally distributed random error term.

He finds that[17]

$$DY_i = \quad 0.42 \quad - \quad .021\beta_i \quad + \quad .031\,AGE_i \quad - \quad .037\,INC_i \quad + \quad .006\,DTR_i.$$
$$\quad\quad (11.01) \quad\quad (-16.03) \quad\quad (6.15) \quad\quad (-2.25) \quad\quad (1.57)$$

The evidence suggests that there is a clientele effect because a significant portion of the observed cross-sectional variation in individual portfolio dividend yields can be explained. However, the study in no way suggests that the market price of a security is determined by the dividend policy followed by the firm.

A second study by Lewellen, Stanley, Lease, and Schlarbaum [1978] was drawn from the same database as the Pettit study but reached different conclusions. They ran a multiple regression to explain the dividend yields of investor portfolios as a function of various investor characteristics. Although the tax rate variable was negatively related to dividend yield and was statistically significant, it implied that a 10% increase in an investor's marginal (imputed) tax bracket was associated with only a .1% decline in the yield of securities held. This suggests only a very weak dividend clientele effect.

Baker and Wurgler [2002] develop a theory in which the decision to pay dividends is driven by investor demand. Specifically, managers cater to investors by initiating dividends when investors put a relatively high stock price on dividend payers and omit dividends when nonpayers are preferred. They empirically test this hypothesis by relating the rates of dividend initiation and the difference between stock prices of payers and nonpayers. Specifically they regress the initiation rate on four measures of investor demands for payers—the difference in the log of the market

---

[17] The numbers in parentheses are t-statistics. The r^2 was .3 for 914 observations.

Table 16.5 Regression Results: Total Debt to Total Capital Ratios vs. Shareholder Characteristics[a]

Independent Variable	Estimated Coefficient $(\times 10^{-2})$	Standard Error $(\times 10^{-2})$	t-statistic
Constant term	45.69	2.72	16.82[c]
Shareholder characteristics			
Sex	2.38	0.72	3.31[c]
Educational level	−0.31	0.08	−3.74[c]
Employment status	1.30	0.64	2.00[b]
Marginal tax rate	−6.81	2.19	−3.11[c]
Age	−0.07	0.03	−2.28[b]
Family size	−0.13	0.24	−0.56
Marital status	0.14	0.76	0.18

a. Variables listed in stepwise entry order: $R^2 = 0.008$, $N = 6,217$, $F = 7.51$.
b. Denotes significance at the 0.05 level.
c. Denotes significance at the 0.01 level.
From E. H. Kim, W. Lewellen, and J. McConnell, "Financial Leverage Clienteles: Theory and Evidence," reprinted with permission of *Journal of Financial Economics*, March 1979, 106. © North-Holland.

to book ratios of payers and nonpayers (the dividend premium), the difference in values between Citizens Utility cash dividend and stock dividend shares, the average announcement effect of recent initiations and the difference between future returns on indices of payers and nonpayers. They find that the dividend premium variable explains 60% of the variation in aggregate initiations. They explore other possible explanations for this result, including the clientele effect, and conclude that catering is the "most natural explanation."

2. Debt Clientele Effects

Investors can choose to borrow on their personal account or to invest in levered firms, thereby using the corporation's tax shelter on debt. In Chapter 15 we discussed the possibility of debt clientele effects. Personal debt will be preferred to corporate debt by individuals in high marginal personal tax brackets, and low-income investors will prefer to invest in firms with high leverage.

Kim, Lewellen, and McConnell [1979] and Harris, Roenfeldt, and Cooley [1983] tested for leverage-related clientele effects. The first study used a data set consisting of 1,140 companies whose stock was owned by at least three investors from among a group of 887. Questionnaires provided demographic and income data for the investors during a three-year period from 1969 to 1971. From these data the marginal tax rates of the investors were determined. Table 16.5 shows the results of a multiple regression that explains the corporate total debt to total capital ratio as a function of various shareholder characteristics. The coefficients of five of the seven independent variables are statistically significant as is the overall significance of the regression ($F = 7.51$). The coefficient of the investor tax rate is the correct sign and is statistically significant, but its magnitude indicates that an increase in an investor's personal tax rate from zero to 70% is associated with an increase of only 5% in the corporate leverage ratio. Kim, Lewellen, and McConnell [1979] suggest, "A relationship that slight has to be interpreted as somewhat less than strongly supportive of the financial leverage clientele hypothesis."

Harris, Roenfeldt, and Cooley [1983] estimate investor-implied tax rates by using the Elton and Gruber procedure, Eq. (16.29). They then examine a sample of large firms, 1968–1976, to see if firms with high leverage have investors with low tax rates, and vice versa. They find that implied tax rates are strongly negatively correlated with corporate financial leverage, thereby lending further support to the leverage clientele hypothesis.

Allen, Bernardo, and Welch [2000] provide a theory of dividends based on tax clienteles. They propose to solve two puzzles. First is the inclination of firms to pay dividends, even in tax regimes that seemingly support repurchases because they are taxed less. For example, in the U.S. from 1984 to 1988, repurchases increased from 6% to 38% of earnings, but dividends increased from 44% to 51%. The second puzzle is the inclination of firms to smooth dividends. The clienteles in the paper are characterized as "untaxed institutions" and "taxed individuals." Managers are assumed to know more about the future of the firm and institutions are assumed to be better able than individuals to discover this information. Therefore dividends attract institutions as clientele, making it more likely that the true information will be revealed in a separating equilibrium.

F. Dividend Announcement Date Effects: The Signaling Hypothesis

The announcement of a dividend will convey information about the future prospects of the firm if the dividend has an unexpected (or "surprise") component. Thus, abnormal rates of return on the *announcement* date are a test of the information signalling content of the dividend. *Ex-date* abnormal returns reflect tax clientele effects that accrue to the shareholder of record on the ex-date. Thus, the total effect of a dividend is the sum of both announcement date and ex-date effects. The previous section of this chapter reviewed ex-date effects, and now we focus our attention on announcement date effects. There is little literature that studies the combined effects. Most firms that pay dividends exhibit behavior that results in constant dividend payouts that are increased only when management is relatively certain that the higher dividend payout can be maintained indefinitely. Given this type of management behavior, it is likely that investors will interpret an increase in current dividend payout as a message that management anticipates permanently higher levels of cash flows from investment. We may therefore expect to observe an increase in share prices associated with public announcement of a dividend increase. The dividend per se does not affect the value of the firm. Instead it serves as a message from management that the firm is anticipated to do better. If dividend changes are to have an impact on share values, it is necessary that they convey information about future cash flows, but it is not sufficient. The same information may be provided to investors via other sources.[18] Therefore it becomes an empirical question whether or not announcements of dividend changes actually affect share value.

The first study to look at this issue was the stock split study of Fama, Fisher, Jensen, and Roll [1969], which was discussed in Chapter 11. They found that when splits were accompanied by dividend announcements, there was an increase in adjusted share prices for the group that announced dividend increases and a decline in share prices for the dividend decrease group. Other studies of the effect of unexpected dividend changes on share prices have been made by Pettit [1972], Watts [1973], Kwan [1981], and Aharony and Swary [1980].

---

[18] Ross [1977] argues that an increase in dividend payout is an unambiguous message because (1) it cannot be mimicked by firms that do not anticipate higher earnings and (2) management has an incentive to "tell the truth."

Watts found a positive dividend announcement effect but concluded that the information content is of no economic significance because it would not enable a trader with monopolistic access to the information to earn abnormal returns after transactions cost. On the other hand, Pettit found clear support for the proposition that the market uses dividend announcements as information for assessing security values. Their methodologies are also different. Watts proceeded in two stages. First, he developed a model to predict dividend changes. It is the same model that Fama and Babiak [1968] found to provide the best prediction of the next period's dividends. It may be written as follows:

$$\Delta Div_t = \beta_1 Div_{t-1} + \beta_2 NI_t + \beta_3 NI_{t-1} + Z_t, \tag{16.33}$$

where

$$\Delta Div_t = \text{the change in dividends in period } t,$$
$$Div_{t-1} = \text{the previous period's dividends,}$$
$$NI_t = \text{this period's earnings,}$$
$$NI_{t-1} = \text{last period's earnings,}$$
$$Z_t = \text{unanticipated dividend changes (the error term).}$$

Using this equation, we are able to estimate unanticipated dividend changes, Z_t. Next, an abnormal performance index that measures departures from the risk-adjusted rate of return can be constructed from the market model,

$$R_{jt} = \alpha + \beta_j R_{mt} + \varepsilon_{jt}, \tag{16.34}$$

where

$$R_{jt} = \text{the total return (dividends and capital gains) on the common stock of the } j\text{th firm,}$$
$$\beta_j = \text{a constant term,}$$
$$R_{mt} = \text{systematic risk,}$$
$$\varepsilon_{jt} = \text{the abnormal performance of the } j\text{th security.}$$

The abnormal performance index (API) for a security is computed as the product of its one-month returns:

$$API = \prod_{t=1}^{T}(1 + \varepsilon_{jt}), \quad T = 1, \ldots, N.$$

Watts looked at the abnormal performance index averaged across 310 firms. The abnormal performance index for 24 months around the dividend announcement for the subsamples of firms that had unanticipated dividend increases or decreases is given in Table 16.6. The performance of firms with dividend increases is better than that of firms with dividend decreases, but the greatest difference between the two samples in the 6 months around the dividend change is only .7% in the month of the dividend. This is a trivial difference.

Pettit used both monthly and daily data to investigate the abnormal performance index of firms that had dividend changes of −1% to −99%, 1% to 10%, 10% to 25%, and over 25%. Figure 16.2

Table 16.6 Abnormal Performance Indices for Subsamples of Firms with Unanticipated Dividend Changes

Month Relative to Last Month of Fiscal Year	API		χ^2 **Statistic for Sign of Stock Return Residual for Month and Dividend Residual for Year**	Total API
	$\hat{z}_{i,t} > 0$	$\hat{z}_{i,t} < 0$		
−11	0.996	0.995	0.2	0.995
−10	0.998	0.997	0.3	0.998
−9	1.003	1.002	1.9	1.002
−8	1.002	1.002	4.0	1.002
−7	1.004	1.001	2.5	1.002
−6	1.004	0.999	2.6	1.001
−5	1.003	1.000	0.6	1.002
−4	1.001	0.999	0.3	1.000
−3	1.000	0.997	0.0	0.998
−2	1.003	1.001	2.6	1.002
−1	1.006	1.001	4.0	1.004
0	1.009	1.002	0.1	1.006
1	1.003	0.996	0.0	1.000
2	1.005	0.999	0.6	1.002
3	1.010	1.005	0.0	1.008
4	1.011	1.004	1.4	1.007
5	1.011	1.004	0.0	1.008
6	1.012	1.003	3.3	1.008
7	1.011	1.003	0.2	1.007
8	1.010	1.001	0.2	1.006
9	1.007	1.000	0.4	1.004
10	1.011	1.002	1.5	1.007
11	1.012	1.006	3.4	1.009
12	1.014	1.006	1.2	1.010

Note: Probability $(\chi^2 > 3.84 \mid x^2 = 0) = .05$ for 1 df; probability $(\chi^2 > 6.64 \mid x^2 = 0) = .01$ for 1 df.
From R. Watts, "The Information Content of Dividends," reprinted from *Journal of Business*, April 1973, 206.

shows the cumulative abnormal performance index using daily data for 135 firms. Most of the price adjustment takes place very quickly either on the dividend announcement date or on the following day. Furthermore, the price changes appear to be significant. This leads Pettit to conclude that substantial information is conveyed by the announcement of dividend changes.

Pettit's results have been criticized because he used the observed dividend changes rather than the *unexpected* dividend changes. Kwan [1981] has improved on Pettit's design by forming portfolios based on unexpected dividend changes, and he finds statistically significant abnormal returns when firms announce unexpectedly large dividend changes. A study by Aharony and Swary [1980] separates the information content of quarterly earnings reports from that of unexpected quarterly

Figure 16.2 Abnormal performance index for dividend announcement effects, using daily data. (From R. Pettit, "Dividend Announcements, Security Performance and Capital Market Efficiency," reprinted with permission of *Journal of Finance*, December 1972, 1004.)

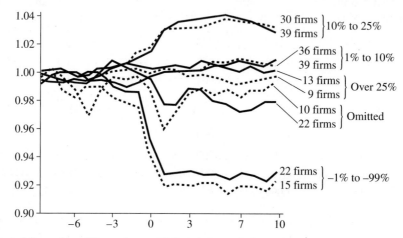

Dashed line, where different from solid line, indicates index performance when companies with announcements other than dividend announcements were eliminated from the sample.

dividend changes. They examine only those quarterly dividend and earnings announcements made public on different dates within any given quarter. Their findings strongly support the hypothesis that changes in quarterly cash dividends provide useful information beyond that provided by corresponding quarterly earnings numbers. Kane, Lee, and Marcus [1984] also select a set of firms whose quarterly dividend and earnings announcements are separated by at least 10 days, build models to predict expected earnings and dividends, and then to test to see if unexpected dividend and earnings announcements corroborate each other—in other words, is there an interaction effect? Their empirical results confirm the earlier studies that found that both earnings and dividend announcements have a significant effect on share price, and in addition they find a significant corroboration effect.

Woolridge [1983] studies the effect of dividend announcements on nonconvertible bonds and nonconvertible preferred stock in an attempt to separate expropriation effects from announcement effects. If dividend payouts to shareholders are viewed as payments of collaterizable assets, and if debt covenants are imperfect protection, then debt holders and preferred shareholders would view dividend increases as bad news and the market value of their claims on the firm would fall upon the announcement of dividend increases. On the other hand, if dividend increases are signals about higher future cash flows, then bondholders and preferred stockholders should feel more secure and the market value of their claims should increase. Woolridge's empirical results support the signaling hypothesis (or at least the conclusion that the signaling effect dominates any expropriation effect). Announcement date abnormal returns are positive given unexpected dividend increases and negative given unexpected dividend decreases. Handjiinicolaou and Kalay [1984] find that for a sample of 255 nonconvertible bonds, prices are unaffected by unexpected dividend increases but react negatively to dividend reductions. They interpret this as evidence consistent with the dividend signaling hypothesis.

Asquith and Mullins [1983] and Richardson, Sefcik, and Thompson [1986] study the effect on shareholder wealth of the initial dividend announcement—the firm's first dividend (most firms had never paid a dividend, although a few had not paid a dividend for 10 years). Both studies find large, statistically significant two-day announcement abnormal returns for initial dividend announcements, 3.7% to 4.0%. In addition, Richardson, Sefcik, and Thompson (and Asquith and Krasker [1985]) study trading volume around the announcement date, and between the announcement and ex-dates. Unusual trading volume may be evidence of clientele changes induced when high-tax-bracket shareholders sell out to low-tax-bracket investors when the higher dividend payout is announced. Both studies find statistically significant abnormal volume increases during the announcement week that are related to the information content of dividends. There is only weak evidence for higher volume following the announcement and hence only weak support for clientele adjustments.

Another way to test the signaling hypothesis is to look for evidence of an abnormal level of insider trading before the dividend announcement. John and Long [1991] do so and find that insider trading immediately prior to the announcement of dividend initiations has significant explanatory power. Given insider selling, the announcement date excess returns are significantly lower than given insider buying.

Brickley [1983] studies the announcement effect of specially designated dividends—those labeled by management as "extra," "special," or "year-end," and compares them to surrounding regular dividend increases. Specially designated dividends are interesting because they are not intended to be a part of continuing higher dividend payout and may therefore not be interpreted by the market as a signal about higher future cash flows. Brickley's results support the opposite conclusion—namely, that the market does react positively to the information content of specially designated dividends but that dollar-for-dollar regular dividends convey more information.

Nissim and Ziv [2001] directly test the relationship between dividend changes and the level of profitability in subsequent years. Instead of modeling expected earnings as a random walk with a drift (a naive approach), they develop and test a model that predicts future earnings changes, deflated by the book value of equity, as a lower function of the rate of change in dividend per share and prior year's ratio of earnings to the book value of equity. They find that dividend changes in the current time period are positively related to unexpected positive earnings changes in each of the following two years. Therefore they conclude that there is strong information content in dividend increases (although their results were not symmetric, i.e., dividend decreases were not related to future profitability).

DeAngelo and DeAngelo [1990] studied the dividend policy adjustments of 80 financially distressed NYSE firms during 1980–1985. Almost all reduced their dividend payout, but unless forced by debt covenants, few omitted dividends altogether. Also, firms that had established long continuous dividend histories were more reluctant to omit dividends than the remainder of the sample.

Fama and French [2001] report a remarkably reduced propensity for industrial firms to pay dividends. During the period 1978–1998 the number of dividend-paying industrials declined over 50%. DeAngelo, DeAngelo, and Skinner [2002] confirm these results and go on to show that in spite of the dramatic reduction in the number of firms paying dividends, the aggregate amount of dividends paid went up 207% in nominal terms and 16% in real terms (1978–2000). Therefore the *concentration* of dividends in the set of large firms increased (see Table 16.7). In 2000, for e~ 75% of total industrial company dividends were paid by just 75 firms. The number of ~ real dividends of $100 million or more increased from 42 in 1978 to 75 in 2000, and

Table 16.7 Concentration of Dividends and Earnings among U.S. Industrial Firms

Dividend Ranking	*Percent of Total Dividends*		*Percent of Total Earnings*	
	1978	**2000**	**1978**	**2000**
Top 100	67.3	81.0	57.5	72.9
101–200	11.8	10.5	13.5	12.5
201–300	6.3	4.1	7.2	6.5
301–400	4.0	2.0	5.1	3.1
401–500	2.8	1.1	3.8	2.3
501–600	1.9	.6	2.5	1.5
601–700	1.4	.4	2.0	.5
701–800	1.0	.2	1.5	.5
801–900	.8	.1	1.4	.3
901–1,000	.6	.0	1.0	.0

Source: DeAngelo, DeAngelo, and Skinner [2000]. (© 2000, with permission from Elsevier.)

paid increased by $10.6 billion. Over the same period 1,069 firms that paid $5 million or less decreased their aggregate payout by $1.1 billion (which was 86% of the total decline in dividends paid). One must conclude that over the past two decades there has been a remarkable increase in the concentration of dividend payout among large firms with commensurate large earnings. Nevertheless, DeAngelo, DeAngelo, and Skinner find, in spite of the fact that fewer firms are paying dividends, that the dividend payout ratio is not significantly changed between 1978 and 2000, both in aggregate and for the subset of firms that do not pay dividends.

In sum the evidence in support of the informational content of dividends is overwhelming. Unexpected dividend changes do convey information to the market about expected future cash flows.

G. The Relationship between Dividends and Value

In Chapter 15 we saw that in a world with only corporate taxes the Miller-Modigliani proposition suggests that dividend policy is irrelevant to value. However, when personal taxes are introduced with a capital gains rate that is less than the rate on ordinary income, the picture changes. Under this set of assumptions the firm should not pay any dividends. One way to test these theories is to look directly at the relationship between dividend payout and the price per share of equity.

Friend and Puckett [1964] use cross-section data to test the effect of dividend payout on share value. Prior to their work, most studies had related stock prices to current dividends and retained earnings, and reported that higher dividend payout was associated with higher price/earnings ratios. The "dividend multiplier" was found to be several times the "retained earnings multiplier." The usual cross-section equation was

$$P_{it} = a + bDiv_{it} + cRE_{it} + \varepsilon_{it}, \qquad (16.35)$$

where

$$P_{it} = \text{the price per share,}$$

$$Div_{it} = \text{aggregate dividends paid out,}$$

$$RE_{it} = \text{retained earnings,}$$

$$\varepsilon_{it} = \text{the error term.}$$

Friend and Puckett criticize the above approach on three major points. First, the equation is misspecified because it assumes that the riskiness of the firm is uncorrelated with dividend payout and price/earnings ratios. However, a look at the data suggests that riskier firms have both lower dividend payout and lower price/earnings ratios. Consequently, the omission of a risk variable may cause an upward bias in the dividend coefficient in Eq. (16.35). Second, there is almost no measurement error in dividends, but there is considerable measurement error in retained earnings. It is well known that accounting measures of income often imprecisely reflect the real economic earnings of the firm. The measurement error in retained earnings will cause its coefficient to be biased downward. Third, Friend and Puckett argue that even if dividends and earnings *do* have different impacts on share prices, we should expect their coefficients in (16.35) to be equal. In equilibrium, firms would change their dividend payout until the marginal effect of dividends is equal to the marginal effect of retained earnings. This will provide the optimum effect on their price per share.

No theory had been developed to allow the pricing of risk when they wrote their paper, but Friend and Puckett were able to eliminate the measurement error on retained earnings by calculating a normalized earnings variable based on a time-series fit of the following equation:

$$\frac{(NI/P)_{it}}{(NI/P)_{kt}} = a_i + b_i t + \varepsilon_{it}, \tag{16.36}$$

where

$$(NI/P)_{it} = \text{the earnings/price ratio for the firm,}$$

$$(NI/P)_{kt} = \text{the average earnings/price ratio for the industry,}$$

$$t = \text{a time index,}$$

$$\varepsilon_{it} = \text{the error term.}$$

When normalized retained earnings were calculated by subtracting dividends from normalized earnings and then used in Eq. (16.35), the difference between the dividend and retained earnings coefficients was reduced. Unfortunately, no test was performed to see whether the difference between the impact of retained earnings and dividends was significant after Friend and Puckett had normalized earnings and controlled for firm effects.

A study by Black and Scholes [1974] uses capital asset pricing theory to control for risk.[19] Their conclusion is quite strong. "It is not possible to demonstrate, using the best empirical methods, that the expected returns on high yield common stocks differ from the expected returns on low yield common stocks either before or after taxes." They begin by pointing out that the assumption that capital gains tax rates are lower than income tax rates does not apply to all classes of investors. Some

---

[19] See Chapter 6 for a complete development of the capital asset pricing model.

classes of investors might logically prefer high dividend yields. They include (1) corporations, because they usually pay higher taxes on realized capital gains than on dividend income (because of the 80% exclusion of dividends); (2) certain trust funds in which one beneficiary receives the dividend income and the other receives capital gains; (3) endowment funds from which only the dividend income may be spent; and (4) investors who are spending from wealth and may find it cheaper and easier to receive dividends than to sell or borrow against their shares. Alternatively, investors who prefer low dividend yield will be those who pay higher taxes on dividend income than on capital gains. With all these diverse investors, it is possible that there are clientele effects that imply that if a firm changes its dividend payout, it may lose some shareholders, but they will be replaced by others who prefer the new policy. Thus dividend payout will have no effect on the value of an individual firm.[20]

The Black-Scholes [1974] study presents empirical evidence that the before-tax returns on common stock are unrelated to corporate dividend payout policy. They adjust for risk by using the CAPM. The CAPM predicts that the expected return on any asset is a linear function of its systematic risk.

$$E\left(\tilde{R}_j\right) = R_f + \left[E(\tilde{R}_m) - R_f\right]\beta_j. \tag{16.37}$$

However, it is derived by assuming, among other things, that there are no differential tax effects that would affect investors' demands for different securities. Brennan [1970] has shown that if effective capital gains tax rates are lower than effective rates on dividend income, then investors will demand a higher rate of return on securities with higher dividend payout. Using annual data, Black and Scholes test this hypothesis by adding a dividend payout term to an empirical version of the CAPM:

$$\tilde{R}_j = \gamma_0 + \left[\tilde{R}_m - \gamma_0\right]\beta_j + \gamma_1(DY_j - DY_m)/DY_m + \varepsilon_j, \tag{16.38}$$

where

$\tilde{R}_j$ = the rate of return on the jth portfolio,

γ_0 = an intercept term that should be equal to the risk-free rate, R_f, according to the CAPM,

$\tilde{R}_m$ = the rate of return on the market portfolio,

β_j = the systematic risk of the jth portfolio,

γ_1 = the dividend impact coefficient,

DY_j = the dividend yield on the jth portfolio, measured as the sum of dividends

   paid during the previous year divided by the end-of-year price,

DY_m = the dividend yield on the market portfolio measured over the prior 12 months,

ε_j = the error term.

---

[20] This does not rule out the possibility that in aggregate there is a desired equilibrium amount of dividend payout. For example, in the United States there are obviously a far greater number of companies with generous dividend payout than without.

Table 16.8 Results from the Black-Scholes Test for Dividend Effects

The Portfolio Estimators for $\widehat{\gamma}_1$				
Period	$\alpha_1 = \widehat{\gamma}_1$	t_α	$\widehat{\beta}_1$	DY_1	DY_m
1936–66	0.0009	0.94	−0.01	0.044	0.048
1947–66	0.0009	0.90	0.08	0.047	0.049
1936–46	0.0011	0.54	−0.01	0.036	0.046
1947–56	0.0002	0.19	0.11	0.054	0.060
1957–66	0.0016	0.99	−0.14	0.040	0.038
1940–45	0.0018	0.34	0.15	0.051	0.052

The Portfolio Estimators for $\widehat{\gamma}_0$				
Period	$\alpha_0 = \widehat{\gamma}_0$	t_α	$\widehat{\beta}_0$	DY_0	DY_m
1936–66	0.0060	3.02	0.02	0.048	0.048
1947–66	0.0073	3.93	0.03	0.049	0.049
1936–46	0.0033	0.72	−0.01	0.046	0.046
1947–56	0.0067	2.55	0.12	0.060	0.060
1957–66	0.0065	2.37	0.10	0.038	0.038

From F. Black and M. Scholes, "The Effects of Dividend Yield and Dividend Policy on Common Stock Prices and Returns," reprinted from *Journal of Financial Economics*, May 1974, 14. © 1974 North-Holland.

If the coefficient, γ_1, of the dividend yield is significantly different from zero, we would reject the null hypothesis that dividend payout has no impact on the required rate of return for securities. The results of Black and Scholes are summarized in Table 16.8. Note that the dividend impact coefficient, $\widehat{\gamma}_1$, is not significantly different from zero (since the t-test is less than the level required to make it significant at the 95% confidence level) across the entire time period, 1936 through 1966, or in any subperiod. This means that the expected returns on high-yield securities are not significantly different from the expected returns on low-yield securities, other things being equal.[21]

The Black-Scholes study has been criticized because their test is not very powerful. Had the null hypothesis been that dividend policy does matter, it could not have been rejected either. Their test is inefficient because they grouped stocks into portfolios instead of using individual stock returns and, perhaps, because they used annual data.

Litzenberger and Ramaswamy [1979] also test the relationship between dividends and security returns. They use the Brennan [1970] model, Eq. (16.15), with monthly data for individual securities:

$$E(\widehat{R}_{jt}) - R_{ft} = a_1 + a_2\beta_j + a_3(DY_{jt} - R_{ft}), \tag{16.39}$$

---

[21] The lower half of Table 16.8 shows that $\widehat{\gamma}_0$ is significantly different from the risk-free rate. This is not important for the conclusion about dividend policy but is consistent with other empirical work (e.g., Black, Jensen, and Scholes [1972]) that shows that the intercept term in the CAPM is different from what theory would predict.

where

$E(\widehat{R}_{jt})$ = the expected before-tax return on the jth security,

R_{ft} = the before-tax return on the risk-free asset,

β_j = the systematic risk of the jth security,

a_1 = the constant term,

a_2 = the marginal effect of systematic risk,

a_3 = the marginal effective tax difference between ordinary income and capital gains rates,

DY_{jt} = the dividend yield (i.e., dividend divided by price) for the jth security.

Litzenberger and Ramaswamy conclude that risk-adjusted returns are higher for securities with higher dividend yields. The implication is that dividends are undesirable; hence higher returns are necessary to compensate investors in order to induce them to hold high dividend yield stocks.

There are (at least) three serious problems with testing for the dividend effect predicted by Eq. (16.39). The first is that investors use dividend announcements to estimate expected returns, $E(\widehat{R}_{jt})$; that is, there is an information effect. The second is that measures of systematic risk, $\widehat{\beta}_j$, are subject to a great deal of error. And the third is that individual security returns (rather than portfolio returns) are needed to obtain statistically powerful results. Litzenberger and Ramaswamy [1979] largely solved the second and third problems but have been criticized by Miller and Scholes [1982] for their handling of the information effect of dividend announcements. When using monthly data, about two thirds of the firms in the sample will have a zero yield because most firms pay dividends on a quarterly basis. Of the firms that pay their dividend (i.e., go ex-dividend) in month t, about 30–40% also announce the dividend in the same month. When the announcement date and the ex-dividend date occur in the same month, the monthly return will contain both the information effect and the tax effect (if any). To avoid confusing these effects, Litzenberger and Ramaswamy computed dividend yields in the following way:

- If a firm declared its dividend prior to month t and went ex-dividend in month t, then the dividend yield, DY_{jt}, was computed using the actual dividend paid in t divided by the share price at the end of the month $t - 1$.

- If a firm both declared and went ex-dividend in month t, then the yield, DY_{jt}, was computed using the last regular dividend, going as far back as one year.

Table 16.9 shows the results of regressions run by Miller and Scholes [1982] using Eq (16.39). Regressions using the actual dividend in month t show that the dividend variable has a coefficient of .317 and is highly significant, but recall that the actual yield confuses announcement effects with dividend tax effects. When the Litzenberger-Ramaswamy measure of dividend yield (called the level-revised yield) was duplicated by Miller and Scholes, the dividend coefficient dropped from .317 to .179 and also dropped in significance.

The third regression in Table 16.9 corrects for a bias not contemplated in the two prior regressions, namely, that some firms are expected to pay a dividend in month t, but for some reason, the board of directors suspends the dividend. Miller and Scholes call this the case of the "dog that didn't bark." Suppose that a $10 stock has a 50/50 chance of either announcing a $2 dividend (in which case the stock price doubles to $20) or suspending the dividend (thereby causing the stock price to fall to $5). The ex ante rate of return (and the average ex post return) is 35%, and

Table 16.9 Cross-Sectional Estimates of the Dividend Yield Effect (Eq. 16.15), 1940–1978

Definition of Expected Dividend Yield	a_1	a_2	a_3
Actual dividend yield	.0059	.0024	.3173
	(4.5)	(1.6)	(10.2)
Level-revised monthly	.0065	.0022	.1794
dividend yield	(4.9)	(1.4)	(6.1)
Dividend yield of 12	.0038	.0019	.0376
months ago	(2.9)	(1.3)	(1.3)
Only firms with dividends	.0043	.0035	.0135
declared in advance	(2.5)	(2.2)	(0.1)

Note: t-statistics are in parentheses. From M. H. Miller and M. Scholes, "Dividends and Taxes: Some Empirical Evidence," *Journal of Political Economy*, December 1982, 1124, 1129.

the ex ante dividend yield is 10%.[22] However, if the level-revised measure of dividend yield is used, then if the firm actually pays the $2 dividend, the yield is 20% and the return is 120%. But if the dividend is passed, the yield is 0% and a −50% return is recorded. Thus the regressions with the level-revised measure tend to show what appears to be a positive association between returns and dividend yields. However, the correlation is spurious. A simple way to correct for the problem is to use the dividend yield of 12 months ago. Shown in the third regression in Table 16.9, the results indicate a small, statistically insignificant relationship between dividend yields and returns.

Another approach, shown in the fourth regression in Table 16.9, is to drop from the sample all firms except those that both paid dividends in month t and announced them in advance. Again the dividend coefficient is insignificant.

Litzenberger and Ramaswamy [1982] have responded to the Miller-Scholes criticism by re-running their regressions. Table 16.10 shows their results. The level-revised dividend yield gave the highest coefficient (a_3), and it is slightly higher than the Miller-Scholes estimate. Instead of using a dividend 12 months ago, Litzenberger and Ramaswamy built a more sophisticated model to predict dividends. Their "predicted dividend yield" model avoids the Miller-Scholes criticism and continues to give a statistically significant estimate of the dividend effect. So, too, does a restricted subsample designed to avoid the Miller-Scholes criticism. Thus the empirical evidence, at this point in time, points toward the conclusion that shareholders express their displeasure with corporate dividend payments by requiring a higher risk-adjusted return (i.e., by paying a lower price) for those stocks that have higher dividend yields.

---

[22] The ex ante return is computed as

$$.5\left(\frac{20-10}{10}\right) + .5\left(\frac{5-10}{10}\right) = .35,$$

and the ex ante dividend yield is

$$.5\left(\frac{2}{10}\right) + .5\left(\frac{0}{10}\right) = .10.$$

Table 16.10 Pooled Time Series and Cross-Section Test of the Dividend Effect, 1940–1960

Definition of Expected Dividend Yield	a_1	a_2	a_3
Level-revised monthly dividend yield	.0031	.0048	.233
	(1.81)	(2.15)	(8.79)
Predicted dividend yield	.0034	.0047	.151
	(1.95)	(2.08)	(5.39)
Restricted subsample	.0010	.0053	.135
	(.052)	(2.33)	(4.38)

Note: t-statistics are in parentheses.
From R. Litzenberger and K. Ramaswamy, "The Effects of Dividends on Common Stock Prices: Tax Effects or Information Effects?" *Journal of Finance*, May 1982, 441. Reprinted with permission.

A more recent study by Naranjo, Nimalendran, and Ryngaert [1998] examines the cross-section of returns as a function of the Fama-French [1992] factors and dividend yield as shown in the empirical model given below:

$$R_{pt} = \lambda_0 + \beta_{1F}[MKT + \lambda_1] + \beta_{2F}[SMB_t + \lambda_2] + \beta_{3F}[HML_t + \lambda_3] + \lambda_4\, d_{pt-1} + \in_{pt},$$

where

MKT = the excess returns on the CRSP value-weighted portfolio,

SMB = the difference between average returns on small minus big equity capitalization portfolios,

HML = the difference between average returns on high minus low book equity to market equity portfolios,

d_{pt-1} = the equally weighted yield of stocks in portfolio p minus the market dividend yield,

λ_i = the risk premium corresponding to the ith risk factor,

λ_4 = the coefficient on the dividend yield measure.

Using the data from July 1963 to December 1994 (378 months) they find that companies with higher dividend yields have higher returns and that the result is statistically significant. They go on to test for a tax effect, but find no evidence for it.

The Friend and Puckett, Black and Scholes, and Miller and Scholes studies tend to support the conclusion that the value of the firm is independent of dividend yield. The Litzenberger and Ramaswamy and the Naranjo, Nimalendran, and Ryngaert studies support the conclusion that dividends are undesirable. The next study to be discussed concludes that dividends are desirable to shareholders; that is, they will require a lower rate of return on shares that pay a high dividend yield.

Long [1978] provides a detailed analysis of two classes of shares issued by Citizens Utilities Company in 1956. They are virtually identical in all respects except for dividend payout. Series A shares pay only stock dividends that are not taxable as ordinary income (due to a special Internal Revenue Service ruling granted to Citizens Utilities). Series B shares pay only cash dividends. Series A shares are freely convertible into Series B shares (on a one-for-one basis) at any time. However, the opposite is not true. Series B shares may not be converted to Series A shares. Historically the directors of Citizens Utilities have semiannually declared stock dividends that

Figure 16.3 The natural log of $P_A/\widehat{P}_B$ plotted monthly for the period April 1956 to December 1976. (From J. Long, Jr., "The Market Valuation of Cash Dividends: A Case to Consider," reprinted with permission from *Journal of Financial Economics*, June–September 1978, 254. © North-Holland.)

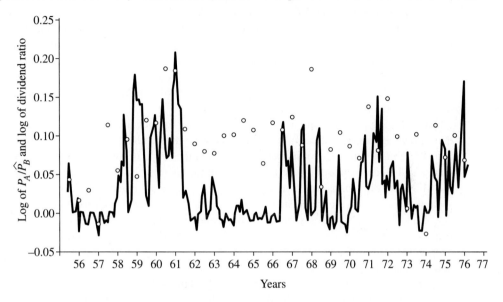

(with a high degree of certainty) are 8% to 10% larger than the corresponding Series B cash dividends (paid on a quarterly basis).

Figure 16.3 shows the natural logarithm of the ratio of the price of Series A to Series B shares on a monthly basis between 1956 and 1977. Note that the price of Series A shares, P_A, never falls significantly below the price of Series B shares, P_B. If it did, then Series A shareholders could immediately profit by converting to Series B. Figure 16.3 also shows, q, the ratio of Series A stock dividends to Series B cash dividends (illustrated by the circles). In a world without taxes the price per share of Series A "should" always equal q times the price per share of Series B stock, that is, $P_{At} = q\,P_{Bt}\,(t = 0, 1, \ldots, N)$. Figure 16.3 indicates that 80% of the dividend ratios, q, between 1962 and 1976 fall in the range 1.07 to 1.137. The ratio of stock prices, however, shows much more variability and is usually below the dividend ratio. How can this be explained?

In a world with taxes, cross-sectional heterogeneity in investor tax rates will cause the price ratio to differ from the dividend ratio. If very few investors face strictly higher taxes on stock dividends than on cash dividends, then the ratio of prices, P_A/P_B, should be greater than the dividend ratio, q. The equilibrium price ratio P_A/P_B will be less than q if there are sufficient numbers of investors who have a strict tax-induced preference for cash dividends over capital gains, and this is what is observed. Therefore Long [1978] concludes that "claims to cash dividends have, if anything, commanded a slight premium in the market to claims to equal amounts (before taxes) of capital gains." The Citizens Utilities case is anomalous because it is the only major study that indicates an investor preference for cash dividends. Furthermore, the strength of Long's conclusion has been weakened by Poterba [1986], who finds (1) that the relative price of the stock dividend shares has been higher since 1976 (the end of Long's sample); (2) that the ratio of stock dividends to cash dividend share prices averaged 1.134 during the 1976–1984 period; and (3) that the cash dividend shares' ex-day price decline is less than their dividend payment, whereas stock dividend shares fall by nearly their full dividend. These results are more consistent with investor preference for capital gains rather than dividends.

According to the Miller-Modigliani irrelevancy proposition, it is also important to know whether or not dividend policy can affect the investment decisions made by managers of the firm. This is a particularly difficult empirical question because the Miller-Modigliani theorem requires only that *dividend payout not affect investment decisions*. However, the opposite causality is not ruled out by Miller and Modigliani. That is, investment decisions can affect dividends. For example, the firm may simply choose to treat dividends as a residual payout after all profitable investment projects have been undertaken. This would not be inconsistent with the Miller-Modigliani proposition that the value of the firm is unaffected by dividend policy.

Fama [1974] uses a sophisticated two-stage least-squares econometric technique in order to determine the direction of causality, if any, between dividend and investment decisions. Because a description of two-stage least-squares is beyond the scope of this book, we refer the interested reader to Fama's article for a detailed exposition. His conclusion, however, is consistent with the Miller-Modigliani assumption that the period-by-period investment decisions of the firm are separable from its dividend decisions. There appears to be no causality in either direction. The data could not reject the hypothesis that investment and dividend decisions are completely independent from each other. Fama's conclusion that investment and dividend decisions are independent is supported by Smirlock and Marshall [1983], who employ causality tests using both firm-specific and aggregate data for 194 firms between 1958 and 1977.

Although the foregoing studies appear to support the Miller-Modigliani irrelevancy proposition from the point of view of an individual firm, they do not necessarily rule out the possibility that there may exist an aggregate equilibrium supply of dividends that will increase if the difference between the ordinary income rate and the capital gains rate declines. This type of situation is implicit in Miller's [1977] paper, "Debt and Taxes," which was discussed at length in Chapter 15.

Some empirical evidence that is consistent with the thesis that the aggregate supply of dividends is sensitive to the differential between the ordinary income and capital gains is contained in a study by Khoury and Smith [1977]. They observed that Canadian corporations significantly increased their dividend payout after a capital gains tax was introduced for the first time in the Canadian tax code. Passed in 1972, it affected the cross-sectional relationship between dividends and capital gains. Prior to 1972 they were imperfect substitutes, but afterward they became more or less perfect substitutes.

H. Corporate Equity Repurchases

Corporations can repurchase their own shares in either of two ways: on the open market or via tender offer. Open market repurchases usually (but not always) involve gradual programs to buy back shares over a period of time. In a tender offer the company usually specifies the number of shares it is offering to repurchase, a tender price, and a period of time during which the offer is in effect. If the number of shares actually tendered by shareholders exceeds the maximum number specified by the company, then purchases are usually made on a pro rata basis. Alternatively, if the tender offer is undersubscribed the firm may decide to cancel the offer or extend the expiration date. Shares tendered during the extension may be purchased on either a pro rata or first-come, first-served basis.

The choice between dividend payout and share repurchase as ways of delivering wealth to shareholders involves many trade-offs. Earlier in the chapter we discussed the tax advantage of share repurchase when capital gains taxes are lower than ordinary income taxes on dividends for the marginal investor. Jaganathan, Stephens, and Weisbach [2000] also point out that repurchases of stock are treated by management as more flexible than dividends. Stock repurchases are pro-cyclical while dividends increase steadily over time. Dividends are paid by firms with higher "permanent" operating income while repurchases are used by firms that have more volatile income with a larger "temporary" component. In general, firms tend to pay increased dividends following good performance and use repurchases following poor performance. Guay and Harford [2000] find similar results, namely, that firms choose dividends to distribute relatively permanent cash flows, while repurchases are chosen to distribute relatively transient income. They also find that the very choice of the method of distribution is a signal to the market. After controlling for payout size and the market expectations about the permanence of the cash flow stock, the price reaction to positive dividend increases is more positive than the reaction to repurchases (in spite of any tax disadvantage).

Dittmar and Dittmar [2002] examine how macroeconomic conditions influence the payout policies of firms. They find that aggregate repurchases increase with both transitory and permanent earnings increases, where the latter variables are obtained from an estimated cointegrating relation between aggregate earnings and several macroeconomic variables including per capita GDP, per capita consumption of nondurable goods and services, and industrial production. They also find that the ratio of repurchases to total payouts are only affected by shifts in transitory earnings, while changes in permanent earnings are the only driver of aggregate changes in dividends. Based on these results, they conclude that repurchases are a way of distributing permanent earnings only.

Tender offers are usually significant corporate events. Dann [1981] reports that for a sample of 143 cash tender offers by 122 different firms between 1962 and 1976, the average cash distributions proposed by the tender represented almost 20% of the market value of the company's pre-tender equity value. The announcement effects of tender offers on the market values of corporate securities have been studied by Masulis [1980], Dann [1981], and Vermaelen [1981].[23] Share repurchases are not just a simple alternative to cash dividends. Tender offers for repurchase are related to (at least) five separate, but not mutually exclusive, hypotheses:

1. *The information or signaling hypothesis.* The cash dividend disbursed to shareholders in a tender offer may represent a signal that the firm is expected to have increased future cash flows, but it may also imply that the firm has exhausted profitable investment opportunities. Therefore the signal may be interpreted as either good or bad news by shareholders.

2. *The leverage tax shield hypothesis.* If the repurchase is financed by issuing debt rather than paying out cash, the leverage of the firm may increase, and if there is a gain to leverage as suggested by Modigliani and Miller [1963], then shareholders may benefit.

3. *The dividend tax avoidance hypothesis.* The tender for share repurchase will be taxed as a capital gain rather than a dividend if (according to Section 302 of the U.S. Internal Revenue Code) the redemption is "substantially disproportionate" to the extent that the individual shareholder must have sold more than 20% of his or her holdings in the tender.[24] This condition is rarely violated; consequently, there may be a tax incentive for repurchases as opposed to large extraordinary dividends.

---

[23] The reader is also referred to studies by Woods and Brigham [1966], Bierman and West [1966], Young [1967], Elton and Gruber [1968], Stewart [1976], Coates and Fredman [1976], and Lane [1976].

[24] According to Vermaelen [1981] only 3 out of 105 tender offers that he studied actually were subject to ordinary income taxes.

Figure 16.4 Schematic representation of average price changes surrounding tender offers for repurchase.

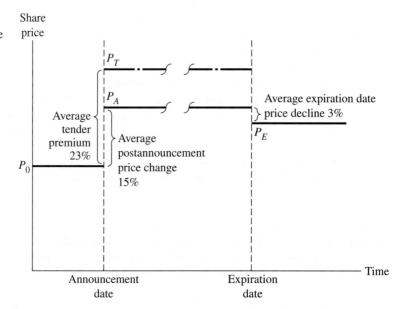

4. *The bondholder expropriation hypothesis.* If the repurchase unexpectedly reduces the asset base of the company, then bondholders are worse off because they have less collateral. Of course, bond indentures serve to protect against this form of expropriation. A direct test of this hypothesis is to look at bond price changes on the repurchase announcement date.

5. *Wealth transfers among shareholders.* Wealth transfers between tendering and nontendering stockholders may occur when there are differential constraints and/or costs across groups of owners. Even when the tender price is substantially above the pre-tender stock price, some shareholders may voluntarily decide not to tender their shares.

A great deal can be learned about these hypotheses if we focus on the price effects on shares, bonds, and preferred stock. Figure 16.4 shows the average pattern of share price changes around the tender announcement date and the expiration date. More or less the same results were reported by Masulis [1980], Dann [1981], and Vermaelen [1981]. The average tender price, P_T, is roughly 23% above the preannouncement price, P_0. If all shares tendered were actually purchased by the firm, then the tender price, P_T, would equal the average postannouncement price, P_A. But because of pro rata repurchases given oversubscribed tenders, we observe that on average $P_A < P_T$. The postannouncement price, P_A, averages 15% above the preannouncement price, P_0. Finally, note that the average postexpiration price, P_E, is only 3% below the average postannouncement price, P_A, and is above the preannouncement price, P_0. This suggests that the tender offer may have increased the market value of the firm's equity.

Unfortunately, the difference between the preannouncement price and the postexpiration price does not measure the information effect of the tender offer. We have to look deeper. Begin by noting that the market value of the firm's equity after expiration, $P_E N_E$, is equal to the pre-announcement value, $P_0 N_0$, minus the cash paid out in the tender, $P_T (N_0 - N_E)$, plus the tender offer effect, ΔW:

$$P_E N_E = P_0 N_0 - P_T (N_0 - N_E) + \Delta W, \tag{16.40}$$

P_E = the postexpiration share price,

N_E = the number of shares outstanding after repurchase,

P_0 = the preannouncement share price,

N_0 = the preannouncement number of shares outstanding,

P_T = the tender price,

ΔW = the shareholder wealth effect attributable to the tender offer.

Note that the change in value attributable to the tender, ΔW, may be caused by (1) personal tax savings, (2) a leverage effect, (3) expropriation of bondholder wealth, or (4) the reassessment of the firm's earnings prospects.

If we define the fraction of shares repurchased, F_p, as

$$F_p = 1 - \frac{N_E}{N_0} \tag{16.41}$$

and divide Eq. (16.40) by N_0, we have

$$P_E(1 - F_p) = P_0 - P_T F_p + \frac{\Delta W}{N_0}. \tag{16.42}$$

Solving for $\Delta W / N_0$ and dividing by P_0 gives

$$\frac{\Delta W}{N_0 P_0} = (1 - F_p)\frac{P_E - P_0}{P_0} + F_p \frac{P_T - P_0}{P_0}. \tag{16.43}$$

Thus the rate of return created by the tender offer has two components. First is the rate of return received by nontendering shareholders weighted by the percentage of untendered shares, $1 - F_p$, and second is the rate of return received by tendering shareholders weighted by the percentage of shares purchased, F_p.

Vermaelen [1981] found that the average wealth effect, $\Delta W / N_0 P_0$, was 15.7% and that only 10.7% of the tender offers experienced a wealth decline. On average, both nontendered shares and tendered shares experienced a wealth increase, although not by equal amounts.

What causes the average 15.7% wealth gain from tender offers? Personal tax savings are a possibility but seem too small to explain the large wealth gain. For example, if 20% of the value of the firm is repurchased and if the marginal investor's tax rate is 40%, then the tax savings would imply a 4% rate of return. This is too small to explain the wealth gain.

The leverage hypothesis suggests that if the repurchase is financed with debt, and if there is a tax gain from leverage, then the shareholders will benefit. Both Masulis [1980] and Vermaelen [1981] find evidence consistent with a leverage effect. Masulis divided his sample into offers with more than 50% debt financing where the average announcement return was 21.9%, and offers with less than 50% debt where the average announcement return was only 17.1%. Vermaelen finds similar results and concludes that while it is not possible to reject the leverage hypothesis outright, it is possible to conclude that it is not the predominant explanation for the observed abnormal returns following the tender offer. Also, if leverage is a signal, then it is not possible to separate the leverage signaling effect from the leverage tax effect.[25]

The best explanation for the shareholder wealth gain from the tender offer is that the offer represents a favorable signal. Vermaelen [1981] finds that the per-share earnings of tendering firms are above what would have been predicted by a time-series model using preannouncement data. Thus the tender offer may be interpreted as an announcement of favorable earnings prospects. Also, the size of the tender premium, the fraction of shares repurchased, and the fraction of insider holdings are all positively related to the wealth gain, ΔW, and explain roughly 60% of its variance. These results are also consistent with interpreting the tender offer as a signal.

Evidence on the bondholder wealth expropriation hypothesis is provided by looking at bond price changes around the announcement date. Dann [1981] found 122 publicly traded debt and preferred stock issues for 51 tender offers. There were 41 issues of straight debt, 34 issues of convertible debt, 9 issues of straight preferred stock, and 38 issues of convertible preferred stock. An analysis of abnormal returns around the announcement date revealed significant positive rates of return for the convertible securities and rates that were insignificantly different from zero for straight debt and preferred. Furthermore, the correlation between common stock returns and straight debt (and preferred) returns was positive. Thus the evidence seems to contradict bondholder expropriation as the dominant effect and seems to support the signaling hypothesis.

Dittmar [2000] empirically investigates the motives behind decisions by firms to repurchase stock over the 1977–1996 time period. In general, she finds that firms repurchase stocks to take advantage of undervaluation and to distribute free cash flow. In addition, she reports that in certain periods repurchases are undertaken to change leverage, as a takeover defense, and to offset the potential dilution effects from the exercise of stock options.

Grullon and Michaely [2002] report what seems to be an increasing propensity in recent years to choose repurchase over dividend payout. Not only have repurchases become more important, but firms are choosing to finance repurchases with funds that would not have otherwise been used to increase dividends. Young firms have a greater propensity to repurchase, and while established firms have not cut dividends, they nevertheless show a greater propensity to repurchase at the margin.

Repurchases via tender offer represent an interesting and significant corporate event. The empirical evidence, although not rejecting leverage effects or dividend tax avoidance effects, seems to most strongly support the hypothesis that the tender offer for repurchase is interpreted by the marketplace as favorable information regarding future prospects of the firm.

I. Other Dividend Policy Issues

1. Dividends and Share Repurchases from the Bondholders' Point of View

Debt contracts, particularly when long-term debt is involved, frequently restrict a firm's ability to pay cash dividends. Such restrictions usually state that (1) future dividends can be paid only out of earnings generated after the signing of the loan agreement (i.e., future dividends cannot be paid out of past retained earnings) and (2) dividends cannot be paid when net working capital (current assets minus current liabilities) is below a prespecified amount.

---

[25] See the discussion of debt for common exchange offers in Chapter 15 for evidence consistent with the hypothesis that higher leverage (repurchases of equity with debt) is a favorable signal about the future prospects of the firm.

One need not restrict the argument to only dividend payout. The effect of share repurchases on bondholders is similar. When any of the assets of a corporation are paid out to shareholders in any type of capital distribution, the effect is to "steal away" a portion of bondholders' collateral. In effect, some of the assets that bondholders could claim, in the event that shareholders decide to default, are paid out to shareholders. This diminishes the value of debt and increases the wealth of shareholders.

Of course, the most common type of capital distribution is a dividend payment. A portion of the firm's assets is paid out in the form of cash dividends to shareholders. The most extreme example of defrauding bondholders would be to simply liquidate the assets of the firm and pay out a single, final dividend to shareholders, thereby leaving bondholders with a claim to nothing. For this very reason, most bond indentures explicitly restrict the dividend policy of shareholders. Usually dividends cannot exceed the current earnings of the firm, and they cannot be paid out of retained earnings.

It is an interesting empirical question whether or not any dividend payment, no matter how huge it is, will affect the market value of bonds. One would expect that the market price of bonds would reflect the risk that future dividend payments or repurchases would lower the asset base that secures debt.[26] However, as changes in the dividend payments are actually realized, there may be changes in the expectations of the bondholders, which in turn would be reflected in the market price of bonds. All other things being equal, we may expect that higher dividend payments or share repurchases will be associated with a decline in the market value of debt. However, rarely do we have a situation where all other things are equal. For example, if announcements about dividend changes are interpreted as information about future cash flows, then a dividend increase means that current debt will be more secure because of the anticipated higher cash flows, and we would observe dividend increases to be positively correlated with increases in the market value of debt.

Maxwell and Stephens [2001] examine the bond price reactions to open market repurchase announcements. They find that bond prices decrease significantly around the announcement of repurchase programs, with the decrease being greater for larger repurchases and for speculative grade debt. These results therefore provide support for the hypothesis that stock repurchases cause a wealth redistribution from bondholders and stockholders.

2. Stock Dividends and Share Repurchase

Stock dividends are often mentioned as part of the dividend policy of the firm. However, a stock dividend is nothing more than a small stock split. It simply increases the number of shares outstanding without changing any of the underlying risk or return characteristics of the firm. Therefore we might expect that it has little or no effect on shareholders' wealth except for the losses associated with the clerical and transactions costs that accompany the stock dividend. Recall, however, that the empirical evidence in Chapter 11 indicated that stock dividend announcements are in fact accompanied by statistically significant abnormal returns on the announcement date. So far, no adequate explanation has been provided for this fact, although Brennan and Copeland [1987] suggest that stock dividends may be used to force the early conversion of convertible debt, convertible preferred, or warrants, because these securities are frequently not protected against stock dividends.

---

[26] Dividend payments do not necessarily change the assets side of the balance sheet. When cash balances are reduced in order to pay dividends, there is an asset effect. However, it is not necessary. Dividends can also be paid by issuing new debt or equity. In this case, assets remain unaffected, and the dividend decision is purely financial in nature.

Another question that often arises is whether share repurchase is preferable to dividend payment as a means of distributing cash to shareholders. Share repurchase allows shareholders to receive the cash payment as a capital gain rather than as dividend income. Any shareholder who pays a higher tax rate on income than on capital gains would prefer share repurchase to dividend payment. But not all classes of shareholders have this preference. Some, like tax-free university endowment funds, are indifferent to income versus capital gains, whereas others, such as corporations with their dividend exclusions, would actually prefer dividends.

To see that share repurchase can result in the same benefit per share, consider the following example. The Universal Sourgum Company earns $4.4 million in 1981 and decides to pay out 50%, or $2.2 million, either as dividends or repurchase. The company has 1,100,000 shares outstanding with a market value of $22 per share. It can pay dividends of $2 per share or repurchase shares at $22 each. We know that the market price for repurchase is $22 rather than $20 because $22 will be the price per share after repurchase. To demonstrate this statement, we know that the current value of the (all-equity) firm is $24.2 million. For $2.2 million in cash it can repurchase 100,000 shares. Therefore after the repurchase the value of the firm falls to $24.2 − 2.2 = $22 million, and with 1,000,000 shares outstanding the price per share is $22. Thus, in theory, there is no price effect from repurchase.

A comparison of shareholders' wealth before taxes shows that it is the same with either payment technique. If dividends are paid, each shareholder receives a $2 dividend, and the ex-dividend price per share is $20 ($22 million ÷ 1.1 million shares). Alternately, as shown above, each share is worth $22 under repurchase, and a shareholder who needs cash can sell off a portion of his or her shares. The preferred form of payment (dividends versus repurchase) will depend on shareholders' tax rates.

In the sample shown above there is no price effect from share repurchase. However, recent empirical studies of repurchases via tender offers have found a positive announcement effect.

Summary

Several valuation models with or without growth and with or without corporate taxes have been developed. Dividend policy is irrelevant in all instances. It has no effect on shareholders' wealth. When personal taxes are introduced, we have a result where dividends matter. For shareholders who pay higher taxes on dividends than on capital gains, the preferred dividend payout is zero; they would rather have the company distribute cash payments via the share repurchase mechanism. Yet corporations do pay dividends. The Rozeff [1982] paper suggests that there appear to be strong cross-sectional regularities in dividend payout. Thus there may be optimal dividend policies that result from a trade-off between the costs and benefits of paying dividends. The list of possible costs includes (1) tax advantages of receiving income in the form of capital gains rather than dividends, (2) the cost of raising external capital if dividends are paid out, and (3) the foregone use of funds for productive investment. The possible benefits of dividend payout are (1) higher perceived corporate value because of the signaling content of dividends, (2) lower agency costs of external equity, and (3) the ability of dividend payments to help complete the markets.

The evidence supporting dividend clientele effects is much stronger than the evidence for capital structure clientele effects. Another issue is the relationship between dividend yield and equity values. The preponderance of empirical evidence seems to favor the conclusion that dividend yield has no strong effect on the required rate of return on equity; however, if there is any effect it is in favor of capital gains over dividends. The Litzenberger and Ramaswamy [1979, 1982] studies found that higher dividend yields required higher rates of return to compensate investors for the disadvantage of dividend payout. The only study that found dividends were desirable was the Citizens Utilities case [Long, 1978], which has been questioned by Poterba [1986]. On the other hand, changes in dividends paid out are interpreted as new information about the future cash flows of the firm. There is strong evidence to support a dividend signaling effect. There appears to be no causal relationship between investment and dividend policy. Finally, empirical evidence on share repurchase via tender offer indicates that the announcement effect is predominantly viewed as favorable news regarding the firm's future cash flows. Little or no expropriation of bondholders' wealth was observed.

PROBLEM SET

16.1 Under what conditions might dividend policy affect the value of the firm?

16.2 According to federal tax law, corporations need not pay taxes on 80% of dividends received from shares held in other corporations. In other words, only 20% of the dividends received by a corporate holder are taxable. Given this fact, how much must the price of a stock fall on the ex-dividend date in order to prevent a corporate holder from making arbitrage profits? Assume that the capital gains rate equals the corporate tax rate, $\tau_c = .5$.

16.3 Empirical evidence supports the existence of a clientele effect. This implies that every time a company revises its dividend policy to pay out a greater (or smaller) percentage of earnings, the characteristics of its shareholders also change. For example, a firm with a higher payout ratio may expect to have more shareholders in lower tax brackets. Suppose that lower-income people are also more risk averse. Would this have an effect on the value of the firm?

16.4 Miller and Scholes [1978] suggest that it is possible to shelter income from taxes in such a way that capital gains rates are paid on dividend income. Furthermore, since capital gains need never be realized, the effective tax rate will become zero. Why would this scheme not be used to shelter income, instead of just dividend income? The implication would be that no one has to pay taxes—*ever*!

16.5 The Pettit study suggests an increase in the price per share of common stock commensurate with an increase in dividends. Can this be taken as evidence that the value of the firm is in fact affected by dividend policy?

16.6 Assume that the XYZ firm has the following parameters in a world with no taxes:

$\sigma = .2$	instantaneous standard deviation,
$T = 4$ years	maturity of debt,
$V = \$2,000$	value of the firm $(V = B + S)$,
$R_f = .06$	risk-free rate,
$D = \$1,000$	face value of debt.

(a) What will be the market value of equity cum dividend (i.e., before any dividend is paid)?

(b) If the shareholders decide to pay themselves a $500 dividend out of cash, what will be the ex-dividend wealth of shareholders? (*Note*: The dividend payment will have two effects.

First, it will decrease the market value of the firm to $1,500. Second, since cash has little or no risk, the instantaneous standard deviation of the firm's assets will increase to .25.)

16.7 The chairman of the board of Alphanull Corporation has announced that the corporation will change its dividend policy from paying a fixed dollar dividend per share. Instead, dividends will be paid out as a residual. That is, any cash flows left over after the firm has undertaken all profitable investments will be paid out to shareholders. This new policy will obviously increase the variability of dividends paid. How do you think it will affect the value of the firm?

16.8 The XYZ Company (an all-equity firm) currently has after-tax operating cash flows of $3.00 per share and pays out 50% of its earnings in dividends. If it expects to keep the same payout ratio, and to earn 20% on future investments forever, what will its current price per share be? Assume that the cost of capital is 15%.

16.9 The balance sheet of the Universal Sour Candy Company is given in Table Q16.9. Assume that all balance sheet items are expressed in terms of market values. The company has decided to pay a $2,000 dividend to shareholders. There are four ways to do it:

1. Pay a cash dividend.
2. Issue $2,000 of new debt and equity in equal proportions ($1,000 each) and use the proceeds to pay the dividend.
3. Issue $2,000 of new equity and use the proceeds to pay the dividend.
4. Use the $2,000 of cash to repurchase equity.

What impact will each of the four policies above have on the following?

(a) The systematic risk of the portfolio of assets held by the firm
(b) The market value of original bondholders' wealth
(c) The market value ratio of debt to equity
(d) The market value of the firm in a world without taxes

Table Q16.9 Balance Sheet as of December 31, 2003

Assets		Liabilities	
Cash	$2,000	Debt	$5,000
Inventory	2,000	Equity	5,000
Property, plant, and equipment	6,000	Total liabilities	$10,000
Total assets	$10,000		

16.10 Prove the following for a firm with no supernormal growth (in a world with only corporate taxes):

$$V^L = \frac{E(EBIT_1)(1 - \tau_c)}{WACC} = V^U + \tau_c B.$$

16.11 How does an increase in the investment (retention rate) affect the anticipated stream of investments that a company will undertake?

16.12 It was suggested that if a firm announces its intention to increase its dividends (paid from cash), the price of common stock increases, presumably because the higher dividend payout represents an unambiguous signal to shareholders that anticipated cash flows from investment are permanently higher. A higher level of cash flows is also beneficial to bondholders because it diminishes the probability of default. If dividends are paid from cash, what does the OPM suggest will happen to the market value of debt?

REFERENCES

Aharony, J., and I. Swary, "Quarterly Dividend and Earnings Announcements and Stockholders' Returns: An Empirical Analysis," *Journal of Finance*, March 1980, 1–12.

Allen, F., A. Bernardo, and I. Welch, "A Theory of Dividends Based on Tax Clienteles," *Journal of Finance*, December 2000, Vol. 55, No. 6, 2444–2536.

Asquith, P., and W. Krasker, "Changes in Dividend Policy, and Stock Trading Volume," working paper, Harvard Business School, October 1985.

Asquith, P., and D. Mullins, Jr., "The Impact of Initiating Dividend Payments on Shareholders' Wealth," *Journal of Business*, January 1983, 77–96.

Austin, D., "Treasury Stock Reacquisition by American Corporations 1961–1967," *Financial Executive*, May 1969, 40–61.

Bajaj, M., and A. Vijh, "Dividend Clienteles and the Information Content of Dividend Changes," *Journal of Financial Economics*, August 1990, Vol. 26, No. 2, 176–192.

Baker, M., and J. Wurgler, "A Catering Theory of Dividends," working paper, Harvard University, 2002.

Bali, R., and G. Hite, "Ex Dividend Day Stock Price Behavior: Discreteness or Tax-Induced Clienteles?" *Journal of Financial Economics*, February 1998, Vol. 47, No. 2, 127–160.

Bar-Yosef, S., and R. Kolodny, "Dividend Policy and Market Theory," *Review of Economics and Statistics*, May 1976, 181–190.

Bell, L., and T. Jenkinson, "New Evidence of the Impact of Dividend Taxation and on the Identity of the Marginal Investor," *Journal of Finance*, June 2002, Vol. 57, No. 3, 1321–1346.

Bernartzi, S., R. Michaely, and R. Thakor, "Do Changes in Dividends Signal the Future or the Past?" *Journal of Finance*, July 1997, Vol. 52, No. 3, 1007–1034.

Bhattacharya, S., "Imperfect Information, Dividend Policy, and 'The Bird in the Hand' Fallacy," *Bell Journal of Economics,* Spring 1979, 259–270.

Bierman, H., and R. West, "The Acquisition of Common Stock by the Corporate Issuer," *Journal of Finance*, December 1966, 687–696.

Black, F., "The Dividend Puzzle," *Journal of Portfolio Management*, Winter 1976, 5–8.

Black, F., M. Jensen, and M. Scholes, "The Capital Asset Pricing Model: Some Empirical Tests," in M. Jensen, ed., *Studies in the Theory of Capital Markets*. Praeger, New York, 1972, 79–124.

Black, F., and M. Scholes, "The Effects of Dividend Yield and Dividend Policy on Common Stock Prices and Returns," *Journal of Financial Economics*, May 1974, 1–22.

Blume, M., "Stock Returns and Dividend Yields: Some More Evidence," *Review of Economics and Statistics*, November 1980, 567–577.

Booth, L., and D. Johnston, "The Ex-Dividend Day Behavior of Canadian Stock Prices: Tax Changes and Clientele Effects," *Journal of Finance*, June 1984, 457–476.

Brav, A., J. Graham, C. Harvey, and R. Michaely, "Payout Policy in the 21st Century," working paper, Duke University, 2003.

Brennan, M., "Taxes, Market Valuation and Corporate Financial Policy," *National Tax Journal*, December 1970, 417–427.

Brennan, M., and Copeland, T., "Stock Splits, Stock Prices, and Transaction Costs," *Journal of Financial Economics*, December 1988.

Brennan, M., and A. Thakor, "Shareholder Preferences and Dividend Policy," *Journal of Finance*, September 1990, Vol. 45, No. 4, 993–1018.

Brickley, J., "Shareholder Wealth, Information Signaling and the Specially Designated Dividend," *Journal of Financial Economics*, August 1983, 187–210.

Charest, G., "Dividend Information, Stock Returns and Market Efficiency," *Journal of Financial Economics*, June–September 1978, 297–330.

Coates, C., and A. Fredman, "Price Behavior Associated with Tender Offers to Repurchase Common Stock," *Financial Executive*, April 1976, 40–44.

Cusatis, P., J. Miles, and J. R. Woolridge, "Restructuring through Spin-offs: The Stock Market Evidence," *Journal of Financial Economics*, June 1993, Vol. 33, No. 3, 264–292.

Daley, L., V. Mehruta, and R. Sivakumar, "Corporate Focus and Value Creation: Evidence from Spin-offs," *Journal of Financial Economics*, August 1997, Vol. 45, No. 2, 224–257.

Dann, L., "Common Stock Repurchases: An Analysis of Returns to Bondholders and Stockholders," *Journal of Financial Economics*, June 1981, 113–138.

DeAngelo, H., and L. DeAngelo, "Dividend Policy and Financial Distress: An Empirical Investigation of Troubled NYSE Firms," *Journal of Finance*, December 1990, Vol. 45, No. 5, 1415–1431.

DeAngelo, H., L. DeAngelo, and D. Skinner, "Special Dividends and the Evolution of Dividend Signaling," *Journal of Financial Economics*, September 2000, Vol. 57, No. 3, 309–354.

———, "Are Dividends Disappearing?: Dividend Concentration and the Consolidation of Earnings," working paper, University of Southern California, July 2002.

Denis, D., "Defensive Changes in Corporate Payout Policy: Share Repurchases and Special Dividends," *Journal of Finance*, December 1990, Vol. 45, No. 5, 1433–1456.

Dielman, T., T. Nantell, and R. Wright, "Price Effects of Stock Repurchasing: A Random Coefficient Regression Approach," *Journal of Financial and Quantitative Analysis*, March 1980, 175–189.

Dittmar, A., "Why Do Firms Repurchase Stock?" *Journal of Business*, Vol. 73, 331–355.

Dittmar, A., and R. Dittmar, "Stock Repurchase Waves: An Explanation of Trends in Aggregate Corporate Payout Policy," working paper, Indiana, University, 2002.

Dobrovolsky, S., *The Economics of Corporation Finance*. McGraw-Hill, New York, 1971.

Eades, K., P. Hess, and E. H. Kim, "On Interpreting Security Returns during the Ex-Dividend Period," *Journal of Financial Economics*, March 1984, 3–34.

———, "Market Rationality and Dividend Announcements," *Journal of Financial Economics*, December 1985, 581–604.

Elton, E. J., and M. J. Gruber, "The Effect of Share Repurchase on the Value of the Firm," *Journal of Finance*, March 1968, 135–149.

———, "Marginal Stockholders' Tax Rates and the Clientele Effect," *Review of Economics and Statistics*, February 1970, 68–74.

Fama, E., "The Empirical Relationship between the Dividend and Investment Decisions of Firms," *American Economic Review*, June 1974, 304–318.

Fama, E., and H. Babiak, "Dividend Policy: An Empirical Analysis," *Journal of the American Statistical Association*, December 1968, 1132–1161.

Fama, E., L. Fisher, M. Jensen, and R. Roll, "The Adjustment of Stock Prices to New Information," *International Economic Review*, February 1969, 1–21.

Fama, E., and K. French, "Disappearing Dividends: Changing Firm Characteristics or Lower Propensity to Pay?" *Journal of Financial Economics*, 2001, Vol. 60, 3–43.

Farrar, D., and L. Selwyn, "Taxes, Corporate Financial Policy and Return to Investors," *National Tax Journal*, December 1967, 444–454.

Feenberg, D., "Does the Investment Interest Limitation Explain the Existence of Dividends?" *Journal of Financial Economics*, September 1981, 265–270.

Frank, M., and R. Jaganathan, "Why Do Stock Prices Drop by Less than the Value of the Dividend? Evidence from a Country without Taxes." *Journal of Financial Economics*, February 1998, Vol. 47, No. 2, 128–160.

Friend, I., and M. Puckett, "Dividends and Stock Prices," *American Economic Review*, September 1964, 656–682.

Gordon, M., "Dividends, Earnings, and Stock Prices," *Review of Economics and Statistics*, May 1959, 99–105.

———, "The Savings, Investment and Valuation of a Corporation," *Review of Economics and Statistics*, February 1962, 37–51.

Gordon, R., and D. Bradford, "Taxation and the Stock Market Valuation of Capital Gains and Dividends," *Journal of Public Economics*, October 1980, 103–136.

Grinblatt, M., R. Masulis, and S. Titman, "The Valuation Effects of Stock Splits and Stock Dividends," *Journal of Financial Economics*, December 1984, 461–490.

Grullon, G., and R. Michaely, "Dividends, Share Repurchase and the Substitution Hypothesis," *Journal of Finance*, August 2002, Vol. 57, No. 4, 1649–1684.

Guay, V., and J. Harford, "The Cash-Flow Performance and Information Content of Dividend Increases versus Repurchases," *Journal of Financial Economics*, September 2000, Vol. 57, No. 3, 385–416.

Hakannson, N., "To Pay or Not to Pay Dividends," *Journal of Finance*, May 1982, 415–428.

Handjiinicolaou, G., and A. Kalay, "Wealth Redistributions or Changes in Firm Value: An Analysis of Returns to Bondholders and Stockholders around Dividend Announcements," *Journal of Financial Economics*, March 1984, 35–64.

Harris, J., Jr., R. Roenfeldt, and P. Cooley, "Evidence of Financial Leverage Clientele," *Journal of Finance*, September 1983, 1125–1132.

Hess, P., "The Ex-Dividend Behavior of Stock Returns: Further Evidence on Tax Effects," *Journal of Finance*, May 1982, 445–456.

Higgins, R., "The Corporate Dividend-Saving Decision," *Journal of Financial and Quantitative Analysis*, March 1972, 1527–1541.

Hite, G., and J. Owners, "Security Price Reactions around Corporate Spin-Off Announcements," *Journal of Financial Economics*, December 1983, 409–436.

Jaganathan, M., C. Stephens, and M. Weisbach, "Financial Flexibility and the Choice between Dividends and Stock Repurchases," *Journal of Financial Economics*, September 2000, Vol. 57, No. 3, 355–384.

John, K., and L. Long, "Insider Trading around Dividend Announcements," *Journal of Finance*, September 1991, Vol. 46, No. 4, 1361–1389.

John, K., and J. Williams, "Dividends, Dilution and Taxes: A Signalling Equilibrium," *Journal of Finance*, September 1985, 1053–1070.

Kalay, A., "Essays in Dividend Policy," Ph.D. dissertation, University of Rochester, 1977.

———, "The Ex-Dividend Behavior of Stock Prices; A Re-examination of the Clientele Effect," *Journal of Financial Economics*, September 1982, 1059–1070.

Kalay, A., and U. Lowenstein, "Predictable Events and Excess Returns: The Case of Dividend Announcements," *Journal of Financial Economics*, September 1985, 423–450.

———, "The Informational Content of the Timing of Dividend Announcements," *Journal of Financial Economics*, July 1986, 373–388.

Kane, A., Y. K. Lee, and A. Marcus, "Signaling, Information Content, and the Reluctance to Cut Dividends," *Journal of Financial and Quantitative Analysis*, November 1980, 855–870.

———, "Earnings and Dividend Announcements: Is There a Corroboration Effect?" *Journal of Finance*, September 1984, 1091–1099.

Kaplanis, C., "Options, Taxes, and Ex-dividend Day Behavior," *Journal of Finance*, June 1986, 411–424.

Keim, D., "Dividend Yields and Stock Returns: Implications of Abnormal January Returns," *Journal of Financial Economics*, September 1985, 473–490.

Khoury, N., and K. Smith, "Dividend Policy and the Capital Gains Tax in Canada," *Journal of Business Administration*, Spring 1977.

Kim, E. H., W. Lewellen, and J. McConnell, "Financial Leverage Clienteles: Theory and Evidence," *Journal of Financial Economics*, March 1979, 83–110.

Krushnaswami, S., and V. Subramanian, "Information Asymmetry, Valuation, and the Corporate Spinoff Decision," *Journal of Financial Economics*, July 1999, Vol. 53, No. 1, 44–72.

Kwan, C., "Efficient Market Tests of the Informational Content of Dividend Announcements: Critique and Extension," *Journal of Financial and Quantitative Analysis,* June 1981, 193–206.

Lakonishok, J., and T. Vermaelen, "Tax Reform and Ex-Dividend Day Behavior," *Journal of Finance*, September 1983, 1157–1179.

———, "Tax-induced Trading around Ex-Dividend Days," *Journal of Financial Economics*, July 1986, 287–320.

Lane, W., "Repurchase of Common Stock and Managerial Discretion," Ph.D. dissertation, University of North Carolina, 1976.

Lewellen, W., K. Stanley, R. Lease, and G. Schlarbaum, "Some Direct Evidence on the Dividend Clientele Phenomenon," *Journal of Finance*, December 1978, 1385–1399.

Lintner, J., "Distribution of Incomes of Corporations among Dividends, Retained Earnings and Taxes," *American Economic Review*, May 1956, 97–113.

———, "Optimal Dividends and Corporate Growth under Uncertainty," *Quarterly Journal of Economics*, February 1964, 49–95.

———, "The Valuation of Risk Assets and the Selection of Risky Investments in Stock Portfolios and Capital Budgets," *Review of Economics and Statistics*, February 1965, 13–37.

Litzenberger, R., and K. Ramaswamy, "The Effect of Personal Taxes and Dividends on Capital Asset Prices: Theory and Empirical Evidence," *Journal of Financial Economics*, June 1979, 163–196.

———, "Dividends, Short-Selling Restrictions, Tax-Induced Investor Clienteles and Market Equilibrium," *Journal of Finance*, May 1980, 469–482.

———, "The Effects of Dividends on Common Stock Prices: Tax Effects or Information Effects?" *Journal of Finance*, May 1982, 429–444.

Loderer, C., and D. Mauer, "Corporate Dividends and Seasoned Equity Issues: An Empirical Investigation," *Journal of Finance*, March 1992, Vol. 47, No. 1, 201–225.

Long, J., Jr., "Efficient Portfolio Choice with Differential Taxation of Dividends and Capital Gains," *Journal of Financial Economics*, August 1977, 25–54.

———, "The Market Valuation of Cash Dividends: A Case to Consider," *Journal of Financial Economics*, June–September 1978, 235–264.

Mackie–Mason, J., "Do Taxes Affect Corporate Financing Decisions?" *Journal of Finance*, December 1990, Vol. 45, No. 5, 1471–1493.

Masulis, R., "Stock Repurchase by Tender Offer: An Analysis of the Causes of Common Stock Price Changes," *Journal of Finance*, May 1980, 305–318.

Masulis, R., and B. Trueman, "Corporate Investment and Dividend Decisions under Differential Personal Taxation," *Journal of Financial and Quantitative Analysis,* December 1988.

Maxwell, W., and C. Stephens, "The Wealth Effects of Repurchases on Bondholders," working paper, University of Missouri, 2001.

McCabe, G., "The Empirical Relationship between Investment and Financing: A New Look," *Journal of Financial and Quantitative Analysis*, March 1979, 119–135.

Miller, M. H., "Debt and Taxes," *Journal of Finance*, May 1977, 261–275.

———, "Dividends and Taxes: Some Empirical Evidence," *Journal of Political Economy*, December 1982, 1118–1141.

Miller, M. H., and F. Modigliani, "Dividend Policy, Growth and the Valuation of Shares," *Journal of Business*, October 1961, 411–433.

Miller, M., and K. Rock, "Dividend Policy under Asymmetric Information," *Journal of Finance*, September 1985, 1031–1051.

Miller, M., and M. Scholes, "Dividends and Taxes," *Journal of Financial Economics*, December 1978, 333–364.

———, "Dividends and Taxes: Some Empirical Evidence," *Journal of Political Economy*, December 1982, 1118–1141.

Modigliani, F., and M. Miller, "Taxes and the Cost of Capital: A Correction," *American Economic Review*, June 1963, 433–443.

Morgan, I. G., "Dividends and Stock Price Behavior in Canada," *Journal of Business Administration*, Fall 1980, 91–106.

Naranjo, A., M. Nimalendran, and M. Ryngaert, "Stock Returns, Dividend Yields and Taxes," *Journal of Finance*, December 1998, Vol. 53, No. 6, 2029–2057.

Nissim, D., and A. Ziv, "Dividend Changes and Future Profitability," *Journal of Finance*, December 2001, Vol. 56, No. 6, 2111–2133.

Noe, T., and M. Rebello, "Asymmetric Information, Managerial Opportunism, Financing, and Payout Policies," *Journal of Finance*, June 1996, Vol. 51, No. 2, 637–660.

Penman, S., "The Predictive Content of Earnings Forecasts and Dividends," *Journal of Finance*, September 1983, 1181–1199.

Pettit, R. R., "Dividend Announcements, Security Performance, and Capital Market Efficiency," *Journal of Finance*, December 1972, 993–1007.

———, "The Impact of Dividend and Earnings Announcements: A Reconciliation," *Journal of Business*, January 1976, 86–96.

———, "Taxes, Transactions Costs and Clientele Effects of Dividends," *Journal of Financial Economics*, December 1977, 419–436.

Poterba, J., "The Market Valuation of Cash Dividends: The Citizens Utilities Case Reconsidered," *Journal of Financial Economics*, March 1986, 395–406.

Poterba, J., and L. Summers, "Taxes, Transactions Costs and Clientele Effects of Dividends," *Journal of Financial Economics*, December 1977, 419–436.

———, "New Evidence That Taxes Affect the Valuation of Dividends," *Journal of Finance*, December 1984, 1397–1415.

Richardson, G., S. Sefcik, and R. Thompson, "A Test of Dividend Irrelevance Using Volume Reactions to a Change in Dividend Policy," *Journal of Financial Economics*, December 1986, 313–334.

Ross, S. A., "The Determination of Financial Structure: The Incentive-Signalling Approach," *Bell Journal of Economics*, Spring 1977, 23–40.

———, "Some Notes on Financial Incentive-Signalling Models, Activity Choice and Risk Preferences," *Journal of Finance*, June 1978, 777–792.

Rozeff, M., "Growth, Beta and Agency Costs as Determinants of Dividend Payout Ratios," *Journal of Financial Research*, Fall 1982, 249–259.

Sheffrin, H., and M. Statman, "Explaining Investor Preference for Cash Dividends," *Journal of Financial Economics*, June 1984, 253–282.

Slavin, M., M. Sushka, and S. Ferraro, "A Comparison of the Information Conveyed by Equity Carve-outs, Spin-offs, and Asset Sell Offs," *Journal of Financial Economics*, January 1995, Vol. 37, No. 1, 68–88.

Smirlock, M., and W. Marshall, "An Examination of the Empirical Relationship between the Dividend and Investment Decisions: A Note," *Journal of Finance*, December 1983, 1659–1667.

Stewart, S., "Should a Corporation Repurchase Its Own Stock?" *Journal of Finance*, June 1976, 911–921.

Van Horne, J., and J. G. McDonald, "Dividend Policy and New Equity Financing," *Journal of Finance*, May 1971, 507–520.

Vermaelen, T., "Common Stock Repurchases and Market Signalling: An Empirical Study," *Journal of Financial Economics*, June 1981, 139–183.

Walter, J. E., *Dividend Policy and Enterprise Valuation*. Wadsworth, Belmont, Calif., 1967.

Watts, R., "The Information Content of Dividends," *Journal of Business,* April 1973, 191–211.

———, "Comments on 'The Impact of Dividend and Earnings Announcements: A Reconciliation,' " *Journal of Business*, January 1976, 81–85.

Woods, D., and E. Brigham, "Stockholder Distribution Decisions: Share Repurchases or Dividends?" *Journal of Financial and Quantitative Analysis*, March 1966, 15–28.

Woolridge, J., "Dividend Changes and Security Prices," *Journal of Finance*, December 1983, 1607–1615.

Young, A., "The Performance of Common Stocks Subsequent to Repurchase," *Financial Analysts Journal*, September–October 1967, 117–121.

Chapter 17

Espoused theories often represent our ideas—indeed our ideals—about effective action. Theories-in-use are what produce real, concrete actions.

—Chris Argyris, *Flawed Advice and the Management Trap*, Oxford Press, 2000.

Applied Issues in Corporate Finance

A. Introduction

T HIS CHAPTER IS A COLLECTION OF TOPICS that are each important to decision making. But they are, for the most part, straightforward applications of the theories found elsewhere in the book. They include the theory of leasing, with the key point being that leasing is a substitute for senior secured debt financing. The right point of view is lease versus borrow, not lease versus buy. Next, we discuss another type of financing, namely, interest rate swaps. We also discuss the complex topic of risk management and hedging—stressing that the correct objective is to maximize the value of the firm rather than to minimize its risk. Fourth is a discussion of the management of the pension obligations of the firm, and finally is a brief section on how to analyze leveraged buyouts (LBOs).

B. Leasing

Lease contracts have long been an important alternative to direct ownership of an asset. For example, one may choose to lease an automobile or rent a house, rather than owning them outright. For the student of finance, leasing is an important applied issue because the use of an asset and the methods of financing it are seemingly intertwined. However, this is an illusion. As we shall see, it is critical to keep the investment decision separate from the financing decision in the analysis. Failure to do so has led many decision makers to make the wrong comparison between the lease/own decision and the lease/borrow decision.

For the purpose of consistency, we shall assume throughout most of this section that there are no transactions costs or economies of scale in financial contracts. Among other things, this implies that there are no flotation costs in issuing financial securities. Thus it would make no difference at all in the percentage of transactions costs whether one issued a bond for $100 or $100,000,000. Additionally, we shall assume (1) that firms possess optimal capital structures without specifying the reason, (2) that firms may have different effective tax rates, and (3) that the Miller-Modigliani [1966] valuation framework is applicable. First, we review a detailed description of the legal and accounting treatment of different types of lease contracts. Then we analyze the economics of the lease/buy decision for noncancelable long-term leases, for cancelable leases, for leveraged leases, and for short-term leases. Finally, the scant empirical literature on leasing is reviewed.

1. The Legal and Accounting Treatment of Leases

TYPES OF LEASES Leases take several different forms, the most important of which are sale and leaseback, service or operating leases, and straight financial leases. These three major types of leases are described below.

Under a *sale and leaseback arrangement*, a firm owning land, buildings, or equipment sells the property to a financial institution and simultaneously executes an agreement to lease the property back for a certain period under specific terms.

Note that the seller, or *lessee*, immediately receives the purchase price put up by the buyer, or lessor. At the same time, the seller-lessee retains the use of the property. This parallel is carried over to the lease payment schedule. Under a mortgage loan arrangement the financial institution receives a series of equal payments just sufficient to amortize the loan and to provide the lender with a specified rate of return on investment. Under a sale and leaseback arrangement the lease payments are set up in the same manner. The payments are sufficient to return the full purchase price to the financial institution in addition to providing it with some return on its investment.

Operating (or service) leases include both financing and maintenance services. IBM is one of the pioneers of the service lease contract. Computers and office copying machines, together with automobiles and trucks, are the primary types of equipment covered by operating leases. The leases ordinarily call for the lessor to maintain and service the leased equipment, and the costs of this maintenance are either built into the lease payments or contracted for separately.

Another important characteristic of the service lease is that it is frequently not fully amortized. In other words the payments required under the lease contract are not sufficient to recover the full cost of the equipment. Obviously, however, the lease contract is written for considerably less than the expected life of the leased equipment, and the lessor expects to recover the cost either in subsequent renewal payments or on disposal of the equipment.

A final feature of the service lease is that it frequently contains a cancelation clause giving the lessee the right to cancel the lease and return the equipment before the expiration of the basic agreement. This is an important consideration for the lessee, who can return the equipment if technological developments render it obsolete or if it simply is no longer needed.

A *strict financial lease* is one that does not provide for maintenance services, is not cancelable, and is fully amortized (i.e., the lessor contracts for rental payments equal to the full price of the leased equipment). The typical arrangement involves the following steps:

1. The user firm selects the specific equipment it requires and negotiates the price and delivery terms with the manufacturer or distributor.

2. Next, the user firm arranges with a bank or leasing company for the latter to buy the equipment from the manufacturer or distributor, simultaneously executing an agreement to lease the equipment from the financial institution. The terms call for full amortization of the financial institution's cost, plus a rate of return on investment. The lessee generally has the option to

renew the lease at a reduced rental on expiration of the basic lease but does not have the right to cancel the basic lease without completely paying off the financial institution.

Financial leases are almost the same as sale and leaseback arrangements, the main difference being that the leased equipment is new and the lessor buys it from a manufacturer or a distributor instead of from the user-lessee. A sale and leaseback can thus be thought of as a special type of financial lease.

TAX TREATMENT The full amount of the annual lease payments is deductible for income tax purposes—provided the Internal Revenue Service (IRS) agrees that a particular contract is a genuine lease and not simply an installment loan called a lease. This makes it important that the lease contract be written in a form acceptable to the IRS. Following are the major requirements for bona fide lease transactions costs from the standpoint of the IRS:

1. The term must be less than 30 years; otherwise the lease is regarded as a form of sale.

2. The rent must represent a reasonable return to the lessor.

3. The renewal option must be bona fide, and this requirement can best be met by giving the lessee the first option to meet an equal bona fide outside offer.

4. There must be no repurchase option; if there is, the lessee should merely be given parity with an equal outside offer.

ACCOUNTING TREATMENT In November 1976 the Financial Accounting Standards Board issued its Statement of Financial Accounting Standards No. 13, *Accounting for Leases*. Like other FASB statements, the standards set forth must be followed by business firms if their financial statements are to receive certification by auditors. FASB Statement No. 13 has implications both for the utilization of leases and for their accounting treatment. Those implications of FASB Statement No. 13 that are most relevant for financial analysis of leases are summarized below.

For some types of leases, this FASB statement requires that the obligation be capitalized on the asset side of the balance sheet with a related lease obligation on the liability side. The accounting treatment depends on the type of lease. The classification is more detailed than the two categories of operating and financial leases described above.

From the lessee's point of view the two accounting categories are *capital leases* and *operating leases*. A lease is classified in Statement No. 13 as a capital lease if it meets one or more of four Paragraph 7 criteria:

1. The lease transfers ownership of the property to the lessee by the end of the lease term.

2. The lease gives the lessee the option to purchase the property at a price sufficiently below the expected fair value of the property that the exercise of the option is highly probable.

3. The lease term is equal to 75% or more of the estimated economic life of the property.

4. The present value of the minimum lease payments exceeds 90% of the fair value of the property at the inception of the lease. The discount factor to be used in calculating the present value is the implicit rate used by the lessor or the lessee's incremental borrowing rate, whichever is lower. (Note that a lower discount factor represents a higher calculated present value for a given pattern of lease payments. Thus, it increases the likelihood that the 90% test will be met and that the lease will be classified as a capital lease.)

From the standpoint of the lessee, if a lease is not a capital lease, it is classified as an operating lease.

From the standpoint of the lessor, four types of leases are defined: (1) *sales-type leases*, (2) *direct financing leases*, (3) *leveraged leases*, and (4) *operating leases*, representing all leases other than the first three types. Sales-type leases and direct financing leases meet one or more of the four Paragraph 7 criteria and both of the Paragraph 8 criteria, which are

1. Collectability of the minimum lease payments is reasonably predictable.
2. No important uncertainties surround the amount of unreimbursable costs yet to be incurred by the lessor under the lease.

Sales-type leases give rise to profit (or loss) to the lessor—the fair value of the leased property at the inception of the lease is greater (or less) than its cost-of-carrying amount. Sales-type leases normally arise when manufacturers or dealers use leasing in marketing their products. Direct financing leases are leases other than leveraged leases for which the cost-of-carrying amount is equal to the fair value of the leased property at the inception of the lease. Leveraged leases are direct financing leases in which substantial financing is provided by a long-term creditor on a nonrecourse basis with respect to the general credit of the lessor.

The actual bookkeeping for lessees is set up in the following way. For operating leases, rentals must be charged to expense over the lease term, with disclosures of future rental obligations in total as well as by each of the following five years. For lessees, capital leases are to be capitalized and shown on the balance sheet both as a fixed asset and as a noncurrent obligation. Capitalization represents the present value of the minimum lease payments minus that portion of lease payments representing executory costs such as insurance, maintenance, and taxes to be paid by the lessor (including any profit return in such charges). As described in Paragraph 7(4), the discount factor is the lower of the implicit rates used by the lessor or the incremental borrowing rate of the lessee.

The asset must be amortized in a manner consistent with the lessee's normal depreciation policy for owned assets. During the lease term, each lease payment is to be allocated between a reduction of the obligation and the interest expense to produce a constant rate of interest on the remaining balance of the obligation. Thus for capital leases the balance sheet includes the terms in Table 17.1.

In addition to the balance sheet capitalization of capital leases, substantial additional footnote disclosures are required for both capital and operating leases. These include a description of leasing arrangements, an analysis of leased property under capital leases by major classes of property, a schedule by years of future minimum lease payments (with executory and interest costs broken out for capital leases), and contingent rentals for operating leases.

FASB Statement No. 13 sets forth requirements for capitalizing capital leases and for standardizing disclosures by lessees for both capital leases and operating leases. Lease commitments therefore do not represent "off-balance-sheet" financing for capital assets, and standard disclosure requirements make general the footnote reporting of information on operating leases. Hence the

Table 17.1 Balance Sheet for Capitalized Leases

Assets	Liabilities
	Current:
Leased property under capital leases	Obligations under capital leases
less accumulated amortization	Noncurrent:
	Obligations under capital leases

argument that leasing represents a form of financing that lenders may not take into account in their analysis of the financial position of firms seeking financing will be even less valid in the future than it is now.

It is unlikely that sophisticated lenders were ever fooled by off-balance-sheet leasing obligations. However, the capitalization of capital leases and the standard disclosure requirements for operating leases will make it easier for general users of financial reports to obtain additional information on firms' leasing obligations. Hence the requirements of FASB Statement No. 13 are useful. Probably the extent to which leasing is used will remain substantially unaltered since the particular circumstances that have provided a basis for its use in the past are not likely to be greatly affected by the increased disclosure requirements.

2. The Theory of Leasing

THE LONG-TERM LEASE FROM THE LESSOR'S POINT OF VIEW The lessor is frequently a financial intermediary such as a commercial bank, an insurance company, or a leasing company. Also equipment manufacturers—for example, GATX (railroad cars), IBM (computers and office equipment), and Xerox (copiers)—are among the largest lessors. However, the institutional arrangements are largely arbitrary. Anyone who owns an asset may also decide to lease it. For example, suppose one owns a car or a house. There is always the choice between owning it and using it for one's own purposes, thereby gaining a direct (nontaxable) stream of consumption of transportation or housing services. Or alternatively, one can lease the asset to a second party. In return one then receives a (taxable) stream of income that can be used for the consumption of transportation and housing (among other things). From the lessee's point of view, the choice to own the asset in the first place was an investment decision. At the same time, there is a separate decision to make—namely, the financing decision. Should use of the asset be financed with debt and equity, or should it be leased? How much of the lease financing can be considered to be debt? How much is equity?

In the analysis that follows it is convenient to divide lease contracts into major categories: (1) *strict financial leases* and (2) *operating leases*. Strict financial leases, along with sale and leaseback arrangements, will be characterized as perfect substitutes for debt capital; in other words, they have exactly the same risk.[1] A lessee may not cancel a strict financial lease, the failure to meet lease payments can force the lessee into bankruptcy (or reorganization), and the lease is fully amortized (i.e., the lessor receives lease payments that repay the full cost of the leased asset). Operating leases are riskier than financial leases. We assume that they may be canceled at the option of the lessee, are usually not fully amortized, and require that the salvage value go to the lessor. Finally, either type of lease may involve a separable contract for various types of maintenance on the leased asset (e.g., automobile servicing). Because the maintenance contract is economically separable, we shall not discuss it in this chapter.

Financial leases and operating leases involve very different risks to the lessor and must therefore be discussed separately. We shall defer a discussion of operating leases until later in the chapter and focus on the much simpler financial lease for the time being. Suppose that the lessor is a commercial bank. Recall that any commercial bank will hold a well-diversified portfolio of corporate debt as its major asset. Obviously it requires that this portfolio earn (at least) the bank's after-tax weighted average cost of capital. On the other hand, what we call the rate of return to the bank is also the

---

[1] This means that debt capital lent to the ith firm and leased to the same firm have the *same* risk. Of course, lending to different firms may have different risks.

cost of debt to the borrowing firm. Therefore if we designate the bank's after-tax weighted average cost of capital as $WACC_B$ and the firm's before-tax cost of debt as k_b, then

$$k_b = \frac{WACC_B}{(1 - \tau_c)},$$

where τ_c is the bank's marginal tax rate.

The Modigliani-Miller model may be employed to compute $WACC_B$, the lessor's after-tax weighted average cost of capital.[2] Designate $\rho(\text{lease})$ as the rate of return required on leasing projects, assuming that the lessor is 100% equity financed. Then, given that B and S are the market values of debt and equity, respectively, the M-M cost of capital is

$$WACC_B = \rho(\text{lease}) \left[1 - \tau_c \frac{B}{B + S}\right].$$

If the required rate of return on the lease project is 9.375% and the leasing firm (the bank) uses 90% debt in its optimal capital structure and has a 40% marginal tax rate, then

$$WACC_B = .09375[1 - .4(.9)] = .06.$$

Thus from the lessor's point of view the lease project will have a 6% after-tax weighted average cost of capital. From the lessee's point of view the before-tax cost of leasing will be

$$k_b = \frac{WACC_B}{1 - \tau_c} = \frac{.06}{1 - .4} = 10\%.$$

As mentioned before, each dollar in a pure financial lease is a perfect substitute for one dollar of debt in the capital structure of the lessee firm. Thus if a lessee is at its optimal capital structure prior to signing a lease contract and wishes to maintain that structure, then it must displace one dollar of debt for each dollar in the lease contract.

What lease fee should the lessor charge for a pure financial lease? Assume the cost of the leased asset is $\$I$, the lessor's tax rate is τ_c, and the annual (straight-line) depreciation write-off on the leased asset is dep_t.[3] Also, assume that there is no salvage value. If the lessor charges an annual lease payment of L_t, then the net present value of the lease to the lessor is[4]

$$NPV \text{ (to lessor)} = -I + \sum_{t=1}^{N} \frac{L_t(1 - \tau_c) + \tau_c dep_t}{(1 + WACC_B)^t} \tag{17.1}$$

The numerator of Eq. 17.1 is the standard definition of after-tax cash flows from an investment, including the depreciation tax shield.[5] To provide a numerical example, let $I = \$10,000$, $\tau_c = 40\%$,

---

[2] See Chapter 15, Eq. (15.12).

[3] Although we have assumed straight-line depreciation for convenience, there is usually an optimal depreciation schedule that maximizes the present value of the depreciation tax shield. Our analysis will not change if, in practice, both the lessor and lessee use the same optimal depreciation schedule.

[4] For convenience, we have assumed that the stream of lease payments is an annuity with the first payment at the end of the first year. Most lease contracts require the first payment to be made immediately.

[5] If there were an investment tax credit, it would also be counted as a cash inflow.

$WACC_B = 6\%$, and the life of the project, N, be 5 years. Given these facts and assuming that the lease fee is competitively determined so that NPV (to lessor) $= 0$, then the minimum lease fee, L_t, is

$$0 = -10,000 + \sum_{t=1}^{5} \frac{L_t(1-.4) + .4(2,000)}{(1+.06)^t}$$

$$0 = -10,000 + L_t(.6)(4.212) + 4(2,000)(4.212)$$

$$\frac{10,000 - .4(2,000)(4.212)}{.6(4.212)} = L_t = \$2,624.$$

If the lessor charges \$2,624, then it will earn a rate of return that just compensates it for taking a debt position in the lessee firm. A higher lease fee would result in a positive NPV.

THE INVESTMENT DECISION Now suppose that, instead of leasing the asset, the *lessor* decides to own it and operate it. What rate of return would be required? Clearly, owning the asset exposes the lessor to more risk than a lending position of an equivalent dollar amount. Owning the project involves the total risk of its cash flows, not merely the risk of a debt position. Suppose we define the required rate of return on the unlevered cash flows from the project as $\rho(\text{project})$. We know that $\rho(\text{project}) > k_b(\text{lease}) \geq WACC_B$. Furthermore, if one borrows to undertake the investment, the Modigliani-Miller definition of the cost of capital can be applied. Then if the project's optimal capital structure is $B/(B+S)$, the appropriate weighted average cost of capital is

$$WACC \text{ (project)} = \rho(\text{project}) \left(1 - \tau_c \frac{B}{B+S}\right). \tag{17.2}$$

Note that this weighted average cost of capital for owning the project is the same no matter who owns it, so long as their marginal tax rates are the same. We assume that the optimal capital structure is project specific. For example, a commercial bank with a 90–95% debt in its capital structure should not apply the same leverage to a wholly owned computer division. Presumably, the computer division has its own optimal leverage, different from (less than) the commercial bank's.

To continue with the numerical example, assume that the unlevered cost of capital, $\rho(\text{project})$, is 14% for the project and that its optimal capital structure is one third debt to total assets, that is, $B/(B+S) = .33$. The required rate of return on the wholly owned project is

$$WACC \text{ (project)} = .14[1 - .4(.33)] = 12.152\%.$$

If the project has a positive net present value when its after-tax operating cash flows are discounted at the appropriate $WACC$, then it is a good investment.

To add realism to the investment decision, assume that the investment project has expected annual sales revenue of $S_t = \$20,000$, and expected annual cash costs of $C_t = \$16,711$. Then the NPV of the investment project is

$$NPV \text{ (investment)} = -I + \sum_{t=1}^{N} \frac{(S_t - C_t)(1 - \tau_c) + \tau_c dep_t}{(1 + WACC)^t}$$

$$= -10,000 + \sum_{t=1}^{5} \frac{.6(20,000 - 16,711) + .4(2,000)}{(1.12152)^t}$$

$$= -10,000 + .6(20,000 - 16,711)(3.5912) + .4(2,000)(3.5912)$$

$$= -10,000 + 7,087 + 2,873$$

$$= -40.$$

Under these assumptions, the project should be rejected.

THE LONG-TERM LEASE CONTRACT FROM THE LESSEE'S POINT OF VIEW As before, we assume that the lease is a perfect substitute for debt because it is assumed to be a strict financial lease. Operating leases are riskier for the lessor and will be discussed later on.

Failure to remember that strict financial leases are perfect substitutes for debt causes much confusion about how to evaluate a lease contract. For example, one often hears the mistaken phrase that leases are 100% debt financing. The advertising of leasing companies invariably points out that lease payments are deductible in full, whereas owners deduct only the machine's depreciation plus that part of the capital costs represented by interest payments. This is nonsense. If all of a project is provided by lease financing, then the lessee firm's debt capacity is reduced by an equivalent dollar amount. Other projects can carry less debt financing. Hence an opportunity cost of leasing is the displacement of the firm's debt capacity, and the associated loss of the tax shield provided by that debt.

The lessee firm must make two decisions. First, is the project acceptable as an investment? Does it have a positive net present value if financed at its optimal capital structure? This analysis was described above. Second, should it be financed by leasing or borrowing? The user firm takes the lease-rental fee, L_t, as an input in making a comparison between the cost of leasing and the cost of borrowing. Myers, Dill, and Bautista [1976] have shown that the costs and benefits of leasing involve an analysis of the following cash flows:

1. A cash saving amounting to the dollar amount of the investment outlay, I, that the firm does not have to incur if it leases.
2. A cash outflow amounting to the present value of the after-tax lease payments, $PV[L_t(1 - \tau_c)]$.
3. The present value of the opportunity cost of the lost depreciation tax shield, $PV[\tau_c dep_t]$ (and lost investment tax credits, which were relevant prior to the 1986 tax code).
4. The present value of the *change* in the interest tax shield on debt that is displaced by the lease financing, $PV[\tau_c \Delta(k_d D_t)]$, where D_t is the remaining book value of debt outstanding in period t.

These four terms are summarized in the following equation:

$$NPV \text{ (to lessee)} = I - PV[(1 - \tau_c)L_t] - PV[\tau_c dep_t] - PV[\tau_c \Delta(k_d D_t)]. \tag{17.3}$$

We have assumed for strict financial leases that debt and lease financing are perfect substitutes. Therefore the fourth term in Eq. (17.3) will reflect a dollar-for-dollar substitution of debt tax shield for leasing tax shield for the portion of the asset that would be debt financed at the project's optimal capital structure. Furthermore, because leasing and debt are perfect substitutes, the cash inflows to the lessor and the cash outflows from the lessee have the same risk. Therefore the appropriate

Table 17.2 NPV (to lessee) Using Eq. (17.5)

(1) Year	(2) dep_t	(3) $\tau_c dep_t$	(4) $(1-\tau_c)L_t$	(5) D_{t-1}	(6) $\Delta k_d D_t$	(7) $\tau_c \Delta k_d D_t$	(8) ΔD_t	(9) CF_t	(10) $(1+k_b)^{-t}$	(11) $PV(CF_t)$
1	2,000	800	1,574.4	10,000	1,000	400.0	1,638	2,774.4	.909	2,521.93
2	2,000	800	1,574.4	8,632	836	334.4	1,802	2,708.8	.826	2,237.47
3	2,000	800	1,574.4	6,560	656	262.4	1,982	2,636.8	.751	1,980.24
4	2,000	800	1,574.4	4,578	458	183.2	2,180	2,557.6	.683	1,746.84
5	2,000	800	1,574.4	2,398	240	96.0	2,398	2,470.4	.621	1,534.12
							10,000			10,020.60

Notes:

L_t = the annual lease fee on a fully amortized lease (i.e., no salvage value),

dep_t = the annual (straight-line) depreciation write-off,

τ_c = the lessee marginal tax rate,

D_{t-1} = the face value of debt displaced by the lease in the previous time period,

k_d = the before-tax cost of the displaced debt capital,

$\Delta k_d D_t$ = the change in the interest payments on debt displaced by the lease,

ΔD_t = the repayment of principal on debt,

CF_t = the cash flow for the lease contract = columns (3) + (4) + (7),

$(1+k_b)^{-t}$ = the present value factor, where k_b is the market rate on debt (bonds).

before-tax discount rate for the cash flows in Eq. (17.3) is k_b, the borrowing rate. Equation (17.3) may be rewritten as

$$NPV \text{ (lessee)} = I - \sum_{t=1}^{N} \frac{L_t(1-\tau_c) + \tau_c\, dep_t + \tau_c \Delta(k_d D_t)}{(1+k_b)^t}. \tag{17.4}$$

Table 17.2 illustrates how the cash flow definitions of Eq. (17.4) can be used to compute the present value of a lease contract. The example in Table 17.2 uses the same numbers we have developed in this chapter. The annual lease fee (assumed to be paid at the end of each year) is $2,624. Except for a rounding error, the NPV of the lease is $0. This is to be expected in a competitive market where the tax rates of the lessor and lessee are identical. There is no advantage to leasing over borrowing in these circumstances.

One problem in applying Eq. (17.4) is that the remaining debt balance, D_t, declines each year as the lease fees amortize the principal. This makes computations more cumbersome than they need be. A much simpler way of looking at the problem was derived by Levy and Sarnat [1979]. Equation (17.4) puts the tax effect of displaced debt in the numerator and discounts at the before-tax rate, k_b. However, it has been our practice throughout the text to account for the tax effect of financing costs by discounting at the after-tax rate in the denominator and writing the numerator in terms of after-tax cash flows net of financing effects. If this is done, Eq. (17.4) is equivalent to Eq. (17.5) below:

$$NPV \text{ (lessee)} = I - \sum_{t=1}^{N} \frac{L_t(1 - \tau_c) + \tau_c \, dep_t}{[1 + (1 - \tau_c)k_b]^t}. \qquad (17.5)$$

Also, recall that $(1 - \tau_c)k_b = WACC_B$. Substituting the numbers from our previous example in order to determine the NPV of the lease and assuming that the tax rate of the lessee is the same as the lessor, namely, 40%, we have

$$NPV \text{ (lessee)} = I - \sum_{t=1}^{N} \frac{L_t(1 - \tau_c) + \tau_c \, dep_t}{[1 + (1 - \tau_c)k_b]^t}$$

$$= 10,000 - \sum_{t=1}^{5} \frac{2,624(1 - .4) + .4(2,000)}{[1 + .6(.10)]^t}$$

$$= 10,000 - 2,624(.6)(4.212) - .4(2,000)(4.212)$$

$$= 10,000 - 6,631 - 3,369$$

$$= 0.$$

The numerical result shows very clearly that the risk and cash flows to the lessor and lessee are identical if they have the same marginal tax rates. There is an equilibrium between the lessor market and the user market. Each term in Eq. (17.5) is identical to the corresponding term in Eq. (17.1) except that the signs are reversed. In other words a cash outflow to the lessee is a cash inflow to the lessor, and vice versa.

THE EFFECT OF DIFFERENT TAX RATES ON THE VALUE OF LEASING Frequently the lessor and lessee have different marginal tax rates. If the lessor has a higher tax rate than the lessee, it may be possible to strike a bargain where the tax shield from owning the asset can be shared between the two. Suppose that we assume the lessor has 40% marginal tax rate and charges a lease fee of $2,624, as before, but that the marginal tax rate of the lessee is only 5%. What is the NPV of the lease contract to the lessee? Substituting into Eq. (17.5), we have

$$NPV \text{ (to lessee)} = 10,000 - \sum_{t=1}^{5} \frac{2,624(1 - .05) + .05(2,000)}{[1 + (1 - .05).10]^t}$$

$$= 10,000 - 2,624(.95)(3.8397) - .05(2,000)(3.8397)$$

$$= 10,000 - 9,571.59 - 383.97$$

$$= 44.44.$$

Now the lease contract has a positive net present value for the lessee.

Actually, the positive net present value created by the difference in the marginal tax rates can be shared between the lessor and lessee unless perfect competition among lessors results in giving the full value of the tax shield to the lessee. Also, note that any positive net present value from the lease contract that accrues to the lessee can be used to augment the net present value of the investment decision. It is conceivable that negative NPV projects might be undertaken if the NPV of the lease contract is large enough. Consider the following example: The lease payments remain at $2,624 per year, but the operating costs (in the lessee's investment decision) are $17,060 rather than $16,711 per year. Given a 5% tax rate, the lessee's weighted average cost of capital is

$$WACC \text{ (project)} = .14[1 - .05(.33)] = 13.77\%,$$

and the NPV of the project becomes

$$NPV = -10,000 + \sum_{t=1}^{5} \frac{.95(20,000 - 17,060) + .05(2,000)}{(1 + .1377)^t}$$

$$= 10,000 + 2,893.00(3.4521)$$

$$= 10,000 + 9,986.93$$

$$= -13.07.$$

If the project is leased, rather than undertaken with debt financing, the NPV (to the lessee) of the lease contract can offset the negative NPV of the investment, namely, $44.44 in our example. The NPV if the firm buys the project is $ − 13.07 but rises to ($ − 13.07 + $44.44 = $31.37) if leased.

Although the above numerical example shows a benefit to the lessee given that the lessor's tax rate is higher, this may not always be true. The tax effect can go either way. As pointed out by Lewellen, Long, and McConnell [1976], the net tax benefit will depend on the specific asset life (lease period), depreciation schedule, capitalization rate, and leverage policies involved.

NONTAX DETERMINANTS OF THE LEASING DECISION While taxes provide strong incentives for leasing rather than owning and can predict which firms will lease, they provide very little understanding of which assets will be leased. For example, why does a company lease some assets and own others when the company's tax rate applies equally to all projects? Smith and Wakeman [1985] provide a useful first look at this issue.[6] They point out, for example, that since lessees have no right to the residual value of the asset, they have less incentive to take care of it. Thus the more sensitive the value of an asset to use and maintenance decisions, the higher is the probability that the asset will be purchased rather than leased. Most automobiles for personal use, for instance, are owned rather than leased. Another factor is the degree that an asset is specialized for use within a given firm. Organization-specific assets generate agency costs in the form of negotiation, administration, and enforcement costs due to conflicts between the lessor and lessee. According to Smith and Wakeman, this may explain why corporations lease office facilities with greater frequency than production or research facilities.

The distinction between long-term leases and short-term leases is not trivial. At one end of the continuum are very short-term leases such as hotel room, automobile, truck, and tool rentals. For these contracts the differences in transactions costs between leasing and owning are likely to be more important for tax considerations. It is much easier to rent a room for a night than to buy it in the afternoon, then sell it back in the morning. On the other hand, for long-term leases, factors of this type are minimized, and consideration of the differences in tax rates is the major consideration. Since we have already discussed tax considerations at some length, it is appropriate to focus on transactions costs and economies of scale from specialization. For a reference on this point of view see Flath [1980].

---

[6] See their article for a more complete description of the many nontax determinants of leasing. Only a few are mentioned here.

Transactions costs may include clerical costs, search costs, and costs of assessing, assuring, and maintaining quality. Leasing transactions costs are different from owning because the set of rights being exchanged differs. A lessee obtains the right to use an asset for a fixed period of time. When this time interval is less than the economic life of the asset, transactions costs become relevant.

Suppose that an individual wishes to use an asset for only a fraction of its economic life. For example, suppose that tuxedos go out of style in five-year cycles, whether they are used or not, and that you plan to wear the tuxedo only one day per year. Then you would be willing to pay anything up to 99.73% ($= 364/365$) of the value of the asset to rent it. Of course, if other people also plan to use tuxedos and if the timing of their use is independent of yours, then it will pay someone else to own the tuxedo and rent it out. Thus if an individual wants to use an asset for an interval considerably shorter than the asset's economic life, then a demand for short-term leasing will arise. If enough people have uncorrelated demand, then the volume of business will be sufficient for someone to specialize in renting the asset, thereby creating a supply.

It is conceivable that even though you want to use a tuxedo for one day, you could buy it at the beginning of the day and sell it at day's end. If so, why is leasing the preferred contract for obtaining short-term use of an asset? A supplier of short-term leases, for example, a hotel owner, could arrange a one-day sale and buyback of a room rather than renting it out. There are, of course, some obvious transactions cost savings from short-term leasing. For example, the transaction's demand for money is much less if people only have to exchange currency worth one day's use of an asset rather than its full value. Also, the need for the user to separately contract for insurance and financing is reduced.

Another consideration that favors short-term leasing over sale and buyback is the cost of evaluating the quality of the leased asset. A lease is a contract for the use of an asset, not its ownership. A potential owner of an asset, for example, an automobile, will wish to have a detailed inspection of the car's quality. On the other hand, a lessee will only need to perform a less costly inspection because the potential loss from using a low-quality asset for one day is less than the loss from owning it. Also, from the owner's point of view the gain from deceiving a customer about an asset's quality is not as great for a short-term lease as for long-term ownership. Thus the lower cost of quality evaluation favors lease contracts over ownership. However, this advantage must be weighed against higher average usage costs. For example, a lessee has less incentive to take proper care of an asset that has an owner. Lessors know this and include a "moral hazard" cost as part of the lease fee. Still, leasing will be preferred if the moral hazard cost is less than the cost of the frequent detailed inspections that would be necessary if ownership were exchanged.

Thus whenever the desired period of usage is less than the economic life of an asset, short-term leasing may be preferred to an ownership market such as a second-hand market.

LEVERAGED LEASING   A leveraged lease is one where the lessor borrows a substantial portion of the purchase price of the asset. Figure 17.1 is a schematic representation of the parties to a leveraged lease. The lender typically holds a first mortgage on the asset. Also, the lessor assigns the lease payments to the lender (or a trustee). The debt interest and principal are deducted by the lender, who then returns the balance of the lease payment, which is kept by the equity holder. Equity may be supplied either directly by the lessor or indirectly by third parties. The loan agreement is now called a nonrecourse loan because its effect is to indemnify the lessor in the event of default. The lessor benefits from the investment tax credit (if any) created when the asset is purchased, the depreciation tax shield, the residual value of the equipment (if any), the interest tax deduction, and the equity payments (if not turned over to third-party equity investors).

Figure 17.1 A schematic representation of a leveraged lease.

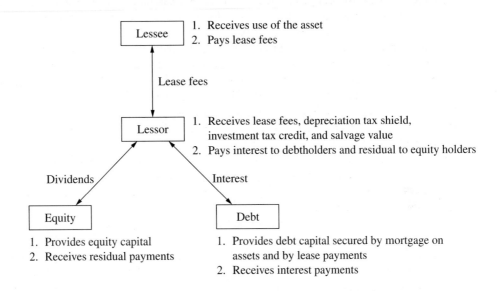

There is not real economic difference between the economics of leveraged lease contracts and strict financial lease contracts, which have already been discussed in detail.[7] In a strict financial lease, the lessor purchases the asset with a combination of debt and equity capital. The same is true in a leveraged lease with the possible exception that a different debt/equity mix may be used.

Leveraged leasing does, however, raise the issue of determining the opportunity cost of debt and equity funds employed in the lease. Suppose a lessor approaches your firm and asks that you lend funds or provide equity participation. What is your minimum acceptable rate of return?

To provide a concrete example we will use the same numerical example as employed earlier in the chapter. Also, as before, we will adopt the Modigliani-Miller valuation framework. Recall that the equipment costs $10,000 and had a five-year life with no salvage value, and there was no investment tax credit. The lease fee was determined to be $2,624. Both the lessor and lessee had marginal tax rates, τ_c, of 40%. The lessor earned 10% before taxes and had a 6% after-tax weighted average cost of capital.

The first question is, What is the cost of debt if it is lent by a third party? For straight financial leases the third party might be a depositor in a commercial bank or debt holders of an insurance company or a leasing company. For leveraged leases debt may be supplied (e.g., by an insurance company). We can get an idea of the rate of return that will be required on debt by noting that the lease payments must be riskier than the debt. In the event of default on a leveraged lease the debt holders are somewhat protected because they own the mortgage on the leased assets. By way of contrast the equity holders, being residual claimants, can lose everything. The lessor charges a

---

[7] The existence of leveraged leases may be explained by various institutional considerations and agency costs. For example, for very large leveraged leases a single bank may be constrained from doing the deal because regulations prohibit it from lending more than a small percentage of its equity to a single firm. Also, leveraged leases match long-term borrowing against long-term lending (i.e., the lease), whereas most of a bank's other loans and deposits are short or intermediate term.

10% before-tax rate of return on the lease. This results in an 8% before-tax cost of borrowing, k_b, which is the rate at which the debt holders will supply capital to the leveraged lease.

The cost of equity depends on the amount of leverage used in the lease. For "blue-chip" leases the ratio of debt to total assets might be 90–95%. We assumed the ratio was 90%. Given these facts, we can employ the Modigliani-Miller cost of capital definitions (from Chapter 15) to compute the cost of equity in the leveraged lease. Recall that we assumed, earlier in the chapter, that the unlevered cost of equity, ρ, was 9.375%. The Modigliani-Miller definition of the cost of equity is

$$k_s = \rho + (\rho - k_b)(1 - \tau_c)\frac{B}{S},$$

where

$\rho = $ the unlevered cost of equity,

$k_b = $ the before-tax cost of borrowing $= 8\%$,

$\tau_c = $ the marginal effective tax rate $= 40\%$,

$\dfrac{B}{S} = $ the market value debt-to-equity ratio $= 9$.

Therefore the required rate of return on equity in the leveraged lease is

$$k_s = .09375 + (.09375 - .08)(1 - .4)9$$

$$= 16.8\%.$$

This is more than double the borrowing rate on the same project and reflects the greater risk accepted by the equity holders in a leveraged lease.

CANCELABLE OPERATING LEASES Unlike straight financial leases, operating leases may be canceled at the option of the lessee. From the point of view of the lessee, capital employed under operating lease contracts becomes a variable cost (rather than a fixed cost) because the lease contract may be terminated (sometimes requiring a penalty to be paid) and the leased asset returned whenever economic conditions become unfavorable. It is like having equipment that can be laid off. From the lessor's point of view cancelable operating leases are riskier than straight financial leases. A straight lease, like a loan, is secured by all the assets in the firm. A cancelable operating lease is not.

The risk that the lessor must bear depends on the economic depreciation of the asset. There is always uncertainty about the ability of an asset to physically withstand wear and tear. In addition, there is obsolescence caused by technological advances that cause the economic value of an asset to decline vis-à-vis newer assets. And finally, there is a risky end-of-period economic value of an asset, which is usually called its salvage value. All these concepts are different descriptions of economic depreciation, which henceforth we shall call *replacement cost* uncertainty.

To focus on replacement cost risk by itself, assume that we know with certainty the future revenue stream that the leased asset will produce as well as other costs unassociated with the economic value of the leased asset. Figure 17.2 shows an example of how the economic value of the asset might change over time. The downward-sloping line illustrates the expected decline in the asset's value due to anticipated wear and tear and obsolescence. Note that the value is expected

Figure 17.2 Changes in replacement value over time.

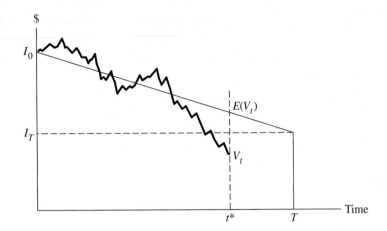

to decline from $\$I_0$ to $\$I_T$ over the life of the contract, T years. The expected salvage value is I_T.[8] It is reasonable to assume that the value of the asset never falls below zero. Given replacement cost uncertainty, the actual cost of the asset at any time $t^* \leq T$ may be greater or less than expected. The particular situation that has been illustrated at t^* in Fig. 17.2 shows that if the value of the asset, V_t, falls far enough below the expected value, $E(V_t)$, it will pay the lessee to terminate the lease.

Thus the cancelation feature is really an option. In particular it is an American put held by the lessee. The present value of the relevant American put is derived by Copeland and Weston [1982], who utilize the binomial option pricing model. They use the following numerical example to illustrate the effect of the put option on leasing fees. Assume that a $10,000 asset is expected to have a three-year economic life and depreciate an equal amount each year (i.e., the replacement value declines in a straight line at the rate of $1 - \theta$ each year, where $\theta = .667$). However, its value may be 50% higher or lower than expected at the end of a given year. Also, the lessor has a tax rate of 40% and will write a two-year lease. If the lease contract were a straight financial lease, it would require a 10% before-tax rate of return (i.e., $k_b = 10\%$). The salvage value is uncertain and requires a 16% risk-adjusted rate of return.[9] Using Eq. (17.1) we can write the competitive net present value of the lease if it were noncancelable as follows:

$$0 = -I + \sum_{t=1}^{2} \frac{(1 - \tau_c)L_t + \tau_c \, dep_t}{\left[1 + (1 - \tau_c)k_b\right]^t} + \frac{E(MV)}{(1 + k_1)^2}, \tag{17.6}$$

where

$$E(MV) = \text{the expected market value of the asset after two years,}$$

$$k_1 = \text{the risk-adjusted discount rate for the salvage value.}$$

---

[8] For papers on how to deal with uncertain salvage values, the reader is referred to Lee, Martin, and Senchack [1980] and to McConnell and Schallheim [1983].

[9] For simplicity we ignore capital gains taxation on the salvage value as well as investment tax credits.

Substituting in the numbers we have

$$0 = -10,000 + \sum_{t=1}^{2} \frac{(1 - .4)L_t + .4(3,333)}{[1 + (1 - .4).10]^t} + \frac{3,333}{(1.16)^2}.$$

Solving, we find that the competitive lease fee is $4,617.

Next, we want to determine the competitive lease payments assuming that the above contract is a cancelable operating lease. Equation (17.6) must be modified by subtracting out the present value of the American put option, P. The new valuation equation is

$$0 = -I + \sum_{t=1}^{2} \frac{(1 - \tau_c)L_t + \tau_c dep_t}{[1 + (1 - \tau_c)k_b]^t} + \frac{E(MV)}{(1 + k_1)^2} - P.$$

The value of the put (see Copeland and Weston [1982]) is determined to be $850. Solving for the cancelable lease fee, we find that it increases to $5,392. The lease fee has increased substantially to reflect the extra risk of possible early cancelation of the operating lease.[10]

The example serves to illustrate that the replacement cost uncertainty borne by the lessor in a cancelable operating lease can have a profound impact on the competitive lease fee. In general the cancelation clause may be thought of as an American put purchased by the lessee. Its cost will increase with (1) greater uncertainty in the replacement value of the leased asset and (2) decreases in the risk-free discount rate.

Grenadier [1995, 1996] uses a real options approach for modeling leasing. An N-year lease is economically equivalent to a portfolio that simultaneously purchases the underlying asset and writes a European call on the asset with expiration date N and zero exercise price.

3. Empirical Testing of Leasing

The empirical evidence on leasing-related issues is scant. There are (at least) four topics of interest. First is whether or not the theory of leasing is sufficiently rich to predict when a firm will use leasing instead of debt financing. Although debt and leasing are very similar, they are not necessarily perfect substitutes. Otherwise the form of financing being used would be randomly distributed across firms. Casual empiricism suggests that patterns of choice do exist. Factors such as tax shield utilization, economies of scale in service contracts, and comparative advantages in resale of equipment may explain the use of lease financing.

A second issue is the extent to which lease financing is a substitute for debt financing *within* a given firm. The theory of leasing logically assumes that each dollar of leasing utilized by the firm will replace one dollar of debt capacity; that is, they are perfect substitutes. Whether or not firms actually behave in this manner is an empirical issue. Bowman [1980] collected a 1973 sample of 92 firms in seven different industries (according to a two-digit SIC code) where both lease and debt financing were reported. A second sample of 158 firms that did not use leasing was also collected. Bowman then ran a cross-section regression to explain the systematic risk of the nonlease sample

---

[10] If a lessee takes the lease fee of $5,392 as an input and tries to compute an internal rate of return (IRR) on the contract using Eq. (17.6), the noncancelable lease formula, the IRR will be approximately 14%. However, the lessee would be mistaken to compare the 14% return on a cancelable lease with 10% on a straight financial lease for comparable debt financing.

as a function of the accounting beta and the debt-to-equity ratio. The results are given below, with t-statistics in parentheses:

$$\beta_i = \quad 1.223 \quad + \quad 0.88\beta_i^A \quad + \quad .104(D/S)_i \quad (\overline{R}^2 = .29),$$
$$(2.51) \qquad\quad (4.19)$$

where

$$\beta_i = \text{the systematic risk of the } i\text{th firm estimated using the last 60 months of data,}$$

$$\beta_i^A = \text{an estimate of the accounting beta for the } i\text{th firm (two versions were tested}$$
$$\text{without obtaining different results: one version used the first difference}$$
$$\text{of net income before extraordinary items and the second used EBIT),}$$

$$(D/S)_i = \text{the book value of debt over the market value of equity.}$$

The association between systematic risk and lease utilization was then tested by first adjusting the beta of the ith firm by using the above estimated coefficients, then regressing the result against a lease utilization variable as shown below:

$$\beta_i - 1.223 - .088\beta_i^A - .104(D/S)_i = \lambda(L/S)_i + \varepsilon_i,$$

where

$$(L/S)_i = \text{the book value of leasing over the market value of equity,}$$

$$\varepsilon_i = \text{the residual.}$$

This research design controls for measurement error and multicollinearity. The relationship between systematic risk, β_i, and the use of leasing, $(L/S)_i$, was positive and statistically significant. This led Bowman to conclude that debt and lease financing both affected the market's estimate of the systematic risk of the firms. Consequently, leasing and debt were recognized as close substitutes.

Ang and Peterson [1984] use cross-sectional data for approximately 600 nonregulated and nonfinancial firms each year between 1976 and 1981. The book value lease to equity ratio was explained as a function of the book value debt to equity ratio, operating leverage, the coefficient of variation of sales, return on net fixed plant, the price/earnings ratio, the book value of assets, and the current ratio. The results indicated a significant positive relationship between leasing and debt. The conclusion is that debt and leases appear to be complements, rather than perfect substitutes as assumed in the theory of leasing.

A third area of empirical interest is whether or not the mandated disclosure of off-balance-sheet leasing had any measurable impact on the real decisions of firms. For example, in order to comply with the accounting disclosure changes, firms had to capitalize their lease obligations and report them on their balance sheets. When this was done, some firms found themselves in technical violation of their debt covenants. Ro [1978] looked at the impact of lease disclosure on bond risk premia and found no impact on security prices. Thus the evidence is mixed. As more empirical research is reported we will obtain a better understanding of how the market reacts (if at all) to the initial disclosure of off-balance-sheet financing.

Finally, studies by Sorensen and Johnson [1977], McGugan and Caves [1974], Gudikunst and Roberts [1975], and Crawford, Harper, and McConnell [1981] have empirically estimated the internal rates of return (i.e., the "yields") on commercial bank leases. They all report that the estimated yields were higher than debt of equivalent risk. If leases and debt are perfect substitutes in straight financial leases, this should not be so. Schallheim, Johnson, Lease, and McConnell [1986] provide a potential explanation for this puzzle. They find that the higher yields on financial leases are related to the discounted value of the leased asset's residual value covariance risk (or to the residual value itself). Franks and Hodges [1986] use a sample of English leasing data and conclude that low-tax firms are lessees and high-tax firms are lessors, but interestingly most of the tax shelter value was captured by the lessor rather than the lessee. Their result implies that the estimated yields on leases would be higher than the debt rate because taxable earnings (owned by lessors) was a scarce resource and lessors had to pay a premium for using it.

4. Summary of Leasing

We have examined the leasing problem from the point of view of the lessee and the lessor. If they have identical tax rates, then a competitive lease fee will have zero net present value to both parties. Yet if their leasing analysis inputs are different—for example, the lessee may have a higher tax rate than the lessor—then it is possible that some negotiated lease fee can have a positive net present value to both parties. They can share the net present value of the tax shield from leasing (if any).

Strict financial leases are assumed to be perfect substitutes for debt capital. There is no such thing as 100% lease financing, just as there is no such thing as 100% debt financing. For each dollar of leasing employed by a firm, one dollar of debt capacity is displaced.

Leveraged leasing is really no different from straight financial leasing. Both employ debt and equity that are used by the lessor to purchase the asset for leasing. If one knows the financing mix that will be used by the lessor, the rate of return on the lease payments, and the (lower) rate of return received by debt holders in the contract, then it is possible to estimate the required rate of return on equity invested in leveraged leases.

Cancelable leases contain a put option sold to the lessee. Often valuable, this option may considerably raise the implied lease cost.

The character of short-term leases is quite different from that of long-term financial leases. In particular the transactions costs and agency costs of short-term leases are important in explaining why we rent hotel rooms instead of buying them for one day and selling them back the next.

The empirical evidence on leasing is scant. What little there is provides mixed evidence on whether or not leasing is viewed by the market as a close substitute for debt financing.

C. Interest Rate Swaps

It has been estimated that a total of at least $79 trillion in interest rate swaps were outstanding globally as of December 2002. First available in the 1970s, interest rate swaps have been a rapidly growing activity.

An interest rate swap is a contract between firms in which interest payments are based on a notational principal amount that is itself never paid or received. Instead the parties agree to pay each other the interest that would be due on the notational principal. Swaps are usually between fixed and floating rate instruments, although floating for floating and fixed for fixed are also possible. The most common swap is where one interest stream, the floating payment, is tied to a short-term

Figure 17.3 An interest rate swap.

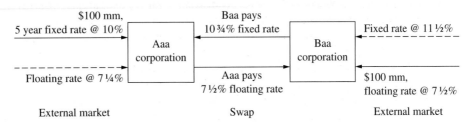

money market rate such as the U.S. Treasury bill rate or to LIBOR (the London Interbank Offer Rate). The other payment stream is fixed for the life of the swap. Both fixed and floating interest payments start accruing on the swap's effective date and cease on the swap's maturity date.

Figure 17.3 illustrates a swap. Suppose that an Aaa-rated firm can borrow five-year fixed-rate debt at 10% and floating-rate debt at the T-bill rate, 7% plus $\frac{1}{2}$%. Thus the short-term quality premium is only $\frac{1}{4}$%, whereas the long-term premium is $1\frac{1}{2}$%.

Suppose the Aaa-rated firm has borrowed $100 million of five-year fixed-rate debt at 10%. A swap can be arranged whereby the Baa-rated firm agrees to pay $10\frac{3}{4}$% on the five-year debt and the Aaa-rated firm pays the T-bill rate plus $\frac{1}{2}$% (i.e., $7\frac{1}{2}$%). The net position of the Aaa-rated firm is a gain of $\frac{1}{2}$%, the extra $\frac{3}{4}$% received on the five-year note less the extra $\frac{1}{4}$% paid on the variable rate loan. The Baa-rated firm borrows $100 million at the T-bill rate plus $\frac{1}{2}$%, receives the same rate from the Aaa-rated firm, and agrees to pay $10\frac{3}{4}$% on the fixed rate debt. Since the rate on the fixed debt is $\frac{3}{4}$% less than the Baa-rated firm would otherwise have to pay, it comes out $\frac{3}{4}$% ahead as a result of the swap. In this example the presumption is that both firms benefit by splitting the difference in the quality spread on short-term variable-rate debt and longer-term fixed-rate debt.

In the absence of market imperfections and comparative advantages among different classes of borrowers, there would be no reason for interest rate swaps. However, in less-than-perfect markets there are a number of possible motivations for engaging in a swap. Henderson and Price [1984], Bicksler and Chen [1985], and Smith, Smithson, and Wakeman [1986] discuss the more frequently mentioned reasons:

1. *Duration matching.* Firms with variable-rate assets and fixed-rate liabilities may end up in a losing position. A swap of fixed-rate for variable-rate debt can help to match the duration of their assets and liabilities and to reduce their interest rate risk.

2. *Quality spread arbitrage.* When the quality spread between short- and long-term debt gets far enough out of line, it may be possible to engage in the quality spread arbitrage, as was illustrated in Fig. 17.3.[11]

3. *Refunding debt.* When debt is noncallable or is privately held, swaps may be used to refund the debt and to simultaneously convert fixed rates to variable.

4. *Tax and regulatory arbitrage.* The introduction of a swap allows an "unbundling" of currency and interest rate exposure from regulation and tax rules in very creative ways. For example, until

---

[11] One of the reasons why the quality yield spread on short-term notes is less than the spread on long-term notes is that the probability of default in a low-quality bond is less in the short run than in the long run. Therefore parties who agree to lock into a long-term swap may be fooling themselves into thinking they are arbitraging the quality spread when in fact the spread on a one-year position rolled over N times should be the same as that on an N-year position.

Figure 17.4 Creating a synthetic deep-discount dollar-denominated bond. (From C. Smith, Jr., C. Smithson, and L. Wakeman, "The Evolving Market for Swaps," *Midland Corporate Finance Journal*, Winter 1986, 25. Reprinted with permission.)

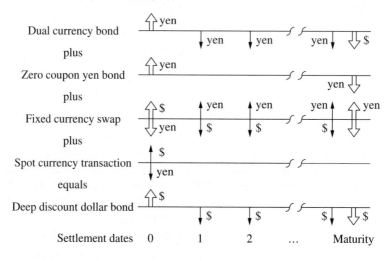

recently, zero-coupon bonds in Japan were not taxed until maturity and then only at the capital gains rate. Furthermore, the Japanese Ministry of Finance limited the amount a pension fund could invest in non-yen-denominated foreign issues to 10% of the fund's portfolio. U.S. firms issued zero-coupon yen bonds plus dual-currency bonds (with interest payments in yen and principal in dollars) and were able to capitalize on the superior tax treatment of zero-coupon bonds in Japan as well as the Japanese funds' desire to diversify their funds internationally because the ministry qualified dual-currency bonds as yen-denominated. To transfer their yen exposure back to a U.S. dollar exposure, the U.S. firms used currency swaps in conjunction with spot currency transactions. See Fig. 17.4 for an illustration of the cash flow pattern.

The economic evaluation of swap decisions requires that we compare the present values of fixed- and variable-rate instruments—not an easy task because of differences in default risk and the difficulty in modeling the term structure of interest rates. Cox, Ingersoll, and Ross [1980] and Ramaswamy and Sundaresan [1986] have shown how to value variable-rate debt given various assumptions. The following example assumes no default risk and a monotonic term structure of interest rates.

The first task, and by no means the easiest, is to model the term structure of interest rates. To keep things simple, assume a three-period world where one-period risk-free interest rates are modeled as binomial trials.[12] The interest rate can move up by a factor of 1.2 or down by a factor of .9. Figure 17.5 shows the term structure assuming that last period's rate was 11.11% and that this period's rate is 10%. Since the up movements are larger than the down movements, the term structure is upward sloping in this example. Once one has an adequate model of the term structure, the next step is to model the actual payouts on both instruments. If the floating-rate bond always paid the current one-period rate, it would adjust perfectly to changes in the interest rate and would

---

[12] See Chapter 9 on option pricing for complete exposition of the binomial model.

Figure 17.5 A binomial model of one-period riskless interest rates for three time periods.

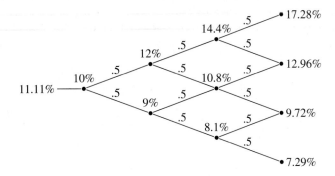

Figure 17.6 Payments on a floating-rate bond where the coupon is an average of rates for the last two periods.

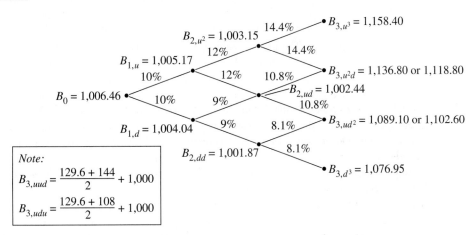

Note:
$$B_{3,uud} = \frac{129.6 + 144}{2} + 1,000$$

$$B_{3,udu} = \frac{129.6 + 108}{2} + 1,000$$

always sell for par. Unfortunately, this is not usually the case. Suppose the floating-rate bond promises to pay a coupon based on the arithmetic average of the current one-period rate and last period's rate. Coupons based on moving-average schemes of this type are common. Figure 17.6 illustrates the coupons that would be paid, contingent on the path of one-period riskless rates. Since there is no default risk involved, we can discount the coupon payments at the one-period riskless rate. The iterative pricing formula is

$$B_{t,s} = \frac{q(coupon_{t,u}) + (1-q)(coupon_{t,d})}{1 + r_{f,t,s}}, \tag{17.7}$$

where t is the time period; s is the state of nature (up or down); $coupon_{t,s}$ is the coupon in period t and state s; q is the probability of an upward movement; and $r_{f,t,s}$ is the riskless rate in period t and state s. To illustrate the use of Eq. (17.7), take the second-highest payoff (state 2) in the third time period (see Fig. 17.6). It was reached in one of three ways: after two upward movements followed by one downward movement in the interest rate; or after one downward and two upward movements; or via an up, a down, and then an upward movement. With the first path, the coupon payment is $136.80 and the face value is $1,000, resulting in a total payment of $1,136.80. Via the

Figure 17.7 The valuation of three-year fixed-rate debt paying a 12% coupon.

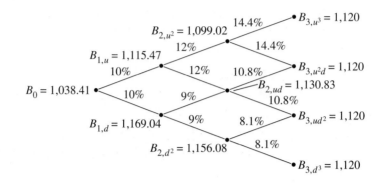

second and third paths, the coupon is $118.80 and the face value is still $1,000. Thus the coupon payment is path dependent. To compute the value of the bond in state 1 of period 2, one averages the payout in state 1 of period 3, $1,158.40, with the payout in state 2 of period 3, which was reached via two upward and one downward movements, $1,136.80, and discounts at 14.4%. The result is $B_{2,u^2} = \$1,003.15$. The present value of the bond in state 1 of time period 2 is the average of the total payoffs (since they are equally likely) discounted at a one-period rate, 14.4%. Given the numbers in our example, the present value of the floating-rate bond (at time 0) is $1,006.46.

Next, suppose that you are the treasurer of an Aaa-rated company that has $100 million of floating-rate debt with exactly the same terms as the instrument we just valued. You are approached by a company that has the same default risk (assume no default risk at all for an Aaa-rated company). They want to swap their three-year fixed-rate, which pays a 12% coupon, with your floating-rate debt. What should you do? The solution of course is to analyze the fixed-rate debt and compare its value with the value of your floating-rate debt. If your debt is worth less than the fixed-rate debt, you would take the offer.

Figure 17.7 shows how to use Eq. (17.7) to value the fixed-rate debt. The procedure is much the same as before. The value of the bond cum coupon is discounted each period at the risk-free rate in the appropriate state of nature. The present value of the 12% fixed-rate bond turns out to be $1,038.41. Since it is worth more than your floating-rate bond, you would be willing to undertake the proposed swap.

Interest rate and foreign exchange swaps are a rapidly growing business. There are many reasons. One is that there are capital market inefficiencies that allow arbitrage using swaps. But another is that the parties involved in the swaps are being fooled because they do not understand how to price the complex instruments involved in the deals—especially floating-rate notes with default risk and with complex terms.

There is little empirical research yet to help answer the question of whether market inefficiencies are driving the growth in swaps. Partly this is so because of the lack of good data and partly because of the difficulty of theoretical models to predict yield premia. More research in both areas is needed.

D. $\mathcal{R}$isk Management

In frictionless markets all risk is appropriately priced in equilibrium so that the risk-return trade-off does not affect the value of the portfolio of businesses. Consequently, financial theory is strained for explanations for why managers would want to manage risk at all. Yet survey data by Bodnar,

Figure 17.8 Breakdown of derivative usage by firm size and industry. (From G. Bodnar, S. Hayt, R. Marston, and C. Smithson, "Wharton Survey of Derivatives Usage by U.S. Nonfinancial Firms," *Financial Managment*, Summer 1995, 104–114.)

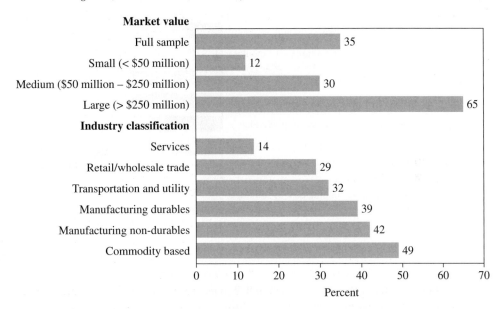

Hayt, Marston, and Smithson [1995] of 530 nonfinancial firms indicated that 65% of large firms used financial derivatives such as futures, forwards, and options (Figs. 17.8 and 17.9) and that the most frequent use was to hedge anticipated transactions.

Stulz [1984] and Smith and Stulz [1985] present a list of valid economic rationales for hedging. They include diversification and hedging as ways of reducing the volatility of operating cash flows in order to benefit from the tax shield provided by a greater debt capacity, and from reduction in the present value of expected disruption costs. Also, better risk management decreases the probability that the firm might have to forgo attractive investment opportunities because it cannot find external financing. Finally, smoothing the firm's stream of cash flows can, in some cases, transfer tax obligations from the current to future time periods.

In addition, there are other reasons for risk management. A change of risk exposure can affect the demand for a product or service and therefore the firm's expected operating cash flows. For example, a company called Metalgesellschaft captured 3% of the U.S. retail energy market by offering highly desirable fixed-price contracts to supply gasoline as far out as 10 years to retail gas stations and municipalities. Metalgesellschaft attempted to hedge the risk by using a "stacked hedge" in the futures market.[13] They failed to hedge properly and ultimately went bankrupt. However, their initial success was a clear indication that customer demand shifts with risk exposure.

Sometimes better risk management enables profitable business opportunities that would otherwise be missed. A consulting firm recommended to the owners of a large Mediterranean refinery that they refuse to take the tolling business of a significant fraction of their customers because they

---

[13] A "stacked hedge" offsets the risk of a T-year sequence of commitments by going short the present value of T one-year contracts (a stack), then rolling it over.

Figure 17.9 Percentage of firms that use derivatives. (From G. Bodnar, S. Hayt, R. Marston, and C. Smithson, "Wharton Survey of Derivatives Usage by U.S. Nonfinancial Firms," *Financial Managment*, Summer 1995, 104–114.)

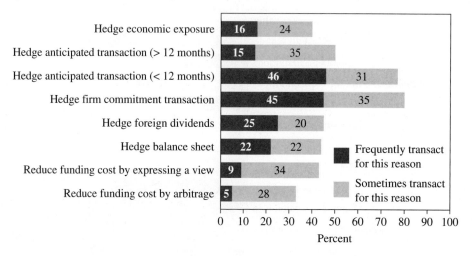

failed to deliver crude oil on time and failed to pay receivables due on finished goods supplied by the refinery.[14] This was a privately owned firm and its owners said that the higher profit (that would come from getting rid of bad tolling customers and by replacing their business by purchasing crude on the spot market, refining it into gasoline and heating oil, and selling them on the market) was not worth the extra risk. It took about three weeks for a molecule of crude oil to go through the refining process and if the prices of the finished goods (gasoline and heating oil) fell during that time, the company would experience a loss. This was the risk that caused the owners to balk. However, this obstacle was removed when they were shown that a hedge in commodity futures could reduce the increase in risk by roughly 70%. Given the hedge, they found the small increase in risk acceptable and went ahead with the recommendation. Thus, although the hedge per se may not have created value, it was nevertheless an enabling device that reversed their decision to change the company's operating policies.

1. Basic Principles of Reward-Risk Management

As we shall see there are four widely used risk management philosophies: transaction hedging, minimizing the variance of the cash flows of the firm, maximizing the value of the firm, and maximizing the value of the firm relative to other firms in the same industry. The first two are suboptimal.

There is a wide gulf between common managerial practices of risk management and best practices. Furthermore, best practices are still being developed. Here are a few practical issues:

- Risk-reward control is affected by operating as well as financial actions.

---

[14] Tolling is charging a fee for processing other people's oil, gasoline, and heating oil, rather than owning the oil and also processing it.

- Any change in risk is associated with changes in return, therefore the proper objective is to maximize the value of the firm.

- Risk-reward analysis should encompass the effects on the whole firm, not merely on anticipated transactions.

- Be sure you understand and appropriately measure the risks.

Let's take a look at each of these issues in the remainder of the section.

UNDERSTANDING HEDGE RATIOS AND HEDGING EFFICIENCY To introduce the basics, let's assume, for the time being, that our objective is simply to reduce risk of operations by hedging with a financial instrument, a futures contract that has a price today of F_0 and an end-of-period price of F_1. The profit, π, of the firm (assuming one unit of production, for convenience) can be written as

$$\tilde{\pi} = \left(\tilde{P}_1 - P_0\right) - h\left(\tilde{F}_1 - F_0\right), \tag{17.8}$$

where P_0 is the current cash flow per unit, $\tilde{P}_1$ is the uncertain future cash flow, and h is a hedge ratio expressed as the number of future contracts per unit of production. Using the basic principles of probability theory, we can write down the mean and variance of Eq. (17.8) as follows:

$$E(\tilde{\pi}) = \left[E(\tilde{P}_1) - P_0\right] - h\left[E(\tilde{F}_1) - F_0\right], \tag{17.9}$$

$$VAR(\tilde{\pi}) = VAR(\tilde{P}) - 2rh\sigma_P\sigma_F + h^2 VAR(\tilde{F}). \tag{17.10}$$

Note that $VAR(.)$ is the variance; r is the correlation coefficient between the two random variables, $\tilde{P}$ and $\tilde{F}$; and σ_P and σ_F are the standard deviations of $\tilde{P}$ and $\tilde{F}$, respectively.

To minimize the variance of profit, we take the derivative of Eq. (17.10) and set it equal to zero, then solve for the choice variable, the optimal hedge ratio, h:

$$\frac{dVAR(\tilde{\pi})}{dh} = -2r\sigma_P\sigma_F + 2h\sigma_F^2 = 0,$$

$$h^* = \frac{r\sigma_P}{\sigma_F}. \tag{17.11}$$

Thus, the optimal hedge ratio, h^*, is estimated as the slope of the regression of cash flows from operations versus cash flows from the hedge. This is illustrated in Fig. 17.10.

By substituting the optimal hedge ratio, h^*, into the variance equation (17.10), we see that the standard deviation of the minimum variance portfolio, $\sigma^*(\pi)$, depends on the r^2 between $\tilde{P}$ and $\tilde{F}$, that is,

$$VAR^*(\tilde{\pi}) = VAR(\tilde{P}) - 2rh^*\sigma_P\sigma_F + h^2 VAR(\tilde{F})$$

$$VAR^*(\tilde{\pi}) = \sigma_P^2 - 2r\left(\frac{r\sigma_P}{\sigma_F}\right)\sigma_P\sigma_F + \left(\frac{r^2\sigma_P^2}{\sigma_F^2}\right)\sigma_F^2$$

$$= \sigma_P^2 - 2r^2\sigma_P^2 + r^2\sigma_P^2$$

$$= \sigma_P^2 - r^2\sigma_P^2 = \sigma_P^2\left(1 - r^2\right)$$

$$\sigma^*(\pi) = \sigma_P\sqrt{1 - r^2}. \tag{17.12}$$

Figure 17.10 Regression of cash flows from operations versus cash flows from a hedge.

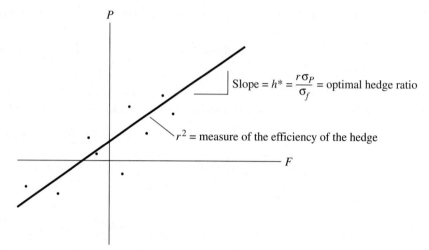

$\text{Slope} = h^* = \dfrac{r\sigma_P}{\sigma_f} = \text{optimal hedge ratio}$

$r^2 = \text{measure of the efficiency of the hedge}$

Figure 17.11 Efficiency of the hedge.

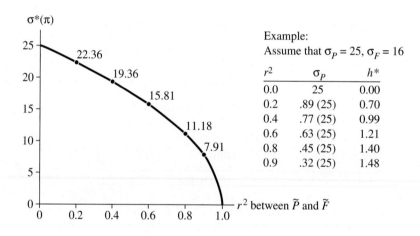

Example:
Assume that $\sigma_P = 25$, $\sigma_F = 16$

r^2	σ_P	h^*
0.0	25	0.00
0.2	.89 (25)	0.70
0.4	.77 (25)	0.99
0.6	.63 (25)	1.21
0.8	.45 (25)	1.40
0.9	.32 (25)	1.48

Thus, we see that the standard deviation of the firm's unhedged position, σ_P, is reduced by $\sqrt{1-r^2}$. The higher the correlation between the end-of-period cash flows and the cash flows from the hedge, the greater will be the *efficiency of the hedge* in reducing risk. Note that the risk is reduced by the square root of $1 - r^2$. The practical implication is that it takes very high r^2 in order to have an efficient hedge. In Fig. 17.11, for example, an r^2 of 0.80 only reduces the standard deviation from 25 to 11.18, a 55% reduction. To achieve an 80% reduction in the standard deviation, one needs a correlation of at least 96%.

2. Hedges Affect the Whole Firm

Recall that a cross-hedging example was discussed in Chapter 5.[15] A company bought a large futures position in contracts on 10-year Treasury bonds. If interest rates fell, the company would profit from its hedge. It turned out that the hedge position was correlated with both the assets and

---

[15] This is now available as a Harvard case called "The Expert Witness Case."

the liabilities side of the balance sheet. The primary assets were real estate holdings. A decrease in interest rates implied a reduction in their value because rates would grow closer. Thus, the T-bond futures hedge was effective in offsetting the risk that a decline in interest rates would decrease the market value of the company's major assets. There was also interest rate risk on the liabilities side of the company's balance sheet because it had roughly $100 million of long-term debt outstanding. It would increase in value if interest rates were to fall. Since the value of the hedge would rise at the same time, it would serve as a hedge against both the asset and the liability exposure to a decline in interest rates—it would be a cross-hedge.

Although it may seem to be obvious that one should set up any hedge by studying its effect on the whole firm, this is rarely done in practice. Figure 17.9 shows that transaction hedging is by far the most common practice.[16] The danger of transaction hedging is that it fails to focus on the total risk of the firm. A good example is what happened to Lufthansa, the German airline, in the fall of 1984. It became obligated to purchase $3 billion of aircraft. To hedge against possible strengthening of the dollar, its treasurer bought roughly $1.5 billion forward.

To see why hedging the specific transaction was inappropriate, one needs only to recognize that as a whole, Lufthansa was already, as a firm, a dollar-denominated risk. It was long the dollar prior to making the Boeing commitment; therefore if the dollar strengthened, the value of Lufthansa's operating cash flows would increase and the value of its obligation to purchase aircraft would also increase. The two positions are offsetting; therefore Lufthansa had a natural hedge. The effect of the forward position was to unhedge Lufthansa—to increase its risk.

Table 17.3 helps to understand why a company domiciled in Germany was really a dollar-denominated risk. First, it is important to know that Lufthansa had a near monopoly on local routes but strong transoceanic competition from competitors that price in dollars. Equipment and fuel costs are primarily in dollars, but personnel and overhead costs are priced in deutsche marks. Suppose that the dollar weakens vis-à-vis the deutsche mark. Ticket prices in Germany can be held constant, but in order to hold market share on its transoceanic routes, Lufthansa must hold dollar prices constant, which implies a deutsche mark decline in ticket prices (see Table 17.3, first row). These actions keep the quantity sold constant but sales revenues, although constant in dollars, decline in deutsche marks. Equipment and fuel costs are constant in dollars but decline in deutsche marks, and personnel, overhead, and other costs, while constant in deutsche marks, will go up in dollars. Total costs are up in dollars and total revenues are constant; therefore if the dollar weakens, dollar cash flows go down. The same weakening of the dollar, when viewed from a deutsche mark point of view, will result in a revenue decline and a proportionate cost decline, but the net effect is a decline in deutsche mark cash flows. The conclusion is that Lufthansa does worse when the dollar weakens and better when it strengthens. Therefore Lufthansa is a dollar-denominated risk. When the dollar weakened in late 1984 and 1985, Lufthansa's operating cash flows declined and it lost on its hedge position. The "hedge" had the net effect of increasing Lufthansa's risk.

3. There Are Many Ways to Hedge

Table 17.4 lists the variety of ways that one may hedge. Many of them are natural hedges that await financial hedging with derivatives. To highlight a few, let's talk about forecasting and operating

---

[16] The choice of what to hedge is important. It is possible to hedge a specific transaction (and consequently ignore cash flow risk of the firm as a whole), to hedge the firm's cash flow this period (to avoid insolvency or business disruption), or to hedge the value of the firm's equity (a stacked dynamic hedge) to prevent the relative price of the equity from falling relative to competitors that might become predators.

Table 17.3 The German Airline as a Dollar-Denominated Risk

	If the Dollar Weakens		If the Dollar Strengthens	
	U.S.$	Home Currency	U.S.$	Home Currency
Ticket pricing decision	Constant	Down	Constant	Up
Quantity sold	Constant	Constant	Constant	Constant
Sales revenues	Constant	Down	Constant	Up
Equipment costs	Constant	Down	Constant	Up
Fuel costs	Constant	Down	Constant	Up
Personnel and overhead	Up	Constant	Down	Constant
Other operating costs	Up	Constant	Down	Constant
Total costs	Up	Down	Down	Up
Cash flow	Down	Down	Up	Up

Notes:
1. Airline had monopoly on local routes but strong transoceanic competition from competitors who price in dollars.
2. Equipment costs in dollars (new aircraft on international routes).
3. Fuel costs in dollars.
4. Personnel and overhead costs priced in the local currency.
5. Other operating costs in various currencies.

Table 17.4 Hedging Techniques

Natural Hedges	Financial Hedges
Borrow in the same currency that your asset risk is denominated in	Futures: commodities, securities
Engineer flexibility into operations	Forwards: commodities, securities
Diversify	Options
Improve forecasting	
Match operating costs and revenues in the same currency	
Optimize insurance policy	
Share risks: joint ventures, sales agreements	

hedges. Recall from the previous section that the efficiency of the hedge depends on the r^2 between operating cash flows and cash flows from the hedge. When hedging a specific transaction (e.g., the commitment to purchase a quantity of Boeing aircraft), it is easy to convince oneself that there is a perfect correlation between the cash foreign exchange exposure on the contract and the offsetting exposure on financial futures or forwards, and in fact there is. However, as we just saw, this is delusionary logic because what counts is the correlation between the total cash flows and cash flows from the hedge.

Many companies hedge their foreign currency receivables, reasoning that if most of their costs are in dollars and receivables are in the foreign currency, then it is only necessary to hedge the foreign currency receivables. This is fine, as far as it goes, yet the greatest practical problem is the company's ability to forecast receivables 12–18 months from now. Poor forecasting implies a low hedge efficiency—and very little variable reduction. Better forecasting can dramatically improve the effectiveness of the hedge.

Other important types of natural hedge include borrowing in the same currency as the risk of operations. For example, a Brazilian aluminum company could borrow locally (in reales), in yen from Japan (because your interest rates are low), or from the United States in dollars. This choice should be governed by the currency exposure of the aluminum business—which is dollars—not yen or reales (the Brazilian currency).

Consider the results of a telephone survey of 10 managers of international equity investment funds (in April 2002). Individually they had assets under management from $100 million to $4 billion, and the total was roughly $10 billion. All 10 stated that beta on foreign exchange risk was outside of their area of competency; therefore they all attempted to hedge currency risk. Eight out of ten calculated their "net currency" exposure in each country as the currency value of long minus short positions, then hedged the "net exposure." Two out of ten simply required that long and short positions be matched by currency.

What are the shortcomings of these two approaches? The fundamental problem is the assumption that the actual currency exposure of a company is the currency of the country where its stock is listed. We already saw that Lufthansa, although domiciled in Germany, is a dollar risk. And if Lufthansa had its own efficient hedge, it might convert its dollar risk into deutsche mark risk. None of the 10 international investment funds understood the basic point, and it would not be difficult to improve their FX hedging policy.

Finally, it is useful to comment on the use of interrelationships among a company's existing businesses as natural hedges. As the CFO of one of Europe's largest power companies put it, "We finally figured out that the first call after a generator goes down should be to our trading floor." What he meant was that the generator failure would create a shortage that would in turn force up the spot price of electricity. By moving quickly the trading floor could take a position to benefit—with profits that often paid for repair of the generator.

4. Maximizing Value Instead of Minimizing Risk

Mello and Parsons [2000] and Copeland and Copeland [1999] point out that the objective of minimizing the volatility of cash flows (i.e., risk minimization) is neither a necessary nor a sufficient condition for maximizing the value of the firm. They model the benefit of risk management as the present value of pushing away the expected time of business disruption. Costs are measured as the present value of expected management time and transactions costs. If the ratio of benefits to costs is greater than one, the company should hedge; otherwise it should not. Later on, we shall see that an important distinction between value maximization and risk minimization is that some companies will hedge and others will not—even within the same industry—given value maximization. But with risk minimization it is always possible to reduce risk, no matter how inefficient the hedge; therefore all companies would hedge.

Figure 17.12 shows the unhedged cash flows of a company modeled as a Gauss-Weiner process (the solid line) and hedged cash flows as a second Gauss-Weiner process (the dashed line). If we designate the hedged cash flows as P_t, the drift per unit time of the hedged cash flows as μ, and σ as the standard deviation, then

$$\frac{dP_t}{P} = \mu dt + \sigma dz, \tag{17.13}$$

$$P_t = P_0 e^{(\mu - \sigma/2)t + \sigma zt}. \tag{17.14}$$

Figure 17.12 Cash flows and a boundary over time.

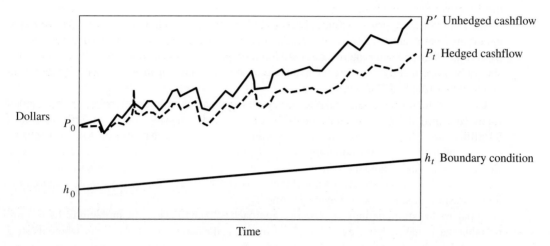

The firm finds its business disrupted when its hedged cash flows touch a lower boundary (the straight solid line):

$$h_t = h_0 e^{rt}. \tag{17.15}$$

The business disruption condition occurs when $P_t = h_t$. This "touching condition" may be written as

$$P_t = h_t \quad \text{iff} \quad \left(\mu - \frac{\sigma^2}{2} - r\right) t + \sigma z_t = \ln \frac{h_0}{P_0}. \tag{17.16}$$

By integration, the expected time to business disruption is

$$E(T) = \frac{b}{a}, \tag{17.17}$$

where

$$a = \frac{\mu}{\sigma} - \frac{\sigma}{2} - \frac{r}{\sigma}, \tag{17.18}$$

$$b = \frac{1}{\sigma} \ln \left[\frac{h_0}{P_0}\right]. \tag{17.19}$$

Substituting (17.18) and (17.19) into (17.17) and simplifying, we get[17]

$$E(T) = \frac{- \ln(P_0/h_0)}{\mu - r - \frac{\sigma^2}{2}}. \tag{17.20}$$

---

[17] In order for $E(T)$ to be finite, $\mu - r < \frac{\sigma^2}{2}$.

The expected time to business disruption increases as the variance of hedged cash flow, σ, decreases. It also increases as the initial cash flows coverage, namely, P_0/h_0, increases, and it increases as the drift in hedged cash flows relative to the drift in the boundary condition, $\mu - r$, increases. These results are intuitive and clearly indicate that variance reduction is not the only consideration for hedging. In fact, even if the hedge reduces σ, it may decrease μ enough to decrease the expected time to ruin. Variance reduction is not sufficient to increase $E(T)$. It is not necessary either if the hedge decreases μ.

Note that the optimal hedge ratio changes slightly from the traditional definition. To see this, write the drift in the firm's unhedged cash flows as

$$\mu = \mu_c - w_x\mu_x, \tag{17.21}$$

where μ_c is the nominal drift in unhedged cash flows, w_x is the dollars of the hedge instrument sold (or bought) per dollar of unhedged cash flows (i.e., the hedge ratio), and μ_x is the ex ante drift in the value of the forward contract (assumed to be the hedge instrument). The variance of the cash flows can be written as

$$\sigma^2 = \sigma_c^2 - 2w_x\rho_{cx}\sigma_c\sigma_x + w_x^2\sigma_x^2, \tag{17.22}$$

where σ_c^2 is the variance of the unhedged cash flows, ρ_{cx} is the correlation between the unhedged cash flows and cash from the hedging instrument, and σ_x^2 is the variance of the cash flows from the hedging instrument.

The optimal hedge ratio is determined by taking the first derivative of Eq. (17.22) with respect to w_x and setting the result equal to zero.[18] Since P_0 and h_0 are constants, this is equivalent to maximizing the denominator of Eq. (17.20), as follows:

$$-2\mu_x + 2\rho_{cx}\sigma_c\sigma_x - 2w_x\sigma_x^2 = 0 \tag{17.23}$$

$$w_x = \frac{\rho_{cx}\sigma_c\sigma_x - \mu_x}{\sigma_x^2} = \beta_x - \frac{\mu_x}{\sigma_x^2}. \tag{17.24}$$

Note that β_x is the traditional definition of a hedge ratio (the slope of a regression between the unhedged cash flows and the hedging cash flows). It is reduced by the rate of drift per unit of variance in the hedging instrument.

The decision about whether or not to hedge at all depends on the benefit of the hedge, namely, the present value of the amount and timing of business disruption costs. For example, they might be 15% of the value of assets and be expected to occur 50 years from now without the hedge and 53 years hence with the hedge. The decision also depends on the costs that must be paid every year for 53 years. They include transaction fees, bid-ask spreads, market impact, and management expenses (often about .5% per year). If the benefit cost ratio is greater than one, the company should hedge using the hedge ratio of Eq. (17.24).

---

[18] Note that the numerator of Eq. (17.20) is a negative constant $(-\ln(P_0/h_0))$ because the initial boundary h_0 is less than P_0, the initial cash flow. Therefore, maximizing the denominator of Eq. (17.20) is the same as maximizing Eq. (17.20) itself.

5. Empirical Evidence

What little empirical evidence that there is has been consistent with the predictions of the value-maximizing hedge that was described in the previous section. Nance, Smith, and Smithson [1993] find that companies are less likely to hedge if they have high boundary conditions—interpreted as high research and development expenses, or as a low ratio of operating cash flow to interest expenses. Bodnor, Hayt, and Marston [1998] found that half of the firms surveyed did not hedge either because their exposure was thought to be low or manageable, or because the costs of hedging exceeded the benefits. Mian [1996] finds that companies with higher liquidity and firms with higher growth are less likely to hedge. Howton and Perfect [1998] find that companies are unlikely to hedge if their ratio of R&D to sales is low, and if financial distress is not a threat. Berkman and Bradbury [1996] also find that companies that are financially healthy (e.g., with high coverage ratios) are less likely to hedge. Geczy, Minton, and Schrand [1997] report that high-growth firms with low levels of accessibility to capital markets are more likely to hedge. Finally, Gay and Nam [1998] find that firms with good investment opportunities, lower liquidity, and a low correlation between cash flow and investment opportunities are less likely to hedge.

E. $\mathscr{P}$ension Fund Management

Pension fund management is a topic that uses prior knowledge of option pricing (Chapter 7), portfolio theory (Chapter 6), and capital structure (Chapter 15). We begin with the history of the enormous growth of pension funds in the United States, then discuss pension fund regulations, and finally turn to the management of pension plans.

1. Overview: Historical Data and Financial Statements

Corporate pension plan liabilities have grown rapidly during the last four decades. For many companies, pension plan liabilities are larger than the book value of all long-term assets. We shall, in turn, discuss various types of pension plans, publicly accepted accounting principles that govern pension plan reporting, the regulation of pension plans by the Employment Retirement Income Security Act (ERISA), and management decision making about various pension plan problems, such as how to use pension fund assets to reduce the tax liabilities of the firm.

A pension plan is a promise by an employer to provide benefits to employees upon their retirement. Contractual pension fund commitments are a liability of the employer and must be disclosed in the firm's financial statements. A pension fund is established on behalf of employees and is managed by a trustee, who collects cash from the firm, manages the assets owned by the fund, and makes disbursements to retired employees. The firm is able to expense pension fund contributions for tax purposes. The fund pays no taxes on its earnings. However, beneficiaries must pay personal taxes upon receiving retirement payments from the fund. Hence pension funds are a tax-favored form of employee compensation because taxes are deferred until retirement.

The composition of pension fund assets is given in Table 17.5. Most pension funds hold their assets in the form of marketable securities: money market accounts, bonds, and stocks. Because pension fund earnings are not taxed, it never pays to hold municipal bonds because their low tax-exempt interest rates are always dominated by the higher interest paid by taxable. Direct investment in real estate (with the possible exception of undeveloped land) is also not advisable because most

Table 17.5 Distribution of Assets of Noninsured Pension Funds (Percentage of the Book Value of Total Assets Invested)

	1950	1960	1970	1980	2002
U.S. government securities	30.5	8.1	3.1	11.0	33.8
Corporate bonds	43.8	47.4	30.6	24.9	32.2
Stocks	17.1	34.7	55.1	50.5	28.0
Mortgages	1.6	3.9	4.3	1.6	0.1
Cash, deposits, other	7.0	5.9	6.9	12.0	5.9
Total	100.0	100.0	100.0	100.0	100.0

Source: U.S. Securities and Exchange Commission.

real estate investments are priced such that the investor must be in a relatively high tax bracket in order to receive a positive after-tax return. Pension funds are in a zero-tax bracket.

Later on in the chapter we shall discuss some of the possible influences that may affect the composition of assets in pension fund portfolios. Although the pension fund can profitably hold taxable securities, it is not immediately clear what percentage should be held in the form of interest-bearing securities (money market funds and bonds) or common stock.

Table 17.6 gives the format for a typical pension fund income statement and balance sheet. Cash inflows to the fund are provided by corporate contributions, employee contributions, dividends and interest earned by the funds' stocks and bonds, and capital gains. Cash outflows are management fees, brokerage expenses, disbursements to beneficiaries, and capital losses. The change in the net fund balance is the difference between inflows and outflows. The fund's profit is not taxable. Marketable securities are the only item in the pension fund balance sheet that is not the result of a present value calculation. The present value of future contributions to the fund is the other major asset. Contributions are received in two forms: cash from the firm and earnings on the fund's assets. A major issue is, What rate of return will be generated from the fund's assets? If the return is high, then the firm can reduce the amount of cash it puts into the fund. As we shall see later in the chapter, the rate of return assumption is a tricky decision.

Liabilities are subdivided into two categories. The present value (PV) of benefits from past service is handled one of two ways. Some companies calculate the present value of vested benefits only. These are the benefits that would be paid if all employees left the firm immediately. However, it is typical that employees become vested in the pension plan only after accumulating a minimum period of seniority, say, five years. If they leave prior to five years, they receive none of their promised pension benefits. An alternative procedure is to calculate the present value of all benefits accrued for past service whether employees are fully vested or not. Hence accrued benefits will usually be larger than vested benefits because not all employees are fully vested. Regardless of how the present value of benefits from past service is handled, total pension liabilities remain unchanged. If only vested benefits are included in the present value of benefits for past service, then unvested benefits are included in the second liability category.

The second major liability item is the present value of benefits for future service. Its computation is complex and depends on actuarial assumptions about the amount of employee turnover, the age and seniority of retiring employees, their life expectancy, and the choice of a discount rate for present value computations.

Table 17.6 Format for a Pension Fund Income Statement and Balance Sheet

Pension Fund Income Statement	Pension Fund Balance Sheet
Funds received	Assets
From employer(s)	Marketable securities
From employees	Cash
From dividends, interest, and	Bonds
capital gains (losses)	Stock
Funds expended	PV of future contributions
Management fees and brokerage costs	Deficit (surplus)
Disbursement to beneficiaries	Liabilities
Change in net fund balance	PV of benefits for past service
	PV of benefits for future service

Table 17.7 Hypothetical 1984 Consolidated Year-End Balance Sheet for Du Pont Showing Vested Pension Liabilities (billions of dollars)

Assets		Liabilities	
Pension fund	$8.4	Pension liability	$7.6
Plant and equipment	14.4	Long-term debt	3.4
Other long-term assets	1.0	Equity	13.0
Current assets	8.7	Other long-term liabilities	3.3
Total assets	$32.5	Current liabilities	5.2
		Total liabilities	$32.5

Of major concern to all parties is the size of the pension fund deficit or surplus. An unfunded deficit is an asset of the pension fund (as shown in Table 17.6) and a liability of the firm, and it can be enormous. For example, had the pension liabilities of Du Pont been included, its balance sheet for the end of its 1984 fiscal year would have looked like Table 17.7. The $7.6 billion pension liability represents the vested liabilities of Du Pont, that is, the liability that would be incurred if all the employees left the firm at the end of 1984. Du Pont's pension was overfunded by $800 million. In principle, this money "belongs" to shareholders. Even though the pension was overfunded, the addition of pension assets and liabilities to the balance sheet raised Du Pont's debt-to-total-assets ratio from 49% to 60%.[19] Clearly, pension fund liabilities are important enough to require full disclosure.

---

[19] The effect of the pension fund on the balance sheet is to increase assets by $8.4 billion, to increase pension liabilities by $7.6 billion, and to increase equity by $0.8 billion (the amount of overfunding). Note that Table 17.7 is purely hypothetical and does conform to the generally accepted accounting practices that are discussed later in the chapter.

2. Pension Fund Regulations: ERISA, FASB, and the IRS

With the rapid growth of pensions as a form of deferred compensation, it became more and more important that firms fully disclose their pension commitments in their financial statements and that various pension practices become regulated by law. The Financial Accounting Standards Board (FASB) has established the generally accepted accounting practices for reporting by pension funds and firms (FASB No. 35 and 36, issued in 1980). In September 1974, President Gerald Ford signed into law the Employment Retirement Income Security Act (ERISA), which regulates various aspects of pension plans, including eligibility, vesting, funding, fiduciary responsibility, reporting and disclosure, and plan termination insurance.

There are two types of pension plans. *Defined contribution plans* consist of funds built up over time via employee and employer contributions, but benefits are not predetermined. Employees are simply paid out the market value of their portion of the pension fund when they retire. The firm has no responsibilities other than paying its share of the contributions and prudent management of the pension fund assets. The second, and more common, type is a *defined benefit plan*. Corporations are required to pay a contractual benefit upon the retirement of a vested employee. When ERISA was signed, defined benefit pensions were converted from corporate promises to liabilities enforceable by law.

The provisions of ERISA are many. No employee older than 25 years and with more than 1 year of service with a company, or hired more than 5 years before normal retirement age, may be excluded from participation in that company's pension plan. Prior to ERISA, unusual vesting practices resulted in many injustices. For example, some plans required 20 or more years of uninterrupted service before an employee became vested. Sometimes workers would be fired in their 19th year simply to prevent vesting them in a pension plan. With the advent of ERISA and the passage of the 1986 tax code, all plans must choose from one of two minimum vesting schedules for the corporate portion of the contributions to the pension plan:

1. Cliff vesting: 100% vesting after 5 years of service.
2. Graded vesting: 20% vesting after 3 years of service and then increasing by 20% per year up to 100% vesting after 7 years of service.

All employee contributions to a pension fund, and investment returns on such contributions, are fully vested from the beginning.

ERISA legislates the minimum funding of defined benefit plans, whereas the IRS sets limits on the maximum corporate contribution. According to ERISA, the minimum contribution is determined as follows: (1) all normal costs attributable to benefit claims deriving from employee services in a given year must be paid by that year; (2) any experience losses (caused by a decline in the value of the securities in the fund, by unexpected changes in employee turnover, or by changes in actuarial assumptions about the discount rate) must be amortized over a period not to exceed 15 years; and (3) supplemental liabilities resulting from increased benefits or unfunded past service costs must be amortized over a period not to exceed 30 years (40 years for companies with pre-ERISA supplemental liabilities). On the other hand, the IRS defines the maximum corporate pension contribution as the actuarially determined normal cost of the plan plus any amount necessary to amortize supplemental and experience losses over a 10-year period. The ERISA and IRS restrictions limit corporate discretion over the amount of funds contributed to a plan.

One of the most important provisions of ERISA was the creation of the Pension Benefit Guaranty Corporation (PBGC). It is a pension insurance fund operated under the supervision of the U.S.

Department of Labor. Corporations must pay the PBGC a fixed annual premium (currently $16.00 per employee per year) for each employee in a pension plan.[20] There is also a variable cost component for underfunded plans that can raise the premium per worker. This central fund is then used to guarantee pension benefits even if a plan fails. A pension plan may be terminated voluntarily by the corporation or involuntarily by the PBGC upon court order. The PBGC may terminate a plan (1) if the plan fails to meet minimum funding standards, (2) if the plan is unable to pay benefits when due, (3) if the plan is administered improperly, or (4) if the liability of the PBGC for fulfilling claims deriving from the plan is likely to increase unreasonably.

If a plan is terminated because it is underfunded, the company is liable for 100% of the deficit up to 30% of the company's net worth. Furthermore, the PBGC may place a lien on corporate assets that has the same priority as federal taxes. Hence unfunded pension liabilities are equivalent to the most senior debt. A bankrupt firm may have few assets to pay to the PBGC; hence a worthy public policy question is whether the PBGC has enough resources of its own to adequately insure pensioners of major corporate bankruptcies. In July 1987 the PBGC had total assets of $3 billion and faced total obligations of $7 billion for people currently retired or who would retire under plans of which it was trustee. The agency also faced cash flow problems because the premium income that it collected from corporations and the dividends from its investments were less than the benefits that it had already undertaken to pay. These were the unrealized liabilities. The present value of the PBGC potential liabilities is much larger. Marcus [1985] estimates the present value of the PBGC insurance liability for a sample of 87 of the Fortune 100 companies based on their 1982 annual reports. His reports range from $6.7 to $14.8 billion.

3. Managerial Decisions Regarding Pension Plans

Most of the foregoing discussion has been descriptive in nature. We have discussed the rapid growth of pension funds, their asset composition, the pension plan financial statements, and pension fund regulation by ERISA and the IRS. Now it is time to ask what types of pension fund decisions confront financial managers and how these decisions will affect the value of shareholders' wealth. Listed by order of presentation, the decisions are

1. Which type of pension plan, defined contribution or defined benefit, should a firm choose?

2. What are the effects of changing the actuarial assumptions of a pension fund?

3. What is the optimal mix of pension fund assets?

4. When, if ever, is it optimal to voluntarily terminate a pension plan? How can termination be accomplished legally?

5. Should the firm manage its pension plan or enter into a contract with an insurance company?

6. Pension plans are a form of remuneration that is a substitute for current salary and bonus compensation. How should one think about the trade-off?

These are common pension plan problems, and every chief financial officer should understand the impact that pension plan decisions will have on the corporation's shareholders.

CHOICE OF PLAN TYPE At first, it might seem that defined contribution plans are better than defined benefit plans because no promise of a predetermined retirement benefit is made to employees. With defined contribution plans they receive payments based on whatever is in

---

[20] There is also a variable cost component for underfunded plans that can bring the premium up to a total of $50 per worker.

the fund at retirement. However, there is a drawback to defined contribution plans, which from the corporation's point of view probably explains why most companies use defined benefit plans instead.

Defined benefit plans allow flexibility for the purpose of tax planning. With defined benefit plans the firm can slow its payments to the plan (down to the minimum allowed by ERISA) during years of low profitability when the cash is needed for other purposes; then, during years of high profitability, payment can be accelerated (up to the limits established by the IRS) as a way of sheltering cash flows from income taxes. Defined contribution plans do not allow similar flexibility because they are established as a fixed percentage of employee compensation. We might expect to see defined benefit plans used by corporations, especially those that can benefit from tax planning. Defined contribution plans are more likely to be used by nontaxable entities and by partnerships.

CHANGING THE ACTUARIAL ASSUMPTIONS In 1973, U.S. Steel increased its reported profits by $47 million by "reducing" its pension costs. This was accomplished by recognizing some appreciation in its $2 billion pension fund. Presumably, cash was then diverted from pension contributions to other uses. In the fourth quarter of 1980, Chrysler changed its assumed discount rate on its employee pension plan from 6% to 7%. Pension costs were reduced, and $50 million was added to profits. Also, in 1980, Bethlehem Steel changed the assumed discount rate for its pension benefits to 10% from 7%.[21] This 3% increase had the effect of decreasing the present value of accumulated pension plan benefits by $713 million (22.5% of total benefits). Before the change, pension plan net assets totaled $1.952 billion and the plan was underfunded by $1.215 billion. After the change, underfunding fell to $502 million, a 58.7% decline. *Accounting Trends and Techniques*, an annual survey of reporting practices of 600 companies, showed that roughly 30% of the companies sampled voluntarily changed their pension fund accounting assumptions at least once between 1975 and 1980.

The economic effect on shareholders' wealth depends on how the accounting changes revised shareholders' expectations about the level and riskiness of the future cash flows of the firm. The value of shareholders' wealth is equal to the market value of the firm, V, minus the market value of its liabilities. For convenience, we shall divide liabilities into pension fund liabilities, PFL, and other debt, B. When ERISA was signed, defined pension liabilities became senior debt of the firm. Equation (17.25) shows S, the value of shareholders' wealth:

$$S = V - PFL - B. \tag{17.25}$$

We are interested in the market value of pension fund liabilities and how they are affected by accounting changes. The market value is the way the marketplace will view the true pension fund deficit and does not have any necessary relationship to the accounting or book value deficit. The market value of the pension fund deficit (or surplus) is given in Eq. (17.26):

$$PFL = - \text{Market value of pension fund assets} \tag{17.26}$$

$$- [PV \text{ (expected contributions)}](1 - \tau_c)$$

$$+ PV \text{ (expected pension fund benefits from past and future service)}.$$

---

[21] FASB Statement No. 36 allows companies to use different interest rate assumptions for disclosure in the annual report and for funding purposes; for example, Bethlehem used 7% for funding and 10% for disclosure. See Regan [1982].

There are two major pension fund assets. First is the current market value of the stocks, bonds, mortgages, and so forth held by the pension fund. Second is the present value of the expected fund contributions, which are multiplied by one minus the corporate tax rate $(1 - \tau_c)$ in order to reflect the fact that pension fund contributions are tax deductible by the firm. As long as the firm is making profits, then pension contributions are "shared" with the government because more contributions mean lower taxes.[22] Balancing the pension fund assets is the pension fund liability, the present value of expected pension fund benefits to be paid to employees.

The main difference between the book value of the pension fund deficit and its market value, or true economic value, *PFL*, is reflected in the rates of return (discount rates). Equation (17.27) further elaborates Eq. (17.26) by showing the present value of the pension fund along with the appropriate market-determined discount rates:

$$PFL = - \text{ Market value of pension fund assets}$$

$$- \sum_{t=1}^{n} \frac{E(\text{contributions in year } t)(1 - \tau_c)}{[1 + k_b(1 - \tau_c)]^t}$$

$$+ \sum_{t=1}^{n} \frac{E(\text{benefits in year } t)}{(1 + k_b)^t}. \tag{17.27}$$

The expected pension benefits are discounted at the pretax cost of senior debt, k_b, because ERISA has made the payment of pension benefits a senior obligation of the firm, second only to tax liabilities.[23] Pension contributions are also discounted at the rate k_b, but on an after-tax basis. Prior to ERISA, the expected benefits would have been discounted at the cost of junior, or subordinated, debt, k_j, which is higher than k_b, the cost of senior debt. One of the major effects of ERISA was to transfer wealth from shareholders to pension beneficiaries by increasing the present value of pension deficits, *PFL*. The transfer was especially large for plans that were seriously underfunded.

The real effect of a change in pension plan actuarial assumptions depends on the cash flow consequences. If the *actuarial* discount rate assumption is raised, then the present value of accumulated benefits in book value terms decreases, as do the normal costs that have to be paid into the fund. This has the effect of decreasing the annual expected contributions into the fund and hence decreasing their present value in Eq. (17.27), because expected contributions decrease, whereas the *market-determined* discount rate, k_b, does not change. The present value of expected benefits, however, remains unchanged. The net effect is to increase the market value of pension liabilities, *PFL*. There is usually no effect on the firm as a whole because the cash flow not put into pension fund contributions may be used either to decrease other liabilities or to increase assets. Either way, the increased pension liability is exactly offset.[24]

---

[22] If one considers Social Security to be a pension plan, then recent changes in the Social Security tax law that require nonprofit organizations to pay Social Security tax for their employees are burdensome. Because nonprofit organizations have no tax shelter, they must bear the full cost of Social Security expenses.

[23] Some have argued that promised pension benefits are subordinated to other debt claims in spite of ERISA because other debt comes due before pension obligations. Pension beneficiaries cannot force the firm into bankruptcy, whereas debt holders can. The existence of large unfunded pension deficits will, in our opinion, cause debt holders to force bankruptcy sooner than they might if there were no pension obligations. Nevertheless, pension liabilities will still be senior claims at the time of bankruptcy.

[24] One sometimes hears that pension contributions can be legitimately cut if the funds are alternatively used to invest in positive net present value projects. This argument confuses the investment decision (take the profitable project) with the

Thus we see that, from the shareholders' point of view, changing the actuarial assumptions in order to change pension contributions is usually an exercise in futility. Even worse, if the funds generated by cutting pension contributions are used for a purpose that is not expensed (e.g., repaying the principal on debt), the effect is to increase taxable income and decrease net cash flows to shareholders. Accounting profits have increased, but the firm has sacrificed the pension contribution tax shield. The net effect (assuming the firm is paying taxes) is to benefit the IRS at the expense of shareholders. Finally, changing actuarial assumptions for disclosure in the annual report but not for funding purposes is chicanery at best and stupid at worst. If taxes are based on actual contributions, then, at best, managers think they can somehow fool the marketplace.

CHOOSING THE MIX OF PENSION PLAN ASSETS As with any other portfolio decision, the choice of assets for a pension plan involves a selection of risk and return. Furthermore, tax considerations and pension fund insurance through ERISA are paramount.

Modeling pension plan payoffs. Before turning to the effect of ERISA and taxes on pension fund investments, let us build a more complete understanding of their risk and return characteristics. Prior to the passage of ERISA, corporate pension liabilities were analogous to risky debt, and the shareholders' position was equivalent to a call option on a leveraged firm.[25] To illustrate this, assume a one-period framework, an all-equity firm that has an uncertain end-of-period value, V_1, and a world with no taxes. The pension fund holds some risky assets with an end-of-period value, A_1, and the pension beneficiaries have been promised an end-of-period benefit, B.

Figure 17.13 shows the end-of-period payoffs to the pension beneficiaries, assuming that the pension fund is uninsured. Along the horizontal axis, we have the market value of the firm plus the market value of the pension assets, $V + A$, whereas dollars of end-of-period payoff are graphed along the vertical axis. The pension beneficiaries will receive the full promised amount if the market value of assets, $V + A$, exceeds the promised benefits, B. But if not, the pension beneficiaries receive $V + A < B$. The solid line OXB in Fig. 17.13 shows the pension beneficiaries' payoff. Because we have assumed the firm has no debt, the shareholders' payoff is simply the residual, as shown in the following equation:

$$\text{Shareholders' payoff} = \text{MAX}[0, (V + A) - B]. \tag{17.28}$$

Referring back to Chapter 7 on options on risky assets, we see that the shareholders' payoff is identical to a call option on a levered firm. The pension beneficiaries' position is equivalent to owning a risk-free bond with an end-of-period value equal to the promised pension benefits, B, and selling a put option, P, on the assets of the firm.[26] In other words, they have a risky debt claim. Figure 17.14 shows that if we vertically sum the payoff from holding a riskless bond and selling a put option (at no cost to shareholders), we do indeed arrive at the pension beneficiaries' position.

The claims of all parties can be summarized by referring to the put-call parity equation (discussed in Chapter 7). Put-call parity said that the current market value of an underlying risky asset

---

way it is financed (cut pension fund contributions). The project can be financed either by cutting pension contributions, which increases pension liabilities, or by borrowing, which increases debt liabilities. Either way, the effect on shareholders' wealth is the same.

[25] For a more complete presentation of pension fund liabilities as options, see Sharpe [1976] and Treynor, Priest, and Regan [1976].

[26] Given that this is a one-period model and that pension benefits are not payable until employees retire at the end of the period, all options in the model are European options. They cannot be exercised before maturity.

Figure 17.13 End-of-period pension fund payoffs.

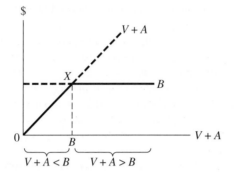

Figure 17.14 The pension beneficiaries' position is equivalent to risky debt (long in a riskless bond and short in a put option).

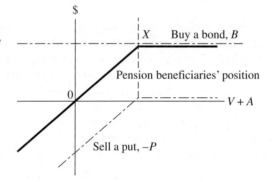

plus the value of a put option written on it (with maturity T periods hence and with an exercise price X) is equal to the value of a riskless bond plus a call option on the risky asset (with the same maturity and exercise price as the put). Using our current notation, the put-call parity expression becomes

$$(V_0 + A_0) + P_0 = B_0 + S_0,$$

$$S_0 = (V_0 + A_0) - (B_0 - P_0). \tag{17.29}$$

The shareholders' position, S_0, is equivalent to a call option on a levered firm. On the right-hand side of Eq. (17.29), we note that $(V_0 + A_0)$ is the present value of the firm and pension fund assets and that $(B_0 - P_0)$ is the present value of risky debt (i.e., the pension benefits).

Considerable insight into pension fund asset mix can be provided by this simple option pricing approach. For example, what happens to shareholders' wealth if the pension trustees change the mix of pension assets from a well-diversified portfolio of equity to being 100% invested in shares of the firm?[27] The effect would be to increase the correlation between V, the value of the firm, and A, the value of the pension assets. Consequently, the variance of the underlying portfolio of assets increases, and the value of shareholders' wealth, S_0, which is a call option on the assets, will also increase. Thus, the effect of any decision that unexpectedly increases the risk of $(V + A)$ is to shift

---

[27] This situation is not unusual. For example, at one time, the Sears pension fund had over 50% of its assets invested in its stock.

wealth to shareholders and away from pension beneficiaries. The only mitigating circumstance, which was pointed out by Sharpe [1976], is that employees may be able to demand higher wages to compensate them for the higher risk they must bear when pension assets are invested in the firm's own stock. Or they might require pension fund insurance.[28]

The effects of ERISA and the PBGC. Now let us look at the effect of government pension fund insurance on the pension fund asset mix but maintain our assumption that there are no taxes. As was mentioned earlier, the Pension Benefit Guaranty Corporation (PBGC) ensures pension fund liabilities. Corporations contribute into PBGC a fixed insurance premium per employee each year. In the event that an underfunded pension plan is terminated, the firm is liable up to 30% of its net worth, and the PBGC guarantees the remainder of the pension fund liability.

If the PBGC were a privately owned insurance company, it would charge premiums based on the probability of corporate default on a pension fund. However, as a government organization, it charges all firms exactly the same insurance premium regardless of the extent of pension plan underfunding or the likelihood of bankruptcy. One implication, of course, is that firms with overfunded pension funds are paying too much to the PBGC relative to those with badly underfunded pension plans. Another implication is that firms threatened with bankruptcy can decide to change their pension plan asset mix to maximize the value of the call option that represents their shareholders' wealth. If they go bankrupt, shareholders receive nothing, and although the PBGC can claim 30% of each firm's net worth, 30% of nothing is still nothing. The PBGC claim on equity is worthless in both Chapter 7 bankruptcy and Chapter 11 reorganization. Consequently, the optimal strategy from the point of view of shareholders is to put all the pension assets into very risky stocks. If they are lucky the risky portfolio may do well and even result in overfunding in the pension fund. If they are unfortunate, then they end up with nothing, which is where they would have been anyway, and the PBGC has to pay off the pension beneficiaries.

Given that the PBGC undercharges for pension fund insurance for underfunded plans, then there is the distinct possibility that corporations facing potential bankruptcy can game the PBGC by shifting pension plan assets to being 100% invested in risky stocks.

An interesting case history of a company in trouble is International Harvester. In May 1982, the *Wall Street Journal* reported that International Harvester Company's pension fund abruptly switched at least $250 million of stock holdings into bonds, chiefly U.S. government issues. Pension industry executives suggested that the company was pursuing a strategy that would let it reduce pension contributions. As of October 31, 1981, Harvester's combined pension assets totaled $1.35 billion.

What are the real economic consequences of Harvester's decision? First, since the company had negative earnings, it is not likely that the tax consequences of the decision were important.[29] Second, by changing the actuarial assumptions of the plan either (1) by realizing gains on the stocks that were sold or (2) by raising the fund rate of return assumption due to the shift from stocks to bonds, Harvester could reduce its planned cash contributions to the fund. We have already seen (in the previous material in this chapter) that the change in actuarial assumptions has no effect on shareholders' wealth at best and a negative effect at worst. Finally, the analysis in this section of the chapter suggests that a shift from stock to bonds (in the absence of tax benefits) decreases shareholders' wealth and benefits pension beneficiaries (and debt holders) of the firm. Although

---

[28] For more on the economics of insuring portfolios of risky assets, see Gatto, Geske, Litzenberger, and Sossin [1980].

[29] The next section of this chapter provides the only rational tax explanation for why Harvester shareholders may have benefited from switching pension assets to bonds.

we have insufficient information to draw a definite conclusion about the Harvester decision, it looks like the net effect was to diminish shareholders' wealth.

The effect of taxes. For most firms, pension fund contributions reduce taxes because they are immediately deductible. At the same time, the pension plan pays no taxes on its earnings. Hence the rapid growth of pensions is largely attributable to the fact that they are a form of tax-deferred compensation.

The pension assets should be invested in those securities that have the most favorable pretax rates of return. Obvious examples of securities that pension managers should *not* invest in are those that are used as tax shelters by investors with high marginal tax rates, such as municipal bonds or real estate with depreciable assets like buildings.

Perhaps the most interesting tax implication for the pension fund asset mix is that pension plans should be fully funded and invested totally in bonds as opposed to equities.[30] The logic is developed in two parts. The first argument is that the return on debt held in a corporate pension fund is passed through the firm to its shareholders in the form of higher share prices because an overfunded pension plan is an asset of the firm.[31] The implication is that the return on debt held in the pension fund is ultimately taxed at the lower personal tax rate on equities. Shareholders will pay less tax than if the debt were held in their personal portfolios. Consequently, shareholders are much better off if the pension funds or corporations are invested in bonds, whereas their personal portfolios are invested in equities. This conclusion is based on the fact that pension plan earnings are not taxed and that bond income is taxed at a higher rate than capital gains.[32] It does not depend on any theoretical gain to leverage (e.g., Chapter 15).

The second reason for investing pension assets in bonds is the potential value of the tax shelter involved when the firm borrows to invest pension assets in bonds. The following example compares two pension investment strategies, the first with all pension assets in stock and the second with all assets in bonds. For the sake of simplicity, we assume a one-period world with two equally likely states of nature. If the economy is good, stocks will yield a 100% rate of return, whereas bonds will yield 10%. If the economy is bad, stocks yield −50% and bonds yield 10%. The risk-free rate is 10%. Note that the expected (or average) return on stocks is 25%, whereas bonds are expected to yield only 10%. Even so, we will see that the bond investment strategy is better for shareholders.

Table 17.8 shows a beginning-of-period market value balance sheet that combines the firm and pension fund assets and liabilities for each of the two pension investment strategies: all stock and all bonds. The firm's defined benefit pension plan promises to pay $220 million at the end of the period. The present value of this liability is $200 million, and it appears on the liabilities side of the corporate balance sheet. On the assets side, the current market value of the pension assets is $200 million (either in stock or bonds). The pension plan is fully funded because the present value of its assets equals that of its liabilities.

If we employ the 100% stock investment strategy for our pension plan, the end-of-period payoffs are as shown in Table 17.9. Using the "good economy" as an example, we see that the pension fund stocks can be sold for $400 million at the end of the year. After paying the $220 million of

---

[30] For the proof of this proposition, the reader is referred to Tepper and Affleck [1974], Black [1980], and especially to Tepper [1981].

[31] The next section of this chapter discusses ways that shareholders can gain access to the assets of overfunded pension plans.

[32] Even though the 1986 tax code makes the scheduled capital gains rate equal to the ordinary income rate, the effective capital gains rate is still lower because of the tax-timing option implicit in the realization of capital gains.

Table 17.8 Beginning Balance Sheets for Two Pension Investment Strategies

100% *Stock Strategy (millions of dollars)*

Assets		Liabilities	
Pension plan		Pension plan	
Bonds, B	0	PV of benefits, PFB	200
Stock, S	200	Corporate	
Corporate, A	800	Debt, D	300
		Equity, E	500
	1,000		1,000

100% *Bond Strategy (millions of dollars)*

Assets		Liabilities	
Pension plan		Pension plan	
Bonds, B	200	PV of benefits, PFB	200
Stock, S	0	Corporate	
Corporate, A	800	Debt, D	400
		Equity, E	400
	1,000		1,000

Table 17.9 Payoffs for the 100% Stock Pension Investment Strategy (millions of dollars)

	State of Nature	
	Good Economy	**Bad Economy**
Sell stock and receive	$400	$100
Pay off defined benefits	−220	−220
Cash to the firm	180	−120
Less taxes at 50%	−90	60
Net cash to shareholders	$90	−$60

pension benefits, shareholders are left with $180 million pretax and $90 million after taxes. In the "bad economy," they suffer a $60 million loss. The expected gain in shareholders' wealth is $15 million, but they are exposed to a great deal of risk. The alternate pension investment strategy is to invest $200 million in bonds. If that is all we did, the end-of-period payoff would be exactly $220 million in either economy, the pension benefits would be paid off, and there would be no gain or loss to shareholders. Their expected gain is zero, but they take no risk at all.

To present a valid comparison of the stock and bond strategies, we need to keep shareholders' risk constant. Then we can compare after-tax expected returns to see which strategy is better, given

Table 17.10 Payoffs for the 100% Bond Pension Investment Strategy (millions of dollars)

	State of Nature	
	Good Economy	**Bad Economy**
Sell bonds and receive	$220	$220
Pay off defined benefits	−220	−220
	0	0
Sell stock (book value = $100)	200	50
Pay off extra bonds	−100	−100
	100	−50
Less interest on bonds	−10	−10
	90	−60
Plus tax shield on interest	5	5
Net cash to shareholders	$95	−$55

equivalent risk. Table 17.8 shows balance sheets that have the same risk for shareholders.[33] On the assets side, $200 million of bonds is less risky than $200 million of stock. Therefore to offset the decline in risk caused by the 100% bond strategy, we increase the firm's financial leverage by borrowing $100 million and using the proceeds to repurchase $100 million in equity.[34] The resulting payoffs are given in Table 17.10.

In the "good economy," the bonds are sold for $220 million and the proceeds are used to pay off the defined benefits. Next the $100 million of repurchased equity is reissued for $200 million (because the stock has appreciated by 100% in the good economy). Half of the $200 million is used to repay the $100 million of borrowing, and $10 million pays the required interest. Note that the interest payments are tax deductible. If the firm is in a 50% tax bracket, then taxes are reduced $5 million below what they otherwise would have been. Net cash available to shareholders in the favorable state of nature is $95 million with the 100% bond strategy but is only $90 million with the 100% equity strategy. The bond strategy also dominates the equity strategy in the unfavorable state of nature (−$55 million versus −$60 million). Hence our example demonstrates the superiority of the bond strategy from the shareholders' point of view. We have increased their return in both states of nature without changing their risk because the range of payoffs is $150 million in either case. Regardless of whether the actual return on stock investments is higher or lower than on bonds, the bond strategy is preferable.

Summarizing, we have seen that investing all pension fund assets in bonds benefits shareholders in two ways. First, the pretax bond rate of return is passed through the firm to its shareholders in the form of higher share prices, which are in turn taxed at the lower capital gains rate. This argument

---

[33] It really does not make any difference, in our example, how risk is measured. Shareholders' risk is equivalent whether one uses the range, the variance, or the beta to measure risk.

[34] In practice, it is not necessary for corporations to actually repurchase shares in order to implement the 100% bond pension investment plan. What is important is that when pension assets are invested in bonds rather than stock, the risk of the corporate asset portfolio is lower. Hence, from the point of view of lenders, there is greater debt capacity. More borrowing provides a debt tax shield.

Figure 17.15 Corner solutions to the pension funding and asset problem.

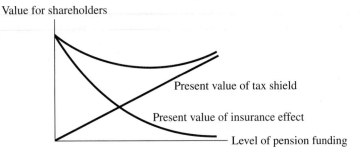

Value for shareholders

Present value of tax shield

Present value of insurance effect

Level of pension funding

applies even if there is no gain to leverage. The second reason for favoring bonds over equity is that there may be a gain to firms that they carry more debt without increasing shareholders' risk— a gain to leverage. We have seen that firms that choose to invest pension assets in bonds actually experience lower total asset risk than firms that put pension assets into stock. The lower risk means a greater debt capacity. If the firm uses this debt capacity and if there is a valuable tax shield created by the deductibility of interest payments, then there is a gain to leverage from investing pension assets in bonds while borrowing to hold shareholders' risk constant.[35]

Empirical evidence by Landsman [1984] covering a large sample of firms for the years 1979 through 1981 shows that on average each dollar contributed to the assets of defined benefit pension funds results in a $1.12 increase in the value of shareholders' equity, other things being held constant. That the increase is significantly greater than $1 means that there may, in fact, be a clear tax advantage resulting from pension assets held by the firm.

Combining the insurance and tax effects. The insurance and tax effects of pension funding on shareholder wealth seem to suggest corner solutions for the choice of the level of funding and the type of assets mix. If a firm is successful and is paying high taxes, then it should make full use of the tax shield provided by pension plans—it should overfund to the maximum extent permitted by law and invest primarily in bonds. Alternatively, if it is losing money, or it is not paying taxes for other reasons, it cannot benefit from the pension fund tax shield and should therefore underfund to the maximum extent permitted by law and put all the pension assets into risky equities. This result is illustrated in Fig. 17.15. Note, however, that if the line representing the present value of the tax shield were steeper, then the plan would be overfunded.

Bicksler and Chen [1985] and Westerfield and Marshall [1983] suggest that this conclusion may be too strong. Rarely do firms actually go to either extreme. And they usually have a mix of debt and equity in their pension fund portfolios. There are two reasons, and they are illustrated in Fig. 17.16. First, there are deadweight losses associated with involuntary pension fund insurance provided by the PBGC from point X to X'. Examples of such costs are legal expenses and higher employee wage demands to offset the probability that their defined pension benefit may not be paid. On the tax side, Bicksler and Chen suggest that the present value of the tax shield diminishes because of the asymmetric structure of the U.S. tax code. Firms pay taxes when their income is positive but cannot count on using all tax credits from carry forwards and carrybacks if income is negative. As illustrated in Fig. 17.16, the joint effects of termination deadweight losses and

---

[35] The gain to leverage is most likely to be valuable for those firms that have higher effective tax rates because their tax shelters from other sources (such as depreciation, research and development expenses, or tax carryback and carry forward) are limited.

Figure 17.16 An interior solution for funding and the choice of asset mix. (From J. Bicksler and A. Chen, "The Integration of Insurance and Taxes in Corporate Pension Strategy," *Journal of Finance*, July 1985, 951. Reprinted with permission.)

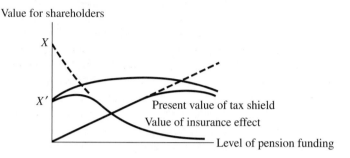

a diminishing tax shelter result in an interior optimum. If the tax effect dominates, the level of pension funding will be higher and more of the fund assets will be in bonds than stocks, and vice versa.

VOLUNTARY TERMINATION OF DEFINED BENEFIT PENSION PLANS
In June 1983, Occidental Petroleum voluntarily terminated four defined benefit pension plans for salaried employees in its oil and chemicals divisions, replacing them with defined contribution plans. All employees covered by the terminated plans received a lump sum payment covering their vested benefits. Because the defined benefit plans were overfunded by approximately $294 million (at the end of 1982), the voluntary termination boosted Occidental's after-tax net income by approximately $100 million, or 64% of its 1982 earnings.

Fortune magazine (December 26, 1983) reported that since 1980, 128 companies have carried out 138 pension reversions where defined benefit plans were canceled. The excess assets, which reverted to use in operating and capital budgets, amounted to $515 million. The Pension Benefit Guarantee Corporation, which has to approve any cancelations, was considering applications that would free up well over $1 billion more in excess assets. Furthermore, an estimated $150 billion in excess assets sits untapped in other private pension plans.

These examples clearly demonstrate that if underfunded pension plans are liabilities of shareholders, then overfunded plans are assets. Although the firm owns the excess assets in the fund, it is restricted greatly in its ability to use them.[36] ERISA states that any residual assets in a terminated plan revert to the employer only if the pension plan explicitly provides for such a distribution upon termination. In many cases, the PBGC has contended that excess assets should go to plan beneficiaries. Consequently, firms must be careful about the process of terminating overfunded pension plans. It should also be noted that ERISA has made it more difficult to borrow against the assets in the pension fund, and that the IRS collects taxes plus a 10% surcharge when an overfunded plan is terminated (see the 1986 Tax Reform Act).

Usually, firms do not consider voluntary termination of underfunded plans because the PBGC can lay claim to 30% of their net worth. However, two questions arise. How is net worth to be measured? And, can a subsidiary with negative net worth terminate its pension plan and relinquish the unfunded liabilities to the PBGC? In answer to the second question, the PBGC has denied

---

[36] For a more complete exposition, the reader is referred to Bulow, Scholes, and Manell [1982].

subsidiaries the right to terminate their plans so long as the parent company shows adequate net worth. Furthermore, the PBGC has argued that in determining net worth it can look beyond book value and use other information to establish the value of the firm as a going concern. Consequently, voluntary termination of underfunded plans is an unlikely strategy.

Most companies replace their defined benefit plans with defined contribution plans, thereby shifting the uncertainties of pension performance from themselves to their employees. The company simply promises to pay a fixed percentage of each employee's salary or wages into the defined contribution plan. Benefits upon retirement depend on the return on pension assets. Sometimes the defined contribution plans are coupled with the 401(k) tax-deferred savings plan authorized by the Internal Revenue Act of 1978. Employee contributions to the plan reduce their tax liabilities and earn tax-free returns until retirement. One drawback, from the company's perspective, is that its contributions to the 401(k) plan are vested immediately.

INSURANCE COMPANY CONTRACTS   About 39% of all nongovernment pension plans were invested with insurance companies. The usual insurance company contract provides "guaranteed" rates of return for a fixed period of time. For example, you may be guaranteed an 8% return for a 10-year period. The insurance companies can provide the guarantee because they invest your pension fund contributions in 10-year government bonds, which, if held to maturity, yield exactly 8%. The catch is that you cannot withdraw your pension plan assets if interest rates change. When market rates of interest rose rapidly during the late 1970s and early 1980s, many firms suddenly realized that a guaranteed rate of return was very different from a riskless return. Market rates of interest of 14% on long-term bonds were not unusual, but those companies whose pension assets were committed to insurance company contracts found they were locked into an 8% return. This is the hard way to learn about opportunity cost (although it is still a fair game).

If your company is large enough to provide its own pension fund accounting for employees, then there is no difference between contributing pension funds to an insurance company plan and directly investing in 8% 10-year bonds yourself. Just bear in mind that long-term bonds are riskier than short-term bonds or money market assets. Some companies have decided to immunize their pension liabilities by purchasing long-term bonds that mature with the same pattern as employee retirements. They know for sure that maturing bonds will pay promised benefits.

4. Summary of Pension Fund Management

The rapid growth of pension funds has made their management one of the primary responsibilities of corporate chief financial officers (CFOs). CFOs must be familiar with accounting regulations governing pension fund reporting practices, with government regulation of defined benefit plans under ERISA, and with a wide range of managerial decisions. We discussed the economic implications of choosing between defined benefit and defined contribution plans, changing the pension fund actuarial assumptions, the choice of asset mix, the implications of voluntary termination of defined benefit plans, and the economics of investing pension plan assets with guaranteed insurance company plans.

There are still some as yet unanswered questions. For example, why were 50.5% of all non-insured pension fund assets invested in common stocks in 1980? The tax advantage of investing in bonds (at least for fully funded plans) seems obvious. Another question is, Why are actuarial changes so frequent when they have no impact on shareholder wealth (at best)?

F. ℒeveraged Buyouts and Management Buyouts

Leveraged buyouts involve management purchase of the entire public stock interest of a firm, or division of a firm. If the shares are owned exclusively by management, the transaction is called "going private," and there is no market for trading its shares. If ownership in the subsequent private firm is shared with third party investors and financed heavily with debt, the transaction is called a "leveraged buyout." The issues raised by leveraged buyouts are many. Why do they happen in the first place? Are they motivated as an attempt by incumbent management to expropriate wealth from minority shareholders—a minority freezeout? Are they done for tax reasons? Who benefits? Who loses and why? How are the deals structured?

1. How to Go Private

There are four commonly used techniques for implementing the going-private transaction. Management may form a shell corporation that combines with the firm via *merger*. Usually merger approval is required by shareholders of the original firm, and the shell corporation may pay with cash or securities. *Asset sales* are similar in that a vote is required, and assets are purchased by a shell corporation owned by management. A *tender offer* does not require a vote and does not require minority shareholders to surrender their shares involuntarily. In a tender offer the firm buys back its own shares, either with cash, debt, or convertible securities. Least common among the methods is a *reverse stock split*. Holders of fractional shares are usually required to sell their ownership back to the corporation. DeAngelo, DeAngelo, and Rice [1984] found that in a sample of 81 going-private proposals between 1973 and 1980, 27 were mergers, 3 were sales of assets, 16 were tenders (or exchange offers), and 1 was a reverse split. The remaining 34 were either leveraged buyouts (LBOs) with third-party participation (28) or unclassified acquisitions (6).

The distinction between a pure going-private transaction and a leveraged buyout with the involvement of third parties is important for leverage changes. De Angelo, DeAngelo, and Rice [1984] report that for those firms where the proxy statement had a forecast of leverage changes, the leveraged buyout book ratio of debt to total assets increased from 11% to 86%, but for the pure going-private transactions it changed very little—26% versus 30%.

2. Gains from Going Private and LBOs

The most obvious gains from going private are the savings from reduced exchange registration and listing costs, and from the elimination of shareholder servicing costs. These savings, which have been estimated to range between $30,000 and $200,000 per annum, can be significant for smaller firms. If capitalized at 10%, the present value of the pretax savings is as high as $2 million—not a trivial number when compared with the median $2 million public capitalization of the DeAngelo, DeAngelo, and Rice sample of pure going-private firms.

Another frequently cited benefit is that management-shareholder agency costs are reduced. Following the transaction, management no longer shares the costs of perquisites or of shirking with outside owners. This may provide a strong incentive for better management performance and may therefore add value to the firm. Furthermore, in LBOs the greatly increased leverage may provide management with much stronger incentives to trim the fat from operating costs.

Along similar lines is the argument that agency costs arising from conflicts between debt and equity claims on the firm may be reduced. One reason is that third-party equity participants have

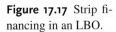

Figure 17.17 Strip financing in an LBO.

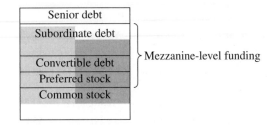

a stronger incentive to monitor management than would diffuse ownership. And second, LBOs are often structured to use *strip financing*. Suppose an LBO creates several layers of nonequity financing such as senior debt, subordinated debt, convertible debt, and preferred stock. Securities between senior debt and equity are often called mezzanine-level financing. Strip financing requires that a buyer who purchases $X\%$ of any mezzanine-level security must purchase $X\%$ of all mezzanine-level securities and some equity. Jensen [1987] points out that this LBO financing technique can be an advantage because as each level of financing senior to equity goes into default, the strip holder automatically receives new rights to intercede in the organization. As a result, it is quicker and less expensive to replace management in an LBO with strip financing. Strip financing also reduces (or even eliminates) conflicts between senior and junior claim holders. Figure 17.17 illustrates strip financing in an LBO. The senior claim is usually bank debt financing. Subordinate to it are the "mezzanine securities" including subordinate debt, convertible debt, and preferred stock. Third-party financiers typically hold strips of the mezzanine as well as equity. Venture capitalists may hold up to 80% of the equity, with management holding the remainder. Because venture capitalists are generally the largest shareholders and control the board of directors, they have both greater ability and stronger incentives to monitor managers than directors representing diffuse public shareholders in the typical public corporation.

LBO targets are frequently firms with relatively stable cash flows and unutilized debt capacity. It may be possible for management to benefit from the greater tax shield provided when the buyout is financed with debt. Thus the value gained from leverage may be an additional motivation for leveraged buyouts.

An example of how transactions might work out for a target company is shown in Table 17.11. Table 17.11 shows how the earnings before interest and taxes grow at 10% a year. The interest payments reflect the amortization of principal that takes place each year. A 40% tax rate is assumed. After deduction of taxes, net income is shown in row 5. Depreciation is added back to obtain the usual definition of cash flow shown in row 7. Row 8 illustrates an amortization schedule for the debt. This results in the cash flow cushion depicted in row 9. With the amortization schedule shown in row 8, we can also indicate how the debt/equity position changes over time. This is illustrated by Table 17.12.

Table 17.12 reflects the amortization program agreed upon. Over the five-year period, debt is reduced from 90% to 0%. We then assume that the company is sold at its book value at the end of year 5. This is a conservative assumption because, with the record it has established, the firm might well sell for a premium over book value. The ratio of the price received to the initial equity investment is 476.5/50, which equals 953%. This represents a five-year annual compounded rate of return on the initial $50,000 investment of 57%. The plausibility of these results is indicated by some published statistics. A *Fortune* magazine article (Ross [1984]) stated that one of the leveraged buyout specialist companies, Kohlberg, Kravis, Roberts, and Co., has earned an average annualized return of 62% on the equity it has invested in its transactions. Another buyout specialist,

Table 17.11 Pro Forma Cash Flows for Leveraged Buyout

	Year 0	Year 1	Year 2	Year 3	Year 4	Year 5
1. EBIT	150.0	165.0	181.5	199.7	219.6	241.6
2. Interest		88.5	76.5	62.2	45.0	24.5
3. EBT		76.5	105.0	137.5	174.6	217.1
4. Taxes @ 40%		30.6	42.0	55.0	69.8	86.8
5. Net income		45.9	63.0	82.5	104.8	130.3
6. Depreciation		30.0	30.0	30.0	30.0	30.0
7. Cash flow		75.9	93.0	112.5	134.8	160.3
8. Amortization of loans		60.9	72.9	87.2	104.4	129.9
9. Cash flow cushion		15.0	20.1	25.3	30.4	35.4

Table 17.12 The Changing Debt Ratio in a Leveraged Buyout

	Year 0	Year 1	Year 2	Year 3	Year 4	Year 5
1. Equity	50.0	95.9	158.9	241.4	346.2	476.5
2. Debt	450.0	389.1	316.2	229.0	124.6	0.0
3. Total assets	500.0	485.0	475.1	469.7	470.1	476.5
4. Percent debt	90%	80%	67%	49%	26%	0%

Carl Ferenbach, has stated that his firm expects an annual return of 50% on its equity investment (DeAngelo, DeAngelo, and Rice [1984]).

Much has been made of the conflict of interest that managers, as insiders, have when engaging in a buyout. If they obtain the best deal for themselves, it may be at the expense of minority shareholders. One would expect managers to try a buyout when they have inside information that indicates that the future of the firm is better than previously expected. Rational expectations theory, however, suggests that shareholders know that insiders have an informational advantage and are not fooled. Therefore they demand a higher price in order to sell their ownership claims. Furthermore, minority shareholders must approve the transaction and often have veto power. A countervailing force is that management frequently has a majority ownership position prior to the transaction. For example, DeAngelo, DeAngelo, and Rice [1984] report that the median management ownership was 51% of the stock in pure going-private transactions and 33% in LBOs with third-party participation. This makes it difficult for raiders to compete to bid away potential management gains. Therefore we might predict that gains from going private are shared between management and minority shareholders.

3. Empirical Evidence on the Announcement Effects

The empirical evidence is unable to separate the effect of favorable insider information from other benefits (e.g., reduced agency costs and reduced shareholder service costs). It can, however, tell us whether minority shareholders benefit and by how much.

DeAngelo, DeAngelo, and Rice [1984] report a highly significant average two-day abnormal return of 22.4% upon the initial announcement of a going-private or LBO transaction. If the announcement period is extended to include information leakage during the 40 trading days prior to the announcement, the cumulative abnormal return increases to 30.4%. They also report that the initial market reaction is well below the 56.3% average premium offered by management. The difference is explained by the relatively high percentage of offers that are withdrawn (18 firms). The two-day abnormal return at the time of the withdrawal announcement was a significantly negative 8.9%. These facts clearly indicate that minority shareholders received significant gains from the transaction. They do not shed any light on what percentage of the total gain was received by management and by minority shareholders. For those buyouts that were consummated, both parties certainly believed they were gaining.

There are many unanswered questions regarding going-private and LBO transactions. For example, how does one evaluate the transaction on a net present value basis before taking action? What determines the best structure for the deal? And how does one estimate the required rates of return on the securities involved? Future research is needed to help answer these thorny problems.

$\mathcal{S}$ummary

This chapter has used the theoretical frameworks set out in Part I of this text to think about some of the more important applied issues in corporate finance. We covered the economics of leasing and saw that the decision is really a financial choice—lease versus borrow, and not lease versus own. Then we investigated interest rate swaps—commonly used to "doctor" the income statement. In the risk management section we differentiated between risk management policies that minimize the variance of cash flows (or of equity returns) and those that maximize value. Pension fund management reviewed regulation of pension funds, and also decisions such as the choice of defined benefit versus defined contribution plans, the effect of changing actuarial assumptions, the choice of the mix of assets in the fund, and the possibility of termination. Finally, we discussed the economics of leveraged buyouts.

PROBLEM SET

17.1 Your firm is considering lease financing for a computer that is expected to have a five-year life and no salvage value (it is a strict financial lease). You have the following facts:

- Your firm's tax rate is 30%. There is no investment tax credit.
- If purchased, the project would require a capital outlay of $100,000.
- The project will be depreciated using the straight-line method.
- Debt of equivalent risk costs 10% before taxes.
- The annual lease fee is $32,000 paid at the beginning of each year for five years.
- The optimal capital structure for the project is 50% to total assets.

Should you use lease financing or not?

17.2 Giveaway State Teacher's College is trying to decide whether to buy a new computer or to lease it from Readi Roller Leasing. The computer costs $500,000. Giveaway has a zero tax rate, whereas Readi Roller enjoys a 40% tax rate. There is no investment tax credit. The computer is expected to last five years and have no salvage value. It will be depreciated using the straight-line method. The college can borrow at a 15% interest rate. The five annual lease fees are $147,577 paid at the end of each year.

    (a) What is the NPV of the lease for Readi Roller Leasing Co.?

    (b) What is the NPV of the lease for Giveaway State?

    (c) What do the results tell you about the lease/buy decision for tax-free institutions?

17.3 This question involves a more realistic set of facts and therefore requires a more detailed analysis of cash flows than contained in the chapter. Your company is going to negotiate a lease contract for manufacturing equipment. You have the following facts:

- The equipment costs $100,000 and is expected to have a five-year life with an expected salvage value of $10,000; however, it can be fully depreciated in four years using the sum-of-the-years digits method of accelerated depreciation.
- Whether leased or owned, the equipment will be sold for $1 at the end of the fifth year, and the owner will pay a capital gains tax equal to one half of the ordinary income tax rate on the difference between $1 and the book value.
- Your firm will pay no taxes for the next two years and then will return to its normal 48% tax rate.
- The leasing firm will require equal annual lease payments paid at the beginning of each year. The leasing firm's tax rate is 48%.
- Your firm can borrow at the prime rate plus 1%, that is, at 17%.

    (a) What is the maximum lease payment that your firm can afford to offer in the negotiations?

    (b) What is the minimum lease payment that you think the leasing company can accept in the negotiations?

17.4 Your firm has been approached to become an equity participant in a leveraged leasing deal. You need to estimate the minimum rate of return on equity that is acceptable. You have collected the following facts:

- The asset to be leased will cost $100 million, of which 90% will be financed with debt and the remaining 10% with equity.
- The debt portion of the financing is to receive a 14% rate of return before taxes.
- Your tax rate is 40%. The lessor's tax rate is 48%.
- The before-tax rate of return that the lessee will be paying is 18%.

    Use the Modigliani-Miller cost of capital assumptions to make your analysis (i.e., assume a world with corporate taxes only).

17.5 The Mortar Bored Company was considering whether to buy a new $100,000 reduction machine or to lease it. It was estimated that the machine would reduce variable costs by $31,000 per year and have an eight-year life with no salvage value. The machine will be depreciated on a straight-line basis, and there is no investment tax credit. The firm's optimal capital structure is 50% debt to total assets, its before-tax costs of debt and equity are 15% and 25%, respectively, and it has a 40% tax rate. If it were to lease, the fees would be $21,400 per year paid at the end of each year.

    (a) What is the NPV of the project if the firm owns the project?

    (b) What is the NPV of the lease to the company?

    (c) Should the company lease the project? Why or why not?

REFERENCES

Abdel-Khalik, A., R. Thompson, and R. Taylor, "The Impact of Reporting Leases Off the Balance Sheet on Bond Risk Premiums: Two Explanatory Studies," Accounting Research Center Working Paper #78-2, University of Florida, February 1978.

American Institute of Certified Public Accountants, *Accounting Trends and Techniques*. AICPA, New York, 1986.

Ang, J., and P. Peterson, "The Leasing Puzzle," *Journal of Finance*, September 1984, 1055–1065.

Arnold, T., "How to Do Interest Rate Swaps," *Harvard Business Review*, September–October 1984, 96–101.

Athanosopoulos, P., and P. Bacon, "The Evaluation of Leveraged Leases," *Financial Management*, Spring 1980, 76–80.

Bagehot, W. (pseud.), "Risk and Reward in Corporate Pension Funds," *Financial Analysts Journal*, January–February 1972, 80–84.

Bank Administration Institute, *Measuring the Investment Performance of Pension Plans*. BAI, Park Ridge, Ill., 1968.

Berkman, H., and M. Bradbury, "Empirical Evidence on the Corporate Use of Derivatives," *Financial Management*, 1996, 5–13.

Bicksler, J., and A. Chen, "The Integration of Insurance and Taxes in Corporate Pension Strategy," *Journal of Finance*, July 1985, 943–955.

———, "An Economic Analysis of Interest Rate Swaps," *Journal of Finance*, July 1986, 645–655.

Black, F., "The Tax Consequences of Long-Run Pension Policy," *Financial Analysts Journal*, July–August 1980, 21–28.

Bodnar, G., G. Hayt, and R. Marston, "1998 Wharton Survey of Financial Risk Management by U.S. Non-Financial Firms," *Financial Management*, Winter 1998, 70–91.

Bower, R., "Issues in Lease Financing," *Financial Management*, Winter 1973, 25–33.

Bowman, R., "The Debt Equivalence of Leases: An Empirical Investigation," *Accounting Review*, April 1980, 237–253.

Brealey, R., and C. Young, "Debt, Taxes and Leasing—A Note," *Journal of Finance*, December 1980, 1245–1250.

Bulow, J., M. Scholes, and P. Manell, "Economic Implications of ERISA," working paper, Graduate School of Business, University of Chicago, March 1982.

Copeland, T., "An Economic Approach to Pension Fund Management," *Midland Corporate Finance Journal*, Spring 1984, 26–39.

Copeland, T., and M. Copeland, "Foreign Exchange Hedging: A Value Maximizing Approach," *Financial Management*, Autumn 1999.

Copeland, T., and J. F. Weston, "A Note on the Evaluation of Cancelable Operating Leases," *Financial Management*, Summer 1982, 60–67.

Cornell, B., "Pricing Interest Rate Swaps: Theory and Empirical Evidence," working paper, Anderson Graduate School of Management, UCLA, April 1986.

Cox, J., J. Ingersoll, and S. Ross, "An Analysis of Variable Rate Loan Contracts," *Journal of Finance*, May 1980, 389–403.

Cox, J., S. Ross, and M. Rubinstein, "Option Pricing: A Simplified Approach," *Journal of Financial Economics*, September 1979, 229–264.

Crawford, P., C. Harper, and J. McConnell, "Further Evidence on the Terms of Financial Leases," *Financial Management*, Autumn 1981, 7–14.

DeAngelo, H., and L. DeAngelo, "Management Buyouts of Publicly Traded Corporations," *Financial Analysts Journal*, May–June 1987, 38–48.

DeAngelo, H., L. DeAngelo, and E. Rice, "Going Private: Minority Freezeouts and Stockholder Wealth," *Journal of Law and Economics*, October 1984, 367–401.

DeAngelo, L., "Accounting Numbers as Market Valuation Substitutes; A Study of Management Buyouts of Public Stockholders," *Accounting Review*, July 1986, 400–420.

Dyl, E., and S. Martin, Jr., "Setting Terms for Leveraged Leases," *Financial Management*, Winter 1977, 20–27.

Elam, R., "The Effect of Lease Data on the Predictive Ability of Financial Ratios," *Accounting Review*, January 1975, 25–43.

Feldstein, M., and S. Seligman, "Pension Funding, Share Prices and National Savings," *Journal of Finance*, September 1981, 801–824.

Financial Accounting Standards Board, Statement of Financial Accounting Standards No. 13, Stamford, Conn., 1976.

Flath, D., "The Economics of Short-Term Leasing," *Economic Inquiry*, April 1980, 247–259.

Franks, J., and S. Hodges, "Valuation of Financial Lease Contracts: A Note," *Journal of Finance*, May 1978, 647–669.

———, "Lease Valuation When Taxable Earnings Are a Scarce Resource," working paper, London Business School, 1986.

Gatto, M., R. Geske, R. Litzenberger, and H. Sossin, "Mutual Fund Insurance," *Journal of Financial Economics*, September 1980, 283–317.

Gay, G., and J. Nam, "The Underinvestment Problem and Corporate Derivatives Use," *Financial Management*, Winter 1998, 53–69.

Geczy, C., B. Minton, and C. Schrand, "Why Firms Use Currency Derivatives," *Journal of Finance*, 1997, 1323–1354.

Grenadier, S., "Valuing Lease Contracts: A Real-Options Approach," *Journal of Financial Economics*, 1995, Vol. 38, 297–331.

———, "Leasing and Credit Risk," *Journal of Financial Economics*, 1996, Vol. 42, 333–364.

Gudikunst, A., and G. Roberts, "Leasing: Analysis of a Theoretic-Pragmatic Dilemma," paper presented at the annual meeting of the Financial Management Association, Kansas City, October 1975.

Haugen, R., and L. Senbet, "Resolving the Agency Costs of External Capital through Options," *Journal of Finance*, June 1981, 629–647.

Heaton, H., "Corporate Taxation and Leasing," *Journal of Financial and Quantitative Analysis*, September 1986, 351–359.

Henderson, S., and J. Price, *Currency and Interest Rate Swaps*. Butterworths and Co., London, 1984.

Howton, S., and S. Perfect, "Currency and Interest-Rate Derivatives Use in U.S. Firms," *Financial Management*, Winter 1998, 111–121.

Idol, C., "A Note on Specifying Debt Displacement and Tax Shield Borrowing Opportunities in Financial Lease Valuation Models," *Financial Management*, Summer 1980, 24–29.

Jensen, M., "Takeovers: Folklore and Science," *Harvard Business Review*, November–December 1984, 109–121.

———, "The Takeover Controversy: Analysis and Evidence," in J. Coffee, L. Lowenstein, and S. Rose-Ackerman, eds., *Takeovers and Contests for Corporate Control*. Oxford University Press, Oxford, 1987.

Johnson, R., and W. Lewellen, "Analysis of the Lease-or-Buy Decision," *Journal of Finance*, September 1972, 815–823.

Kim, E., W. Lewellen, and J. McConnell, "Sale and Leaseback Agreements and Enterprise Valuation," *Journal of Financial and Quantitative Analysis*, December 1978, 871–883.

Korpprasch, R., J. MacFarlane, D. Ross, and J. Showers, "The Interest Rate Swap Market Yield Mathematics, Terminology and Conventions," Salomon Brothers, 1985.

Landsman, W., "An Investigation of Pension Fund Property Rights," Ph.D. dissertation, Stanford University, 1984.

Lee, W., J. Martin, and A. J. Senchack, "An Option Pricing Approach to the Evaluation of Salvage Values in Financial Lease Agreements," working paper, University of Texas at Austin, September 1980.

Levy, H., and M. Sarnat, "Leasing, Borrowing and Financial Risk," *Financial Management*, Winter 1979, 47–54.

Lewellen, W., M. Long, and J. McConnell, "Asset Leasing in Competitive Capital Markets," *Journal of Finance*, June 1976, 787–798.

Long, M., "Leasing and the Cost of Capital," *Journal of Financial and Quantitative Analysis*, November 1977, 579–598.

Marcus, A., "Spinoff/Terminations and the Value of Pension Insurance," *Journal of Finance*, July 1985, 911–924.

McConnell, J., and J. Schallheim, "Valuation of Asset Leasing Contracts," *Journal of Financial Economics*, August 1983, 237–262.

McGugan, V., and R. Caves, "Interpretation and Competition in the Equipment Leasing Industry," *Journal of Business*, July 1974, 382–396.

Mello, A., and J. Parsons, "Hedging and Liquidity," *Review of Financial Studies*, 2000, Vol. 13, No. 1, 127–153.

Mian, S., "Evidence on Corporate Hedging Policy," *Journal of Financial and Quantitative Analysis*, 1996, 419–439.

Miller, M., and F. Modigliani, "Some Estimates of the Cost of Capital to the Electric Utility Industry, 1954–57," *American Economic Review*, June 1966, 333–391.

Miller, M., and C. Upton, "Leasing, Buying and the Cost of Capital Services," *Journal of Finance*, June 1976, 761–786.

Myers, S., "Interactions of Corporate Financing and Investment Decisions—Implications for Capital Budgeting," *Journal of Finance*, March 1974, 1–25.

Myers, S., D. Dill, and A. Bautista, "Valuation of Financial Lease Contracts," *Journal of Finance*, June 1976, 799–819.

Nance, D., C. Smith, Jr., and C. Smithson, "Determinants of Corporate Hedging," *Journal of Finance*, Vol. 48, 1993, 267–284.

Ofer, A., "The Evaluation of the Lease versus Purchase Alternatives," *Financial Management*, Summer 1976, 67–72.

Perg, W., "Leveraged Leasing: The Problem of Changing Leverage," *Financial Management*, Autumn 1978, 45–51.

Pesando, J., "The Usefulness of the Wind-up Measure of Pension Liabilities: A Labor Market Perspective," *Journal of Finance*, July 1985, 927–940.

Ramaswamy, K., and S. M. Sundaresan, "The Valuation of Floating Rate Instruments," *Journal of Financial Economics*, December 1986, 251–272.

Regan, P., "Reasons for the Improving Pension Fund Figures," *Financial Analysts Journal*, March–April 1982, 14–15.

Ro, B., "The Disclosure of Capitalized Lease Information and Stock Prices," *Journal of Accounting Research*, Autumn 1978, 315–340.

Roberts, G., and A. Gudikunst, "Equipment Financial Leasing Practices and Costs: Comment," *Financial Management*, Summer 1978, 79–81.

Ross, I., "How the Champs Do Leveraged Buyouts," *Fortune*, January 23, 1984, 70–72, 74, 78.

Schall, L., "Asset Valuation, Firm Investment, and Firm Diversification," *Journal of Business*, January 1972, 11–28.

———, "The Lease-or-Buy and Asset Acquisition Decisions," *Journal of Finance*, September 1974, 1203–1214.

Schallheim, J., R. Johnson, R. Lease, and J. McConnell, "The Determinants of Yields on Financial Leasing Contracts," working paper, University of Utah, 1986.

Sharpe, W., "Corporate Pension Funding Policy," *Journal of Financial Economics*, June 1976, 183–194.

Smith, C., and R. Stulz, "The Determinants of a Firm's Hedging Policies," *Journal of Financial and Quantitative Analysis*, December 1985, 391–403.

Smith, C., Jr., C. Smithson, and L. Wakeman, "The Evolving Market for Swaps," *Midland Corporate Finance Review*, Spring 1986, 16–31.

Smith, C., Jr., and L. Wakeman, "Determinants of Corporate Leasing Policy," *Journal of Finance*, July 1985, 896–908.

Snyder, N., "Financial Leases," in J. F. Weston and M. Goudzwaard, eds., *The Treasurer's Handbook*. Dow-Jones Irwin, Homewood, Ill., 1976, 783–822.

Sorensen, I., and R. Johnson, "Equipment Financial Leasing Practices and Costs: An Empirical Study," *Financial Management*, Spring 1977, 33–40.

Stickney, C., R. Weil, and M. Wolfson, "Income Taxes and Tax Transfer Leases," *Accounting Review*, April 1983, 439–459.

Stulz, R., "Optimal Hedging Policies," *Journal of Financial and Quantitative Analysis*, June 1984, 127–140.

Taylor, D., "Technological or Economic Obsolescence: Computer Purchase vs. Lease," *Management Accounting*, September 1968.

Tepper, I., "Taxation and Corporate Pension Policy," *Journal of Finance,* March 1981, 1–13.

———, "The Future of Private Pension Funding," *Financial Analysts Journal*, 1982, 25–31.

Tepper, I., and A. Affleck, "Pension Plan Liabilities and Corporate Financial Strategies," *Journal of Finance*, December 1974, 1549–1564.

Treynor, J., "The Principles of Corporate Pension Finance," *Journal of Finance*, May 1977, 627–638.

Treynor, J., W. Priest, and P. Regan, *The Financial Reality of Funding under ERISA*. Dow Jones-Irwin, Homewood, Ill., 1976.

Vancil, R., "Lease or Borrow—New Method Analysis," *Harvard Business Review*, September–October 1961.

Vanderwicken, P., "The Powerful Logic of the Leasing Boom," *Fortune*, November 1973, 136–140.

Westerfield, R., and W. Marshall, "Pension Funding Decisions and Corporate Shareholder Value: A New Model and Some Empirical Results," mimeo, September 1983.

Chapter 18

To some, M&As, restructuring, and corporate control activities represent a new force that will lead economies that provide these arts to new heights of creativity and productivity. To others, these same activities are regarded as a blight.

—Weston, J. F., K. Chung, J. Siu, *Takeovers, Restructuring, and Corporate Governance*, second edition, Prentice-Hall, Upper Saddle River, N.J., 1990.

Acquisitions, Divestitures, Restructuring, and Corporate Governance

MERGERS AND ACQUISITIONS (M&As) perform important functions for both economies and individual firms. M&As involve central aspects of finance theory and corporate financial policy. However, our subject is broader than M&As. We also discuss how value may be created by shrinking the firm. Therefore we have chosen to entitle the chapter "Acquisitions, Divestitures, Restructuring, and Corporate Governance."

A. Merger Activity

Data on merger activity in the United States since 1975 is presented in Table 18.1. The peak year in terms of the number of mergers announced was 2000. The 9,566 announcements in 2000 were nearly three times the previous peak in 1986. The peak (in terms of 1996 dollars) took place in 1999 at $1.363 trillion, representing 4.42 times the previous peak value in 1988. After two years of declines, the 2001 values were more than double the previous 1988 peak. Notable is the number of billion dollar deals from 1997 through 2001—more than 100 in every year. Deals of $100 million or more exceeded 1,000 in 1999 and 2000.

Worldwide merger activity paralleled the U.S. experience as shown in Table 18.2. The peak was reached in 2000 at $3.444 trillion. Activity in 2001 and 2002 declined in both the U.S. and the rest of the world. The economic downturn and the decline in stock prices that began in early 2000 caused a sharp decline in M&A activity in 2001 and 2002.

B. Alternative Growth Strategies

Mergers and acquisitions are a form of external investments. However, interactions take place between mergers (and other forms of external investments) and internal expansion, restructuring,

Table 18.1 Merger Announcements

Year	Total Dollar Value Paid ($ Billion)	Number Total	Number of Transactions Valued at		GDP Deflator (1996 = 100)	1996 Constant Dollar Consideration	Percent Change
			$100 Million or More	$1 Billion or More			
1975	11.8	2,297	14	0	40.0	29.5	
1976	20.0	2,276	39	0	42.3	47.3	60
1977	21.9	2,224	41	1	45.0	48.7	3
1978	34.2	2,106	80	0	48.2	70.9	46
1979	43.5	2,128	83	3	52.2	83.3	17
1980	44.3	1,889	94	4	57.0	77.7	−7
1981	82.6	2,395	113	12	62.4	132.4	71
1982	53.8	2,346	116	6	66.3	81.2	−39
1983	73.1	2,533	138	11	68.9	106.2	31
1984	122.2	2,543	200	18	71.4	171.1	61
1985	179.8	3,011	270	36	73.7	244.0	43
1986	173.1	3,336	346	27	75.3	229.8	−6
1987	163.7	2,032	301	36	77.6	211.0	−8
1988	246.9	2,258	369	45	80.2	307.8	46
1989	221.1	2,366	328	35	83.3	265.5	−14
1990	108.2	2,074	181	21	86.5	125.1	−53
1991	71.2	1,877	150	13	89.7	79.4	−36
1992	96.7	2,574	200	18	91.8	105.3	33
1993	176.4	2,663	242	27	94.0	187.6	78
1994	226.7	2,997	383	51	96.0	236.1	26
1995	356.0	3,510	462	74	98.1	362.9	54
1996	495.0	5,848	640	94	100.0	495.0	36
1997	657.1	7,800	873	120	101.9	644.6	30
1998	1,191.9	7,809	906	158	103.2	1,154.9	79
1999	1,425.9	9,278	1,097	195	104.6	1,362.6	18
2000	1,325.7	9,566	1,150	206	107.0	1,238.6	−9
2001	699.4	8,290	703	121	109.4	639.5	−48
2002	440.7	7,303	608	72	110.7	398.2	−38

Source: Mergerstat Review.

Table 18.2 Worldwide M&A Activity, 1998–2002 ($ Billion)

	1998	1999	2000	2001	2002
U.S	$1,373.3	$1,433.7	$1,792.2	$1,148.4	$612.6
Rest of world*	$659.3	$917.3	$1,652.2	$821.8	$623.7
World	$2,032.6	$2,351.0	$3,444.4	$1,970.2	$1,236.3
U.S. percent of world	67.6%	61.0%	52.0%	58.3%	49.6%

* Non-U.S. targets and acquirers
Source: Mergers & Acquisitions, 2003 Almanac, February 2003.

Table 18.3 Alternative Ownership Strategies

A. **Growth Strategies**

   1.   **Mergers**—Any transaction that forms one economic unit from two or more previous units

      a.   **Tender offers**—A method of making a takeover via a direct offer to target firm shareholders

      b.   **Pooling of interest**—A method of merger that combines the financial statements of two (or more) firms

   2.   **Joint ventures**—A combination of subsets of assets contributed by two (or more) business entities for a specific business purpose and a limited duration

   3.   **Other forms of collaboration**

      a.   **Supplier networks**—Long-term cooperative relationships

      b.   **Alliances**—More informal interbusiness relations

      c.   **Investments**—A stake, but not control in another organization

      d.   **Franchising**—Contracts for the use of name, reputation, business format

B. **Shrinkage Strategies**

   1.   **Divestitures**—Sale of a segment of a company (assets, a product line, a subsidiary) to a third party for cash and/or securities

   2.   **Equity carveouts**—A transaction in which a parent firm offers some of a subsidiary's common stock to the general public, to bring in a cash infusion without loss of control

   3.   **Spin-offs**—A transaction in which a company distributes on a pro rata basis all of the shares it owns in a subsidiary to its own shareholders; creates a new public company with (initially) the same proportional equity ownership as the parent company

   4.   **Tracking stock**—A separate class of common stock of a company that tracks the performance of a particular segment or division

and financing. Table 18.3 sets forth and briefly describes strategies for value creation via growth or shrinkage. The alternatives range from growth via mergers and acquisitions joint ventures, alliances, investments, and franchising to shrinkage via divestment, equity carveout, spin-offs, and tracking stock. Or the ownership structure may be altered. Table 18.4 describes financial engineering, and Table 18.5 describes changes in authority relationships or architecture for more efficient decision making. Of increasing importance is management of agency conflicts and stakeholders' relationships covered in Table 18.5. The disastrous consequences of corporate misrepresentation

Table 18.4 Financial Engineering and Changes in Ownership Structure

1. **Exchange offers**—The right or option to exchange one class of a security for another (e.g., an exchange of common stock for debt)

2. **Share repurchases**—A public corporation buys its own shares (a) by tender offer, (b) on the open market, or (c) in negotiated buybacks

3. **Leveraged buyouts (LBOs, MBOs)**—The purchase of a company by a small group of investors, financed largely by debt

4. **Leveraged recapitalizations**—A large increase in the leverage ratio to finance the return of cash to shareholders

5. **Employee stock ownership plans (ESOPs)**—A defined contribution pension plan designed to invest primarily in the stock of the employer firm

6. **Dual-class recapitalizations**—Creation of two classes of common stock, with the superior-vote stock concentrated in the hands of management

Table 18.5 Governance—Control of Decision Powers

1. **Compensation arrangements**—Payment forms to align interests of managers, owners, and employees

2. **Proxy contest**—An attempt by a dissident group of shareholders to gain representation on a firm's board of directors

3. **Premium buy-backs (greenmail)**—The repurchase of specified shares, usually from a party seeking to take over a firm

4. **Takeover defenses**—Methods employed by targets to prevent the success of bidders' efforts

5. **Stakeholder relationships**

6. **Ethics and reputation**

and fraud have also increased the importance of strengthening the reputation of a firm for honest and ethical behavior.

It has long been recognized that individual mergers are best understood within the framework of merger programs over time (Schipper and Thompson [1983]). This is also true of many other M&A activities described in Table 18.4. For example, many companies have had open market share repurchases that have taken place year after year (IBM, Coca-Cola).

C. M&As as an Adjustment Process

Reviews of the M&A activity of the 1990s suggest that M&A activities in this period have reflected powerful change forces in the world economy.[1] Ten change forces are commonly identified: (1) the pace of technological change has accelerated; (2) the costs of communication and transportation

---

[1] The peaking of heightened merger activity was accompanied by a number of assessments of its significance (Wasserstein [1998, 2000], Flom [2000], Lipton [2001], Holmstrom and Kaplan [2001] Andrade, Mitchell, and Stafford [2001], Geis and Geis [2001], Pautler [2001], and Tichy [2001, 2002]). Wasserstein analyzes the business rationale for mergers in a number of industries in which he was involved as an investment banker with a legal background. Flom (Skadden, Arps,

have been greatly reduced; (3) markets have become international in scope; (4) the forms, sources, and intensity of competition have expanded; (5) new industries have emerged; (6) while regulations have increased in some areas, deregulation has taken place in other industries; (7) favorable economic and financial environments persisted from 1982 to 1990 and from 1992 to mid-2000; (8) within a general environment of strong economic growth, problems have developed in individual economies and industries; (9) inequalities in income and wealth have been widening; and (10) valuation relationships and equity returns for most of the 1990s had risen to levels significantly above long-term historical patterns.

Overriding all are technological changes, which include personal computers, computer services, software, servers, and the many advances in information systems, including the Internet. Improvements in communication and transportation have created a global economy. Nations have adopted international agreements such as the General Agreement on Tariffs and Trade (GATT) that have resulted in freer trade. The growing forces of competition have produced deregulation in major industries such as financial services, airlines, and medical services.

The next set of factors relates to efficiency of operations. Economies of scale spread the large fixed cost of investing in machinery or computer systems over a larger number of units. Economies of scope refer to cost reductions from operations in related activities. In the information industry, these would represent economies of activities in personal computer (PC) hardware, PC software, server hardware, server software, the Internet, and other related activities. Another efficiency gain is achieved by combining complementary activities—for example, combining a company strong in research with one strong in marketing.

As a consequence of the pervasive change forces, industry structures have changed. Table 18.6 summarizes representative sources of change in industry structures plus industry examples. We begin with industry transformation. The computer industry was vertically integrated in the 1970s, when mainframes were the major product. It was referred to as IBM and the seven dwarfs. IBM produced the chips, the hardware, the operating systems, other application software, the sales and distribution systems, and organization of service and maintenance engineers. By the 1990s, horizontal value chains had developed with multiple competitors. Chips were produced by Intel, Advanced Micro Devices, Motorola, and others. PC producers included IBM, Dell, Compaq, Apple, and Hewlett Packard. Microsoft dominated operating systems. The computer industry occupied only part of the value chains of the broader information industry. Servers, routers, and network businesses were further developed as the Internet evolved. Cable and digital satellite systems were created. Wireless telecommunication developed. New companies included Oracle, Sun Microsystems, Cisco, 3Com, Qualcomm, Vodafone, and Nokia. Older companies like Ericsson moved from traditional telephone products to wireless.

Slate, Meagher & Flom LLP) and Lipton (Wachtell, Lipton, Rosen & Katz), senior partners in two of the leading U.S. law firms, have been insightful writers on developments leading to merger activity during 1980–2000. Holmstrom and Kaplan focus on the developments on corporate governance supporting increased M&A activity during the 20-year period. Andrade, Mitchell, and Stafford develop further the earlier paper by Mitchell and Mulherin [1996] in which a shock theory of mergers is set forth. Geis and Geis build on case studies of leading firms in the high-technology area to set forth best practices for strategies and structuring successful deals. Pautler, an economist with the Federal Trade Commission, reviews a wide range of literature on the market power effects of horizontal mergers, finding mixed results. Tichy, in a comprehensive survey, compiles evidence that acquiring firms lose in the long run, but expresses concerns about the anticompetitive effects of mergers.

Table 18.6 Sources of Change in Industry Structure

Source of Change	Industries	
Industry transformation	Computers	Media
Technology change	Broadcasting, entertainment	Telecommunications
	Internet	Tire and rubber
	Packaging and containers	Retailing
Globalization	Apparels, textiles	Packaging and containers
	Metal and mining	Tire and rubber
Commoditization	Chemical	Telecommunications
	Pharmaceuticals	
Low growth	Grocery stores	
	Toiletries and cosmetics	
Attractive high growth	Computers	Wireless
	Software	Hotels and gaming
	Servers, networks, Internet	
Chronic excess capacity (consolidation)	Automobiles	Integrated steel
	Food processing	
Fragmentation (rollups)	Staffing services	Facility services
	Rental equipment	Electrical contracting
Large capital investment subject to high risks	Pharmaceuticals	
Price volatility	Coal, uranium, geothermal	Petroleum producing
	Integrated petroleum	
	Oilfield services	
Unrelated activities	Food companies	
	Oil companies	
Demand shifts	Defense	
New entries	Groceries	
	Drugstores	
Deregulation	Air transport	Medical services
	Broadcasting, entertainment	Natural gas
	Truck and transport leasing	

The other categories in Table 18.6 could also be used to describe the industry adjustments required. Of the hundreds of possible reasons for mergers, Table 18.7 lists 10. It also includes the critical and different managerial issues involved in making different kinds of mergers succeed. The leading challenge in mergers is combining different organizations and cultures. Change forces impact industries and cause individual firms to make adjustments. Success is difficult to achieve. Multiple adjustment processes are required.

Table 18.7 Merger Types and Management Implications

	Examples		
Types	**Industries**	**Firms**	**Critical Managerial Issues**
Leader in new technologies	Internet infrastructure	Cisco, Nortel, Lucent	—A strategic vision for the company that provided the candidate a criteria framework for list —Rapid integration
Develop critical size mass for industry leadership	Internet as an efficient marketplace	Ebay, Yahoo!, Amazon, AOL	—Balance growth and profitability
Adjusting to changes in technology	Telecom, computers	AT&T, IBM	—Leveraging strengths into related markets
Economics of size	Pharmaceuticals, aerospace	Pfizer, Novartis, GlaxoSmithKline	—Large costs of developing new products —Broaden new product potential
Industry consolidation	Oil, chemicals, autos, steel, foods	ExxonMobil, BP, Dow	—Improve operating margins —Eliminate plant capacity and people quickly —Can't be a merger of equals —New authority relationships —But keep key capabilities; shut down less efficient operations; spread best practices
Industry roll-ups	Banking, food, dairy	Norwest/Wells Fargo, NationsBank/BankAmerica	—Operations local, but economies of management functions —Add valuable corporate assistance to operating managers —Evolve new cultures that respect and blend diversity
Product and market extension; more complete product line	Food, autos, household products	General Mills, Proctor & Gamble	—Managing related but diverse activities —Leveraging relatedness —Relatively small incremental additions to deal with cultural and organization differences
Cross-border combinations	Telecom, financial, pharmaceuticals, autos, utilities	Vodafone, Vivendi, Daimler Chrysler	—Learn new technologies —Leverage product differentiation advantages —Gain knowledge of different geographic markets with different laws and cultures —Phased economies of scale
Industry convergence	Computers, telecom, media	AOL Time Warner, Tribune/Times Mirror, Viacom/CBS	—Preserve strengths in core industries —Anticipate cross-benefits but avoid distortions —Considerable independence of parts but work toward cross-fertilization
Adjustments to deregulation	Airlines, banking, telecom	AT&T	—Identifying sources of economies —testing theories of cross-selling

Table 18.8 Pattern of Gains Related to Takeover Theories

Motive	(1) Total Gains	(2) Gains to Target	(3) Gains to Acquirer
I. Efficiency and/or synergy	+	+	+
II. Hubris (winner's curse, overpay)	0	+	−
III. Agency problems or mistakes	−	+	−

Source: Berkovitch and Narayanan [1993]. © 1995 by University of Washington. Reprinted with permission of the *Journal of Financial and Quantitative Analysis.*

D. $\mathcal{T}$heories of Mergers, Implications, and Empirical Evidence

Many individual theories or explanations for mergers and takeovers have been formulated. They can be summarized into three major categories as shown by Table 18.8 (Berkovitch and Narayanan, [1993]). The first column of Table 18.8 lists the three major motives for mergers and takeovers on the basis of whether value changes are positive, zero, or negative. The value changes refer to movements in the prices of the securities of companies as a result of changes in ownership.

Total gains can be positive because of efficiency improvements, synergy, or increased market power. The hubris theory (Roll [1986]) postulates that total gains are zero and that the acquiring firms overpay. Total gains may be negative as a result of agency problems or mistakes. When agency factors motivate an acquisition or merger, managers take the action in their own self-interest even to the detriment of the company.

By definition, total gains are positive for synergy, zero for hubris, and negative for agency problems. Column 2 of Table 18.8 lists gains to targets. All empirical studies show positive gains for groups of targets. We next consider the gains to the acquirer. With synergy or efficiency, the total gains from the merger are positive. If the value increases are shared to any degree, the gains to both the target and the bidder would be positive. Of course, when the total gains are positive, it is possible that the premium paid by the bidder could be greater than the total gains, resulting in negative gains to the bidder. But overpaying puts us in the second category of hubris, in which gains to targets are positive but the gains to bidders are negative. Because gains to targets are positive, the returns to the acquirer or bidding firm would necessarily be negative.

Table 18.8 provides a beginning framework for analyzing the reasons for mergers and takeovers. It centers attention on the very important issue of whether the total gains are positive, negative, or negligible. But some redistribution elements are not encompassed by it. Table 18.9 summarizes various hypotheses that might explain the wealth effects in Table 18.8.

1. Efficiency Increases (Restructuring)

Efficiency improvements can result from combining firms of unequal managerial capabilities. A relatively efficient bidder may acquire a relatively inefficient target. Value can be increased by improving the efficiency of the target via restructuring its operations. Or the bidder may seek a merger with a target firm because the management of the target firm can improve the efficiency of the bidder. Neither of these efficiency increases require operating synergies. But, there may be other synergies. Sometimes growth opportunities are enhanced. Sometimes the combination will achieve a more efficient critical mass. The investments in expensive specialized machinery may be

Table 18.9 Theories of M&As

A. Total value increased

    1.   Efficiency increases
    2.   Operating synergy
    3.   Financial synergy
    4.   Strategic realignments
    5.   The q-ratio
    6.   Information
    7.   Signaling

B. Hubris: Acquirer overpays for target

C. Agency: Managers make value-decreasing mergers to increase size of firm

D. Redistribution

    1.   Taxes—redistribution from government
    2.   Market power—redistribution from consumers
    3.   Redistribution from bondholders
    4.   Labor—wage renegotiation
    5.   Pension reversions

E. Conglomerate mergers

large. Combining firms may achieve better utilization of large fixed investments. Plants that have old or inefficient-sized equipment may be shut down after the merger.

Anslinger and Copeland [1996] study a small sample of ex post successful nonsynergistic merger programs and conclude that seemingly unrelated acquisitions always had a theme. For example, Emerson Electric bought unrelated businesses but always cut costs. Sara Lee also was unconcerned with synergies, but always worked to create value via successful branding of the acquired products.

2. Operating Synergies

The theory based on operating synergies assumes that economies of scale and scope do exist in the industry and that prior to the merger the firms are operating at levels of activity that fall short of achieving the potential for economies of scale. Economies of scale arise because of indivisibilities, such as people, equipment, and overhead, that result in lower costs if spread over a large number of units of output. Thus, in manufacturing operations, heavy investments in plant and equipment typically produce such economies. For example, costly machinery such as the large presses used to produce automobile bodies requires optimal utilization. The research and development departments of chemical and pharmaceutical companies must have a large staff of highly competent scientists who can develop and oversee a larger number of product areas. In marketing, having one organization cover the entire United States may yield economies of scale because of the increase in the ratio of calling-on-customer time to traveling time, which in turn is due to the higher density of customers who can be called on by the same number of salespeople.

One potential problem in merging firms with existing organizations is the question of how to combine and coordinate the good parts of the organizations and eliminate what is not required.

The merger announcement may say that firm A is strong in research and development but weak in marketing, while firm B is strong in marketing but weak in research and development, and the two firms combined will complement each other. Analytically, this implies underutilization of some existing factors and inadequate investment in other factors of production. (Because the economies are jointly achieved, the assignment of the contributions of each firm to the merger is difficult both in theory and in practice.)

Managerial economies of production, research, marketing, or finance are sometimes referred to as economies in the specific management functions. It has also been suggested that economies may be achieved in generic management activity such as the planning and control functions of the firm. It is argued that firms of even moderate size need at least a minimum number of corporate officers. The corporate staff with capabilities for planning and control is therefore assumed to be underutilized to some degree. Acquisitions of firms just approaching the size where they need to add corporate staff would provide for fuller utilization of the corporate staff of the acquiring firm and avoid the necessity of firing staff for the other firm.

Another area in which operating economies may be achieved is in vertical integration. Combining firms at different stages of an industry may achieve more efficient coordination of the different levels. The argument here is that costs of communication and various forms of bargaining can be avoided by vertical integration (Arrow [1975], Klein, Crawford, and Alchian [1978], and Williamson [1975]).

3. Financial Synergy

One source of financial synergy is the lower costs of internal financing in comparison with external financing. Firms with large internal cash flows and small investment opportunities have excess cash flows. Firms with low internal funds generation and large growth opportunities have a need for additional financing. Combining the two may result in advantages from the lower costs of internal funds availability.[2]

Previous empirical findings appear to support this internal funds effect. Nielsen and Melicher [1973] found that the rate of premium paid to the acquired firm as an approximation to the merger gain was greater when the cash flow rate of the acquiring firm was greater than that of the acquired firm. This implied that there was redeployment of capital from the acquiring to the acquiring firm's industry. The investment literature also indicates that internal cash flows affect the rate of investment of firms (Nickell [1978]).

Another proposition is that the debt capacity of the combined firm can be greater than the sum of the two firms' capacities before their merger, and this provides tax savings on investment income. Still another possible dimension is economies of scale in flotation and transaction costs of securities (Levy and Sarnat [1970]). Changes in the economic and financial environments may permit higher levels of debt than those employed historically. Debt ratios increased during the 1980s in an economy of sustained growth and large tax advantages to debt. Tax law changes after 1986 and the recession of 1989 and 1990 resulted in more equity financing and a reduction in book leverage ratios in the early 1990s (McCauley, Ruud, and Iacono [1999], Chapter 5).

A second type of financial synergy is simply the ability to underpay (i.e., to purchase at bargain basement prices). One theory is that companies are successful at buying when the q-ratio is low. The q-ratio is defined as the ratio of the market value of the firm's securities to the replacement costs

---

[2] The opposite, called financial anergy, takes the form of an agency cost—the cross-subsidization of underperforming business units.

of its assets. One frequently discussed reason that firms stepped up acquisition programs in the late 1970s was that entry in new market areas could be accomplished on a bargain basis. Inflation had a double-barreled impact. For various reasons, including inflation, stock prices were depressed during the 1970s and did not recover until the latter part of 1982 as the level of inflation dropped and business prospects improved. The second impact of inflation was to cause current replacement costs of assets to be substantially higher than their recorded historical book values. These twin effects resulted in a decline of the q-ratio because the market value of the firm's securities fell and the replacement costs of its assets increased.

In the late 1970s and early 1980s the q-ratio had been running between 0.5 and 0.6. If a company wished to add to capacity in producing a particular product, it could acquire the additional capacity more cheaply by buying a company that produced the product rather than building brick-and-mortar from scratch. If firm A sought to add capacity, this implied that its marginal q-ratio was greater than 1. But if other firms in its industry had average q-ratios of less than 1, it was efficient for firm A to add capacity by purchasing other firms. For example, if the q-ratio was 0.6 and if in a merger the premium paid over market value was even as high as 50%, the resulting price would still be 10% below the current replacement costs of the assets acquired. This potential advantage would provide a broad basis for the operation of the undervaluation theory in years when the q-ratio was low.

When a firm's q-ratio is high, this implies superior management. A high q-ratio firm may be bought by a low q-ratio firm seeking to augment its managerial capabilities.

4. Information

The shares of the target firm in a tender often experience upward revaluation even if the offer turns out to be unsuccessful (Bradley [1980]; Dodd and Ruback [1977]). A hypothesis based on this empirical observation posits that new information is generated as a result of the tender offer and the revaluation is permanent. Two forms of this information hypothesis can be distinguished. One is that the tender offer disseminates information that the target shares are undervalued, and the offer prompts the market to revalue those shares. No particular action by the target firm or any others is necessary to cause the revaluation. This has been called the "sitting-on-a-goldmine" explanation (Bradley, Desai, and Kim [1983]). The other is that the offer inspires target firm management to implement a more efficient business strategy on its own. This is the "kick-in-the-pants" explanation. No outside input other than the offer itself is required for the upward revaluation.

An opposing view holds that the increase in share value of the target firm involved in an unsuccessful offer is due to the expectation that the target firm will subsequently be acquired by another firm. The latter would have some specialized resources to apply to the target resources. Bradley, Desai, and Kim [1983, 1988] examined the data to determine whether the information hypothesis or the latter (synergy) explanation is acceptable. They found that the share prices of the target firms that did not subsequently receive acquisition offers within five years of the initial unsuccessful offer fell back to their preoffer level. The share prices of those targets that received a subsequent bid increased further. They interpret this result as indicating that the information hypothesis is not valid. A permanent revaluation of the target shares occurs when the target resources are combined with the resources of the firm, or at least when the control of the target resources is transferred to the acquiring firm.

But Roll [1987] suggested that the data were equally consistent with an information explanation. He observed that the appearance of a rival bid increased the probability that there existed positive nonpublic information about the target firm. It also decreased the probability that the initial bidder had exclusive possession of the information.

A distinction may be drawn between information and signaling. When a firm receives a tender offer, this conveys information to the market that a bidder sees value in the firm greater than its prevailing market price. The information conveyed to the market by the bid did not represent the motive of the bidder, which was to make an advantageous purchase. On the other hand, in a share repurchase when management holds a significant proportion of the stock and does not tender stock at the premium in the repurchase price, it is signaling that the company's shares are undervalued. It would not be advantageous for an acquiring company with overvalued stock to pay a premium in a share repurchase because it would not recoup the premium paid.

5. Hubris and the Winner's Curse

The winner's curse has a long history in the literature on auction. When there are many bidders or competitors for an object of highly uncertain value, a wide range of bids is likely to result. For example, suppose that many oil companies are bidding on the drilling rights to a particular parcel of land. Given the difficulty of estimating the actual amount of oil in the land, the estimates of the oil companies will vary greatly. The highest bidder will bid and typically pay in excess of the expected value of the oil on the property. The winning bidder is, therefore, "cursed" in the sense that its bid exceeds the value of the tract, so the firm loses money. Capen, Clapp, and Campbell [1971], based on their analysis of sealed-bid competitive lease sales, presented a diagram that depicted the ratio of high estimate to true value as a function of the degree of uncertainty and the number of bidders. For example, with 10 bidders for leases on a large-uncertainty oil project (Arctic), the ratio of high estimate (bid) to true value was about 3.5 times.

Roll [1986] analyzed the effect in takeover activity. Postulating strong market efficiency in all markets, the prevailing market price of the target already reflected the full value of the firm. The higher valuation of the bidders (over the target's true economic value), he states, resulted from *hubris*—their excessive self-confidence (pride, arrogance). Hubris is one of the factors that caused the winner's curse phenomenon to occur. Even if there were synergies, the competition of other bidders could cause the winning bidder to pay too much.

6. Agency Problems

Jensen and Meckling [1976] formulated the implications of agency problems. This was discussed in Chapter 12. An agency problem arises when managers own only a fraction of the ownership shares of the firm. This partial ownership may cause managers to work less vigorously than otherwise and/or to consume more perquisites (luxurious offices, company cars, memberships in clubs) because the majority owners bear most of the cost. Furthermore, the argument goes, in large corporations with widely dispersed ownership there is not sufficient incentive for individual owners to expend the substantial resources required to monitor the behavior of managers.

Agency problems arise basically because contracts between managers (decision or control agents) and owners (risk bearers) cannot be written and enforced at no cost. Resulting (agency) costs include (1) costs of structuring a set of contracts, (2) costs of monitoring and controlling the behavior of agents by principals, (3) costs of bonding to guarantee that agents will make optimal decisions or principals will be compensated for the consequences of suboptimal decisions, and (4) the residual loss, that is, the welfare loss experienced by principals, arising from the divergence between agents' decisions and decisions to maximize principals' welfare. This residual loss can arise because the costs of full enforcement of contracts exceed the benefits.

CHANGES IN OWNERSHIP AS A SOLUTION TO AGENCY PROBLEMS The agency problems may be efficiently controlled by some organizational and market mechanisms. Fama and Jensen [1983] hypothesize that when a firm is characterized by separation of ownership and control, decision systems of the firm separate decision management (initiation and implementation) from decision control (ratification and monitoring) in order to limit the power of individual decision agents to expropriate shareholders' interests. Control functions are delegated to a board of directors by the shareholders, who retain approval rights on important matters, including board membership, mergers, and new stock issues.

Compensation arrangements and the market for managers may also mitigate the agency problem (Fama [1980]). Compensation can be tied to performance through such devices as bonuses and executive stock options. Managers carry their own reputation, and the labor market sets their wage levels based on performance reputation.

The stock market gives rise to an external monitoring device because stock prices summarize the implications of decisions made by managers. Low stock prices exert pressure on managers to change their behavior and to stay in line with the interests of shareholders (Fama and Jensen [1983]).

When these mechanisms are not sufficient to control agency problems, the market for takeovers provides an external control device of last resort (Manne [1965]). A takeover through a tender offer or a proxy fight enables outside managers to gain control of the decision processes of the target while circumventing existing managers and the board of directors. Manne emphasized mergers as a threat of takeover if a firm's management lagged in performance either because of inefficiency or because of agency problems.

Spin-offs can also solve agency problems. For example, AT&T acknowledged that it was cross-subsidizing NCR, a major division, by an annual amount that exceeded $1 billion. There was little that shareholders could do. But when AT&T announced the spin-off of NCR, it effectively eliminated any possibility of further cross-subsidization. Termination of this agency cost caused the stock price to rise on the announcement.

MANAGERIALISM In contrast to the view that mergers occur to control agency problems, some observers consider mergers as a manifestation of agency problems rather than as a solution. The managerialism explanation for conglomerate mergers was set forth most fully by Mueller [1969], who hypothesized that managers are motivated to increase the size of their firms. He assumes that the compensation to managers is a function of the size (sales) of the firm, and he argues that managers therefore adopt a lower investment hurdle rate. In a study critical of earlier evidence, Lewellen and Huntsman [1970] present findings that managers' compensation is significantly correlated with the firm's profit rate, not its level of sales. Thus, the basic premise of the Mueller theory may not be valid.

The modern theory of the firm exists because the market is not frictionless. Economies of scale arise out of indivisibilities. Managements are organized as teams based on firm-specific information on individual characteristics. Firm reputation is valuable because information is costly. Transaction costs lead to integration of operations. The existence of these imperfections (indivisibilities, information costs, and transaction costs) make it inefficient to have individual productive inputs move individually and separately across firms. Takeovers and mergers may be one means of efficiently redeploying corporate resources across firms while minimizing transaction costs and preserving organizational values. Product and labor market efficiency would not automatically result in changing market conditions and would require reallocation of resources across economic activities. Mergers and takeovers may represent one of the reallocation processes necessary to maintain or restore efficiency.

THE FREE CASH FLOW HYPOTHESIS The problem of agency costs discussed in the preceding section also gives rise to the free cash flow hypothesis (FCFH). Jensen [1986, 1988] considered the agency costs associated with conflicts between managers and shareholders over the payout of free cash flow to be a major cause of takeover activity. According to Jensen, shareholders and managers (who are their agents) have serious conflicts of interest over the choice of corporate strategy. Agency costs resulting from these conflicts of interest can never be resolved perfectly. When these costs are large, takeovers may help reduce them, according to Jensen.

Jensen's free cash flow hypothesis is that the payout of free cash flow can serve an important role in dealing with conflict between managers and shareholders. Jensen defines free cash flow as cash flow in excess of the amounts required to fund all projects that have positive net present values when discounted at the applicable cost of capital. He states that such free cash flow must be paid out to shareholders if the firm is to be efficient and to maximize its share price. The payout of free cash flow (FCF) reduces the amount of resources under the control of managers and thereby reduces their power. In addition, they are then more likely to be subject to monitoring by the capital markets when they seek to finance additional investments with new capital.

In addition to paying out the current amount of excess cash, Jensen considers it important that managers bond their promise to pay out future cash flows. An effective way to do this is by debt creation without retention of the proceeds of the issue. Jensen argues that by issuing debt in exchange for stock, for example, managers bond their promise to pay out future cash flows more effectively than any announced dividend policy could achieve. Jensen emphasizes that the control function of debt is most important in organizations that generate large cash flows but whose outlook involves low growth or an actual reduction in size.

Jensen recognizes that increased leverage involves costs. It increases the risk of bankruptcy costs. There are agency costs of debt as well. One is for the firm to take on highly risky projects that benefit shareholders at the expense of bondholders. He defines an optimal debt-to-equity ratio where the marginal costs of debt are equal to the marginal benefits of debt.

Jensen argues that, in virtually all of the 32 cases he summarizes, the direction of the effect on share price agreed with the predictions of the free cash flow hypothesis. Jensen states that his predictions do not apply to firms that have more profitable projects than cash flow to fund them. Nor does the theory apply to growth firms, only to firms that should be exiting some of their activities. Similarly, Jensen argues that in leveraged buyouts (LBOs) the high debt ratios taken on caused the increase in share price. But successful LBOs usually involved a turnaround—an improvement in company performance (Kaplan [1989]). Also, in LBOs the executive group was provided with a large ownership stake in the company, which would have substantial value if the LBO succeeded. It is likely that the incentives provided by the strong ownership stake and other characteristics of LBO situations accounted for the rise in value in addition to the bonding effects of the high debt ratios.

7. Redistribution

The Berkovitch and Narayanan (BN) framework shown in Table 18.8 does not include forms of redistribution such as taxes, market power, or breach of trust (redistribution) with respect to bondholders and labor.

TAX GAINS Tax savings may be another motive for mergers, representing a form of redistribution from the government or public at large. The empirical evidence establishes that tax benefits from a merger may be substantial. However, the evidence also establishes that tax advantages are not likely to be the major reason. Successful mergers are based on sound business and economic principles. Taxes are likely to be a reinforcing influence rather than the major force in a sound merger.

An example of a tax gain is that when a firm that has accrued net operating loss carry forwards (NOLs) acquires a profitable firm, it can consolidate for tax purposes, thereby accelerating the use of its NOLs. Thus the earnings of the acquired firm and the present value of the free cash flows increase. (By the way, the opposite is not true, namely, a profitable acquiring firm cannot shelter its taxes with the NOLs of an acquired firm.)

MARKET POWER An objection that is often raised to permitting a firm to increase its market share by merger is that the result will be "undue concentration" in the industry. The argument in brief is that if four or fewer firms account for a substantial percentage of an industry's sales, these firms will recognize the impact of their actions and policies on one another. This recognized interdependence will lead to a consideration of actions and reactions to changes in policy that will tend toward "tacit collusion." As a result, the prices and profits of the firms will contain monopoly elements. Thus, if economies from mergers cannot be established, it is assumed that the resulting increases in concentration may lead to monopoly returns. If economies can be demonstrated, then a comparison of increased efficiencies versus the effects of increased concentration must be made.

While some economists hold that high concentration, however measured, leads to some degree of monopoly, other economists hold that increased concentration is generally the *result* of active and intense competition. They argue further that the intense competition continues among large firms in concentrated industries because the dimensions of decision making with respect to prices, outputs, types of product, quality of product, service, and so on are so numerous and of so many gradations that neither tacit nor overt collusion could possibly be achieved.

When the antitrust authorities determine a merger to be anticompetitive in some sense, they can prevent the merger. They can also block the merger by delays. Or they can approve it only if certain conditions are met, such as selling off part of the assets acquired. Ellert [1975, 1976] analyzed data for 205 defendants in antimerger complaints initiated by the Justice Department and Federal Trade Commission (FTC) under Section 7 of the Clayton Act for the period 1950–1972. Of the complaints, 121 were issued by the Justice Department and 84 by the FTC. Ellert observes that the government had not lost a single Supreme Court merger case after the 1950 revision to the Clayton Act. In 60% of the cases studied, defendants canceled merger plans or were ordered to divest part or all of the assets previously acquired. The average duration of litigation measured by the interval between the filing of the complaint and the entry of the last judicial order was 34 months.

Ellert analyzes the behavior of the data for the 205 defendants and also for the two groups broken into 123 defendants ordered to divest acquired assets and 82 defendants not required to divest assets. For both groups of defendants for a period preceding the filing of a merger complaint by four years, the residual performance was positive and statistically significant. The cumulative average residual was over 18% for defendants ordered to divest and about 13% for defendants not required to divest. For the 48 months prior to the filing of the merger complaint, defendants required to divest achieved a further positive residual that was statistically significant. For the same 48 months proximate to the filing of the merger complaint, defendants not required to divest had returns that were not statistically different from the average for the market. In the 12 months preceding the merger complaint the residual performance was statistically significant for both classes of defendants.

On the filing of the merger complaint the average portfolio residual declines by 1.86% for defendants ordered to divest and 1.79% for defendants not required to divest. While these percentages are small, they represent substantial absolute amounts when applied to the large dollar amount of assets involved. In the postwar period these percentages translate into an average dollar loss per respondent of about $7.5 million.

Both Stillman [1983] and Eckbo [1981] analyze the residuals of the rivals to firms participating in mergers. They sought to distinguish between the possible efficiency versus monopolization effects of mergers. The problem is somewhat complex because at the theoretical level alternative hypotheses can be formulated. The complexity is illustrated in Table 18.10, where three events are identified: the announcement of the merger, the announcement of its challenge by the antitrust authorities, and the announcement of the government decision. For firms participating in the merger the second column of Table 18.10 indicates that the predicted signs of the cumulative average residuals (CARs) are the same for the collusion versus efficiency hypotheses at the times of the announcements of the merger and its challenge. It was for the purpose of sharpening the analysis that the residuals for rival firms were analyzed. But as the final column of Table 18.10 indicates, there is considerable overlap in the predicted signs for the alternative collusion and efficiency hypotheses. Nevertheless, the pattern of these relationships is such that some judgments can be formulated.

Specifically, at the merger announcement date, if the sign of the effect on rivals is not positive, this is consistent with efficiency because efficiency can have a negative or zero sign. Similarly, at the date of the merger challenge, if the effect on the abnormal returns of rivals is not negative, this also is consistent with efficiency, which can also take on a positive or zero sign. In general, when the effect on the CARs is the same for both participants and rivals, it is not possible to distinguish between collusion and efficiency. If the signs differ, then the two groups are affected differently, which tends to rule out the collusion hypothesis. However, at the decision date the results are more difficult to interpret. This is because the effects on rivals can take any of the three possible signs for either outcome. In the light of the general framework presented, let us now look at the empirical results that have been compiled.

Stillman [1983] found that the effect of 30 major challenged horizontal mergers on the residuals of rivals was not statistically significant. The concentration-collusion theory argues that positive residuals should have been observed when the merger was observed both in relation to the original merger proposal and when it was challenged. Since the effect on rivals was not statistically significant, this casts doubt on the concentration-collusion theory that the mergers were in fact viewed as opportunities for increased possibilities of collusion among the firm's major rivals in the industry.

Eckbo [1981] extended the Stillman study, using a larger sample and a "control" sample of vertical mergers. Eckbo finds that on the announcement of the mergers there are positive residuals both for the participants and their major rivals. This appears to be consistent with the monopoly theory. It is not unambiguous though, because one could also argue that the announcement of the proposed merger conveys information to rivals of opportunities for increased efficiency by expanding scale. Eckbo further finds that at the announcement of the filing of a suit by the antitrust authorities, there is not much effect on the residuals of either the participants or their rivals; in fact, in cases brought by the Federal Trade Commission the effect on rivals is slightly positive. This is consistent with the explanation that the merger partners would have been more efficient and the rivals are protected from this increased efficiency by the Federal Trade Commission suit blocking

Table 18.10 Alternative Hypotheses of Merger Effects

	Participating Firms	*Rival Firms*
I. Announcement of Merger		
Collusion	+ Higher profits from colluding	+ Are part of the collusion
Efficiency	+ External investment with large positive NPV	+ Demonstrate how to achieve greater efficiency
		− Tougher competition
		0 Competition in marketplace unaffected by purchase of undervalued firm
II. Announcement of Challenge		
Collusion	− Collusion prevented	− Collusion prevented
Efficiency	− Prevents a positive NPV investment, also litigation costs	+ Threat of more efficient rivals reduced
		− Also prevented from mergers for efficiency
	0 Could do same thing internally	0 Can do internally
III. Announcement of Decision		
Collusion	− Collusion definitely prevented	− Collusion prevented
		+ Defendants prevented from being more efficient
	0 (1) Negative impact already, at challenge date	0 (1) Negative impact already, at challenge date
	(2) Leakage of likely judicial decision during trial	(2) Leakage of likely judicial decision during trial
	(3) Underlying economics of the industry not affected	(3) Underlying economics of the industry not affected
Efficiency	+ Increased efficiency	+ Can now legally merge for efficiency
		− Tougher competition
		0 Could have accomplished the same thing internally

the merger. Eckbo concludes that the positive performance of rivals of challenged mergers at the time of the original merger announcement reflects information conveyed by the proposed merger that efficiencies can be achieved by expanding scale either internally or externally.

In an extension of Eckbo's earlier work, Eckbo and Wier [1985] paid particular attention to mergers challenged after 1978—that is, following passage of the Hart-Scott-Rodino Antitrust Improvements Act of 1976, which was intended to improve the likelihood that mergers selected for prosecution were truly anticompetitive. Eckbo and Wier found little evidence of improvement; the 17 post-1978 mergers in their study were "economically efficient" and "apparently would not have harmed competition" (Eckbo and Wier [1985], 139). They lay the blame for this failure on the case selection criteria, that is, inappropriate application of the Department of Justice

Merger Guidelines of 1968 and 1982, including the Herfindahl-Hirschman index, which, while representing an advance of economic thinking, are still dominated by the older "structural theory" of antitrust, which holds that the degree of concentration determines industry conduct and behavior.

The studies appear to support the efficiency basis for mergers. Ellert emphasized that acquiring firms had positive residuals in prior years and acquired firms had negative residuals in prior years. Stillman's evidence was that rival firms did not benefit from the announcement of proposed mergers, which is inconsistent with the concentration-collusion hypothesis. Eckbo [1981] and Eckbo and Wier [1985] found positive residuals on the merger announcement but no negative effects on rivals when it appeared that the merger would be blocked by the antitrust authorities. He interprets this pattern of relationships as indicating that the main effect of the merger is to signal the possibility for achieving economies for merging firms, providing information to rivals that such economies may also be available to them.

REDISTRIBUTION FROM BONDHOLDERS   Most of the studies find no evidence that shareholders gain in mergers and tender offers at the expense of bondholders (Asquith and Kim [1982]; Dennis and McConnell [1986]; Kim and McConnell [1977]). Even in debt-for-common-stock exchanges, most of the evidence indicates that there is no negative impact on bondholders even though leverage has been increased. However, in leveraged buyouts in which debt is increased by very high orders of magnitude, there is evidence of negative impacts on bondholders (McDaniel [1986]; Warga and Welch [1993]). There is also dramatic evidence of negative effects on bondholders in individual cases and in patterns of downgrading (*Wall Street Journal*, October 25, 1998). But the losses to bondholders, on average, represent only a small fraction from the gains to shareholders.

REDISTRIBUTION FROM LABOR   Redistribution from labor to shareholders has also received attention (Shleifer and Summers [1988]). The problem was formalized by Williamson [1988]. The issues can be delineated by a case example based on the TWA-Icahn study outlined by Shleifer and Summers and covered in some detail in the press.

Whether "breach of trust" or redistribution occurs depends on a number of variables. The labor costs that were subsequently reduced could have reflected union power, the firm-specific productivity of the employees, or a form of management inefficiency. Another set of variables that influences the interpretation of the case is whether the product markets in which airline services were being sold were competitive, monopolized, or operated under government regulation. A third set of variables to consider is whether, as a consequence of a takeover, the quality of the product services sold went down, went up, or remained the same.

In their analysis of the case, Shleifer and Summers [1988] gave emphasis to the interpretation that the high labor costs may have reflected the firm-specific productivity developed by the employees. With deregulation, new airline entrants hired employees at much lower rates than unionized airlines such as TWA were paying. But if the unionized employees at TWA were more efficient because of their firm-specific skills, the real cost of labor would not necessarily be any higher for TWA than for its nonunionized rivals. Under this scenario, Shleifer and Summers observed that a breach of trust is involved. This says that as a consequence of the takeover, investments made by employees to develop firm-specific skills are not paid their full value when previous labor contracts are broken by the new control group. If breach of trust is involved, then employees would take this into account when writing contracts in the future. It would affect their supply price. The consequence would be that labor costs in the airline industry would rise and prices to airline passengers and other users would be increased in the long run.

Whether the value increases associated with mergers and takeovers represent redistribution, particularly from labor, depends on which scenario is correct. If union power is reflected in monopoly rents to employees, then the employee cost reductions do not represent a breach of trust. They represent a movement from monopoly elements to competitive elements in the industry. If management inefficiency is involved, the introduction of efficient managers moves the industry from inefficiency to efficiency gains. Thus, whether breach of contract or other forms of expropriation are involved depends on the facts of the individual industry circumstances.

PENSION FUND REVERSIONS Pontiff, Shleifer, and Weisbach (PSW) [1990] studied another aspect of breach of trust. Their sample of 413 successful tender offers executed from March 1981 through May 1988 was taken from Jarrell [1988]. This sample was matched to a list of pension plan reversions over $1 million from the Pension Benefit Guarantee Corporation (PBGC). In the two years following hostile takeovers, 15.1% of acquirers executed pension asset reversions compared with 8.4% in friendly takeovers.

Reversions occurred mostly in unit-benefit plans in which pension benefits are based on final wages (a pension bond). Reversions are less likely in flat-benefit plans based on number of years worked (no pension bond). Viewing the pension plan agreement as an implicit contract, terminations or returning excess funding to the firm benefits shareholders, and workers lose. Event return analysis finds positive returns to shareholders at the announcement of a pension plan termination. Pontiff, Shleifer, and Weisbach [1990] suggest that the stock market is surprised by this transfer of cash to the shareholders and expects that the funds will be used in positive net present value (NPV) projects. Similarly, share prices rise on reversion announcements, indicating that the market expects the funds to be used more in the shareholders' interest. Reversions, on average, account for about 11% of the takeover premium in cases in which they actually occurred. Pontiff, Shleifer, and Weisbach conclude that reversions are not a major source of takeover gains.

MERGER PREMIUMS: VALUE RELATIVE TO THE NEXT-BEST ALTERNATIVE The decision of what to bid should always be made relative to the next best alternative. Consider the example illustrated in Table 18.11. The government of a developing nation wishes to sell bank D, the fourth largest bank. Although it is currently worth $60 million, once restructured after the sale, its value will rise to $90 million. Three larger banks, A, B, and C, all wish to bid on D. Their stand-alone values, V_1, are given in the first column and their postmerger values with D (and without D) are given in the remaining three columns.

How much should bank C bid to acquire D? Although the synergies with D and the opportunity to restructure it are important, the next-best alternative is the value of C assuming that a competitor wins the bid. If C loses, its value will fall by $15 million because it will be a subscale competitor to either AD or BD. Therefore, it can afford to pay a price that is the sum of (1) the current value

Table 18.11 Stand-Alone and Merged Firm Value Example

	Stand-Alone Value	Value with D		
		A	B	C
A	100	190	90	90
B	80	70	170	70
C	70	55	55	160
D	60	0	0	0

of D ($60 million) plus (2) the value of restructuring D ($30 million) plus its value decline should it lose the bidding ($15 million). If C bids $105 for D, it will win, its value with D will be $55 (the same as if it had lost the bid), and the values of A and B will decline $10 million each.[3] In this example the values of all the bidders fall.

E. $\mathscr{P}$otential Sources of Synergy in Conglomerate Mergers

From the mid-1950s through 1968, economists and managers offered a number of reasons other than the ones discussed above to explain how economies might be achieved in conglomerate mergers. During this period, formal long-range enterprise planning developed, and computer technology began to be adapted to the management of the firm. Financial planning and control systems were extended with further improvements in the use of balanced, centralized-decentralized management control systems. Further, World War II and the Korean conflict had stimulated new technologies, resulting in an uneven diffusion of and wide variations in advanced technological capabilities among firms.

The major conceptual point here is that the role of the general management functions (planning, control, organizing, information systems) and functions centralized at top management levels (research, finance, legal) increased in importance in the management of enterprises. As a consequence the costs of managing large, diversified firms were substantially reduced relative to potential operating economies. This is the broader theoretical basis explaining the formation of conglomerates. However, there is considerable disagreement about whether synergy is achieved in conglomerate mergers from the sources just described. Most of the theoretical literature of finance has assumed no synergy in conglomerate mergers and has analyzed pure financial effects. For a theory of pure conglomerate mergers, see Chung [1982].

1. Pure Financial Theories of Conglomerate Firms

The popular justification of conglomerate mergers was synergy—the $2 + 2 = 5$ effect. But other theories of conglomerate firms were set forth that did not require the assumption of synergy. Lewellen [1971], for example, offered a purely financial rationale for conglomerate mergers. His theory may be summarized initially in terms of the numerical examples he provides, concluding with his general statement of conditions.

Let us consider two firms, A and B, whose annual cash flows are independent (correlation coefficient is zero) and each distributed as shown in columns (1) through (3) of Table 18.12.

It is assumed that each firm has incurred borrowings to the point that its annual cash contractual obligation amounts to $240. The probability, $P(D)$, that one or both firms will be unable to meet their debt service obligations of $240 each is

$$P(D) = P(Y_A < 240) + P(Y_B < 240) - P(Y_A < 240, Y_B < 240)$$

$$= .1 + .1 - (.1)(.1) = .19.$$

---

[3] Bank C could win the bid with as little as $100 million plus one penny. Why?

Table 18.12 Cash Flow Distribution Example

(1) State (s_1)	(2) $P(s_1)$	(3) Y_1
1	.1	100
2	.2	250
3	.7	500

Note: s_1 = alternative future state of the world; $P(s_1)$ = probability of alternative states; Y_1 = annual cash flow outcomes under alternative states.

Table 18.13 Distribution of Joint Returns Example

		.1	.2	.7
.1	Joint probability	.01	.02	.07
	Amount	200.00	350.00	600.00
.2	Joint probability	.02	.04	.14
	Amount	350.00	500.00	750.00
.7	Joint probability	.07	.14	.49
	Amount	600.00	750.00	1,000.00

If the two firms merge, the distribution of their joint returns can be calculated as shown in the matrix in Table 18.13. The distribution of their joint returns would therefore become

Y_m	200	350	500	600	750	1,000
$P(Y_m)$	.01	.04	.04	.14	.28	.49

Since their aggregate debt burden would become $480 per annum, the probability of default now drops to .05 as compared with .19 before the merger.

The foregoing was based on the assumption of zero correlation between the two returns. If the correlation were −1, the gains from merger would be even greater. If the correlation were +1, reducing the probability of default would require other differences such as differences in the size of debt obligations. Thus if we assume the same distribution of returns for the two firms as before, but assume a correlation of +1 between the two and debt obligations of A and B to be $255 and $240, respectively, the before-merger probability of default would be

$$P(D) = .3 + .1 - .1 = .3.$$

After merger the total debt obligations would be $495, and they would be related to the following combined cash flow pattern:

Y_m	200	500	1,000
$P(Y_m)$	.1	.2	.7

The probability of default would therefore fall to only .01.

Levy and Sarnat [1970, 801] set forth a similar argument. They state: "A somewhat stronger case can be made for conglomerate mergers when economies in capital costs are considered . . . large firms have better access to the capital markets and also enjoy significant cost savings when securing their financial needs. . . . These cost savings presumably reflect, at least in part, the reduction in lenders' risk achieved through diversification."

Galai and Masulis [1976] point out the confusion involved between the value of the merged firm and the positions of the debt and equity holders. They argue that the value of the merged firm is the simple sum of the constituent firms. "This can be seen once one recognizes that investors in the marketplace could have created an identical financial position by purchasing equal proportions of the debt and equity of the two firms" (Galai and Masulis [1976, 68]). The OPM establishes that the relative position of the creditors and the equity holders of the firms will be changed. If the correlation between the returns of the merging firms is less than 1, the variance in the rate of return of the merged firm will be lower than the variance of the rates of return of the merging firms (assumed to be equal). (For numerical illustrations see Problems 18.2, 18.3, and 18.4 at the end of the chapter.)

It follows from the OPM that the value of the equity of the merged firm will be less than the sum of the constituent equity values and the value of the debt will be higher. According to the OPM, increased variability increases the value of the option, and conversely. Since the equity is an option on the face value of the debt outstanding, its value will fall with a decrease in volatility. "What is taking place, as Rubinstein points out, is that the bondholders receive more protection since the stockholders of each firm have to back the claims of the bondholders of both companies. The stockholders are hurt since their limited liability is weakened" (Galai and Masulis [1976, 68]).

Thus a pure diversification rationale for conglomerate mergers is not valid. Reducing the risk to bondholders represents a redistribution of value from shareholders, leaving the total value of the firm unchanged.

However, a number of alternatives could be used to return the wealth of different classes of security holders to the original position they held prior to the merger. One solution would be to increase the amount of the face value of debt and use the proceeds to retire equity. This process is continued until the original bondholders' holdings have a market value equal to their constituent sum prior to the merger. The debt-to-equity ratio of the merged firm can be increased to offset the decrease in the volatility of the merged firm's rate of return. The increased amount of debt implies that the total value of the firm is increased through merger due to the tax deductibility of interest payments. Galai and Masulis suggest that this may explain some conglomerate mergers.

2. Shastri's Extension of the Analysis of the Effects of Mergers on Corporate Security Values

Shastri [1982] extends the Galai-Masulis (G-M) study by allowing the two firms to have different variances, different debt ratios, and different debt maturities. Shastri's results for the effects of mergers on shareholder values versus bondholders' positions under these more general conditions are presented in Table 18.14. Because the correlation between the cash flow streams of the two firms can be either positive or negative, the resulting combined firm variance may be less than the variance of the individual firms or greater than one of the firms and less than the other firm. However, the leverage effects and maturity effects are simply weighted average effects. The combined firm will simply have a weighted average of the leverage or maturity pattern of the combining firms.

Table 18.14 The Effects of the Merger on Firm Security Values

		Bond A	Bond B	$S_C - (S_A + S_B)$ Common Stock*
Variance effect	$\sigma_A > \sigma_C > \sigma_B$	> 0	< 0	$\lessgtr 0$
	$\sigma_A < \sigma_C < \sigma_B$	< 0	> 0	$\lessgtr 0$
	$\sigma_A, \sigma_B > \sigma_B$	> 0	> 0	< 0
Leverage effect	$M_A/V_A > M_B/V_B$	> 0	< 0	< 0
	$M_A/V_A < M_B/V_B$	< 0	> 0	< 0
Maturity effect		> 0	$\lessgtr 0$	< 0

* The effect of the merger on each individual firm's stock would depend on the merger terms.

The other relationship that stands out in the table is that the value of the common stock of the combined firm may under some conditions be larger than the addition of the premerger stock values of the two firms even in a pure conglomerate merger, assuming no synergy. The reasons for Shastri's conclusions are reviewed next.

There are three possibilities under the variance effect. The variance of the combined firm may be less than the variance of either of the individual firms before the merger. This is the G-M result where the variance effect is positive for the bonds of both firm A and B and negative for both stocks. However, the variance of the combined firm may be greater than one of the firms and lower than the other. For example, when $\sigma_A > \sigma_C > \sigma_B$, the securities of firm B become riskier with the merger, and conversely with firm A. So there is a positive impact on the bonds of A and the stock of B, negative on the bonds of B and the stock of A. The effects on the value of the stock of the combined firm compared with the sum of the premerger stock values is ambiguous depending on the relative magnitudes of the premerger stock A and stock B values.

Shastri defines the leverage ratio as the ratio of the face value of debt to firm value. If the leverage ratio of firm A is greater than the ratio for B, the combined firm has a leverage ratio less than that of firm A and greater than that of firm B. The merger results in a decrease in the leverage-ratio-related risk for bond A, with the opposite result for bond B. This implies an increase in the value of bond A and a decrease in the value of bond B. When the leverage ratio of A is lower than that of B, the opposite results follow. Because of an ambiguous increase in the bankruptcy-related risk for the combined equity, the leverage effect is always negative for the combined common stock.

The maturity effect has two components. Assume that the maturity of bond A is shorter than the maturity of bond B. The effect of a merger from the point of view of bond B is equivalent to having the firm issue new debt with a shorter maturity. Thus bond A is paid in full ahead of bond B and in some sense becomes "senior" to bond B. This seniority effect would be positive for bond A and negative for bond B.

The second effect is a bankruptcy effect. If bankruptcy occurs at bond A's maturity date, debt B also shares in the proceeds of the bankruptcy and so gains from the merger. Hence the bankruptcy component of the maturity effect is negative for debt A and positive for debt B.

The size of these two effects depends on both the probability of bankruptcy and the bankruptcy sharing rules. Shastri argues that the first effect will dominate the second for bond A so that it always gains in a merger. But the net effect on debt B is ambiguous. From the point of view of debt B, the "new debt issue" is always accompanied by a change in firm value by an amount generally greater than the face value of the "new issue." So the maturity effect on debt B value is ambiguous. The effect on the combined stock value is always negative. This is essentially because with a merger the option that a shareholder of B had of buying out debt of B is no longer available directly because debt A has to be paid off first. This loss of an option leads to a decline in the combined stock price.

Thus Shastri's extension of previous work yields some different empirical predictions. The value of the stock of the combined firm may, under certain conditions, exceed the combined premerger stock values of the combined firms. In addition, all three of the effects under certain conditions can be negative on at least one of the bonds, leading to a decline in value. So bonds do not necessarily gain in a merger. This explains why bond indentures may include covenants restricting the freedom of the firm to engage in mergers. Thus, in general, the extension by Shastri results in a generalization of predictions of the effects of mergers.

3. Tests of the Performance of Conglomerate Firms

Empirical studies of conglomerate performance have been of two kinds. The first was a concern with their operating characteristics. In a study whose data ended in the early 1960s, Reid [1968] concluded that conglomerate mergers satisfied the desires of managers for larger firms but did not increase earnings or market prices. For a later period, 1958–1968, Weston and Mansinghka [1971] found that conglomerates as a group raised the depressed premerger rates of return on total assets up to the average for all firms. In the Melicher and Rush [1974] study for 1960–1969, conglomerates acquired more profitable firms than nonconglomerate acquirers and increased the utilization of latent debt capacity.

A second type of empirical study focused on conglomerate performance within the context of the CAPM. Weston, Smith, and Shrieves [1972] compared conglomerates with mutual funds (using annual data for 1960–1969), finding that conglomerates provided higher ratios of return to systematic risk. Melicher and Rush [1973] analyzed conglomerates against a matched sample of nonconglomerates. Operating comparisons were based on annual data, whereas market comparisons utilized monthly data over the period 1965–1971. Conglomerates exhibited higher levels of systematic risk but did not achieve significantly different rates of return or other performance measures. Joehnk and Nielsen [1974] compared levels of systematic risk and coefficients of determination for 21 conglomerates and 23 nonconglomerates (1962–1969). The market response for three years before and three years after each merger was not significantly different. Mason and Goudzwaard [1976] compared 22 conglomerates against randomly selected portfolios having similar asset structures for the years 1962–1967. They concluded that conglomerates performed statistically worse, on the basis of both return on assets and return on equity, compared with an unmanaged portfolio of similar industry investments.

In a later study, Smith and Weston [1977] retested their 1972 results, using monthly data and extending the coverage through 1973. Their research broadened the comparisons of Melicher and Rush [1973] by including mutual funds and closed-end investment companies as well as nonconglomerate firms. They studied a sample of 38 conglomerate firms. Conglomerates from their 1972 study were included for which complete data of monthly prices and dividends were available for the 10 years from 1964 through 1973. Similar data were available for 35 nonconglomerate firms that were part of a larger sample (matched by major industry) as developed by Melicher and Rush [1973]. Standard and Poor's Composite Stock Price Index was used as a surrogate for the overall stock market. For comparisons of managed portfolios, they compiled data for 104 mutual funds and also for 17 closed-end investment companies.

The risk-adjusted performance of conglomerates was found to be significantly better than that of the mutual funds. The higher-beta conglomerates performed better during the rising market but less well during the flat market. However, on theoretical grounds, the risk-adjusted performance measure should not show better performance for higher-risk securities during an up-market or worse performance during a down-market situation. As discussed by Friend and Blume [1970] and Black, Jensen, and Scholes [1972], a possible reason for the early differentially better performance of conglomerates is that the CAPM from which the risk-adjusted performance measures are derived is misspecified. An alternative explanation is expectation errors coupled with institutional changes. The attitudes toward conglomerates changed considerably over time, exhibiting overoptimism about their potential during 1964–1968. During the second period, 1969–1973, some unfavorable institutional changes took place. Accounting rules were changed, adverse tax treatment was legislated, and antitrust suits were filed by the Department of Justice. Also, the aerospace industry, which spawned many of the conglomerates as a form of defensive diversification, suffered from excess capacity and sharp product shifts with the escalation of the Vietnam war. Tests of operating effectiveness suggest an initial overoptimism about the potentials for management performance of conglomerates. Following 1969, conglomerates began to be viewed with considerable pessimism. These expectation changes are consistent with the risk-adjusted performance exhibited by the conglomerates.

As experience with conglomerates grew, investors were able to develop a more dependable basis for forming expectations with respect to their performance. We would expect conglomerates to continue to exhibit high betas because of the characteristics of the product markets of the conglomerate firms. Risk-adjusted measures of conglomerate performance are not likely to be significantly different from those of other firms and portfolios.

4. The Diversification Discount Issue

A substantial literature has developed on the conglomerate or diversification discount. One definition is that diversified firms trade at values at a discount relative to an "equivalent" firm simulated by a weighted average of single-segment firms in the same lines of business as the conglomerates. Both the theories and empirical evidence are mixed. Theories to support a diversification discount include (1) inefficient internal capital markets (Scharfstein [1998]; Scharfstein and Stein [2000]; Rajan, Servaes, and Zingales [2000]); (2) agency problems such as inefficient use of excess cash for empire building (Jensen [1986]); (3) information asymmetry when managers have information not shared with the market (Krishnaswami and Subramaniam [1999]; Myers and Majluf [1984]); (4) analyst specialization (Gilson, Healy, Noe, and Palepu [2001]).

Theories to support a diversification premium include (1) economies of scope (Panzar and Willig [1979]; Teece [1980, 1982]); (2) combining uncorrelated cash flows (Lewellen [1971]); and (3) efficient internal capital markets (Alchian [1969]; Weston [1970]; Williamson [1975]).

Early empirical studies found a diversification discount (Lang and Stulz [1994]; Berger and Ofek [1995]; Servaes [1996]). Correcting for sample selection bias, later studies found a diversification premium (Villalonga [1999]; Campa and Kedia [2002]). Whited [2001] demonstrated that the earlier empirical findings were caused by errors in measuring Tobin's q. Using census data at the establishment level, Villalonga [2003] obtains a diversification premium on a sample that gives a discount using segment data.

A fundamental challenge to the theory and evidence arguing for a diversification discount is that a firm could eliminate it by restructuring through the use of divestitures or spin-offs. If existing management failed to do this, the market for corporate control (acquisitions followed by bust-ups) would do it.

F. 𝒯he Performance of M&As

1. Studies of Event Returns

Many studies have calculated merger performance using event study methods. Tables summarizing these studies are found in Chapter 8 of *Takeovers, Restructuring, and Corporate Governance* (Weston, Mitchell, and Mulherin [2004]). Here we summarize the detailed tables presented. In stock-for-stock mergers, target firms gain on average about 15–20%. When the method of payment is cash, the abnormal returns to targets are 25–30%. Two reasons have been suggested for the higher event returns to targets in cash acquisitions. One is that when targets receive stock in the acquiring company as payment they share in the future performance and risks of a combined enterprise. Two, the buyer who pays cash is showing greater confidence in the value of the target; in a stock-for-stock deal, the buyer may be using shares that are relatively overvalued. When there are multiple bidders, returns can be 5–10 percentage points higher resulting from the competition.

On average, bidders have zero abnormal returns, which implies that the market expects them to earn only their cost of capital. In negotiated mergers, bidders on average may have abnormal returns of 1–2%. All studies show that combined returns are positive for the samples of mergers and acquisitions studied. In a study of 364 of the largest mergers between 1992 and 1998, accounting for about 50% of the total value of transactions, Weston and Johnson [1999] found that the combined event returns were positive in 65.4% of the deals. When the negative combined event returns are deducted, the net overall returns for the total sample are positive, suggesting that the combinations were value increasing.

2. Longer-Run Performance Studies

Some question the reliability of event studies on grounds that it is longer-term results that matter. However, event returns represent the market's best judgment of the long-run prospects of an announced merger, divestiture, restructuring, or other adjustment activities. But longer-term studies may be confounded by changes in general economic conditions as well as competitive developments. Market prices reflect expectations of future developments that are likely to require revisions. Nevertheless, substantial evidence supports the usefulness of event studies.

Healy, Palepu, and Ruback [1992] studied the postacquisition performance of the 50 largest U.S. mergers between 1979 and 1984. They used accounting data primarily but tested their results by using market valuation measures as well. They analyzed both operating characteristics and investment characteristics. The first two measures of operating characteristics are the cash flow margin on sales and asset turnover. When these two measures are multiplied, they obtain the margin on the market value of assets.

Their third variable measures the effect of the merger on employment. They calculate the change in the number of employees during a given year as a percentage of the number of employees in the previous year. This is to test the hypothesis that gains in mergers are achieved by downsizing and reducing the number of employees.

Their fourth measure is pension expense per employee. Again, this is to test whether gains from mergers come at the expense of reducing pension protection for employees.

Next, they consider a number of effects on investment. Here they are testing whether gains may come from underinvesting for the future, from selling off assets, or from reducing research and development activities.

They looked at the results for the firms themselves and then made a further adjustment. They made an industry adjustment to test whether the changes in the variables occurred because of industry effects as distinguished from the effects of the mergers on the individual firms. For example, the merged firms may have reduced employment. But if employment reduction in nonmerging firms in the same industry was even greater, then industry-adjusted employment in the merged firms would have increased.

Their data show that industry-adjusted employment decreased. This implies that the merging firms did more restructuring and reorganization than other firms in the industry. But the cash flow margin on sales did not significantly change. However, asset turnover significantly improved. The return on the market value of assets also improved significantly. However, the fact that the cash flow margin on sales had not changed implies that the improvement in the return on assets did not come from the reduction of employment costs, which would have increased the cash flow margin on sales. It was better asset management that increased the return on assets. Pension expense per employee was reduced somewhat but not by a statistically significant degree; none of the investment characteristics were significantly changed on the basis of industry-adjusted performance, except asset sales measured at book value.

These results imply that industry-adjusted performance of the merging firms had improved. The improvement came not at the expense of labor income but by improving the management of assets. The investments in capital equipment and investments in research and development were not significantly changed.

One of the important findings in this study related to the event returns calculated as described in connection with the previous studies summarized in this chapter: The event returns for the firms are significantly correlated with the subsequent accounting returns during the postmerger period. This is evidence that on average, for their sample, event returns correctly forecast postmerger performance.

Agrawal, Jaffe, and Mandelker [1992] also studied postmerger performance. They developed a larger sample of 937 mergers and 227 tender offers. Their sample included firms smaller than those of the Healy et al. study, which focused on the 50 largest mergers. They adjusted for size effect and for beta-weighted market returns. They found that shareholders of acquiring firms experienced a wealth loss of about 10% over the five years following the merger completion.

This finding has some interesting implications. First, it represents an anomaly in the sense that it provides an opportunity for a positive abnormal investment return. If acquiring firms always lose after a merger, this suggests that investors short the acquiring firm on a long-term basis at the time of a merger announcement. Of course, over time this anomaly should be wiped out.

Another implication may be explored. Healy, Palepu, and Ruback [1992] found that industry-adjusted postmerger performance was positive. Agrawal, Jaffe, and Mandelker [1992] found that marketwide or economy-wide adjustments result in negative returns. These two results together imply that merger activity took place mainly in industries where performance was subpar compared to the market or the economy as a whole.

Franks, Harris, and Titman [1991] found that postmerger share price performance is sensitive to the benchmark employed. Using an equally weighted index, their findings confirmed earlier studies that found negative postmerger performance. However, the use of the value-weighted benchmark results in positive postmerger performance. When various multiportfolio benchmarks are employed, no statistically significant abnormal performance is found.

Table 18.15 Long-Term Compound Annual Returns (5 Years)

	Compound Annual Returns	
	Mergers	**Tender Offers**
Stock		
Acquirer	9.9%	0.9%
Control	10.7%	10.7%
Cash		
Acquirer	15.2%	20.3%
Control	11.1%	13.1%

Source: Table V, Loughran and Vikh [1997], 1780. (© 1992 Blackwell Publishing. Reprinted with permission.)

Ghosh [2001] extended the earlier Healy et al. [1992] study. He uses a sample of 315 of the largest acquisitions during the period 1981–1995. He initially replicates the Healy et al. [1992] results that cash flow margins are higher than industry-median benchmarks after acquisitions. But he finds that the merging firms also have superior preacquisition performance; when he adjusts for this in his regression model, the cash flow margins are no longer higher. Alternatively, when control firms are matched by performance and size from preevent years, the merging firms no longer show superior performance. For cash acquisitions, cash flows improve 3% per year (significant), with the improvements coming from higher sales growth rather than cost reductions. In stock acquisitions, he finds that both operating cash flow margins and sales growth decline, but not significantly. The Ghosh study confirms the Healy et al. results, which also reinforces their finding that the initial event returns were consistent with the longer-term accounting performance.

The Loughran and Vijh [1997] paper studies the long-term returns by acquirers compared with a control group. The key data are summarized in Table 18.15. In cash mergers, the five-year compound annual returns for acquirers are much higher than for the control firms. In stock mergers, the returns are approximately equal. In stock tender offers, acquirers have clearly subnormal returns. The results are strongly supportive of acquirers' positive performance except for tender offers made with stock. Possible explanations for the negative performance of stock-for-stock transactions would begin with the presumption that the stock of the acquirer was overvalued. Another possibility is that on average acquirers overpaid.

Rau and Vermaelen [1998] use the Fama-French size and book-to-market factors as controls in their sample of 3,169 mergers and 348 tender offers between January 1, 1980, and December 31, 1991. They test performance over a subsequent three-year period controlling for size and the book-to-market ratio. Value bidders (high book-to-market) achieve significantly superior returns of 8% in mergers (stock) and 16% in tender offers (cash). Glamour bidders (low book-to-market or growth stocks) earn negative returns of 17% in mergers (stock) and nonsignificant positive returns of 4% in tender offers (cash).

These last two studies make it clear that mergers overall do not fail. The method of payment and the initial book-to-market ratios greatly influence the results. But the Anslinger and Copeland [1996] study found that how the combination is managed is another important variable. They studied the unpromising area of nonsynergistic acquisitions. They developed data on 21 companies that made 829 acquisitions during 1985–1994. Their group of eight corporate acquirers operated 50 different lines of business, experiencing a compound annual revenue growth of 12%, and outperformed the S&P 500 index by an average of almost 50%. The group of 13 financial buyers reported capital of more than $16 billion and achieved estimated returns of about 25% annually for their funds. Anslinger and Copeland proposed seven key operating principles that achieved the superior results even in areas where other acquirers had failed.

3. Bad Bidders Become Good Targets

Mitchell and Lehn [1990] studied stock price reactions to acquisitions during the period 1982–1986. One sample was composed of firms that became targets of takeovers after they had made acquisitions. A control group consisted of acquiring firms that did not subsequently become targets of takeover bids. The stock prices of acquirers that became targets declined significantly when they announced acquisitions. The stock prices of acquiring firms that did not become subsequent targets increased significantly when they announced acquisitions.

Furthermore, they found that for the entire sample of acquisitions, those that were subsequently divested had significantly negative event returns. Acquisitions that were not subsequently divested had significantly positive event returns. This suggests that when companies announce acquisitions, the event returns forecast the likelihood that the assets will ultimately be divested. Mitchell and Lehn point out that in the aggregate the returns to acquiring firms were approximately zero. But when acquiring firms experienced negative event returns, they were subsequently likely to become takeover targets. Bidders that experienced positive event returns were less likely to become targets. Event returns were able to discriminate between "bad" bidders and "good" bidders.

4. Efficiency Pressures

Early studies found that as high as two-thirds of acquisitions did not earn the bidders' cost of capital. Later studies suggest that the failure rate has dropped to the 50% level. But the greatest positive benefits of M&A activity have come because every firm has become a potential takeover target. If a firm underperforms, it is likely to become a takeover target. The availability of financing for bidders since the early 1980s has put pressure on all firms to become lean, mean, and efficient. A fundamental role of mergers is to discipline management. An active market for corporate control increases efficiencies and contributes to favorable economic performance overall.

G. Joint Ventures

1. The Use of Joint Ventures

A joint venture is a separate business entity that usually involves only a fraction of the activities of the participating organizations. The participants in a joint venture continue as separate firms, but create a new corporation, partnership, or other business form. Joint ventures are limited in scope and duration.

There are several objectives that may be achieved by a joint venture. The participating firms obtain an opportunity to share risks. Working with other firms reduces the investment costs of entering potentially risky new areas. Even though investment requirements are less than solely internal operations, the joint venture may still enjoy the benefits of economies of scale, critical mass, and the learning curve. Also, joint ventures allow firms the opportunity to gain knowledge. Firms may share or exchange technology to accomplish what one firm could not do alone. There is a potential for sharing managerial skills in organization, planning, and control.

Joint ventures have proved to be particularly advantageous in the international setting. In some situations, local governments may not allow an acquisition. A joint venture presents an opportunity to combine some assets without violating such a regulation. International joint ventures usually reduce risks of firms operating in foreign countries. In addition, joint ventures have been used as a means of circumventing certain international trade barriers.

When a firm buys a segment divested by another firm, it may have a high uncertainty about its future performance under the buyer's management. This uncertainty might make it difficult for the parties to agree on a price. Joint ventures can serve a useful function as an interim step. A common pattern is for the acquirer to pay cash for 40–45% of the divested segment it is buying as its contribution to the formation of the joint venture. The joint venture may be used as a device for the selling firm to convey knowledge of manufacturing and/or distribution. The motivations and the incentives are all in the right directions. The better the selling firm does in teaching the acquirer the potentials of the segment, the more the segment will be worth. As a consequence, after a year or two, the buyer may complete the purchase of the percentage of the joint venture it does not own. Typically, the price paid for the second segment is substantially higher than for the first segment because the acquirer better understands the potentials of the business. Value is created by minimizing employee turnover and avoiding the impairment of supplier and distribution networks.

Requirements for successful joint ventures can be summarized in the following:

1. Each has something to offer.
2. Careful preplanning.
3. Key executive assigned to implement.
4. May be used for information for an acquisition.
5. Preplan termination; often provisions are made for a buyout by one of the parties.

2. Event Returns for Joint Ventures

The performance of joint ventures was examined by McConnell and Nantell [1985] using residual analysis. Their study covered a selection from all joint ventures reported in *Mergers and Acquisitions* for the period 1972–1979. Their sample consisted of 210 firms engaged in 136 joint ventures. The average size of the joint ventures was about $5 million. The two-day announcement period abnormal return was 0.73%, which was significant at the .01 level. The cumulative average residual (abnormal return) over the 62-day period ending on the event day (announcement day) was 2.15%, significant at the .10 level. The cumulative average residual (CAR) remains at 2.15% after 60 days subsequent to the joint venture announcement, indicating no further valuation effect following the initial announcement.

McConnell and Nantell compared the size of the abnormal return with the results for companies involved in mergers using a representative study of mergers by Asquith [1983]. Asquith found excess returns for the two days ending in the announcement to be 6.5% for the target firm and 0.3% for the bidding firm. Because joint ventures do not identify the acquiring and acquired firm, their results should fall between the two, which they do. Asquith found that over a 60-day period prior to the merger announcement the CAR increased by 11% for acquired firms and was unchanged for the acquiring companies. Again the CAR for joint ventures lay between the CARs for the individual firms.

Because real estate and entertainment joint ventures constituted 23% of their sample, McConnell and Nantell also tested for overrepresentation by calculating results without this group.

Their results were similar. They also eliminated firms for which other information was released near the joint venture announcement date. Again the results were unchanged.

McConnell and Nantell also studied the relative size effect. They noted that in mergers the dollar value of gains appears to be evenly divided between the two companies. But if the acquiring company is 20 times as large as the target that gains 10% in market value, the acquiring company will gain only 0.5% in stock value. Accordingly, the firms in their joint venture sample were divided into large and small groups based on the total market value of their common stock 61 trading days before the announcement of the joint venture. Information was available to do this for 65 joint ventures but not for 80 other companies that were placed into a third, "all other," category. The statistical tests were repeated for the three groups. The small firms gained 1.10%, the large firms gained 0.63%, and all others gained 0.57%—all of these statistically significant. The dollar gain to the small-firm sample was $4.538 million, and to the large-firm sample $6.651 million. Thus, as in mergers, the dollar gain was about evenly divided, but the percentage gains were much higher for the smaller firms.

When the dollar gains are scaled by the amounts invested in the joint venture, the average premium is 23% (after removing one outlier). This result lies in the range of premiums observed in mergers and tender offers. McConnell and Nantell observe that the gains in mergers and tender offers could be from either synergy or the displacement of less effective management. Because joint ventures do not change the management of the parents, McConnell and Nantell [1985] conclude that "we are inclined to interpret our results as supportive of the synergy hypothesis as the source of gains in other types of corporate combinations" (p. 535).

H. Alliances and Partnerships

The change forces in the world economy have become so powerful they have accelerated the pace of change. Potentials for accelerating product developments and new products are increased, causing product life cycles to become shorter. Industry boundaries are blurred so that companies have opportunities in a wider range of industries and are impacted by competitors from more distant product-market activities. In these new industrial dynamics, alliances and partnerships have increasingly been used.

Alliances are less formal than joint ventures. A new entity need not be created. A formal contract may not be written. The relative size of participants may be highly unequal. Partner firms pool resources, expertise, and ideas so that the partners will have a continuing need for one another. Evolving relationships require adaptability and change over time. The alliance may involve multiple partners. Since the relationships are less legalistic, mutual trust is required. The speed of change in a relationship may be rapid. Firms may modify and move to other alliances as attractive possibilities emerge. Some creative people do not wish to be in the environment of large firms. But large firms may increase their access to creative people by alliances with small firms.

Alliances may have some advantages over mergers or joint ventures. They are more informal and provide flexibility. They may provide a firm with access to new markets and technologies with relatively small investments. Alliances provide the ability to create and disband projects with minimal formality. Working with partners possessing multiple skills can create major synergies.

Alliances vary in their characteristics. Greater ambiguity and uncertainty are involved. The partner relationship evolves in ways that are difficult to predict. Today's ally may be tomorrow's rival—or may be a current rival in some other market. Managing the alliance relationship over

Table 18.16 Acquisitions versus Joint Ventures versus Strategic Alliances

Acquisition	Joint Venture	Strategic Alliance
Allows 100% control; no need for interfirm consensus	Firms intersect over narrow, well-defined segments	Useful for creation of complex systems between multiple firms
• Less flexible	• Exploit distinctive or narrow opportunities	• Blurs corporate boundaries
– Larger commitment of resources	– Generally only two firms involved	– Partner is usually larger than JVs (10/1 versus 5/1)
– Risky	– Limited risk	– Allows firms to focus on fewer core competencies
• Often requires more than is needed	• Joint production of single products	• Less clear contributions and benefits
• May cause upheaval in corporate culture	• Combines known resources	• Difficult to anticipate consequences
– May require accommodating different management systems	– Requires high-level management interaction	– Gives firms access to people who would not work directly for them
	– Rarely used in new markets or technologies	
– Requires combining, harmonizing information systems	– Can be used to reduce risk in a Merger transaction	– Often small resource commitment
		Limited time duration
– Requires combining different corporate cultures	– Often across borders	– Must be managed actively by senior executives
• Requires rapid, effective integration	• Tensions: Your firm wants to learn as much as possible, but not to convey too much	• The relationship is likely to evolve in directions not initially planned
• Remedy for strategic miscalculations		
• Most cost-cutting possible		• Managing over time requires adaptability to change and new knowledge
• Can have partial investments as an interim step		• Especially useful across borders given government prohibitions of cross-border mergers
• Can be across borders		

time may be more important than crafting the initial partnership. Thus, initial understandings may have less to do with future success than adaptability to change.

The advantages and limitations on a comparative basis of acquisitions versus joint ventures versus strategic alliances are summarized in Table 18.16. Acquisitions involve greater risks and greater potential gains or losses. Joint ventures involve smaller investments. They may be of temporary duration, moving toward broader long-term goals. Strategic alliances can create complex relationships between multiple firms. The initial resource commitment may be quite small. The exchange of ideas may be valuable for the multiple partnering firms.

Some successful firms have used all of the above forms of acquisitions, joint ventures, and alliances to increase their growth opportunities. It is reported that companies like Oracle have more than 10,000 business alliances. Announcement of new alliances occur almost daily in the press—this is of course true for mergers, takeovers, and joint ventures as well.

1. Event Returns for Alliances

Dyer, Kale, and Singh [2001] report the results of a study of 200 corporations involved in 1,572 alliances (including joint ventures) over the period 1993–97. They report that the companies' stock price increases by almost 1% with each announcement of a new alliance, representing an increase in market value of $54 million per alliance. For companies that have a dedicated alliance function in the organization structure to guide and coordinate alliance-related activities, the average abnormal announcement return is 1.35%. For companies without such a dedicated function, the average abnormal event return is only 0.18%. They observe that returns to alliance activity are superior to event returns for acquirers in mergers and takeovers. Their later study confirms these results (Kale, Dyer, and Singh [2002]).

I. *S*hedding Assets to Create Value

The main techniques for shrinking to create value are (1) divestitures, (2) equity carveouts, (3) spin-offs, (4) split-ups, and (5) tracking stocks. We shall discuss each in turn.

1. Divestitures

Divestitures represent the sale of a segment of a company to another entity. The divestiture by a seller generally represents focusing on a narrower core of activities. The buying firm seeks to strengthen its strategic programs. For example, in April 1998, Cooper Industries sold its auto parts business, Cooper Automotive, to Federal Mogul. This transaction reflected competitive forces in the auto business. Cost-cutting pressure from auto manufacturers pushed the auto parts makers to deliver complete systems of parts, rather than individual items. Cooper's strategy was to focus on its strengths in tools and hardware, along with electrical products. Federal Mogul had a five-year strategic acquisition program that would enable it to manufacture complete engine systems. In addition, the crown jewel of the deal was Cooper's brake and friction product business, which would help Federal Mogul become a major supplier of brake systems.

During the 1980s acquisitions that represented divestitures from another firm ranged from 35% to 45% of total acquisitions. This represented a part of the process of unwinding the conglomerate, unrelated acquisitions during the 1960s. During the strategic mergers between 1995 and 2001, the percentage of acquisitions representing divestitures ranged from 25% to 35% (*Mergerstat Review*, 2002, p. 30).

The key reason for divestitures is that they are worth more as a part of the buyer's organization than as a part of the seller's. Often the seller seeks to shed unrelated activities or activities it feels that it is not managing effectively. The buyer is seeking to further strengthen an existing business.

Kaplan and Weisbach [1992] study a sample of 271 acquisitions of at least 100 million 1982 dollars during 1971–1982. By 1989, 119 had been divested after a median holding period of seven years. Almost 60% of the acquisitions in which the acquirer and target were not highly related had been divested. Fewer than 20% of the highly related acquisitions were divested over the same time period. Only 44% of the acquirers who reported to an accounting result for the divestiture reported a loss on sale. The remaining 56% reported a gain or no loss. The purchase price was about 60% higher than the pretakeover value. The sale price was about 72% higher. Deflated, the sale price is

Table 18.17 Returns to Shareholders from Divestitures

Authors	Year Published	Period Covered	Event Window in Days unless Noted	Sample Size	Mean Event Returns to Parent
Gleason, Mathur, and Singh	2000	1980–1996	−1, 0	244 divestitures by U.S. multinational corporations	0.65% ***
Mulherin and Boone	2000	1990–1998	−1, +1	370 divestitures: 106 spin-offs, 125 carveouts, 139 asset sales	3.04% *** 4.51% *** 2.27% *** 2.60% ***
Lang, Poulsen, and Stulz	1995	1984–1989	−5, +5	93 asset sales: 40 pay out proceeds, 53 reinvest in firm	2.80% *** 5.65% *** 0.65%

*** Significant at the 1% level
** Significant at the 5% level
* Significant at the 10% level

only 43% higher than the pretakeover value. Thus, compared with the original pretakeover value, the predeflated sale price represents 43% gain over the pretakeover value. So although value was added, the acquirer paid too much in the sense that the deflated value of the sale price was only 90% of the purchase price. If the acquisition price had been 10% lower, the acquirers would have earned the 20% rise in the S&P 500 over the average seven-year holding period.

Table 18.17 summarizes event returns from divestitures to shareholders of selling firms. For all the studies the event returns from divestitures of all types are positive. The Lang, Poulsen, and Stulz [1995] study shows that when proceeds of assets sales are paid out to shareholders, the event returns were relatively high, 5.65%. When the proceeds were reinvested in the firm, the event returns were small and not statistically significant.

2. Equity Carveouts and Spin-Offs

Equity carveouts are usually followed by spin-offs. A company sells up to 20% of the stock of a segment to raise funds followed by a tax-free spin-off. Examples include the equity carveouts of GM and of DuPont. In 1998, Delphi was created by a decision of the GM board of directors and was incorporated in September in Delaware. On January 1, 1999, GM supplied Delphi with the assets and liabilities that had been the Delphi Automotive Systems segment of GM. In February, an equity carveout of 17.7% of the Delphi stock was made, with GM holding the remaining 82.7%. In the following April, substantially all of the remaining shares of Delphi were distributed in a spin-off as a dividend of 0.7 share of Delphi per share of GM common stock. Upon completion of the spin-off, executives of GM on Delphi's board resigned. Delphi became a fully independent, publicly traded company.

The DuPont spin-off of Conoco involved a share exchange. In its initial equity carveout, DuPont sold 150 million A shares at $23, raising $3.45 billion. The spin-off of the remainder of Conoco was made through a share exchange at the option of the DuPont shareholders, who would receive 2.95 shares of class B stock of Conoco. Each share of the class B stock carried five votes; class A shares had only one vote per share.

Table 18.18 Returns to Shareholders from Equity Carveouts

Authors	Year Published	Period Covered	Event Window in Days unless Noted	Sample Size	Mean Event Returns to Parent
Hulbert, Miles, and Woolridge	2002	1981–1994	−1, +1	183 carveouts:	1.92% ***
				153 cross-industry,	2.10% ***
				30 own-industry	−0.39%
Vijh	2002	1980–1997	−251, −2	336 carveouts	14.88% ***
			−1, +1		1.94% ***
Schill and Zhou	2001	1996–2000	−1, +1	11 Internet subsidiary carveouts	11.30% *
Mulherin and Boone	2000	1990–1998	−1, +1	125 carveouts	2.27% ***
Allen	1998	1983–1995	−1, 0	12 carveouts of Thermo Electron	−0.09%
Allen and McConnell	1998	1978–1993	−1, +1	186 carveouts:	1.90% ***
				54 pay out proceeds,	6.63% ***
				60 retain proceeds,	−0.01%
				72 no indication	0.85%
Michaely and Shaw	1995	1981–1988	−2, +2	9 MLP spin-offs,	4.46% *
				28 MLP carveouts	0.40%
Slovin, Sushka, and Ferraro	1995	1980–1991	0, 1	32 carveouts	1.23% ***
Klein, Rosenfeld, and Beranek	1991	1966–1983	−4, 0	52 carveouts	2.75% ***
Schipper and Smith	1986	1965–1983	−4, 0	76 carveouts,	1.83% **
				39 seasoned equity offerings	−3.50% ***

*** Significant at the 1% level
** Significant at the 5% level
* Significant at the 10% level

The two examples illustrate the general characteristics of equity carveouts. The Conoco carveout and spin-off created a separate petroleum company and focused DuPont more on the chemical business. DuPont raised a substantial sum in the process. In addition to the $3.45 billion from the IPO, Conoco repaid debt of $9.22 billion to DuPont, and in the share exchange, DuPont received $11.95 billion share value.

We discuss carveouts first since they are often the prelude to spin-offs. Table 18.18 presents event returns to shareholders from equity carveouts. The event returns are almost uniformly positive, suggesting that the firm is engaging in some form of refocusing or restructuring. The negative return observed in the Hulburt, Miles, and Woolridge [2002] study is for 30 carveouts in which the parent and subsidiary were in the same industry. Thus the refocusing motive is not present. Also, industry problems are a possibility. The events returns are not significant, suggesting that the own-industry carveouts did not achieve refocusing benefits. The 12 carveouts of Thermo Electron were not statistically significant. In the Allen and McConnell [1998] study, carveouts had positive returns only if the proceeds were paid out to shareholders of the parent. In the Schipper and Smith [1986] study, the positive event returns from carveouts are contrasted with the negative returns from seasoned equity offerings in which overvalued stock may be sold to time the market.

Table 18.19 presents results of studies (after 1990) of returns to shareholders from spin-offs. In general, returns from spin-offs are positive. The Desai and Jain [1999] study shows that the returns are higher when the spin-offs are focus increasing. Similarly, the Daley, Mehrotra, and Sivakumar [1997] study shows that when the subsidiary and parent are in the same industry, the event returns are not significant. The Alli, Ramirez, and Yung [2001] study finds nonsignificant

Table 18.19 Returns to Shareholders from Spin-Offs

Authors	Year Published	Period Covered	Event Window in Days unless Noted	Sample Size	Mean Event Returns to Parent
Alli, Ramirez, and Yung	2001	1984–1994	−1, +1	47 spin-offs later withdrawn:	−1.05%
				26 withdrawn with stated reason,	2.68% **
				21 withdrawn without stated reason	−5.67%
Wruck and Wruck	2001	1985–1995	−1, 0	172 spin-offs	3.58% N/S
Desai and Jain	1999	1975–1991	−1, 1	144 total spin-offs:	3.84% ***
				103 focus increasing,	4.45% ***
				41 non-focus increasing	2.17% ***
Krishnaswami and Subramaniam	1999	1979–1993	−1, 0	118 spin-offs	3.15% ***
Best, Best, and Agapos	1998	1979–1993	−1, 0	72 spin-offs	3.41% ***
Daley, Mehrotra, and Sivakumar	1997	1975–1991	−1, 0	85 spin-offs:	3.40% ***
				25 own industry,	1.40%
				60 cross industry	4.30% ***
Allen, Lummer, McConnell, and Reed	1995	1962–1991	−1, 0	94 spin-offs of prior acquisitions	2.15% ***
Michaely and Shaw	1995	1981–1988	−2, +2	9 MLP spin-offs,	4.46% *
				28 MLP carveouts	0.40%
Vijh	1994	1964–1990	−1, 0	113 spin-offs	2.90% ***
Gerard and Silberman	1994	1979–1986	−5, +5	146 spin-offs	4.4% ***
			−1, 0		4.1% ***

*** Significant at the 1% level
** Significant at the 5% level
* Significant at the 10% level
N/S Significance data not stated

negative returns for spin-offs later withdrawn. However, for those withdrawn with stated reasons, the event returns are positive and significant.

Economic logic supports the positive market response to equity carveouts and to spin-offs. In the equity carveout, substantial funds are raised. The parent can focus more directly on its core business. Each segment can improve efficiency by focus. In the segment spun off, performance of managers can be measured directly. Compensation can be tied to performance. Motivation and incentives are strengthened.

3. Tracking Stocks

Tracking stocks are separate classes of the common stock of the parent corporation. They were first issued in 1984 when GM used a tracking stock to buy EDS, creating a class of common identified as E stock (called a letter stock at the time). Similarly, in 1985, when GM acquired Hughes Aircraft, a new class called H was used. In May 1991, the U.S. Steel Company became USX for the steel business and created a USX-Marathon stock for the oil business (called a target stock at the time). In September 1992, USX created a third tracking stock when it sold shares of the USX-Delphi group stock in an IPO. Each tracking stock is regarded as common stock of the parent for voting purposes. The tracking stock company is usually assigned its own name.

Table 18.20 Returns to Shareholders from Tracking Stocks

Authors	Year Published	Period Covered	Event Window in Days unless Noted	Sample Size	Mean Event Returns to Parent
Billett and Mauer	2000	1984–1996	−1, 0 −1, +1	23 tracking stocks	2.55% *** 1.58%
D'Souza and Jacob	2000	1984–1999	−1, 0 −2, 0	12 tracking stocks	3.67% *** 3.61% ***
Elder and Westra	2000	1984–1999	−5, 0 −1, 0	35 tracking stocks	3.9% *** 3.1% ***
Logue, Seward, and Walsh	1996	1991–1995	−1, 0	8 tracking stocks	2.9% N/S

*** Significant at the 1% level
** Significant at the 5% level
* Significant at the 10% level
N/S Significance data not stated

Tracking stock is similar to a spin-off in that financial results of the parent and the tracking stock companies are reported separately. An important difference is that in the tracking stock relationship, the board of the parent continues to control the activities of the tracking segment; in contrast, a spin-off becomes an independent company. Tracking stock companies trade separately so dividends paid to shareholders of each company can be based on their individual cash flows. The performance and compensation of managers can be measured at the tracking stock company level. Managerial compensation can be based on performance of the tracking stock company and its stock price behavior. One of the criticisms of tracking stocks is that the subsidiary is still subject to control of the parent.

Table 18.20 summarizes the studies on event returns at the announcement of the establishment of a tracking stock. For relatively short windows, the abnormal returns to the parent company average about 3% positive. The number of firms in each study is relatively small, only eight in the Logue, Seward, and Walsh [1996] study. In fact, the largest number of firms in Elder and Westra [2000] represents the universe of usable companies. They started with 51 announcements but excluded 16 because the tracking stock was used for an acquisition or other significant simultaneous events. Over half of the announcements took place during 1998 and 1999 in technology-oriented industries near the peak of the bubble. This evidence suggests that the use of tracking stocks was relatively limited because of the potential conflict of interests resulting from the continuing control by the parent.

4. Split-Ups

In some cases, a simple spin-off, carveout, or restructuring of assets is not enough to change the trajectory of a firm's strategy. In these cases, management may seek to split the company into smaller pieces through a series of restructuring techniques, including initial equity carveouts and subsequent spin-offs. We present the following cases as examples of firms that have undergone split-ups. Table 18.21 summarizes the event returns of these split-ups.

These results are difficult to generalize. Each has its own story. US West offered local phone services in 14 western states, which were relatively sparsely populated with low growth. It moved

Table 18.21 Split-Up Announcements Returns

Firm	Announcement Date	CAR $(-10, 10)$	CAR $(-1, 0)$
ITT (three-way 1995 split)	6/13/1995	4.02%	3.98%
AT&T (1995—Lucent, NCR)	9/20/1995	12.91%	10.19%
ITT (planned defense—not completed)	7/16/1997	−3.12%	5.72%
US West (MediaOne)	10/27/1997	13.47%	−1.84%
Hewlett-Packard (Agilent)	3/2/1999	−9.91%	5.02%
AT&T (2000—wireless, broadband)	10/25/2000	−18.75%	−9.07%
	Average	−0.23%	2.33%

into cable television, creating a tracking stock in 1995. In 1997, the cable operations were split off into MediaOne. Within two years after the split-up both companies became takeover targets.

The split-up of AT&T in 1995 was accomplished by spin-offs of two segments. The long-distance business continued with the AT&T name. The equipment company became Lucent. The computer business was initially Global Information Solutions and then later renamed back to NCR. This split-up was viewed optimistically and had positive event returns. The split-up in 2000 was viewed rather pessimistically.

On November 18, 1999, Hewlett-Packard Company (HP) completed a $2.2 billion initial public offering of its test-and-measurement equipment subsidiary, Agilent Technologies. This split-up was initially viewed favorably because it could bring greater focus to HP. However, HP's problems were not solved. In 2001, the controversial decision to merge with Compaq was announced.

When Harold Geneen became the head of ITT in 1959, ITT was heavily dependent on operating telephone companies in foreign countries subject to high political risk. Geneen embarked on a program of domestic acquisitions for diversification. Geneen was succeeded by Rand V. Araskog in 1979, who proceeded to sell off 250 business units by 1994. Araskog also made acquisitions involving the Madison Square Garden, the New York Knicks, and the New York Rangers, to all of which the market reacted negatively. In December 1994, ITT acquired Caesar's World. On June 13, 1995, ITT announced a split into three companies. ITT Holdings, headed by Araskog, would manage hotels, casinos, and entertainment companies. A second company would include finance and the Hartford Insurance Company. The third was ITT Industries including automotive, valves, and pumps. This split-up did not perform well, and ITT Holdings became a takeover target. After ITT rejected several informal offers from Hilton Hotels, on January 27, 1997, Hilton announced a hostile bid. ITT resisted and announced a broad restructuring and recapitalization plan. After litigation, which Hilton won, ITT found a white knight in Starwood Hotels, a real estate investment trust. A bidding war ensued, with Hilton terminating its offer on November 12, 1997. After Starwood's acquisition, it sold ITT's gaming division to Park Place Entertainment, a Hilton spin-off. The casino operations of ITT had been Hilton's main interest. Both of ITT's split-ups were defensive because of lagging stock prices. The bidding war resulted in a favorable sale to Starwood, but with a large stock component that substantially declined in value.

The record of split-ups is mixed. They may represent attempts to solve difficult problems due to unfavorable industry developments or individual company unsound diversification efforts.

5. The Choice of Restructuring Methods

Spin-offs are best when the main business of the parent is not likely to make substantial contributions to the segment. Clearly, GM's automotive business did not inherently contribute to the computer processing and data analysis business of EDS, which subsequently was spun off. In some cases, a conflict of interest may be involved. This was the reason that Lucent was one of the spin-offs in the 1995–1996 split-up of AT&T. A major part of Lucent was the old Western Electric, which manufactured central station telephone exchange equipment as well as other products sold to the operating companies, which after 1984 had become competitors to their former parent. Also, a segment with high margins and high growth can command higher stock price multiples when its performance might be made less certain by less favorable prospects for the parent. The converse could be true as well.

Tracking stocks can also isolate subsidiaries with high profit and growth opportunities. Tracking stock subsidiaries can benefit from the strong financial position of the parent. Tracking stocks may be useful for companies with segments that share significant synergies. If a parent of a tracking stock company has losses, overall corporate taxes can be reduced. Since the parent continues to control the tracking stock subsidiary, potential conflicts of interest raise some concerns.

J. Changes in Ownership Structure

1. Leveraged Buyouts

The most complete form of ownership change is represented by taking a public company private through a leveraged buyout (LBO). When the former managers are the prime movers in the transaction, it is called a management buyout (MBO). The basic idea is to raise the necessary funds to purchase control from the existing public shareholders, using financing with a large percentage debt component, providing management with a high percentage of the remaining small equity base. A turnaround was usually involved in the sense that fundamental operating changes were made to increase profitability and value.

Highly leveraged transactions have been used prior to the 1980s, when LBOs became substantial in dollar volume. But the high degree of diversification activity that took place during the conglomerate merger movement of the 1960s resulted in many firms having segments that did not receive informed guidance by top management. During the 1980s, LBOs were one of the methods for unwinding the diversification of the 1960s.

Table 18.22 presents data on the value of LBO transactions in relation to total merger activity between 1982 and 1999. In the 1986–1989 period, LBOs represented over 20% of the total dollar value of completed mergers. While the $62 billion value of LBOs in 1999 was almost back to the $65.7 billion peak in 1989, the LBO percentage of total mergers was still only 4.4%.

As Table 18.22 suggests, LBOs went through three distinct periods. The first period was from 1982–1989, when strong growth occurred. Many segments were being shed by companies with valuations in the range of three to five times EBITDA. With new management or previous management energized and motivated by their substantial equity positions, efficiency and profitability were improved. These LBOs were mainly in consumer nondurable goods industries with stable cash flows, such as food and retailing. Within three to four years, debt was reduced from as high as 90% of total capitalization from the stable cash flows. With profitability restored and attractive growth opportunities, the company could be sold in a secondary public offering (SIPO). The data show that a substantial portion of the proceeds received by the company were used to further reduce

Table 18.22 Value of LBO Transactions ($ Billions)

Year	Total Value Offered All M&As	Leveraged Buyouts	% of Total Mergers
1982	53.8	3.5	6.5
1983	73.1	4.5	6.2
1984	122.2	18.7	15.3
1985	179.8	19.7	11.0
1986	173.1	45.2	26.1
1987	163.7	36.2	22.1
1988	246.9	47.0	19.0
1989	221.1	65.7	29.7
1990	108.2	15.2	14.1
1991	71.2	7.0	9.8
1992	96.7	9.6	9.9
1993	176.4	11.0	6.2
1994	226.7	13.0	5.7
1995	356.0	20.0	5.6
1996	495.0	29.0	5.9
1997	657.1	28.7	4.4
1998	1,191.9	41.0	3.4
1999	1,425.9	62.0	4.3
2000	1,325.7	51.5	3.9
2001	699.4	18.6	2.7
Yearly Averages			
1982–1985	107.2	11.6	9.7
1986–1989	201.2	48.5	24.2
1990–1992	92.0	10.6	11.3
1993–1995	253.0	14.7	5.9
1996–2000	1,019.1	42.4	4.4
2001	699.4	18.6	2.7

Source: Mergers & Acquisitions Almanac Issues, Mergerstat Review, 2002.

the debt to almost normal industry standards. The value of shares held by management had greatly increased in value. While debt was substantial in the initial LBO financing and provided valuable tax shields to the company, the main motivation was to provide management with the incentives from owning a substantial portion of the relatively small equity base. Management ownership of equity typically moved from 1–2% to as high as 15–20%.

Debt also played a significant role in the initial stage of taking the company private. Often a commercial bank or insurance company provided the senior debt financing, often secured. The other sources between common equity and the senior debt were called mezzanine financing, consisting of senior unsecured debt, subordinated debt, and preferred stock. Sometimes the mezzanine financing required some options to buy equity as compensation for their junior position.

LBO activity was highly successful during this initial period from 1982 to 1989. The numerous empirical studies agreed in finding annual returns above 25%, with many even higher. The reasons for the success in the early stages of the LBO movement can be enumerated. First, segments were available at relatively low valuation multiples. Second, the firms and segments taken over in LBOs and MBOs were not performing up to their potentials. Third, managers were given substantial equity stakes in entities whose performance could be measured and evaluated as independent entities. Fourth, investors and managers benefited from harvesting the gains in secondary public offerings or sales to public companies.

The successes during this initial period attracted a substantial flow of capital into the activity. The large pool of funds from both operating firms as strategic buyers as well as financial buyers reached several hundred billions. Well-known financial buyers with capital to invest of over $1 billion included Kohlberg, Kravis, & Roberts; Morgan Stanley Capital Partners; E. M. Warburg, Pincus & Company; Clayton, Dubilier, & Rice; Thomas H. Lee Company; GS Capital Venture Partners; The Blackstone Group; Forstmann Little & Company; and Hicks, Muse, Tate, & Furst. But there were many others as well, so that the total funds available for LBOs far exceeded the opportunities for profitable investments. This competition pushed valuation multiples from the three to five times EBITDA to over ten and higher; often the difference between the winning bid and others was exceedingly high. In addition, the unwinding of the diversification activities of the 1960s sharply reduced the opportunities. The demise of the dominant investment banking firm in LBOs, Drexel Burnham Lambert, was disruptive. New federal legislation required that investments in below-investment-grade debt securities (junk bonds) by financial institutions such as the savings and loan companies had to be marked down to market. This aggravated the already adverse developments in the junk bond market. As shown in Table 18.22, leveraged buyout activity in 1991 and 1992 dropped below $10 billion a year.

The third period of LBO activity began after 1992. The economy experienced sustained economic growth, stock prices moved continuously higher, and interest rate levels were favorable. This more favorable economic environment helped stimulate the resurgence in LBOs. Innovative approaches were developed by LBO sponsor companies and financial buyers. LBOs were applied increasingly beyond industries with stable earnings to high-growth technology-driven industries.

2. Leveraged Recapitalizations

Substantial ownership changes also take place in leveraged recapitalizations. Historically, leveraged recapitalizations substituted for the acquisition of a company that would create substantial goodwill whose write-off would burden reported future earnings. A typical pattern was to issue a large amount of debt whose proceeds are used to pay a large cash dividend to existing stockholders. The cash dividend may be in excess of the preactivity market price of the stock. Essentially, a substantial stock buyback has taken place for the shareholders. The result is a highly leveraged company with a debt-to-equity ratio as high as five to one, whose equity shares sell at a small fraction of their preactivity level. These shares are referred to as "stubs." Existing management may take additional shares of common stock in lieu of the cash dividend payments, substantially increasing their ownership fraction. Thus, the ownership control has been substantially changed without creating the requirement of future goodwill write-offs.

Another variation is for a financial buyer to become the majority owner. As before, the target company issues a large amount of debt, whose proceeds are used to pay a cash dividend to existing shareholders or used in a stock buyback program. The financial buyer acquires sufficient shares to own 80%, with 20% owned by the original shareholders. The deal can be structured so that, from an accounting standpoint, the transaction is a recapitalization of the target, with no goodwill at the target level. If the financial buyer uses a new shell company as an acquisition vehicle, it may record the goodwill.

In both of the examples described above, the transaction can avoid the creation of goodwill that will reduce the reported earnings of the subject company. So the leveraged recapitalization is an alternative to an outright acquisition or merger as a method of changing ownership control.

3. Dual-Class Recapitalizations

In dual-class recapitalizations (DCRs), firms create a second class of common stock with inferior voting rights and higher dividend payments. An illustrative DCR creates class A shares with one vote per share, but with a higher dividend rate. The class B shares have a lower dividend rate, but can cast multiple votes, as high as 10 per share. As a result of a DCR, the control group will own about 60% of the common stock voting rights, but have a claim of only about 25% of the dividends paid. Often the control group represents founding families or their descendants with two or more of the top executives related by either blood or marriage.

The main reason for DCRs is for top management to maintain control so that long-term programs can be pursued. The pressure to show improving results quarter by quarter is reduced. If the operations of the firm are relatively complicated, it would be especially difficult to evaluate managerial performance. Another reason is that managers develop firm-specific capabilities. The managers would be subject to the risk that outside shareholders would support an acquisition offer before the longer-term plans have come to fruition. Shareholder approval is required for a DCR. Apparently, the higher dividend and the prospect of higher future stock values result in shareholder approval.

Empirical studies support the value-increasing motives of DCRs. Compared with LBO firms, DCRs achieve higher growth rates in sales and number of employees. The DCRs have higher ratios of R&D expenditures to sales. They also use a higher percentage of their cash flows for capital expenditures than the LBO firms. Dual-class firms have lower leverage ratios and do not change them as a consequence of the recap. Also a large proportion of the dual-class firms sell more equity following the recap. On balance it appears that the superior voting shares are used by the control group to improve firm performance.

K. ℳerger Defenses

Along with the economic, financial, and technological forces that stimulated takeovers and restructuring, counterforces developed in the form of merger defenses. The many types of merger defenses may be grouped into five categories: (1) defensive restructuring, (2) poison pills, (3) poison puts, (4) antitakeover amendments, and (5) golden parachutes.

The first major form is defensive restructuring of six types. One is a scorched earth policy by incurring large debt and selling off attractive segments of the company and using the newly acquired funds to declare a large dividend to existing shareholders. Two involves selling off the crown jewels by disposing of those segments of the business in which the bidder is most interested. Three is to consolidate a voting block allied with target management. This may involve dilution of the bidder's voting percentage by issuing substantial new equity. Four is share repurchase without management sale. This simultaneously increases leverage and increases the equity position of management, which may enable management to have enough shares to defeat a takeover bid. Five is to issue new securities to parties friendly to management. Six is to create barriers specific to the bidder. For example, antitrust suits may be filed against the bidder, or the firm may purchase assets or other firms that will create antitrust issues for the bidder.

A second major type of defense against takeovers is the use of poison pills. Poison pills are warrants issued to existing shareholders that give them the right to purchase surviving firm securities at very low prices in the event of a merger. Typical triggering events are the acquisition of 10–20% of the firm's shares or a tender offer for 20–30% or more of the firm's shares. The aim of poison pills is to seriously impair the control and wealth position of the bidding firm. The risk and expense of a poison pill challenge may induce bidders to make offers conditional on the withdrawal of the poison pill. At a minimum the poison pill gives incumbent management considerable bargaining power since it can also set aside the warrants if, for example, a very attractive price is offered to the shareholders and perhaps other inducements offered to existing management.

A third type of merger defense, poison puts, were stimulated by the decline in bond values as a result of the RJR-Nabisco leveraged buyout in December 1988. It permits the bondholders to put (sell) the bonds to the issuer corporation or its successor at par or at par plus some premium.

A fourth group of merger defenses consists of many types of antitakeover amendments. Fair price provisions provide that all shareholders must receive a uniform, fair price. This is aimed as a defense against two-tier offers. Supermajority amendments require 67–80% (or more) shareholder approval for a change of control. A staggered or classified board of directors may be used to delay the effective transfer of control. For example, the provision may require that only one third of the board is elected each year. Another type of charter amendment is to provide for reincorporation in a state with laws more protective against takeovers. Or the charter amendment may provide for the creation of a new class of securities (often privately placed) whose approval is required for takeover. In addition, lock-in amendments may be enacted to make it difficult to void the previously passed antitakeover amendments. While the enactment of antitakeover amendments typically is associated with negative impacts on stock prices, shareholders have approved 90% of proposed amendments. The passage of antitakeover amendments may also sometimes have positive effects on stock prices.

The fifth major type of merger defense is golden parachutes. Golden parachutes are separation provisions of an employment contract that provide for payments to managers under a change-of-control clause. Usually a lump sum payment is involved. The rationale is to help reduce the conflict of interest between shareholders and managers in change-of-control situations. While the dollar amounts are large, the cost in most cases is less than 1% of the total takeover value. Recent changes in tax laws have limited tax deductions to the corporation for golden parachute payments and have imposed penalties upon the recipient. A theoretical argument for golden parachutes is that they encourage managers to make firm-specific investments of their human capital and encourage them to take the longer-term view for the corporation.

The effect on shareholder returns of the use of takeover defenses is relatively small. Takeover defenses can be grouped on the basis of whether or not shareholder approval is required. Anti-takeover charter amendments (fair-price, classified board of directors, supermajority voting) require shareholder approval. The earlier studies indicated no significant effect on shareholder wealth. Later studies indicate negative wealth effects of about 1%. A wide range of shareholder rights plans such as poison pills do not require shareholder approval. Earlier studies found negative event returns of about 3%. Later studies found that the negative event effects are less than 1%.

Clearly, the measured initial impact of announcement of takeover defenses is relatively small. We believe this is because a number of counterforces are operating. When a firm gets on a "rumor list" as a possible takeover target, the potential premium or future improvements might stimulate positive stock price reactions. But this is attenuated by the fractional probability that an offer will actually be made. A further attenuation effect is the probability that some antitakeover measure will be adopted in an effort to block the takeover. There is some probability factor that the antitakeover measure will be adopted and another probability of the extent to which it will be effective. These joint probabilities will then need to be multiplied times the loss or the potential gain or improvement from the takeover.

If the antitakeover measure is effective, a new set of probabilities must be considered. In the years subsequent to the initial takeover rumor and the defenses thereby stimulated, will internal restructuring efforts by the target succeed? Or will the market for corporate control produce other bidders in the ultimate takeover of the target? Given all the possibilities and their associated probability factors, it appears that attenuation effects and offsetting influences are operating. The net result is relatively small event return impacts from the announcement of plans for the adoption or elimination of antitakeover measures.

L. *A*ccounting Aspects

The Financial Accounting Standards Board (FASB) issued two statements in June 2001 that made fundamental changes in accounting for mergers and acquisitions. Statement of Financial Accounting Standards No. 141 on Business Combinations abolishes the use of the pooling of interest method (pooling method). FASB No. 141 requires that all business combinations be accounted for by a single method—the purchase method. Statement of Financial Accounting Standards No. 142 on Goodwill and Other Intangible Assets sets forth procedures for accounting for acquired goodwill and other intangible assets.

1. Pooling of Interests Accounting

Since the pooling method was relatively simple, we provide a brief explanation to facilitate understanding of the issues involved. We illustrate the method by the Dow Chemical/Union Carbide merger announced August 4, 1999. Table 18.23 presents a summary of the pro forma balance sheet taken from the merger proxy statement. Pooling of interests accounting was used. All asset and liability items of the two companies are added. In Table 18.23, total assets of the combined firm pro forma are the addition of the total assets of the individual firms, and similarly for total liabilities. For stockholders' equity, the common stock of the acquired firm is eliminated by a debit to the common stock account of Union Carbide. Union Carbide had 133 million shares outstanding premerger. The terms of the deal gave 0.537 shares of Dow for 1 share of Union Carbide. Hence, 71 million shares of Dow were issued to Union Carbide shareholders. The par value of the Dow common stock was $2.50. So a total of $177 million par value was paid to Union Carbide. This is the credit entry. A balancing debit of $20 million is made to the paid-in capital account, representing a "plug" entry.

Table 18.23 Completed Pro Forma Balance Sheet ($ Millions)
Dow Chemical (DOW)/Union Carbide (UK)

	Dow Chemical	Union Carbide	Pro Forma Adjustments	Combined Pro Forma
Total assets	$23,105	$7,465		$30,570
Total liabilities	$15,411	$5,024		$20,435
Stockholders' equity:				
Common stock (Dow par value = $2.50)	818	157	(157)[1]	818
Additional paid-in capital	891	114	(20)[3]	985
Retained earnings	13,242	3,404		16,646
Unearned employee compensation—ESOP and other equity adjustments		(58)		(58)
Accumulated other comprehensive loss	(300)	(157)		(457)
Treasury stock, at cost	(6,957)	(1,019)	177[2]	(7,799)
Net stockholders' equity	7,694	2,441		10,135
Total liabilities and stockholders' equity	$23,105	$7,465		$30,570

Adjustments:

1. Debt of $157 million to eliminate Union Carbide common stock.
2. Credit of $177 million for Dow stock being given to Union Carbide stockholders (71 million UK shares * $2.50 par Dow stock = $177 million).
3. Balancing entry of $20 million debt to additional paid-in capital.

If the par value paid by the acquirer were less than the debit to eliminate the common stock of the acquired firm, the plug entry would have been a credit to the paid-in capital account.

One of the attractions of the pooling method was that no goodwill had to be recorded and then written off against reported net income. Twelve conditions had to be met to qualify for pooling of interests accounting. In Statement No. 141, FASB noted that the "twelve criteria did not distinguish economic dissimilar transactions" resulting in accounting reports that were not comparable. In addition, the pooling method simply added historical numbers without reflecting the current realities that had been revealed by a marketplace transaction.

2. Purchase Accounting

We illustrate the purchase method by use of the pro forma accounting statements contained in the proxy to shareholders in connection with the AOL/Time Warner (TWX) transaction. The merger was announced on January 10, 2000. The main purchase accounting adjustment entries were

Debit ($ Billion)	
TWX shareholders' book equity	$10.0
Other miscellaneous adjustments, net	(30.9)
Goodwill and other intangibles	174.0
Total pro forma debit adjustments	$153.1

Credit (\$ Billion)	
AOL common stock at par issued to pay for TWX	\$0.1
Addition to AOL paid in capital	153.0
Total pro forma credit adjustments	\$153.1

Before the merger announcement, AOL had 2.6 billion shares outstanding, trading at \$72.88 per share. TWX had 1.4 billion shares outstanding, trading at \$64.75. AOL exchanged 1.5 of its shares for each TWX share, paying a total of 2.1 billion shares. Multiplying this amount times the AOL share price of \$72.88 gives a market value paid of \$153.1 billion, which needs to be allocated.

The basic entries for purchase accounting are the following: Eliminate TWX book equity by a debit of \$10 billion. Next, miscellaneous adjustments of a negative debit of \$30.9 billion were made. The total increase in goodwill is \$174 billion. So the sum of the pro forma debit adjustments equals the market value of AOL stock (\$153.1 billion) paid for TWX. We next consider the credits. The AOL common stock at par issued to pay for the purchase of TWX is a credit of \$0.1 billion (rounded). This is deducted from the amount paid for TWX to obtain \$153.1 billion, which becomes the addition to AOL paid in capital.

The effects on the asset structures of AOL and TWX are shown in Table 18.24. Only 4% of AOL's assets were goodwill. For TWX the ratio of tangible assets to intangibles was slightly over 1. AOL paid \$153.1 billion for the Time Warner book equity of \$10.3 billion. So the goodwill account of the combined firm was greatly increased. As a consequence, the ratio of tangible assets to total assets in the combined company dropped to about 15%.

The effects on leverage are summarized in Table 18.25. Before the transaction, AOL had only about \$68 liabilities for every \$100 of shareholders' equity. For TWX, liabilities were \$389 to \$100. With the huge increase in the equity of the combined firm as a consequence of the \$109.32 per share (\$72.88 × 1.5) paid for TWX in relation to the penny per share par value of the AOL shares used in payment, the paid-in capital account of the combined company increased by a huge amount.

On January 30, 2003, AOL Time Warner announced its financial results for its fiscal year ended December 31, 2002. From the financial statements we are able to extend the results in Tables 18.24 and 18.25. In Tables 18.26 and 18.27, we see that the total assets had declined from \$235 billion to \$209 billion by December 31, 2001. By December 31, 2002, total assets had further declined to \$115 billion. Tangible assets remained virtually the same. But goodwill and other intangibles had declined by \$91.2 billion, recognizing their impairment as required by FASB No. 142. AOL Time Warner adopted FASB No. 142 effective January 1, 2002. AOL Time Warner had announced

Table 18.24 Asset Structure Changes in AOL and TWX (\$ Millions)

	Premerger				Pro Forma Postmerger	
	AOL		TWX		Combined	
	Amount	%	Amount	%	Amount	%
Total assets	\$10,789	100.0	\$50,213	100.0	\$235,388	100.0
Less goodwill + other intangibles	\$432	4.0	\$24,507	48.8	\$199,325	84.7
Tangible assets	\$10,357	96.0	\$25,706	51.2	\$36,063	15.3

Table 18.25 Leverage Changes in the AOL and TWX Merger ($ Millions)

	Premerger				Pro Forma Postmerger Combined	
	AOL		TWX			
	Amount	%	Amount	%	Amount	%
Total liabilities	$4,370	40.5	$39,949	79.6	$79,095	33.6
Shareholders' equity	$6,419	59.5	$10,264	20.4	$156,293	66.4
Total claims	$10,789	100.0	$50,213	100.0	$235,388	100.0
Liabilities/equity		68.1		389.2		50.6

Table 18.26 Asset Structure Changes in AOL and TWX ($ Millions)

	Premerger				Postmerger					
					Pro Forma		Actual			
	AOL		TWX		(6/23/00)		(12/31/01)		(12/31/02)	
	Amount	%	Amount	%	Amount	%	Amount	%	Amount	%
Total assets	$10,789	100.0	$50,213	100.0	$235,388	100.0	$208,504	100.0	$115,450	100.0
Less goodwill + other intangibles	$432	4.0	$24,507	48.8	$199,325	84.7	$172,417	82.7	$81,192	70.3
Tangible assets	$10,357	96.0	$25,706	51.2	$36,063	15.3	$36,087	17.3	$34,258	29.7

Table 18.27 Leverage Changes in the AOL and TWX Merger ($ Millions)

	Premerger				Postmerger					
					Pro Forma		Actual			
	AOL		TWX		(6/23/00)		(12/31/01)		(12/31/02)	
	Amount	%	Amount	%	Amount	%	Amount	%	Amount	%
Total liabilities	$4,370	40.5	$39,949	79.6	$79,095	33.6	$56,477	27.1	$62,633	54.3
Shareholders' equity	$6,419	59.5	$10,264	20.4	$156,293	66.4	$152,027	72.9	$52,817	45.7
Total claims	$10,789	100.0	$50,213	100.0	$235,388	100.0	$208,504	100.0	$115,450	100.0
Liabilities/equity		68.1		389.2		50.6		37.1		118.6

accounting changes including goodwill impairment of $54.2 billion during the first quarter of fiscal 2002 in addition to the fourth quarter impairment of $44.7 billion, a total for the year of $98.9 billion. Other adjustments of a positive $7.7 billion reconciles to the $91.2 billion net change.

We distinguish between the types of amortization to clarify the impairment rules. This example is based on the types of amortization described in Appendix C of FASB No. 141. Alpha acquired Beta on June 30, 20XX. The purchase price was $9.4 billion. Tangible assets acquired net of debt were $2.3 billion. The $7.1 billion was allocated as follows: to goodwill $2.2 billion, to intangible assets not subject to amortization $1.4 billion (registered trademarks), $1.0 billion to research and development in process, and the remaining $2.5 billion of acquired intangible assets were to be amortized (patents and computer software) over their weighted average useful life. The R&D in process can be immediately written off, included in general and administrative expenses. In the AOL Time Warner balance sheets, the three remaining categories are shown. Between December 31, 2001, and December 31, 2002, intangible assets subject to amortization decreased from $7.3 to $7.1 billion. Intangible assets not subject to amortization decreased from $37.7 to $37.1 billion. Goodwill decreased from $127.4 to $37.0 billion—a substantial impairment.

In the income statement the amortization of goodwill and other intangible assets is shown as a deduction before operating income. The impairment of goodwill and other intangibles is also a deduction before operating income. The reported net income before income taxes, discontinued operations, and accounting changes was a negative $44.5 billion. Adding the cumulative effect of the accounting changes, the reported net income of AOL Time Warner was a $98.7 billion loss.

In the statement of cash flows the accounting changes plus impairment charges of $99.7 billion are added back to net income; the other items representing depreciation and amortization plus changes in operating assets and liabilities result in reported cash provided by operations of a plus $7.0 billion.

The AOL Time Warner example illustrates the application of the new accounting rules set forth in FASB No. 141 and 142. It also illustrates the relationships between income statements, balance sheets, and cash flow statements. The example also demonstrates that the use of purchase accounting has some strange results. The higher the ratio of the price paid to the book equity acquired, the greater the degree to which a high book-leverage company will become a lower book-leverage company.

The rules for measuring impairment set forth in FASB No. 142 are equivalent to standard valuation methods. The emphasis is on comparable transactions and applications of discounted cash flow methodologies.

3. Earnings Dilution

The board of directors always asks how an acquisition will affect the company's earnings per share. In particular, they want to avoid earnings dilution. Occasionally, when earnings dilution is judged to be too large, the board rejects the deal, even when the overall economics looks good.

Before launching into a discourse about why earnings dilution is irrelevant, let us first understand what it is and how it is calculated.

Table 18.28 shows the calculation of the new earnings per share. Suppose that the acquirer has $100 million of net income and the target has $40 million, and that their market values are $1 billion and $800 million, respectively. The larger company has 10 million shares outstanding, and the smaller company has 5 million. Therefore their EPS numbers, premerger, were $10.00 per share for the acquirer and $8 for the target; their stock prices are $100 and $160, respectively. If after-tax synergies amount to $10 million, and the acquirer pays $800 million plus a $40 million premium, which it borrows at 10% interest (after-tax), the net income of the combined

Table 18.28 How to Calculate Earnings Dilution

Forecast Earnings of New Entity	New Number of Shares of Acquirer
Net income of acquirer	
+ net income of target	Shares of acquirer
+ after-tax revenue and cost synergies	+ additional shares issued
− after-tax deal and integration costs	= new total shares of acquirer
− after-tax goodwill amortization	
− additional after-tax interest expense	
= net income of combined company	

$$\text{New EPS} = \frac{\text{net income of the combined company}}{\text{new total shares}}$$

company will be $65 million.[4] When divided by 10 million shares, EPS turns out to decrease from $10.00 to $6.50 and the deal is dilutive. Had the acquirer decided to pay for the deal by issuing new shares instead of borrowing to pay cash, it would have had to issue 8.4 million additional shares, pay $4 million of deal costs after-taxes, and its new net income would be $145 million. Its EPS would decline from $10.00 to $7.88 and the deal would be dilutive, as shown in Table 18.29.

Next suppose the smaller company pays the $100 million plus the $40 million premium to buy the big company. If it borrowed to pay cash, the net income of the combined company would be $45. When divided by the 5 million shares of the small company, EPS goes from $8.00 to $9.00. If the smaller company issues an additional 130 million shares (to pay $1,040 million in stock for A), the combined earnings will be $144 million and there will be 135 million shares; therefore EPS will be $1.07—making the deal dilutive. The deal is accretive only if SmallCo buys BigCo with cash. Nevertheless, the market cap of the combined company is the same regardless of approach. This example demonstrates that earnings accretion or dilution has nothing to do with the economics of the deal.

---

[4]

	BigCo buys SmallCo		SmallCo buys BigCo	
Calculation of net income	Cash	Stock	Cash	Stock
NI of BigCo	100	100	100	100
+ NI of SmallCo	40	40	40	40
+ after-tax synergies	10	10	10	10
− transactions costs	0	−4	0	−5
− increase in interest (AT)	−84	0	−104	0
− increase in goodwill*	−1	−1	−1	−1
= combined net income	65	145	45	144
Shares outstanding	10	18.4	5	135

* Assumes 40-year write-off of $40 million

Table 18.29 Earnings per Share Accretion and Dilution (EPS before the deal: BigCo $10 and SmallCo $8) ($ Millions)

	Combined Market Cap	Net Income	Number of Shares	EPS	P/E	P/Share
If BigCo acquires SmallCo with cash	$2,200	$ 65	10	6.50	33.85	$220.00
with stock	2,200	145	18.4	7.88	15.17	119.57
If SmallCo acquires BigCo with cash	2,200	45	5	9.00	48.89	440.00
with stock	2,200	144	135	1.07	15.23	16.30

Table 18.30 70 Largest Deals, 1995–96

Analyst Reaction	No. of Stocks	Dilutive	Neutral	Accretive
Positively perceived	20	40%	10%	50%
Immaterial reaction	24	—	—	—
Negatively perceived	26	62%	19%	19%
	70			

We looked at the 20 largest deals in the United States in 1995 and 1996 and built a simple 3×3 table. The market reaction to the announcement of a deal was defined as positive if the increase in total return to shareholders (adjusted by subtracting the market effect) was positive 1.5% or greater on the day after the announcement than the day before. The deal was defined as accretive if there was an increase in analyst expectations (before restructuring charges) for the following fiscal year. The results are shown in Table 18.30. At best there is only a weak correlation between earnings dilution and a negative market perception of the deal. Forty percent of the deals that were viewed favorably by the market were dilutive.

M. *C*orporate Governance

As the economy began to move into a recession in early 2000, stock prices declined. The drop in stock prices was aggravated by disclosures of unethical behavior in a number of companies. Illustrative examples are set forth in Table 18.31. In addition to outright fraud, executive self-dealing was criticized. *Fortune* magazine exposed these practices in its article of September 2, 2002, entitled, "You Bought. They Sold." They listed 26 companies whose stock price declined 75% or more from their peak during the period January 1999 through May 2002 in which the top executives "walked away" with $66 billion.

Earlier examples of fraud were studied by Agrawal, Jaffe, and Karpoff [1999]. They identified 103 firms accused of fraud from the Wall Street Journal Index from 1981 to 1992. They also developed 103 matched control firms with the same two-digit Compustat primary SIC code, with net sales close to the fraud firm. The firms in the fraud sample have significantly more frauds than the control group in the two years before and two years after the year of the fraud event keyed upon this study. The operating performance changes around the fraud events were not statistically significant between the two groups.

Table 18.31 Forms of Corporate Fraud

Company Name	Type of Fraud
Sunbeam	Goods shipped on consignment were included in sales.
Enron	1. Special-purpose entities (SPEs) used to understate liabilities and to book artificial profits for both the SPEs and Enron. 2. Contracts extending over multiple years were booked in the first year, understanding costs and overstating profits.
Dynegy	Engaged in cross-selling with Enron and others at artificially high prices to manipulate energy prices and to book artificial profits for each.
WorldCom	1. Treated operating expenses as capital expenses. 2. Large loans to top executives were not repaid.
Adelphia	1. Value of cable companies based on number of customers, so signed contracts with imaginary customers—inflated share prices. 2. Top executives looted the company.
Tyco	1. Manipulated accounting to show high profits. 2. Multiple acquisitions have differentially higher P/E ratios to create artificial earnings growth. 3. Unapproved loans to executives and unapproved cancelations.
ImClone	Insider trading days before public information that one of its major drugs would not receive FDA approval.

With respect to managerial turnover, they "find no evidence that the revelation of fraud leads to a subsequent change in leadership structure," as defined by the single top executive—the CEO and chairman are the same individual. But turnover is also measured for persons holding the three top positions of chairman, CEO, and president. In year -1 relative to the keyed fraud, an average of 1.57 individuals hold these top positions among the fraud firms; 1.61 for the control firms. Higher turnover occurs for the fraud sample mainly in years $+2$ and $+3$, consistent with early studies that managerial turnover and takeovers lag poor firm performance. During the year of the keyed fraud and the three years following, the fraud firms reduced their board size slightly, decreasing both inside and outside directors; the control firms increased their outside board representation slightly but not significantly. These results are surprising since fraud would surely injure the reputation of the firm. The relatively modest impacts of fraud reported in this study may reflect the favorable economic and financial characteristics of the 1981–1992 period of the study.

Book-length treatments of corporate fraud have also been published. Howard Schilit published the first edition of his book entitled *Financial Shenanigans* in 1993. He established a Center for Financial Research and Analysis (CFRA) to detect early warning signs of operating problems or accounting "anomalies." In his 2002 edition, he lists 30 techniques of financial shenanigans, defined as practices that intentionally distort a company's reported financial performance or condition. Examples of these practices for public companies are presented. A similar book with many other examples was published by Mulford and Comiskey [2002].

These disclosures caused widespread indignation and resulted in the passage of the Sarbanes-Oxley Act (SOA) on July 30, 2002. The SOA covers 11 main areas:

1. PCAOB. Title 1 provides for the establishment of the Public Company Accounting Oversight Board (PCAOB). The PCAOB is not an agency of the U.S. government. It is a private nonprofit corporation subject to SEC regulation and oversight. The PCAOB is responsible for overseeing the auditing of public companies and for establishing standards for audit reports. Every auditing firm must be registered with the PCAOB. There are also greater responsibilities for company audit committees. Each company is required to report that its audit committee is comprised of at least one member who is a financial expert as defined by the SEC.

2. Auditor independence. Title 2 outlines the requirements for auditor independence. Audit firms are prohibited from providing nonaudit services such as consulting. Audit partner rotation is required every five years. Auditor reports should be made to audit committees rather than management. The auditing firm shall have not employed an accounting or financial officer of the audited company during the one-year period preceding the initiation of an audit.

3. Certification. The CEO and CFO must certify, as to each 10-K and 10-Q, that the report complies with SEC regulations and fairly presents the financial position of the company (Section 906). It is a crime punishable by up to $1 million and up to 10 years in prison to give the certification knowing that it is false, and a crime punishable by up to $5 million and up to 20 years in prison to willingly give the certification knowing that it is false.

4. Disclosure. Each annual and quarterly report filed with the SEC is required to disclose all material off-balance-sheet transactions. Pro forma financial statements should not be untrue or misleading. The filing deadline for the occurrence of a disclosable event is shortened to two days.

5. Insider trading. Insider trading in their company's securities is considered a disclosable event to be reported on a Form 4 within two days. This supersedes the previous rule of the 10th day of the month following the transaction. Form 4 is to be filed electronically. During any blackout period imposed under a 401(k) or other profit sharing or retirement plans, insiders are prohibited from trading any equity securities of the company.

6. Conflicts of interest. Personal loans to officers and directors by corporations are prohibited. To improve the objectivity of research and to provide investors with reliable information, new rules should be reasonably designed to address conflicts of interest that can arise when security analysts recommend equity securities.

7. Professional responsibility. New SEC rules will establish minimum standards for professional conduct of attorneys who practice before the SEC. The rules will require that an attorney report evidence of securities law violations to the company's CEO or chief legal officer.

8. Studies and reports. A wide range of GAO and commission studies shall be conducted.

9. Fraud accountability. Destruction, alteration, or falsification of records in federal investigations and bankruptcy is criminal fraud. Debts are nondischargeable if incurred in violation of securities fraud laws. Protections for whistle blowers are strengthened.

10. Penalties. All audit or work papers shall be maintained for five years. Violators shall be fined or imprisoned for up to ten years. False certification or falsifying financial reports shall result in fines of up to $5 million and/or imprisonment of no more than 20 years. The statute of limitations for securities fraud is extended.

11. SEC powers. Any person who has violated the antifraud provision of federal securities law may be prohibited by the SEC from serving as an officer or director. During investigations of possible violations of the federal securities laws, the SEC may petition a court to freeze extraordinary payments by the company.

On August 16, 2002, the New York Stock Exchange (NYSE) submitted revised listing requirements to the SEC for final approval. The NYSE new listing rules go beyond the auditor independence requirements of SOA. The company must have an ongoing independent audit committee with at least three directors. The committee must have a written charter covering the committee's activities. Detailed specifications of board independence are set forth. Within two years the majority of the board of directors must be independent. Nonmanagement directors must meet periodically without management. Within two years boards must have wholly independent compensation and nominating committees. Shareholders must vote on all stock option plans. Each listed company is required to adopt a set of governance guidelines. With regard to directors, the guidelines must cover their qualifications, responsibilities, compensation, and access to management. Each listed company must disclose a code of business conduct and ethics.

The passage of SOA and the NYSE new listing requirements addressed the perceived deficiencies in corporate governance. The governance failures sought to be corrected can be inferred from their content. Board members were not independent. Audit committees did not have sufficient powers independent of management. Auditing firms had conflicts of interests resulting from providing nonaudit services such as consulting. The CEOs and CFOs used aggressive accounting and did not take responsibility for the accuracy or reliability of financial reports. Off-balance-sheet transactions were not adequately disclosed. Personal loans to officers and directors were not justified. The reports of security analysts were flawed by conflicts of interest. The professional conduct of attorneys did not meet minimum standards. Top management dominated the selection of directors who performed more as their cronies rather than representatives of shareholders. The unrestrained power of top executives enabled them to award themselves excessive bonuses and to engage in other forms of self-dealing. Whether the new laws and regulations will repair corporate governance deficiencies remains to be seen. Effective corporate governance in the United States remains a work in progress.

N. Corporate Governance in Germany and Japan

In contrast to dispersed shareholders in the United States, in Germany large shareholders, major banks and insurance companies, exercise control over large firms through equity ownerships (Franks and Mayer [1998]). In addition, they are major lenders. They have not been effective in performing their monitoring responsibilities (Bradley, Schipani, Sundaram, and Walsh [1999]; Logue and Seward [1999]). Small investors have limited participation in the stock market (Shleifer and Vishny [1997]).

Japan is characterized by *keiretsu*, in which a financial group has controlling investments in a collection of firms. Groups of firms also become linked through cross shareholdings (Kaplan [1994]). Participation by small investors is more widespread than in Germany.

In theory, the large equity positions of sophisticated owner-lenders should motivate effective monitoring. In a survey of corporate governance, *The Economist* (January 29, 1994) questioned the effectiveness of the German and Japanese corporate governance model. They cited studies with evidence that the owner-lenders became active only when their client firms severely under-performed. *The Economist* also argued that American corporate governance was improved by merger and takeover activity. An active market for corporate control makes governance ultimately market-based. But the examples of widespread corporate misconduct in the United States during 2000–2002 raise questions about its effectiveness.

Summary

This chapter views business finance decisions in the dynamic framework of M&A activities. It describes the major change forces behind the worldwide growth in M&A activities. Growth oppor-tunities can be enhanced by both internal and external strategies. Multiple growth strategies include M&As, joint ventures, alliances, partnerships, investments, licensing, and exclusive agreements.

Restructuring can also increase value. The main forms of restructuring are divestitures, equity carveouts, spin-offs, split-ups, and tracking stocks. Divestitures move resources to the higher-value users. Equity carveouts raise funds for the parent firm and prepare the way for the spin-offs to shareholders of the remaining shares. Split-ups use divestitures, spin-offs, and acquisitions to change the product-market configuration of firms. Tracking stocks result in separate reporting, but the parent continues to control the tracking segment.

Changed ownership structures include LBOs, leveraged recapitalizations, and dual-class re-capitalizations. LBOs take a company private, make initial heavy use of debt financing, usually involve an improvement in operations, and increase the ownership position of management to strengthen motivation. Leveraged recapitalizations use substantial debt increases to make large cash dividends or share repurchases; management ownership positions are increased. A financial buyer is often involved in LBOs and leveraged recaps. Dual-class recapitalizations provide top management with magnified voting rights and the other shareholders with larger claims to divi-dends to support programs with longer-term payoffs. Merger defenses can have diverse motives. Defenses may be used as a negotiating device to improve the deal terms for the target. Defenses may be used to seek to entrench underperforming management. Defenses may also be used be-cause shareholders and management judge that the long-run performance would be superior as an independent firm.

A summary of event studies is presented in Table 18.32. The wide range of M&As generally represents value increasing activities. The positive event returns shown are generally significant except for returns to acquiring firms, which are statistically not different from zero. All of the figures presented represent mean values, with wide dispersions.

The pooling method can no longer be used in accounting for business combinations. The purchase method credit adjustments begin with the par or stated value of equity issued by the buyer. The excess of purchase price over this credit is assigned to paid-in capital.

The debits in the purchase method include elimination of the seller book equity. The purchase market value less this debit is assigned to four types of accounts: purchased R&D, intangible assets subject to amortization, intangibles assets not subject to amortization, and goodwill. Purchased R&D can be written off in the year of the transaction. Intangible assets subject to amortization are amortized over their estimated lives. Intangible assets not subject to amortization do not have definite lives. This category and goodwill are subject to a periodic impairment review. If their carrying values are determined to be below their fair values, the difference is a deduction in the

Table 18.32 Results from Event Studies

M&A Form	Returns
A. Mergers	
1. Sellers	
a. Stock-for-stock	15–20%
b. Cash	25–30%
2. Buyers	1–2% *
B. Tender offers	
1. Sellers	35%
2. Buyers	1–2%*
C. Restructuring forms	
1. Divestitures	
a. Sellers	0.5–2.5%
b. Buyers	0.34%
2. Equity carveouts	2%
3. Spin-offs	2–4%
4. Tracking stocks	2–3%
D. Changes in ownership structure	
1. Leveraged buyouts	10–15%
2. Leveraged recapitalizations	3–5%
3. Dual class recapitalizations	1–2%
E. Control contests	
1. Proxy contests	5–7%
2. Antitakover actions	1–1.5%
F. Alliances and joint ventures	0.18–1.35%

* Not statistically significant.

income statement before income from continuing operations (FASB No. 142, Paragraph 43). The asset accounts are reduced by corresponding amounts (credits).

The valuation methodology of Chapter 14 can be applied to merger transactions. The DCF methodology is applied in both spreadsheet and formula examples. The process requires the formulation of judgments on the magnitude of the projected value drivers based on a business economic analysis of the industry and the position of the merged firm in it. The comparables methodology is illustrated by the use of market multiples and other supplementary techniques.

The chapter concludes with a discussion of corporate governance issues. It describes some fraudulent practices that led to the passage of new legislation and revised listing requirements in 2002. Dispersed ownership in the United States is contrasted with more concentrated ownership in Germany and Japan. None of the three countries has succeeded in achieving effective corporate governance systems.

PROBLEM SET

18.1 Differential P/E games: This is a problem that illustrates how the differential P/E games have been played by companies like Tyco. We first present the basic input data in Table Q18.1.

   (a) Complete the table.

   (b) Discuss the general implications suggested by this model.

Table Q18.1 Model of Differential P/E Ratios

	Acquirer (A)	Target (T)	Combined
1. Net income	$100	$100	$200
2. Number of shares	100	100	140
3. EPS (old)	$1	$1	$1.43
4. P/E ratio	50x	10x	50x
5. Price/share	$50	$10	$71.43 (new)
6. Total market value (old)	$5,000	$1,000	$6,000
7. Proportions (old)	83.3%	16.7%	
8. Terms paid (A for T)	0.4A/1	$20	
9. Premium to T		100%	
10. EPS (new)	_____	_____	
11. EPS (% change)	_____	_____	
12. Total market values (new)	_____	_____	_____
13. Market values (% change)	_____	_____	
14. Proportions (new)	_____	_____	

18.2 For this problem and the next, assume the following:

   (a) We are dealing with a world where there are no taxes.

   (b) The changes in the parameters affecting value are unanticipated; therefore redistribution effects are possible.

   (c) Firms A and B initially have the following parameters:

$$\sigma_A = \sigma_B = .2 \qquad \text{Instantaneous standard deviation}$$
$$T_A = T_B = 4 \text{ years} \qquad \text{Maturity of debt}$$
$$V_A = V_B = \$2,000 \qquad \text{Value of the firm, } V = B + S$$
$$R_f = .06 \qquad \text{Risk-free rate}$$
$$D_A = D_B = \$1,000 \qquad \text{Face value of debt}$$

The correlation between the cash flows of firms A and B is .6. If they merge, the resultant firm will be worth $4,000 = V_A + V_B$, but its new instantaneous variance will be

$$\sigma_{AB}^2 = \left(\frac{1}{2}\right)^2 \sigma_A^2 + 2\left(\frac{1}{2}\right)\left(\frac{1}{2}\right) r_{AB}\sigma_A\sigma_B + \left(\frac{1}{2}\right)^2 \sigma_B^2$$

$$= (.25)(.2)^2 + 2(.5)(.5)(.6)(.2)(.2) + (.25)(.25)^2$$

$$= .01 + .012 + .01 = .032$$

$$\sigma_{AB} = .179.$$

What will be the market value of debt and equity in the merged firm? If there were no other merger effects, would shareholders agree to the merger?

18.3 Given the results of Problem 18.2, suppose that the merged firm has 1,000 shares outstanding. Furthermore, suppose that the shareholders decide to issue $1,000 of new debt (which is not subordinate to outstanding debt), maturing in four years, and invest the proceeds in marketable securities, so that the new value of the merged firm is $5,000. What will be the new price per share? Assume the merged firm's instantaneous variance is unchanged by this investment.

18.4 You are given the following information:

	Firm A	Firm B
Value prior to merger	$1,000	$1,000
Face value of debt	500	500

In addition, the value of equity for firm A equals the value of equity for firm B, and the variance of returns for firms A and B are also equal. Using a risk-free rate of 8%, an appropriate time horizon of five years, and a variance for each firm of 10%, apply the OPM to calculate the value of equity of the two firms before the merger. Under the further assumption that the correlation between the percentage returns on firms A and B is zero, calculate the value of equity and the value of debt of the merged firm, using the OPM.

(a) How does the new market value of equity and debt of the merged firm compare with the sum of the values of equity and debt of the constituent firms that combined in the merger?

(b) How much additional debt would the merged firm have to issue to restore equity holders to their original position?

18.5 Empirical studies have established that the betas of conglomerate firms have been significantly above 1. What does this imply about diversification as a strong motive for conglomerate mergers?

18.6 Over a long period of time would you expect the risk-adjusted performance of conglomerate firms to be significantly different from the risk-adjusted performance of a broad market index? Explain.

18.7 Some argue that if two firms merge and thus decrease the probability of default on their debt, the stockholders are actually hurt, since they have assumed some of the risk previously borne by the bondholders. Why might nonowner managers of a firm be motivated to transfer risk from bondholders to stockholders in this manner?

18.8 Alternative strategies for growth: Six alternative strategies for growth are listed at the top of the columns in Table Q18.8. The seven rows are identified as strengths or benefits for each of the growth strategies.

(a) Fill in the blanks with your judgment of whether the benefits for the strategy are **High**, **Medium**, or **Low**.

(b) Compare the relative kinds of benefits for each of the growth strategies.

Table Q18.8 Multiple Strategies for Growth

	Internal	Merger	JV	Alliance	Licensing	Investment
Speed	_____	_____	_____	_____	_____	_____
Cost known	_____	_____	_____	_____	_____	_____
Add capabilities	_____	_____	_____	_____	_____	_____
Add products	_____	_____	_____	_____	_____	_____
Add markets	_____	_____	_____	_____	_____	_____
Avoid antitrust	_____	_____	_____	_____	_____	_____
Clarity	_____	_____	_____	_____	_____	_____

18.9 Asset restructuring: Four alternative asset restructuring strategies are listed at the top of the columns in Table Q18.9. The five rows are identified as strengths or benefits for each of the strategies.

(a) Fill in the blanks with your judgment of whether the benefits for the strategy are **High**, **Medium**, or **Low**.

(b) Compare the relative kinds of benefits for each of the strategies.

Table Q18.9 Asset Restructuring

	Divestiture	Equity Carveout	Spin-Off	Tracking Stock
Raise funds	_____	_____	_____	_____
Improve efficiency by focus	_____	_____	_____	_____
Measure performance better	_____	_____	_____	_____
Tie compensation to performance	_____	_____	_____	_____
Parent focus on core business	_____	_____	_____	_____

18.10 Changes in ownership structure: Five alternative changes in ownership structure strategies are listed at the top of the columns in Table Q18.10. The seven rows are identified as strengths or benefits for each of the strategies.

(a) Fill in the blanks with your judgment of whether the benefits for the strategy are **High**, **Medium**, or **Low**.

(b) Compare the relative kinds of benefits for each of the strategies.

Table Q18.10 Changes in Ownership Structure (Financial Engineering)

	Leveraged Recap	LBL or MBO	Share Repurchase	Proxy Contest
Infusion of new capital	_____	_____	_____	_____
Achieve a turnaround	_____	_____	_____	_____
Tax benefits	_____	_____	_____	_____
Takeover defense	_____	_____	_____	_____
Leverage is increased	_____	_____	_____	_____
Maintain control	_____	_____	_____	_____
Management incentives	_____	_____	_____	_____

18.11 The Watro Personal Computer Company is considering merger to achieve better growth and profitability. It has narrowed potential merger candidates to two firms. The Alber Company, a producer of PBXs, has a strong research department and a good record of internal profitability. The Saben Company operates a chain of variety stores and has a very high expansion rate. Data on all three firms are given below:

	Watro	Alber	Saben
Book value per share	$10	$10	$10
Number of shares (millions)	5	2.0	2.0
Debt/equity ratio	1	1	1
Internal profitability rate, r (after tax)	.09	.18	.15
Investment rate, K	1.0	1.0	1.5
Growth rate, $g = Kr$	.09	.18	.225
WACC	9%	11%	12%

Each firm pays 15% interest on its debt and has a 40% tax rate. Ten years of supernormal growth are forecast, followed by no growth.

    (a) What are the total assets of each firm?

    (b) What is each company's NOI if it earns its before-tax r on total assets?

    (c) What is the indicated market value of each firm?

    (d) Compare Watro's increase in value as a result of merger at market value with the cost of acquiring Alber or Saben if the combined firms have the following financial parameters:

	Watro-Alber	Watro-Saben
Net operating income	$30 million	$23 million
Internal profitability rate, r	20.09%	16%
WACC	11%	12%
Investment rate, K	1.1	1.0
Growth rate, $g = Kr$	.221	.16

18.12 The Jordan Corporation is a manufacturer of heavy-duty trucks. Because of a low internal profitability rate and lack of favorable investment opportunities in the existing line of business, Jordan is considering merger to achieve more favorable growth and profitability opportunities. It has made an extensive search of a large number of corporations and has narrowed the candidates to two firms. The Konrad Corporation is a manufacturer of materials handling equipment and is strong in research and marketing. It has had higher internal profitability than the other firm being considered and has had substantial investment opportunities.

The Loomis Company is a manufacturer of food and candles. It has a better profitability record than Konrad. Data on all three firms are given in Table Q18.12. Additional information on market parameters includes a risk-free rate of 6% and an expected return on the market, $E(R_m)$, of 11%. Each firm pays a 10% interest rate on its debt. The tax rate, τ_c, of each is 40%. Ten years is estimated for the duration of supernormal growth. Use the continuing value formula from Chapter 17 to estimate supernormal growth.

(a) Prepare the accounting balance sheets for the three firms.
(b) If each company earns the before-tax r on total assets in the current year, what is the net operating income for each company?

Table Q18.12

	Book Value per Share $	Price/Earnings Ratio, PE	Number of Shares (Millions)	Debt Ratio, B/S	β for Existing Leverage	Internal Profitability Rate, r	Investment Rate, K	Growth Rate, g
Jordan	20.00	6	4	1	1.4	.06	0.5	.03
Konrad	20.00	15	2	1	1.2	.12	1.5	.18
Loomis	20.00	12	2	1	1.5	.15	1.0	.15

(a) Given the indicated price/earnings ratios, what is the market price of the common stock for each company?
(b) What will be the immediate effects on the earnings per share of Jordan if it acquires Konrad or Loomis at their current market prices by the exchange of stock based on the current market prices of each of the companies?
(c) Compare Jordan's new beta and required return on equity if it merges with Konrad with the same parameters that would result from its merger with Loomis.
(d) Calculate the new required cost of capital for a Jordan-Konrad combination and for a Jordan-Loomis combination, respectively.
(e) Compare the increase in value of Jordan as a result of a merger at market values with the cost of acquiring either Konrad or Loomis if the combined firms have the following financial parameters:

	EBIT	r	WACC	K	g
Jordan/Konrad	32	.16	9.3%	1.0	.16
Jordan/Loomis	36	.13	10%	1.0	.13

REFERENCES

Agrawal, A., J. F. Jaffe, and J. M. Karpoff, "Management Turnover and Governance Changes Following the Revelation of Fraud," *Journal of Law and Economics*, April 1999, Vol. 42, 309–342.

Agrawal, A., J. F. Jaffe, and G. N. Mandelker, "The Post-Merger Performance of Acquiring Firms: A Re-Examination of an Anomaly," *Journal of Finance*, September 1992, Vol. 47, 1605–1622.

Alchian, A. A., "Corporate Management and Property Rights," in H. Manne, ed., *Economic Policy and the Regulation of Corporate Securities*. American Enterprise Institute, Washington D.C., 1969, 337–360.

Allen, J. A., "Capital Markets and Corporate Structure: The Equity Carve-Outs of Thermo Electron," *Journal of Financial Economics*, April 1998, Vol. 48, 99–124.

Allen, J. W., S. L. Lummer, J. J. McConnell, and D. K. Reed, "Can Takeover Losses Explain Spin-Off Gains?" *Journal of Financial and Quantitative Analysis*, 1995, Vol. 30, No. 4, 465–485.

Allen, J. W., and J. J. McConnell, "Equity Carve-Outs and Managerial Discretion," *Journal of Finance*, February 1998, Vol. 53, 163–186.

Alli, K., G. G. Ramirez, and K. K. Yung, "Withdrawn Spin-Offs: An Empirical Analysis," *Journal of Financial Research*, 2001, Vol. 24, No. 4, 603–616.

Andrade, G., M. Mitchell, and E. Stafford, "New Evidence and Perspectives on Mergers," *Journal of Economic Perspectives*, Spring 2001, Vol. 15, 103–120.

Anslinger, P. L., and T. E. Copeland, "Growth through Acquisitions: A Fresh Look," *Harvard Business Review*, January/February 1996, Vol. 74, 126–135.

Arrow, K. J., "Vertical Integration and Communication," *Bell Journal of Economics*, 1975, Vol. 6, 173–183.

Asquith, P., "Merger Bids, Uncertainty, and Stockholder Returns," *Journal of Financial Economics*, 1983, Vol. 11, No. 1, 51–83.

Asquith, P., and E. H. Kim, "The Impact of Merger Bids on the Participating Firms' Security Holders," *Journal of Finance*, 1982, Vol. 37, 1209–1228.

Berger, P. G., and E. Ofek, "Diversification's Effect on Firm Value," *Journal of Financial Economics*, 1995, Vol. 37, 39–65.

Berkovitch, E., and M. P. Narayanan, "Motives for Takeovers: an Empirical Investigation," *Journal of Financial and Quantitative Analysis*, September 1993, Vol. 28, 347–362.

Best, R. W., R. J. Best, and A. M. Agapos, "Earnings Forecasts and the Information Contained in Spinoff Announcements," *Financial Review*, August 1998, Vol. 33, 53–68.

Billett, M. T., and D. C. Mauer, "Diversification and the Value of Internal Capital Markets: The Case of Tracking Stock," *Journal of Banking and Finance*, September 2000, Vol. 24, 1457–1490.

Black, F., M. Jensen, and M. Scholes, "The Capital Asset Pricing Model: Some Empirical Tests," in M. Jensen, ed., *Studies in the Theory of Capital Markets*. Praeger, New York, 1972.

Bradley, M., "Interfirm Tender Offers and the Market for Corporate Control," *Journal of Business*, 1980, Vol. 53, 345–376.

Bradley, M., A. Desai, and E. H. Kim, "The Rationale behind Interfirm Tender Offers: Information or Synergy," *Journal of Financial Economics*, April 1983, Vol. 11, 183–206.

———, "Synergistic Gains from Corporate Acquisitions and Their Division between the Stockholders of Target and Acquiring Firms," *Journal of Financial Economics*, 1988, Vol. 21, No. 1, 3–40.

Bradley, M., C. A. Schipani, A. K. Sundaram, and J. P. Walsh, "The Purposes and Accountability of the Corporation in Contemporary Society: Corporate Governance at a Crossroads," *Law and Contemporary Problems*, Summer 1999, Vol. 62, 9–86.

Campa, J. M., and S. Kedia, "Explaining the Diversification Discount," *Journal of Finance*, 2002, Vol. 57, 1731–1762.

Capen, E. C., R. V. Clapp, and W. M. Campbell, "Competitive Bidding in High Risk Situations," *Journal of Petroleum Technology*, June 1971, Vol. 23, 641–653.

Chung, K. S., "Investment Opportunities, Synergies, and Conglomerate Mergers," dissertation, Graduate School of Management, University of California, Los Angeles, 1982.

Copeland, T., T. Koller, and J. Murrin, *Valuation: Measuring and Managing the Values of Companies*, third ed., John Wiley and Sons, New York, 2000.

Cornell, B., "Is the Response of Analysts to Information Consistent with Fundamental Valuation? The Case of Intel," *Financial Management*, Spring 2001, Vol. 30, 113–136.

Cusatis, P. J., J. A. Miles, and J. R. Woolridge, "Restructuring through Spinoffs: The Stock Market Evidence," *Journal of Financial Economics*, 1993, Vol. 33, No. 3, 293–311.

Daley, L., V. Mehrotra, and R. Sivakumar, "Corporate Focus and Value Creation: Evidence from Spinoffs," *Journal of Financial Economics*, August 1997, Vol. 45, 257–281.

Dennis, D. K., and J. J. McConnell, "Corporate Mergers and Security Returns," *Journal of Financial Economics*, 1986, Vol. 16, 143–187.

Desai, H., and P. C. Jain, "Firm Performance and Focus: Long-Run Stock Market Performance Following Spinoffs," *Journal of Financial Economics*, October 1999, Vol. 54, 75–101.

Dodd, P., and R. Ruback, "Tender Offers and Stockholder Returns: An Empirical Analysis," *Journal of Financial Economics*, December 1977, Vol. 5, 351–374.

D'Souza, J., and J. Jacob, "Why Firms Issue Targeted Stock," *Journal of Financial Economics*, June 2000, Vol. 56, 459–483.

Dyer, J. H., P. Kale, and H. Singh, "How to Make Strategic Alliances Work," *MIT Sloan Management Review*, Summer 2001, Vol. 42, 37–43.

Eckbo, B. E., "Examining the Anti-Competitive Significance of Large Horizontal Mergers," Ph.D. dissertation, University of Rochester, 1981.

Eckbo, B. E., and P. Wier, "Antimerger Policy under the Hart-Scott-Rodino Act: A Reexamination of the Market Power Hypothesis," *Journal of Law and Economics*, April 1985, Vol. 28, 119–150.

The Economist, "A Survey of Corporate Governance," January 29, 1994, special supplement, 1–18.

Elder, J., and P. Westra, "The Reaction of Security Prices to Tracking Stock Announcements," *Journal of Economics and Finance*, Spring 2000, Vol. 24, 36–55.

Ellert, J. C., "Antitrust Enforcement and the Behavior of Stock Prices," Ph.D dissertation, Graduate School of Business, University of Chicago, 1975.

———, "Mergers, Antitrust Law Enforcement and Stockholder Returns," *Journal of Finance*, May 1976, Vol. 31, 715–732.

Fama, E. F., "Agency Problems and the Theory of the Firm," *Journal of Political Economy*, April 1980, Vol. 88, 288–307.

Fama, E. F., and M. C. Jensen, "Separation of Ownership and Control," *Journal of Law and Economics*, 1983, Vol. 26, 301–325.

Financial Accounting Standards Board, *Statement of Financial Accounting Standards No. 141: Business Combinations*, June 2001a.

———, *Statement of Financial Accounting Standards No. 142: Goodwill and Other Intangible Assets*, June 2001b.

Flom, J. H., "Mergers & Acquisitions: The Decade in Review," *University of Miami Law Review*, July 2000, Vol. 54, 753–781.

Franks, J., R. Harris, and S. Titman, "The Postmerger Share-Price Performance of Acquiring Firms," *Journal of Financial Economics*, 1991, Vol. 29, 81–96.

Franks, J., and C. Mayer, "Bank Control, Takeovers and Corporate Governance in Germany," *Journal of Banking and Finance*, October 1998, Vol. 22, 1385–1403.

Friend, I., and M. Blume, "Measurement of Portfolio Performance under Uncertainty," *American Economic Review*, September 1970, Vol. 60, 561–575.

Galai, D., and R. W. Masulis, "The Option Pricing Model and the Risk Factor of Stock," *Journal of Financial Economics*, January–March 1976, Vol. 3, 53–82.

Geis, G. T., and G. S. Geis, *Digital Deals: Strategies for Selecting and Structuring Partnerships*, McGraw-Hill, New York, 2001.

Gerard, B., and M. L. Silberman, "Spinoff Gains and Economic Efficiency: The Operating Performance of Parents and Spun Off Subsidiaries," working paper, Department of Finance and Business Economics, University of Southern California, Los Angeles, 1994.

Ghosh, A., "Does Operating Performance Really Improve Following Corporate Acquisitions?" *Journal of Corporate Finance*, June 2001, Vol. 7, 151–178.

Gilson, S. C., P. H. Healy, C. F. Noe, and K. Palepu, "Analyst Specialization and Conglomerate Stock Breakups," *Journal of Accounting Research*, 2001, Vol. 39, 565–582.

Gleason, K. C., I. Mathur, and M. Singh, "Wealth Effects for Acquirers and Divestors Related to Foreign Divested Assets," *International Review of Financial Analysis*, 2000, Vol. 9, No. 1, 5–20.

Healy, P. M., K. G. Palepu, and R. S. Ruback, "Does Corporate Performance Improve after Mergers?" *Journal of Financial Economics*, April 1992, Vol. 31, 135–176.

Holmstrom, B., and S. N. Kaplan, "Corporate Governance and Merger Activity in the United States: Making Sense of the 1980s and 1990s," *Journal of Economic Perspectives*, Spring 2001, Vol. 15, 121–144.

Hulburt, H. M., J. A. Miles, and J. R. Woolridge, "Value Creation from Equity Carve-Outs," *Financial Management*, Spring 2002, Vol. 31, 5–22.

Jarrell, G. A., *Testimony in the Case of RP Acquisition Corp. v. Staley Continental and Michael Harkins*. Testimony in the United States District Court for the District of Delaware (Civil Action No. 88-190), 1988.

Jensen, M. C., "Agency Costs of Free Cash Flow, Corporate Finance, and Takeovers," *American Economic Review*, May 1986, Vol. 76, 323–329.

———, "The Takeover Controversy: Analysis and Evidence," Chapter 20 in J. C. Coffee, Jr., L. Lowenstein, and S. Rose-Ackerman, eds., *Knights, Raiders, and Targets*, Oxford University Press, New York, 1988.

Jensen, M. C., and W. H. Meckling, "Theory of the Firm: Managerial Behavior, Agency Costs and Ownership Structure," *Journal of Financial Economics*, October 1976, Vol. 3, 305–360.

Joehnk, M. D., and J. F. Nielsen, "The Effects of Conglomerate Merger Activity on Systematic Risk," *Journal of Financial and Quantitative Analysis*, March 1974, Vol. 9, 215–225.

Kale, P., J. H. Dyer, and H. Singh, "Alliance Capability, Stock Market Response, and Long-Term Alliance Success: The Role of the Alliance Function," *Strategic Management Journal*, 2002, Vol. 23, 747–767.

Kaplan, S., "The Effects of Management Buyouts on Operating Performance and Value," *Journal of Financial Economics*, 1989, Vol. 24, 217–254.

———, "Top Executive Rewards and Firm Performance: A Comparison of Japan and the United States," *Journal of Political Economy*, June 1994, Vol. 102, 510–546.

Kaplan, S., and M. S. Weisbach, "The Success of Acquisitions: Evidence from Divestitures," *Journal of Finance*, March 1992, Vol. 47, 107–138.

Kim, E. H., and J. J. McConnell, "Corporate Mergers and the Co-Insurance of Corporate Debt," *Journal of Finance*, 1977, Vol. 32, 349–365.

Klein, A., J. Rosenfeld, and W. Beranek, "The Two Stages of an Equity Carve-Out and the Price Response of Parent and Subsidiary Stock," *Managerial and Decision Economics*, December 1991, Vol. 12, 449–460.

Klein, B., R. G. Crawford, and A. A. Alchian, "Vertical Integration, Appropriate Rents, and the Competitive Contracting Process," *Journal of Law and Economics*, October 1978, Vol. 21, 297–326.

Krishnaswami, S., and V. Subramaniam, "Information Asymmetry, Valuation, and the Corporate Spin-Off Decision," *Journal of Financial Economics*, July 1999, Vol. 53, 73–112.

Lang, L., A. Poulsen, and R. Stulz, "Asset Sales, Firm Performance, and the Agency Costs of Managerial Discretion," *Journal of Financial Economics*, January 1995, Vol. 37, 3–37.

Lang, L. H. P., and R. M. Stulz, "Tobin's q, Corporate Diversification, and Firm Performance," *Journal of Political Economy*, 1994, Vol. 102, 1248–1280.

Levy, H., and M. Sarnat, "Diversification, Portfolio Analysis and the Uneasy Case for Conglomerate Mergers," *Journal of Finance*, September 1970, 795–802.

Lewellen, W. G., "A Pure Financial Rationale for the Conglomerate Merger," *Journal of Finance*, May 1971, Vol. 26, 521–545.

Lewellen, W. G., and B. Huntsman, "Managerial Pay and Corporate Performance," *American Economic Review*, September 1970, Vol. 60, 710–720.

Lipton, M., "Mergers: Past, Present and Future," manuscript Wachtell, Lipton, Rosen & Katz, January 10, 2001.

Logue, D. E., and J. K. Seward, "Anatomy of a Governance Transformation: The Case of Daimler-Benz," *Law and Contemporary Problems*, Summer 1999, Vol. 62, 87–112.

Logue, D. E., J. K. Seward, and J. P. Walsh, "Rearranging Residual Claims: A Case for Targeted Stock," *Financial Management*, Spring 1996, Vol. 25, 43–61.

Loughran, T., and A. M. Vijh, "Do Long-Term Shareholders Benefit from Capital Acquisitions?" *Journal of Finance*, December 1997, Vol. 52, 1765–1790.

Malkiel, B. G., "Equity Yields, Growth, and the Structure of Share Prices," *American Economic Review*, December 1963, Vol. 53, 1004–1031.

Manne, H. G., "Mergers and the Market for Corporate Control," *Journal of Political Economy*, April 1965, Vol. 73, 110–120.

Mason, R. H., and M. B. Goudzwaard, "Performance of Conglomerate Firms: A Portfolio Approach," *Journal of Finance*, March 1976, Vol. 31, 39–48.

McCauley, R. N., J. S. Ruud, and F. Iacono, *Dodging Bullets*. MIT Press, Cambridge, Mass., 1999.

McConnell, J. J., and T. J. Nantell, "Corporate Combinations and Common Stock Returns: The Case of Joint Ventures," *Journal of Finance*, June 1985, Vol. 40, 519–536.

McDaniel, M. W., "Bondholders and Corporate Governance," *The Business Lawyer*, February 1986, Vol. 41, 413–460.

Melicher, R. W., and D. F. Rush, "The Performance of Conglomerate Firms: Recent Risk and Return Experience," *Journal of Finance*, May 1973, Vol. 28, 381–388.

———, "Evidence on the Acquisition-Related Performance of Conglomerate Firms," *Journal of Finance*, March 1974, Vol. 29, 141–149.

Michaely, R., and W. H. Shaw, "The Choice of Going Public: Spin-offs vs. Carve-Outs," *Financial Management*, Autumn 1995, Vol. 24, 5–21.

Miller, M. H., and F. Modigliani, "Dividend Policy, Growth, and the Valuation of Shares," *Journal of Business*, October 1961, Vol. 34, 411–433.

Mitchell, M. L., and K. Lehn, "Do Bad Bidders Become Good Targets?" *Journal of Political Economy*, April 1990, Vol. 98, 372–398.

Mitchell, M. L., and J. H. Mulherin, "The Impact of Industry Shocks on Takeover and Restructuring Activity," *Journal of Financial Economics*, June 1996, Vol. 41, 193–229.

Mueller, D. C., "A Theory of Conglomerate Mergers," *Quarterly Journal of Economics*, 1969, Vol. 83, 643–659.

Mulford, C. W., and E. E. Comiskey, *The Financial Numbers Game: Detecting Creative Accounting Practices*. John Wiley and Sons, New York, 2002.

Mulherin, J. H., and A. L. Boone, "Comparing Acquisitions and Divestitures," *Journal of Corporate Finance*, July 2000, Vol. 6, 117–139.

Myers, S. C., and N. S. Majluf, "Corporate Financing and Investment Decisions When Firms Have Information That Investors Do Not Have," *Journal of Financial Economics*, 1984, Vol. 13, No. 2, 187–221.

Nickell, S. J., *The Investment Decisions of Firms*. Cambridge University Press, Oxford, 1978.

Nielsen, J. F., and R. W. Melicher, "A Financial Analysis of Acquisition and Merger Premiums," *Journal of Financial and Quantitative Analysis*, March 1973, Vol. 8, 139–162.

Panzar, J. C., and R. D. Willig, "Economics of Scope," *American Economic Review*, 1981, Vol. 71, 268–272.

Pautler, P. A., "Evidence on Mergers and Acquisitions," Working Paper No. 243, Bureau of Economics, Federal Trade Commission, Washington, D.C., September 25, 2001.

Pontiff, J., A. Shleifer, and M. S. Weisbach, "Reversions of Excess Pension Assets after Takeovers," *RAND Journal of Economics*, Winter 1990, Vol. 21, 600–613.

Rajan, R., H. Servaes, and L. Zingales, "The Cost of Diversity: The Diversification Discount and Inefficient Investment," *Journal of Finance*, 2000, Vol. 60, 35–80.

Rappaport, A., *Creating Shareholder Value: A Guide for Managers and Investors*, second edition. The Free Press, New York, 1998.

Rau, P. R., and T. Vermaelen, "Glamour, Value and the Post-Acquisition Performance of Acquiring Firms," *Journal of Financial Economics*, August 1998, Vol. 49, 223–253.

Reid, S. R., *Mergers, Managers, and the Economy*. McGraw-Hill, New York, 1968.

Roll, R., "The Hubris Hypothesis of Corporate Takeovers," *Journal of Business*, April 1986, Vol. 59, 197–216.

———, "Empirical Evidence on Takeover Activity and Shareholder Wealth," Chapter 5 in T. E. Copeland, ed., *Modern Finance and Industrial Economics*, Basil Blackwell, New York, 1987, 74–91.

Ruback, R. S., "Capital Cash Flows: A Simple Approach to Valuing Risky Cash Flows," *Financial Management*, Summer 2002, Vol. 31, 85–103.

Scharfstein, D. F., "The Dark Side of Internal Capital Markets II: Evidence from Diversified Conglomerates," Working Paper 6352, National Bureau of Economic Research, Cambridge, Mass., 1998.

Scharfstein, D. S., and J. C. Stein, "The Dark Side of Internal Capital Markets: Divisional Rent-Seeking and Inefficient Investment," *Journal of Finance*, 2000, Vol. 55, 2537–2564.

Schilit, H., *Financial Shenanigans*, second edition. McGraw-Hill, New York, 2002.

Schill, M. J., and C. Zhou, "Pricing an Emerging Industry: Evidence from Internet Subsidiary Carve-Outs," *Financial Management*, Autumn 2001, Vol. 30, 5–33.

Schipper, K., and A. Smith, "A Comparison of Equity Carve-Outs and Seasoned Equity Offerings: Share Price Effects and Corporate Restructuring," *Journal of Financial Economics*, January/February 1986, Vol. 15, 153–186.

Schipper, K., and R. Thompson, "Evidence on the Capitalized Value of Merger Activity for Acquiring Firms," *Journal of Financial Economics*, 1983, Vol. 11, No. 1, 85–119.

Servaes, H., "The Value of Diversification during the Conglomerate Merger Wave," *Journal of Finance*, 1996, Vol. 51, No. 4, 1207–1225.

Shastri, K., "Valuing Corporate Securities: Some Effects of Mergers by Exchange Offers," Working Paper #S17, University of Pittsburgh, revised January 1982.

Shleifer, A., and L. H. Summers, "Breach of Trust in Hostile Takeovers," Chapter 2 in A. J. Auerbach, ed., *Corporate Takeovers: Causes and Consequences*, University of Chicago Press, Chicago, 1988.

Shleifer, A., and R. W. Vishny, "A Survey of Corporate Governance," *Journal of Finance*, June 1997, Vol. 52, 737–783.

Slovin, M. B., M. E. Sushka, and S. R. Ferraro, "A Comparison of the Information Conveyed by Equity Carve-Outs, Spin-Offs, and Asset Sell-Offs," *Journal of Financial Economics*, January 1995, Vol. 37, 89–104.

Smith, K. V., and J. F. Weston, "Further Evaluation of Conglomerate Performance," *Journal of Business Research*, March 1977, 5–14.

Spence, M., "Job Market Signaling," *Quarterly Journal of Economics*, 1973, Vol. 87, 355–379.

———, "Competitive and Optimal Responses to Signals: An Analysis of Efficiency and Distribution," *Journal of Economic Theory*, March 1974, Vol. 7, 296–332.

Stillman, R., "Examining Antitrust Policy Towards Horizontal Mergers," *Journal of Financial Economics*, April 1983, Vol. 11, 225–240.

Teece, D. J., "Economics of Scope and the Scope of the Enterprise," *The Journal of Economic Behavior and Organization*, 1980, Vol. 1, 223–247.

———, "Toward an Economic Theory of the Multiproduct Firm," *Journal of Economic Behavior and Organization*, 1982, Vol. 3, 39–63.

Tichy, G., "What Do We Know about Success and Failure of Mergers?" *Journal of Industry, Competition and Trade*, December 2001a, 347–394.

———, "What Do We Know about Success and Failure of Mergers?—Rejoinder," *Journal of Industry, Competition and Trade*, December 2001b, 423–430.

Vijh, A. M., "The Spinoff and Merger Ex-Date Effects," *Journal of Finance*, 1994, Vol. 49, No. 2, 581–609.

———, "The Positive Announcement-Period Returns of Equity Carveouts: Asymmetric Information or Divestiture Gains?" *Journal of Business*, January 2002, Vol. 75, 153–190.

Villalonga, B., "Does Diversification Cause the 'Diversification Discount'?" working paper, University of California, Los Angeles, 1999.

———, "Diversification Discount or Premium? New Evidence from BITS Establishment-Level Data," *Journal of Finance*, forthcoming, 2003.

Warga, A., and I. Welch, "Bondholder Losses in Leveraged Buyouts," *Review of Financial Studies*, 1993, Vol. 6, 959–982.

Wasserstein, B., *Big Deal: 2000 and Beyond*. Warner Books, New York, 1998, 2000.

Weston, J. F., "The Nature and Significance of Conglomerate Firms," *St. John's Law Review*, 1970, Vol. 44, 66–80.

———, "The Exxon-Mobil Merger: An Archetype," *Journal of Applied Finance*, Spring/Summer 2002, 69–88.

Weston, J. F., and B. Johnson, "What It Takes for a Deal to Win Stock Market Approval," *Mergers & Acquisitions*, September/October 1999, Vol. 34, 43–48.

Weston, J. F., and S. K. Mansinghka, "Tests of the Efficiency Performance of Conglomerate Firms," *Journal of Finance*, September 1971, Vol. 26, 919–936.

Weston, J. F., M. Mitchell, and J. H. Mulherin, *Takeovers, Restructuring, and Corporate Governance*, fourth ed. Prentice-Hall, Upper Saddle River, N.J., 2004.

Weston, J. F., K. V. Smith, and R. E. Shrieves, "Conglomerate Performance Using the Capital Asset Pricing Model," *Review of Economics and Statistics*, 1972, Vol. 54, 357–363.

Whited, T. M., "Is It Inefficient Investment That Causes the Diversification Discount?" *Journal of Finance*, 2001, Vol. 56, 1667–1691.

Williamson, O. E., *Markets and Hierarchies: Analysis and Antitrust Implications*. Free Press, New York, 1975.

———, "Comment," Chapter 2 in A. J. Auerbach, ed., *Corporate Takeovers: Cause and Consequences*, University of Chicago Press, Chicago, 1988, 61–67.

Wruck, E. G., and K. H. Wruck, "Restructuring Top Management: Evidence from Corporate Spinoffs," working paper, Ohio State University, October 2001.

Chapter 19

Like the traffic lights in a city, the international monetary system is taken for granted until it begins to malfunction and to disrupt people's daily lives.

—Robert Solomon, *The International Monetary System, 1945–1976, An Insider's View*, Harper and Row, New York, 1977, 1.

International Financial Management

I N THIS CHAPTER WE ANALYZE the international dimension of financial theory and corporate policy.* We live in a world in which transactions take place across nations with different characteristics and different currencies. Multinational corporations (MNCs) are not all giant firms. More than half are small firms with less than 100 employees. Even firms and individuals not directly engaged in international business may be affected by the relative values of domestic versus foreign currencies.

This chapter discusses the continued high volatility in foreign exchange rates, the evolution of the international financial systems, the analysis of international transactions, the international parity relationships, exchange rate forecasting, management of foreign exchange risks, international asset pricing models, and the cost of capital and currency risk.

A. Volatility in Exchange Rates

International financial managers are responsible for handling the continued high volatility of the relative values of currencies. Figure 19.1 illustrates that the trade-weighted average index (the base of the index is March 1973) in relationship to the currency values of a group of major foreign countries has changed significantly over time. Between January 1973 and January 1981 it fluctuated within a relatively narrow range between 90 and 110. The U.S. dollar strengthened relative to the comparison currencies by more than 50% between 1981 and 1985, but the index then declined from 140 to under 80 by 1995. The value of the U.S. dollar in relationship to the other currencies then increased in value to a high of 109 in 2002, declining to 95 in early 2003.

---

*Juan Siu and Paul Alapat contributed to the chapter.

Figure 19.1 Trade-weighted value of the U.S. dollar, major currencies index (base March 1973 = 100).

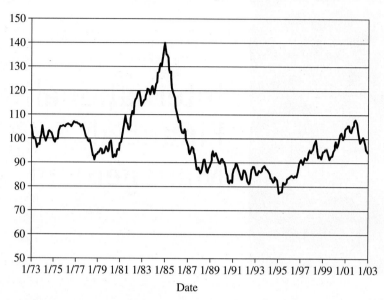

Note: includes currencies of the euro area, Australia, Canada, Japan, Sweden, Switzerland, and the U.K.

Fluctuations in individual currencies are even greater. Figure 19.2 provides some evidence. The number of Japanese yen per dollar was as high as 145 in 1998, dropping to almost 100 in late 1999. The number of British pounds per dollar moved from almost 0.72 to 0.61 between 2001 and early 2003. The number of Canadian dollars per U.S. dollar was about 1.42 in 1998 and reached a level of 1.60 in early 2002. The number of euros per dollar was less than 0.85 in 1998, rose to over 1.15 in 2000, and dropped to under 0.95 in 2003.

Fluctuations in foreign exchange rates often cause changes in the amounts realized in the home currency. For example, suppose a Japanese auto producer needs to receive 2 million yen per car to cover costs plus the required return on capital. When the exchange rate was 265 yen to the dollar, as it was in early 1985, the Japanese producer would have to receive $7,547 per car. At 100 yen to the dollar, the Japanese producer would have to receive $20,000 per car. So when the yen is strong, the price charged in dollars by Japanese auto sellers has to be higher or profit margins lower. Conversely, at a weak yen of 200 to the dollar, the price per car can drop to $10,000 per car, while maintaining margins.

The nature of risks in an international financial setting must be considered along with other risks. We shall focus on corporate financial policies to manage these risks. In addition to the pattern of cash inflows and cash outflows, we examine the changes in its balance sheet in terms of monetary versus nonmonetary net positions. We also examine the use of the forward markets for dealing with foreign exchange fluctuations and analyze whether the benefits of limiting the risk of exchange rate fluctuations are worth the cost.

We will emphasize some basic propositions in international finance that are the key to measuring returns and costs in international financial activities. But, these basic relations are best understood after background materials on the adjustment processes in international finance have been developed.

Figure 19.2 U.S. dollar against foreign currencies, monthly average values.

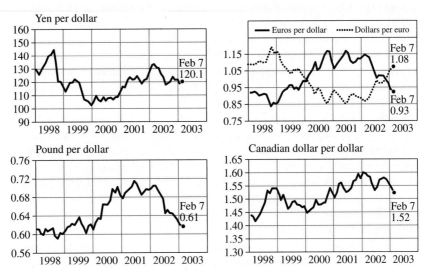

Sources: National sources, Federal Reserve Board of Governors, Bank of International Settlements.

B. International Financial Systems

The international financial markets as a part of a general system of financial intermediation increase efficiency of the production and exchange of goods and services. Money and prices convey information and guide the choices about economic alternatives. International finance, like financial intermediation in general, provides for shifting patterns of investments and savings that increase productivity. Surplus savings postpones consumption and deficit savings increases the output of real goods via investments that utilize these savings.

1. The Economic Basis for International Transactions

The fundamental basis for international trade is the *principle of comparative advantage*. The law of comparative advantage states that trade will be mutually advantageous if one country is *relatively* more efficient in producing some products and other countries are *relatively* more efficient in producing others. A classic illustration would be if you were a better typist than your secretary. Nevertheless, you hire your secretary because your comparative advantage is your knowledge of other things (e.g., international finance). To illustrate the opportunities for gain from trade, consider the following example.

Let us postulate that opportunity costs in country A are reflected in prices of $3 for product X and $1 for product Y, whereas opportunity costs in country B result in prices of 12 foreign currency units (FC) for X and FC6 for Y. The pattern is

	X	Y
Country A	$3	$1
Country B	FC12	FC6

At more than FC6 per dollar, both goods X and Y would be cheaper in country B. Country B would export both X and Y and import neither. For example, at FC8 = $1, B could sell X in A for $1.50 and Y in A for $0.75. On the other hand, a rate of less than FC4 per dollar would make both goods cheaper in country A. Country A would export both and import neither. For example, at FC2 = $1, A could sell X in B for FC6 and Y in B for FC2. To achieve equilibrium between the two countries the exchange rate would have to fall somewhere between 6 and 4 FC per dollar. For example, at FC5 = $1, B can sell X in A for $2.40, and A can sell Y in B for FC5. A basis for trade would now exist.

In the example, the relative prices of X and Y are 3:1 in country A and 2:1 in country B. With a large number of products the cheaper one country's currency is in relation to other currencies, the larger the range of that country's products that are underselling foreign products of the same type. As a result the importing country will need greater amounts per unit of time of the exporting country's currency in order to buy its relatively cheap goods. Differences in the patterns of relative prices result from differences among countries in resources, skills, and tastes and in social and political conditions, which in turn lead to comparative advantages in different kinds of activities. As a consequence, there will be profit incentives to engage in trade. These private benefits will, in turn, lead to social gains as the theory describes. Foreign exchange rates can bring the trade between countries to levels where the exports and imports of individual countries will be in balance in their own currency.

However, the overall balance is also affected by the existence of short- and long-term capital flows associated with borrowing and lending activities, shifts in the comparative rates of development of individual industries in different countries, and differences in the domestic and government monetary, fiscal, and investment policies among individual countries. Possible imbalances in international activities can be restored to equilibrium by adjustment processes via two alternative exchange mechanisms. One is a gold standard with fixed exchange rates; the other is a system of flexible exchange rates.

2. Gold Standard and Fixed Exchange Rates

The mechanism governing the relationship of prices to the flow of gold was first formulated in the mid-18th century. Suppose that country A runs an export surplus, whereas country B runs a deficit. Hence gold flows into A while it flows out of B. Domestic prices in A rise, the prices in B fall. Country A is an attractive market in which to increase sales from other countries, and A's imports increase. Country A's goods are more expensive in other countries, so its export sales decrease. Thus A's export surplus will be reduced or reversed until equilibrium between the relative price relationships of the countries is restored.[1] The flow of gold operates through prices to function as an adjustment mechanism for international balances of trade and payments as well as to regulate the price relationships between countries.

In addition to price changes, income and employment may also affect the adjustment process. If the surplus country was not functioning at full employment, the export surplus increases its income and employment. Income and employment decline in the deficit country. Also, in the adjustment process, employment may decline in A and increase in B.

Under the gold standard, exchange rates are said to remain "fixed" through the adjustment process because gold would flow to prevent exchange rates from moving beyond the "gold points."

---

[1] Of course if the real rate of productivity growth in B is perpetually higher, the "equilibrium" described here will not occur. There may even be a "permanent" export balance deficit for country B.

For example, suppose that the British pound contains four times as much gold as the U.S. dollar (the dollar contains .05 ounce of gold, whereas the British pound contains .2 ounce of gold). A U.S. trade deficit vis-à-vis the United Kingdom would increase the demand for pounds to pay for the imports from the United Kingdom, and the dollar price (value) of pounds would therefore rise, say, to $4.10. We could take $1,000 to the U.S. Treasury to receive 50 ounces of gold since $1 contains .05 ounce of gold. Next we could transport the 50 ounces of gold to the United Kingdom where we would receive £250 in exchange: 50/.2 = 250. With the rate of exchange of $4.10 to £1 less a $0.02 cost of transportation and insurance of gold flows, we would net $4.08 for each pound. Multiplying $4.08 times £250 yields $1,020, or a profit of $20. Thus at any rate of exchange above $4.02 or below $3.98 (the gold points), the actions of gold arbitrageurs would force a return to equilibrium.

To the extent that a gold standard with fixed exchange rates worked, it was because two-way convertibility between a nation's monetary unit and a fixed amount of gold was a policy goal that received great emphasis and a high priority. So long as it was recognized that convertibility was a major policy goal, speculative capital movements were more likely to be stabilizing rather than destabilizing. In other words, the general expectation that the convertibility of the currency would be maintained was so strong that when a gold standard currency did weaken almost to its gold export points, one could reasonably assume that it would not drop much lower and would probably rise. Speculators would then take positions based on the expectations that a rise in the value of the currency was imminent, and this would strengthen the currency.

3. The Adjustment Process under Flexible Exchange Rates

Under a regime of flexible exchange rates no attempt is made to tie the value of a currency to gold or to any one foreign currency. The exchanges of currencies that take place in the international financial markets are based on the forces of demand and supply for the currencies. Exchange rates would be related to the purchasing power of goods and services of the respective currencies.

To illustrate the operation of the adjustment process, assume an initial relationship of 1 dollar to 1.4 Swiss francs: $1 = SF 1.4. Next, assume that the volume of imports into the United States exceeds exports in relationship to countries whose currency is the SF. The demand for SF relative to dollars increases. The foreign exchange value of the dollar falls; the foreign exchange value of the SF rises. For purposes of illustration, let us now assume $1 = SF 1.0.

At the new exchange rate, the prices of U.S. imports in dollars rise. For example, suppose that the shipment of pharmaceuticals sold in the United States for $2,000 when the exchange rate is $1 to SF 1.4. A sale at $2,000 provided the Swiss exporter with SF 2,800. At the new exchange rate the Swiss exporter still seeks to receive SF 2,800. But at the new exchange rates the exporter needs to receive $2,800 for the shipment of pharmaceuticals.

Similarly, at the old exchange rate the price of grain (a U.S. export good) was $4 per bushel. To obtain this price the U.S. export firm needs to receive SF 5.6 per bushel. At the new exchange rates, in order to receive $4 per bushel, the U.S. firm needs to receive only SF 4 per bushel. The prices of exports in the foreign currency fall.

In the United States at the new exchange rates, import purchases would have to be made at higher prices and export sales could be made at lower prices than before. Conversely, for foreign countries with stronger currencies, import prices are lower and export prices are higher. Purchase prices from the United States would decrease and export prices would have to be increased. The original deficit in trade in the United States would tend to be corrected.

An argument for the use of flexible exchange rates is that the relations between the prices of domestic and foreign goods adjust through exchange rates. The prices of internationally traded goods carry most of the adjustment process. It is argued that under the gold standard with fixed exchange rates a disequilibrium exchange rate is adjusted not by changing exchange rates but by adjusting all other things. Under flexible exchange rates, when exchange rates are out of line, the correction takes place in the exchange rates themselves. If wages and prices are relatively inflexible, they do not make the necessary adjustments. However, exchange rates do not have the same built-in institutional barriers to flexibility and can make the required adjustments.

4. Toward Coordinated Intervention

The fundamental problem with a fixed gold standard was that it tied the world monetary base to the supply of gold. The supply of gold was greatly influenced by chance discoveries that were not necessarily related to the needs of the international currency requirements. Another difficulty was that the rate of economic development in different countries could be so unequal that some countries were subject to substantial gold drains that were deflationary. As a consequence, individual countries would seek to protect their gold reserves by a wide variety of policies such as tariffs and various restrictions against imports and subsidies to exports. These nationalistic economic policies restricted the growth of international trade and represented an economic drag on all nations. The result was to aggravate the worldwide recession of 1929 to 1933.

AUTHORIZATION AND MANAGEMENT OF INTERVENTION OPERATIONS Today, the U.S. Treasury and Federal Reserve each have independent legal authority to intervene in the foreign exchange markets. The Treasury is authorized to intervene by the Gold Reserve Act of 1934 and the Bretton Woods Agreement Act of 1944. The Federal Reserve is authorized to intervene by the Federal Reserve Act of 1913. Intervention is usually done in close cooperation between the two U.S. authorities. All U.S. foreign exchange market operations on behalf of the U.S. monetary authorities are conducted by the Foreign Exchange Desk of the Federal Reserve Bank of New York.

The Treasury's foreign exchange operations are financed through the Exchange Stabilization Fund (ESF). The Federal Reserve's foreign exchange operations are financed through a system account in which all 12 Federal Reserve banks participate under the auspices of the Federal Open Market Committee (FOMC).

The Federal Reserve Bank of New York has used various intervention techniques depending on the policy objective, market conditions, and effectiveness. In recent years, most of the intervention has been operated openly and directly with a number of commercial banks and other interbank market participants.

STERILIZATION The dollar amount of any intervention is routinely sterilized. Any intervention in the currency markets by policy authorities has two effects—first, on the exchange rate, and second, on the domestic money supply. *Sterilization* is the effort to neutralize the effect on the domestic money supply. Any expansion or contraction in the monetary base resulting from the intervention would be automatically offset by the Fed's domestic monetary action. For example, if the Fed wants to strengthen the euro, it would (1) exchange dollars for euros, and (2) sell some of its holdings of Treasury securities for dollars. The dollar flows resulting from the exchange of currencies is offset by the exchange of Treasury securities for dollars. The net effect is an increase in the supply of publicly held Treasury securities and a decrease in the supply of publicly held euro-denominated securities.

Since the 1980s, the U.S. authorities have built up their international reserves. The U.S. increased its total international reserve balances (excluding gold) from $37 billion in 1988 to $68 billion by 2002 (*International Financial Statistics*, IFS, April 2003). However, the level of U.S. holdings, measured relative to imports or size of economy, still remains well below many other major industrial nations. For example, Japan holds total reserve balances of $461 billion, of which $451 billion is foreign currencies (*IFS*, April 2003).

5. The History of the Euro

Against this background of international efforts to arrive at a workable set of rules for international monetary relationships, cooperation among European nations was developing. As a part of a broader movement toward a European Union (EU), efforts were made to coordinate economic policies and exchange rate fluctuations.

The history of the euro goes back to the 1957 Treaty of Rome that advocated a common market in Europe as a means of increasing economic prosperity. Actual implementation of a common currency began in 1990 with cooperation among banks of the EMU to narrow the bands of the foreign exchange rates. Next, in 1994 a central European bank was created. Soon it began to set interest rates and maintain price stability in the EMU. In 1999 the euro was launched as an electronic currency and finally, in 2002, national currencies were replaced with the euro as legal tender.

As the European monetary union succeeds, the transaction costs of exchanging currencies will be reduced, thereby encouraging trade and economic activity. This in turn will lower the costs of financing. It creates a larger entity in relation to the dominant position of the United States in the international financial market and will increase competition. To succeed, member countries will be constrained to coordinate their fiscal and monetary policies. Economic growth patterns will have to be harmonized.

To summarize this background material we observe that exchange standards have moved toward floating or flexible exchange rates within coordinated boundaries. Competition between financial markets has increased. Instability has occurred periodically in major segments of the world financial markets. These include the difficulties of the Mexican peso in 1994–95, the East Asia crisis of 1997–98, and crisis conditions in Argentina and Venezuela in 2002–2003.

As a foundation for understanding relationships between foreign exchange rates we next discuss the topic of the analysis of the international financial accounts of individual countries.

C. Analysis of International Transactions

In recent years the U.S. Department of Commerce has stopped using the term *balance of payments* in favor of the more general expression *U.S. international transactions*. The balance of payments of a nation is a double-entry accounting statement of its transactions with the rest of the world. Inflows are recorded as a plus. (Sometimes the words *receipts* or *credits* are used, but the terms plus and minus are preferred as being more neutral in their implications.) Outflows are a minus (sometimes called *debits* or *payments*).

The basic entries in the balance of payments statement can be summarized into four categories, as shown in Table 19.1. This summary indicates how the adjustment process can be complicated by a number of relationships going in different directions. For example, if a country runs a deficit by having an excess of imports over exports, instead of settling the balance by payments in the

Table 19.1 Effects on the Balance of Payments

Plus	Minus
Exports and income receipts	Imports and income payments
Increase liabilities of foreigners	Decrease liabilities to foreigners
Decrease claims on foreigners:	Increase claims on foreigners:
Decrease investments	Increase investments
Sell assets	Buy assets

foreign country, a number of other offsets may take place. As shown in Table 19.1 the offsets can take the form of increasing liabilities to foreigners, decreasing claims on foreigners, liquidating assets, or decreasing other foreign investments. Consequently, there will be a lag in pressures that would result if payments in foreign currencies had to be made immediately. This lag will postpone the contraction in the money supply and/or incomes of the deficit country.

Similarly, a country that is increasing its investments abroad will improve its investment position, but it will be creating minus entries in its current balance of payments statement. The long-run outlook for a country that is making substantial foreign investments, however, may be favorable as a result of the future income that may be generated from those investments.

In Table 19.2 we have selected lines from the Table of U.S. International Transactions by the Bureau of Economic Analysis of the U.S. Department of Commerce, published both in the *Survey of Current Business* and in the *Federal Reserve Bulletin*. The lines omitted are individual accounts whose totals are captured by the lines presented in Table 19.2. From lines 2 and 19, the balance of goods and services is calculated to be a negative $358 billion in 2001 (line 73). Another relationship of interest is the current account balance (line 76), which is the sum of lines 1, 18, and 35. The current account balance in 2001 was a negative $393 billion. The current account balance is also equal to the sum of lines 41, 50, 56, 63, and 70. These accounts provide an analytical framework for the determinants of the current account balance. We will use the symbols defined in Table 19.3.

U.S. private lending is an outflow $(-)$ in the transaction accounts; private borrowing is an inflow $(+)$. An increase in U.S. official reserve assets is an outflow while an increase in foreign official assets held in the United States is an inflow. The relationships can be expressed as an identity:

$$\Delta PL_{US} \quad +\Delta PB_{US} \quad +\Delta ORA_{US} \quad +\Delta ORA_F \quad +SD \quad \equiv -CA$$
$$-366 \quad\quad +748 \quad\quad\quad -5 \quad\quad\quad\quad +5 \quad\quad +11 \quad \equiv +393$$

The identity has policy implications. If the current account balance is negative, the sum of private and government lending and borrowing will be an offsetting positive (and conversely). The data in Table 19.2 show that the increase of direct and portfolio investments by foreigners resulting in an increase in foreign-owned assets in the United States offsets the increase of direct and portfolio investments representing the change in U.S. private assets held in foreign countries. If private investors had not been motivated to invest in the U.S. (lending) to offset the current account deficit, downward pressure would have been created on the foreign exchange value of the U.S. dollar. If the dollar became cheaper that would encourage exports by the U.S. and discourage imports into the U.S. by foreigners. This in time would reduce the current account deficit, other

Table 19.2 U.S. International Transactions (Billions of Dollars)

Line	Item	2001
	Current Account	
1	**Exports of goods and services and income receipts**	**1,282**
2	Exports of goods and services	998
12	Income receipts	284
18	**Imports of goods and services and income payments**	**−1,626**
19	Imports of goods and services	−1,356
29	Income payments	−269
35	**Unilateral current transfers, net**	**−49**
	Capital and Financial Account	
40	**U.S.-owned assets abroad, net**	
	(increase/financial outflow (−))	**−371**
41	U.S. official reserve assets, net	−5
46	U.S. government assets	
	other than official reserve assets, net	0
50	U.S. private assets, net	−366
55	**Foreign-owned assets in the United States, net**	
	(increase/financial inflow (+))	**753**
56	Foreign official assets in the United States, net	5
63	Other foreign assets in the United States, net	748
70	**Statistical discrepancy**	**11**
	Memoranda:	
73	**Balance on goods and services**	
	(lines 2 and 19) ($998 − $1,356)	**−358**
76	**Balance on current account**	
	(lines 1, 18, and 35) ($1,282 − $1,626 − $49)	**−393**

Source: U.S. Department of Commerce, Bureau of Economic Analysis, *Survey of Current Business*, January 2003.

things being equal. If the U.S. government, for policy reasons, did not want the foreign exchange value of the U.S. dollar to decrease, it could have relieved the pressure by using (reducing) the U.S. official reserve assets to buy U.S. dollars in the foreign exchange market.

These relationships can be clarified by relating them to the national product accounts. The basic equation for the national income accounts is

$$Y = C + I + G + NX, \tag{19.1}$$

Table 19.3 Key Transaction Categories

Category	Symbol	Sign	Amount in 2001 (Billions of Dollars)	Line in Table 19.2
U.S. private lending	ΔPL_{US}	$(-)$	-366	50
U.S. private borrowing	ΔPB_{US}	$(+)$	$+748$	63
U.S. official reserve assets	ΔORA_{US}	$(-)$	-5	41
Foreign official assets in U.S.	ΔORA_F	$(+)$	$+5$	56
Statistical discrepancy	SD	$(+, -)$	$+11$	70
Current asset balance	CA	$(+, -)$	-393	76

where

$$Y = \text{output or gross domestic product,}$$

$$C = \text{consumer expenditures,}$$

$$I = \text{investment,}$$

$$G = \text{government spending,}$$

$$NX = \text{net exports.}$$

Rearranging Eq. (19.1) gives us

$$Y - C - G = I + NX. \tag{19.2}$$

The left-hand side of Eq. (19.2) is "national saving." National saving (S) is that portion of current product or income not consumed by either the households or government. The right-hand side of Eq. (19.2) expresses national saving in another form. It can also be written as

$$NX = S - I. \tag{19.3}$$

This defines the nature of net exports. If the savings of a country are less than its domestic investment, it will have negative net exports. Since the balance on current account in the United States has been negative (as shown in Table 19.2), this implies that investment has exceeded savings in the United States; the United States has liquidated assets abroad or foreign assets in the United States have increased to cover the U.S. savings gap. From the basic identity in Eq. (19.3), it therefore follows that the $393 billion current account deficit represents the excess of domestic investment over national savings for the same time period. This would also represent the excess of domestic expenditures over domestic output. This means that in 2001 the United States consumed $393 billion more than it produced. This excess consumption was provided by net imports, which had to be financed by changes in the international financial or capital accounts of the United States.

In summary, while government reports on U.S. international transactions avoid the concept of balance of payments, it is still measured. The pattern in recent years for the United States has been a very substantial negative balance on current account. In terms of Table 19.2, the negative balance has been further increased by accumulating U.S. private assets abroad. However, a very substantial buildup of offsetting foreign private investments in the United States has also taken place.

The significance of alternative measures of "the balance of payments" depends on the circumstances of an individual country and the pattern of international economic developments taking place. One must analyze as many components of information as possible, including the more general economic developments taking place in individual countries. The balance of payments along with other information sources may be analyzed within a more general economic framework to develop judgments about adjustment processes taking place that will have implications for changes in foreign exchange rates as well. It is this kind of analysis that is required for formulating corporate financial policies of firms substantially affected by changes in foreign exchange rates. We next analyze some of the fundamental relationships that reflect the broad economic adjustment forces reflected in statements of international transactions.

D. *T*he International Parity Relationships

Sound decision making in managing foreign exchange (FX) risks requires an understanding of the key equilibrium relations involving international prices, interest rates, inflation rates, and spot versus forward exchange rates. For example, MNCs often value their foreign operations in dollars with the implication that cash flows originally forecasted in the local currency must be converted to dollars at the forward FX rate on a year-by-year basis. This section provides a basic understanding of the theory of FX.

The analysis begins with assumptions required to establish the fundamental propositions, which can then be modified as applications require. The basic assumptions are those required for perfect markets, namely:

A1. Financial markets are perfect. (Numerous buyers and sellers; no taxes, no information asymmetry or transactions costs, and no government controls.)

A2. Goods and markets are perfect. (Numerous buyers and sellers; no transportation costs, no barriers to trade.)

A3. There is a consumption basket common to all.

A4. The future is known with certainty.

A5. The competitive markets are in equilibrium.

The following equilibrium relationships can then be established:

1. Purchasing power parity (PPP)

2. Interest rate parity (IRP)

3. Fisher relation (FR)

4. International Fisher effect (IFE)

5. Forward exchange expectations (FEE)

International business transactions are conducted in many different currencies. However, a U.S. exporter selling to a foreigner expects to be paid in dollars. Conversely, a foreign importer buying from an American exporter may prefer to pay in his or her own currency. The existence of the foreign exchange markets allows buyers and sellers to deal in the currencies of their preference. The foreign exchange markets consist of individual brokers, the large international money banks, and many commercial banks that facilitate transactions on behalf of their customers. Payments may be made in one currency by an importer and received in another by the exporter.

Table 19.4 Illustrative Exchange Rates

Country	Monetary Unit	Feb. 27, 2003
Australia*	Dollar	0.6054
Brazil	Real	3.5660
Canada	Dollar	1.4954
China, P.R.	Yuan	8.2775
Denmark	Krone	6.9030
EMU Members*	Euro	1.0763
Hong Kong	Dollar	7.7991
India	Rupee	47.6600
Japan	Yen	117.5800
Malaysia	Ringgit	3.8000
Mexico	Peso	11.0230
New Zealand*	Dollar	0.5620
Norway	Krone	7.1980
Singapore	Dollar	1.7361
South Africa	Rand	8.0200
South Korea	Won	1,186.0000
Sri Lanka	Rupee	96.9000
Sweden	Krona	8.4820
Switzerland	Franc	1.3598
Taiwan	Dollar	34.7500
Thailand	Baht	42.6800
United Kingdom*	Pound	1.5798
Venezuela	Bolivar	1,600.0000

Note: Rates in currency units per U.S. dollar except as noted by *.
Source: Federal Reserve Statistical Release H. 10, February 27, 2003.

Foreign exchange rates can be expressed in foreign currency (FC) units per dollar such as FC/$ or in dollars per FC units such as $/FC. A list of illustrative exchange rates and their values is given in Table 19.4. Note that for four of the countries their rates are expressed as $/FC. For all the others, the relationship is expressed as FC/$. Since the conventions are not consistent in practice, we shall generally use both forms, making explicit the direction of the measurement.

In the foreign exchange rate literature the symbols S and F are used to refer to spot and future exchange rates. However, it is sometimes ambiguous whether it represents the units of foreign currency per dollar or the dollar value of the foreign currency. Therefore, always subscript the S and F to make clear the relationships between the currencies involved. Table 19.5 lists the key input items utilized in the following discussion of the parity relationships.

Table 19.5 Symbol Definitions and Inputs

Symbol	Definition	Illustrative Input
$S_{\$/€,0}$	Spot exchange rate, dollars per euro	$1.1/€
$_0F_{\$/€,T}$	Foreign exchange rate $t = 0$, for dollars per euro at $t = T$	$1.07944/€
$P_{\$,1}/P_{\$,0}$	Rate of price level change in U.S.	1.02547
$P_{€,1}/P_{€,0}$	Rate of price level change in euro	1.0450
$_0R_{\$,T}$	U.S. nominal interest rate from $t = 0$ to T	5% per annum
$_0R_{€,T}$	Euro nominal interest rate from $t = 0$ to T	7% per annum
$_0r_T$	Real rate of interest from $t = 0$ to T	

1. Purchasing Power Parity (PPP)

ABSOLUTE PPP The *purchasing power parity* doctrine is an expression of the law of one price. In competitive markets the exchange-adjusted prices of identical tradable goods and financial assets must be equal worldwide (taking account of information and transaction costs). PPP deals with the rates at which domestic goods are exchanged for foreign goods. A formal expression of the absolute version of PPP is

$$P_{\$,0} = P_{€,0} \times S_{\$/€,0}. \tag{19.4}$$

An illustration is

$$P_{\$,0} = €10 \times (\$1.1/€)$$

$$= \$11.$$

Thus if 10 U.K. pounds buys a quantity of wheat in the United Kingdom and the spot exchange rate is $1.625/£, the same quantity of wheat will sell for $16.25 in the United States.

The purchasing power parity doctrine states that people will value currencies for what they will buy. If an American dollar buys the same basket of goods and services as five units of a foreign currency, we should have an exchange rate of five foreign currency units to the dollar, or each foreign currency unit should be worth $0.20. An attempt to compare price indices to computed purchasing power parity assumes that it is possible to compile comparable baskets of goods in different countries. As a practical matter, the purchasing power parity rate is estimated from changes in the purchasing power of two currencies with reference to some past base period when the exchange rate was (theoretically) in equilibrium.

RELATIVE PPP In using the PPP we formulate it as a statement that *changes* in exchange rates reflect *changes* in the relative prices between two countries. In formal terms the relative PPP may be stated as follows:

$$\frac{E(S_{\$/€,T})}{S_{\$/€,0}} = \frac{P_{\$,T}/P_{\$,0}}{P_{€,T}/P_{€,0}}, \tag{19.5}$$

where the terms are as defined in Table 19.5 and E is the expectation operator. An example is

$$E(S_{\$/\mathord{\text{€}},1}) = S_{\$/\mathord{\text{€}},0} \times \frac{P_{\$,1}/P_{\$,0}}{P_{\mathord{\text{€}},1}/P_{\mathord{\text{€}},0}}$$

$$= \$1.1/\mathord{\text{€}} \times \frac{1.02547}{1.0450}$$

$$= \$1.07944.$$

For the country with the higher expected inflation rate, the expected future spot exchange rate will fall. More general numerical examples will illustrate some of the implications of the purchasing power parity doctrine. Let us assume that for a given time period foreign price levels have risen by 32%, whereas domestic price levels have risen by 20%. If the initial exchange rate is FC 10 to \$1, the subsequent new exchange rate will be

$$E(S_{FC/\$,1}) = S_{FC/\$,0} \times \frac{P_{FC,0}}{P_{\$,1}/P_{\$,0}} = 10 \times \frac{1.32}{1.20} = 11 \, \text{FC/\$}.$$

It will now take 10% more foreign currency units to equal \$1 because the relative inflation rate has been higher in the foreign country. Alternatively, with an exchange rate of FC 10 to \$1, let us assume that foreign prices have risen by 17% while domestic prices have risen by 30%. The expected new exchange rate would be

$$E(S_{FC/\$,1}) = S_{FC/\$,0} \times \frac{P_{FC,1}/P_{FC,0}}{P_{\$,1}/P_{\$,0}} = 10 \times \frac{1.17}{1.30} = 9 \, \text{FC/\$}.$$

In this example the number of foreign currency units needed to buy \$1 would drop by 10%. Thus the value of the foreign currency has increased due to the differential rates of inflation in domestic versus foreign prices.

Empirical studies indicate that while the purchasing power parity relationship does not hold perfectly, it holds in the long run (Solnik [2000], Levich [2001], Madura [2003]). More fundamentally, the doctrine predicts that an equilibrium rate between two currencies will reflect market forces and that random deviations from the central tendency will tend to be self-correcting; that is, it suggests the existence of some strong equilibrating forces. Furthermore, it argues that the relations between exchange rates will not be haphazard but will reflect underlying economic conditions and changes in these conditions. The relationships are not precise because of a number of factors. These include differences in incomes or other endowments between the two countries, differences in tastes and/or market baskets consumed, changes in government policies, transportation costs, lags in market responses, differences between the two countries in the price ratios of internationally traded goods to domestically traded goods, and the effect of a risk premium.

2. Interest Rate Parity (IRP)

Interest rate parity holds that the ratio of the forward and spot exchange rates will equal the ratio of foreign and domestic nominal interest rates. The formal statement of IRP is

$$\frac{{}_0F_{\$/\mathord{\text{€}},T}}{S_{\$/\mathord{\text{€}},0}} = \frac{1 + {}_0R_{\$,T}}{1 + {}_0R_{\mathord{\text{€}},T}}, \tag{19.6}$$

where the terms are as defined in Table 19.5. Adding 1 to the left and right side of Eq. (19.6), an equivalent expression for the IRP is

$$\frac{{}_0F_{\$/€,T} - S_{\$/€,0}}{S_{\$/€,0}} = \frac{{}_0R_{\$,T} - {}_0R_{€,T}}{1 + {}_0R_{€,T}}. \tag{19.6a}$$

The general expression for the IRP in Eq. (19.6a) provides a basis for some illustrative examples. In Table 19.6 we present an example of interest rate parity between the euro and U.S. dollar. At time 0, \$100 can be invested for one year in bonds denominated either in euros or U.S. dollars. We use annual rates for simplicity. If the \$100 is invested at the U.S. interest rate, its end-of-year value would be \$105. Alternatively, the \$100 can be converted into euros, invested in a euro security, at the same time buying a euro forward contract to receive dollars in the future. Converting the \$100 into euros provides €90.909, invested at the euro rate of 7% to obtain an end of the year €97.273. The forward contract converts this amount to \$105. This is a parity relationship in which the forward discount on the euro of 1.869% is equal to the discounted interest rate differential as shown in Table 19.6.

Table 19.6 Example of Interest Rate Parity Equilibrium, Euro and U.S. Dollar, ${}_0F_{\$/€,1} = \$1.07944/€$

$$S_{\$/€,0} = \$1.1/€$$

$${}_0F_{\$/€,1} = \$1.07944/€$$

$${}_0R_{\$,1} = 5\% \text{ per annum}$$

$${}_0R_{€,1} = 7\% \text{ per annum}$$

	Year 0	**Year 1**
Dollar	\$100	$\$100 \times (1 + {}_0R_{\$,1}) = \$100 \times 1.05 = \$105.00$
		in €: €90.909 × $(1 + {}_0R_{€,1})$
		= €90.909 × 1.07 = €97.273
Euro	$\$100 \times (1/S_{\$/€,0})$	
	= \$100 × (€1/\$1.1) = €90.909	in \$: €97.273 × ${}_0F_{\$/€,1}$
		= €97.273 × \$1.07944/€ = \$105.0

$$\frac{{}_0F_{\$/€,1} - S_{\$/€,0}}{S_{\$/€,0}} = \frac{{}_0R_{\$,1} - {}_0R_{€,1}}{1 + {}_0R_{€,1}}$$

$$\frac{1.09744 - 1.1}{1.1} = \frac{0.05 - 0.07}{1.07}$$

$$\frac{-0.02056}{1.1} = \frac{-0.02}{1.07}$$

$$-0.01869 = -0.01869$$

If interest rate parity does not hold, Table 19.7 demonstrates how *covered interest arbitrage* will move the market towards parity. In Table 19.7, the forward rate is higher than the spot rate so the euro is at a forward premium. Since this is an example of arbitrage, a $100 U.S. security is sold short, equivalent to borrowing $100. At the end of the year, $105 must be repaid. Alternatively, the $100 can be invested in a euro security at the spot exchange rate. We sell a euro forward contract to receive $1.15/€ at the end of the year. The euros received and what they earn is the same as in Table 19.6. But now the forward rate at which the euros are converted into dollars is higher so that the $105 borrowed can be repaid and yield a profit of $6.864 per $100 invested with a present value of $6.415. The premium rate on the euro in the forward market plus the discount in the investment market, as shown in Table 19.7, sums to the same profit level of 6.415%.

Table 19.7 Example of Covered Interest Arbitrage, U.S. Dollars to Euros, $_0F_{\$/€,1} = \$1.15/€$

$$S_{\$/€,0} = \$1.1/€$$

$$_0F_{\$/€,1} = \$1.15/€$$

$$_0R_{\$,1} = 5\% \text{ per annum}$$

$$_0R_{€,1} = 7\% \text{ per annum}$$

	Year 0	**Year 1**
Borrow (short) $100. Repay at $_0R_{\$,1}$.	−$100	$-\$100 \times (1 + {_0R_{\$,1}}) = -\$100 \times 1.05$ $= -\$105.0$
Buy euro spot. Invest (long) euro at $_0R_{€,1}$. Sell euro forward.	$\$100 \times (1/S_{\$/€,0})$ $= \$100 \times (€1/\$1.1) = €90.909$	in €: $€90.909 \times (1 + {_0R_{€,1}})$ $= €90.909 \times 1.07 = €97.273$ in $: $€97.273 \times {_0F_{\$/€,1}}$ $= €97.273 \times \$1.15/€ = \$111.864$
Net dollar position	$0	$-\$105.0 + \$111.864 = \$6.864$
PV net dollar position at $_0R_{€,1}$	$0	$\$6.864/(1.07) = \$6.415$

$$d = \frac{_0F_{\$/€,1} - S_{\$/€,0}}{S_{\$/€,0}} - \frac{_0R_{\$,1} - {_0R_{€,1}}}{1 + {_0R_{€,1}}}$$

$$= \frac{1.15 - 1.1}{1.1} - \frac{0.05 - 0.07}{1.07}$$

$$= \frac{0.05}{1.1} - \frac{-0.02}{1.07}$$

$$= 0.04546 - (-0.01869)$$

$$= 0.06415$$

3. Fisher Relation (FR)

The *Fisher relation* describes how price changes in a single country cause a difference between real and nominal interest rates. When pairs of countries are involved, the *international Fisher effect* describes relationships between interest rate differences across countries and expected exchange rate changes.

The Fisher relation can be stated as

$$E\left(\frac{P_1}{P_0}\right) = \frac{1+R}{1+r}. \tag{19.7}$$

In words, expected inflation is equal to the ratio of nominal to real interest rates.

While the Fisher relation can be stated in a number of forms, its nature can be conveyed by a simple numerical example. Over a given period of time, if the price index is expected to rise 10% and the real rate of interest is 7%, then by rearranging Eq. (19.7), we find that the current nominal rate of interest is

$$R = (1+r)E(P_1/P_0) - 1 \tag{19.7a}$$

$$R = [(1.07)(1.10)] - 1 = 17.7\%.$$

Similarly, if the nominal rate of interest is 12% and the price index is expected to rise 10% over a given time period, the current real rate of interest is

$$r = [1.12(100/110)] - 1 = 1.018 - 1 = 0.018 = 1.8\%. \tag{19.7b}$$

4. International Fisher Effect (IFE)

The domestic version of the Fisher effect states that nominal interest rates will reflect both real rates and rates of price changes. The *international Fisher effect* (IFE) recognizes that differences in nominal interest rate levels will have an impact on expected foreign exchange rates. The derivation of the IFE is based on arbitrage activities under the assumptions of perfect capital markets. The analysis is similar to what we used in Table 19.6 in developing interest rate parity relations. To illustrate, assume that an investor can invest $100 in a U.S. security that pays 5% per one period. His ending wealth will be $100 \times 1.05 = \$105$. Alternatively, if the $100 is invested in a euro security, the investor would first convert the $100 at the spot exchange rate of $1.1 per euro to obtain €90.909. (See Table 19.6.) The ending wealth will be

$$(\$100 \times 1€/\$1.1)(1 + 0.07)E(S_{\$/€,1}).$$

Under the perfect capital market assumptions, each investment should produce the same ending wealth. For this to be true, the expected future spot price would have to be $1.0794/€. In general terms, the expected future spot exchange rate or the expected exchange rate percent change must equal the percent interest differential. This gives us

$$\frac{E(S_{\$/€,T}) - S_{\$/€,0}}{S_{\$/€,0}} = \frac{{}_0R_{\$,T} - {}_0R_{€,T}}{1 + {}_0R_{€,T}} \tag{19.8}$$

Equation (19.8) differs from Eq. (19.6a) because the four terms in Eq. (19.6a) can all be observed at the time of the arbitrage investment; however, in Eq. (19.8) only three terms can be observed since the expected future spot rate is not realized until the end of the period. Hence ex post, the IFE represents borrowing or investing on an uncovered basis. If the expectations with respect to the future spot rate are not realized, the investor would have gains or losses. Capital does not flow into high interest rate countries if the differential reflects high expected inflation and currency depreciation. Similarly, capital does not flow out of low interest rate countries with low expected inflation and strong currencies.

5. Forward Rate Unbiased (FRU)

Under perfect capital market assumptions, the IFE will hold. The forward exchange premium or discount will equal the expected percentage change in the exchange rates:

$$\frac{_0F_{\$/€,T} - S_{\$/€,0}}{S_{\$/€,0}} = \frac{E(S_{\$/€,T}) - S_{\$/€,0}}{S_{\$/€,0}} \tag{19.9}$$

or

$$_0F_{\$/€,T} = E(S_{\$/€,T}). \tag{19.9a}$$

Under actual real-world market conditions, risk premia and expectational errors are likely to cause inequalities between short-term movements in expected exchange rates changes and percent changes in the forward premium or discount. If over time these differences between the beginning period forward rate and the ending period actual spot exchange rate are small, on average, the forward rate is an unbiased predictor of the future spot rate.

6. Parity Relationships

Under the assumptions of perfect market conditions, we have derived the parity relationships in international finance: purchasing power parity, interest rate parity, international Fisher effect, and the forward rate unbiased theory. The relationships are summarized in Table 19.8. PPP represents an equilibrium condition based on the arbitrage of goods sold in different countries and priced in different currencies. Interest rate parity results from arbitrage between interest rate differentials on securities and the relation between forward and spot exchange rates. The international Fisher effect differs from IRP in that the expected future spot rate substitutes for the current forward rate.

In the preceding discussion of the parity conditions, the euro was the reference currency and postulated to have the relatively higher interest rates. In Problem 19.1 at the end of the chapter, we present the data for conducting the analysis with the dollar as the reference currency with the relatively lower interest rates in relation to Mexico. The problem seeks to reinforce the concepts and demonstrates the symmetry of the analysis and results.

Table 19.8 Parity Relationships in International Finance (Dollars per Euro)

Purchasing power parity (PPP)

    Absolute version

$$P_{\$/0} = P_{\euro,0} \times S_{\$/\euro,0} \tag{19.4}$$

    Relative version

$$\frac{E(S_{\$/\euro,T})}{S_{\$/\euro,0}} = \frac{P_{\$,T}/P_{\$,0}}{P_{\euro,T}/P_{\euro,0}} \tag{19.5}$$

Interest rate parity (IRP)

$$\frac{_0F_{\$/\euro,T}}{S_{\$/\euro,0}} = \frac{1+{_0}R_{\$,T}}{1+{_0}R_{\euro,T}} \tag{19.6}$$

$$\frac{_0F_{\$/\euro,T} - S_{\$/\euro,0}}{S_{\$/\euro,0}} = \frac{_0R_{\$,T} - {_0}R_{\euro,T}}{1+{_0}R_{\euro,T}} \tag{19.6a}$$

Fisher relation (FR)

$$E\left(\frac{P_{\$,T}}{P_{\$,0}}\right) = \frac{1+{_0}R_{\$,T}}{1+{_0}r_T} \tag{19.7}$$

$$_0R_{\$,T} = (1+{_0}r_T) \times E\left(\frac{P_{\$,T}}{P_{\$,0}}\right) - 1 \tag{19.7a}$$

$$_0r_T = (1+{_0}R_{\$,T}) \times \frac{1}{E(P_{\$,T}/P_{\$,0})} - 1 \tag{19.7b}$$

International Fisher effect (IFE)

$$\frac{E(S_{\$/\euro,T}) - S_{\$,\euro,0}}{S_{\$/\euro,0}} = \frac{_0R_{\$,T} - {_0}R_{\euro,T}}{1+{_0}R_{\euro,T}} \tag{19.8}$$

Forward rate unbiased (FRU)

$$\frac{_0F_{\$/\euro,T} - S_{\$/\euro,0}}{S_{\$,\euro,0}} = \frac{E(S_{\$,\euro,T}) - S_{\$/\euro,0}}{S_{\$/\euro,0}} \tag{19.9}$$

$$_0F_{\$/\euro,T} = E(S_{\$/\euro,T}) \tag{19.9a}$$

E. *Empirical* Evidence and Exchange Rate Forecasting

In all of the parity relationships only three sets of prices are involved: the prices of goods, the interest rates on securities, and the relative prices of currencies. An implicit assumption is that the influence of all economic variables is embedded in the three price measures. If we depart from perfect capital market assumptions, many other economic, political, and cultural forces will impact these prices in different and changing ways. Among these are uncertainties, changes in government fiscal and monetary policies, relative productivity among countries, national income levels, changes in beliefs or expectations, unexpected shocks that are economy wide or affect individual industries, and so on.

    With so many variables, uncertainties, and changing expectations and beliefs, it is predictable that the parity conditions do not hold at any point in time. Empirical studies summarize considerable evidence of persistent departures from parity conditions (Caves, Frankel, and Jones [2002],

Levich [2001], Madura [2003], and Solnik [2000]). But empirical studies summarized in the same sources also establish that there are long-run tendencies to move to parity relationships.

With regard to PPP, Rogoff [1996] summarizes a number of studies, finding a consensus result that the half-life of PPP deviations is 3–5 years. Furthermore, he finds that the speed of converge to PPP is "extremely slow." Deviations from PPP are corrected at a rate of roughly 15% per year.

Similarly departures were found for interest parity relations. Under uncovered interest parity, the interest rate differential between two countries is an unbiased estimate of the future exchange rate change if expectations are rational. In fact, under risk neutrality and rational expectations, the forward discount (the difference between the current forward and spot exchange rates) should also be an unbiased estimate of subsequent exchange rate changes.

The unbiasedness can be tested by a regression of the following form:

$$\ln S_{t+k} - \ln S_t = \alpha + \beta(\ln F_{t,t+k} - \ln S_t) + \eta_{t+k}, \tag{19.10}$$

where $\ln S_{t+k} - \ln S_t$ is the change in log of the spot price of foreign exchange over k periods, $F_{t,t+k}$ is the current k-period forward rate, $\ln F_{t,t+k} - \ln S_t$ is the forward discount, and η_{t+k} is the random error term. In Eq. (19.10), the null hypothesis is that $\beta = 1$ under unbiasedness. A failure of the regression to yield $\beta = 1$ is often referred to as the forward discount bias.

Many studies have tested the unbiasedness hypothesis and found the coefficient of β to be less than one. The average coefficient across some 75 published estimates is -0.88 (Froot [1990]). A negative β implies that investors are better off investing in the currency with the higher interest rate.

Two possible explanations for the bias are common in the literature (Froot and Thaler [1990]). One is that $\beta < 1$ is evidence of a risk premium on foreign exchange. If investors are risk averse and foreign exchange risk is not fully diversifiable, the interest differential or the forward rate discount is no longer a pure estimate of the expected change in future exchange rates, but the sum of the expected change in the exchange rate plus a risk premium. When the dollar interest rate rises, investments in dollar assets become more risky. Another explanation is that the bias is evidence of expectational errors.

Investment banks have sought to develop models forecasting foreign exchange rates based on short-run departures from parity relationships. Deutsche Bank explains the forward rate bias as resulting from investors' risk aversion to short-term losses that can be substantial (Deutsche Bank, *FX Weekly*, January 24, 2003, pp. 4–7). Hence, currencies trading at a forward discount (premium), on average, tend to weaken (rise) less than what is implied by the forward discount (premium). Currencies trading at a forward discount tend to outperform those trading at a forward premium. This bias could be exploited by taking long positions in currencies that trade at a forward discount and short currencies that trade at a forward premium. In theory, in the long run, this arbitrage opportunity will disappear as investors make such trades. But because of risk aversion, the forward rate bias persists.

The Deutsche Bank investment strategy is to go long in the three highest-yielding (highest forward discount) currencies and to go short in the three lowest-yielding (highest forward premium) currencies. This is called going long in the forward rate bias trades. This strategy is combined with a daily optimized technical moving-average model that yields a trading rule on when to move in and out of the forward rate bias trades, that is, whether to go long in the forward rate bias trade or to close the position and do nothing.

Merrill Lynch has developed a model based on departures from PPP (Merrill Lynch, *Global FX Paper #2: Navigating for Currency Value—ML FX COMPASS*, March 17, 2003). The Merrill Lynch model is based on the Fundamental Equilibrium Exchange Rate (FEER) methodology developed by Williamson [1994]. FEER is the exchange rate that would achieve internal and external balance. The exchange rates would adjust so that a country's trade shortfall (surplus) can be satisfied by foreign capital inflows (outflows) over a long-term horizon. For example, if trade deficits and foreign capital needs are high, the equilibrium exchange rate needs to be lower. This cheapens exports, imports are more expensive, the country's trade position improves, and the need for foreign capital is lower.

Merrill Lynch has named its model FX COMPASS, which seeks to implement the FEER methodology. Estimates are obtained for an equilibrium real exchange rate based on a complete model of the current account and sustainable capital flows. Three steps are used for implementation. First, detailed equations for the components of the current account are estimated to determine the historical sensitivity of trade flows to income and exchange rate movements. Second, the structural position of trade is separated from the cyclical swings in trade. A country's structural position is estimated based on assumptions of internal equilibrium (output at trend and inflation at target). A country's long-term capital demands or supplies are determined once the structural trade balance and net asset/liability position are defined. Third, the equilibrium exchange rate is estimated. This is the rate that ensures the structural position of the current account is consistent with sustainable capital flows based on long-term projections. The FX COMPASS approach allows for scenario analyses and gives a macroeconomics explanation for the optimal real exchange rate. A trading rule can be developed based on identifying countries with significant imbalances in their real exchange rate.

For decisions involving long-term time horizons, the parity conditions offer useful planning guides. Departures from parity relationships may offer opportunities for speculative gains. However, departures can be uncertain in size and duration, and turning points are likely to be difficult to predict.

Commercial forecasting models such as the Deutsche Bank and Merrill Lynch efforts do not guarantee success. The underlying difficulties reflect the wide range of economic, financial, and speculative variables influencing exchange rate behavior. Forecasters with superior judgments may succeed at least temporarily. The slow rate at which foreign exchange rates move toward parity conditions suggests that the biases are not eliminated. This conclusion has implications for operating business firms. They face currency risks. Firms may use multiple methods in reducing currency risks, but costs are involved. We discuss methods of managing currency risks in the following section.

F. *M*anagement of Foreign Exchange Risks

The first issue is whether the parity conditions preclude the necessity of dealing with foreign exchange risk. Dufey and Srinvasulu [1983] address this question and point to a number of market imperfections that must be taken into account such as incomplete securities markets, positive transactions and information costs, the deadweight costs of financial distress, and agency costs. Hence, the departures from parity conditions and their slow rates of correction make it desirable for corporate management to seek to cope with exchange risk.

1. Empirical Studies of Foreign Exchange Exposure

A number of articles have dealt with the issue of how to measure *foreign exchange exposure*. Hekman [1985] develops a model of foreign exchange exposure defined as the sensitivity of an investment's value in a reference currency to changes in exchange rate forecasts; this sensitivity is because some share of the cash flows from the investment are denominated in foreign currency. Also, a share of cash flows denominated in a reference currency affected by future exchange rates will also generate sensitivity.

Kaufold and Smirlock [1986] measure uncertainty about the domestic currency value of a corporation's net foreign exchange position as a function of the duration of the cash flows and unanticipated changes in foreign interest and exchange rates. They assert that despite the expanding opportunities for the use of interest rate swaps and currency swaps, it is often not possible to completely eliminate net foreign exposures of firms. It may not always be possible to find firms with exactly offsetting positions; also, the forward and futures currency markets may not be operative for the requisite maturities involved. They develop illustrations of how to hedge a U.S. firm's foreign currency exposure using the domestic interest rate futures contract and the relevant currency futures contract. They observe that complete hedging requires that both domestic and foreign interest rates be related to the domestic risk-free rate without error.

Adler and Dumas [1984] take a market approach to the nature of currency risk exposure. They reason that the exposure to exchange risk is essentially the same as exposure to market risk. They propose that a portfolio's average exposure to exchange risk can be measured on a historical basis by regressing its total dollar value on a vector of exchange rates. The resulting partial regression coefficients represent the exposure to each currency. In principle, if the same relationships hold in the future, these exposures could be hedged. They recognize that as exposures vary over time, it would be necessary to seek to derive multiperiod hedging rules.

Johnson and Walther [1984] measure the effectiveness of portfolio hedges in currency forward markets. To hedge the exposed cash position using portfolio theory, the firm takes an offsetting position in the forward market. The portion of the spot market holding to be offset in the forward market equals the variance-minimizing portfolio hedging ratio.[2] This is the subjective covariance between the forward market price changes and the spot market price changes to the variance of the forward market price changes. The portfolio approach is compared with a naive hedge in which the exposure is offset completely in the forward market and the gain or loss is determined by the difference between the forward market rate and the future spot rate of the foreign currency. They conclude that the naive hedge is superior but that neither achieves complete elimination of foreign currency price risk.

Copeland and Copeland [1999] introduce a value-maximizing approach to hedging by trading off reductions in the expected cost of business disruption against the expected cost of the hedge. They evaluate FX management programs that estimate the probability of business disruption within a specified time period. The solution to the time to disruption calculation demonstrates that, in addition to the variance of hedged cash flows, other variables should be analyzed. One is the ratio of operating cash flows to cash outflow levels that represent the business disruption boundary— a coverage ratio. For firms with a high coverage ratio, the probability of business disruption is so low that hedging is unnecessary. A second is the reduction in the drift in operating cash flows caused by FX hedging costs. The optimal hedge ratio is the variance-reducing hedge adjusted by

---

[2] See the discussion of FX hedging in Chapter 17, where we discuss the efficiency of the hedge, the hedge ratio, and why variance minimization is not the appropriate objective function.

transaction costs per unit of variance in the FX contract. In a case study, transaction costs of only 14 basis points per quarter reduced the optimal hedge ratio by 20%.

2. Expected Net Monetary Asset Position Exposure

With the background of empirical studies of a number of dimensions of foreign exchange exposure, we next turn to some managerial techniques for reducing or limiting such exposure. The exposure of a business firm to foreign exchange risks is determined by the patterns of its cash flow and asset-liability positions, which in turn depend upon uncertain patterns of future receipts and payments and the patterns of the firm's net monetary asset position. Monetary assets are those assets denominated in a fixed number of units of money such as cash, marketable securities, accounts receivable, tax refunds receivable, notes receivable, and prepaid insurance. Monetary liabilities are those liabilities expressed in fixed monetary terms, such as accounts payable, notes payable, tax liability reserves, bonds, and preferred stock.

The effects of a net monetary position exposure can be formulated as follows:

$$C_p = [(MA - ML)/X_0 - (MA - ML)/X_1](1 - t_{u.s.}) \qquad (19.11)$$

$$= (E_0 - E_1)(MA - ML)(1 - t_{u.s.})$$

$$= (E_0 - E_1)(NMP)(1 - t_{u.s.}),$$

where

C_p = cost of net monetary position (NMP) due to exchange rate changes,

MA = monetary assets,

ML = monetary liabilities,

E_0 = exchange rate at the beginning in \$/FC,

E_1 = exchange rate a period later in \$/FC,

X_0 = exchange rate at the beginning in FC/\$ = $1/E_0$,

X_1 = exchange rate a period later in FC/\$ = $1/E_1$,

$t_{u.s.}$ = tax rate in the United States.

The effects of a decline in foreign currency value are that a net FC monetary creditor loses and a net FC monetary debtor gains. Note, however, that the NMP is today's estimate of the firm's expected exposure at a future date. If we assume a world of perfect certainty, we can set up a perfect hedge by first eliminating the NMP, then finding a way of taking the opposite position—the hedge.

To illustrate, postulate:

$$MA = FC200,000 \quad X_0 = FC4/\$ \quad E_0 = \$0.25/FC$$
$$ML = FC100,000 \quad X_1 = FC5/\$ \quad E_1 = \$0.20/FC$$

We calculate the net monetary loss (ignoring taxes for simplicity):

$$C_p = NMP(E_0 - E_1) = (FC200,000 - FC100,000)(\$0.25/FC - \$0.20/FC)$$

$$= \$5,000.$$

Our calculations show an expected decrease in the dollar value of our asset position—that is, a loss of $5,000. The hedging position would have an expected net monetary profit of −$5,000. We can accomplish this result if we let $ML = $ FC300,000. Then

$$NMP = MA - ML = \text{FC}200,000 - \text{FC}300,000 = -\text{FC}100,000,$$

and

$$C_p = NMP(E_0 - E_1) = -\text{FC}100,000(\$0.25/\text{FC} - \$0.20/\text{FC})$$

$$= -\$5,000.$$

The net amount owed is decreased by $5,000, representing a gain.

The expected effects of an increase in FC value are the opposite. The net monetary debtor loses and the net monetary creditor gains.

If the normal pattern of operations will put the firm in an exposed position, the adjustments required may involve costs. For example, one strategy may be to rearrange the pattern of payments and the pattern of holdings of monetary assets and liabilities in foreign currencies to achieve perfect balance so that the net exposure is zero. But changes in the flow of receipts and payments or in the holdings of monetary assets and liabilities may represent departures from the firm's normal operations. Such artificial changes from the firm's normal patterns may involve costs. To determine whether such adjustments are better than alternative methods of limiting exposure requires that management calculate the cost of altering the patterns of cash flows or of its net monetary position. This may be a rather complex undertaking for an individual firm, but is nonetheless necessary if the firm is to make a rational choice among alternatives.

A firm seeking protection against the foreign exchange risk exposure may employ alternative methods. One is the use of the forward market. Another is the use of the money and capital markets. Still another is to use foreign currency options. If the interest rate parity relationship holds, it is a matter of indifference as to which of the first two methods is employed. For example, if the amount of foreign currency involved is 100,000 FC units, then the cost of hedging in the foreign market, C_f, is

$$C_f = (E_0 - E_f)(\text{FC exposure})$$

$$= (\$0.25/\text{FC} - \$0.20/\text{FC})(\text{FC}100,000)$$

$$= \$5,000.$$

The logic here is that if the current forward rate correctly reflects the expected future spot rate, the net exposure loss has already taken place. The economic benefit of the hedge is that the loss is limited—it is like an insurance payment. If the future spot rate turned out to be lower than the current forward, a dollar value of the foreign currency of $0.18 rather than $0.20, the loss from the FX exposure has been fixed in advance. However, as Chapter 17 discussed, locking in the rate of exchange solves only part of the risk management problem. The quantity of foreign currency exposure is also a random variable. An example might be the dividends that a MNC expects to receive from a foreign subsidiary. We can hedge the risk of a change in the FX rate between the foreign currency and the dollar, but the number of FC units in the dividend is also uncertain and can be perfectly hedged only if the dividend is known with certainty. Therefore, better forecasting techniques that reduce the uncertainty of future cash flows are an effective way of reducing the quantity risk of the hedge.

3. Interest Rate Swaps (International Setting)

An interest rate swap is an agreement between two parties for the exchange of a series of cash payments, one on a fixed-rate liability and the other on a floating-rate liability. For example, a financial institution (FI) has a portfolio of assets consisting of long-term fixed-rate mortgages. Its liabilities are shorter-term deposits and money market certificates. It faces the risk of a rise in interest rates on its shorter-duration liabilities.

An interest rate swap can reduce its risk exposure. For example, the intermediary may be a European bank acting on behalf of a corporate customer seeking floating-rate funding in dollars. The FI agrees to make fixed interest payments to the intermediary, which in turn agrees to make variable interest payments to the FI. The interest rates paid to each other are negotiated. Although both parties swap net interest payments on their underlying liabilities, the principal amounts are not exchanged.

Another source of interest rate swaps results from different comparative advantages in generating funds in either the fixed- or floating-rate interest markets. An example would be a low-rated company seeking fixed-rate long-term credit but with access to variable interest rate funds at a margin of $1\frac{1}{2}\%$ over the London Interbank Offer Rate (LIBOR), whereas its direct borrowing costs in a fixed-rate public market would be 13%. A high-rated company may have access to fixed-rate funds in the Euro-dollar bond market at 11% and variable-rate funds at LIBOR $+ \frac{1}{2}\%$. Thus it has a relatively greater advantage in the fixed-rate market. The high-rated company would borrow fixed-rate funds at 11% in the Eurobond market while the low-rated company borrows an identical amount of variable-rate funds at $1\frac{1}{2}\%$ over LIBOR. They swap the payment streams, negotiating the interest rate savings. A commercial bank or other financial intermediary can act as the counterparty to each side of the transaction, often guaranteeing it and saving both parties interest costs on their preferred debt service flow.

4. Currency Swaps

In currency swaps the two debt service flows are denominated in different currencies, and principal amounts may also be exchanged. A U.S. corporation may seek fixed-rate funds in euros, whereas a German corporation may desire variable-rate dollar financing. A bank intermediary may arrange a currency swap. The U.S. company borrows variable-rate funds in dollars, whereas the German company borrows fixed-rate funds in euros. The two companies swap. Both exchange rate and interest rate risks are thereby managed at cost savings to both parties because they borrow initially in the market where they have a comparative advantage, then swap for their preferred liability.

Currency swaps illustrate the basic principle of international transactions in that all parties benefit as a result of their differing comparative advantage. They then swap for the preferred liability. It enables firms to manage their portfolios at lowered transactions costs.

5. Foreign Currency Translation

In December 1981, the Financial Accounting Standards Board (FASB) issued FASB No. 52, *Foreign Currency Translation*, superseding FASB No. 8, which had been issued in 1976. In general, translation gains or losses are carried directly to the equity account on the balance sheet and do not affect net income. Individual transaction gains or losses net of hedging costs and net of translation gains or losses do enter into the calculations that determine net income. Also, the method of translation is changed from the temporal method to the use of the current exchange rate for all balance sheet items and the use of the average exchange rate for the period for the income statement.

However, the temporal method will continue to be applied to operations in highly inflationary economies, defined as those in which the price level doubles within a three-year period of time.

Since the temporal method of currency translation continues to be applied in the circumstances indicated, it will be useful to explain and illustrate both methods. The temporal method was essentially the monetary-nonmonetary method with one change. Under the monetary-nonmonetary method, the logic of defining exposure by the net monetary position was followed. Monetary assets and liabilities were translated at current exchange rates, whereas nonmonetary assets and liabilities were translated at the applicable historical exchange rates. Under the monetary-nonmonetary method of translation, inventories were treated as real assets to which the applicable historical exchange rate was applied. The temporal method recognized that alternative inventory valuation methods may be used. For example, FIFO charges the income statement for the historical costs of inventory flows, resulting in balance sheet values that are closer to current values. The use of LIFO has the opposite effect. Thus if FIFO is used, the current exchange rate should be applied to the balance sheet inventory account; with LIFO an applicable historical rate should be used. This was the distinction recognized by the temporal method. The two methods are now illustrated by a numerical example.

In this example (see Table 19.9) the Canadian subsidiary of a U.S. company with a Canadian dollar functional currency started business and acquired fixed assets at the beginning of the year when the Canadian $/U.S. $ exchange rate was .95. The average exchange rate for the period was .90, the rate at the end of the period was .85, and the historical rate for inventory was .91. The LIFO inventory valuation method is employed.

Table 19.9 illustrates two ways of accounting for the transaction. The temporal method used in FASB No. 8 and for inflationary economies in FASB No. 52 applies the current (end-of-period) rate to monetary assets and liabilities. It uses the applicable historical rates for the nonmonetary assets and liabilities. Since LIFO is used, the balance sheet inventory account reflects historical costs, and the historical rate for inventories is used. In the income statement the applicable average rates are applied to all items except cost of goods sold and depreciation. Depreciation expense in the income statement would employ the same rate as fixed assets on the balance sheet.

In contrast, FASB No. 52 applies the current rate to all balance sheet items except common stock to which the historical rate is applied. The average rate is applied to all income statement items. The net income figure that results is reflected in the translated retained earnings account. Total assets and claims are brought into balance by a translation adjustment account.

The use of the current method of FASB No. 52 results in financial ratios that are unchanged from their relationships in the foreign currency before translation. This is claimed to be an advantage of the new method. But if the underlying reality is a change in the ratios, preserving them is a distortion. The logic of the temporal method captures the underlying economic determinants of exposure as demonstrated in the previous discussion of the net monetary creditor or debtor position of the foreign subsidiary.

G. *International* Asset Pricing Models

Investors, whether they be firms or individuals, often consider the possibility of expanding beyond the geographical limits of their own countries, if only because of the greater number and diversity of investment possibilities available. If the universe of assets available for investment is larger than just the assets in one country (even a country as large as the United States), investors may be able

Table 19.9 Translation of Canadian Subsidiary Financial Statements

		FASB No. 8		FASB No. 52	
Balance Sheet	**Canadian Dollars**	**Rates Used**	**U.S. Dollars**	**Rates Used**	**U.S. Dollars**
Cash and receivables, net	100	.85	$ 85	.85	$ 85
Inventory	300	.91	273	.85	255
Fixed assets, net	600	.95	570	.85	510
	1,000		$928		$850
Current liabilities	180	.85	$153	.85	$153
Long-term debt	700	.85	595	.85	595
Stockholders' equity:					
Common stock	100	.95	95	.95	95
Retained earnings	20		85		18
Equity adjustment from foreign					
currency translation	—		—		(11)
	1,000		$928		$850
Income statement					
Revenue	130	.90	$117	.90	$117
Cost of goods sold	(60)	.93*	(56)	.90	(54)
Depreciation	(20)	.95*	(19)	.90	(18)
Other expenses, net	(10)	.90	(9)	.90	(9)
Foreign exchange gain	—		70		—
Income before taxes	40		$103		$36
Income taxes	(20)	.90	(18)	.90	(18)
Net income	20		$ 85		$ 18
Ratios					
Net income to revenue	.15		.73		.15
Gross profit	.54		.52		.54
Debt to equity	5.83		3.31		5.83

* Historical rates for cost of goods sold and depreciation of fixed assets.
From Peat, Marwick, Mitchell, and Company, *Statement of Financial Accounting Standards, No. 52, Foreign Currency Translation*, December 1981, 52. Reprinted with permission.

to reduce the risk of their investment portfolios by diversifying across countries. Solnik [1974b] provides empirical estimates for the risk of an internationally diversified portfolio compared with a diversified portfolio that is purely domestic. Using weekly data on stocks in eight major European countries and the United States, he found that an internationally diversified portfolio would be one tenth as risky as a typical security and one half as risky as a well-diversified portfolio of U.S.

stocks alone, using the variance of returns as a measure of risk. He also found that interindustry diversification within the United States was inferior to intercountry diversification.

In a related study, Jacquillat and Solnik [1978] compared the performance of multinational corporations with that of an internationally diversified portfolio. By the same risk measure as above, a portfolio of U.S. multinational firms had about 90% of the standard deviation of a purely domestic U.S. portfolio. Internationally diversified portfolios had only about 30% to 50% of the risk of the U.S. domestic portfolio. This is suggestive evidence that the international dimension had not yet been fully exploited by multinational corporations (MNCs). A portfolio of MNC stocks is a poor substitute to the investor for a truly internationally diversified portfolio.

Maldonado and Saunders [1983] concluded that their empirical evidence "supports capital market efficiency and the law of one price for internationally traded stocks." This casts doubt on the benefits of international diversification. But Philippatos, Christofi, and Christofi [1983] argued that the above study and an earlier one (Maldonado and Saunders [1981]) were influenced by the methodologies and samples employed. They agreed with other studies that find ex ante gains from international diversification. Later studies confirmed gains from international diversification (Levitch [2001], Solnik [2000]).

1. The ICAPM

Asset pricing models, similar in form and spirit to the CAPM, have been derived for international financial assets. In a manner analogous to the standard CAPM derivations in continuous time, Solnik [1974a, 1974d] developed an international asset pricing model (ICAPM) and tested it. A market portfolio, with properties similar to that in the CAPM, is constructed by using markct value-weighted stocks, and a portfolio of risk-free assets of the various countries in the world. Relative weights in the portfolio depend on net foreign investment positions in each country and the relative risk aversions of citizens of each country. A risk-pricing relationship similar in form to the standard CAPM is derived:

$$E(r_i) - R_i = \beta_i[E(r_m) - R_m],$$

where

r_i = the return on security i,

R_i = the riskless rate in the country of security i in terms of the currency of country i,

R_m = an average riskless rate, with weights as in the market portfolio,

r_m = the return on the world market portfolio,

β_i = the *international* systematic risk coefficient of security i.

In his empirical tests, Solnik [1974a, 1974d] used daily data on stocks of eight European countries and of the United States. The results are weakly consistent with his ICAPM. Solnik [1974d] also used the Solnik IAPM to test whether assets are best regarded as being traded in national (segmented) or in international (integrated) markets. This test is a simple extension of his IAPM tests. He found some evidence that markets are integrated, in that the IAPM performs better than a purely national specification.

Grauer, Litzenberger, and Stehle [1976] also derive an international asset pricing model but under the assumptions of identical tastes across countries. Building on that work, Stehle [1977]

improved upon Solnik's specification of the integration hypothesis and corrected some econometric problems with Solnik's methodology. He also found weak evidence in support of integration.

2. Use of Consumption Opportunity Sets

Breeden [1979] developed an asset pricing model that explicitly noted that individuals derive their utility from consumption. Maximizing lifetime utility from consumption, Breeden developed a more complete model for asset pricing, wherein pricing of an asset depended on covariances with aggregate consumption rather than any "market" index or portfolio. Such a model is more general than standard market models because, under certain conditions, a consumption-based model is equivalent to a multibeta model where an asset's pricing is allowed to depend on many state variables. In the field of international finance, Stulz [1981] used Breeden's results to develop an asset pricing theory, much as Solnik [1974c] had followed Merton's [1973] lead.

Stulz [1981] extended Solnik's model essentially by allowing consumption opportunities to differ across countries, at least temporarily, until arbitrage through trade flows equalizes them. Stulz noted that Solnik's model requires the exchange rate to be perfectly correlated with the relative price of the two countries' imports (the terms of trade). The empirical evidence is that although a correlation exists, it is not perfect (Isard [1978]). Stulz allowed the consumption opportunity set to differ across countries. By "consumption opportunity set" is meant the set of goods available for consumptions, current prices, and the distribution of future prices of these goods. It is assumed that prices of commodities and the exchange rate itself follow a stochastic Itô process. All assets are assumed to be traded, but all commodities are not.

Stulz shows that the forward exchange rate is inversely proportional to the covariance between the changes in the exchange rate and changes in the real-world consumption rate. This is the first full model to permit the forward rate to change through time, always remaining in equilibrium. Stulz finally notes that this more general model of asset pricing in international financial markets may explain why some previous models seemed to find the international financial markets to be segmented: If changes in the world consumption rate are not perfectly correlated with the market indices used by previous researchers, spurious results may flow from the misspecification of the tested models.

3. Difficulties of Testing IAPM

The IAPM is subject to the same sort of problem in empirical testing that Roll [1977] had noted with the conventional CAPM. Strongly influenced by Roll's critique, Solnik [1977] pointed out that testing the IAPM in a satisfactory manner is an essentially impossible task. All the problems in testing methodology observed by Roll continue to plague the testing of the IAPM—after all, merely a variant of the CAPM.

In addition, the IAPM has its own problems. Solnik makes two points. First, it is well documented that the covariance between national indices is quite low. In that case, even if markets were *completely* segmented and assets priced *entirely* in domestic markets, with no influence of the international financial markets, an "optimal" portfolio, artificially constructed by the researcher without regard to actual feasibility, will always end up being well diversified internationally. Such a portfolio will be mean-variance efficient, and an IAPM-type test will "succeed," using this "optimal" portfolio as a proxy for the "world market portfolio." This is a direct consequence of Roll's insight about the role of the index. So the success of the test tells us nothing about how assets are actually priced. Second, even if there were no conceptual problems as above, there is a practical problem. In Solnik's derivation of the IAPM, the world market portfolio turns out to include a portfolio he calls a "pure exchange risk asset." Weights of the nominally riskless securities of different countries in this portfolio are shown to be dependent on the net foreign investment positions in the different countries, and the relative risk aversions of citizens of the different countries. This specification would be difficult to implement in practice.

These general results continue to hold in later studies. For an update of the literature, see Chapters 4 and 5 in Solnik [2000].

H. The Cost of Capital and Currency Risk

The cost of capital is relevant for decisions such as capital budgeting for foreign projects, and for valuing foreign subsidiaries and foreign investments such as cross-border mergers. We begin with a simple procedure to estimate the cost of capital to use in a capital budgeting example and then compare alternative methods of calculating the cost of equity.

1. The Cost of Debt Relationships

We begin with an example of how to calculate the cost of debt. We find that the spot price of the Mexican peso is 9.52 pesos per dollar and that the one-year forward rate is 10.75 pesos per dollar. So it takes more pesos to buy a dollar in the futures market than in the spot market. We use a U.S. prime rate of 9% as an indication of the borrowing cost to a prime business customer in the United States. We now apply the interest rate parity relation to obtain the current foreign interest rate. We have

$$\frac{{}_0F_{p/\$,1}}{S_{p/\$,0}} = \frac{10.75}{9.52} = \frac{1 + {}_0R_{p,1}}{1.09}.$$

Solving for ${}_0R_{p,1}$, we obtain 1.23 or a Mexican interest rate to a prime borrower in Mexico of 23%.

There are many real-world frictions that cause departures from parity conditions in the short run. But these are the relationships toward which international financial markets are always moving. Experience and empirical evidence teach us that the parity conditions provide a useful guide to business executives. For an individual manager to believe that he can outguess the international financial markets, which reflect the judgments of many players, is hubris in the extreme. He puts his company at the peril of severe losses.

2. The Cost of Equity and the Cost of Capital

We begin with the basic idea behind the capital asset pricing model (CAPM), widely used to calculate the cost of equity. CAPM states that the cost of equity capital is the risk-free return plus a risk adjustment that is the product of the return on the market as a whole multiplied by the beta risk measure of the individual firm or project. How the market is defined depends on whether the global capital market is integrated or segmented. If integrated, investments are made globally and systematic risk is measured relative to a world market index. If capital markets are segmented, investments are predominantly made in a particular segment or country and systematic risk is measured relative to a domestic index. With the rise of large financial institutions investing worldwide and mutual funds that facilitate international or foreign investments, the world is moving toward a globally integrated capital market.

But we are not there yet because of the home bias phenomenon—investors place only a relatively small part of their funds abroad. For recent data, see Hulbert [2000]. The reasons are not fully understood. One possibility is there may be extra costs of obtaining and digesting information. Another possibility is the greater uncertainty associated with placing investments under the jurisdiction of another country whose authorities may change the rules of the game. If capital markets are not fully integrated, there are gains from international diversification. A multinational corporation (MNC) would apply a lower cost of capital to a foreign investment than would a local (foreign) company (see Chan, Karolyi, and Stulz [1992]; Stulz [1995a, 1995b]; Stulz and Wasserfallen [1995]; Godfrey and Espinosa [1996]).

Let us continue with the Mexico example. A firm domiciled in Mexico would have a beta based on expected market returns for investments in Mexico. An MNC domiciled outside Mexico will have a cost of equity capital related to its beta measured with respect to the markets in which it operates. A world market index might be a reasonable approximation.

If we calculated the cost of equity for an investment in Mexico in nominal peso terms, it would necessarily reflect a risk differential above the cost of debt borrowing in Mexico. If the cost of debt borrowing in Mexico is about 23% based on our prior analysis, then the cost of equity is likely to be at least four to seven percentage points higher. Assuming a leverage ratio of debt to enterprise market value of 50%, a cost of equity of 30%, and a tax rate of 40%, we can calculate the weighted cost as follows:

$$WACC = (0.23)(0.6)(0.5) + (0.30)(0.5) = 0.219$$

We could use this discount factor of approximately 22% in calculating the present value of an investment in Mexico. The cash flows expressed in pesos discounted by the peso cost of capital would give us a present value expressed in pesos. This present value converted to dollars at the spot rate should give us the net present value of the investment in dollars.

We should get the same result by beginning with the cash flows in pesos, converting them to dollars over time (by using estimated forward FX rates), and discounting them by the WACC of the U.S. firm. We illustrate this second method. The project yields cash flows over a five-year period, at the end of which it can be sold to a local buyer. First we calculate the expected foreign exchange rate expressed in the number of pesos per dollar.

We start with the spot rate of 9.5 pesos per dollar. From purchase power parity, for each subsequent year t, we multiply the 9.5 times $(1.16/1.03)^t$, the relative rates of price level changes, as shown in Table 19.10. These are inputs that we use in Table 19.11, the calculation of the present value of the firm or project, expressed in dollars.

Table 19.10 Calculation of Expected Future Exchange Rates (i.e., the Forward Rates)

Year	Relative Rates of Price Level Changes	$E(S_{p/\$,t})$
0	$S_{p/\$,0}$ = pesos per dollar	9.50
1	$9.5(1.16/1.03)$	10.70
2	$9.5(1.16/1.03)^2$	12.05
3	$9.5(1.16/1.03)^3$	13.57
4	$9.5(1.16/1.03)^4$	15.28
5	$9.5(1.16/1.03)^5$	17.21

Table 19.11 Calculation of Present Value Dollars

				Year			
	0	1	2	3	4	5	5*
1. Initial expected cash flows in pesos		1,000	1,100	1,200	1,400	1,600	10,000
2. Probability (risk) factors		0.9	0.9	0.8	0.8	0.6	0.5
3. Risk-adjusted expected peso cash flow		900	990	960	1,120	960	5,000
4. Exchange rate in year $t(S_{p/\$,t})$		10.7	12.05	13.57	15.28	17.21	17.21
5. Expected dollar cash flows		$84	$82	$71	$73	$56	$291
6. Applicable discount factor @10%		1.10	1.21	1.33	1.46	1.61	1.61
7. Discounted dollar cash flows		$76.47	$67.90	$53.15	$50.06	$34.64	$180.40
8. Present value	$462.61						

* Sale of assets for 10,000 pesos in year 5.

Line 1 represents the preliminary estimates of cash flows from the firm or project expressed in pesos. In line 2 we recognize that these projections are subject to error. We are particularly concerned that the foreign country may change the rules of the game. Political instability might bring a government with an anti foreign business philosophy into power. Discriminatory taxes might be imposed. Restrictions on repatriation of funds might be enacted. Militant unions might raise wage costs, reducing net cash flows. We feel it is better to explicitly recognize these risk adjustments in the cash flows, rather than fudge the discount factor. The discount factor should reflect systematic risk and not the idiosyncratic factors described.

Line 3 therefore represents the risk-adjusted expected peso cash flows. In line 4 we list the results from Table 19.10, where the expected future exchange rates were calculated. In line 5 the exchange rates are applied to the expected peso cash flows of line 3 to give us the expected cash flows expressed in dollars.

In line 6 we apply a discount factor. In the discussion of interest rate parity, we assumed a before-tax cost of debt for the U.S. firm of 9%. We postulate further a cost of equity, leverage, and tax rates to yield a *WACC* of 10%. Since we already covered these procedures in Chapter 14, we can streamline this discussion to focus on the foreign investment issues. Line 7 presents the discounted dollar cash flows using the data in lines 5 and 6. In line 8 the present values from line 7 are summed to obtain the total present value of the firm or project of $463 million. The U.S. firm could incur investment outlays with a present value of up to $463 million to earn its cost of capital.

We have illustrated a systematic methodology for valuing foreign acquisitions or making direct investments. The numbers used in the example were simplified to facilitate the exposition. The underlying principles and concepts would be the same if we were using a complex sophisticated computer program. The method is similar to the valuation of domestic investments. The complications are mainly foreign exchange risks and foreign country risks. The parity relationships provide useful guidelines for thinking about foreign exchange rates, relative inflation, and relative interest rates.

In Table 19.11 we did not mean to imply that the risk factors applied in line 2 were to be approached passively. A company can use a wide range of strategies to minimize unfavorable possibilities. A sound project or the purchase of a foreign firm can contribute to increased employment, productivity, and output in the foreign country. The technological and management practices the parent brings to the subsidiary may make its continued participation indispensable. Also, the foreign operations can be so organized that it could not function without the unique parts provided by the parents. Another possibility is that the investment be a part of an international agency program to develop the infrastructure of the host country. Arbitrary changes in the rules of the game could injure the reputation and reduce future international support of a self-serving government.

3. Alternative Formulations of the Cost of Equity for Foreign Valuations

We next consider alternative approaches for measuring the cost of equity in an international context.

COPELAND, KOLLER, AND MURRIN [2000] Copeland, Koller, and Murrin [2000] provide a detailed treatment. They make a distinction between valuation for developed countries and for emerging countries. For developed countries, the basic approach would be the same as in Chapter 14. Multinational enterprises that sell their products globally with similar geographic patterns whose shares are traded on the U.S. and other major stock exchanges should have similar costs of capital. However, Copeland, Koller, and Murrin [2000] present an exhibit that shows that the realized premiums on stock market indexes compared with government bond returns for a number of European countries vary substantially. They cite a study by Roll [1992] that shows that most European stock market indices had less than 100 stocks with high industry concentrations. Roll [1992] also demonstrated that on average 50% of the equity returns could be explained by the industry composition of the index.

The ideal global market risk premium would be based on a global index. However, global indices cannot be calculated over a large number of years. They recommend use of the U.S. market, which is highly diversified and has a long history of data. They recommend use of a global market risk premium in the same range as that of the U.S., 4.5% to 5%. Company betas measured against a global market index are available in U.S. dollars. They note that smaller firms have higher returns than larger companies and that the average company size is smaller in many countries than in the United States. They describe how to make an appropriate adjustment for an average Danish company that has a beta of 1 on a Danish CAPM line. Because the company is smaller than an average U.S. company, they use a beta relative to the U.S. index of 1.3. The cost of equity relative to the U.S. market with a risk-free rate of 6% and a U.S. market risk premium of 5% will be 12.5% (6% + 5% × 1.3). Alternatively, the cost of equity could be calculated relative to the Danish market. Since the result should still be 12.5%, the market risk premium for the Danish market must be 6.5%, when expressed in U.S. dollars (6% + 6.5% × 1.0).

For emerging markets, valuation presents greater difficulties. These countries have relatively illiquid capital markets and higher levels of sovereign risk, macroeconomic uncertainties, and political risks. The approach by Copeland, Koller, and Murrin [2000] is to start with discounted cash flows with probability scenarios that explicitly model the risks faced by business firms for the numerator. This result is a DCF approach with a country inflation premium included in the cost of capital measurement. A third method is valuation based on comparable multiples.

In using the first method, calculations are made in both real and nominal terms since each has some limitations. A calculation in real terms would make errors in calculating taxes since they are based on nominal data. A problem with calculations in nominal terms is that revenues will immediately reflect inflation but fixed property, plant, and equipment will lag at least to some degree. This kind of problem carries over into the influence of exchange rates. For example, an oil exporter will have revenues determined by the dollar price of oil while labor costs and local purchases are in the local currency. They point out that exchange rates can deviate from purchasing

Figure 19.3 Estimating the cost of equity in Brazil.

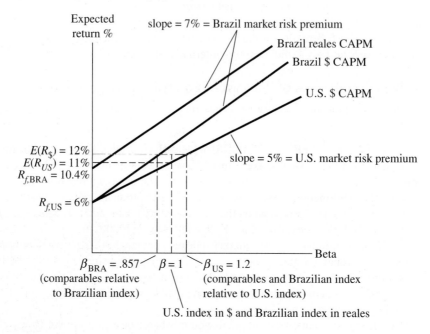

U.S. index in $ and Brazilian index in reales

power parity by substantial percentages for extended periods of time, reflecting the results of empirical studies we cited earlier.

The cost of debt is measured by the global industry cost of debt adjusted for the company's target capital structure and inflation. Copeland, Koller, and Murrin [2000] illustrate their method by the use of a major Brazilian supermarket (see Figure 19.3). The global debt rating for the particular industry is their starting point. The illustrative calculation starts with the dollar-based yield to maturity for a 10-year U.S. government bond of 6%. A Brazilian 10-year inflation differential of 4.4% is added to obtain a 10.4% estimate of the risk-free rate for Brazil, denominated in reales. A 3.6% yield differential over a 10-year U.S. government bond for a U.S. B+ corporate debt instrument is added to obtain 14% as the local, reales-denominated before-tax cost of debt for the company in Brazil.

Calculating the cost of equity for a Brazilian firm proceeds as follows:

1. Calculate the required return on equity in dollars for a set of U.S. comparable companies starting with a U.S.-based dollar-denominated CAPM.

   - Required dollar return $= E(R_\$) =$ risk-free rate for the U.S. $(R_{f,US})+$ market risk premium for the U.S. $(MRP_{US}) \times$ beta relative to the U.S. index for the comparable companies (β_{US}).
   - β_{US} calculated to average 1.2 and MRP_{US} is 5%.[3]
   - The 10-year U.S. government bond rate of 6% is used for the risk-free rate.
   - The required dollar return $= 0.06 + 0.05(1.2) = 12\%$.

---

[3] These are unlevered betas and have to be releveraged using the marginal corporate tax rate and target capital structure of the Brazilian company (see Chapter 15). To simplify this example, we have assumed no debt.

Their calculation of the local cost of equity for Brazil proceeds as follows.

2. Estimate the risk-free rate for Brazil in dollars.

• Obtain yield on dollar-denominated 10-year Brady bonds issued by the government of Brazil.	13.9%
• Remove Brazilian government credit risk spread.	−7.9%
• Result is dollar-denominated risk-free rate, $R_{f,US}$, given U.S. inflation.	6.0%

3. Convert dollar-denominated risk-free rate to Brazilian reales by adding expected inflation.

• Add a forecast of a 10-year inflation differential per annum.	+4.4%
• Result is local currency risk-free rate $R_{f,BRA}$, in reales.	10.4%

4. Calculate beta of U.S.-comparable companies relative to Brazilian index (β_{BRA}).

- The Brazilian market risk premium (expressed in dollars) is estimated to be 7% based on a premium of 2% over the U.S. market risk premium of 5%.
- The 2% premium is based on the average return spread between the second and ninth size deciles of NYSE companies. The average market capitalization of companies in the Brazilian index falls in the ninth size decile while the S&P 500 companies fall in the second size decile. The philosophy behind the approach is that components of the same size have the same expected return, regardless of location. Thus the Brazilian market index has a beta of 1.2 relative to the U.S. market index—the same beta as the set of comparables relative to the U.S. index. The expected return (dollar-denominated) for the Brazilian index is 12%. To establish a Brazilian dollar-denominated CAPM, we constrain the Brazilian market index to have the same 12% return and a beta of 1.0. This implies a Brazilian dollar-denominated CAPM with an interest rate at $R_f = 6\%$ and a MRP of 7%.
- The set of U.S. comparables had an expected return of 12% on the Brazilian dollar-denominated CAPM. This implies a beta, β_{BRA}, of $E(R_\$) = 0.12 = 0.06 + 0.07\beta_{BRA}$.
- Solving for β_{BRA} gives 0.857.

For the final step we move to the CAPM for Brazil, which is reales-denominated. Due to the 4.4% inflation differential between the United States and Brazil (over the next 10 years), it has an intercept at 10.4% and a slope of 7%.

5. Calculate the cost of equity in reales.

• Required return in dollars, $E(R_\$)$.	12.0%
• Add inflation differential.	4.4%
• Required return in reales, $E(R_{reales})$.	16.4%
• Or $E(R_{reales}) = R_{f,BRA} + MRP_{BRA}\,\beta_{BRA} = 10.4\% + 7\% \times 0.857$	= 16.4%

In performing a DCF valuation, Copeland, Koller, and Murrin [2000] consider the question of whether to include country risks in the cash flows (the numerator) or in the discount rate (the denominator). They recommend accounting for this risk in the cash flows through probability-weighted scenarios. They argue that the discount rate in the CAPM framework reflects only systematic risks and that idiosyncratic risks are generally diversifiable. In applying this methodology to a sample of Brazilian companies, they discounted their forecast of cash flows based on alternative scenarios using an industry-specific global cost of capital, adjusted for capital structure differences. They found that their valuation estimates related closely to market values.

Having the cost of debt and the cost of equity, the calculation of the weighted cost of capital proceeds in the standard way.

ERB, HARVEY, AND VISKANTA (EHV) [1996] Harvey [2001] begins with a review of earlier studies of the cost of capital in international markets. For developed equity markets, systematic risks in both single-factor and multiple-factor models are significantly related to expected returns (Ferson and Harvey [1993, 1994]). However, for developing markets Harvey [1995] finds no relation between expected returns and betas measured with respect to a world market portfolio. He considers the interpretation that the prices in emerging markets were too high but the model was correct—the model expected returns were much lower than the realized returns. In Harvey [2000], he studies emerging market stock price levels after financial crises that caused significant declines. The CAPM model performs better but variances of country returns are superior in explaining returns across emerging markets.

Harvey [2001] summarizes an external ex ante risk measure based on country credit ratings (Erb, Harvey, and Viskanta [1996]). The Institutional Investor publishes country credit ratings based on a semiannual survey of 75 to 100 bankers who rate each country on a scale of 0 to 100, with 100 measuring the smallest default risk. The higher the credit risk of a borrower home country, the higher the rate of interest the borrower is required to pay. There are many factors that simultaneously influence a country credit rating: "political and other expropriation risk, inflation, exchange-rate volatility and controls, the nation's industrial portfolio, its economic viability, and its sensitivity to global economic shocks" (p. 7). The credit rating may proxy for these fundamental risks and has the virtue of estimating future risk.

In implementation, the EHV model recognizes that for the United States with "little or no country risk," the company-idiosyncratic risk should be incorporated in the cash flows (the numerator of the valuation equation). For emerging markets, country risk ratings are reflected in the denominator for the countrywide effect. The cash flows can be further adjusted to reflect company-specific probabilities. An example is presented of valuing a project in industry A. If the industry is located in the United States, the expected cash flows are a $100 perpetuity with an applicable discount rate of 10% to give a value of $1,000. When the spreadsheet model of the EHV gives a 20% discount rate reflecting the emerging country risk, the value becomes $100/0.20 = $500. The alternative they present is to use the lower discount rate but adjust the cash flows by the same factor to obtain $50/0.10 = $500. They state that this makes it possible to back out the 20% discount factor for country risk to apply to the $100 cash flows that only reflect firm-specific risks.

The EHV model is specified as

$$R_j = a_0 + a_1 \ln(CCR_j) + \varepsilon_j$$

where R_j is the semiannual return in U.S. dollars for country j and $\ln(CCR_j)$ is the natural logarithm of the country credit rating. The coefficient is the worldwide reward for risk and is not specific to a particular country. They find that the higher CCR (lower risk) is associated with lower expected returns for the period 1990–1997 with an R^2 of 30%. Erb, Harvey, and Viskanta [1998] find an 81% correlation between the country credit ratings and the sovereign yield spreads (U.S.-denominated dollar bonds issued in emerging markets minus the U.S. Treasury yields). They state that the credit ratings measure the country risk embedded in the spread.

This high correlation suggests an alternative specification with sovereign yield spreads as the explanatory variable. The advantage of the sovereign yield spreads is that they represent market measures. In addition these are market measures based on expectations over a broad set of economic factors with future time horizons. Herding patterns in credit analyst subjective judgments could cause them to miss important turning points (Bikhchandani, Hirshleifer, and Welch [1992, 1998]).

SOLNIK [2000] The Solnik [2000] discussion of the cost of capital in an international setting extends his earlier work on the development of an international asset pricing model. He begins with a risk pricing relation in the spirit of a multifactor model whose theoretical foundations are found in the arbitrage pricing theory (APT) initially set forth by Ross [1976]. In this model the expected returns of a security are a function of the probability distribution of unanticipated inflation and unanticipated changes in real activity and other macroeconomic changes, the interest rate credit risk spread between government bonds and corporate bonds, the term structure spread between short and long maturities, and so on. Only the betas associated with each factor are priced so that the expected return on a security is a linear function of the betas:

$$E(R) = R_0 + \beta_1 RP_1 + \beta_2 RP_2 + \ldots + \beta_k RP_k, \tag{19.12}$$

where R_0 is the risk-free rate and RP_i is the risk premium associated with each factor.

In the international risk pricing relation, additional risk premia must be added to reflect the covariance of asset returns with exchange rate movements. If there are $k + 1$ countries, there will be k additional risk premia. Hence, each security is influenced by its domestic market factor, which in turn is influenced by a single world market factor and currency risk factors:

$$E(R_i) = R_0 + \beta_{iw} RP_w + \gamma_{i1} RP_1 + \gamma_{i2} RP_2 + \ldots + \gamma_{ik} RP_k \tag{19.13}$$

where

R_0	is the risk-free interest rate,
β_{iw}	is the sensitivity of asset i to market movements,
RP_w	is the world market risk premium equal to $E(R_w) - R_0$,
γ_{i1} to γ_{ik}	are the sensitivities of asset i to the currencies 1 to k,
RP_1 to RP_k	are the risk premia on currencies 1 to k.

National market risk can be decomposed into a risk caused by world factors and a country-specific risk. The world beta of a security (β_{iw}) is the product of its domestic beta (β_i) and the sensitivity of the domestic country factor to the world market factor (β_{cw}).

A numerical illustration is presented by Solnik [2000]. An international asset pricing model (IAPM) formulates the expected return (in dollars) on a stock ABC in a country P whose national currency is the franc:

$$E(R_i) = R_0 + \beta_i \beta_{cw} RP_w + \gamma_{i1} RP_1 \tag{19.14}$$

$$= 6\% + 1.2 \times 1 \times 4\% + 0.4 \times 1\% = 11.2\%.$$

The dollar risk-free rate is given as 6%. The stock market in P is estimated to have a sensitivity of 1 to the world market factor ($\beta_{cw} = 1$). ABC has a β_i relative to the country P index equal to 1.2. The estimated world market risk premium RP_w is 4%. P trades mostly with the United States. All currency exposures of ABC are reflected by the sensitivity to the exchange rate between the franc and the dollar (γ_{i1}). The ABC stock price in P has an elasticity of 0.6 when the P franc depreciates relative to the dollar. This implies that the dollar currency exposure for an investment in ABC is $1 - 0.6$ or 0.4. The investor estimates the currency risk premium on the P franc (RP_1) to be 1%. The example assumes that ABC is exposed to currency risk.

The example illustrates that the Solnik IAPM is based on a multifactor model. The illustration also demonstrates that the measurement requirements are formidable as Solnik himself recognizes. But it provides a methodology based on prevailing asset pricing theory.

In theory, if ABC sells its final products mostly to the United States, a U.S. investor does not face currency risk and the term drops out. If, however, ABC sells mostly in countries other than the United States, the currency risk premium would be a weighted average of the currency by currency risk premium on the FC multiplied by the associated beta, the sensitivity of the dollar return to changes in the FC value expressed in each of the currencies in the markets in which it sells its products (Solnik [2000]). The weighted average is calculated by the percentage of ABC sales in each of the currencies in the markets in which its sales are made.

The country or sovereign risk is taken into account in the numerator of the return calculation. This is an estimate that involves subjective judgments. One approach would be a scenario analysis in which alternative macroeconomic and microeconomic variables are taken into account.

$\mathscr{S}$ummary

The foreign exchange values of currencies have continued to exhibit high levels of volatility. The euro was worth $1.18 in late 1998, dropped to $0.85 by mid-2001, and by early 2003 had risen to $1.08, representing a 27% rise in relation to the dollar. The number of yen per dollar had fallen to almost 100 by late 1999, rose to 133 by early 2002, and then fell back to 119 by early 2003. The fluctuations in exchange rates have greatly affected the terms of trade. The causes and consequences of exchange rate fluctuations continue to be of importance to economies and business firms.

Over time international financial systems have evolved. The gold standard with fixed exchange rates had been the prevailing mechanism since the 1700s. By 1879 virtually all major industrial countries had adopted the gold standard. With the outbreak of World War I in 1914 most European governments did not permit their currencies to be convertible into either gold or other currencies. The United States remained on the gold standard with an official gold price or mint parity at $20.67 per ounce. A return to the gold standard for most European countries took place during the 1920s. However, the worldwide depression of 1929–1933 was attributed in part to the rigidities of the gold standard. At the end of World War II the Bretton Woods Agreement established the International Monetary Fund (IMF) and sought to establish stable but adjustable exchange rates. The par value of domestic currencies was established in terms of gold or a currency tied to gold. In the short run the exchange rate was held within 1% of its par value; in the long run the par value could be adjusted with the concurrence with the IMF. This system evolved into a fixed-rate dollar exchange standard during the period 1950–1970. In 1973 the United States no longer provided convertibility at the official price of $35 per ounce, which had been established in 1933.

The international exchange mechanism continued to evolve into a program of coordinated intervention. The United States, as did other major countries, built up its international reserve balances in the form of holdings of foreign currencies, a reserve position in the IMF, and special drawing rights. Intervention was accompanied by sterilization to reduce disruptions in domestic monetary policies.

Analysis of the international transactions of countries is made to determine whether imbalances are developing. The current account receives close attention. Deficits in the current accounts usually mean that a country is saving less than it invests. Capital inflows are required to offset current account deficits. But numerous studies fail to find that the current account balance measure provides reliable predictions. The influence of GDP growth rates, productivity rates, fiscal policies, monetary policies, interest rates levels, and relative inflation rates make it impossible to predict the impact of current account balance developments.

International parity conditions have established equilibrium relationships for the impact of price level changes on interest rate levels and foreign exchange rates. The purchasing power parity relationships measure the impact of different levels of price changes on the relation between current spot rates and expected future spot rates. Interest rate parity relationships analyze relations between interest rate levels in different countries and the premium or discount in the current forward exchange rate.

Empirical studies find substantial short-run departures from purchasing power parity. The half life of PPP deviations is 3–5 years, with correction rates of only 15% per year. With regard to interest rate parity, the forward discount or premium should be an unbiased estimate of subsequent exchange rate changes. Theory predicts that the regression coefficient calculated for the two relationships should be a positive 1. The empirical literature finds the coefficient to be less than 1, with an average coefficient across a large number of published studies of −0.88. Because the lags are unpredictable and the movements in currency markets extremely volatile, many retail investors may find it difficult to profitably exploit these imbalances (the forward bias). Investment advisors seek to exploit the slow correction by going long in a group of the highest yielding (higher forward discount) currencies and short in a group of the lowest yielding (higher forward premium) currencies. The investors get the benefits of averaging over a group of securities. This is similar to a value investor going long on a portfolio of low market-to-book securities and going short on high market-to-book securities. In addition, the investor reviews general economic developments and technical factors to be sure that special influences will not result in a prolonged continuation of the disequilibrium relations.

Despite efforts to forecast foreign exchange behavior, a wide range of economic, financial, and speculative instabilities create major uncertainties. Considerable empirical evidence establishes that departures from parity conditions are large and movements toward equilibrium are slow. Hence business firms face foreign exchange risk.

Monetary assets decrease in value with inflation; monetary liabilities are reduced with inflation. One method of risk management is to seek balance in monetary assets and liabilities. Real assets rise in monetary units with inflation. Business firms can also seek to balance production and sales patterns in relation to currency risk. If these practices involve substantial departures from normal firm operations, costs are incurred. Hedging activities by the use of forward and futures markets are also costly. The use of swaps and options has payoffs achieved by incurring costs. Hence, as Solnik [2000, 167] observed, the world market portfolio is sensitive to currency risk; since "the world market portfolio has to be held in *aggregate*, . . . world market risk has to be borne by investors."

This result affects asset pricing models. Multinational enterprises that sell their products globally with shares traded on the U.S. and other major stock exchanges should have similar costs of capital. Valuation methodology employs the same general principles as discussed in Chapter 14. However, for companies in emerging countries, valuation presents greater challenges. Sovereign and political risks must be reflected in the cash flows. The cost of capital in dollars considers the company's beta for comparable companies in the United States. In theory, the cost of equity calculation reflects currency risks in the spirit of a multifactor model.

PROBLEM SET

19.1 Interest rate parity for FC/$: With the input data in Table Q19.1:

(a) Using Case A, illustrate interest rate parity conditions as in the text.

(b) Using Case B, illustrate interest rate arbitrage required.

(c) Using Case C, illustrate interest rate arbitrage required.

Table Q19.1 Symbol Definitions and Inputs

Symbol	Definition	Inputs
$_0R_{\$,1}$	U.S. nominal interest rate	5% per annum
$_0R_{p,1}$	Mexican nominal interest rate	9% per annum
$S_{p/\$,0}$	Spot exchange rate, pesos per dollar	10.0 p/$
$_0F_{p/\$,1}$	Forward exchange rate, pesos per dollar	Case A: 10.381 p/$
		Case B: 10.5 p/$
		Case C: 9.8 p/$

19.2 Empirical studies find a forward exchange rate bias, which means that future spot rates are different from those predicted by current forward rates. For example, if country B has a higher nominal interest rate structure than country A, this implies higher expected future inflation in country B than in A so that the forward exchange rate of country A should be at a premium over the current spot rate. The expected future spot rate should also be higher than the current spot rate by the same percent as the forward premium. Over a large number of empirical studies, often the actual future spot rate is lower than the current spot rate.

(a) What are some possible explanations for the forward rate bias?

(b) How do forecasters seek to profit from the bias?

19.3 Considerable progress has been made toward a European Monetary Union (EMU). A European Central Bank has been established seeking to influence member nations toward convergence of their economic and monetary policies. A new common currency, the euro, has been launched.

(a) What are the potential benefits of a monetary union?

(b) What are the potential costs?

(c) What on balance determines whether a monetary union achieves benefits greater than its costs?

19.4 Since the parity conditions do not generally hold in the short run, do they fail to add to our understanding of the behavior of foreign exchange rates?

19.5 You are given the prices of products in two countries as shown below:

	Product	
	X	**Y**
Country A	$3	$1
Country B	FC12	FC6

At an exchange rate of 5 foreign currency units per dollar, describe the pattern of exports and imports between countries A and B.

19.6 Country A and country B are each on a full gold standard with fixed exchange rates. Country A runs an export surplus, whereas country B runs an export balance deficit. Describe the adjustment process that will restore balance to the flow of trade between the two countries.

19.7 Country A and country B are on the gold standard. The currency of country A contains 1 ounce of gold, whereas the currency of country B contains 0.025 ounce of gold. What will be the par exchange rate between the two countries?

19.8 Consider two countries C and D operating in a world with completely flexible exchange rates. Country C runs a substantial export surplus to country D, which experiences a substantial trade deficit. Assuming no initial offsetting capital flows, explain the adjustment process to bring the trade between the two countries into balance.

19.9 Keep in mind Table Q19.9 listing the effects of individual transactions on the balance of payments. Indicate the plus entry and the minus entry for the following transactions. For example, the country exports goods in the amount of $1,000 paid for by the importer by a check on a foreign bank. The entry would be

P1 $1,000   M3 $1,000

Table Q19.9 Effects on the Balance of Payments, Country A

Plus (P)	Minus (M)
1. Exports and income receipts	1. Imports and income payments
2. Increase in liabilities to foreigners	2. Decrease liabilities to foreigners
3. Decrease claims on foreigners	3. Increase claims on foreigners
3a. Decrease investments	3a. Increase investments
3b. Sell assets	3b. Buy assets

(a) Country A exports $10,000 of goods to country I paid for by the exporter by a check on his account with a bank in country A.

(b) Country A imports $5,000 worth of merchandise paid for by a check on a bank in country A.

(c) Direct investment income of $2,000 was received by a firm in country A from a foreign subsidiary, which paid by drawing a check on a bank in its own country F.

(d) A multinational firm domiciled in country A made an investment of $1 million on a direct basis to establish a foreign subsidiary in country G. Payment was made by drawing on its bank account in country A.

(e) A citizen of country A made a gift of $3,000 to a friend in a foreign country who deposited the check drawn on a bank in country A in his own bank in country M.

(f) A citizen in country A bought an airline ticket to Europe that he purchased from Lufthansa Airlines by a check for $500 drawn on a bank in country A.

19.10 In January 2004 (when FC3 = $1) it was expected that by the end of 2004 the price level in the United States would have risen by 10% and in the foreign currency by 5%. The real rate of interest in both countries is 4%.

(a) Use the PPP to project the expected FCs per $1 at the end of 2004 (the expected future spot rate of FCs per $1).

(b) Use the Fisher relation to estimate the nominal interest rates in each country that make it possible for investments in each country to earn their real rate of interest.

(c) Use the IRP to estimate the current one-year forward rate of FCs per $1.

(d) Compare your estimate of the current forward rate in (c) with your estimate of the expected future spot rate in (a).

(e) Prove analytically that the Fisher effect and the IRP guarantee consistency with the PPP relation when real interest rates in the different countries are equal. (Assume that all the fundamental relations hold.)

19.11 Agrimex, S.A., a Mexican corporation, borrowed $1 million in dollars at a 10% interest rate when the exchange rate was 10 pesos per dollar. When the company repaid the loan plus interest one year later, the exchange rate was 10.5 pesos to the dollar.

(a) What was the rate of interest on the loan based on the pesos received and paid back by Agrimex?

(b) Use the interest rate parity theorem to illustrate this result.

19.12 An American manufacturing company has imported industrial machinery at a price of FC4.6 million. The machinery will be delivered and paid for in six months. For planning purposes, the American company wants to establish what the payment (in dollars) will be in six months. It decides to use the forward market to accomplish its objective. The company contacts its New York bank, which provides the following quotations:

	FC	$
Six-month Eurocurrency rates	8%	7%
Spot exchange rates	2.08 FC/$	$0.48/FC

The bank states that it will charge a commission of .25% on any transaction.

(a) Does the American company enter the forward market to go long or short of forward FC?

(b) What is the equilibrium forward rate for the foreign currency expressed as FC/$?

(c) Does the commission increase or decrease the number of FC/$ in the transaction?

(d) What price in dollars can the American company establish by using the forward market in foreign currency units?

19.13 A foreign company buys industrial machinery from a U.S. company at a price of $10 million. The machinery will be delivered and paid for in six months. The foreign company seeks to establish its costs in FCs. It decides to use the forward market to accomplish its objective. The company contacts its bank, which provides the following quotations:

	FC	$
Six-month rates	8%	9%
Spot exchange rates	2.041FC/$	$0.49/FC

The bank states that it will charge a commission of .25% on any transaction.

(a) Does the foreign company enter the forward market to go long or short forward dollars?

(b) What is the equilibrium forward rate for the foreign currency expressed as $/FC?

(c) Does the commission increase or decrease the dollar value of the foreign currency?

(d) What price in foreign currency units can the foreign company establish by using the forward market in dollars?

19.14 Globalcorp makes a sale of goods to a foreign firm and will receive FC380,000 three months later. Globalcorp has incurred costs in dollars and wishes to make definite the amount of dollars it will receive in three months. It plans to approach a foreign bank to borrow an amount of local currency such that the principal plus interest will equal the amount Globalcorp expects to receive. The interest rate it must pay on its loan is 28%. With the borrowed funds, Globalcorp purchases dollars at the current spot rate that are invested in the United States at an interest rate of 8%. When Globalcorp receives the FC380,000 at the end of three months, it uses the funds to liquidate the loan at the foreign bank. The effective tax rate in both countries is 40%.

(a) What is the net amount that Globalcorp will receive if the current spot rate is FC1.90 to the dollar?

(b) How much less is this than the amount Globalcorp would have received if the remittance had been made immediately instead of three months later?

(c) At what forward rate of exchange would the amount received by Globalcorp have been the same as what would have been obtained using the capital markets? Would Globalcorp have sold the FC forward short or long to hedge its position?

(d) If a speculator took the opposite position from Globalcorp in the forward market for FC, would the speculator sell long or short? If the speculator received a risk premium for holding this position, would this place the current forward rate in FC above or below the expected future spot rate in FC per dollar?

19.15 Transcorp has made a purchase of goods from a foreign firm that will require payment of FC380,000 six months later. Transcorp wishes to make definite the amount of dollars it will need to pay the FC380,000 on the due date. The foreign firm is domiciled in a country whose currency has been rising in relation to the dollar in recent years. The tax rate in both countries is 40%. Transcorp plans to borrow an amount in dollars from a U.S. bank to immediately exchange into FCs to buy securities in the foreign country, which with interest, will equal FC380,000 six months later. The interest rate that will be paid in the United States is 12%; the interest rate that will be earned on the foreign securities is 8%. When at the end of six months Transcorp is required to make the payment in FC, it will use the funds from the maturing foreign securities in FCs to meet its obligation in FCs. At the same time it will pay off the loan plus interest in the United States in dollars.

(a) What is the net amount that Transcorp pays to meet the obligation of FC380,000 in six months if the current spot rate is FC2.00 to the dollar?

(b) How much more is this than the amount Transcorp would have paid if payment had been made immediately instead of six months later?

(c) At what forward rate of exchange would the amount paid by Transcorp have been the same as what it would have paid using the capital markets? Would Transcorp have taken the long position in the forward FC or have sold the FC forward short to hedge its position?

(d) If a speculator took the opposite position from Transcorp in the forward market for FCs, would the speculator be long or short? If the speculator received a risk premium for holding this position, would this place the current forward rate in FCs above or below the expected future spot rate in FCs per dollar?

REFERENCES

Adler, M., and B. Dumas, "Exposure to Currency Risk: Definition and Measurement," *Financial Management*, 1984, Vol. 13, No. 2, 41–50.

Bikhchandani, S., D. Hirshleifer, and I. Welch, "A Theory of Fads, Fashion, Custom, and Cultural Change as Informational Cascades," *Journal of Political Economy*, 1992, Vol. 100, 992–1026.

———, "Learning from the Behavior of Others: Conformity, Fads, and Informational Cascades," *Journal of Economic Perspectives*, Summer 1998, Vol. 12, 151–170.

Breeden, D. T., "An Intertemporal Asset Pricing Model with Stochastic Consumption and Investment Opportunities," *Journal of Financial Economics*, 1979, Vol. 7, No. 3, 265–296.

Caves, R. E., J. A. Frankel, and R. W. Jones, *World Trade and Payments: An Introduction*, ninth edition. Addison Wesley, Boston, 2002.

Chan, K. C., G. A. Karolyi, and R. M. Stulz, "Global Financial Markets and the Risk Premium on U.S. Equity," *Journal of Financial Economics*, 1992, Vol. 32, 137–168.

Copeland, T., and M. Copeland, "Managing Corporate FX Risk: A Value-Maximizing Approach," *Financial Management*, Autumn 1999, Vol. 28, 68–75.

Copeland, T., T. Koller, and J. Murrin, *Valuation: Measuring and Managing the Value of Companies*, third edition. John Wiley and Sons, New York, 2000.

Cross, S. Y., "All about . . . the Foreign Exchange Market in the United States," Federal Reserve Bank of New York, 1998.

Dufey, G., and S. L. Srinivasulu, "The Case for Corporate Management of Foreign Exchange Risk," *Financial Management*, 1983, Vol. 12, No. 4, 54–62.

Erb, C., C. R. Harvey, and T. Viskanta, "Expected Returns and Volatility in 135 Countries," *Journal of Portfolio Management*, Spring 1996, 46–58.

———, *Country Risk in Global Financial Management*. Research Foundation of the AIMR, 1998.

Ferson, W. E., and C. R. Harvey, "The Risk and Predictability of International Equity Returns," *Review of Financial Studies*, 1993, Vol. 6, 527–566.

———, "Sources of Risk and Expected Returns in Global Equity Markets," *Journal of Banking and Finance*, 1994, Vol. 18, 775–803.

Froot, K. A., "Short Rates and Expected Asset Returns," NBER Working Paper No. 3247, January 1990.

Froot, K. A., and R. H. Thaler, "Anomalies: Foreign Exchange," *Journal of Economic Perspectives*, Summer 1990, Vol. 4, 179–192.

Godfrey, S., and R. Espinosa, "A Practical Approach to Calculating Costs of Equity for Investment in Emerging Markets," *Journal of Applied Corporate Finance*, Fall 1996, Vol. 9, 80–89.

Grauer, F. L. A., R. H. Litzenberger, and R. E. Stehle, "Sharing Rules and Equilibrium in an International Market under Uncertainty," *Journal of Financial Economics*, June 1976, Vol. 3, No. 3, 233–256.

Harvey, C. R., "Predictable Risk and Returns in Emerging Markets," *Review of Financial Studies*, 1995, Vol. 8, 773–816.

———, "Drivers of Expected Returns in International Markets," *Emerging Market Quarterly*, 2000, Vol. 4, 32–49.

Harvey, C. R., "International Cost of Capital and Risk Calculator (ICCRC)," working paper, July 25, 2001.

Hekman, C. R., "A Model of Foreign Exchange Exposure," *Journal of International Business Studies*, 1985, 85–99.

Hulbert, M., "A Plan to Overcome Investors' Home Bias," *New York Times*, January 23, 2000, Sec. 3, p. 9.

Isard, P., "Exchange Rate Determination: A Survey of Popular Views and Recent Models," *Princeton Studies in International Finance*, 1978, Vol. 42.

Jacquillat, B., and B. Solnik, "Multinationals Are Poor Tools for Diversification," *Journal of Portfolio Management*, Winter 1978, Vol. 4, No. 2, 8–12.

Johnson, L. J., and C. H. Walther, "New Evidence of the Effectiveness of Portfolio Hedges in Currency Forward Markets," *Management International Review*, 1984, 15–23.

Kaufold, H., and M. Smirlock, "Managing Corporate Exchange and Interest Rate Exposure," *Financial Management*, Autumn 1986, Vol. 15, No. 3, 64–72.

Levich, R. M., *International Financial Markets: Price and Policies*, second edition. McGraw-Hill Irwin, New York, 2001.

Madura, J., *International Financial Management*, seventh edition. Thomson South-Western, Mason, Ohio, 2003.

Maldonado, R., and A. Saunders, "International Portfolio Diversification and the Inter-Temporal Stability of International Stock Market Relationships, 1957–1978," *Financial Management*, Autumn 1981, Vol. 10, No. 3, 54–63.

———, "Foreign Exchange Futures and the Law of One Price," *Financial Management*, Spring 1983, Vol. 12, No. 1, 19–23.

McKinnon, R. I., "The Rules of the Game: International Money in Historical Perspective," *Journal of Economic Literature*, March 1993, Vol. 31, 1–44.

Merton, R. C., "An Intertemporal Capital Asset Pricing Model," *Econometrica*, September 1973, Vol. 41, No. 5, 867–888.

Philippatos, G. C., A. Christofi, and P. Christofi, "The Inter-Temporal Stability of International Stock Market Relationships: Another View," *Financial Management*, Winter 1983, Vol. 12, No. 4, 63–69.

Rogoff, K., "The Purchasing Power Parity Puzzle," *Journal of Economic Literature*, June 1996, Vol. 34, 647–668.

Roll, R., "A Critique of the Asset Pricing Theory's Tests: Part I: On Past and Potential Testability of Theory," *Journal of Financial Economics*, March 1977, Vol. 4, No. 2, 129–176.

———, "Industrial Structure and the Comparative Behavior of International Stock Market Indices," *Journal of Finance*, March 1992, 3–42.

Ross, S. A., "The Arbitrage Theory of Capital Asset Pricing," *Journal of Economic Theory*, December 1976, Vol. 13, 341–360.

Solnik, B. H., "The International Pricing of Risk: An Empirical Investigation of the World Capital Market Structure," *Journal of Finance*, May 1974a, Vol. 29, No. 2, 365–378.

———, "Why Not Diversify Internationally Rather than Domestically?" *Financial Analyst Journal*, May 1974b, Vol. 30, No. 4, 48–54.

———, "An Equilibrium Model of the International Capital Market," *Journal of Economic Theory*, August 1974c, Vol. 8, No. 4, 500–524.

———, "An International Market Model of Security Price Behavior," *Journal of Financial and Quantitative Analysis*, September 1974d, Vol. 9, No. 4, 537–554.

———, "Testing International Asset Pricing: Some Pessimistic Views," *Journal of Finance*, May 1977, Vol. 32, No. 2, 503–512.

———, *International Investments*, fourth edition. Addison-Wesley, Reading, Mass., 2000.

Stehle, R., "An Empirical Test of the Alternative Hypotheses of National and International Pricing of Risky Assets," *Journal of Finance*, May 1977, Vol. 32, No. 2, 493–502.

Stulz, R. M., "A Model of International Asset Pricing," *Journal of Financial Economics*, 1981, Vol. 9, No. 4, 383–406.

———, "Globalization of Capital Markets and the Cost of Capital: The Case of Nestle," *Journal of Applied Corporate Finance*, Fall 1995b, Vol. 8, 30–38.

————, "The Cost of Capital in Internationally Integrated Markets: The Case of Nestle," *European Financial Management*, March 1995a, Vol. 1, 11–22.

Stulz, R. M., and W. Wasserfallen, "Foreign Equity Investment Restrictions, Capital Flight, and Shareholder Wealth Maximization: Theory and Evidence," *Review of Financial Studies*, Winter 1995, Vol. 8, 1019–1057.

Williamson, J., "Estimates of FEERs," in J. Williams, ed., *Estimating Equilibrium Exchange Rates*, Institute for International Economics, 1994.

Chapter 20

Forever am I conscious, moving here,

That should I step a little space aside

I pass the boundary of some glorified

Invisible domain—it lies so near!

—Thomas Bailey Aldrich,
"The Undiscovered Country,"
from *XXVI Sonnets*, 1882.

That's one small step for (a) man;

one giant leap for mankind.

—Neil Armstrong, 1969.

Unsolved Issues, Undiscovered Territory, and the Future of Finance

COLLECTIVELY THE THREE COAUTHORS of this book represent over 100 years of teaching and research, have published about 120 refereed papers, written 15 books, and chaired 80 doctoral theses. We have been and will continue to be enthusiastic about the field of financial economics. One of us has often been quoted as saying that it is one of the few social sciences where there is actually enough data to reject some theories—meaning that the scientific method can be applied. As old theories are rejected and replaced with newer theories that fit reality better, the field advances. Partially for this reason, finance has proven to be one of the most practical and impactful of the social sciences.[1]

The topics for discussion are categorized into major groupings. We begin with corporate finance—a section that includes integrative issues that might be called the theory of the firm, then investment decisions, financing decisions, and managerial finance issues such as performance measurement and incentive design. What follows are valuation, risk management, regulation, performance measurement, capital markets, individual decision making, and experimental economics. Ideas about theory and empirical evidence are commingled within each section.

This chapter represents our unconstrained thinking on what might prove for some of you a map of future paths of research. Many of our ideas are only half-baked. But that leaves room for you to better formulate them, and encourages you to make your own list of unanswered questions. We welcome you to help push back the frontiers and hope that among you is a potential Nobel laureate, the chief financial officer of a major firm, a successful arbiteur, a federal judge, a congressperson, or someone that simply has fun with ideas. For our fellow academics, especially those of you who are doctoral students, we hope some of these ideas can be developed into publishable research. Doctoral theses can be roughly separated into three categories—those that solve classic questions that have been around for a long time, those that ask and find answers to questions that no one

---

[1] See, for example, Peter Bernstein [1996].

had thought to ask yet, and those that are extensions of existing theories or new empirical results that push back the frontiers. We will point out those classic questions that remain unanswered, completely miss those that we can't see, and try to help a little with all others.

A. Corporate Finance

The theory of the firm starts with the objective of maximizing the market value of the firm by choosing the correct investment and financing decisions. But there are also managerial aspects of concern to practitioners—issues such as how shall I measure the performance of business units, how shall I design incentives, and how do I think about the planning and budgeting process?

We start with the firm as a whole. Our first observation is that flexibility on the assets side of the balance sheet is a substitute for flexibility in financing. This provides a basis for a new theory of the firm that may explain the cross-sectional regularities in capital structure. Next, we revisit the divided puzzle. Then we argue that a theory of implicit contracts may improve corporate governance and therefore guide corporate decision making better than theories of explicit contracts that are the basis of current thinking. Finally, dynamic finance is shown to have the potential to better explain significant firm-specific events such as acquisitions and divestitures.

1. Flexibility, Investment Decisions, and Capital Structure

Modigliani and Miller [1958, 1963] started modern corporate finance with the conclusion that the mix of debt and equity, its capital structure, had no effect on the entity value. Soon the debate moved to the trade-off between the value of the tax deductibility of interest payments on debt versus bankruptcy costs (e.g., Baxter [1967]). The most modern literature in this area (e.g., Leland [1994] and Leland and Toft [1996]) has refined the topic to describe the value of the levered firm as its value as unlevered, plus the present value of two tax terms, one without default risk and a second negative term reflecting the present value of tax shield that is lost as more debt is added to the capital structure mix due to the increased probability of default, and finally the present value of business disruption costs. Modigliani and Miller had maintained the assumption that greater debt loads did not affect the operating profits of the firm (its EBIT). When relaxed, this assumption becomes important because operating and financial flows are no longer treated as independent. Optimal capital structure can result. But can the trade-off between the value gained by the tax shield provided by debt and the greater likelihood of incurring business disruption costs explain cross-sectional regularities in capital structure? This is a classic, unsolved question. We believe that this trade-off, while important within an industry, cannot explain cross-sectional differences in capital structure across industries. There must be a better theory.

Black and Scholes [1973] likened the equity in a levered firm to a call option written on the value of the firm with the face value of debt as its exercise price. This helped with the pricing of risky debt and levered equity, but left as unexplored the value of the underlying unlevered firm.

We suggest that the theory of the firm should model it as a "three-layer cake." First is the firm's investment opportunity set, treated as a perpetual sequence of capital investments, with their own distinguishing characteristics (e.g., life of each asset, revenue growth rate, operating margin, and salvage value). This layer of the cake is precommitted (i.e., inflexible) and is bounded above by a capacity cap in the form of a call option written by the firm. Thus, for any project

Figure 20.1 Flexibility in investment and financing are substitutes.

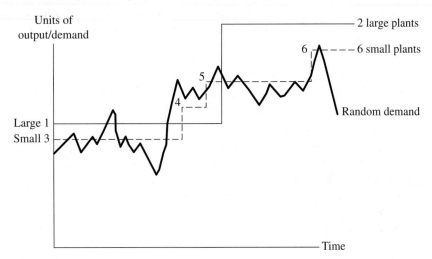

there is an initial cost of excess capacity during its early life (assuming growing revenues), and later on, there is the opportunity cost of the capacity cap. The second layer of the cake is a portfolio of call options to expand and put options to shrink the firm. When exercised properly, these real options create flexibility that has value. One may, for example, choose to build a series of small, less operationally efficient facilities rather than a large, more efficient facility because, being more modular, the small facilities are more flexible and can respond to fluctuations in demand. This flexibility can be valuable enough to offset economies of scale. Third is the "financial layer" of the cake—the fact that equity is a call option on the two aforementioned layers.

Once completed, this new theory of the firm demonstrates that flexibility in investment and in financing are substitutes for each other. Figure 20.1 shows the quantity demanded of the firm as a geometric Brownian motion process. Large investments, being less flexible, are subject to greater cash flow volatility and require more financial flexibility—less debt and more equity. Smaller, more modular investments allow more debt (less flexibility) because they generate more cash flow flexibility. Although their operating efficiency may be lower, their greater modularity provides a better fit to random demand. The value of their enhanced flexibility can easily dominate inferior economies of scale.

This new paradigm has interactive boundary conditions—more equity permits more fixed investment, and less fixed investment permits more equity.

2. Dividend Policy

Black [1976] called it the dividend puzzle. The assumption is that changing dividend policy cannot, in and of itself, destroy or create value. Rather, it is merely a choice about how to deliver value already created by the operations of the firm and with the choices being either share repurchases or dividends. Since share repurchase is seemingly more tax effective, it is a better delivery mechanism. So why do firms pay dividends at all? Why not simply carry extra cash within the firm, thereby creating a low or even negative net debt while carrying debt liabilities that are a tax-deductible source of capital? Is it possible that the commitment to pay dividends affects the feasibility of the firm's investment opportunity set? Or do firms deliberately cut dividend payout on a temporary basis in order to maintain planned investment? If dividend policy is not actually independent of investment policy, then the theory must be rewritten. It would be useful, however, to have empirical results first. We note also that excess cash benefits bondholders by enhancing the firm's credit rating and by providing a reservoir of non-operating value that can be paid out to bondholders should operating cash flows diminish. Given debt covenants that restrict dividend payout, shareholders may prefer dividend payout that prevents too much excess cash.

3. The Role of Contracts

An alternative approach to the theory of the firm is presented by Zingales [2000], who argues that existing theories are inapplicable to new types of firms that are emerging. He seeks to demonstrate his central propositions with analysis of the three main areas of corporate finance identified as financing, governance, and valuation.

He argues that the earlier theories view the firm as a nexus of explicit contracts (Alchian and Demsetz [1972]; Jensen and Meckling [1976]). With regard to capital structure, a firm cannot be worth more than the sum of the individual contracts that compose it. The irrelevance theorem of Modigliani and Miller [1958] applies. With regard to corporate governance, the only residual claim is equity—shareholders deserve the right to make decisions (shareholders' supremacy). Valuation is performed by the cash-flow-to-entity approach using discounted cash flow analysis (Copeland, Koller, and Murrin [1994]).

However, in the newer view, the firm is regarded as a nexus of explicit and implicit contracts (Baker, Gibbons, and Murphy [1999]). This is a view that no one has tried before. A firm can be worth more or less than the sum of its parts, with the difference being the net of the value of organizational assets and liabilities (organizational capital). A temporary shock (such as financial distress) may have very long-term consequences on the value of the firm. To illustrate, he cites Titman [1984], in which capital structure choices affect the implicit contracts a firm makes to service its customers. With regard to corporate governance, there are other claimants besides equity holders who may need to be protected. Valuation must recognize the existence of multiple organization assets and liabilities.

In the "new firm," physical assets are no longer the source of economic rents. The globalization of competition has increased its intensity, increasing pressures for innovation by talented employees. He states that increased competition at the intermediate goods level has provided market performance benchmarks exposing the cost of cross-subsidies in vertically integrated firms. He concludes that the increased role of human capital has changed the nature of the firm. In the new firm, an entrepreneur controls a critical resource around which a web of specific investments can be built. Because this organization "cannot be reproduced instantaneously," potential competing entrepreneurs and others are willing to be employed and make further firm-specific investments because "their rewards are greater" (Zingales [2000], pp. 1645–1646). Zingales then sketches the resulting implications for corporate governance and valuation.

The diffusion of power according to Zingales requires that corporate governance confront the issue of allocation of de jure control rights versus "multiple sources of de facto control rights."

His solution is to "argue that de jure control rights should be given to the party who has de facto power to minimize the amount of resources in fighting" (p. 1648). Because of the fragmentation of power in the new firm, no party is the sole residual claimant and "nobody fully internalizes the preservation of organizational capital " (p. 1648). The resulting "governance overhang" will result in failure to exploit growth opportunities and their rewards. However, the earlier paper by Fama [1980] calls to question the theory set forth by Zingales [2000]. Fama [1980] argues that the market for managers and the post-settling-up process work efficiently well to make managers function effectively in financing decisions, governance, and valuation.

4. Dynamic Finance

Others have addressed the state of corporate finance theory. See Barclay and Smith [1996], Bradley, Schipani, Sundaram, and Walsh [1999], Brennan [1995], Gertner and Scharfstein [1991], Harris and Raviv [1991], La Porta et al. [1997, 1999, 2000], Myers [2000], Rajan and Zingales [2001], Shleifer and Vishny [1997], and Zingales [1995, 1998, 2000]. Yet these writings do not fully explore the implications of the vast growth in M&A activities since 1980.

Table 20.1 shows that each of the adjustment activities described in Chapter 18 has implications for one or more of the seven major areas of finance. For example, consider the impact of mergers. The choice of method of payment will affect capital structure. The combined firm will necessarily reassess dividend policy, which is a part of the broader subject of returning cash to the firm's investors. Mergers are a form of capital budgeting. Changed investment opportunities are likely in the combined firm. Premiums paid and the possibilities of synergies impact valuation. The size and cash flow generation of the combined firm will affect compensation and governance. Accounting and information systems have to be combined or accommodated. The increased pace of change has generally stimulated firms like Cisco, with a high rate of acquisitions, to develop real-time financial planning and control systems.

Divestitures and spin-offs alter the boundaries of the firm. Often they are part of a restructuring process in which the firm improves its operating effectiveness in a number of ways. It moves to product areas in which growth opportunities are most favorable. It augments its managerial capabilities. It manages its resources better as measured by reducing investments in receivables, inventories, and plant and equipment in relation to sales activity.

Similarly, in the third category covered by Table 20.1, exchange offers, share repurchases, leveraged recapitalizations, and buyouts have implications for all the main areas of financial decision making. Changes in ownership structures have similar implications. These activities are closely related to governance issues as indicated by the fourth category of adjustment activities.

Most importantly, the adjustment processes discussed in Chapter 18 and listed in Table 20.1 need to be viewed in a multiperiod context. The literature focuses on the effects on individual acquisitions or divestitures. Our studies of individual companies since 1980 show yearly patterns of multiple acquisitions, divestitures, buybacks, alliances, joint ventures, licensing, and repeated minority investment in other firms. To view any merger and divestiture as a single event is to miss the multiyear strategic horizons in which these decisions are made. Capital structure is also dynamic, being pushed away from its firm-specific equilibrium, then gradually adjusting back. The literature has a few papers on this dynamic process, but much remains to be done.

Table 20.1 Finance Impacts of Adjustment Activities

	Capital Structure	Dividend Policy	Capital Budgeting	Valuation	Compensation	Governance	Financial Planning & Control
I. Expansion	X	X	X	X	X	X	X
A. Mergers	X	X	X	X	X	X	X
B. Tender offers	X	X	X	X	X	X	X
C. Joint ventures	X	X	X	X	X	X	X
D. Supplier networks	X	X	X	X	X	X	X
E. Alliances	X	X	X	X	X	X	X
F. Investments	X	X	X	X	X	X	X
G. Franchising	X	X	X	X	X	X	X
II. Restructuring	X	X	X	X	X	X	X
A. Equity carveouts	X	X		X	X	X	X
B. Spin-offs	X	X	X	X	X	X	X
C. Divestitures	X	X	X	X			
D. Tracking stock	X	X	X	X	X	X	X
III. Financial Engineering and Changes in Ownership Structure							
A. Exchange offers	X	X		X	X	X	X
B. Share repurchases	X	X	X	X	X	X	X
C. Leveraged buyouts (LBOs, MBOs)	X	X	X	X	X	X	X
D. Leveraged recapitalizations	X	X	X	X	X	X	X
E. Employee stock ownership plans (ESOPs)	X	X	X	X	X	X	X
F. Dual-class recapitalizations	X	X	X	X	X	X	X
IV. Governance							
A. Compensation arrangements				X	X	X	X
B. Proxy contest						X	
C. Premium buy-backs						X	
D. Takeover defenses	X	X	X	X	X	X	X

B. *R*isk Management

It is easy—too easy—to focus entirely on risk management when it is always risk-reward management and where the objective is to maximize the value of the firm. We still seek a multiperiod, multirisk, firmwide perspective about what to actually do. Most practitioners hedge the risk of a single transaction at a time when they should take a corporate-wide point of view. Hedging a single transaction can easily unhedge the firm if one fails to take other cash flows of the firm into account. Therefore, it may be possible to find a hedge that minimizes the variance of operating cash flows, but the efficiency of the hedge is limited by the correlation between the cash flows from the hedge and the cash flows of the firm. But why stop there? Instead of trying to hedge the firm's cash flows, why not hedge the market value of the equity? Presumably this would involve a dynamic hedge that is unwound as the firm's operating margin goes up, and laid on (up to the optimal hedge ratio) as its operating margin decreases. The big question is not whether a firm chooses one method of hedging over another at a particular time, but why. We need better theory and some empirical evidence that is consistent with it. Why do some firms in an industry hedge while others in the same industry do not?

Banks have experimented with using allocations of risk equity to business units in an effort to obtain risk-adjusted measures of performance. One popular system is called RAROC, risk-adjusted return on capital. A system that successfully accomplishes this goal need not attempt to estimate risk-adjusted costs of capital on a business unit basis because the allocation of risk equity would theoretically equalize the risk-adjusted required rates of return. Unfortunately, RAROC does not take the covariance between the risks of business units into account. Is there a better system?

C. Managerial Finance

Often the decisions that managers confront as "top of mind" issues are not the stuff of which textbooks are made. Corporate finance textbooks are seemingly silent about how to measure performance, and how to design incentive structure. We have done our best to cover these topics in Chapter 13, but there are some tough questions to be answered. How do firms handle the problem of reputation building as it relates to communicating with the market? Is more open or less open discourse the better path for top management as they decide how to communicate and how much information to convey? And what about compensation and incentive design? What factors determine the equilibrium wage necessary to attract and retain the desired quality of executives? How should the bonus system be designed—especially in a multiperiod context?

And what about transfer pricing? If it is not designed exclusively for tax purposes, what are the general principles involved? How should transfer pricing policy be organized and administrated? What effect does it have on real decisions?

D. Real Option Pricing

Even though there has been a great deal of successful research into the pricing of all types of financial options, there has been much less work on real options. If we stick to this topic for the time being, we note that no one has provided any evidence that real options are priced correctly in the marketplace. Both empirical and experimental evidence are needed. Next, many real option applications take place in a competitive game situation. If so, it becomes necessary to combine real options with game theory. Papers by Smit amd Ankum [1993] and Grenadier [2000] have made some progress, but much more is needed.

The treatment of variance and techniques for estimating it are essential for the application of real options, and little has been published on this issue. The most common assumption is wrong—namely, most academic papers assume that the variance of the factor that drives risk is the correct variance. This is wrong because decisions are based on the value of the project, not on a single value driver. Therefore the relevant variance is the variance of the value of the project, not of the input variable that drives risk.

Isn't information a real option? Why can we not apply real options to information theory? Isn't the definition of a real option the right but not the obligation to take an action *upon the receipt of information* at a point of time in the future? Philosophers tell us that we are entering the "information age." First came hunting and gathering, then agrarian, then industrial, then service economies. In fact, the United States is counted as roughly 75% services—with airlines, telecommunications, banking and finance, restaurants, and transportation all counted as services. But the new growth firms are often thought of as information companies—Microsoft, Oracle, Accenture, and IBM are a few names that come to mind. A common, but incomplete, way of thinking about information is as a store or inventory of knowledge—a library or database. However, a much more complete definition of the value of information is that it is the right to take an action upon the receipt of a message at a future point in time. In other words, one can think of the value of information as a real option?

Chief financial officers often describe flexibility as something of real value. For example, leasing is described as more flexible than debt financing—why? Is their intuition right? Is there something that the theory is missing? And what about the premium for control (e.g., majority ownership in a joint venture)? Doesn't it provide greater flexibility? Might it be possible to use real options to value that flexibility?

E. Valuation—Expert Systems and Neural Networks

Valuation is the lingua franca of financial economics. Individuals are supposed to maximize their personal wealth, and managers, acting as agents for owners, are supposed to maximize the value of the firm. Yet practitioners need anywhere from a few hours to over a week to do the valuation of a single company. Furthermore, it has been only recently that academic attention has been focused on testing the validity of DCF valuation (e.g., Kaplan and Ruback [1995]). The problem from a practical point of view is that it takes too long to do a valuation. If it were possible to build an expert system that provides valuations that are statistically valid, then it would be possible to value thousands of companies overnight.

Other valuation-related issues include topics such as, How do we estimate the cost of capital in developing countries? What about the market risk premium? Is there a country risk premium? How large is it? How do you estimate the cost of debt for a company or a country when there are no priced bonds outstanding? How do you value firms where financing is part of operations, for example, banks and insurance companies?

F. Regulation

Regulation sets caps on the allowed rate of return, strands assets that have extremely low returns, and sets allowed price maximums. Each of these regulatory constraints may be modeled as an option and priced accordingly. Might it be useful to think of these regulations as real options and thereby to recast the theory of regulation in an option pricing setting? How would this change the regulators' view of idiosyncratic risk?

G. Empirical Studies

1. Explaining the Residuals

Goodness knows that there have been thousands of empirical studies on every topic in finance. Yet the field remains wide open with much to be done. For example, we know (Korwar and

Masulis [1983]) that average announcement date residuals are negative upon the announcement of a leverage-decreasing recap of the firm. However, no one has tried to explain the sign and magnitude of the residual on the announcement date. If the weighted average cost of capital curve is really U-shaped, then companies that voluntarily reduce their leverage from very high to more normal levels may experience positive residuals.

We suggest that there is much to be learned from explaining the residuals. Why do some companies have higher residuals than others upon announcement of stock splits (see Brennan and Copeland [1989]), at the date of spin-offs, at changes in the capital gains tax rate, when investments are announced, at earnings announcements, and on and on?

2. New Data Fields to Be Mined

International finance is rapidly developing as the nations that generate the data are also developing. Many questions are being addressed. Is foreign exchange risk a priced factor in the ICAPM? Are country risk premia a reality, or is there a better disaggregated point of view?

What are the issues that cross the interdisciplinary barrier between development economics and finance? Do liquid capital markets, as embodied in stock exchanges and bond exchanges, actually facilitate development, or are they mainly a place for the rich to manipulate stock prices? How efficient are they?

What about the relationship between the nexus of socioeconomic features such as unemployment policy, the ability to reallocate human and physical capital, and the savings rate—or the ability to compete—or GDP growth?

H. Security Markets and Market Microstructure

In the first course in economics we learn of supply and demand—the classical Walrasian tatonnement. Equilibrium price and quantity are determined by the intersection of a downward-sloping demand curve and an upward-sloping cost curve. But even a casual observer can ask, How does one describe trading volume in such a setting? The answer is that you cannot. We do not have a complete theory of asset trading—one that simultaneously describes price, quantity demanded, quantity traded, and bid-ask spreads.

I. The Cross-Section of Returns

1. The Fama-French Three-Factor Model

The three-factor model of Fama and French (FF) [1989, 1992, 1993, 1995, 1996a, 1996b, 1997, 1998a, 1998b, 1999, 2000] consists of beta, size effects, and the book to market (B/M) ratio. They interpret the B/M ratio as a risk factor, positively related to stock returns.

Subsequent papers on the B/M influence give mixed results. Kothari, Shanken, and Sloan [1995] do not find a significant relation between B/M and returns. They conclude that this result is a serious challenge to the FF empirical results. Loughran [1997] finds that the B/M effect in FF is really low returns on small firms outside of January plus a January effect for value firms. Kim [1997], after correcting for the errors-in-variables bias, finds support for the B/M effect.

Using established statistical procedures for studies of this kind, Roll [1995] formed eight portfolios from the CRSP database over the decade April 1984 through March 1994. The portfolios

Table 20.2 Raw Returns for Eight Style Portfolios, April 1984 to March 1994

Rank	Compound Annual Return (%)	Size	E/P	B/M
1	21.22	Low	High	High
2	18.24	High	High	High
3	17.81	Low	High	Low
S&P 500	14.75	—	—	—
4	13.31	High	High	Low
5	11.80	High	Low	Low
6	10.69	High	Low	High
7	7.28	Low	Low	High
8	5.07	Low	Low	Low

Source: Roll, R., "Style Return Differentials: Illusions, Risk Premiums, or Investment Opportunities," in T. D. Coggin and F. J. Fabozzi, eds., *Handbook of Equity Style Management*, Frank J. Fabozzi Associates, New Hope, Penn., 1995, 99–128.

were formed by classifying individual stocks on the basis of three style dimensions: size, earning-to-price ratio (E/P), and book-to-market. The raw returns are summarized in Table 20.2. The portfolio with the highest compound annual return for the period was LHH: small market cap, high E/P, and high B/M, representing a "value" portfolio of small stocks. The difference between rank 1 and rank 8 (LLL) was 16.15% compound annual returns. Rank 1 outperformed the S&P 500 by 6.47% compound annual returns.

These results are not adjusted for risk. When a single market factor measured by the S&P 500 is introduced into pooled time-series/cross-section regressions, the size variable is no longer significant. The significance of the E/P variable increases. The B/M variable declines and is marginally significant.

Roll next put the analysis in an arbitrage pricing theory (APT) framework. The returns from the eight style portfolios on five APT risk factors are calculated using pooled time-series/cross-section regressions. Again size is no longer statistically significant. The significance levels of the E/P and B/M variables increase. These findings of Roll appeared as a chapter in a book on equity investment styles, but were not ever put in the journal literature. But its implications are startling because it holds that neither B/M or E/P are risk factors, since the influence on risk has already been captured by the five APT factors used by Roll. Hence, FF may be confounding B/M with risk because it is correlated with one or more of the APT risk factors.

The methodology of the Roll study differs from the FF studies. Roll's initial raw results, not adjusting for risks, find that size, E/P, and B/M significantly influence returns. When the Roll study accounts for APT risks, size is no longer significant and B/M has about half the influence of E/P.

2. International Finance

With continued improvements in transportation and communication, markets are becoming increasingly globalized. With international markets, international finance takes on increased importance. The literature on international economics and finance has become increasingly enriched. Governments increasingly intervene to manage the international values of their currencies. Yet international financial crises recur with increased frequency. The literature on the international parity conditions confirms their theoretical validity in the long run, but substantial departures occur and adjustments take place with lags. Governments and private forecasting firms, however, find it useful to use parity conditions as relationships toward which foreign exchange rates move. The theoretical materials are rich and informative. Their applications require much empirical analysis and considerable judgment.

3. Forward-Looking Factors

Examples of forward-looking factors that might explain the cross-section of returns are analyst expectations, the credit spread, implied volatility (e.g., the VIX index), and GDP forecasts. Why has the literature spent so much time testing for the relationship between total return to shareholders and backward or contemporaneous factors such as the market capitalization and book-to-market ratio? One of us has co-authored a paper (Copeland, Dolgoff, and Moel [2003]) that finds r^2 of up to 50% using changes in analyst expectations to explain the cross-section of returns. Extensions can probably do much better.

J. $\mathscr{I}$ndividual Decision-Making

1. Behavioral Finance

Both behavioral finance and experimental economics have received recognition with the awards of the 2002 Nobel Prize in economics to Daniel Kahneman and Vernon Smith. Kahneman and Tversky [1974, 1979, 2000] presented empirical evidence in support of models of bounded rationality and how individuals form expectations and make choices. They also modeled prospect theory, which holds that inventors focus more on risk (losses) than on benefits (gains).

Shiller [1981, 2003] and De Bondt and Thaler [1985, 1987] argued that stock prices overreact to economic developments. Barberis and Thaler [2003] and Hirshleifer [2001] have presented exhaustive analysis of the rich literature that has developed. Hirshleifer's study contains 20 pages of references. In addition to variations in human behavior based on psychological concepts, it has also been argued that the limits of arbitrage can result in mispricing (Shleifer and Vishny [1997]; Shleifer [2000]).

Counterarguments have been presented by Fama [1970, 1998], Rubinstein [2001], and Malkiel [2003]. They observe that the characteristics of markets protect it from aggregating the irrationalities of individuals into prices (Rubinstein [2001]). Malkiel [2003] observes that the stock market is remarkably efficient in its utilization of information. Both sides of the argument agree that prices can be wrong without creating opportunities for abnormal returns. However, misallocation of economic resources could occur.

Even more disturbing is evidence of dishonesty by corporate executives. Most notorious was the collapse of Enron, whose stock price was $90 per share in August 2000, but entered bankruptcy in December 2001, only a 15-month interval. Among the activities alleged, Enron entered into long-term contracts, but booked sales in the first year with arbitrarily underestimated costs to report overstated profits. Special-purpose entities were created by Enron executives to engage in transactions with Enron to book artificial profits for both. Dynegy participated in cross-selling with Enron and other companies at inflated prices to book high phantom profits for each. WorldCom classified operating expenses as capital outlays to overstate profits. Tyco manipulated accounting to show high P/E ratios, which enabled them to report earnings accretion for its many acquisitions; top executives received large cash bonuses and loans that were subsequently canceled. Adelphia signed contracts with imaginary customers to inflate share prices, and top executives looted the company.

Accounting manipulations of these kinds distort accounting reports and shake the foundations of confidence in information flows to the public. Pathological activities of these types are difficult to fit into behavioral theory or efficient markets theory.

2. Incentive Design

The design of incentive contracts to solve the principal-agent problem is in its infancy. The incentive structure actually changes depending on the level of the executive being evaluated, whether the executive is line or staff, whether she or he is at the start of a career or near retirement, and changes with the expected frequency of job category changes. When designing incentives not one size fits all. Not only is the theory underdeveloped, but the empirical evidence is weak—often focusing on the level of compensation, rather than on the pay-at-risk, and often missing large parts of compensation. Cross-sectional studies of the relationship between governance structure and compensation are fruitful territory to explore.

K. Experimental Economics

Sometimes when empirical data is nonexistent, it is reasonable to create your own data via an experiment. Much of what we know about the efficiency of capital markets comes from experiments—many of them having been described in Chapters 10 and 11. Experimental evidence provided proof that futures markets help spot markets to aggregate individual information, for example.

There are more than a few opportunities to design experiments that can test otherwise untestable hypotheses. For example, which model better explains new capital expenditure decisions—the net present value approach or the real options approach? What is the effect of a short sales constraint on the pricing of securities? How do various regulations on the dissemination of information affect securities pricing?

Summary

This chapter has covered some of our predictions about where research might go over the next decade in the field of financial economics. As a parting thought, there are fusions with other fields that show promise as well. Certainly human behavior and what has come to be called behavioral finance is a combination of different fields. Frankly, a financial angle on the history of economics would be interesting. Surely, statistics and mathematics will continue to contribute to the field of economics. We wish the reader good luck and good fortune in pursuing these endeavors.

REFERENCES

Alchian, A., and H. Demsetz, "Production, Information Costs, and Economic Organization," *American Economic Review*, 1972, Vol. 62, 777–795.

Baker, G., R. Gibbons, and K. Murphy, "Information Authority in Organizations," *Journal of Law, Economics and Organization*, 1999, Vol. 15, 56–73.

Barberis, N., and R. Thaler, "A Survey of Behavioral Finance," Chapter 18 in G. M. Constantinides, M. Harris, and R. Stulz, eds., *Handbook of the Economics of Finance*, Elsevier Science B.V., 2003.

Barclay, M., and C. Smith, Jr., "On Financial Architecture: Leverage, Maturity, and Priority," *Journal of Applied Corporate Finance*, 1996, Vol. 8, 4–17.

Baxter, N., "Leverage, Risk of Ruin, and the Cost of Capital," *Journal of Finance*, September 1967, 395–403.

Bernstein, P., *Against the Gods: The Remarkable Story of Risk*, John Wiley & Sons, Inc., 1996.

Black, F., "The Dividend Puzzle," *Journal of Portfolio Management*, Winter 1976, 5–8.

Black, F., and M. Scholes, "The Pricing of Options and Corporate Liabilities," *Journal of Political Economy*, May–June 1973, 637–659.

Bradley, M., C. Schipani, A. Sundaram, and J. Walsh, "The Purposes and Accountability of the Corporation in Contemporary Society: Corporate Governance at a Crossroads," *Law and Contemporary Problems*, 1999, Vol. 62, 9–86.

Brennan, M., "Corporate Finance over the Past 25 Years," *Financial Management*, 1995, Vol. 24, 9–22.

Brennan, M., and T. Copeland, "Beta Changes around Stock Splits: A Note," *The Journal of Finance*, September 1988, Vol. 43, No. 4, 1009–1013.

Copeland, T., A. Dolgoff, A. Moel, "The Role of Expectations in the Cross-Section of Returns," working paper, Monitor Group, 2003.

Copeland, T., T. Koller, and J. Murrin, *Valuation: Measuring and Managing the Value of Companies*, McKinsey & Company, New York, second edition, 1994.

De Bondt, W., and R. Thaler, "Does the Stock Market Overreact?" *Journal of Finance*, 1985, Vol. 40, No. 3, 793–805.

———, "Further Evidence on Investor Overreaction and Stock Market Seasonality," *Journal of Finance*, 1987, Vol. 42, No. 3, 557–581.

Fama, E., "Efficient Capital Markets: A Review of Theory and Empirical Work," *Journal of Finance*, 1970, Vol. 25, 383–417.

———, "Agency Problems and the Theory of the Firm," *Journal of Political Economy*, 1980, Vol. 88, 288–307.

———, "Market Efficiency, Long-Term Returns, and Behavioral Finance," *Journal of Financial Economics*, September 1998, Vol. 49, 283–306.

Fama, E. F., and K. R. French, "Business Conditions and Expected Returns on Stocks and Bonds," *Journal of Financial Economics*, November 1989, Vol. 25, No. 1, 23–49.

———, "The Cross-Section of Expected Stock Returns," *Journal of Finance*, June 1992, Vol. 47, No. 2, 427–466.

———, "Common Risk Factors in the Returns on Stocks and Bonds," *Journal of Financial Economics*, February 1993, Vol. 33, No. 1, 3–56.

———, "Size and Book-to-Market Factors in Earnings and Returns," *Journal of Finance*, March 1995, Vol. 50, No. 1, 131–155.

———, "Multifactor Explanation of Asset Pricing Anomalies," *Journal of Finance*, March 1996a, Vol. 51, No. 1, 55–84.

———, "The CAPM Is Wanted, Dead or Alive," *Journal of Finance*, December 1996b, Vol. 51, No. 5, 1947–1958.

———, "Industry Costs of Equity," *Journal of Financial Economics*, February 1997, Vol. 43, No. 2, 153–193.

———, "Taxes, Financing Decisions, and Firm Value," *Journal of Finance*, June 1998a, Vol. 53, No. 3, 819–849.

———, "Value versus Growth: The International Evidence," *Journal of Finance*, December 1998b, Vol. 53, No. 6, 1975–1999.

———, "The Corporate Cost of Capital and the Return on Corporate Investment," *Journal of Finance*, December, 1999, Vol. 54, No. 6, 1939–1967.

———, "Forecasting Profitability and Earnings," *Journal of Business,* April 2000, Vol. 73, No. 2, 161–175.

Gertner, R., and D. Scharfstein, "A Theory of Workouts and the Effects of Reorganization Law," *Journal of Finance*, 1991, Vol. 46, 1189–1222.

Grenadier, S., ed., *Game Choices: The Intersection of Real Options and Game Theory*, Risk Books, 2000.

Harris, M., and A. Raviv, "The Theory of Capital Structure," *Journal of Finance*, 1991, Vol. 46, 297–356.

Hirshleifer, D., "Investor Psychology and Asset Pricing," *Journal of Finance*, August 2001, Vol. 56, 1533–1597.

Jensen, M. C., and W. H. Meckling, "Theory of the Firm: Managerial Behavior, Agency Costs and Ownership Structure," *Journal of Financial Economics*, 1976, Vol. 3, 305–360.

Kahneman, D., and A. Tversky, "Judgment under Uncertainty: Heuristics and Biases," *Science*, 1974, Vol. 185, 1124–1131.

———, "Prospect Theory: An Analysis of Decision under Risk," *Econometrica*, 1979, Vol. 47, No. 2, 263–292.

———, eds., *Choices, Values and Frames*, Cambridge University Press, 2000.

Kaplan, S., and R. Ruback, "The Valuation of Cash Flow Forecasts: An Empirical Analysis," *Journal of Finance*, 1995, Vol. 50, No. 4, 1059–1093.

Kim, D., "A Reexamination of Firm Size, Book-to-Market, and Earnings Price in the Cross-Section of Expected Stock Returns," *Journal of Financial and Quantitative Analysis*, December 1997, Vol. 32, No. 4, 463–489.

Kothari, S. P., J. Shanken, and R. Sloan, "Another Look at the Cross-Section of Expected Stock Returns," *Journal of Finance*, March 1995, Vol. 50, No. 1, 185–224.

La Porta, R., J. Lakonishok, A. Shleifer, and R. Vishny, "Good News for Value Stocks: Further Evidence on Market Efficiency," *Journal of Finance*, 1997, Vol. 52, 859–874.

La Porta, R., F. Lopez-de-Silanes, and A. Shleifer, "Corporate Ownership around the World," *Journal of Finance*, 1999, Vol. 54, 471–518.

La Porta, R., F. Lopez-de-Silanes, A. Shleifer, and R. Vishny, "Investor Protection and Corporate Governance," *Journal of Financial Economics*, 2000, Vol. 58, 3–27.

Leland, H., "Corporate Debt Value, Bond Covenants, and Optimal Capital Structure," *Journal of Finance*, September 1994, Vol. 49, No. 4, 1213–1252.

Leland, H., and K. Toft, "Optimal Capital Structure, Endogenous Bankruptcy, and the Term Structure of Credit Spreads," *Journal of Finance*, 1996, Vol. 51, No. 3, 982–1019.

Loughran, T., "Book-to-Market across Firm Size, Exchange, and Seasonality: Is There an Effect?" *Journal of Financial and Quantitative Analysis*, September 1997, Vol. 32, No. 3, 249–268.

Malkiel, B. G., "The Efficient Market Hypothesis and Its Critics," *Journal of Economic Perspectives*, Winter 2003, Vol. 17, 59–82.

Masulis, R., and A. Korwar, "Seasoned Equity Offerings: An Empirical Investigation," *Journal of Financial Economics*, January–February 1986, 91–118.

Modigliani, F., and M. Miller, "The Cost of Capital, Corporation Finance, and the Theory of Investment," *American Economic Review*, 1958, Vol. 48, 261–297.

———, "Corporate Income Taxes and the Cost of Capital: A Correction," *American Economic Review*, June 1963, 433–442.

Myers, S., "Outside Equity," *Journal of Finance*, 2000, Vol. 55, 1005–1037.

Rajan, R., and L. Zingales, "The Influence of the Financial Revolution on the Nature of Firms," The Center for Research in Security Prices, Working Paper No. 525, February 2001.

Roll, R., "Style Return Differentials: Illusions, Risk Premiums, or Investment Opportunities," in T. D. Coggin and F. J. Fabozzi, eds., *Handbook of Equity Style Management*, Frank J. Fabozzi Associates, New Hope, Penn., 1995, 99–128.

Rubinstein, M., "Rational Markets: Yes or No? The Affirmative Case," *Financial Analysts Journal*, May/June 2001, Vol. 57, 15–29.

Shiller, R., "Do Stock Prices Move Too Much to Be Justified by Subsequent Changes in Dividends?" *American Economic Review*, 1981, Vol. 71, 421–436.

———, "From Efficient Markets Theory to Behavioral Finance," *Journal of Economic Perspectives*, Winter 2003, Vol. 17, 83–104.

Shleifer, A., *Inefficient Markets: An Introduction to Behavioral Finance*, Oxford University Press, 2000.

Shleifer, A., and R. Vishny, "A Survey of Corporate Governance," *Journal of Finance*, 1997, Vol. 52, 737–783.

———, "The Limits of Arbitrage," *Journal of Finance*, March 1997, Vol. 52, 25–55.

Smit, H., and L. Ankum, "A Real Options and Game-Theoretic Approach to Corporate Investment Strategy under Competition," *Financial Management*, Autumn 1993, 241–250.

Titman, S., "The Effect of Capital Structure on a Firm's Liquidation Decision," *Journal of Financial Economics*, 1984, Vol. 13, 137–151.

Zingales, L., "What Determines the Value of Corporate Votes," *Quarterly Journal of Economics*, 1995, Vol. 110, 1047–1073.

———, "Corporate Governance," in Peter Newman, ed., *The New Palgrave Dictionary of Economics and the Law*, Stockton Press, London, 1998.

———, "In Search of New Foundations," *Journal of Finance*, 2000, Vol. 55, 1623–1653.

Discounting

A. $\mathcal{I}$ntroduction

In any economy, capitalist or socialist, we find positive rates of interest. This reflects two underlying influences: the productivity of economic goods and time preference. Capital goods are goods used in the production of other goods and services. Some capital goods are specialized machinery and others are materials—such as iron, copper, or textiles—used in the production of machinery to produce other goods. More basically, our productive efforts may be used to produce goods that we consume immediately or to produce goods that will produce other goods and services for future use. One reason to use some of our productive efforts to have goods that will produce future goods is that the postponement of current consumption will enable us to have more wealth in the future than we would have otherwise. For example, we can consume grains now or plant them to harvest future crops that will represent larger quantities than the seeds with which we started. Because of the productivity of goods, they have a time value. A bushel of seeds today will become several bushels of grain in the future. So productivity is one basis for the time value of money and positive rates of interest.

A second basis is time preference. Would we rather have the use of an automobile now or wait five years? Clearly, it is more advantageous to have the use of goods now than to wait for them.

B. $\mathcal{T}$he Time Value of Money: Discrete Compounding

1. Compound Future Sums

Because of the productivity and time preference, a positive rate of interest is a universal phenomenon. It is a necessary guide to present versus future uses of goods and to the allocation of goods among alternative uses when time is involved. Since a positive rate of interest is a general phenomenon, future sums will be greater than present values. For example, assume that if a company received funds immediately, it could earn a 10% return on those funds. We could then state the problem as follows: Let

$$P = \text{principal, or beginning amount} \quad = \$1{,}000,$$
$$r = \text{interest rate} \quad = 10\% = .10,$$
$$n = \text{number of years} \quad = 5,$$
$$S_n = \text{the value at the end of year } n.$$

We can readily derive the applicable compound interest formula. The amount received at the end of the first year is $P(1+r)$. This is again compounded to determine the amount received at the end of the second year, and so on.

	End of Year 1	End of Year 2	End of Year 3	...	End of Year n
Amount received	$P(1+r)$	$P(1+r)(1+r)$	$P(1+r)(1+r)(1+r)$	...	
	$P(1+r)$	$P(1+r)^2$	$P(1+r)^3$	...	$P(1+r)^n$

The result is the compound interest formula. In general terms it may be stated as follows:

$$S_n = P(1+r)^n. \tag{A.1}$$

We now have all the information needed to compute the value at the end of the fifth year, using a pocket calculator:

$$S_5 = \$1{,}000(1.10)^5 = \$1{,}000(1.611) = \$1{,}611$$

A dollar over a five-year period grows to $1,611. Since the amount we have is $1,000, it is multiplied by 1.011.

Therefore, if the firm can earn 10% on the money, it is indifferent between the $1,000 today and $1,611 at the end of the fifth year.

2. Future Amounts and Their Present Values

A similar type of problem occurs when a company is offered an amount to be received in the future. It is desirable to compare that amount with the value of whatever amount could be received today. This requires the computation of the present value of the amount to be received in the future. The determination of present values involves the same formula except that it is solved for P, representing present value, instead of S_n, which, in this situation, is known. By simple algebra the required formula would be

$$P = \frac{S_n}{(1+r)^n}. \tag{A.2a}$$

Using our previous example, we determined S_n to be $1,611. Since the appropriate interest rate is 10% and the number of years is five, this is what is required to determine P. This can be done by using our previous information and making a division. We would be dividing $1,611 by 1.611 to obtain the result, $1,000. In this case the formula is

$$P = S_n(1+r)^{-n}. \tag{A.2b}$$

We can now insert the numbers:

$$P = \$1,611(0.621)$$

$$= \$1,000.$$

The results of compound interest and present value computations are just two different ways of looking at the same relationship.

3. Constant Payment Annuities

An annuity is a series of periodic payments made over a span of time. This is a frequently encountered type of compound interest situation. For example, a firm may sell some goods that will be paid for in installments. A basic question is, What is the present value of those installment payments? Or the firm makes an investment from which it expects to receive a series of cash returns over a period of years. At an appropriate discount rate, what would the series of future income receipts be worth today? The firm needs this information in order to determine whether it is worthwhile to make the investment.

Some specific examples will further illustrate these ideas. The firm makes an investment. It is promised the payment of $1,000 per year (paid at the end of the year—and called an annuity in arrears) for 10 years with an interest rate of 10%. What is the present value of such a series of payments?

The basic formula involved is the present value of an annuity:

$$A_{n,r} = a \left[\frac{1 - (1+r)^{-n}}{r} \right], \tag{A.3}$$

where

$$A = \text{present value of an annuity,}$$

$$a = \text{amount of the periodic annuity payment,}$$

$$r = \text{interest factor,}$$

$$n = \text{number of annuity payments.}$$

Equation (A.3) is derived by discounting the stream of payments, the first of which is made at the end of the first year. Mathematically, this is

$$A_{n,r} = \frac{a}{1+r} + \frac{a}{(1+r)^2} + \frac{a}{(1+r)^3} + \dots + \frac{a}{(1+r)^n}.$$

If we let $u = [1/(1+r)]$, this becomes

$$A_{n,r} = au + au^2 + au^3 + \cdots + au^n. \tag{A.4}$$

Multiplying Eq. (A.4) by u and subtracting the result from Eq. (A.4) yields

$$A_{n,r} - uA_{n,r} = au - au^{n+1},$$

$$A_{n,r} = \frac{au(1 - u^n)}{1 - u}.$$

Substituting back the value of u we have

$$A_{n,r} = \frac{a\left(\frac{1}{1+r}\right)\left[1 - \frac{1}{(1+r)^n}\right]}{\left(1 - \frac{1}{1+r}\right)}$$

$$= \frac{a\left[1 - (1+r)^{-n}\right]}{(1+r)\left(\frac{1+r-1}{1+r}\right)}$$

$$= a\left[\frac{1 - (1+r)^{-n}}{r}\right],$$

which gives us Eq. (A.3).

Note that if the number of payments is infinite, then the present value of the annuity becomes

$$\lim_{n \to \infty} A_{n,r} = \frac{a}{r}, \tag{A.5}$$

since we know that when $r > 0$, then the limit of $(1 + r)^{-n}$ as n approaches infinity is zero. An example of an annuity with an infinite number of constant payments is a *consol* bond. It pays a coupon at the end of each time period (usually a year) and never matures.

The expression in brackets in Eq. (A.3) is rather cumbersome. For convenience, then, instead of the cumbersome expression set out above, we shall use the symbol $P_{n,r}$, where $P_{n,r}$ = present value of an annuity factor for n years at r percent. Equation (A.3) can therefore be rewritten as

$$A_{n,r} = aP_{n,r}.$$

Substituting actual numbers, we would have the following for an annuity of $1,000 per year for 10 years at 10%:

$$A_{n,r} = A_{10,10\%} = \$1,000\left[\frac{1 - (1 + .1)^{-10}}{.1}\right]$$

$$A_{n,r} = \$6,145 = \$1,000(6.145).$$

In other words, applying an interest factor of 10%, a series of payments of $1,000 received for 10 years would be worth $6,145 today. Hence if the amount of investment we were required to make were $8,000, for example, or any amount greater than $6,145, we would be receiving a return of less than 10% on our investment. Conversely, if the investment necessary to earn annual payments of $1,000 for 10 years at 10% were $5,000 or any amount less than $6,145, we would be earning a return greater than 10%.

A number of other questions can be answered using these same relationships. Suppose the decision facing the firm requires determining the rate of return on an investment. For example, suppose we would have $6,145 to invest and that an investment opportunity promises an annual return of $1,000 for 10 years. What is the indicated rate of return on our investment? Exactly the same relationship is involved, but we are now solving for the interest rate. We can therefore rewrite our equation as follows:

$$P_{10,10\%} = \frac{A_{10,10\%}}{a}.$$

We can now substitute the appropriate figures:

$$P_{10,10\%} = \frac{\$6,145}{\$1,000} = 6.145 = \left[\frac{1 - (1+r)^{-10}}{r} \right]$$

This problem is solved (by your pocket calculator) iteratively by trying different values of r until the expression in brackets equals 6.145. This rate turns out to be 10%. We are earning a 10% return on our investment.

Let us consider another situation. Suppose that we are going to receive a return of $2,000 per year for five years from an investment of $8,424. What is the return on our investment? This is generally referred to as the internal rate of return on the investment, or it is also referred to as the DCF (discounted cash flow) approach to valuing an investment.

We follow the same procedure as before:

$$P_{5,r} = \frac{\$8,424}{\$2,000}$$

$$= 4.212.$$

We again use our pocket calculator and find that the return on that investment is 6%. If our required rate of return were 10%, we would not find this investment attractive. On the other hand, if the required return on our investment were only 5%, we would consider the investment attractive.

These relationships can be used in still another way. Taking the facts of the preceding illustration, we may ask the following question: Given an investment that yields $2,000 per year for five years, at an appropriate discount factor (or cost of capital) of 6%, what is the investment worth today? What is the present value of a series of future income flows? For example, if a firm were to make a sale of goods on an open account with a down payment of $1,000 plus yearly payments of $2,000 for five years, what would the present value of all the payments be at a 6% interest rate? From our previous calculations we know that the series of payments of $2,000 for five years at a 6% interest rate is worth $8,424 today. When we add the $1,000 down payment to this figure, we would have a total of $9,424.

4. Compound Sum of an Annuity

We may need to know the future value or future sum to which a series of payments will accumulate. The reason may be to determine the amount of funds required to repay an obligation in the future.

The sum of an annuity can be determined from the following basic relationship:[1]

$$S_{n,r} = a \left[\frac{(1+r)^n - 1}{r} \right],$$ (A.6)

where

$S_{n,r}$ = the future sum of an annuity in n years at rate r,

a = the amount of the annuity payment.

Suppose the firm were to receive annual payments of $1,000 a year for 10 years and is earning an interest rate of 10%. What will be the amount that the firm will have at the end of 10 years? Utilizing equation (A.6), we would have

$$S_{n,r} = \$1,000(15.937)$$

$$= \$15,937.$$

The 10 payments of $1,000 with interest would amount to $15,937 by the end of the 10th year. Thus if we had to make a payment of $15,937 in 10 years, we would be able to do it by making annual payments of $1,000 per year into a fund that earns interest at 10% per year.

5. Calculations for a Series of Unequal Receipts or Payments

In all the previous illustrations we have assumed that the receipts flowing in or the payments to be made are of equal amounts. This simplifies the calculations. However, if unequal receipts or unequal payments are involved, the principles are again the same, but the calculations must be somewhat extended. For example, suppose that the firm makes an investment from which it will receive the following amounts:

Year	Receipts	×	Discount Factor (15%)	=	Present Value
1	$100		.870		$87.00
2	200		.756		151.20
3	600		.658		394.80
4	300		.572		171.60
			PV of the investment	=	$804.60

Using your pocket calculator and Eq. (A.2b) (with $r = .15$) you will obtain the amounts indicated above. The interest factor is multiplied by the receipts to provide the amounts in the

---

[1] Note that the present value of an annuity can be obtained by discounting the expression back to the present:

$$A_{n,r} = a \left[\frac{(1+r)^n - 1}{r(1+r)^n} \right].$$

Now divide the numerator and the denominator by $(1+r)^n$. We have

$$A_{n,r} = a \left[\frac{1 - (1+r)^{-n}}{r} \right].$$

This is now in the form of Eq. (A.3), the present value of an annuity.

present value column. The amounts for each year are then summed to provide the present value of the investment, which in this example is $804.60. What we are doing in this example is illustrating how a series of unequal payments can be handled by breaking the problem into a series of one-year payments received at successively later time periods.

6. Annuities with Growing Payments

Previously we had assumed that annuity payments were constant through time. Now we consider the case where the payments are assumed to be growing at the constant rate g. This is a more realistic assumption if, for example, we are modeling the growing dividends paid out by a firm. Let d_0 be the current dividend per share and assume that it was paid just yesterday, so that it does not enter into the present value computations. The stream of growing dividends to be received starts with the first end-of-period dividend, $d_1 = d_0(1 + g)$. The dividend at the end of the second year is $d_2 = d_0(1 + g)^2$. The stream of payments is assumed to grow at a constant rate for n years; therefore its present value, PV, is

$$PV = \frac{d_1}{1+r} + \frac{d_2}{(1+r)^2} + \frac{d_3}{(1+r)^3} + \cdots \frac{d_n}{(1+r)^n}$$

$$= \frac{d_0(1+g)}{1+r} + \frac{d_0(1+g)^2}{(1+r)^2} + \frac{d_0(1+g)^3}{(1+r)^3} + \cdots \frac{d_0(1+g)^n}{(1+r)^n}.$$

If we let $u = (1 + g)/(1 + r)$, this can be rewritten as

$$PV = d_0 u + d_0 u^2 + d_0 u^3 + \cdots + d_0 u^n$$

$$= u d_0 (1 + u + u^2 + u^3 + \cdots + u^{n-1}). \tag{A.7}$$

By multiplying Eq. (A.7) by u and subtracting the result from Eq. (A.7), we obtain

$$PV - uPV = u d_0 (1 - u^n),$$

and solving for the present value of the growing annuity, we have

$$PV = \frac{u d_0 (1 - u^n)}{(1 - u)}.$$

Substituting back the value of u gives us

$$PV = \frac{\left(\frac{1+g}{1+r}\right) d_0 \left[1 - \left(\frac{1+g}{1+r}\right)^n\right]}{1 - \left(\frac{1+g}{1+r}\right)}.$$

By rearranging terms and recalling that $d_0(1 + g) = d_1$, we obtain

$$PV = \frac{d_1 \left[1 - \left(\frac{1+g}{1+r}\right)^n\right]}{r - g}. \tag{A.8}$$

Equation (A.8) is the present value of n annuity payments that start at a level of d_0 and grow at a constant rate g.

Note that if the number of payments is infinite, we can obtain a finite present value if we assume that the growth rate in dividends, g, is less than the time value of money, r. If $g < r$, then the fraction in the numerator of Eq. (A.8) goes to zero in the limit as n approaches infinity:

$$\lim_{n \to \infty} \left(\frac{1+g}{1+r} \right)^n = 0, \quad \text{if} \quad g < r.$$

Therefore the present value of an infinite number of growing dividends is

$$\lim_{n \to \infty} PV = \frac{d_1}{r-g}. \tag{A.9}$$

Equation (A.9) is used frequently in the text, where it is called the *Gordon growth model*. It provides us with an estimate of the present value of a share of common stock where the stream of dividends received from it is assumed to grow at a constant rate that is assumed to be less than the discount rate (which in this case would be cost of capital, k_s).

7. Compounding Periods within One Year

In the illustrations set forth thus far, the examples have been for returns that were received annually. If the interest rates are calculated for periods of time within one year, a simple relationship can be followed, utilizing the principles already set forth. For compounding within one year, we simply divide the interest rate by the number of compoundings within a year and multiply the annual periods by the same factor. For example, in our first equation for compound interest we had the following:

$$S_n = P(1+r)^n.$$

This was for annual compounding. For semiannual compounding we would follow the rule just set forth. The equation would become

$$S_n = P \left(1 + \frac{r}{m} \right)^{nm}, \tag{A.10a}$$

where $m =$ the number of compoundings during a year.

We may apply this in a numerical illustration. Suppose the initial question is, "To how much would $1,000 at a 6% interest rate accumulate over a five-year period?" The answer is $1,338. Now we apply semiannual compounding. The equation would appear as follows:

$$S_{5/2} = \$1,000 \left(1 + \frac{.06}{2} \right)^{5(2)}.$$

Thus the new expression is equivalent to compounding the $1,000 at 3% for 10 periods. Our equation would therefore read:

$$S_{5/2} = \$1,000(1 + .03)^{10},$$

$$= \$1,344.$$

It will be noted that with semiannual compounding the future sum amounts to $1,344 as compared with the $1,338 we had before. Frequent compounding provides compound interest paid on compound interest, so the amount is higher. Thus we would expect that daily compounding, as some financial institutions advertise, or continuous compounding, as is employed under some assumptions, would give somewhat larger amounts than annual or semiannual compounding. But the basic ideas are unchanged.

The same logic is equally applicable to all the categories of relationships we have described. For example, suppose a problem on the present value of an annuity was stated as the payment of $1,000 a year for 10 years with an interest rate of 10% compounded annually. If the compounding is semiannual, we would employ an interest rate of 5% and apply the compounding to a period of 20 years. When we compound semiannually we also have to divide the annual payment by the number of times the compounding takes place within the year. We would have the following expression:

$$A_{nm,r/m} = \$500\left(P_{nm,r/m}\right)$$

$$= \$500\left[P_{10(2),10\%/2}\right]$$

$$= \$500\left(P_{20,5\%}\right)$$

$$= \$500\left[\frac{1 - (1 + .05)^{-20}}{.05}\right]$$

$$= \$500(12.462)$$

$$= \$6,231.$$

It will be noted that with annual compounding the present value of the annuity was $6,145. With semiannual compounding the present value is $6,231. With more frequent compounding the resulting amounts will be somewhat higher because interest is compounded on interest more often.

C. The Time Value of Money: Continuous Compounding

1. Compound Sums and Present Values

Continuous compounding simply extends the ideas involved in compounding periods within one year. Let us restate Eq. (A.10a) in somewhat more general symbols:

$$V_t = P_0\left(1 + \frac{k}{q}\right)^{qt}. \tag{A.10b}$$

Since we can multiply qt by k/k, we can set $qt = (q/k)(kt)$ and rewrite Eq. (A.10b) as

$$V_t = P_0\left[\left(1 + \frac{k}{q}\right)^{(q/k)}\right]^{kt}. \tag{A.11a}$$

Define $m = q/k$ and rewrite Eq. (A.11a) as

$$V_r = P_0\left[\left(1 + \frac{1}{m}\right)^{m}\right]^{kt}. \tag{A.11b}$$

As the number of compounding periods, q, increases, m also increases; this causes the term in brackets in Eq. (A.11b) to increase. At the limit, when q and m approach infinity (and compounding is instantaneous, or continuous), the term in brackets approaches the value 2.718 . . . . The value e is defined as this limiting case:

$$e = \lim_{m \to \infty} \left(1 + \frac{1}{m}\right)^m = 2.718 \ldots .$$

We may substitute e for the bracketed term:

$$V_t = P_0 e^{kt}. \tag{A.12}$$

Equation (A.12) is the expression for the case of continuous compounding (or continuous growth).

For example, suppose our problem is to determine the future value of $1,000 compounded continuously at 10% for eight years. Then $t = 8$ and $k = .10$, so $kt = .80$. Therefore, we have

$$V_t = 1,000 e^{.8}$$

$$= \$1,000 (2.2256)$$

$$= \$2,226$$

This compares with $2,144 with compounding on an annual basis.

Equation (A.12) can be transformed into Eq. (A.13) and used to determine present values under continuous compounding. Using k as the discount rate, we obtain

$$PV = \frac{V_t}{e^{kt}} = V_t e^{-kt}. \tag{A.13}$$

Thus if $2,225 is due in eight years and if the appropriate continuous discount rate k is 10%, the present value of this future payment is

$$PV = \frac{\$2,225}{2.225} = \$1,000.$$

2. Continuous Payment Annuities

If we assume that an asset pays a constant continuous amount per unit time, then we can write that the payment at any point in time, a_t, is a constant, a_0:

$$a_t = a_0. \tag{A.14}$$

Using basic integral calculus (discussed in Appendix D), we can express the present value of a constant payment stream as the discounted value of the payment function given in Eq. (A.14):

$$PV = \int_0^n a_t e^{-kt} dt. \tag{A.15}$$

Note that we have employed Eq. (A.13) to discount each payment. The stream of payments is assumed to start immediately ($t = 0$) and continue for n time periods. Hence the limits of integration in Eq. (A.15) are 0 to n. Following the applicable rules of integral calculus to evaluate the definite integral, we obtain

$$PV = a_0 \int_0^n e^{-kt} dt$$

$$= a_0 \left[\frac{-e^{-kt}}{k} \right]\Big|_0^n$$

$$= a_0 \left[\frac{-e^{-kn}}{k} - \frac{-e^0}{k} \right]$$

$$= a_0 \left[\frac{1 - e^{-kn}}{k} \right]. \tag{A.16}$$

Equation (A.16) is the continuous-time analogue to Eq. (A.3), which was the discrete time version of the present value of an annuity of constant payments. Note that the continuous discount factor e^{-kn} in Eq. (A.16) is roughly equivalent to the discrete discount factor $(1 + r)^{-n}$ in Eq. (A.3).

If we want the present value of an infinite stream of constant, continuously compounded payments, we take the limit of Eq. (A.16) as n becomes infinite:

$$\lim_{n \to \infty} PV = \frac{a_0}{k}. \tag{A.17}$$

Equation (A.20) is exactly equal to Eq. (A.5).

3. Annuities with Growing Payments

For a stream of growing payments, we can see from Eq. (A.12) that the payment function is

$$a_t = a_0 e^{gt}. \tag{A.18}$$

The present value of such a stream is

$$PV = \int_0^n a_t e^{-kt} dt$$

$$= a_0 \int_0^n e^{gt} e^{-kt} dt.$$

Combining terms, we have

$$PV = a_0 \int_0^n e^{-(k-g)t} dt.$$

Using the rules of integral calculus, the solution to this integral is

$$PV = a_0 \left[\frac{-e^{-(k-g)t}}{k-g} \right] \Big|_0^n$$

$$= a_0 \left[\frac{-e^{-(k-g)n}}{k-g} - \left(\frac{-e^0}{k-g} \right) \right]$$

$$= a_0 \left[\frac{1 - e^{-(k-g)n}}{k-g} \right]. \qquad (A.19)$$

Equation (A.19) is analogous to Eq. (A.8), the discrete compounding version of the present value of an annuity of growing payments that lasts for n years.

As before, the present value of an infinite stream of payments is obtained by taking the limit of Eq. (A.19) as n approaches infinity:

$$\lim_{n \to \infty} PV = \frac{a_0}{k-g}, \quad \text{if} \quad g < k. \qquad (A.20)$$

Summary

Consumption is allocated over time by "the" interest rate. Positive rates of interest induce people to postpone consumption and save part of their income. The pool of savings at any given time is used for investments that yield output in the form of goods that may be consumed at future dates.

The combined preferences of all members of society and the society's technology together determine the pattern of interest rates that will allocate consumption over time optimally. The structure of interest rates guides individuals into making investment decisions that are most desired by the society as a whole.

Present value or future value calculations at appropriately chosen interest rates, given the riskiness of the project, will tell an investor whether the future receipts are sufficient to justify the current investment. Since the pattern of interest rates is determined by the behavior of all members of society, a positive net present value means not only that the project will yield a profit to the investor but also that no member of the society has a superior use for the resources being invested. If many other investment rate opportunities were to appear that were superior to the one in question, the interest rate appropriate for the present value calculation would rise, and the present value of the project might then appear to be negative.

To evaluate projects with cash flows distributed over time it is necessary to express all flows in terms of their value at one specific point in time. Expressing them in terms of value today is discounting to net present value; expressing them at their value on some future date is compounding to future value. There is conceptually no difference between the two approaches.

Interest rates are traditionally expressed per annum, but cash flows may occur at discrete periods during the year or may even be continuous. However, the continuous form expressions are often more convenient for complex valuation problems. For example, some models of option pricing assume that stock behavior is continuous, and consequently most option valuation expressions are in continuous form.

Matrix Algebra

A. Matrices and Vectors

A matrix is a rectangular array of numbers. The following are examples of matrices:

$$\underset{(3 \times 2)}{A} = \begin{pmatrix} 1 & 2 \\ 0 & 1 \\ -1 & 4 \end{pmatrix},$$

$$\underset{(3 \times 4)}{B} = \begin{pmatrix} 2 & 3 & 1.5 & 0 \\ -1 & 4 & -1 & -1 \\ 3 & 1.1 & 2 & -5 \end{pmatrix},$$

$$\underset{(2 \times 2)}{C} = \begin{pmatrix} 2 & 1 \\ 1 & -2 \end{pmatrix}.$$

The matrix A is a 3×2 matrix because it has three rows and two columns. The matrix B is a 3×4 matrix because it has three rows and four columns. The matrix C is a 2×2 square matrix because it has two rows and two columns.

Each number in a matrix is called an element. The element on the ith row and the jth column of matrix A is designated by a_{ij}. For example, in the matrix A above, $a_{11} = 1$, $a_{12} = 2$, $a_{21} = 0$, and so on. Similarly, in the matrix B, $b_{12} = 3$, $b_{32} = 1.1$.

We say that two $m \times n$ matrices are equal if all their corresponding elements are identical. In other words, if both R and S are $m \times n$ matrices, then $R = S$ if and only if $r_{ij} = s_{ij}$ for all $i = 1, 2, \ldots, m$ and $j = 1, 2, \ldots, n$. For example,

$$\begin{pmatrix} 1 & 2 \\ -1 & 1 \end{pmatrix} = \begin{pmatrix} 1 & 2 \\ -1 & 1 \end{pmatrix} \quad \text{but} \quad \begin{pmatrix} 1 & 1 \\ 0 & 1 \end{pmatrix} \neq \begin{pmatrix} 1 & 0 \\ 1 & 1 \end{pmatrix}.$$

Vectors are matrices with only one row or one column. A $1 \times m$ matrix is called a row vector, and a $m \times 1$ matrix is called a column vector. For example,

$$\underset{(1 \times 3)}{a} = (1 \quad -1 \quad 1), \qquad \underset{(1 \times 4)}{b} = (1 \quad 2 \quad 0 \quad 1)$$

are row vectors and

$$\underset{(2 \times 1)}{c} = \begin{pmatrix} 1 \\ -1 \end{pmatrix}, \qquad \underset{(3 \times 1)}{d} = \begin{pmatrix} 1 \\ 3 \\ 2 \end{pmatrix}$$

are column vectors. Each number in a vector is called a component of that vector. The ith component of the vector a is designated by a_i. So, $a_1 = 1$, $a_2 = -1$, $a_3 = 1$ in the vector above.

Two $1 \times n$ row vectors or two $m \times 1$ column vectors are equal if all the corresponding components are the same. For example,

$$\begin{pmatrix} 1 \\ 2 \end{pmatrix} = \begin{pmatrix} 1 \\ 2 \end{pmatrix}, \qquad (3 \quad 1 \quad 2) = (3 \quad 1 \quad 2),$$

but

$$\begin{pmatrix} 1 \\ 2 \end{pmatrix} \neq (1 \quad 2), \qquad \begin{pmatrix} 1 \\ 2 \end{pmatrix} \neq \begin{pmatrix} 2 \\ 1 \end{pmatrix}, \qquad \begin{pmatrix} 1 \\ 2 \end{pmatrix} \neq \begin{pmatrix} 1 \\ 2 \\ 3 \end{pmatrix}.$$

B. The Operations of Matrices

Addition and subtraction of two matrices A and B can be performed if A and B have the same dimension—that is, if the number of rows and the number of columns are the same. Addition and subtraction are carried out on each corresponding pair of elements. If $A + B = C$, then $a_{ij} + b_{ij} = c_{ij}$. For example,

$$\begin{pmatrix} 1 & 2 \\ 3 & 4 \end{pmatrix} + \begin{pmatrix} -1 & 1 \\ 2 & -1 \end{pmatrix} = \begin{pmatrix} 1-1 & 2+1 \\ 3+2 & 4-1 \end{pmatrix} = \begin{pmatrix} 0 & 3 \\ 5 & 3 \end{pmatrix},$$

$$\begin{pmatrix} 1 & 2 \\ 3 & 4 \end{pmatrix} - \begin{pmatrix} -1 & 1 \\ 2 & -1 \end{pmatrix} = \begin{pmatrix} 1-(-1) & 2-1 \\ 3-2 & 4-(-1) \end{pmatrix} = \begin{pmatrix} 2 & 1 \\ 1 & 5 \end{pmatrix},$$

$$\begin{pmatrix} 1 \\ 2 \end{pmatrix} - \begin{pmatrix} 1 \\ 1 \end{pmatrix} = \begin{pmatrix} 0 \\ 1 \end{pmatrix}, \qquad \begin{pmatrix} 1 \\ 2 \end{pmatrix} + \begin{pmatrix} 1 \\ 1 \end{pmatrix} = \begin{pmatrix} 2 \\ 3 \end{pmatrix}.$$

If we multiply a matrix A by a scalar, the resultant matrix is obtained by multiplying each element of A by that scalar. So if

$$A = \begin{pmatrix} 1 & 2 & 3 \\ -1 & 1 & 2 \end{pmatrix},$$

then

$$2A = \begin{pmatrix} 2 & 4 & 6 \\ -2 & 2 & 4 \end{pmatrix}, \qquad -3A = \begin{pmatrix} -3 & -6 & -9 \\ 3 & -3 & -6 \end{pmatrix}.$$

We can also multiply two matrices together provided that the number of columns in the first matrix is equal to the number of rows in the second matrix. To form the product AB of the two matrices A and B, the number of columns of A must be equal to the number of rows of B. If we designate the result of the matrix multiplication AB by C, then C is again a matrix and C has the same number of rows as A and the same number of columns as B. To summarize: if A is an $m \times n$ matrix and B a $p \times q$ matrix, then the product AB can be formed only if $n = p$; further, if $C = AB$, then C is an $m \times q$ matrix.

To complete our definition of matrix multiplication, we have to describe how the elements of C are obtained. The following rule specifies c_{ij}, the element in the ith row and jth column of the resultant matrix C, in terms of elements A and B:

$$c_{ij} = a_{i1} + b_{1j} + a_{i2}b_{2j} + \ldots + a_{in}b_{nj} = \sum_{k=1}^{n} a_{ik}b_{kj}, \tag{B.1}$$

where $n = $ number of columns of $A = $ number of rows of B.

Equation (B.1) tells us that c_{ij} is a sum of products. Each product consists of an element from the ith row of A and an element from the jth column of B. We multiply the first element in the ith row of A with the first element in the jth column of B, the second element in the ith row of A with the second element in the jth column of B—and so on until the last element in the ith row of A is multiplied with the last element in the jth column of B—and then sum all the products. Another way to look at this: to obtain c_{ij}, we "multiply" the ith row of A with the jth column of B.

An example further clarifies Eq. (B.1). Consider $C = AB$, where

$$A = \begin{pmatrix} 1 & 2 & 3 \\ 1 & 0 & 1 \end{pmatrix}, \qquad B = \begin{pmatrix} -1 & 3 & 0 & 0 \\ 2 & 1 & 1 & 0 \\ 1 & 0 & 0 & 1 \end{pmatrix}.$$

Since A is 2×3 and B is 3×4, the product AB can be formed and C would be 2×4. According to Eq. (B.1),

$$c_{11} = a_{11}b_{11} + a_{12}b_{21} + a_{13}b_{31} = 1 \times (-1) + 2 \times 2 + 3 \times 1 = 6,$$

$$c_{12} = a_{11}b_{12} + a_{12}b_{22} + a_{13}b_{32} = 1 \times 3 + 2 \times 1 + 3 \times 0 = 5,$$

and so on. The result $AB = C$ is

$$\begin{pmatrix} 1 & 2 & 3 \\ 1 & 0 & 1 \end{pmatrix} \begin{pmatrix} -1 & 3 & 0 & 0 \\ 2 & 1 & 1 & 0 \\ 1 & 0 & 0 & 1 \end{pmatrix} = \begin{pmatrix} 6 & 5 & 2 & 3 \\ 0 & 3 & 0 & 1 \end{pmatrix}.$$

We should emphasize at this point that the product BA may not be defined even though AB is. We can take the above as an example: A is 2×3 and B is 3×4, so AB is defined, but BA is not, since $4 \neq 2$. In the event that BA is also defined, $BA \neq AB$ in general. For example, let

$$A = \begin{pmatrix} 1 & 1 \\ 0 & 1 \end{pmatrix}, \qquad B = \begin{pmatrix} 1 & 0 \\ 1 & 1 \end{pmatrix},$$

then

$$AB = \begin{pmatrix} 2 & 1 \\ 1 & 1 \end{pmatrix}, \quad \text{but} \quad BA = \begin{pmatrix} 1 & 1 \\ 1 & 2 \end{pmatrix}.$$

C. $\mathcal{L}$inear Equations in Matrix Form

A system of linear equations can be expressed in matrix form. First, let us consider one simple linear equation, say, $X_1 - 2X_2 + 2X_3 = 4$. Using matrix multiplication, the matrix will be expressed as

$$(1 \quad -2 \quad 2) \begin{pmatrix} X_1 \\ X_2 \\ X_3 \end{pmatrix} = 1X_1 + (-2)X_2 + 2X_3 = 4.$$

Suppose we now have the following system of three equations:

$$X_1 - 2X_2 + 2X_3 = 4,$$
$$X_1 + X_2 + X_3 = 5,$$
$$-X_1 + 5X_2 - 3X_3 = 1.$$

Using matrix multiplication, this is equivalent to

$$\underbrace{\begin{pmatrix} 1 & -2 & 2 \\ 1 & 1 & 1 \\ -1 & 5 & -3 \end{pmatrix}}_{3 \times 3} \underbrace{\begin{pmatrix} X_1 \\ X_2 \\ X_3 \end{pmatrix}}_{3 \times 1} = \begin{pmatrix} 1 \cdot X_1 - 2 \cdot X_2 + 2 \cdot X_3 \\ 1 \cdot X_1 + 1 \cdot X_2 + 1 \cdot X_3 \\ -1 \cdot X_1 + 5 \cdot X_2 - 3 \cdot X_3 \end{pmatrix} = \underbrace{\begin{pmatrix} 4 \\ 5 \\ 1 \end{pmatrix}}_{3 \times 1}$$

And because of the equality definition of vectors, we must equate $(1 \cdot X_1 - 2 \cdot X_2 + 2 \cdot X_3)$ to 4 and $(1 \cdot X_1 + 1 \cdot X_2 + 1 \cdot X_3)$ to 5 and $(-1 \cdot X_1 + 5 \cdot X_2 - 3 \cdot X_3)$ to 1, which shows that the matrix formulation

$$\begin{pmatrix} 1 & -2 & 2 \\ 1 & 1 & 1 \\ -1 & 5 & -3 \end{pmatrix} \begin{pmatrix} X_1 \\ X_2 \\ X_3 \end{pmatrix} = \begin{pmatrix} 4 \\ 5 \\ 1 \end{pmatrix} \tag{B.2}$$

is equivalent to the system of linear equations. In general, Eq. (B.2) is written as $Ax = b$, where

$$A = \begin{pmatrix} 1 & -2 & 2 \\ 1 & 1 & 1 \\ -1 & 5 & -3 \end{pmatrix}, \quad x = \begin{pmatrix} X_1 \\ X_2 \\ X_3 \end{pmatrix}, \quad b = \begin{pmatrix} 4 \\ 5 \\ 1 \end{pmatrix}.$$

A is called the coefficient matrix, x is the vector of unknowns, and b is the vector of constants. Finding the solution to a system of linear equations is equivalent to solving for the unknown vector x in the matrix equation $Ax = b$. We will come back to solving $Ax = b$ in a later section.

D. Special Matrices

There are special types of matrices that possess useful properties. Here we list some of the more important ones.

The zero (or null) matrix is a matrix with all elements (or components) being zero. For example,

$$\begin{pmatrix} 0 & 0 \\ 0 & 0 \end{pmatrix}, \qquad \begin{pmatrix} 0 & 0 & 0 & 0 \\ 0 & 0 & 0 & 0 \\ 0 & 0 & 0 & 0 \end{pmatrix}$$

are null matrices of dimensions 2×2 and 3×4. The zero matrix $\mathbf{0}$ possesses the property that

$$A + \mathbf{0} = \mathbf{0} + A = A$$

for any matrix A of the same dimension.

A diagonal matrix is a square matrix whose elements are all zeros except on the *main diagonal*—that is, D is a diagonal matrix if $d_{ij} = 0$ for $i \neq j$. For example,

$$\begin{pmatrix} 1 & 0 \\ 0 & 2 \end{pmatrix}, \qquad \begin{pmatrix} 1 & 0 & 0 \\ 0 & 3 & 0 \\ 0 & 0 & 4 \end{pmatrix}$$

are diagonal matrices. The elements $d_{11}, d_{22}, \ldots, d_{nn}$ are called elements on the main diagonal. Note that all diagonal matrices are square by definition.

The identity matrix, I, is a diagonal matrix that has ones on the main diagonal and zeros everywhere else. For example,

$$\begin{pmatrix} 1 & 0 \\ 0 & 1 \end{pmatrix}, \begin{pmatrix} 1 & 0 & 0 \\ 0 & 1 & 0 \\ 0 & 0 & 1 \end{pmatrix}, \begin{pmatrix} 1 & 0 & 0 & 0 \\ 0 & 1 & 0 & 0 \\ 0 & 0 & 1 & 0 \\ 0 & 0 & 0 & 1 \end{pmatrix}$$

are identity matrices of dimensions 2×2, 3×3, 4×4. The identity matrix has the useful property that

$$AI = A, \qquad IB = B.$$

for all matrices A and B provided the matrix multiplication is defined; that is, A and B must be of appropriate dimensions.

E. Matrix Inversion Defined

Now, given a square matrix A, there may exist a matrix B, such that

$$AB = BA = I.$$

If such matrix B exists, then A is said to be nonsingular and the matrix B is called the multiplicative *inverse* of A. We usually write B as A^{-1} to denote inverse. A^{-1} plays a significant role in solving the matrix equation $Ax = b$. If A^{-1} is known, we can premultiply both sides of the matrix equation by A^{-1} to get

$$A^{-1}Ax = A^{-1}b.$$

Since $A^{-1}A = I$, the equation becomes

$$Ix = A^{-1}b.$$

But $Ix = x$, where x is an $(m \times 1)$ matrix; therefore

$$x = A^{-1}b.$$

The system can now be solved for the unknown vector, x, by carrying out the matrix multiplication, $A^{-1}b$.

F. *M*atrix Transposition

Before we describe how to compute A^{-1}, we must first define the transpose of a matrix. For a given matrix A, the transpose of A, denoted by A', is obtained from A by writing the columns of A as rows of A'. Formally, we have $a'_{ij} = a_{ji}$. For example, if

$$A = \begin{pmatrix} 1 & 2 & 3 \\ 3 & 2 & 1 \\ 4 & 3 & 2 \end{pmatrix}, \quad \text{then} \quad A' = \begin{pmatrix} 1 & 3 & 4 \\ 2 & 2 & 3 \\ 3 & 1 & 2 \end{pmatrix}$$

Finally, if $A = A'$, then we say that A is a symmetric matrix. For example,

$$A = \begin{pmatrix} 1 & -1 & 4 \\ -1 & 2 & 5 \\ 4 & 5 & 3 \end{pmatrix}$$

is a symmetric matrix. Notice that the entries of A are symmetric across the main diagonal; hence all diagonal matrices are symmetric.

The class of symmetric matrices is very important and arises very often in many real-life problems. The covariance matrix in portfolio theory is a symmetric matrix. Furthermore, algebraic systems involving symmetric matrices are in general easier to solve.

G. *D*eterminants

Given $x = A^{-1}b$ and A, the first step in finding A^{-1} is to determine if A is nonsingular. To do that, we make use of the determinant function that is defined for all square matrices.

The determinant of a square matrix A, denoted by $|A|$, is a unique number associated with that matrix. For a 2×2 matrix

$$A = \begin{pmatrix} a_{11} & a_{12} \\ a_{21} & a_{22} \end{pmatrix}, \quad |A| = a_{11}a_{22} - a_{12}a_{21}.$$

For example,

$$\begin{vmatrix} 2 & 1 \\ 3 & 4 \end{vmatrix} = (2 \times 4) - (1 \times 3) = 8 - 3 = 5.$$

So the determinant of the matrix is 5.

The definition of a determinant of a 3×3 or higher-order square matrix involves the notion of minors and cofactors of elements of the matrix. The minor of a_{ij}, denoted by $|M_{ij}|$, is the determinant of the *submatrix* of A obtained by deleting the ith row and jth column of A. Suppose

$$A = \begin{pmatrix} a_{11} & a_{12} & a_{13} \\ a_{21} & a_{22} & a_{23} \\ a_{31} & a_{32} & a_{33} \end{pmatrix};$$

then

$$|M_{11}| = \begin{vmatrix} a_{11} & a_{12} & a_{13} \\ a_{21} & a_{22} & a_{23} \\ a_{31} & a_{32} & a_{33} \end{vmatrix} = \begin{vmatrix} a_{22} & a_{23} \\ a_{32} & a_{33} \end{vmatrix} = a_{22}a_{33} - a_{23}a_{32},$$

$$|M_{21}| = \begin{vmatrix} a_{11} & a_{12} & a_{13} \\ a_{21} & a_{22} & a_{23} \\ a_{31} & a_{32} & a_{33} \end{vmatrix} = \begin{vmatrix} a_{12} & a_{13} \\ a_{32} & a_{33} \end{vmatrix} = a_{12}a_{33} - a_{13}a_{32},$$

and so on. The cofactor of a_{ij}, denoted by $|C_{ij}|$, is equal to $(-1)^{i+j} |M_{ij}|$. That is why sometimes cofactors are called signed minors. Whenever $i + j$ is even, $|C_{ij}| = |M_{ij}|$, and whenever $i + j$ is odd, $|C_{ij}| = - |M_{ij}|$. Take the 3×3 matrix A:

$$A = \begin{pmatrix} 1 & 2 & 1 \\ 3 & 0 & 4 \\ 0 & 1 & 5 \end{pmatrix}, \qquad \text{then} \qquad |M_{11}| = \begin{vmatrix} 0 & 4 \\ 1 & 5 \end{vmatrix} = -4,$$

$$|M_{12}| = \begin{vmatrix} 3 & 4 \\ 0 & 5 \end{vmatrix} = 15, \qquad |M_{13}| = \begin{vmatrix} 3 & 0 \\ 0 & 1 \end{vmatrix} = 3.$$

The reader may check that $|M_{21}| = 9$, $|M_{22}| = 5$, $|M_{23}| = 1$, $|M_{31}| = 8$, $|M_{32}| = 1$, $|M_{33}| = -6$. Hence

$$|C_{11}| = -4, |C_{12}| = -15, |C_{13}| = 3,$$

$$|C_{21}| = -9, |C_{22}| = 5, |C_{23}| = -1,$$

$$|C_{31}| = 8, |C_{32}| = -1, |C_{33}| = -6.$$

The determinant of a general $n \times n$ matrix can now be defined in terms of minors, which are themselves determinants of $(n - 1) \times (n - 1)$ matrices. The rule is

$$|A| = a_{i1}(-1)^{i+1} |M_{i1}| + a_{12}(-1)^{i+2} |M_{12}| + \ldots + a_{in}(-1)^{i+n} |M_{in}|$$

$$= \sum_{j=1}^{n} a_{ij}(-1)^{i+j} |M_{ij}|. \tag{B.3a}$$

The operation described is known as finding the determinant by expansion by the ith row of A. It is possible to expand by any row or column in A to find $|A|$; hence, expanding by the jth column, we have

$$|A| = a_{1j}(-1)^{1+j}\,|M_{1j}| + a_{2j}(-1)^{2+j}\,|M_{2j}| + \ldots + a_{nj}(-1)^{n+j}\,|M_{nj}|$$

$$= \sum_{i=1}^{n} a_{ij}(-1)^{i+j}\,|M_{ij}|. \tag{B.3b}$$

Although Eq. (B.3a) and Eq. (B.3b) may look rather complicated at first glance, they are in fact quite simple. Each term of the sum in Eq. (B.3a) simply consists of an element in the ith row and its (signed minor). An example will clarify this further. Let

$$A = \begin{pmatrix} 1 & 2 & 1 \\ 3 & 0 & 4 \\ 0 & 1 & 5 \end{pmatrix}.$$

From Eq. (B.3a), taking $i = 1$, and expanding by the ith row,

$$|A| = a_{11}(-1)^{1+1}|M_{11}| + a_{12}(-1)^{1+2}|M_{12}| + + a_{13}(-1)^{1+3}|M_{13}|$$

$$= 1 \cdot (-1)^2 \cdot \begin{vmatrix} 3 & 4 \\ 0 & 5 \end{vmatrix} + 0 \cdot (-1)^4 \begin{vmatrix} 1 & 1 \\ 0 & 5 \end{vmatrix} + 1(-1)^5 \begin{vmatrix} 1 & 1 \\ 3 & 4 \end{vmatrix}$$

$$= -30 + 0 + (-1) = -31,$$

which agrees with our previous result.

A key observation regarding the definition of the determinant of an $n \times n$ matrix is that we can express it in terms of determinants of $(n-1) \times (n-1)$ matrices (the minors). As in the above example, we reduce the determinant of a 3×3 matrix into a sum of terms involving determinants, and the problem is solved. Now to evaluate a 4×4 determinant, we must first use Eq. (B.3a) or Eq. (B.3b) to reduce it in terms of 3×3 determinants, then use Eq. (B.3a) or Eq. (B.3b) again to reduce each 3×3 determinant to a sum of 2×2 determinants, and then evaluate. So the reduction goes on, and we can now evaluate determinants of any size.

A well-known theorem in matrix algebra states that a square matrix A is nonsingular if and only if $|A| \neq 0$. So the matrix in the previous example has a multiplicative inverse because $|A| = -31 \neq 0$.

H. *The* Inverse of a Square Matrix

Given a nonsingular square matrix A, construct a new matrix B of the same dimension with $b_{ij} = |C_{ij}|$, the cofactor of a_{ij}. Then transpose B and call the resultant matrix the adjoint of A, "adj A." That is, adj $A = B'$. It can be shown that

$$(\text{adj } A)(A) = |A| \cdot I.$$

Since the nonsingularity of A implies $|A| \neq 0$, we can divide both sides by the scalar $|A|$:

$$\frac{1}{|A|}(\text{adj } A)(A) = I;$$

since $A^{-1}A = I$, it is immediately evident that $(1/|A|)(\text{adj } A)(A) = A^{-1}$.

As an example take the 3×3 matrix A from the previous section. We have already computed the determinant as well as all the cofactors, so

$$B = \begin{pmatrix} C_{11} & C_{12} & C_{13} \\ C_{21} & C_{22} & C_{23} \\ C_{31} & C_{32} & C_{33} \end{pmatrix} = \begin{pmatrix} -4 & -15 & 3 \\ -9 & 5 & -1 \\ 8 & -1 & -6 \end{pmatrix},$$

$$\text{adj } A = B' = \begin{pmatrix} -4 & -9 & 8 \\ -15 & 5 & -1 \\ 3 & -1 & -6 \end{pmatrix}.$$

Since $|A| = -31$, the inverse of A is simply

$$A^{-1}\frac{1}{|A|} \text{ adj } A = \begin{pmatrix} \dfrac{4}{31} & \dfrac{9}{31} & -\dfrac{8}{31} \\ \dfrac{15}{31} & -\dfrac{5}{31} & \dfrac{1}{31} \\ -\dfrac{3}{31} & \dfrac{1}{31} & \dfrac{6}{31} \end{pmatrix}.$$

The curious reader may verify that $A^{-1}A = I = AA^{-1}$, or

$$\begin{pmatrix} \dfrac{4}{31} & \dfrac{9}{31} & -\dfrac{8}{31} \\ \dfrac{15}{31} & -\dfrac{5}{31} & \dfrac{1}{31} \\ -\dfrac{3}{31} & \dfrac{1}{31} & \dfrac{6}{31} \end{pmatrix} \begin{pmatrix} 1 & 2 & 1 \\ 3 & 0 & 4 \\ 0 & 1 & 5 \end{pmatrix} = \begin{pmatrix} 1 & 0 & 0 \\ 0 & 1 & 0 \\ 0 & 0 & 1 \end{pmatrix} = \begin{pmatrix} 1 & 2 & 1 \\ 3 & 0 & 4 \\ 0 & 1 & 5 \end{pmatrix} \begin{pmatrix} \dfrac{4}{31} & \dfrac{9}{31} & -\dfrac{8}{31} \\ \dfrac{15}{31} & -\dfrac{5}{31} & \dfrac{1}{31} \\ -\dfrac{3}{31} & \dfrac{1}{31} & \dfrac{6}{31} \end{pmatrix}$$

I. Solving Linear Equation Systems

Now suppose we have a system of linear equations:

$$\begin{aligned} X_1 &+ 2X_2 &+ X_3 &= 1, \\ 3X_1 & & + 4X_3 &= -1, \\ & X_2 &+ 5X_3 &= 2. \end{aligned}$$

The matrix formulation would look like $Ax = b$, or

$$\begin{pmatrix} 1 & 2 & 1 \\ 3 & 0 & 4 \\ 0 & 1 & 5 \end{pmatrix} \begin{pmatrix} X_1 \\ X_2 \\ X_3 \end{pmatrix} = \begin{pmatrix} 1 \\ -1 \\ 2 \end{pmatrix}.$$

We know what A^{-1} is, and we know that the solution of the system is $x = A^{-1}b$; therefore

$$
\begin{pmatrix} X_1 \\ X_2 \\ X_3 \end{pmatrix} = \underbrace{\begin{pmatrix} \dfrac{4}{31} & \dfrac{9}{31} & -\dfrac{8}{31} \\ \dfrac{15}{31} & -\dfrac{5}{31} & \dfrac{1}{31} \\ -\dfrac{3}{31} & \dfrac{1}{31} & \dfrac{6}{31} \end{pmatrix}}_{3 \times 3} \underbrace{\begin{pmatrix} 1 \\ -1 \\ 2 \end{pmatrix}}_{3 \times 1} = \underbrace{\begin{pmatrix} -\dfrac{21}{31} \\ \dfrac{22}{31} \\ \dfrac{8}{31} \end{pmatrix}}_{3 \times 1}
$$

or

$$
X_1 = -\frac{21}{31}, \quad X_2 = \frac{22}{31}, \quad X_3 = \frac{8}{31}.
$$

As a check on the solution, we insert the values into the original equation system:

$$
-\frac{21}{31} + \frac{44}{31} + \frac{8}{31} = 1,
$$

$$
-\frac{63}{31} + 0 + \frac{32}{31} = -1,
$$

$$
0 + \frac{22}{31} + \frac{40}{41} = 2.
$$

J. *Cramer's Rule*

A direct but not obvious corollary to our derivation of A^{-1} is Cramer's rule for the solution of a linear equation. The rule states that

$$
X_i = \frac{|\widehat{A}_i|}{|A|},
$$

where $\widehat{A}_i$ is the matrix obtained from A by replacing the ith column with the *constant vector*. Using the same example and applying Cramer's rule, we first substitute the constant vector for the first column in the numerator and then expand by the first row. Recall that the sign changes are the result of converting minors to cofactors.

$$
X_1 = \frac{\begin{vmatrix} 1 & 2 & 1 \\ -1 & 0 & 4 \\ 2 & 1 & 5 \end{vmatrix}}{|A|} = \frac{1 \cdot \begin{vmatrix} 0 & 4 \\ 1 & 5 \end{vmatrix} - 2 \cdot \begin{vmatrix} -1 & 4 \\ 2 & 5 \end{vmatrix} + 1 \cdot \begin{vmatrix} -1 & 0 \\ 2 & 1 \end{vmatrix}}{-31}
$$

$$
= \frac{-4 + 26 - 1}{-31} = -\frac{21}{31}.
$$

Next we replace the second column of the original numerator by the constant vector and again expand by the first row:

$$X_2 = \frac{\begin{vmatrix} 1 & 1 & 1 \\ 3 & -1 & 4 \\ 0 & 2 & 5 \end{vmatrix}}{-31} = \frac{1 \cdot \begin{vmatrix} -1 & 4 \\ 2 & 5 \end{vmatrix} - 1 \cdot \begin{vmatrix} 3 & 4 \\ 0 & 5 \end{vmatrix} + 1 \cdot \begin{vmatrix} 3 & -1 \\ 0 & 2 \end{vmatrix}}{-31}$$

$$= \frac{-13 - 15 + 6}{-31} = -\frac{22}{31},$$

and again for the third column,

$$X_3 = \frac{\begin{vmatrix} 1 & 2 & 1 \\ 3 & 0 & -1 \\ 0 & 1 & 2 \end{vmatrix}}{-31} = \frac{1 \cdot \begin{vmatrix} 0 & -1 \\ 1 & 2 \end{vmatrix} - 2 \cdot \begin{vmatrix} 3 & -1 \\ 0 & 2 \end{vmatrix} + 1 \cdot \begin{vmatrix} 3 & 0 \\ 0 & 1 \end{vmatrix}}{-31}$$

$$= \frac{1 - 12 + 3}{-31} = \frac{8}{31}.$$

This agrees with the previous result. All the determinants above were evaluated by expanding the first row.

K. Applications

In this section we present two applications of matrix algebra in the theory of finance.

1. Minimum-Variance Portfolio

Suppose we are considering investing in three securities: X_1, X_2, and X_3, and we want to form the portfolio that minimizes the variance of return. Let σ_1^2, σ_2^2, σ_3^2 be individual variances of return, and x_1, x_2, x_3 be weights of investment in the portfolio of securities X_1, X_2, X_3, respectively. So $x_1 + x_2 + x_3 = 1$. Furthermore, let $\sigma_{12} = \sigma_{21}$ be the covariance of return between X_1 and X_2, $\sigma_{13} = \sigma_{31}$ the covariance of return between X_1 and X_3, $\sigma_{23} = \sigma_{32}$ the covariance of return between X_2 and X_3. Constructing the covariance matrix A, we wish to solve for the weight vector X that will minimize the variance. Let

$$\underset{(3 \times 3)}{A} = \begin{pmatrix} \sigma_1^2 & \sigma_{12} & \sigma_{13} \\ \sigma_{21} & \sigma_2^2 & \sigma_{23} \\ \sigma_{31} & \sigma_{32} & \sigma_3^2 \end{pmatrix}, \qquad \underset{(3 \times 1)}{X} = \begin{pmatrix} x_1 \\ x_2 \\ x_3 \end{pmatrix}.$$

The variance of the portfolio with x_1 of X_1, x_2 of X_2, x_3 of X_3 can be expressed in matrix form as $\sigma_p^2 = X'AX$. To minimize the variance of the portfolio is equivalent to minimizing σ_p^2 subject to the weight constraint $x_1 + x_2 + x_3 = 1$. This constrained optimization problem can be solved by the method of the Lagrange multiplier.[1] Let

$$g\left(x_1, x_2, x_3, \lambda'\right) = \sigma_p^2 + \lambda'(1 - x_1 - x_2 - x_3)$$

$$= X'AX + \lambda'(1 - x_1 - x_2 - x_3),$$

---

[1] Readers unfamiliar with the method of solving constrained optimization problems using Lagrange multipliers should consult Appendix D.

where $X'AX$ is the variance-covariance matrix of the portfolio and $(1 - x_1 - x_2 - x_3)$ is the implicit expression of the constraint that requires that the sum of the weights equal one. Then the first-order conditions for an extremum are attained by setting all the partial derivatives of g equal to zero:

$$\frac{\partial g}{\partial x_1} = 0, \tag{B.4a}$$

$$\frac{\partial g}{\partial x_2} = 0, \tag{B.4b}$$

$$\frac{\partial g}{\partial x_3} = 0, \tag{B.4c}$$

$$\frac{\partial g}{\partial \lambda'} = 0. \tag{B.4d}$$

Eqs. (B.4a), (B.4b), (B.4c) can be expressed in matrix notation as

$$AX = \lambda \mathbf{e}, \quad \text{where} \quad \mathbf{e} = \begin{pmatrix} 1 \\ 1 \\ 1 \end{pmatrix} \quad \text{and} \quad \lambda = \lambda'/2, \tag{B.5}$$

and (B.4d) is simply the reiteration of the constraint $x_1 + x_2 + x_3 = 1$. The solution to the matrix Eq. (B.5) will give us the answer in terms of λ, and the constraint condition will give us the value of λ, hence the complete solution.

As a numerical example, take

$$A = \begin{pmatrix} 2 & -1 & 0 \\ -1 & 2 & -1 \\ 0 & -1 & 2 \end{pmatrix}$$

as the covariance matrix for securities X_1, X_2, X_3. Then (B.5) becomes

$$\begin{pmatrix} 2 & -1 & 0 \\ -1 & 2 & -1 \\ 0 & -1 & 2 \end{pmatrix} \begin{pmatrix} X_1 \\ X_2 \\ X_3 \end{pmatrix} = \lambda \begin{pmatrix} 1 \\ 1 \\ 1 \end{pmatrix} = \begin{pmatrix} \lambda \\ \lambda \\ \lambda \end{pmatrix}.$$

Using Cramer's rule, substituting the λ vector for the first column, and expanding both numerator and denominator by the first column, we have

$$X_1 = \frac{\lambda \begin{vmatrix} 2 & -1 \\ -1 & 2 \end{vmatrix} - \lambda \begin{vmatrix} -1 & 0 \\ -1 & 2 \end{vmatrix} + \lambda \begin{vmatrix} -1 & 0 \\ 2 & -1 \end{vmatrix}}{2 \begin{vmatrix} 2 & -1 \\ -1 & 2 \end{vmatrix} + 1 \begin{vmatrix} -1 & 0 \\ -1 & 2 \end{vmatrix} + 0} = \frac{3\lambda + 2\lambda + \lambda}{6 - 2} = \frac{6\lambda}{4} = \frac{3}{2}\lambda.$$

Then substituting the vector λ in column 2 and expanding by column 1,

$$X_2 = \frac{\lambda \begin{vmatrix} \lambda & -1 \\ \lambda & 2 \end{vmatrix} + 1 \begin{vmatrix} \lambda & 0 \\ \lambda & 2 \end{vmatrix} + 0}{4} = \frac{6\lambda + 2\lambda}{4} = \frac{8\lambda}{4} = 2\lambda.$$

And finally substituting the vector λ in column 3,

$$X_3 = \frac{2\begin{vmatrix} 2 & \lambda \\ -1 & \lambda \end{vmatrix} + 1\begin{vmatrix} -1 & \lambda \\ -1 & \lambda \end{vmatrix} + 0}{4} = \frac{6\lambda + 0}{4} = \frac{6\lambda}{4} = \frac{3}{2}\lambda.$$

Since

$$1 = x_1 + x_2 + x_3 = \frac{3}{2}\lambda + 2\lambda + \frac{3}{2}\lambda = 5\lambda,$$

we have

$$\lambda = \frac{1}{5}.$$

Hence,

$$x_1 = \frac{3}{10}, \; x_2 = \frac{2}{5}, \; x_3 = \frac{3}{10}.$$

In other words, if you have \$1,000 to invest, you should put \$300 in X_1, \$400 in X_2, and \$300 in X_3 to form the minimum-variance portfolio. Note that we have not actually established that this is the minimum-variance portfolio. We have merely determined an extreme point that may be either a maximum or a minimum. To guarantee that this is the minimum-variance portfolio, we would need to examine the second-order conditions. (For a discussion, see Appendix D.)

2. Linear Regression

Very often, when we consider a security, we like to know how its return varies as the market fluctuates. Suppose we have the data in Table B.1. Can we discern any pattern or simple relation between the return on security A and the market?

First, we put the data on a graph, as in Fig. B.1. We can see that an approximately linear pattern exists. The following question naturally arises: What is the equation of the straight line that "best" fits the data points? In mathematical terms, this is equivalent to finding the values of two constants a and b such that whenever the return on the market is given, then the expression [$a + b\times$ (return on market)] will give the "best overall" predictive value of the return on security A. In symbols, let X_i, $i = 1, 2, 3, 4, 5, 6$, be the returns on the market given the various states of the world; let Y_i be the returns on security A; and let $\widehat{Y}_i = a + bX_i$, the predicted return on security A using the best-fitting straight line. We call $e_i = Y_i - \widehat{Y}_i$, which is the difference between the observed value and the predicted value of return on security A, the error term. These error terms can be positive or negative. To find the best-fitting straight line is equivalent to minimizing the magnitude of the

Table B.1 Security A and Market Returns

			Return (in %)			
Security A	9	9.5	10.5	10.5	11	12
Market	8	9	10	11	12	13
State	1	2	3	4	5	6

Figure B.1 Graph of joint security and market returns.

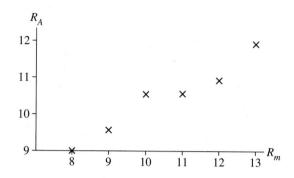

error terms in a certain sense. The technique of minimizing the sum of the squares of the error terms is called linear regression. In our example above with six different states, we have six error terms. Let

$$g(a, b) = \sum_{i=1}^{6} e_i^2 = \sum_{i=1}^{6} (Y_i - \widehat{Y}_i)^2 = \sum_{t=1}^{6} (Y_i - a - bX_i)^2$$

be the sum of the squares of the error terms. The first-order conditions for minimizing $g(a, b)$ are

$$\frac{\partial g}{\partial a} = 0, \qquad\qquad\qquad (B.6a)$$

$$\frac{\partial g}{\partial b} = 0. \qquad\qquad\qquad (B.6b)$$

Equations (B.6a) and (B.6b) written in matrix form turn out to be

$$\begin{pmatrix} 1 & 1 & 1 & 1 & 1 & 1 \\ X_1 & X_2 & X_3 & X_4 & X_5 & X_6 \end{pmatrix} \begin{pmatrix} 1 & X_1 \\ 1 & X_2 \\ 1 & X_3 \\ 1 & X_4 \\ 1 & X_5 \\ 1 & X_6 \end{pmatrix} \begin{pmatrix} a \\ b \end{pmatrix} = \begin{pmatrix} 1 & 1 & 1 & 1 & 1 & 1 \\ X_1 & X_2 & X_3 & X_4 & X_5 & X_6 \end{pmatrix} \begin{pmatrix} Y_1 \\ Y_2 \\ Y_3 \\ Y_4 \\ Y_5 \\ Y_6 \end{pmatrix}$$

Performing matrix multiplication, as explained earlier, we get

$$\begin{pmatrix} 6 & \sum_{i=1}^{6} X_i \\ \sum_{i=1}^{6} X_i & \sum_{i=1}^{6} X_i^2 \end{pmatrix} \begin{pmatrix} a \\ b \end{pmatrix} = \begin{pmatrix} \sum_{i=1}^{6} Y_i \\ \sum_{i=1}^{6} X_i Y_i \end{pmatrix}.$$

This is equivalent to two equations and two unknowns (a and b). As a numerical example, let us take the data from Table B.1:

$$\sum_{i=1}^{6} X_i = 8 + 9 + 10 + 11 + 12 + 13 = 63,$$

$$\sum_{i=1}^{6} X_i^2 = 8^2 + 9^2 + 10^2 + 11^2 + 12^2 + 13^2 = 679,$$

$$\sum_{i=1}^{6} Y_i = 9 + 9.5 + 10.5 + 10.5 + 11 + 12 = 62.5,$$

$$\sum_{i=1}^{6} X_i Y_i = 8 \times 9 + 9 \times 9.5 + 10 \times 10.5 + 11 \times 10.5 + 12 \times 11 + 13 \times 12 = 666,$$

so

$$\begin{pmatrix} 6 & 63 \\ 63 & 679 \end{pmatrix} \begin{pmatrix} a \\ b \end{pmatrix} = \begin{pmatrix} 62.5 \\ 666.0 \end{pmatrix}.$$

By Cramer's rule, we have

$$a = \frac{\begin{vmatrix} 62.5 & 63 \\ 666.0 & 679 \end{vmatrix}}{\begin{vmatrix} 6 & 63 \\ 63 & 679 \end{vmatrix}} = \frac{479.5}{105} = 4.57,$$

$$b = \frac{\begin{vmatrix} 6 & 62.5 \\ 63 & 666.0 \end{vmatrix}}{\begin{vmatrix} 6 & 63 \\ 63 & 679 \end{vmatrix}} = \frac{58.5}{105} = 0.56.$$

Therefore the equation of the best-fitting straight line is $Y = 4.57 + 0.56X$. Note that b is the slope of the straight line. Both the sign and the magnitude of b contain important information. If b is positive, we would expect that the return on security A moves with the market, whereas a negative b implies that the return on security A and the market generally move in the opposite directions. The magnitude of b measures the degree of volatility of security A. The larger the magnitude of b, the more volatile the return on security A.

An Introduction to Multiple Regression

B USINESS STUDENTS ARE FREQUENTLY CONFRONTED with journal articles that are riddled with econometrics. Econometrics courses, however, assume prior knowledge of matrix algebra and calculus and therefore present a formidable barrier to the curious. This appendix is written to provide an overview of multiple regression techniques that assumes only the rudimentary knowledge of calculus and matrix algebra provided in the other appendices. Although not a substitute for a good econometrics course, this appendix enables the reader to understand and interpret the computer output from a typical multiple regression software package and to have an introductory level of understanding of some of the typical errors made in econometric studies.

A. *O*rdinary Least Squares, Linear Estimation

If we are trying to explain the distribution of sales revenue for the XYZ Company given a forecast of gross national product, we might choose a linear model like

$$\widetilde{Y}_t = a + bX_t + \widetilde{\varepsilon}_i, \tag{C.1}$$

where

$\widetilde{Y}_t =$ sales revenue in year t,

$X_t =$ forecast of gross national product for year t,

$\widetilde{\varepsilon}_i =$ error term (the difference between actual sales revenue and that predicted by the model).

Linear relationships have the virtue that they are simple and robust. Many natural phenomena are not linearly related, but linear approximations usually work very well within a limited range.

Figure C.1 Revenues versus forecast GNP.

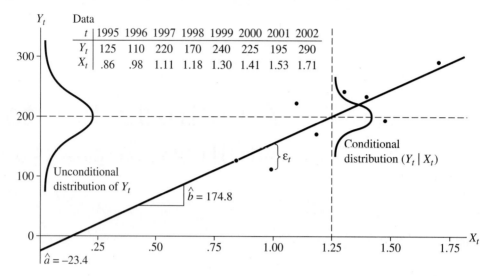

The object is to find the set of weights (a and b) in Eq. (C.1) that provide the best unbiased estimate of revenue given GNP. If GNP has any explanatory power, the conditional distributions of revenues, $\widetilde{Y}_t \mid X_t$, will be different from their unconditional distribution. This is illustrated in Fig. C.1. The mean and standard deviation of the unconditional distribution of Y_t are \$196.90 and \$60.10. The unconditional probability distribution of revenues is plotted along the y-axis. The conditional distribution of $Y_t \mid X_t$ is the distribution of error terms, ε_t. For example, given that $X_t = \$.126$ (its mean), then the estimated revenue is \$196.90 (its mean) and the standard deviation of the estimate is \$33.73. Notice that the conditional distribution has lower variance than the unconditional distribution. This is because knowledge of predicted GNP allows us to refine our estimate of sales revenue.

To obtain the best linear model to predict Y_t given X_t, we want to find the equation that minimizes the squared error terms. The error term is the difference between the actual revenue and the revenue predicted by the linear model. If we minimize the squared error terms, we are in effect minimizing the variance of the conditional distribution. To see how this is accomplished, rewrite Eq. (C.1) as follows:

$$\varepsilon_t = Y_t - a - bX_t.$$

The variance of the error terms is[1]

$$\sigma_\varepsilon^2 = E\left[(Y_t - a - bX_t) - \left(\overline{Y} - a - b\overline{X} \right) \right]^2, \tag{C.2}$$

$$\sigma_\varepsilon^2 = E\left[\left(Y_t - \overline{Y} \right) - b\left(X_t - \overline{X} \right) \right]^2,$$

$$\sigma_\varepsilon^2 = \sigma_Y^2 - 2b\mathrm{COV}(Y, X) + b^2\sigma_X^2.$$

---

[1] This result follows from the properties of random variables discussed in Chapter 6.

We want to choose the slope, b, and the intercept, a, that minimize the squared error terms. To do this, take the derivative of σ_ε^2 with respect to b and set the result equal to zero:

$$\frac{d\sigma_\varepsilon^2}{db} = -2\text{COV}(Y, X) + 2b\sigma_X^2 = 0.$$

Solving for $\widehat{b}$, the estimated slope term, we have

$$\widehat{b} = \frac{\text{COV}(Y, X)}{\sigma_X^2}. \tag{C.3}$$

The intercept is determined by the fact that the line must pass through the mean values for both $\overline{Y}$ and $\overline{X}$. At that point, we have

$$\overline{Y} = \widehat{a} + \widehat{b}\,\overline{X}. \tag{C.4}$$

Therefore, solving for $\widehat{a}$, we have

$$\widehat{a} = \overline{Y} - \widehat{b}\,\overline{X}.$$

The estimated slope and intercept terms are computed in Table C.1.

Having obtained estimates of the slope and intercept that minimize the squared error terms, we now have the following linear equation:

$$\widehat{Y}_t = -23.42 + 174.84 X_t.$$

It can be used to predict sales revenue when given a forecast of GNP. The difference between predicted revenue and actual revenue in any given year is the error of estimate, often called the residual:

$$\varepsilon_t = Y_t - \widehat{Y}_t.$$

Note that in Table C.1 the average error term $\overline{\varepsilon}_t$ (except for rounding error in the calculations) is zero. This implies that the linear estimate is unbiased. In other words, on average, there is no error of estimate.

In linear regression the residual errors indicate the extent of movement in the dependent variable (the variable on the left-hand side of the regression equation) that is not explained by the independent variable(s) (the variable(s) on the right-hand side). If the residuals are small relative to the total movement in the dependent variable, then it follows that a major part of the movement has been explained. We define the summary statistic known as the squared multiple correlation coefficient, r^2, as the percentage of the total variation in the dependent variable that is explained by the regression equation. The square of the correlation coefficient is

$$r^2 = \frac{\text{variation explained by the regression equation}}{\text{total variation of the dependent variable}}$$

$$= \frac{\sum(Y - \overline{Y})^2 - \sum(\varepsilon - \overline{\varepsilon})^2}{\sum(Y - \overline{Y})^2}. \tag{C.5}$$

Note that $\sum(Y - \overline{Y})^2$ is the variance of the dependent variable, σ_Y^2, in our example. Note also that $\sum(\varepsilon - \overline{\varepsilon})^2$ is the variance of the residuals. Furthermore, the average error term, $\overline{\varepsilon}$, is always zero; therefore we can rewrite the square correlation coefficient as zero.[2] To do this we can calculate t-statistics in order to test the significance of the slope and intercept terms.

The t-statistics are defined as the estimates of the intercept, $\widehat{a}$, or the slope, $\widehat{b}$, divided by their respective standard errors of estimate:[3]

$$t_a = \frac{\widehat{a}}{se(\widehat{a})}, \qquad t_b = \frac{\widehat{b}}{se(\widehat{b})}. \tag{C.6}$$

We shall assume that the independent variable, X, can be treated as a constant in repeated samplings. In fact, this is where regression analysis derives its name. We say that Y is regressed on X. We also assume that the error terms are generated by random selection from a stationary statistical distribution with a mean of zero and a constant variance, σ_ε^2. Also, the error terms in

---

[2] An important relationship, which is used in Chapter 6, is that

$$r = \frac{\text{COV}(Y, X)}{\sigma_Y \sigma_X}.$$

Proof follows from the definitions of r^2, σ_ε^2, and b. First, rewrite r^2 and the definition of b

$$r^2 = \frac{\sigma_Y^2 - \sigma_\varepsilon^2}{\sigma_Y^2}, \qquad b = \frac{\text{COV}(Y, X)}{\sigma_X^2}.$$

From Eq. (C.2), we have

$$\sigma_\varepsilon^2 = \sigma_Y^2 - 2b\text{COV}(Y, X) + b^2\sigma_X^2.$$

Substituting in the value of b, we have

$$\sigma_X^2 = \sigma_Y^2 - 2\left(\frac{\text{COV}(Y, X)}{\sigma_X^2}\right)\text{COV}(Y, X) + \left(\frac{\text{COV}(Y, X)}{\sigma_X^2}\right)^2 \sigma_X^2$$

$$= \sigma_Y^2 - \frac{[\text{COV}(Y, X)]^2}{\sigma_X^2}.$$

Substituting this result into the definition of r^2 gives

$$r^2 = \frac{\sigma_Y^2 - \sigma_Y^2 + \frac{[\text{COV}(Y,X)]^2}{\sigma_X^2}}{\sigma_Y^2}$$

$$r^2 = \frac{[\text{COV}(Y, X)]^2}{\sigma_X^2 \sigma_Y^2}.$$

Therefore, taking the square root,

$$r = \frac{\text{COV}(Y, X)}{\sigma_X \sigma_Y}. \qquad \text{QED}$$

[3] A good reference to the t-statistics is Hoel [1954, 274–283].

Table C.1 Simple Regression Computations

t	Y	$Y - \overline{Y}$	$(Y - \overline{Y})^2$	X	$X - \overline{X}$	$(X - \overline{X})^2$	$(Y - \overline{Y})(X - \overline{X})$	$\varepsilon = \widehat{Y} - Y$	ε^2
1995	125	−71.875	5,166.01	.86	−.40	.1600	8.750	−1.94	3.7636
1996	110	−88.875	7,547.27	.98	−.28	.0784	24.325	−37.92	1437.9264
1997	220	23.125	534.76	1.11	−.15	.0225	−3.469	49.35	2435.4225
1998	170	−26.875	722.27	1.18	−.08	.0064	2.150	−12.89	166.1521
1999	240	43.125	1,859.76	1.30	.04	.0016	1.725	36.13	1305.3769
2000	225	28.125	791.02	1.41	.15	.0225	4.219	1.90	3.6100
2001	195	−1.875	3.52	1.53	.27	.0729	−.506	−49.09	2409.8281
2002	290	93.125	8,672.27	1.71	.45	.2025	41.906	14.44	208.5136
Sum	1575		25,296.89	10.08		.5668	99.100	−.02 ≈ 0	7970.5932

$$\overline{Y} = \frac{\sum Y}{N} = \frac{1575}{8} = 196.875 \qquad\qquad \overline{X} = \frac{\sum X}{N} = \frac{10.08}{8} = 1.26$$

$$\sigma_Y^2 = \frac{\sum(Y - \overline{Y})^2}{N - 1} = \frac{25,296.89}{7} = 3,613.84 \qquad \sigma_X^2 = \frac{\sum(X - \overline{X})^2}{N - 1} = \frac{.5668}{7} = .08097914$$

$$\sigma_Y = \sqrt{\sigma_Y^2} = \sqrt{3,613.84} = 60.12 \qquad\qquad \sigma_X = \sqrt{\sigma_X^2} = .2846$$

$$\text{COV}(Y, X) = \frac{\sum(Y - \overline{Y})(X - \overline{X})}{N - 1} = \frac{99.10}{7} = 14.16$$

$$\widehat{b} = \frac{\text{COV}(Y, X)}{\sigma_X^2} = \frac{14.16}{.0809714} = 174.88$$

$$\widehat{a} = \overline{Y} - \widehat{b}\,\overline{X} = 196.876 - 174.84(1.26) = -23.42$$

Symbol definitions:

$$\begin{aligned}
\overline{Y}, \overline{X} &= \text{the means of revenue and GNP, respectively,} \\
N &= \text{the number of observations in the sample,} \\
\sigma_Y^2, \sigma_X^2 &= \text{the variances of revenue and GNP, respectively,} \\
\text{COV}(Y, X) &= \text{the covariance between revenue and GNP,} \\
\widehat{a}, \widehat{b} &= \text{the intercept and slope estimates,} \\
\varepsilon &= \text{the error term.}
\end{aligned}$$

successive samplings are independent. This specification of the error-generating process may be stated as

$$E(\varepsilon) = 0, \tag{C.7}$$

$$\text{VAR}(\varepsilon) = E\,[\varepsilon - E(\varepsilon)]^2 = E(\varepsilon)^2 = \sigma_\varepsilon^2, \tag{C.8}$$

$$\text{COV}(\varepsilon_t, \varepsilon_{t-1}) = 0. \tag{C.9}$$

To determine the standard error of estimate for $\widehat{b}$, recall the definition given in Eq. (C.3):

$$\widehat{b} = \frac{\text{COV}(Y, X)}{\sigma_X^2}.$$

We also know that observed values of Y are

$$Y = a + bX + \varepsilon.$$

Rewriting Eq. (C.3), using the definitions of $\text{COV}(Y, X)$ and σ_X^2, we have

$$b = \frac{\sum \left[(X - \overline{X})(Y - \overline{Y})\right]}{\sum \left[(X - \overline{X})(X - \overline{X})\right]}.$$

Substituting in Y yields

$$\widehat{b} = \frac{\sum \left[(X - \overline{X})(a + bX + \varepsilon - \overline{a} - \overline{b}X)\right]}{\sum \left[(X - \overline{X})(X - \overline{X})\right]}$$

$$= \frac{\sum \left[(X - \overline{X})(Y - \overline{Y}) + (X - \overline{X})\varepsilon\right]}{\sum \left[(X - \overline{X})(X - \overline{X})\right]}$$

$$= \frac{\sum \left[(X - \overline{X})(Y - \overline{Y})\right]}{\sum \left[(X - \overline{X})(X - \overline{X})\right]} + \frac{\sum \left[(X - \overline{X})\varepsilon\right]}{\sum \left[(X - \overline{X})(X - \overline{X})\right]}$$

$$= b + \frac{\sum \left[(X - \overline{X})\varepsilon\right]}{\sum \left[(X - \overline{X})^2\right]}. \tag{C.10}$$

Equation (C.10) tells us that the estimated slope, $\widehat{b}$, is equal to the true slope, b, plus a term that depends on the variance of X (in the denominator) and the error terms (in the numerator). The expected value of $\widehat{b}$ is

$$E(\widehat{b}) = b, \quad \text{since } E(\varepsilon) = 0. \tag{C.11}$$

Note that the expected value of the slope is equal to the true slope. Therefore we can say that the slope estimate is unbiased. The variance of $\widehat{b}$ is

$$\text{VAR}(\widehat{b}) = E\left[\widehat{b} - E(\widehat{b})\right]^2$$

$$= E\left[\overline{b} + \frac{\sum \left[(X_i - \overline{X})\varepsilon_i\right]}{\sum \left[(X_i - \overline{X})^2\right]} - \overline{b}\right]^2$$

$$= E\left[\frac{\sum \left[(X_i - \overline{X})\varepsilon_i\right]}{\sum \left[(X_i - \overline{X})^2\right]}\right]^2,$$

and since X is assumed to be a constant, we have

$$\text{VAR}(\widehat{b}) = \left[\frac{1}{\sum\left[(X_i - \overline{X})^2\right]} \right]^2 E\left[\sum (X_i - \overline{X})\varepsilon_i\right]^2.$$

Expanding the second term yields

$$E\left[\sum (X_i - \overline{X})\varepsilon_i\right]^2 = E[(X_1 - \overline{X})^2\varepsilon_1^2 + (X_2 - \overline{X})^2\varepsilon_2^2 + \cdots$$

$$+ 2(X_1 - \overline{X})(X_2 - \overline{X})\varepsilon_1\varepsilon_2 + \cdots]$$

$$= (X_1 - \overline{X})^2 E\left(\varepsilon_1^2\right) + \left(X_2 - \overline{X}\right)^2 E\left(\varepsilon_2^2\right) + \cdots$$

$$+ 2(X_1 - \overline{X})(X_2 - \overline{X})E(\varepsilon_1\varepsilon_2) + \cdots.$$

Using Eqs. (C.8) and (C.9), the above result can be reduced to

$$E\left[\sum (X_i - \overline{X})\varepsilon_i\right]^2 = \left[\sum (X_i - \overline{X})^2\right]\sigma_\varepsilon^2.$$

This means that the variance of the estimate of b can be written as

$$\text{VAR}(\widehat{b}) = \frac{\sum (X - \overline{X})^2}{\left[\sum (X - \overline{X})^2\right]^2}\sigma_\varepsilon^2$$

$$= \frac{\sigma_\varepsilon^2}{\sum (X - \overline{X})^2}. \tag{C.12}$$

We now have the result that the slope estimate, $\widehat{b}$, is distributed normally with a mean of b and a variance of $\sigma_\varepsilon^2/\sigma_X^2$. The variance of the estimate of b provides a measure of the precision of the estimate. The larger the variance of the estimate, the more widespread the distribution and the smaller the precision of the estimate.

A similar derivation would show that the intercept estimate, $\widehat{a}$, is also normally distributed with a mean of

$$E(\widehat{a}) = a \tag{C.13}$$

and a variance of

$$\text{VAR}(\widehat{a}) = \frac{\left(\sum X^2\right)/\sigma_\varepsilon^2}{N \sum (X - \overline{X})^2}, \qquad se(\widehat{a}) = \sqrt{\text{VAR}(\widehat{a})}, \tag{C.14}$$

where N is the number of observations in the sample.

Using Eqs. (C.12) and (C.14) for the sample problem of Table C.1, and given that the t-statistics defined in Eq. (C.6) have $n - m$ degrees of freedom (where $N = 8 =$ the number of observations and $m = 2 =$ the number of independent variables including the constant term), we can compute the appropriate significance tests for the slope and intercept. The standard error term for the slope term is

$$se(\widehat{b}) = \sqrt{\frac{\sigma_\varepsilon^2}{\sum(X - \overline{X})^2}} = \sqrt{\frac{7970.5932/(8 - 2)}{.5668}} = 48.41,$$

and the t-statistic for b is

$$t(\widehat{b}) = \frac{\widehat{b}}{se(\widehat{b})} = \frac{174.84}{48.41} = 3.61.$$

We refer to the table of t-statistics (Table C.2) for $8 - 2 = 6$ degrees of freedom and a 95% confidence interval (in a two-tail t-test). That table shows that the t-statistic must be greater than 2.447 in order to reject the null hypothesis that the slope coefficient is not significantly different from zero. It is. Therefore we can say that predicted GNP, the independent variable, is a significant explanatory variable for sales revenue, given our sample data.

Next, compute the t-test to determine whether or not the intercept estimate, $\widehat{a}$, is significantly different from zero. The standard error of $\widehat{a}$ is

$$se(\widehat{a}) = \left[\frac{(\sum X^2)\sigma_\varepsilon^2}{N\sum(X - \overline{X})^2}\right]^{1/2}$$

$$= \left[\frac{(13.2676)(7,970.5932/6)}{8(.5668)}\right]^{1/2} = 62.35,$$

and the t-statistic is

$$t(\widehat{a}) = \frac{\widehat{a}}{se(\widehat{a})} = \frac{-23.42}{62.35} = -.375.$$

The t-statistic for $\widehat{a}$ is less than 2.447, the required level for significance. Therefore we cannot conclude that the intercept term is significantly different from zero.

Summarizing, up to this point we can write the results of the regression analysis as follows:

$$Y_t = -23.42 + 174.84X, \quad r^2 = .6849,$$
$$(-.38) \qquad (3.61) \qquad df = 6.$$

The numbers in parentheses are the appropriate t-statistics, and df designates the degrees of freedom.

B. $\mathcal{B}$ias and Efficiency

1. The Mean Square Error Criterion

The researcher is always interested in the bias and efficiency of the estimated regression equations. Unbiased estimates have the property that on average the sample statistic equals the true value of the underlying population parameter. The most efficient statistic equals the true value of the underlying parameter. The most efficient estimate is the one with the lowest possible variance of estimation. Frequently there is a trade-off between bias and efficiency. One rule that weighs both of these

Table C.2 *t*-Statistics

Degrees of Freedom	Probability of a Value Greater in Value than the Table Entry					
	0.005	0.01	0.025	0.05	0.1	0.15
1	63.657	31.821	12.706	6.314	3.078	1.963
2	9.925	6.965	4.303	2.920	1.886	1.386
3	5.841	5.541	3.182	2.353	1.638	1.250
4	4.604	3.747	2.776	2.132	1.533	1.190
5	4.032	3.365	2.571	2.015	1.476	1.156
6	3.707	3.143	2.447	1.943	1.440	1.134
7	3.499	2.998	2.365	1.895	1.415	1.119
8	3.355	2.896	2.306	1.860	1.397	1.108
9	3.250	2.821	2.262	1.833	1.383	1.100
10	3.169	2.764	2.228	1.812	1.372	1.093
11	3.106	2.718	2.201	1.796	1.363	1.088
12	3.055	2.681	2.179	1.782	1.356	1.083
13	3.012	2.650	2.160	1.771	1.350	1.079
14	2.977	2.624	2.145	1.761	1.345	1.076
15	2.947	2.602	2.131	1.753	1.341	1.074
16	2.921	2.583	2.120	1.746	1.337	1.071
17	2.898	2.567	2.110	1.740	1.333	1.069
18	2.878	2.552	2.101	1.734	1.330	1.067
19	2.861	2.539	2.093	1.729	1.328	1.066
20	2.845	2.528	2.086	1.725	1.325	1.064
21	2.831	2.518	2.080	1.721	1.323	1.063
22	2.819	2.508	2.074	1.717	1.321	1.060
23	2.807	2.500	2.069	1.714	1.319	1.060
24	2.797	2.492	2.064	1.711	1.318	1.059
25	2.787	2.485	2.060	1.708	1.316	1.058
26	2.779	2.479	2.056	1.706	1.315	1.058
27	2.771	2.473	2.052	1.703	1.314	1.057
28	2.763	2.467	2.048	1.701	1.313	1.056
29	2.756	2.462	2.045	1.699	1.311	1.055
30	2.750	2.457	2.042	1.697	1.310	1.055
∞	2.576	2.326	1.960	1.645	1.282	1.036

aspects is the concept of "quadratic loss." The expected value of the distribution of quadratic loss is called the mean square error. It may be formally defined as

$$\text{MSE}(\widehat{\theta}) = E\left(\widehat{\theta} - \theta\right)^2, \tag{C.15}$$

where θ is the population parameter $\widehat{\theta}$ and is the estimate of that parameter.

The mean square error can be expressed in terms of the variance and the bias of the estimate by first adding and then subtracting $E(\theta)$ in Eq. (C.15). The result is

$$\text{MSE}(\theta) = E\left[\theta - E(\widehat{\theta}) + E(\widehat{\theta}) - \theta\right]^2$$

$$= E\left[\widehat{\theta} - E(\widehat{\theta})\right]^2 + \left[E(\widehat{\theta}) - \theta\right]^2$$

because the cross-product term has a zero expected value. Therefore the mean square error can be written as

$$\text{MSE}(\widehat{\theta}) = \text{Variance}(\widehat{\theta}) + \left[\text{bias}(\widehat{\theta})\right]^2. \tag{C.16}$$

Minimizing the MSE imposes an arbitrary judgment as to the relative importance of bias and variance. If it is thought that minimizing bias is of paramount importance, then the MSE may be inappropriate.

2. Sources of Bias

LEFT-OUT VARIABLES One of the most frequently encountered problems of regression analysis is that the empirical model is not founded on a sound theoretical footing. When this happens we say that the model is misspecified. If an important explanatory variable is left out of the regression equation, then the estimates of the coefficients for the variables included in the equations can be biased. This was one of the empirical difficulties in the early attempt to test for relationships between capital structure and value (see Chapter 15). The empirical work was done before a theoretical model of value had been derived. Therefore relevant variables were often left out, and the empirical results were biased.

Suppose that the true theoretical relationship is

$$Y_t = a + b_1 X_{1t} + b_2 X_{2t} + \varepsilon_t, \tag{C.17}$$

but that the researcher mistakenly estimates the following regression equation:

$$Y_t = a + \widetilde{b} X_{1t} + U_t. \tag{C.18}$$

From Eq. (C.3) the ordinary least squares estimate of $\widetilde{b}_1$ is

$$\widetilde{b}_1 = \frac{\sum (X_1 - \overline{X}_1)(Y - \overline{Y})}{\sum (X_1 - \overline{X}_1)(X_1 - \overline{X}_1)}. \tag{C.19}$$

By substituting the true relation for Y from Eq. (C.17) into Eq. (C.19), we obtain

$$\tilde{b}_1 = \frac{\sum (X_1 - \overline{X}_1)(a + b_1 X_1 + b_2 X_2 + \varepsilon - a - b_1 \overline{X}_1 - b_2 \overline{X}_2)}{\sum (X_1 - \overline{X}_1)(X_1 - \overline{X}_1)}$$

$$= \frac{\sum (X_1 - \overline{X}_1)(a + b_1 X_1 - a - b_1 \overline{X}_1)}{\sum (X_1 - \overline{X}_1)^2}$$

$$+ \frac{\sum (X_1 - \overline{X}_1)(b_2 X_2 - b_2 \overline{X}_2)}{\sum (X_1 - \overline{X}_1)^2} + \frac{\sum (X_1 - \overline{X}_1)\varepsilon}{\sum (X_1 - \overline{X}_1)^2},$$

and because the error terms are assumed to follow Eqs. (C.7), (C.8), and (C.9), we have

$$\tilde{b}_1 = b_1 + b_2 \frac{\sum (X_1 - \overline{X}_1)(X_2 - \overline{X}_2)}{\sum (X_1 - \overline{X}_1)^2}. \tag{C.20}$$

Equation (C.20) shows that, when a relevant variable is left out of the equation specification, the slope estimate, $\tilde{b}$, is biased. The direction of the bias depends on the sign of b_2 (the relationship between Y and X_2) and on $\sum (X_1 - \overline{X}_1)(X_2 - \overline{X}_2)$ (the relationship between the independent variables, X_1 and X_2). If X_1, X_2, and Y are all positively related, then b will be biased upward. In general the only way to eliminate misspecification bias is to be sure that the empirical test is appropriately founded on sound theory, rather than going on an ad hoc "fishing trip."

ERRORS IN VARIABLES There is almost always some measurement error involved when taking sample statistics. The degree of accuracy in estimating both independent and dependent variables can vary considerably, and unfortunately this problem also results in bias. For example, in Chapter 16, Friend and Puckett showed that measurement error is important when trying to estimate the relative effect of dividends and retained earnings on the price of common stock. The estimated equation was

$$P_{it} = a + b D_{it} + c R_{it} + \varepsilon_{it},$$

where

$$P_{it} = \text{the price per share,}$$

$$D_{it} = \text{the aggregate dividends paid out,}$$

$$R_{it} = \text{the retained earnings of the firm,}$$

$$\varepsilon_{it} = \text{the error term.}$$

Dividends can be measured without any error whatsoever, but retained earnings (the difference between accounting earnings and dividends paid) is only an estimate of true economic retained earnings on which value is based. Thus retained earnings possesses a great deal of measurement error. Consequently, the estimate of the effect of retained earnings on the price per share was biased downward. This led earlier researchers to incorrectly conclude that dividends had a greater effect on price per share than retained earnings.

To demonstrate the effect of measurement error, suppose that both the independent and dependent variables have sampling error. This may be written as

$$X = x + w, \tag{C.21}$$

$$Y = y + v, \tag{C.22}$$

where X and Y indicate observations, x and y are the true values, and w and v are the measurement errors. Suppose, further, that the true variables have the following relationship:

$$y = a + bx. \tag{C.23}$$

We would like to have unbiased estimates of a and b.

Substituting Eqs. (C.21) and (C.22) into Eq. (C.23) gives

$$Y = a + bX + z,$$

where $z = v - bw$. From Eq. (C.3), the estimate of b is

$$\widehat{b} = \frac{\sum (X - \overline{X})(Y - \overline{Y})}{\sum (X - \overline{X})(X - \overline{X})}$$

$$= \frac{\sum (x + w - \overline{x} - \overline{w})(y + v - \overline{y} - \overline{v})}{\sum (x + w - \overline{x} - \overline{w})^2}$$

$$= \frac{\sum (x - \overline{x})(y - \overline{y}) + \sum (x - \overline{x})(v - \overline{v}) + \sum (y - \overline{y})(w - \overline{w}) + \sum (w - \overline{w})(v - \overline{v})}{\sum (x - \overline{x})^2 + 2\sum (x - \overline{x})(w - \overline{w}) + \sum (w - \overline{w})^2}.$$

Given that the measurement errors, w and v, are distributed independently of each other and of the true parameters, then the last three terms in the numerator and the middle term in the denominator vanish as the sample size becomes large. Therefore the limiting value of b is

$$\text{plim } \widehat{b} = \frac{\sum (x - \overline{x})(y - \overline{y})}{\sum (x - \overline{x})^2 + \sum (w - \overline{w})^2}.$$

Dividing numerator and denominator by $\sum (x - \overline{x})^2$, we have

$$\widehat{b} = \frac{b}{1 + \left[\sum (w - \overline{w})^2 / \sum (x - \overline{x})^2\right]}. \tag{C.24}$$

Equation (C.24) shows that even if the errors of measurement are assumed to be mutually independent, independent of the true values, and have constant variance, the estimate, $\widehat{b}$, will be biased downward. The greater the measurement error, the greater the downward bias.

There are two generally accepted techniques for overcoming the problem of errors in variables: (1) grouping and (2) instrumental variables. Grouping procedures can reduce measurement error because when grouped the errors of individual observations tend to be canceled out by their mutual independence. Hence there is less measurement in a group average than there would be if sample data were not grouped. An instrumental variable is one that is highly correlated with the independent variable but that is independent of the errors w and v in Eqs. (C.21) and (C.22). This was the technique employed by Friend and Puckett in testing dividend policy. Instead of using the accounting measurement of earnings, they used normalized earnings (a time-series estimate of predicted earnings) to eliminate most of the measurement error bias.

3. Loss of Efficiency

MULTICOLLINEARITY When two or more independent variables are highly correlated, it frequently becomes difficult to distinguish their separate effects on the dependent variable. In fact, if they are perfectly correlated, it is impossible to distinguish. For example, consider the following equation:

$$S_t = a + b_1 R_t + b_2 L_t + b_3 O_t + \varepsilon_t,$$

where S_t is the sales revenue of a ski shop, R_t and L_t are the sales of left and right downhill skis, and O_t is the sales of other items. The estimated coefficient b_1 is supposed to measure the impact of the sale of the right skis, holding all other variables constant. Of course this is nonsense, since right and left skis are sold simultaneously.

The usual multicollinearity problem occurs when two independent variables are highly, but not perfectly, correlated. And usually the effect is to reduce the efficiency of estimates of b_1 and b_2 by increasing the standard error of estimate. The best remedy for the problem is larger sample sizes.

SERIAL CORRELATION One of the important assumptions for linear regression, Eq. (C.9), is that samplings are drawn *independently* from the same multivariate distribution. In other words, successive error terms should be independent. If this is not the case, we still obtain unbiased estimates of the slope and intercept terms, but there is a loss of efficiency because the sampling variances of these estimates may be unduly large.

Consider the following two variable cases. Suppose that

$$Y_t = a + bX_t + \varepsilon_t,$$

but that the error term follows a first-order autoregressive scheme such as

$$\varepsilon_t = K\varepsilon_{t-1} + U_t,$$

where $|K| < 1$ and U_t satisfies the assumptions

$$E(U_t) = 0,$$

$$E(U_t U_{t-N}) = \begin{cases} \sigma_U^2 & \text{if } N = 0 \\ 0 & \text{if } N \neq 0. \end{cases}$$

In general the tth error term can be written as

$$\varepsilon_t = K\varepsilon_{t-1} + U_t$$
$$= K(K\varepsilon_{t-2} + U_{t-1}) + U_t$$
$$= U_t + KU_{t-1} + K^2 U_{t-2} + \cdots K^n U_{t-n}$$
$$= \sum_{t=0}^{\infty} K^\tau U_{t-\tau},$$

$$E(\varepsilon_t) = 0 \quad \text{since } E(U_t) = 0 \text{ for all } t.$$

The expected value of the squared error terms is

$$E(\varepsilon_t^2) = E(U_t^2) + K^2 E(U_{t-1}^2) + K^4 E(U_{t-2}^2) + \cdots,$$

since the error terms U_t are serially independent. Consequently,

$$E(\varepsilon_t^2) = \sigma_t^2 = (1 + K^2 + K^4 + \cdots)\sigma_U^2.$$

This is a geometric series that reduces to

$$E(\varepsilon_t^2) = \sigma_\varepsilon^2 = \frac{\sigma_U^2}{1 + K^2}. \tag{C.25}$$

Equation (C.25) shows that the closer the relationship between ε_t and ε_{t-1}, the closer K is to unity and the greater will be the estimated error term and the loss of efficiency.

We can test for serial correlation by using the Durbin-Watson d-statistic. If ε_t are the residuals from a fitted least squares equation, then d is defined as

$$d = \frac{\displaystyle\sum_{t=2}^{n}(\varepsilon_t - \varepsilon_{t-1})^2}{\displaystyle\sum_{t=1}^{n}\varepsilon_t^2}.$$

Durbin and Watson have tabulated upper and lower bounds d_u and d_l for various numbers of observations, n, and numbers of independent variables, K.

When the error terms are serially independent, the d-statistic has a theoretical distribution with a mean of 2, but sampling fluctuations may lead to a different estimate even when the errors are not autocorrelated. Table C.3 provides critical values for the d-statistic. If the computed d is smaller than the lower critical value, d_l, or above the critical value $(4 - d_l)$, then the null hypothesis of serial independence is rejected. When the statistic is larger than d_u but smaller than $(4 - d_u)$, then the null hypothesis is accepted. When neither of these two cases is true, then the test is inconclusive.

For the set of sample data in Table C.1, the estimated d-statistic is computed in Table C.4. From Table C.3 the critical values for the Durbin-Watson test are $d_l = .95$ and $d_u = 1.23$. Since our computed value is neither below $d_l = .95$ nor above the critical value of $(4 - d_l) = 3.05$, the null hypothesis of serial independence cannot be rejected. However, because $d = 2.88$ is greater than $d_u = 1.23$ but not smaller than $(4 - d_u) = 2.77$, we cannot accept the null hypothesis. Because serial correlation cannot be either accepted or rejected, the test is inconclusive in this case.

*S*ummary

This has been an extremely brief overview of linear regression analysis. We have shown how to estimate the slope, the intercept, the standard errors of each, their t-statistics, and the correlation coefficient for a two-variable case. Multivariate estimates of the same variables in a multiple regression equation have the same interpretation and are provided by many different computer software packages. The summary statistics for the example problem of Table C.1 would appear in a computer printout in something like the following form:

$$Y_t = -23.42 \quad +174.84X_t \quad r^2 = .6849 \quad d = 2.88$$
$$(-.38) \qquad (3.61) \qquad df = 6$$

Table C.3 Critical Values for the Durbin-Watson Test: 5% Significance Points of d_t and d_u in the Two-Tailed Tests

n	$k' = 1$ d_t	d_u	$k' = 2$ d_t	d_u	$k' = 3$ d_t	d_u	$k' = 4$ d_t	d_u	$k' = 5$ d_t	d_u
15	0.95	1.23	0.83	1.40	0.71	1.61	0.59	1.84	0.48	2.09
16	0.98	1.24	0.86	1.40	0.75	1.59	0.64	1.80	0.53	2.03
17	1.01	1.25	0.90	1.40	0.79	1.58	0.68	1.77	0.57	1.98
18	1.03	1.26	0.93	1.40	0.82	1.56	0.72	1.74	0.62	1.93
19	1.06	1.28	0.96	1.41	0.86	1.55	0.76	1.72	0.66	1.90
20	1.08	1.28	0.99	1.41	0.89	1.55	0.79	1.70	0.70	1.87
21	1.10	1.30	1.01	1.41	0.92	1.54	0.83	1.69	0.73	1.84
22	1.12	1.31	1.04	1.42	0.95	1.54	0.86	1.68	0.77	1.82
23	1.14	1.32	1.06	1.42	0.97	1.54	0.89	1.67	0.80	1.80
24	1.16	1.33	1.08	1.43	1.00	1.54	0.91	1.66	0.83	1.79
25	1.18	1.34	1.10	1.43	1.02	1.54	0.94	1.65	0.86	1.77
26	1.19	1.35	1.12	1.44	1.04	1.54	0.96	1.65	0.88	1.76
27	1.21	1.36	1.13	1.44	1.06	1.54	0.99	1.64	0.91	1.75
28	1.24	1.37	1.15	1.45	1.08	1.54	1.01	1.64	0.93	1.74
29	1.25	1.38	1.17	1.45	1.10	1.54	1.03	1.63	0.96	1.73
30	1.26	1.38	1.18	1.46	1.12	1.54	1.05	1.63	0.98	1.73
31	1.27	1.39	1.20	1.47	1.13	1.55	1.07	1.63	1.00	1.72
32	1.28	1.40	1.21	1.47	1.15	1.55	1.08	1.63	1.02	1.71
33	1.29	1.41	1.22	1.48	1.16	1.55	1.10	1.63	1.04	1.71
34	1.30	1.41	1.24	1.48	1.17	1.55	1.12	1.63	1.06	1.70
35	1.31	1.42	1.25	1.48	1.19	1.55	1.13	1.63	1.07	1.70
36	1.32	1.43	1.26	1.49	1.20	1.56	1.15	1.63	1.09	1.70
37	1.33	1.43	1.27	1.49	1.21	1.56	1.16	1.62	1.10	1.70
38	1.34	1.44	1.28	1.50	1.23	1.56	1.17	1.62	1.12	1.70
39	1.35	1.44	1.29	1.50	1.24	1.56	1.19	1.63	1.13	1.69
40	1.39	1.45	1.30	1.51	1.25	1.57	1.20	1.63	1.15	1.69
45	1.42	1.48	1.34	1.53	1.30	1.58	1.25	1.63	1.21	1.69
50	1.45	1.50	1.38	1.54	1.34	1.59	1.30	1.64	1.26	1.69
55	1.45	1.52	1.41	1.56	1.37	1.60	1.33	1.64	1.30	1.69
60	1.47	1.54	1.44	1.57	1.40	1.61	1.37	1.65	1.33	1.69
65	1.49	1.55	1.46	1.59	1.43	1.62	1.40	1.66	1.36	1.69
70	1.51	1.57	1.48	1.60	1.45	1.63	1.42	1.66	1.39	1.70
75	1.53	1.58	1.50	1.61	1.47	1.64	1.45	1.66	1.42	1.70
80	1.54	1.59	1.52	1.62	1.49	1.65	1.47	1.67	1.44	1.70
85	1.56	1.60	1.53	1.63	1.51	1.65	1.49	1.68	1.46	1.71
90	1.57	1.61	1.55	1.64	1.53	1.66	1.50	1.69	1.48	1.71
95	1.58	1.62	1.56	1.65	1.54	1.67	1.52	1.69	1.50	1.71
100	1.59	1.63	1.57	1.65	1.55	1.67	1.53	1.70	1.51	1.72

Table C.4 Durbin-Watson Statistic for Data in Table C.1

t	ε_t	$\varepsilon_t - \varepsilon_{t-1}$	ε_t^2	$\left(\varepsilon_t - \varepsilon_{t-1}\right)^2$
1976	14.44	63.53	208.5136	4,036.0609
1975	−49.09	−50.99	2,409.8281	2,599.9801
1974	1.90	−34.23	3.6100	1,171.6929
1973	36.13	49.02	1,305.3769	2,402.9604
1972	−12.89	−62.24	166.1521	3,873.8176
1971	49.35	87.27	2,435.4225	7,616.0529
1970	−37.92	−35.98	1,437.9264	1,294.5604
1969	−1.94	—	3.7764	—
Sum			7,970.5932	22,995.1252

$d = \frac{22,995.1252}{7,970.5932} = .288.$

We can infer that sales revenue is significantly related to predicted GNP, with an intercept term insignificantly different from zero and a significant slope term. Because the Durbin-Watson test is inconclusive, we cannot be sure whether or not serial correlation has reduced the efficiency of our estimates. Furthermore, additional testing would be necessary to determine whether or not left-out variables have caused a biased estimate of b_1.

The mean square error criterion is one way of trading off bias and loss of efficiency. It may be desirable, for example, to accept a small bias in order to gain much greater efficiency. Although we have not discussed all the causes of bias or inefficiency, a few of the more important ones were covered. The interested reader should refer to an econometrics text for a more rigorous and detailed presentation.

REFERENCES

Christ, C. G., *Econometric Models and Methods*. Wiley, New York, 1966.

Dhrymes, P. J., *Econometrics: Statistical Foundations and Applications*. Harper & Row, New York, 1970.

Goldberger, A. S., *Econometric Theory*. Wiley, New York, 1964.

Hoel, P. G., *Introduction to Mathematical Statistics*, third edition, Wiley, New York, 1954.

Johnston, J., *Econometric Methods*. McGraw-Hill, New York, 1963.

Rao, P., and L. Miller, *Applied Econometrics*. Wadsworth, Belmont, Calif., 1971.

Wonnacott, R. J., and T. H. Wonnacott, *Econometrics*. Wiley, New York, 1970.

Calculus and Optimization

O PTIMIZING OR MAXIMIZING are concepts basic to finance theory as well as to economics. In this brief review, we shall summarize the main concepts drawn on in the text. These include functions, differential calculus, optimization, series, and integral calculus.

A. *F*unctions

A fundamental notion used in finance is the concept of a function. There are three ways to express functions: as (1) mathematical equations, (2) graphs, and (3) tables.

EXAMPLE Suppose a variable Y is related to a variable X by the following mathematical equation:

$$Y = 2X^2 - 3X + 6.$$

A shorthand way of expressing this relationship is to write $Y = f(X)$, which is read "Y is a function of the variable X" and where Y is the range and X is the domain of the function. X is also called the independent variable and Y the dependent variable, since Y's value $\left[f(X)\right]$ is *posited* to depend on X's value.

We can also express the function in a tabular and graphical manner. Thus the equation enables us to construct a range of Y values for a given table of X values. The data in the table can then be plotted in a graph as in Fig. D.1.

DEFINITION The *dimension* of a function is determined by the number of independent variables in the domain of the function.

Figure D.1 Example of a (quadratic) function.

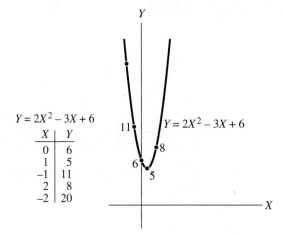

$Y = 2X^2 - 3X + 6$

X	Y
0	6
1	5
−1	11
2	8
−2	20

$Y = 2X^2 - 3X + 6$

EXAMPLE $Y = f(X, Z)$ is a two-dimensional function.

$Y = f(X_1, X_2, \ldots, X_n)$ is an n-dimensional function.

EXAMPLE   From basic capital budgeting concepts (see Chapter 2), we know that the net present value (*NPV*) of an investment project is equal to

$$NPV = \sum_{t=1}^{N} \frac{FCF_t}{(1+k)^t} - I_0,$$

where

$$FCF_t = \text{free cash flow in time period } t,$$
$$I_0 = \text{the project's initial cash outlay,}$$
$$k = \text{the firm's cost of capital,}$$
$$N = \text{the number of years in the project.}$$

We can express this relationship functionally as

$$NPV = f(FCF_t, I_0 k, N) \quad t = 1, \ldots N.$$

Given values for the right-hand-side independent variables, we can determine the left-hand-side dependent variable, NPV. The functional relationship tells us that for every X that is in the domain of the function a unique value of Y can be determined.

1. Inverse Functions

How about going the other way? Given Y, can we determine X? Yes, we can.

DEFINITION   The function that expresses the variable X in terms of the variable Y is called the *inverse function* and is denoted $X = f^{-1}(Y)$.

Figure D.2 y graphed as the inverse of X.

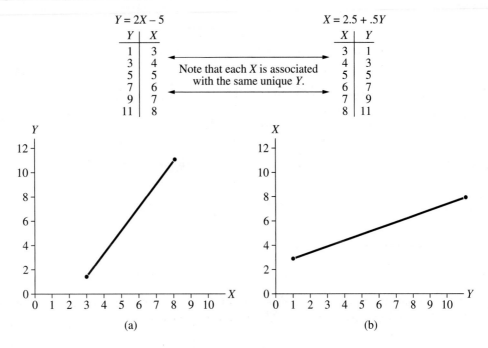

EXAMPLE $Y = f(X) = 2X - 5.$

Solving for X in terms of Y,

$$X = \frac{Y+5}{2} = 2.5 + 2.5Y = f^{-1}(Y).$$

The inverse relationship can be seen more clearly if we graph the two functions (Fig. D.2). The inverse function, however, does not exist for all functions. But the inverse of a function always exists when we are dealing with one-to-one functions.

2. Linear Functions

An important type of function consists of *linear functions* of the form

$$Y = a_1 X_1 + a_2 X_2 + \cdots + a_n X_n.$$

These functions are used in regression and in the CAPM. In two dimensions a linear function is a straight line, usually written as $Y = a + bX$, where a is the intercept on the y-axis and b is the *slope* of the line:

$$b = \frac{Y_1 - Y_2}{X_1 - X_2} = \frac{\Delta Y}{\Delta X}$$

$$= \frac{\text{change in } Y}{\text{change in } X} = \frac{\text{rise}}{\text{run}}.$$

Figure D.3 Linear function (a); and an example (security market line) (b)

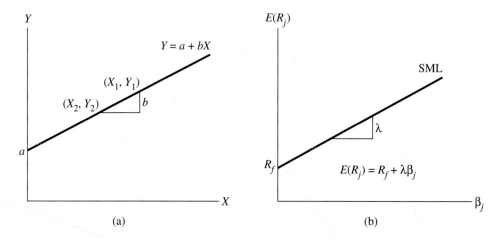

(a)   (b)

Figure D.4 Examples of the slopes of linear functions.

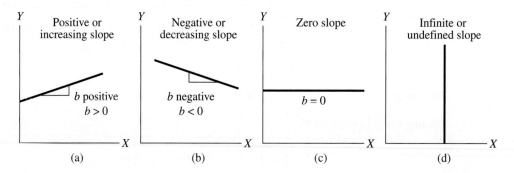

(a)   (b)   (c)   (d)

The CAPM is of the form $Y = a + bX$, where $E(R_j) = R_f + \lambda \beta_j$. This equation plots like the relationship in Fig. D.3(a), as we see in Fig. D.3(b). The slope of the security market line in Fig. D.3(b) is $[E(R_m) - R_f]$, which is the market risk premium, λ.

The slope of a function is an important concept: it tells us the change in Y per unit change in X. The various types of slopes are pictured in Fig. D.4.

EXAMPLE   Straight-line depreciation is a simple linear function:

$$BV = c - \left(\frac{c}{N} \right) X,$$

BV = book value of the asset,

c = original cost of the asset,

N = estimated economic life of the asset,

X = number of years that have elapsed,

so that the book value after two years is $BV = c - (c/N)2$.

Figure D.5 Examples of exponential functions.

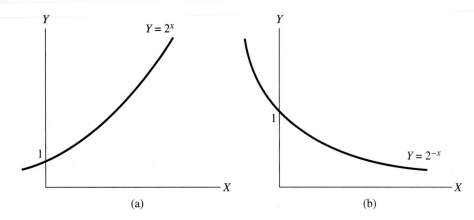

(a)   (b)

3. Exponential Functions

As their name suggests, exponential functions are those in which independent variable X appears as an exponent. They are useful for describing growth and compound interest. More formally:

DEFINITION   The equation $Y = ma^X$ (a always > 0) is called an exponential function, and a is called the base.

Some properties of the exponential function are

1. If $m > 0$, $a > 0$, then the function lies above the x-axis.
2. If $m < 0$, $a > 0$, then the function lies below the x-axis.
3. If $a > 1$, $m > 0$, then the curve rises to the right.
4. If $a < 1$, $m > 0$, then the curve rises to the left.

EXAMPLE   An example of properties 3 and 4 appears in Fig. D.5.

EXAMPLE   Compound interest can be shown to be an exponential function. If you invest Z dollars in a bank that pays $r\%$ compound annual interest, then

$$Y_1 = Z + Zr = Z(1+r)$$

$$= \text{cumulative amount of money by the end of the first year,}$$

$$Y_2 = Z(1+r) + [Z(1+r)]r = Z(1+r)(1+r)$$

$$= Z(1+r)^2 = \text{cumulative amount of money by the end of the second year,}$$

$$\vdots$$

$$Y_n = Z(1+r)^n = \text{amount taken at the end of } n \text{ years.}$$

This last expression is simply an exponential function:

$$Y_n = Z(1+r)^n$$

$$Y = ma^X, \text{ where the base is } (1+r) \text{ and only } n \text{ can vary.}$$

Figure D.6 Percent and future value functions.

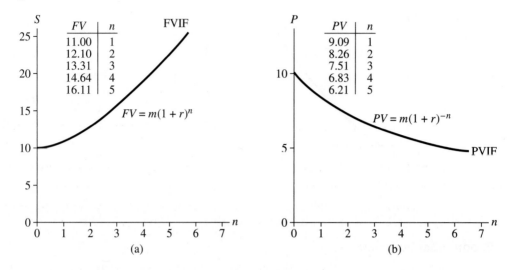

(a)   (b)

Note that money grows exponentially, as in Fig. D.6(a), when it is paid compound interest.

EXAMPLE Both future value interest factors (FVIF) and present value interest factors (PVIF) are exponential functions. Consider the case of compounding and discounting $10 for five periods when the appropriate interest rate is 10%.

Future Value	Present Value
$Y = ma^X$	$Y = ma^{-X}$
$FV = m(1+r)^n$	$PV = m(1+r)^{-n}$
$a = (1+r) > 1$	$a = (1+r)^{-1} < 1$
$n = 1, 2, \ldots, N$	$n = 1, 2, \ldots, N$
For $r = 10\%$	For $r = 10\%$
$m = \$10$	$m = \$10$
$n = 1, 2, \ldots, 5$	$n = 1, 2, \ldots, 5$
Then $FV = 10 \cdot (1+r)^n$	Then $PV = 10 \cdot (1+r)^{-n}$
$=$ future value of $10 at the end of the nth period.	$=$ present value of $10.

4. Logarithmic Functions

DEFINITION If $N = b^r$, where both $n > 0$, $b > 0$, then we define $r = \log_b N$, which is read "r is the log to the base b of N."

In other words, $\log_b N$ is the number to which b has to be raised exponentially in order to equal N. So a log is simply an exponent.

EXAMPLES

$$100 = 10^2$$

so $\log_{10} 100 = 2.$

$$\frac{1}{2} = 2^{-1}$$

so $\log_2 \frac{1}{2} = -1.$

The two most widely used bases for logarithms are base 10 and base e, where e is an irrational number equal to 2.7182818 . . .

DEFINITION   The logarithm to the base 10 of N is called the "common logarithm of N." It is usually designated log N.

DEFINITION   The logarithm to the base e of N is called the "natural logarithm of N." To differentiate it from the common log, the natural log is designated ln N.

DEFINITION   The function $Y = \log_b X$ is called a *logarithmic function*.

Since by definition $Y = \log_b X$ if and only if $X = b^Y$, we see that the exponential and logarithmic functions are inverse functions of each other:

$$X = 10^Y \Longleftrightarrow Y = \log_{10} X,$$

$$X = e^Y \Longleftrightarrow Y = \ln X.$$

The logarithmic function $Y = \ln X$ is graphed in Fig. D.7.

Some properties of the logarithmic function $Y = \log_b X$ are as follows:

1. The function equals zero when $X = 1$.
2. The function is an increasing function (i.e., it rises to the right) for all $b > 1$.
3. The function is a decreasing function (i.e., it falls to the right) for $0 < b < 1$. See Fig. D.8.
4. The function is negative when $0 < X < 1$ and $b > 1$.
5. The function is positive when $1 < X < \infty$.
6. The function is not defined when X is negative.

Figure D.7 Natural logarithm of X.

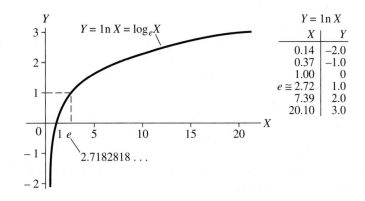

$Y = \ln X$	
X	Y
0.14	−2.0
0.37	−1.0
1.00	0
$e \cong 2.72$	1.0
7.39	2.0
20.10	3.0

Figure D.8 Log base 0.5 of X.

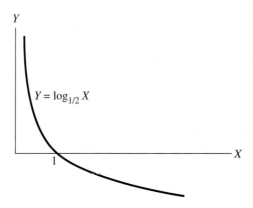

$$X = 2^{-Y} = \frac{1}{2^Y} = \left(\frac{1}{2}\right)^2,$$

so $Y = \log_{1/2} X$.

Since logarithms are simply exponents, the rules of logs simply mirror the rules of exponents:

Exponents	**Logarithms**
$a^m \cdot a^n = a^{m+n}$	$\log_a(XY) = \log_a X + \log_a Y$
$\frac{a^m}{a^n} = a^{m-n}$ if $m > n$	$\log_a \frac{X}{Y} = \log_a X - \log_a Y$
$(a^m)^n = a^{mn}$	$\log_a(X^n) = n \log_a X$

B. *D*ifferential Calculus

1. Limits

The central idea in calculus is the concept of the limit of a function. Often we want to know how the values of a function, $f(X)$, behave as the independent variable X approaches some particular point, a. If as $X \to a$ (read "X approaches a"), $f(X)$ approaches some number L, then we say that the *limit* of $f(X)$ as X approaches a is L. This is written more compactly as

$$\lim_{X \to a} f(X) = L.$$

Intuitively, the existence of a limit L means that the function of $f(X)$ will take on a value as close to L as one may desire, given that the independent variable takes a value that is sufficiently close to a.

EXAMPLE   Many times we are interested in just what happens to a function as X increases without bound, that is, when $X \to \infty$ (read "X approaches infinity"). For instance, what is lim as $X \to \infty$ of $[(X + 1)/X]$? The way to evaluate this limit is to observe the behavior of $f(X)$ as X gets larger and larger. From the table and the graph in Fig. D.9, we see that $f(X)$ approaches

Figure D.9 Lim of
$(X + 1)/X$ as $X \to \infty$.

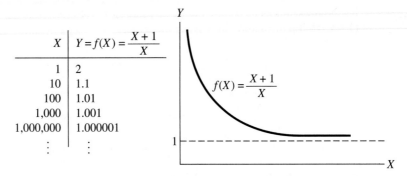

X	$Y = f(X) = \dfrac{X+1}{X}$
1	2
10	1.1
100	1.01
1,000	1.001
1,000,000	1.000001
$\vdots$	$\vdots$

Figure D.10 Lim of
$(3X/X^2)$ as $X \to 0$.

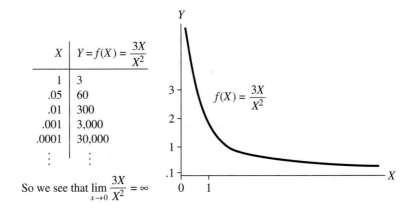

X	$Y = f(X) = \dfrac{3X}{X^2}$
1	3
.05	60
.01	300
.001	3,000
.0001	30,000
$\vdots$	$\vdots$

So we see that $\lim\limits_{x \to 0} \dfrac{3X}{X^2} = \infty$

1 as $X \to \infty$, so we can write lim as $X \to \infty$ of $[(X + 1)/X] = 1$. Intuitively, as X gets very large, the fact that the numerator is greater by one than the denominator does not matter "much," so we have $X/X = 1$.

EXAMPLE   As we will see next, we are often interested in what happens to $f(X)$ as X gets very small, i.e., when $X \to 0$. For instance, what is the lim as $X \to 0$ of $(3X/X^2)$? Again, to evaluate this limit we see what happens to $f(X)$ as $X \to 0$ (Fig. D.10).

EXAMPLE   Generally we assume that compounding and discounting occur discretely in annual periods. If the compounding is more than once a year, the compound value interest factor is changed from $(1 + r)^n$ to $(1 + r/m)^{nm}$, where m is the number of times per year compounding occurs. We can now see with limits what the relationship is between the continuous compounding rate and the discrete compounding rate. Continuous compounding means

$$\lim_{m \to \infty} \left[\left(1 + \frac{r}{m} \right)^{nm} \right] = e^{rn} \quad \text{by definition of } e.$$

If r_c = the continuous compounding rate and r_d = the discrete compounding rate, then $e^{r_c n}$ = $(1 + r_d)^n$. Taking natural logs:

$$\ln\left[e^{r_c n}\right] = \ln\left(1 + r_d\right)^d,$$

$$r_c n \ln e = n \ln(1 + r_d),$$

$$r_c n = n \ln(1 + r_d) \qquad \text{since } \ln e \equiv 1,$$

$$r_c = \ln(1 + r_d).$$

So 5.25% continuously compounded is equal to 5.39% compounded annually. That is, if $r_c = 5.25\%$, then using $\ln(1 + r_d) = 5.25\%$, r_d must be 5.39%.

2. Derivatives

The rate of change of a function (the change in Y per unit change in X) is an important concept in mathematics. It is referred to as the *derivative* of Y with respect to X. In finance and economics the rate of change is called "marginal." For example, the marginal cost of capital (MCC) is the rate of change of the total cost of capital per change in new capital raised. Analytically, the marginal quantities are simply the *slopes* of the total quantities.

The derivative is usually denoted as dY/dX, or $f'(X)$. The advantage of the $f'(X)$ notation is that it reminds us that the *derivative is itself a function:* the value of the derivative depends on where it is evaluated. Fortunately there are special rules of differentiation that can be used to guide calculations.

3. Rules of Differentiation

1. $f(X) = c$, where c is a constant, $f'(X) = 0$. This rule states that the slope of a horizontal line is zero, since by definition Y does not change when X changes.
2. $f(X) = X^n$, $f'(X) = nX^{n-1}$. In order to differentiate X^n, reduce the exponent by one and multiply by n.
3. $f(X) = g(X) \cdot h(X)$, $f'(X) = g'(X) \cdot h(X) + h'(X) \cdot g(X)$. The derivative of $g(X) \cdot h(X)$ equals $h(X)$ times the derivative of $g(X)$ plus $g(X)$ times the derivative of $h(X)$.
4. $f(X) = g(X)/h(X)$, $\left[h(X) \neq 0\right]$, $f'(X) = \left[g'(X)h(X) - g(X)h'(X)/h(X)\right]^2$.
5. $f(X) = c \cdot g(X)$, where c is a constant, $f'(X) = c \cdot g'(X)$.
6. $f(X) = g(X) + h(X)$, $f'(X) = g'(X) + h'(X)$.
7. $f(X) = \ln X$, $f'(X) = 1/X$.
8. $f(X) = e^{g(X)}$, $f'(X) = 1/X$.
9. $f(X) = X$, $f'(X) = 1$.
10. $f(X) = a^X$, $f'(X) = a^X \cdot \ln a$.
11. $f(X) = \log_b X$, $f'(X) = 1/(X \ln b)$.
12. $f(X) = \log\left[g(X)\right]$, $f'(X) = g'(X)/g(X)$.

EXAMPLES

1.
$$Y = 6X^3 - 3X^2 + 4X + 7,$$

$$\frac{dY}{dX} = 6 \cdot \frac{d}{dX}(X^3) - 3 \cdot \frac{d}{dX}(X^2) + 4 \cdot \frac{d}{dX}(X) + \frac{d}{dX}(7)$$

$$= 6(3X^2) - 3(2X) + 4(1) + 0$$

$$= 18X^2 - 6X + 4.$$

2.
$$Y = X^2(X + 3),$$

$$\frac{dY}{dX} = \left[\frac{d}{dX}\left(X^2\right)\right](X + 3) + \left[\frac{d}{dX}(X + 3)\right]X^2$$

$$= 2X(X + 3) + (1)X^2 = 3X^2 + 6X.$$

3.
$$Y = X^{-4},$$

$$\frac{dY}{dX} = -4X^{-5} = \frac{-4}{X^5}.$$

4.
$$Y = \frac{(2X^2 + 6)}{X^3},$$

$$\frac{dY}{dX} = \frac{4X(X^3) - (2X^2 + 6)(3X^2)}{(X^3)^2} = \frac{-2X^4 - 18X^2}{X^6}.$$

5.
$$Y = \frac{2}{\sqrt{X}} = 2X^{-1/2},$$

$$\frac{dY}{dX} = 2 \cdot -\frac{1}{2} \cdot X^{-3/2} = -X^{-3/2} = \frac{-1}{X^{3/2}} = \frac{-1}{\sqrt{X^3}}.$$

4. Chain Rule

An extremely useful and powerful tool in differential calculus is the chain rule, or the function of a function rule. Suppose Y is a function of a variable Z:

$$Y = f(Z),$$

but Z is in turn a function of another variable X:

$$Z = g(X).$$

Because Y depends on Z, and in turn depends on X, Y *is also a function of* X. We can express this fact by writing Y as a composite function (i.e., a function of a function) of X: $Y = f[g(X)]$.

To determine the change in Y from a change in X, the chain rule says:

$$\frac{dY}{dX} = \frac{dY}{dZ}\frac{dZ}{dX} = f'(Z) \cdot g'(X).$$

Intuitively the chain rule says, "Take the derivative of the outside (function) and multiply it by the derivative of the inside (function)." The reason behind the name "chain" rule is that there is a chain reaction relationship between X, Z, and Y:

$$\Delta X \xrightarrow{\text{via } g} \Delta Z \xrightarrow{\text{via } f} \Delta Y.$$

In words, a change in X has an ultimate impact on Y by causing a change in Z via function g, and this change in Z will in turn cause a change in Y by function f.

There is a temptation to look at the chain rule by canceling the intermediate dZ term:

$$\frac{dY}{dX} = \frac{dY}{dZ} \cdot \frac{dZ}{dX} = \frac{dY}{dX}.$$

This is incorrect! It is no more valid than canceling the 3s in

$$3 = \frac{\cancel{3}9}{1\cancel{3}} \neq \frac{9}{1} \neq 9.$$

The usefulness of the chain rule can best be seen by considering some examples in which it is used.

EXAMPLE   Suppose we want to differentiate

$$Y = (3 + 6X^2)^{10}.$$

We could, by a considerable amount of work, expand $(3 + 6X^2)^{10}$ and differentiate term by term. Instead we can use the chain rule. Note that if we wanted to simply differentiate $Z = (3 + 6X^2)$, that would pose no problem:

$$\frac{dZ}{dX} = \frac{d}{dX}(3) + \frac{d(6X^2)}{dX}$$
$$= 0 + 12X,$$
$$= 12X.$$

Likewise, if we let

$$Y = (Z)^{10},$$

then we can differentiate easily:

$$\frac{dY}{dZ} = \frac{d(Z)^{10}}{dZ} = 10Z^{10-1} = 10 \cdot Z^9.$$

The chain rule says to simply multiply these two results together to get dY/dX:

$$\frac{dY}{dX} = \frac{dY}{dZ} \cdot \frac{dZ}{dX}$$

$$= \left[10 \cdot Z^9\right] 12X$$

$$= \left[10 \cdot (3 + 6X^2)^9\right] 12X$$

$$= 120X(3 + 6X^2)^9.$$

Intuitively, the chain rule says to take the derivative of the function outside the parentheses—in this case, $10 \cdot (\ )^9$—and multiply it by the derivative of what is inside the parentheses—i.e., $12X$. So what seemed to be at first a rather forbidding problem turns out to be very easy to solve.

EXAMPLES

$$\frac{d}{dX}\left(\sqrt[3]{5X + 7}\right) = \frac{d}{dX}(5X + 7)^{1/3}$$

$$= \frac{1}{3}(5X + 7)^{-2/3} \cdot 5$$

$$= \frac{5}{3}\frac{1}{\left(\sqrt[3]{5X + 7}\right)^2}$$

$$= \frac{5}{3(5X + 7)^{2/3}}.$$

$$\frac{d}{dX}(e^{3X-4}) = e^{3X-4} \cdot 3$$

$$= 3e^{3X-4}.$$

5. Higher-Order Derivatives

In our development of derivatives we have emphasized that the derivative of a function is also a function. That is, the value of the derivative depends on the point X at which it is being evaluated. Like $f(X)$, $f'(X)$ is also a function of X.

EXAMPLE Consider the function

$$f(X) = -10X^2 + 2{,}400X - 8{,}500, \quad \text{then}$$

$$f'(X) = -20X + 2{,}400.$$

The value of this derivative depends on the point at which it is being evaluated:

$$f'(120) = -20(120) + 2{,}400 = 0,$$

$$f'(60) = -20(60) + 2{,}400 = 1{,}200.$$

Table D.1

	$f'(X)$	$f''(X)$	$f(X)$ **is**
(a)	>0	>0	Increasing at an increasing rate
(b)	>0	<0	Increasing at a decreasing rate
(c)	<0	<0	Decreasing at an increasing rate
(d)	<0	>0	Decreasing at a decreasing rate

Because it is also a function of X, we can take the derivative of $f'(X)$. This new function, $f''(X)$, is called the *second derivative* of the original function, $f(X)$. The *third derivative* is the derivative of the second derivative and is written $f'''(X)$. In principle we can go on forever and form derivatives of as high order as we like. Notationally these higher-order derivatives are symbolized in the same manner as the second derivative:

$$f'''(X), f^{(4)}(X), f^{(5)}(X), \ldots, f^{(n)}(X),$$

$$\frac{d^3Y}{dX^3}, \frac{d^4Y}{dX^4}, \frac{d^5Y}{dX^5}, \ldots, \frac{d^nY}{dX^n}.$$

EXAMPLE

$$Y = f(X) = X^3 - 7X^2 + 6X - 5,$$

$$f'(X) = 3X^2 - 14X + 6,$$

$$f''(X) = 6X - 14,$$

$$f'''(X) = 6,$$

$$f^{(4)}(X) = 0,$$

$$f^{(5)}(X) = 0,$$

$$\vdots$$

$$f^{(n)}(X) = 0.$$

As we shall see, higher-order derivatives play an important role in Taylor and MacLaurin series (see Section D of this appendix). The most important of the higher-order derivatives is the second derivative. Understanding the meaning of the second derivative is crucial. We know that the first derivative of a function, $f'(X)$, is the slope of a function or the rate of change of Y as a result of a change in X. The second derivative, $f''(X)$, is the rate of change of the slope of $f(X)$; that is, it is the rate of change of the rate of change of the original function, $f(X)$. Table D.1 and Fig. D.11 show various combinations of signs for $f'(X)$ and $f''(X)$ and the implied shape of the graph of fX).

EXAMPLE   In developing the theory of investor choice under uncertainty, cardinal utility functions [$U(W)$] are used. These utility functions should have the following property: $U'(W) > 0$, $U''(W) < 0$. That is, they should look like Fig. D.11(b). Check to see if and when the following four functions have this property:

Figure D.11 Utility functions and their derivatives.

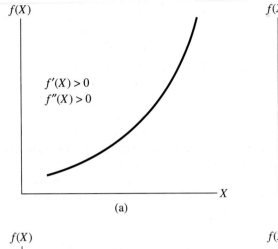

$f(X)$

$f'(X) > 0$
$f''(X) > 0$

X

(a)

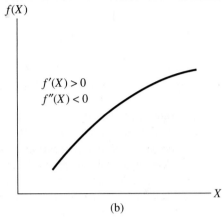

$f(X)$

$f'(X) > 0$
$f''(X) < 0$

X

(b)

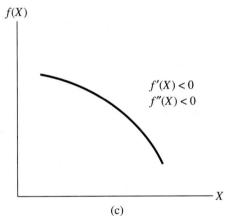

$f(X)$

$f'(X) < 0$
$f''(X) < 0$

X

(c)

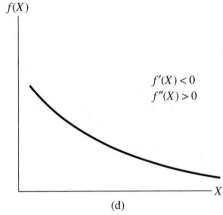

$f(X)$

$f'(X) < 0$
$f''(X) > 0$

X

(d)

1. $U(W) = aw - bw^2$ (quadratic utility function),

     $U'(W) = a - 2bw > 0$ when $a > 2bw$,

     $U''(W) = -2b < 0$ when $b > 0$.

2. $U(W) = \ln W$ (logarithmic utility function),

     $U'(W) = \dfrac{1}{W} > 0$ W is always > 0 by definition of log function,

     $U''(W) = \dfrac{-1}{W^2} < 0.$

3. $U(W) = -e^{-aW}$ (exponential utility function),

     $U'(W) = -(-a)e^{-aW} = ae^{-aW} > 0$ if $a > 0$,

     $U''(W) = -a^2 e^{-aW} < 0.$

4. $U(W) = W^a$ (power utility function),

     $U'(W) = aW^{a-1} > 0,$

     $U''(W) = a(a-1)W^{a-2} < 0$ when $a < 1.$

EXAMPLE   Given the following linear demand function:

$$p = 100 - 10q,$$

where

$$p = \text{price per unit sold (i.e., average revenue),}$$

$$q = \text{quantity sold,}$$

(note that p is the dependent variable here), we can obtain the total revenue function by multiplying through by q: $TR = pq = 100q - 10q^2$, which is a quadratic equation. The first derivative of total revenue tells us how total revenue responds to changes in the quantity sold. Economists call this function the marginal revenue:

$$MR \equiv \frac{d(TR)}{dq} = 100 - 20q.$$

If we want to know by how much marginal revenue itself varies when quantity sold varies, we compute the slope of the marginal revenue. This is the second derivative of the total revenue function:

$$\frac{d(MR)}{dq} = \frac{d^2(TR)}{dq^2} = -20.$$

So marginal revenue declines at a constant rate of -20 per unit increase in quantity sold. Graphically the relationship between total, average, and marginal revenue is shown in Fig. D.12.

DEFINITION   An important class of functions are those functions whose first derivative is positive for all values of the independent variable. Such functions are called *monotonically increasing* functions. Likewise, functions whose first derivative is negative for all values of the independent variable are *monotonically decreasing*.

6. Differentials

Let $Y = f(X)$; then the differential, dY, is defined as

$$dY = f'(X)dX.$$

If we regard $dX \equiv \Delta X$, a small increment in the independent variable X, then we can see that dY is an approximation to ΔY induced by ΔY because $f'(X) = \lim$ as $\Delta X \to 0$ of $(\Delta Y / \Delta X)$.

EXAMPLE   Let $Y = 2X^2 + X + 2$. Then $dY = (4X + 1)dX$. The concept of differentials is very useful when we consider integration later in Section E.

7. Partial Differentiation

So far we have only considered differentiation of functions of one independent variable. In practice, functions of two or more independent variables do arise quite frequently. Since each independent variable influences the function differently, when we consider the instantaneous rate

Figure D.12 Total revenue, marginal revenue, and average revenue.

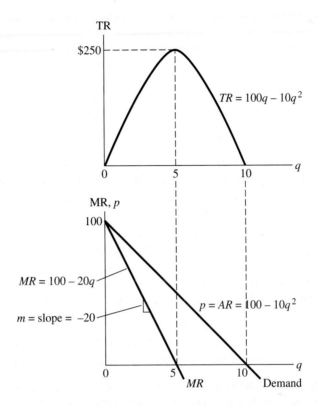

of change of the function, we have to isolate the effect of each of the independent variables. Let $W = f(X, Y, Z)$. When we consider how W changes as X changes, we want to hold the variables Y and Z constant. This gives rise to the concept of partial differentiation. Note that only the variable X is changing, while both Y and Z remain constant. The rules for partial differentiation and ordinary differentiation are exactly the same except that when we are taking partial derivative of one independent variable, we regard *all other independent variables as constants.*

EXAMPLES

1. $(W) = XY + YZ + XZ$

$$\frac{\partial W}{\partial X} = Y + 0 + Z = Y + Z,$$

$$\frac{\partial W}{\partial Y} = X + Z + 0 = X + Z,$$

$$\frac{\partial W}{\partial Z} = 0 + Y + X = Y + X.$$

2. $W = X^2 Y Z^3 + e^X + \ln Y Z,$

$$\frac{\partial W}{\partial X} = 2XYZ^3 + e^X,$$

$$\frac{\partial W}{\partial Y} = X^2 Z^3 + \frac{1}{YZ} \cdot Z = X^2 Z^3 + \frac{1}{Y},$$

$$\frac{\partial W}{\partial Z} = 3X^2 Y Z^2 + \frac{1}{YZ} \cdot Z = 3X^2 Y Z^2 + \frac{1}{Z}.$$

Figure D.13 Function with multiple local maxima and minima.

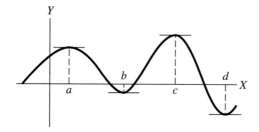

C. $\mathcal{O}$ptimization

A company seeks to maximize its profit. A production unit seeks to minimize its cost for a given level of output. An individual investor seeks to maximize his or her utility when choosing among investment alternatives. Indeed, we are all engaged in big and small optimization problems every day at work or in leisure. If we have a mathematical objective function, then we can solve our optimization problem using calculus. The procedure is divided into two steps:

1. Locate all *relative* maxima and minima of the objective function.

2. Compare the function value at the relative maxima and minima and at the boundary points (to be explained later) to pick the highest (lowest) value to be the *global* maximum (minimum).

To accomplish step 1, let us first consider the graph of a function $f(X)$ that appears in Fig. D.13. At the point $X = a$, the function $f(X)$ is said to have a relative maximum because $f(a) > f(Z)$ for all Z sufficiently close to a. Similarly, $f(X)$ has a relative maximum at $X = c$, and $f(X)$ has relative minima at $X = b$ and $X = d$. One common characteristic those four points share is the slope of $f(X)$ at those points. If we draw tangent lines to $f(X)$ at $X = a, b, c, d$, then all the tangent lines must be perfectly horizontal. In other words the slopes $f'(a) = f'(b) = f'(c) = f'(d) = 0$. Thus we have the following theorem:

THEOREM If $f(X)$ has a relative maximum or minimum at $X = a$, then $f'(a) = 0$.

Note that the theorem does *not* say that if $f'(a) = 0$, then $X = a$ is a relative maximum or minimum. It says that if $f'(a) = 0$ then $X = a$ is a *candidate* for a relative maximum or minimum. There exist points for which the derivative of $f(X)$ is zero, but the points are neither relative maxima nor minima. Nevertheless, to locate all relative maxima and minima, we differentiate $f(X)$, set the result to zero, and solve for X. That is, find all the solutions to the equation

$$f'(X) = 0.$$

The above equation is called the first-order condition. The solutions are candidates for relative maxima and minima. To determine which of these solutions are indeed relative maxima or minima, we need the so-called second-order conditions. Consider the relative maximum shown in Fig. D.14(a). The slope, $f'(X)$, is zero at the top, positive to the left of the top, and negative to the right of the top. Therefore as X increases from left to right, the slope, $f'(X)$, is decreasing from positive to zero to negative. We know from the previous section that if $f'(X)$ is decreasing, then the derivative of $f'(X)$, $f''(X)$, is *negative*. The condition $f''(X) < 0$ is called the second-

Figure D.14 Max and min as defined by the change in slope.

      (a)   (b)

Figure D.15 Max and min can occur at a boundary.

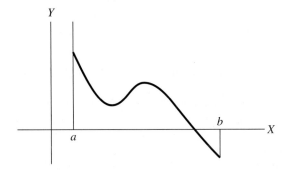

order condition for relative maxima. Similar reasoning would indicate that at a relative minimum, $f''(X) > 0$. We can now summarize step 1: Find all the X such that $f'(X) = 0$; then for each of those X, if $f''(X) > 0$, it is a relative minimum; if $f''(X) < 0$, it is a relative maximum; if $f''(X) = 0$, we cannot tell (and have to use more sophisticated techniques).

Step 2 requires us to compare the function value at the relative maxima and minima and the boundary points to determine the global optimum. Boundary points exist because we generally wish to optimize $f(X)$ in some interval, say, $a \leq X \leq b$, then a and b are boundary points. Sometimes the global maximum or minimum occurs at the boundary (see Fig. D.15). That is why we want to evaluate $f(X)$ at the boundary.

EXAMPLE A monopolist faces a downward-sloping demand curve given by $p(X) = 100 - 2X$, where X is the quantity and $p(X)$ is the price at that quantity. Suppose the fixed cost of production is 10 and variable cost is constant at 8 per unit. How many units should the monopolist produce to maximize profit?

$$Profit = \text{total revenue} - \text{total cost}$$

$$= \text{price} \times \text{quantity} - (\text{total variable cost} + \text{fixed cost}),$$

$$\pi(X) = (100 - 2X)X - (8X + 10)$$

$$= 100X - 2X^2 - 8X - 10$$

$$= -92X - 2X^2 - 10,$$

$$\pi'(X) = 92 - 4X = 0 \text{ (first-order condition)},$$

so

$$92 = 4X \quad \text{or} \quad X = 23,$$

$$\pi''(X) = -4;$$

hence

$$\pi''(X) < 0 \text{ (second-order condition)}.$$

Therefore $X = 23$ is a relative maximum. Implicit in this problem is the boundary $X \geq 0$. So $X = 0$ is a boundary. Obviously $\pi(0) = 0$ because this is a decision of not getting into the business at all. $\pi(23) = 92 \times 23 - 2 \times (23)^2 - 10 = 1{,}048 > \pi(0)$. The solution to this problem is therefore $X = 23$. The monopolist should produce 23 units. If we change the original problem by making the fixed cost 1,060 instead of 10, then $X = 23$ is still the only relative maximum. But not $\pi(23) = -2 < \pi(0)$. So the monopolist is better off not getting into the business at all. Here the optimum point occurs at the boundary.

If our objective function has two independent variables, then we have to resort to partial derivatives. Suppose $Z = f(X, Y)$, and let

$$f_x = \frac{\partial Z}{\partial X}, \qquad f_y = \frac{\partial Z}{\partial Y}, \qquad f_{xx} = \frac{\partial}{\partial X}\left(\frac{\partial Z}{\partial X}\right)$$

(taking partial derivative twice with respect to X), and

$$f_{yy} = \frac{\partial}{\partial Y}\left(\frac{\partial Z}{\partial Y}\right), f_{xy} = f_{yx} = \frac{\partial}{\partial X}\left(\frac{\partial Z}{\partial X = Y}\right)$$

(taking partial derivative twice, first with respect to Y, then with respect to X). The conditions for relative maxima and minima are

$$\left.\begin{array}{l} f_x = 0 \\ f_y = 0 \end{array}\right\} \qquad \text{(first-order conditions)}.$$

In addition, if $f_{xx}f_{yy} > f_{xy}^2$, then the point is either a relative maximum or minimum. To distinguish relative maximum and minimum, we have

$$\left.\begin{array}{ll} f_{xx}, f_{yy} < 0 & \text{maximum} \\ f_{xx}f_{yy} > 0 & \text{minimum} \end{array}\right\} \qquad \text{(second-order conditions)}.$$

An example of using partial derivatives to find the optimum point is given in the application section of Appendix B.

1. Constrained Optimization

Very often, a business entity operates under certain constraints. They may be budgetary, technological, or physical constraints. To solve this constrained optimization problem, we can use the method of Lagrange multipliers if the constraints are given as equations. For example, the production function of a firm may be $F(X, Y) = 2XY$, where X represents units of labor and Y represents units of capital. The budgetary constraint may look like

$$g(X, Y) = 100 - 2X - 10Y = 0,$$

where 100 represents the maximum amount of money to be spent on this production and 2 and 100 represent unit costs of labor and capital, respectively. To use the method of Lagrange multipliers, we first construct a new function of three independent variables:

$$L(X, Y, \lambda) = f(X, Y) + \lambda g(X, Y)$$
$$= 2XY + \lambda(100 - 2X - 10Y),$$

where λ is a new variable that is called the Lagrange multiplier. The constrained optimum will appear as a solution to the first-order condition:

$$\left. \begin{array}{l} \dfrac{\partial L}{\partial X} = L_x = 0 \\[2mm] \dfrac{\partial L}{\partial Y} = L_y = 0 \\[2mm] \dfrac{\partial L}{\partial \lambda} = L_\lambda = 0 \end{array} \right\} \quad \text{(first-order conditions).}$$

Let

$$H = \begin{pmatrix} 0 & g_x & g_y \\ g_x & L_{xx} & L_{xy} \\ g_y & L_{yx} & L_{yy} \end{pmatrix} \quad \text{and} \quad |H| = \text{determinant of } H \text{ (defined in Appendix B);}$$

then

$$\left. \begin{array}{ll} |H| < 0 & \text{relative minimum} \\ |H| > 0 & \text{relative maximum} \end{array} \right\} \quad \text{(second-order conditions).}$$

EXAMPLE   Take the production function and the budgetary constraint above and find the optimal combination of labor and capital.

$$L(X, Y, \lambda) = 2XY + \lambda(100 - 2X - 10Y)$$

$$\left. \begin{array}{ll} L_x = & 2Y - 2\lambda = 0 \\ L_y = & 2X - 10\lambda = 0 \\ L_\lambda = & 100 - 2X - 10Y = 0 \end{array} \right\} \quad \text{(first-order conditions).}$$

Solving these equations simultaneously gives us $X = 25$, $Y = 5$, $\lambda = 5$. (For a discussion of methods of solving a system of linear equations, see Appendix B.) Therefore under the budgetary constraint the maximum output level is $f(25, 5) = 2 \times 25 = 250$ when we employ 25 units of labor and 5 units of capital. We know that this must be the maximum point before computing the second-order condition because a relative maximum is the only sensible solution. The interested reader may check that

$$|H| = \begin{vmatrix} 0 & -2 & -10 \\ -2 & 0 & 2 \\ -10 & 2 & 0 \end{vmatrix} = 80 > 0.$$

Another example of using the method of the Lagrange multiplier can be found in the application section of Appendix B regarding the minimum-variance portfolio.

2. The Meaning of λ

The solution of λ also has a meaning. The magnitude of λ measures how much the optimum changes as we relax the constraint. In the above example the solution of λ is 5. That means if we relax the budgetary constraint 1 unit from 100 to 101, the optimal level of output would increase approximately 5 units to 255.

If the solution to λ is equal to zero, then the constraint is not binding. That means the constrained optimum is equal to the unconstrained optimum.

D. $\mathcal{T}$aylor and MacLaurin Series

The Taylor and MacLaurin series are widely used in economics and finance. Their most important use is to help evaluate the function around a certain point. Suppose we are interested in evaluating the function $Y = f(X)$ around a point a in its domain. Then we can make use of Taylor's theorem:

TAYLOR'S THEOREM   In the one-dimensional case we can evaluate the function $Y = f(X)$ around a point a in terms of its derivatives as follows:

$$f(X) = f(a) + f'(a)(X - a) + \frac{f''(a)(X - a)^2}{2!}$$

$$+ \frac{f'''(a)(X - a)^3}{3!} + \cdots + \frac{f^{(n)}(a)(X - a)^n}{n!}.$$

Alternatively, if we let $h = (X - a)$, then the Taylor series is

$$f(a + h) = f(a) + f'(a)h + \frac{f''(a)h^2}{2!}$$

$$+ \frac{f'''(a)h^3}{3!} + \cdots + \frac{f^{(n)}(a)h^n}{n!},$$

where $f(a)$ = value of the function at point a (Pratt [1964] uses this). This is called the *Taylor series*.

DEFINITION   If we evaluate the function around zero (i.e., if $a = 0$ above), then we have what is called a *MacLaurin series:*

$$f(X) = f(0) + f'(0) \cdot X + \frac{f''(0)}{2!} \cdot X^2 + \frac{f'''(0)}{3!} \cdot X^3 + \cdots + \frac{f^{(n)}(0)}{n!} \cdot X^n.$$

DEFINITION   The symbol $n!$ (read "n factorial") represents the product of all positive integers from 1 to n (or vice versa). That is,

$$n! = n \cdot (n - 1) \cdot n - 2 \cdot (n - 3) \cdot (n - 4) \cdots 4 \cdot 3 \cdot 2 \cdot 1.$$

EXAMPLES $5! = 5 \cdot 4 \cdot 3 \cdot 2 \cdot 1 = 1 \cdot 2 \cdot 3 \cdot 4 \cdot 5 = 120,$

$$10! = 10 \cdot 9 \cdot 8 \cdot 7 \cdot 6 \cdot 5 \cdot 4 \cdot 3 \cdot 2 \cdot 1 = 3{,}628{,}000,$$

$$(n - r)! = (n - r) \cdot (n - r - 1) \cdot (n - r - 2) \cdot (n - r - 3) \cdots 4 \cdot 3 \cdot 2 \cdot 1,$$

$$1! = 0! = 1 \text{ (by definition)}.$$

Intuitively, what the Taylor series is trying to do is to approximate the function $f(X)$ with the following polynomial:

$$f(X) \approx T_0 + T_1(X - a) + T_2(X - a)^2 + T_3(X - a)^3 + \cdots. \tag{D.1}$$

The problem is to find the values of the coefficients (the Ts) of this polynomial. To find them, take the higher-order derivatives of Eq. (D.1):

$$f'(X) = T_1 + T_2 \cdot 2(X - a) + T_3 \cdot 3(X - a)^2 + \cdots \tag{D.2}$$

$$f''(X) = 2T_2 + T_3 \cdot 2 \cdot 3(x - a) + T_4 \cdot 4 \cdot 3(x - a)^2 + \cdots \tag{D.3}$$

$$f'''(X) = 2 \cdot 3T_3 + T_4 \cdot 4 \cdot 3 \cdot 2(X - a) + T_5 \cdot 5 \cdot 4 \cdot 3(X - a)^2 + \cdots \tag{D.4}$$

$$\vdots$$

If we evaluate (D.1) through (D.4) at $X = a$, then $(X - a) = 0$, so all terms involving $(X - a)$ will vanish:

$$\left.\begin{aligned} f(X) &= T_0 \\ F'(X) &= T_1 \\ f''(X) &= 2 \cdot T_2 \\ \\ f'''(X) &= 2 \cdot 3T_3 \end{aligned}\right\} \quad \text{Solving for the } T\text{s} \quad \left\{\begin{aligned} T_0 &= & f(X) \\ T_1 &= & f'(X) \\ T_2 &= & \frac{f''(X)}{2} = \frac{f''(X)}{2 \cdot 1} = \frac{f''(X)}{2!} \\ T_3 &= & \frac{f'''(X)}{3 \cdot 2} = \frac{f'''(X)}{3 \cdot 2 \cdot 1} = \frac{f'''(X)}{3!} \\ \vdots & \vdots & \vdots \quad\quad \vdots \end{aligned}\right.$$

Plugging these values of the Ts into Eq. (D.1) results in the Taylor series we stated earlier. The usefulness of the Taylor series can best be seen with the help of a numerical example.

EXAMPLE   Expand the function $f(X) = 1/X$ around 1, for $n = 0, 1, 2, 3$. Computing the derivatives:

$$f(X) = \frac{1}{X} \qquad \text{so} \qquad f(1) = \frac{1}{1} = 1,$$

$$f'(X) = \frac{-1}{X^2} \qquad \text{so} \qquad f'(1) = \frac{-1}{(1)^2} = -1,$$

$$f''(X) = \frac{2}{X^3} \qquad \text{so} \qquad f''(1) = \frac{2}{(1)^3} = 2,$$

$$f'''(X) = \frac{-6}{X^4} \qquad \text{so} \qquad f'''(1) = \frac{-6}{(1)^4} = -6.$$

The Taylor series approximation when $n = 0$ is

$$T_0(X) = f(a), \qquad \text{since } a = 1(\text{ we are expanding around } 1)$$
$$T_0(X) = f(1) = 1.$$

The Taylor approximation when $n = 1$ is

$$T_1 = f(a) + f'(a)(X - a)$$
$$= f(1) + (-1)(X - 1)$$
$$= 1 - (X - 1).$$

The approximation when $n = 2$ is

$$T_2(X) = f(a) + f'(a)(X - a) + \frac{f''(a)}{2!}(X - a)^2$$
$$= f(1) + (-1)(X - 1) + \frac{2}{2 \cdot 1}(X - 1)^2$$
$$= 1 - (X - 1) + (X - 1)^2.$$

The approximation when $n = 3$ is

$$T_3(X) = f(a) + f'(a)(X - a) + \frac{f''(a)}{2!}(x - a)^2 + \frac{f'''(a)}{3!}(X - a)^3$$
$$= 1 - (X - 1) + (X - 1)^2 + \frac{-6}{3 \cdot 2 \cdot 1}(X - 1)^3$$
$$= 1 - (X - 1) + (X - 1)^2 - (X - 1)^3.$$

Expanding and rearranging the polynomials:

$T_0(X) = 1$ (constant),

$T_1(X) = 1 - (X - 1) = -X + 2$ (straight line),

$T_2(X) = 1 - (X - 1) + (X - 1)^2 = X^2 - 3X + 3$ (parabola),

$T_3(X) = 1 - (X + 1) + (X - 1)^2 - (X - 1)^3 = -X^3 + 4X^2 - 6X + 4$ (cubic).

Figure D.16 graphs the function $f(X) = 1/X$ and each of the approximating polynomials:

$$\frac{dT_2(X)}{dX} = 2X - 3 = 0, \quad X = 1.5 = \min,$$

$$\frac{dT_3(X)}{dX} = -3X^2 + 8X - 6 = 0$$

$$= (-3X + 2)(X - 3) \quad \text{inflection point} > 1.$$

From the graph we see that each successive Taylor series does a better job of approximating $f(X) = 1/X$ in the vicinity of 1; see Fig. D.17.

Figure D.16 Taylor's series approximations.

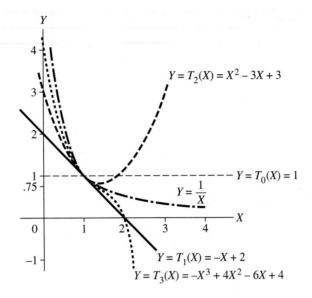

$$Y = T_2(X) = X^2 - 3X + 3$$

$$Y = T_0(X) = 1$$

$$Y = \frac{1}{X}$$

$$Y = T_1(X) = -X + 2$$

$$Y = T_3(X) = -X^3 + 4X^2 - 6X + 4$$

Figure D.17 Approximation of $f(x) = 1/X$ in the vicinity of 1.

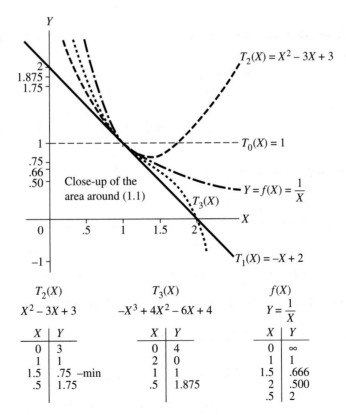

$$T_2(X) = X^2 - 3X + 3$$

$$T_0(X) = 1$$

$$Y = f(X) = \frac{1}{X}$$

$T_3(X)$

Close-up of the area around (1.1)

$$T_1(X) = -X + 2$$

$T_2(X)$		$T_3(X)$		$f(X)$	
$X^2 - 3X + 3$		$-X^3 + 4X^2 - 6X + 4$		$Y = \dfrac{1}{X}$	
X	Y	X	Y	X	Y
0	3	0	4	0	∞
1	1	2	0	1	1
1.5	.75 –min	1	1	1.5	.666
.5	1.75	.5	1.875	2	.500
				.5	2

EXAMPLE   Pratt [1964] uses the Taylor series to derive a measure of absolute relative risk aversion. Let

$$X = \text{amount of wealth,}$$

$$U = \text{acceptable utility function,}$$

$$\pi = \text{risk premium, } \pi \text{ is a function, } \pi(X, \tilde{Z}),$$

$$\tilde{Z} = \text{a gamble (and a random variable),}$$

$$\tilde{Z} \sim E(\tilde{Z}) - \pi(X, \tilde{Z}).$$

$$E\{U(X + \tilde{Z}\} = U[X + E(\tilde{Z}) - \pi(X, \tilde{Z})] \tag{D.5}$$

by choosing an actuarially neutral risk $E(\tilde{Z}) = 0$. So

$$E\{U(X + \tilde{Z})\} = U[X - \pi(X, \tilde{Z})]. \tag{D.6}$$

Expand the right-hand side of Eq. (D.6) using Taylor series:

$$U(X - \pi) = U(X) + \pi \cdot U'(X) - \frac{\pi^2}{2!} U''(X) - \cdots$$

Pratt assumes second-order and higher terms are insignificant. Expand the left-hand side of Eq. (D.6) using Taylor series:

$$E\{U(X) + \tilde{Z}\} = E\{U(X)\} + \tilde{Z}U'(X) + \frac{\tilde{Z}^2}{2!} U''(X) + \cdots \searrow \approx 0$$

$$= E\{U(X)\} + E(\tilde{Z})U'(X) + \frac{E(\tilde{Z}^2)}{2!} U''(X).$$

But

$$E\{U(X)\} = U(X) \qquad \text{not a random variable,}$$

$$E\{\tilde{Z}\} = 0,$$

$$E\{\tilde{Z}^2\} = \sigma_Z^2 \qquad \text{since } \sigma_Z^2 = \underset{0}{Zp_i[Z_i - E(Z_i)]^2} = \sum p_i Z_i^2 = E(Z_i^2).$$

So

$$E\{U(X) + \tilde{Z}\} = U(X) + 0 + \frac{\sigma_Z^2}{2} U''(X).$$

Putting the left-hand and right-hand sides together:

$$U(X) + \frac{\sigma_Z^2}{2} U''(X) = U(X) - \pi U'(X).$$

Solving for π, the risk premium:

$$\pi = \frac{1}{2} \sigma_Z^2 \left[-\frac{U''(X)}{U'(X)} \right]$$

Note that this is a function of $\widetilde{Z}$ and X, and that it is always positive by the definition of variance. The term in brackets is a measure of absolute risk aversion.

E. Integral Calculus

1. Indefinite Integrals

Integration is the reverse process to differentiation. Given a function $f(X)$, the indefinite integral of $f(X)$, denoted by $\int f(X)dX$, is a function whose derivative is $f(X)$. In other words,

$$\int f(X)dX = F(X) \quad \text{iff} \quad F'(X) = f(X).$$

A peculiar feature regarding the indefinite integral of $f(X)$ is that it is not unique. Observe the following fact: if $F'(X) = f(X)$, so is $[F(X) + C]' = F(X) + 0 = f(X)$, where C is an arbitrary constant. Therefore both $F(X)$ and $F(X) + C$ can be indefinite integrals of $f(X)$. So, in general, we write

$$\int f(X)dX = F(X) + C$$

to indicate that an arbitrary constant may be added to the answer.

We also have rules of integration that correspond very closely with those of differentiation.

2. Rules of Integration

1. $\int X^n dX = \frac{1}{n+1} X^{n+1} + C. \quad (n \neq -1)$
2. $\int \frac{1}{X} dX = \ln X + C. \quad (X > 0)$
3. $\int e^X dX = e^X + C.$
4. $\int c \cdot g(X)dX = c \cdot \int g(X)dX. \qquad (c = \text{constant})$
5. $\int [g(X) + h(X)dX = \int g(X)dX + \int h(X)dX.$
6. $\int a^X dX = \frac{1}{\ln a} a^X + C.$
7. Method of substitution (counterpart of the chain rule in differentiation):

$$\int g(u)\frac{du}{dX}dX = \int g(u)du.$$

EXAMPLE $\int e^{2X} dX$. To compute this integral, we first substitute $u = 2X$, then $du = 2 \cdot dX$ (recall $du = (du/dX) \cdot dX$, the differential); therefore $dX = (du/2)$. Hence $\int e^{2X} dX = \int e^u (du/2)$, by substituting u for $2X$ and $(du/2)$ for dX. But $\int e^u (du/2) = \frac{1}{2} \int e^u du$ (by rule 4) $= \frac{1}{2} e^u + C$ (by rule 3)$= \frac{1}{2} e^{2X} + C$ (by substituting back $2X$ for u). This example shows the essence of the method of substitution. When it is not obvious how to integrate directly, we substitute u for part of the expression, we write everything in terms of u and du, and hopefully we come up with an expression in u that is easier to integrate (see also examples below).

EXAMPLES

1.

$$\int 2X^2 + 3X + 1 dX = 2 \int X^2 dX + 3 \int X dX + \int 1 dX$$

$$= 2 \cdot \frac{X^3}{3} + 3\frac{X^2}{2} + X + C$$

$$= \frac{2}{3}X^3 + \frac{3}{2}X^2 + X + C.$$

2. For

$$\int \frac{2X+1}{X^2+X} dX,$$

we have to use the method of substitution again. Let $u = X^2 + X$, then $du = (2X + 1)dX$.

$$\int \frac{2X+1}{X^2+X} dX = \int \frac{1}{u} du = \ln u + C = \ln(X^2 + X) + C.$$

3. For

$$\int X\sqrt{X^2 + 1} dX,$$

we let $u = X^2 + 1$, then $du = 2X \, dX$ or $dX = (du/2X)$.

$$\int X\sqrt{X^2 + 1} dX = \int X\sqrt{u}\frac{du}{2X} = \int \frac{1}{2}\sqrt{u} du$$

$$= \frac{1}{2} \int u^{1/2} du = \frac{1}{2} \cdot \frac{1}{3/2} u^{3/2} + C$$

$$= \frac{1}{3}(X^2 + 1)^{3/2} + C.$$

3. Definite Integrals

A typical definite integral looks like

$$\int_a^b f(X) dX$$

(read "integral of $f(X)$ from a to b"). Here $f(X)$ is called the integrand, a is called the lower limit, and b is called the upper limit of integration. The main difference between an indefinite and a definite integral is that the result of indefinite integration is a function, whereas the result of definite integration is a number. The meaning of that number is as follows.

Let

$$\int_a^b f(X) dX = A.$$

Figure D.18 Examples of definite integrals.

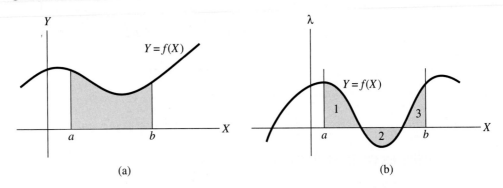

(a)   (b)

If $f(X) \geq 0$, then A is simply the area under the curve $Y = f(X)$ from a to b, shown in Fig. D.18(a). That area is equal to

$$\int_a^b f(X)dX.$$

Suppose now $f(X)$ is both positive and negative in the range of $a \leq X \leq b$, then A, the result of

$$\int_a^b f(X)dX,$$

is the *signed* area "under" $f(X)$ from a to b. By "signed area," we mean that the area above the X-axis is assigned a positive sign and the area below the x-axis is assigned a negative sign. Then A is the sum of all the positive and negative area. If the curve of the $f(X)$ is the one in Fig. D.18(b), then

$$\int_a^b f(X)dX = A = \text{area } 1 = \text{area } 2 + \text{area } 3.$$

The link between the definite integral and the indefinite integral is given by the next theorem, which is called the Fundamental Theorem of Calculus.

THEOREM   Let $F(X)$ be an indefinite integral of $f(X)$, then

$$\int_a^b f(X)dX = F(b) - F(a).$$

The theorem shows us a way to evaluate the definite integral. We need only to find the indefinite integral of the integrand and then substitute the upper and lower limits and find the difference. Although the indefinite integral of a function is not unique, the theorem says that any one will do, as long as it is the same one in which you substitute the upper and lower limits.

EXAMPLES

1.
$$\int_1^2 (X+2)dX = \left(\frac{X^2}{2} + 2X\right)\Big|_1^2 = \left[\frac{2^2}{2} + 2(2)\right] - \left[\frac{1^2}{2} + 2\cdot 1\right]$$

$$= (2+4) - \left(\frac{1}{2} + 2\right) = 3\frac{1}{2}.$$

2.
$$\int_0^1 e^X dX = e^X\Big|_0^1 = [e^1] - [e^0] = e - 1.$$

PROPERTIES OF DEFINITE INTEGRALS

1. $\int_a^a f(X)dX = 0.$
2. $\int_a^b f(X)dX = -\int_b^a f(X)dX.$
3. If $a < c < b$, then $\int_a^b f(X)dX = \int_a^c f(X)dX + \int_c^b f(X)dX.$
4. $\int_a^b cf(X)dX = c\int_a^b f(X)dX.$
5. $\int_a^b \left[f(X) + g(X)\right]dX = \int_a^b f(X)dX + \int_a^b g(X)dX.$

4. Applications

EXAMPLE   Let the fixed cost of production be 100 and let marginal cost be $10/\sqrt{X}$ per unit. What is the total cost function for producing q units?

$$\text{total cost} = \text{fixed cost} + \text{variable cost}$$

$$= 100 + \int_0^q 10/\sqrt{X}dX$$

$$= 100 + \int_0^q 10X^{-1/2}dX$$

$$= 100 + 10\frac{1}{1/2} \cdot X^{1/2}\Big|_0^q$$

$$= 100 + [20\sqrt{q}] - [20\sqrt{0}]$$

$$= 100 + 20\sqrt{q}.$$

EXAMPLE   Suppose an income stream of 10,000/year is coming in continuously for the next 10 years. How much is it worth today if the discount rate is 5%?

$$\text{present value} = \int_0^{10} 10,000e^{-0.5t}dt$$

$$= 10,000 \times \frac{-1}{.05}e^{-.05t}\Big|_0^{10}$$

$$= 10,000 \times \left(-\frac{1}{.05}\right)\left[e^{-.05\times 10} - e^{-.05\times 0}\right]$$

$$= 100 + 10 \frac{1}{1/2} \cdot X^{1/2} \Big|_0^q$$

$$= -200,000[0.06065 - 1]$$

$$= 78,700.$$

Note that the formula for the present value of continuous discounting of a continuous flow is

$$\int_0^T (CF) e^{-rt} dt,$$

where CF = cash flow per time unit, T = time when cash flow ends, and r = discount rate.

5. Improper Integrals

Sometimes the limits of integration may be $-\infty$ or $+\infty$. Such a definite integral is called an improper integral. To evaluate an improper integral, we do not substitute $-\infty$ or $+\infty$ into the indefinite integral, but rather we substitute a variable b in place of $+\infty$ (or $-\infty$) and let $b \to \infty$ (or $-\infty$). In other words:

$$\int_a^\infty f(X) dX = \lim_{b \to \infty} \int_a^b f(X) dX,$$

$$\int_{-\infty}^a f(X) dX = \lim_{b \to -\infty} \int_b^a f(X) dX,$$

$$\int_{-\infty}^\infty f(X) dX = \lim_{\substack{a \to -\infty \\ b \to +\infty}} \int_b^a f(X) dX,$$

EXAMPLE Suppose the income stream in the previous example is perpetual; then the present value would be

$$PV = \int_0^\infty 10,000 e^{-.05t} dt$$

$$= \lim_{b \to \infty} \int_0^b 10,000 e^{-.05} dt$$

$$= \lim_{b \to \infty} 10,000 \left(-\frac{1}{.05}\right) [e^{-.05b} - e^{-.05 \times 0}]$$

$$= 10,000 \times (-20)[0 - 1], \qquad \text{since } e^{-.05b} \to 0 \text{ as } b \to \infty,$$

$$= \$200,000.$$

Note that for a perpetual stream, we also have

$$PV = \frac{CF}{i} = \frac{10,000}{.05} = \$200,000 \qquad \text{where } CF \text{ is the cash flow.}$$

REFERENCE

Pratt, J. W., "Risk Aversion in the Small and in the Large," *Econometrica*, January–April 1964, 122–136.

Stochastic Calculus

S TOCHASTIC CALCULUS PROVIDES a set of rules that can be used for the differentiation, integration, and expansion of functions of random variables. This appendix provides an introduction to differentiation, integration, and series expansions in a stochastic environment. Specific topics discussed will include stochastic differential equations, Itô integrals, and Itô's lemma.*

To consider the difference between "deterministic" calculus and stochastic calculus, consider the following example where $y = f(x)$. The Taylor series expansion of $f(x)$ around x_0 would be given by

$$f(x) = f(x_0) + \frac{\partial f(x_0)}{\partial x}\left(x - x_0\right) + \frac{1}{2}\frac{\partial^2 f(x_0)}{\partial x^2}\left(x - x_0\right)^2 + \frac{1}{6}\frac{\partial^3 f(x_0)}{\partial x^3}(x - x_0)^3 + r(x_0), \quad \text{(E.1)}$$

where $r(x_0)$ is the remainder of the Taylor series expansion that contains differentials of $f(x)$ and power terms of $\left(x - x_0\right)$ of order four or more.

If x is defined as $x_0 + \Delta x$ and terms of order three or more are ignored in Eq. (E.1), the Taylor series approximation for $f(x)$ is given by

$$f(x_0 + \Delta x) - f(x_0) = \frac{\partial f(x_0)}{\partial x}\Delta x + \frac{1}{2}\frac{\partial^2 f(x_0)}{\partial x^2}\left(\Delta x\right)^2. \quad \text{(E.2)}$$

If the variable x is deterministic and if Δx is small (but nonnegligible), then it can be assumed that $(\Delta x)^2$ is negligible and Eq. (E.2) can be written as

$$f(x_0 + \Delta x) - f(x_0) = \frac{\partial f(x_0)}{\partial x}\Delta x. \quad \text{(E.3)}$$

---

* For a more detailed discussion of these topics, see Malliaris and Brock [1982] and Neftci [2000].

This implies that if the variable x is deterministic, dividing both sides by Δx in Eq. (E.3) and taking limits yields the equation for the first differential of $f(x)$, that is,

$$\lim_{\Delta x \to 0} \frac{f(x_0 + \Delta x) - f(x_0)}{\Delta x} = \frac{\partial f(x_0)}{\partial x}. \tag{E.4}$$

In contrast, if x is random, then Δx is random and even if the mean of Δx is zero ($E(\Delta x) = 0$), the variance of Δx will be positive ($\sigma^2_{\Delta x} > 0$). This implies that $E(\Delta x)^2$ is greater than zero and we cannot ignore the $(\Delta x)^2$ term in Eq. (E.2). Thus, as suggested in Neftci [2000], a possible candidate for defining a derivative when x is random is

$$\lim_{\Delta x \to 0} \frac{f(x_0 + \Delta x) - f(x_0)}{\Delta x} = \frac{\partial f(x_0)}{\partial x} + \frac{1}{2} \frac{\partial^2 f(x_0)}{\partial x^2} \lim_{\Delta x \to 0} \frac{(\Delta x)^2}{\Delta x}. \tag{E.5}$$

As can be seen from a comparison of Eqs. (E.4) and (E.5), differentiation cannot be handled the same way with stochastic variables as compared to deterministic variables. The remainder of this appendix is organized as follows. Section A provides a discussion of stochastic differential equations, Itô integrals are discussed in Section B, and finally a derivation of Itô's lemma is contained in Section C.

A. $\mathscr{S}$tochastic Differential Equations

This section provides a derivation of the differential equation that governs innovations in a random variable. Consider a random variable x_t, where t belongs to the time interval $[0, T]$. Further assume that the time interval $[0, T]$ is divided into k equal increments of length Δt ($T = k\Delta t$). The value of the random variable at time t_i is denoted by $x_{t_i} = x(i \Delta t) = x_i$. The innovation in the random variable over interval i is given by

$$\Delta x_i = x(i \Delta t) - x((i-1)\Delta t) = x_i - x_{i-1}. \tag{E.6}$$

The expected value of the innovation conditional on information available at the beginning of interval i is denoted by

$$E\left[x(i \Delta t) - x((i-1)\Delta t)\right] = E(x_i - x_{i-1}) = E(\Delta x_i).$$

The innovations are assumed to be uncorrelated over the various time intervals. Define a random variable Δv_i such that

$$\Delta v_i = \Delta x_i - E(\Delta x_i). \tag{E.7}$$

Equation (E.7) implies that given the information set available at the beginning of interval i, $E(\Delta v_i) = 0$. On the other hand, $E(\Delta v_i)^2 > 0$ and we need to account for the $(\Delta v_i)^2$ term in stochastic differentiation and obtain an approximation to it. The approximation is derived here using the approach in Merton [1992] and Neftci [2000].

Let the variance of Δv_i be denoted by Λ_i; that is,

$$E(\Delta v_i)^2 = \Lambda_i.$$

This implies that the variance of cumulative errors over the time interval $[0, T]$ would be given by

$$\Lambda = E\left[\sum_{i=1}^{k} \Delta v_i\right]^2 = E\left[\sum_{i=1}^{k} \Delta v_i^2\right] + E\left[2\sum_{i=1}^{k-1}\sum_{j=i+1}^{k} \Delta v_i \Delta v_j\right]. \tag{E.8}$$

Since the errors Δv_i are uncorrelated across the time intervals i, $i = 1, \ldots, k$, this implies that $E(\Delta v_i \Delta v_j) = 0$ for all $i, j = 1, \ldots, k$ and $i \neq j$. Substituting this independence property in Eq. (E.8) yields

$$\Lambda = E\left[\sum_{i=1}^{k} \Delta v_i^2\right] = \sum_{i=1}^{k} E\left[\Delta v_i^2\right] = \sum_{i=1}^{k} \Lambda_i. \tag{E.9}$$

Now assume that the volatility over the interval $[0, T]$, Λ, is bounded above and below by $\overline{\Lambda}$ and $\underline{\Lambda}$, respectively; that is, $0 < \underline{\Lambda} < \Lambda < \overline{\Lambda} < \infty$ and that there is some minimum volatility in every time interval, that is, $\Lambda_i > \alpha \Lambda_{MAX}$, where $\Lambda_{MAX} = Max\left[\Lambda_1, \Lambda_2, \ldots, \Lambda_k\right]$ is the volatility in the most volatile interval and $0 < \alpha < 1$. Under these assumptions, the variance of Δv_i is proportional to Δt; that is, $\Lambda_i = \sigma_i^2 \Delta t$, where σ_i^2 is a constant that is independent of Δt.

To see this, sum the assumption that $\Lambda_i > \alpha \Lambda_{MAX}$ over all intervals to get

$$\sum_{i=1}^{k} \Lambda_i > k\alpha \Lambda_{MAX} \text{ or } \Lambda > k\alpha \Lambda_{MAX}. \tag{E.10}$$

Since the variance of cumulative errors is bounded above by $\overline{\Lambda}$, Eq. (E.10) implies that

$$\overline{\Lambda} > k\alpha \Lambda_{MAX} \text{ or } \frac{\overline{\Lambda}}{k\alpha} > \Lambda_{MAX} > \Lambda_j, \text{ or } \Lambda_i < \frac{\overline{\Lambda}}{k\alpha} = \frac{\Delta t}{T}\frac{\overline{\Lambda}}{\alpha}. \tag{E.11}$$

Equation (E.11) implies that there is an upper bound on Λ_i that depends on the choice of Δt only.

Similarly, a lower bound on Λ_i can be established. Since $\underline{\Lambda} < \Lambda$ and $\Lambda < k\Lambda_{MAX}$, this implies that $\underline{\Lambda} < k\Lambda_{MAX}$ or

$$\frac{\underline{\Lambda}}{k} = \frac{\Delta t}{T}\underline{\Lambda} < \Lambda_{MAX}. \tag{E.12}$$

Since $\Lambda_i > \alpha \Lambda_{MAX}$, substituting this condition in Eq. (E.12) yields

$$\frac{\Delta t}{T}\underline{\Lambda} < \frac{\Lambda_i}{\alpha} \text{ or } \Lambda_i > \frac{\Delta t}{T}\alpha\underline{\Lambda}. \tag{E.13}$$

Equation (E.13) establishes a lower bound on Λ_i that depends on the choice of Δt only. Combining Eqs. (E.11) and (E.13) yields

$$\frac{\alpha\underline{\Lambda}}{T}\Delta t < \Lambda_i < \frac{\overline{\Lambda}}{\alpha T}\Delta t. \tag{E.14}$$

Equation (E.14) implies that there should be a constant σ_i^2 depending on i such that Λ_i is proportional to Δt. This implies that

$$\Lambda_i = \sigma_i^2 \Delta t. \tag{E.15}$$

This implies that we can use Eq. (E.15) to rewrite Eq. (E.6) as

$$\Delta x_i = E(\Delta x_i) + \sigma_i \Delta z_i, \tag{E.16}$$

where Δz_i has a mean of zero and a variance of Δt. Now consider the term $E(\Delta x_i)$. This term represents the expectation for the innovation in the variable x conditional on the information that is available at the beginning of time interval i. Thus $E(\Delta x_i)$ is a function of the length of the time interval Δt and the information available at the beginning of the time interval i, I_i. Denote this function by $\Psi(I_i, \Delta t) = E(\Delta x_i)$. Consider the Taylor series expansion of $\Psi(\bullet)$ around $\Delta t = 0$. It is

$$\Psi(I_i, \Delta t) = \Psi(I_i, 0) + \frac{\partial \Psi(I_i, 0)}{\partial(\Delta t)} \Delta t + r(I_i, \Delta t). \tag{E.17}$$

Since $\Psi(I_i, 0) = 0$ and we can ignore all terms involving Δt with power of two or higher, that is, $r(I_i, \Delta t) \simeq 0$, Eq. (E.17) can be written as

$$E(\Delta x_i) = \Psi(I_i, \Delta t) \simeq \mu(I_i, i\Delta t)\Delta t, \tag{E.18}$$

where

$$\mu(I_i, i\Delta t) = \frac{\partial \Psi(I_i, 0)}{\partial(\Delta t)}.$$

Substituting Eq. (E.18) into Eq. (E.16) yields the *stochastic difference equation:*

$$\Delta x_i = \mu(I_i, i\Delta t)\Delta t + \sigma_i \Delta z_i. \tag{E.19}$$

Letting $\Delta t \to 0$ yields the *stochastic differential equation:*

$$dx_t = \mu(I_t, t)dt + \sigma_t dz_t. \tag{E.20}$$

Equation (E.20) implies that the change in a random variable can be decomposed into a predictable part (the drift) and an unpredictable part (the diffusion).

B. $\mathscr{T}$he Itô Integral

The Itô integral helps define the sum of random increments over time. For example, consider the stochastic differential equation defined in Eq. (E.20). If both sides of the equation are integrated over the time interval $(0, T)$, the resulting equation would be

$$\int_0^T dx_t = \int_0^T \mu(I_t, t)dt + \int_0^T \sigma_t dz_t. \tag{E.21}$$

The last term in Eq. (E.21) is an integral with respect to innovations in the process z_t and would be solved with the help of the Itô integral.

To define an Itô integral, consider the stochastic difference equation specified in Eq. (E.19). If σ_i is *nonanticipative*, that is, it is independent of the future, and

$$\int_0^T \sigma_i^2 dt < \infty,$$

then the Itô integral

$$\int_0^T \sigma_t dz_t$$

is the mean-square limit of

$$\sum_{i=1}^k \sigma_i \Delta z_i$$

as $\Delta t \to 0$.[1]

Consider an application of the Itô integral to evaluate the integral

$$\int_0^T x_t dx_t$$

with the initial condition that x_0 is zero. If x_t is a deterministic variable, the solution would be $0.5x_T^2$. To obtain this solution, define k time intervals of length Δt ($k\Delta t = T$) and the sums

$$S_k = \sum_{i=0}^{k-1} x_{i+1} (x_{i+1} - x_i) = \sum_{i=0}^{k-1} x_{i+1}\Delta x_{i+1}, \qquad (E.22)$$

where x_i is the value of the variable x in interval i. The solution is the value of the sum as k goes to ∞.

If x_t is stochastic, then the sums are modified to

$$S_k = \sum_{i=0}^{k-1} x_i (x_{i+1} - x_i) = \sum_{i=0}^{k-1} x_i\Delta x_{i+1}. \qquad (E.23)$$

Specifically a comparison of Eqs. (E.22) and (E.23) indicates that in the latter equation the first term is x_i and not x_{i+1}. This follows from the fact that this term has to be *nonanticipative* and x_i is known but x_{i+1} is not at time i.

To determine the mean-square limit of S_k, we need to find the variable S that satisfies the property

$$\lim_{k\to\infty} E(S_k - S)^2 = 0 \text{ or } \lim_{k\to\infty} E\left[\sum_{i=0}^{k-1} x_i\Delta x_{i+1} - S\right]^2 = 0. \qquad (E.24)$$

---

[1] Let $x_0, x_1, \ldots, x_k$ be a sequence of random variables. x is the mean square limit of x_k if $\lim_{k\to\infty} E(x_k - x)^2 = 0$.

To evaluate Eq. (E.24), consider the definition of S_k and substitute

$$x_i \Delta x_{i+1} = \frac{1}{2} \left[x_{i+1}^2 - x_i^2 - \Delta x_{i+1}^2 \right]$$

into Eq. (E.23) to get

$$S_k = \frac{1}{2} \sum_{i=0}^{k-1} \left[x_{i+1}^2 - x_i^2 - \Delta x_{i+1}^2 \right] = \frac{1}{2} \left[\sum_{i=0}^{k-1} x_{i+1}^2 - \sum_{i=0}^{k-1} x_i^2 - \sum_{i=0}^{k-1} \Delta x_{i+1}^2 \right]. \tag{E.25}$$

Changing the range of the summation in the first term yields

$$S_k = \frac{1}{2} \left[\sum_{j=1}^{k} x_j^2 - \sum_{i=0}^{k-1} x_i^2 - \sum_{i=0}^{k-1} \Delta x_{i+1}^2 \right] = \frac{1}{2} \left[x_T^2 - \sum_{i=0}^{k-1} \Delta x_{i+1}^2 \right]. \tag{E.26}$$

The second equality follows from the fact that

$$\sum_{j=1}^{k} x_j^2 = x_T^2 + \sum_{i=1}^{k-1} x_i^2 = x_T^2 + \sum_{i=0}^{k-1} x_i^2 - x_0^2$$

and $x_0 = 0$.

Equation (E.26) indicates that the limit of S_k can be obtained from the limit of

$$\sum_{i=0}^{k-1} \Delta x_{i+1}^2.$$

To find this limit consider the variable

$$E \left[\sum_{i=0}^{k-1} \Delta x_{i+1}^2 \right].$$

Taking the expectation inside the summation yields

$$E \left[\sum_{i=0}^{k-1} \Delta x_{i+1}^2 \right] = \sum_{i=0}^{k-1} E \left[\Delta x_{i+1}^2 \right] = \sum_{i=0}^{k-1} \Delta t = T. \tag{E.27}$$

To determine whether T is the mean square limit of

$$\sum_{i=0}^{k-1} \Delta x_{i+1}^2,$$

we need to show that

$$E \left[\sum_{i=0}^{k-1} \Delta x_{i+1}^2 - T \right]^2 = 0.$$

To show this, expand the square to get

$$E\left[\sum_{i=0}^{k-1}\Delta x_{i+1}^4 + 2\sum_{i=0}^{k-2}\sum_{j=1}^{k-1}\Delta x_{i+1}^2\Delta x_{j+1}^2 + T^2 - 2T\sum_{i=0}^{k-1}\Delta x_{i+1}^2\right]. \tag{E.28}$$

The first term in Eq. (E.28) can be written as

$$\sum_{i=0}^{k-1}E\left[\Delta x_{i+1}^4\right] = \sum_{i=0}^{k-1}E\left[\Delta x_{i+1}^2\Delta x_{i+1}^2\right] = \sum_{i=0}^{k-1}3\,(\Delta t)^2 = 3k\,(\Delta t)^2.$$

Since the innovations are independent across time intervals,

$$E\left[\sum_{i=0}^{k-2}\sum_{j=1}^{k-1}\Delta x_{i+1}^2\Delta x_{j+1}^2\right] = \sum_{i=0}^{k-2}\sum_{j=1}^{k-1}E\left[\Delta x_{i+1}^2\right]E\left[\Delta x_{j+1}^2\right] = \sum_{i=0}^{k-2}\sum_{j=1}^{k-1}(\Delta t)^2 = \frac{k(k-1)}{2}(\Delta t)^2.$$

Finally,

$$T = k\,\Delta t$$

and

$$E\left[\sum_{i=0}^{k-1}\Delta x_{i+1}^2\right] = k\,\Delta t.$$

Substituting these four expressions in Eq. (E.28) yields

$$E\left[\sum_{i=0}^{k-1}\Delta x_{i+1}^2 - T\right]^2 = 3k\,(\Delta t)^2 + k(k-1)\,(\Delta t)^2 + k^2\,(\Delta t)^2 - 2k^2\,(\Delta t)^2 = 3k\,(\Delta t)^2 = \frac{3T^2}{k}. \tag{E.29}$$

Therefore,

$$\lim_{k\to\infty}E\left[\sum_{i=0}^{k-1}\Delta x_{i+1}^2 - T\right]^2 = \lim_{k\to\infty}\frac{3T^2}{k} = 0. \tag{E.30}$$

This implies that T is the mean square limit of

$$\sum_{i=0}^{k-1}\Delta x_{i+1}^2.$$

Therefore the mean square limit of S_k is $\frac{1}{2}x_T^2 - T$. Thus the Itô integral

$$\int_0^T x_t\,dx_t$$

is $\frac{1}{2}x_T^2 - T$, while that for "deterministic" integration is $\frac{1}{2}x_T^2$.

It should also be noted that this example shows that $(dz_t)^2 = dt$. To see this, consider the integral

$$\int_0^T (dx_t)^2.$$

Using Itô's integral,

$$\lim_{k \to \infty} E \left[\sum_{i=0}^{k-1} \Delta x_{i+1}^2 - \int_0^T (dx_t)^2 \right]^2 = 0 = \lim_{k \to \infty} E \left[\sum_{i=0}^{k-1} \Delta x_{i+1}^2 - T \right]^2, \tag{E.31}$$

where the last part of the equality follows from Eq. (E.30). This implies that

$$\int_0^T (dx_t)^2 = T. \tag{E.32}$$

But, since

$$T = \int_0^T dt,$$

substitution into Eq. (E.32) yields

$$\int_0^T (dx_t)^2 = \int_0^T dt \text{ or } (dx_t)^2 = dt. \tag{E.33}$$

This implies that in applications involving stochastic calculus, one can replace $(dz_t)^2$ by dt if dz_t is a mean zero process with variance of dt.

C. $\mathcal{I}$tô's Lemma

Consider a function $f(x_t, t)$. If the variables are deterministic, the chain rule states that

$$\frac{df(x_t, t)}{dt} = \frac{\partial f(x_t, t)}{\partial x_t} \frac{dx_t}{dt} + \frac{\partial f(x_t, t)}{\partial t} = f_x \frac{dx}{dt} + f_t. \tag{E.34}$$

The equivalent of Eq. (E.34) in stochastic calculus is called Itô's lemma. To derive Itô's lemma, consider the function $f(x_i, i)$ but with x_i being a random variable with innovations given by the stochastic difference equation $\Delta x_i = \mu_i \Delta t + \sigma_i \Delta z_i$.

Consider a Taylor series expansion of $f(x_i, i)$ around $(x_{i-1}, i-1)$:

$$f(x_i, i) = f(x_{i-1}, i-1) + f_x (x_i - x_{i-1}) + f_t \Delta t + \frac{1}{2} f_{xx} (x_i - x_{i-1})^2$$

$$+ \frac{1}{2} f_{tt} (\Delta t)^2 + f_{xt} (x_i - x_{i-1}) \Delta t + r, \tag{E.35}$$

where r is the remainder.

Substituting $\Delta f_i = f(x_i, i) - f(x_{i-1}, i-1)$ and $\Delta x_i = x_i - x_{i-1} = \mu_i \Delta t + \sigma_i \Delta z_i$ in Eq. (E.35) yields

$$\Delta f_i = f_x \left(\mu_i \Delta t + \sigma_i \Delta z_i\right) + f_t \Delta t + \frac{1}{2} f_{xx} \left(\mu_i \Delta t + \sigma_i \Delta z_i\right)^2 + \frac{1}{2} f_{tt} (\Delta t)^2 + f_{xt} \left(\mu_i \Delta t + \sigma_i \Delta z_i\right) \Delta t + r.$$

(E.36)

Grouping terms together we get

$$\Delta f_i = (f_x \mu_i + f_t) \Delta t + f_x \sigma_i \Delta z_i + \frac{1}{2} \left(f_{xx} \mu_i^2 + +2 f_{xt} \mu_i + f_{tt}\right) (\Delta t)^2 + (f_{xx} \mu_i \sigma_i + f_{xt} \sigma_i) \Delta t \Delta z_i$$

$$+ \frac{1}{2} f_{xx} \sigma_i^2 \Delta z_i^2 + r.$$

(E.37)

Since $(dz_t)^2$ can be replaced by dt, substituting in Eq. (E.37) yields

$$\Delta f_i = (f_x \mu_i + f_t + \frac{1}{2} f_{xx} \sigma_i^2) \Delta t + f_x \sigma_i \Delta z_i + \frac{1}{2} \left(f_{xx} \mu_i^2 + +2 f_{xt} \mu_i + f_{tt}\right) (\Delta t)^2$$

$$+ (f_{xx} \mu_i \sigma_i + f_{xt} \sigma_i) \Delta t \Delta z_i + r.$$

(E.38)

Ignoring all terms of magnitude larger than Δt, that is, $(\Delta t)^2$ and $\Delta t \Delta z_i$ (of magnitude $(\Delta t)^{\frac{3}{2}}$) and the remainder, yields

$$\Delta f_i = (f_x \mu_i + f_t + \frac{1}{2} f_{xx} \sigma_i^2) \Delta t + f_x \sigma_i \Delta z_i$$

(E.39)

or

$$df_i = (f_x \mu_i + f_t + \frac{1}{2} f_{xx} \sigma_i^2) dt + f_x \sigma_i dz_i.$$

(E.40)

As can be seen from Eq. (E.40), Itô's lemma provides a tool to transform a stochastic differential equation for a random variable x to a stochastic differential equation for a function of the random variable $f(x, t)$. As shown in Chapter 7, the Black-Scholes differential equation is a direct application of Itô's lemma.

If the function under consideration is bivariate in random variables, that is, $f(x, y, t)$, where x and y are random variables that follow the stochastic differential equations,

$$\begin{bmatrix} dx \\ dy \end{bmatrix} = \begin{bmatrix} \mu_x \\ \mu_y \end{bmatrix} dt + \begin{bmatrix} \sigma_{xx} & \rho_{xy} \sigma_x \sigma_y \\ \rho_{xy} \sigma_x \sigma_y & \sigma_{yy} \end{bmatrix} \begin{bmatrix} dz_x \\ dz_y \end{bmatrix},$$

(E.41)

then Itô's lemma would suggest that

$$df_i = (f_x \mu_x + f_y \mu_y + f_t + \frac{1}{2} f_{xx} \sigma_x^2 + \frac{1}{2} f_{yy} \sigma_y^2 + f_{xy} \rho_{xy} \sigma_x \sigma_y) dt + f_x \sigma_x dz_x + f_y \sigma_y dz_y.$$

(E.42)

As can be seen above, Itô's lemma can be easily extended to a multivariate scenario.

REFERENCES

Malliaris, A. G., and W. A. Brock, *Stochastic Methods in Economics and Finance*, first edition. North-Holland, Amsterdam, 1982.

Merton, R. C., *Continuous Time Finance*, second edition. Blackwell Publishers, Oxford, 1992.

Neftci, S. N., *An Introduction to the Mathematics of Financial Derivatives*, second edition. Academic Press, San Diego, 2000.

Wilmott, P., S. Howison, and J. Dewynne, *The Mathematics of Financial Derivatives*, first edition. Cambridge University Press, Cambridge, 1995.

Author Index

Subject Index

About the Authors

Tom Copeland is Managing Director of Corporate Finance at Monitor Group, a top-management consulting company with 1,200 consultants located in 26 offices around the world. He has a BA from Johns Hopkins University, an MBA from Wharton, where he graduated second in his class, and a Ph.D. in applied economics from The University of Pennsylvania. He was a member of the finance faculty at UCLA from 1973–1987, a full professor and department chairman. From 1987-1998 he was a partner and co-leader of the corporate finance practice at McKinsey & Co. in New York. He was an adjunct professor of finance at NYU from 1988 to 1988, at MIT in 2001 and at the Harvard Business School in 2002. He has written five books that collectively have sold over 400,000 copies, and have been translated into 12 languages. They include *Real Options: A Practitioner's Guide, Valuation: Measuring and Managing the Value of Companies,* and *Managerial Finance*. He is among the top 100 authors cited in the top three finance journals over the last 25 years, a member of the Financial Economists Roundtable, and member of the practitioners board of directors of the Financial Management Association.

J. Fred Weston is Professor Emeritus Recalled of Managerial Economics and Finance at the John E. Anderson Graduate School of Management at UCLA. He received his Ph.D. degree from the University of Chicago in 1948. He has published 31 books, 147 journal articles, and chaired 32 doctoral dissertations. Since 1968 he has been Director of the UCLA Research Program on Takeovers and Restructuring.

Dr. Weston has served as President of the American Finance Association, President of the Western Economic Association, President of the Financial Management Association, and member of the American Economic U.S. Census Advisory Committee. In 1978, he was selected as one of five outstanding teachers on the UCLA campus and in 1994 received the Dean's Award for Outstanding Instruction in the Anderson School at UCLA. He served as an associate editor on 14 journals. He has been a consultant to business firms and governments on financial and economic policies since 1950. He has been selected as a Fellow of the American Finance Association, of the Financial Management Association, and of the National Association of Business Economists.

Kuldeep Shastri holds the Roger Ahlbrandt, Sr. Endowed Chair in Finance and is Professor of Business Administration at University of Pittsburgh's Katz Graduate School of Business. He completed his doctoral studies in Financial Economics at the University of California–Los Angeles in 1982. He has an MBA from the University of Pittsburgh (1976) and a Bachelor of Technology in Electrical Engineering from the Indian Institute of Technology–Delhi (1975). Dr. Shastri teaches in the areas of corporate finance, derivatives, financial engineering and market microstructure. He has received Distinguished Teaching awards from the 1984, 1989, and 1995 Executive MBA and the 2002 Brazil International Executive MBA classes at the Katz School and the 1990 MBA class at the International Management Center in Budapest. In addition to teaching at the Katz School,

Dr. Shastri has lectured extensively in Central and Eastern Europe and Southeast Asia, and has held visiting positions at the Czech Management Center in Prague, the International Management Center in Budapest, Thammasat University in Bangkok, and Universidad Tecnica Federico Santa Maria in Guayaquil. Dr. Shastri has published over 40 articles in a variety of finance journals and made over 60 presentations at national and international conferences. He is currently an Academic Director of the Financial Management Association International and was a past President of the Eastern Finance Association.